Ex Líbrís

BATTLES AND LEADERS OF THE CIVIL WAR

VOLUME ONE

THE BUGLE CALL.

FROM THE PAINTING BY WILLIAM M. HUNT.

BATTLES AND LEADERS OF THE CIVIL WAR

VOLUME I

BEING FOR THE MOST PART CONTRIBUTIONS
BY UNION AND CONFEDERATE OFFICERS.
BASED UPON "THE CENTURY WAR SERIES."
EDITED BY ROBERT UNDERWOOD JOHNSON
AND CLARENCE CLOUGH BUEL, OF THE EDI-
TORIAL STAFF OF "THE CENTURY MAGAZINE."

CASTLE

CAMP GOSSIP. FROM A PHOTOGRAPH.

PREFACE.

WITH the main purpose in its origin of interesting veterans in their own memories and of instructing the generation which has grown up since the War for the Union, the "Century War Series," through peculiar circumstances, has exerted an influence in bringing about a better understanding between the soldiers who were opposed in that conflict. This influence, of which substantial evidence has been given, North and South, lends additional historical interest to the present work. Many commanders and subordinates have here contributed to the history of the heroic deeds of which they were a part. General Grant, who, in accord with the well-known purpose of President Lincoln, began at Appomattox the work of reconciliation, contributed to the War Series four papers on his greatest campaigns, and these are here included. They were written before his severe illness, and became the foundation of his "Personal Memoirs." The narrative of his battles, continued under the tragic circumstances of the last year of his life, retrieved his fortunes and added a new laurel to his fame. The good temper and the unpartisan character of his articles, and of the papers by the leading writers on both sides, are the most significant signs in these pages. For the most part, each side has confined controversy to its own ranks, and both have emphasized the benefit as well as the glory of the issue. Coincident with the progress of the series during the past three years, may be noted a marked increase in the number of fraternal meetings between Union and Confederate veterans, enforcing the conviction that the nation is restored in spirit as in fact, and that each side is contributing its share to the new heritage of manhood and peace.

On the 17th of July, 1883, Mr. Buel, Assistant-Editor of "The Century" magazine, proposed in detail a magazine series by prominent generals of both sides. The original suggestion (based upon the success of two articles from different points of view on the John Brown raid, in "The Century" for that month) was of eight or ten articles on the decisive battles of the war, and included in the main the features of the expanded series. Mr. R. W. Gilder, the Editor-in-Chief, at once cordially adopted the suggestion, committing the charge of its execution to Mr. Johnson, the Associate-Editor, assisted by Mr. Buel; from the start Mr. Gilder has aided the work by his counsel, and by the support of his confidence in its success and public usefulness—ends which could not have been attained except for the liberal and continued support of Roswell Smith, Esq., President of The Century Co. The elaboration of the first plan, the securing of the contributions, and the shaping and editing of the series were shared by Mr. Johnson and Mr. Buel, the former devoting the more time to the work during the months of organization, and the latter having entire charge of the editing for nearly the whole of the second year. The course of the series in magazine form was from November, 1884, to November, 1887.

That the plan and the time of the enterprise were alike fortunate, may be estimated from the unprecedented success of the articles. Within six months from the appearance of the first battle paper, the circulation of "The Century" advanced from 127,000 to 225,000 copies, or to a reading audience estimated at two millions. A part of this gain was the natural growth of the periodical. The still further increase of the regular monthly issue during the first year of the serial publication of Messrs. Nicolay and Hay's Life of Lincoln (1886–87) has proved the permanent character of the interest in important contributions to the history of the Civil War.

The present work is a natural sequence of the magazine series, and was provided for before the publication of the first paper. Both the series and this expansion of it in book form are, in idea as well as in execution, an outgrowth of the methods and convictions belonging to the editorial habit of "The Century" magazine. The chief motive has been strict fairness to the testimony of both sides, and the chief endeavors have been to prove every important statement by the "Official Records" and other trustworthy documents, and to spare no pains in the interest of elucidation and accuracy. These ends could not have been attained without the cordial coöperation as writers, and assistance as interested actors, of the soldiers of both sides; in these respects the aid rendered by veterans, from the highest rank to the lowest, has been unstinted, and would be deserving of particular mention if such were possible within the bounds of an ordinary preface. Nearly every writer in the work, and very many others whose names do not appear, have been willing sources of suggestion and information. Special aid has been received from General James B. Fry, from the late Colonel Robert N. Scott, who was the editorial head of the "War Records" office, and from his successor, Colonel H. M. Lazelle; and thanks are due to General Adam Badeau, George E. Pond, Colonel John P. Nicholson, Colonel G. C. Kniffin, and to General Marcus J. Wright, Agent of the War Department for the Collection of Confederate Records.

Material for the illustrations, which form a most striking and not the least important feature of the work, has been received from all sides, as will be noted in the table of contents. Special acknowledgment is due to the Massachusetts Commandery of the Loyal Legion, to whose complete set of the Gardner and the Brady photographs, as well as to other material, access has been had from the beginning of the series. Colonel Arnold A. Rand, Recorder of the Massachusetts Commandery, and General Albert Ordway have rendered valuable aid in connection with the Brady and the Gardner photographs and in other ways. The importance of accuracy has been kept constantly in view in the preparation of the illustrations—a laborious work which has been executed under the direction of Mr. Alexander W. Drake, Superintendent, and Mr. W. Lewis Fraser, Manager, of the Art Department of The Century Co.

THE EDITORS.

NEW YORK, November, 1887.

CORRECTIONS IN THE FIRST EDITION.

Page 5. For Admiral Charles A. Davis (so printed in part of the edition), read Admiral Charles H. Davis.

Page 6 and page 108. For Charles G. Memminger, read Christopher G. Memminger.

Page 41. "From Moultrie to Sumter," by General Doubleday. Concerning the statement that Major Robert Anderson, of Kentucky, " was a regular officer and owner of a slave plantation in Georgia," Major Anderson's widow writes to the Editors that he never owned a plantation anywhere, and that he never resided in Georgia. She adds, "He inherited slaves in Kentucky from his father, Colonel Richard Clough Anderson, and these he liberated immediately on coming into possession of them, which was a few years after he was graduated at the Military Academy of West Point." General Doubleday will modify the statement for other editions.

Page 81. For Lieutenant James A. Yates (so printed in part of the edition), read Lieutenant Joseph A. Yates.

Page 236. For Sergeant Thomas Shumate (so printed in part of the edition), read Sergeant Joseph Shumate.

Page 261. "The Confederate Commissariat at Manassas," by Colonel Northrup. Near the middle of the second column — for " Lieutenant-Colonel Robert B. Lee was added," read " Lieutenant-Colonel Richard B. Lee was added."

Page 438. In the foot-note: For General George W. Cullom (so printed in part of the edition), read General George W. Cullum.

Page 576. "The Campaign of Shiloh," by General G. T. Beauregard. Line 27 — for the 13th of February, read the 13th of March.

Page 669. Title to portrait. For Colonel Zebulon B. Vance, read Brigadier-General Robert B. Vance.

FORT SUMTER.

PAGE

FROM MOULTRIE TO SUMTER.................*GENERAL ABNER DOUBLEDAY*....... 40

ILLUSTRATIONS: View of Charleston from Castle Pinckney *(T. R. Davis)* — Major Robert Anderson, from Brady photo.— Major Anderson and his Officers, from Cook photo.— The Sea-battery at Fort Moultrie, from photo.— Map of Charleston Harbor *(Jacob Wells)* — The Hot-shot Furnace, Fort Moultrie, from photo.— Major Anderson's Men Crossing to Fort Sumter *(Theo. R. Davis)*.

INSIDE SUMTER IN '61......................*CAPTAIN JAMES CHESTER* 50

ILLUSTRATIONS: South-west or Gorge Front of Fort Sumter, from photo. lent by the Washington Light Infantry, Charleston, S. C. *(W. Taber)* — The Sally-port of Fort Sumter, from photo.— Ground Plan of Fort Sumter *(F. E. Sitts)* — Interior of Fort Sumter after the Surrender, from photo. *(W. Taber)* — Interior of Fort Sumter after the Bombardment, showing the Gate and the Gorge Wall, from photo.— Interior of Fort Sumter, showing the 10-inch Columbiad bearing on Charleston, from photo. lent by G. L. G. Cook *(W. Taber)* — Effect of the Bombardment on the Barbette Guns, from photo. lent by the Rev. John Johnson *(E. J. Meeker)* — The Sumter Garrison Watching the Firing on the "Star of the West" *(T. R. Davis)* — Confederate Floating Battery in Action *(T. R. Davis)* — Plan of the Floating Battery, from a Sketch by Colonel Joseph A. Yates — Sergeant Carmody Firing the Barbette Guns of Sumter *(T. R. Davis)* —A Casemate Gun during the Conflagration *(T. R. Davis)* — Ruins of the Casemates and of the Barbette Tier of Guns, from photo's.

THE FIRST STEP IN THE WAR.................*GENERAL STEPHEN D. LEE*......... 74

ILLUSTRATIONS: Bursting of the Signal-shell from Fort Johnson over Fort Sumter *(T. R. Davis)* — Governor Francis W. Pickens, from photo. lent by Louis Manigault — Confederate Mortar-battery on Morris Island, from photo.— General G. T. Beauregard, from Anderson-Cook photo.— Secession Hall, Charleston, from Cook photo. *(E. J. Meeker)* — Fort Sumter at the close of the Bombardment *(T. R. Davis)* —Jefferson Davis, from Brady photo.—View of Cumming's Point *(T. R. Davis)*.

NOTES ON THE SURRENDER OF FORT SUMTER...*COLONEL A. R. CHISOLM*............ 82

ORGANIZING FOR THE CONFLICT.

WAR PREPARATIONS IN THE NORTH............*GENERAL JACOB D. COX*............ 84

ILLUSTRATIONS: The Awkward Squad *(W. Taber)* — Life-mask of Stephen A. Douglas, from photo.— Portrait of Stephen A. Douglas, from daguerreotype taken in 1852 — Major-General George B. McClellan, from photo. by R. W. Addis — Major-General Gordon Granger, from Brady photo.— Camp Dennison, near Cincinnati, based upon photo. *(W. Taber)*.

THE CONFEDERATE GOVERNMENT AT MONT-⎫
GOMERY. By the Editor of the Charleston ⎬ *R. BARNWELL RHETT*............. 99
"Mercury" in 1860-2..................⎭

ILLUSTRATIONS: Montgomery, Alabama, in 1861, showing the Confederate Capitol *(T. R. Davis)* — Alexander H. Stephens, from Brady photo.— William L. Yancey, from Cook photo.— Robert Toombs, from photo.— Leroy Pope Walker, from Brady photo.—R. Barnwell Rhett, from Cook photo.— Howell Cobb, from photo. lent by General Marcus J. Wright — Stephen R. Mallory, from daguerreotype — Judah P. Benjamin, from photo. lent by James Blair — Charles G. Memminger and John H. Reagan, from photos.

FIRST OPERATIONS IN VIRGINIA.

JACKSON AT HARPER'S FERRY IN 1861 ....*GENERAL JOHN D. IMBODEN* 111

ILLUSTRATIONS: Richmond, Va., in 1861 *(Theo. R. Davis)* — Palmetto Regiment parading in Charleston, S. C., *en route* for Richmond *(Theo. R. Davis)* — Map of Virginia, West Virginia, and Maryland *(Jacob Wells)* — Court-house, Charleston, Va., where John Brown and his Associates were Tried and Sentenced, from photo. by W. G. Reed *(Harry Fenn)* — Map of Harper's Ferry *(G. H. Brown)* — Portrait of John Brown, from photo. by J. W. Black & Co. (with Autograph) — Engine-house, Harper's Ferry *(Joseph Pennell)* — Portrait of Colonel Robert E. Lee, from photo. taken before the War, lent by General G. W. C. Lee — View of Harper's Ferry looking down the Potomac, from photo. *(W. Taber)* — Harper's Ferry from the Maryland side, from photo. *(W. Taber)* — Lieut.-General Thomas J. ("Stonewall") Jackson, C. S. A., from photo. by Tanner & Van Ness — General Jackson in 1861, from pen sketch lent by Mrs. Harriet Coxe Bledsoe *(A. J. Volck)* — Colonel Roger Jones, from Brady photo.

PAGE

McCLELLAN IN WEST VIRGINIA .... *GENERAL JACOB D. COX* 126

ILLUSTRATIONS: An Affair of Outposts (*W. Taber*) — Major-General Lew Wallace, from Brady photo.— Map of Campaigns in West Virginia (*Jacob Wells*) — Brig.-General T. A. Morris, from Brady photo.— Plan of Combat at Rich Mountain (*J. Wells*) — Brig.-General John Pegram, C. S. A., from Anderson-Cook photo.— Brig.-General R. S. Garnett, C. S. A., from photo.— Major-General W. S. Rose-crans, from photo. by Bogardus — Brig.-General H. A. Wise, C. S. A., from Brady photo.— Brig.-General J. B. Floyd, C. S. A., from photo.— Post-hospital and Wagon-shop at Kanawha Falls, from photo. lent by General J. D. Cox (*Harry Fenn*) — Plan of Gauley Bridge and Vicinity (*Jacob Wells*) — View of Gauley Bridge and New River Cliffs, from photo's lent by General J. D. Cox (*Harry Fenn*) — Plan of Affair at Carnifex Ferry (*Jacob Wells*) — Floyd's Command Recrossing the Gauley River, and Preparing to Shell Rosecrans's Camp at Gauley Bridge, from sketches by W. D. Washington owned by J. F. Gibson (*W. L. Sheppard*) — View of Romney, Va. (*A. R. Waud*).

FIRESIDE AND FIELD OF BATTLE.

GOING TO THE FRONT (Recollections of a Private — 1). *WARREN LEE GOSS* 149

ILLUSTRATIONS: Fac-simile of the Conclusion of General Dix's "American Flag" Dispatch, from the original lent by the Rev. Morgan Dix, D. D.— Arrival of the New York 7th at Annapolis (*Theo. R. Davis*) — Uniform of the 6th Massachusetts (*H. A. Ogden*) — "And the Corporal did" (*E. W. Kemble*) — A Mother's Parting Gift (*E. W. Kemble*) — Militia Uniform of '61, from photo. of the statue by J. Q. A. Ward — The New York 7th Marching down Broadway (*W. Taber*) — Federal Hill, Baltimore (*F. H. Schell*) — Pennsylvania Avenue, Washington, in '61 (*Theo. R. Davis*) — The New York 7th at Camp Cameron, Washington (*M. J. Burns*).

VIRGINIA SCENES IN '61 .... *MRS. BURTON HARRISON* 160

ILLUSTRATIONS: Confederate Battle-flag, from original flag lent by Mrs. Harrison (*E. J. Meeker*) — A Virginia Homestead, from sketch lent by Mrs. Harrison (*E. J. Meeker*) — Confederates on the Way to Manassas (*E. W. Kemble*) — Listening for the First Gun (*E. W. Kemble*) — Fac-simile of Autographic Copy of the First Stanza of "My Maryland."

CAMPAIGN OF THE FIRST BULL RUN.

McDOWELL'S ADVANCE TO BULL RUN .... *GENERAL JAMES B. FRY* 167

ILLUSTRATIONS: Scrutinizing a Pass at the Long Bridge, based on photo. (*W. H. Shelton*) — Uniform of the 14th New York at Bull Run (*W. Taber*) — Simon Cameron, Secretary of War, from Brady photo. — Uniform of the 1st Massachusetts at Bull Run (*H. A. Ogden*) — General Irvin McDowell, from photo. by Fredericks — Uniform of the 2d Ohio at Bull Run (*H. A. Ogden*) — Map of the Defenses of Washington, July, 1861 (*Jacob Wells*) — Fac-simile of a Washington Pass of 1861 (obverse and reverse), lent by Murat Halstead — View of Washington from the Signal Camp, two cuts (*Theo. R. Davis*) — The Stone Church, Centreville, from Gardner photo. (*Harry Fenn*) — Uniform of the 11th New York (Fire Zouaves) at Bull Run (*H. A. Ogden*) — Outline Map of the Battle-field of Bull Run (*Jacob Wells*) — Sudley Springs Hotel (*Joseph Pennell*) — Sudley Springs Ford in 1884 (*Joseph Pennell*) — Sudley Springs Ford, from Gardner photo. (*Harry Fenn*) — The Stone Bridge over Bull Run (*Joseph Pennell*) — Fatigue Uniform and Kilts of the 79th New York (*H. A. Ogden*) — The Sudley Springs Road, from photo. by Captain J. E. Barr (*J. D. Woodward*) — Major-General Charles Griffin, and Major-General James B. Ricketts, from photo's lent by General James B. Fry — The Contest for the Henry Hill (*W. Taber*) — Uniform of the Garibaldi Guards (*H. A. Ogden*) — Uniform of Blenker's 8th New York Volunteers (*H. A. Ogden*) — Brig.-General Louis Blenker, from Brady photo.

THE OPPOSING ARMIES AT THE FIRST BULL RUN. Table of Strength, Composition, and Losses 194

THE FIRST BATTLE OF BULL RUN .... *GENERAL G. T. BEAUREGARD* 196

ILLUSTRATIONS: A Louisiana "Tiger" (*A. C. Redwood*) — Arlington, the Home of General Robert E. Lee (*J. H. Cocks*) — Map of the Bull Run Campaign (*Jacob Wells*) — The McLean House, General Beauregard's Headquarters, near Manassas, from Gardner photo. (*W. Taber*) — Topographical Map of the Bull Run Battle-field (*Jacob Wells*) — Rallying the Troops of Bee, Bartow, and Evans behind the Robinson House (*T. de Thulstrup*) — A Louisiana "Pelican" (*A. C. Redwood*) — The Robinson House, from Gardner photo. (*J. D. Woodward*) — The Main Battle-ground, two views, from photo's (*Harry Fenn*) — Colonel F. S. Bartow, from photo. lent by Georgia Historical Society — Fairfax Court-house, from Gardner photo. (*W. Taber*) — Ruins of the Stone Bridge, looking along the Warrenton Turnpike toward the Battle-field, from Gardner photo.— Confederate Quaker Guns, from Gardner photo. (*A. C. Redwood*) — Generals R. E. Lee and J. E. Johnston, from photo. by D. J. Ryan (with Autographs).

PAGE

INCIDENTS OF THE FIRST BULL RUN ....*GENERAL JOHN D. IMBODEN*........229

    ILLUSTRATIONS: The New Henry, House and the Monument of the First Battle, from photo. (*W. Taber*) — Confederate Fortifications about Manassas Junction, and the Stone House on the Warrenton Turnpike, from Gardner photo's (*Harry Fenn*) — Plan of the Bull Run Battle-field (*Jacob Wells*) — Brigadier-General Barnard E. Bee, from photo. by Tucker & Perkins.

RESPONSIBILITIES OF THE FIRST BULL RUN......*GENERAL JOSEPH E. JOHNSTON*....240

    ILLUSTRATIONS: Quaker Gun found in the Confederate Works at Manassas, from Gardner photo. (*W. Taber*) — General Samuel Cooper, from photo. by Davis lent by General Marcus J. Wright — Lieutenant-General Richard S. Ewell, from Anderson-Cook photo. — "Stonewall" Jackson as First-Lieutenant of Artillery, from daguerreotype lent by his niece, Miss Alice E. Underwood.

GENERAL EWELL AT BULL RUN................*MAJOR CAMPBELL BROWN*........259

THE CONFEDERATE COMMISSARIAT AT MANASSAS.....*COLONEL L. B. NORTHROP*.....261

WILSON'S CREEK, LEXINGTON, AND PEA RIDGE.

THE FIRST YEAR OF THE WAR IN MISSOURI.....*COLONEL THOMAS L. SNEAD*.......262

    ILLUSTRATIONS: A Very Raw Recruit (*E. W. Kemble*) — Map of Operations in Missouri, 1861 (*Jacob Wells*) — Governor Claiborne F. Jackson, from phototype lent by General Marcus J. Wright — Brigadier-General D. M. Frost, from photo. by Scholten — Fac-simile of Missouri War Scrip, lent by R. I. Holcombe — Major-General Sterling Price, from Anderson-Cook photo. — Major-General David Hunter, from Brady photo. — Major-General Henry W. Halleck, from photo.

IN COMMAND IN MISSOURI.....................*GENERAL JOHN C. FRÉMONT*........278

    ILLUSTRATIONS: Off to the War (*W. Taber*) — Major-General F. P. Blair, Jr., from Brady photo. — Brig.-General Nathaniel Lyon, from Brady photo. — Major-General Franz Sigel, from photo. — Major-General John C. Frémont, from steel portrait lent by Mrs. Frémont.

WILSON'S CREEK, AND THE DEATH OF LYON....*GENERAL WILLIAM M. WHERRY*.....289

    ILLUSTRATIONS: Cavalryman of the United States Regulars in 1861 (*H. A. Ogden*) — Map of Wilson's Creek, or Oak Hills (*Jacob Wells*) — Major-General John M. Schofield, from Brady photo. — Battle-field of Wilson's Creek from behind Pearce's Camp, from photo's (*E. J. Meeker*) — Brigadier-General N. B. Pearce, C. S. A., from Brady photo.

ARKANSAS TROOPS IN THE BATTLE }
   OF WILSON'S CREEK......... } ....*GENERAL N. B. PEARCE*.............298

    ILLUSTRATIONS: Bloody Hill from the East, from photo. by Sittler lent by R. I. Holcombe (*W. Taber*) — Major-General Ben. McCulloch, C. S. A., from photo. — Brigadier-General W. Y. Slack, C. S. A., from Brady photo.

THE FLANKING COLUMN AT WILSON'S CREEK....*GENERAL FRANZ SIGEL*.............304

THE OPPOSING FORCES AT WILSON'S CREEK, MO. Composition, Strength, and Losses 306

THE SIEGE OF LEXINGTON ....*COLONEL JAMES A. MULLIGAN*......307

    ILLUSTRATIONS: Confederates Fighting behind Hemp-bales (*W. Taber*) — Map of the Siege of Lexington (*Jacob Wells*) — Battle of Lexington, as seen from Parsons's position, after sketch by F. B. Wilkie in "Frank Leslie's" (*F. H. Schell*) — Colonel James A. Mulligan, from photo. (*Sidney L. Smith*).

THE PEA RIDGE CAMPAIGN.....................*GENERAL FRANZ SIGEL*..............314

    ILLUSTRATIONS: Uniform of the United States Regulars in 1861, from photo. (*H. A. Ogden*) — Major-General Samuel R. Curtis, from photo. — Major-General Earl Van Dorn, C. S. A., from photo. by Earle & Son (with Autograph) — Map of the Battle-field of Pea Ridge, or Elkhorn Tavern (*Jacob Wells*) — Major-General Peter J. Osterhaus, from photo. by Fredericks — Major-General Eugene A. Carr, from Brady photo. — Brigadier-General James McIntosh, C. S. A., from photo. — The Union Right under General Carr at Pratt's Store, Second Day of the Battle — and Last Hour of the Battle of Pea Ridge, from paintings by Hunt P. Wilson owned by Southern Historical Society of St. Louis (*Schell and Hogan*) — Brigadier-General Albert Pike, C. S. A., from photo. by Scholl, and Brigadier-General Stand Waitie, C. S. A., from photo's lent by General Marcus J. Wright.

PAGE

UNION AND CONFEDERATE INDIANS }
IN THE CIVIL WAR............ } ....*WILEY BRITTON*....................335

ILLUSTRATION: Elkhorn Tavern, Pea Ridge, from photo. (*W. Taber*).

THE OPPOSING FORCES AT PEA RIDGE. Composition, Strength, and Losses...............337

BELMONT AND FORT HENRY.

RECOLLECTIONS OF FOOTE AND THE GUN-BOATS..*CAPTAIN JAMES B. EADS*...........338

ILLUSTRATIONS: Building the Eads Gun-boats at Carondelet (*Theo. R. Davis*) — The "De Kalb," formerly the "St. Louis" (Type of the "Carondelet," "Cincinnati," "Louisville," "Mound City," "Cairo," and "Pittsburgh"), from photo. lent by Captain Eads — Captain James B. Eads, from photo.— The "Osage" (Twin of the "Neosho") — and the "Chickasaw" (Type of the "Milwaukee," "Winnebago," and "Kickapoo"), from photo's lent by Captain Eads (*E. J. Meeker*) — Rear-Admiral Andrew Hull Foote, from photo. by E. Anthony — Rear-Admiral Henry Walke, from ambrotype.

NOTES ON THE LIFE OF ADMIRAL FOOTE. }
By his Brother..................... } .....*JOHN A. FOOTE*....................347

GENERAL POLK AND THE BATTLE OF BELMONT. }
By his Son................................ } *CAPTAIN WILLIAM M. POLK*.........348

[From the MS. of the "Life of Leonidas Polk" (unpublished).]

ILLUSTRATIONS: Portraits of Confederate Privates of the West, from ambrotypes (*H. A. Ogden*) — Map of the Battle-field near Belmont, Mo. (*J. S. Kemp*) — Lieutenant-General Leonidas Polk, Bishop of Louisiana, from photo. by Morse — Brigadier-General U. S. Grant (1861), from photo. lent by O. Hufeland — The Gun-boats "Tyler" and "Lexington" fighting the Columbus Batteries during the Battle of Belmont, from drawing by Rear-Admiral Walke (*F. H. Schell and T. Hogan*) — Confederate Fortifications at Columbus, Ky., from sketch made for "Frank Leslie's" and lent by G. N. Putnam (*J. D. Woodward*) — Captain John A. Rawlins (1861), from photo. lent by O. Hufeland — Reëmbarkation of Grant's Troops after the Battle, from drawing by Rear-Admiral Walke (*F. H. Schell and T. Hogan*).

THE GUN-BOATS AT BELMONT AND FORT HENRY..*REAR-ADMIRAL HENRY WALKE*.....358

ILLUSTRATIONS: Army Transports at the Cairo Levee (*Theo. R. Davis*) — Flag-Officer Foote in the Wheel-house of the "Cincinnati" at Fort Henry (*W. Taber*) — Wharf-boat at Cairo, from photo. lent by Major J. H. Benton (*W. Goater*) — The Gun-boats "Tyler" and "Lexington" engaging the Batteries of Columbus, from sketch by Rear-Admiral Walke (*Harry Fenn*) — Map of the Region of Foote's Operations (*Jacob Wells*) — United States Gun-boat "Tyler," from drawing by Rear-Admiral Walke — Map of Fort Henry (*Jacob Wells*) — Cross-section of a Confederate Torpedo found in the Tennessee River (*E. J. Meeker*) — Between Decks: Serving the Guns, from drawing by Rear-Admiral Walke (*A. C. Redwood*) — General Lloyd Tilghman, from photo.

THE DEFENSE OF FORT HENRY..................*CAPTAIN JESSE TAYLOR*............368

ILLUSTRATION: The Attack upon Fort Henry, from drawing by Rear-Admiral Walke.

MILL SPRINGS, THE BIG SANDY, AND FORT DONELSON.

HOLDING KENTUCKY FOR THE UNION..........*COLONEL R. M. KELLY*.............373

ILLUSTRATIONS: Military Water-sled (*Frank H. Schell*) — Rev. Robert J. Breckinridge, D. D., from steel portrait — Major-General William Nelson, from Brady photo. — Major-General John C. Breckinridge, C. S. A., from daguerreotype lent by Anson Maltby — Map of Kentucky and Tennessee (*Jacob Wells*) — John C. Crittenden, from daguerreotype — Camp Dick Robinson — The Farm-house, from sketch lent by Mrs. M. B. Robinson — Major-General Lovell H. Rousseau, from Brady photo. — Major-General George B. Crittenden, C. S. A., from photo. — Major-General D. C. Buell, from photo. lent by General James B. Fry — Map of the Battle of Logan's Cross Roads, or Mill Springs, Ky. (*Jacob Wells*) — Brigadier-General Felix K. Zollicoffer, C. S. A., from photo. — Brigadier-General Speed S. Fry, from photo. taken in 1862 — National Cemetery at Logan's Cross Roads, from photo. (*E. J. Meeker*) — View on the Battle-field of Logan's Cross Roads, from photo. (*E. J. Meeker*).

THE OPPOSING FORCES AT LOGAN'S CROSS ROADS, KY. (MILL SPRINGS OR FISHING CREEK). Composition, Strength, and Losses 392

MARSHALL AND GARFIELD IN } EASTERN KENTUCKY..... } .... *REV. EDWARD O. GUERRANT* 393

    ILLUSTRATIONS : Confederate Private, from ambrotype *(Frank Day)* — Map of Big Sandy River and Middle Creek Battle-field *(Jacob Wells)* — Brigadier-General James A. Garfield, from Brady photo. — Brigadier-General Humphrey Marshall, C. S. A., from photo.

THE CAPTURE OF FORT DONELSON............. *GENERAL LEW WALLACE* 398

    ILLUSTRATIONS: Headquarters in the Field *(R. F. Zogbaum)* — the Town of Dover from Robinson's Hill, from photo. *(W. H. Drake)* — Map of Fort Donelson as Invested by General Grant *(Jacob Wells)* — Glimpse of the Cumberland River where the Gun-boats first appeared, from photo. *(Harry Fenn)* — Major-General John A. McClernand, from photo. — Major-General Simon B. Buckner, C. S. A., from photo. by Anthony — Dover Tavern, General Buckner's Headquarters and the Scene of the Surrender, from photo. *(Harry Fenn)* — Major-General Morgan L. Smith, from photo. lent by Miss D. Morgan Smith — Major-General C. F. Smith, from Brady photo. — The Crisp Farm — General Grant's Headquarters — Front View of Mrs. Crisp's House, from photo's *(W. H. Drake)* — The Position of the Gun-boats and the West Bank, from photo's *(Harry Fenn)* — The Bivouac in the Snow on the Line of Battle *(R. F. Zogbaum)* — Branch of Hickman's Creek near James Crisp's House, the Left of General C. F. Smith's Line, from photo. *(Harry Fenn)* — McAllister's Battery in Action *(W. Taber)* — View on the Line of Pillow's Defenses in front of McClernand, showing Water in the Old Trenches, from photo. *(Harry Fenn)* — Major-General Gideon J. Pillow, C. S. A., from Anderson-Cook photo. — Rowlett's Mill, from photo. *(W. Taber)* — Fac-simile of the original "Unconditional Surrender" Dispatch — View from the National Cemetery, from photo. *(C. H. Stephens)*.

THE OPPOSING FORCES AT FORT DONELSON, TENN. Composition, Strength, and Losses...429

THE RIVER GUN-BOATS FROM FORT DONELSON TO NEW MADRID.

THE WESTERN FLOTILLA AT FORT } DONELSON, ISLAND NUMBER TEN, } ...... *REAR-ADMIRAL HENRY WALKE* ...... 430 FORT PILLOW, AND MEMPHIS.... }

    ILLUSTRATIONS: The "Carondelet" Fighting Fort Donelson, from sketch by Rear-Admiral Walke *(F. H. Schell and T. Hogan)* — Explosion of a Gun on board the "Carondelet" during the Attack on Fort Donelson, from sketch by Rear-Admiral Walke *(M. J. Burns)* — The Gun-boats at Fort Donelson — The Land Attack in the Distance, from sketch by Rear-Admiral Walke *(Harry Fenn)* — Map of the Region of the Flotilla Operations *(Jacob Wells)* — Map of Military and Naval Operations about Island Number Ten *(Jacob Wells)* — The Mortar-boats at Island Number Ten *(E. J. Meeker)* — The "Carondelet" Running the Confederate Batteries at Island Number Ten, from sketch by Rear-Admiral Walke *(Harry Fenn)* — The Levee at New Madrid *(A. R. Waud)* — Major-General John Pope, from Brady photo. — Brigadier-General W. W. Mackall, C. S. A., from photo. by G. W. Davis — The "Carondelet" and "Pittsburgh" Capturing the Confederate Batteries below New Madrid, from drawing by Rear-Admiral Walke *(F. H. Schell and T. Hogan)* — Flag-Officer Charles Henry Davis, from Brady photo. — Fort Pillow and the Water-battery, and the Battle of Fort Pillow, from sketches by Rear-Admiral Walke *(F. H. Schell and T. Hogan)* — The Battle of Memphis (looking South), from drawing by Rear-Admiral Walke *(Frank H. Schell)* — Brigadier-General M. Jeff. Thompson, C. S. A., from photo.

ELLET AND HIS STEAM-RAMS AT MEMPHIS....... *GENERAL ALFRED W. ELLET* 453

    ILLUSTRATIONS: The Battle of Memphis (looking North) — Retreat of the Confederate Fleet, from drawing by Rear-Admiral Walke *(F. H. Schell and T. Hogan)* — Colonel Charles Ellet, Jr., from photo. by Rehn & Hurn — Close of the Battle of Memphis, from drawing by Rear-Admiral Walke *(F. H. Schell and T. Hogan)* — Practicing on a River Picket *(W. Taber)*.

SAWING OUT THE CHANNEL ABOVE ISLAND } NUMBER TEN....................... } ....*COLONEL J. W. BISSELL*............460

    ILLUSTRATIONS: Method of Cutting the Channel *(W. Taber)* — Map of the Corrected Line of the Channel above Island Number Ten, cut by the Engineer Regiment *(Jacob Wells)*.

COMMENT ON COLONEL BISSELL'S PAPER........ *GENERAL SCHUYLER HAMILTON* 462

THE OPPOSING FORCES AT NEW MADRID (ISLAND NUMBER TEN), FORT PILLOW, AND MEMPHIS. Composition, Strength, and Losses......................................463

SHILOH.

PAGE

THE BATTLE OF SHILOH . . . . *GENERAL ULYSSES S. GRANT* 465

ILLUSTRATIONS: General U. S. Grant, from photo. (with Autograph) — On the Skirmish Line *(W. Taber)* — Outline Map of the Shiloh Campaign *(Jacob Wells)* — Mrs. Crump's House and the Landing below the House, from photo's *(George Gibson)* — New Shiloh Church and Shiloh Spring, in the Ravine South of the Chapel, from photo's *(W. H. Drake)* — Map of the Field of Shiloh, from General Grant's "Memoirs" — First Position of Waterhouse's Battery, from sketch by E. W. Andrews, M. D. *(E. J. Meeker)* — Confederate Charge upon Prentiss's Camp on Sunday Morning *(A. C. Redwood)* — Checking the Confederate Advance on the Evening of the First Day *(Edwin Forbes)* — Present Aspect of the Old Hamburg Road which led up to the "Hornets' Nest," from photo. *(Fred. B. Schell)* — Major-General B. M. Prentiss, from Brady photo. — Brigadier-General W. H. L. Wallace, from photo. — Ford where the Hamburg Road Crosses Lick Creek, from photo. *(Fred. B. Schell)* — Bridge over Snake Creek by which General Lew Wallace's Troops reached the Field, from photo. *(Fred. B. Schell)* — Bivouac of the Federal Troops *(T. de Thulstrup)* — Wounded and Stragglers on the Way to the Landing *(T. de Thulstrup)* — Above the Landing: The Store, and a part of the National Cemetery, from photo. lent by Captain A. T. Andreas *(E. J. Meeker)*.

SHILOH REVIEWED . . . . *GENERAL DON CARLOS BUELL* 487

ILLUSTRATIONS: Battery Forward! *(W. Taber)* — Pittsburg Landing, viewed from the Ferry Landing on the opposite Shore, from photo. lent by Captain A. T. Andreas *(E. J. Meeker)* — Pittsburg Landing, from photo. lent by W. H. Chamberlin *(J. O. Davidson)* — The Landing at Savannah, from photo. *(F. B. Schell)* — Major-General Alexander McD. McCook, from Brady photo. — Pittsburg Landing in the Summer of 1884, from photo. *(F. B. Schell)* — Map Showing the Union Camps at Shiloh, fac-simile of original — Map of the Field of Shiloh, revised and amended by General Buell *(Jacob Wells)* — The "Hornets' Nest": Prentiss's Troops and Hickenlooper's Battery repulsing Hardee's Troops, and Gibson's Brigade charging Hurlbut's Troops in the "Hornets' Nest," from the Cyclorama of Shiloh at Chicago *(H. A. Ogden)* — The Official, or Thom, Map of the Battle of Shiloh *(Jacob Wells)* — In the "Hornets Nest" (two views on W. H. L. Wallace's Line), from the Cyclorama at Chicago *(H. C. Edwards)* — The Siege-battery, above the Landing, from photo. lent by W. H. Chamberlin *(W. Taber)* — Buell's Troops debarking at Pittsburg Landing *(T. de Thulstrup)* — Major-General Thomas J. Wood, from steel portrait, by permission of D. Van Nostrand — Major General Thomas L. Crittenden, from Brady photo. — Capture of a Confederate Battery *(T. de Thulstrup)* — Scene in a Union Field-hospital *(A. C. Redwood)*.

SKIRMISHING IN SHERMAN'S FRONT . . . . *ROBERT W. MEDKIRK* 537

THE OPPOSING FORCES AT SHILOH. Composition, Strength, and Losses 537

ALBERT SIDNEY JOHNSTON AT SHILOH. } . . . . . . *COL. WILLIAM PRESTON JOHNSTON* . . 540
By his Son . . . . }

ILLUSTRATIONS: Albert Sidney Johnston at the Age of Thirty-five, from miniature — General Albert Sidney Johnston at the Age of Fifty-seven, from photo. — Fac-simile of Autograph found inside the Cover of General Johnston's Pocket-map of Tennessee — Birthplace of Albert Sidney Johnston, Washington, Ky., from photo. *(C. A. Vanderhoof)* — Fort Anderson, Paducah, in April, 1862, after lithograph from sketch by A. E. Mathews *(H. C. Edwards)* — Camp Burgess, Bowling Green, after lithograph from sketch by A. E. Mathews *(E. J. Meeker)* — Map of Kentucky and Tennessee *(Jacob Wells)* — Battle of Logan's Cross Roads, or Mill Springs, after lithograph from drawing by A. E. Mathews *(W. Taber)* — Colonel Schoepf's Troops crossing Fishing Creek on the way to join General Thomas, after lithograph from sketch by A. E. Mathews *(E. J. Meeker)* — Confederate Types of 1862 *(A. C. Redwood)* — Map used by the Confederate Generals at Shiloh, by permission of D. Appleton & Co. — Lieutenant-General W. J. Hardee, C. S. A., from photo. lent by Colonel Charles C. Jones, Jr. — Map of Battle of Shiloh (Part I.) and Map of Battle of Shiloh (Part II.), by permission of D. Appleton & Co. — Vicinity of the "Hornets' Nest," from photo's lent by Captain A. T. Andreas *(W. L. Lathrop)* — Scene of General Albert Sidney Johnston's Death, from photo. *(W. Taber)* — Map of Battle of Shiloh (Part III.), by permission of D. Appleton & Co.

THE CAMPAIGN OF SHILOH . . . . *GENERAL G. T. BEAUREGARD* 569

ILLUSTRATIONS: Preaching at the Union Camp Dick Robinson, Kentucky, after lithograph from sketch by A. E. Mathews *(E. J. Meeker)* — Lieutenant-General John C. Breckinridge, C. S. A., from Anderson-Cook photo. — Slaves Laboring at Night on the Confederate Earth-works at Corinth *(W. L. Sheppard)* — Five Corinth Dwellings, from photo's *(W. J. Fenn)* — Major-General Bushrod R. Johnson, C. S. A., from Anderson-Cook photo. — The "Hornets' Nest," from photo. lent by Captain A. T. Andreas *(E. J. Meeker)* — The Union Gun-boats at Shiloh on the Evening of the First Day, after lithograph from sketch by A. E. Mathews *(H. M. Eaton)*.

NOTES OF A CONFEDERATE STAFF-OFFICER } . . . *GENERAL THOMAS JORDAN* 594
AT SHILOH . . . . }

ILLUSTRATIONS: A Confederate Private of the West, from ambrotype — A Union Battery taken by Surprise *(R. F. Zogbaum)* — The Last Stand made by the Confederate Line *(R. F. Zogbaum)*.

PAGE

SURPRISE AND WITHDRAWAL AT SHILOH.......*COLONEL S. H. LOCKETT*..........604
    ILLUSTRATION: Initial (*R. F. Zogbaum*).

THE SHILOH BATTLE ORDER AND THE ⎫ ....*COLONEL A. R. CHISOLM*..........606
    WITHDRAWAL SUNDAY EVENING.. ⎭

THE MARCH OF LEW WALLACE'S DIVISION TO SHILOH,
    With Documents submitted by General Lew Wallace 607
    Map of the Routes by which General Grant was reënforced (*Jacob Wells*).

NAVAL PREPARATIONS.

THE UNION AND CONFEDERATE NAVIES.........*PROFESSOR J. R. SOLEY*............611
    ILLUSTRATIONS: A Frigate of the Olden Time: the "Independence," built in 1814, from photo. (*Granville Perkins*) — Roman War Galley — Line-of-battle Ship of the 17th Century — The U. S. Frigate "Merrimac" before and after Conversion into an Iron-clad (*J. O. Davidson*) — The Navy Yard, Washington, in 1861, from war-time sketch (*A. R. Waud*) — The Old Navy Department Building, Washington, from photo. (*W. Taber*) — Launch of the "Dictator," from photo. lent by Delamater & Co. (*W. Taber*) — Monitor "Weehawken" in a Storm (*Granville Perkins*) — Gideon Welles, Secretary of the U. S. Navy, from Brady photo.— Gustavus V. Fox, Assistant-Secretary of the U. S. Navy, from photo.— William Faxon, Chief Clerk of the U. S. Navy Department during the War, from photo. by Prescott & White.

COAST OPERATIONS IN THE CAROLINAS.

EARLY COAST OPERATIONS IN NORTH CAROLINA..*GENERAL RUSH C. HAWKINS*.......632
    (Including Capture and Defense of Hatteras Island, Land and Water Fighting at Roanoke Island, the Two Squadrons at Elizabeth City, Battle of New Berne, Siege of Fort Macon, Battle of South Mills, and other Operations.)
    ILLUSTRATIONS: Uniform of Hawkins's Zouaves, from photo. (*H. A. Ogden*) — Rear-Admiral Silas H. Stringham, from Brady photo.— Map of Early Coast Operations in North Carolina (*Jacob Wells*) — Forts Hatteras and Clark, from war-time sketch (*A. R. Waud*) — The "Cumberland" Sailing into Action, and Union Fleet Bombarding Forts Hatteras and Clark, from war-time sketches (*F. H. Schell and Thomas Hogan*) — Retreat of the Confederates to their Boats after their Attack upon Hatteras (*W. Taber*) — Landing of the Union Troops at Hatteras, from war-time sketch (*A. R. Waud*) — Map of the Operations at Roanoke Island, from Official Records — Map of the Battle-field of Roanoke Island, from Official Records — Union Assault upon the Three-gun Battery, Roanoke Island, from war-time sketch (*F. H. Schell*) — Vice-Admiral S. C. Rowan, from Brady photo.— Brigadier-General L. O'B. Branch, from photo.— Bombardment of Fort Thompson during the Battle of New Berne, from war-time sketch (*F. H. Schell*) — Major-General John G. Foster, from Brady photo.— Map of Operations in the Battle of New Berne (*Jacob Wells*) — Assault of Union Troops upon Fort Thompson, from war-time sketch (*F. H. Schell*) — Fort Macon after its Capture by the Union Forces, from war-time sketch by F. H. Schell (*Thomas Hogan*) — Map of the Engagement at South Mills (*Fred. E. Sitts*) — Passage of the Union Boats through the Dismal Swamp Canal, from war-time sketch by Horatio L. Wait (*E. J. Meeker*).

THE BURNSIDE EXPEDITION ....*GENERAL A. E. BURNSIDE*. 660
    ILLUSTRATIONS: Union Lookout, Hatteras Beach, from war-time sketch (*A. R. Waud*) — Uniform of the First Rhode Island (*H. A. Ogden*) — Brevet Brigadier-General Rush C. Hawkins, from Brady photo.— Rear-Admiral L. M. Goldsborough, from photo. lent by Henry Carey Baird — General Burnside's Headquarters, Roanoke Island, from war-time sketch by F. H. Schell (*Thomas Hogan*) — General Burnside at the Confederate Cotton Battery, New Berne, from war-time sketch by F. H. Schell (*Thomas Hogan*) — Brigadier-General Robert B. Vance, from tintype.

THE OPPOSING FORCES AT ROANOKE ISLAND AND NEW BERNE, NORTH CAROLINA 670

DU PONT AND THE PORT ROYAL EXPEDITION....*REAR-ADMIRAL DANIEL AMMEN*....671
    ILLUSTRATIONS: General View of Hilton Head after its Capture by the Union Forces and View of Post-Office, Hilton Head, from war-time sketches (*Xanthus Smith*) — Brevet Major-General Thomas W. Sherman, from Brady photo.— Map of the Coast of South Carolina and part of North Carolina (*Jacob Wells*) — Rear-Admiral Samuel F. Du Pont, from photo. lent by Horatio L. Wait — Gun-boat "Seneca" and Sloop of War "Vandalia," from war-time sketches (*Xanthus Smith*) — Map of Naval Attack at Hilton

Head, Nov. 7, 1861— United States Gun-boat "Mohawk," the Guard-ship at Port Royal— Attack of the Union Fleet at Hilton Head— Ten-inch Shell-gun which threw the Opening Shot from the Flag-ship "Wabash"— Bay Point and Fort Beauregard after Capture, and Rifle-gun at Fort Beauregard, five pictures from war-time sketches (*Xanthus Smith*)— Battle of the Union Fleet with Forts Beauregard and Walker, and Hoisting the Stars and Stripes over Fort Walker, from war-time sketches (*Frank H. Schell*)— Brigadier-General Thomas F. Drayton, C. S. A., from Brady photo.— Captain Percival Drayton, U. S. N., from Brady photo.— Old Headquarters, Hilton Head, and Pope's House, Hilton Head, used by the Union Army as Signal Station, from war-time sketches (*Xanthus Smith*)— Union Signal Station, Beaufort, S. C., House of J. G. Barnwell and Fuller's House, Beaufort, S. C., from Gardner photo's (*T. F. Moessner*).

THE OPPOSING FORCES AT PORT ROYAL. Composition and Losses......................691

"MONITOR" AND "MERRIMAC."

THE FIRST FIGHT OF IRON-CLADS...............*COLONEL JOHN TAYLOR WOOD*....692

ILLUSTRATIONS: Head-piece (*W. H. Drake*)— Burning of Frigate "Merrimac" and of Gosport Navy Yard, and Remodeling "Merrimac" at Gosport Navy Yard (*J. O. Davidson*)— Fac-simile of sketch of "Merrimac" made the day before the fight by Lieutenant B. L. Blackford— Lieutenant Catesby ap R. Jones, from photo. by Courret Hermans, Lima, Peru— Admiral Franklin Buchanan, C. S. N., and Commodore Josiah Tattnall, C. S. N., from photo. by D. J. Ryan— Colonel John Taylor Wood, from oil-portrait by Galt— Map of Hampton Roads and Adjacent Shores (*Jacob Wells*)— The "Merrimac" ramming the "Cumberland" (*J. O. Davidson*)— Lieutenant George U. Morris, from photo.— The "Merrimac" driving the "Congress" from her anchorage (*J. O. Davidson*)— Escape of part of the Crew of the "Congress" (*J. O. Davidson*)— Explosion on the burning "Congress" (*J. O. Davidson*)— Lieutenant Joseph B. Smith, from photo. by Black and Batchelder— Encounter between the "Monitor" and the "Merrimac" at short range (*J. O. Davidson*)— Captain G. J. Van Brunt, from photo.— The "Monitor" in Battle-trim, from tracing lent by Commander S. D. Greene.

WATCHING THE "MERRIMAC"...... ....*GENERAL R. E. COLSTON*...........712

ILLUSTRATION: The "Merrimac" passing the Confederate Battery on Craney Island (*J. O. Davidson*).

HOW THE GUN-BOAT "ZOUAVE" AIDED THE "CONGRESS" ....} *ACTING MASTER HENRY REANEY*...714

THE PLAN AND CONSTRUCTION OF THE "MERRIMAC" ....{ *COMMANDER JOHN M. BROOKE*.....715
} *CONSTRUCTOR JOHN L. PORTER*...716

ILLUSTRATION: Cross-section of the "Merrimac," from a drawing by John L. Porter.

NOTES ON THE "MONITOR"-"MERRIMAC" FIGHT..*SURGEON DINWIDDIE B. PHILLIPS*...718

IN THE "MONITOR" TURRET ....*COMMANDER S. DANA GREENE*......719

ILLUSTRATIONS: Arrival of the "Monitor" at Hampton Roads (*J. O. Davidson*)— Rear-Admiral John L. Worden, from photo.— Side Elevation and Deck-plan of the "Monitor," lent by Captain John Ericsson— Bird's-eye view of "Monitor"-"Merrimac" Fight (*J. O. Davidson*)— Part of the Crew of the "Monitor," from Gardner photo.— Commander Samuel Dana Greene, from photo. by Halleck.

THE BUILDING OF THE "MONITOR".............*CAPTAIN JOHN ERICSSON*...........730

ILLUSTRATIONS: Captain John Ericsson, from Brady photo.— Longitudinal Plan through Center Line of Original Monitor: 1, aft section; 2, central section; 3, forward section— Plan of Berth-deck of Original Monitor— and Transverse Section of Hull of Original Monitor, from drawings lent by Captain Ericsson— View showing Effect of Shot on the "Monitor" Turret, from Gardner photo.— Side Elevation of Floating Revolving Circular Tower, published by Abraham Bloodgood in 1807— Floating Circular Citadel submitted to French Directory in 1798, from "Engineering" (*W. Taber*)— Side Elevation and Transverse Section of Iron-clad Steam Battery proposed by Captain Ericsson to Napoleon III. in 1854, lent by Captain Ericsson— Engineer Isaac Newton, from medallion portrait by Launt Thompson— Transverse section of the "Monitor" through the center of the turret, lent by Captain Ericsson— Sinking of the "Monitor," December 22, 1862 (*J. O. Davidson*).

THE LOSS OF THE "MONITOR"................*FRANCIS B. BUTTS*..................745

NEGOTIATIONS FOR THE BUILDING OF THE "MONITOR"............................748

(Including Letters from C. S. Bushnell, Captain John Ericsson, and Secretary Gideon S. Welles.)
ILLUSTRATION: Union Soldier's Candlestick (*W. Taber*).

MAPS.

PAGE

THE UNITED STATES { Showing posts occupied by U. S. troops Jan. 1, 1861; limit of territory controlled by U. S. forces July, 1861; and blockade stations.. 8

PENSACOLA HARBOR, FLORIDA, MAY 27, 1861 28

CHARLESTON HARBOR AND VICINITY, SOUTH CAROLINA 44

EASTERN VIRGINIA AND MARYLAND.. 113

HARPER'S FERRY, VIRGINIA 115

CAMPAIGNS IN WEST VIRGINIA, 1861.. 129

COMBAT AT RICH MOUNTAIN, WEST VIRGINIA 131

GAULEY BRIDGE AND VICINITY, WEST VIRGINIA............................... 142

AFFAIR AT CARNIFEX FERRY, WEST VIRGINIA 145

DEFENSES OF WASHINGTON, D. C., JULY, 1861 172

OUTLINE MAP OF THE FIRST BULL RUN BATTLE-FIELD 180

THE FIRST BULL RUN CAMPAIGN 199

TOPOGRAPHICAL MAP OF THE FIRST BULL RUN BATTLE-FIELD 204

PLAN OF THE FIRST BULL RUN BATTLE-FIELD 233

OPERATIONS IN MISSOURI, 1861 263

BATTLE OF WILSON'S CREEK, OR OAK HILLS, MISSOURI......................... 290

SIEGE OF LEXINGTON, MISSOURI.. 309

BATTLE OF PEA RIDGE, OR ELKHORN TAVERN, ARKANSAS 322

BATTLE-FIELD NEAR BELMONT, MISSOURI 350

REGION OF FOOTE'S OPERATIONS 361

FORT HENRY, TENNESSEE 363

KENTUCKY AND TENNESSEE... 378

BATTLE OF LOGAN'S CROSS ROADS, OR MILL SPRINGS, KENTUCKY 388

BIG SANDY RIVER AND MIDDLE-CREEK BATTLE-FIELD, KENTUCKY 394

FORT DONELSON, TENNESSEE 402

REGION OF THE OPERATIONS OF THE WESTERN FLOTILLA 436

MILITARY AND NAVAL OPERATIONS ABOUT ISLAND NUMBER TEN, MISSISSIPPI RIVER, 437

CORRECTED LINE OF THE CHANNEL ABOVE ISLAND NUMBER TEN.................. 461

OUTLINE MAP OF THE SHILOH CAMPAIGN, WEST TENNESSEE 466

THE FIELD OF SHILOH. From General Grant's "Personal Memoirs." 470

LOCATION OF THE UNION CAMPS AT SHILOH ....496—497

THE FIELD OF SHILOH. From the Official Map, revised and amended by Gen. D. C. Buell, 502—503

OFFICIAL, OR THOM, MAP OF SHILOH 508

KENTUCKY AND TENNESSEE... 545

MAP USED BY THE CONFEDERATE GENERALS AT SHILOH 551

BATTLE OF SHILOH. PART I. From Col. W. P. Johnston's "Life of Gen. A. S. Johnston." 556

  "   "   "   " II.   "   "   "   "   " 560

  "   "   "   " III.   "   "   "   "   " 566

ROUTES BY WHICH GENERAL GRANT WAS REËNFORCED AT PITTSBURG LANDING ... 608

EARLY COAST OPERATIONS IN NORTH CAROLINA 634

OPERATIONS AT ROANOKE ISLAND, NORTH CAROLINA 641

BATTLE-FIELD OF ROANOKE ISLAND 643

BATTLE OF NEW BERNE, NORTH CAROLINA...................................... 651

CONTENTS OF VOLUME ONE.

PAGE

ENGAGEMENT AT SOUTH MILLS, NORTH CAROLINA 656

COAST OF NORTH AND SOUTH CAROLINA 673

NAVAL ATTACK AT HILTON HEAD, SOUTH CAROLINA 678

HAMPTON ROADS, VIRGINIA, AND ADJACENT SHORES 699

ARTISTS.

BRIDWELL, H. L.

BURNS, M. J.

COCKS, J. H.

DAVIDSON, J. O.

DAVIS, THEO. R.

DAY, FRANK

DRAKE, WILL. H.

EATON, HUGH M.

EDWARDS, G. W.

EDWARDS, H. C.

FENN, HARRY

FENN, WALTER J.

FORBES, EDWIN

GIBSON, GEORGE

GOATER, WALTER H.

HOGAN, THOMAS

HOSIER, ABRAM

HUNT, WILLIAM M.

KEMBLE, E. W.

LATHROP, W. L.

MEEKER, EDWIN J.

MOESSNER, T. F.

OGDEN, HENRY A.

PENNELL, JOSEPH

PERKINS, GRANVILLE

REDWOOD, ALLEN C.

SCHELL, FRANK H.

SCHELL, FRED. B.

SHELTON, W. H.

SHEPPARD, W. L.

SMITH, SIDNEY L.

SMITH, XANTHUS

STEPHENS, C. H.

TABER, WALTON

THULSTRUP, T. DE

VANDERHOOF, C. A.

VOLCK, A. J.

WALKE, HENRY,
    U. S. N.

WAUD, ALFRED R.

WAUD, WILLIAM

WOODWARD, J. D.

ZOGBAUM, RUFUS F.

DRAUGHTSMEN.

BROWN, G. H.

KEMP, J. S.

SITTS, FRED. E.

WELLS, JACOB

ENGRAVERS.

AITKEN, PETER

ANDREWS, JOHN

ATWOOD, K. C.

BABCOCK, H. E.

BARTLE, G. P.

BOGERT, J. A.

BUTLER, T. A.

CLEMENT, E.

CLEMENT, J.

COLE, TIMOTHY

COLLINS, R. C.

DANA, W. J.

DAVIDSON, H.

DAVIS, SAMUEL

ERTZ, EDWARD

EVANS, J. W.

FAY, GASTON

FILLEBROWN, F. E.

GARDNER, E. D.

HAYMAN, ARTHUR

HEARD, T. H.

HEINEMANN, E.

HELD, E. C.

HIRSCHMANN, W. A.

HOSKINS, ROBERT

IRWIN, ALLEN

JOHNSON, THOMAS

JUNGLING, J. F.

KARST, JOHN

KILBURN, S. S.

KINGSLEY, ELBRIDGE

KLASEN, W.

KRUELL, G.

LINDSAY, A.

LOCKHARDT, A.

MOLLIER, WILLIAM

MORSE, WILLIAM H.

MULLER, R. A.

NAYLOR, JESSIE

NEGRI, A.

NICHOLS, DAVID

OWENS, MARY L.

PECKWELL, H. W.

POWELL, C. A.

REED, C. H.

ROBERTS, W.

SCHUSSLER, T.

SCHWARTZBURGER, C.

SPIEGLE, CHARLES

STATE, CHARLES

SYLVESTER, H. E.

TICHENOR, E. R.

TIETZE, R. G.

TYNAN, JAMES

VELTEN, H.

WHITNEY, J. H. E.

WILLIAMS, G. P.

WINHAM, E. A.

WOLF, HENRY

WRIGHT, C.

PRELIMINARY EVENTS.

FROM THE CHARLESTON CONVENTION TO THE FIRST BATTLE OF BULL RUN.

1860.

APRIL 23. The National Convention of the Democratic Party assembled at Charleston, S. C. Dissensions arising in regard to the question of congressional protection of slavery in the territories, the Southern delegates withdrew, organized another convention in Charleston, and adjourned May 4th, to meet in Richmond, Va., June 11th.

May 3. The Douglas, or Northern, wing of the Convention adjourned, to reassemble at Baltimore, Md., June 18th.

May 9. The Convention of the Constitutional Union Party (formerly the American, or "Know-Nothing," Party), held at Baltimore, Md., nominated John Bell, of Tennessee, for President, and Edward Everett, of Massachusetts, for Vice-President, and adopted a platform evading the slavery issue.

May 18. The National Convention of the Republican Party, held at Chicago, nominated Abraham Lincoln, of Illinois, for President, and Hannibal Hamlin, of Maine, for Vice-President, and pronounced in favor of congressional prohibition of slavery in the territories.

June 23. The Northern "Democratic National Convention," nominated Stephen A. Douglas, of Illinois, for President, and Benjamin Fitzpatrick, for Vice-President. (The latter declined, and the National Committee substituted Herschel V. Johnson, of Georgia.) The convention declared in favor of leaving the question of slavery in the territories to the people of the territories, or to the Supreme Court of the United States.

June 28. The Southern "Democratic National Convention" (adjourned from Richmond) nominated, at Baltimore, Md., John C. Breckinridge, of Kentucky, for President, and Joseph Lane, of Oregon, for Vice-President. The convention declared that neither Congress nor a territorial legislature had the right to prohibit slavery in a territory, and that it was the duty of the Federal Government, in all its depart-

ments, to protect slavery in the territories when necessary.

November 6. Presidential election, resulting as follows :

	States.	Electoral Votes.	Popular Vote.
Lincoln	17	180	1,866,352
Breckinridge	11	72	845,763
Douglas	2	12	1,375,157
Bell	3	39	589,581

December 3. Meeting of Congress. Message from President Buchanan arguing against the right of secession, but expressing doubt as to the constitutional power of Congress to make war upon a State.

December 6. Select Committee of Thirty-three appointed by the House of Representatives to take measures for the perpetuity of the Union. (See "February 28.")

December 10. Resignation of Howell Cobb, of Georgia, Secretary of the Treasury.

December 12. Arrival of General Winfield Scott in Washington, to advise with the President.

December 14. Resignation of Lewis Cass, of Michigan, Secretary of State.

December 20. Ordinance of secession adopted in South Carolina by a convention called by the Legislature of the State.

December 26. United States troops, under Major Robert Anderson, transferred from Fort Moultrie to Fort Sumter, S. C.

December 27. Castle Pinckney and Fort Moultrie, Charleston Harbor, seized by the South Carolina authorities.

December 27. Surrender of the United States Revenue cutter *William Aiken* to the authorities of South Carolina.

December 27. Arrival in Washington of Messrs. Barnwell, Orr, and Adams, Commissioners from South Carolina, to treat with the administration.

December 29. Resignation of John B. Floyd, of Virginia, Secretary of War.

December 30. United States Arsenal, at Charleston, S. C., seized by the State authorities.

1861.

January 2. Fort Johnson, Charleston Harbor, seized by State authorities.

January 3. Fort Pulaski, Ga., seized by State authorities.

January 4. United States Arsenal, at Mt. Vernon, Ala., seized by State authorities.

January 5. Forts Morgan and Gaines, Mobile Bay, Ala., seized by State authorities.

January 5. Departure of first expedition for relief of Fort Sumter, S. C., from N. Y. Harbor.

January 6. United States Arsenal, at Apalachicola, Fla., seized by State authorities.

January 7. Fort Marion, St. Augustine, Fla., seized by State authorities.

January 8. Resignation of Jacob Thompson, of Mississippi, Secretary of the Interior.

January 9. Ordinance of secession adopted in Mississippi.

January 9. Fort Johnston, N. C., seized by citizens of Smithville.

January 9. The *Star of the West*, conveying relief to Fort Sumter, fired upon at the entrance to Charleston Harbor and driven back.

January 10. Fort Caswell, N. C., seized by citizens of Smithville and Wilmington.

January 10. Ordinance of secession adopted in Florida.

January 10. United States troops, under Lieut. Adam J. Slemmer, transferred from Barrancas Barracks to Fort Pickens, Pensacola, Fla.

January 10. Reënforcements for the troops at Pensacola sailed from Boston, Mass.

January 10. United States Arsenal and Barracks at Baton Rouge, La., seized by State authorities.

January 11. Ordinance of secession adopted in Alabama.

January 11. Surrender of Fort Sumter, S. C., demanded by Governor Pickens, of South Carolina, and refused by Major Anderson.

January 11. Forts Jackson and St. Philip, La., seized by State authorities.

January 11. United States Marine Hospital, near New Orleans, La., seized by State authorities.

January 12. Barrancas Barracks, Forts Barrancas and McRee, and the Navy Yard at Pensacola, Fla., seized by State authorities.

January 12. Surrender of Fort Pickens, Fla., demanded by the Governors of Florida and Alabama and refused by Lieutenant Slemmer.

January 14. Fort Taylor, Key West, Fla., garrisoned by United States troops.

January 14. Fort Pike, La., seized by State authorities.

January 15. United States Coast Survey steamer *Dana* seized at St. Augustine, Fla.

January 15. Second demand for the surrender of Fort Pickens, Fla.

January 18. Third demand for the surrender of Fort Pickens, Fla.

January 19. Ordinance of secession adopted in Georgia.

January 20. Fort on Ship Island, Miss., seized by State authorities.

January 24. Reënforcements for Fort Pickens, Fla., sailed from Fort Monroe, Va.

January 24. United States Arsenal, at Augusta, Ga., seized by State authorities.

January 26. Oglethorpe Barracks and Fort Jackson, Ga., seized by State authorities.

January 26. Ordinance of secession adopted in Louisiana.

January 28. Fort Macomb, La., seized by State authorities.

January 28. United States property in hands of army officers seized at New Orleans, La.

February 1. Ordinance of secession adopted in Texas.

February 1. United States Mint and Custom House, at New Orleans, La., seized by State authorities.

February 4. Meeting at Washington of a Peace Conference, representing 13 Free and 7 Border States, called at the request of the Virginia Legislature. (See " February 28.")

February 4. Convention of seceded States met at Montgomery, Ala.

February 6. The *Brooklyn* arrived off Pensacola with reënforcements for Fort Pickens, Fla.

February 7. The Choctaw Nation of Indians declared its adherence to the Southern States.

February 8. United States Arsenal, at Little Rock, Ark., seized by State authorities.

February 8. A "Constitution for the Provisional Government of the Confederate States of America" adopted at Montgomery, Ala., by deputies from the States of Alabama, Florida, Georgia, Louisiana, Mississippi, and South Carolina.

February 9. Jefferson Davis, of Mississippi, elected President, and Alexander H. Stephens, of Georgia, Vice-President, of " the Confederate States of America," by the Montgomery Convention, or Provisional Congress.

February 13. Abraham Lincoln and Hannibal Hamlin officially declared elected President and Vice-President of the United States.

February 15. Resolution passed by Confederate Congress for appointment of Commissioners to the Government of the United States.

February 16. United States Arsenal and Barracks at San Antonio, Tex., seized by State authorities.

February 18. All United States military posts in Texas surrendered to the State authorities by General David E. Twiggs, U. S. Army.

February 18. Jefferson Davis and Alexander H. Stephens inaugurated at Montgomery, Ala.

February 20. Act passed by Confederate Congress to provide munitions of war.

February 21. Camp Cooper, Texas, abandoned by United States troops. (During the next six months other United States military posts in Texas and New Mexico were abandoned.— See map, page 8.)

February 23. Abraham Lincoln arrived in Washington.

February 26. Act passed by Confederate Congress to organize a general staff for the army.

February 28. Adoption by the United States House of Representatives of the amendment offered by the Committee of Thirty-three, forbidding any interference by Congress with slavery in the States. (This amendment was adopted by the Senate March 2, but was never adopted by the necessary number of States.)

February 28. Act passed by Confederate Congress to raise provisional forces.

March 1. The President of the Confederate States assumed control of military affairs in the States of Alabama, Florida, Georgia, Louisiana, Mississippi, South Carolina, and Texas.

March 2. United States Revenue cutter *Dodge* seized at Galveston, Tex., by State authorities.

March 2. Texas admitted as a member of the Confederate States of America.

March 3. Brig.-General G. T. Beauregard, C. S. Army, assumed command at Charleston, S. C.

March 4. Abraham Lincoln inaugurated as President of the United States.

March 6. Confederate Congress passed act for the establishment of an army, not to exceed 100,000 men, for 12 months' service.

March 7. Ringgold Barracks, Tex., abandoned.

March 7. Camp Verde, Tex., abandoned.

March 11. Brig.-General Braxton Bragg assumed command of the Confederate forces in Florida.

March 11. Adoption of the "Constitution of the Confederate States of America," at Montgomery, Ala., following in general the Constitution of the United States, but prohibiting the passage of any "law denying or impairing the right of property in negro slaves"; prohibiting "the importation of negroes of the African race from any foreign country other than the slave-holding States and territories of the United States of America," and giving to the Confederate Congress "power to prohibit the introduction of slaves from any State not a member of, or territory not belonging to," the Confederacy. The preamble included a declaration of the "sovereign and independent character" of each State.

March 15. Confederate Congress passed act authorizing the construction or purchase of ten gun-boats.

April 7. Reënforcements for Fort Pickens sailed from New York.

April 10. Second expedition for the relief of Fort Sumter sailed from New York.

April 11. Evacuation of Fort Sumter demanded by General Beauregard.

April 12. Reënforcements from Fort Monroe, Va., landed at Fort Pickens, Fla.

April 12. Bombardment of Fort Sumter commenced.

April 13. Fort Sumter surrendered.

April 14. Fort Sumter evacuated by its garrison and occupied by Confederate troops.

April 15. President Lincoln issued a call for 75,000 militia for 3 months' service, and a summons to Congress to assemble on July 4th.

April 15. Fort Macon, N. C., seized by State authorities.

April 16. Forts Caswell and Johnston, N.C., seized by State authorities.

April 17. Reënforcements from New York landed at Fort Pickens, Fla.

April 17. Confederate President called for 32,000 troops, and offered letters of marque against United States commerce.

April 17. Ordinance of secession adopted in Virginia by Convention, subject to popular vote.

April 18. United States Armory at Harper's Ferry abandoned and burned.

April 19. President Lincoln announced the blockade of Southern ports, from South Carolina to Texas inclusive.

April 19. Conflict between U. S. troops and mob in Baltimore, Md.

April 19. Major-General Robert Patterson, Pennsylvania Militia, assigned to command over the States of Delaware, Pennsylvania, and Maryland, and the District of Columbia.

April 20. Expedition from Fort Monroe to destroy dry-dock at Norfolk, Va.

April 20. United States Arsenal at Liberty, Mo., seized by armed secessionists.

April 21. United States Branch Mint at Charlotte, N. C., seized by State authorities.

April 21. Colonel Earl Van Dorn, C. S. Army, assumed command in Texas.

April 22. United States Arsenal at Fayetteville, N. C., seized by State authorities.

April 23. Fort Smith, Ark., seized by State authorities.

April 23. United States army officers at San Antonio, Tex., seized as prisoners of war.

April 23. Company of 8th U. S. Infantry (Lee's) captured near San Antonio, Tex.

April 23. Captain Nathaniel Lyon, U. S. Army, assumed temporary command of the Department of the West.

April 23. Major-General Robert E. Lee assigned to the command of the forces of Virginia.

April 26. Major-General Joseph E. Johnston, Virginia Volunteers, assigned to command of the State forces in and about Richmond, Va.

April 27. Blockade of Virginia and North Carolina ports announced.

April 27. Major-General Robert Patterson, Pennsylvania Militia, assigned to command of the Department of Pennsylvania.

April 27. Brig.-General B. F. Butler, Massachusetts Militia, assigned to command of the Department of Annapolis.

April 27. Colonel J. K. F. Mansfield, U. S. Army, assigned to command of the Department of Washington.

April 27. Colonel T. J. Jackson, Virginia Volunteers, assigned to command at Harper's Ferry.

May 1. Volunteer forces called for by the Governor of Virginia.

May 3. Additional forces called for in Virginia.

May 3. President Lincoln issued call for volunteers to serve three years; ordered the regular army to be increased, and directed the enlistment of additional seamen.

May 4. Colonel G. A. Porterfield, Virginia Vols., assigned to command in Northwestern Virginia.

May 6. Ordinance of secession adopted in Arkansas.

May 6. Confederate Congress passed act "recognizing the existence of war between the United States and the Confederate States, and concerning letters of marque, prizes, and prize goods."

May 7. Tennessee entered into military league with the Confederate States.

May 7. Arlington Heights, Va., occupied by Virginia troops.

May 7. Virginia admitted as a member of the Confederate States of America.

May 9. Exchange of shots between U. S. steamer *Yankee* and the batteries at Gloucester Point, Va.

May 10. Major-General Robert E. Lee assigned to command of Confederate forces in Virginia.

May 10. Camp Jackson, St. Louis, Mo., captured by U. S. forces under Captain Nathaniel Lyon.

May 11. Riot in St. Louis, Mo.

May 11. Brig.-General W. S. Harney, U. S. Army, resumed command of the Department of the West.

May 13. Brig.-General Ben. McCulloch, C. S. Army, assigned to command in the Indian Territory.

May 13. Baltimore occupied by General Butler.

May 13. Major-General G. B. McClellan, U. S. Army, assigned to command of the Department of Ohio, including a portion of West Virginia.

May 15. Brig.-General J. E. Johnston, C. S. Army, assigned to command near Harper's Ferry, Va.

May 15. Brevet Major-General George Cadwalader, Pennsylvania Militia, superseded General Butler in the Department of Annapolis.

May 17. Acts passed by Confederate Congress providing, upon certain conditions, for the admission of North Carolina and Tennessee as members of the Confederate States of America.

May 18. Naval attack on batteries at Sewell's Point, Va.

May 20. Ordinance of secession adopted in North Carolina.

May 21. Brig.-General M. L. Bonham, C. S. Army, assigned to command on the "Alexandria Line," Va.

May 21. Colonel J. B. Magruder, Provisional Army of Virginia, assigned to command at Yorktown.

May 21. Convention between General Harney, U. S. Army, and General Sterling Price, Missouri State Guard, with a view to the preservation of order in the State.

May 22. Brig.-General B. F. Butler assigned to command at Fort Monroe, Va.

May 23. Demonstration against Hampton, Va.

May 23. Brig.-General Benj. Huger, Virginia Volunteers, assigned to command at Norfolk, Va.

May 24. Resolutions of mediation and neutrality adopted in Kentucky.

May 24. Union troops advanced into Virginia and occupied Arlington Heights and Alexandria.

May 26-30. Union troops advanced from the Ohio River and occupied Grafton, West Virginia.

May 27-29. Union troops advanced from Fort Monroe and occupied Newport News, Va.

May 28. Brig.-General Irvin McDowell, U. S. Army, assumed command of the Department of Northeastern Virginia.

May 31. Brig.-General Nathaniel Lyon superseded General W. S. Harney in command of the Department of the West.

May 31. Naval attack on batteries at Aquia Creek, Va.

June 1. Skirmishes at Arlington Mills and Fairfax Court House, Va.

June 2. Brig.-General Beauregard superseded General Bonham in command on the "Alexandria Line."

June 3. Action at Philippi, W. Va.

June 5. Naval attack on batteries at Pig Point, Va.

June 6. Brig.-General Henry A. Wise, C. S. Army, ordered to command in the Kanawha Valley, W. Va.

June 6. Virginia State military and naval forces transferred to the Confederate States.

June 7. Confederate reconnoissance from Yorktown to Newport News, Va.

June 8. Brig.-General R. S. Garnett, C. S. Army, assigned to command in Northwestern Va.

June 10. Engagement at Big Bethel, or Bethel Church, Va.

June 10. Brig.-General Beauregard in command of all Confederate forces in Prince William, Fairfax, and Loudoun counties, Va.

June 11. Maj.-General Cadwalader superseded by Maj.-General Banks in Department of Annapolis.

June 13. Descent of Union troops upon Romney, W. Va.

June 15. Harper's Ferry, Va., evacuated by Confederate forces.

June 17. Engagement at Booneville, Mo.

June 17. Action at Camp Cole, Mo.

June 17. Action at Vienna, Va.

July 2. General Patterson's command crossed the Potomac at Williamsport.

July 2. Advance of General George H. Thomas's command, and engagement at Falling Waters, Va.

July 5. Engagement near Carthage, Mo.

July 8. Brig.-General Henry H. Sibley, C. S. Army, ordered to Texas to expel Union forces from New Mexico.

July 9. Skirmish at Vienna, Va.

July 10. Skirmish at Laurel Hill, W. Va.

July 11. Engagement at Rich Mountain, W. Va.

July 13. Major-General Leonidas Polk, C. S. Army, assumed command of Department No. 2, with headquarters at Memphis.

July 13. Action at Carrick's Ford, W. Va.

July 13. Surrender of Pegram's Confederate forces in Western Virginia.

July 14. Brig.-General H. R. Jackson ordered to command of Confederate forces in Western Va.

July 15. Military forces, stores, etc., of Arkansas transferred to the Confederate States.

July 16. Union advance toward Manassas, Va.

July 17. Confederate army retired to the line of Bull Run, Va.

July 17. Skirmish at Fairfax Court House, Va.

July 18. Skirmish at Mitchell's Ford, Va.

July 18. Action at Blackburn's Ford, Va.

July 18-21. Confederate forces from the Shenandoah Valley, under General Joseph E. Johnston, reënforced the army of General Beauregard at Manassas, Va.

July 20. Brig.-General William W. Loring, C. S. Army, assigned to command of "Northwestern Army" (Western Virginia).

July 21. Battle of Bull Run, or Manassas, Va.

ORGANIZATION OF THE TWO GOVERNMENTS.

THE UNITED STATES GOVERNMENT.

I. THE BUCHANAN ADMINISTRATION.
(1857–1861.)

President: JAMES BUCHANAN (Pa.)
Vice-President: JOHN C. BRECKINRIDGE* (Ky.)
Secretary of State: LEWIS CASS (Mich.); JEREMIAH S. BLACK (Pa.), appointed Dec. 17, 1860.
Secretary of War: JOHN B. FLOYD* (Va.); JOSEPH HOLT (Ky.) *(ad interim)*, Dec. 31, 1860; regularly appointed Jan. 18, 1861.
Secretary of the Navy: ISAAC TOUCEY (Conn.)
Secretary of the Treasury: HOWELL COBB* (Georgia); PHILIP F. THOMAS (Md.), appointed Dec. 12, 1860; JOHN A. DIX (N. Y.), appointed Jan. 11, 1861.
Attorney-General: JEREMIAH S. BLACK; EDWIN M. STANTON (Pa.), appointed Dec. 20, 1860.
Secretary of the Interior: JACOB THOMPSON* (Miss.)
Postmaster-General: AARON V. BROWN (Tenn.), died Mar. 8, 1859; JOSEPH HOLT (Ky.), appointed Mar. 14, 1859; HORATIO KING (Maine), appointed Feb. 12, 1861.

II. THE LINCOLN ADMINISTRATION.
(1861–1865.)

President: ABRAHAM LINCOLN (Ill.)
Vice-President: HANNIBAL HAMLIN (Maine).
Secretary of State: WILLIAM H. SEWARD (New York).
Secretary of War: SIMON CAMERON (Pa.); EDWIN M. STANTON (Pa.), appointed Jan. 15, 1862.
Secretary of the Navy: GIDEON WELLES (Conn.)
Secretary of the Treasury: SALMON P. CHASE (Ohio); W. P. FESSENDEN (Maine), appointed July 1, 1864; HUGH McCULLOCH (Ind.), appointed March 7, 1865.
Secretary of the Interior: CALEB B. SMITH (Ind.); JOHN P. USHER (Ind.), appointed January 8, 1863.
Attorney-General: EDWARD BATES (Mo.); JAMES SPEED (Ky.), appointed Dec. 2, 1864.
Postmaster-General: MONTGOMERY BLAIR (Md.); WILLIAM DENNISON (Ohio), appointed September 24, 1864.

THE UNITED STATES WAR DEPARTMENT.

Secretary of War: JOSEPH HOLT (appointed Jan. 18, 1861); SIMON CAMERON (appointed March 5, 1861); EDWIN M. STANTON (appointed January 15, 1862).
Assistant Secretaries of War: THOMAS A. SCOTT (appointed Aug. 3, 1861; PETER H. WATSON (appointed Jan. 24, 1862); JOHN TUCKER (appointed Jan. 29, 1862); CHRISTOPHER P. WOLCOTT (appointed June 12, 1862; resigned Jan. 23, 1863); CHARLES A. DANA (appointed August, 1863). (Colonel Scott was regularly commissioned under the act of August 3, 1861, authorizing the appointment of one assistant secretary of war. Subsequently three assistant secretaries were authorized by law.)
Adjutant-General's Department: Colonel SAMUEL COOPER* (resigned March 7, 1861); Brig.-Gen. LORENZO THOMAS (assigned to other duty March 23, 1863); Colonel EDWARD D. TOWNSEND.
Quartermaster's Department: Brig.-Gen. JOSEPH E. JOHNSTON* (resigned April 22, 1861); Brig.-Gen. MONTGOMERY C. MEIGS.
Subsistence Department: Colonel GEORGE GIBSON (died Sept. 29, 1861); Brig.-Gen. JOSEPH P. TAYLOR (died Jan. 29, 1864); Brig.-Gen. AMOS B. EATON.
Medical Department: Colonel THOMAS LAWSON (died May 15, 1861); Colonel CLEMENT A. FINLEY (retired April 14, 1862); Brig.-Gen. WILLIAM A. HAMMOND; Brig.-Gen. JOSEPH K. BARNES (appointed Aug. 22, 1864).
Pay Department: Colonel BENJAMIN F. LARNED (died Sept. 6, 1862); Colonel TIMOTHY P. ANDREWS (retired Nov. 29, 1864); Brig.-Gen. BENJAMIN W. BRICE.
Corps of Topographical Engineers: Colonel JOHN J. ABERT (retired Sept. 9, 1861); Colonel STEPHEN H. LONG. (This corps was consolidated with the "Corps of Engineers," under act of March 3, 1863.)
Corps of Engineers: Brig.-Gen. JOSEPH G. TOTTEN (died April 22, 1864); Brig.-Gen. RICHARD DELAFIELD.
Ordnance Department: Colonel HENRY K. CRAIG (until April 23, 1861); Brig.-Gen. JAMES W. RIPLEY (retired Sept. 15, 1863); Brig.-Gen. GEORGE D. RAMSAY (retired Sept. 12, 1864); Brig.-Gen. ALEXANDER B. DYER.
Bureau of Military Justice: Major JOHN F. LEE (resigned Sept. 4, 1862); Brig.-Gen. JOSEPH HOLT.
Bureau of the Provost Marshal General (created by act of March 3, 1863): Brig.-Gen. JAMES B. FRY.
General Officers of the United States Army, January 1, 1861: Brevet Lieut.-Gen. WINFIELD SCOTT (General-in-chief); Brig.-Generals: JOHN E. WOOL, DAVID E. TWIGGS,* WILLIAM S. HARNEY. (NOTE.— E. V. Sumner was promoted Brigadier-General March 16, 1861, *vice* David E. Twiggs, dismissed March 1, 1861.)

THE UNITED STATES NAVY DEPARTMENT.

Secretary of the Navy: GIDEON WELLES.
Assistant Secretary: GUSTAVUS V. FOX.
Yards and Docks: Rear-Admiral JOSEPH SMITH.
Ordnance and Hydrography: Captain GEORGE A. MAGRUDER (dismissed April 22, 1861); Captain ANDREW A. HARWOOD (relieved July 22, 1862); Rear-Admiral JOHN A. DAHLGREN (relieved June 24, 1863); Commander HENRY A. WISE. (By act of Congress of July 5, 1862, "Hydrography" was transferred to the Bureau of Navigation.)
Navigation (established by act of July 5, 1862): Rear-Admiral CHARLES H. DAVIS.
Equipment and Recruiting (established by act of July 5, 1862): Rear-Admiral ANDREW H. FOOTE (relieved June 3, 1863); Commander ALBERT N. SMITH.
Construction, Equipment, and Repair: Chief Naval Constructor JOHN LENTHALL. (By act of July 5, 1862, the "Equipment and Recruiting" Bureau was organized, and thereafter the old bureau was designated as "Construction and Repair.")
Provisions and Clothing: Pay-Director HORATIO BRIDGE.
Medicine and Surgery: Surgeon WILLIAM WHELAN.
Steam-Engineering (established by act of July 5, 1862): Engineer-in-Chief BENJAMIN F. ISHERWOOD.

* Afterward in the Confederate service.

THE CONFEDERATE STATES GOVERNMENT.

President: JEFFERSON DAVIS (Miss.)   *Vice-President:* ALEXANDER H. STEPHENS (Ga.)

I. PROVISIONAL ORGANIZATION.

(Feb. 8, 1861.)

Secretary of State: ROBERT TOOMBS (Ga.), Feb. 21, 1861; R. M. T. HUNTER, (Va.) July 24, 1861.

Secretary of War: LEROY P. WALKER (Ala.), Feb. 21, 1861; JUDAH P. BENJAMIN (La.), Sept. 17, 1861.

Secretary of the Navy: STEPHEN R. MALLORY (Fla.), Feb. 25, 1861.

Secretary of the Treasury: CHRISTOPHER G. MEM- MINGER (S. C.), Feb. 21, 1861.

Attorney-General: JUDAH P. BENJAMIN, Feb. 25, 1861; THOMAS BRAGG, (Ala.), Sept. 17, 1861.

Postmaster-General: J. H. REAGAN (Texas), March 6, 1861.

II. REORGANIZATION.

(Feb. 22, 1862, to April, 1865.)

Secretary of State: R. M. T. HUNTER, July 24, 1861; JUDAH P. BENJAMIN, March 17, 1862.

Secretary of War: JUDAH P. BENJAMIN, Sept. 17, 1861; GEORGE W. RANDOLPH, March 17, 1862; GUSTAVUS W. SMITH, acting, Nov. 17, 1862; JAMES A. SEDDON, Nov. 20, 1862; JOHN C. BRECKINRIDGE, Jan. 28, 1865.

Secretary of the Navy: STEPHEN R. MALLORY.

Secretary of the Treasury: C. G. MEMMINGER; GEORGE A. TRENHOLM, June, 1864.

Attorney-General: THOMAS BRAGG; THOMAS H. WATTS (Ala), March 17, 1862; GEORGE DAVIS (N. C.), 1864-5.

Postmaster-General: JOHN H. REAGAN.

THE CONFEDERATE STATES WAR DEPARTMENT.

Secretary of War: (see above).

Assistant Secretary of War: ALBERT T. BLEDSOE (April 1, 1862); JOHN A. CAMPBELL (October 20, 1862).

Adjt. and Insp.-Gen's Dep't: General SAMUEL COOPER.

Quartermaster-General's Dep't: Colonel ABRAM C. MYERS (March 15, 1861); Brig.-Gen. A. R. LAWTON (Aug. 10, 1863).

Commissary-General's Dep't: Colonel LUCIUS B. NOR- THROP (March 16, 1861); Brig.-Gen. I. M. ST. JOHN (Feb- ruary 16, 1865).

Ordnance Dep't: Brig.-Gen. JOSIAH GORGAS.

Engineer Bureau: Maj.-Gen. JEREMY F. GILMER.

Medical Dep't: Brig.-Gen. SAMUEL P. MOORE.

Nitre and Mining Bureau: Brig.-Gen. I. M. ST. JOHN; Colonel RICHARD MORTON (Feb. 16, 1865).

Conscription Bureau: Brig.-Gen. JOHN S. PRESTON, Chief; Col. T. P. AUGUST, Supt.

Prison Camps: Brig.-Gen. JOHN H. WINDER.

Exchange of Prisoners: Col. ROBERT OULD, Chief.

Commissioner of Patents: RUFUS R. RHODES.

THE CONFEDERATE STATES NAVY DEPARTMENT.

Secretary of the Navy: STEPHEN R. MALLORY.

Orders and Detail: Captain FRENCH FORREST; Com- mander JOHN K. MITCHELL.

Ordnance and Hydrography: Commander GEORGE MINOR; Commander JOHN M. BROOKE.

Provisions and Clothing: Assis't Surgeon JOHN DE BREE.

Medicine and Surgery: Surgeon W. A. W. SPOTS- WOOD.

GOVERNORS OF THE STATES DURING THE WAR.

UNION STATES: *California,* JOHN G. DOWNEY (1860-1), LELAND STANFORD (1861-3), FREDERICK F. LOW (1863-8); *Connecticut,* WILLIAM A. BUCKINGHAM (1858-66); *Delaware,* WILLIAM BURTON (1859-63), WILLIAM CANNON (1863-7); *Illinois,* RICHARD YATES (1861-5); *Indiana,* OLIVER P. MORTON (1861-7); *Iowa,* SAMUEL J. KIRKWOOD (1860-4), WILLIAM M. STONE (1864-8); *Kansas,* CHARLES ROBINSON (1861-3), THOMAS CARNEY (1863-5); *Maine,* IS- RAEL WASHBURN, JR. (1861-3), ABNER COBURN (1863-4), SAMUEL CONY (1864-7); *Massachusetts,* JOHN A. ANDREW (1861-6); *Michigan,* AUSTIN BLAIR (1861-4), HENRY H. CRAPO (1865-9); *Minnesota,* ALEXANDER RAMSEY (1859-63), STEPHEN MILLER (1863-6); *Nevada* (State admitted 1864), HENRY G. BLASDELL (1864-71); *New Hampshire,* ICHA- BOD GOODWIN (1859-61), NATHANIEL S. BERRY (1861-3), JOSEPH A. GILMORE (1863-5); *New Jersey,* CHARLES S. OLDEN (1860-3), JOEL PARKER (1863-6); *New York,* EDWIN D. MORGAN (1859-63), HORATIO SEYMOUR (1863-5), REU- BEN E. FENTON (1865-9); *Ohio,* WILLIAM DENNISON (1860-2), DAVID TOD (1862-4), JOHN BROUGH (1864-5); *Oregon,* JOHN WHITTAKER (1859-62), ADDISON C. GIBBS (1862-6); *Pennsylvania,* ANDREW G. CURTIN (1861-7); *Rhode Island,* WILLIAM SPRAGUE (1860-1), JOHN R. BART- LETT, acting (1861-2), WILLIAM C. COZZENS, acting (1863). JAMES Y. SMITH (1863-5); *Vermont,* ERASTUS FAIRBANKS (1860-1), FREDERIC HOLBROOK (1861-3), J. GREGORY SMITH (1863-5); *West Virginia* (admitted 1863), Provi- sional Governor, FRANCIS H. PEIRPOINT (1861-3), AR- THUR I. BOREMAN (1863-9); *Wisconsin,* ALEXANDER W. RANDALL (1857-61), LOUIS P. HARVEY (1861-2), EDWARD SALOMON (1862-3), JAMES T. LEWIS (1863-6).

CONFEDERATE STATES: *Alabama,* ANDREW B. MOORE (1857-61), JOHN GILL SHORTER (1861-3), THOMAS H. WATTS (1863-5); *Arkansas,* HENRY M. RECTOR (1860-3), HARRIS FLANAGIN (1863-4), ISAAC MURPHY (1864-8); *Florida,* MADISON S. PERRY (1857-61), JOHN MILTON (1861-5); *Georgia,* JOSEPH E. BROWN (1857-65); *Louisiana,* THOMAS O. MOORE (1860-4), HENRY W. ALLEN (1864-5); Union Military Governors, GEORGE F. SHEPLEY (1862-4), MICHAEL HAHN (1864-5); *Mississippi,* JOHN J. PETTUS (1860-2), CHARLES CLARKE (1863), JACOB THOMPSON (1863-4); *North Carolina,* JOHN W. ELLIS (1859-61), H. T. CLARK, acting (1861-2), ZEBULON B. VANCE (1862-5); *South Carolina,* FRANCIS W. PICKENS (1860-2), M. L. BONHAM (1862-4), A. G. MAGRATH (1864-5); *Tennessee,* ISHAM G. HARRIS (1857-65), ANDREW JOHNSON, Union Military Governor (1862-5); *Texas,* SAMUEL HOUSTON (1859-61), EDWARD CLARK, acting (1861), FRANCIS R. LUBBOCK 1861-3), PENDLETON MURRAH (1863-5); *Virginia,* JOHN LETCHER (1860-4), WILLIAM SMITH, (1864-5).

BORDER STATES: *Kentucky,* BERIAH MAGOFFIN (1859-62), JAMES F. ROBINSON (1862-3); THOMAS E. BRAM- LETTE (1863-7); *Maryland,* THOMAS H. HICKS (1857-61), A. W. BRADFORD (1861-5); *Missouri,* C. F. JACKSON (1861); Union, H. R. GAMBLE (1861-4), T. C. FLETCHER (1864-8).

N. B.— The Confederate Government of Kentucky was provisional in its character. George W. Johnson was elected Governor by the Russellville Convention in November, 1861. He served until he was killed in action at the battle of Shiloh. Richard Hawes was elected by the Provisional Council of Kentucky to succeed him, and acted as the Confederate Provisional Governor of Kentucky from 1862 until the close of the war.— In Missouri Thomas C. Reynolds was the Confederate Governor from 1862 to 1865; but after 1861 a Confederate Governor of Missouri was little more than a name.— In Tennessee, Governor Harris being ineligible for a fourth term, Robert L. Caruthers was elected Governor in August, 1863. Tennessee and her capital being then occupied by the United States forces, Mr. Caruthers was never inaugurated, and Governor Harris held over under the law.

WASHINGTON ON THE EVE OF THE WAR.

BY CHARLES P. STONE, BRIGADIER-GENERAL, U. S. V.

ROTUNDA OF THE CAPITOL IN 1861.

ALL who knew Washington in the days of December, 1860, know what thoughts reigned in the minds of thinking men. Whatever their daily occupations, they went about them with their thoughts always bent on the possible disasters of the near future. The country was in a curious and alarming condition: South Carolina had already passed an ordinance of secession, and other States were preparing to follow her lead. The only regular troops near the capital of the country were 300 or 400 marines at the marine barracks, and 3 officers and 53 men of ordnance at the Washington arsenal. The old militia system had been abandoned (without being legally abolished), and Congress had passed no law establishing a new one. The only armed volunteer organizations in the District of Columbia were: The Potomac Light Infantry, 1 company, at Georgetown; the National Rifles, 1 company, in Washington; the Washington Light Infantry, of about 160 men, and another small organization called the National Guard Battalion. It had been evident for months that, on assembling in December, Congress would have far different work to consider than the organization of the District of Columbia militia. Nor in the delicate position of affairs would it be the policy of President Buchanan, at the outset of the session, to propose the military organization of the Federal District. It was also evident that, should he be so disposed, the senators and representatives of the Southern States would oppose and denounce the project.

What force, then, would the Government have at its disposal in the Federal District for the simple maintenance of order in case of need? Evidently but a handful; and as to calling thither promptly any regular troops, that was out of the question, since they had already all been distributed by the Southern sympathizers to the distant frontiers of the Indian country,— Texas, Utah, New Mexico, Oregon, and Washington Territory.☆ Months would have been

☆ In December, 1860, the military forces of the United States consisted of 1108 officers and 15,-259 men of the regular army; total, 16,367. The distribution of the army may be inferred from the map printed on page 8, and from the following "memorandum" (made on the 6th of December, 1875), by Adjutant-General E. D. Townsend, exhibiting "certain changes in the stations of troops made under the orders of the Secretary of War, John B. Floyd, during the years 1858-60":

"After the removal of the troops to Kansas and Utah at the close of Indian hostilities in Florida, in June, 1858, there were left in the country east of the Mississippi River 16 companies of artillery. From that time (June, 1858) till Decem-

ber 31, 1860, some changes of stations occurred, by which the Department of the East gained 3 companies (2 of artillery and 1 of engineers), so that at the end of 1860 there were 18 companies of artillery and 1 of engineers serving east of the Mississippi River. There were no troops in the neighborhood of Washington during the whole of Secretary Floyd's term of office. In the spring and summer of 1860 the force in Utah was reduced to 3 companies of dragoons, 3 companies of artillery, and 4 companies of infantry. The remainder (13 companies of infantry and 2 of dragoons) were sent to New Mexico, relieving 1 regiment of infantry already there, which thereupon proceeded to Texas. No other changes of importance were made during the period in question."— EDITORS.

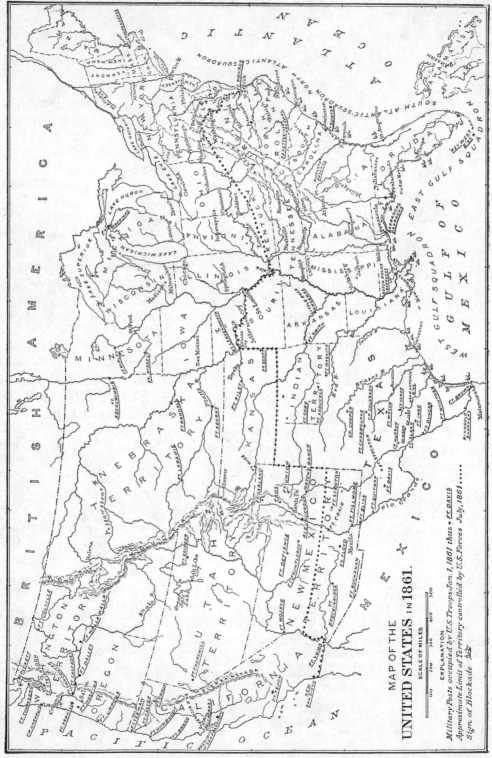

MAP OF THE
UNITED STATES IN 1861.

SCALE OF MILES

100   200   300   400   500

EXPLANATION

Military Posts occupied by U.S.Troops Jan.1, 1861 thus +Ft.Davis
Approximate Limit of Territory controlled by U.S.Forces July,1861......
Sign of Blockade ...

necessary to concentrate at Washington, in that season, a force of three thousand regular troops. Even had President Buchanan been desirous of bringing troops to the capital, the feverish condition of the public mind would, as the executive believed, have been badly affected by any movement of the kind, and the approaching crisis might have been precipitated. I saw at once that the only force which could be readily made of service was a volunteer force raised from among the well-disposed men of the District, and that this must be organized, if at all, under the old law of 1799. By consultation with gentlemen well acquainted with the various classes of Washington society, I endeavored to learn what proportion of the able-bodied population could be counted on to sustain the Government should it need support from the armed and organized citizens.

On the 31st of December, 1860, Lieutenant-General Scott, General-in-Chief of the army (who had his headquarters in New York), was in Washington. The President, at last thoroughly alarmed at the results of continued concessions to secession, had summoned him for consultation. On the evening of that day I went to pay my respects to my old commander, and was received by him at Wormley's hotel. He chatted pleasantly with me for a few minutes, recalling past service in the Mexican war, etc.; and when the occasion presented itself, I remarked that I was glad to see him in good spirits, for that proved to me that he took a more cheerful view of the state of public affairs than he had on his arrival — more cheerful than we of Washington had dared to take during the past few days.

UNIFORM OF THE NATIONAL RIFLES. FROM A PHOTOGRAPH.

"Yes, my young friend," said the general, "I feel more cheerful about the affairs of the country than I did this morning; for I believe that a safer policy than has hitherto been followed will now be adopted. The policy of entire conciliation, which has so far been pursued, would soon have led to ruin. We are now in such a state that a policy of pure force would precipitate a crisis for which we are not prepared. A mixed policy of force and conciliation is now necessary, and I believe it will be adopted and carried out." He then looked at his watch, rose, and said: "I must be with the President in a quarter of an hour," and ordered his carriage. He walked up and down the dining-room, but suddenly stopped and faced me, saying: "How is the feeling in the District of Columbia? What proportion of the population would sustain the Government by force, if necessary?"

UNIFORM OF THE POTOMAC LIGHT INFANTRY. FROM A PHOTOGRAPH.

"It is my belief, General," I replied, "that two-thirds of

WINFIELD SCOTT, BREVET LIEUTENANT-GENERAL, U. S. A.   FROM A PHOTOGRAPH.

General Scott was General-in-Chief of the army until November 1, 1861, when he was placed upon the
retired list on his own application, and was succeeded by Major-General George B. McClellan.
He died at West Point in May, 1866, in his eightieth year.

the fighting stock of this population would sustain the Government in defending itself, if called upon. But they are uncertain as to what can be done or
what the Government desires to have done, and they have no rallying-point."

The general walked the room again in silence. The carriage came to the
door, and I accompanied him toward it. As he was leaving, he turned suddenly, looked me in the face, placed his hand on my shoulder, and said:

"These people have no rallying-point. Make yourself that rallying-point!"

The next day I was commissioned by the President colonel in the staff and Inspector-General of the District of Columbia. I was mustered into the service of the United States from the 2d day of January, 1861, on the special requisition of the General-in-Chief, and thus was the first of two and a half millions called into the military service of the Government to defend it against secession.

I immediately entered upon my duties, commencing by inspections in detail of the existing organizations of volunteers. The Potomac Light Infantry company, of Georgetown, I found fairly drilled, well armed, and, from careful information, it seemed to

HEADQUARTERS OF GENERAL WINFIELD SCOTT, WASHINGTON.
FROM A WAR-TIME SKETCH.

me certain that the majority of its members could be depended upon in case of need, but not all of them.

On the 2d of January, I met, at the entrance of the Metropolitan Hotel, Captain Schaeffer, of the "National Rifles" of Washington, and I spoke to him about his company, which was remarkable for drill. Schaeffer had been a lieutenant in the Third United States Artillery, and was an excellent drill-master.

He had evidently not yet heard of my appointment as Inspector-General, and he replied to my complimentary remarks on his company:

"Yes, it is a good company, and I suppose I shall soon have to lead it to the banks of the Susquehanna!"

"Why so?" I asked.

"Why! To guard the frontier of Maryland and help to keep the Yankees from coming down to coerce the South!"

I said to him quietly that I thought it very imprudent in him, an employee of the Department of the Interior and captain of a company of District of Columbia volunteers, to use such expressions. He replied that most of his men were Marylanders, and would have to defend Maryland. I told him that he would soon learn that he had been imprudent, and advised him to think more seriously of his position, but did not inform him of my appointment, which he would be certain to learn the following morning from the newspapers.

It must be admitted that this was not a very cheerful beginning.

On inspecting the "National Rifles," I found that Schaeffer had more than 100 men on his rolls, and was almost daily adding to the number, and that he had a full supply of rifles with 200 rounds of ball cartridges, two mountain

howitzers with harness and carriages, a supply of sabers and of revolvers and ammunition, all drawn from the United States arsenal. I went to the Chief of Ordnance, to learn how it was that this company of riflemen happened to be so unusually armed; and I found at the Ordnance Office that an order had been given by the late Secretary of War (John B. Floyd) directing the

THE WASHINGTON ARSENAL. FROM A WAR-TIME PHOTOGRAPH.

Chief of Ordnance to cause to be issued to Captain Schaeffer "all the ordnance and ordnance stores that he might require for his company!" I ascertained also that Floyd had nominated Captain Schaeffer to the President for the commission of major in the District of Columbia militia, and that the commission had already been sent to the President for his signature.

I immediately presented the matter to the new Secretary of War (Joseph Holt), and procured from him two orders,—one, an order to the Chief of Ordnance to issue no arms to any militia or volunteers in the District of Columbia unless the requisition should be countersigned by the Inspector-General; the other, an order that all commissions issued to officers of the District of Columbia should be sent to the Inspector-General for delivery.

An office was assigned me in the War Department, convenient to the army-registers and near the Secretary of War, who kindly gave orders that I should at all times be admitted to his cabinet without waiting, and room was made for me in the office of Major-General Weightman, the senior major-general of the District, where each day I passed several hours in order to confer with him, and to be able promptly to obtain his authority for any necessary order.

The Washington Light Infantry organization and the National Guard were old volunteers composed of Washington people, and were almost to a man faithful to the Government. Of their officers, Major-General Weightman, though aged, and Major-General Force, aged and infirm, were active, and true as steel; Brigadier-Generals Bacon and Carrington were young, active, and true. Brigadier-General Robert Ould, who took no part in the preparations of the winter, joined the Confederates as soon as Virginia passed her ordinance of secession, and his known sentiments precluded consultation with him.

Having thus studied the ground, and taken the first necessary steps toward security, I commenced the work of providing a force of volunteers. I addressed individual letters to some forty well-known and esteemed gentlemen of the District, informing each one that it would be agreeable to the Government should he in his neighborhood raise and organize a company of volunteers for the preservation of order in the District. To some of these letters I received no replies; to some I received replies courteously declining the service; to some I received letters sarcastically declining; but to many I received replies enthusiastically accepting the service. In about six weeks thirty-three companies of infantry and riflemen and two troops of cavalry were on the lists of the District volunteer force; and all had been uniformed, equipped, and put under frequent drill.

The Northern Liberties fire companies brought their quota; the Lafayette Hose Company was prompt to enroll; the masons, the carpenters, the stonecutters, the painters, and the German turners responded: each corporation formed its companies and drilled industriously. Petty rivalries disappeared, and each company strove to excel the others in drill and discipline. While the newly organized companies thus strove to perfect themselves, the older organizations resumed their drills and filled their ranks with good recruits.

The National Rifles company (Captain Schaeffer's) was carefully observed, and it was found that its ranks received constant accessions, including the most openly declared secessionists and even members of Congress from the Southern States. This company was very frequently drilled in its armory, and its recruits were drilled nearly every night.

Having, as Inspector-General, a secret service force at my disposition, I placed a detective in the company, and had regular reports of the proceedings of its captain. He was evidently pushing for an independent command of infantry, artillery, and cavalry, having his rifles, cannon, sabers, and revolvers stored in his armory. He also began to prepare for action, ordering his men to take their rifles and equipments home with them, with a supply of ammunition, so that even should his armory be occupied, they could assemble on short notice, ready for action. Meantime, his commission as major was signed by the President and sent to me.

I reported these matters to General Scott, who ordered me to watch these proceedings carefully, and to be ready to suppress any attempt at violence; but to avoid, if possible, any shock, for, said he, "We are now in such a state that a dog-fight might cause the gutters of the capital to run with blood."

While the volunteer force for the support of the Government

THE COLUMBIAN ARMORY, WASHINGTON. FROM A WAR-TIME SKETCH.

was organizing, another force with exactly the opposite purpose was in course of formation. I learned that the great hall over Beach's livery stable was nightly filled with men who were actively drilled. Doctor B——, of well-known secession tendencies, was the moving spirit of these men, and he was assisted by other citizens of high standing, among whom was a connection of Governor Letcher of Virginia. The numbers of these occupants of Beach's hall increased rapidly, and I found it well to have a skillful New York detective officer, who had been placed at my disposition, enrolled among them. These men called themselves "National Volunteers," and in their meetings openly discussed the seizure of the national capital at the proper moment. They drilled industriously, and had regular business meetings, full reports of which were regularly laid before me every following morning by "the New York member." In the meeting at which the uniform to be adopted was discussed, the vote was for gray Kentucky jeans, with the Maryland button. A cautious member suggested that they must remember that, in order to procure

JOSEPH HOLT. SECRETARY OF WAR FROM DEC. 31, 1860, UNTIL MARCH 4, 1861. FROM A PHOTOGRAPH.

arms, it would be "necessary to get the requisition signed by 'Old Stone,' and if he saw that they had adopted the Maryland button, and not that of the United States, he might suspect them and refuse the issue of arms!" Doctor B—— supported the idea of the Maryland button, and said that, if Stone refused the arms, the Governor of Virginia would see them furnished, etc. These gentlemen probably little thought that a full report of their remarks would be read the next morning by "Old Stone" to the General-in-Chief.

The procuring of arms was a difficult matter for them, for it required the election of officers, the regular enrolling of men, the certificate of elections, and the muster-rolls, all to be reported to the Inspector-General. The subject was long discussed by them, and it was finally arranged that, out of the 360 men, a pretended company should be organized, officers elected, and the demand for arms made. This project was carried out, and *my* member brought to me early the next morning the report of the proceedings, informing me that Doctor B—— had been elected captain, and would call on the Inspector-General for arms. Sure enough Doctor B—— presented himself in my office and informed me that he had raised a company of volunteers, and desired an order for arms. He produced a certificate of election in due form. I received him courteously, and informed him that I could not give an order for arms without having a muster-roll of his men, proving that a full one hundred had signed the rolls. It was desirable to have the names of men holding such sentiments and nursing such projects as were known to be theirs.

He returned, I think, on the following day, with a muster-roll in due form, containing the names of one hundred men. This was all that I wanted. I looked him full in the face, smiled, and locked the muster-roll in a drawer of my desk, saying:

"Doctor B——, I am very happy to have obtained this list, and I wish you good-morning."

The gallant doctor evidently understood me. He smiled, bowed, and left the office, to which he never returned. He subsequently proved the sincerity of his principles by abandoning his pleasant home in Washington, his large and valuable property, and giving his earnest service to the Confederate cause. The "National Volunteer" organization broke up without further trouble.

Next came the turn of Captain Schaeffer. He entered my office one day with the air of an injured man, holding in his hand a requisition for arms and ammunition, and saying, that, on presenting it at the Ordnance Office, he had been informed that no arms could be issued to him without my approval. I informed him that that was certainly correct, and that the order of the Secretary of War was general. I told him that he had already in his possession more rifles than were required for a company, and that he could have no more. He then said, sulkily, that with his company he could easily *take* the arms he wanted. I asked him, "Where?" and he replied:

"You have only four soldiers guarding the Columbian armory, where there are plenty of arms, and those four men could not prevent my taking them."

"Ah!" I replied, "in what part of the armory are those arms kept?" He said they were on the upper floor, which was true.

"Well," said I, "you seem to be well informed. If you think it best, just try taking the arms by force. I assure you that if you do you shall be fired on by 150 soldiers as you come out of the armory."

The fact was, that only two enlisted men of ordnance were on duty at the Columbian armory, so feeble was the military force at the time. But Barry's battery had just arrived at the Washington arsenal, and on my application General Scott had ordered the company of sappers and miners at West Point to come to Washington to guard the armory; but they had not yet arrived. The precautions taken in ordering them were thus clearly proved advisable.

The time had evidently come to disarm Captain Schaeffer; and when he reached his office after leaving mine, he found there an order directing him to deposit in the Columbian armory, before sunset on that day, the two howitzers with their carriages which he had in his possession, as well as the sabers and revolvers, as these weapons formed no part of the proper armament of a company of riflemen. He was taken by surprise, and had not time to call together men enough to resist; so that nothing was left to him but to comply with the order. He obeyed it, well knowing that if he did not I was prepared to take the guns from his armory by means of other troops.

Having obeyed, he presented himself again in my office, and before he had time to speak I informed him that I had a commission of major for his name. He was much pleased, and said: "Yes, I heard that I had been appointed." I then handed him a slip of paper on which I had written out the form of oath which the old law required to be taken by officers, that law never having been repealed, and said to him:

"Here is the form of oath you are to take. You will find a justice of the peace on the next floor. Please qualify, sign the form in duplicate, and bring both to me. One will be filed with your letter of acceptance, the other will be filed in the clerk's office of the Circuit Court of the District."

He took the paper with a sober look, and stood near my table several minutes looking at the form of oath and turning the paper over, while I, apparently very busy with my papers, was observing him closely. I then said:

"Ah, Schaeffer, have you already taken the oath?"

"No," said he.

"Well, please be quick about it, as I have no time to spare."

He hesitated, and said slowly:

"In ordinary times I would not mind taking it, but in these times ——"

"Ah!" said I, "you decline to accept your commission of major.

JAMES BUCHANAN, PRESIDENT OF THE UNITED STATES FROM MARCH 4, 1857, UNTIL MARCH 4, 1861. FROM A PHOTOGRAPH.

Very well!" and I returned his commission to the drawer and locked it in.

"Oh, no," said Schaeffer, "I want the commission."

"But, sir, you cannot have it. Do you suppose that, in these times, which are not, as you say, 'ordinary times,' I would think of delivering a commission of field-officer to a man who hesitates about taking the oath of office? Do you think that the Government of the United States is stupid enough to allow a man to march armed men about the Federal District under its authority, when that man hesitates to take the simple oath of office? No, sir, you cannot have this commission; and more than that, I now inform you that you hold no office in the District of Columbia volunteers."

"Yes, I do; I am captain, and have my commission as such, signed by the President and delivered to me by the major-general."

"I am aware that such a paper was delivered to you, but you failed legally to accept it."

"I wrote a letter of acceptance to the adjutant-general, and forwarded it through the major-general."

"Yes, I am aware that you did; but I know also that you failed to inclose in that letter, according to law, the form of oath required to accompany all letters of acceptance; and on the register of the War Department, while the issuance of your commission is recorded, the acceptance is not recorded. You have never legally accepted your commission, and it is now too late. The oath of a man who hesitates to take it will not now be accepted."

So Captain Schaeffer left the "National Rifles," and with him left the

CHARLES P. STONE, BRIGADIER-GENERAL, U. S. V.
FROM A PHOTOGRAPH.

secession members of the company. I induced quite a number of true men to join its ranks; a new election was ordered, and a strong, loyal man (Lieutenant Smead of the 2d Artillery) was elected its captain. Smead was then on duty in the office of the Coast Survey, and I easily procured from the War Department permission for him to accept the position.

If my information was correct, the plan had been formed for seizing the public departments at the proper moment and obtaining possession of the seals of the Government. Schaeffer's part, with the battalion he was to form, was to take possession of the Treasury Department for the benefit of the new Provisional Government. Whatever may have been the project, it was effectually foiled. With the breaking up of the "National Volunteers"; with the transformation of the secession company of "National Rifles" into a thoroughly faithful and admirably drilled company ready for the service of the Government; with the arrival from West Point of the company of sappers and miners, and, later, the arrival of the Military Academy battery under Griffin; and with the formation in the District of thirty new companies of infantry and riflemen from among the citizens of Washington and Georgetown, the face of things in the capital had much changed before the 4th of March.

I must now go back a little in time, to mention one fact which will show in how weak and dangerous a condition our Government was in the latter part of January and the early part of February, 1861. The invitations which I had issued for the raising of companies of volunteers had, as already stated, been enthusiastically responded to, and companies were rapidly organized. The preparatory drills were carried on every night, and I soon found that the men were sufficiently advanced to receive their arms. I began to approve the requisitions for arms; but, to my great astonishment, the captains who first received the orders came back to me, stating that the Ordnance Department had refused to issue any arms! On referring to the Ordnance Office, I was informed by the Chief of Ordnance that he had received, the day before, an order not to issue any arms to the District of Columbia troops, and that this order had come from the President!

I went immediately to the Secretary of War (Mr. Holt) and informed him of the state of affairs, telling him at the same time that I did not feel disposed to be employed in child's play, organizing troops which could not be armed, and that unless the order in question should be immediately revoked there was no use for me in my place, and that I must at once resign. Mr. Holt told me that I was perfectly right; that unless the order should be revoked there was no use in my holding my place, and he added, with a smile, "and I will also say, Colonel, there will be no use in my holding my place any longer. Go to the President, Colonel, and talk to him as you have talked to me."

I went to the White House, and was received by Mr. Buchanan. I found him sitting at his writing-table, in his dressing-gown, wearied and worried.

I opened at once the subject of arms, and stated the necessity of immediate issue, as the refusal of arms would not only stop the instruction of the volunteers, which they needed sadly, but would make them lose all confidence in the Government and break up the organizations. I closed by saying that, while I begged his pardon for saying it, in case he declined to revoke his order I must ask him to accept my resignation at once.

Mr. Buchanan was evidently in distress of mind, and said:

"Colonel, I gave that order acting on the advice of the District Attorney, Mr. Robert Ould."

"Then, Mr. President," I replied, "the District Attorney has advised your Excellency very badly."

"But, Colonel, the District Attorney is an old resident of Washington, and he knows all the little jealousies which exist here. He tells me that you have organized a company from the Northern Liberty Fire Company."

"Not only one, but two excellent companies in the Northern Liberty, your Excellency."

"And then, the District Attorney tells me you have organized another company from among the members of the Lafayette Hose Company."

A. Lincoln

FROM AN AMBROTYPE TAKEN FOR MARCUS L. WARD (AFTERWARD GOVERNOR OF NEW JERSEY) IN
SPRINGFIELD, ILL., MAY 20, 1860, TWO DAYS AFTER MR. LINCOLN'S FIRST NOMINATION.

" Yes, your Excellency, another excellent company."

"And the District Attorney tells me, Colonel, that there is a strong feeling of enmity between those fire companies, and, if arms are put in their hands, there will be danger of bloodshed in the city."

" Will your Excellency excuse me if I say that the District Attorney talks nonsense, or worse, to you ? If the Northern Liberties and the Lafayette Hose men wish to fight, can they not procure hundreds of arms in the shops along the avenue ? Be assured, Mr. President, that the people of this District are thinking now of other things than old ward feuds. They are thinking whether or not the Government of the United States is to allow itself to crumble out of existence by its own weakness. And I believe that the District Attorney knows that as well as I do. If the companies of volunteers are not armed, they will disband, and the Government will have nothing to protect it in case of even a little disturbance. Is it not better for the public peace, your Excellency, even if the bloody feud exists (which I believe is forgotten in a greater question),— is it not better to have these men organized and under the discipline of the Government ?"

The President hesitated a moment, and then said :

"I don't know that you are not right, Colonel; but you must take the responsibility on you that no bloodshed results from arming these men."

I willingly accepted this responsibility. The prohibitory order was revoked. My companies received their arms, and made good use of them, learning the manual of arms in a surprisingly short time. Later, they made good use of them in sustaining the Government which had furnished them against the faction which soon became its public enemy, including Mr. Robert Ould, who, following his convictions (no doubt as honestly as I was following mine), gave his earnest services to his State against the Federal Government.

I think that the country has never properly appreciated the services of those District of Columbia volunteers. It certainly has not appreciated the difficulties surmounted in their organization. Those volunteers were citizens of the Federal District, and therefore had not at the time, nor have they ever had since, the powerful stimulant of State feeling, nor the powerful support of a State government, a State's pride, a State press to set forth and make much of their services. They did their duty quietly, and they did it well and faithfully. Although not mustered into the service and placed on pay until after the fatal day when the flag was fired upon at Sumter, yet they rendered great service before that time in giving confidence to the Union men, to members of the national legislature, and also to the President in the knowledge that there was at least a small force at its disposition ready to respond at any moment to his call. It should also be remembered of them, that the first troops mustered into the service were sixteen companies of these volunteers ; and that, during the dark days when Washington was cut off from communication with the North, when railway bridges were burned and tracks torn up, when the Potomac was blockaded, these troops were the only reliance of the Government for guarding the public departments, for preserving order and for holding the bridges and other outposts; that these were the troops which recovered possession of the railway from Washington to Annapolis Junction and made practicable the reopening of communications. They also formed the advance guard of the force which first crossed the Potomac into Virginia and captured the city of Alexandria.

Moreover, these were the troops which insured the regular inauguration on the steps of the Capitol of the constitutionally elected President. I firmly believe that without them Mr. Lincoln would never have been inaugurated. I believe that tumults would have been created, during which he would have been killed, and that we should have found ourselves engaged in a struggle, without preparation, and without a recognized head at the capital. In this I may be mistaken, of course, as any other man may be mistaken; but it was then my opinion, when I had many sources of information at my command, and it remains my opinion now, when, after the lapse of many years and a somewhat large experience, I look back in cool blood upon those days of political madness.

HANNIBAL HAMLIN, VICE-PRESIDENT OF THE UNITED STATES FROM MARCH 4, 1861, TO MARCH 4, 1865. FROM A PHOTOGRAPH.

One day, after the official declaration of the election of Mr. Lincoln, my duties called me to the House of Representatives; and while standing in the lobby waiting for the member with whom I had business, I conversed with a distinguished officer from New York. We were leaning against the sill of a window which overlooked the steps of the Capitol, where the President-elect usually stands to take the oath of office. The gentleman grew excited as we discussed the election of Mr. Lincoln, and pointing to the portico he exclaimed:

"He will never be inaugurated on those steps!"

"Mr. Lincoln," I replied, "has been constitutionally elected President of the United States. You may be sure that, if he lives until the fourth day of March, he will be inaugurated on those steps."

As I spoke, I noticed for the first time how perfectly the wings of the Capitol flanked the steps in question; and on the morning of the 4th of March I saw to it that each window of the two wings was occupied by two riflemen.

I received daily numerous communications from various parts of the country, informing me of plots to prevent the arrival of the President-elect at the capital. These warnings came from St. Louis, from Chicago, from Cincinnati, from Pittsburgh, from New York, from Philadelphia, and especially from Baltimore. Every morning I reported to General Scott on the occurrences of the night and the information received by the morning's mail; and every evening I rendered an account of the day's work and received instructions for the night. General Scott also received numerous warnings of danger to the President-elect, which he would give me to study and compare. Many of the communications were anonymous and vague. But, on the other hand, many were from calm and wise men, one of whom became, shortly afterward, a cabinet minister; one was a railway president, another a distinguished ex-governor of a State, etc. In every case where the indications were distinct, they were followed up to learn if real danger existed.

SOUTH OR GARDEN SIDE OF THE WHITE HOUSE.— TREASURY BUILDING IN THE DISTANCE.

So many clear indications pointed to Baltimore, that three good detectives of the New York police force were constantly employed there. These men reported frequently to me, and their statements were constantly compared with the information received from independent sources.

Doubtless, Mr. Lincoln, at his home in Springfield, Ill., received many and contradictory reports from the capital, for he took his own way of obtaining information. One night, between 11 o'clock and midnight, while I was busy in my study over the papers of the day and evening, a card was brought to me, bearing the name "Mr. Leonard Swett," and upon it was written in the well-known hand of General Scott, "Colonel Stone, Inspector-General, may converse freely with Mr. Swett." Soon a tall gentleman of marked features entered my room. At first I thought it was Mr. Lincoln himself, so much, at first glance, did Mr. Swett's face resemble the portraits I had seen of Mr. Lincoln, and so nearly did his height correspond with that attributed to the President-elect. But I quickly found that the gentleman's card bore his true name, and that Mr. Swett had come directly from Mr. Lincoln, having his full confidence, to see for him the state of affairs in Washington, and report to him in person.

Mr. Swett remained several days in the capital, had frequent and long conversations with General Scott and myself (and I suppose also with many others), and with me visited the armories of some of the volunteer companies. As he drove with me to the railway station on his departure, Mr. Swett said:

"Mr. Lincoln, and in fact almost everybody, is ignorant of the vast amount of careful work which has been done here this winter, by General Scott and yourself, to insure the existence of the Government and to render certain and safe the inauguration of Mr. Lincoln. He will be very grateful to both."

I replied, with more sincerity than tact:

"Mr. Lincoln has no cause to be grateful to me. I was opposed to his election, and believed in advance that it would bring on what is evidently coming, a fearful war. The work which I have done has not been done for him, and he need feel under no obligations to me. I have done my best toward saving the Government of the country and to insure the regular inauguration of the constitutionally elected President on the 4th of next month."

As President Lincoln approached the capital, it became certain that desperate attempts would be made to prevent his arriving there. To be thoroughly informed as to what might be expected in Baltimore, I directed a detective to be constantly near the chief of police and to keep up relations with him; while two others were instructed to watch, without the knowledge and independent of the chief of police. The officer who was near the chief of police reported regularly, until near the last, that there was no danger in Baltimore; but the others discovered a band of desperate men plotting for the destruction of Mr. Lincoln during his passage through the city, and by affiliating with them, these detectives obtained the details of the plot.

Mr. Lincoln passed through Baltimore in advance of the time announced for the journey (in accordance with advice given by me to Mr. Seward and

THE WHITE HOUSE AT NIGHT.

INAUGURATION OF ABRAHAM LINCOLN, MARCH 4, 1861.   PROCESS REPRODUCTION OF AN IMPERFECT PHOTOGRAPH.

which was carried by Mr. Frederick W. Seward to Mr. Lincoln), and arrived safe at Washington on the morning of the day he was to have passed through Baltimore. But the plotting to prevent his inauguration continued; and there was only too good reason to fear that an attempt would be made against his life during the passage of the inaugural procession from Willard's hotel, where Mr. Lincoln lodged, to the Capitol.

On the afternoon of the 3d of March, General Scott held a conference at his headquarters, there being present his staff, General Sumner, and myself, and then was arranged the programme of the procession. President Buchanan was to drive to Willard's hotel, and call upon the President-elect. The two were to ride in the same carriage, between double files of a squadron of the District of Columbia cavalry. The company of sappers and miners were to march in front of the presidential carriage, and the infantry and riflemen of the District of Columbia were to follow it. Riflemen in squads were to be placed on the roofs of certain commanding houses which I had selected, along Pennsylvania Avenue, with orders to watch the windows on the opposite side and to fire upon them in case any attempt should be made to fire from those windows on the presidential carriage. The small force of regular cavalry which had arrived was to guard the side-street crossings of Pennsylvania Avenue, and to move from one to another during the passage of the procession. A battalion of District of Columbia troops were to be placed near the steps of the Capitol, and riflemen in the windows of the wings of the Capitol. On the arrival of the presidential party at the Capitol, the troops were to be stationed so as to return in the same order after the ceremony.

To illustrate the state of uncertainty in which we were at that time concerning men, I may here state that the lieutenant-colonel, military secretary of the General-in-Chief, who that afternoon recorded the conclusions of the General in conference, and who afterward wrote out for me the instructions regarding the disposition of troops, resigned his commission that very night, and departed for the South, where he joined the Confederate army.

During the night of the 3d of March, notice was brought me that an attempt would be made to blow up the platform on which the President would stand to take the oath of office. I immediately placed men under the steps, and at daybreak a trusted battalion of District troops (if I remember rightly, it was the National Guard, under Colonel Tait) formed in a semicircle at the foot of the great stairway, and prevented all entrance from without. When the crowd began to assemble in front of the portico, a large number of policemen in plain clothes were scattered through the mass to observe closely, to place themselves near any person who might act suspiciously, and to strike down any hand which might raise a weapon.

At the appointed hour, Mr. Buchanan was escorted to Willard's hotel, which he entered. There I found a number of mounted " marshals of the day," and posted them around the carriage, within the cavalry guard. The two Presidents were saluted by the troops as they came out of the hotel and took their places in the carriage. The procession started. During the march to the Capitol I rode near the carriage, and by an apparently clumsy use of my spurs managed to keep the horses of the cavalry in an uneasy state, so that it would have been very difficult for even a good marksman to get an aim at one of the inmates of the carriage between the prancing horses.

After the inaugural ceremony, the President and the ex-President were escorted in the same order to the White House. Arrived there, Mr. Buchanan walked to the door with Mr. Lincoln, and there bade him welcome to the House and good-morning. The infantry escort formed in line from the gate of the White House to the house of Mr. Ould, whither Mr. Buchanan drove, and the cavalry escorted his carriage. The infantry line presented arms to the ex-President as he passed, and the cavalry escort saluted as he left the carriage and entered the house. Mr. Buchanan turned on the steps, and gracefully acknowledged the salute. The District of Columbia volunteers had given to President Lincoln his first military salute and to Mr. Buchanan his last.

FORT McREE. THE "POWHATAN." FORT PICKENS, SANTA ROSA ISLAND.

PENSACOLA HARBOR FROM THE BAR. FROM A SKETCH MADE IN MAY, 1862.

WITH SLEMMER IN PENSACOLA HARBOR.

BY J. H. GILMAN, BREVET LIEUTENANT-COLONEL, U. S. A. ↓

WILLIAM CONWAY, THE MAN WHO REFUSED TO HAUL DOWN THE UNION FLAG AT THE PENSACOLA NAVY YARD. FROM A SKETCH FROM LIFE BY WILLIAM WAUD.

ENTERING Pensacola Harbor from the Gulf of Mexico, one sees as he crosses the bar, immediately to his left, Fort McRee on the mainland, or west shore of the bay, and to his right Fort Pickens on the western extremity of Santa Rosa Island, which is about forty miles in length, nearly parallel to the shore of the mainland, and separated from it by Pensacola Bay. On the mainland, directly opposite Fort Pickens, about a mile and a half from it and two miles north-east of Fort McRee, stands Fort Barrancas, and, now forming a part of it, the little old Spanish fort, San Carlos de Barrancas. About a mile and a half east of this is the village of Warrington, adjoining the Navy Yard, and seven miles farther up the bay is the town of Pensacola. Near Fort Barrancas, and between it and the Navy Yard, is the post of Barrancas Barracks, and there, in January, 1861, was stationed Company G, 1st United States Artillery, the sole force of the United States army in the harbor to guard and hold, as best it might, the property of the United States. The captain of this company, John H. Winder (afterward brigadier-general in the Confederate army, and widely known in connection with the military prisons in the South), and the senior first lieutenant, A. R. Eddy, were absent

↓ Lieut. Slemmer's report says of Lieut. Gilman: "During the whole affair we have stood side by side, and if any credit is due for the course pursued, he is entitled [to it] equally with myself."—EDITORS.

on leave, and the only officers with it were First Lieutenant Adam J. Slemmer and the writer of this sketch,— then the second lieutenant of the company, who, by virtue of that high rank, was also the post treasurer, post quartermaster, post commissary, and post adjutant.

With the new year, 1861, came to us at that quiet little post the startling news of the seizure of United States property at various points by State troops, and by January 7th rumors, to us still more startling, reached our ears, to the effect that the Navy Yard and forts in Pensacola Harbor were to be seized by troops already preparing, in Florida and Alabama, to march against us. As yet no orders had come to Lieutenant Slemmer for his guidance in this emergency, and, as may be imagined, we had frequent conversations as to what should or could properly be done. As it would be useless to attempt to hold Barrancas, the occupation of Fort Pickens was suggested and considered; but Lieutenant Slemmer, thinking that he would not be justified in changing his station without authority, decided to remain where he was.

On January 8th the first step indicating to outsiders an intention on our part to resist was taken, by the removal of the powder from the Spanish fort to Fort Barrancas, where on the same night a guard was placed with loaded muskets. It was none too soon, for about midnight a party of twenty men came to the fort, evidently with the intention of taking possession, expecting to find it unoccupied as usual. Being challenged and not answering nor halting when ordered, the party was fired upon by the guard and ran in the direction of Warrington, their footsteps resounding on the plank walk as the long roll ceased and our company started for the fort at double-quick. This, I believe, was the first gun in the war fired on our side.

Next day, January 9th, an order came from General Scott to Lieutenant Slemmer to do all in his power to prevent the seizure of the public property and to coöperate with Commodore James Armstrong at the yard. The latter received orders on the same day to coöperate with the army; but he was already so greatly under the influence of Captain Ebenezer Farrand and other secessionist officers of his command that he dared not take any very active part in aiding us, not even so far as to let us have the marines, as he had promised. The excitement at the yard and in the village of Warrington was intense and was increasing daily, and the commodore was nearly distracted. He was desirous of doing his duty, and apparently saw it clearly while we were with him; but as soon as we left, became demoralized, and was thwarted in his plans by his own officers and others about him, who advised and warned him not to inaugurate civil war and bloodshed by aiding us in what they called the mad scheme of resisting the State authorities.

Fearing that, as soon as the determination to occupy Pickens became known, attempts would be made to prevent it, Lieutenant Slemmer decided to move at once, and the commodore promised to have the *Wyandotte* at Barrancas to take us across at 1 P. M. that day. She did not come, however, and we had to visit the commodore twice more that day to counteract the influence of those about him. The steamer was again promised at 5 P. M., but did not arrive until next morning. In a large flat-boat or scow, and several small boats loaded with our men, provisions, brass field-pieces, ammunition, tools, and whatever public property was most needed and could be carried, including, I remember, an old mule and cart (which afterward proved of great service to us), we were towed over to Pickens and landed there about 10 A. M. January 10th, 1861, the day that Florida seceded from the Union.

Lieutenant Slemmer's family and mine were sent on board the storeship *Supply*, on which, a few days later, they sailed for New York. All our men

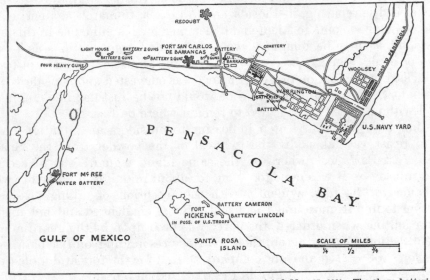

This map shows the Union and Confederate batteries as they existed May 27, 1861. The shore batteries were constructed by the Confederates after Slemmer's crossing to Fort Pickens. Two other Union batteries near Fort Pickens — batteries Scott and Totten — were added after the date of this map.

were compelled to leave behind more or less personal property, those who were married leaving their houses and families as they were. Under such circumstances, when so many inducements were held out for men to desert, and when so many men in higher places failed, it speaks well for their character, loyalty, and discipline that none of our men deserted. No company of men could work better or with more enthusiasm, and they were not at all disposed to give information to those outside. The day before we left, a civilian, visiting the post to see what news he could gather, asked one of them: " What is all this stir about ? You men are not going to fight, are you ?" " Faith, you needn't ask me; I'm not the man that gives orders here!" " What are they moving these gun-carriages out for ?" " Well, sir, I hear they are to be painted to-morrow." " How many men are there here now ?" " Sure, I'm not the baker, and don't know how many he bakes for."

Next to the commodore, the most thoroughly excited and demoralized man I saw was our old Spanish friend, Francisco Gomez, who was well known in all that region, and had long lived in a little cottage just in front of the barracks. He was the friend of all army officers, but his *hero* was General Jackson, and his great delight was to spin yarns to us about Jackson's capture of Pensacola from the British. Gomez was a true " original Jackson man," having as a youth seen him at Pensacola. The morning we left, I met him walking to and fro in front of his cottage, and said: "Good-bye, Mr. Gomez; *you* must take care of things here now!" He replied, with upturned eyes, "My God! My God! it is awful; nothing can be saved; we shall all be killed — everything destroyed. I am afraid to say anything. How I wish General Jackson was here." And the old man straightened himself up as if the mere mention of the name gave him strength and courage.

On the 12th we saw the flag at the Navy Yard lowered, and then knew that it had been quietly and tamely surrendered. Seeing our flag thus lowered to an enemy caused intense excitement and emotion, a mingled feeling of shame, anger, and defiance. Not yet having a flag-staff up, we hung our flag over the north-west bastion of the fort, that all might see "that our flag was still there." The *Supply* (Captain Henry Walke) immediately hoisted extra flags, and soon after was towed out of the harbor by the *Wyandotte* (Captain O. H. Berryman). With the capture of the Navy Yard everything on shore fell into the enemy's hands, including the large fine dry dock — the workshops, material, and supplies of all sorts. Fortunately, the *Supply* and *Wyandotte*, the only United States vessels in the harbor, were commanded by loyal men, and were saved.

We now felt sure that an attack on the fort would not long be delayed. The enemy was in possession of everything on the mainland, and Fort Pickens alone was left, and it was in a very dilapidated condition, not having been occupied since the Mexican war. We numbered, all told, including the 30 ordinary seamen, only 81 men. Our first attention was given to the flank casemate guns, loading with grape and canister such as could be worked, and at other points closing the embrasures.

Just before sundown that evening, four gentlemen landed, and demanded of the corporal on guard, outside the gate, admittance to the fort as "citizens of Florida and Alabama." Lieutenant Slemmer and myself went to the gate and found Mr. Abert, civil engineer of the yard, whom we knew very well, and three officers, strangers to us, whom he introduced as Captain Randolph, Major Marks, and Lieutenant Rutledge. Captain Randolph said: "We have been sent by the governors of Florida and Alabama to demand a peaceable surrender of this fort." Lieutenant Slemmer replied: "I am here by authority of the President of the United States, and I do not recognize the authority of any governor to demand the surrender of United States property,— a governor is nobody here." One of them exclaimed sharply: "Do you say the governor of Florida is nobody, the governor of Alabama nobody?" Lieutenant Slemmer replied: "I know neither of them, and I mean to say that they are nothing to me." They soon left, the conference being very short.

The next night (the 13th) a small party of armed men was discovered near the fort by our patrol, and a few shots were fired. We had little fear of an attack by day, but had every reason to expect a night attack, an attempt to surprise us and carry the place by storm. All the men had to work by day mounting guns, preparing fire-balls, hand-grenades, etc., and by night do picket or patrol duty or stand by the guns. They were nearly tired out

CONFEDERATE WATER BATTERY NEAR WARRINGTON, PENSACOLA HARBOR.
FROM A WAR-TIME PHOTOGRAPH CAPTURED AT MOBILE IN 1864 BY ADMIRAL FARRAGUT.

with hard work and want of sleep, not having had a night's rest since the night of January 7th.

On the 15th Colonel W. H. Chase, commanding the enemy's forces at the yard and Barrancas, came over in a small boat with Captain Farrand (late of the United States navy, and next in rank at the yard to Commodore Armstrong) and landed at the Pickens wharf, where Lieutenant Slemmer and myself met them, and the following conversation took place:

Colonel Chase: "I have come on business which may occupy some time, and, if you have no objection, we had better go inside to your quarters."

Lieutenant Slemmer: "I have objections, and it could hardly be expected that I would take you into the fort."

Colonel Chase: "As I built the fort and know all its weak and strong points, I would learn nothing new by going in, and had no such object in proposing it."

Lieutenant Slemmer: "I understand that perfectly, but it would be improper for me to take you in; and, however well you may have known the fort before, you do not know what it now contains, nor what I have done inside."

Colonel Chase: "That is true, and I will state my business here. It is a most distressing duty to me. I have come to ask of you young officers, officers of the same army in which I have spent the best and happiest years of my life, the surrender of this fort. I would not ask it if I did not believe it right and necessary to save bloodshed; and fearing that I might not be able to say it as I ought, and in order, also, that you may have it in proper form, I have put it in writing and will read it."

He then took the manuscript from his pocket and began to read, but, after reading a few lines, his voice shook, and his eyes filled with tears. He stamped his foot, as if ashamed of exhibiting such weakness, and said, "I can't read it. Here, Farrand, you read it." Captain Farrand took it, and, remarking that he hadn't his glasses and his eyes were poor (they looked watery), passed the paper to me, saying, "Here, Gilman, you have good eyes; please read it." I took the paper and read aloud the demand for the surrender. As soon as I finished, I handed the paper to Lieutenant Slemmer, when he and I went a few paces away; and, after talking the matter over, it was decided, in order to gain time and give our men a night's rest, to ask until next day to consider the matter. We returned to Colonel Chase, and the following conversation took place:

LIEUTENANT ADAM J. SLEMMER, U. S. A.
FROM A PHOTOGRAPH.

Lieutenant Slemmer: "Colonel, how many men have you?"

Colonel Chase: "To-night I shall have 800 or 900."

Lieutenant Slemmer: "Do you imagine you could take this fort with that number?"

Colonel Chase: "I certainly do. I could carry it by storm. I know every inch of this fort and its condition."

Lieutenant Slemmer: "With your knowledge of the fort and of your troops, what proportion of them, do you imagine, would be killed in such an attack?"

Colonel Chase (shrugging his shoulders): "If you have made the best possible preparations, as I suppose you have, and should defend it, as I presume you would, I might lose one-half of my men."

Lieutenant Slemmer: "At least, and I don't believe you are prepared to sacrifice that many men for such a purpose."

Colonel Chase: "You must know very well that, with your small force, you are not expected to, and cannot, hold this fort. Florida cannot permit it, and the troops here are determined to have it; and if not surrendered peaceably, an attack and the inauguration of civil war cannot be prevented. If it is a question of numbers, and eight hundred is not enough, I can easily bring thousands more."

Lieutenant Slemmer: "I will give this letter due consideration, and as I wish to consult with the captains of the *Supply* and *Wyandotte* before replying, I will give you my answer to-morrow morning."

The next day the reply, refusing to surrender, was sent, Captain Berryman of the *Wyandotte* taking it to the yard. Immediately after, the *Wyandotte* steamed out of the harbor, and, the same day, I think, the *Supply* sailed for New York.

On the 18th another, and the last, demand for surrender was received from Colonel Chase, and next day Lieutenant Slemmer sent the following reply: "In reply to your communication of yesterday, I have the honor to state that, as yet, I know of no reason why my answer of the 16th inst. should be changed, and I therefore very respectfully refer you to that reply for an answer to this."

With his small command, Lieutenant Slemmer continued to hold Fort Pickens until he was reënforced about the middle of April. He remained there until about the middle of May, when our company, on the recommendation of the surgeon, the men being much broken down by the severe labor, incessant watching, exposure, and want of proper food of the past four months, was ordered to Fort Hamilton, New York Harbor, to recruit. The order was a humane one, and came none too soon, as scurvy had already appeared among the men. On the way North one of them died, and few of them ever entirely recovered from the effects of the severe physical and mental strain they had endured with Slemmer in Pensacola Harbor.

During the remainder of the war Fort Pickens continued to be held by the United States troops, assisted by various vessels of the blockading squadron. Lieutenant Slemmer was reënforced on the 6th of February by one company under Captain Israel Vogdes in the *Brooklyn*, and on the 17th of April by five companies in the *Atlantic*, under Colonel Harvey Brown, who had been appointed to the command of the Department of Florida, with headquarters at Fort Pickens, and continued in command until February 22d, 1862, when he was succeeded by General Lewis G. Arnold. The Confederates continued to hold the opposite shore until the 9th of May, 1862, when it was evacuated by them, the Union forces taking possession the next day. On the 11th of March, 1861, General Braxton Bragg assumed command of the Confederate forces. He was succeeded in command of the Army of Pensacola on the 27th of January, 1862, by General Samuel Jones, who, on the 8th of March, was succeeded in command of the post by Colonel Thomas M. Jones, under whom the evacuation took place, whereupon the position was occupied by the United States troops, and the headquarters of the West Gulf Squadron, which had been at Ship Island, were transferred to Pensacola. The harbor was considered the best on the Gulf.

The chief events during the Confederate occupation were:

September 2d, 1861. Destruction of the dry-dock at Pensacola by order of Colonel Harvey Brown.

September 14th. Destruction of the Confederate war schooner *Judah* by a night expedition. The *Judah* was moored to the wharf at the Navy Yard under the protection of a battery and a columbiad, and was armed with a pivot and four broadside guns. The expedition, which was matured by Captain Theodorus Bailey of the *Colorado*, consisted of 100 men in 4 boats, under the command of Lieutenant John H. Russell, U. S. Navy. Lieutenant Sproston and Gunner Borton, from one of the boats, succeeded in spiking the columbiad.

Lieutenants Russell and Blake with two boats, after receiving a volley from the *Judah*, boarded her, and, joined later by their comrades, engaged in a hand-to-hand conflict with her crew of 75 men, who made a brave resistance, but were driven off to the wharf, where they rallied, and, reënforced, kept up a continuous fire upon the vessel, which had been ignited in several places by Lieutenant Russell's men. The alarm roll was sounded, and rockets were sent up by the Confederates. The enemy's forces being aroused, the *Colorado's* boats pulled away, rallying at a short distance from the shore to fire six charges of canister from their howitzers, under cover of which they returned to the fort. The *Judah* burned to the water's edge, and, having been set free from her moorings by the fire, drifted down opposite Fort Barrancas, where she sank. The Union loss was 3 men killed and 13 wounded. Lieutenant Russell's gallantry was the subject of official mention.

October 9th. Night attack by a Confederate force of one thousand men, under General R. H. Anderson, upon the camp of Colonel William Wilson's 6th New York (Zouave) regiment on Santa Rosa Island. The Confederates landed on the island at 2 A. M., burned a part of the camp four miles from Fort Pickens, and retired to their boats after encountering Union reënforcements from the fort. The losses in killed, wounded, and missing were: Union, 67; Confederate, 87.

November 22d and 23d. Bombardment of the Confederate lines by the United States vessels *Niagara* (Flag-Officer McKean) and *Richmond* (Captain Ellison), and by Fort Pickens and the neighboring Union batteries. Although Fort McRee was so badly injured that General Bragg entertained the idea of abandoning it, the plan of the Union commanders to "take and destroy" it was not executed.

January 1st, 1862. Bombardment of Forts McRee and Barrancas by Union batteries.

May 9th. Burning and evacuation of Pensacola.
                                                    EDITORS.

RECOLLECTIONS OF THE TWIGGS SURRENDER.

BY MRS. CAROLINE BALDWIN DARROW.

A TEXAS RANGER — FROM AN AMBROTYPE.

EARLY in December, 1860, a rumor reached San Antonio, Texas, that Captain John R. Baylor, well known throughout the State, was organizing a company of one thousand men for a buffalo-hunt. ☆ As Captain Baylor's secession sentiments were well known, this was believed to be a mere pretense, and his real design to be to surprise and seize the arsenal in San Antonio, in time to prevent any resistance on the part of the United States, should Texas go out of the Union. The Union citizens, alarmed lest the few soldiers stationed there should prove insufficient, appealed to General David E. Twiggs, then commanding the Department of Texas, to increase the force. He accordingly furnished several hundred men, consisting of Knights of the Golden Circle (a secret secession organization), the Alamo Rifles, two other citizen companies, and an Irish and a German company. This quieted apprehension for a time, but in January these troops were quietly withdrawn. At this time General Twiggs's loyalty to the United States Government began to be questioned, as he was known to be often in consultation with prominent secessionists, some of them ladies. Toward the end of January the Union men again appealed to General Twiggs, but nothing was accomplished, whereupon they armed themselves, waiting with undefined dread for the next move. Meanwhile no one trusted his neighbor, since spies and informers abounded, and to add to the terror, there were fears of insurrection among the negroes, some of whom were arrested; while all of them were forbidden to walk or talk together on the streets, or to assemble as they had been accustomed to do.

Late in January was held the election for delegates to a State convention which should consider the question of secession. San Antonio was crowded. Women vied with each other in distributing the little yellow ballots, on which were printed in large type, "For Secession," or "Against Secession." Many an ignorant Mexican received instructions that the ballot "with the longest words" was the right one. The *carteros* from New Mexico, who were in town with their wagon-trains, were bought by the secessionists, and some were known to have voted three times. It was well known that the Federal civil officers were loyal; the French and German citizens were emphatically so; and

---

☆ August 2d, 1861, John R. Baylor, then Lieutenant-Colonel, commanding the Confederate army in New Mexico, organized that part of the Territory lying south of the thirty-fourth parallel, as the Confederate Territory of Arizona, the seat of government being at Mesilla, and the authority of governor being assumed by him. This action was approved by General Henry H. Sibley, then in command of the Confederate department.— EDITORS.

yet against the will of the people, " by superior political diplomacy," secession triumphed in San Antonio by a small majority. Many Germans gave up their business and left the town, taking refuge in New Braunfels, 31 miles away. Many of these men were political refugees of rare culture and scholarly attainments.

On the 1st of February, the ordinance of secession was adopted by the Texas Convention,⌡ and on the 4th commissioners were appointed " to confer with General Twiggs, with regard to the public arms, stores, munitions of war, etc., under his control, and belonging to the United States, with power to demand [them] in the name of the people of the State of Texas." To meet this commission, which consisted of Thomas J. Devine, P. N. Luckett,⌖ and Samuel A. Maverick,⌡ on the 9th of February General Twiggs appointed a commission consisting of Major David H. Vinton, Major Sackfield Maclin (secessionist), and Captain R. H. K. Whiteley. By this time the news of General Twiggs's disaffection had reached the Government, and Colonel C. A. Waite was sent to supersede him.

One day, accidentally overhearing parts of a conversation between General Twiggs and a prominent Southern lady, I felt no longer any doubt that he was about to betray his trust, and reported the matter to Major Vinton. He sought an interview with General Twiggs, and told me that he could find no suspicion of disloyalty, and that I was entirely mistaken. Getting information a few days later, which led me to believe that the day for the surrender was fixed, I again informed Major Vinton. He then decided to remove at once from his safe all papers that would give valuable information to the State authorities, and the moneys belonging to the Government, and he intrusted them to his confidential clerk, Charles Darrow. They were sent at midnight to his wife,⌐ who was waiting to receive them, and who buried part of them in a deserted garden; the rest, secreted in the ashes of an unused stove and in the tester of a bed, were guarded by her till the information was no longer valuable.

General Twiggs had succeeded in completely blinding his brother-officers as to his plans; but he now had no time to lose before Colonel Waite's arrival.

On the 15th news came that some of the passengers on the mail-coach had alighted at the crossing of the Salado and joined a large company of Texas Rangers who, under the command of Ben McCulloch, had been encamped there for several days. Captain Baylor's buffalo-hunt had at last assumed a tangible shape.

To be prepared for any emergency, for many nights we had kept our fire-arms beside us. On the night of the 15th, worn out with anxious watching, we fell asleep, to be suddenly roused about 4 o'clock by the screams of the negroes, who were coming home from market, " We're all going to be

---

⌡ The secession of Texas was not legally completed until the ratification of this ordinance by the people, February 23d, but the secession party considered the authority of the convention sufficient for the prior seizure of United States property.— EDITORS.

⌖ James H. Rogers, also appointed, was a commissioner, but it appears from the Official Records that he did not serve.— EDITORS.

⌡ From whom stray cattle were styled "Mavericks."

⌐ The writer.

killed!" I grasped my revolver, and, springing to my feet, looked out upon the plaza. In the dim light I saw the revolutionists appearing, two by two, on muleback and horseback, mounted and on foot,—a motley though quite orderly crowd, carrying the Lone Star flag before them, and surrounded and supported by armed men. The nights had been cold, and a week on the Salado without comforts had not added to their valorous appearance. Some had coats, but others were in their shirt-sleeves, and not a few were wrapped in old shawls and sad-dle-blankets. Their arms were of every description. By daylight more had appeared, perhaps a thousand in all, and so great was the enthusiasm of two women who had aided General Twiggs in his arrangements that they mounted their horses, in male attire, and with pistols in their belts rode out to meet their friends. Coffee and refreshments had been provided, and blankets and clothing were lavishly dis-tributed. All the stores were closed; men, women, and children

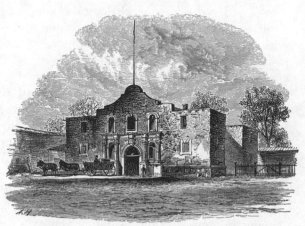

THE ALAMO, SAN ANTONIO.

armed themselves, and the excitement was intense. Companies of Union citizens, well drilled and well armed, were marching and countermarching, presenting an imposing contrast to the other party, and a conflict seemed inevitable. The arsenal building had been opened and was swarming with Rangers. Early in the morning General Twiggs drove down to the main plaza, where he was instantly surrounded by secessionists demanding the Government property, whereupon he went through the form of refusing their request. He then held a conference with Major W. A. Nichols, his assistant adjutant-general, and Ben McCulloch, and was given six hours in which to reconsider. By noon he had surrendered all the United States posts and stores in Texas. When the result was known there was great indignation against him among the citizens. Two or three hours later he left for New Orleans, where he was received with public honors.

Orders were sent to all the outposts to turn over the military property to the State. The officers and men were widely scattered, and many of them were taken completely by surprise. The Federal troops in town gave their parole "not to take up arms" against the Confederacy, and were ordered to leave the post in the afternoon. By this time the German company had refused to act against the United States, and the citizen companies had dis-banded. The Irish company had twice torn down the Stars and Stripes from the Alamo, and had raised the Lone Star flag in its place. An attempt was made to disarm the troops, but they declared that they would kill any man who interfered, and marched away under Major Larkin Smith and Captain

John H. King, with the stained and bullet-riddled old flag of the 8th Regiment flying over them, while the band played national airs. Strong men wept; the people cheered them along the streets, and many followed them to the head of the San Pedro, where they encamped. By 6 o'clock the Rangers had returned to their camp on the Salado, and the day ended without further excitement.

About 2 o'clock that afternoon, Colonel Robert E. Lee arrived in his ambulance from Fort Mason, Texas, on his way to Washington, whither he had been ordered by General Scott. As he approached the Read House I went out to greet him. At the same time some of the Rangers gathered around his wagons, and, attracted, no doubt, by their insignia of rank, the red flannel strips sewed on their shoulders, he asked, "Who are those men?" "They are McCulloch's," I answered. "General Twiggs surrendered everything to the State this morning, and we are all prisoners of war." I shall never forget his look of astonishment, as with his lips trembling and his eyes full of tears, he exclaimed, "Has it come so soon as this?" In a short time I saw him crossing the plaza on his way to headquarters, and noticed particularly that he was in citizen's dress. He returned at night and shut himself in his room, which was over mine, and I heard his footsteps through the night, and sometimes the murmur of his voice, as if he were praying. He remained at the hotel a week, and in conversations declared that the position he held was a neutral one. When he left it was my firm belief that no one could persuade or compel him to change his decision.

During the next two days the Rangers were drinking and shouting about the streets, recklessly shooting any one who happened to displease them. From this time on, Union men were in danger, and Northerners sent their families away. Some who were outspoken were imprisoned and barely escaped with their lives; among them, Charles Anderson, brother of Robert Anderson.

On the 26th of February a dozen men of the State troops were stationed on guard over the offices of the disbursing officers, and the occupants were ordered to leave, but forbidden to take away papers or effects, though allowed to keep the keys to their safes. Colonel Waite had now arrived and assumed command, and the secessionist commissioners made a second demand for

On this point Captain R. M. Potter, U. S. A., says: "I saw General Lee (then Colonel Lee) when he took leave of his friends to depart for Washington some days after the surrender of Twiggs. I have seldom seen a more distressed man. He said, 'When I get to Virginia I think the world will have one soldier less. I shall resign and go to planting corn.'" Colonel Charles Anderson, U. S. V., who is referred to above, and who talked with General Lee on the same day, thus gives the substance of his parting words (see "Texas Before and on the Eve of the Rebellion." Cincinnati, 1884): "I still think . . . that my loyalty to Virginia ought to take precedence over that which is due to the Federal Government, and I shall so report myself at Washington. If Virginia stands by the old Union, so will I. But if she secedes (though I do not believe in secession as a constitutional right, nor that there is a sufficient cause for revolution), then I will still follow my native State with my sword, and, if need be, with my life. I know you think and feel very differently, but I can't help it. These are my principles, and I must follow them." Colonel Anderson, in the course of a high tribute to General Lee's character, gives General Scott as his authority for the statement that the command of the United States forces (under Scott) was offered to Lee, and was declined by him on the same ground,—that he must be guided wholly in his action by that of Virginia. Colonel Albert G. Brackett, U. S. A., says: "When the civil war broke out, Lee was filled with sorrow at the condition of affairs, and, in a letter to me deploring the war in which we were about to engage, he made use of these words: 'I fear the liberties of our country will be buried in the tomb of a great nation.'"—EDITORS.

"a statement of the amount of indebtedness and funds on hand and required a promise from each officer that he would pay outstanding debts with funds and turn the balance over to the State": it being very desirable to the enemy to possess the Government records, which exhibited the number of troops and the condition of the whole department. Imprisonment and death were to be the penalty in case of refusal; but Major Vinton of the quartermaster's

COLONEL DANIEL H. VINTON, U. S. A.
FROM A PHOTOGRAPH.

department declared that he did not fear either, would do nothing dishonorable and would not comply. Major Daniel Mc-Clure of the pay department ☆ and Captain Whiteley of the ordnance department also refused, but several officers did comply and were returned to their offices. The larger responsibilities of the quartermaster's department detained Major Vinton after the above-named officers had left, and thus he fought his battle almost alone. His office was transferred to his own house, where with the aid of Mr. Darrow he transacted his business. He soon became so ill that it was impossible for him to leave his bed. Both were afterward arrested and given ten days in which to surrender the papers and funds

or be shot. These threats were not executed, for on the morning of the tenth day we were gladdened by the news that United States troops from the different outposts were within a few miles of the town, having been three weeks on the way. They were met at the San Pedro and paroled not to take arms against the Confederacy or serve in any capacity during the war. These troops, representing the army in Texas, were loyal almost to a man, while all but forty of the officers went over to the Confederacy. The commissioners had promised to furnish facilities for the transportation of these troops to the coast, but so great had been the confusion and so many supplies had been carried off, that the soldiers were left almost destitute. I visited their camp and found them cursing the man who had placed them in this position.

Major Vinton and family, with my husband and myself, were the last to leave. On the morning of our departure, the 11th of May, as the ambulances and baggage wagons stood at the door, to add to the gloom, a storm broke over the city, enveloping us in midnight darkness. The thunder and lightning was so loud and incessant as to seem like the noise of battle. For two weeks we journeyed over the park-like prairies, fragrant and brilliant with

---

☆ Captain Potter says: "The officers detained in San Antonio were much indebted to Major McClure for his successful efforts to raise money, on his own responsibility, for the pay of his brother officers, when no public funds were accessible. He, of course, had no office in which to transact business, and paid the officers covertly in holes and corners."

flowers. We forded streams and rivers, crossed the Brazos by a rope ferry, and, taking the railroad train from Harrisburg to Galveston, caught the last steamer before the blockade of New Orleans. We went up the Mississippi in the steamer *Hiawatha*, which was crowded with refugees, who made no sign until, in answer to a shot from shore at Cairo, the steamer rounded to and we found ourselves once more under the protection of our own flag.

On the 13th of December, 1860, General David E. Twiggs, of the United States Army, who had served with distinction in the war with Mexico, and who was at that date in command of the Department of Texas, wrote the following letter to General Scott from San Antonio:

"I think there can be no doubt that many of the Southern States will secede from the Union. The State of Texas will be among the number, and, from all appearances at present, it will be at an early day; certainly before the 4th of March next. What is to be done with public property in charge of the army? The arsenal at this place has some ordnance and other munitions of war. I do not expect an order for the present for the disposition of them, but I would be pleased to receive your views and suggestions. My course, as respects myself, will be to remain at my post and protect this frontier as long as I can, and then when turned adrift make my way home, if I have one. I would be pleased to hear from you at your earliest convenience."

At this time it took from ten to fifteen days for a letter to pass between San Antonio and army headquarters. December 28th, General Scott replied:

"In cases of political disturbance involving local conflict with the authority of the general government, the general-in-chief considers that the military questions, such as you suggest, contain a political element, with due regard to which, and in due deference to the chief executive authority, no extraordinary instructions concerning them must be issued without the consent of such authority. He has labored hard in suggesting and urging proper measures to vindicate the laws and protect the property of the United States without waging war or acting offensively against any State or community. All such suggestions, though long since made in good time to have been peaceably and efficiently carried out, have failed to secure the favorable attention of the Government. The President has listened to him with due friendliness and respect, but the War Department has been little communicative. [Mr. Floyd was then Secretary of War.] Up to this time he has not been shown the written instructions of Major Anderson, nor been informed of the purport of those more recently conveyed to Fort Moultrie verbally by Major Buell. Probably the policy of the Government in regard to the forts and depots within the limits of seceding States will have been clearly indicated before events can have caused a practical issue to be made up in Texas. The general does not see, at this moment, that he can tender you any special advice, but leaves the administration of your command in your own hands, with the laws and regulations to guide, in the full confidence that your discretion, firmness, and patriotism will effect all of good that the sad state of the times may permit."

December 27th, and January 2d, 7th, and 23d, General Twiggs wrote similar letters to army headquarters, making urgent requests for instructions. January 15th, after the receipt of the above letter from General Scott, General Twiggs wrote to him again, this time expressing sympathy with the secession movement, and asking to be relieved from command of the department on or before the 4th of March. The order relieving him, and appointing Colonel Waite as his successor, is dated January 28th, and was received by General Twiggs on the 15th of February. Meanwhile the secession party in Texas had made decided progress toward carrying the State out of the Union. Late in January an election had been held for delegates to a State convention to consider the question of secession. This convention had met on the 28th of January, at Austin, and on the 1st of February had passed an ordinance of secession which was to take effect on the 2d of March, if it should be ratified by the people on the 23d of February. General Twiggs did not wait till the ordinance was in operation, or even till its ratification, to surrender the military posts and public property under his charge. February 9th he appointed a military commission to treat with a commission from the convention,— as his order of that date announced, "to transact such business as relates to the disposition of the public property upon the demand of the State of Texas." February 16th, three days before the arrival of Colonel Waite, the actual surrender took place, nominally to superior forces under Colonel Ben McCulloch, then in command of 1000 to 1500 men, and acting under the authority, not of the governor (General Sam Houston, a Union man), but of the commissioners appointed by the convention.* On the 17th the State Commissioners wrote to General Twiggs:

"In our communication of the 16th instant we required a delivery up by you of the positions held and public property held by or under your control as commander

---

* Captain Potter (before quoted), in a written memorandum to the Editors, says:

"It was on the evening before McCulloch entered San Antonio, or, perhaps, two evenings before, that I met General Twiggs at a wedding party. He said to me: 'It is rumored that Ben McCulloch has been in town; have you seen him?' I replied, no. After a few more words on the state of affairs, he said: 'There is no need of sending him to coerce me. If an old woman with a broomstick should come with full authority from the State of Texas to demand the public property, I would give it up to her.'" Captain Potter further says: "From the date of Twiggs's return from New Orleans [about the 27th of November] there was no doubt of his intention not to withstand any insurrectionary movement on the part of the State. He constantly said that the break-up was coming, and that there was no one living who could resist the secession movement successfully."

On the same point, Colonel Charles Anderson says: "It must be remembered distinctly, on this, my testimony, and that of very many others, that from the time of his return, with increasing frequency and vehemence of his speeches, General Twiggs had not only declared that he 'would *never* fire on American citizens under *any* circumstances,' but that he would surrender the United States property in his department to the *State* of Texas *whenever it was demanded*."— ("Texas, Before and on the Eve of the Rebellion.")

in this department. As no reply save your verbal declaration (which declaration was that you 'gave up everything') has been given to our note, . . . we again demand the surrender . . ."

To this General Twiggs replied the same day:

"I have to say that you are already aware of my views in regard to the delivery of the public property of this department, and I now repeat that I will direct the positions held by the Federal troops to be turned over to the authorized agents of the State of Texas, provided the troops retain their arms and clothing, camp and garrison equipage, quartermaster's stores, subsistence, medical, hospital stores, and such means of transportation of every kind as may be necessary for an efficient and orderly movement of the troops from Texas, prepared for attack or defense against aggression from any source."

The commissioners then wrote, making two further conditions: that the troops should leave Texas by way of the coast, and that they should there surrender all means of transportation as well as the artillery. General Twiggs responded, consenting to the first condition, but objecting to the second so far as it related to the guns of the light batteries, and it was to that extent waived by the commissioners. Thus the formal surrender was consummated on the 18th of February, five days before the ratification of the ordinance of secession by the people of Texas. In a letter to Mr. Davis, dated New Orleans, February 25th, 1861, General Braxton Bragg says: "General Twiggs was ordered to turn over the command to Colonel Waite, a Northern man, but preferred surrendering to Texas." March 1st, General Twiggs was dismissed from the United States army. He was appointed major-general in the Confederate service, and was placed in command at New Orleans. He died September 15th, 1862, at Augusta, Georgia, his own State.

On the 28th of January, General Twiggs's successor, Colonel Waite, was in command at Camp Verde, 65 miles from San Antonio. In a letter of that date to General Twiggs's assistant adjutant-general at San Antonio, Colonel Waite said:

"For the purpose of making some defensive arrangements, I have deemed it proper to order the remainder of Captain Brackett's company to this place without waiting for further instructions from your office. . . . I respectfully request that 1 or 2 pieces of artillery . . . may be sent here as early as practicable. In making this application I assume that there is a probability, or at least a possibility, that a mob of reckless men may attempt to seize the public property here, the most valuable of which consists of 53 camels, . . . worth some $20,000. . . . I hold it to be the duty of every commanding officer to be at all times, and under all circumstances, prepared as far as possible for any and every emergency. To this end he must anticipate his wants and take timely measures to meet them."

February 12th, he wrote again:

"Being desirous of concentrating my regiment (the 1st Infantry) so as to bring the companies more under my control, I respectfully request permission to move out of the department with the five companies now serving here and join the remainder of the regiment which is in the Department of the West."

February 26th, in his report of the situation after he had assumed command, he says:

"To concentrate a sufficient number [of troops] to make a successful resistance after the Texans had taken the field was not practicable. Besides, we had no large depot of provisions to move upon, and the means of transportation at the posts were so limited that the troops could have taken with them a supply for only a few days. An attempt to bring them together under these circumstances would have no doubt resulted in their being cut up in detail before they could get out of the country. Under these circumstances, I felt it my duty to comply with the agreement entered into by General Twiggs, and remove the troops from the country as early as possible."

For this purpose Colonel Waite continued at San Antonio. The troops (except those mentioned below) marched to the coast, where vessels chartered by the United States awaited them.

Concerning the advantages which General Twiggs's surrender conferred upon the cause of secession, Colonel Charles Anderson says:

"Of its successes, the first was that it carried the so-called election five days afterward. Without this brilliant coup de main (the first victory of rebellion) the majority would have surely been in Texas for the Union cause. As it was, only 42,000 votes (less than half the total vote of the State) was polled, of which 13,000 votes were given by the now confounded and dismayed Unionists. [The exact vote was: for ratification, 34,794; against, 11,235.—EDITORS.] And just here (a second and great success) was the beginning of that series of flockings pari passu, with every disaster to the Union cause, of our Douglas Democrats, and our Bell and Everett men to the winning side—the Breckinridge Democrats. . . . A third gain to the rebellion was the immense money and military values of the public arms and other war properties on the very verge of the coming war, which it hastened, if it did not determine. Fourthly, our national prestige lost was a vast and instant impulse to secession and rebellion in every slave State."

The number of posts surrendered was 19. The number of troops "to be removed, in compliance with General Twiggs's agreement," was reported by Colonel Waite, February 26th, at 2328. This agreement was not respected by the Confederate authorities, who, on the 11th of April, on the ground "that hostility exists between the United States and Confederate States," gave instructions to Colonel Earl Van Dorn "to intercept and prevent the movement of the United States troops from the State of Texas." Under these orders 815 officers and men were captured, including Colonel Waite and his staff, who accepted parole under protest. Many of the private soldiers were kept in confinement for nearly two years. The San Antonio "Herald," of February 23d, 1861, estimated the total value of the property surrendered at $1,209,500, "exclusive of public buildings to which the Federal Government has a title." This property included mules, wagons, horses, harness, tools, corn, clothing, commissary and ordnance stores.

In the main the authority for the foregoing statements is Volume I. of the "Official Records of the Union and Confederate Armies," issued by the War Department, under the editorship of Lieutenant-Colonel Robert N. Scott, U. S. A. This work will be referred to hereafter in these pages as "Official Records."—EDITORS.

VIEW OF CHARLESTON FROM THE RAMPART OF CASTLE PINCKNEY.—FROM A SKETCH MADE IN 1861.

FROM MOULTRIE TO SUMTER.

BY ABNER DOUBLEDAY, BREVET MAJOR-GENERAL, U. S. A., RETIRED.

AS senior captain of the 1st Regiment of United States Artillery, I had been stationed at Fort Moultrie, Charleston Harbor, two or three years previous to the outbreak of 1861. There were two other forts in the harbor. Of these, Fort Sumter was unoccupied, being in an unfinished state, while Castle Pinckney was in charge of a single ordnance sergeant. The garrison of Fort Moultrie consisted of 2 companies that had been reduced to 65 men, who with the band raised the number in the post to 73. Fort Moultrie had no strength; it was merely a sea battery. No one ever imagined it would be attacked by our own people; and if assailed by foreigners, it was supposed that an army of citizen-soldiery would be there to defend it. It was very low, the walls having about the height of an ordinary room. It was little more, in fact, than the old fort of Revolutionary time of which the father of Major Robert Anderson had been a defender. The sand had drifted from the sea against the wall, so that cows would actually scale the ramparts. In 1860 we applied to have the fort put in order, but the quartermaster-general, afterward the famous Joseph E. Johnston, said the matter did not pertain to his department. We were then apprehending trouble, for the signs of the times indicated that the South was drifting toward secession, though the Northern people could not be made to believe this, and regarded our representation to this effect as nonsense. I remember that at that time our engineer officer, Captain J. G. Foster, was alone, of the officers, in thinking there would be no trouble. We were commanded by a Northern man of advanced age, Colonel John L. Gardner, who had been wounded in the war of 1812 and had served with credit in Florida and Mexico. November 15th, 1860, Mr.

Floyd, the Secretary of War, relieved him and put in command Major Robert Anderson of Kentucky, who was a regular officer. Floyd thought the new commander could be relied upon to carry out the Southern programme, but we never believed that Anderson took command with a knowledge of that programme or a desire that it should succeed. He simply obeyed orders, he had to obey or leave the army. Anderson was a Union man and, in the incipiency, was perfectly willing to chastise South Carolina in case she should attempt any revolutionary measures. His feeling as to coercion changed when he found that all the Southern States had joined South Carolina, for he looked upon the conquest of the South as hopeless.

Soon after his arrival, which took place on the 21st of November, Anderson wanted the sand removed from the walls of Moultrie, and urged that it be done. Suddenly the Secretary of War seemed to adopt this view. He pretended there was danger of war with England, with reference to Mexico, which was absurd; and under this pretext was seized with a sudden zeal to put the harbor of Charleston in con-

MAJOR ROBERT ANDERSON.   FROM A PHOTOGRAPH.

dition,— to be turned over to the Confederate forces. He appropriated $150,-000 for Moultrie and $80,000 to finish Sumter. There was not much to be made out of Fort Moultrie, with all our efforts, because it was hardly defensible; but Major Anderson strove to strengthen it. He put up heavy gates to prevent Charleston secessionists from entering, and made a little man-hole through which visitors had to crawl in and out.

We could get no additional ammunition, but Colonel Gardner had managed to procure a six months' supply of food from the North before the trouble

BREV.-CAPT. TRUMAN SEYMOUR.   LIEUT. G. W. SNYDER.   LIEUT. JEFF. C. DAVIS.   2D LIEUT. R. K. MEADE, JR.   LIEUT. THEO. TALBOT.

CAPT. ABNER DOUBLEDAY.   MAJOR ROBERT ANDERSON.   SURGEON S. W. CRAWFORD.   CAPT. J. G. FOSTER.

ANDERSON AND HIS OFFICERS. PROCESS REPRODUCTION OF AN IMPERFECT PHOTOGRAPH.

Second Lieutenant Norman J. Hall, who was present at the bombardment, was absent when the photograph was taken. Lieutenant Talbot had been sent to Washington, and had returned with a message from President Lincoln announcing to Governor Pickens that the Government would attempt to provision Sumter; he was not permitted to rejoin Anderson. The picture, though dim, has the value of a fac-simile.

came. The Secretary of War would not let us have a man in the way of reënforcement, the plea being that reënforcements would irritate the people. The secessionists could hardly be restrained from attacking us, but the leaders kept them back, knowing that our workmen were laboring in their interests, at the expense of the United States. When Captain Truman Seymour was sent with a party to the United States arsenal in Charleston to get some friction primers and a little ammunition, a crowd interfered and drove his men back. It became evident, as I told Anderson, that we could not defend the fort, because the houses around us on Sullivan's Island looked down into Moultrie, and could be occupied by our enemies. At last it was rumored that two thousand riflemen had been detailed to shoot us down from the tops of those houses. I proposed to anticipate the enemy and burn the dwellings, but Anderson would not take so decided a step at a time when the North did not believe there was going to be war. It was plain that the only thing to be done was to slip over the water to Fort Sumter, but Anderson said he had been assigned to Fort Moultrie, and that he must stay there. We were then in a very peculiar position. It was commonly believed that we would not be supported even by the North, as the Democrats had been bitterly opposed to the election of Lincoln; that at the first sign of war twenty thousand men in sympathy with the South would rise in New York. Moreover, the one to whom we soldiers always looked up as to a father,—the Secretary of War, seemed to be devising arrangements to have us made away with. We believed that in the event of an outbreak from Charleston few of us would survive; but it did not greatly concern us, since that risk was merely a part of our business, and we intended to make the best fight we could. The officers, upon talking the matter over, thought they might control any demonstration at Charleston by throwing shells into the city from Castle Pinckney. But, with only sixty-four soldiers and a brass band, we could not detach any force in that direction.

Finally, Captain Foster, who had misapprehended the whole situation, and who had orders to put both Moultrie and Sumter in perfect order, brought several hundred workmen from Baltimore. Unfortunately, these were nearly all in sympathy with the Charlestonians, many even wearing secession badges.

Bands of secessionists were now patrolling near us by day

THE SEA BATTERY OF FORT MOULTRIE.
FROM A PHOTOGRAPH TAKEN BEFORE THE WAR.

and night. We were so worn out with guard-duty—watching them—that on one occasion my wife and Captain Seymour's relieved us on guard, all that was needed being some one to give the alarm in case there was an attempt to break in. Foster thought that out of his several hundred workmen he could get a few Union men to drill at the guns as a garrison in Castle Pinckney, but they rebelled the moment they found they were expected to act as artillerists, and said that they were not there as warriors. It was said that when the enemy took possession of the castle, some of these workmen were hauled from under beds and from other hiding-places.

The day before Christmas I asked Major Anderson for wire to make an entanglement in front of my part of the fort, so that any one who should charge would tumble over the wires and could be shot at our leisure. I had already caused a sloping picket fence to be projected over the parapet on my side of the works so that scaling-ladders could not be raised against us. The discussion in Charleston over our proceedings was of an amusing character. This wooden *fraise* puzzled the Charleston militia and editors; one of the latter said, "Make ready your sharpened stakes, but you will not intimidate freemen."

When I asked Anderson for the wire, he said I should have a mile of it, with a peculiar smile that puzzled me for the moment. He then sent for Hall, the post quartermaster, bound him to secrecy, and told him to take three schooners and some barges which had been chartered for the purpose of taking the women and children and six months' supply of provisions to Fort Johnson, opposite Charleston. He was instructed when the secession patrols should

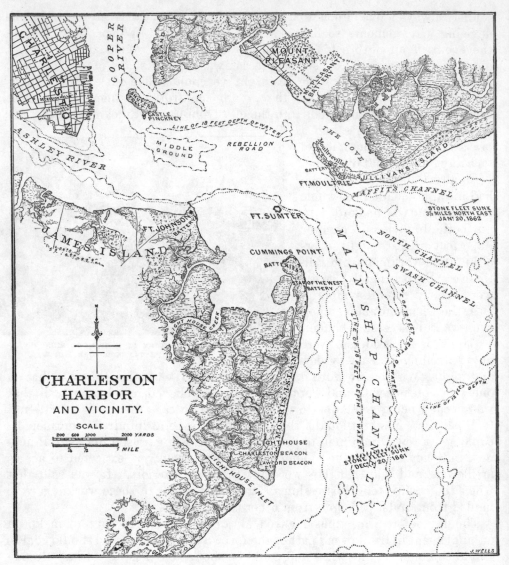

CHARLESTON
HARBOR
AND VICINITY.

SCALE

ask what this meant, to tell them we were sending off the families of the
officers and men to the North because they were in the way. The excuse
was plausible, and no one interfered. We were so closely watched that we
could make no movement without demands being made as to the reason
of it. On the day we left—the day after Christmas—Anderson gave up
his own mess, and came to live with me as my guest. In the evening of
that day I went to notify the major that tea was ready. Upon going to
the parapet for that purpose, I found all the officers there, and noticed
something strange in their manner. The problem was solved when Anderson walked up to me and said: "Captain, in twenty minutes you will leave
this fort with your company for Fort Sumter." The order was startling and
unexpected, and I thought of the immediate hostilities of which the movement

would be the occasion. I rushed over to my company quarters and informed my men, so that they might put on their knapsacks and have everything in readiness. This took about ten minutes. Then I went to my house, told my wife that there might be fighting, and that she must get out of the fort as soon as she could and take refuge behind the sand-hills. I put her trunks out of the sally-port, and she followed them. Then I started with my company to join Captain Seymour and his men. We had to go a quarter of a mile through the little town of Moultrieville to reach the point of embarkation. It was about sunset, the hour of the siesta, and fortunately the Charleston militia were taking their afternoon nap. We saw nobody, and soon reached a low line of sea-wall under which were hidden the boats in charge of the three engineers, for Lieutenants Snyder and Meade had been sent by Floyd to help Captain Foster do the work on the forts. The boats had been used in going back and forward in the work of construction, manned by ordinary workmen, who now vacated them for our use. Lieutenant Snyder said to me in a low tone: "Captain, those boats are for your men." So saying, he started with his own party up the coast. When my thirty men were embarked I went straight for Fort Sumter. It was getting dusk. I made slow work in crossing over, for my men were not expert oarsmen. Soon I saw the lights of the secession guard-boat coming down on us. I told the men to take off their coats and cover up their muskets, and I threw my own coat open to conceal my buttons. I wished to give the impression that it was an officer in charge of laborers. The guard-ship stopped its paddles and inspected us in the gathering darkness, but concluded we were all right and passed on. My party was the first to reach Fort Sumter.

We went up the steps of the wharf in the face of an excited band of secession workmen, some of whom were armed with pistols. One or two Union men among them cheered, but some of the others said angrily: "What are these soldiers doing here? what is the meaning of this?" Ordering my men to charge bayonets, we drove the workmen into the center of the fort. I took possession of the guard-room commanding the main entrance and placed sentinels. Twenty minutes after, Seymour arrived with the rest of the men. Meantime Anderson had crossed in one of the engineer boats. As soon as the troops were all in we fired a cannon, to give notice of our arrival to the quartermaster, who had anchored at Fort Johnson with the schooners carrying the women and children. He immediately sailed up to the wharf and landed his passengers and stores. Then the workmen of secession sympathies were sent aboard the schooners to be taken ashore.

Lieutenant Jefferson C. Davis of my company had been left with a rear-guard at Moultrie. These, with Captain Foster and Assistant-Surgeon Crawford, stood at loaded columbiads during our passage, with orders to fire upon the guard-boats and sink them if they tried to run us down. On withdrawing, the rear-guard spiked the guns of the fort, burned the gun-carriages on the front looking toward Sumter, and cut down the flag-staff. Mrs. Doubleday first took refuge at the house of the post sutler, and afterward with the family of Chaplain Harris, with whom she sought shelter behind the sand-hills.

When all was quiet they paced the beach, anxiously watching Fort Sumter. Finding that the South Carolinians were ignorant of what had happened, we sent the boats back to procure additional supplies.|

The next morning Charleston was furious. Messengers were sent out to ring every door-bell and convey the news to every family. The governor sent two or three of his aides to demand that we return to Moultrie. Anderson replied in my hearing that he was a Southern man, but that he had been assigned to the defense of Charleston Harbor, and intended to defend it.

Chaplain Harris was a spirited old man. He had lived at Charleston most of his life and knew the South Carolinians well. He visited Fort Sumter on our first day there and made a prayer at the raising of the flag, after which he returned to his home at Moultrieville. One day he went to the commander of Fort Moultrie and said to him: "Will any impediment be put in the way of my going over to Fort Sumter?" The reply was: "Oh, no, parson; I reckon we'll give you a pass." The chaplain answered: "I didn't ask you for a pass, sir. I am a United States officer, and will go to any United States fort without your permission. I asked you a different question: whether you would prevent my going by force." He was not allowed to cross, after that.

We had no light and were obliged to procure some if possible, for the winter nights were long. There was much money due the workmen who had been discharged, and the secessionists sent them over to demand their pay. Mrs. Doubleday came in the same boat with them, and managed to ship us a box of candles at the same time; she also brought a bandbox full of matches. At the same time Mrs. Seymour reached us stealthily in a boat rowed by two little boys. Mrs. Foster was already there. Anderson thought there was going to be trouble, so he requested the ladies to return to Moultrieville that night. The next day they went to a Charleston hotel, where they were obliged to keep very quiet and have their meals served privately in their rooms. After a day or two they left for the North, on account of the feeling in the city.

From December 26th until April 12th we busied ourselves in preparing for the expected attack, and our enemies did the same on all sides of us. Anderson apparently did not want reënforcements, and he shrank from civil war. He endured all kinds of hostile proceedings on the part of the secessionists, in the hope that Congress would make some compromise that would save slavery and the Union together.

Soon after daylight on the 9th of January, with my glass I saw a large steamer pass the bar and enter the Morris Island Channel. It was the *Star of the West*, with reënforcements and supplies for us. When she came near the upper part of the island the secessionists fired a shot at her. I hastened

---

| I will give an incident here to show how completely even our own people were deceived by the celerity and secrecy of Major Anderson's movement. Lieutenant Davis and some other officers had a mess, which was in charge of the wife of one of the soldiers. She had prepared the evening meal as usual and was amazed that no one came to eat it. When the officers, after their successful transit to Fort Sumter, went back to Moultrie in small boats to procure additional supplies, Davis walked over to the mess. He was received very indignantly by the woman, for coming to supper when everything was cold. Nothing could exceed her astonishment when she learned that the entire garrison was in Fort Sumter. Davis carried her and her pots and kettles back with him.

to Major Anderson's room, and was ordered by him to have the long roll beaten and to post the men at the barbette guns. By the time we reached the parapet the transport coming to our relief had approached so near that Moultrie opened fire. Major Anderson would not allow us to return the fire, so the transport turned about and steamed seaward. Anderson asked for an explanation of the firing from Governor Pickens, and announced that he would allow no vessel to pass within range of the guns of Sumter if the answer was unsatisfactory. Governor Pickens replied that he would renew the firing under like circumstances. I think Major Anderson had received an intimation that the *Star of the West* was coming, but did not believe it. He thought General Scott would send a man-of-war instead of a merchant vessel. Great secrecy was observed in loading her, but the purpose of the expedition got into the newspapers, and, of course, was telegraphed to Charleston. Bishop Stevens of the Methodist Church stated in a speech made by him on Memorial Day in the Academy of Music, New York, that he aimed the first gun against the *Star of the West*. I aimed the first gun on our side in reply to the attack on Fort Sumter.

Sure that we would all be tasked to the utmost in the coming conflict, and be kept on the alert by day and night, I desired to get all the sleep I could beforehand, and lay down on a cot bedstead in the magazine nearest to Morris Island,— one of the few places that would be shell-proof when the fire opened. About 4 A. M. on the 12th, Major Anderson came to me as his executive officer, and informed me that the enemy would fire upon us as soon as it was light enough to see the fort. He said he would not return it until it was broad daylight, the idea being that he did not desire to waste his ammunition.

We have not been in the habit of regarding the signal shell fired from Fort Johnson as the first gun of the conflict, although it was undoubtedly aimed at Fort Sumter. Edmund Ruffin of Virginia is usually credited with opening the attack by firing the first gun from the iron-clad battery on Morris Island. The ball from that gun struck the wall of the magazine where I was lying, penetrated the masonry, and burst very near my head. As the smoke from this explosion came in through the ventilators of the magazine, and as the floor was strewn with powder where the flannel cartridges had been filled, I thought for a moment the place was on fire.

When it was fully light we took breakfast leisurely before going to the guns, our food consisting of pork and water.

The first night after the bombardment we expected that the naval vessels outside would take advantage of the darkness to send a fleet of boats with reënforcements of men and supplies of provisions, and as it was altogether probable that the enemy would also improvise a fleet of small boats to meet those of the navy, it became an interesting question, in case parties came to us in this way, to decide whether we were admitting friends or enemies. However, the night passed quietly away without any demonstration.

Captain Chester, in his paper which follows, has omitted a fact that I will mention. As the fire against us came from all directions, a shot from

THE HOT-SHOT FURNACE, FORT MOULTRIE — FROM A PHOTOGRAPH.

Sullivan's Island struck near the lock of the magazine, and bent the copper door, so that all access to the few cartridges we had there was cut off. Just previous to this the officers had been engaged, amid a shower of shells, in vigorous efforts to cut away wood-work which was dangerously near the magazine.

After the surrender we were allowed to salute our flag with a hundred guns before marching out, but it was very dangerous and difficult to do so; for, owing to the recent conflagration, there were fire and sparks all around the cannon, and it was not easy to find a safe place of deposit for the cartridges. It happened that some flakes of fire had entered the muzzle of one of the guns after it was sponged. Of course, when the gunner attempted to ram the cartridge down it exploded prematurely, killing Private Daniel Hough instantly, and setting fire to a pile of cartridges underneath, which also exploded, seriously wounding five men. Fifty guns were fired in the salute.

With banners flying, and with drums beating "Yankee Doodle," we marched on board the transport that was to take us to the steamship *Baltic*, which drew too much water to pass the bar and was anchored outside. We were soon on our way to New York.

With the first shot against Sumter the whole North became united. Mobs went about New York and made every doubtful newspaper and private house display the Stars and Stripes. When we reached that city we had a royal reception. The streets were alive with banners. Our men and officers were seized and forced to ride on the shoulders of crowds wild with enthusiasm. When we purchased anything, merchants generally refused all compensation.

Fort Hamilton, where we were stationed, was besieged with visitors, many of whom were among the most highly distinguished in all walks of life. The Chamber of Commerce of New York voted a bronze medal to each officer and soldier of the garrison.

We were soon called upon to take an active part in the war, and the two Sumter companies were sent under my command to reënforce General Patterson's column, which was to serve in the Shenandoah Valley. Our march through Pennsylvania was a continuous ovation. Flowers, fruits, and delicacies of all kinds were showered upon us, and the hearts of the people seemed overflowing with gratitude for the very little we had been able to accomplish.

Major Anderson was made a brigadier-general in the regular army, and assigned to command in his native State, Kentucky; but his system had been undermined by his great responsibilities; he was threatened with softening of the brain, and was obliged to retire from active service. The other officers were engaged in battles and skirmishes in many parts of the field of war. Anderson, Foster, Seymour, Crawford, Davis, and myself became major-generals of volunteers. Norman J. Hall, who rendered brilliant service at Gettysburg, became a colonel, and would doubtless have risen higher had he not been compelled by ill health to retire. Talbot became an assistant adjutant-general with the rank of captain, but died before the war had fairly begun. He was not with us during the bombardment, as he had been sent as a special messenger to Washington with dispatches. Lieutenant Snyder of the engineers, a most promising young officer, also died at the very commencement of hostilities.

Only one of our number left us and joined the Confederacy,—Lieutenant R. K. Meade of the engineers, a Virginian. His death occurred soon after.

SUMTER.   GUARD-BOAT.   CHARLESTON.   CASTLE PINCKNEY.   MOULTRIE.

MAJOR ANDERSON'S MEN CROSSING IN BOATS TO FORT SUMTER. FROM A WAR-TIME SKETCH.

THE SOUTH-WEST OR GORGE FRONT OF FORT SUMTER, SHOWING THE GATE WHARF, AND ESPLANADE, MACHICOULIS GALLERIES ON THE PARAPET, AND THE EFFECT OF THE FIRE FROM CUMMING'S POINT AND FORT JOHNSON.   FROM A PHOTOGRAPH.

INSIDE SUMTER IN '61.

BY JAMES CHESTER, CAPTAIN THIRD ARTILLERY, U. S. A.

TOWARD the close of 1860, the national defenses of Charleston Harbor, consisting of Castle Pinckney, Fort Moultrie, and Fort Sumter, were garrisoned by an army of 65 men instead of the 1050 men that were required. Fort Moultrie alone, where the 65 soldiers were stationed, required 300 men for its defense, and Fort Sumter, to which they were ultimately transferred, was designed for a garrison of 650.

Fort Moultrie, at the time of which we write, was considered a rather pleasant station, Sullivan's Island being a favorite summer resort. Many of the wealthy citizens of Charleston had their summer residences there, and indeed some of them lived there all the year round. There was a large summer hotel on the beach half-way up the island, and a horse railway connected the steamboat wharf and the hotel. The military reservation stretched across the island from the front to the back beach, like a waistbelt of moderate width, and the fort looked like a big buckle at the front end. It was a brick structure, or rather an earthen structure revetted with brick. It was bastioned on the land side, and had a scarp wall perhaps fifteen feet high; but the sand had drifted against it at some points so as almost to bury its masonry. With its full complement of men it could hardly have been held against a numerous and enterprising enemy, and with 65 men it was plainly untenable.

This garrison consisted of two skeleton companies and the regimental band of the 1st Artillery. They had occupied the fort since 1857, and were fairly well acquainted in the neighborhood. Indeed, several of the men had been enlisted at the post, and were native Carolinians. As the political pot began to boil toward the close of 1860 and secession was openly discussed, the social position of the garrison became anomalous. Army officers had always been favorites in the South; and as they were discreet and agreeable, it is not surprising, perhaps, that their society continued to be sought after, even by the most outspoken secessionists, up to the actual commencement of hostilities. But enlisted men, even in the South, were social outcasts. It was rather surprising, therefore, to find them receiving attentions from civilians. But the fact is that the soldiers of the army were never before treated with such consideration in the South as on the eve of the rebellion. ☆   The secession-

☆ An amusing incident which illustrates this occurred during the election excitement in November, 1860. Elections in South Carolina were always peculiar. It could hardly be said that there were two parties, but there generally were two candidates for every office in the State. In

ists were determined to have the fort, and they wanted to get it without bloodshed. They had failed with the commissioned officers, and they had no better success with the soldiers: every enlisted man remained faithful to the Union.

The old commander of Fort Moultrie, Colonel John L. Gardner, was removed; the new one, Major Robert Anderson of Kentucky, arrived on November 21st. As a Southern man, he was expected to be reasonable. If he had scruples upon the question of qualified allegiance, he might surrender on demand, on purely professional grounds. No one doubted Major Anderson's professional ability, and of course he could see the hopelessness of his situation at Moultrie. Moreover, he was a humane man, and would be unwilling to shed blood needlessly. But his actions clearly indicated that he would not surrender on demand. He continued defensive preparations with as much energy and zeal as his predecessor, and manifestly meant to fight. This was very discouraging to the preachers of bloodless secession, and when he transferred his command to Sumter their occupation was completely gone. Nothing but war would now get him out. Hence the efforts to get him ordered back again by President Buchanan—efforts which almost succeeded.

The transfer of Major Anderson's command from Moultrie to Sumter was neatly executed early in the evening of December 26th, 1860. It was a few minutes after sunset when the troops left Moultrie; the short twilight was about over when they reached the boats; fifteen or twenty minutes more carried them to Sumter. The workmen had just settled down to an evening's enjoyment when armed men at the door startled them. There was no parleying, no explaining; nothing but stern commands, silent astonishment, and prompt obedience. The workmen were on the wharf, outside the fort, before they were certain whether their captors were secessionists or Yankees.

Meantime the newly arrived troops were busy enough. Guards were posted, embrasures secured, and, as far as practicable, the place was put in a defensible condition against any storming-party which chagrin might drive the guard-boat people to send against it. Such an attempt was perfectly feasible. The night was very dark; the soldiers were on unknown ground

such cases the candidates would each give a barbecue or feast of some kind to the voters, at which stump speeches were delivered in a somewhat florid style. The whole body of voters attended both entertainments, and it is to be feared decided rather upon the merits of the feast than the fitness of the candidate. At one of these entertainments on Sullivan's Island, the regimental band attended,—hired as an attraction,—and such soldiers as were on pass gathered around the outskirts of the crowd which surrounded the open-air supper table. The supper was over, and the speaking had begun. Everything eatable had been devoured except a remnant of ham which rested on a platter in front of the chairman — who perhaps was also the candidate — at one end of the long table. The chairman was speaking, and the audience was enthusiastic. A storm of applause had just broken out at something the speaker had said, when a soldier, who had had his eyes on the fragment of ham for some time, deliberately mounted the table at the lower end, and carefully picking his steps among the dishes, walked to the chairman's end, picked up the coveted fragment, and started on the return trip. The audacity of the man stunned the audience for a moment, but indignation soon got the better of astonishment, and the soldier was in some danger of rough treatment. But the chairman had his revolver out in a second, and holding it aloft proclaimed: "I'll shoot the first man who interferes with that soldier." And the soldier carried off the fragment. Of course he was drunk; but he could not have done the same thing without a drubbing in 1859. This anecdote — and others might be related — indicates the policy and perhaps the expectations of the secessionists in connection with the soldiers of Fort Moultrie.—J. C.

and could not find their way about readily; many of the embrasures could not be closed; and there were at least a hundred willing guides and helpers already on the wharf and in a fine frame of mind for such work. But nothing was attempted, and when the soldiers felt themselves in a position to repel any attempt against them that night, two guns were fired as a signal to friends that the occupation had been successfully accomplished, and that they might proceed with their part of the programme. This was the first intimation the guard-boat people had of the transfer; and, indeed, it told them nothing, except that some soldiers must have got into Sumter. But they blew their alarm-whistle all the same, and burned blue-lights; signal-rockets were sent up from various points, and there was great excitement everywhere in the harbor until morning.

When the signal-guns were fired, the officer in charge of the two schooners which had carried provisions and ammunition to Fort Johnson (under the pretense that they were subsistence for the women and children, whom he had also carried there as a cloak) cast loose his lines and made all speed for Sumter, and the old sergeant who had been left in Moultrie for the purpose set fire to the combustibles which had been heaped around the gun-carriages, while another man spiked the guns. The garrison from the ramparts of its new nest grimly approved of the destruction of the old one.

At dawn of December 27th the men were up and ready for any emergency; indeed, most of them had been up all night. Captain Foster had been specially busy with his former employees. Among them he found several loyal men, and also some doubtful ones who were willing to share the fortunes of the garrison. These constituted an acceptable addition to our working strength, although those classed as doubtful would have been an element of weakness in case of a fight. However, they did much good work before hostilities began, and the worst ones were weeded out before we were closely invested. Those who remained to the end were excellent men. They endured the hardships of the siege and the dangers of the bombardment without a murmur, and left Sumter with the garrison — one of them, John Swearer, severely wounded — with little besides the clothes they stood in. They were the first volunteers for the Union, but were barred from the benefits secured by legislation for the national soldiers, having never been "mustered in."

Fort Sumter was unfinished, and the interior was filled with building materials, guns, carriages, shot, shell, derricks, timbers, blocks and tackle, and coils of rope in great confusion. Few guns were mounted, and these few were chiefly on the lowest tier. The work was intended for three tiers of guns, but the embrasures of the second tier were incomplete, and guns could be mounted on the first and third tiers only.

The complete armament of the work had not yet arrived, but there were more guns on hand than we could mount or man. The first thing to be considered was immediate defense. The possibility of a sudden dash by the enemy, under cover of darkness and guided by the discharged workmen then in Charleston, demanded instant attention. It was impossible to spread 65 men over ground intended for 650, so some of the embrasures had to be bricked up. Selecting those, therefore, essential to artillery defense, and mounting guns in them, Anderson closed the rest. This was the work of many days; but we were in no immediate danger of an artillery attack. The armament of Moultrie was destroyed; its guns were spiked, and their carriages burned; and it would take a longer time to put them in condition than it would to mount the guns of Sumter.

On the parade were quantities of flag-stones standing on end in masses and columns everywhere. We dared not leave them where they were, even if they had not been in the way, because mortar shells bursting among them would have made the very bomb-proofs untenable. A happy idea occurred to some one in authority, and the flag-stones were arranged two tiers high in front of the casemates, and just under the arches, thus partly closing the casemates and making excellent splinter-proofs. This arrangement, no doubt,

THE SALLY-PORT OF FORT SUMTER.
FROM A PHOTOGRAPH TAKEN FROM THE WHARF.

saved the garrison from many wounds similar to that inflicted on John Swearer, for it was in passing an opening unprotected by the screen that he was struck by a fragment of shell.

Moving such immense quantities of material, mounting guns, distributing shot, and bricking up embrasures kept us busy for many weeks. But order was coming out of chaos every day, and the soldiers began to feel that they were a match for their adversaries. Still, they could not shut their eyes to the fact that formidable works were growing up around them. The secessionists were busy too, and they had the advantage of unlimited labor and material. Fort Moultrie had its armament again in position, and was receiving the framework of logs which formed the foundation for its sandbag bomb-proofs. The Stevens' Point floating battery was being made impregnable by an overcoat of railroad iron; and batteries on Morris, James, and Sullivan's islands were approaching completion. But our preparations were more advanced than theirs; and if we had been permitted to open on them at this time, the bombardment of Sumter would have had a very different termination. But our hands were tied by policy and instructions.

The heaviest guns in Sumter were three ten-inch columbiads—considered very big guns in those days. They weighed fifteen thousand pounds each, and were intended for the gorge and salient angles of the work. We found them skidded on the parade ground. Besides these there was a large number of eight-inch columbiads—more than we could mount or man—and a full supply of 42, 32, and 24-pounders, and some eight-inch sea-coast howitzers.

There was an ample supply of shot and shell, and plenty of powder in the magazines, but friction primers were not abundant and cartridge-bags were scarce. The scarcity of cartridge-bags drove us to some strange makeshifts. During the bombardment several tailors were kept busy making cartridge-bags out of soldiers' flannel shirts, and we fired away several dozen pairs of woolen socks belonging to Major Anderson. In the matter of friction primers strict economy had to be observed, as we had no means of improvising a substitute.

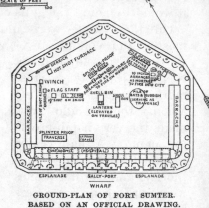

GROUND-PLAN OF FORT SUMTER.
BASED ON AN OFFICIAL DRAWING.

Our first efforts in preparation were directed toward mounting the necessary guns on the lowest tier. These consisted of 42 and 32-pounders, and as the necessary trucks, gins, and tackle were on hand, the work went on rapidly. The men were in fine condition and as yet well fed; besides, they had the assistance of the engineer workmen, who soon became experts at this kind of work. Meantime a party of mechanics were making the main gate secure. This was situated at the middle of the gorge or base of the pentagon (the trace of the work was pentagonal), which was also the south-west side. It was closed by two heavy iron-studded gates, the outer a folding pair, and the inner arranged on pulleys, so that it could be raised or lowered at will. It was clear that the enemy, if he meant to bombard us, would erect batteries on Morris Island, and thus would be able to deliver an oblique fire on the gate sufficient to demolish it in a very few minutes. The gate once demolished, a night assault would become practicable.

To meet this possible emergency the main entrance was closed by a substantial brick wall, with a man-hole in the middle two feet wide and opposite to the man-hole in the gate. This wall was about six feet high, and to increase the security and sweep the wharf, an eight-inch sea-coast howitzer was mounted on its upper carriage without any chassis, so as to fire through the man-hole. The howitzer was kept loaded with double canister. To induce the belief that the folding gates were our sole dependence at this point, their outer surface was covered with iron.

The lower tier of guns being mounted, the more difficult operation of sending guns up to the third tier began. The terre-plein of the work was about fifty feet above parade level,— a considerable hoist,— but a pair of shears being already in position, and our tackle equal to the weight of eight-inch columbiads, the work went on amidst much good humor until all the guns of that caliber were in position.

We had now reached a problem more difficult to solve, namely, sending up our ten-inch columbiads. We were extremely desirous to have them—or at least two of them—on the upper tier. They were more powerful guns than any the enemy had at that time, and the only ones in our possession capable of smashing the iron-clad defenses which might be constructed against us. We had rumors that an iron-clad floating battery was being built in Charleston, which the enemy proposed to anchor in some convenient position so as to breach Sumter at his leisure. We had no faith in the penetrating power of the eight-inch guns, and if we wished to demolish this floating adversary, it was necessary that the ten-inch guns should be mounted. Besides, an iron-clad battery was well on the road to completion at Cumming's Point (twelve hundred yards from the weakest side of Sumter), which, from what we could see of it, would be impervious to any less powerful gun.

There was in the fort a large coil of very heavy rope, new, and strong enough to sustain fifteen thousand pounds, but some of the doubtful workmen had cut several strands of it at various points on the outside of the coil; at least we could account in no other way for the damage. Besides, we had no blocks large enough to receive the rope even if it had been uninjured. The rope was uncoiled and examined. The portion on the inner side of the coil was found uninjured, and a few splices gave rope enough for a triple tackle sixty feet long. The improvisation of blocks of sufficient size and strength now became the sole remaining difficulty, and it was overcome in this way: the gun-carriages of those days were made of well-seasoned oak, and one of them was cut up and the material used for the construction of blocks. When the blocks were finished the iron-clad battery was shorn of half its terrors.

The tackle thus improvised was rigged on the shears, the first gun was rolled into position for hoisting, the sling was attached, and the windlass was manned. After carefully inspecting every knot and lashing, the officer in charge gave the word, " Heave away," and the men bent to their work steadily and earnestly, feeling, no doubt, that the battle with the iron-clad had really begun. Every eye watched the ropes as they began to take the strain, and when the gun had fairly left the skids, and there was no accident, the song which anxiety had suspended was resumed, all hands joining in the chorus, " On the plains of Mexico," with a sonorous heartiness that might well have been heard at Fort Moultrie. The gun made the vertical passage of fifty feet successfully, and was safely landed on the terre-plein. The chassis and carriage were then sent up, transported to the proper emplacement, and put in position, and the gun was mounted.

The ten-inch columbiad threw a shot weighing one hundred and twenty-eight pounds, and it was now necessary that a supply of such shot should be raised. Of course, they could have been sent up at the derrick, but that would have been a slow process, and, moreover, it would have required the derrick and the men, when they were needed for other work. So after retreat roll-call, when the day's work was over, the men were bantered by some designing sergeant as to their ability to carry a ten-inch shot up the stairway. Some of the soldiers, full of confidence and energy, shouldered a shot each and started. They accomplished the feat, and the less confident, unwilling to be outdone by comrades no bigger than themselves, shouldered a shot each and made the passage. In a few minutes sixty shot were deposited near the gun ; and it became the custom to carry up a ten-inch shot after retreat—just for fun—as long as there were any to carry.

These trivial incidents serve to show the spirit and humor of the men better than any description. There never was a happier or more contented set of men in any garrison than the Sumter soldiers. There was no sulkiness among them, and no grumbling until they had to try their teeth on spun yarn as a substitute for tobacco. This occurred long before the ration was reduced, and it produced some of the loudest grumbling ever listened to.

The second ten-inch columbiad was less fortunate than its fellow. It reached the level of the terre-plein without accident, but almost at the first haul on the watch tackle to swing it in, it broke away and fell with a dull thud. There was no mirth in the faces of the men at the watch tackle as they looked over the edge of the parade wall to see how many of the men at the windlass were left. The gun had descended, breech first, like a bolt from a catapult, and had buried itself in the sand up to the trunnions; but beyond breaking the transoms of the derrick, no damage was done. The cause of the accident was easily discovered. The amateur block-maker, unwilling to weaken the blocks by too much trimming, had left their upper edges too sharp, and the strap of the upper block had been cut in consequence. In four days the derrick was repaired, and the gun safely landed on the terre-plein.

The third ten-inch columbiad was not sent up. It was mounted as a mortar on the parade, for the purpose of shelling Charleston should that become advisable. A mortar platform already existed there. A ten-inch top carriage was placed on it and the gun mounted pointing toward the city.

A laughable incident occurred in connection with this gun soon after it was mounted. Some of the officers were anxious to try how it would work, and perhaps to see how true its alignment was, and to advertise to the enemy the fact that we had at least one formidable mortar in Fort Sumter. At any rate they obtained permission from Major Anderson to try the gun with a " very small charge." So, one afternoon the gun was loaded with a blind shell, and what was considered a " very small charge" of powder. The regulation charge for the gun, as a gun, was eighteen pounds. On this occasion two pounds only were used. It was not expected that the shell would be thrown over a thousand yards, and as the bay was clear no danger was anticipated. Everything being in readiness, the gun was fired, and the eyes of the garrison followed the shell as it described its graceful curve in the direction of the city. By the time it reached the summit of its trajectory, the fact that the charge used was not a " very small" one for the gun fired as a mortar became painfully apparent to every observer, and fears were entertained by some that the shell would reach the city, or at least the shipping near the wharves. But fortunately it fell short, and did no damage beyond scaring the secessionist guard-boat then leaving the wharf for her nightly post of observation. The guard-boat put back and Sumter was visited by a flag of truce, perhaps to find out the meaning of our performance. No doubt the explanations given were satisfactory. No more experiments for range were tried with that gun, but we knew that Charleston was within range.

Although the full armament of Sumter was not on hand, there were many more guns than places to put them. This resulted from the fact that no guns were mounted on the second tier, and because many embrasures on the first tier were bricked up. There were four unplaced eight-inch columbiads after the fort had been satisfactorily garnished with guns. But we were entirely without mortars. Perhaps this serious defect in our armament, and perhaps our success with the ten-inch gun mounted as a mortar, induced Major Anderson to mount his extra eight-inch guns in that way. Morris Island, twelve hundred yards away, was the nearest terra firma to Fort Sumter, and there the enemy would plant his most important batteries. The more searching and severe the fire that could be brought to bear upon that island, therefore, the better. So the four extra columbiads were mounted as mortars to fire in that direction. We had no carriages for the guns and no platforms. So a trench

INTERIOR OF SUMTER AFTER THE SURRENDER, SHOWING THE 8-INCH COLUMBIADS PLANTED AS MORTARS, AND THE CONFEDERATE FLAG FLYING FROM THE DERRICK BY WHICH THE GUNS WERE RAISED TO THE UPPER TIER. FROM A PHOTOGRAPH.

was dug in the parade at right angles to the proposed line of fire. A heavy timber was then embedded in the sand at the bottom of the trench, and another on the Morris Island side of it, in such a way that a gun resting on the one and leaning on the other would be supported at an angle of forty-five degrees. The guns were then placed in notches at equal intervals along the trench. We had no opportunity to try this novel mortar battery, but everybody was satisfied that it could have done good service.

It was expected that the walls of Fort Sumter would be able to withstand the guns which we knew the enemy possessed, but we did not anticipate importations from abroad. During the bombardment a Whitworth gun of small caliber, just received from England, was mounted in one of the Morris Island batteries, and in a few rounds demonstrated its ability to breach the work. Fortunately its supply of ammunition was limited, and the fire stopped short of an actual breach. But a few hours more of that Whitworth 12-pounder would have knocked a hole in our defenses.

A breach was not dreaded by the garrison, for, weak as it was, it could have given a good account of itself defending a breach. The greatest danger was a simultaneous attack on all sides. Sixty-four men could not be made very effective at a dozen different points. The possibility of the enemy, under cover of darkness, getting a foothold in force on the narrow bit of riprapping between tide-water and the foundation of the scarp was ever present in our minds.

The most likely place to land was the wharf, a stone structure in front of the main entrance. There an assaulting column might be formed and the main gate stormed, while the bulk of the garrison was defending the embrasures. To checkmate any such attempt, means of blowing the wharf out of existence were devised. Two five-gallon demijohns filled with powder were planted as mines, well under the wharf pavement, in such a way as to insure the total demolition of the structure by their explosion. These mines were arranged so that both should explode at the same instant. The means of firing were twofold: first, a powder-hose leading from the mines through a wooden trough buried under the pavement, and terminating in a dry well just inside the gate; second, a long lanyard connected with friction primers inserted in the corks of the powder demijohns, and extending through the trough into the well, whence it branched like a bell wire to convenient points inside the fort.

Another place offering special advantages to a storming party was the esplanade. This was a broad promenade extending the whole length of the gorge wall on the outside, and paved with immense blocks of dressed granite. As Fort Sumter was not designed to resist attack by storm, the esplanade was unswept by any fire. To remedy this defect the stone fougasse was resorted to. To the uninitiated the "fougasse" looked like a harmless pile of stones resting against the scarp wall. The only thing that would be likely to attract his attention was the bin-like inclosure of solid masonry open at the outer side, which looked like an immense dust-pan, and which he might think was a rather elaborate arrangement to hold merely a pile of stones together. There was nothing to indicate that beneath the stones, in the angle close to the scarp wall, a magazine of gunpowder lay concealed, and that behind were arrangements for firing it from the inside of the works. These harmless-looking piles of stones were mines of the deadliest kind. In addition, two eight-inch sea-coast howitzers were mounted on their upper carriages only, and placed in front of the main entrance, pointing to the right and left so as to sweep the esplanade.

The possibility of a hostile landing on the narrow strip of riprapping between the scarp wall and tide-water still remained to be provided for. Before secondary defenses were constructed, this was a continuous dead space on which a thousand men could have found a safe lodgment perfectly screened from fire and observation. The danger from such a lodgment was, that from it all our embrasures could have been assaulted at the same time. It was all-important, therefore, that the entrance by an embrasure should be made as difficult as possible. The ledge of riprapping was little more than four feet below the sills of the embrasures, and there would have been no difficulty in stepping in, if the two or three guards inside were disposed of. This fact was well known to the enemy, and we felt certain that, if he decided to attempt an assault in this way, he would consider scaling-ladders unnecessary. In order

INTERIOR OF SUMTER AFTER THE BOMBARDMENT, SHOWING THE GATE AND THE GORGE WALL; ALSO ONE
OF THE 8-INCH COLUMBIADS SET AS MORTARS, BEARING ON MORRIS ISLAND. FROM A PHOTOGRAPH.

to disappoint him, therefore, we removed the riprapping in front of each
embrasure to the depth of four or five feet, rolling the large stones into the
water. This gave a height of eight or nine feet to the embrasure sills.

Machicoulis galleries were also erected on all the flanks and faces of the
work. The machicoulis when completed looked like an immense dry-goods
box, set upon the parapet so as to project over the wall some three or four
feet. The beams upon which it rested extended inward to the terre-plein
and were securely anchored down. But the dry-goods box was deceptive.
Inside it was lined with heavy iron plates to make it bullet-proof. That portion
of the bottom which projected beyond the wall was loop-holed for musketry,
and a marksman in the machicoulis could shoot a man, however close he
might be to the scarp wall. But musketry from the machicoulis could hardly
be expected to beat off a determined assault upon the flanks and faces of
the work. To meet this difficulty, hand-grenades were improvised. Shells of
all sizes, from 12-pounders to 10-inch, were loaded, and the fuse-holes stopped
with wooden plugs. The plugs were then bored through with a gimlet, and
friction primers inserted. Behind the parapet at short intervals, and
wherever it was thought they might be useful, numbers of these shell-grenades
were stored under safe cover in readiness for any emergency. The method
of throwing them was simple. Lanyards of sufficient length to reach to
within about four feet of the riprapping were prepared, and fastened securely
at the handle end near the piles of shell-grenades. To throw a grenade, the
soldier lifted it on the parapet, hooked the lanyard into the eye of the friction
primer, and threw the shell over the parapet. When the lanyard reached
its length, the shell exploded. Thus a very few men would be more than a
match for all that could assemble on the riprapping.

Another contrivance, the "flying fougasse," or bursting barrel, a device of Captain Truman Seymour, consisted of an ordinary cask or barrel filled with broken stones, and having in its center a canister of powder, sufficient to burst the barrel and scatter its contents with considerable force. A fuse connected the powder in the canister with a friction primer in the bung, and the barrel was exploded by attaching a lanyard to the eye of the primer, and letting the barrel roll over the parapet, as in the case of the shell-grenade. If one experiment can justify an opinion, the flying fougasse would have been a success. When it became known in the fort that one of the barrels was about to be fired as an experiment, the novelty of the thing attracted most of the men to the place, and the little crowd attracted the attention of the enemy. No doubt glasses were focused on the party from every battery within sight. When everything was ready the barrel was allowed to roll over the parapet, and an instant afterward a terrific explosion took place. The stones were thrown in every direction, and the surface of the water was lashed into foam for a considerable distance. The effect as seen by the secessionists must have appeared greater than it did to us, although we thought it quite satisfactory. The Charleston newspapers described the effect of the "infernal machine" as simply terrific. Only three of them were constructed, yet for moral effect an empty barrel set upon the parapet would have been just as good.

In war, plan as we may, much depends upon accident, and the moral effect of very insignificant incidents is often considerable. For this reason "Wittyman's Masterpiece" deserves to be mentioned. Wittyman was a German carpenter, not very familiar with English, and wholly ignorant of military engineering. His captain had conceived the idea that a *cheval-de-frise* across the riprapping at the salient angles of the fort would confine the enemy on whatever face he landed until he had been treated liberally with shell-grenades. So Wittyman was ordered to build a *cheval-de-frise* at the angle of the gorge nearest Morris Island. It was easy to see that Wittyman was not familiar with *chevaux-de-frise*, so the captain explained and roughly illustrated the construction. At last Wittyman seemed to grasp the idea and went to work upon it forthwith. Perhaps the work was not examined during construction, nor seen by any one but Wittyman until it was placed. But from that day forward it was the fountain of amusement for the men. No matter how sick or sad a man might be, let him look at the masterpiece and his ailments were forgotten. Not a steamer passed,—and they were passing almost every hour,—but every glass on board was leveled at the masterpiece. But it baffled every one of them. Not one could guess what it was, or what it was intended to be; and after the bombardment was over we learned, quite accidentally, that it had been set down by the enemy as a means of exploding the mines.

Any description of the siege of Sumter would be incomplete without some sort of reference to the *Star of the West* fiasco. At reveille on the 9th of January, it became generally known among the men that a large steamer flying the United States flag was off the bar, seemingly at anchor. There had been some talk among the men, based upon rumors from Charleston, that the garrison would either be withdrawn from the harbor or returned to

Fort Moultrie; and there were some who believed the rumors. These believers were now confident that withdrawal had been determined on, and that the steamer off the bar was the transport come to take them away. There was no denying that appearances favored the theory, yet there was no enthusiasm. The men were beginning to feel that they were a match for their adversaries, and they were loath to leave without proving it. And, indeed, at that time Sumter was master of the situation. Moultrie had very few guns mounted,—only one, according to report,—and that fact ought to have been known to the people on the *Star of the West*. It was known officially in Washington that fourteen days previously Major Anderson had spiked the guns and burned the carriages at Moultrie, and gun-carriages cannot be replaced in two weeks when they have to be fabricated. Hence Moultrie could not have been formidable, and as soon as it should have passed the battery on Morris Island, it would have been comparatively safe.

INTERIOR OF FORT SUMTER — THE 10-INCH COLUMBIAD BEARING ON CHARLESTON. FROM A PHOTOGRAPH.

When the *Star of the West* was seen standing in, the novelty of a steamer carrying the national flag had more attractions for the men than the breakfast table. They soon made her out to be a merchant steamer, as the walking-beam, plainly visible as she rounded into the channel, was unknown on a man-of-war. She had taken the Morris Island channel, and was approaching at a fair rate of speed. Perhaps every man in Sumter was on the ramparts, but there was no excitement. But when the blue puff of smoke from a hidden battery on Morris Island advertised the fact that she was being fired on, there was great scurrying and scampering among the men. The long roll was beaten, and the batteries were manned almost before the guns of the hidden battery had fired their second shot. As she approached, a single gun at Fort Moultrie opened at extreme long range, its shot falling over half a mile short. There seemed to be much perplexity among our officers, and Major Anderson had a conference with some of them in a room used as a laundry which opened on the terre-plein of the sea-flank. The conference was an impromptu one, as Captain Doubleday and Lieutenant Davis were not of it. But Captain Foster was there, and by his actions demonstrated his disappointment at the result. He left the laundry, bounding up the two or three steps that led to the terre-plein, smashing his hat, and muttering something about the flag, of which the words "trample on it" reached the ears of the men at the guns, and let them know that there was to be no fighting, on their part at least. Meantime the steamer had worn ship, and was standing out again, receiving the fire of the hidden battery in passing. This is about all the men saw or knew about the strange vessel at the time, although she came near enough for them to look down upon her decks and see that there were no troops visible on her.☆

With the exception of the mounting of the guns, the preparations described were chiefly intended to ward off assault. The actions of the enemy now indicated that he proposed to bombard the work at an early day. If we would meet Moultrie, and the numerous batteries which were being constructed against us, on anything like even terms, we must be prepared to shoot accurately.

Few artillerymen, without actual experience, have any idea of the difficulty of aiming a gun during a bombardment. They may be able to hit a target in ordinary practice with absolute certainty, and yet be unable to deliver a single satisfactory shot in a bombardment. The error from smoke is difficult to deal with, because it is a variable, depending upon the density of the smoke clouds which envelop your own and your adversary's batteries. (Within the writer's experience, a thin veil of fog protected a mass of army wagons—900, it was said—from the fire of some 8 or 10 guns, during a whole forenoon, although the guns were within easy range, and the wagons could be distinctly seen. Refraction saved them, every shot going over.) Then danger and its consequent excitement are also disturbing elements, especially where delicate instruments have to be used. It is easier to lead a forlorn hope than to set a vernier under a heavy artillery fire. Fortunately, we had officers of experience in Sumter, and fortunately, too, we had very few instruments; one gunner's level and two old quadrants being the extent of the outfit, with perhaps some breech-sights and tangent-scales. The paucity of aiming-instruments, and perhaps the experience of some of the officers, led to the devising of instruments and methods which neither smoke nor excitement could disturb; and as some of them, in a much more perfect form, have since been adopted, the rude originals may as well be described here. Aiming cannon consists of two distinct operations: namely, alignment and elevation. In the former, according to instructions and practice, the gunner depends upon his eye and the cannon-sights. But for night firing or when the enemy is enveloped in smoke,—as he is sure to be in any artillery duel,— the eye cannot be depended on. Visual aiming in a bombardment is a delusion and a snare. To overcome this difficulty, on clear days, when all the conditions were favorable to accuracy, and we could work at our leisure, every gun in the armament was carefully aimed at all the prominent objects within its field of fire, and its position marked on the traverse circle, the index being a pointer securely fastened to the traverse fork. After this had been done, alignment became as easy as setting a watch, and could be done by night or day, by the least intelligent soldier in the garrison.

The elevation was more difficult to deal with. The ordinary method by the use of a breech-sight could not be depended on, even if there had been a

☆ The troops on the *Star of the West* consisted of 200 men, under Lieut. Charles R. Woods.—EDITORS.

sufficient supply of such instruments, because darkness or smoke would render it inapplicable or inaccurate; and the two quadrants in the outfit could not be distributed all over the fort.

Before the correct elevation to carry a shot to a given object can be determined, it is necessary to know the exact distance of the object. This was obtained from the coast-survey chart of the harbor. The necessary elevation was then calculated, or taken from the tables, and the gun elevated accordingly by means of the quadrant. The question then became, How can the gunner bring the gun to this elevation in the heat of action, and without the use of a quadrant? There was an abundance of brass rods, perhaps a quarter-inch in diameter, in the fort. Pieces of such rods, eighteen inches long, were prepared by shaping one end to fit into a socket on the cheek of

EFFECT OF THE BOMBARDMENT ON THE BARBETTE GUNS OF THE SEA FRONT OF SUMTER. FROM A PHOTOGRAPH.

the carriage, and the other into a chisel edge. They were called by the men pointing rods. A vertical line was then drawn on the right breech of the gun, and painted white. The non-commissioned officer who attended to this preparation, having carefully elevated the gun with the quadrant for a particular object, set the pointing rod in the socket, and brought its chisel end down on the vertical line. The point thus cut was marked and the initials of the object to be struck with that elevation written opposite. These arrangements, which originated with Captain Doubleday, were of great value during the bombardment.

The preparation of Sumter for defense afforded a fine field for ingenuity, because nothing connected with its equipment was complete. As another illustration of this ingenuity, the following is in point. It might become desirable to continue a bombardment into the night, and the casemates, owing to the partial closing up of the arches with flagstones, were as dark as dungeons, even on very clear nights. Lights of some kind were absolutely necessary, but there were no candles and no lamps. There was a light-house on the fort, however, and the light-keeper had several barrels of oil on hand. Small tubes of tin, to receive wicks, were made, and fitted into disks of cork sufficiently large to float them on the surface of the oil. Coffee-cups were then filled with oil and the floats laid on the surface.

Among the many incidents of the siege may be mentioned the mishap of an ice-laden Yankee schooner that strayed within range of the secession batteries; the accidental solid shot fired at Fort Sumter by an impatient secessionist in the Cumming's Point battery, and the daring generosity of McInerny, a

THE "STAR OF THE WEST."

THE SUMTER GARRISON WATCHING THE FIRING ON THE "STAR OF THE WEST."
Fort Moultrie is shown on the left, and the smoke of the Morris Island battery on the extreme right.

warm-hearted and loyal Irishman, who did not "cross the broad Atlantic to become the citizen of only one Shtate," and who cheerfully risked his life and ruined his Sunday shirt by tearing a white flag from it, that he might be able to deliver in person his donation of tobacco to the besieged soldiers. There is one other incident which should find a place in these reminiscences.

Major Anderson was fully impressed with the solemn responsibilities which rested upon him when he transferred his command to Sumter. When he reached Sumter there were no halliards to the flag-staff, and as there was more pressing work on hand for several days, some time elapsed before it became possible to display the national flag. At length, however, halliards were rigged, and everything was ready for the flag. The usual method of proceeding in such a case would have been to order the sergeant of the guard to send up the flag, but it was otherwise arranged on this occasion. A dress-parade was ordered, and the little garrison formed around the flag-staff, the officers in the center. Presently Major Anderson, with Chaplain Harris of Fort Moultrie, who perhaps had been summoned for the purpose, approached the flag-staff, and the command was brought to "Attention." The flag, already bent to the halliards, was held by one officer, and another held the hoisting end of the halliards. The chaplain then, in a few words, invited those present to join with him in prayer, and Major Anderson, receiving the halliards from the officer who till that time had held them, knelt beside the chaplain, most of the officers and some of the men in the ranks following his example. Prayers being ended, all rose, and the flag of

Fort Sumter was raised by Major Anderson, and the halliards secured. He then turned toward the officers and directed that the companies be dismissed. If any of those who doubted the loyalty to the Union of Major Anderson could have had but one glimpse of that impressive scene, they would have doubted no longer.

The weary waiting for war or deliverance which filled up the few weeks that intervened between the preparations and the actual bombardment developed no discontent among the men, although food and fuel were getting scarce. The latter was replenished from time to time by tearing down sheds and temporary workshops, but the former was a constantly diminishing quantity, and the men could count on their fingers the number of days between them and starvation. It was a favorite belief among the secessionists that the pinchings of hunger would arouse a spirit of mutiny among the soldiers, and compel Major Anderson to propose terms of evacuation. But no such spirit manifested itself. On the contrary, the men exhibited a devotion to their Government and the officers appointed over them which surprised their enemies, but attracted little attention from their friends.⎪

The opening of the bombardment was a somewhat dramatic event. A relieving fleet was approaching, all unknown to the Sumter garrison, and General Beauregard, perhaps with the hope of tying Major Anderson's hands in the expected fight with that fleet, had opened negotiations with him on the 11th of April looking toward the evacuation of the fort. But Major Anderson declined to evacuate his post till compelled by hunger. The last ounce of breadstuffs had been consumed, and matters were manifestly approaching a crisis. It was evident from the activity of the enemy that something important was in the wind. That night we retired as usual. Toward half-past three on the morning of the 12th we were startled by a gun fired in the immediate vicinity of the fort, and many rose to see what was the matter. It was soon learned that a steamer from the enemy desired to communicate with Major Anderson, and a small boat under a flag of truce was received and delivered the message. Although no formal announcement of the fact was made, it became generally known among the men that in one hour General Beauregard would open his batteries on Sumter.

The men waited about for some time in expectation of orders, but received none, except an informal order to go to bed, and the information that reveille would be sounded at the usual hour. This was daylight, fully two hours off, so some of the men did retire. The majority perhaps remained up, anxious to see the opening, for which purpose they had all gone on the ramparts. Except that the flag was hoisted, and a glimmer of light was visible at the guard-house, the fort looked so dark and silent as to seem deserted. The morning was dark and raw. Some of the watchers surmised that Beauregard was " bluffing," and that there would be no bombardment. But

⎪ So faithful and true have the soldiers of the army always been that even very striking exhibitions of these qualities are not considered worthy of notice. There were military posts in 1861 which were abandoned by all the commissioned officers, at which not one of the enlisted men proved untrue. The loyalty of the latter has never been properly appreciated. — J. C.

CONFEDERATE FLOATING BATTERY IN ACTION AT THE WEST END OF SULLIVAN'S ISLAND.

Colonel Joseph A. Yates, who was a lieutenant in the attack on Fort Sumter, says in a letter accompanying the plan on the next page: "I send a rough sketch of the floating battery which I commanded; it is rough, but from my recollection it is very like her. The battery was substantially built, flat, heavily timbered on her shield, with railroad iron laid on it—two courses of rails turned inward and outward, so as to form a pretty smooth surface. The bags of sand represented on the deck were to counterweigh the guns, which were 32 and 42-pounders. She was struck many times, several shot going entirely through the shield."

promptly at 4:30 A. M. a flash as of distant lightning in the direction of Mount Pleasant, followed by the dull roar of a mortar, told us that the bombardment had begun. The eyes of the watchers easily detected and followed the burning fuse which marked the course of the shell as it mounted among the stars, and then descended with ever-increasing velocity, until it landed inside the fort and burst. It was a capital shot. Then the batteries opened on all sides, and shot and shell went screaming over Sumter as if an army of devils were swooping around it. As a rule the guns were aimed too high, but all the mortar practice was good. In a few minutes the novelty disappeared in a realizing sense of danger, and the watchers retired to the bomb-proofs, where they discussed probabilities until reveille.

Habits of discipline are strong among old soldiers. If it had not been for orders to the contrary, the men would have formed for roll-call on the open parade, as it was their custom to do, although mortar-shells were bursting there at the lively rate of about one a minute. But they were formed under the bomb-proofs, and the roll was called as if nothing unusual was going on. They were then directed to get breakfast, and be ready to fall in when "assembly" was beaten. The breakfast part of the order was considered a grim joke, as the fare was reduced to the solitary item of fat pork, very rusty indeed. But most of the men worried down a little of it, and were "ready" when the drum called them to their work.

By this time it was daylight, and the effects of the bombardment became visible. No serious damage was being done to the fort. The enemy had concentrated their fire on the barbette batteries, but, like most inexperienced gunners, they were firing too high. After daylight their shooting improved, until at 7:30 A. M., when "assembly" was beaten in Sumter, it had become fairly good. At "assembly" the men were again paraded, and the orders of the day announced. The garrison was divided into two reliefs, and the tour of duty at the guns was to be four hours. Captain Doubleday being the senior captain, his battery took the first tour.

There were three points to be fired upon,— the Morris Island batteries, the James Island batteries, and the Sullivan's Island batteries. With these last was included the famous iron-clad floating battery, which had taken up a position off the western end of Sullivan's Island to command the left flank of Sumter. Captain Doubleday divided his men into three parties: the first, under his own immediate command, was marched to the casemate guns bearing on Morris Island; the second, under Lieutenant Jefferson C. Davis, manned the casemate guns bearing on the James Island batteries; and the third—without a commissioned officer until Dr. Crawford joined it—was marched by a sergeant ⚓ to the guns bearing on Sullivan's Island. The guns in the lower tier, which were the only ones used during the bombardment,—except surreptitiously without orders,—were 32 and 42-pounders, and some curiosity was felt as to the effect of such shot on the iron-clad battery. The gunners made excellent practice, but the shot were seen to bounce off its sides like pease. After battering it for about an hour and a half, no visible effect had been produced, although it had perceptibly slackened its fire, perhaps to save ammunition. But it was evident that throwing 32-pounder shot at it, at a mile range, was a waste of iron, and the attention of the gunners was transferred to Fort Moultrie.

Moultrie was, perhaps, a less satisfactory target than the iron-clad. It was literally buried under sand-bags, the very throats of the embrasures being closed with cotton-bales. The use of cotton-bales was very effective as against shot, but would have been less so against shell. The fact that the embrasures were thus closed was not known in Sumter till after the bombardment. It explained what was otherwise inexplicable. Shot would be seen to strike an embrasure,

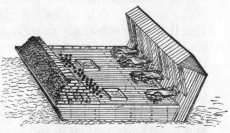

THE IRON-CLAD FLOATING BATTERY.
FROM A PLAN BY COLONEL JOSEPH A. YATES.

and the gunner would feel that he had settled one gun for certain, but even while he was receiving the congratulations of his comrades the supposed

⚓ The non-commissioned officers in Fort Sumter were Ordnance-Sergeant James Kearney, U. S. A., Quartermaster-Sergeant William H. Hammer, 1st U. S. Artillery; Regimental Band, 1st Artillery: Sergeant James E. Galway, Corporal Andrew Smith; Company E, 1st Artillery: First Sergeant Eugene Scheibner, Sergeants Thomas Kirnan, William A. Harn, and James Chester, Corporals Owen M'Guire, Francis J. Oakes, Charles Bringhurst, and Henry Ellerbrook; Company H, 1st Artillery: First Sergeant John Renehan, Sergeants James M'Mahon, John Carmody, and John Otto, Corporal Christopher Costolan. — EDITORS.

disabled gun would reply. That the cotton-bales could not be seen from Sumter is not surprising. The sand-bag casemates which covered the guns were at least eighteen feet thick, and the cotton-bale shutter was no doubt arranged to slide up and down like a portcullis inside the pile of sand-bags. The gunners of Sumter, not knowing of the existence of these shutters, directed their shot either on the embrasures for the purpose of disabling the enemy's guns, or so as to graze the sand-bag parapet for the purpose of reaching the interior of the work. The practice was very good, but the effect, for reasons already stated, was inconsiderable.

At the end of the first four hours, Doubleday's men were relieved from the guns and had an opportunity to look about them. Not a man was visible near any of the batteries, but a large party, apparently of non-combatants, had collected on the beach of Sullivan's Island, well out of the line of fire, to witness the duel between Sumter and Moultrie. Doubleday's men were not in the best of temper. They were irritated at the thought that they had been unable to inflict any serious damage on their adversary, and although they had suffered no damage in return they were dissatisfied. The crowd of unsympathetic spectators was more than they could bear, and two veteran sergeants determined to stir them up a little. For this purpose they directed two 42-pounders on the crowd, and, when no officer was near, fired. The first shot struck about fifty yards short, and, bounding over the heads of the astonished spectators, went crashing through the Moultrie House. The second followed an almost identical course, doing no damage except to the Moultrie House, and the spectators scampered off in a rather undignified manner. The Moultrie House was flying a yellow flag at the time, and the Charleston newspapers discoursed upon the barbarity of firing upon a hospital flag, forgetting, perhaps, that we also had a hospital in Sumter, which they treated to red-hot shot during the bombardment. Of course, none of the officers of Sumter knew anything about the two 42-pounder shot.

The smoke which enveloped the Confederate batteries during the first day, while not so thick as entirely to obscure them, was sufficiently so to make visual aiming extremely unreliable; and during the second day, when Sumter was on fire, nothing could be seen beyond the muzzles of our own guns. But the aiming arrangements, due to the foresight and ingenuity of Captain Doubleday, enabled us to fire with as much accuracy when we could not see the object as when we could.

Early on the first day several vessels of the fleet were observed off the bar, and orders were given to dip the flag to them. This was done, and the salute was returned, but while our flag was being hoisted after the third dip, a shell burst near the flag-staff and cut the halliards. This accident put the flag beyond our control. It ran down until the kinky halliards jammed in the pulley at the mast-head, and the flag remained at about half-staff. This has been interpreted as a signal of distress, but it was only an accident. There was no special distress in Sumter, and no signal to that effect was intended.

Major Anderson had given orders that only the casemate batteries should be manned. While this was undoubtedly prompted by a desire to save his men, it operated also, in some degree, to save the Confederates. Our most powerful batteries and all our shell guns were on the barbette tier, and, being forbidden their use, we were compelled to oppose a destructive shell fire with solid shot alone. This, especially as we had no mortars, was a great disadvantage.

SERGEANT JOHN CARMODY FIRING THE BARBETTE GUNS.

Had we been permitted to use our shell guns we could have set fire to the barracks and quarters in Moultrie; for, as it was, we wrecked them badly with solid shot, although we could not see them. Then the cotton-bale shutters would have been destroyed, and we could have made it much livelier generally for our adversaries. This was so apparent to the men, that one of them — a man named Carmody — stole up on the ramparts and deliberately fired every barbette gun in position on the Moultrie side of the work. The guns were already loaded and roughly aimed, and Carmody simply discharged them in succession; hence, the effect was less than it would have been if the aim had been carefully rectified. But Carmody's effort aroused the enemy to a sense of his danger. He supposed, no doubt, that Major Anderson had determined to open his barbette batteries, so he directed every gun to bear on the barbette tier of Fort Sumter, and probably believed that the vigor of his fire induced Major Anderson to change his mind. But the contest was merely Carmody against the Confederate States; and Carmody had to back down, not because he was beaten, but because he was unable, single-handed, to reload his guns.

Another amusing incident in this line occurred on the Morris Island side of the fort. There, in the gorge angle, a ten-inch columbiad was mounted, *en barbette*, and as the 42-pounders of the casemate battery were making no impression on the Cumming's Point iron battery, the two veteran sergeants who had surreptitiously fired upon the spectators, as already related, determined to try a shot at the iron battery from the big gun. As this was a direct violation of orders, caution was necessary. Making sure that the major was out of the way, and that no officers were near, the two sergeants stole upstairs to the ten-inch gun. It was loaded and aimed already, they very well knew, so all they would have to do was to fire it. This was the work of a few seconds only. The gun was fired, and those in the secret down below watched the flight of the shot in great expectations of decided results. Unfortunately the shot missed; not a bad shot—almost grazing the crest of the battery— but a miss. A little less elevation, a very little, and the battery would have been smashed: so thought the sergeants, for they had great faith in the power of their gun; and they determined to try a second shot. The gun was reloaded, a feat of some difficulty for two men, but to run it "in battery" was beyond their powers. It required the united efforts of six men to throw the carriage "in gear," and the two sergeants could not budge it. Things were getting desperate around them. The secessionists had noticed the first shot, and had now turned every gun that would bear on that ten-inch gun. They were just getting the range, and it was beginning to be uncomfortable for the sergeants, who in a fit of desperation determined to fire the gun "as she was." The elevating screw was given half a turn less elevation, and the primer was inserted in the vent. Then one of the sergeants ran down the spiral stairs to see if the coast were clear, leaving his comrade in a very uncomfortable position at the end of the lanyard, and lying flat on the floor. It was getting hotter up there every second, and a perfect hurricane of shot was sweeping over the prostrate soldier. Human nature could stand it no longer. The lanyard was pulled and the gun was fired. The other sergeant was hastening up the stairway, and had almost reached the top, when he met the gun coming down, or at least trying to. Having been fired "from battery," it had recoiled over the counter-hurters, and, turning a back somersault, had landed across the head of the stairway. Realizing in a moment what had happened, and what would be to pay if they were found out, the second sergeant crept to the head of the stairway and called his comrade, who, scared almost to death,— not at the danger he was in, but at the accident,—was still hugging the floor with the lanyard in his hand. Both got safely down, swearing eternal secrecy to each other; and it is doubtful if Major Anderson ever knew how that ten-inch gun came to be dismounted. It is proper to add that the shot was a capital one, striking just under the middle embrasure of the iron battery and half covering it with sand. If it had been a trifle higher it would have entered the embrasure.

The first night of the bombardment was one of great anxiety. The fleet might send reënforcements; the enemy might attempt an assault. Both would come in boats; both would answer in English. It would be horrible to fire upon friends; it would be fatal not to fire upon enemies. The night was dark and chilly. Shells were dropping into the fort at regular intervals, and the men were tired, hungry, and out of temper. Any party that approached that night would have been rated as enemies upon general principles. Fortunately nobody appeared; reveille sounded, and the men oiled their appetites with the fat pork at the usual hour by way of breakfast.

The second day's bombardment began at the same hour as did the first; that is, on the Sumter side. The enemy's mortars had kept up a very slow fire all night, which gradually warmed up after daylight as their batteries seemed to awaken, until its vigor was about equal to their fire of the day before. The fleet was still off the bar—perhaps waiting to see the end. Fire broke out once or twice in the officers' quarters, and was extinguished. It broke out again in several places at once, and we realized the truth and let the quarters burn. They were firing red-hot shot. This was about 9 o'clock. As soon as Sumter was noticed to be on fire the secessionists increased the fire of their batteries to a maximum. In the perfect storm of shot and shell that beat upon us from all sides, the flag-staff was shot down, but the old flag was rescued and nailed to a new staff. This, with much difficulty, was carried to the ramparts and lashed to some chassis piled up there for a traverse.

A CASEMATE GUN DURING THE CONFLAGRATION.

We were not sorry to see the quarters burn. They were a nuisance. Built for fire-proof buildings, they were not fire-proof. Neither would they burn up in a cheerful way. The principal cisterns were large iron tanks immediately under the roof. These had been riddled, and the quarters below had been deluged with water. Everything was wet and burned badly, yielding an amount of pungent piney smoke which almost suffocated the garrison.

The scene inside the fort as the fire gained headway and threatened the magazine was an exciting one. It had already reached some of our stores of loaded shells and shell-grenades. These must be saved at all hazard. Soldiers brought their blankets and covered the precious projectiles, and thus the most of them were saved. But the magazine itself was in danger. Already it was full of smoke, and the flames were rapidly closing in upon it. It was evident that it must be closed, and it would be many hours before it could be opened again. During these hours the fire must be maintained with such powder as we could secure outside the magazine. A number of barrels were rolled out for this purpose, and the magazine door—already almost too hot to handle—was closed.

It was the intention to store the powder taken from the magazine in several safe corners, covering it with damp soldiers' blankets. But safe corners were hard to find, and most of the blankets were already in use covering loaded shells. The fire was raging more fiercely than ever, and safety demanded that the uncovered powder be thrown overboard. This was instantly done, and if the tide had been high we should have been well rid of it. But the tide was low, and the pile of powder-barrels rested on the riprapping in front of the embrasure. This was observed by the enemy, and some shell guns were turned upon the pile, producing an explosion which blew the gun at that embrasure clear out of battery, but did no further damage.

The fire had now enveloped the magazine, and the danger of an explosion was imminent. Powder had been carried out all the previous day, and it was more than likely that enough had sifted through the cartridge-bags to carry the fire into the powder-chamber. Major Anderson, his head erect as if on parade, called the men around him;

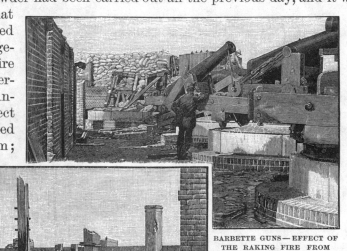

BARBETTE GUNS — EFFECT OF THE RAKING FIRE FROM FORT MOULTRIE.

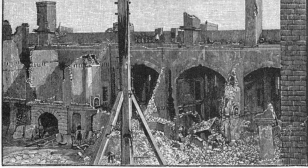

RUINS OF THE CASEMATES NEAR THE SALLY-PORT, AND OF THE FLAG-STAFF. FROM PHOTOGRAPHS.

directed that a shot be fired every five minutes; and mentioned that there was some danger of the magazine exploding. Some of the men, as soon as they learned what the real danger was, rushed to the door of the magazine and hurriedly dug a trench in front of it, which they kept filled with water until the danger was considered over.

It was during this excitement that ex-Senator Wigfall of Texas visited the fort. It came the turn of one of the guns on the left face of the work to fire,— we were now firing once in five minutes,— and as the cannoneer approached for the purpose of loading, he discovered a man looking in at the embrasure. The man must have raised himself to the level of the embrasure by grasping the sill with his hands. A short but lively altercation ensued between the man and the cannoneer, the man pleading to be taken in lest he should be killed with his own shot and shell. He was hauled in, Thompson, the cannoneer, first receiving his sword, to the point of which a white handkerchief was attached, not by way of surrender, but for convenience. Once inside, the bearer asked to see Major Anderson. The major was soon on the spot and opened the conversation by asking, "To what am I indebted for this visit?" The visitor replied, "I am Colonel Wigfall, of General Beauregard's staff. For God's sake, Major, let this thing stop. There has been enough bloodshed already." To which the major replied, "There has been none on my side, and besides, your batteries are still firing on me." At which Wigfall exclaimed, "I'll soon stop that," and turning to Thompson, who still held the sword under his arm, he said, pointing to the handkerchief, "Wave that out there." Thompson then handed the sword to Wigfall, saying, in substance, "Wave it yourself." Wigfall received back his sword and took a few steps toward the embrasure, when the major called him back, saying, "If you desire that to be seen you had better send it to the parapet." There was a good deal more said on the subject of the white flag both by Wigfall and the major which the writer cannot recall, but the end of it all was that a white flag was ordered to be displayed from the parapet at the request of Colonel Wigfall, and pending negotiations with him, which was instantly done, a hospital sheet being used for the purpose. Then the firing gradually ceased, and the major and his officers and Colonel Wigfall retired into the hospital bomb-proof, the only habitable room left. This was about 3 o'clock in the afternoon.

Wigfall's conference was not of long duration. He left the fort in the small boat which brought him from Morris Island, and which was manned by negroes. Shortly after his departure another small boat from Sullivan's Island, containing officers in full uniform (Wigfall wore citizen's dress with the sword), approached the fort. The officers in this boat were very much astonished and annoyed at being warned off by the sentinel, and compelled to show a white flag before they were permitted to approach. They were received by the officer of the day, who apologized for not meeting them afloat, saying that all our boats had been destroyed by shot or burned up. They were indignant at their reception, and demanded to know whether or not the fort had surrendered. What was said in reply was not distinctly heard by the writer, but it was believed to be a negative. The officer then asked what the white flag meant, and Wigfall's name was mentioned in reply, About this time Major Anderson made his appearance, and the visitors, still talking in an indignant tone, addressed themselves to him. What was said seemed to be a repetition of what had just been said to the officer of the day. The major's replies were inaudible where the writer of this stood, except when he raised his hand in a sweeping sort of gesture in the direction of Fort Moultrie, and said, "Very well, gentlemen, you can return to your batteries." They did not return, however, immediately, but were conducted into the hospital where Wigfall had been, and remained there some time. When they left we learned that there would be no more firing until General Beauregard had time to hear from his Government at Montgomery.

About 7 o'clock in the evening another white flag brought the announcement that the terms agreed upon between General Beauregard and Major Anderson had been confirmed, and that we would leave Fort Sumter the following day; which we did, after saluting our flag with fifty guns.

FORT JOHNSON. IRON-CLAD BATTERY, CUMMING'S POINT. FORT SUMTER. FORT MOULTRIE.

BURSTING OF THE SIGNAL-SHELL FROM FORT JOHNSON OVER FORT SUMTER.

THE FIRST STEP IN THE WAR.

BY STEPHEN D. LEE, LIEUTENANT-GENERAL, C. S. A.

IN the month of December, 1860, the South itself had no more realizing sense than the North of the magnitude of events about to be entered into so lightly. Even the Southern leaders did not realize that there could be any obstacle to "peaceable secession." Many at the North were willing to "let the wayward sisters depart in peace." Only a few on either side expected that blood would be shed. When, in the first Confederate Congress at Montgomery, one prudent debater exclaimed, "What if we really have a war?" the general response was, "There will be no war." "But," he persisted, "if there *is* a war, what are our resources?" and when one man in reply expressed his conviction that if the worst came, the South could put fifty thousand men into the field, he was looked upon as an enthusiast. The expectation of "peaceable secession" was the delusion that precipitated matters in the South; and it was on this expectation, when the crisis came, that South Carolina seceded. Her first step was to organize troops and assert the sovereignty in which she believed, by the occupation of her territory.

After the evacuation of Fort Moultrie, although Major Anderson was not permitted by the South Carolina authorities to receive any large supply of provisions, yet he received a daily mail, and fresh beef and vegetables from the city of Charleston, and was unmolested at Fort Sumter. He continued industriously to strengthen the fort. The military authorities of South Carolina, and afterward of the Confederate States, took possession of Fort Moultrie, Castle Pinckney, the arsenal, and other United States property in the vicinity. They also remounted the guns at Fort Moultrie, and constructed batteries on Sullivan's, Morris, and James islands, and at other places, looking to the reduction of Fort Sumter if it should become necessary; meantime leaving no stone unturned to secure from the authorities at Washington a quiet evacuation of the fort. Several arrangements to accomplish this purpose were almost reached, but failed. Two attempts were made to reënforce and supply the garrison: one by the steamer *Star of the West*, which tried to reach the fort, January 9th, 1861, and was driven back by a battery on Morris Island, manned by South Carolina troops; the other just before the bombardment of Sumter, April 12th. The feeling of the Confederate authorities was that a peaceful issue would finally be arrived at; but they had a fixed determination to use force, if necessary, to occupy the fort. They did not desire or intend to take the initiative, if it could be avoided. So soon, however, as it was clearly understood that the authorities at Washington had abandoned peaceful views, and would assert the power of the United States to supply Fort Sumter, General Beauregard, the commander of the Confederate forces at Charleston, in obedience to the command of his Government at Montgomery, proceeded to reduce the fort. His arrangements were about complete, and on April 11th he demanded of Major Anderson the evacuation of Fort Sumter. He offered to transport Major Anderson and his command to any port in the United States; and to allow him to move out of the fort with company arms and property, and all private property, and to salute his flag in lowering it. This demand was delivered to Major Anderson at 3:45 P. M., by two aides of General Beauregard, James Chesnut, Jr., and myself. At 4:30 P. M. he handed us his reply, refusing to accede to the demand; but added, "Gentlemen, if you do not batter the fort to pieces about us, we shall be starved out in a few days."

The reply of Major Anderson was put in General Beauregard's hands at 5:15 P. M., and he was also told of this informal remark. Anderson's reply and remark were communicated to the Confederate authorities at Montgomery. The Secretary of War, L. P. Walker, replied to Beauregard as follows:

"Do not desire needlessly to bombard Fort Sumter. If Major Anderson will state the time at which, as indicated by him, he will evacuate, and agree that in the meantime he will not use his guns against us, unless ours should be employed against Fort Sumter, you are authorized thus to avoid the effusion of blood. If this, or its equivalent, be refused, reduce the fort as your judgment decides to be most practicable."

FRANCIS W. PICKENS, GOVERNOR OF SOUTH CAROLINA, 1861. FROM A PHOTOGRAPH.

The same aides bore a second communication to Major Anderson, based on the above instructions, which was placed in his hands at 12:45 A. M., April 12th. His reply indicated that he would evacuate the fort on the 15th, provided he did not in the meantime receive contradictory instructions from his Government, or additional supplies, but he declined to agree not to open his guns upon the Confederate troops, in the event of any hostile demonstration on their part against his flag. Major Anderson made every possible effort to retain the aides till daylight, making one excuse and then another for not replying. Finally, at 3:15 A.M., he delivered his reply. In accordance with their instructions, the aides read it and, finding it unsatisfactory, gave Major Anderson this notification:

"FORT SUMTER, S. C., April 12, 1861, 3:20 A. M.—SIR: By authority of Brigadier-General Beauregard, commanding the Provisional Forces of the Confederate States, we have the honor to notify you that he will open the fire of his batteries on Fort Sumter in one hour from this time. We have the honor to be very respectfully, Your obedient servants, JAMES CHESNUT, JR., *Aide-de-camp.* STEPHEN D. LEE, *Captain C. S. Army, Aide-de-camp.*"

The above note was written in one of the casemates of the fort, and in the presence of Major Anderson and several of his officers. On receiving it,

CONFEDERATE MORTAR-BATTERY ON MORRIS ISLAND, COMMANDED BY LIEUTENANT C. R. HOLMES. FROM A PHOTOGRAPH.

he was much affected. He seemed to realize the full import of the consequences, and the great responsibility of his position. Escorting us to the boat at the wharf, he cordially pressed our hands in farewell, remarking, "If we never meet in this world again, God grant that we may meet in the next."

The boat containing the two aides and also Roger A. Pryor, of Virginia, and A. R. Chisolm, of South Carolina, who were also members of General Beauregard's staff, went immediately to Fort Johnson on James Island, and the order to fire the signal gun was given to Captain George S. James, commanding the battery at that point. It was then 4 A. M. Captain James at once aroused his command, and arranged to carry out the order. He was a great admirer of Roger A. Pryor, and said to him, "You are the only man to whom I would give up the honor of firing the first gun of the war"; and he offered to allow him to fire it. Pryor, on receiving the offer, was very much agitated. With a husky voice he said, "I could not fire the first gun of the war." His manner was almost similar to that of Major Anderson as we left him a few moments before on the wharf at Fort Sumter. Captain James would allow no one else but himself to fire the gun.☆

The boat with the aides of General Beauregard left Fort Johnson before arrangements were complete for the firing of the gun, and laid on its oars, about one-third the distance between the fort and Sumter, there to witness the firing of "the first gun of the war" between the States. It was fired from a ten-inch mortar at 4:30 A. M., April 12th, 1861. Captain James was a skillful officer, and the firing of the shell was a success. It burst immediately over the fort, apparently about one hundred feet above. The firing of the

---

☆ When the *Star of the West* arrived, on the 9th of January, the first shot, aimed across her bow, was fired by G. E. Haynsworth, and the second, aimed directly at her, by Cadet Horlbeck. It is claimed that before this date a hostile shot from a 4-pounder had been fired from Vicksburg by Horace Miller at a passing United States vessel, supposed to be carrying a supply of arms and ammunition to New Orleans. (See also pp. 27 and 47.)—EDITORS.

mortar woke the echoes from every nook and corner of the harbor, and in this the dead hour of night, before dawn, that shot was a sound of alarm that brought every soldier in the harbor to his feet, and every man, woman,

and child in the city of Charleston from their beds. A thrill went through the whole city. It was felt that the Rubicon was passed. No one thought of going home; unused as their ears were to the appalling sounds, or the vivid flashes from the batteries, they stood for hours fascinated with horror. After the second shell the different batteries opened their fire on Fort Sumter, and by 4:45 A. M. the firing was general and regular. It was a hazy, foggy morning. About daylight, the boat with the aides reached Charleston, and they reported to General Beauregard.

Fort Sumter did not respond with her guns till 7:30 A. M. The firing from this fort, during the entire bombardment, was slow and deliberate, and marked with little

FROM A PHOTOGRAPH TAKEN IN 1863.

accuracy. The firing continued without intermission during the 12th, and more slowly during the night of the 12th and 13th. No material change was noticed till 8 A. M. on the 13th, when the barracks in Fort Sumter were set on fire by hot shot from the guns of Fort Moultrie. As soon as

SECESSION HALL, CHARLESTON, SCENE OF THE PASSAGE
OF THE ORDINANCE OF SECESSION.
FROM A PHOTOGRAPH.

this was discovered, the Confederate batteries redoubled their efforts, to prevent the fire being extinguished. Fort Sumter fired at little longer intervals, to enable the garrison to fight the flames. This brave action, under such a trying ordeal, aroused great sympathy and admiration on the part of the Confederates for Major Anderson and his gallant garrison; this feeling was shown by cheers whenever a gun was fired from Sumter. It was shown also by loud reflections on the "men-of-war" outside the harbor.⚓

About 12:30 the flag-staff of Fort Sumter was shot down, but it was soon replaced. As soon as General Beauregard heard that the flag was no longer flying, he sent three of his aides, William Porcher Miles, Roger A. Pryor, and myself, to offer, and also to see if Major Anderson would receive or needed, assistance, in subduing the flames inside the fort. Before we reached it, we saw the United States flag again floating over it, and began to return to the city. Before going far, however, we saw the Stars and Stripes replaced by a white flag. We turned about at once and rowed rapidly to the fort. We were directed, from an embrasure, not to go to the wharf, as it was mined, and the fire was near it. We were assisted through an embrasure and conducted to Major Anderson. Our mission being made known to him, he replied, "Present my compliments to General Beauregard, and say to him I thank him for his kindness, but need no assistance." He further remarked that he hoped the worst was over, that the fire had settled over the magazine, and, as it had not exploded, he thought the real danger was about over. Continuing, he said, "Gentlemen, do I understand you come direct from General Beauregard?" The reply was in the affirmative. He then said, "Why! Colonel Wigfall has just been here as an aide too, and by authority of General Beauregard, and

⚓ These vessels, part of the second expedition for the relief of Fort Sumter, were the *Baltic* (no guns), the *Pawnee* (8 9-inch guns), and the *Harriet Lane* (1 8-inch gun and 4 32-pounders). The *Pocahontas* did not arrive till the afternoon of the 13th. The expedition was in charge of Captain Gustavus V. Fox (afterward Assistant Secretary of the Navy), who had visited the fort on the 21st of March. It had been understood between Secretary Welles and Captain Fox that the movement should be supported by the *Powhatan* (1 11-inch and 10 9-inch guns); but, unknown to Mr. Welles, and perhaps without full understanding of this plan, President Lincoln had consented to the dispatch of the ship to the relief of Fort Pickens, for which destination it had sailed from New York, April 6th, under command of Lieutenant David D. Porter. This conflict of plans deprived Captain Fox of the ship which he calls the "fighting portion" of his fleet; and to this circumstance he attributed the failure of the expedition.

EDITORS.

proposed the same terms of evacuation offered on the 11th instant." We informed the major that we were not authorized to offer terms; that we were direct from General Beauregard, and that Colonel Wigfall, although an aide-de-camp to the general, had been detached, and had not seen the general for several days. Major Anderson at once stated, "There is a misunderstanding on my part, and I will at once run up my flag and open fire again." After consultation, we requested him not to do so, until the matter was explained to General Beauregard, and requested Major Anderson to reduce to writing his understanding with Colonel Wigfall, which he did. However, before we left the fort, a boat arrived from Charleston, bearing Major D. R. Jones, assistant adjutant-general on General Beauregard's staff, who offered substantially the same terms to Major Anderson as those offered on the 11th, and also by Colonel Wigfall, and which were now accepted.

Thus fell Fort Sumter, April 13th, 1861. At this time fire was still raging in the barracks, and settling steadily over the magazine. All egress was cut off except through the lower embrasures. Many shells from the Confederate batteries, which had fallen in the fort and had not exploded, as well as the hand-grenades used for defense, were exploding as they were reached by the fire. The wind was driving the heat and smoke down into the fort and into the casemates, almost causing suffocation. Major Anderson, his officers, and men were blackened by smoke and cinders, and showed signs of fatigue and exhaustion, from the trying ordeal through which they had passed.

It was soon discovered, by conversation, that it was a bloodless battle; not a man had been killed or seriously wounded on either side during the entire bombardment of nearly forty hours. Congratulations were exchanged on so happy a result. Major Anderson stated that he had instructed his officers only to fire on the batteries and forts, and not to fire on private property.

The terms of evacuation offered by General Beauregard were generous, and were appreciated by Major Anderson. The garrison was to embark on the 14th, after running up and saluting the United States flag, and to be carried

FORT SUMTER AFTER THE BOMBARDMENT. FROM A SKETCH MADE IN APRIL, 1861.

JEFFERSON DAVIS, PRESIDENT OF THE CONFEDERATE STATES OF AMERICA.
FROM A PHOTOGRAPH.

to the United States fleet. A soldier killed during the salute was buried inside the fort, the new Confederate garrison uncovering during the impressive ceremonies. Major Anderson and his command left the harbor, bearing with them the respect and admiration of the Confederate soldiers.↓ It was conceded that he had done his duty as a soldier holding a most delicate trust.

This first bombardment of Sumter was but its "baptism of fire." During subsequent attacks by land and water, it was battered by the heaviest Union artillery. Its walls were completely crushed, but the tons of iron projectiles imbedded in its ruins added strength to the inaccessible mass that surrounded it and made it impregnable. It was never taken, but the operations of General Sherman, after his march to the sea, compelled its evacuation, and the Stars and Stripes were again raised over it, April 14th, 1865. ♭

↓The officers, under General Beauregard, of the batteries surrounding Fort Sumter were:

SULLIVAN'S ISLAND, Brigadier-General R. G. M. Dunovant commanding, Lieutenant-Colonel Roswell S. Ripley, commanding the artillery: *Five-gun Battery* (east of Fort Moultrie), Captain S. Y. Tupper; *Maffit Channel Battery* (2 guns) and *Mortar Battery No.* 2 (2 10-inch mortars), Captain William Butler, Lieutenant J. A. Huguenin; *Fort Moultrie* (30 guns), Captain W. R. Calhoun: consisting of Channel Battery, Lieutenants Thomas M. Wagner, Preston, and Sitgreaves, Sumter Battery, Lieutenants Alfred Rhett and John Mitchell, and Oblique Battery, Lieutenant C. W. Parker; *Mortar Battery* No. 1 (2 10-inch mortars) and *Enfilade Battery* (4 guns), Captain James H. Hallonquist, Lieutenants Flemming, Jacob Valentine, and B. S. Burnet; the *Point Battery* (1 9-inch Dahlgren) and the *Floating Iron-clad Battery* (2 42-pounders and 2 32-pounders), Captain John R. Hamilton and Lieutenant Joseph A. Yates; the *Mount Pleasant Battery* (2 10-inch mortars), Captain Robert Martin, Lieutenant George N. Reynolds.

MORRIS ISLAND, Brigadier-General James Simons commanding, Lieutenant-Colonel Wilmot G. De Saussure, commanding the artillery: Major P. F. Stevens, commanding *Cumming's Point Battery*

(Blakely gun, which arrived from Liverpool April 9th, Captain J. P. Thomas; 2 42-pounders, Lieutenant T. Sumter Brownfield; and 3 10-inch mortars, Lieutenants C. R. Holmes and N. Armstrong) and the *Stevens Iron-clad Battery* (3 8-inch columbiads), Captain George B. Cuthbert, Lieutenant G. L. Buist; *Trapier Battery* (3 10-inch mortars), Captain J. Gadsden King, Lieutenants W. D. H. Kirkwood, J. P. Strohecker, A. M. Huger, and E. L. Parker.

JAMES ISLAND, Major N. G. Evans commanding; *Fort Johnson* (battery of 24-pounders), Captain George S. James; *Mortar Battery*, Lieutenants W. H. Gibbes, H. S. Farley, J. E. McP. Washington, and T. B. Hayne; *Upper Battery* (2 10-inch mortars), *Lower Battery* (2 10-inch mortars), Captain S. C. Thayer.— EDITORS.

♭ Under an order from Secretary Stanton, the same flag that was lowered, April 14th, 1861, was raised again over Sumter, by Major (then General) Anderson, on April 14th, 1865, the day President Lincoln was shot. Of Major Anderson's former officers, Generals Abner Doubleday and Norman J. Hall and Chaplain Matthias Harris were present. The Rev. Henry Ward Beecher delivered an oration, and other prominent anti-slavery men attended the ceremony.— EDITORS.

VIEW OF CUMMING'S POINT. FROM A SKETCH MADE AFTER THE BOMBARDMENT.

NOTES ON THE SURRENDER OF FORT SUMTER.

BY A. R. CHISOLM, COLONEL, C. S. A.

VERY soon after Major Robert Anderson moved with his command into Fort Sumter from Fort Moultrie, Governor Francis W. Pickens sent James Fraser, of the Charleston Light Dragoons, to me at my plantation, fifty miles south of Charleston, with the request that I would assist with my negroes in constructing batteries on Morris Island. Taking my own negro men and others from the plantation of my uncle, Robert Chisolm, and that of Nathaniel Heyward, I was engaged in this work when General Beauregard arrived to take command. I then informed the governor that it would be necessary for General Beauregard to have an aide-de-camp who was familiar with the harbor and with boating; that I was the owner of a large six-oared boat and six superior oarsmen, that were at his service free of cost. I was thereupon commissioned lieutenant-colonel, and ordered to report to General Beauregard.

Having visited Fort Sumter five times under a flag of truce, and once after the surrender, I became well acquainted with most of its officers. During a visit in company with Captain Samuel W. Ferguson, the officers jokingly complained of being short of cigars and like luxuries. With General Beauregard's approval, the next time duty called us to the fort we presented them with several cases of claret and boxes of cigars.

April 12th, 1861, I visited the fort in company with James Chesnut, Jr., and Captain Stephen D. Lee with the demand for its surrender, and heard Major Anderson say in conversation with us, "I shall await the first shot, and if you do not batter us to pieces we shall be starved out in a few days." These words being communicated to General Beauregard, we were again sent to the fort, arriving there about 1:30 A. M., April 12th. After waiting nearly two hours for a reply, we sent word to Major Anderson that our orders did not admit of our waiting any longer. He came to where we were in the guard-room, and informed us " that we had twice fired on his flag, and that if we did so again he would open his fire on our batteries." Under our instructions this reply admitted of no other answer than the one dated April 12th, 1861, 3:20 A. M. [see page 76], which was dictated by Chesnut, written by Lee, and copied by me. Roger A. Pryor was with us on the second visit, but did not enter the fort, giving me as a reason that his State, Virginia, had not yet seceded. For the same reason he declined to fire the signal shot. Moreover, I believe he was then a member of Congress, and may have been unwilling to compromise himself.

The facts of the surrender of Fort Sumter to ex-Senator Wigfall are these: General Beauregard, seeing the fort on fire, sent me with a note to General James Simons, commanding on Morris Island, in which he directed him, if he could do so without risk to his command, to offer assistance in extinguishing the fire. I passed down between Fort Sumter and our batteries; delivering my dispatches, I volunteered to go to Fort Sumter, which offer was accepted.

Colonel Wigfall, of Texas, volunteered to accompany me. While bringing my boat from its moorings in a creek, Wigfall, who was very much excited, jumped into a small skiff. The flag of the fort, which had been shot away, reappeared, and Wigfall was ordered to return, but he was out of hearing. I was ordered to return, and obeyed. Colonel Wigfall climbed through an embrasure, and, assuming authority from General Beauregard, called upon Major Anderson to surrender. Major Anderson did not realize the unauthorized nature of Wigfall's mission until the arrival of Captain Stephen D. Lee, William Porcher Miles, and Roger A. Pryor with an offer direct from General Beauregard, similar to the one General Simons was authorized to make. Major Anderson was about to renew the action, when Major David R. Jones arrived with the offer of terms for the surrender of the fort, which were virtually almost anything that Anderson might ask, in order that we might get possession before the fleet could reënforce and provision the garrison.

I have always been of the opinion that Major Anderson should not have surrendered when he did. The fire only consumed the officers' and men's quarters; the two magazines were uninjured, only one man had been wounded, the walls were secure, and he still had provisions which would have sustained his small command until the fleet could both have provisioned and reënforced him. I was present with Captain Hartstene during the evacuation, and was astonished to see barrels of pork\ being rolled out and shipped on board the *Isabel*, the steamer furnished by General Beauregard to transport Anderson's men to the fleet. My duty often required that I should pass Fort Sumter and our guard-boats at night to visit Hartstene, who commanded the poor boats we used. I was rarely seen and had such a contempt for our guards that on one occasion, having a strong tide in my favor, we did not halt when shots were fired at us. In fact, we were seldom seen until close to the guards of the boat we sought. Captain Hartstene was well aware how easy it was to pass to Fort Sumter and expressed to me his uneasiness on this point; in fact, one bold officer in command of a navy barge, armed with a boat howitzer, could have easily cleared the way for a hundred barges with men and supplies to pass to the fort. The night but one previous to the surrender was very dark. I was ordered to Hartstene between the fort and the fleet in the main ship-channel, and my boat touched his guards before it was seen. Later in the war, when Beauregard defended the fort, one of the bravest officers in his command pronounced the work untenable. Beauregard then informed me that if necessary he would go there and hold the fort with his staff; that on no condition would he consent to give it up to General Gillmore. It was after this that General (then Major) Stephen Elliott made his gallant defense of the ruins; when, with the exception of some guns buried under the ruins of the casemate facing Fort Moultrie, but one small gun remained mounted, and that was pointed toward the city, being used merely to fire the salutes.

\ Captain J. G. Foster in his report says that the supply of bread in Sumter failed April 10th, and that the last of the damaged rice was served at breakfast on the 13th. "The want of provisions," he adds, "would soon have caused the surrender of the fort, but with plenty of cartridges [referring to the lack of material for cartridge-bags] the men would have cheerfully fought five or six days, and, if necessary, much longer, on pork alone, of which we had a sufficient supply."— EDITORS.

THE AWKWARD SQUAD.

WAR PREPARATIONS IN THE NORTH.

BY JACOB D. COX, MAJOR-GENERAL, U. S. V., EX-GOVERNOR OF OHIO,
EX-SECRETARY OF THE INTERIOR.

THE wonderful outburst of national feeling in the North in the spring of
1861 has always been a thrilling and almost supernatural thing to those
who participated in it. The classic myth that the resistless terror which sometimes unaccountably seized upon an army was the work of the god Pan might
seem to have its counterpart in the work of a national divinity rousing a
whole people, not to terror, but to a sublime enthusiasm of self-devotion.
To picture it as a whole is impossible. A new generation can only approximate a knowledge of the feelings of that time by studying in detail some separate scenes of the drama that had a continent for its stage. The writer can
only tell what happened under his eye. The like was happening everywhere
from Maine to Kansas. What is told is simply a type of the rest.

On Friday, the twelfth day of April, 1861, the Senate of Ohio was in session,
trying to go on in the ordinary routine of business, but with a sense of
anxiety and strain which was caused by the troubled condition of national

In those opening days of the war, the National
Government seemed for the moment to be subor-
dinated to the governments of the States. A revolution in the seceding South had half destroyed
the national legislature, and the national executive
was left without a treasury, without an army, and
without laws adequate to create these at once. At
no time since the thirteen colonies declared their
independence have the State governors and the
State legislators found so important a field of duty
as then. A little hesitation, a little lukewarmness,
would have ended all. Then it was that the intense zeal and high spirit of Governor Andrew of
Massachusetts led all New England, and was ready
to lead the nation, as the men of Concord and Lex-

ington had led in 1775. Then it was that Governor Morton of Indiana came to the front with a
masculine energy and burly weight of character
and of will which was typical of the force which
the Great West could throw into the struggle.
    Ohio was so situated with regard to West Vir-
ginia and Kentucky that the keystone of the Union
might be said to be now west of the mountains.
Governor Dennison mediated, like the statesman
he was, between East and West; and Tod and
Brough, following him by the will of the people
in votes that ran up to majorities of near a hundred thousand, gave that vigorous support to Mr.
Lincoln which showed the earnest nationality of
the "war Democrats" of that day. — J. D. C.

affairs. The passage of "ordinances of secession" by one after another of the Southern States, and even the assembling of a provisional Confederate government at Montgomery, had not wholly destroyed the hope that some peaceful way out of our troubles would be found; yet the gathering of an army on the sands opposite Fort Sumter was really war, and if a hostile gun were fired, we knew it would mean the end of all effort at arrangement. Hoping almost against hope that blood would not be shed, and that the pageant of military array and of a secession government would pass by, we tried to give our thoughts to business; but there was no heart in it, and the "morning hour" lagged, for we could not work in earnest, and we were unwilling to adjourn.

Suddenly a senator came in from the lobby in an excited way, and, catching the chairman's eye, exclaimed, "Mr. President, the telegraph announces that the secessionists are bombarding Fort Sumter!" There was a solemn and painful hush, but it was broken in a moment by a woman's shrill voice from the spectators' seats, crying, "Glory to God!" It startled every one, almost as if the enemy were in the midst. But it was the voice of a radical friend of the slave, Abby Kelly Foster, who, after a lifetime of public agitation, believed that only through blood could his freedom be won, and who had shouted the fierce cry of joy that the question had been submitted to the decision of the sword. With most of us, the gloomy thought that civil war had begun in our own land overshadowed everything else; this seemed too great a price to pay for any good,— a scourge to be borne only in preference to yielding what was to us the very groundwork of our republicanism, the right to enforce a fair interpretation of the Constitution through the election of President and Congress.

The next day we learned that Major Anderson had surrendered, and the telegraphic news from all the Northern States showed plain evidence of a popular outburst of loyalty to the Union, following a brief moment of dismay. That was the period when the flag—*The Flag*—flew out to the wind from every housetop in our great cities, and when, in New York, wildly excited crowds marched the streets demanding that the suspected or the lukewarm should show the symbol of nationality as a committal to the country's cause. He that is not for us is against us, was the deep, instinctive feeling.

Judge Thomas M. Key of Cincinnati, ⚓ chairman of the Judiciary Committee, was the recognized leader of the Democratic party in the Senate, and at an early hour moved an adjournment to the following Tuesday, in order, as he said, that the senators might have the opportunity to go home and consult their constituents in the perilous crisis of public affairs. No objection was made to the adjournment, and the representatives took a similar recess. All were in a state of most anxious suspense,— the Republicans to know what initiative the Administration at Washington would take, and the Democrats to determine what course they should follow if the President should call for troops to put down the insurrection.

⚓ Afterward aide-de-camp and acting judge-advocate on General McClellan's staff.

Before we met again, Mr. Lincoln's proclamation and call for 75,000 men for three months' service had been issued, and the great mass of the people of the North, forgetting all party distinctions, answered with an enthusiasm that swept politicians off their feet. When we met again on Tuesday morning, Judge Key, taking my arm and pacing the floor outside the railing, broke out impetuously, "Mr. Cox, the people have gone stark mad!"—"I knew they would if a blow were struck against the flag," said I, reminding him of some previous conversations we had had on the subject. He, with most of the politicians of the day, partly by sympathy with the overwhelming current of public opinion, and partly by the reaction of their own hearts against the theories which had encouraged the secessionists, determined to support the war measures of the Government and to make no factious opposition to such State legislation as might be necessary to sustain the Federal Administration.

The attitude of Mr. Key is only a type of many others, and marks one of the most striking features of the time. On the 8th of January the usual Democratic convention and celebration of the battle of New Orleans had taken place, and a series of resolutions had been passed, in which, professing to speak in the name of "200,000 Democrats of Ohio," the convention had very significantly intimated that this vast organization of men would be found in the way of any attempt to put down secession until the demands of the South in respect to slavery were complied with. A few days afterward I was returning to Columbus from my home in Trumbull county, and meeting upon the railway train with David Tod, then an active Democratic politician, but afterward one of our loyal "war governors," the conversation turned on the action of the convention which had just adjourned. Mr. Tod and I were personal friends and neighbors, and I freely expressed my surprise that the convention should have committed itself to what must be interpreted as a threat of insurrection in the North, if the Administration should, in opposing secession by force, follow the example of Andrew Jackson, in whose honor they had assembled. He rather vehemently reasserted the substance of the resolution, saying that we Republicans would find the 200,000 Ohio Democrats in front of us, if we attempted to cross the Ohio River. My answer was, "We will give up the contest if we cannot carry your 200,000 over the heads of you leaders."

The result proved how hollow the party assertions had been, or, perhaps, I should say, how superficial was the hold of such doctrines upon the mass of men in a great political organization. At the first shot from Beauregard's guns in Charleston Harbor these men crowded to the recruiting stations to enlist for the defense of the national flag and the national union. It was a popular torrent which no leaders could resist; but many of these should be credited with the same patriotic impulse, and it made them nobly oblivious of party consistency. A few days after the surrender of Sumter, Stephen A. Douglas passed through Columbus on his way to Washington, and, in response to the calls of a spontaneous gathering of people, spoke to them from the window of his bedroom in the hotel. There had been no thought for any of the common surroundings of a public meeting. There were no torches, no music.

A dark mass of men filled full the dimly lit street, and called for Douglas with an earnestness of tone wholly different from the enthusiasm of common political gatherings. He came half-dressed to his window, and, without any light near him, spoke solemnly to the people upon the terrible crisis which had come upon the nation. Men of all parties were there: his own followers to get some light as to their duty; the Breckinridge Democrats ready, most of them, repentantly to follow a Northern leader now that their Southern associates were in armed opposition to the Government; the Republicans eager to know whether so potent an influence was to be unreservedly on the side of the nation. I remember well the serious solicitude with which I listened to his opening sentences as I leaned against the railing of the State House park, trying in vain to see more than a dim outline of the man as he stood at the unlighted window. His deep, sonorous tones rolled down through the darkness from above us, an earnest, measured voice, the more solemn, the more impressive, because we could not see the speaker, and it came to us literally as " a voice in the night,"—the night of our country's unspeakable trial. There was no uncertainty in his tone; the Union must be preserved and the insurrection must be crushed; he pledged his hearty support to Mr. Lincoln's administration in doing this; other questions must stand aside till the national authority should be everywhere recognized. I do not think we greatly cheered him,—it was, rather, a deep Amen that went up from the crowd. We went home breathing more freely in the assurance we now felt that, for a time at least, no organized opposition to the Federal Government and its policy of coercion could be formidable in the North.

Yet the situation hung upon us like a nightmare. Garfield and I were lodging together at the time, our wives being kept at home by family cares, and when we reached our sitting-room, after an evening session of the Senate, we often found ourselves involuntarily groaning, " Civil war in *our* land!" The shame, the folly, the outrage, seemed too great to believe, and we half hoped to wake from it as

LIFE-MASK OF STEPHEN A. DOUGLAS. TAKEN BY LEONARD VOLK SHORTLY BEFORE THE LINCOLN-DOUGLAS DEBATES OF 1858.

from a dream. Among the painful remembrances of those days is the ever-present weight at the heart which never left me till I found relief in the active duties of camp life at the close of the month. I went about my duties (and I am sure most of those with whom I associated did the same) with the half-choking sense of a grief I dared not think of: like one who is

STEPHEN A. DOUGLAS. FROM A DAGUERREOTYPE TAKEN IN 1852.

dragging himself to the ordinary labors of life from some terrible and recent bereavement.

We talked of our personal duty, and though both Garfield and myself had young families, we were agreed that our activity in the organization and support of the Republican party made the duty of supporting the Government by military service come peculiarly home to us. He was, for the moment, somewhat trammeled by his half-clerical position, but he very soon cut the knot. My own path seemed unmistakably plain. He, more careful for his friend than for himself, urged upon me his doubts whether my physical strength was equal to the strain that would be put upon it. "I," said he, "am big and strong, and if my relations to the church and the college can be loosened, I shall have no excuse for not enlisting; but you are slender and will break down." It is true I then looked slender for a man six feet high ; yet I had confidence in the elasticity of my constitution, and the result justified me, while it also showed how liable one is to mistake in such things. Garfield found that he had a tendency to weakness of the alimentary system, which broke him down on every campaign in which he served, and led to his retiring from the army at the close of 1863. My own health, on the other hand, was strengthened by outdoor life and exposure, and I served to the end with growing physical vigor.

When Mr. Lincoln issued his first call for troops, the existing laws made it necessary that these should be fully organized and officered by the several States. Then, the treasury was in no condition to bear the burden of war expenditures, and, till Congress could assemble, the President was forced to rely on the States for means to equip and transport their own men. This threw upon the governors and legislatures of the loyal States responsibilities of a kind wholly unprecedented. A long period of profound peace had made every military organization seem almost farcical. A few independent companies formed the merest shadow of an army, and the State militia proper was only a nominal thing. It happened, however, that I held a commission as brigadier in this State militia, and my intimacy with Governor Dennison led him to call upon me for such assistance as I could render in the first enrollment and organization of the Ohio quota. Arranging to be called to the Senate chamber when my vote might be needed, I gave my time chiefly to such military matters as the governor appointed. Although, as I have said, my military commission had been a nominal thing, and in fact I had never worn a uniform, I had not wholly neglected theoretic preparation for such work. For some years, the possibility of a war of secession had been one of the things which were forced upon the thoughts of reflecting people, and I had given some careful study to such books of tactics and of strategy as were within easy reach. I had especially been led to read military history with critical care, and had carried away many valuable ideas from that most useful means of military education. I had, therefore, some notion of the work before us, and could approach its problems with less loss of time, at least, than if I had been wholly ignorant.

My commission as brigadier-general in the Ohio quota in national service was dated the 23d of April. Just about the same time Captain George B. McClellan was requested by Governor Dennison to come to Columbus for consultation, and, by the governor's request, I met him at the railway station and took him to the State House. I think Mr. Lars Anderson (brother of Major Robert Anderson) and Mr. L'Hommedieu of Cincinnati were with him. The intimation had been given me that he would probably be made major-general of the Ohio contingent, and this, naturally, made me scan him closely. He was rather under the medium height, but muscularly formed, with broad shoulders and a well-poised head, active and graceful in motion. His whole appearance was quiet and modest, but when drawn out he showed no lack of confidence in himself. He was dressed in a plain traveling dress and wore a narrow-rimmed soft felt hat. In short, he seemed what he was, a railway superintendent in his business clothes.   At the time, his name was a good deal associated with Beauregard's, and they were spoken of as young men of similar standing in the engineer corps of the army, and great things were expected of them both because of their scientific knowledge of their profession, though McClellan had been in civil life for some years. McClellan's report on the Crimean war was one of the few important memoirs our old army had produced, and was valuable enough to give a just reputation for comprehensive understanding of military organization, and the promise of ability to conduct the operations of an army.

I was present at the interview which the governor had with him.   The destitution of the State of everything like military material and equipment was very plainly put, and the magnitude of the task of building up a small army out of nothing was not blinked.   The governor spoke of the embarrassment he felt at every step from the lack of practical military experience in his staff, and of his desire to have some one on whom he could properly throw the details of military work.   McClellan showed that he fully understood the difficulties there would be before him, and said no man could wholly master them at once, although he had confidence that if a few weeks' time for preparation were given, he would be able to put the Ohio division into reasonable form for taking the field.   The command was then formally tendered and accepted. All of us who were present felt that the selection was one full of promise and hope, and that the governor had done the wisest thing practicable at the time.

The next morning McClellan requested me to accompany him to the State arsenal, to see what arms and material might be there.   We found a few boxes of smooth-bore muskets which had once been issued to militia companies and had been returned rusted and damaged.   No belts, cartridge-boxes, or other accouterments were with them.   There were two or three smooth-bore brass field-pieces, 6-pounders, which had been honey-combed by firing salutes, and of which the vents had been worn out, bushed, and worn out again.   In a heap in one corner lay a confused pile of mildewed harness which had been once used for artillery horses, but was now not worth carrying away.   There had for many years been no money appropriated to buy military material or even to protect the little the State had.   The Federal Government had occasionally distributed some arms which were in the hands of the independent uniformed militia, and the arsenal was simply an empty store-house.   It did not take long to complete our inspection.   At the door, as we were leaving the building, McClellan turned, and, looking back into its emptiness, remarked, half humorously and half sadly, "A fine stock of munitions on which to begin a great war!"

We went back to the State House where a room was assigned us, and we sat down to work.   The first task was to make out detailed schedules and estimates of what would be needed to equip ten thousand men for the field. This was a unit which could be used by the governor and Legislature in estimating the appropriations needed then or subsequently.   Intervals in this labor were used in discussing the general situation and plans of campaign. Before the close of the week McClellan drew up a paper embodying his own views, and forwarded it to Lieutenant-General Scott. He read it to me, and my recollection of it is that he suggested two principal lines of movement in the West: one to move eastward by the Kanawha Valley with a heavy column to coöperate with an army in front of Washington; the other to march directly southward and to open the Valley of the Mississippi. Scott's answer was appreciative and flattering, without distinctly approving his plan, and I have never doubted that the paper prepared the way for his appointment in the regular army, which followed at an early day.↓

But in trying to give a connected idea of the first military organization of the State, I have outrun some incidents of those days which are worth recollection. From the hour the call for troops was published, enlistments began, and recruits were parading the streets continually. At the capitol the restless impulse to be doing something military seized even upon the members of the Legislature, and a good many of them assembled every evening upon the east terrace of the State House to be drilled in marching and facing by one or two of their own number who had some knowledge of company tactics. Most of the uniformed independent companies in the cities of the State immediately tendered their services and began to recruit their numbers to the hundred men required for acceptance. There was no time to procure uniforms, nor was it desirable; for these companies had chosen their own, and would have to change it for that of the United States as soon as this could be furnished. For some days companies could be seen marching and drilling, of which part would be uniformed in some gaudy style such as is apt to prevail in holiday parades in time of peace, while another part would be dressed in the ordinary working garb of citizens of all degrees. The uniformed files would also be armed and accoutered, the others would be without arms or equipments, and as awkward a squad as could well be imagined. The material, however, was magnificent and soon began to take shape. The fancy uniforms were left at home, and some approximation to a simple and useful costume was made. The recent popular outburst in Italy furnished a useful idea, and the " Garibaldi uniform " of a red flannel shirt with broad falling collar, with blue trousers held by a leathern waist-belt, and a soft felt hat for the head, was extensively copied and served an excellent purpose. It could be made by the wives and sisters at home, and was all the more acceptable for that. The spring was opening and a heavy coat would not be much needed, so that with some sort of overcoat and a good blanket in an improvised knapsack, the new company was not badly provided. The warm scarlet color reflected from their enthusiastic faces as they stood in line made a picture that never failed to impress the mustering officers with the splendid character of the men.

The officering of these new troops was a difficult and delicate task, and, so far as company officers were concerned, there seemed no better way at the beginning than to let the enlisted men elect their own, as was in fact done. In most cases where entirely new companies were raised, it had been by the

↓ Scott's answer was dated May 3d, and is given by General E. D. Townsend (then on Scott's staff), in his " Anecdotes of the Civil War."

MAJOR-GENERAL GEORGE B. McCLELLAN. FROM A WAR-TIME PHOTOGRAPH.

enthusiastic efforts of some energetic volunteers who were naturally made the commissioned officers. But not always. There were numerous examples of self-denial by men who remained in the ranks after expending much labor and money in recruiting, modestly refusing the honors, and giving way to some one supposed to have military knowledge or experience. The war in Mexico in 1846–7 had been our latest conflict with a civilized people, and to have served in it was a sure passport to confidence. It had often been a service more in name than in fact; but the young volunteers felt so deeply their own ignorance that they were ready to yield to any pretense of superior knowledge, and generously to trust themselves to any one who would offer to lead them. Hosts of charlatans and incompetents were thus put into responsible places at the beginning, but the sifting work went on fast after the troops were once in the field. The election of field-officers, however, ought not to have been allowed. Companies were necessarily regimented together of which each could have little personal knowledge of the officers of the others; intrigue and demagogy soon came into play, and almost fatal mistakes were made in selection. The evil worked its cure, but the ill effects of it were long visible.

The immediate need of troops to protect Washington caused most of the uniformed companies to be united into the first two regiments, which were quickly dispatched to the East. These off, companies began to stream in from all parts of the State. On their first arrival they were quartered wherever shelter could be had, as there were no tents or sheds to make a camp for them. Going to my evening work at the State House, as I crossed the rotunda I saw a company marching in by the south door, and another disposing itself for the night upon the marble pavement near the east entrance; as I passed on to the north hall, I saw another that had come a little earlier holding a prayer-meeting, the stone arches echoing with the excited supplications of some one who was borne out of himself by the terrible pressure of events around him, while, mingling with his pathetic, beseeching tones as he prayed for his country, came the shrill notes of the fife and the thundering din of the ubiquitous bass-drum from the company marching in on the other side. In the Senate chamber a company was quartered, and the senators were supplying them with paper and pens with which "the boys" were writing their farewells to mothers and sweethearts, whom they hardly dared hope they should see again. A similar scene was going on in the Representatives' hall, another in the Supreme Court-room. In the executive office sat the governor, the unwonted noises, when the door was opened, breaking in on the quiet, business-like air of the room,—he meanwhile dictating dispatches, indicating answers to others, receiving committees of citizens, giving directions to officers of companies and regiments, accommodating himself to the willful democracy of our institutions which insists upon seeing the man in chief command, and will not take its answer from a subordinate, until in the small hours of the night the noises were hushed, and after a brief hour of effective, undisturbed work upon the matters of chief importance, he could leave the glare of his gas-lighted office and seek a few hours' rest, only to renew his wearing labors on the morrow.

On the streets the excitement was of a rougher if not more intense character. A minority of unthinking partisans could not understand the strength and sweep of the great popular movement, and would sometimes venture to speak out their sympathy with the rebellion, or their sneers at some party friend who had enlisted. In the boiling temper of the time the quick answer was a blow; and it was one of the common incidents of the day for those who came into the State House to tell of a knock-down that had occurred here or there, when this popular punishment had been administered to some indiscreet "rebel-sympathizer."

Various duties brought young army officers of the regular service to the State capital, and others sought a brief leave of absence to come and offer their services to the governor of their native State.   General Scott had planted himself firmly on the theory that the regular army must be the principal reliance for severe work, and that the volunteers could only be auxiliaries around this solid nucleus which would show them the way to perform their duty, and take the brunt of every encounter.   The young regulars who asked leave to accept commissions in State regiments were therefore refused, and were ordered to their own subaltern positions and posts.   There can be no doubt that the true policy would have been to encourage the whole of this younger class to enter at once the volunteer service.   They would have been field-officers in the new regiments, and would have impressed discipline and system upon the organization from the beginning.   The Confederates really profited by having no regular army.   They gave to the officers who left our service, it is true, commissions in their so-called "provisional" army, to encourage them to expect permanent military positions if the war should end in the independence of the South; but this was only a nominal organization, and their real army was made up (as ours turned out practically to be) from the regiments of State volunteers.   Less than a year afterward we changed our policy, but it was then too late to induce many of the regular officers to take regimental positions in the volunteer troops.   I hesitate to declare that this was not, after all, for the best; for, although the organization of our army would have been more rapidly perfected, there are other considerations which have much weight.   The army would not have been the popular thing it was, its close identification with the people's movement would have been weakened, and it, perhaps, would not so readily have melted again into the mass of the nation at the close of the war.

On the 29th of April I was ordered by McClellan to proceed next morning to Camp Dennison, near Cincinnati, where he had fixed the site for a permanent camp of instruction.   I took with me one full regiment and half of another.   The day was a fair one, and when about noon our railway train reached the camping ground, it seemed an excellent place for our work.   The drawback was that the land was planted in wheat and corn, instead of being meadow or pasture land.   Captain Rosecrans (later the well-known general) met us as McClellan's engineer officer, coming from Cincinnati with a train-load of lumber.   With his compass and chain, and by the help of a small detail of men, he soon laid off the two regimental camps, and the general lines of the whole encampment for a dozen regiments.   The men of the regiments shouldered the pine boards, and carried them up to the lines of the company streets which were close to the hills skirting the valley, and which opened into the parade and drill ground along the railway.   Vigorous work housed all the men before night, and it was well that it did so, for the weather changed in the evening, a cold rain came on, and the next morning was a chill and dreary one.   My own headquarters were in a little brick school-house of one story, and with a single aide (my only staff-officer) we bestowed ourselves for the night in the little spaces between the pupils' desks and the teacher's pulpit.   The windy, cheerless night was a long one, but gave place at last to a fickle, changeable day of drifting showers and occasional sunshine, and we were roused by our first reveille in camp. A breakfast was made from some cooked provisions brought with us, and we resumed the duty of organizing and instructing the camp. With the vigorous outdoor life and the full physical and mental employment, the depression which had weighed upon me since the news of the guns at Sumter passed away, never to return.

New battalions arrived from day to day, the cantonments were built by themselves, like the first, and the business of instruction and drill was systematized. The men were not yet armed, so there was no temptation to begin too soon with the manual of the musket, and they were kept industriously employed in marching in single line, by file, in changing direction, in forming column of fours from double line, etc., before their guns were put into their hands. Each regiment was treated as a separate camp with its own chain of sentinels, and the officers of the guard were constantly busy inspecting the sentinels on post and teaching guard and picket duty theoretically to the reliefs off duty. Schools were established in each regiment for field and staff as well as for company officers, and Hardee's "Tactics" was in the hands of everybody who could procure a copy. One of the proofs of the unprecedented scale of our war preparation is found in the fact that the supply of the authorized "Tactics" was soon exhausted, making it difficult to get the means of instruction in the company schools. The arriving regiments sometimes had their first taste of camp life under circumstances well calculated to dampen their ardor. The 4th Ohio, under Colonel Lorin Andrews, president of Kenyon College, came just before a thunderstorm one evening, and the bivouac that night was as rough a one as his men were likely to experience for many a day. They made shelter by placing boards from the fence-tops to the ground, but the fields were level and soon became a mire under the pouring rain, so that they were a queer-looking lot when they crawled out in the morning. The sun was then shining bright, however, and they had better cover for their heads by the next night. The 7th Ohio, which was recruited in Cleveland and on the "Western Reserve," sent a party in advance to build some of their huts, and though they too came in a rain-storm, they were less uncomfortable than some of the others. In the course of a fortnight all the regiments of the Ohio contingent were in the camp, except the two that had been hurried to Washington. They were organized into three brigades. The brigadiers, besides myself, were Generals J. H. Bates and Newton Schleich. General Bates, who was the senior, and as such assumed command of the camp in McClellan's absence, was a graduate of West Point who had served some years in the regular army, but had resigned and adopted the profession of law. General Schleich was a Democratic senator, who had been in the State militia, and had been one of the drill-masters of the Legislative Squad, which had drilled upon the Capitol terrace. McClellan had intended to make his own headquarters in the camp; but the convenience of attending to official business in Cincinnati kept him in the city. His purpose was to make the brigade organizations permanent, and to take them as a division to the field when they were a little prepared for the work. Like many other good plans, it failed to be carried out. I was the only one of the brigadiers who remained in the service after the first enlistment for ninety days, and it was my fate to take the field with new regiments, only one of which had been in my brigade in camp. After General Bates's arrival my own hut was built on the slope of the hillside behind my brigade, close under the wooded ridge, and here for the next six weeks was my home. The morning brought its hour of business correspondence relating to the command; then came the drill, when the parade ground was full of marching companies and squads. Officers' drill followed, with sword exercise and pistol practice, and the evening was allotted to schools of theoretic tactics, outpost duty, and the like.

The first fortnight in camp was the hardest for the troops. The plowed fields became deep with mud which nothing could remove till steady good weather should allow them to be packed hard under the continued tramp of thousands of men. The organization of camp-kitchens had to be learned by the hardest experience also, and the men who had some aptitude for cooking had to be found by a slow process of natural selection, during which many an unpalatable meal had to be eaten. A disagreeable bit of information soon came to us in the proof that more than half the men had never had the contagious diseases of infancy. The measles broke out, and we had to organize a camp-hospital at once. A large barn near by was taken for this purpose, and the surgeons had their hands full of cases, which, however trivial they might seem at home, were here aggravated into dangerous illness by the unwonted surroundings, and the impossibility of securing the needed protection from exposure. The good women of Cincinnati took promptly in hand the task of providing nurses for the sick and proper diet and delicacies for hospital use. The Sisters of Charity, under the lead of Sister Anthony, a noble woman, came out in force, and their black and white robes harmonized picturesquely with the military surroundings, as they flitted about under the rough timber framing of the old barn, carrying comfort and hope from one rude couch to another.

As to supplies, hardly a man in a regiment knew how to make out a requisition for rations or for clothing, and, easy as it is to rail at "red-tape," the necessity of keeping a check upon embezzlement and wastefulness justified the staff-bureaus at Washington in insisting upon regular vouchers to support the quartermasters' and commissaries' accounts. But here, too, men were gradually found who had special talent for the work. Where everybody had to learn a new business, it would have been miraculous if grave errors had not frequently occurred. Looking back at it, the wonder is that the blunders and mishaps had not been tenfold more numerous than they were.

By the middle of May the confusion had given way to reasonable system, but we now were obliged to meet the embarrassments of reorganization for three years, under the President's second call for troops (May 3d). In every company some discontented spirits wanted to go home, and, to avoid the odium of going alone, they became mischief-makers, seeking to prevent the whole company from reënlisting. The growing discipline was relaxed or lost in the solicitations, the electioneering, the speech-making, and the other common arts of persuasion. In spite of all these discouragements, however, the daily drills and instruction went on with some approach to regularity, and our raw volunteers began to look more like soldiers. Captain Gordon Granger, of the regular army, came to muster the reënlisted regiments into the three-years service, and as he stood at the right of the 4th Ohio, looking down the line of a thousand stalwart men, all in their Garibaldi shirts (for we had not yet got our uniforms), he turned to me and exclaimed, "My God! that such men should be food for powder!" It certainly was a display of manliness and intelligence such as had hardly ever been seen in the ranks of an army. There were in camp at that time, three if not four companies in different regiments that were wholly made up of under-graduates of colleges, who had enlisted together, their officers being their tutors and professors. And where there was not so striking evidence as this of the enlistment of the best of our youth, every company could still show that it was largely recruited from the best nurtured and most promising young men of the community.

MAJOR-GENERAL GORDON GRANGER.
FROM A PHOTOGRAPH.

Granger had been in the South-west when the secession movement began, and had seen the formation of military companies everywhere, and the incessant drilling which had been going on all winter; while we, in a strange condition of political paralysis, had been doing nothing. His information was eagerly sought by us all, and he lost no opportunity of impressing upon us the fact that the South was nearly six months ahead of us in organization and preparation. He did not conceal his belief that we were likely to find the war a much longer and more serious piece of business than was commonly expected, and that, unless we pushed hard our drilling and instruction, we should find ourselves at a disadvantage in our earlier encounters. What he said had a good effect in making officers and men take more willingly to the laborious routine of the parade ground and the regimental school; for such opinions as his soon ran through a camp, and they were commented upon by the enlisted men quite as earnestly as among the officers. Still, hope kept the upper hand, and I believe that three-fourths of us still cherished the belief that a single campaign would end the war.

Though most of our men were native Ohioans, we had in camp two regiments made up of other material. The 9th Ohio was recruited from the Germans of Cincinnati, and was commanded by Colonel Robert McCook. In camp, the drilling of the regiment fell almost completely into the hands of the adjutant, Lieutenant August Willich (afterward a general of division), and McCook, who humorously exaggerated his own lack of military knowledge, used to say that he was only "clerk for a thousand Dutchmen," so completely did the care of equipping and providing for his regiment engross his time and labor. The 10th Ohio was an Irish regiment, also from Cincinnati, and its men were proud to call themselves the "Bloody Tinth." The brilliant Lytle was its commander, and his control over them, even in the beginning of their service and near the city of their home, showed that they had fallen into competent hands. It happened, of course, that the guard-house pretty frequently contained representatives of the 10th, who, on the short furloughs that were allowed them, took a parting glass too many with their friends in the city, and came to camp boisterously drunk. But the men of the regiment got it into their heads that the 13th, which lay just opposite them across the railroad, took a malicious pleasure in filling the guard-house with the Irishmen. Some threats had been made that they would go over and "clean out" the 13th, and one fine evening these came to a head. I suddenly got orders from General Bates to form my brigade and march them at once between the 10th and 13th to prevent a collision that seemed imminent. The long-roll was beaten as if the drummers realized the full importance of the first opportunity to sound that warlike signal. We marched by the moonlight into the space between the belligerent regiments; but Lytle already had got his own men under control, and the less mercurial 13th were not disposed to be aggressive, so that we were soon dismissed, with a compliment for our promptness.

The six weeks of our stay in Camp Dennison seem like months in the retrospect, so full were they crowded with new experiences. The change came in an unexpected way. The initiative taken by the Confederates in West Virginia had to be met by prompt action, and McClellan was forced to drop his own plans and meet the exigency. The organization and equipment of the regiments for the three-years service was still incomplete, and the brigades were broken up, to take across the Ohio the regiments best prepared to go. This was discouraging to a brigade commander, for, even with veteran troops, acquaintanceship between the officer and his command is a necessary condition of confidence and a most important element of strength. My own assignment to the Great Kanawha district was one I had every reason to be content with, except that for several months I felt the disadvantage I suffered from having command of troops which I had never seen till we met in the field.

CAMP DENNISON, NEAR CINCINNATI.

VIEW OF MONTGOMERY, ALABAMA, SHOWING THE STATE CAPITOL.
FROM A SKETCH MADE IN 1861.

THE CONFEDERATE GOVERNMENT AT MONTGOMERY.

BY R. BARNWELL RHETT (EDITOR OF THE CHARLESTON "MERCURY," 1860–62).

TWENTY-SIX years have passed since the delegates of six States of the South that had seceded from the Union met in a convention or Provisional Congress, at the Capitol, at Montgomery, Alabama. Twenty-one years have elapsed since the close of the war between the States of the North and the eleven States of the South that entered the Confederate Government then and there organized. Most of the men who participated in the deliberations of that convention are dead, and the few now left will before long be laid away. Of the debates of that body there is no record, and the proceedings in secret session have never been published. In Washington the proceedings of the Congress of the United States were open, and at the North there was an intelligent, well-informed, powerful public opinion throughout the war. Not so at the South. Secret sessions were commenced at Montgomery, and at Richmond almost all important business was transacted away from the knowledge and thus beyond the criticism of the people. Latterly, accounts of the battles fought have been written from every standpoint; but of the course and policy of the Confederate Government, which held in its hands all the resources of the Southern people, and directed their affairs, diplomatic, financial, naval, and military, little has been said. During the war scarcely anything was known except results, and when the war terminated, the people of the South, though greatly dissatisfied, were generally as ignorant of the management of Confederate affairs as the people of the North. The arrest and long imprisonment of the President of the Confederacy made of him a representative martyr, and silenced the voice of criticism at the South. And up to this time little has been done to point out the causes of the events which occurred, or to develop the truth of history in this direction. It very well suits men at the South who opposed secession to compliment their own sagacity by assuming that the end was inevitable. Nor do men identified with the Confederacy by office, or feeling obligation for its appreciation of their personal merits, find it hard to persuade themselves that all was done that could be done in "the lost cause." And, in general, it may be an agreeable sop to Southern pride to take for granted that superior numbers alone effected the result. Yet, in the great wars of the world, nothing is so little proved as that the more numerous always and necessarily prevail. On the contrary, the facts of history show that brains have ever

been more potent than brawn. The career of the Confederate States exhibits no exception to this rule. Eliminate the good sense and unselfish earnestness of Mr. Lincoln, and the great ability and practical energy of Seward and Adams, and of Stanton and Chase from the control of the affairs of the United States; conceive a management of third-rate and incompetent men in their places—will any one doubt that matters would have ended differently? To many it may be unpalatable to hear that at the South all was not done that might have been done and that cardinal blunders were made. But what is pleasing is not always true, and there can be no good excuse now for suppressing important facts or perverting history. The time has come when public attention may with propriety be directed to the realities of that momentous period at the South.

ALEXANDER H. STEPHENS, VICE-PRESIDENT OF THE CONFEDERACY. FROM A PHOTOGRAPH.

On the 20th of December, 1860, South Carolina passed unanimously the first ordinance of secession, in these words:

"We, the people of the State of South Carolina in convention assembled, do declare and ordain, and it is hereby declared and ordained, that the ordinance adopted by us in convention on the twenty-third day of May, in the year of our Lord one thousand seven hundred and eighty-eight, whereby the Constitution of the United States of America was ratified, and also, all Acts and parts of Acts of the General Assembly of this State, ratifying amendments of the said Constitution, are hereby repealed; and that the Union now subsisting between South Carolina and other States, under the name of 'the United States of America,' is hereby dissolved."

On her invitation, six other Southern States sent delegates to a convention in Montgomery, Alabama, for the purpose of organizing a Confederacy. On the 4th of February, 1861, this convention assembled. The material which constituted it was of a mixed character. There were members who were constitutionally timid and unfit by character and temperament to participate in such work as was on hand. Others had little knowledge of public affairs on a large scale, and had studied neither the resources of the South nor the conduct of the movement. A number of them, however, were men of ripe experience and statesmanlike grasp of the situation — men of large knowledge, with calm, strong, clear views of the policies to be pursued. Alexander H. Stephens characterized this convention as "the ablest body with which he ever served, and singularly free from revolutionary spirit." ¦

In the organization of the convention, Howell Cobb was chosen to preside, and J. J. Hooper, of Montgomery, to act as secretary. It was decided to organize a provisional government under a provisional constitution, which was adopted on the 8th of February. On the 9th a provisional President and Vice-President were elected, who were installed in office on the 18th to carry the government into effect. In regard to this election, it was agreed that when four delegations out of the six should settle upon men, the election should take place. Jefferson Davis was put forward by the Mississippi delegation and Howell Cobb by that of Georgia. The Florida delegation proposed to vote for whomsoever South Carolina should support. The South Carolina delegation offered no candidate and held no meeting to confer upon the matter. The chairman, Mr. R. Barnwell Rhett, ⚓ did not call them together. Mr. Barnwell, however, was an active supporter of Mr. Davis, and it was afterward said that while in Washington in December, as a commissioner to treat for the evacuation of Fort Sumter, he had committed himself to Mr. Davis. At any rate, he was zealous. Colonel Keitt afterward stated to the writer and others in Charleston that

WILLIAM L. YANCEY, MEMBER OF THE CONFEDERATE SENATE, CONFEDERATE COMMISSIONER TO EUROPE IN 1861. FROM A PHOTOGRAPH.

¦ The deputies elected to meet at the Montgomery convention were: SOUTH CAROLINA, R. Barnwell Rhett, Lawrence M. Keitt, C. G. Memminger, Thomas J. Withers, Robert W. Barnwell, James Chesnut, Jr., W. Porcher Miles, and William W. Boyce; FLORIDA, Jackson Morton, James B. Owens, and J. Patton Anderson; MISSISSIPPI, Wiley P. Harris, W. S. Wilson, Walker Brooke, Alexander M. Clayton, James T. Harrison, William S. Barry, and J. A. P. Campbell; ALABAMA, Richard W. Walker, Colin J. McRae, William P. Chilton, David P. Lewis, Robert H. Smith, John Gill Shorter, Stephen F. Hale, Thomas Fearn, and Jabez L. M. Curry; GEORGIA, Robert Toombs, Martin J. Crawford, Benjamin H. Hill, Augustus R. Wright, Augustus H. Kenan, Francis S. Bartow, Eugenius A. Nisbet, Howell Cobb, Thomas R. R. Cobb, and Alexander H. Stephens; LOUISIANA, John Perkins, Jr., Charles M. Conrad, Edward Sparrow, Alexander De Clouet, Duncan F. Kenner, and Henry Marshall. The Texas delegates were not appointed until February 14th.

These delegates had been appointed by the conventions of their respective States on the ground that the people had intrusted the State conventions with unlimited powers. They constituted

⚓ Father of the writer. — EDITORS.

a majority of the delegation were opposed to Mr. Davis, but that, not having compared opinions, they did not understand one another, and that Mr. Davis received the vote of South Carolina, and was elected, by the casting vote of Mr. Rhett. Personally Mr. Rhett knew little of Mr. Davis. He regarded him

ROBERT TOOMBS, FIRST SECRETARY OF STATE OF THE
CONFEDERACY; MEMBER OF THE CONFEDERATE
SENATE; BRIGADIER-GENERAL, C. S. A.
FROM A PHOTOGRAPH.

as an accomplished man, but egotistical, arrogant, and vindictive, without depth or statesmanship. Besides this, he judged him not sufficiently in accord with the movement to lead it. His speech on the 4th of July, 1858, between New York and Boston, was reported as denunciatory of secessionists, and as comparing them to " mosquitoes around the horns of an ox, who could annoy, but could do no harm." The strong Union sentiments uttered in his New England electioneering tour, which secured to him the vote of B. F. Butler and others at the Democratic convention at Charleston, in 1860, were confirmatory of the newspaper report. As late as November 10th, 1860, after the South Carolina convention was called, Mr. Davis had written a letter, within the cognizance of Mr. Rhett, and published by himself since the war, in which he unmistakably indicated the opinion that, if South Carolina seceded, neither Georgia, nor Alabama, nor Mississippi, nor Louisiana, nor any other State would secede unless

both the convention that organized the Confederacy and its Provisional Congress. On the 8th of February the Provisional Constitution was adopted, to be in force one year. On the 9th was passed the first enactment, providing "That all the laws of the United States of America in force and in use in the Confederate States of America on the first day of November last, and not inconsistent with the Constitution of the Confederate States, be and the same are hereby continued in force until altered or repealed by the Congress." The next act, adopted February 14th, continued in office until April 1st all officers connected with the collection of customs, and the assistant treasurers, with the same powers and functions as under the Government of the United States. An act of the 25th of February declared the peaceful navigation of the Mississippi River free to the citizens of any of the States upon its borders, or upon the borders of its navigable tributaries. On the 25th of February a commission to the Government of the United States, for the purpose of

negotiating friendly relations and for the settlement of all questions of disagreement between the two governments, was appointed and confirmed. The commissioners were A. B. Roman, of Louisiana, Martin J. Crawford, of Georgia, and John Forsyth, of Alabama. An act of February 26th provided for the repeal of all laws which forbade the employment in the coasting trade of vessels not enrolled or licensed, and all laws imposing discriminating duties on foreign vessels or goods imported in them. This Provisional Congress of one House held four sessions, as follows: I. February 4th–March 16th, 1861; II. April 29th–May 22d, 1861; III. July 20th–August 22d, 1861; IV. November 18th, 1861–February 17th, 1862; the first and second of these at Montgomery, the third and fourth at Richmond, whither the Executive Department was removed late in May, 1861,—because of "the hostile demonstrations of the United States Government against Virginia," as Mr Davis says in his "Rise and Fall of the Confederate Government."— EDITORS.

LEROY POPE WALKER, FIRST CONFEDERATE
SECRETARY OF WAR.
FROM A PHOTOGRAPH.

the United States Government should attempt to coerce South Carolina back into the Union, or to blockade her ports. His expectation, at that late period, apparently was that South Carolina would be left out of the Union alone, and that the United States Government would simply collect duties off the bars of her seaports; and he expressed himself "in favor of seeking to bring those [the planting States] into coöperation before asking for a popular decision upon a new policy and relation to the nations of the earth." These views did not strengthen him with Mr. Rhett for the executive head of the Southern Confederacy; nor did the published report of his shedding tears on retiring from the United States Senate after the secession of Mississippi. But Mr. Rhett's cotemporary and second cousin, Mr. Barnwell, called three times to solicit his vote for Mr. Davis. The impression was produced upon his mind that he, Mr. Rhett, was the only man in the delegation opposed to Mr. Davis. In reply to objections suggested by Mr. Rhett, Mr. Barnwell said that Mr. Rhett's standard of the statesmanship requisite was higher than he might be able to get. He added that he knew Mr. Davis, and although he considered him not a man of great ability, yet he believed him just and honorable, and that he would utilize the best ability of the country, as Monroe and Polk and others had done, and would administer the powers intrusted to him as President, with an eye single to the interests of the Confederacy. Upon this presentment Mr. Rhett concluded to forego his own mistrust, and to give his vote for Mr. Davis, along with the rest, as he supposed. On taking the vote in the convention (February 9th) Georgia gave

ROBERT BARNWELL RHETT, CHAIRMAN OF COMMITTEE
ON FOREIGN AFFAIRS, CONFEDERATE PROVISIONAL
CONGRESS. FROM A PHOTOGRAPH.

hers to Mr. Cobb, and the other States theirs to Mr. Davis. Georgia then changed her vote, which elected Mr. Davis unanimously. Mr. Alexander H.

Stephens was chosen Vice-President. ↓ Mr. Rhett was made chairman of the committee to notify the President-elect, and to present him to the convention for inauguration. This office he performed in complimentary style, reflecting the estimate of Mr. Barnwell rather than his own fears. Within six weeks the Provisional Congress found out that they had made a mistake, and that there was danger of a division into an administration and an anti-administration party, which might paralyze the Government. To avoid this, and to confer all power on the President, they resorted to secret sessions.

Mr. Davis offered the office of Secretary of State to Mr. Barnwell, but he declined it, and recommended Mr. C. G. Memminger, also of South Carolina, for the Treasury portfolio, which was promptly accorded to him. Both of these gentlemen had been coöperationists, and up to the last had opposed secession. Mr. Barnwell would not have been sent to the State convention from Beaufort but for the efforts of Edmund Rhett, an influential State senator. Of Mr. Memminger it was said that when a bill was on its passage through the Legislature of South Carolina in 1859, appropriating a sum of money for the purchase of arms, he had slipped in an amendment which had operated to prevent Governor Gist from drawing the money and procuring the arms. In Charleston he was known as an active friend of the free-school system and orphan house, a moral and charitable Episcopalian, and a lawyer, industrious, shrewd, and thrifty. As chairman of the Committee on Ways and Means in the House of Representatives, he was familiar with the cut-and-dried plan of raising the small revenue necessary to carry on the government of South Carolina. Such was his record and experience when appointed to the cabinet of Mr. Davis. Mr. Memminger received no recommendation for this office from the South Carolina delegation; nor did the delegation from any State, so far as known, attempt to influence the President in the choice of his cabinet.

Mr. Robert Toombs, of Georgia, was appointed Secretary of State. This was in deference to the importance of his State and the public appreciation of his great mental powers and thorough earnestness, not for the active part he had taken in the State convention in behalf of secession. In public too fond of sensational oratory, in counsel he was a man of large and wise views.

Mr. Leroy Pope Walker, of Alabama, was appointed Secretary of War on the recommendation of Mr. William L. Yancey. Ambitious, without any special fitness for this post, and overloaded, he accepted the office with the understanding that Mr. Davis would direct and control its business, which he did. After differing with the President as to the number of arms to be imported, and the number of men to be placed in camp in the winter of 1861–62 (being in favor of very many more than the President), he wisely resigned.

Mr. Stephen R. Mallory, of Florida, was appointed Secretary of the Navy. He was a gentleman of unpretending manners and ordinary good sense, who had served in the Senate with Mr. Davis, and had been chairman of the Committee

↓ The choice was provisional only, but was made permanent on the 6th of November, 1861, when Mr. Davis and Mr. Stephens were unanimously elected for six years. The Confederate Constitution made them ineligible to reëlection. — EDITORS.

on Naval Affairs. With some acquaintance with officers of the United States Navy, and some knowledge of nautical matters, he had small comprehension of the responsibilities of the office. His efforts were feeble and dilatory, and he utterly failed to provide for keeping open the seaports of the Confederacy. But he was one of the few who remained in the cabinet to the end.

Mr. Judah P. Benjamin, of Louisiana, was appointed Attorney-General, and held that office until the resignation of Mr. Walker, when he was transferred to the post of Secretary of War. Upon the fall of New Orleans, public indignation compelled a change, and he was made Secretary of State. A man of great fertility of mind and resource and of facile character, he was the factotum of the President, performed his bidding in various ways, and gave him the benefit of his brains in furtherance of the views of Mr. Davis.[

Although a provisional government was more free to meet emergencies and correct mistakes, it was determined to proceed to the formation of a permanent government. It was apprehended that in the lapse of time and

HOWELL COBB, PRESIDENT OF THE FIRST CONFEDERATE CONGRESS; MAJOR-GENERAL, C. S. A. FROM A PHOTOGRAPH.

[Mr. Davis's reasons for the selection of the members of the first Cabinet are given in his " Rise and Fall of the Confederate Government" (New York: D. Appleton & Co., 1881), Vol. I., pp. 241–3, in these words:

"After being inaugurated, I proceeded to the formation of my Cabinet, that is, the heads of the executive departments authorized by the laws of the Provisional Congress. The unanimity existing among our people made this a much easier and more agreeable task than where the rivalries in the party of an executive have to be consulted and accommodated, often at the expense of the highest capacity and fitness. Unencumbered by

any other consideration than the public welfare, having no friends to reward or enemies to punish, it resulted that not one of those who formed my first Cabinet had borne to me the relation of close personal friendship, or had political claims upon me; indeed, with two of them I had no previous acquaintance.

"It was my wish that the Hon. Robert W. Barnwell, of South Carolina, should be Secretary of State. I had known him intimately during a trying period of our joint service in the United States Senate, and he had won alike my esteem and regard. Before making known to him my wish in this connection, the delegation of South Carolina, of which he was a member, had resolved to recommend one of their number to be Secretary of the Treasury, and Mr. Barnwell, with

change of circumstances and of men, the cardinal points for which the South had contended, and on which the separation of sections had occurred. might be lost sight of; so it was decided to impress at once upon the new government the constitutional amendments regarded as essential.

STEPHEN R. MALLORY, SECRETARY OF THE NAVY TO THE CONFEDERACY. FROM A PHOTOGRAPH.

The committee, of which Mr. Rhett was chairman, agreed at its first meeting that the Constitution of the United States should be adopted, with only such alterations as experience had proved desirable, and to avoid latitudinarian constructions. Most of the important amendments were adopted on motion of the chairman. But the limits of this paper do not permit a specific statement of their character and scope. ⸮

The permanent constitution was adopted on the 11th of March, 1861, and went into operation, with the permanent government, at Richmond, on the 18th of February, 1862, when the Provisional Congress expired.

Those men who had studied the situation felt great anxiety about the keeping open of the ports of the Confederacy. Much was said and published about the immediate

characteristic delicacy, declined to accept my offer to him.

"I had intended to offer the Treasury Department to Mr. Toombs, of Georgia, whose knowledge on subjects of finance had particularly attracted my notice when we served together in the United States Senate. Mr. Barnwell having declined the State Department, and a colleague of his, said to be peculiarly qualified for the Treasury Department, having been recommended for it, Mr. Toombs was offered the State Department, for which others believed him to be well qualified.

"Mr. Mallory, of Florida, had been chairman of the Committee on Naval Affairs in the United States Senate, was extensively acquainted with the officers of the navy, and for a landsman had much knowledge of nautical affairs; therefore he was selected for Secretary of the Navy.

"Mr. Benjamin, of Louisiana, had a very high reputation as a lawyer, and my acquaintance with him in the Senate had impressed me with the lucidity of his intellect, his systematic habits and capacity for labor. He was therefore invited to the post of Attorney-General.

"Mr. Reagan, of Texas, I had known for a sturdy, honest Representative in the United States Congress, and his acquaintance with the territory included in the Confederate States was both extensive and accurate. These, together with his industry and ability to labor, indicated him as peculiarly fit for the office of Postmaster-General.

"Mr. Memminger, of South Carolina, had a high reputation for knowledge of finance. He bore an unimpeachable character for integrity and close attention to duties, and, on the recommendation of the delegation from South Carolina, he was appointed Secretary of the Treasury, and proved himself entirely worthy of the trust.

"Mr. Walker, of Alabama, was a distinguished member of the bar of north Alabama, and was eminent among the politicians of that section. He was earnestly recommended by gentlemen intimately and favorably known to me, and was therefore selected for the War Department. His was the only name presented from Alabama."

EDITORS.

⸮ One of them, offered by Mr. Rhett, and unanimously adopted, relates to civil-service reform, and is in the following words:

"The principal officer in each of the executive departments, and all persons connected with the diplomatic service, may be removed from office at the pleasure of the President. All other civil officers of the executive department may be removed at any time by the President or other appointing power, when their services are unnecessary, or for dishonesty, incapacity, inefficiency, misconduct, or neglect of duty; and when so removed, the removal shall be reported to the Senate, together with the reasons therefor."

R. B. R.

necessity of providing gun-boats and shipping suitable for that purpose. In the winter of 1861 Mr. C. K. Prioleau, of the firm of John Fraser & Co., of Liverpool, found a fleet of ten first-class East Indiamen, available to a buyer at less than half their cost. They belonged to the East India Company, and had been built in Great Britain for armament if required, or for moving troops and carrying valuable cargoes and treasure. Four of them were vessels of great size and power and of the very first class; and there were six others, which, although smaller, were scarcely inferior for the required purpose. On surrendering their powers to the British throne, the company had these steamships for sale. Mr. Prioleau secured the refusal of this fleet. The total cost of buying, arming, and fitting out the ten ships and putting them on the Southern coast ready for action was estimated at $10,000,000, or, say, 40,000 bales of cotton. The harbor of Port Royal, selected before the war as a coaling station for the United States Navy, with 26 feet of water at mean low tide, was admirably adapted for a rendezvous and point of supply. Brunswick, Georgia, was another good harbor, fit for such a fleet. The proposal was submitted to the Government through a partner of Mr. Prioleau in Charleston, Mr. George A. Trenholm, who forwarded the proposition by his son, William L. Trenholm. Its importance was not at all comprehended, and it was rejected by the executive. Captain J. D. Bulloch, the secret naval agent in Europe, who had the *Alabama* built, states that "the Confederate Government wanted ships to cruise and to destroy the enemy's mercantile marine." It was of infinitely more importance to keep Southern ports open, but this does not seem to have been understood until too late. The opportunity of obtaining these ships was thrown away. They were engaged by the British Government.

To show the narrow spirit of those in office, an incident concerning Captain Maffit, who figured afterward in command of the *Florida*, may be mentioned. In May, after the reduction of Fort Sumter, Maffit came from Washington to offer his services, and when he met the writer was in a state of indignation and disgust. He said that after having been caressed and offered a command in the Pacific, he had sneaked away from Washington to join the Confederacy, and that he had been received by the Secretary of the Navy as if he (Maffit) had designs upon him.

JUDAH P. BENJAMIN, CONFEDERATE ATTORNEY-GENERAL UNTIL SEPT. 17TH, 1861; SECOND SECRETARY OF WAR; THIRD SECRETARY OF STATE. FROM A PHOTOGRAPH.

The Secretary of War has stated that before the Government moved from Montgomery 360,000 men, the flower of the South, had tendered their services in the army. Only a small fraction of the number were received. The Secretary was worn out with personal applications of ardent officers, and himself stated that in May, 1861, he was constantly waylaid, in walking the back way from his office to the Exchange Hotel, by men offering their lives in the Confederate cause.

Another instance of narrowness may be named in the case of William Cutting Heyward. He was a wealthy rice-planter and an eminently practical and efficient man, a graduate at West Point in the class with Mr. Davis. He went to Montgomery to tender a regiment. He sent in his card to the President and waited for days in the lobby without obtaining an interview, and then returned home. He finally died from exposure, performing the duties of a private in the Home Guard at Charleston. The reason alleged for not accepting more men was the want of arms, and Mr. Davis's book is an apology for not procuring them. Insisting that a great war was probable, and in-

CHRISTOPHER G. MEMMINGER, FIRST SECRETARY OF THE TREASURY OF THE CONFEDERACY.

augurated on the 18th of February,— there was no declaration of war before the middle of April and no efficient blockade of the ports for many months,— yet it was in May that he started Major Huse over to England with instructions to purchase 10,000 Enfield rifles! By these facts may be gauged his estimate of the emergency or of the purchasing ability of the Confederate States. The provisional constitution provided that "Congress shall appropriate no money from the Treasury unless it be asked and estimated for by the President or some one of the heads of departments, except for the purpose of paying its own expenses and contingencies." The Congress could, therefore, do nothing about the purchase of arms without a call from the executive.

But for the Treaty of Paris in 1778, made by Benjamin Franklin, Silas Dean, and Arthur Lee, with France, the independence of the thirteen original States would not have been established. It was deemed important in the Provisional Congress of the Confederate States to send commissioners abroad to negotiate for a recognition of their independence, and, in case of war with the States of the North, perhaps for assistance. The chairman of the Committee on Foreign Affairs, Mr. Rhett, reported such a resolution, which was unanimously adopted. As the treaty-making power of the Government belonged to the President, Congress could not dictate to him the limit of authority that should be conferred upon the commissioners, in the negotiations desired. But all those who had reflected upon the subject expected the President to give extensive authority for making treaties. The views held by the chairman were that the commissioners should be authorized to propose to Great Britain, France, and other European nations, upon the conditions of recognition and alliance, that the Confederate States for twenty years would agree to lay no higher duties on productions imported than fifteen or twenty per cent. *ad valorem;* that for this period, no tonnage duties would be laid on their shipping, entering or leaving Confederate ports, but such as should be imposed to keep in order the harbors and rivers; that the navigation between the ports of the Confederate States for the same time should be free to the nations entering into alliance with the Confederate States, while upon the productions and tonnage of all nations refusing to recognize their independence and enter into treaty with them, a discriminating duty of ten per cent. would be imposed. He believed, moreover, that they should be authorized to make an offensive and defensive league, with special guarantees, as was done in 1778. Here was a direct and powerful appeal to the interests of foreign nations, especially England. Would any British Minister have dared to reject a treaty offering such vast advantages to his country? And if so, when the fact became known to Parliament, could he have retained his place?

Up to September, 1862, the United States Government was committed, both by diplomatic dispatches and by the action of Congress, to the declaration that the war was made solely to preserve the Union and with the purpose of maintaining the institutions of the seceded States, unimpaired and unaltered. Hence, at this period, the issue of slavery had not been injected into diplomacy, and was no obstacle to negotiating treaties.

When Mr. Yancey received the appointment at the head of the commission, Mr. Rhett conferred with him at length, and found that the commissioner fully concurred in the views just mentioned. But he surprised Mr. Rhett by the statement that the President had given no powers whatever to make commercial treaties, or to give

JOHN H. REAGAN, CONFEDERATE POSTMASTER-GENERAL.

any special interest in Confederate trade or navigation to any foreign nations, but relied upon the idea that "Cotton is King." "Then," rejoined Mr. Rhett, "if you will take my advice, as your friend, do not accept the appointment. For you will have nothing to propose and nothing to treat about, and must necessarily fail. Demand of the President the powers essential to the success of your mission, or stay at home."

On the reassembling of the Provisional Congress in April, ascertaining that these powers had not been conferred upon the commission, Mr. Rhett prepared a resolution requesting the President to empower the commissioners to propose to European nations, as the basis of a commercial treaty, a tariff of duties for 20 years no higher than 20 per cent. *ad valorem* on their imports into the Confederate States.   This he submitted to Mr. Toombs, the Secretary of State, who promptly approved it and appeared before the Committee on Foreign Affairs to urge it. It was reported, with the indorsement of the committee, to the Congress, and was not opposed in debate; but Mr. Perkins moved, as an amendment, six years instead of twenty. As this was carried, Mr. Rhett moved to lay the resolution on the table, which was done ; and this was the only effort made to appeal to the interests of foreign nations, to secure recognition of the independence of the Confederate States, or to obtain assistance. Upon his return from abroad, Mr. Yancey met Mr. Rhett and said: "You were right, sir. I went on a fool's errand." In December, 1863, at Richmond, James L. Orr, chairman of the Committee on Foreign Affairs of the Senate, said to the writer, "The Confederate States have had no diplomacy."

In March, 1863, proposals were made for a loan of $15,000,000 on 7 per cent. bonds, secured by an engagement of the Confederate Government to deliver cotton at 12 cents per pound within 6 months after peace. The loan stood in the London market at 5 per cent. premium ; and the applications for it exceeded $75,000,000. In the Provisional Congress at Montgomery, Mr. Stephens proposed that the Confederate Government should purchase cotton at 8 cents per pound, paying in 8 per cent. bonds, running 20 or 30 years. He believed that 2,000,000 bales of the crop of 1860 could be obtained in that way from the planters, and that, of the crop of 1861, 2,000,000 more bales might be obtained afterward. By using this cotton as security, or shipping it abroad, he maintained the finances of the Confederate States could at once be placed on a solid basis. His plan met with much favor, but was opposed by the administration and was not carried through. Money for the long war was to be raised by loans from Confederate citizens on bonds supplemented by the issue of Treasury notes and by a duty on exported cotton.

In April, 1865, after the collapse of the Confederacy, Mr. Barnwell, who had steadfastly supported Mr. Davis in the Confederate Senate, met the writer at Greenville, S. C., where Governor Magrath had summoned the Legislature of the State to assemble. There, in conversation, Mr. Barnwell explicitly expressed his judgment in the following words: "Mr. Davis never had any policy; he drifted, from the beginning to the end of the war."

For practical regret at the issue of the secession movement, the time has long passed by. The people of the South have reconciled themselves to the restoration of the Union and to the abolishment of slavery. They have bravely and strenuously endeavored to go through the transition period of an enormous change without wreck. In complete harmony with the destinies of the Union, they are working out the future of the United States faithfully.

This is set down to prevent the suppression of important facts in history, and in justice to eminent men, now dead, who have been much misunderstood.

RICHMOND, VIRGINIA, IN 1861. FROM A SKETCH.

JACKSON AT HARPER'S FERRY IN 1861.

BY JOHN D. IMBODEN, BRIGADIER-GENERAL, C. S. A.

THE movement to capture Harper's Ferry, Virginia, and the fire-arms manufactured and stored there was organized at the Exchange Hotel in Richmond on the night of April 16th, 1861. Ex-Governor Henry A. Wise was at the head of this purely impromptu affair. The Virginia Secession Convention, then sitting, was by a large majority "Union" in its sentiment till Sumter was fired on and captured, and Mr. Lincoln called for seventy-five thousand men to enforce the laws in certain Southern States. Virginia was then, as it were, forced to "take sides," and she did not hesitate. I had been one of the candidates for a seat in that convention from Augusta county, but had been overwhelmingly defeated by the "Union" candidates, because I favored secession as the only "peace measure" Virginia could then adopt, our aim being to put the State in an independent position to negotiate between the United States and the seceded Gulf and Cotton States for a new Union, to be formed on a compromise of the slavery question by a convention to be held for that purpose.

Late on April 15th I received a telegram from "Nat" Tyler, the editor of the "Richmond Enquirer," summoning me to Richmond, where I arrived the next day. Before reaching the Exchange Hotel I met ex-Governor Wise on the street. He asked me to find as many officers of the armed and equipped volunteers of the inland towns and counties as I could, and request them to be at the hotel by 7 in the evening to confer about a military movement which he deemed important. Not many such officers were in town, but I found Captains Turner Ashby and Richard Ashby of Fauquier county, Oliver R. Funsten of Clarke county, all commanders of volunteer companies of cavalry; also Captain John A. Harman of Staunton—my home—and Alfred M. Barbour, the latter ex-civil superintendent of the Government works at Harper's Ferry.☆ These persons, with myself, promptly joined ex-Governor Wise, and a plan

☆ See page 125 for a letter of Mr. Barbour, regarding the security of the armory.—EDITORS.

111

for the capture of Harper's Ferry was at once discussed and settled upon. The movement, it was agreed, should commence the next day, the 17th, as soon as the convention voted to secede,—provided we could get railway transportation and the concurrence of Governor Letcher. Colonel Edmund Fontaine, president of the Virginia Central railroad, and John S. Barbour, president of the Orange and Alexandria and Manassas Gap railroads, were sent for, and joined us at the hotel near midnight. They agreed to put the necessary trains in readiness next day to obey any request of Governor Letcher for the movement of troops.

THE PALMETTO REGIMENT PARADING IN CHARLESTON, S. C., EN ROUTE FOR RICHMOND. FROM A SKETCH.

A committee, of which I was chairman, waited on Governor Letcher after midnight, and, arousing him from his bed, laid the scheme before him. He stated that he would take no step till officially informed that the ordinance of secession was passed by the convention. He was then asked if contingent upon the event he would next day order the movement by telegraph. He consented. We then informed him what companies would be under arms ready to move at a moment's notice. All the persons I have named above are now dead, except John S. Barbour, "Nat" Tyler, and myself.

On returning to the hotel and reporting Governor Letcher's promise, it was decided to telegraph the captains of companies along the railroads mentioned to be ready next day for orders from the governor. In that way I ordered the Staunton Artillery, which I commanded, to assemble at their armory by 4 P. M. on the 17th, to receive orders from the governor to aid in the capture of the Portsmouth Navy Yard. This destination had been indicated in all our dispatches, to deceive the Government at Washington in case there should be a "leak" in the telegraph offices. Early in the evening a message had been received by ex-Governor Wise from his son-in-law Doctor Garnett of Washington, to the effect that a Massachusetts regiment, one thousand strong, had been ordered to Harper's Ferry. Without this reënforcement we knew the guard there consisted of only forty-five men, who could be captured or driven away, perhaps without firing a shot, if we could reach the place secretly.

The Ashbys, Funsten, Harman, and I remained up the entire night. The superintendent and commandant of the Virginia Armory at Richmond, Captain Charles Dimmock, a Northern man by birth and a West Point graduate, was in full sympathy with us, and that night filled our requisitions for ammunition and moved it to the railway station before sunrise. He also granted one hundred stand of arms for the Martinsburg Light Infantry, a

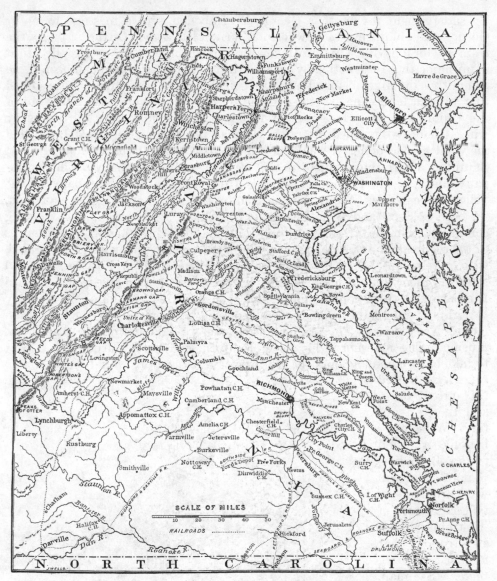

new company just formed. All these I receipted for and saw placed on the
train. Just before we moved out of the depot, Alfred Barbour made an
unguarded remark in the car, which was overheard by a Northern traveler, who
immediately wrote a message to President Lincoln and paid a negro a dollar
to take it to the telegraph office. This act was discovered by one of our party,
who induced a friend to follow the negro and take the dispatch from him.
This perhaps prevented troops being sent to head us off.

My telegram to the Staunton Artillery produced wild excitement, that spread
rapidly through the county, and brought thousands of people to Staunton
during the day. Augusta had been a strong Union county, and a doubt was
raised by some whether I was acting under the orders of Governor Letcher.

To satisfy them, my brother, George W. Imboden, sent a message to me at Gordonsville, inquiring under whose authority I had acted. On the arrival of the train at Gordonsville, Captain Harman received the message and replied to it in my name, that I was acting by order of the governor. Harman had been of the committee, the night before, that waited on Governor Letcher, and he assumed that by that hour—noon—the convention must have voted the State out of the Union, and that the governor had kept his promise to send orders by wire. Before we reached Staunton, Harman handed me the dispatch and told me what he had done. I was annoyed by his action till the train drew up at Staunton, where thousands of people were assembled, and my artillery company and the West Augusta Guards (the finest infantry company in the valley) were in line. Major-General Kenton Harper, a native of Pennsylvania, "a born soldier," and Brigadier-General William H. Harman, both holding commissions in the Virginia militia,—and both of whom had won their spurs in the regiment the State had sent to the Mexican war,—met me as I alighted, with a telegram from Governor Letcher ordering them into service, and referring them to me for information as to our destination and troops. Until I imparted to them confidentially what had occurred the night before, they thought, as did all the people assembled, that we were bound for the Portsmouth Navy Yard. For prudential reasons, we said nothing to dispel this illusion. The governor in his dispatch informed General Harper that he was to take chief command, and that full written instructions would reach him *en route.* He waited till after dark, and then set out for Winchester behind a good team. Brigadier-General Harman was ordered to take command of the trains and of all troops that might report *en route.* (See map, page 113.)

About sunset we took train ; our departure was an exciting and affecting scene. At Charlottesville, in

THE COURT-HOUSE, CHARLESTOWN, VA., WHERE JOHN BROWN AND HIS ASSOCIATES
WERE TRIED AND SENTENCED. FROM A PHOTOGRAPH.

the night, the Monticello Guards, Captain W. B. Mallory, and the Albemarle Rifles, under Captain R. T. W. Duke, came aboard. At Culpeper a rifle company joined us, and just as the sun rose on the 18th we reached Manassas.

The Ashbys and Funsten had gone on the day before to collect their cavalry companies, and also the famous "Black Horse Cavalry," a superb body of men and horses, under Captains John Scott and Welby Carter of Fauquier. By marching across the Blue Ridge, they were to rendezvous near

Harper's Ferry. Ashby had sent men on the night of the 17th to cut the wires between Manassas Junction and Alexandria, and to keep them cut for several days.

Our arrival at Manassas Junction startled the quiet people of the village. General Harman at once "impressed" the Manassas

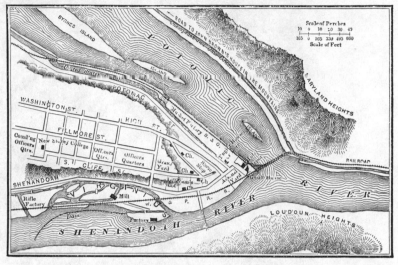

MAP OF HARPER'S FERRY.

Gap train to take the lead, and switched two or three other trains to that line in order to proceed to Strasburg. I was put in command of the foremost train. We had not gone five miles when I discovered that the engineer could not be trusted. He let his fire go down, and came to a dead standstill on a slight ascending grade. A cocked pistol induced him to fire up and go ahead. From there to Strasburg I rode in the engine-cab, and we made full forty miles an hour with the aid of good dry wood and a navy revolver.

At Strasburg we left the cars, and before 10 o'clock the infantry companies took up the line of march for Winchester. I now had to procure horses for my guns. The farmers were in their corn-fields, and some of them agreed to hire us horses as far as Winchester, eighteen miles, while others refused. The situation being urgent, we took the horses by force, under threats of being indicted by the next grand jury of the county. By noon we had a sufficient number of teams. We followed the infantry down the Valley Turnpike, reaching Winchester just at nightfall. The people generally received us very coldly. The war spirit that bore them up through four years of trial and privation had not yet been aroused.

General Harper was at Winchester, and had sent forward his infantry by rail to Charlestown, eight miles from Harper's Ferry. In a short time a train returned for my battery. The farmers got their horses and went home rejoicing, and we set out for our destination. The infantry moved out of Charlestown about midnight. We kept to our train as far as Halltown, only four miles from the ferry. There we set down our guns to be run forward by hand to Bolivar Heights, west of the town, from which we could shell the place if necessary.

FROM A PHOTOGRAPH.

John Brown

The well-known raid of John Brown upon Harper's Ferry, Virginia, for the purpose of freeing slaves by force of arms, occurred on the evening of Sunday, the 17th of October, 1859. His party, including himself and five negroes (three of whom were fugitive slaves), consisted of 22 men, three of whom remained at the rendezvous on the Maryland side of the Potomac. The others crossed by the bridge and seized the United States armory and arsenal, and during the next eighteen hours were busy in arousing slaves, cutting telegraph wires, providing defenses against attack, and imprisoning citizens. They were at last besieged in the engine-house by a large number of citizens and militia, to

A little before dawn of the next day, April 18th, a brilliant light arose from near the point of confluence of the Shenandoah and Potomac rivers. General Harper, who up to that moment had expected a conflict with the Massachusetts regiment supposed to be at Harper's Ferry, was making his dispositions for an attack at daybreak, when this light convinced him that the enemy had fired the arsenal and fled. He marched in and took possession, but too late to extinguish the flames. Nearly twenty thousand rifles and pistols were destroyed. The workshops had not been fired. The people of the town told us the catastrophe, for such it was to us, was owing to declarations made the day before by the ex-superintendent, Alfred Barbour. He reached Harper's Ferry, *via* Washington, on the 17th about noon, and, collecting the mechanics in groups, informed them that the place would be captured within twenty-four hours by Virginia troops. He urged them to protect the property, and join the Southern cause, promising, if war ensued, that the place would be held by the South, and that they would be continued at work on high wages. His influence with the men was great, and most of them decided to accept his advice. But Lieutenant Roger Jones, who commanded the little guard of forty-five men, hearing what was going on, at once took measures to destroy the place if necessary. Trains of gunpowder

THE ENGINE-HOUSE, HARPER'S FERRY —"JOHN BROWN'S FORT," IN WHICH HE WAS CAPTURED.

whom were added, on the morning of Tuesday, a force of United States marines, sent from Washington under Colonel Robert E. Lee and Lieutenants Green and J. E. B. Stuart. The marines battered down the door of the engine-house and captured the insurgents, after a brave resistance. In the conflict John Brown was wounded; his sons Watson and Oliver were mortally wounded, and eight others of the party were killed. Five, including another son, Owen Brown, escaped. Seven were captured, and, after trial and conviction, were hanged at Charlestown, Virginia,— John Brown on the 2d of December, 1859; John E. Cook, Edwin Coppoc, John A. Copeland (a mulatto), and Shields Green (a negro) on the 16th of December; and Aaron D. Stevens and Albert Hazlett on the 16th of the following March. Three citizens and a number of negroes were killed by the insurgents, and others were wounded.

EDITORS.

COLONEL ROBERT E. LEE.
FROM A PHOTOGRAPH TAKEN BEFORE THE WAR.

April 23d, 1861, Robert E. Lee, with the rank of major-general, was appointed by Governor Letcher commander-in-chief of the military and naval forces of the State of Virginia, and assumed charge of the military defenses of the State. June 8th, 1861, in accordance with the proclamation of Governor Letcher, he transferred the command to the Confederate States, but he remained the ranking officer of the Virginia military forces.

were laid through the buildings to be fired. In the shops the workmen of Southern sympathies managed to wet the powder in many places during the night, rendering it harmless. Jones's troops, however, held the arsenal buildings and stores, and when their commander was advised of Harper's rapid approach the gunpowder was fired, and he crossed into Maryland with his handful of men. So we secured only the machinery and the gun and pistol barrels and locks, which, however, were sent to Richmond and Columbia, South Carolina, and were worked over into excellent arms. [See note, page 125.]

Within a week about thirteen hundred Virginia volunteers had assembled there. As these companies were, in fact, a part of the State militia, they were legally under command of the three brigadiers and one major-general of militia, who had authority over this, that, or the other organization. These generals surrounded themselves with a numerous staff, material for which was abundant in the rank and file of the volunteers; for instance, in my battery there were at least a dozen college graduates of and below the grade of corporal. Every fair afternoon the official display in Harper's Ferry of "fuss and feathers" would have done no discredit to the Champs Élysées.

One afternoon, six or eight days after our occupation, General Harper sent for me, as the senior artillery officer (we then had three batteries, but all without horses), to say he had been told that a number of trains on the Baltimore and Ohio railroad would try to pass us in the night, transporting troops from the West to Washington, and that he had decided to prevent them at the risk of bringing on a battle. He ordered the posting of guns so as to command the road for half a mile or more, all to be accurately trained on the track by the light of day, and ready to be discharged at any moment. Infantry companies were stationed to fire into the trains, if the artillery failed to stop them. Pickets were posted out two or three miles, with orders to fire signal-guns as soon as the first troop-laden train should pass. About 1 o'clock at night we heard the rumbling of an approaching train. The long roll was beat; the men assembled at their assigned positions and in silence awaited the sound of the signal-guns. A nervous cavalryman was the vedette. As the train passed him (it was the regular mail) he thought he saw soldiers in it, and fired. *Pop! pop! pop!* came down the road from successive sentries. Primers were inserted and lan-

MARYLAND HEIGHTS.   LOUDOUN HEIGHTS.

HARPER'S FERRY, LOOKING DOWN THE POTOMAC.
FROM A PHOTOGRAPH TAKEN FROM THE HILL ABOVE THE TOWN.

yards held taut, to be pulled when the engine should turn a certain point four hundred yards distant from the battery. By great good luck Colonel William S. H. Baylor, commanding the 5th Virginia regiment, was with some of his men stationed a little beyond the point, and, seeing no troops aboard the train, signaled it to stop. It did so, not one hundred yards beyond where the artillery would have opened on it. When the first excitement was over, he demanded of the conductor what troops, if any, were on board, and was told there was "one old fellow in uniform asleep on the mail-bags in the first car." Entering that car with a file of soldiers, he secured the third prisoner of war taken in Virginia. It proved to be Brigadier-General W. S. Harney, of the United States army, on his way from the West to Washington, to resign his commission and go to Europe rather than engage in a fratricidal war. He surrendered with a pleasant remark, and was taken to General Harper's headquarters, where he spent the night. On his assurance that he knew of no troops coming from the West, Harper ordered us all to quarters. Next morning General Harney was paroled to report in Richmond, and was escorted to a train about to leave for Winchester. He was a fine-looking old soldier, and as he walked down the street to the depot he saw all our forces except the cavalry. He was accompanied socially by two or three of our generals and a swarm of staff-officers. He cast his glance over the few hundred men in sight, and turning to General Harper, I heard him inquire, with a merry twinkle in his eye, "Where is your army encamped, general?" Harper's face crimsoned as he replied, "Excuse me from giving information." Harney smiled, and said politely, "Pardon me for asking an improper question, but I had forgotten I was a prisoner." He went on to Richmond, was treated with marked courtesy, and in a day or two proceeded to Washington.

In a few days our forces began to increase by the arrival of fresh volunteer companies. Being only a captain, I was kept very busy in trying to get my battery into the best condition. We had no caissons and but insufficient harness. For the latter I sent to Baltimore, purchasing on my private credit. In the same way I ordered from Richmond red flannel shirts and other clothing for all my men, our uniforms being too fine for camp life. The governor subsequently ordered these bills to be paid by the State treasurer. We found at the armory a large number of very strong horse-carts. In my battery were thirty or more excellent young mechanics. By using the wheels and axles of the carts they soon constructed good caissons, which served us till after the first battle of Bull Run.

We had no telegraph line to Richmond except *via* Washington, and the time of communication by mail was two days. General Harper found it so difficult to obtain needed munitions and supplies, that about the last of April he decided to send me to the governor, who was my intimate friend, with a requisition for all we needed, and verbal instructions to make to him a full statement of our necessitous and defenseless condition, in case General Robert Patterson, who was reported with a Federal force at Chambersburg, should move against us. When I arrived in Richmond, General Robert E. Lee had been placed in command of all the Virginia forces by the governor, and by an ordinance every militia officer in the State above the rank of captain had been decapitated, and the governor and his military council had been authorized to fill vacancies thus created.

HARPER'S FERRY, FROM THE MARYLAND SIDE.

The railway bridge was destroyed by the Confederates on the 13th of June, 1861. Two days later, on the approach of Union forces under General Robert Patterson, near Williamsport, and under Colonel Lew Wallace at Romney (see footnote page 127), General Joseph E. Johnston (who had succeeded Colonel Jackson in command on the 23d of May), considering the position untenable, withdrew the Confederate army to Winchester.

This was a disastrous blow to "the pomp and circumstance of glorious war" at Harper's Ferry. Militia generals and the brilliant "staff" were stricken down, and their functions devolved, according to Governor Letcher's order of April 27th, upon Thomas J. Jackson, colonel commandant, and James W.

Massie, major and assistant adjutant-general, who arrived during the first week of May.

This was "Stonewall" Jackson's first appearance on the theater of the war. I spent one day and night in Richmond, and then returned to camp, arriving about 2 P. M. What a revolution three or four days had wrought! I could scarcely realize the change. The militia generals were all gone, and the staff had vanished. The commanding colonel and his adjutant had arrived, and were occupying a small room in the little wayside hotel near the railroad bridge. Knowing them both, I immediately sought an interview, and delivered a letter and some papers I had brought from General Lee. Jackson and his adjutant were at a little pine table figuring upon the rolls of the troops present. They were dressed in well-worn, dingy uniforms of professors in the Virginia Military Institute, where both had recently occupied chairs. Colonel Jackson had issued and sent to the camps a short, simple order assuming the command, but had had no intercourse with the troops. The deposed officers had nearly all left for home or for Richmond in a high state of indignation. After an interview of perhaps a half hour I proceeded to my camp on the hill, and found the men of the 5th Virginia regiment, from my own county, in assembly, and greatly excited. They were deeply attached to their field-officers, and regarded the ordinance of the convention as an outrage on freemen and volunteers, and were discussing the propriety of passing denunciatory resolutions. On seeing me they called

GENERAL THOMAS J. ("STONEWALL") JACKSON. FROM A PHOTOGRAPH.

for a speech. As I did not belong to the regiment, I declined to say anything, but ordered the men of the Staunton Artillery to fall into line. Then I briefly told them that we were required to muster into service either for twelve months or during the war, at our option, and urged them to go in for the full period of the war, as such action would be most creditable to them, and a good example to others. They unanimously shouted, "For the war! For the war!" Before they were dismissed the ceremony of mustering in was completed, and I proudly took the roll down to Colonel Jackson with the remark, "There, colonel, is the roll of your first company mustered in for the war." He looked it over, and, rising, shook my hand, saying, "Thank you, captain — thank you; and please thank your men for me." He had heard that there was dissatisfaction in the camps, and asked me to act as mustering officer for two other artillery companies present. Before sunset the rolls were returned. This prompt action of the batteries was emulated the next day by the other troops, and all were mustered in. Within a week Governor Letcher wisely appointed Major-General Harper colonel of the 5th Virginia, Brigadier-General Harman lieutenant-colonel, and Colonel Baylor major, and I venture to say no regiment in either army was better officered, as the fame it won in the "Stonewall" brigade will prove. The presence of a master mind was visible in the changed condition of the camp. Perfect order reigned everywhere. Instruction in the details of military duties occupied Jackson's whole time. He urged the officers to call upon him for information about even the minutest details of duty, often remarking that it was no discredit to a civilian to be ignorant of military matters. He was a rigid disciplinarian, and yet as gentle and kind as a woman. He was the easiest man in our army to get along with pleasantly so long as one did his duty, but as inexorable as fate in exacting the performance of it; yet he would overlook serious faults if he saw they were the result of ignorance, and would instruct the offender in a kindly way. He was as courteous to the humblest private who sought an interview for any purpose as to the highest officer in his command. He despised superciliousness and self-assertion, and nothing angered him so quickly as to see an officer wound the feelings of those under him by irony or sarcasm.

When Jackson found we were without artillery horses, he went into no red-tape correspondence with the circumlocution offices in Richmond, but ordered his quartermaster, Major John A. Harman, to proceed with men to the Quaker settlements in the rich county of Loudoun, famous for its good horses, and buy or impress as many as we needed. Harman executed his orders with such energy and dispatch that he won Jackson's confidence, and remained his chief quartermaster till the day of Jackson's death.

By Jackson's orders I took possession of the bridge across the Potomac at Point of Rocks, twelve miles below Harper's Ferry, and fortified the Virginia end of the bridge, as we expected a visit any night from General B. F. Butler, who was at the Relay House on the Baltimore and Ohio railroad. It was my habit to keep awake all night to be ready for emergencies, and to sleep in the day-time, making daily reports, night and morning, to Jackson. One Sunday afternoon, a little over a week after we occupied this post, I was aroused from my nap by one of my men, who said there were two men in blue uniforms (we had not yet adopted the gray) riding about our camp, and looking so closely at everything that he believed they were spies. I went out to see who they were, and found Jackson and one of his staff. As I approached them, he put his finger on his lips and shook his head as a signal for silence. In a low tone he said he preferred it should not be known he had come there. He approved of all I had done, and soon galloped away. I afterward suspected that the visit was simply to familiarize himself with the line of the canal and railroad from Point of Rocks to Harper's Ferry preparatory to a sharp bit of strategy which he practiced a few days later.

From the very beginning of the war the Confederacy was greatly in need of rolling-stock for the railroads. We were particularly short of locomotives, and were without the shops to build them. Jackson, appreciating this, hit upon a plan to obtain a good supply from the Baltimore and Ohio road. Its line was double-tracked, at least from Point of Rocks to Martinsburg, a distance of 25 or 30 miles. We had not interfered with the running

PEN SKETCH OF GENERAL JACKSON, DRAWN
FROM LIFE, NEAR BALL'S BLUFF,
PROBABLY IN 1861.

of trains, except on the occasion of the arrest of General Harney. The coal traffic from Cumberland was immense, as the Washington government was accumulating supplies of coal on the seaboard. These coal trains passed Harper's Ferry at all hours of the day and night, and thus furnished Jackson with a pretext for arranging a brilliant " scoop." When he sent me to Point of Rocks, he ordered Colonel Harper with the 5th Virginia Infantry to Martinsburg. He then complained to President Garrett, of the Baltimore and Ohio, that the night trains, eastward bound, disturbed the repose of his camp, and requested a change of schedule that would pass all east-bound trains by Harper's Ferry between 11 and 1 o'clock in the day-time. Mr. Garrett complied, and thereafter for several days we heard the constant roar of passing trains for an hour before and an hour after noon. But since the " empties" were sent up the road at night, Jackson again complained that the nuisance was as great as ever, and, as the road had two tracks, said he must insist that the west-bound trains should pass during the same two hours as those going east. Mr. Garrett promptly complied, and we then had, for two hours every day, the liveliest railroad in America. One night, as soon as the schedule was working at its best, Jackson sent me an order to take a force of men across to the Maryland side of the river the next day at 11 o'clock, and, letting all west-bound trains pass till 12 o'clock, to permit none to go east, and at 12 o'clock to obstruct the road so that it would require several days to repair it. He ordered the reverse to be done at Martinsburg. Thus he caught all the trains that were going east or west between those points, and these he ran up to Winchester, thirty-two miles on the branch road, where they were safe, and whence they were removed by horse-power to the railway at Strasburg. I do not remember the number of trains captured, but the loss crippled the Baltimore and Ohio road seriously for some time, and the gain to our scantily stocked Virginia roads of the same gauge was invaluable.

While we held the Point of Rocks bridge, J. E. B. Stuart (afterward so famous as a cavalry leader) was commissioned lieutenant-colonel, and reported to Colonel Jackson for assignment to duty. Jackson ordered the consolidation of all the cavalry companies into a battalion to be commanded by Stuart, who then appeared more like a well-grown, manly youth than the mature man he really was. This order was very offensive to Captain Turner Ashby, at that time the idol of all the troopers in the field, as well he might be, for a more brave and chivalrous officer never rode at the head of well-mounted troopers. Ashby was older than Stuart, and he thought, and we all believed, that he was entitled to first promotion. When not absent scouting, Ashby spent his nights with me at the bridge. He told me of Jackson's order, and that he would reply to it with his resignation. I expostulated with him, although he had all my sympathies. I urged him to call upon Colonel Jackson that night. It was only twelve miles by the tow-path of the canal, and on his black Arabian he could make it in less than an hour. I believed Jackson would respect his feelings and leave his company out of Stuart's battalion. I

COLONEL ROGER JONES. FROM A PHOTOGRAPH.

ventured to write a private letter to Jackson, appealing in the strongest terms for the saving of Ashby to the service. The result of his night ride was that Jackson not only relieved him from the obnoxious order, but agreed to divide the companies between him and Stuart, and to ask for his immediate promotion, forming thus the nuclei of two regiments of cavalry, to be filled as rapidly as new companies came to the front. One of these regiments was commanded at first by Colonel Angus McDonald, with Ashby as lieutenant-colonel, and in a few months Ashby was promoted to its full command. Ashby got back to Point of Rocks about 2 in the morning, as happy a man as I ever saw, and completely enraptured with Jackson. From that night on, the affection and confidence of the two men were remarkable. A trip Ashby had made a few days before to Chambersburg and the encampment of General Robert Patterson was the real reason for Jackson's favor. Ashby had rigged himself in a farmer's suit of homespun that he had borrowed, and, hiring a plow-horse, had personated a rustic horse-doctor. With his saddle-bags full of some remedy for spavin or ringbone, he had gone to Chambersburg, and had returned in the night with an immense amount of information. The career of Ashby was a romance from that time on till he fell, shot through the heart, two days before the battle of Cross Keys.

May 23d, 1861, Colonel Jackson was superseded in command at Harper's Ferry by Brigadier-General Joseph E. Johnston. When General Johnston arrived several thousand men had been assembled there, representing nearly all the seceded States east of the Mississippi River. Johnston at once began the work of organization on a larger scale than Jackson had attempted. He brigaded the troops, and assigned Colonel Jackson to the command of the exclusively Virginian brigade. The latter was almost immediately commissioned brigadier-general, and when on the 15th of June Johnston withdrew from Harper's Ferry to Winchester, he kept Jackson at the front along the Baltimore and Ohio road to observe General Patterson's preparations. Nothing of much importance occurred for several weeks, beyond a little affair near Martinsburg in which Jackson captured about forty men of a reconnoitering party sent out by Patterson. His vigilance was ceaseless, and General Johnston felt sure, at Winchester, of ample warning of any aggressive movement of the enemy.

On the 2d of January, 1861, Alfred M. Barbour (mentioned in the foregoing paper), Superintendent of the United States Armory at Harper's Ferry, wrote to Captain William Maynadier of the Ordnance Bureau, Washington, in part as follows:

"I have reason to apprehend that some assault will be made upon the United States Armory at Harper's Ferry. My reasons I do not feel at liberty to disclose. They may or they may not be well founded. I deem it my duty to inform you that there is no regularly organized defense for the post. The armorers have been formed into volunteer companies, and arms and ammunition furnished them. . . . But the armory might be taken and destroyed; the arms might be abstracted and removed or destroyed; vast amount of damage might be done to the Government property before the companies could be notified or rallied. . . . I cannot be held responsible for consequences at present, unless the Government itself sees to the protection of its property by placing reliable regularly drilled forces to sustain me. I do not look to personal consequences at all. I look to the duty of protecting the property of the Federal Government now under my charge."

The next day Major (now General) Henry J. Hunt was assigned to command at Harper's Ferry, and Lieutenant Roger Jones was ordered to report to him with a small force from Carlisle Barracks, Pennsylvania. Major Hunt, in response to his request for instructions, accompanied by a statement of the weakness of his position, was directed by the Secretary of War (Holt) to avoid all needless irritation of the public mind. April 2d Major Hunt was ordered to other service, and the command devolved upon Lieutenant Jones (now Colonel and Inspector-General, U. S. A.), who, in a letter to the Editors, gives the following account of the destruction of the armory:

"From an early day after I reported with my detachment of sixty men from Carlisle, it became evident that a defense of the valuable Government interests at Harper's Ferry would be impracticable unless large reënforcements were sent there; and as there was every reason for believing that this would not be done, I early became convinced that there was but one course to pursue,— viz., to destroy what could not be defended. The chances for the capture or destruction of my small force — reduced on April 18th to 45 men — were overwhelming, but I counted on the unorganized and undisciplined state of the troops to be sent against me, on their surprise and bitter disappointment, as circumstances favoring our escape.

"On the Sunday preceding the seizure of the armory, a wealthy miller of the village came to me and offered to be the bearer of any message I might care to send to the Secretary of War [Mr. Simon Cameron], saying he knew him intimately and that he believed Mr. Cameron would heed and give due consideration to any representation coming from him. Having full confidence in the gentleman, I intrusted him with a message to Mr. Cameron, to the effect that if he would save for the Government the arms, etc., etc., at the armory, troops must be sent there at once and by the thousand. I further charged this gentleman to go to Washington that night, and not delay until the next morning, as he had intended — all of which he promised to do and none of which he did. But of his failure and change of purpose I was ignorant until his return to the Ferry Wednesday evening, when I learned that fear of the consequences of his mission, voluntarily assumed, had made him abandon it. Monday was passed in anxious expectation; the silence of Tuesday added to my anxiety, which culminated on the following morning, when Ex-Superintendent Barbour, fresh from the convention at Richmond, appeared upon the scene, told what had been done, and announced that within twenty-four hours the forces of the State of Virinia would be in possession of the armory.

"As I was acting entirely on my own judgment and responsibility, it was apparent I must not act prematurely, before the danger was self-evident and imminent. As the evening advanced, nearer and nearer came the troops from Halltown, and finally, shortly after 9 o'clock, when they had advanced to within less than a mile of the armory,— in time less than five minutes,— the torch was applied, and before I could withdraw my men from the village, the two arsenal buildings, containing about twenty thousand stand of rifles and rifle muskets, were ablaze. But very few of these arms were saved, for the constantly recurring explosions of powder which had been distributed through the buildings kept the crowd aloof. The fire in the shops was extinguished, but the arms, which were then of incalculable value, were destroyed. The spirit, devotion, and loyalty of my men, except two deserters, were admirable; four of them were captured at their posts, but they all eventually escaped,— one by swimming the river,— and reported to me at Carlisle. I have heard that within a few minutes after my command had crossed the Potomac to the Maryland side of the river, a train was heard starting off for Baltimore, and that it was assumed by the Virginia troops and their officers that my command had been taken off by that train, and that, consequently, pursuit was useless."

Lieutenant Jones's action was warmly approved by the President in a congratulatory letter from Secretary Cameron.

Governor Letcher estimated the value of the property secured to the State by the seizure of the Gosport Navy Yard and the Harper's Ferry Arsenal at $25,000,000 to $30,000,000.

EDITORS.

"AN AFFAIR OF OUTPOSTS."

McCLELLAN IN WEST VIRGINIA.

BY JACOB D. COX, MAJOR-GENERAL, U. S. V.

THE reasons which made it important to occupy West Virginia with National troops were twofold—political and strategic. The people were strongly attached to the Union, and had opposed the secession of Virginia, of which State they were then a part. But few slaves were owned by them, and all their interests bound them more to Ohio and Pennsylvania than to eastern Virginia. Under the influence of Lincoln's administration, strongly backed, and, indeed, chiefly represented, by Governor Dennison of Ohio, a movement was on foot to organize a loyal Virginia government, repudiating that of Governor Letcher and the State convention as self-destroyed by the act of secession. Governor Dennison had been urging McClellan to cross the Ohio to protect and encourage the loyal men when, on the 26th of May, news came that the Confederates had taken the initiative, and that some bridges had been burned on the Baltimore and Ohio railroad a little west of Grafton, the crossing of the Monongahela River, where the two western branches of the railroad unite, viz., the line from Wheeling and that from Parkersburg. [See map, p. 129.] The great line of communication between Washington and the west had thus been cut, and action on our part was made necessary. Governor Dennison had anticipated the need of more troops than the thirteen regiments which had been organized as Ohio's quota under the President's first call. He had organized nine other regiments, numbering them consecutively with those mustered into the national service, and had put them in camps near the Ohio River, where they could occupy Wheeling, Parkersburg, and the mouth of the Great Kanawha at a moment's notice. Two Union regiments were also organizing in West Virginia itself, at Wheeling and Parkersburg, of which the first was commanded by Colonel (afterward General) B. F. Kelley. West Virginia was in McClellan's department, and the formal authority to act had come from Washington on the 24th, in the shape of an inquiry from General Scott whether the enemy's force at Grafton could be counteracted.

The dispatch directed McClellan to "act promptly." On the 27th Colonel Kelley was sent by rail from Wheeling to drive off the enemy and protect the railroad. The hostile parties withdrew at Kelley's approach, and the bridges were quickly rebuilt. At the same time several of the Ohio regiments were ordered across the river, and a brigade of Indiana volunteers under Brigadier-General Thomas A. Morris was sent forward by rail from Indianapolis. Morris reached Grafton on the 1st of June, and was intrusted with the command of all the troops in West Virginia. He found that Colonel Kelley had already planned an expedition against the enemy, who had retired southward to Philippi, about thirty miles from Grafton. Morris approved the plan, but enlarged it by sending another column under Colonel Ebenezer Dumont of the 7th Indiana to coöperate with Kelley. Both columns were directed to make a night march, starting from points on the railroad about twelve miles apart, and converging on Philippi, which they were to attack at daybreak of June 3d. Each column consisted of about 1500 men, and Dumont's had with it 2 field-pieces of artillery, smooth 6-pounders.

The Confederate force was commanded by Colonel G. A. Porterfield, of the Virginia volunteers, and was something less than a thousand strong, about one-fourth cavalry.↓

The night was dark and stormy, and Porterfield's raw troops had not learned picket duty. The concerted movement against them was more successful than such marches commonly are, and Porterfield's first notice of danger was the opening of the artillery upon his sleeping troops. It had been expected that the two columns would inclose the enemy's camp and capture the whole; but, though in disorderly rout, Porterfield succeeded, by personal coolness and courage, in getting them off with but few casualties and the loss of a few arms. The camp equipage and supplies were, of course, captured. Colonel Kelley was wounded by a pistol-shot in the breast, which was the only injury reported on the National side; no prisoners were taken, nor did any dead or wounded fall into our hands. Porterfield retreated to Beverly, some thirty miles farther to the south-east, and the National forces occupied Philippi. The telegraphic reports had put the Confederate force at 2000 and their loss at 15

MAJOR-GENERAL LEW WALLACE.↓
FROM A WAR-TIME PHOTOGRAPH.

↓ A Confederate Court of Inquiry reported that he had "600 effective infantry (or thereabouts) and 173 cavalry (or thereabouts)." — OFFICIAL RECORDS, II., p. 72.

↓ The 11th Indiana Zouaves, Colonel Lew Wallace, passed through Cincinnati June 7th on their way to the front. They belonged to General Morris's First Indiana Brigade (which also included the 6th, 7th, 8th, 9th, and 10th Indiana regiments), but were placed on detached service at Cumberland, on the Potomac. Under instructions from General Robert Patterson, Colonel Wallace led an

killed. This implied a considerable list of wounded and prisoners also, and the newspapers gave it the air of a considerable victory. The campaign thus opened with apparent *éclat* for McClellan, and the "Philippi races," as they were locally called, greatly encouraged the Union men of West Virginia and correspondingly depressed the secessionists.

McClellan, however, was still of the opinion that his most promising line of operations would be by the Great Kanawha Valley, and he retained in their camp of instruction the Ohio regiments which were mustered into the service of the United States, sending into Virginia only those known as the State forces. Another reason for this was that the older regiments were now nearly at the end of their three-months' enlistment, and were trying to reorganize under the President's second call, which required enlistment for "three years or the war."↓ Nearly a month elapsed, when, having received reports that forces of the enemy were gathering at Beverly, McClellan determined to proceed in person to that region with his best-prepared troops, postponing his Kanawha plan till north-western Virginia should be cleared of hostile forces.

Reference to the map will show that as the Potomac route was usually in the hands of the Northern forces, a Confederate occupation of West Virginia must be made either by the Staunton and Beverly road, or by the Kanawha route, of which the key-point west of the mountains was Gauley Bridge.

General Lee determined to send columns upon both these lines — General Henry A. Wise upon the Kanawha route, and General Robert S. Garnett to Beverly. Upon Porterfield's retreat to Beverly after the "Philippi races," Garnett, who had been an officer in the United States army, was ordered to Beverly to assume command and to stimulate the recruiting and organization of regiments from the secession element of the population. Some Virginia regiments, raised on the eastern slope of the mountains, were sent with him,

expedition against a force of about five hundred Confederates at Romney, which influenced General J. E. Johnston in his decision to evacuate Harper's Ferry (see note, page 120). In his report of the Romney engagement Colonel Wallace says:

"I left Cumberland at 10 o'clock on the night of the 12th June with 8 companies, in all about 500 men, and by railway went to New Creek station, 21 miles distant. A little after 4 o'clock I started my men across the mountains, 23 miles off, intending to reach the town by 6 o'clock in the morning. The road was very fatiguing and rough. . . . With the utmost industry I did not get near Romney until about 8 o'clock. . . . I afterward learned that they had notice of my coming full an hour before my arrival. In approaching the place, it was necessary for me to cross a bridge over the South Branch of the Potomac. A reconnaissance satisfied me that the passage of the bridge would be the chief obstacle in my way, although I could distinctly see the enemy drawn up on the bluff, which is the town site, supporting a battery of two guns, planted so as to sweep the road completely. I directed my advance guard to cross the bridge on the run, leap down an embankment at the farther entrance, and observe the windows of a large brick house not farther off than seventy-five yards. Their appearance was the signal for an assault. A warm fire opened from the house, which the guard returned, with no other loss than the wounding of a sergeant. The firing continued several minutes. I led a second company across the bridge, and by following up a ravine got them

into a position that soon drove the enemy from the house and into a mountain to its rear. My attention was then turned to the battery on the hill. . . . I pushed five companies in skirmishing order, and at double-quick time, up a hill to the right, intending to get around the left flank of the enemy, and cut off their retreat. . . . Between their position and that of my men was a deep, precipitous gorge, the crossing of which occupied about ten minutes. When the opposite ridge was gained we discovered the rebels indiscriminately blent, with a mass of women and children, flying as for life from the town. Having no horse, pursuit of the cannoneers was impossible. . . . After searching the town for arms, camp equipage, etc., I returned to Cumberland by the same road, reaching camp at 11 o'clock at night."

EDITORS.

↓ It is necessary to remember that at this time the Virginia State Government at Richmond was trying to keep up an appearance of independence, and that Robert E. Lee had been made major-general of Virginia troops, conducting a campaign ostensibly under the direction of Governor Letcher, and not of the Confederate authorities. A simulacrum of neutrality was still preserved, and a shadow of doubt regarding Virginia's ultimate attitude had some effect in delaying active operations along the Ohio as well as upon the Potomac. — J. D. C.

and to these was soon added the 1st Georgia. On the 1st of July he reported his force as 4500 men, but declared that his efforts to recruit had proven a complete failure, only 23 having joined. The West Virginians, he says, " are thoroughly imbued with an ignorant and bigoted Union sentiment." Other reënforcements were promised Garnett, but none reached him except the 44th Virginia regiment, which arrived at Beverly the very day of the action, but which did not take part in the fighting.

Tygart's Valley, in which Beverly lies, is between Cheat Mountain

CAMPAIGNS IN
WEST VIRGINIA.
1861.
SCALE OF MILES

on the east, and Rich Mountain on the west. The river, of the same name as the valley, flows north-ward about fifteen miles, then turns westward, breaking through the ridge, passes by Philippi, and afterward crosses the railroad at Grafton. The Staunton and Parkersburg Turnpike divides at Beverly, the Parkersburg route passing over a saddle in Rich Mountain, and the Wheeling route following the river to Philippi. The ridge north of the river at the gap is known as Laurel Mountain, and the road passes over a spur of it. Garnett regarded the two positions at Rich Mountain and Laurel Mountain as the gates to all the region beyond, and to the West. A rough mountain road, barely passable, connected the Laurel Mountain position with Cheat River on the east, and it was possible to go by this way northward through St. George to the Northwestern Turnpike, turning the mountain ranges. [See map, p. 131.]

Garnett thought the pass over Rich Mountain much the stronger and more easily held, and he therefore intrenched there about 1300 of his men and

4 cannon, under command of Lieutenant-Colonel Pegram. The position chosen was on a spur of the mountain near its western base, and it was rudely fortified with breastworks of logs covered with an abattis of slashed timber along its front. The remainder of his force he placed in a similar fortified position on the road at Laurel Mountain, where he also had four guns, of which one was rifled. Here he commanded in person. His depot of supplies was at Beverly, which was 16 miles from the Laurel Mountain position and 5 from that at Rich Mountain. He was pretty accurately informed of McClellan's forces and movements, and his preparations had barely been completed by the 9th of July, when the Union general appeared in his front.

McClellan entered West Virginia in person on the 22d of June, and on the 23d issued from Grafton a proclamation to the inhabitants. He had gradually collected his forces along the Baltimore and Ohio railroad, which, at the time of the affair at Rich Mountain, consisted of 16 Ohio regiments,

BRIGADIER-GENERAL THOMAS A. MORRIS.
FROM A PHOTOGRAPH.

9 from Indiana and 2 from West Virginia; in all, 27 regiments with 4 batteries of artillery of 6 guns each, 2 troops of cavalry, and an independent company of riflemen. Of his batteries, one was of the regular army, and another, a company of regulars (Company I, 4th U. S. Artillery), was with him awaiting mountain howitzers, which arrived a little later. ⦆ The regiments varied somewhat in strength, but all were recently organized, and must have averaged at least 700 men each, making the whole force about 20,000. Of these, about 5000 were guarding the railroad and its bridges for some 200 miles, under the command of Brigadier-General C. W. Hill, of the Ohio Militia; a strong brigade under Brigadier-General Morris, of Indiana, was at Philippi, and the rest were in three brigades forming the immediate command of McClellan, the brigadiers being General W. S. Rosecrans, U. S. A., General Newton Schleich, of Ohio, and Colonel Robert L. McCook, of Ohio. On the date of his proclamation McClellan intended, as he informed General Scott, to move his principal column to Buckhannon on June 25th, and thence at once upon Beverly; but delays occurred, and it was not till July 2d that he reached Buckhannon, which is 24 miles west of Beverly, on the Parkersburg branch

⦆ As part of the troops were State troops not mustered into the United States service, no report of them is found in the War Department; but the following are the numbers of the regiments found named as present in the correspondence and reports,—viz., 3d, 4th, 5th, 6th, 7th, 8th, 9th, 10th, 13th, 14th, 15th, 16th, 17th, 18th, 19th, 20th, and 22d Ohio; 6th, 7th, 8th, 9th, 10th, 11th, 13th, 14th, 15th Indiana, and 1st and 2d Virginia; also Howe's United States battery, Barnett's Ohio battery, Loomis's Michigan battery, and Daum's Virginia battery; the cavalry were Burdsal's Ohio Dragoons and Barker's Illinois Cavalry.—J. D. C.

of the turnpike. Before leaving Grafton the rumors he heard had made him estimate Garnett's force at 6000 or 7000 men, of which the larger part were at Laurel Mountain in front of General Morris. On the 6th of July he moved McCook with two regiments to Middle Fork Bridge, about half-way to Beverly, and on the same day ordered Morris to march with his brigade from Philippi to a position one and a half miles in front of Garnett's principal camp, which was promptly done. Three days later, McClellan concentrated the three brigades of his own column at Roaring Creek, about two miles from Colonel Pegram's position at the base of Rich Mountain. The advance on both lines had been made with only a skirmishing resistance, the Confederates being aware of McClellan's great superiority in numbers, and choosing to await his attack in their fortified positions. The National commander was now convinced that his opponent was 10,000 strong, of which about 2000 were before him at Rich Mountain. A reconnoissance made on the 10th showed that Pegram's position would be difficult to assail in front, but preparations were made to attack the next day, while Morris was directed to hold firmly his position before Garnett, watching for the effect of the attack at Rich Mountain. In the evening Rosecrans took to McClellan a young man named Hart, whose father lived on the top of the mountain two miles in rear of Pegram, and who thought he could guide a column of infantry to his father's farm by a circuit around Pegram's left flank south of the turnpike. The paths were so difficult that cannon could not go by them, but Rosecrans offered to lead a column of infantry and seize the road at the Hart farm. After some discussion McClellan adopted the suggestion, and it was arranged that Rosecrans should march at daybreak of the 11th with about two thousand men, including a troop of horse, and that upon the sound of his engagement in the rear of Pegram, McClellan would attack in force in front. By a blunder in one of the regimental camps, the reveille and assembly were sounded at midnight, and Pegram was put on the *qui vive*. He, however, believed that the attempt to turn his position would be by a path or country road passing round his right, between him and Garnett (of which the latter had warned him), and his attention was diverted from Rosecrans's actual route, which he thought impracticable. The alert which had occurred at midnight made Rosecrans think it best to make a longer circuit

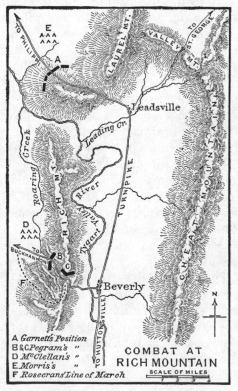

A *Garnett's Position*
B & C *Pegram's* "
D *McClellan's* "
E *Morris's* "
F *Rosecrans' Line of March*

COMBAT AT
RICH MOUNTAIN
SCALE OF MILES

than he at first intended, and it took ten hours of severe marching and mountain climbing to reach the Hart farm. The turning movement was made, but he found an enemy opposing him. Pegram had detached about 350 men from the 1300 which he had, and had ordered them to guard the road at the mountain summit. He sent with them a single cannon from the four which constituted his only battery, and they threw together a breastwork of logs. The turnpike at Hart's runs in a depression of the summit, and as Rosecrans, early in the afternoon, came out upon the road, he was warmly received by both musketry and cannon. The ground was rough, the men were for the first time under fire, and the skirmishing combat varied through two or three hours, when a charge by part of Rosecrans's line, aided by a few heavy volleys from another portion of his forces which had secured a good position, broke the enemy's line. Reënforcements from Pegram were nearly at hand, with another cannon, but they did not come into action, and the runaway team of the caisson on the hill-top, dashing into the gun that was coming up, capsized it down the mountain-side where the descending road was

BRIGADIER-GENERAL JOHN PEGRAM, C. S. A. (KILLED AT HATCHER'S RUN, NEAR PETERSBURG, FEBRUARY 6, 1865). FROM A PHOTOGRAPH.

scarped diagonally along it. Both guns fell into Rosecrans's hands, and he was in possession of the field. The march and the assault had been made in rain and storm. Nothing was heard from McClellan, and the enemy, rallying on their reënforcements, made such show of resistance on the crest a little farther on, that Rosecrans directed his men to rest upon their arms till next morning. When day broke on the 12th, the enemy had disappeared from the mountain-top, and Rosecrans, feeling his way down to the rear of Pegram's position, found it also abandoned, the two remaining cannon being spiked, and a few sick and wounded being left in charge of a surgeon. Still nothing was seen of McClellan, and Rosecrans sent word to him, in his camp beyond Roaring Creek, that he was in possession of the enemy's position. Rosecrans's loss had been 12 killed and 49 wounded. The Confederates left 20 wounded on the field, and 63 were surrendered at the lower camp, including the sick. No trustworthy report of their dead was made.

The noise of the engagement had been heard in McClellan's camp, and he formed his troops for attack, but the long continuance of the cannonade and some signs of exultation in Pegram's camp seem to have made him think Rosecrans had been repulsed. The failure to attack in accordance with the plan has never been explained. Rosecrans's messengers had failed to reach McClellan during the 11th, but the sound of the battle was sufficient notice that he had gained the summit and was engaged; and he was, in fact, left to win his own battle or to get out of his embarrassment as he could. Toward evening McClellan began to cut a road for artillery to a neighboring height, from which he hoped his twelve guns would make Pegram's position untenable; but his lines were withdrawn again beyond Roaring Creek at nightfall, and further action was postponed to the next day.

About half of Pegram's men had succeeded in passing around Rosecrans's right flank during the night and had gained Beverly. These, with the newly arrived Confederate regiment, fled southward on the Staunton road. Garnett had learned in the evening by messenger from Beverly that Rich Mountain summit was carried, and evacuated his camp in front of Morris about midnight. He first marched toward Beverly, and was within five miles of that place when he received information (false at the time) that the National forces already occupied it. He then retraced his steps nearly to his camp, and, leaving the turnpike at Leadsville, he turned off upon a country road over Cheat Mountain into Cheat River Valley, following the stream northward toward St. George and West Union, in the forlorn hope of turning the mountains at the north end of the ridges and regaining his communications by a very long detour. He might have continued southward through Beverly almost at leisure, for McClellan did not enter the town till past noon on the 12th.

Morris learned of Garnett's retreat at dawn, and started in pursuit as soon as rations could be issued. He marched first to Leadsville, where he halted to communicate with McClellan at Beverly and get further orders. These reached him in the night, and at daybreak of the 13th he resumed the pursuit. His advance-guard of three regiments, accompanied by Captain H. W. Benham of the Engineers, overtook the rear of the Confederate column about noon and continued a skirmishing pursuit for some two hours. Garnett himself handled his rear-guard with skill, and at Carrick's Ford a lively encounter was had. A mile or two farther, at another ford and when the skirmishing was very slight, he was killed while withdrawing his skirmishers from behind a pile of driftwood which he had used as a barricade. One of his cannon had become stalled in the ford, and, with about forty wagons, fell into Morris's hands. The direct pursuit was here discontinued, but McClellan had sent a dispatch to General Hill at Grafton, to collect the garrisons along the railway and block the way of the Confederates where they must pass around the northern spurs of the mountains.

His military telegraph terminated at the Roaring Creek camp, and the dispatch written in the evening of the 12th was not forwarded to Hill till near noon of the 13th. This officer immediately ordered the collection of the greater part of his detachments at Oakland and called upon the railway officials for special trains to hurry them to the rendezvous. About one thousand men under Colonel James Irvine of the 16th Ohio were at West Union where the St. George road reaches the Northwestern Turnpike, and Hill's information was that a detachment of these held Red House, a crossing several miles in advance by which the retreating enemy might go. Irvine was directed to hold his positions at all hazards till he could be reënforced. Hill himself hastened with the first train from Grafton to Oakland with about 500 men and 3 cannon, reached his destination at nightfall, and hurried his detachment forward by a night march to Irvine, 10 or 12 miles over rough roads. It turned out that Irvine did not occupy Red House, and the prevalent belief that the enemy was about eight thousand in number, with the uncertainty of the road he would take, made it proper to keep the little force concentrated till reënforcements should come. The first of these reached Irvine about 6 o'clock on the morning of the 14th, raising his command to 1500, but a few moments after their arrival he learned that the enemy had passed Red House soon after daylight. He gave chase, but did not overtake them.

Meanwhile, General Hill had spent the night in trying to hasten forward the railway trains, but none were able to reach Oakland till morning, and Garnett's forces had now more than twenty miles the start, and were on fairly good roads, moving southward on the eastern side of the mountains. McClellan still telegraphed that Hill had the one opportunity of a lifetime to cap-

BRIGADIER-GENERAL ROBERT SELDEN GARNETT, C. S. A. (KILLED JULY 13, 1861). FROM A PHOTOGRAPH.

ture the fleeing army, and that officer hastened in pursuit, though unprovided with wagons or extra rations. When, however, the Union commander learned that the enemy had fairly turned the mountains, he ordered the pursuit stopped. Hill had used both intelligence and energy in his attempt to concentrate his troops, but it proved simply impossible for the railroad to carry them to Oakland before the enemy had passed the turning-point, twenty miles to the southward.

During the 12th Pegram's situation and movements were unknown. He had intended, when he evacuated his camp, to follow the line of retreat taken by the detachment already near the mountain-top, but, in the darkness of the night and in the tangled woods and thickets of the mountain-side, his column got divided, and, with the rear portion of it, he wandered all day on the 12th, seeking to make his way to Garnett. He halted at evening at the Tygart Valley River, six miles north of Beverly, and learned from some country people of Garnett's retreat. It was still possible to reach the mountains east of the valley, but beyond was a hundred miles of wilderness and half a dozen mountain ridges on which little, if any, food could be found for his men. He called a council of war, and, by advice of his officers, sent to McClellan, at Beverly, an offer of surrender. This was received on the 13th, and Pegram brought in 30 officers and 525 men. McClellan then moved southward himself, following the Staunton road, by which the remnant of Pegram's little force had escaped, and on the 14th occupied Huttonsville. Two regiments of Confederate troops were hastening from Staunton to reënforce Garnett. These were halted at Monterey, east of the principal ridge of the Alleghanies, and upon them the retreating forces rallied. Brigadier-General H. R. Jackson was assigned to command in Garnett's place, and both Governor Letcher and General Lee made strenuous efforts to increase this army to a force sufficient to resume aggressive operations. On McClellan's part nothing further was attempted, till, on the 22d, he was summoned to Washington to assume command of the army which had retreated to the capital after the panic of the first Bull Run battle.

The affair at Rich Mountain and the subsequent movements were among the minor events of a great war, and would not warrant a detailed description, were it not for the momentous effect they had upon the conduct of the war, by being the occasion of McClellan's promotion to the command of the Potomac army. The narrative which has been given contains the "unvarnished tale," as nearly as official records of both sides can give it, and it is a curious task to compare it with the picture of the campaign and its results which was then given to the world in the series of proclamations and dispatches of the young general, beginning with his first occupation of the country and ending with his congratulations to his troops, in which he announced that they had "annihilated two armies, commanded by educated and experienced soldiers, intrenched in mountain fastnesses fortified at their leisure." The country was eager for good news, and took it as literally true. McClellan was the hero of the moment, and when, but a week later, his success was followed by the disaster to McDowell at Bull Run, he seemed pointed out by Providence as the ideal chieftain, who could repair the misfortune and lead our armies to certain victory. His personal intercourse with those about him was so kindly, and his bearing so modest, that his dispatches, proclamations, and correspondence are a psychological study, more puzzling to those who knew him well than to strangers. Their turgid rhetoric and exaggerated pretense did not seem natural to him. In them he seemed to be composing for stage effect, something to be spoken in character by a quite different person from the sensible and genial man we knew in daily life and conversation. The career of the great Napoleon had been the study and the absorbing admiration of young American soldiers, and it was, perhaps, not strange that when real war came they should copy his bulletins and even his personal bearing. It was, for the moment, the bent of the people to be pleased with McClellan's rendering of the rôle; they dubbed him the young Napoleon, and the photographers got him to stand with folded arms, in the historic pose. For two or three weeks his dispatches and letters were all on fire with enthusiastic energy. He appeared to be in a morbid condition of mental exaltation. When he came out of it, he was as genial as ever, as can be seen by the contrast between his official communications and that private letter to General Burnside, written just after the evacuation of Yorktown, which, oddly enough, has found its way into the official records of the war.\ The assumed dash

---

\ Letter of May 21st, 1862. "My Dear Burn: Your dispatch and kind letter received. I have instructed Seth [Williams] to reply to the official letter, and now acknowledge the kind private note. It always does me good, in the midst of my cares and perplexities, to see your wretched old scrawling. I have terrible troubles to contend with, but have met them with a good heart, like your good old self, and have thus far struggled through successfully. . . . The crisis cannot long be deferred. I pray for God's blessing on our arms, and rely far more on his goodness than I do on my own poor intellect. I sometimes think now that I can almost realize that Mahomet was sincere. When I see the hand of God guarding one so weak as myself, I can almost think myself a chosen instrument to carry out his schemes. Would that a better man had been selected. . . . Good-bye, and God bless you, Burn. With the sincere hope that we may soon shake hands, I am as ever,

Your sincere friend, McClellan."—J. D. C.

MAJOR-GENERAL W. S. ROSECRANS. FROM A WAR-TIME PHOTOGRAPH.

and energy of his first campaign made the disappointment and the reaction more painful, when the excessive caution of his conduct in command of the Army of the Potomac was seen. But the Rich Mountain affair, when analyzed, shows the same characteristics which became well known later. There was the same overestimate of the enemy, the same tendency to interpret unfavorably the sights and sounds in front, the same hesitancy to throw in his whole force when he knew that his subordinate was engaged. If Garnett had been as strong as McClellan believed him, he had abundant time and means to overwhelm Morris, who lay four days in easy striking distance, while the National commander delayed attacking Pegram; and had Morris been beaten, Garnett would have been as near Clarksburg as his opponent, and there would have been a race for the railroad. But, happily, Garnett was less strong and less enterprising than he was credited with being. Pegram was dislodged, and the Confederates made a precipitate retreat.

THE KANAWHA VALLEY.

WHEN McClellan reached Buckhannon, on the 2d of July, the rumors he heard of Garnett's strength, and the news of the presence of General Wise with a considerable force in the Great Kanawha Valley, made him conclude to order a brigade to that region for the purpose of holding the lower part of the valley defensively till he might try to cut off Wise's army after Garnett should be disposed of. This duty was assigned to me. The brigade which I had organized had all been taken for his own campaign, except the 11th Ohio (only five companies present), but the 12th Ohio, which was still at Camp Dennison, was ordered to report to me, and these two regiments were to be sent by rail to Gallipolis as soon as the railways could furnish transportation. At Gallipolis we should find the 21st Ohio militia, and the 1st and 2d Kentucky volunteers were also to join me there, coming by steamboat from Cincinnati. The two Kentucky regiments had been organized in Cincinnati, and were made up chiefly of steamboat crews and "longshoremen" thrown out of employment by the stoppage of commerce on the river. There were in them some companies of other material, but these gave the distinctive character to the regiments as a whole. The colonels and part of the field-officers were Kentuckians, but the organizations were Ohio regiments in nearly everything but the name. The men were mostly of a rough and reckless class, and gave a good deal of trouble by insubordination; but they did not lack courage, and, after they had been under discipline for a while, became good fighting regiments.

The troops moved the moment transportation could be furnished, and those going by rail were at Gallipolis and Point Pleasant (the mouth of the Great Kanawha) on the 10th. My only artillery was a section of 2 bronze rifles, altered from smooth 6-pounders, and my only cavalry some 30 raw recruits, useful only as messengers. Meanwhile, my orders had been changed, and in accordance with them I directed the 2d Kentucky to land at Guyandotte, on the Ohio, about 70 miles below the Kanawha, the

1st Kentucky to proceed to Ripley, landing at Ravenswood, about 50 miles above, while with two and a half regiments I myself should move up the Kanawha Valley. The two detachments would join me after a time by lateral roads. My total force, when assembled, would be a little over three thousand men, the regiments having the same average strength as those with McClellan. The opposing force under General Wise was four thousand by the time the campaign was fully opened, though somewhat less at the beginning.☆

The Kanawha River was navigable for small steamboats about 70 miles, to a point 10 or 12 miles above Charleston, the only important town of the region and lying at the confluence of the Kanawha and Elk rivers. Steamboats were plenty, owing to the interruption of trade, and wagons were wholly lacking, so that my column was accompanied and partly carried by a fleet of stern-wheel steamers.

On the 11th of July the movement from Point Pleasant began. An advance-guard was sent out on each side of the

BRIGADIER-GENERAL HENRY A. WISE, C. S. A.,
EX-GOVERNOR OF VIRGINIA.
FROM A PHOTOGRAPH.

river, marching upon the roads which were near its banks. The few horsemen were divided and sent with them as messengers, and the boats followed, steaming slowly along in rear of the marching men. Most of two regiments were carried on the steamers, to save fatigue to the men, who were as yet unused to their work, and many of whom were footsore from their first long march of 25 miles to Gallipolis, from the station where they left the railway. The arrangement was also a good one in a military point of view, for if an enemy were met on either bank of the stream, the boats could land in a moment and the troops disembark without delay.

Our first day's sail was thirteen miles up the river, and it was the very romance of campaigning. I took my station on top of the pilot-house of the leading boat, so that I might see over the banks of the stream and across the bottom-lands which bounded the valley. The afternoon was a lovely one. Summer clouds lazily drifted across the sky, the boats were dressed in their colors, and swarmed with men as a hive with bees. The bands played national tunes, and as we passed the houses of Union citizens, the inmates would wave their handkerchiefs to us and were answered by cheers from the troops. The scenery was picturesque, the gently winding river making beautiful reaches that opened new scenes upon us at every turn. On either

☆ Wise reported his force on 17th July as 3500 "effective" men and 10 cannon, and says he received "perhaps 300" in reënforcements on the 18th. When he abandoned the valley ten days later he reported his force 4000 in round numbers.—J. D. C.

side the advance-guard could be seen in the distance, the main body in the road, with skirmishers exploring the way in front and flankers on the sides. Now and then a horseman would bring some message to the shore from the front, and a small boat would be sent to receive it, giving us the rumors with which the country was rife, and which gave just enough of excitement and of the spice of possible danger to make this our first day in the enemy's country key everybody to a pitch that doubled the vividness of every sensation. The landscape seemed more beautiful, the sunshine more bright, and the exhilaration of outdoor life more joyous than any we had ever before known.

Our first night's camp was in a picturesque spot in keeping with the beauties of the day's progress, and was enlivened by a report that the enemy was advancing to attack us in force. It was only a rumor, based upon the actual approach of a reconnoitering party of cavalry, and the camp was not allowed to be disturbed except to send a small reconnoissance forward on our own part. Two more days' advance, in the face of a slight skirmishing resistance, brought us to the Pocotalico, a stream entering the Kanawha from the north.

Wise had placed his principal camp at Tyler Mountain, a bold spur which reaches the river on the northern side (on which is also the turnpike road) about 12 miles above my position, while he occupied the south side with a detachment above Scary Creek some 3 miles from us. The hills closing in nearer to the river make it easy to stop steamboat navigation with a small force, and it became necessary to halt a little and await the arrival of the wagons which had not yet been sent me, and of the 2d Kentucky regiment, which was marching to me from Barboursville, where one wing of it, commanded by Lieutenant-Colonel Neff, had a brilliant little affair with a body of Confederate recruits occupying the place. On the afternoon of the 17th, the Kentuckians having arrived, and a reconnoissance having been made of the Scary Creek position, which was found to be held by about 500 of the enemy with 1 or 2 cannon, Colonel John W. Lowe of the 12th Ohio was ferried over the river with his own regiment and 2 companies of the 21st Ohio with our 2 cannon, and directed to occupy the attention of the enemy in front at the creek, which was unfordable at its mouth, while he tried to turn the position with part of his command. The enemy at first retreated, leaving one cannon disabled, but, being reënforced, they rallied, and, no good crossing of the creek being found, Lowe was foiled in his effort to dislodge them after a sharp engagement across the stream.

The wagons reached us a few at a time, but by the 24th I was able to move from our strong position behind Pocotalico, and, taking circuitous country roads among the hills, to come upon the rear of Wise's camp at Tyler Mountain. The march was a long and difficult one, but was successful. As soon as his outposts were driven in, the enemy decamped in a panic, leaving his camp-kettles and supper over the fires. We had also cut off a steamboat with troops which was just below us as we came to the bluff, and which, under the fire of our cannon, was run ashore and burned, while the detachments on the other side of the river hastened by country roads to rejoin Wise at Charleston. It was now nightfall, and we bivouacked upon the mountain-side. Wise

abandoned Charleston in the night and retreated toward Gauley Bridge. On the 25th
I occupied Charleston without resistance, and
moved on, ordering the 1st Kentucky up from
Ripley to garrison the place and establish my
depot there.

At every mile above Charleston the scenery
grows wilder, the mountains crowding in
upon the river, often with high, beetling cliffs
overhanging it, and offering numerous positions where a small detachment might hold
an army in check. Wise, however, made no
resistance worth naming, except to fell timber
into the road, and he passed the Gauley, burning the important bridge there and continuing his hasty retreat to the White Sulphur
Springs, hurried, no doubt, by the fear that
McClellan might intercept him by way of
Huntersville and Lewisburg. McClellan had
recognized the fact that he was asking me to
face the enemy with no odds in my favor, and as soon as he heard that
Wise was disposed to make a stand, he had directed me not to risk attacking
him in front, but rather to await the result of his own movement toward
the Upper Kanawha. Rosecrans did the same when he assumed command; but I knew the hope had been that I could reach Gauley Bridge,
and I felt warranted, as soon as wagons reached me, in attempting the turning
movement which seems to have thrown Wise into a panic from which he
did not recover till he got out of the valley. Rosecrans ordered me to
remain on the defensive at Charleston, but his dispatches did not reach me,
fortunately, till I was close to Gauley Bridge, some forty miles above Charleston, and was quite sure of my ability to take possession of that defile, as I did
on the 29th of July. Another reason for haste was that the time of enlistment of the 21st Ohio had expired, and I was ordered by the governor to send
it back to Ohio for reorganization, which would make a reduction of one-
fourth of my numbers.

At my first night's encampment above Charleston, in a lovely nook
between spurs of the hills, I was treated to a little surprise on the part of
three of my subordinates which was an unexpected enlargement of my military experience, and which is worth preserving to show some of the conditions attending the beginning of a war with undisciplined troops. The
camp was nicely organized for the night and supper was over, when I was
waited upon at my tent by these gentlemen. Their spokesman informed me
that after consultation they had concluded that it was foolhardy to follow
the Confederates into the gorge we were traveling, and, unless I could show
them satisfactory reasons for changing their opinion, they would not lead
their commands farther into it. I dryly asked if he was quite sure he under-

BRIGADIER-GENERAL JOHN B. FLOYD, C. S. A.,
SECRETARY OF WAR UNDER PRESIDENT
BUCHANAN. FROM A PHOTOGRAPH.

stood the nature of his communication. There was probably something in the tone of my question which was not altogether expected, and his companions began to look a little uneasy. He then protested that they meant no disrespect, but, as their military experience was about as extensive as my own, they thought I ought to make no movement but on consultation with them and by their consent. The others seemed better pleased with this way of putting it. My answer was that whether they meant it or not, their action was mutinous, and only their ignorance of military law could palliate it. The responsibility for the movement of the army was with me, and, while glad to confer freely with them, I should call no council of war and submit nothing to vote till I felt incompetent to decide for myself. If they apologized for their conduct and showed earnestness in military obedience, what they had now said would be overlooked, but on any recurrence of insubordination I should enforce my power by arresting the offender at once. I dismissed them with this, and immediately sent out orders through my adjutant-general to march early next morning. Before they slept, one of the three had come to me with an earnest apology for his part in the matter, and a short time made them all as subordinate as I could wish. The incident could not have occurred in the brigade which had been under my command at Camp Dennison, and was the natural result of the sudden assembling of inexperienced men under a brigade commander of whom they knew nothing except that at the beginning of the war he had been a civilian like themselves.

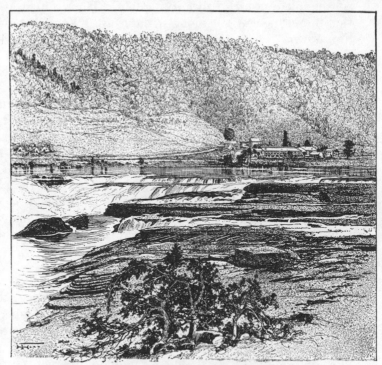

POST HOSPITAL AND WAGON-SHOP AT KANAWHA FALLS, NEAR GAULEY BRIDGE. FROM A PHOTOGRAPH.

The same march enabled me to make the acquaintance of another army "institution,"—the newspaper correspondent. At Charleston I was joined by two men representing influential newspapers, who wished to know on what terms they might accompany the column. The answer was that the quartermaster would furnish them with a tent and with transportation, and that their letters should be submitted to one of the staff to protect us from the publication of facts which

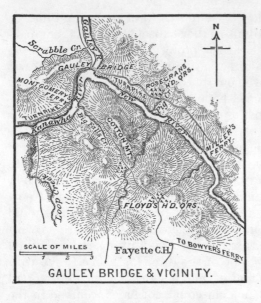

GAULEY BRIDGE & VICINITY.

might aid the enemy. This seemed unsatisfactory, and they intimated that they expected to be taken into my mess, and to be announced as volunteer aides with military rank. They were told that military position or rank could only be given by authority much higher than mine, and that they could be more honestly independent if free from personal obligation and from temptation to repay favors with flattery. My only purpose was to put the matter upon the foundation of public right and of mutual self-respect. The day before we reached Gauley Bridge they opened the matter again to my adjutant-general, but were informed that I had decided it upon a principle by which I meant to abide. Their reply was, "Very well; General Cox thinks he can get along without us. We will show him. We will write him down!" They left the camp the same evening and wrote letters to their papers, describing the army as a rabble of ruffians, burning houses, ravishing women, robbing and destroying property, and the commander as totally incompetent. As to the troops, more baseless slander was never uttered. Their march had been orderly, no willful injury had been done to private property, and no case of personal violence to any non-combatant, man or woman, had been even charged. Yet the publication of such communications in widely read journals was likely to be as damaging as if it were true. My nomination as brigadier-general was then before the Senate for confirmation, and "the pen" would probably have proved "'mightier than the sword" but for McClellan's knowledge of the nature of the task we had accomplished, as he was then in the flood-tide of power at Washington, and had expressed his satisfaction at the performance of our part of the campaign which he had planned.

ROSECRANS IN COMMAND.

General Rosecrans had succeeded McClellan as ranking officer in West Virginia, but it was not until the beginning of November, 1861, that the region was made a department and he was regularly assigned to command. Meanwhile the three-months' enlistments were expiring, many regiments were sent home, new ones were received, and a complete reorganization of his forces took place. Besides holding the railroad, he fortified the Cheat Mountain Pass looking toward Staunton, and the pass at Elkwater on the mountain summit between Huttonsville and Huntersville. In similar manner I was directed to fortify the camp at Gauley Bridge, and to cover the front in every direction with active detachments, constantly moving from the central position.

By the middle of August, Rosecrans had established a chain of posts, with a regiment or two at each, on a line upon which he afterward marched from Weston, by way of Bulltown, Sutton, and Summersville, to Gauley Bridge.

The Confederates had also been straining every nerve to collect a force that might give us an effective return blow, and Robert E. Lee was expected to lead their forces in person. After ten days' quiet occupation of Gauley Bridge, in which I had reconnoitered the country nearly forty miles in front and on each flank, we learned that General John B. Floyd had joined Wise with a brigade, and that both were moving toward the Kanawha. At the same time the militia of Raleigh, Mercer, and Fayette counties were called out, making a force of two thousand men under General Chapman. The total force confronting us was thus about eight thousand. ⏐ To resist these I kept 2 regiments at Gauley Bridge, an advance-guard of 8 companies vigorously skirmishing toward Sewell Mountain, a regiment distributed on the Kanawha to cover the steamboat communications, and some West Virginia recruits organizing at the mouth of the river. By extreme activity these were able to baffle the enemy and impose upon him the belief that our numbers were

GAULEY BRIDGE, LOOKING DOWN STREAM.
FROM A PHOTOGRAPH.

more than double our actual force. Rosecrans had informed me of his purpose to march a strong column to join me as soon as Lee's plans were fully developed, and I accumulated supplies and munitions at Gauley Bridge, determined to stand a siege if necessary. On the 13th of August the 7th Ohio, Colonel E. B. Tyler, was ordered by Rosecrans to Cross Lanes, covering Carnifex Ferry on the Gauley River about twenty miles above us, where a road from Lewisburg meets that going up the Gauley to Summersville. I was authorized to call Tyler to me if seriously attacked. On the 20th Wise made a strong demonstration in front, but was met at Pig Creek, three miles up the

New River, and easily repulsed. On the 26th Floyd, having raised two flat-boats which Tyler had sunk, crossed the Gauley at Carnifex Ferry with 2000 or 3000 men, and surprised him, routing the regiment with a loss to us of 15 killed and about 100 captured, of which 50 were wounded. The greater part of the regiment was rallied by Major Casement, and led over the

⏐ On the 14th of August Wise reported to General Lee that he had 2000 ready to move, and could have 2500 ready in 5 days; that 550 of his cavalry were with Floyd, besides an artillery detachment of 50. This makes his total force 3100. At that time he gives Floyd's force at 1200, with 2 strong regiments coming up, besides 2000 militia under General Chapman, as stated above. The aggregate force operating on the Kanawha line he gives as 7800, Sept. 9th.—J. D. C.

NEW RIVER CLIFFS, NEAR GAULEY BRIDGE.
FROM A PHOTOGRAPH.

mountains to Elk River, and thence to Charleston. Floyd intrenched his position, and built a foot-bridge to connect it with the eastern side of the wild gorge. Wise's failure to coöperate was Floyd's reason for abandoning his announced purpose of marching upon my rear; but he was on my northern line of communication with Rosecrans, and the latter hastened his preparations to come to my relief.

On the 3d of September, Wise and Chapman attempted a concerted attack upon Gauley Bridge, the first pushing in upon the turnpike, while Chapman advanced from Fayette by Cotton Hill and a road to the river a little below Kanawha Falls. Wise was again met at Pig Creek and driven back; Chapman reached the bluffs overlooking the river in rear of us, driving in our outposts, but did us little mischief, except to throw a few shells into our lower camp, and on Wise's repulse he also withdrew. Our detachments followed them up on both lines with daily warm skirmishes, and the advance-guard ambushed and punished the enemy's cavalry in a very demoralizing way. Efforts to reach the river and stop our steamboats, kept the posts and detachments below us on the alert, and an expedition of half the 1st Kentucky, under Lieutenant-Colonel D. A. Enyart, sent to break up a Confederate militia encampment at Boone Court House, 40 miles southward, routed the enemy, who left 25 dead upon the field. The march and attack had been swift and vigorous, and the terror of the blow kept that region quiet for some time afterward.

I was puzzled at Floyd's inaction at Carnifex Ferry, but the mystery is partly solved by the publication of the Confederate records. There was no coöperation between the commanders, and Wise refused the assistance Floyd demanded, nor could even the authority of Lee reduce the ex-governor of Virginia to real subordination. The letters of Wise show a capacity for keeping a command in hot water which was unique. If he had been half as troublesome to me as he was to Floyd, I should, indeed, have had a hot time of it. But he did me royal service by preventing anything approaching unity of action between the two principal Confederate columns.

Rosecrans now began his march from Clarksburg with three brigades, having left the Upper Potomac line in command of General Kelley, and the Cheat Mountain region in command of General J. J. Reynolds. His route (already indicated) was a rough one, and the portion of it between Sutton and Summersville, over Birch Mountain, was very wild and difficult. He left his bivouac on the morning of the 10th of September, before daybreak, and, marching through Summersville, reached Cross Lanes about 2 o'clock in the afternoon. Floyd's position was now about two miles distant, and waiting only for his column to close up, he again pressed forward. General Benham's brigade was in front, and soon met the enemy's pickets. Getting the impression that Floyd was in retreat, Benham pressed forward rather rashly, deploying to the left, and coming under a sharp fire from the right of the enemy's works. The woods were dense and tangled, it was too late for a proper reconnoissance, and Rosecrans could only hasten the advance and deployment of the other brigades under Colonels McCook and Scammon. Benham had sent a howitzer battery and two rifled cannon with his head of column at the left, and these soon got a position, from which, in fact, they enfiladed part of Floyd's line, though it was impossible to see much of the situation. Charges were made by portions of Benham's and McCook's brigades as they came up, but they lacked

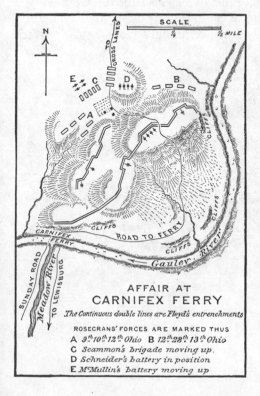

AFFAIR AT
CARNIFEX FERRY
The Continuous double lines are Floyd's entrenchments

ROSECRANS' FORCES ARE MARKED THUS
A 9th 10th 12th Ohio B 12th 28th 13th Ohio
C Scammon's brigade moving up.
D Schneider's battery in position
E McMullin's battery moving up

unity, and Rosecrans was dissatisfied that his head of column should be engaged before he had time to plan an attack. Colonel Lowe, of the 12th Ohio, had been killed at the head of his regiment, and Colonel W. H. Lytle, of the 10th, had been severely wounded; darkness was rapidly coming on, and Rosecrans ordered the troops withdrawn from fire, till positions could be rectified, and the attack renewed in the morning. Seventeen had been killed and 141 had been wounded in the sharp but irregular combat. Floyd, however, had learned that his position could be subjected to a destructive cannonade; he was himself slightly wounded, and his officers and men were discouraged. He therefore retreated across the Gauley in the night, having great difficulty in carrying his artillery down the cliffs by a wretched road in the darkness. He had built a slight foot-bridge for infantry, in the bit of smooth water known as the Ferry, though both above and below the stream is an impassable mountain torrent. Once over, the bridge was broken up and the flat-boats were destroyed. He reported but twenty casualties, and threw much of the responsibility upon Wise, who had not obeyed orders to reënforce him. His hospital, containing the wounded prisoners taken from Tyler, fell into Rosecrans's hands.

On the 12th of September we first heard, at Gauley Bridge, of the engagement at Carnifex Ferry, and I at once moved with two regiments to attack Wise, who retired as we advanced, till I occupied the junction of the turnpike with the Sunday road. The whole hostile force had retreated to Sewell Mountain, and Rosecrans halted me until he could create means of crossing the Gauley.

McCook's brigade joined me on the 16th of September, and my own command was increased by bringing up another of my regiments from below. With

FLOYD'S COMMAND RECROSSING THE GAULEY RIVER AFTER THE FIGHT OF SEPTEMBER 10TH,
AT CARNIFEX FERRY. AFTER A SKETCH MADE AT THE TIME.

the two brigades I advanced to Spy Rock, a strong position overlooking a valley several miles broad, beyond which was Big Sewell Mountain, the crest of which we occupied with an advance-guard on the 20th and in force on the 24th. Before the 1st of October Rosecrans had concentrated his force at the mountain, the four brigades being so reduced by sickness and by detachments that he reported the whole as making only 5200 effective men. Immediately in front, across a deep gorge, lay the united forces of Floyd and Wise, commanded by Lee

A DETACHMENT FROM GENERAL FLOYD'S COMMAND PREPARING TO SHELL GENERAL ROSECRANS'S CAMP AT GAULEY BRIDGE. FROM A SKETCH MADE AT THE TIME.

in person. The autumn rains set in upon the very day of Rosecrans's arrival, and continued without intermission. The roads became so difficult that the animals of the wagon trains were being destroyed in the effort to supply the command. The camp was 35 miles from Gauley Bridge, and our stores were landed from steamboats 25 miles below that post, making 60 miles of wagoning. The enemy was as badly off, and no aggressive operations were possible on either side. This became so evident that on the 5th of October Rosecrans withdrew his forces to camps within 3 or 4 miles of Gauley Bridge.

Lee had directed an effort to be made by General Loring, his subordinate on the Staunton line, to test the strength of the posts under Reynolds at Cheat Mountain and Elkwater, and lively combats had resulted on the 12th and 14th of September. Reynolds held firm, and Rosecrans had not been diverted from his own plans. On October 2d Reynolds delivered a return blow upon the Confederate position at Greenbrier River, but found it too strong to be carried. Both parties now remained in observation till the end of October. Floyd reported to his Government that the eleven days of cold storms at Sewell Mountain had "cost more men, sick and dead, than the battle of Manassas Plains." More enterprising in plans than resolute or skillful in carrying them out, he determined upon another effort, with Lee's consent. Taking advantage of Rosecrans's neglect to occupy Fayette Court House and Cotton Hill, a mountainous mass in the angle of the Kanawha and New rivers, he moved with a column of about five thousand men across New River and down its left bank, and startled the Union commander by opening with cannon upon the post at Gauley Bridge on the 1st of November. The demonstration was more noisy than dangerous, for Floyd had no means of crossing the river. The ordnance stores at the post were moved into a gorge out of the range of fire, and a battery was established high up on Gauley Mount to reply to the enemy. Rosecrans had hopes of capturing Floyd, by turning his position from below by Benham's and Robert C. Schenck's (formerly Scammon's) brigades. Delays occurred which Rosecrans attributed to failure to obey orders on the part of Benham. On the 10th detachments from my brigade at Gauley Bridge crossed the river and scaled the heights, attacking Floyd in front and securing a position on the top of the mountain. Floyd withdrew his artillery, and on the 12th, learning that Schenck and Benham were moving toward his rear, decamped, and did not cease his retreat till he reached the Holston Valley railroad.

Lee returned to Richmond, and portions of the troops on both sides were sent to other fields, where military operations in winter were thought to be more practicable. The remnant went into winter quarters, and though some combats occurred, the most noteworthy of which was Milroy's attack upon the Confederates in front of Cheat Mountain Pass in December, these engagements did not change the situation. West Virginia had organized as a free State within the Union, and this substantial result of the campaign crowned it with success. The line of the Alleghanies became the northern frontier of the Confederacy in Virginia, and was never again seriously broken.

VIEW OF ROMNEY, VA. FROM A WAR-TIME SKETCH.

On October 26th, 1861, Brigadier-General B. F. Kelley, with a small force of infantry and cavalry, advanced upon Romney from New Creek Station, 26 miles distant, on the Potomac (see map, page 129). After a sharp engagement, the Confederates were driven from their intrenchments and the town was captured. The Union forces lost 1 killed and 20 wounded. In the sketch are shown the camps of General Kelley's troops.

If any one attempts to haul down the American flag, shoot him on the spot. —

John A. Dix
Secretary of the Treasury.

GOING TO THE FRONT.

RECOLLECTIONS OF A PRIVATE — I. BY WARREN LEE GOSS.

BEFORE I reached the point of enlisting, I had read and been "enthused" by General Dix's famous "shoot him on the spot" dispatch; I had attended flag-raisings, and had heard orators declaim of "undying devotion to the Union." One speaker to whom I listened declared that "human life must be cheapened"; but I never learned that he helped on the work experimentally. When men by the hundred walked soberly to the front and signed the enlistment papers, he was not one of them. As I came out of the hall, with conflicting emotions, feeling as though I should have to go finally or forfeit my birthright as an American citizen, one of the orators who stood at the door, glowing with enthusiasm and patriotism, and shaking hands effusively with those who enlisted, said to me:

"Did you enlist?" "No," I said. "Did you?"

"No; they won't take me. I have got a lame leg and a widowed mother to take care of."

I remember another enthusiast who was eager to enlist others. He declared that the family of no man who went to the front should suffer. After

☆ January 18th, 1861, three days after he had entered on his duties as Secretary of the Treasury to President Buchanan, General Dix sent W. Hemphill Jones, chief clerk of one of the Treasury bureaus, to the South, for the purpose of saving the revenue-cutters at New Orleans, Mobile, and Galveston. January 29th, Mr. Jones telegraphed from New Orleans that the captain of the revenue-cutter *McClelland* refused to obey the Secretary's orders. It was seven in the evening when the dispatch was received. Immediately, Secretary Dix wrote the following reply: "Treasury Department, January 29, 1861. Tell Lieutenant Caldwell to arrest Captain Breshwood, assume command of the cutter, and obey the order I gave through you. If Captain Breshwood, after arrest, undertakes to interfere with the command of the cutter, tell Lieutenant Caldwell to consider him as a mutineer, and treat him accordingly. If any one attempts to haul down the American flag, shoot him on the spot. JOHN A. DIX, Secretary of the Treasury."— EDITORS.

149

ARRIVAL OF THE SEVENTH NEW YORK AT ANNAPOLIS, APRIL 20, 1861, ON THE WAY TO WASHINGTON.
FROM A SKETCH MADE AT THE TIME.

the war he was prominent among those who at town-meeting voted to refund the money to such as had expended it to procure substitutes. He has, moreover, been fierce and uncompromising toward the ex-Confederates since the war.

From the first I did not believe the trouble would blow over in "sixty days"; ⸗ nor did I consider eleven dollars a month, ⚓ and the promised glory, large pay for the services of an able-bodied young man.

It was the news that the 6th Massachusetts regiment had been mobbed by roughs on their passage through Baltimore which gave me the war fever. ⸗

⸗ Mr. Seward, speaking in New York two days after the secession of South Carolina, said : "Sixty days' more suns will give you a much brighter and more cheerful atmosphere."

⚓ The monthly pay of Union privates was: cavalry $12, artillery and infantry $11; from August 6th, 1861, $13 for all arms, and from May 1st, 1864, $16. Confederate privates received: in the cavalry and light batteries $12; in the artillery and infantry $11; increased June 9th, 1864, to $19 and $18 per month for a period of one year from that date. — EDITORS.

⸗ Concerning this encounter Colonel Edward F. Jones, of the 6th Massachusetts, says in his report:

"After leaving Philadelphia I received intimation that our passage through the city of Baltimore would be resisted. I caused ammunition to be distributed and arms loaded, and went personally through the cars, and issued the following order, viz., 'The regiment will march through Baltimore in column of sections, arms at will. You will undoubtedly be insulted, abused, and perhaps assaulted, to which you must pay no attention whatever, but march with your faces square to the front and pay no attention to the mob, even if they throw stones, bricks, or other missiles; but if you are fired upon and any one of you is hit, your officers will order you to fire. Do not fire into any promiscuous crowds, but select any man whom you may see aiming at you, and be sure you drop him.' Reaching Baltimore, horses were attached the instant that the locomotive was detached, and the cars were driven at a rapid pace across the city. After the cars containing seven companies had reached the Washington depot the track behind them was barricaded, and the cars containing . . . the following companies, viz., Company C, of Lowell, Captain Follansbee; Company

D, of Lowell, Captain Hart; Company I, of Lawrence, Captain Pickering, and Company L, of Stoneham, Captain Dike, were vacated, and they proceeded but a short distance before they were furiously attacked by a shower of missiles, which came faster as they advanced. They increased their steps to double-quick, which seemed to infuriate the mob, as it evidently impressed the mob with the idea that the soldiers dared not fire or had no ammunition, and pistol-shots were numerously fired into the ranks, and one soldier fell dead. The order 'Fire' was given, and it was executed. In consequence, several of the mob fell, and the soldiers again advanced hastily. The mayor of Baltimore placed himself at the head of the column beside Captain Follansbee, and proceeded with them a short distance." . . .

The Hon. George William Brown, then mayor of Baltimore, in his volume entitled "Baltimore and the 19th of April, 1861," thus describes the march of the soldiers after he joined the column:

"They were firing wildly, sometimes backward, over their shoulders. So rapid was the march that they could not stop to take aim. The mob, which was not very large, as it seemed to me, was pursuing with shouts and stones, and, I think, an occasional pistol-shot. The uproar was furious. I ran at once to the head of the column, some persons in the crowd shouting, 'Here comes the mayor.' I shook hands with the officer in command, Captain Follansbee, saying, as I did so, 'I am the mayor of Baltimore.' The captain greeted me cordially. I at once objected to the double-quick, which was immediately stopped. I placed myself by his side, and marched with him. He said, 'We have been attacked without provocation,' or words to that effect. I replied, 'You must defend yourselves.' I expected that he would face his men to the rear, and, after giving warning, would fire if necessary. But I said no more, for I immediately felt that, as mayor of the city, it was

And yet when I read Governor John A. Andrew's instructions to have the hero martyrs "preserved in ice and tenderly sent forward," somehow, though I felt the pathos of it, I could not reconcile myself to the ice. Ice in connection with patriotism did not give me agreeable impressions of war, and when I came to think of it, the stoning of the heroic "Sixth" didn't suit me; it detracted from my desire to die a soldier's death.

I lay awake all night thinking the matter over, with the "ice" and "brick-bats" before my mind. However, the fever culminated that night, and I resolved to enlist.

"Cold chills" ran up and down my back as I got out of bed after the sleepless night, and shaved, preparatory to other desperate deeds of valor. I was twenty years of age, and when anything unusual was to be done, like fighting or courting, I shaved.

With a nervous tremor convulsing my system, and my heart thumping like muffled drum-beats, I stood before the door of the recruiting-office, and, before turning the knob to enter, read and re-read the advertisement for recruits posted thereon, until I knew all its peculiarities. The promised chances for "travel and promo-

UNIFORM OF THE SIXTH MASSACHUSETTS.
FROM A PHOTOGRAPH.

not my province to volunteer such advice. Once before in my life I had taken part in opposing a formidable riot, and had learned by experience that the safest and most humane manner of quelling a mob is to meet it at the beginning with armed resistance. The column continued its march. There was neither concert of action nor organization among the rioters. They were armed only with such stones or missiles as they could pick up, and a few pistols. My presence for a short time had some effect, but very soon the attack was renewed with greater violence. The mob grew bolder. Stones flew thick and fast. Rioters rushed at the soldiers and attempted to snatch their muskets, and at least on two occasions succeeded. With one of these muskets a soldier was killed. Men fell on both sides. A young lawyer, then and now known as a quiet citizen, seized a flag of one of the companies and nearly tore it from its staff. He was shot through the thigh, and was carried home apparently a dying man, but he survived to enter the army of the Confederacy, where he rose to the rank of captain, and he afterward returned to Baltimore, where he still lives. The soldiers fired at will. There was no firing by platoons, and I heard no order given to fire. I remember that at the corner of South street several citizens standing in a group fell, either killed or wounded. It was impossible for the troops to discriminate between the rioters and the by-standers, but the latter seemed to suffer most. . . . Marshal Kane, with about fifty policemen (as I then supposed, but I have since ascertained that, in fact, there were not so many), came at a run from the direction of the Camden street station, and throwing themselves in the rear of the troops, they formed a line in front of the mob, and with drawn revolvers kept it back. This was between Light and Charles streets. Marshal Kane's voice shouted, 'Keep back, men, or I shoot!' This movement, which I saw myself, was gallantly executed, and was perfectly successful. The mob recoiled like water from a rock. One of the leading rioters, then a young man, now a peaceful merchant, tried, as he has himself told me, to pass the line, but the marshal seized him, and

vowed he would shoot if the attempt was made. This nearly ended the fight, and the column passed on under the protection of the police, without serious molestation, to Camden station "

Sumner H. Needham, of Lawrence, Addison O. Whitney and Luther C. Ladd, of Lowell, and Charles A. Taylor were the killed, and thirty-six of their comrades were wounded. Twelve citizens were killed, and an unknown number were wounded. Col. Jones continues:

"As the men went into the cars I caused the blinds to the cars to be closed, and took every precaution to prevent any shadow of offense to the people of Baltimore; but still the stones flew thick and fast into the train, and it was with the utmost difficulty that I could prevent the troops from leaving the cars and revenging the death of their comrades. . . . On reaching Washington we were quartered at the Capitol, in the Senate Chamber."

This regiment, the 6th Massachusetts, were the first armed troops to reach Washington in response to the call of the President.

The 27th Pennsylvania Regiment (unarmed) arrived at Baltimore by the same train as the Massachusetts troops. It was attacked by a mob and obliged to remain at the President street station, from which point it was sent back the same day in the direction of Philadelphia. The same night, by order of the Board of Police Commissioners, with the concurrence of Governor Hicks and Mayor Brown, the railways from the north were obstructed, so that the 8th Massachusetts, with General B. F. Butler, and the 7th New York were compelled to go to Annapolis by water and march thence to Washington.—EDITORS.

tion" seemed good, and I thought I might have made a mistake in considering war so serious after all. "Chances for travel!" I must confess now, after four years of soldiering, that the "chances for travel" were no myth; but "promotion" was a little uncertain and slow.

I was in no hurry to open the door. Though determined to enlist, I was half inclined to put it off awhile; I had a fluctuation of desires; I was faint-hearted and brave; I wanted to enlist, and yet —— Here I turned the knob, and was relieved. I had been more prompt, with all my hesitation, than the officer in his duty; he wasn't in. Finally he came, and said: "What do you want, my boy?" "I want to enlist," I responded, blushing deeply with upwelling patriotism and bashfulness. Then the surgeon came to strip and examine me. In justice to myself, it must be stated that I signed the rolls without a tremor. It is common to the most of humanity, I believe, that, when confronted with actual danger, men have less fear than in its contemplation. I will, however, make one exception in favor of the first shell I heard uttering its blood-curdling hisses, as though a steam locomotive were traveling the air. With this exception I have found the actual dangers of war always less terrible face to face than on the night before the battle.

"AND THE CORPORAL DID!"

My first uniform was a bad fit: my trousers were too long by three or four inches; the flannel shirt was coarse and unpleasant, too large at the neck and too short elsewhere. The forage cap was an ungainly bag with pasteboard top and leather visor; the blouse was the only part which seemed decent; while the overcoat made me feel like a little nubbin of corn in a large preponderance of husk. Nothing except "Virginia mud" ever took down my ideas of military pomp quite so low.

After enlisting I did not seem of so much consequence as I had expected. There was not so much excitement on account of my military appearance as I deemed justly my due. I was taught my facings, and at the time I thought the drill-master needlessly fussy about shouldering, ordering, and presenting arms. At this time men were often drilled in company and regimental evolutions long before they learned the manual of arms, because of the difficulty of obtaining muskets. These we obtained at an early day, but we would willingly have resigned them after carrying them for a few hours. The musket, after an hour's drill, seemed heavier and less ornamental than it had looked to be. The first day I went out to drill, getting tired of doing the same things over and over, I said to the drill-sergeant: "Let's stop this fooling and go over to the grocery." His only reply was addressed to a corporal: "Corporal, take this man out and drill him like h—l"; and the corporal did! I found that suggestions were not so well appreciated in the army as in private life, and that no wisdom was equal to a drill-master's "Right face," "Left wheel," and "Right, oblique, march." It takes a raw recruit some time to learn that he is not to think or suggest, but obey. Some never do learn. I acquired it at last, in humility and mud, but it was tough. Yet I doubt if my patriotism, during my first three weeks' drill, was quite knee-high. Drilling looks easy to a spectator, but it isn't. Old soldiers who read this will remember their green recruithood and smile assent. After a time I had cut down my uniform so that I could see out of it, and had conquered the drill sufficiently to see through it. Then the word came: On to Washington!

Our company was quartered at a large hotel near the railway station in the town in which it had been recruited. Bunks had been fitted up within a part of the hotel but little used. We took our meals at the public table, and found fault with the style. Six months later we would have considered ourselves aristocratic to have slept in the hotel stables with the meal-bin for a dining-table. One morning there was great excitement at the report that we were going to be sent to the front. Most of us obtained a limited pass and went to see our friends for the last time, returning the same night. Many of our schoolmates came in tears to say good-bye. We took leave of them all with heavy hearts, for, lightly as I may here seem to treat the subject, it was no light thing for a boy of twenty to start out for three years into the unknown dangers of a civil war. Our mothers — God bless them! — had brought us something good to eat, — pies, cakes, doughnuts, and jellies. It was one way in which a mother's heart found utterance. The young ladies (sisters, of course) brought an invention, usually made of leather or cloth, containing needles, pins, thread, buttons, and scissors, so that nearly every recruit had an embryo tailor's shop, with the goose outside. One old lady, in the innocence of her heart, brought her son an umbrella. We did not see

A MOTHER'S PARTING GIFT.

anything particularly laughable about it at the time, but our old drill-sergeant did. Finally we were ready to move; our tears were wiped away, our buttons were polished, and our muskets were as bright as emery paper could make them.

"Wad" Rider, a member of our company, had come from a neighboring State to enlist with us. He was about eighteen years of age, red-headed, freckled-faced, good-natured and rough, with a wonderful aptitude for crying or laughing from sympathy. Another comrade, whom I will call Jack, was honored with a call from his mother, a little woman, hardly reaching up to his shoulder, with a sweet, motherly, care-worn face. At the last moment, though she had tried hard to preserve her composure, as is the habit of New England people, she threw her arms around her boy's neck, and with an outburst of sobbing and crying, said: "My dear boy, my dear boy, what will

your poor old mother do without you? You are going to fight for your country. Don't forget your mother, Jack; God bless you, God bless you!" We felt as if the mother's tears and blessing were a benediction over us all. There was a touch of nature in her homely sorrow and solicitude over her big boy, which drew tears of sympathy from my eyes as I thought of my own sorrowing mother at home. The sympathetic Wad Rider burst into tears and sobs. His eyes refused, as he expressed it, to "dry up," until, as we were moving off, Jack's mother, rushing toward him with a bundle tied like a wheat-sheaf, called out in a most pathetic voice, "Jack! Jack! you've forgotten to take your pennyroyal." We all laughed, and so did Jack, and I think the laugh helped him more than the cry did. Everybody had said his last word, and the cars were off. Handkerchiefs were waved at us from all the houses we passed; we cheered till we were hoarse, and then settled back and swung our handkerchiefs.

Just here let me name over the contents of my knapsack, as a fair sample of what all the volunteers started with. There were in it a pair of trousers, two pairs of drawers, a pair of thick boots, four pairs of stockings, four flannel shirts, a blouse, a looking-glass, a can of peaches, a bottle of cough-mixture, a button-stick, chalk, razor and strop, the "tailor's shop"

A MILITIA UNIFORM OF '61. — AFTER THE NEW YORK SEVENTH'S MEMORIAL STATUE IN THE CENTRAL PARK.

THE NEW YORK SEVENTH MARCHING DOWN BROADWAY, APRIL 19, 1861.

spoken of above, a Bible, a small volume of Shakspere, and writing utensils. To its top was strapped a double woolen blanket and a rubber one. Many other things were left behind because of lack of room in or about the knapsack. ♭

On our arrival in Boston we were marched through the streets — the first march of any consequence we had taken with our knapsacks and equipments. Our dress consisted of a belt about the body, which held a cartridge-box and bayonet, a cross-belt, also a haversack and tin drinking-cup, a canteen, and, last but not least, the knapsack strapped to the back. The straps ran over, around, and about one, in confusion most perplexing to our unsophisticated shoulders, the knapsack constantly giving the wearer the feeling that he was being pulled over backward. My canteen banged against my bayonet, both tin cup and bayonet badly interfered with the butt of my musket, while my cartridge-box and haversack were constantly flopping up and down — the whole jangling like loose harness and chains on a runaway horse. As we marched into Boston Common, I involuntarily cast my eye about for a bench. But for a former experience in offering advice, I should have proposed to the captain to "chip in" and hire a team to carry our equipments. Such was my first experience in war harness. Afterward, with hardened muscles, rendered athletic by long marches and invigorated by hardships, I could look back upon those days and smile, while carrying a knapsack as lightly as my heart. That morning my heart was as heavy as my knapsack. At last the welcome

♭ It is said by one of the "Monticello Guards," that most of its members started for Bull Run with a trunk and an abundant supply of fine linen shirts.—EDITORS.

FEDERAL HILL, BALTIMORE. FROM A SKETCH MADE ON THE DAY OF THE OCCUPATION BY GENERAL BUTLER.

On the 27th of April, 1861, General B. F. Butler was assigned to the command of the Department of Annapolis, which did not include Baltimore. On the 5th of May, with two regiments and a battery of artillery, he moved from Washington to the Relay House, on the Baltimore and Ohio Railway, 7 miles from Baltimore, at the junction of the Washington branch. He fortified this position, and on the 13th entered Baltimore and occupied and fortified Federal Hill, overlooking the harbor and commanding the city. On the 15th he was followed in command of the Department by General George Cadwalader, who was succeeded on the 11th of June by General N. P. Banks, who administered the Department until succeeded by General John A. Dix, July 23d, 1861. On the 22d of May General Butler assumed command at Fort Monroe, Va.

orders came: "Prepare to open ranks! Rear, open order, march! Right dress! Front! Order arms! Fix bayonets! Stack arms! Unsling knapsacks! In place, rest!"

The tendency of raw soldiers at first is to overload themselves. On the first long march the reaction sets in, and the recruit goes to the opposite extreme, not carrying enough, and thereby becoming dependent upon his comrades. Old soldiers preserve a happy medium. I have seen a new regiment start out with a lot of indescribable material, including sheet-iron stoves, and come back after a long march covered with more mud than baggage, stripped of everything except blankets, haversacks, canteens, muskets, and cartridge-boxes.

During that afternoon in Boston, after marching and countermarching, or, as one of our farmer-boy recruits expressed it, after "hawing and geeing" about the streets, we were sent to Fort Independence for the night for safe-keeping. A company of regulars held the fort, and the guards walked their post with an uprightness that was astonishing. Our first impression of them was that there was a needless amount of "wheel about and turn about, and walk just so," and of saluting, and presenting arms. We were all marched to our quarters within the fort, where we unslung our knapsacks. After the first day's struggle with a knapsack, the general verdict was, " got too much of it." At supper-time we were marched to the dining-barracks, where our bill of fare was beefsteak, coffee, wheat bread, and potatoes, but not a sign of milk or butter. It struck me as queer when I heard that the army was never provided with butter and milk.

The next day we started for Washington, by rail. We marched through New York's crowded streets without awakening the enthusiasm we thought our due; for we had read of the exciting scenes attending the departure of the New York 7th for Washington, on the day the 6th Massachusetts was mobbed in Baltimore, and also of the march of the 12th Massachusetts down Broadway on the 24th of July, when the regiment sang the then new and always thrilling lyric, "John Brown's Body." The following morning we took breakfast in Philadelphia, where we were attended by matrons and maidens, who waited upon us with thoughtful tenderness, as if they had been our own mothers and sweethearts instead of strangers. They feasted us and then filled our haversacks. God bless them! If we did not quite appreciate them then, we did afterward. After embarking on the cars at Philadelphia, the waving of handkerchiefs was less and less noticeable along the route. We arrived in Baltimore late at night; Union troops now controlled the city, and we marched through its deserted streets unmolested. On our arrival at Washington the next morning, we were marched to barracks, dignified by the name of " Soldiers' Retreat," where each man received a half loaf of " soft-tack," as we had already begun to call wheat bread, with a piece of " salt junk," about as big and tough as the heel of my government shoe, and a quart of coffee,—which constituted our breakfast. Our first day in Washington was spent in shaving, washing, polishing our brasses and buttons, and cleaning-up for inspection. A day or two later we moved to quarters not far from the armory, looking out on the broad Potomac, within sight of Long Bridge and the city of Alexandria.

Here and there the sound of a gun broke the serenity, but otherwise the quiet seemed inconsistent with the war preparations going on around us. In the distance, across the wide river, we could see the steeples and towers of the city of Alexandria, while up stream, on the right, was the Long Bridge. Here and there was to be seen the moving panorama of armed men, as a regiment crossed the bridge; a flash of sunlight on the polished muskets revealed them to the eye; while the white-topped army baggage-wagons filed over in constant procession, looking like sections of whitewashed fence in motion. The overgrown country village of that period, called Washington, can be described in a few words. There were wide streets stretching out from a common center like a spider's web. The Capitol, with its unfinished dome; the Patent Office, the Treasury, and the other public buildings, were in marked and classic contrast with the dilapidated, tumble-down, shabby look of the average homes, stores, groceries, and groggeries, which increased in shabbiness and dirty dilapidation as they approached the suburbs. The climate of Washington was genial, but in the winter months the mud was fearful. I have drilled in it,

PENNSYLVANIA AVENUE, WASHINGTON. FROM A SKETCH MADE IN 1861.

marched in it, and run from the provost-guard in it, and I think I appreciate it from actual and familiar knowledge. In the lower quarter of the city there was not a piece of sidewalk. Even Pennsylvania Avenue, with its side-walks, was extremely dirty; and the cavalcade of teams, artillery caissons, and baggage-wagons, with their heavy wheels, stirred the mud into a stiff batter for the pedestrian.

Officers in tinsel and gold lace were so thick on Pennsylvania Avenue that it was a severe trial for a private to walk there. The salute exacted by officers, of bringing the hand to the visor of the cap, extending the arm to its full length, and then letting it drop by the side, was tiresome when followed up with the industry required by this horde. Perhaps I exaggerate, but in a half-hour's walk on the avenue I think I have saluted two hundred officers. Brigadier-generals were more numerous there than I ever knew them to be at the front. These officers, many of whom won their positions by political wire-pulling at Washington, we privates thought the great bane of the war; they ought to have been sent to the front rank of battle, to serve as privates until they had learned the duties of a soldier. Mingled with these gaudy, useless officers were citizens in search of fat contracts, privates, "non-com's" and officers whose uniforms were well worn and faded, showing that they were from encampments and active service. Occasionally a regiment passed through the streets, on the way to camp; all surged up and down wide Pennsylvania Avenue.

The soldiers of this period were eager to collect mementoes of the war. One of my acquaintances in another regiment made sketches of the different camps he had visited around Washington, including " Brightwood " and Camp

Cameron; the latter he termed "a nursery for brigadier-generals." Another friend hoarded specimens of official signatures and passes issued in Washington, conspicuous among which was a pass with the well-known John-Hancock-like signature of Drake De Kay. (See page 173.)

Before enlisting, and while on a visit to a neighboring town, I was one evening at the village store, when the talk turned upon the duration of the war. Jim Tinkham, the clerk of the grocery store, announced his belief in a sixty days' war. I modestly asked him for more time. The older ones agreed with Jim and argued, as was common at that time, that the Government would soon blockade all the rebel ports and starve them out. Tinkham proposed to wager a supper for those present, if the rebels did not surrender before snow came that year. I accepted. Neither of us put up any money, and in the excitement of the weeks which followed I had forgotten the wager. During my first week in Washington, whom should I meet but Jim Tinkham, the apostle of the sixty-day theory. He was brown with sunburn, and clad in a rusty uniform which showed service in the field. He was a veteran, for he had been at the battle of Bull Run. He confidentially declared that after getting the order to retreat at that battle, he should not have stopped short of Boston if he had not been halted by a soldier with a musket, after crossing Long Bridge.

THE SEVENTH NEW YORK AT CAMP CAMERON, WASHINGTON.

VIRGINIA SCENES IN '61.

BY CONSTANCE CARY HARRISON.

CONFEDERATE BATTLE-FLAG.　SEE PAGE 167.

THE only association I have with my old home in Virginia that is not one of unmixed happiness relates to the time immediately succeeding the execution of John Brown at Harper's Ferry. Our homestead was in Fairfax County, at some distance from the theater of that tragic episode; and, belonging as we did to a family among the first in the State to manumit slaves,—our grandfather having set free those that came to him by inheritance, and the people who served us being hired from their owners and remaining in our employ through years of kindliest relations,— there seemed to be no especial reason for us to share in the apprehension of an uprising of the blacks. But there was the fear — unspoken, or pooh-poohed at by the men who were mouth-pieces for our community—dark, boding, oppressive, and altogether hateful. I can remember taking it to bed with me at night, and awaking suddenly oftentimes to confront it through a vigil of nervous terror, of which it never occurred to me to speak to any one. The notes of whip-poor-wills in the sweet-gum swamp near the stable, the mutterings of a distant thunder-storm, even the rustle of the night wind in the oaks that shaded my window, filled me with nameless dread. In the daytime it seemed impossible to associate suspicion with those familiar tawny or sable faces that surrounded us. We had seen them for so many years smiling or saddening with the family joys or sorrows; they were so guileless, so patient, so satisfied. What subtle influence was at work that should transform them into tigers thirsting for our blood? The idea was preposterous. But when evening came again, and with it the hour when the colored people (who in summer and autumn weather kept astir half the night) assembled themselves together for dance or prayer-meeting, the ghost that refused to be laid was again at one's elbow. Rusty bolts were drawn and rusty fire-arms loaded. A watch was set where never before had eye or ear been lent to such a service. In short, peace had flown from the borders of Virginia.

Although the newspapers were full of secession talk and the matter was eagerly discussed at our tables, I cannot remember that, as late as Christmas-time of the year 1860, coming events had cast any definite shadow on our homes. The people in our neighborhood, of one opinion with their dear and honored friend, Colonel Robert E. Lee, of Arlington, were slow to accept the startling suggestion of disruption of the Union. At any rate, we enjoyed the usual holiday gathering of kinsfolk in the usual fashion. The old Vaucluse house, known for many years past as a center of cheerful hospitality in the county, threw wide open its doors to receive all the members who could be gathered there of a large family circle. The woods about were despoiled of

"VAUCLUSE"—A VIRGINIA HOMESTEAD.

holly and spruce, pine and cedar, to deck the walls and wreathe the picture-frames. On Christmas Eve we had a grand rally of youths and boys belonging to the "clan," as they loved to call it, to roll in a yule log, which was deposited upon a glowing bed of coals in the big "red-parlor" fire-place, and sit about it afterward, welcoming the Christmas in with goblets of egg-nog and apple-toddy.

"Where shall we be a year hence?" some one asked at a pause in the merry chat; and, in the brief silence that followed, arose a sudden spectral thought of war. All felt its presence; no one cared to speak first of its grim possibilities.

On Christmas Eve of the following year the old house lay in ruins, a sacrifice by Union troops to military necessity; the forest giants that kept watch around her walls had been cut down and made to serve as breastworks for a fort erected on the Vaucluse property as part of the defenses of Washington. Of the young men and boys who took part in that holiday festivity, all were in the active service of the South,— one of them, alas! soon to fall under a rain of shot and shell beside his gun at Fredericksburg; the youngest of the number had left his mother's knee to fight at Manassas, and found himself, before the year was out, a midshipman aboard the Confederate steamer *Nashville*, on her cruise in distant seas!

My first vivid impression of war-days was during a ramble in the neighboring woods one Sunday afternoon in spring, when the young people in a happy band set out in search of wild flowers. Pink honeysuckles, blue lupine, beds of fairy flax, anemones, and ferns in abundance sprung under the canopy of young leaves on the forest boughs, and the air was full of the song of birds and the music of running waters. We knew every mossy path far and near in those woods; every tree had been watched and cherished by those who went before us, and dearer than any other spot on earth was our tranquil, sweet Vaucluse. Suddenly the shrill whistle of a locomotive struck the ear, an unwonted sound on Sunday. "Do you know what that means?" said one of the older cousins who accompanied the party. "It is the special train carrying Alexandria volunteers to Manassas, and to-morrow I shall follow with my company." Silence fell upon our little band. A cloud seemed to come between us and the sun. It was the begininng of the end too soon to come.

The story of one broken circle is the story of another at the outset of such a war. Before the week was over, the scattering of our household, which no one then believed to be more than temporary, had begun. Living as we did upon ground likely to be in the track of armies gathering to confront each other, it was deemed advisable to send the children and young girls into a place more remote from chances of danger. Some weeks later the heads of the household, two widowed sisters whose sons were at Manassas, drove away from their home in their carriage at early morning, having spent the previous night in company with a half-grown lad digging in the cellar hasty graves for the interment of two boxes of old English silver-ware, heirlooms in the family, for which there was no time to provide otherwise. Although the enemy were long encamped immediately above it after the house was burnt the following year, this silver was found there when the war had ended; it was lying loose in the earth, the boxes having rotted away.

The point at which our family reunited within the Confederate lines was Bristoe, the station next beyond Manassas, a cheerless railway inn; a part of the premises was used as a country grocery store; and there quarters were secured for us with a view to being near the army. By this time all our kith and kin of fighting age had joined the volunteers. One cannot picture accommodations more forlorn than these eagerly taken for us and for other families attracted to Bristoe by the same powerful magnet. The summer sun poured its burning rays upon whitewashed walls unshaded by a tree. Our bedrooms were almost uninhabitable by day or night, our fare the plainest. From the windows we beheld only a flat, uncultivated country, crossed by red-clay roads, then ankle-deep in dust. We learned to look for all excitement to the glittering lines of railway track, along which continually thundered trains bound to and from the front. It was impossible to allow such a train to pass without running out upon the platform to salute it, for in this way we greeted many an old friend or relative buttoned up in the smart gray uniform, speeding with high hope to the scene of coming conflict. Such shouts as went up from sturdy throats while we stood waving hands, handkerchiefs, or the rough woolen garments we were at work upon! Then fairly awoke the spirit that made of Southern women the inspiration of Southern men throughout the war. Most of the young fellows we knew and were cheering onward wore the uniform of privates, and for the right to wear it had left homes of

ON THE WAY TO MANASSAS.

ease and luxury. To such we gave our best homage; and from that time forth the youth who was lukewarm in the cause or unambitious of military glory fared uncomfortably in the presence of the average Confederate maiden.

Thanks to our own carriage, we were able during those rallying days of June to drive frequently to visit "the boys" in camp, timing the expeditions to include battalion drill and dress parade, and taking tea afterward in the different tents. Then were the gala days of war, and our proud hosts hastened to produce home dainties dispatched from the far-away plantations— tears and blessings interspersed amid the packing, we were sure; though I have seen a pretty girl persist in declining other fare, to make her meal upon raw biscuit and huckleberry pie compounded by the bright-eyed amateur cook of a well-beloved mess. Feminine heroism could no farther go.

And so the days wore on until the 17th of July, when a rumor from the front sent an electric shock through our circle. The enemy were moving forward! On the morning of the 18th those who had been able to sleep at all awoke early to listen for the first guns of the engagement of Blackburn's Ford. Deserted as the women at Bristoe were by every male creature old enough to gather news, there was, for us, no way of knowing the progress of events during the long, long day of waiting, of watching, of weeping, of praying, of rushing out upon the railway track to walk as far as we dared in the direction whence came that intolerable booming of artillery. The cloud of dun smoke arising over Manassas became heavier in volume as the day progressed. Still, not a word of tidings, till toward afternoon there came limping up a single, very dirty, soldier with his arm in a sling. What a heaven-send he was, if only as an escape-valve for our pent-up sympathies! We seized him, we washed him, we cried over him, we glorified him until the man was fairly bewildered. Our best endeavors could only develop a pin-scratch of a wound on his right hand; but when our hero had laid in a substantial meal of bread and meat, we plied him with trembling questions, each asking news of some staff or regiment or company. It has since oc-curred to me that he was a humorist in disguise. His invariable reply, as he looked from one to the other of his satellites, was: "The —— Virginia, marm? Why, of coase. They warn't no two ways o' thinkin' 'bout that ar reg'ment. They just *kivered* tharselves with glory!"

A little later two wagon-loads of slightly wounded claimed our care, and with them came authentic news of the day. Most of us re-ceived notes on paper torn

LISTENING FOR THE FIRST GUN.

from a soldier's pocket-book and grimed with gunpowder, containing assurance of the safety of our own. At nightfall a train carrying more wounded to the hospitals at Culpeper made a halt at Bristoe; and, preceded by men holding lanterns, we went in among the stretchers with milk, food, and water to the sufferers. One of the first discoveries I made, bending over in that fitful light, was a young officer whom I knew to be a special object of solicitude with one of my comrades in the search; but he was badly hurt, and neither he nor she knew the other was near until the train had moved on. The next day, and the next, were full of burning excitement over the impend-ing general engagement, which people then said would decide the fate of the young Confederacy. Fresh troops came by with every train, and we lived only to turn from one scene to another of welcome and farewell. On Saturday even-ing arrived a message from General Beauregard, saying that early on Sunday an engine and car would be put at our disposal, to take us to some point more remote from danger. We looked at one another, and, tacitly agreeing the gal-lant general had sent not an order but a suggestion, declined his kind proposal.

Another unspeakably long day, full of the straining anguish of suspense. Dawning bright and fair, it closed under a sky darkened by cannon-smoke. The roar of guns seemed never to cease. First, a long sullen boom; then a sharper rattling fire, painfully distinct; then stragglers from the field, with varying rumors; at last, the news of victory; and, as before, the wounded, to force our numbed faculties into service. One of our group, the mother of an only son barely fifteen years of age, heard that her boy, after being in action all the early part of the day, had through sheer fatigue fallen asleep upon the ground, where he was found resting peacefully amidst the roar of the guns.

A few days later we rode over the field. The trampled grass had begun to spring again, and wild flowers were blooming around carelessly made graves. From one of these imperfect mounds of clay I saw a hand extended; and when, years afterward, I visited the tomb of Rousseau beneath the Panthéon in Paris, where a sculptured hand bearing a torch protrudes from the sarcophagus, I thought of that mournful spectacle upon the field of Manassas. Fences were everywhere thrown down; the undergrowth of the woods was riddled with shot; here and there we came upon spiked guns, disabled gun-carriages, cannon-balls, blood-stained blankets, and dead horses. We were glad enough to turn away and gallop homeward.

With August heats and lack of water, Bristoe was forsaken for quarters near Culpeper, where my mother went into the soldiers' barracks, sharing soldiers' accommodations, to nurse the wounded. In September quite a party of us, upon invitation, visited the different headquarters. We stopped over-night at Manassas, five ladies, sleeping upon a couch made of rolls of car-tridge-flannel, in a tent guarded by a faithful sentry. I remember the comical effect of the five bird-cages (of a kind without which no self-respecting young woman of that day would present herself in public) suspended upon a line running across the upper part of our tent, after we had reluctantly removed them in order to adjust ourselves for repose. Our progress during that mem-orable visit was royal; an ambulance with a picked troop of cavalrymen had been placed at our service, and the convoy was "personally conducted" by a pleasing variety of distinguished officers. It was at this time, after a supper at the headquarters of the "Maryland line" at Fairfax, that the afterward uni-versal war-song, "My Maryland!" was put afloat upon the tide of army favor. We were sitting outside a tent in the warm starlight of an early autumn night, when music was proposed. At once we struck up Randall's verses to the tune of the old college song, "Lauriger Horatius,"—a young lady of the party, Jennie Cary, of Baltimore, having recently set them to this music before leaving home to share the fortunes of the Confederacy. All joined in the ring-ing chorus; and, when we finished, a burst of applause came from some soldiers listening in the darkness behind a belt of trees. Next day the melody was hummed far and near through the camps, and in due time it had gained the place of favorite song in the army. Other songs sung that evening, which afterward had a great vogue, were one beginning "By blue Patapsco's billowy dash," and "The years glide slowly by, Lorena."

Another incident of note, during the autumn of '61, was that to my cousins, Hetty and Jennie Cary, and to me was intrusted the making of the first three battle-flags of the Confederacy. They were jaunty squares of scarlet crossed with dark blue edged with white, the cross bearing stars to indicate the number of the seceded States. We set our best stitches upon them, edged them with golden fringes, and, when they were finished, dispatched one to Johnston, another to Beauregard, and the third to Earl Van Dorn, then commanding infantry at Manassas. The banners were received with all possible enthusiasm; were toasted, fêted, and cheered abundantly. After two years, when Van Dorn had been killed in Tennessee, mine came back to me, tattered and storm-stained from long and honorable service in the field. But it was only a little while after it had been bestowed that there arrived one day at our lodgings in Culpeper a huge, bashful Mississippi scout,—one of the most daring in the army,—with the frame of a Hercules and the face of a child. He had been bidden to come there by his general, he said, to ask, if I would not give him an order to fetch some cherished object from my dear old home—something that would prove to me "how much they thought of the maker of that flag!" A week later I was the astonished recipient of a lamented bit of finery left "within the lines," a wrap, brought to us by Dillon himself, with a beaming face. Mounted on a load of fire-wood, he had gone through the Union pickets, and while peddling poultry had presented himself at the house of my uncle, Dr. Fairfax, in Alexandria, whence he carried off his prize in triumph, with a letter in its folds telling us how relatives left behind longed to be sharing the joys and sorrows of those at large in the Confederacy.

The despot's heel is on thy shore,
  Maryland!
His torch is at thy temple door,
  Maryland!

Avenge the patriotic gore
That flecked the streets of Baltimore,
And be the battle-queen of yore,
  Maryland! My Maryland!

FAC-SIMILE OF AUTOGRAPHIC COPY OF THE FIRST STANZA OF "MY MARYLAND!"

Written in the Parish of Pointe Coupée,
La, April 1861 by

James R. Randall

SCRUTINIZING A PASS AT THE WASHINGTON END OF THE LONG BRIDGE.

McDOWELL'S ADVANCE TO BULL RUN.

BY JAMES B. FRY, BREVET MAJOR-GENERAL, U. S. A. (AT BULL RUN, CAPTAIN AND ASSISTANT
ADJUTANT-GENERAL ON McDOWELL'S STAFF).

AS President Buchanan's administration was drawing to a close, he was forced by the action of the South to decide whether the power of the general Government should be used to coerce into submission States that had attempted to secede from the Union. His opinion was that the contingency was not provided for, that while a State had no right to secede, the Constitution gave no authority to coerce, and that he had no right to do anything except hold the property and enforce the laws of the United States.

Before he went out of office the capital of the nation seemed to be in danger of seizure. For its protection, and in order to consult about holding Southern forts and arsenals, General Scott was in December called to Washington, from which he had been absent since the inauguration of Pierce, who had defeated him for the presidency. Jefferson Davis, Pierce's Secretary of War, and General Scott had quarreled, and the genius of acrimony controlled the correspondence which took place

UNIFORM OF THE 14TH NEW YORK
AT BULL RUN.

The battle of Bull Run was notable in a minor way for the variety of uniforms worn on both sides — a variety greater than was shown in any later engagement. The Federal blue had not yet been issued, and the troops wore either the uniforms of their militia organizations (including various patterns of Zouave dress) or those furnished by their several States. The Confederate uniforms exhibited similar variety; some regiments were in citizens' dress, and several of the general officers who had been in the old service — including, we are informed, Generals Johnston, Beauregard, and Longstreet — still wore the dress of the United States Army.— EDITORS.

between them. Notwithstanding the fact that on account of his age and infirmities he was soon overwhelmed by the rush of events, General Scott's laurels had not withered at the outbreak of the war, and he brought to the emergency ability, experience, and prestige. A high light in the whole military world, he towered above the rest of our army at that time professionally as he did physically. As the effect of his unusual stature was increased by contrast with a short aide-de-camp (purposely chosen, it was suspected), so was his exalted character marked by one or two conspicuous but not very harmful foibles. With much learning, great military ability, a strict sense of justice, and a kind heart, he was vain and somewhat petulant. He loved the Union and hated Jefferson Davis.

By authority of President Buchanan, Scott assembled a small force of regulars in the capital, and for the first time in the history of the country the electoral count was made and a President was inaugurated under the protection of soldiery. But before the inauguration of Lincoln, March 4th, the secession movement had spread through the "cotton-belt" and delegates from the secession States had met as a congress at Montgomery, Alabama, February 4th. On the 8th they had organized the "Provisional Government of the Confederate States of

SIMON CAMERON, SECRETARY OF WAR FROM MARCH 4, 1861, UNTIL JAN. 15, 1862. FROM A PHOTOGRAPH.

America," and on the 9th had elected Jefferson Davis President and Alexander H. Stephens Vice-President.

When the news of the firing upon Sumter reached Washington, President Lincoln prepared a proclamation, and issued it April 15th, convening Congress and calling forth 75,000 three-months militia to suppress combinations against the Government. The Federal situation was alarming. Sumter fell on the 13th of April, and was evacuated on the 14th. Virginia seceded on the 17th, and seized Harper's Ferry on the 18th and the Norfolk Navy Yard on the 20th. On the 19th a mob in Baltimore assaulted the 6th Massachusetts volunteers as it passed through to Washington, and at once bridges were burned and railway communication was cut off between Washington and the North.

Lincoln had had no experience as a party leader or executive officer, and was without knowledge of military affairs or acquaintance with military men. Davis at the head of the Confederacy was an experienced and acknowledged Southern leader; he was a graduate of the Military Academy; had commanded a regiment in the Mexican war; had been Secretary of War under President Pierce, and had been chairman of the Military Committee in the United States Senate up to the time he left Congress to take part with the South.

He was not only well versed in everything relating to war, but was thoroughly informed concerning the character and capacity of prominent and promising officers of the army. There was nothing experimental in his choice of high military commanders. With but few exceptions, those appointed at the beginning retained command until they lost their lives or the war closed.

The Southern States, all claiming to be independent republics after secession, with all their governmental machinery, including militia and volunteer organizations, in complete working order, transferred themselves as States from the Union to the Confederacy. The organization of a general government from such elements, with war as its immediate purpose, was a simple matter. Davis had only to accept and arrange, according to his ample information and well-matured judgment, the abundant and ambitious material at hand in the way that he thought would best secure his purposes. Lincoln had to adapt the machinery of a conservative old government, some of it unsuitable, some unsound, to sudden demands for which it was not designed. The talents of Simon Cameron, his first Secretary of War, were political, not military. He was a kind, gentle, placid man, gifted with powers to persuade, not to command. Shrewd and skilled in the management of business and personal matters, he had no knowledge of military affairs, and could not give the President much assistance in assembling and organizing for war the earnest and impatient, but unmilitary people of the North.

Officers from all departments of the Federal civil service hurried to the Confederacy and placed themselves at the disposal of Davis, and officers from all the corps of the regular army, most of them full of vigor, with the same education and experience as those who remained, went South and awaited assignment to the duties for which Davis might regard them as best qualified. All Confederate offices were vacant, and the Confederate President had large if not absolute power in filling them. On the other hand, the civil offices under Lincoln were occupied or controlled by party, and in the small regular army of the Union the law required that vacancies should as a rule be filled by seniority. There was no retired list for the disabled, and the army was weighed down by longevity; by venerated traditions; by prerogatives of service

UNIFORM OF THE 1ST MASS.
AT BULL RUN. FROM
A PHOTOGRAPH.

rendered in former wars; by the firmly tied red-tape of military bureauism, and by the deep-seated and well-founded fear of the auditors and comptrollers of the treasury. Nothing but time and experience—possibly nothing but disaster—could remove from the path of the Union President difficulties from which the Confederate President was, by the situation, quite free. In the beginning of the war, the military advantage was on the side of the Confederates, notwithstanding the greater resources of the North, which produced their effect only as the contest was prolonged.

FROM A PHOTOGRAPH.

After the firing of the first gun upon Sumter, the two sides were equally active in marshaling their forces on a line along the border States from the Atlantic coast of Virginia in the east to Kansas in the west. Many of the earlier collisions along this line were due rather to special causes or local feeling than to general military considerations. The prompt advance of the Union forces under McClellan to West Virginia was to protect that new-born free State. Patterson's movement to Hagerstown and thence to Harper's Ferry was to prevent Maryland from joining or aiding the rebellion, to re-open the Baltimore and Ohio railroad, and prevent invasion from the Shenandoah Valley. The Southerners having left the Union and set up the Confederacy upon the principle of State rights, in violation of that principle invaded the State of Kentucky in opposition to her apparent purpose of armed neutrality. That made Kentucky a field of early hostilities and helped to anchor her to the Union. Missouri was rescued from secession through the energy of General F. P. Blair and her other Union men, and by the indomitable will of Captain Lyon of the regular army, whose great work was accomplished under many disadvantages. In illustration of the difficulty with which the new condition of affairs penetrated the case-hardened bureauism of long peace, it may be mentioned that the venerable adjutant-general of the army, when a crisis was at hand in Missouri, came from a consultation with the President and Secretary Cameron, and with a sorry expression of countenance and an ominous shake of the head exclaimed, "It's bad, very bad; we're giving that young man Lyon a great deal too much power in Missouri."

Early in the contest another young Union officer came to the front. Major Irvin McDowell was appointed brigadier-general May 14th. He was forty-three years of age, of unexceptionable habits and great physical powers. His education, begun in France, was continued at the United States Military Academy, from which he was graduated in 1838. Always a close student, he was well informed outside as well as inside his profession. Distinguished in the Mexican war, intensely Union in his sentiments, full of energy and patriotism, outspoken in his opinions, highly esteemed by General Scott, on whose staff he had served, he at once secured the confidence of the President and the Secretary of War, under whose observation he was serving in Washington. Without political antecedents or

UNIFORM OF THE 2D OHIO AT BULL RUN. FROM A PHOTOGRAPH.

acquaintances, he was chosen for advancement on account of his record, his ability, and his vigor.

Northern forces had hastened to Washington upon the call of President Lincoln, but prior to May 24th they had been held rigidly on the north side of the Potomac. On the night of May 23d–24th, the Confederate pickets being then in sight of the Capitol, three columns were thrown across the river by General J. K. F. Mansfield, then commanding the Department of Washington, and a line from Alexandria below to chain-bridge above Washington was intrenched under guidance of able engineers. On the 27th Brigadier-General Irvin McDowell was placed in command south of the Potomac.‡

By the 1st of June the Southern Government had been transferred from Montgomery to Richmond, and the capitals of the Union and of the Confederacy stood defiantly confronting each other. General Scott was in chief command of the Union forces, with McDowell south of the Potomac, confronted by his old classmate, Beauregard, hot from the capture of Fort Sumter.

‡ The aspect of affairs was so threatening after President Lincoln's call of April 15th for 75,000 three-months militia, and General Scott was so averse to undertaking any active operations with such short-term troops, that, as early as May 3d, and without waiting for the meeting of Congress, the President entered upon the creation of an additional volunteer army to be composed of 42,034 three-years men, together with an increase of 22,714 regulars and 18,000 seamen.—J. B. F.

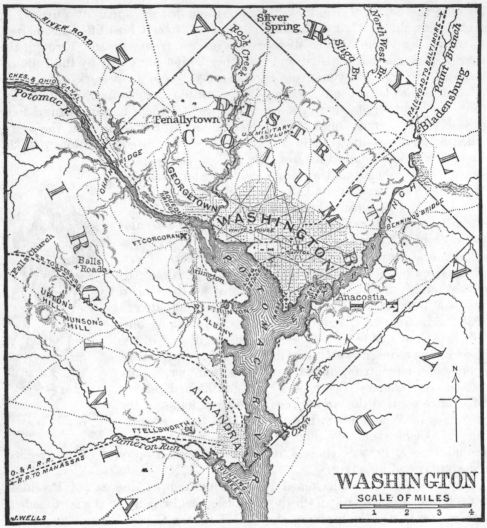

MAP OF THE VICINITY OF WASHINGTON, JULY, 1861.

General Patterson, of Pennsylvania, a veteran of the war of 1812 and the war with Mexico, was in command near Harper's Ferry, opposed by General Joseph E. Johnston. The Confederate President, Davis, then in Richmond, with General R. E. Lee as military adviser, exercised in person general military control of the Southern forces. The enemy to be engaged by McDowell occupied what was called the "Alexandria line," with headquarters at Manassas, the junction of the Orange and Alexandria with the Manassas Gap railroad. The stream known as Bull Run, some three miles in front of Manassas, was the line of defense. On Beauregard's right, 30 miles away, at the mouth of Aquia Creek, there was a Confederate brigade of 3000 men and 6 guns under General Holmes. The approach to Richmond from the Lower Chesapeake, threatened by General B. F. Butler, was guarded by Confederates under Generals Huger and Magruder.

On Beauregard's left, sixty miles distant, in the Lower Shenandoah Valley and separated from him by the Blue Ridge Mountains, was the Confederate army of the Shenandoah under command of General Johnston. Beauregard's authority did not extend over the forces of Johnston, Huger, Magruder, or Holmes, but Holmes was with him before the battle of Bull Run, and so was Johnston, who, as will appear more fully hereafter, joined at a decisive moment.

Early in June Patterson was pushing his column against Harper's Ferry, and on the 3d of that month McDowell was called upon by General Scott to submit "an estimate of the number and composition of a column to be pushed toward Manassas Junction and perhaps the Gap, say in 4 or 5 days, to favor Patterson's attack upon Harper's Ferry." McDowell had then been in command at Arlington less than a week, his raw regiments south of the Potomac were not yet brigaded, and this was the first

Head Quarters,
Military Department of
Washington, June 25th, 1861.

Pass Mr. Hubbard Esq.
over the Bridges & within the lines

By order of General Mansfield, Commanding.

Drake De Kay
Aide-de-Comp.

TURN OVER

FAC-SIMILE OF THE FACE OF A WASHINGTON PASS OF 1861.

The bold signature of "Drake De Kay" on the passes issued by General Mansfield while commanding the Department at Washington, gave celebrity to the young aide-de-camp whose duty it was to sign them. At the outbreak of the war Drake De Kay, who was the son of Commodore George C. De Kay, closed his shipping and commission office in New York, with no more ceremony than to pin to the door the statement, "Gone to Washington. Back at close of war." He took with

intimation he had of offensive operations. He reported, June 4th, that 12,000 infantry, 2 batteries, 6 or 8 companies of cavalry, and a reserve of 5000 ready to move from Alexandria would be required. Johnston, however, gave up Harper's Ferry to Patterson, and the diversion by McDowell was not ordered. But the public demand for an advance became imperative—stimulated perhaps by the successful dash of fifty men of the 2d United States Cavalry, under Lieutenant C. H. Tompkins, through the enemy's outposts at Fairfax Court House on the night of June 1st, and by the unfortunate result of the movement of a regiment under General Schenck toward Vienna, June 9th, as well as by a disaster to some of General Butler's troops on the 10th at Big Bethel, near Fort Monroe. On the 24th of June, in compliance with verbal instructions from General Scott, McDowell submitted a "plan of operations and the composition of the force required to carry it into effect." He estimated the Confederate force at Manassas Junction and its dependencies at 25,000 men, assumed that his movements could not be kept secret and that the enemy

him a detachment of his employees and offered his own and their services to General Scott "free of charge." Of course he was not allowed to bear the expense of his contingent, but his services were accepted, and he received as lieutenant the first appointment to the army from civil life during the war. He accepted a position on General Mansfield's staff and accompanied that officer to Newport News, where, as captain on the staff, he distinguished himself in several daring adventures, sometimes undertaken with the object of getting information of the enemy. In the second Bull Run campaign he was aide-de-camp to General Pope. Afterward he joined his regiment, the 14th Regulars, and he was brevetted major and lieutenant-colonel for gallant service at the Wilderness and at Spotsylvania.

We are indebted to Mr. Murat Halstead, editor of the Cincinnati "Commercial Gazette," for the "Drake De Kay Pass," here reproduced in fac-simile. Of the uses of a bold signature on the passes, Mr. Halstead writes with a characteristic touch of humor: "A statement I have heard, that the famous Drake De Kay passes were written to be read by torchlight at picket posts, reminds me that I have preserved one among

It is understood that the within named and subscriber accepts this pass on his word of honor that he is and will be ever loyal to the United States; and if hereafter found in arms against the Union, or in any way aiding her enemies, the penalty will be death.

M. Halstead

FAC-SIMILE OF THE BACK OF THE PASS.

my papers. It is inclosed. My recollection is that the pass was gotten up in this style that it might not be easily imitated. It was intended to supersede all other passes, and did so. The effect was to check the promiscuous running through the lines. It was regarded at the time as something oracular and formidable, and as likely to convey a salutary impression of the power and majesty of the United States of America. It was said that General Winfield Scott was much impressed by it."—EDITORS.

would call up additional forces from all quarters, and added: "If General J. E. Johnston's force is kept engaged by Major-General Patterson, and Major-General Butler occupies the force now in his vicinity, I think they will not be able to bring up more than 10,000 men, so we may calculate upon having to do with about 35,000 men." And as it turned out, that was about the number he "had to do with." For the advance, McDowell asked "a force of 30,000 of all arms, with a reserve of 10,000." He knew that Beauregard had batteries in position at several places in front of Bull Run and defensive works behind the Run and at Manassas Junction. The stream being fordable at many places, McDowell proposed in his plan of operations to turn the enemy's position and force him out of it by seizing or threatening his communications. Nevertheless, he said in his report:

"Believing the chances are greatly in favor of the enemy's accepting battle between this and the Junction and that the consequences of that battle will be of the greatest importance to the country, as establishing the prestige in this contest, on the one side or the other,—the more so as the two sections will be fairly represented by regiments from almost every State,—I think it of great consequence that, as for the most part our regiments are exceedingly raw and the best of them, with few exceptions, not over steady in line, they be organized into as many small fixed brigades as the number of regular colonels will admit, . . . so that the men may have as fair a chance as the nature of things and the comparative inexperience of most will allow."

This remarkably sound report was approved, and McDowell was directed to carry his plan into effect July 8th. But the government machinery worked slowly and there was jealousy in the way, so that the troops to bring his army up to the strength agreed upon did not reach him until the 16th.

Beauregard's Army of the Potomac at Manassas consisted of the brigades of Holmes, Bonham, Ewell, D. R. Jones, Longstreet, Cocke and Early, and of 3 regiments of infantry, 1 regiment and 3 battalions of cavalry, and 6 batteries of artillery, containing in all 27 guns, making an aggregate available force on the field of Bull Run of about 23,000 men. Johnston's army from the Shenandoah consisted of the brigades of Jackson, Bee, Bartow, and Kirby Smith, 2 regiments of infantry not brigaded, 1 regiment of cavalry (12 companies), and 5 batteries (20 guns), making an aggregate at Bull Run of 8340. ♭

McDowell's army consisted of 5 divisions, Tyler's First Division, containing 4 brigades (Keyes's, Schenck's, W. T. Sherman's, and Richardson's); Hunter's Second Division, containing 2 brigades (Andrew Porter's and Burnside's); Heintzelman's Third Division, containing 3 brigades (Franklin's, Willcox's, and Howard's); Runyon's Fourth Division (9 regiments not brigaded); and Miles's Fifth Division, containing 2 brigades (Blenker's and Davies's),—10 batteries of artillery, besides 2 guns attached to infantry regiments, 49 guns in all, and 7

♭ Beauregard himself has said that on the 18th of July he had along the line of Bull Run about 17,000 men; that on the 19th General Holmes joined him with about 3000 men; and that he "received from Richmond between the 18th and 21st about 2000 more"; and that Johnston brought about 8000 more, the advance arriving "on the morning of the 20th and the remainder about noon of the 21st," making his whole force, as he states it, "nearly 30,000 men of all arms." The figures are probably under the mark, as Hampton's Legion, McRea's regiment, a North Carolina "regiment and two battalions of Mississippi and Alabama" joined between the 17th and 21st. Beauregard's force may fairly be placed at 32,000; and the opposing armies, both in the aggregate and in the parts engaged, were nearer equal in that than in any other battle in Virginia.— J. B. F.

CAPITOL.

WHITE HOUSE.   CANAL.   WASHINGTON MONUMENT.

VIEW OF WASHINGTON FROM THE SIGNAL CAMP, GEORGETOWN HEIGHTS.—I.

companies of regular cavalry. Of the foregoing forces, 9 of the batteries and 8 companies of infantry were regulars, and 1 small battalion was marines. The aggregate force was about 35,000 men. Runyon's Fourth Division was 6 or 7 miles in the rear guarding the road to Alexandria, and, though counted in the aggregate, was not embraced in McDowell's order for battle.ꜟ

There was an ill-suppressed feeling of sympathy with the Confederacy in the Southern element of Washington society; but the halls of Congress resounded with the eloquence of Union speakers. Martial music filled the air, and war was the topic wherever men met. By day and night the tramp of soldiers was heard, and staff-officers and orderlies galloped through the streets between the headquarters of Generals Scott and McDowell. Northern enthusiasm was unbounded. "On to Richmond" was the war-cry. Public sentiment was irresistible, and in response to it the army advanced. It was a glorious spectacle. The various regiments were brilliantly uniformed according to the æsthetic taste of peace, and the silken banners they flung to the breeze were unsoiled and untorn. The bitter realities of war were nearer than we knew.

McDowell marched on the afternoon of July 16th, the men carrying three days' rations in their haversacks; provision wagons were to follow from Alexandria the next day. On the morning of the 18th his forces were concentrated at Centreville, a point about 20 miles west of the Potomac and

ꜟ The average length of service of McDowell's men prior to the battle was about sixty days. The longest in service were the three-months men, and of these he had fourteen regiments.— J. B. F.

ALEXANDRIA.   ARLINGTON.

LONG BRIDGE.   GEORGETOWN OBSERVATORY.

VIEW FROM THE SIGNAL CAMP.—II. FROM A SKETCH MADE AT THE TIME.

6 or 7 miles east of Manassas Junction. Beauregard's outposts fell back without resistance. Bull Run, flowing south-easterly, is about half-way between Centreville and Manassas Junction, and, owing to its abrupt banks, the timber with which it was fringed, and some artificial defenses at the fords, was a formidable obstacle. The stream was fordable, but all the crossings for eight miles, from Union Mills on the south to the Stone Bridge on the north, were defended by Beauregard's forces. [See map, page 180.] The Warrenton Turnpike, passing through Centreville, leads nearly due west, crossing Bull Run at the Stone Bridge. The direct road from Centreville to Manassas crosses Bull Run at Mitchell's Ford, half a mile or so above another crossing known as Blackburn's Ford. Union Mills was covered by Ewell's brigade, supported after the 18th by Holmes's brigade; McLean's Ford, next to the north, was covered by D. R. Jones's brigade; Blackburn's Ford was defended by Longstreet's brigade, supported by Early's brigade; Mitchell's Ford was held by Bonham's brigade, with an outpost of two guns and an infantry support east of Bull Run; the stream between Mitchell's Ford and the Stone Bridge was covered by Cocke's brigade; the Stone Bridge on the Confederate left was held by Evans with 1 regiment and Wheat's special battalion of infantry, 1 battery of 4 guns, and 2 companies of cavalry. ☆

☆ The state of General Beauregard's mind at the time is indicated by the following telegram on the 17th of July from him to Jefferson Davis: "The enemy has assaulted my outposts in heavy force. I have fallen back on the line of Bull Run and will make a stand at Mitchell's Ford. If his force is over-

THE STONE CHURCH, CENTREVILLE. FROM A PHOTOGRAPH TAKEN IN MARCH, 1862.

McDowell was compelled to wait at Centreville until his provision wagons arrived and he could issue rations. His orders having carried his leading division under Tyler no farther than Centreville, he wrote that officer at 8:15 A. M. on the 18th, "Observe well the roads to Bull Run and to Warrenton. Do not bring on an engagement, but keep up the impression that we are moving on Manassas." McDowell then went to the extreme left of his line to examine the country with reference to a sudden movement of the army to turn the enemy's right flank. The reconnoissance showed him that the country was unfavorable to the movement, and he abandoned it. While he was gone to the left, Tyler, presumably to " keep up the impression that we were moving on Manassas," went forward from Centreville with a squadron of cavalry and two companies of infantry for the purpose of making a reconnoissance of Mitchell's and Blackburn's fords along the direct road to Manassas. The force of the enemy at these fords has just been given. Reaching the crest of the ridge overlooking the valley of Bull Run and a mile or so from the stream, the enemy was seen on the opposite bank, and Tyler brought up Benjamin's artillery, 2 20-pounder rifled guns, Ayres's field battery of 6 guns, and Richardson's brigade of infantry. The 20-pounders opened from the ridge and a few shots were exchanged with the enemy's batteries. Desiring more information than the long-range cannonade afforded,

whelming, I shall retire to Rappahannock railroad bridge, saving my command for defense there and future operations. Please inform Johnston of this *via* Staunton, and also Holmes. Send forward any reënforcements at the earliest possible instant and by every possible means." The alarm in this dispatch and the apprehension it shows of McDowell's "overwhelming" strength are not in harmony with the more recent assurance of the Confederate commander, that through sources in Washington treasonable to the Union, and in other ways, he "was almost as well informed of the strength of the hostile army in my [his] front as its commander."—J. B. F.

Tyler ordered Richardson's brigade and a section of Ayres's battery, supported by a squadron of cavalry, to move from the ridge across the open bottom of Bull Run and take position near the stream and have skirmishers "scour the thick woods" which skirted it. Two regiments of infantry, 2 pieces of artillery, and a squadron of cavalry moved down the slope into the woods and opened fire, driving Bonham's outpost to the cover of intrenchments across the stream. The brigades of Bonham and Longstreet, the latter being reën-forced for the occasion by Early's brigade, responded at short range to the fire of the Federal reconnoitering force and drove it back in disorder. Tyler reported that having satisfied himself "that the enemy was in force," and ascertained "the position of his batteries," he withdrew.| This unauthorized reconnoissance, called by the Federals the affair at Blackburn's Ford, was regarded at the time by the Confederates as a serious attack, and was dignified by the name of the "battle of Bull Run," the engagement of the 21st being called by them the battle of Manassas. The Confederates, feeling that they had repulsed a heavy and real attack, were encouraged by the result. The Federal troops, on the other hand, were greatly depressed. The regiment which suffered most was completely demoralized, and McDowell thought that the depression of the repulse was felt throughout his army and produced its effect upon the Pennsylvania regiment and the New York battery which insisted (their terms having expired) upon their discharge, and on the 21st, as he expressed it, "marched to the rear to the sound of the enemy's cannon." Even

UNIFORM OF THE 11TH NEW YORK (FIRE ZOUAVES) AT BULL RUN. FROM A PHOTOGRAPH. ⚓

Tyler himself felt the depressing effect of his repulse, if we may judge by his cautious and feeble action on the 21st when dash was required.

The operations of the 18th confirmed McDowell in his opinion that with his raw troops the Confederate position should be turned instead of attacked in front. Careful examination had satisfied him that the country did not favor a movement to turn the enemy's right. On the night of the 18th

---

| The casualties in the affair were: Union, 1 officer and 18 enlisted men killed; 1 officer and 37 enlisted men wounded; 26 enlisted men missing,— aggregate, 83. Confederate (Beauregard in his official report of 1861), "15 killed and 53 wounded men, several of whom have since died."— J. B. F.

⚓ The 11th New York, or "The First Fire Zouaves," was recruited in April, 1861, from among the firemen of New York City by Colonel E. Elmer Ellsworth, a young man of twenty-four, who, before the war, had organized in Chicago a fine body of Zouaves and exhibited the Zouave drill in several cities of the North. President Lincoln, who had been escorted to Washington by Ellsworth, appointed him to a second lieutenancy in the regular army. On the morning of May 24th, when the Union forces crossed into Virginia, Ellsworth's Zouaves occupied the city of Alexandria. The colonel, with the secretary and the chaplain of the regiment, a correspondent of the New York "Tribune," and a sergeant's squad were proceeding toward the center of the town, when they saw a secession flag flying from the Marshall house. With his two companions Ellsworth ascended to the roof, leaving Private Francis E. Brownell at the foot of the garret stairs. On descending those stairs with the flag in his hands, Ellsworth was shot through the heart by James T. Jackson, the keeper of the hotel, who emptied the second barrel of his shot-gun at Brownell. The latter, who was not hit, shot Jackson through the head. Colonel Ellsworth had endeared himself to President Lincoln, who was deeply affected by his death. For several hours the remains lay in state in the East Room of the White House. His death made a profound impression and greatly stimulated the war feeling in the North.— EDITORS.

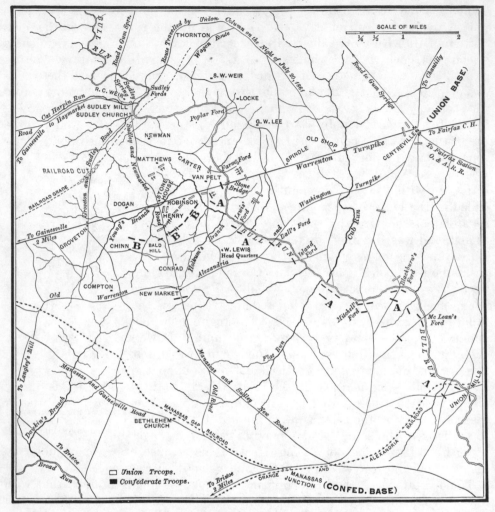

OUTLINE MAP OF THE BATTLE-FIELD OF BULL RUN.

A, A, A, A, A. General line of Confederate dispositions during the skirmish at Mitchell's and Blackburn's
Fords (July 18th), and until the morning of the main
engagement (July 21st).

B, B, B. General line of Confederate dispositions,
made to repel McDowell's flank attack by the Sudley
and Newmarket Road.

The Union dispositions are represented as they
were at the climax of the fighting on the Henry
plateau.

the haversacks of his men were empty, and had to be replenished from the
provision wagons, which were late in getting up. Nor had he yet determined
upon his point or plan of attack. While resting and provisioning his men,
he devoted the 19th and 20th to a careful examination by his engineers of
the enemy's position and the intervening country. His men, not soldiers,
but civilians in uniform, unused to marching, hot, weary, and footsore,
dropped down as they had halted and bivouacked on the roads about Centreville. Notwithstanding Beauregard's elation over the affair at Blackburn's
Ford on the 18th, he permitted the 19th and 20th to pass without a movement to follow up the advantage he had gained. During these two days,
McDowell carefully examined the Confederate position, and made his plan

to manœuvre the enemy out of it. Beauregard ordered no aggressive movement until the 21st, and then, as appears from his own statement, through miscarriage of orders and lack of apprehension on the part of subordinates, the effort was a complete *fiasco*, with the comical result of frightening his own troops, who, late in the afternoon, mistook the return of one of their brigades for an attack by McDowell's left, and the serious result of interfering with the pursuit after he had gained the battle of the 21st.

But Beauregard, though not aggressive on the 19th and 20th, was not idle within his own lines. The Confederate President had authorized Johnston, Beauregard's senior, to use his discretion in moving to the support of Manassas, and Beauregard, urging Johnston to do so, sent railway transportation for the Shenandoah forces. But, as he states, "he at the same time submitted the alternative proposition to Johnston that, having passed the Blue Ridge, he should assemble his forces, press forward by way of Aldie, north-west of Manassas, and fall upon McDowell's right rear," while he, Beauregard, "prepared for the operation at the first sound of the conflict, should strenuously assume the offensive in front." "The situation and circumstances specially favored the signal success of such an operation," says Beauregard. An attack by two armies moving from opposite points upon an enemy, with the time of attack for one depending upon the sound of the other's cannon, is hazardous even with well-disciplined and well-seasoned troops, and is next to fatal with raw levies. Johnston chose the wiser course of moving by rail to Manassas, thus preserving the benefit of "interior lines," which, Beauregard says, was the "sole military advantage at the moment that the Confederates possessed."

SUDLEY SPRINGS HOTEL, ON THE LINE OF McDOWELL'S FLANK ATTACK UPON THE CONFEDERATE FORCES. SKETCHED FROM THE MILL, A FEW RODS ABOVE THE FORD.

The campaign which General Scott required McDowell to make was undertaken with the understanding that Johnston should be prevented from joining Beauregard. With no lack of confidence in himself, McDowell was dominated by the feeling of subordination and deference to General Scott which at that time pervaded the whole army, and General Scott, who controlled both McDowell and Patterson, assured McDowell that Johnston should not join Beauregard without having "Patterson on his heels." Yet Johnston's army, nearly nine thousand strong, joined Beauregard, Bee's brigade and Johnston in person arriving on the morning of the 20th, the remainder

SUDLEY SPRINGS FORD, LOOKING NORTH. FROM A SKETCH MADE IN 1884.

This stream is the Cat Harpin Run, which empties into Bull Run a short distance below the Sudley Springs Ford. In making the flank movement the Union troops, under Generals Hunter and Heintzelman, crossed this ford, followed later in the day by the ambulances and munition wagons. The retreat, also, was largely by this ford. The ruins of the Sudley Sulphur Spring House are shown on the left. The Sudley church, which was the main hospital after the fight, is a short distance south.— EDITORS.

about noon on the 21st. Although the enforced delay at Centreville enabled McDowell to provision his troops and gain information upon which to base an excellent plan of attack, it proved fatal by affording time for a junction of the opposing forces. On the 21st of July General Scott addressed a dispatch to McDowell, saying: "It is known that a strong reënforcement left Winchester on the afternoon of the 18th, which you will also have to beat. Four new regiments will leave to-day to be at Fairfax Station to-night. Others shall follow to-morrow — twice the number if necessary." When this dispatch was penned, McDowell was fighting the "strong reënforcement" which left Winchester on the 18th. General Scott's report that Beauregard had been reënforced, the information that four regiments had been sent to McDowell, and the promise that twice the number would be sent *if necessary*, all came too late — and Patterson came not at all. ↓

↓ On the 17th of July Patterson, with some 16,000 three-months men, whose terms began to expire on the 24th, was at Charlestown, and Johnston, with about the same number, was at Winchester. On that day General Scott telegraphed Patterson, "McDowell's first day's work has driven the enemy behind Fairfax Court House. Do not let the enemy amuse and delay you with a small force in front while he reënforces the Junction with his main body." To this Patterson replied at half-past 1 o'clock in the morning of the 18th, stating his difficulties and asking, "Shall I attack?" General Scott answered on the same day: "I have certainly been expecting you to beat the enemy," or that you "at least had occupied him by threats and demonstrations. You have been at least his equal and I suppose superior in numbers. Has he not stolen a march and sent reënforcements toward Manassas Junction?" Patterson replied on the same day (18th), "The enemy has stolen no march

During the 19th and 20th the bivouacs of McDowell's army at Centreville, almost within cannon range of the enemy, were thronged by visitors, official and unofficial, who came in carriages from Washington, bringing their own supplies. They were under no military restraint, and passed to and fro among the troops as they pleased, giving the scene the appearance of a monster military picnic. ♭ Among others, the venerable Secretary of War, Cameron, called upon McDowell. Whether due to a naturally serious expression, to a sense of responsibility, to a premonition of the fate of his brother who fell upon the field on the 21st, or to other cause, his countenance showed apprehension of evil; but men generally were confident and jovial.

SUDLEY SPRINGS FORD, LOOKING TOWARD THE BATTLE-FIELD. FROM A WAR-TIME PHOTOGRAPH.

On the right are the ruins of the Sudley Sulphur Spring House. The building on the hill is Sudley Church. It is a mile by the Sudley and Manassas road from the ford to where the battle began.—EDITORS.

McDowell's plan of battle promulgated on the 20th, was to turn the enemy's left, force him from his defensive position, and, "if possible, destroy the railroad leading from Manassas to the Valley of Virginia, where the enemy has a large force." He did not know when he issued this order that Johnston had joined Beauregard, though he suspected it. Miles's Fifth Division, with Richardson's brigade of Tyler's division, and a strong force of artillery was to

upon me. I have caused him to be reënforced"; and at 1 o'clock P. M. on that day he added: "I have succeeded, in accordance with the wishes of the General-in-Chief, in keeping General Johnston's force at Winchester." At the very hour that Patterson was writing this dispatch Johnston's advance was leaving Winchester. On the 18th Johnston telegraphed to Richmond that Patterson was at Charlestown, and said: "Unless he prevents it, we shall move toward General Beauregard to-day." He moved accordingly, and the Confederate armies were united for battle. It rested, however, with higher authority than Patterson to establish between his army and McDowell's the relations that the occasion called for. In considering the requirements for McDowell's movement against Manassas, General Scott gave great weight to the general and irresistible fear then prevailing in Washington that the capital might be seized by a dash. Its direct defense was the first purpose of the three-months militia. The Potomac at Washington was itself a strong barrier, and with the field-works on its south bank afforded security in that quarter. The danger was thought to be from the Shenandoah, and that induced the Government to keep Patterson in the valley. Indeed, on the 30th of June Colonel C. P. Stone's command was ordered from Point of Rocks to Patterson at Martinsburg, where it arrived on the 8th of July; whereas the offensive campaign against Manassas, ordered soon after, required Patterson to go to

Stone, as he proposed to do June 21st, instead of Stone to Patterson. The campaign of McDowell was forced upon General Scott by public opinion, but did not relieve the authorities from the fear that Johnston might rush down and seize Washington. General Scott, under the pressure of the offensive in one quarter and the defensive in another, imposed upon Patterson the double task, difficult if not impossible, of preventing Johnston from moving on the capital and from joining Beauregard. If that task was possible, it could have been accomplished only by persistent fighting, and that General Scott was unwilling to order; though in his dispatch of the 18th in reply to Patterson's question, "Shall I attack?" he said, "I have certainly been expecting you to beat the enemy." Prior to that, his instructions to Patterson had enjoined caution. As soon as McDowell advanced, Patterson was upon an exterior line and in a false military position. Admitting that he might have done more to detain Johnston, bad strategy was probably more to blame for the result than any action or lack of action on Patterson's part.—J. B. F.

♭ The presence of senators, congressmen, and other civilians upon the field on the 21st gave rise to extravagant and absurd stories, in which alleged forethought and valor among them are contrasted with a lack of these qualities in the troops. The plain truth is that the non-combatants and their vehicles merely increased the confusion and demoralization of the retreat.—J. B. F.

remain in reserve at Centreville, prepare defensive works there and threaten Blackburn's Ford. Tyler's First Division, which was on the turnpike in advance, was to move at 2:30 A. M., threaten the Stone Bridge and open fire upon it at daybreak. This demonstration was to be vigorous, its first purpose being to divert attention from the movements of the turning column.

As soon as Tyler's troops cleared the way, Hunter's Second Division, followed by Heintzelman's Third Division, was to move to a point on the Warrenton Turnpike about 1 or 2 miles east of Stone Bridge and there take a country road to the right, cross the Run at Sudley Springs, come down upon the flank and rear of the enemy at the Stone Bridge, and force him to open the way for Tyler's division to cross there and attack, fresh and in full force.

Tyler's start was so late and his advance was so slow as to hold Hunter and Heintzelman 2 or 3 hours on the mile or two of the turnpike between

THE STONE BRIDGE OVER BULL RUN, LOOKING TOWARD CENTREVILLE. FROM A SKETCH MADE IN 1884.

their camps and the point at which they were to turn off for the flank march. This delay, and the fact that the flank march proved difficult and some 12 miles instead of about 6 as was expected, were of serious moment. The flanking column did not cross at Sudley Springs until 9:30 instead of 7, the long march, with its many interruptions, tired out the men, and the delay gave the enemy time to discover the turning movement. Tyler's operations against the Stone Bridge were feeble and ineffective. By 8 o'clock Evans was satisfied that he was in no danger in front, and perceived the movement to turn his position. He was on the left of the Confederate line, guarding the point where the Warrenton Turnpike, the great highway to the field, crossed Bull Run, the Confederate line of defense. He had no instructions to guide him in the emergency that had arisen. But he did not hesitate. Reporting his information and purpose to the adjoining commander, Cocke, and leaving 4 companies of infantry to deceive and hold Tyler at the bridge, Evans before 9 o'clock turned his back upon the point he was set to guard, marched a mile away, and, seizing the high ground to the north of Young's Branch of Bull Run, formed line of battle at right angles to his former line, his left resting near the Sudley Springs road, by which Burnside with the head of the turning column was approaching, thus covering the Warrenton Turnpike and opposing a determined front to the Federal advance upon the Confederate left and rear.\ In his rear to the south lay the valley of Young's Branch, and rising from that was the higher ridge or plateau on which the Robinson house and the Henry house were situated, and on which the main action took place in the afternoon. Burnside, finding Evans across his path, promptly formed line of battle and attacked about 9:45 A. M. Hunter, the division commander, who was at the head of Burnside's brigade directing the formation of the first skirmish line, was severely wounded and taken to the rear at the opening of the action. Evans not only repulsed but pursued the troops that made the attack upon him. Andrew Porter's brigade of Hunter's division followed Burnside closely and came to his support. In the mean time Bee had formed a Confederate line of battle with his and Bartow's brigades of Johnston's army on the Henry house plateau, a stronger position than the one held by Evans, and desired Evans to fall back to that line; but Evans, probably feeling bound to cover the Warrenton Turnpike and hold it against Tyler as well as against the flanking column, insisted that Bee should move across the valley to his support, which was done.

After Bee joined Evans, the preliminary battle continued to rage upon the ground chosen by the latter. The opposing forces were Burnside's and Porter's brigades, with one regiment of Heintzelman's division on the Federal side, and Evans's, Bee's, and Bartow's brigades on the Confederate side. The Confederates were dislodged and driven back to the Henry house

FATIGUE UNIFORM AND KILTS OF THE 79TH NEW YORK. ☆

plateau, where Bee had previously formed line and where what Beauregard called "the mingled remnants of Bee's, Bartow's, and Evans's commands" were re-formed under cover of Stonewall Jackson's brigade of Johnston's army.

\ Evans's action was probably one of the best pieces of soldiership on either side during the campaign, but it seems to have received no special commendation from his superiors.—J. B. F.

☆ William Todd, of Company B, 79th New York (Highlanders), writing to correct a statement to the effect "that the 79th New York wore the Highland dress at the battle of Bull Run," says: "If by that is meant the 'kilts,' it is an error. It is true that all the officers and many of the men did wear that uniform when we left the city in June, 1861, and on dress-parade occasions in Washington, but when we went into Virginia it was laid aside, together with the plaid trousers worn by all the men on ordinary occasions, and we donned the ordinary blue. Captain —— was the only one who insisted on wearing the kilts on the march to Bull Run, but the day before we reached Centreville the kilts were the cause of his drawing upon himself much ridicule, and when we started for the battle-field on that Sunday morning he, also, appeared in ordinary blue uniform."—EDITORS.

THE SUDLEY SPRINGS ROAD, LOOKING NORTH FROM THE SLOPE OF THE HENRY HOUSE HILL.

In the middle-ground on the Warrenton turnpike stands the Stone house, a central landmark in both battles of Bull Run. The bank in the right foreground was a cover during the first battle for some of the supports of Griffin's and Ricketts's batteries that were on the Henry house hill, the crest of which is two hundred and fifty yards from the right of the picture. In the first battle the fighting began on the Matthews hill, seen in the background behind the Stone house, and was most desperate on the Henry hill. Young's Branch (see map, page 180) crosses the Sudley road near its junction with the turnpike, and flows near the Stone house.

The time of this repulse, as proved by so accurate an authority as Stonewall Jackson, was before 11:30 A. M., and this is substantially confirmed by Beauregard's official report made at the time. Sherman and Keyes had nothing to do with it. They did not begin to cross Bull Run until noon. Thus, after nearly two hours' stubborn fighting with the forces of Johnston, which General Scott had promised should be kept away, McDowell won the first advantage; but Johnston had cost him dearly.

During all this time Johnston and Beauregard had been waiting near Mitchell's Ford for the development of the attack they had ordered by their right upon McDowell at Centreville. The gravity of the situation upon their left had not yet dawned upon them. What might the result have been if the Union column had not been detained by Tyler's delay in moving out in the early morning, or if Johnston's army, to which Bee, Bartow, and Jackson belonged, had not arrived?

But the heavy firing on the left soon diverted Johnston and Beauregard from all thought of an offensive movement with their right, and decided them, as Beauregard has said, "to hurry up all available reënforcements, including the reserves that were to have moved upon Centreville, to our left, and fight the battle out in that quarter." Thereupon Beauregard ordered "Ewell, Jones, and Longstreet to make a strong demonstration all along their front on the other side of Bull Run, and ordered the reserves, Holmes's brigade with six guns, and Early's brigade, to move swiftly to the left," and he and Johnston set out at full speed for the point of conflict, which they reached while Bee was attempting to rally his men about Jackson's brigade on the Henry house plateau. McDowell had waited in the morning at the point on the Warrenton Turnpike where his flanking column turned to the right, until the troops, except Howard's brigade, which he halted at that point, had passed. He gazed silently and with evident pride upon the gay regiments as they filed briskly but quietly past in the freshness of the early morning, and then, remarking to his staff, "Gentlemen, that is a big force," he mounted and moved forward to the field by way of Sudley Springs. He reached the scene of actual conflict somewhat earlier than Johnston and Beauregard did, and, seeing the enemy driven across the valley of Young's Branch and behind the Warrenton Turnpike, at once sent a swift aide-de-camp to Tyler with orders to "press the attack" at the Stone Bridge. Tyler acknowledged that he received this order by 11 o'clock. It was Tyler's division upon which McDowell relied for the decisive fighting of the day. He knew that the march of the turning column would be fatiguing, and when by a sturdy fight it had cleared the Warrenton Turnpike for the advance of Tyler's division, it had, in fact, done more than its fair proportion of the work. But Tyler did not attempt to force the passage of the Stone Bridge, which, after about 8 o'clock, was defended by only four companies of infantry, though he admitted that by the plan of battle, when Hunter and Heintzelman had attacked the enemy in the vicinity of the Stone Bridge, "he was to force the passage of Bull Run at that point and attack the enemy in flank."⌡ Soon after McDowell's arrival at the front, Burnside rode up to him and said that his brigade had borne the brunt of the battle, that it was out of ammunition, and that he wanted permission to withdraw, refit and fill cartridge-boxes. McDowell in the excitement of the occasion gave reluctant consent, and the brigade, which certainly had done nobly, marched to the rear, stacked arms, and took no further part in the fight. Having sent the order to Tyler to press his attack and orders to the rear of the turning column to hurry forward, McDowell, like Beauregard, rushed in person into the conflict, and by the force of circumstances became for the time the commander of the turning column and the force actually engaged, rather than the commander of his whole army. With the exception of sending his adjutant-general to find and hurry Tyler forward, his subsequent orders were mainly or wholly to the troops under his own observation. Unlike Beauregard, he had no Johnston in rear with full authority and knowledge of the situation to throw forward reserves and reënforcements. It was not until 12 o'clock that Sherman received orders from Tyler to cross the stream, which he did at a ford above the Stone Bridge, going to the assistance of Hunter. Sherman reported to McDowell

⌡ After the affair at Blackburn's Ford on the 18th and Tyler's action in the battle of the 21st, a bitterness between Tyler and McDowell grew up which lasted till they died. As late as 1884, McDowell, writing to me of Tyler's criticism of him after the war, said, "How I have been punished for my leniency to that man! If there is anything clearer to me than anything else with reference to our operations in that campaign, it is that if we had had another commander for our right we should have had a complete and brilliant success."— J. B. F.

CAPTAIN CHARLES GRIFFIN, AFTERWARD
MAJOR-GENERAL.

on the field and joined in the pursuit of Bee's forces across the valley of Young's Branch. Keyes's brigade, accompanied by Tyler in person, followed across the stream where Sherman forded, but without uniting with the other forces on the field, made a feeble advance upon the slope of the plateau toward the Robinson house, and then about 2 o'clock filed off by flank to its left and, sheltered by the east front of the bluff that forms the plateau, marched down Young's Branch out of sight of the enemy and took no further part in the engagement. McDowell did not know where it was, nor did he then know that Schenck's brigade of Tyler's division did not cross the Run at all.

The line taken up by Stonewall Jackson upon which Bee, Bartow, and Evans rallied on the southern part of the plateau was a very strong one. The ground was high and afforded the cover of a curvilinear wood with the concave side toward the Federal line of attack. According to Beauregard's official report made at the time, he had upon this part of the field, at the beginning, 6500 infantry, 13 pieces of artillery, and 2 companies of cavalry, and this line was continuously reënforced from Beauregard's own reserves and by the arrival of the troops from the Shenandoah Valley.

To carry this formidable position, McDowell had at hand the brigades of Franklin, Willcox, Sherman, and Porter, Palmer's battalion of regular cavalry, and Ricketts's and Griffin's regular batteries. Porter's brigade had been reduced and shaken by the morning fight. Howard's brigade was in reserve and only came into action late in the afternoon. The men, unused to field service, and not yet over the hot and dusty march from the Potomac, had been under arms since midnight. The plateau, however, was promptly assaulted, the northern part of it was carried, the batteries of Ricketts and Griffin were planted near the Henry house, and McDowell clambered to the upper story of that structure to get a glance at the whole field. Upon the Henry house plateau, of which the Confederates held the southern and the Federals the northern part, the tide of battle ebbed and flowed as McDowell pushed in Franklin's, Willcox's, Sherman's, Porter's, and at last Howard's brigades, and as Beauregard put into action reserves which Johnston sent from the right and reënforcements which he hurried forward from the Shenandoah Valley as they arrived by cars. On the plateau, Beauregard says, the disadvantage of his "smooth-bore guns was reduced by the shortness of range." The short range was due to the Federal advance, and the several struggles for the plateau were at close quarters and gallant on both sides. The batteries of Ricketts and Griffin, by their fine discipline, wonderful daring, and matchless skill, were the prime features in the fight. The battle was not lost till they were lost. When in their advanced and perilous position, and just after their infantry supports had been driven over the slopes, a fatal mistake occurred. A regiment of infantry came out of the woods on Griffin's right, and as he was in the act of opening upon it with canister, he was deterred by the assurance of Major Barry, the chief of artillery, that it "was a regiment sent by Colonel Heintzelman to support the battery."⚓ A moment more and the doubtful regiment proved its identity by a deadly volley, and, as Griffin states in his official report, "every cannoneer was cut down and a large number of horses killed,

CAPTAIN JAMES B. RICKETTS, AFTERWARD MAJOR-GENERAL.

leaving the battery (which was without support excepting in name) perfectly helpless." The effect upon Ricketts was equally fatal. He, desperately wounded, and Ramsay, his lieutenant, killed, lay in the wreck of the battery. Beauregard speaks of his last advance on the plateau as "leaving in our final possession the Robinson and Henry houses, with most of Ricketts's and Griffin's batteries, the men of which were mostly shot down where they bravely stood by their guns." Having become separated from McDowell, I fell in with Barnard, his chief engineer, and while together we observed the New York Fire Zouaves, who had been supporting Griffin's battery, fleeing to the rear in their gaudy uniforms, in utter confusion. Thereupon

⚓ Griffin himself told me so as we rode together after leaving Centreville. He and I were classmates and warm friends.— J. B. F.

Major Wm. F. Barry gives, in his report, this explanation of the disaster to the batteries:

"Returning to the position occupied by Ricketts' and Griffin's batteries, I received an order from General McDowell to advance two batteries to an eminence [the Henry Hill] specially designated by him, about eight hundred yards in front of the line previously occupied by our artillery, and very near the position first occupied by the enemy's batteries. I therefore ordered these two batteries to move forward at once, and, as soon as they were in motion, went for and procured as supports the 11th (Fire Zouaves) and the 14th (Brooklyn) New York regiments. I accompanied the former regiment to guide it to its proper position, and Colonel Heintzelman, 17th U. S. Infantry, performed the same service for the 14th, on the right of the 11th. A squadron of United States cavalry under Captain Colburn, 1st Cavalry, was subsequently ordered as additional support. We were soon upon the ground designated, and the two batteries at once opened a very effective fire upon the enemy's left. The new position had scarcely been occupied when a

troop of the enemy's cavalry, debouching from a piece of woods close upon our right flank, charged down upon the New York 11th. The Zouaves, catching sight of the cavalry a few moments before they were upon them, broke ranks to such a degree that the cavalry dashed through without doing them much harm. The Zouaves gave them a scattering fire as they passed, which emptied five saddles and killed three horses. A few minutes afterward a regiment of the enemy's infantry, covered by a high fence, presented itself in line on the left and front of the two batteries at not more than sixty or seventy yards' distance, and delivered a volley full upon the batteries and their supports. Lieutenant Ramsay, 1st Artillery, was killed, and Captain Ricketts, 1st Artillery, was wounded, and a number of men and horses were killed or disabled by this close and well-directed volley. The 11th and 14th regiments instantly broke and fled in confusion to the rear, and in spite of the repeated and earnest efforts of Colonel Heintzelman with the latter, and myself with the former, refused to rally and return to the support of the batteries. The enemy, seeing the guns thus abandoned by their supports, rushed upon them, and driving off the cannoneers, who, with their officers, stood bravely at their posts until the last moment, captured them, ten in number. These were the only guns taken by the enemy on the field."—EDITORS.

THE CONTEST FOR THE HENRY HILL.

Colonel William T. Sherman, who commanded the Third Brigade of Tyler's division, describes as follows some of the efforts to regain the Henry Hill after the capture of Griffin's and Ricketts's batteries: "Before reaching the crest of this [Henry] hill, the roadway [see picture, page 186] was worn deep enough to afford shelter, and I kept the several regiments in it as long as possible; but when the Wisconsin 2d was abreast of the enemy, by order of Major Wadsworth, of General McDowell's staff, I ordered it to leave the roadway by the left flank, and to attack the enemy. This regiment ascended to the brow of the hill steadily, received the severe fire of the enemy, returned it with spirit, and advanced delivering its fire. This regiment is uniformed in gray cloth, almost identical with that of the great bulk of the secession army, and when the regiment fell into confusion and retreated toward the road, there was an universal cry that they were being fired on by our own men. The regiment rallied again, passed the brow of the hill a second time, but was again repulsed in disorder. By this time the New York 79th had closed up, and in like manner it was ordered to cross the brow of the hill and drive the enemy from cover. It was impossible to get a good view of this ground. In it there was one battery of artillery, which poured an incessant fire upon our advancing columns, and the ground was very irregular, with small clusters of pines, affording shelter, of which the enemy took good advantage. The fire of rifles and musketry was very severe. The 79th, headed by its colonel (Cameron), charged across the hill, and for a short time the contest was severe. They rallied several times under fire, but finally broke and gained the cover of the hill. This left the field open to the New York 69th, Colonel Corcoran, who in his turn led his regiment over the crest, and had in full open view the ground so severely contested. The firing was very severe, and the roar of cannon, muskets, and rifles incessant. It was manifest the enemy was here in great force, far superior to us at that point. The 69th held the ground for some time, but finally fell back in disorder. . . . Here, about 3:30 P. M., began the scene of confusion and disorder that characterized the remainder of the day."

I rode back to where I knew Burnside's brigade was at rest, and stated to Burnside the condition of affairs, with the suggestion that he form and move his brigade to the front. Returning, I again met Barnard, and as the battle seemed to him and me to be going against us, and not knowing where McDowell was, with the concurrence of Barnard, as stated in his official report, I immediately sent a note to Miles, telling him to move two brigades of his reserve up to the Stone Bridge and telegraph to Washington to send forward all the troops that could be spared.

After the arrival of Howard's brigade, McDowell for the last time pressed up the slope to the plateau, forced back the Confederate line, and regained possession of the Henry and Robinson houses and of the lost batteries. But there were no longer cannoneers to man or horses to move these guns that had done so much. By the arrival upon this part of the field of his own reserves and Kirby Smith's brigade of Johnston's army about half-past 3,

Beauregard extended his left to outflank McDowell's shattered, shortened, and disconnected line, and the Federals left the field about half-past 4. Until then they had fought wonderfully well for raw troops. There were no fresh forces on

the field to support or encourage them, and the men seemed to be seized simultaneously by the conviction that it was no use to do anything more and they might as well start home. Cohesion was lost, the organizations with some exceptions being disintegrated, and the men quietly walked off. There was no special excitement except that arising from the frantic efforts of officers to stop men who paid little or no attention to anything that was said. On the high ground by the Matthews house, about where Evans had taken position in the morning to check Burnside, McDowell and his staff, aided by other officers, made a desperate but futile effort to arrest the masses and form them into line. There, I went to Arnold's battery as it came by, and advised that he unlimber and make a stand as a rallying-point, which he did, saying he was in fair condition and ready to fight as long as there was any fighting to be done. But all efforts failed. The stragglers moved past the guns, in spite of all that could be done, and, as

UNIFORM OF THE GARI-
BALDI GUARDS,
COLONEL D'UTASSY.

stated in his report, Arnold at my direction joined Sykes's battalion of infantry of Porter's brigade and Palmer's battalion of cavalry, all of the regular army, to cover the rear, as the men trooped back in great disorder across Bull Run. There were some hours of daylight for the Confederates to gather the fruits of victory, but a few rounds of shell and canister checked all the pursuit that was attempted, and the occasion called for no sacrifices or valorous deeds by the stanch regulars of the rear-guard. There was no panic, in the ordinary meaning of the word, until the retiring soldiers, guns, wagons, congressmen, and carriages were fired upon, on the road east of Bull Run. Then the panic began, and the bridge over Cub Run being rendered impassable for vehicles by a wagon that was upset upon it, utter confusion set in: pleasure-carriages, gun-carriages, and ammunition wagons which could not be put across the Run were abandoned and blocked the way, and stragglers broke and threw aside their muskets and cut horses from their harness and rode off upon them. In leaving the field the men took the same routes, in a general way, by which they had reached it. Hence when the men of Hunter's and Heintzelman's divisions got back to Cen-

UNIFORM OF BLENKER'S 8TH
NEW YORK VOLUNTEERS.

treville, they had walked about 25 miles. That night they walked back to the Potomac, an additional distance of 20 miles; so that these undisciplined and unseasoned men within 36 hours walked fully 45 miles, besides fighting from about 10 A. M. until 4 P. M. on a hot and dusty day in July. McDowell in person reached Centreville before sunset, ↓ and found there Miles's division with Richardson's brigade and 3 regiments of Runyon's division, and Hunt's, Tidball's, Ayres's, and Greene's batteries and 1 or 2 fragments of batteries, making about 20 guns. It was a formidable force, but there was a lack of food and the mass of the army was completely demoralized.   Beauregard had about an equal force which had not been in the fight, consisting of Ewell's, Jones's, and Longstreet's brigades and some troops of other brigades. McDowell consulted the division and brigade commanders who were at hand upon the question of making a stand or retreating. The verdict was in favor of the latter, but a decision of officers one way or the other was of no moment; the men had already decided for themselves and were streaming away to the rear, in spite of all that could be done. They had no interest or treasure in Centreville, and their hearts were not there. Their tents, provisions, baggage, and letters from home were upon the

BRIGADIER-GENERAL LOUIS BLENKER. ♭
FROM A PHOTOGRAPH.

banks of the Potomac, and no power could have stopped them short of the camps they had left less than a week before. As before stated, most of them were sovereigns in uniform, not soldiers. McDowell accepted the situation, detailed Richardson's and Blenker's brigades to cover the retreat, and the army, a disorganized mass, with some creditable exceptions, drifted

↓ I left the field with General Franklin. His brigade had dissolved. We moved first northerly, crossed Bull Run below the Sudley Spring Ford, and then bore south and east. Learning by inquiries of the men I passed that McDowell was ahead of me, I left Franklin and hurried on to Centreville, where I found McDowell, just after sunset, rearranging the positions of his reserves.— J. B. F.

♭ Colonel Louis Blenker, commanding the First Brigade of Miles's division, covered the retreat of the army from Centreville, which he describes as follows: "In this position the brigade remained until about 4 o'clock P. M., when I received orders to advance upon the road from Centreville to Warrenton. This order was executed with great difficulty, as the road was nearly choked up by the retreating baggage-wagons of several divisions, and by the vast numbers of flying soldiers belonging to various regiments. . . . The 8th [New York Volunteer] Regiment took position one and a half miles south of Centreville, on both sides of the road leading to Bull Run. The 29th [New York] Regiment stood half a mile behind the 8th, en échiquier by companies. The Garibaldi Guard stood

as reserve in line behind the 29th Regiment. The retreat of great numbers of flying soldiers continued till 9 o'clock in the evening, the great majority in wild confusion, but few in collected bodies. Soon afterward several squadrons of the enemy's cavalry advanced along the road and appeared before the outposts. They were challenged by 'Who comes there?' and remaining without any answer, I, being just present at the outposts, called, 'Union forever.' Whereupon the officer of the enemy's cavalry commanded, ' En avant; en avant. Knock him down!' Now the skirmishers fired, when the enemy turned around, leaving several killed and wounded on the spot. About nine prisoners, who were already in their hands, were liberated by this action. Afterward we were several times molested from various sides by the enemy's cavalry. At about midnight the command to leave the position and march to Washington was given by General McDowell. The brigade retired in perfect order, and ready to repel any attack on the road from Centreville to Fairfax Court House, Annandale to Washington."— EDITORS.

as the men pleased away from the scene of action. There was no pursuit, and the march from Centreville was as barren of opportunities for the rear-guard as the withdrawal from the field of battle had been.\ When McDowell reached Fairfax Court House in the night, he was in communication with Washington and exchanged telegrams with General Scott, in one of which the old hero said, "We are not discouraged"; but that dispatch did not lighten the gloom in which it was received. McDowell was so tired that while sitting on the ground writing a dispatch he fell asleep, pencil in hand, in the middle of a sentence. His adjutant-general aroused him; the dispatch was finished, and the weary ride to the Potomac resumed. When the unfortunate commander dismounted at Arlington next forenoon in a soaking rain, after 32 hours in the saddle, his disastrous campaign of 6 days was closed.

The first martial effervescence of the country was over. The three-months men went home, and the three-months chapter of the war ended — with the South triumphant and confident; the North disappointed but determined.

\ The revised losses are as follows: Federal, 16 officers and 444 enlisted men killed; 78 officers and 1046 enlisted men wounded; 50 officers and 1262 enlisted men missing; 25 pieces of artillery and a large quantity of small arms. Confederate, 25 officers and 362 enlisted men killed; 63 officers and 1519 enlisted men wounded; 1 officer and 12 enlisted men missing.—J. B. F.

* The scene in Washington after the battle has been graphically described by Walt Whitman, from whose "Specimen Days and Collect" (Philadelphia: Rees, Welch & Co.) we make these extracts:

"The defeated troops commenced pouring into Washington over the Long Bridge at daylight on Monday, 22d — day drizzling all through with rain. The Saturday and Sunday of the battle (20th, 21st) had been parched and hot to an extreme — the dust, the grime and smoke, in layers, sweated in, follow'd by other layers again sweated in, absorb'd by those excited souls — their clothes all saturated with the clay-powder filling the air — stirr'd up everywhere on the dry roads and trodden fields by the regiments, swarming wagons, artillery, etc.— all the men with this coating of murk and sweat and rain, now recoiling back, pouring over the Long Bridge — a horrible march of twenty miles, returning to Washington baffled, humiliated, panic-struck. Where are the vaunts and the proud boasts with which you went forth? Where are your banners, and your bands of music, and your ropes to bring back your prisoners? Well, there isn't a band playing — and there isn't a flag but clings ashamed and lank to its staff.

" The sun rises, but shines not. The men appear, at first spar'sely and shame-faced enough, then thicker, in the streets of Washington — appear in Pennsylvania Avenue, and on the steps and basement entrances. They come along in disorderly mobs, some in squads, stragglers, companies. Occasionally, a rare regiment, in perfect order, with its officers (some gaps, dead, the true braves), marching in silence, with lowering faces, stern, weary to sinking, all black and dirty, but every man with his musket, and stepping alive; but these are the exceptions. Sidewalks of Pennsylvania Avenue, Fourteenth street, etc., crowded, jamm'd with citizens, darkies, clerks, everybody, lookers-on; women in the windows, curious expressions from faces, as those swarms of dirt-cover'd return'd soldiers there (Will they never end?) move by; but nothing said, no comments, (half our lookers-on 'secesh' of the most venomous kind — they say nothing; but the devil snickers in their faces). During the forenoon, Washington gets all over motley with these defeated soldiers — queer-looking objects, strange eyes and faces, drench'd (the steady rain drizzles on all day) and fearfully worn, hungry, haggard, blister'd in the feet. Good people (but not over-many of them either) hurry up something for their grub. They put wash-kettles on the fire, for soup, for coffee. They set tables on the sidewalks — wagon-loads of bread are purchas'd, swiftly cut in stout chunks. Here are two aged ladies, beautiful, the first in the city for culture and charm, they stand with store of eating and drink at an improvis'd table of rough plank, and give food, and have the store replenish'd from their house every half-hour all that day; and there in the rain they stand, active, silent, white-hair'd, and give food, though the tears stream down their cheeks, almost without intermission, the whole time. Amid the deep excitement, crowds and motion, and desperate eagerness, it seems strange to see many, very many, of the soldiers sleeping — in the midst of all, sleeping sound. They drop down anywhere, on the steps of houses, up close by the basements or fences, on the sidewalk, aside on some vacant lot, and deeply sleep. A poor seventeen or eighteen year old boy lies there, on the stoop of a grand house; he sleeps so calmly, so profoundly. Some clutch their muskets firmly even in sleep. Some in squads; comrades, brothers, close together — and on them, as they lay, sulkily drips the rain. . . .

"But the hour, the day, the night pass'd, and whatever returns, an hour, a day, a night like that can never again return. The President, recovering himself, begins that very night — sternly, rapidly sets about the task of reorganizing his forces, and placing himself in positions for future and surer work. If there were nothing else of Abraham Lincoln for history to stamp him with, it is enough to send him with his wreath to the memory of all future time, that he endured that hour, that day, bitterer than gall — indeed a crucifixion day — that it did not conquer him — that he unflinchingly stemm'd it, and resolv'd to lift himself and the Union out of it."

THE OPPOSING ARMIES AT THE FIRST BULL RUN.

The composition and losses of each army as here stated give the gist of all the data obtainable in the Official Records. K stands for killed; w for wounded; m for captured or missing; c for captured.—EDITORS.

COMPOSITION AND LOSSES OF THE UNION ARMY.

Brig.-Gen. Irvin McDowell. Staff loss: w, 1. (Capt. O. H. Tillinghast, mortally wounded.)

FIRST DIVISION, Brig.-Gen. Daniel Tyler. Staff loss: w, 2. *First Brigade,* Col. Erasmus D. Keyes: 2d Me., Col. C. D. Jameson; 1st Conn., Col. G. S. Burnham; 2d Conn., Col. A. H. Terry; 3d Conn., Col. John L. Chatfield. Brigade loss: k, 19; w, 50; m, 154 = 223. *Second Brigade,* Brig.-Gen. Robert C. Schenck: 2d N.Y. (militia), Col. G. W. B. Tompkins; 1st Ohio, Col. A. McD. McCook; 2d Ohio, Lieut.-Col. Rodney Mason; E, 2d U. S. Arty., Capt. J. H. Carlisle. Brigade loss: k, 21; w, 25; m, 52 = 98. *Third Brigade,* Col. W. T. Sherman: 13th N. Y., Col. I. F. Quinby; 69th N. Y., Col. M. Corcoran (w and c), Capt. James Kelly; 79th N. Y., Col. James Cameron (k); 2d Wis., Lieut.-Col. H. W. Peck; E, 3d U. S. Arty., Capt. R. B. Ayres. Brigade loss: k, 107; w, 205; m, 293 = 605. *Fourth Brigade,* Col. Israel B. Richardson: 1st Mass., Col. Robert Cowdin; 12th N. Y., Col. Ezra L. Walrath; 2d Mich., Major A. W. Williams; 3d Mich., Col. Daniel McConnell; G, 1st U. S. Arty., Lieut. John Edwards; M, 2d U. S. Arty., Capt. Henry J. Hunt. This brigade was only slightly engaged in front of Blackburn's Ford, with the loss of one officer killed.

SECOND DIVISION, Col. D. Hunter (w), Col. Andrew Porter. Staff loss: w, 1; m, 1 = 2. *First Brigade,* Col. Andrew Porter: 8th N. Y. (militia), Col. Geo. Lyons; 14th N. Y. (militia), Col. A. M. Wood (w and c), Lieut.-Col. E. B. Fowler; 27th N. Y., Col. H. W. Slocum (w), Major J. J. Bartlett; Battalion U. S. Infantry, Major George Sykes; Battalion U. S. Marines, Major J. G. Reynolds; Battalion U. S. Cavalry, Major I. N. Palmer; D, 5th U. S. Arty., Capt. Charles Griffin. Brigade loss: k, 86; w, 177; m, 201 = 464. *Second Brigade,* Col. Ambrose E. Burnside: 2d N. H., Col. Gilman Marston (w), Lieut.-Col. F. S. Fiske; 1st R. I., Major J. P. Balch; 2d R. I. (with battery), Col. John S. Slocum (k), Lieut.-Col. Frank Wheaton; 71st N. Y. (with two howitzers), Col. H. P. Martin. Brigade loss: k, 58; w, 171; m, 134 = 363.

THIRD DIVISION, Col. Samuel P. Heintzelman. *First Brigade,* Col. W. B. Franklin: 5th Mass., Col. S. C. Lawrence; 11th Mass., Col. George Clark, Jr.; 1st Minn., Col. W. A. Gorman; I, 1st U. S. Arty., Capt. J. B. Ricketts (w and c), Lieut. Edmund Kirby. Brigade loss: k, 70; w, 197; m, 92 = 359. *Second Brigade,* Col. Orlando B. Willcox (w and c), Col. J. H. H. Ward: 11th N. Y., Lieut.-Col. N. L. Farnham; 38th N. Y., Col. J. H. H. Ward, Lieut.-Col. A. Farnsworth; 1st Mich., Major A. F. Bidwell; 4th Michigan, Col. D. A. Woodbury; D, 2d U. S. Arty., Capt. Richard Arnold. Brigade loss: k, 65; w, 177; m, 190 = 432. *Third Brigade,* Col. Oliver O. Howard: 3d Me., Major H. G. Staples; 4th Me., Col. H. G. Berry; 5th Me., Col. M. H. Dunnell; 2d Vt., Col. Henry Whiting. Brigade loss: k, 27; w, 100; m, 98 = 225.

FOURTH (RESERVE) DIVISION. [Not on the field of battle.] Brig.-Gen. Theodore Runyon. *Militia:* 1st N. J., Col. A. J. Johnson; 2d N. J., Col. H. M. Baker; 3d N. J., Col. Wm Napton; 4th N. J., Col. Matthew Miller, Jr. *Volunteers:* 1st N. J., Col. W. R. Montgomery; 2d N. J., Col. Geo. W. McLean; 3d N. J., Col. George W. Taylor; 41st N. Y., Col. Leopold von Gilsa.

FIFTH DIVISION. [In reserve at Centreville and not engaged in the battle proper. It had some skirmishing during the day and while covering the retreat of the army.] Col. Dixon S. Miles. *First Brigade,* Col. Louis Blenker: 8th N. Y. (Vols.) Lieut.-Col. Julius Stahel; 29th N. Y., Col. Adolph von Steinwehr; 39th N. Y. (Garibaldi Guards), Col. F. G. D'Utassy; 27th Penna., Col. Max Einstein; A, 2d U. S. Arty., Capt. John C. Tidball; Bookwood's N. Y. battery, Captain Charles Bookwood. Brigade loss: k, 6; w, 16; m, 96 = 118. *Second Brigade,* Col. Thomas A. Davies: 16th N.Y., Lieut.-Col. Samuel Marsh; 18th N.Y., Col. W. A. Jackson; 31st N Y., Col. C. E. Pratt; 32d N. Y., Col. R. Matheson; G, 2d U. S. Arty., Lieut. O. D. Greene. Brigade loss: w, 2; m, 1 = 3.

Total loss of the Union army: killed, 460; wounded, 1124; captured or missing, 1312,—grand total, 2896.

STRENGTH OF THE UNION ARMY.

General James B. Fry, who was General McDowell's adjutant-general, prepared in October, 1884, a statement of the strength of the army, in brief as follows:

"It was not practicable at the time to ascertain the strength of the army with accuracy; and it is impossible now to make a return which can be pronounced absolutely correct.

"The abstract which appears on page 309, vol. ii., 'Official Records,' is not a return of McDowell's army at the battle of Bull Run, and was not prepared by me, but, as I understand, has been compiled since the war. It purports to give the strength of the 'Department of Northeastern Virginia,' July 16th and 17th, not of McDowell's army, July 21st. It does not show the losses resulting from the discharge of the 4th Pennsylvania Infantry and Varian's New York battery, which marched to the rear on the morning of the 21st, nor the heavy losses incident to the march of the army from the Potomac; it embraces two regiments—the 21st and 25th New York Infantry—which were not with the army in the field; and it contains the strength of Company E, Second United States Cavalry, as a special item, whereas that company is embraced in the strength of the Second (Hunter's) Division, to which it, with the rest of the cavalry, belonged.

"In his report of the battle (p. 324, vol. ii., 'Official Records') General McDowell says he crossed Bull Run 'with about eighteen thousand men.' I collected information to that effect for him at the time. His statement is substantially correct. The following is an exhibit in detail of the forces actually engaged:

COMMANDS.	Officers.	Enlisted men.
General staff	19	
First Division, two brigades	284	5,068
Second Division, two brigades	252	5,717
Third Division, three brigades	341	6,891
Total — seven brigades	896	17,676

"Only Keyes's and Sherman's brigades of the four brigades of the First Division crossed Bull Run.

"The Fifth Division, with Richardson's brigade of the First Division attached, was in reserve at and in front of Centreville. Some of it was lightly engaged on our side of Bull Run in repelling a feeble advance of the enemy. The Fourth (Reserve) Division was left to guard our communications with the Potomac, its advance being seven miles in rear of Centreville.

"That is to say, McDowell crossed Bull Run with 896 officers, 17,676 rank and file, and 24 pieces of artillery.

"The artillerymen who crossed Bull Run are embraced in the figures of the foregoing table. The guns were as follows: Ricketts's Battery, 6 10-pounder rifle guns; Griffin's Battery, 4 10-pounder rifle guns, 2 12-pounder howitzers; Arnold's Battery, 2 13-pounder rifle guns, 2 6-pounder smooth-bores; R. I. Battery, 6 13-pounder rifles; 71st N. Y. Reg't's Battery, 2 Dahlgren howitzers.

"The artillery, in addition to that which crossed Bull Run, was as follows: Hunt's Battery, 4 12-pounder rifle guns; Carlisle's Battery, 2 13-pounder rifle guns, 2 6-pounder smooth-bore guns; Tidball's Battery, 2 6-pounder smooth-bore guns, 2 12-pounder howitzers; Greene's Battery, 4 10-pounder rifle guns; Ayres's Battery, 2 10-pounder rifle guns, 2 6-pounder smooth-bore guns, 2 12-pounder howitzers; Edwards's Battery, 2 20-pounder rifle guns, 1 30-pounder rifle gun."

COMPOSITION AND LOSSES OF THE CONFEDERATE ARMY

General Joseph E. Johnston.

ARMY OF THE POTOMAC, Brig.-Gen. G. T. Beauregard. *First Brigade,* Brig.-Gen. M. L. Bonham: 11th N. C., Col. W. W. Kirkland; 2d S. C., Col. J. B. Kershaw; 3d S. C., Col. J. H. Williams; 7th S. C., Col. Thomas G. Bacon; 8th S. C., Col. E. B. C. Cash. Loss: k, 10; w, 66 = 76. *Second Brigade* [not actively engaged], Brig.-Gen. R. S. Ewell: 5th Ala., Col. R. E. Rodes; 6th Ala., Col. J. J. Seibels; 6th La., Col. J. G. Seymour. *Third Brigade,* Brig.-Gen. D. R. Jones: 17th Miss., Col. W. S. Featherston; 18th Miss., Col. E. R. Burt; 5th S. C., Col. M. Jenkins. Loss: k, 13; w, 62 = 75. *Fourth Brigade* [not actively engaged], Brig.-Gen. James Longstreet: 5th N. C., Lieut.-Col. Jones; 1st Va., Major F. G. Skinner; 11th Va., Col. S. Garland, Jr.; 17th Va., Col. M. D. Corse. Loss: k, 2; w, 12 = 14. *Fifth Brigade,* Col. P. St. Geo. Cocke: 8th Va., Col. Eppa Hunton; 18th Va., Col. R. E. Withers; 19th Va., Lieut.-Col. J. B. Strange; 28th Va., Col. R. T. Preston; 49th Va. (3 cos.), Col. Wm. Smith. Loss: k, 23; w, 79; m, 2 = 104. *Sixth Brigade,* Col. Jubal A. Early: 7th La., Col. Harry T. Hays; 13th Miss., Col. Wm. Barksdale; 7th Va., Col. J. L. Kemper; 24th Va., Lieut.-Col. P. Hairston, Jr. Loss: k, 12; w, 67 = 79. *Evans's command* (temporarily organized), Col. N. G. Evans: 1st La. Battalion, Major C. R. Wheat (w); 4th S. C., Col. J. B. E. Sloan; Cavalry, Capt. W. R. Terry; Artillery, Lieut. G. S. Davidson. Loss: k, 20; w, 118; m, 8 = 146. *Reserve Brigade* [not actively engaged], Brig.-Gen. T. H. Holmes: 1st Arkansas and 2d Tennessee. *Unattached Infantry.* 8th La.: Col. H. B. Kelly; Hampton's (S. C.) Legion, Col. Wade Hampton.

Loss: k, 19; w, 100; m, 2 = 121. *Cavalry:* 30th Virginia, Col. R. C. W. Radford; Harrison's Battalion; Ten independent companies. Loss: k, 5; w, 8 = 13. *Artillery:* Battalion Washington Artillery (La.), Major J. B. Walton; Alexandria (Va.) Battery, Capt. Del Kemper; Latham's (Va.) Battery, Capt. H. G. Latham; Loudoun (Va.) Artillery, Capt. Arthur L. Rogers; Shields's (Va.) Battery, Capt. J. C. Shields. Loss: k, 2; w, 8 = 10. Total loss Army of the Potomac: k, 105; w, 519; m, 12 = 636.

ARMY OF THE SHENANDOAH, General Joseph E. Johnston. *First Brigade,* Brig.-Gen. T. J. Jackson: 2d Va., Col. J. W. Allen; 4th Va., Col. J. F. Preston; 5th Va., Col. Kenton Harper; 27th Va., Lieut.-Col. John Echols; 33d Va., Col. A. C. Cummings. Loss: k, 119; w, 442 = 561. *Second Brigade,* Col. F. S. Bartow (k): 7th Ga., Col. Lucius J. Gartrell; 8th Ga., Lieut.-Col. W. M. Gardner. Loss: k, 60; w, 293 = 353. *Third Brigade,* Brig.-Gen. B. E. Bee (k): 4th Ala., Col. Jones (k), Col. S. R. Gist; 2d Miss., Col. W. C. Falkner; 11th Miss. (2 cos.), Lieut.-Col. P. F. Liddell; 6th N. C., Col. C. F. Fisher (k). Loss: k, 95; w, 309; m, 1 = 405. *Fourth Brigade,* Brig.-Gen. E. K. Smith (w), Col. Arnold Elzey: 1st Md. Battalion, Lieut.-Col. George H. Steuart; 3d Tennessee, Col. John C. Vaughn; 10th Va., Col. S. B. Gibbons; 13th Va., Col. A. P. Hill. Loss: k, 8; w, 19 = 27. *Artillery:* Imboden's, Stanard's, Pendleton's, Alburtis's, and Beckham's batteries. *Cavalry:* 1st Va., Col. J. E. B. Stuart. (Loss not specifically reported.) Total loss Army of the Shenandoah: k, 282; w, 1063; m, 1 = 1346.

Total loss of the Confederate Army: killed, 387; wounded, 1582; captured or missing, 13,— grand total, 1982.

STRENGTH OF THE CONFEDERATE ARMY.

In October, 1884, General Thomas Jordan, who was General Beauregard's adjutant-general, prepared a statement of the strength of the Confederate army at Bull Run or Manassas, of which the following is a condensation:

"So far as the troops of Beauregard's immediate Army of the Potomac are concerned, this statement is condensed from two that I prepared with the sub-returns of all the commands before me as the adjutant-general of that army, September 25th, 1861, and I will vouch for its exactness. In respect to the Army of the Shenandoah, I have been obliged to present an estimate of 8340 as the total of the rank and file of Johnston's army, my authority for which is a statement written by me in the official report of the battle, and based, as I distinctly recollect, upon official documents and returns in my hands at the time, of the accuracy of which I was and am satisfied. The totals of General Beauregard's Army of the Potomac are:

ARMY OF THE POTOMAC AVAILABLE ON THE FIELD.

Generals and Staff	37
Infantry, Rank and File	19,569
Cavalry, " "	1,468
Artillery, " "	826
	21,900
Field Guns	27

ARMY OF THE POTOMAC ACTIVELY ENGAGED.

Generals and Staff	10
Infantry, Rank and File	8,415
Cavalry, " "	1,000
Artillery, " "	288
	9,713
Field Guns	17

RECAPITULATION.

	Infantry.	Cavalry.	Artillery.	Staff.	Total.
Army of the Potomac — Rank and File engaged	8,415	1,000	288	10	9,713
" " Shenandoah, " " " (estimated)	7,684	300	350	6	8,340
Total Rank and File, both Confederate armies, engaged	16,099	1,300	638	16	18,053"

THE FIRST BATTLE OF BULL RUN.

BY G. T. BEAUREGARD, GENERAL, C. S. A.

SOON after the first conflict between the authorities of the Federal Union and those of the Confederate States had occurred in Charleston Harbor, by the bombardment of Fort Sumter,—which, beginning at 4:30 A. M. on the 12th of April, 1861, forced the surrender of that fortress within thirty hours thereafter into my hands,—I was called to Richmond, which by that time had become the Confederate seat of government, and was directed to "assume command of the Confederate troops on the Alexandria line." Arriving at Manassas Junction, I took command on the 2d of June, forty-nine days after the evacuation of Fort Sumter.

A LOUISIANA "TIGER."

Although the position at the time was strategically of commanding importance to the Confederates, the mere *terrain* was not only without natural defensive advantages, but, on the contrary, was absolutely unfavorable. Its strategic value was that, being close to the Federal capital, it held in observation the chief army then being assembled near Arlington by General McDowell, under the immediate eye of the commander-in-chief, General Scott, for an offensive movement against Richmond; and while it had a railway approach in its rear for the easy accumulation of reënforcements and all the necessary munitions of war from the southward, at the same time another (the Manassas Gap) railway, diverging laterally to the left from that point, gave rapid communications with the fertile valley of the Shenandoah, then teeming with live stock and cereal subsistence, as well as with other resources essential to the Confederates. There was this further value in the position to the Confederate army: that during the period of accumulation, seasoning, and training, it might be fed from the fat fields, pastures, and garners of Loudoun, Fauquier, and the Lower Shenandoah Valley counties, which otherwise must have fallen into the hands of the enemy. But, on the other hand, Bull Run, a petty stream, was of little or no defensive strength; for it abounded in fords, and although for the most part its banks were rocky and abrupt, the side from which it would be approached offensively in most places commanded the opposite ground.

At the time of my arrival at Manassas, a Confederate army under General Joseph E. Johnston was in occupation of the Lower Shenandoah Valley, along the line of the Upper Potomac, chiefly at Harper's Ferry, which was regarded as the gateway of the valley and of one of the possible approaches to Richmond; a position from which he was speedily forced to retire, however, by a flank movement of a Federal army, under the veteran General Patterson, thrown across the Potomac at or about Martinsburg. On my other or right flank, so to speak, a Confederate force of some 2500 men under General

Holmes occupied the position of Aquia Creek on the lower Potomac, upon the line of approach to Richmond from that direction through Fredericksburg. The other approach, that by way of the James River, was held by Confederate troops under Generals Huger and Magruder. Establishing small outposts at Leesburg to observe the crossings of the Potomac in that quarter, and at Fairfax Court House in observation of Arlington, with other detachments in advance of Manassas toward Alexandria on the south side of the railroad, from the very outset I was anxiously aware that the sole military advantage at the moment to the Confederates was that of holding the *interior lines.* On the Federal or hostile side were all material advantages, including superior numbers,

ARLINGTON, THE HOME OF GENERAL ROBERT E. LEE.

largely drawn from the old militia organizations of the great cities of the North, decidedly better armed and equipped than the troops under me, and strengthened by a small but incomparable body of regular infantry as well as a number of batteries of regular field artillery of the highest class, and a very large and thoroughly organized staff corps, besides a numerous body of professionally educated officers in command of volunteer regiments, ⸗ all precious military elements at such a juncture.

Happily, through the foresight of Colonel Thomas Jordan,—whom General Lee had placed as the adjutant-general of the forces there assembled before my arrival,—arrangements were made which enabled me to receive regularly, from private persons at the Federal capital, most accurate information, of which politicians high in council, as well as War Department clerks, were the unconscious ducts. On the 4th of July, my pickets happened upon and captured a soldier of the regulars, who proved to be a clerk in the adjutant-general's office of General McDowell, intrusted with the special duty of compiling returns of his army—a work which he confessed, without reluctance, he had just executed, showing the forces under McDowell about the 1st of July. His statement of the strength and composition of that force tallied so closely with that which had been acquired through my Washington agencies, already mentioned, as well as through the leading Northern newspapers (regular files of which were also transmitted to my headquarters from the Federal capital), that I could not doubt them.

⸗ The professionally educated officers on the Confederate side at Bull Run included Generals Johnston, Beauregard, Stonewall Jackson, Longstreet, Kirby Smith, Ewell, Early, Bee, D. R. Jones, Holmes, Evans, Elzey, and Jordan, all in high positions, besides others not so prominent.— EDITORS.

In these several ways, therefore, I was almost as well advised of the strength of the hostile army in my front as its commander, who, I may mention, had been a classmate of mine at West Point. Under those circumstances I had become satisfied that a well-equipped, well-constituted Federal army at least 50,000 strong, of all arms, confronted me at or about Arlington, ready and on the very eve of an offensive operation against me, and to meet which I could muster barely 18,000 men with 29 field-guns. ⚓

Previously,—indeed, as early as the middle of June,—it had become apparent to my mind that through only one course of action could there be a well-grounded hope of ability on the part of the Confederates to encounter successfully the offensive operations for which the Federal authorities were then vigorously preparing in my immediate front, with so consummate a strategist and military administrator as Lieutenant-General Scott in general command at Washington, aided by his accomplished heads of the large General Staff Corps of the United States Army. This course was to make the most enterprising, warlike use of the interior lines which we possessed, for the swift concentration at the critical instant of every available Confederate force upon the menaced position, at the risk, if need were, of sacrificing all minor places to the one clearly of major military value—there to meet our adversary so offensively as to overwhelm him, under circumstances that must assure immediate ability to assume the general offensive even upon his territory, and thus conquer an early peace by a few well-delivered blows.

My views of such import had been already earnestly communicated to the proper authorities; but about the middle of July, satisfied that McDowell was on the eve of taking the offensive against me, I dispatched Colonel James Chesnut, of South Carolina, a volunteer aide-de-camp on my staff who had served on an intimate footing with Mr. Davis in the Senate of the United States, to urge in substance the necessity for the immediate concentration of the larger part of the forces of Johnston and Holmes at Manassas, so that the moment McDowell should be sufficiently far detached from Washington, I would be enabled to move rapidly round his more convenient flank upon his rear and his communications, and attack him in reverse, or get between his forces, then separated, thus cutting off his retreat upon Arlington in the event of his defeat, and insuring as an immediate consequence the crushing of Patterson, the liberation of Maryland, and the capture of Washington.

This plan was rejected by Mr. Davis and his military advisers (Adjutant-General Cooper and General Lee), who characterized it as " brilliant and comprehensive," but essentially impracticable. Furthermore, Colonel Chesnut came back impressed with the views entertained at Richmond,— as he communicated at once to my adjutant-general,— that should the Federal army soon move offensively upon my position, my best course would be to retire behind the Rappahannock and accept battle there instead of at Manassas. In effect, it was regarded as best to sever communications between the two chief Confederate armies, that of the Potomac and that of the Shenandoah, with the

⚓ For the forces actually engaged in the campaign and on the field, see pp. 194-5.—EDITORS.

inevitable immediate result that Johnston would be forced to leave Patterson in possession of the Lower Shenandoah Valley, abandoning to the enemy so

MAP OF THE BULL RUN CAMPAIGN.

large a part of the most resourceful sections of Virginia, and to retreat southward by way of the Luray Valley, pass across the Blue Ridge at Thornton's Gap and unite with me after all, but at Fredericksburg, much nearer Richmond than Manassas. These views, however, were not made known to me at the time, and happily my mind was left free to the grave problem imposed upon me by the rejection of my plan for the immediate concentration of a materially larger force,— i. e., the problem of placing and using my resources for a successful encounter behind Bull Run with the Federal army, which I was not permitted to doubt was about to take the field against me.

It is almost needless to say that I had caused to be made a thorough reconnoissance of all the ground in my front and flanks, and had made myself personally acquainted with the most material points, including the region of Sudley's Church on my left, where a small detachment was posted in observation. Left now to my own resources, of course the contingency of defeat had to be considered and provided for. Among the measures of precaution for such a result, I ordered the destruction of the railroad bridge across Bull Run at Union Mills, on my right, in order that the enemy, in the event of my defeat, should not have the immediate use of the railroad in following up their movement against Richmond — a railroad which could have had no corresponding value to us eastward beyond Manassas in any operations on our side with Washington as the objective, inasmuch as any such operations must have been made by the way of the Upper Potomac and upon the rear of that city.

Just before Colonel Chesnut was dispatched on the mission of which I have spoken, a former clerk in one of the departments at Washington, well known to him, had volunteered to return thither and bring back the latest information of the military and political situation from our most trusted friends. His loyalty to our cause, his intelligence, and his desire to be of service being vouched for, he was at once sent across the Potomac below Alexandria, merely accredited by a small scrap of paper bearing in Colonel Jordan's cipher the two words, "Trust bearer," with which he was to call at a certain house in

Washington within easy rifle-range of the White House, ask for the lady of the house, and present it only to her. This delicate mission was as fortunately as it was deftly executed. In the early morning, as the newsboys were crying in the empty streets of Washington the intelligence that the order was given for the Federal army to move at once upon my position, that scrap of paper reached the hands of the one person in all that city who could extract any meaning from it. With no more delay than was necessary for a hurried breakfast and the writing in cipher by Mrs. G—— of the words, "Order issued for McDowell to march upon Manassas to-night," my agent was placed in communication with another friend, who carried him in a buggy with a relay of horses as swiftly as possible down the eastern shore of the Potomac to our regular ferry across that river. Without untoward incident the momentous dispatch was quickly delivered into the hands of a cavalry courier, and by means of relays it was in my hands between 8 and 9 o'clock that night. Within half an hour my outpost commanders, advised of what was impending, were directed, at the first evidence of the near presence of the enemy in their front, to fall back in the manner and to positions already prescribed in anticipation of such a contingency in an order confidentially communicated to them four weeks before, and the detachment at Leesburg was directed to join me by forced marches. Having thus cleared my decks for action, I next acquainted Mr. Davis with the situation, and ventured once more to suggest that the Army of the Shenandoah, with the brigade at Fredericksburg or Aquia Creek, should be ordered to reënforce me,— suggestions that were at once heeded so far that General Holmes was ordered to carry his command to my aid, and General Johnston was given discretion to do likewise. After some telegraphic discussion with me, General Johnston was induced to exercise this discretion in favor of the swift march of the Army of the Shenandoah to my relief; and to facilitate that vital movement, I hastened to accumulate all possible means of railway transport at a designated point on the Manassas Gap railroad at the eastern foot of the Blue Ridge, to which Johnston's troops directed their march. However, at the same time, I had submitted the alternative proposition to General Johnston, that, having passed the Blue Ridge, he should assemble his forces, press forward by way of Aldie, north-west of Manassas, and fall upon McDowell's right rear; while I, prepared for the operation, at the first sound of the conflict, should strenuously assume the offensive in my front. The situation and circumstances specially favored the signal success of such an operation. The march to the point of attack could have been accomplished as soon as the forces were brought ultimately by rail to Manassas Junction; our enemy, thus attacked so nearly simultaneously on his right flank, his rear, and his front, naturally would suppose that I had been able to turn his flank while attacking him in front, and therefore, that I must have an overwhelming superiority of numbers; and his forces, being new troops, most of them under fire for the first time, must have soon fallen into a disastrous panic. Moreover, such an operation must have resulted advantageously to the Confederates, in the event that McDowell should, as might have been anticipated, attempt to strike the Manassas Gap railway to my left, and thus cut off railway communications between Johnston's forces and my own, instead of the mere effort to strike my left flank which he actually essayed.↓

It seemed, however, as though the deferred attempt at concentration was to go for naught, for on the morning of the 18th the Federal forces were massed around Centreville, but three miles from Mitchell's Ford, and soon were seen advancing upon the roads leading to that and Blackburn's Ford. [See map, page 180.] My order of battle, issued in the night of the 17th, contemplated an offensive return, particularly from the strong brigades on the right and right center. The Federal artillery opened in front of both fords, and the infantry,

THE McLEAN HOUSE, GENERAL BEAUREGARD'S HEADQUARTERS
NEAR MANASSAS. FROM A PHOTOGRAPH.

while demonstrating in front of Mitchell's Ford, endeavored to force a passage at Blackburn's. Their column of attack, Tyler's division, was opposed by Longstreet's forces, to the reënforcement of which Early's brigade, the reserve line at McLean's Ford, was ordered up. The Federals, after several attempts to force a passage, met a final repulse and retreated. After their infantry attack had ceased, about 1 o'clock, the contest lapsed into an artillery duel, in which the Washington Artillery of New Orleans won credit against the renowned batteries of the United States regular army. A comical effect of this artillery fight was the destruction of the dinner of myself and staff by a Federal shell that fell into the fire-place of my headquarters at the McLean House. ↓

Our success in this first limited collision was of special prestige to my army of new troops, and, moreover, of decisive importance by so increasing General McDowell's caution as to give time for the arrival of some of General

↓ "I am, however, inclined to believe he [the enemy] may attempt to turn my left flank by a movement in the direction of Vienna, Frying-pan Church, and, possibly, Gum Spring, and thus cut off Johnston's line of retreat and communication with this place [Manassas Junction] *via* the Manassas Gap railroad, while threatening my own communications with Richmond and depots of supply by the Alexandria and Orange railroad, and opening his communica-tions with the Potomac through Leesburg and Edward's Ferry."—(Extract from a letter addressed by General Beauregard to Jefferson Davis, July 11th, 1861.)

↓ It is denied that a serious attempt "to force a passage" was made on the 18th. (See page 178.) This engagement was called by the Confederates the battle of Bull Run, the main fight on the 21st being known in the South as the battle of Manassas (pronounced Ma-nass'-sa).—EDITORS.

Johnston's forces.   But while on the 19th I was awaiting a renewed and general attack by the Federal army, I received a telegram from the Richmond military authorities, urging me to withdraw my call on General Johnston on account of the supposed impracticability of the concentration — an abiding conviction which had been but momentarily shaken by the alarm caused by McDowell's march upon Richmond.⸘ As this was not an order in terms, but an urgency which, notwithstanding its superior source, left me technically free and could define me as responsible for any misevent, I preferred to keep both the situation and the responsibility, and continued every effort for the prompt arrival of the Shenandoah forces, being resolved, should they come before General McDowell again attacked, to take myself the offensive.   General McDowell, fortunately for my plans, spent the 19th and 20th in reconnoissances; ☆ and, meanwhile, General Johnston brought 8340 men from the Shenandoah Valley, with 20 guns, and General Holmes 1265 rank and file, with 6 pieces of artillery, from Aquia Creek.   As these forces arrived (most of them in the afternoon of the 20th) I placed them chiefly so as to strengthen my left center and left, the latter being weak from lack of available troops.

The disposition of the entire force was now as follows [see map, page 180]: At Union Mills Ford, Ewell's brigade, supported by Holmes's; at McLean's Ford, D. R. Jones's brigade, supported by Early's; at Blackburn's Ford, Longstreet's brigade; at Mitchell's Ford, Bonham's brigade. Cocke's brigade held the line in front and rear of Bull Run from Bonham's left, covering Lewis's, Ball's, and Island fords, to the right of Evans's demi-brigade, which covered the Stone Bridge and a farm ford about a mile above, and formed part also of Cocke's command. The Shenandoah forces were placed in reserve — Bee's and Bartow's brigades between McLean's and Blackburn's fords, and Jackson's between Blackburn's and Mitchell's fords. This force mustered 29,188 rank and file and 55 guns, of which 21,923 infantry, cavalry, and artillery, with 29 guns, belonged to my immediate forces, *i. e.*, the Army of the Potomac.

The preparation, in front of an ever-threatening enemy, of a wholly volunteer army, composed of men very few of whom had ever belonged to any military organization, had been a work of many cares not incident to the command of a regular army. These were increased by the insufficiency of my staff organization, an inefficient management of the quartermaster's department at Richmond, and the preposterous mismanagement of the commissary-general, who not only failed to furnish rations, but caused the removal of the army commissaries, who, under my orders, procured food from

⸘ [TELEGRAM.]   RICHMOND, July 19, 1861.
GENERAL BEAUREGARD, Manassas, Va.

We have no intelligence from General Johnston. If the enemy in front of you has abandoned an immediate attack, and General Johnston has not moved, you had better withdraw your call upon him, so that he may be left to his full discretion. All the troops arriving at Lynchburg are ordered to join you. From this place we will send as fast as transportation permits. The enemy is advised at Washington of the projected movement of Generals Johnston and Holmes, and may vary his plans in conformity thereto.

S. COOPER, Adjutant-General.

☆ Lack of rations, as well as the necessity for information, detained McDowell at Centreville during these two days.— EDITORS.

the country in front of us to keep the army from absolute want—supplies that were otherwise exposed to be gathered by the enemy. So specially severe had been the recent duties at headquarters, aggravated not a little by night alarms arising from the enemy's immediate presence, that, in the evening of the 20th, I found my chief-of-staff sunken upon the papers that covered his table, asleep in sheer exhaustion from the overstraining and almost slumberless labor of the last days and nights. I covered his door with a guard to secure his rest against any interruption, after which the army had the benefit of his usual active and provident services.

There was much in this decisive conflict about to open, not involved in any after battle, which pervaded the two armies and the people behind them and colored the responsibility of the respective commanders. The political hostilities of a generation were now face to face with weapons instead of words. Defeat to either side would be a deep mortification, but defeat to the South must turn its claim of independence into an empty vaunt; and the defeated commander on either side might expect, though not the personal fate awarded by the Carthaginians to an unfortunate commander, at least a moral fate quite similar. Though disappointed that the concentration I had sought had not been permitted at the moment and for the purpose preferred by me, and notwithstanding the non-arrival of some five thousand troops of the Shenandoah forces, my strength was now so increased that I had good hope of successfully meeting my adversary.

General Johnston was the ranking officer, and entitled, therefore, to assume command of the united forces; but as the extensive field of operations was one which I had occupied since the beginning of June, and with which I was thoroughly familiar in all its extent and military bearings, while he was wholly unacquainted with it, and, moreover, as I had made my plans and dispositions for the maintenance of the position, General Johnston, in view of the gravity of the impending issue, preferred not to assume the responsibilities of the chief direction of the forces during the battle, but to assist me upon the field. Thereupon, I explained my plans and purposes, to which he agreed.⌡

SUNDAY, July 21st, bearing the fate of the new-born Confederacy, broke brightly over the fields and woods that held the hostile forces. My scouts, thrown out in the night toward Centreville along the Warrenton Turnpike, had reported that the enemy was concentrating along the latter. This fact, together with the failure of the Federals in their attack upon my center at Mitchell's and Blackburn's fords, had caused me to apprehend that they would attempt my left flank at the Stone Bridge, and orders were accordingly issued by half-past 4 o'clock to the brigade commanders to hold their forces in readiness to move at a moment's notice, together with the suggestion that the Federal attack might be expected in that quarter. Shortly afterward the enemy was reported to be advancing from Centreville on the Warrenton

⌡ See General Beauregard's postscript (page 226), and General Johnston's consideration of the same topic in the paper to follow (page 245), and his postscript (page 258).— EDITORS.

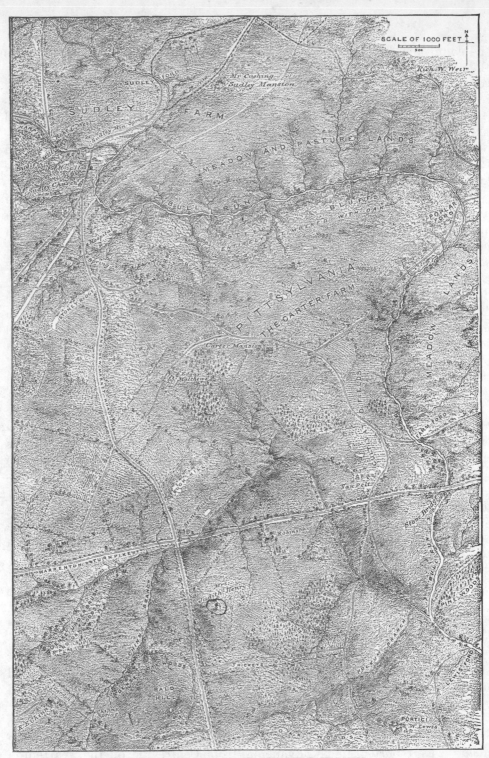

TOPOGRAPHICAL MAP OF THE BULL RUN BATTLE-FIELD.

The original of this map was made for General Beauregard, soon after the battle, from actual surveys by
Captain D. B. Harris, assisted by Mr. John Grant.

Turnpike, and at half-past 5 o'clock as deploying a force in front of Evans. As their movement against my left developed the opportunity I desired, I immediately sent orders to the brigade commanders, both front and reserves, on my right and center to advance and vigorously attack the Federal left flank and rear at Centreville, while my left, under Cocke and Evans with their supports, would sustain the Federal attack in the quarter of the Stone Bridge, which they were directed to do to the last extremity. The center was likewise to advance and engage the enemy in front, and directions were given to the reserves, when without orders, to move toward the sound of the heaviest firing. The ground in our front on the other side of Bull Run afforded particular advantage for these tactics. Centreville was the apex of a triangle — its short side running by the Warrenton Turnpike to Stone Bridge, its base Bull Run, its long side a road that ran from Union Mills along the front of my other Bull Run positions and trended off to the rear of Centreville, where McDowell had massed his main forces; branch roads led up to this one from the fords between Union Mills and Mitchell's. My forces to the right of the latter ford were to advance, pivoting on that position; Bonham was in advance from Mitchell's Ford, Longstreet from Blackburn's, D. R. Jones from McLean's, and Ewell from Union Mills by the Centreville road. Ewell, as having the longest march, was to begin the movement, and each brigade was to be followed by its reserve. In anticipation of this method of attack, and to prevent accidents, the subordinate commanders had been carefully instructed in the movement by me, as they were all new to the responsibilities of command. They were to establish close communication with each other before making the attack. About half-past 8 o'clock I set out with General Johnston for a convenient position,— a hill in rear of Mitchell's Ford,— where we waited for the opening of the attack on our right, from which I expected a decisive victory by midday, with the result of cutting off the Federal army from retreat upon Washington.

Meanwhile, about half-past 5 o'clock, the peal of a heavy rifled gun was heard in front of the Stone Bridge, its second shot striking through the tent of my signal-officer, Captain E. P. Alexander; and at 6 o'clock a full rifled battery opened against Evans and then against Cocke, to which our artillery remained dumb, as it had not sufficient range to reply. But later, as the Federal skirmish-line advanced, it was engaged by ours, thrown well forward on the other side of the Run. A scattering musketry fire followed, and meanwhile, about 7 o'clock, I ordered Jackson's brigade, with Imboden's and five guns of Walton's battery, to the left, with orders to support Cocke as well as Bonham; and the brigades of Bee and Bartow, under the command of the former, were also sent to the support of the left.

At half-past 8 o'clock Evans, seeing that the Federal attack did not increase in boldness and vigor, and observing a lengthening line of dust above the trees to the left of the Warrenton Turnpike, became satisfied that the attack in his front was but a feint, and that a column of the enemy was moving around through the woods to fall on his flank from the direction of Sudley Ford. Informing his immediate commander, Cocke, of the enemy's movement, and of his own dispositions to meet it, he left 4 companies under cover at the Stone Bridge, and led the remainder of his force, 6 companies of Sloan's 4th South Carolina and Wheat's battalion of Louisiana Tigers, with 2 6-pounder howitzers, across the valley of Young's Branch to the high ground beyond it. Resting his left on the Sudley road, he distributed his troops on each side of a small copse, with such cover as the ground afforded, and looking over the open fields and a reach of the Sudley road which the Federals must cover in their approach. His two howitzers were placed one at each end of his position, and here he silently awaited the enemy now drawing near.

The Federal turning column, about 18,000 strong, with 24 pieces of artillery, had moved down from Centreville by the Warrenton Turnpike, and after passing Cub Run had struck to the right by a forest road to cross Bull Run at Sudley Ford, about 3 miles above the Stone Bridge, moving by a long circuit for the purpose of attacking my left flank. The head of the column, Burnside's brigade of Hunter's division, at about 9:45 A. M. debouched from the woods into the open fields, in front of Evans. Wheat at once engaged their skirmishers, and as the Second Rhode Island regiment advanced, supported by its splendid battery of 6 rifled guns, the fronting thicket held by Evans's South Carolinians poured forth its sudden volleys, while the 2 howitzers flung their grape-shot upon the attacking line, which was soon shattered and driven back into the woods behind. Major Wheat, after handling his battalion with the utmost determination, had fallen severely wounded in the lungs. Burnside's entire brigade was now sent forward in a second charge, supported by 8 guns; but they encountered again the unflinching fire of Evans's line, and were once more driven back to the woods, from the cover of which they continued the attack, reënforced after a time by the arrival of 8 companies of United States regular infantry, under Major Sykes, with 6 pieces of artillery, quickly followed by the remaining regiments of Andrew Porter's brigade of the same division. The contest here lasted fully an hour; meanwhile Wheat's battalion, having lost its leader, had gradually lost its organization, and Evans, though still opposing these heavy odds with undiminished firmness, sought reënforcement from the troops in his rear.

General Bee, of South Carolina, a man of marked character, whose command lay in reserve in rear of Cocke, near the Stone Bridge, intelligently applying the general order given to the reserves, had already moved toward the neighboring point of conflict, and taken a position with his own and Bartow's brigades on the high plateau which stands in rear of Bull Run in the quarter of the Stone Bridge, and overlooking the scene of engagement upon the stretch of high ground from which it was separated by the valley of Young's Branch. This plateau is inclosed on three sides by two small watercourses, which empty into Bull Run within a few yards of each other, a half mile to the south of the Stone Bridge. Rising to an elevation of quite 100 feet above the level of Bull Run at the bridge, it falls off on three sides to the level of the inclosing streams in gentle slopes, but furrowed by ravines of irregular directions and length, and studded with clumps and patches of young pine and oaks. The general direction of the crest of the plateau is oblique to the course of Bull Run in that quarter and to the Sudley and turnpike roads, which intersect each other at right angles. On the north-western brow, overlooking Young's Branch, and near the Sudley road, as the latter climbs over the plateau, stood the house of the widow Henry, while to its right and forward on a projecting spur stood the house and sheds of the free negro Robinson, just behind the turnpike, densely embowered in trees and shrubbery and environed by a double row of fences on two sides. Around the eastern and southern brow of the plateau an almost unbroken fringe of second-growth pines gave excellent shelter for our marksmen, who availed themselves of it with the most satisfactory skill. To the west, adjoining the fields that surrounded the houses mentioned, a broad belt of oaks extends directly across the crest on both sides of the Sudley road, in which, during the battle, the hostile forces contended for the mastery. General Bee, with a soldier's eye to the situation, skillfully disposed his forces. His two brigades on either side of Imboden's battery — which he had borrowed from his neighboring reserve, Jackson's brigade — were placed in a small depression of the plateau in advance of the Henry house, whence he had a full view of the contest on the opposite height across the valley of Young's Branch. Opening with his artillery upon the Federal batteries, he answered Evans's request by advising him to withdraw to his own position on the height; but Evans, full of the spirit that would not retreat, renewed his appeal that the forces in rear would come to help him hold his ground. The newly arrived forces had given the Federals such superiority at this point as to dwarf Evans's means of resistance, and General Bee, generously yielding his own better judgment to Evans's persistence, led the two brigades across the valley under the fire of the enemy's artillery, and threw them into action — 1 regiment in the copse held by Colonel Evans, 2 along a fence on the right, and 2 under General Bartow on the prolonged right of this line, but extended forward at a right angle and along the edge of a wood not more than 100 yards from that held by the enemy's left, where the contest at short range became sharp and deadly, bringing many casualties to both sides. The Federal infantry, though still in superior numbers, failed to make any headway against this sturdy van, notwithstanding Bee's whole line was hammered also by the enemy's powerful batteries, until Heintzelman's division of 2 strong brigades, arriving from Sudley Ford, extended the fire on the Federal right, while its battery of 6 10-pounder rifled guns took an immediately effective part from a position behind the Sudley road. Against these odds the Confederate force was still endeavoring to hold its ground, when a new enemy came into the field upon its right. Major Wheat, with characteristic daring and restlessness, had crossed Bull Run alone by a small ford above the Stone Bridge, in order to reconnoiter, when he and Evans had first moved to the left, and, falling on some Federal scouts, had shouted a taunting defiance and withdrawn, not, however, without his place of crossing having been observed. This dis-

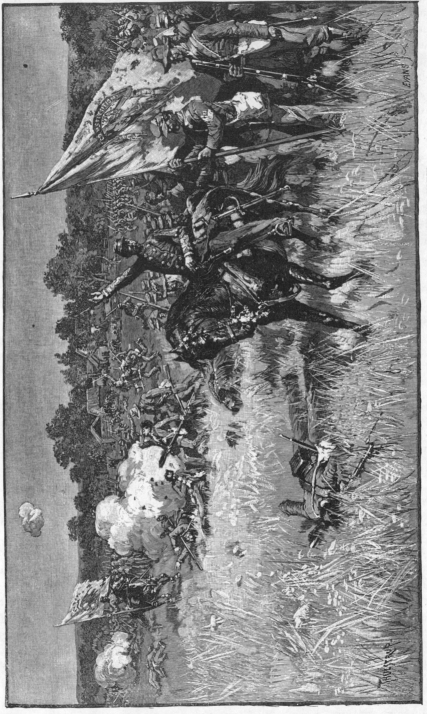

RALLYING THE TROOPS OF BEE, BARTOW, AND EVANS, BEHIND THE ROBINSON HOUSE.

closure was now utilized by Sherman's (W. T.) and Keyes's brigades of Tyler's division; crossing at this point, they appeared over the high bank of the stream and moved into position on the Federal left. There was no choice now for Bee but to retire — a movement, however, to be accomplished under different circumstances than when urged by him upon Evans. The three leaders endeavored to preserve the stead-iness of the ranks as they withdrew over the open fields, aided by the fire of Im-boden's guns on the plateau and the retiring howitzers; but the troops were thrown into confusion, and the greater part soon fell into rout across Young's Branch and around the base of the height in the rear of the Stone Bridge.

A LOUISIANA "PELICAN."

Meanwhile, in rear of Mitchell's Ford, I had been waiting with General John-ston for the sound of conflict to open in the quarter of Centreville upon the Fed-eral left flank and rear (making allow-ance, however, for the delays possible to commands unused to battle), when I was chagrined to hear from General D. R. Jones that, while he had been long ready for the movement upon Centre-ville, General Ewell had not come up to form on his right, though he had sent him between 7 and 8 o'clock a copy of his own order which recited that Ewell had been already ordered to begin the movement. I dispatched an immediate order to Ewell to advance; but within a quarter of an hour, just as I received a dispatch from him informing me that he had received no order to advance in the morning, the firing on the left began to increase so intensely as to indi-cate a severe attack, whereupon General Johnston said that he would go personally to that quarter.

After weighing attentively the firing, which seemed rapidly and heavily increasing, it appeared to me that the troops on the right would be unable to get into position before the Federal offensive should have made too much progress on our left, and that it would be better to abandon it altogether, maintaining only a strong demonstration so as to detain the enemy in front of our right and center, and hurry up all available reënforcements — includ-ing the reserves that were to have moved upon Centreville — to our left and fight the battle out in that quarter. Communicating this view to General Johnston, who approved it (giving his advice, as he said, for what it was worth, as he was not acquainted with the country), I ordered Ewell, Jones, and Longstreet to make a strong demonstration all along their front on the other side of the Run, and ordered the reserves below our position, Holmes's brigade with 6 guns, and Early's brigade, also 2 regiments of Bonham's brigade, near at hand, to move swiftly to the left. General Johnston and I now set out at full speed for the point of conflict. We arrived there just as Bee's troops, after giving way, were fleeing in disorder behind the height in rear of the Stone Bridge. They had come around between the base of the hill and the Stone Bridge into a shallow ravine which ran up to a point on the crest where Jackson had already formed his brigade along the edge of the woods. We found the commanders resolutely stemming the further flight of the routed forces, but vainly endeavoring to restore order, and our own efforts were as futile. Every segment of line we succeeded in forming was again dissolved while another was being formed; more than two thousand men were shouting each some suggestion to his neighbor, their voices mingling with the noise of the shells hurtling through the trees overhead, and all word of command drowned in the confusion and uproar. It was at this moment that General Bee used the famous expression, "Look at Jackson's brigade! It stands there like a stone wall"—a name that passed from the brigade to its immortal commander. The disorder seemed irretrievable, but happily the thought came to me that if their colors were planted out to the front the men might rally on them, and I gave the order to carry the standards forward some forty yards, which was promptly executed by the regimental officers, thus drawing the common eye of the troops. They now received easily the orders to advance and form on the line of their colors, which they obeyed with a general movement; and as General Johnston and myself rode forward shortly after with the colors of the 4th Alabama by our side, the line that had fought all morning, and had fled, routed and disordered, now advanced again into position as steadily as veterans. The 4th Alabama had previously lost all its field-officers; and noticing Colonel S. R. Gist, an aide to General Bee, a young man whom I had known as adjutant-general of South Carolina, and whom I greatly esteemed, I presented him as an able and brave commander to the stricken regiment, who cheered their new leader, and maintained under him, to the end of the day, their previous gallant behavior. We had come none too soon, as the enemy's forces, flushed with the belief of accomplished victory, were already advancing across the valley of Young's Branch and up the slope, where they had encountered for a while the fire of the Hampton Legion, which had been led forward toward the Robinson house and the turnpike in front, covering the retreat and helping materially to check the panic of Bee's routed forces.

As soon as order was restored I requested General Johnston to go back to Portici (the Lewis house), and from that point — which I considered most favorable for the purpose — forward me the reënforcements as they would come from the Bull Run lines below and those that were expected to arrive from Manassas, while I should direct the field. General Johnston was disinclined to leave the battle-field for that position. As I had been compelled to leave my chief-of-staff, Colonel Jordan, at Manassas to forward any troops arriving there, I felt it was a necessity that one of us should go to this duty, and that it was his place to do so, as I felt I was responsible for the battle. He considerately yielded to my urgency, and we had the benefit of his energy and sagacity in so directing the reënforcements toward the field, as to be readily and effectively assistant to my pressing needs and insure the success of the day.

As General Johnston departed for Portici, I hastened to form our line of battle against the on-coming enemy. I ordered up the 49th and 8th Virginia regiments from Cocke's neighboring brigade in the Bull Run lines. Gartrell's 7th Georgia I placed in position on the left of Jackson's brigade, along the belt of pines occupied by the latter on the eastern rim of the plateau. As the 49th Virginia rapidly came up, its colonel, ex-Governor William Smith, was encouraging them with cheery word and manner, and, as they approached, indicated to them the immediate presence of the commander. As the regiment raised a loud cheer, the name was caught by some of the troops of Jackson's brigade in the immediate wood, who rushed out, calling for General Beauregard. Hastily acknowledging these happy signs of sympathy and confidence, which reënforce alike the capacity of commander and troops, I placed the 49th Virginia in position on the extreme left next to Gartrell, and as I paused to say a few words to Jackson, while hurrying back to the right, my horse was killed under me by a bursting shell, a fragment of which carried away part of the heel of my boot. The Hampton Legion, which had suffered greatly, was placed on the right of Jackson's brigade, and Hunton's 8th Virginia, as it arrived, upon the right of Hampton; the two latter being drawn somewhat to the rear so as to form with Jackson's right regiment a reserve, and be ready likewise to make defense against any advance from the direction of the Stone Bridge, whence there was imminent peril from the enemy's heavy forces, as I had just stripped that position almost entirely of troops to meet the active crisis on the plateau, leaving this quarter now covered only by a few men, whose defense was otherwise assisted solely by the obstruction of an abatis.

With 6500 men and 13 pieces of artillery, I now awaited the onset of the enemy, who were pressing forward 20,000 strong, ⚓ with 24 pieces of superior artillery and 7 companies of regular cavalry. They soon appeared over the farther rim of the plateau, seizing the Robinson house on my right and the Henry house opposite my left center. Near the latter they placed in position the two powerful batteries of Ricketts and Griffin of the regular army, and pushed forward up the Sudley road, the slope of which was cut so deep below the adjacent ground as to afford a covered way up to the plateau. Supported by the formidable lines of Federal musketry, these 2 batteries lost no time in making themselves felt, while 3 more batteries in rear on the high ground beyond the Sudley and Warrenton cross-roads swelled the shower of shell that fell among our ranks.

⚓ According to General Fry (page 188), the Union force in the seizure of the Henry hill consisted of four brigades, a cavalry battalion, and two batteries, or (as we deduce from General Fry's statements of the strength of McDowell's forces, page 195) about 11,000 men.— EDITORS.

Our own batteries, Imboden's, Stanard's, five of Walton's guns, reënforced later by Pendleton's and Alburtis's (their disadvantage being reduced by the shortness of range), swept the surface of the plateau from their position on the eastern rim. I felt that, after the accidents of the morning, much depended on maintaining the steadiness of the troops against the first heavy onslaught, and rode along the lines encouraging the men to unflinching behavior, meeting, as I passed each command, a cheering response. The steady fire of their musketry told severely on the Federal ranks, and the splendid action of our batteries was a fit preface to the marked skill exhibited by our artillerists during the war. The enemy suffered particularly from the musketry on our left, now further reënforced by the 2d Mississippi — the troops in this quarter confronting each other at very short range. Here two companies of Stuart's cavalry charged through the Federal ranks that filled the Sudley road, increasing the disorder wrought upon that flank of the enemy. But with superior numbers the Federals were pushing on new regiments in the attempt to flank my position, and several guns, in the effort to enfilade ours, were thrust forward so near the 33d Virginia that some of its men sprang forward and captured them, but were driven back by an overpowering force of Federal musketry. Although the enemy were held well at bay, their pressure became so strong that I resolved to take the offensive, and ordered a charge on my right for the purpose of recovering the plateau. The movement, made with alacrity and force by the commands of Bee, Bartow, Evans, and Hampton, thrilled the entire line, Jackson's brigade piercing the enemy's center, and the left of the line under Gartrell and Smith following up the charge, also, in that quarter, so that the whole of the open surface of the plateau was swept clear of the Federals.

Apart from its impressions on the enemy, the effect of this brilliant onset was to give a short breathing-spell to our troops from the immediate strain of conflict, and encourage them in withstanding the still more strenuous offensive that was soon to bear upon them. Reorganizing our line of battle under the unremitting fire of the Federal batteries opposite, I prepared to meet the new attack which the enemy were about to make, largely reënforced by the troops of Howard's brigade, newly arrived on the field. The Federals again pushed up the slope, the face of which partly afforded good cover by the numerous ravines that scored it and the clumps of young pines and oaks with which it was studded, while the sunken Sudley road formed a good ditch and parapet for their aggressive advance upon my left flank and rear. Gradually they pressed our lines back and regained possession of their lost ground and guns. With the Henry and Robinson houses once more in their possession, they resumed the offensive, urged forward by their commanders with conspicuous gallantry.

The conflict now became very severe for the final possession of this position, which was the key to victory. The Federal numbers enabled them so to extend their lines through the woods beyond the Sudley road as to outreach my left flank, which I was compelled partly to throw back, so as to meet the attack from that quarter; meanwhile their numbers equally enabled them to outflank my right in the direction of the Stone Bridge, imposing anxious watchfulness in that direction. I knew that I was safe if I could hold out till the arrival of reënforcements, which was but a matter of time; and, with the full sense of my own responsibility, I was determined to hold the line of the plateau, even if surrounded on all sides, until assistance should come, unless my forces were sooner overtaken by annihilation.

It was now between half-past 2 and 3 o'clock; a scorching sun increased the oppression of the troops, exhausted from incessant fighting, many of

them having been engaged since the morning. Fearing lest the Federal offensive should secure too firm a grip, and knowing the fatal result that might spring from any grave infraction of my line, I determined to make another effort for the recovery of the plateau, and ordered a charge of the entire line of battle, including the reserves, which at this

THE ROBINSON HOUSE. FROM A WAR-TIME PHOTOGRAPH.

crisis I myself led into action. The movement was made with such keeping and dash that the whole plateau was swept clear of the enemy, who were driven down the slope and across the turnpike on our right and the valley of Young's Branch on our left, leaving in our final possession the Robinson and Henry houses, with most of Ricketts's and Griffin's batteries, the men of which were mostly shot down where they bravely stood by their guns. Fisher's 6th North Carolina, directed to the Lewis house by Colonel Jordan from Manassas, where it had just arrived, and thence to the field by General Johnston, came up in happy time to join in this charge on the left. Withers's 18th Virginia, which I had ordered up from Cocke's brigade, was also on hand in time to follow and give additional effect to the charge, capturing, by aid of the Hampton Legion, several guns, which were immediately turned and served upon the broken ranks of the enemy by some of our officers. This handsome work, which broke the Federal fortunes of the day, was done, however, at severe cost. The soldierly Bee, and the gallant, impetuous Bartow, whose day of strong deeds was about to close with such credit, fell a few rods back of the Henry house, near the very spot whence in the morning they had first looked forth upon Evans's struggle with the enemy. Colonel Fisher also fell at the very head of his troops. Seeing Captain Ricketts, who was badly wounded in the leg, and having known him in the old army, I paused from my anxious duties to ask him whether I could do anything for him. He answered that he wanted to be sent back to Washington. As some of our prisoners were there held under threats of not being treated as prisoners of war, I replied that that must depend upon how our prisoners were treated, and ordered him to be carried to the rear. I mention this, because the report of the Federal Committee on the Conduct of the War exhibits Captain Ricketts as testifying that I only approached him to say that he would be treated as our prisoners might be treated. I sent my own surgeons to care for him, and allowed his wife to cross the lines and accompany him to Richmond; and my adjutant-general, Colonel Jordan, escorting her to the car that carried them to that city, personally attended to the comfortable placing of the wounded enemy for the journey.

That part of the enemy who occupied the woods beyond our left and across the Sudley road had not been reached by the headlong charge which had swept their comrades from the plateau; but the now arriving reënforcements (Kershaw's 2d and Cash's 8th South Carolina) were led into that quarter. Kemper's battery also came up, preceded by its commander, who, while alone, fell into the hands of a number of the enemy, who took him prisoner, until a few moments later, when he handed them over to some of our own troops accompanying his battery. A small plateau, within the south-west angle of the Sudley and turnpike cross-roads, was still held by a strong Federal brigade — Howard's troops, together with Sykes's battalion of regulars; and while Kershaw and Cash, after passing through the skirts of the oak wood along the Sudley road, engaged this force, Kemper's battery was sent forward by Kershaw along the same road, into position near where a hostile battery had been captured, and whence it played upon the enemy in the open field.

Quickly following these regiments came Preston's 28th Virginia, which, passing through the woods, encountered and drove back some Michigan troops, capturing Brigadier-General Willcox. It was now about 3 o'clock, when another important reënforcement came to our aid — Elzey's brigade, 1700 strong, of the Army of the Shenandoah, which, coming from Piedmont by railroad, had arrived at Manassas station, 6 miles in rear of the battle-field, at noon, and had been without delay directed thence toward the field by Colonel Jordan, aided by Major T. G. Rhett, who that morning had passed from General Bonham's to General Johnston's staff. Upon nearing the vicinity of the Lewis house, the brigade was directed by a staff-officer sent by General Johnston toward the left of the field. As it reached the oak wood, just across the Sudley road, led by General Kirby Smith, the latter fell severely wounded; but the command devolved upon Colonel Elzey, an excellent officer, who was now guided by Captain D. B. Harris of the Engineers, a highly accomplished officer of my staff, still farther to the left and through the woods, so as to form in extension of the line of the preceding reënforcements. Beckham's battery, of the same command, was hurried forward by the Sudley road and around the woods into position near the Chinn house; from a well-selected point of action, in full view of the enemy that filled the open fields west of the Sudley road, it played with deadly and decisive effect upon their ranks, already under the fire of Elzey's brigade. Keyes's Federal brigade, which had made its way across the turn-pike in rear of the Stone Bridge, was lurking along under cover of the ridges and a wood in order to turn my line on the right, but was easily repulsed by Latham's battery, already placed in position over that approach by Captain Harris, aided by Alburtis's battery, opportunely sent to Latham's left by General Jackson, and supported by fragments of troops collected by staff-officers. Meanwhile, the enemy had formed a line of battle of formidable proportions on the opposite height, and stretching in crescent outline, with flanks advanced, from the Pittsylvania (Carter) mansion on their left across the Sudley road in rear of Dogan's and reaching toward the Chinn house. They offered a fine spectacle as they threw forward a cloud of skirmishers down the opposite slope, preparatory to a new assault against the line on the plateau. But their right was now severely pressed by the troops that had successively arrived; the force in the south-west angle of the Sudley and Warrenton cross-roads were driven from their position, and, as Early's brigade, which, by direction of General Johnston, had swept around by the rear of the woods through which Elzey had passed, appeared on the field, his line of march bore upon the flank of the enemy, now retiring in that quarter.

This movement by my extreme left was masked by the trend of the woods from many of our forces on the plateau; and bidding those of my staff and escort around me raise a loud cheer, I dispatched the information to the several commands, with orders to go forward in a common charge. Before the full advance of the Confederate ranks the enemy's whole line, whose right was already yielding, irretrievably broke, fleeing across Bull Run by every available direction. Major Sykes's regulars, aided by Sherman's brigade, made a steady and handsome withdrawal, protecting the rear of the routed forces, and enabling many to escape by the Stone Bridge. Having ordered in pursuit all the troops on the field, I went to the Lewis house, and, the battle being ended, turned over the command to General Johnston. Mounting a fresh horse,—the fourth on that day,—I started to press the pursuit which was being made by our infantry and cavalry, some of the latter having been sent by General Johnston from Lewis's Ford to intercept the enemy on the turnpike. I was soon overtaken, however, by a courier bearing a message from Major T. G. Rhett, General Johnston's chief-of-staff on duty at Manassas railroad station, informing me of a report that a large Federal force, having pierced our lower line on Bull Run, was moving upon Camp Pickens, my depot of supplies near Manassas. I returned, and com-municated this important news to General Johnston. Upon consultation it was deemed best that I should take Ewell's and Holmes's brigades, which were hastening up to the battle-field, but too late for the action, and fall on this force of the enemy, while reënforcements should be sent me from the pursuing forces, who were to be recalled for that purpose. To head off the danger and gain time, I hastily mounted a force of infantry behind the cavalrymen then present, but, on approaching the line of march near McLean's Ford, which the Federals must have taken, I learned that the news

THE MAIN BATTLE-GROUND.—NO. I.

View of the Henry house, looking west from the spot where General Bee fell. The Bull Run mountains and Thoroughfare Gap appear in the distance. The Sudley road, a few rods beyond the house, under the hill, runs parallel with the rail fence (in the middle ground on the left). Just within the rail fence is where Griffin's and Ricketts's batteries were planted. Near the house stands the Union Monument, commemorating the battle.

was a false alarm caught from the return of General Jones's forces to this side of the Run, the similarity of the uniforms and the direction of their march having convinced some nervous person that they were a force of the enemy. It was now almost dark, and too late to resume the broken pursuit; on my return I met the coming forces, and, as they were very tired, I ordered them to halt and bivouac for the night where they were. After giving such attention as I could to the troops, I started for Manassas, where I arrived about 10 o'clock, and found Mr. Davis at my headquarters with General Johnston. Arriving from Richmond late in the afternoon, Mr. Davis had immediately galloped to the field, accompanied by Colonel Jordan. They had met between Manassas and the battle-field the usual number of stragglers to the rear, whose appearance belied the determined array then sweeping the enemy before it, but Mr. Davis had the happiness to arrive in time to witness the last of the Federals disappearing beyond Bull Run. The next morning I received from his hand at our breakfast-table my commission, dated July 21st, as General in the Army of the Confederate States, and after his return to Richmond the kind congratulations of the Secretary of War and of General Lee, then acting as military adviser to the President.

It was a point made at the time at the North that, just as the Confederate troops were about to break and flee, the Federal troops anticipated them by doing so, being struck into this precipitation by the arrival upon their flank

THE MAIN BATTLE-GROUND.— NO. 2.

View of the Robinson house, looking north from the spot on the Henry plateau where General Bee fell. At 1 P. M. this ground lay between the hostile lines, which were (roughly speaking) parallel with the sides of the picture : Confederates on the right, Union forces on the left. The foreground was between the centers of the positions.

As these two views are taken from the same spot, the reader will best understand their relation by holding the pages at a right angle to each other.

of the Shenandoah forces marching from railroad trains halted *en route* with that aim — errors' that have been repeated by a number of writers, and by an ambitious but superficial French author.

There were certain sentiments of a personal character clustering about this first battle, and personal anxiety as to its issue, that gladly accepted this theory. To this may be added the general readiness to accept a sentimental or ultra-dramatic explanation — a sorcery wrought by the delay or arrival of some force, or the death or coming of somebody, or any other single magical event — whereby history is easily caught, rather than to seek an understanding of that which is but the gradual result of the operation of many forces, both of opposing design and actual collision, modified more or less by the falls of chance. The personal sentiment, though natural enough at the time, has no place in any military estimate, or place of any kind at this day. The battle of Manassas was, like any other battle, a progression and development from the deliberate counter-employment of the military resources in hand, affected by accidents, as always, but of a kind very different from those referred to. My line of battle, which twice had not only withstood the enemy's attack, but had taken the offensive and driven him back in disorder, was becoming momentarily stronger from the arrival, at last, of the reënforcements provided for; and if the enemy had remained on the field till the arrival of Ewell and

Holmes, they would have been so strongly outflanked that many who escaped would have been destroyed or captured.

Though my adversary's plan of battle was a good one as against a passive defensive opponent, such as he may have deemed I must be from the respective numbers and positions of our forces, it would, in my judgment, have been much better if, with more dash, the flank attack had been made by the Stone Bridge itself and the ford immediately above it. The plan adopted, however, favored above all things the easy execution of the offensive operations I had designed and ordered against his left flank and rear at Centreville. His turning column — 18,000 strong, and presumably his best troops — was thrown off by a long ellipse through a narrow forest road to Sudley Ford, from which it moved down upon my left flank, and was thus dislocated from his main body. This severed movement of his forces not only left his exposed left and rear at Centreville weak against the simultaneous offensive of my heaviest forces upon it, which I had ordered, but the movement of his returning

COLONEL F. S. BARTOW.   FROM A PHOTOGRAPH.

column would have been disconcerted and paralyzed by the early sound of this heavy conflict in its rear, and it could not even have made its way back so as to be available for manœuvre before the Centreville fraction had been thrown back upon it in disorder. A new army is very liable to panic, and, in view of the actual result of the battle, the conclusion can hardly be resisted that the panic which fell on the Federal army would thus have seized it early in the day, and with my forces in such a position as wholly to cut off its retreat upon Washington. But the commander of the front line on my right, who had been ordered to hold himself in readiness to initiate the offensive at a moment's notice, did not make the move expected of him because through accident he failed to receive his own immediate order to advance.↓ The Federal commander's flanking movement, being thus uninterrupted by such a counter-movement as I had projected, was further assisted through the rawness and inadequacy of our staff organization through which I was left unacquainted with the actual state of affairs on my left. The Federal attack, already thus greatly favored, and encouraged, moreover, by the rout of General Bee's advanced line, failed for two reasons : their forces were not handled with concert of masses (a fault often made later on both sides), and the individual action of the Confederate troops was superior, and for a very palpable reason. That one army was fighting for union and the other for disunion is a political expression ; the actual fact on the battle-field, in the face of cannon and musket, was that the Federal troops came as invaders,

↓General R. S. Ewell.   See statement of Major Campbell Brown, page 259.—EDITORS.

and the Southern troops stood as defenders of their homes, and further than this we need not go. The armies were vastly greater than had ever before fought on this continent, and were the largest volunteer armies ever assembled since the era of regular armies. The personal material on both sides was of exceptionally good character, and collectively superior to that of any subsequent period of the war.♭ The Confederate army was filled with generous youths who had answered the first call to arms. For certain kinds of field duty they were not as yet adapted, many of them having at first come with their baggage and servants; these they had to dispense with, but, not to offend their susceptibilities, I then exacted the least work from them, apart from military drills, even to the prejudice of important field-works, when I could not get sufficient negro labor; they "had come to fight, and not to handle the pick and shovel," and their fighting redeemed well their shortcomings as intrenchers. Before I left that gallant army, however, it had learned how readily the humbler could aid the nobler duty.

As to immediate results and trophies, we captured a great many stands of arms, batteries, equipments, standards, and flags, one of which was sent to me, through General Longstreet, as a personal compliment by the Texan "crack shot," Colonel B. F. Terry, who lowered it from its mast at Fairfax Court House, by cutting the halyards by means of his unerring rifle, as our troops next morning reoccupied that place. We captured also many prisoners, including a number of surgeons, whom (the first time in war) we treated not as prisoners, but as guests. Calling attention to their brave devotion to their wounded, I recommended to the War Department that they be sent home without exchange, together with some other prisoners, who had shown personal kindness to Colonel Jones, of the 4th Alabama, who had been mortally wounded early in the day.

SUBSEQUENT RELATIONS OF MR. DAVIS AND THE WRITER.

THE military result of the victory was far short of what it should have been. It established as an accomplished fact, on the indispensable basis of military success, the Government of the Confederate States, which before was but a political assertion; but it should have reached much further. The immediate pursuit, but for the false alarm which checked it, would have continued as far as the Potomac, but must have stopped there with no greater result than the capture of more prisoners and material. The true immediate fruits of the victory should have been the dispersion of all the Federal forces south of Baltimore and east of the Alleghanies, the liberation of the State of Maryland, and the capture of Washington, which could have been made only by the Upper Potomac. And from the high source of this achievement other decisive results would have continued to flow. From my experience in the

♭ This battle was noteworthy for the number of participants whose names are now prominently associated with the war. On the Confederate side, besides Generals Johnston and Beauregard, were Generals Stonewall Jackson, Longstreet, Ewell, Early, J. E. B. Stuart, Kirby Smith, Wade Hampton, Fitzhugh Lee, Thomas Jordan, R. E. Rodes, E. P. Alexander, and others. On the Federal side were Generals McDowell, W. T. Sherman, Burnside, Hunter, Heintzelman, Howard, Franklin, Slocum, Keyes, Hunt, Barry, Fry, Sykes, Barnard, Wadsworth, and others. —EDITORS.

Mexican war I had great confidence in intelligent volunteer troops, if rightly handled; and with such an active and victorious war-engine as the Confederate Army of the Potomac could have immediately been made,— reënforced, as time went, by numbers and discipline,— the Federal military power in the East could never have reached the head it took when McClellan was allowed to organize and discipline at leisure the powerful army that,

in the end, wore out the South. In war one success makes another easier, and its right use is as the step to another, until final achievement. This was the use besought by me in the plan of campaign I have mentioned as presented to Mr. Davis on the 14th of July, a few days before the battle, but rejected by him as impracticable, and as rather offering opportunity

FAIRFAX COURT HOUSE. FROM A WAR-TIME PHOTOGRAPH.

to the enemy to crush us. To supply the deficiency of transportation (our vehicles being few in number, and many so poor as to break down in ordinary camp service), I myself had assigned to special duty Colonel (since Governor) James L. Kemper, of Virginia, who quickly obtained for me some two hundred good wagons, to which number I had limited him so as not to arouse again the jealousy of the President's staff. If my plan of operations for the capture of Washington had been adopted, I should have considered myself thereby authorized and free to obtain, as I readily could have done, the transportation necessary. As it was—though the difficult part of this "impracticable" plan of operations had been proven feasible, that is, the concentration of the Shenandoah forces with mine (wrung later than the eleventh hour through the alarm over the march upon Richmond, and discountenanced again nervously at the twelfth hour by another alarm as to how "the enemy may vary his plans" in consequence), followed by the decisive defeat of the main Federal forces — nevertheless the army remained rooted in the spot, although we had more than fifteen thousand troops who had been not at all or but little in the battle and were perfectly organized, while the remaining commands, in the high spirits of victory, could have been reorganized at the tap of the drum, and many with improved captured arms and equipments. I had already urged my views with unusual persistency, and acted on them against all but an express order to the contrary; and as they had been deliberately rejected in their ultimate scope by Mr. Davis as the commander-in-chief, I did not feel authorized to urge them further than their execution had been allowed, unless the subject were broached anew by himself. But there was no intimation of any such change of purpose, and the army, consistently with this inertia, was left unprovided for manœuvre with transportation for its ammunition; its fortitude, moreover, as a new and volunteer army, while spending sometimes 24 hours without food, being only less wonderful than the commissary administration at Richmond, from which such a state of affairs could proceed even two weeks after the battle of Manassas. Although certain political superstitions about not consolidating the North may then have weighed against the action I proposed, they would have been light against a true military policy, if such had existed in the head of the Government. Apart from an active material ally, such as the colonies had afield and on sea in the War of Independence with Great Britain, a country in fatal war must depend on the vigor of its warfare; the more inferior the country, the bolder and more enterprising the use of its resources, especially if its frontiers are convenient to the enemy. I was convinced that our success lay in a short, quick war of decisive blows, before the Federals, with their vast resources, could build up a great military power; to which end a concerted use of our forces, immediate and sustained, was necessary, so that, weaker though we were at all separate points, we might nevertheless strike with superior strength at some chosen decisive point, and after victory there reach for victory now made easier elsewhere, and thus sum up success. Instead of this, which in war we call concentration, our actual policy was diffusion, an inferior Confederate force at each separate point defensively confronting a superior Federal force; our power daily shrinking, that of the enemy increasing; the avowed Federal policy being that of "attrition," their bigger masses grinding our smaller, one by one, to naught. Out of this state we never emerged, when the direction of the Government was, as almost always, necessary, excepting when "Richmond" was immediately in danger.

Thus, in the fall of 1861, about three months after the battle of Manassas,—after throwing my whole force forward to Fairfax Court House, with outposts flaunting our flags on the hills in sight of Washington, in order to chafe the Federals to another battle, but without success,—I proposed that the army should be raised to an effective of 60,000 men, by drawing 20,000 for the immediate enterprise from several points along the seaboard, not even at that time threatened, and from our advanced position be swiftly thrown across the Potomac at a point which I had had carefully surveyed for that purpose, and moved upon the rear of Washington, thus forcing McClellan to a decisive engagement before his organization (new enlistments) was completed, and while our own army had the advantage of discipline and prestige — seasoned soldiers, whose term, however, would expire in the early part of the coming summer. This plan, approved by General Gustavus W. Smith (then immediately commanding General Johnston's own forces) as well as by General Johnston, was submitted to Mr. Davis in a conference at my headquarters, but rejected because he would not venture to strip those points of the troops we required. Even if those points had been captured, though none were then even threatened, they must have reverted as a direct consequence to so decisive a success. I was willing, then, should it have come to that, to exchange even Richmond temporarily for Washington. Yet it was precisely from similar combinations and elements that the army was made up, to enable it the next spring, under General Lee, to encounter McClellan at the very door of Richmond. If that which was accepted as a last defensive resort against an overwhelming aggressive army had been used in an enterprising offensive against that same army while yet in the raw, the same venture had been made at less general risk, less cost of valuable lives, and with greater certain results. The Federal army would have had no chance meanwhile to become tempered to that magnificent military machine which, through all its defeats and losses, remained sound, and was stronger, with its readily assimilating new strength, at the end of the war than ever before; the pressure would have been lifted from Kentucky and Missouri, and we should have maintained what is called an active defensive warfare, that is, should have taken and kept the offensive against the enemy, enforcing peace.

No people ever warred for independence with more relative advantages than the Confederates; and if, as a military question, they must have failed, then no country must aim at freedom by means of war. We were one in sentiment as in territory, starting out, not with a struggling administration of doubtful authority, but with our ancient State governments and a fully organized central government. As a military question, it was in no sense a civil war, but a war between two countries—for conquest on one side, for self-preservation on the other. The South, with its great material resources, its defensive means of mountains, rivers, railroads, and telegraph, with the immense advantage of the interior lines of war, would be open to discredit as a people if its failure could not be explained otherwise than by mere material contrast. The great Frederick, at the head of a little people, not only beat back a combination of several great military powers, but conquered and kept territory; and Napoleon held combined Europe at the feet of France till his blind ambition overleaped itself. It may be said that the South had no Fredericks or Napoleons; but it had at least as good commanders as its adversary. Nor was it the fault of our soldiers or people. Our soldiers were as brave and intelligent as ever bore arms; and, if only for reasons already mentioned, they did not lack in determination. Our people bore a devotion to the cause never surpassed, and which no war-making monarch ever had for his support; they gave their all—even the last striplings under the family roofs filling the ranks voided by the fall of their fathers and brothers. But the narrow military view of the head of the Government, which illustrated itself at the outset by ordering from Europe, not 100,000 or 1,000,000, but 10,000 stands of arms, as an increase upon 8000, its first estimate, was equally narrow and timid in its employment of our armies.

The moral and material forces actually engaged in the war made our success a moral certainty, but for the timid policy which—ignoring strategy as a science and boldness of enterprise as its ally—could never be brought to view the whole theater of war as one subject, of which all points were but integral parts, or to hazard for the time points relatively unimportant for the purpose of gathering for an overwhelming and rapid stroke at some decisive point; and which, again, with characteristic mis-elation, would push a victorious force directly forward into unsupported and disastrous operations, instead of using its victory to spare from it strength sufficient to secure an equally important success in another quarter. The great principles of war are truths, and the same to-day as in the time of Cæsar or Napoleon, notwithstanding the ideas of some thoughtless persons—their applications being but intensified by the scientific discoveries affecting transportation and communication of intelligence. These principles are few and simple, however various their deductions and application. Skill in strategy consists in seeing through the intricacies of the whole situation, and bringing into proper combination forces and influences, though seemingly unrelated, so as to apply these principles, and with boldness of decision and execution appearing with the utmost force, and, if possible, superior odds, before the enemy at some strategic, that is, decisive point. And although a sound military plan may not be always so readily conceived, yet any plan that offers decisive results, if it agree with the principles of war, is as plain and intelligible as these principles themselves, and no more to be rejected than they. There still remains, of course, the hazard of accident in execution, and the apprehension of the enemy's movements upsetting your own; but hazard may also favor as well as disfavor, and will not unbefriend the enterprising any more than the timid. It was this fear of possible consequences that kept our forces scattered in inferior relative strength at all points of the compass, each holding its bit of ground till by slow local process our territory was taken and our separate forces destroyed, or, if captured, retained by the enemy without exchange in their process of attrition. To stop the slow consumption of this passive mode of warfare I tried my part, and, at certain critical junctures, proposed to the Government active plans of operation looking to such results as I have described,—sometimes, it is true, in relation to the employment of forces not under my control, as I was the soldier of a cause and people, not of a monarch nor even of a government. Two occasions there were when certain of the most noted Federal operations, from their isolated or opportune character, might, with energy and intelligent venture on the Confederate side, have been turned into fatal disaster; among them Grant's movement in front of Vicksburg, and his change of base from the north to the south of the James River, where I was in command, in his last campaign against Richmond. I urged particularly that our warfare was sure of final defeat unless we attempted decisive strokes that might be followed up to the end, and that, even if earlier defeat might chance from the risk involved in the execution of the necessary combinations, we ought to take that risk and thereby either win or end an otherwise useless struggle. But, in addition to the radical divergence of military ideas,—the passive defensive of an intellect timid of risk and not at home in war, and the active defensive reaching for success through enterprise and boldness, according to the lessons taught us in the campaigns of the great masters,—there was a personal feeling that now gave

RUINS OF THE STONE BRIDGE, LOOKING ALONG THE WARRENTON TURNPIKE TOWARD THE BATTLE-FIELD.

This view is from a photograph taken in March, 1862, the region having been left open to the Union forces by the withdrawal of the Confederates. The Confederate battery which in the first battle of Bull Run commanded the bridge was placed on the left in the felled timber, which formed an abatis across the road. The battle was opened from beyond the small house, Van Pelt's, on the right, by the Rhode Island troops.— EDITORS.

cold hearing, or none, to any recommendations of mine. Mr. Davis's friendship, warm at the early period of the war, was changed, some time after the battle of Manassas, to a corresponding hostility from several personal causes, direct and indirect, of which I need mention but one. My report of Manassas having contained, as part of its history, a statement of the submission of the full plan of campaign for concentrating our forces, crushing successively McDowell and Patterson and capturing Washington, Mr. Davis strangely took offense thereat; and, now that events had demonstrated the practicability of that plan, he sought to get rid of his self-accused responsibility for rejecting it, by denying that any such had been submitted — an issue, for that matter, easily settled by my production of the contemporaneous report of Colonel James Chesnut, the bearer of the mission, who, moreover, at the time of this controversy was on Mr. Davis's own staff, where he remained. Mr. Davis made an endeavor to suppress the publication of my report of the battle of Manassas. The matter came up in a secret debate in the Confederate Congress, where a host of friends were ready to sustain me; but I sent a telegram disclaiming any desire for its publication, and advising that the safety of the country should be our solicitude, and not personal ends.

Thenceforth Mr. Davis's hostility was watchful and adroit, neglecting no opportunity, great or small; and though, from motives all its opposite, it was not exposed during the war by any murmurs of mine, it bruited sometimes in certain quarters of its own force. Thus, when in January, 1862, the Western representatives expressed a desire that I should separate myself for a time from my Virginia forces and go to the defense of the Mississippi Valley from the impending offensive of Halleck and Grant, it was furthered by the Executive with inducements which I trusted,—in disregard of Senator Toombs's sagacious warning, that under this furtherance lurked a purpose to effect my downfall, urged in one of his communications through his son-in-law, Mr. Alexander, in words as impressive as they proved prophetic : " Urge General Beauregard to decline all proposals and solicitations. The Blade of Joab. *Verbum Sapienti.*" After going through the campaign of Shiloh and Corinth, not only with those inducements unfulfilled, but with vital drawbacks from the Government, including the refusal of necessary rank to competent subordinates to assist in organizing my hastily collected and mostly raw troops, I was forced, the following June, in deferred obedience to the positive order of my physicians, to withdraw from my immediate camp to another point in my department for recovery from illness, leaving under the care of my lieutenant, General Bragg, my army, then unmenaced and under reorganization with a view to an immediate offensive I had purposed. In anticipation and exclusion of the receipt of full dispatches following my telegram, the latter was tortuously misread, in a manner not creditable to a school-boy and repugnant to Mr. Davis's exact knowledge of syntax, so as to give pretext to the shocking charge that I had abandoned my army, and a telegram was sent in naked haste directly to General Bragg, telling him to retain the permanent command of the army. The " Blade of Joab " had given its thrust. The representatives in Congress from the West and South-west applied to Mr. Davis in a body for my restoration ; and when, disregarding his sheer pretext that I had abandoned my army, they still insisted, Mr. Davis declared that I should not be restored *if the whole world should ask it !* This machination went to such length that it was given out in Richmond that I had softening of the brain and had gone crazy. So carefully was this report fostered (one of its tales being that I would sit all day stroking a pheasant ⸿) that a friend of mine, a member of the Confederate Congress, thought it his duty to write me a special letter respecting the device, advising me to come directly to Richmond to confound it by my presence — a proceeding which I disdained to take. I had not only then, but from later, still more offensive provocation, imperative cause to resign, and would have done so but for a sense of public obligation. Indeed, in my after fields of action the same hostility was more and more active in its various embarrassments, reckless that the strains inflicted upon me bore upon the troops and country depending on me and relatively upon the cause, so that I often

⸿ This silly tale was borrowed from an incident of Shiloh. Toward the end of the first day's battle a soldier had found a pheasant cowering, apparently paralyzed under the ceaseless din, and brought it to my headquarters as a present to me. It was a beautiful bird, and I gave directions to place it in a cage, as I intended sending it as a pleasant token of the battle to the family of Judge Milton Brown, of Jackson, Tennessee, from whom I had received as their guest, while occupying that place, the kindest attentions ; but in the second day's conflict the poor waif was lost.— G. T. B.

dreaded failure more from my own Government behind me than from the
enemy in my front; and, when success came in spite of this, it was acknowledged only by some censorious official "inquiry" contrasting with the repeated
thanks of the Congress. I was, however, not the only one of the highest
military rank with whom Mr. Davis's relations were habitually unwholesome.
It is an extraordinary fact that during the four years of war Mr. Davis did
not call together the five generals [see page 241] with a view to determining
the best military policy or settling upon a decisive plan of operations involving the whole theater of war, though there was often ample opportunity for it.
We needed for President either a military man of a high order, or a politician of
the first class without military pretensions, such as Howell Cobb. The South
did not fall crushed by the mere weight of the North; but it was nibbled
away at all sides and ends because its executive head never gathered and
wielded its great strength under the ready advantages that greatly reduced
or neutralized its adversary's naked physical superiority. It is but another
of the many proofs that timid direction may readily go with physical courage, and that the passive defensive policy may make a long agony, but can
never win a war.

POSTSCRIPT.— Since the publication of the foregoing pages in "The Century"
for November, 1884, General J. E. Johnston, in the course of a paper also contributed to "The Century" [see page 240], took occasion, for the first time, to
set up with positiveness and circumstantiality the claim to having exercised
a controlling connection with the tactics of all the phases of the battle of the 21st
of July, 1861. Respecting such a pretension I shall be content for the present
to recall that, while entirely at variance with the part I have ascribed to him
in relation to that field, it is logically untenable, at this day, when confronted
with the records of the period. In my own official report of the battle closely
contemporaneous with the events narrated — a report that was placed in his
hands for perusal before transmission — it is distinctly related that for certain
reasons, chiefly military, General Johnston had left in my hands for the
impending conflict the command of the Confederate forces. The precise circumstances of my direct conduct of and responsibility for the battle are
stated in such terms that, had I not been in actual direction of the day's
operations on the part of the Confederates, General Johnston must have made
the issue squarely then and there in his own official report. And all the more
incumbent upon him was the making of such an issue, it seems to me, then
or never, in view of the fact that the Confederate Secretary of War on the
24th of July, 1861, wrote me in these words:

"MY DEAR GENERAL: Accept my congratulations for the glorious and most brilliant victory
achieved by you. The country will bless and honor you for it. Believe me, dear General,
        "Truly your friend, L. P. WALKER."

Further, General Lee thus addressed me:

"MY DEAR GENERAL: I cannot express the joy I feel at the brilliant victory of the 21st. The
skill, courage, and endurance displayed by yourself excite my highest admiration. You and
your troops have the gratitude of the whole country, and I offer to all my heartfelt congratulations at their success. . . . Very truly yours, R. E. LEE."

Of the exact purport of these two letters General Johnston could not have been ignorant when he wrote his report of the battle. Nor could he have been unaware that the leading Southern newspapers had in effect attributed to me the chief direction of that battle on the Confederate side. Therefore, if it were the gross historical error which, twenty odd years after the affair, General Johnston characterizes it to be, and one that imputed to him the shirking of a duty which he could not have left unassumed without personal baseness, certainly that was the time for him by a few explicit words in his official report to dispose of so affronting an error. In that report, however, no such exigent, peremptory statement of his relation to the battle is to be found. On the other hand, upon page 57 of his "Narrative" published in 1874 (D. Appleton & Co.), may be found, I fear, the clew to the motive of his actual waiver of command in this curious paragraph:

"If the tactics of the Federals had been equal to their strategy, we should have been beaten. If, instead of being brought into action in detail, their troops had been formed in two lines, with a proper reserve, and had assailed Bee and Jackson in that order, the two Southern brigades must have been swept from the field in a few minutes, or enveloped. General McDowell would have made such a formation, probably, had he not greatly underestimated the strength of his enemy."

Coupled with the disquieting, ever-apprehensive tenor of his whole correspondence with the Confederate War Department, from the day he assumed command in the Valley of Virginia in May, 1861, down to the close of the struggle in 1865, the fair inference from such language as that just cited from his "Narrative" is that General Johnston came to Manassas beset with the idea that our united forces would not be able to cope with the Federal army, and that we should be beaten— a catastrophe in which he was not solicitous to figure on the pages of history as the leading and responsible actor. Originally and until 1875, I had regarded it as a generous though natural act on the part of General Johnston, in such a juncture, to leave me in command and responsible for what might occur. The history of military operations abounds in instances of notable soldiers who have found it proper to waive chief command under similar conditions.

CONFEDERATE QUAKER GUNS. FROM A PHOTOGRAPH.

Confederate fortifications, near Centreville, after their evacuation in the spring of 1862. The muzzle of the log was painted black and the breech was covered with brush to conceal its character from observation by balloon.

FROM A PHOTOGRAPH TAKEN AFTER THE WAR.

THE NEW HENRY HOUSE AND THE MONUMENT OF THE FIRST BATTLE. FROM A PHOTOGRAPH TAKEN IN 1884.

INCIDENTS OF THE FIRST BULL RUN.

BY JOHN D. IMBODEN, BRIGADIER-GENERAL, C. S. A.

FROM the day of his arrival at Winchester [see page 124], General John-ston was ceaseless in his labors to improve the efficiency of his little army, in which he was greatly assisted by several staff-officers who afterward rose to high distinction. The two most active of these subordinates were Majors W. H. C. Whiting and E. Kirby Smith, the former of whom as a major-general fell mortally wounded at the capture of Fort Fisher in North Carolina, and the latter as a lieutenant-general commanded the Trans-Mississippi army when the final collapse came. During our withdrawal from Harper's Ferry, on June 16th, we were deflected from our direct line of march, and held in line of battle a day at Bunker Hill, a few miles north of Winchester, to receive an expected assault from General Patterson, who had crossed the Potomac, but went back without attacking us. Again on July 2d we were marched to Darksville, about midway to Martinsburg, to meet Patterson, where we lay in line of battle till the 5th, when General Patterson, after a slight "brush" with Jackson, again recrossed the Potomac. We returned to Winchester, and to our arduous drilling.

After midnight of July 17th, General Bee, my brigade commander, sent for me to go with him to headquarters, whither he had been summoned. Several brigade commanders were assembled in a room with General Johnston, and a conference of one or two hours was held. When General Bee joined me on the porch to return to our quarters, I saw he was excited, and I asked him, "What is up?" He took my arm, and, as we walked away, told me we would march next day to the support of General Beauregard. He repeated a telegram General Johnston had received from Adjutant-General Cooper about mid-night. This was the famous dispatch that has led to so much controversy between Mr. Davis and General Johnston, as to whether it was a peremptory order, or simply permission to Johnston to go to Beauregard's support. I quote it, and leave the reader to his own construction:

"General Beauregard is attacked; to strike the enemy a decisive blow, a junction of all your effective force will be needed. If practicable, make the movement, sending your sick and baggage to Culpeper Court House, either by railroad or by Warrenton. In all the arrange-ments exercise your discretion."

On the next day, the 18th of July, we left Winchester for Manassas. It was late in the afternoon before my battery took up the line of march—as I now recollect, with the rear-guard, as had been the case when we left Harper's Ferry a month before. It was thought probable that Patterson, who was south of the Potomac, and only a few miles distant, would follow us. But J. E. B. Stuart and Ashby with the cavalry so completely masked our movement that it was not suspected by Patterson until July 20th, the day before the Bull Run fight, and then it was too late for him to interfere.

On the second day of the march an order reached me at Rectortown, Virginia, through Brigadier-General Barnard E. Bee, to collect the four field-batteries of Johnston's army into one column, and, as senior artillery captain, to march them by country roads that were unobstructed by infantry or trains as rapidly as possible to Manassas Junction, and to report my arrival, at any hour, day or night, to General Bee, who was going forward by rail with his brigade. Having assembled the batteries in the night, I began the march at dawn of Saturday, July 20th, the day before the battle. About 8 in the morning we reached a village in Fauquier county — Salem, I think it was. The whole population turned out to greet us. Men, women, and children brought us baskets, trays, and plates loaded with their own family breakfasts. With the improvidence of raw campaigners, we had finished the night before our three days' cooked rations; so I ordered a halt for thirty minutes to enjoy the feast. The Staunton Artillery↲ (my own battery) was at the head of the column, and, being largely composed of young men of high social standing, was especially honored by the ladies of the village, conspicuous among whom were the young daughters of Colonel John A. Washington, late of Mount Vernon. I noticed that some of the young fellows of the battery, lingering round the baskets borne by these young ladies, who bade them die or conquer in the fight, seemed very miserable during the remainder of the march. No doubt many of them, during the battle, felt that it would be better to die on the field than retreat and live to meet those enthusiastic girls again. I make special note of that breakfast because it was the last food any of us tasted till the first Bull Run had been fought and won, 36 hours later.

It was 1 o'clock that night when the head of my little column reached General Bee's headquarters, about one mile north-east of Manassas Junction. He was established in the log-cabin to which afterward he was brought when he was mortally wounded, and to which I shall again allude. General Bee ordered us to unharness the horses and bivouac in the fence corners, adding, "You will need all the rest you can get, for a great battle will begin in the morning."

A little after daybreak we were aroused by the sharp, ringing report of a great Parrott gun across Bull Run, two miles away, and the whizzing of a 30-pounder elongated shell over the tree-tops, 400 or 500 yards to our left. Instantly every man was on his feet, and in five minutes the horses were

↲ It numbered 140 officers and men. Six were college graduates, and several had left college to enter the army. The majority were young men of leisure or mercantile clerks. About forty were young mechanics, whose mechanical skill was of much service. I had provided them with red flannel shirts at Harper's Ferry, because our uniforms were too fine for camp life and for service in the field.—J. D. I.

harnessed and hitched to the guns and caissons. General Bee beckoned to me to come up to the porch, where he was standing in his shirt-sleeves, having also been aroused by the shot. He rapidly informed me of the disposition of our troops of Johnston's army so far as they had arrived at Manassas. His own brigade had been brought forward by rail the evening before. Above all, he was dissatisfied at the prospect of not participating prominently in the battle, saying that he had been ordered to the Stone Bridge, three or four miles away on our extreme left, to cover the left flank of the army from any movement that might be made against it. And as he had been directed to take a battery with him, he had selected mine, and wished me to move at once. He gave me a guide, and said he would follow immediately with his infantry. When I told him we had been 24 hours without food for men or horses, he said he would order supplies to follow, remarking, "You will have plenty of time to cook and eat, to the music of a battle in which we shall probably take little or no part."

Away we went, retracing our steps to the Junction, and by a westerly détour striking into the Sudley road, at a point half-way between the Junction and the scene of the battle. After an hour or so we ascended the hill to the Lewis house, or "Portici." Here a courier at full speed met us with news that the whole Federal army seemed to be marching north-westerly on the other side of Bull Run. Halting my men, I rode to the top of the hill, and had a full view of a long column of glittering bayonets moving up on the north side of the creek. Glancing down the valley, I saw Bee's brigade advancing, and galloped to meet him and report what I had seen. He divined the plans of

CONFEDERATE FORTIFICATIONS ABOUT MANASSAS JUNCTION.

This view is from a photograph taken in March, 1862. It represents the works substantially as they were at the time of the battle.

THE STONE HOUSE
ON THE WARRENTON TURNPIKE.
FROM A PHOTOGRAPH TAKEN IN MARCH, 1862.

The stream in the foreground is Young's Branch.
The Sudley road crosses a little to the left of
the picture. See map, page 204.

McDowell, and, asking me to accompany him, rode rapidly past the Lewis house, across the hollow beyond it, and up the next hill through the pines, emerging on the summit immediately east of the Henry house. As the beautiful open landscape in front burst upon his vision, he exclaimed with enthusiasm: " Here is the battle-field, and we are in for it ! Bring up your guns as quickly as possible, and I'll look round for a good position."

In less than twenty minutes I and my battery had passed the Lewis house, when I discovered Bee coming out of the pines. He stopped, and, placing his cap on his sword-point, waved it almost frantically as a signal to hurry forward. We went at a gallop, and were guided to a depression in the ground about one hundred yards to the north-east of the Henry house, where we unlimbered. With his keen military eye, General Bee had chosen the best possible position for a battery on all that field. We were almost under cover by reason of a slight swell in the ground immediately in our front, and not fifty feet away. Our shot passed not six inches above the surface of the ground on this " swell," and the recoil ran the guns back to still lower ground, where as we loaded only the heads of my men were visible to the enemy.

We went into position none too soon; for, by the time we had unlimbered, Captain Ricketts, appearing on the crest of the opposite hill, came beautifully and gallantly into battery at a gallop, a short distance from the Matthews house on our side of the Sudley road, and about fifteen hundred yards to our front. I wanted to open on him while he was unlimbering, but General Bee objected till we had received a fire, and had thus ascertained the character and caliber of the enemy's guns. Mine, four in number, were all brass smooth-bore 6-pounders. The first round or two from the enemy went high over us. Seeing this, General Bee directed us to fire low and ricochet our shot and shrapnel on the hard, smooth, open field that sloped toward the Warrenton turnpike in the valley between us. We did this, and the effect was very destructive to the enemy.

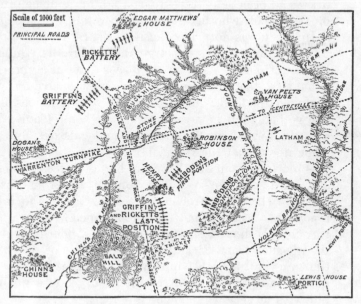

PLAN OF THE BULL RUN BATTLE-FIELD.

Imboden's second position is on the line of the Confederate front as formed by Jackson. Finally the Confederate line reached from behind the Robinson house to the left along the edge of the pines, and (as reënforcements came up) made a concave arc to a point behind the Chinn house. General Imboden counted twenty-six Confederate guns in the semicircle east of the Sudley road, when Griffin and Ricketts had taken position near the Henry house.—EDITORS.

The rapid massing of Federal troops in our front soon led to very heavy fighting. My little battery was under a pitiless fire for a long time. Two guns from an Alexandria battery— Latham's, I think — took part in the conflict on the north side of Young's Branch to our right and across the turnpike, so long as Bee, Bartow, Evans, and Wheat were on that side, we firing over their heads; and about 11 o'clock two brass 12-pounder Napoleons from the New Orleans Washington Artillery unlimbered on our right, retiring, however, after a few rounds.

We were hardly more than fairly engaged with Ricketts when Griffin's splendid battery came to his aid, and took position full five hundred yards nearer to us, in a field on the left of the Sudley road. Ricketts had 6 Parrott guns, and Griffin had as many more, and, I think, 2 12-pounder howitzers besides. These last hurt us more than all the rifles of both batteries, since the shot and shell of the rifles, striking the ground at any angle over 15 or 20 degrees, almost without exception bored their way in several feet and did no harm. It is no exaggeration to say that hundreds of shells from these fine rifle-guns exploded in front of and around my battery on that day, but so deep in the ground that the fragments never came out. After the action the ground looked as though it had been rooted up by hogs. ⚓

⚓ I venture the opinion, after a good deal of observation during the war, that in open ground, at 1000 yards, a 6-pounder battery of smooth guns, or, at 1500 to 1800 yards, a similar battery of 12-pounder Napoleons, well handled, will in one hour discomfit double the number of the best rifles ever

For at least a half-hour after our forces were driven across Young's Branch no Confederate soldier was visible from our position near the Henry house. The Staunton Artillery, so far as we could see, was "alone in its glory." General Bee's order had been, "Stay here till you are ordered away." To my surprise, no orders had come, though, as I afterward learned, orders to withdraw had been sent three-quarters of an hour before through Major Howard, of Bee's staff, who had fallen, desperately wounded, on the way.

Infantry was now massing near the Stone house on the turnpike, not five hundred yards away, to charge and capture us. On making this discovery and learning from the sergeants of pieces that our ammunition was almost entirely exhausted, there remained but one way to save our guns, and that was to run them off the field. More than half of our horses had been killed, only one or two being left in several of my six-horse teams. Those that we had were quickly divided among the guns and caissons, and we limbered up and fled. Then it was that the Henry house was riddled, and the old lady, Mrs. Henry, was mortally wounded;↓ for our line of retreat was so chosen that for 200 or 300 yards the house would conceal us from Griffin's battery, and, in a measure, shelter us from the dreaded fire of the infantry when they should reach the crest we had just abandoned. Several of Griffin's shot passed through the house, scattering shingles, boards, and splinters all around us. A rifle-shot from Ricketts broke the axle of one of our guns and dropped the gun in the field, but we saved the limber. The charging infantry gained the crest in front of the Henry house in time to give us one volley, but with no serious damage.

We crossed the summit at the edge of the pines, midway behind the Henry and Robinson houses, and there met "Stonewall" Jackson at the head of his brigade, marching by the flank at a double-quick. Johnston and Beauregard had arrived upon the field, and were hurrying troops into position, but we had not yet seen them.

When I met Jackson I felt very angry at what I then regarded as bad treatment from General Bee, in leaving us so long exposed to capture, and I expressed myself with some profanity, which I could see was displeasing to Jackson. He remarked, "I'll support your battery. Unlimber right here." We did so, when a perfect lull in the conflict ensued for 20 or 30 minutes — at least in that part of the field.

It was at this time that McDowell committed, as I think, the fatal blunder of the day, by ordering both Ricketts's and Griffin's batteries to cease firing and move across the turnpike to the top of the Henry Hill, and take position on the west side of the house. The short time required to effect the change enabled Beauregard to arrange his new line of battle on the highest crest of the hill,

---

put in the field. A smooth-bore gun never buries its projectiles in the ground, as the rifle does invariably when fired against sloping ground. Of course, this advantage of the smooth-bore gun is limited to its shorter range, and to an open field fight, defensive works not being considered.— J. D. I.

↓ Mrs. Judith Henry, bedridden from old age, was living in the house with her children. When the battle opened near the Matthews house, Mrs. Henry was carried into a ravine below the Sudley road. A little later the house seemed to be the safest place, and she was carried back to her bed. For a time the house was in the line of the artillery fire from both sides. Mrs. Henry received five wounds from fragments of shells, and died two hours after the battle.— EDITORS.

BRIG.-GEN. BARNARD E. BEE (IN THE UNIFORM OF A
CAPTAIN OF INFANTRY OF THE OLD SERVICE).
FROM A PHOTOGRAPH.

south-east of the Henry and Robinson houses, in the edge of the pines. If one of the Federal batteries had been left north of Young's Branch, it could have so swept the hill-top where we re-formed, that it would have greatly delayed, if not wholly have prevented, us from occupying the position. And if we had been forced back to the next hill, on which stands the Lewis house, Sherman, who had crossed Bull Run not far above the Stone Bridge at a farm ford, would have had a fair swing at our right flank, to say nothing of the effect of the artillery playing upon us from beyond Bull Run.

When my retiring battery met Jackson, and he assumed command of us, I reported that I had remaining only three rounds of ammunition for a single gun, and suggested that the caissons be sent to the rear for a supply. He said, "No, not now — wait till other guns get here, and then you can withdraw your battery, as it has been so torn to pieces, and let your men rest."

During the lull in front, my men lay about, exhausted from want of water and food, and black with powder, smoke, and dust. Lieutenant Harman and I had amused ourselves training one of the guns on a heavy column of the enemy, who were advancing toward us, in the direction of the Chinn house, but were still 1200 to 1500 yards away. While we were thus engaged, General Jackson rode up and said that three or four batteries were approaching rapidly, and that we might soon retire. I asked permission to fire the three rounds of shrapnel left to us, and he said, "Go ahead." I picked up a charge (the fuse was cut and ready) and rammed it home myself, remarking to Harman, "Tom, put in the primer and pull her off." I forgot to step back far enough from the muzzle, and, as I wanted to see the shell strike, I squatted to be under the smoke, and gave the word "Fire." Heavens! what a report. Finding myself full twenty feet away, I thought the gun had burst. But it was only the pent-up gas, that, escaping sideways as the shot cleared the muzzle, had struck my side and head with great violence. I recovered in time to see the shell explode in the enemy's ranks. The blood gushed out of my left ear, and from that day to this it has been totally deaf. The men fired the other two rounds, and limbered up and moved away, just as the Rockbridge Artillery, under Lieutenant Brockenbrough, came into position, followed a moment later by the Leesburg Artillery, under Lieutenant Henry Heaton. Pendleton, supposed by me still to be captain of the first, as Rogers was of the second, were not with their batteries when they unlimbered.⟩ But Heaton and Brockenbrough were equal to the occasion. Heaton had been under my command with his battery at the Point of Rocks, below Harper's Ferry, the previous May, and was a brave and skillful young officer. Several other batteries soon came into line, so that by the time Griffin and Ricketts were in position near the Henry house, we had, as I now remember, 26 fresh guns ready for them.

The contest that ensued was terrific. Jackson ordered me to go from battery to battery and see that the guns were properly aimed and the fuses cut the right length. This was the work of but a few minutes. On returning to the left of the line of guns, I stopped to ask General Jackson's permission to rejoin my battery. The fight was just then hot enough to make him feel well. His eyes fairly blazed. He had a way of throwing up his left hand with the open palm toward the person he was addressing. And as he told me to go, he made this gesture. The air was full of flying missiles, and as he spoke he jerked down his hand, and I saw that blood was streaming from it. I exclaimed, "General, you are wounded." He replied, as he drew a handkerchief from his breast-pocket, and began to bind it up, "Only a scratch — a mere scratch," and galloped away along his line.

To save my horse, I had hitched him in a little gully some fifty yards or more in the rear. And to reach him, I had to pass the six hundred infantry of Hampton's Legion, who were lying down in supporting distance of our artillery, then all in full play. While I was untying my horse, a shell exploded in the midst of Hampton's infantry, killing several and stampeding 15 or 20 nearest the spot. I tried to rally them; but one huge fellow, musket in hand, and with bayonet fixed, had started on a run. I threw myself in his front with drawn sword, and threatened to cut him down, whereupon he made a lunge at me. I threw up my left arm to ward off the blow, and the bayonet-point ran under the wristband of my red flannel shirt, and raked the skin of my arm from wrist to shoulder. The blow knocked me sprawling on the ground, and the fellow got away. I tore off the dangling shirt-sleeve, and was bare-armed as to my left, the remainder of the fight.

I overtook my battery on the hill near the Lewis house, which was used as a hospital. In a field in front I saw General Johnston and his staff grouped on their horses, and under fire from numerous shells that reached that hill. I rode up to him, reported our ammunition all gone, and requested to know where I could find the ordnance wagons and get a fresh supply. Observing the sorry plight of the battery and the condition of the surviving men and horses, he directed me to remove them farther to the rear to a place of perfect safety, and return myself to the field, where I might be of some service.

I took the battery back perhaps a mile, where we found a welcome little stream of water. Being greatly exhausted, I rested for perhaps an hour, and returned to the front with Sergeant Joseph Shumate.

⟩ Captain, afterward General, Pendleton had recently been made a colonel and chief of artillery to General Johnston, which separated him from the Rockbridge Artillery. Captain Rogers, I also learn, had a section somewhere lower down on Bull Run with the troops at the fords.— J. D. I.

When we regained the crest of the Henry plateau, the enemy had been swept from it, and the retreat had begun all along the line. We gazed upon the scene for a time, and, hearing firing between the Lewis house and the Stone Bridge, we rode back to see what it meant. Captain Lindsay Walker had arrived from Fredericksburg with his six-Parrott-gun battery, and from a high hill was shelling the fugitives beyond Bull Run as they were fleeing in wild disorder to the shelter of the nearest woods. Colonel J. E. B. Stuart, at the head of a body of yelling cavalry with drawn sabers, was sweeping round the base of the hill we were on, to cross the Run and fall upon the enemy.

When Stuart disappeared in the distance, Shumate and I rode slowly back toward the battery. Nearing the Lewis house, we saw General Johnston and his staff coming toward us slowly, preceded a little by a gentleman on horseback, who was lifting his hat to every one he met. From the likeness I had seen of President Jefferson Davis, I instantly recognized him and told Shumate who it was. With the impulsiveness of his nature, Shumate dashed up to the President, seized his hand, and huzzaed at the top of his voice. I could see that Mr. Davis was greatly amused, and I was convulsed with laughter. When they came within twenty steps of me, where I had halted to let the group pass, Shumate exclaimed, to the great amusement of all who heard him : " Mr. President, there's my captain, and I want to introduce you to him." The President eyed me for a moment, as if he thought I was an odd-looking captain. I had on a battered slouch hat, a red flannel shirt with only one sleeve, corduroy trousers, and heavy cavalry boots, and was begrimed with burnt powder, dust, and the blood from my ear and arm, and must have been about as hard-looking a specimen of a captain as was ever seen. Nevertheless, the President grasped my hand with a cordial salutation, and after a few words passed on.

We found our battery refreshing themselves on fat bacon and bread. After a hasty meal, I threw myself on a bag of oats, and slept till broad daylight next morning, notwithstanding a drenching rain which beat upon me during the night.

In fact, I was aroused in the morning by a messenger from ex-Governor Alston, of South Carolina, summoning me to the side of my gallant commander, Brigadier-General Bee, who had been mortally wounded near the Henry house, where Bartow had been instantly killed almost at the same moment. When I reached General Bee, who had been carried back to the cabin where I had joined him the night before, he was unconscious; in a few minutes, while I was holding his hand, he died. Some one during the night had told him that I had reflected on him for leaving our battery so long exposed to capture; and, at his request, messengers had been for hours hunting me in the darkness, to bring me to him, that I might learn from his own lips that he had sent Major Howard to order me to withdraw, when he was driven back across Young's Branch and the turnpike. I was grieved deeply not to have seen him sooner. Possibly the failure of his order to reach me was providential. For full three-quarters of an hour we had kept up a fire that delayed the enemy's movement across Young's Branch. But for that, they might have gained the Henry plateau, before Jackson and Hampton came up, and before Bee and Bartow had rallied their disorganized troops. Minutes count as hours under such circumstances, and trifles often turn the scale in great battles.

General Jackson's wound became very serious when inflammation set in. On hearing, three days after the fight, that he was suffering with it, I rode to his quarters, a little farm-house near Centreville. Although it was barely sunrise, he was out under the trees, bathing the hand with spring water. It was much swollen and very painful, but he bore himself stoically. His wife had arrived the night before. Of course, the battle was the only topic discussed at breakfast. I remarked, in Mrs. Jackson's hearing, "General, how is it that you can keep so cool, and appear so utterly insensible to danger in such a storm of shell and bullets as rained about you when your hand was hit?" He instantly became grave and reverential in his manner, and answered, in a low tone of great earnestness: "Captain, my religious belief teaches me to feel as safe in battle as in bed. God has fixed the time for my death. I do not concern myself about *that*, but to be always ready, no matter when it may overtake me." He added, after a pause, looking me full in the face: "Captain, that is the way all men should live, and then all would be equally brave."

I felt that this last remark was intended as a rebuke for my profanity, when I had complained to him on the field of the apparent abandonment of my battery to capture, and I apologized. He heard me, and simply said, "Nothing can justify profanity." ⸣

The battle was mainly fought by Johnston's troops from the Shenandoah. Two-thirds of the killed and wounded were his men and officers. Beauregard's troops were strung out for several miles down the valley of Bull Run, and did not get up to our aid till near the end of the day. General Beauregard himself, who was in the thickest of the fight, came upon the field long before any of his troops arrived, except those he had posted under Evans to guard the Stone Bridge, and which, with Bee's troops, bore the brunt of the first attack.

⸥ I never knew Jackson to let profanity pass without a rebuke but once. The incident was reported to me by the chief actor in it, Major John A. Harman, who was Jackson's chief quartermaster. It happened at Edwards Ferry, on the Potomac, when our army was crossing into Maryland in the Antietam campaign. On the march to the river, for some infraction of orders about the manner of marching his division, Major-General A. P. Hill had been ordered in arrest by Jackson. This probably had put Jackson in a ruffled frame of mind. The day was very hot, and the ford was completely blocked with a wagon train, either of Hill's or some other division. On seeing the state of affairs, Jackson turned to Major Harman, and ordered him to clear the ford. Harman dashed in among the wagoners, kicking mules, and apparently inextricable mass of wagons, and, in the voice of a stentor, poured out a volume of oaths that would have excited the admiration of the most scientific mule-driver. The effect was electrical. The drivers were frightened and swore as best they could, but far below the major's standard. The mules caught the inspiration from a chorus of familiar words, and all at once made a break for the Maryland shore, and in five minutes the ford was cleared, Jackson witnessed and heard it all. Harman rode back to join him, expecting a lecture, and, touching his hat, said: "The ford is clear, general! There's only one language that will make mules understand on a hot day that they must get out of the water." The general smiled, and said: "Thank you, major," and dashed into the water at the head of his staff, and rode across.— J. D. I.

The uninformed, North and South, have wondered why Johnston and Beauregard did not follow on to Washington. General Johnston, in his "Narrative," has clearly and conclusively answered that question. It was simply impossible. We had neither the food nor transportation at Manassas necessary to a forward movement. This subject was the cause of sharp irritation between our commanding generals at Manassas on the one hand, and Mr. Davis and his Secretary of War, Mr. Benjamin, on the other. There was a disposition in the quartermaster's and commissary departments at Richmond to deny the extent of the destitution of our army immediately after the battle. To ascertain the exact facts of the case, General Johnston organized a board of officers to investigate and report the condition of the transportation and commissariat of the army at Manassas on the 21st of July, and their daily condition for two weeks thereafter. That Board was composed of Lieutenant-Colonel Robert B. Lee (a cousin of General R. E. Lee), representing the commissary department, Major (afterward Major-General) W. L. Cabell, representing the quartermaster's department, and myself from the line. My associates on this Board were old United States army officers of acknowledged ability and large experience. We organized early in August, and made an exhaustive investigation and detailed report. I have a distinct recollection that we found that on the morning of the battle there was not at Manassas one full day's rations for the combined armies of Johnston and Beauregard, and that on no single day for the succeeding two weeks was there as much as a three days' supply there. We found that there were not wagons and teams enough at any time to have transported three days' supplies for the troops if they had been put in motion away from the railroad. We found that for weeks preceding the 21st of July General Beauregard had been urgent and almost importunate in his demands on the quartermaster and commissary generals at Richmond for adequate supplies. We found that Colonel Northrop, the commissary general, had not only failed to send forward adequate supplies for such an emergency as arose when General Johnston brought his army from the valley, but that he had interfered with and interdicted the efforts of officers of the department who were with General Beauregard to collect supplies from the rich and abundant region lying between the hostile armies. After reporting the facts, we unanimously concurred in the opinion that they proved the impossibility of a successful and rapid pursuit of the defeated enemy to Washington. This report, elaborately written out and signed, was forwarded to Richmond, and in a few days was returned by Mr. Judah P. Benjamin, Secretary of War, with an indorsement to the effect that the Board had transcended its powers by expressing an opinion as to what the facts did or did not prove, and sharply ordering us to strike out all that part of the report, and send only the facts ascertained by us. We met and complied with this order, though indignant at the reprimand, and returned our amended report. This was the last I ever heard of it. It never saw daylight. Who suppressed it I do not know.☆

☆ See statement from Colonel Northrop, page 261.—EDITORS.

RESPONSIBILITIES OF THE FIRST BULL RUN.

BY JOSEPH E. JOHNSTON, GENERAL, C. S. A.

QUAKER GUN FOUND IN THE CONFEDERATE WORKS AT MANASSAS. FROM A PHOTOGRAPH.

WHEN the State of Virginia seceded, being a citizen of that State, I resigned my office in the United States Army; and as I had seen a good deal of military service, in the Seminole and Mexican wars and in the West, the President of the Confederacy offered me a commission in the highest grade in his army. I accepted the offer because the invasion of the South was inevitable. But I soon incurred Mr. Davis's displeasure by protesting against an illegal act of his by which I was greatly wronged. Still he retained me in important positions, although his official letters were harsh. In 1864, however, he degraded me to the utmost of his power by summarily removing me from a high command. Believing that he was prompted to this act by animosity, and not by dispassionate opinion, I undertake to prove this animosity by many extracts from his "Rise and Fall of the Confederacy" (D. Appleton & Co.: 1881), and my comments thereon.

Mr. Davis recites ("R. and F.," I., p. 307) the law securing to officers who might leave the United States Army to enter that of the Confederacy the same relative rank in the latter which they had in the former, provided their resignations had been offered in the six months next following the 14th of March, and then adds:

"The provisions hereof are in the view entertained that the army was of the States, not of the Government, and was to secure to officers adhering to the Confederate States the same relative rank which they had before those States had withdrawn from the Union. . . .

"How well the Government of the Confederacy observed both the letter and spirit of the law will be seen by reference to its action in the matter of appointments."

Those of the five generals were the most prominent, of course. All had resigned within the time prescribed. Their relative rank in the United States

---

The letter of protest covered nine sheets of letter-paper, and the ninth sheet (to quote from the original) sums up the matter in these words:

"My commission is made to bear such a date that my once inferiors in the service of the United States and of the Confederate States shall be above me. But it must not be dated as of the 21st of July nor be suggestive of the victory of Manassas. I return to my first position. I repeat that my right to my rank as General is established by the Acts of Congress of the 14th of March, 1861, and the 16th of May, 1861, and not by the nomination and confirmation of the 31st of August, 1861. To deprive me of that rank it was necessary for Congress to repeal those laws. That could be done by express legislative act alone. It was not done, it could not be done, by a mere vote in secret session upon a list of nominations. If the action against which I have protested be legal, it is not for me to question the expediency of degrading one who has served laboriously from the commencement of the war on this frontier, and borne a prominent part in the only great event of that war for the benefit of persons neither of whom has yet struck a blow for this Confederacy. These views and the freedom with which they are presented may be unusual. So likewise is the occasion which calls them forth. I have the honor to be, very respectfully, your obedient servant,

"J. E. JOHNSTON, General.

"To His Excellency, Jefferson Davis, President of the Confederate States, Richmond."

This ninth sheet is all of the original letter that can be found by the present owner, Mrs. Bledsoe, widow of Dr. Albert T. Bledsoe, who, at the time the letter was written, was Assistant-Secretary of War. Dr. Bledsoe told his wife that President Davis handed the letter to him, with the remark that it would not go upon the official files, and that he might keep it if he liked.— EDITORS.

Army just before secession had been: 1st, J. E. Johnston, Brigadier-General; 2d, Samuel Cooper, Colonel; 3d, A. S. Johnston, Colonel; 4th, R. E. Lee, Lieutenant-Colonel; and 5th, G. T. Beauregard, Major. All of them but the third had had previous appointments, when, on the 31st of August, the Confederate Government announced new ones: Cooper's being dated May 16th, A. S. Johnston's May 28th, Lee's June 14th, J. E. Johnston's July 4th, and Beauregard's July 21st. So the law was violated, 1st, by disregarding existing commissions; 2d, by giving different instead of the same dates to commissions; and 3d, by not recognizing previous rank in the United States Army. The only effect of this triple violation of law was to reduce J. E. Johnston from the first to the fourth place, which, of course, must have been its object. Mr. Davis continues:

GENERAL SAMUEL COOPER, ADJUTANT AND INSPECTOR-GENERAL, C. S. A., RANKING OFFICER IN THE CONFEDERATE ARMY. FROM A PHOTOGRAPH.

"It is a noteworthy fact that the three highest officers in rank . . . were all so indifferent to any question of personal interest that they had received their appointment before they were aware it was to be conferred" (p. 307).

This implies that the conduct described was unusual. On the contrary, it was that of the body of officers who left the United States Army to enter that of the Confederacy. It is strange that the author should disparage so many honorable men. He states ("R. and F.," I., 309) that General Lee, when ordered from Richmond to the South for the first time, asked what rank he held in the army: "So wholly had his heart and his mind been consecrated to the public service that he had not remembered, if he ever knew, of his advancement."

As each grade has its duties, an officer cannot know his duty if ignorant of his rank. Therefore General Lee always knew his rank, for he never failed in his duty. Besides, his official correspondence at the time referred to shows that he knew that he was major-general of the Virginia forces until May 25th, 1861, and a Confederate general after that date.

Describing the events which immediately preceded the battle of Manassas, Mr. Davis says ("Rise and Fall," I., 340):

"The forces there assembled [in Virginia] were divided into three armies, at positions the most important and threatened: one, under General J. E. Johnston, at Harper's Ferry, covering the valley of the Shenandoah. . . . Harper's Ferry was an important position both for military and political considerations. . . . The demonstrations of General Patterson, commanding the Federal army in that region, caused General Johnston earnestly to insist on being allowed to retire to a position nearer to Winchester."

Harper's Ferry is 22 miles east of the route into the Shenandoah Valley, and could be held only by an army strong enough to drive an enemy from the heights north and east of it. So it is anything but an important position. These objections were expressed to the Government two days after my arrival, and I suggested the being permitted to move the troops as might be necessary. All this before Patterson had advanced from Chambersburg.

On page 341, "R. and F.," Mr. Davis quotes from an official letter to me from General Cooper, dated June 13th, 1861, which began thus:

"The opinions expressed by Major Whiting in his letter to you, and on which you have indorsed your concurrence, have been duly considered. You had been heretofore instructed to exercise your discretion as to retiring from your position at Harper's Ferry." ⚓

This latter statement is incorrect. No such instructions had been given. The last instructions on the subject received by me were in General Lee's letter of June 7th. ↓ On page 341 Mr. Davis says:

"The temporary occupation [of Harper's Ferry] was especially needful for the removal of the valuable machinery and material in the armory located there."

The removal of the machinery was not an object referred to in General Cooper's letter. But the presence of our army anywhere in the Valley within a day's march of the position, would have protected that removal. That letter (page 341) was received two days after the army left Harper's Ferry to meet General McClellan's troops, believed by intelligent people of Winchester to be approaching from the west.

On page 345 Mr. Davis says it was a difficult problem to know which army, whether Beauregard's at Manassas or Johnston's in the Valley, should be reënforced by the other, because these generals were "each asking reënforcements from the other." All that was written by me on the subject is in the letter (page 345) dated July 9th:

"I have not asked for reënforcements because I supposed that the War Department, informed of the state of affairs everywhere, could best judge where the troops at its disposal

---

⚓ This letter of Major Whiting to General Johnston, and General Johnston's letter (probably referred to as the indorsement), are both dated May 28th, 1861. The phrase of General Cooper, "You had been heretofore instructed," should have read either, "You had been *theretofore* [before May 28th] instructed," or, "You *have* been heretofore [before June 13th] instructed." The latter is probably what was meant, as the only letter of instructions to General Johnston received at Har-

per's Ferry giving him permission to use his discretion which is to be found in the Official Records, is the one of June 7th from General Lee, in which he says: "It is hoped that you will be able to be timely informed of the approach of troops against you, and retire, provided they cannot be successfully opposed. You must exercise your discretion and judgment in this respect."— EDITORS.

↓ "Official Records," II., 910.

are most required. . . . If it is proposed to strengthen us against the attack I suggest as soon to be made, it seems to me that General Beauregard might with *great expedition* furnish 5000 or 6000 men for a few days."

Mr. Davis says, after quoting from this letter:

" As soon as I became satisfied that Manassas was the objective point of the enemy's movement, I wrote to General Johnston urging him to make preparations for a junction with General Beauregard."

There is abundant evidence that the Southern President never thought of transferring the troops in the "Valley" to Manassas until the proper time to do it came — that is, when McDowell was known to be advancing. This fact is shown by the anxiety he expressed to increase the number of those troops. ♭ And General Lee, writing [from South Carolina] to Mr. Davis, November 24th, 1861 ("Official Records," II., 515), says in regard to General Beauregard's suggestion that he be reënforced from my army:

" You decided that the movements of the enemy in and about Alexandria were not sufficiently demonstrative to warrant the withdrawing of any of the forces from the Shenandoah Valley. A few days afterward, however,— I think three or four,— the reports from General Beauregard showed so clearly the enemy's purpose, that you ordered General Johnston, with his effective force, to march at once to the support of General Beauregard."

This letter is in reply to one from Mr. Davis, to the effect that statements had been widely published to show that General Beauregard's forces had been held inactive by his (Mr. Davis's) rejection of plans for vigorous offensive operations proposed to him by the general, and desiring to know of General Lee what those plans were, and why they were rejected.

"On the 17th of July, 1861," says Mr. Davis ("R. and F." I., 346), "the following telegram was sent by the adjutant-general" to General Johnston, Winchester, Va.:

" General Beauregard is attacked. To strike the enemy a decisive blow, a junction of all your effective force will be needed. If practicable, make the movement, sending your sick and baggage to Culpeper Court House, either by railroad or by Warrenton. In all the arrangements exercise your discretion. S. COOPER, Adjutant and Inspector-General."

Mr. Davis asserts that I claim that discretion was given me by the words " all the arrangements." I claimed it from what he terms the only positive part of the order, viz., "If practicable, make the movement, sending your sick to Culpeper Court House." Mr. Davis adds:

" The sending the sick to Culpeper Court House might have been after or before the effective force had moved to the execution of the main and only positive part of the order."

"Make the movement" would have been a positive order, but "if practicable" deprived it of that character, and gave the officer receiving it a certain discretion. But, as the movement desired was made promptly, it was surely idle to discuss, twenty years after, whether the officer could lawfully have done what he *did not do*. At the time the decision of such a question might have been necessary; but, as Mr. Davis will give no more orders to generals, and as the officer concerned will execute no more, such a discussion

♭ See "Official Records," II., 924, 935, 940, 973, 976-977.

is idle now. The use of the wagons required in the march of the army would have been necessary to remove the sick to the railroad station at Strasburg, eighteen miles distant; so this removal could *not* have been made *after* the march. There being seventeen hundred sick, this part of their transportation would have required more time than the transfer of the troops to Manassas, which was the important thing. The sick were, therefore, properly and quickly provided for in Winchester. I was the only judge of the "practicable"; and "if practicable" refers to the whole sentence—as much to sending the sick to Culpeper as to "make the movement." Still he says ("R. and F.," I., 347):

"His [my] letters of the 12th and 15th expressed his doubts about his power to retire from before the superior force of General Patterson. Therefore, the word 'practicable' was in that connection the equivalent of 'possible.'"

It is immaterial whether "if practicable" or "if possible" was written. I was the only judge of the possibility or practicability; and, if General Patterson had not changed his position after the telegram was received, I might have thought it necessary to attack him, to "make the movement practicable." But as to my power to retire. On the 15th General Patterson's forces were half a day's march from us, and on the 12th more than a day's march; and, as Stuart's cavalry did not permit the enemy to observe us, retreat would have been easy, and I could not possibly have written to the contrary.

As to Mr. Davis's telegram ("R. and F.," I., 348)☆, and the anxiety in Mr. Davis's mind lest there should be some unfortunate misunderstanding between General Beauregard and me,—my inquiry was intended and calculated to establish beyond dispute our relative positions. As a Confederate brigadier-general I had been junior to General Beauregard, but had been created general by act of Congress. But, as this had not been published to the army, it was not certain that it was known at Manassas. If it was not, the President's telegram gave the information, and prevented what he seems to have apprehended.

THE BATTLE OF BULL RUN.

On page 349, to the end of the chapter, the President describes his visit to the field of battle near Manassas. "As we advanced," he says, "the storm of battle was rolling westward." But, in fact, the fighting had ceased before he left Manassas. He then mentions meeting me on a hill which commanded a general view of the field, and proceeding farther west, where he saw a Federal "column," which a Confederate squadron charged and put to flight. But the

Mr. Davis has a few words of praise for General Johnston, which, in this connection, will be of interest to the reader: "It gives me pleasure to state that, from all the accounts received at the time, the plans of General Johnston for masking his withdrawal to form a junction with General Beauregard were conducted with marked skill" ("R. and F.," I., 347).—EDITORS.

☆ This telegram, sent in response to an inquiry from General Johnston, read as follows:

"Richmond, July 20, 1861. General J. E. Johnston, Manassas Junction, Virginia: You are a general in the Confederate Army, possessed of the power attaching to that rank. You will know how to make the exact knowledge of Brigadier-General Beauregard, as well of the ground as of the troops and preparation, avail for the success of the object in which you coöperate. The zeal of both assures me of harmonious action. JEFFERSON DAVIS."

captain in command of this squadron ⚓ says in his report that the column seen was a party of our troops. Mr. Davis also dilates on the suffering of our troops for want of supplies and camp equipage, and on his efforts to have them provided for. After the battle ended, officers were duly directed by me to have food brought to the ground where the troops were to pass the night.

I was not in the conference described by Mr. Davis ("R. and F.," I., 353, 354, 355). Having left the field after 10 o'clock, and ridden in the dark slowly, it was about half-past 11 when I found the President and General Beauregard together, in the latter's quarters at Manassas. We three conversed an hour or more without referring to pursuit or an advance upon Washington. The "conference" described by him must have occurred before my arrival, and Mr. Davis may very well have forgotten that I was not present then.

But, when the President wrote, he had forgotten the subject of the conference he described; for the result, as he states it, was an order, not for pursuit by the army, but for the detail of two parties to collect wounded men and abandoned property near the field of battle. This order (pages 355, 356) is "to the same effect," Mr. Davis says, as the one he wrote, and which he terms a direction to pursue the Federal army at early dawn.

It is asserted ("R. and F.," I., 354)‡ that I left the command over both Confederate armies in General Beauregard's hands during the engagement. Such conduct would have been as base as flight from the field in the heat of battle, and would have brought upon me the contempt of every honorable soldier. It is disproved by the fact that General Beauregard was willing to serve under me there, and again in North Carolina, near the close of the war; and that he associated with me. As this accusation is published by the Southern President, and indorsed by General Beauregard, it requires my contradiction.

Instead of leaving the command in General Beauregard's hands, I assumed it over both armies immediately after my arrival on the 20th, showing General Beauregard as my warrant the President's telegram defining my position. The usual order ♭ assuming command was written and sent to General Beauregard's office for distribution. He was then told that as General Patterson would no doubt hasten to join General McDowell as soon as he discovered my movement, we must attack the Federal army next morning. General Beauregard then pointed out on a map of the neighborhood the roads leading to the enemy's camp at Centreville from the different parts of our line south of the stream, and the positions of the brigades near each road; and a simple order of march, by which our troops would unite near the Federal position, was sketched. Having had neither sleep nor recumbent rest since the morning of the 17th, I begged General Beauregard to put this order of march on paper, and have the necessary copies made and sent to me for inspection in a grove, near, where I expected to be resting—this in time

⚓ Captain John F. Lay. See "Official Records," II., 573.— EDITORS.

‡ Not by Mr. Davis, but in a letter from General Thomas Jordan, quoted by Mr. Davis for another purpose.— EDITORS.

♭ General J. A. Early, in his narrative of these events, says: "During the 20th, General Johnston arrived at Manassas Junction by the railroad, and that day we received the order from him assuming command of the combined armies of General Beauregard and himself."— J. E. J.

for distribution before night. This distribution was to be by him, the immediate commander of most of the troops. Seeing that 8 brigades were on the right of the line to Centreville, and but 1 to the left of it at a distance of 4 miles, I desired General Beauregard to have Bee's and Jackson's brigades placed in this interval near the detached brigade.

The papers were brought to me a little before sunrise next morning. They differed greatly from the order sketched the day before; but as they would have put the troops in motion if distributed, it would have been easy then to direct the course of each division. By the order sketched the day before, all our forces would have been concentrated near Centreville, to attack the Federal army. By that prepared by General Beauregard but 4 brigades were directed "to the attack of Centreville," of which one and a half had not yet arrived from the Valley, while 6 brigades were to move forward to the Union Mills and Centreville road, there to hold themselves in readiness to support the attack on Centreville, or to move, 2 to Sangster's cross-roads, 2 to Fairfax Station, and 2 to Fairfax Court House. The two and a half brigades on the ground, even supported by the half brigade of the reserve also on the ground, in all probability would have been defeated by the whole Federal army before the three bodies of 2 brigades each could have come to their aid, over distances of from 3 to 5 miles. Then, if the enemy had providentially been defeated by one-sixth or one-eighth of their number, Sangster's cross-roads and Fairfax Station would have been out of their line of retreat.

Soon after sunrise on the 21st, it was reported that a large body of Federal troops was approaching on the Warrenton Turnpike. This offensive movement of the enemy would have *frustrated our plan of the day before*, if the orders for it had been delivered to the troops. It appears from the reports of the commanders of the six brigades on the right that but one of them, General Longstreet, received it. Learning that Bee's and Jackson's brigades were still on the right, I again desired General Beauregard to transfer them to the left, which he did, giving the same orders to Hampton's Legion, just arrived. These, with Cocke's brigade then near the turnpike, would necessarily receive the threatened attack.

General Beauregard then suggested that all our troops on the right should move rapidly to the left and assail the attacking Federal troops in flank. This suggestion was accepted; and together we joined those troops. Three of the four brigades of the first line, at Mitchell's, Blackburn's, and McLean's fords, reported strong bodies of United States troops on the wooded heights before them. This *frustrated the second plan*. Two Federal batteries—one in front of Bonham's brigade at Mitchell's Ford, the other before Longstreet's at Blackburn's Ford—were annoying us, although their firing was slow.

About 8 o'clock, after receiving such information as scouts could give, I left General Beauregard near Longstreet's position, and placed myself on Lookout Hill, in rear of Mitchell's Ford, to await the development of the enemy's designs. About 9 o'clock the signal officer, Captain Alexander, reported that a column of Federal troops could be seen crossing the valley of Bull Run, two miles beyond our left.

General McDowell had been instructed by his general-in-chief to pass the Confederate right and seize the railroad in our rear. But, learning that the district to be passed through was rugged and covered with woods, and therefore unfavorable to a large army, he determined, after devoting three days to reconnoissance, to operate on the open and favorable ground to his right, and turn our left. He had another object in this second plan, and an important one—that this course would place his between the two Confederate armies, and prevent their junction; and if it had been made a day or two sooner, this manœuvre would have accomplished that object.

General McDowell marched from Centreville by the Warrenton Turnpike with three divisions, sending a fourth division to deceive us by demonstrations in front of our main body. Leaving the turnpike a half mile from the Stone Bridge, he made a long détour to Sudley Ford, where he crossed Bull Run and turned toward Manassas. Colonel Evans, who commanded fourteen companies near the Stone Bridge, discovered this manœuvre, and moved with his little force along the base of the hill north of the turnpike, to place it before the enemy near the Sudley and Manassas road. Here he was assailed by greatly superior numbers, which he resisted obstinately.

General Beauregard had joined me on Lookout Hill, and we could distinctly hear the sounds and see the smoke of the fight. But they indicated no hostile force that Evans's troops and those of Bee, Hampton, and Jackson, which we could see hurrying toward the conflict in that order, were not adequate to resist.

On reaching the broad, level top of the hill south of the turnpike, Bee, appreciating the strength of the position, formed his troops (half of his own and half of Bartow's brigade) on that ground. But seeing Evans struggling against great odds, he crossed the valley and formed on the right and a little in advance of him. Here the 5 or 6 regiments, with 6 field-pieces, held their ground for an hour against 10,000 or 12,000 United States troops,⸙ when, finding they were overlapped on each flank by the continually arriving enemy, General Bee fell back to the position from which he had moved to rescue Evans — crossing the valley, closely pressed by the Federal army.

Hampton with his Legion reached the valley as the retrograde movement began. Forming it promptly, he joined in the action, and contributed greatly to the orderly character of the retreat by his courage and admirable soldiership, seconded by the excellent conduct of the gentlemen composing his command. Imboden and his battery did excellent service on this trying occasion. Bee met Jackson at the head of his brigade, on the position he had first taken, and he began to re-form and Jackson to deploy at the same time.

In the mean time I had been waiting with General Beauregard on Lookout Hill for evidence of General McDowell's design. The violence of the firing on the left indicated a battle, but the large bodies of troops reported by chosen scouts to be facing our right kept me in doubt. But near 11 o'clock reports that those troops were felling trees showed that they were standing on the

⸙ General Fry (page 185) states that these troops were Andrew Porter's and Burnside's brigades, and one regiment of Heintzelman's division. Reckoning by the estimate of strength given by General Fry on page 194 these would have made a total of about 6500 men.—EDITORS.

defensive; and new clouds of dust on the left proved that a large body of Federal troops was arriving on the field. It thus appeared that the enemy's great effort was to be against our left. I expressed this to General Beauregard, and the necessity of reënforcing the brigades engaged, and desired him to send immediate orders to Early and Holmes, of the second line, to hasten to the conflict with their brigades. General Bonham, who was near me, was desired to send up two regiments and a battery. I then set off at a rapid gallop to the scene of action. General Beauregard joined me without a word. Passing on the way Colonel Pendleton with two batteries, I directed him to follow with them as fast as possible.

It now seemed that a battle was to be fought entirely different in place and circumstance from the two plans previously adopted and abandoned as impracticable. Instead of taking the initiative and operating in front of our line, we were compelled to fight on the defensive more than a mile in rear of that line, and at right angles to it, on a field selected by Bee,— with no other plans than those suggested by the changing events of battle.

While we were riding forward General Beauregard suggested to me to assign him to the immediate command of the troops engaged, so that my supervision of the whole field might not be interrupted, to which I assented. So he commanded those troops under me; as elsewhere, lieutenant-generals commanded corps, and major-generals divisions, under me.

When we were near the ground where Bee was re-forming and Jackson deploying his brigade, I saw a regiment in line with ordered arms and facing to the front, but 200 or 300 yards in rear of its proper place. On inquiry I learned that it had lost all its field-officers; so, riding on its left flank, I easily marched it to its place. It was the 4th Alabama, an excellent regiment; and I mention this because the circumstance has been greatly exaggerated.

After the troops were in good battle order I turned to the supervision of the whole field. The enemy's great numerical superiority was discouraging. Yet, from strong faith in Beauregard's capacity and courage, and the high soldierly qualities of Bee and Jackson, I hoped that the fight would be maintained until I could bring adequate reënforcements to their aid. For this Holmes and Early were urged to hasten their march, and Ewell was ordered to follow them with his brigade with all speed. Broken troops were reorganized and led back into the fight with the help of my own and part of General Beauregard's staff. Cocke's brigade was held in rear of the right to observe a large body of Federal troops in a position from which Bee's right flank could have been struck in a few minutes.

After these additions had been made to our troops then engaged, we had 9 regiments of infantry, 5 batteries, and 300 cavalry of the Army of the Shenandoah, and about 2 regiments and a half of infantry, 6 companies of cavalry, and 6 field-pieces of the Army of the Potomac, holding at bay 3 divisions of the enemy. The Southern soldiers had, however, two great advantages in the contest: greater skill in the use of fire-arms, and the standing on the defensive, by which they escaped such disorder as advancing under fire produced in the ranks of their adversaries, undisciplined like themselves.

A report received about 2 o'clock from General Beauregard's office that another United States army was approaching from the north-west, and but a few miles from us, caused me to send orders to Bonham, Longstreet, and Jones to hold their brigades south of Bull Run, and ready to move.

When Bonham's two regiments appeared soon after, Cocke's brigade was ordered into action on our right. Fisher's North Carolina regiment coming up, Bonham's two regiments were directed against the Federal right, and Fisher's was afterward sent in the same direction; for the enemy's strongest efforts seemed to be directed against our left, as if to separate us from Manassas Junction.

About 3:30 o'clock, General E. K. Smith arrived with three regiments of Elzey's brigade, coming from Manassas Junction. He was instructed, through a staff-officer sent forward to meet him, to form on the left of our line, his left thrown forward, and to attack the enemy in flank. At his request I joined him, directed his course, and gave him these instructions. Before the formation was completed, he fell severely wounded, and while falling from his horse directed Colonel Elzey to take command. That officer appreciated the manœuvre and executed it gallantly and well. General Beauregard promptly seized the opportunity it afforded, and threw forward the whole line. The enemy was driven from the long-contested hill, and the tide of battle at length turned. But the first Federal line driven into the valley was there rallied on a second, the two united presenting a formidable aspect. In the mean time, however, Colonel Early had come upon the field with his brigade. He was instructed by me to make a détour to the left and assail the Federal right in flank. He reached the ground in time, accompanied by Stuart's cavalry and Beckham's battery, and made his attack with a skill and courage which routed the Federal right in a moment. General Beauregard, charging in front, made the rout complete. The Federal right fled in confusion toward the Sudley Ford, and the center and left marched off rapidly by the turnpike.

Stuart pursued the fugitives on the Sudley road, and Colonel Radford, with two squadrons which I had held in reserve near me during the day, was directed to cross Bull Run at Ball's Ford, and strike the column on the turnpike in flank. The number of prisoners taken by these parties of cavalry greatly exceeded their own numbers. But they were too weak to make a serious impression on an army, although a defeated one.

At twenty minutes before 5, when the retreat of the enemy toward Centreville began, I sent orders to Brigadier-General Bonham by Lieutenant-Colonel Lay, of his staff, who happened to be with me, to march with his own and Longstreet's brigade (which were nearest Bull Run and the Stone Bridge), by the quickest route to the turnpike, and form them across it to intercept the retreat of the Federal troops. But he found so little appearance of rout in those troops as to make the execution of his instructions seem impracticable; so the two brigades returned to their camps. When the retreat began, the body of United States troops that had passed the day on the Centreville side of Bull Run made a demonstration on the rear of our right; which was repelled by Holmes's brigade just arrived.

Soon after the firing ceased, General Ewell reported to me, saying that his brigade was about midway from its camp near Union Mills. He had ridden forward to see the part of the field on which he might be required to serve, to prepare himself to act intelligently.

The victory was as complete as one gained in an open country by infantry and artillery can be. Our cavalry pursued as far as they could effectively; but when they encountered the main column, after dispersing or capturing little parties and stragglers, they could make no impression.

General Beauregard's first plan of attack was delivered to me by his aide-de-camp, Colonel Chisolm, when I was thirty-four miles from Manassas. It was, that I should leave the railroad at Piedmont station, thirty-six miles from the enemy at Centreville, and attack him in rear, and when our artillery announced that we had begun the fight, General Beauregard would move up from Bull Run and assail the enemy on that side. I rejected the plan, because such a one would enable an officer of ordinary sense and vigor to defeat our two armies one after the other. For McDowell, by his numerical superiority, could have disposed of my forces in less than two hours; that is to say, before Beauregard could have come up, when he also could have been defeated and the campaign ended.

An opinion seems to prevail with some persons who have written about the battle, that important plans of General Beauregard were executed by him. It is a mistake; the first intention, announced to General Beauregard by me when we met, was to attack the enemy at Centreville as early as possible on the 21st. This was anticipated by McDowell's early advance. The second, to attack the Federals in flank near the turnpike with our main force, suggested by General Beauregard, was prevented by the enemy's occupation of the high ground in front of our right.

As fought, the battle was made by me; Bee's and Jackson's brigades were transferred to the left by me. I decided that the battle was to be there, and directed the measures necessary to maintain it; a most important one being the assignment of General Beauregard to the immediate command of this left, which he held. In like manner the senior officer on the right would have commanded there, if the Federal left had attacked.

These facts in relation to the battle are my defense against the accusation indorsed by General Beauregard and published by Mr. Davis.

In an account of the battle published in "The Century" for November, 1884, General Beauregard mentions offensive operations which he "had designed and ordered against his [adversary's] left flank and rear at Centreville," and censures my friend General R. S. Ewell for their failure. At the time referred to, three of the four Federal divisions were near Bull Run, above the turnpike, and the fourth facing our right, so that troops of ours, going to Centreville then, if not prevented by the Federal division facing them, would have found no enemy. And General Ewell was not, as he reports, "instructed in the plan of attack"; for he says in his official report: ". . . I first received orders to hold myself in readiness to advance at a moment's notice. I next received a copy of an order sent to General Jones and furnished me by him,

LIEUTENANT-GENERAL RICHARD S. EWELL, C. S. A. FROM A PHOTOGRAPH.

in which it was stated I had been ordered at once to proceed to his support."
Three other orders, he says, followed, each contradictory of its predecessor.
General Ewell knew that a battle was raging; but knew, too, that between
him and it were other unengaged brigades, and that his commander was near
enough to give him orders. But he had no reason to suppose that his commander desired him to move to Centreville, where there was then no enemy.
There could have been no greater mistake on General Ewell's part than making the movement to Centreville.

A brief passage in my official report of this battle displeased President
Davis. In referring to his telegraphic order I gave its meaning very briefly,
but accurately—"directing me, if practicable, to go to [General Beauregard's]
assistance, after sending my sick to Culpeper Court House." Mr. Davis
objected to the word *after*. Being informed of this by a friend, I cheerfully
consented to his expunging the word, because that would not affect the
meaning of the sentence. But the word is still in his harsh indorsement. He
also had this passage stricken out: "The delay of sending the sick, nearly

seventeen hundred in number, to Culpeper, would have made it impossible to arrive at Manassas in time. They were therefore provided for in Winchester"; and substituted this: "Our sick, nearly seventeen hundred in number, were provided for in Winchester." Being ordered to send the sick to Culpeper as well as to move to Manassas, it was necessary to account for disobedience, which my words did, and which his substitute for them did not.

Mr. Davis ("R. and F.," I., 359) expresses indignation that, as he says, "among the articles abandoned by the enemy . . . were handcuffs, the fit appendage of a policeman, but not of a soldier." I saw none, nor did I see any one who had seen them.

Mr. Davis says (page 359): "On the night of the 22d, I held a second conference with Generals Johnston and Beauregard." I was in no conference like that of which account is given on page 360. And one that he had with me on that day proved conclusively that he had no thought of sending our army against Washington; for in it he offered me the command in West Virginia, promising to increase the forces there adequately from those around us. He says (page 361):

"What discoveries would have been made, and what results would have ensued from the establishment of our guns upon the south bank of the river to open fire upon the capital, are speculative questions upon which it would be useless to enter."

Mr. Davis seems to have forgotten what was as well known then as now — that our army was more disorganized by victory than that of the United States by defeat; that there were strong fortifications, well manned, to cover the approaches to Washington and prevent the establishment of our guns on the south bank of the river. He knew, too, that we had no means of cannonading the capital, nor a disposition to make barbarous war. He says ("R. and F.," I., 362):

"When the smoke of battle had lifted from the field . . . some . . . censoriously asked why the fruits of the victory had not been gathered by the capture of Washington City. Then some indiscreet friends of the generals commanding in that battle . . . induced the allegation that the President had prevented the generals from making an immediate and vigorous pursuit of the routed enemy."

Mr. Davis has no ground for this assertion; the generals were attacked first and most severely. It was not until the newspapers had exhausted themselves upon us that some of them turned upon him. On November 3d he wrote to me that reports were circulated to the effect that he

"prevented General Beauregard from pursuing the enemy after the battle of Manassas, and had subsequently restrained him from advancing upon Washington City. . . . I call upon you, as the commanding general, and as a party to all the conferences held by me on the 21st and 22d of July, to say whether I obstructed the pursuit of the enemy after the victory at Manassas, or have ever objected to an advance or other active operation which it was feasible for the army to undertake." ("R. and F.," I., 363.)

I replied on the 10th, answering the first question in the negative, and added an explanation which put the responsibility on myself. I replied to the second question, that it had never been feasible for the army to advance farther toward Washington than it had done, and referred to a conference at Fairfax Court House [October 1st, 1861] in reference to leading the army into Maryland, in which he informed the three senior officers that he had not the means of giving the army the strength which they considered necessary for offensive operations.

Mr. Davis was displeased by my second reply, because in his mind there was but one question in his letter. I maintain that there are two; namely, (1) Did he obstruct the pursuit of the enemy after the victory at Manassas? (2) Had he ever objected to an advance or other active operation which it was feasible for the army to undertake?

The second matter is utterly unconnected with the battle of Manassas, and as the question of advance or other active operation had been discussed nowhere by him, to my knowledge, but at the conference at Fairfax Court House, I supposed that he referred to it. He was dissatisfied with my silence in regard to the conferences which he avers took place on July 21st and 22d, the first knowledge of which I have derived from his book.

THE WITHDRAWAL FROM CENTREVILLE TO THE PENINSULA.

Mr. Davis refers ("Rise and Fall," I., 444–5) to the instructions for the reorganization of the army given by him to the three general officers whom he met in conference at Fairfax Court House on October 1st, 1861. But the correspondence urging the carrying out of the orders was carried on with Generals Beauregard and G. W. Smith (my subordinates) in that same October. He neither conversed nor corresponded with me on the subject then, the letter to me being dated May 10th, 1862. The original order was dated October 22d, 1861, to be executed "as soon as, in the judgment of the commanding general, it can be safely done under present exigencies." As the enemy was then nearer to our center than that center to either flank of our army, and another advance upon us by the Federal army was not improbable on any day, it seemed to me unsafe to make the reorganization then. From May 10th to 26th, when the President renewed the subject, we were in the immediate presence of the enemy, when reorganization would have been infinitely dangerous, as was duly represented by me. But, alluding to this conference at Fairfax Court House, he says (p. 449): "When, at that time and place, I met General Johnston for conference, he called in the two generals next in rank to himself, Beauregard and G. W. Smith." These officers were with Mr. Davis in the quarters of General Beauregard, whose guest he was, when I was summoned to him. I had not power to bring any officer into the conference. If such authority had belonged to my office, the personal relations lately established between us by the President would not have permitted me to use it.

He says (pp. 448–9): "I will now proceed to notice the allegation that I was responsible for inaction of the Army of the Potomac in the latter part of 1861 and in the early part of 1862." I think Mr. Davis is here fighting a shadow. I have never seen or heard of the "allegation" referred to; I believe that

that conference attracted no public attention, and brought criticism upon no one. I have seen no notice of it in print, except the merely historical one in a publication made by me in 1874, ☆ without criticism or comment.

In the same paragraph Mr. Davis expresses surprise at the weakness of the army. He has forgotten that in Richmond he was well informed of the strength of the army by periodical reports, which showed him the prevalence of epidemics which, in August and part of September, kept almost thirty per cent. of our number sick. He must have forgotten, too, his anxiety on this subject, which induced him to send a very able physician, Dr. Cartwright, to find some remedy or preventive.

He asserts also that "the generals" had made previous suggestions of a "purpose to advance into Maryland." There had been no such purpose. On the contrary, in my letter to the Secretary of War, suggesting the conference, I wrote:

"Thus far the numbers and condition of this army have at no time justified our assuming the offensive. . . . The difficulty of obtaining the means of establishing a battery near Evansport ⸗ . . . has given me the impression that you cannot at present put this army in condition to assume the offensive. If I am mistaken in this, and you can furnish those means, I think it important that either his Excellency the President, yourself, or some one representing you, should here, upon the ground, confer with me on this all-important question."

In a letter dated September 29th, 1861, the Secretary wrote that the President would reach my camp in a day or two for conference. He came for that object September 30th, and the next evening, *by his appointment*, he was waited on by Generals Beauregard, Gustavus W. Smith, and myself. In discussing the question of giving our army strength enough to assume the offensive in Maryland, it was proposed to bring to it from the South troops enough to raise it to the required strength. The President asked what was that strength. General Smith thought 50,000 men, General Beauregard 60,000, and I 60,000, all of us specifying soldiers like those around us. The President replied that such reënforcements could not be furnished; he could give only as many recruits as we could arm. This decided the question. Mr. Davis then proposed an expedition against Hooker's division, consisting, we believed, of 10,000 men. It was posted on the Maryland shore of the Potomac, opposite Dumfries. [See map, p. 199.] But I objected that we had no means of ferrying an equal number of men across the river in a day, even if undisturbed by ships of war, which controlled the river; so that, even if we should succeed in landing, those vessels of war would inevitably destroy or capture our party returning. This terminated the conference. Mr. Davis says, in regard to the reënforcements asked for ("R. and F.," I., 449): "I had no power to make such an addition to that army without a total disregard of the safety of other threatened positions." We had no threatened positions; and we could always discover promptly the fitting out of naval expeditions against us. And he adds (p. 451), with reference to my request for a conference in regard to reënforcements:

☆ See "Johnston's Narrative" (New York: D. Appleton & Co.), pp. 78, 79.
⸗ Evansport is on the Potomac below Alexandria, at the mouth of Quantico Creek.

"Very little experience, or a fair amount of modesty without any experience, would serve to prevent one from announcing his conclusion that troops could be withdrawn from a place or places without knowing how many were there, and what was the necessity for their presence."

The refutation of this is in General G. W. Smith's memorandum of the discussion : "General Johnston said that he did not feel at liberty to express an opinion of the practicability of reducing the strength of our forces at points not within the limits of his command." On page 452 [referring to possible minor offensive operations. — EDITORS] Mr. Davis says he

"STONEWALL" JACKSON AS FIRST LIEUTENANT OF ARTILLERY, U. S. A.
FROM A DAGUERREOTYPE TAKEN JULY 19, 1848.

"particularly indicated the lower part of Maryland, where a small force was said to be ravaging the country."

He suggested nothing so impossible. Troops of ours could not have been ferried across the broad Potomac then. We had no steamer on that river, nor could we have used one. Mr. Davis says ("R. and F.," I., 452) :

". . . Previously, General Johnston's attention had been called to possibilities in the Valley of the Shenandoah, and that these and other like things were not done, was surely due to other causes than 'the policy of the Administration.'" . . .

Then he quotes from a letter to me, dated August 1st, 1861, as follows :

". . . The movement of Banks ‡ will require your attention. It may be a *ruse*, but if a real movement, when your army has the requisite strength and mobility, you will probably find an opportunity, by a rapid movement through the passes, to strike him in rear or flank."

It is matter of public notoriety that no incursion into the "Valley" worth the notice of a Confederate company was made until March, 1862. That the

‡ By orders dated July 19th, 1861, General N. P. Banks had been assigned to the command of the Department of the Shenandoah, relieving General Patterson in command of the army at Harper's Ferry, General Patterson being by the same orders "honorably discharged from the service of the United States," on the expiration of his term of duty.—EDITORS.

Confederate President should be ignorant of this is inconceivable. Mr. Davis says (p. 462):

" . . . I received from General Johnston notice that his position [at Centreville] was considered unsafe. Many of his letters to me have been lost, and I have thus far not been able to find the one giving the notice referred to, but the reply which is annexed clearly indicates the substance of the letter which was answered: 'General J. E. Johnston: . . . Your opinion that your position may be turned whenever the enemy chooses to advance,' etc."

The sentence omitted by him after my name in his letter from which he quotes as above contains the dates of three letters of mine, in neither of which is there allusion to the safety (or reverse) of the position. They are dated 22d, 23d, and 25th of February, and contain complaints on my part of the dreadful condition of the country, and of the vast accumulation by the Government of superfluous stores at Manassas. There is another omission in the President's letter quoted, and the omission is this:

" . . . with your present force, you cannot secure your communications from the enemy, and may at any time, when he can pass to your rear, be compelled to retreat at the sacrifice of your siege train and army stores. . . . Threatened as we are by a large force on the south-east, you must see the hazard of your position, by its liability to isolation and attack in rear."

By a singular freak of the President's memory, it transferred the substance of these passages from his letter to my three.

Referring again to the conference at Fairfax Court House [October 1st], Mr. Davis says (p. 464):

"Soon thereafter, the army withdrew to Centreville, a better position for defense, but not for attack, and thereby suggestive of the abandonment of an intention to advance."

The President forgets that in that conference the intention to advance was abandoned by him first. He says on the same page:

"On the 10th of March I telegraphed to General Johnston: 'Further assurance given to me this day that you shall be promptly and adequately reënforced, so as to enable you to maintain your position, and resume first policy when the roads will permit.' The first policy was to carry the war beyond our own border."

The roads then permitted the marching of armies, so we had just left Manassas. ♭

On the 20th of February, after a discussion in Richmond, his Cabinet being present, the President had directed me to prepare to fall back from Manassas, and do so as soon as the condition of the country should make the marching of troops practicable. I returned to Manassas February 21st, and on the 22d ordered the proper officers to remove the public property, which was begun on the 23d, the superintendent of the railroad devoting himself to the work under the direction of its president, the Hon. John S. Barbour. The Government had collected three million and a quarter pounds of provisions there, I insisting on a supply of but a million and a half. It also had two million pounds in a meat-curing establishment near at hand, and herds of

♭ Between the 7th and 11th of March, 1862, the Confederate forces in north-eastern Virginia, under General Johnston, were withdrawn to the line of the Rappahannock. On the 11–12th Stonewall Jackson evacuated Winchester and fell back to Strasburg.— EDITORS.

live stock besides. On the 9th of March, when the ground had become firm enough for military operations, I ordered the army to march that night, thinking then, as I do now, that the space of fifteen days was time enough in which to subordinate an army to the Commissary Department. About one million pounds of this provision was abandoned, and half as much more was spoiled for want of shelter. This loss is represented ("R. and F.," I., 468) as so great as to embarrass us to the end of the war, although it was only a six days' supply for the troops then in Virginia. Ten times as much was in North Carolina railroad stations at the end of the war. Mr. Davis says (p. 467):

"It was regretted that earlier and more effective means were not employed for the mobilization of the army, . . . or at least that the withdrawal was not so deliberate as to secure the removal of our ordnance, subsistence, and quartermaster's stores."

The quartermaster's and ordnance stores were brought off; and as to subsistence, the Government, which collected immediately on the frontier five times the quantity of provisions wanted, is responsible for the losses. The President suggested the time of the withdrawal himself, in the interview in his office that has been mentioned. The means taken was the only one available,— the Virginia Midland Railroad. Mr. Davis says ("R. and F.," I., 465):

"To further inquiry from General Johnston as to where he should take position, I replied that I would go to his headquarters in the field, and found him on the south bank of the river, to which he had retired, in a position possessing great natural advantages."

There was no correspondence in relation to selecting a defensive position. I was not seeking one; but, instead, convenient camping-grounds, from which my troops could certainly unite with other Confederate forces to meet McClellan's invasion. I had found and was occupying such grounds, one division being north of Orange Court House, another a mile or two south of it, and two others some six miles east of that place; a division on the south bank of the Rappahannock, and the cavalry beyond the river, and about 13,000 troops in the vicinity of Fredericksburg. Mr. Davis's narrative [of a visit to Fredericksburg at this time, the middle of March.— EDITORS] that follows is disposed of by the proof that, after the army left Manassas, the President did not visit it until about the 14th of May.☆ But such a visit, if made, could not have brought him to the conclusion that the weakness of Fredericksburg as a military position made it unnecessary to find a strong one for the army.

Mr. Davis ("R. and F.," II., 81) credits me with expecting an attack which he shows General McClellan never had in his mind:

"In a previous chapter, the retreat of our army from Centreville has been described, and reference has been made to the anticipation of the commanding general, J. E. Johnston, that the enemy would soon advance to attack that position."

This refers, I suppose, to a previous assertion ("R. and F.," I., 462), my comments upon which prove that this "anticipation" was expressed in the

<hr>

Not by Mr. Davis, but in a statement quoted at the above page from General J. A. Early, who said, "The loss . . . was a very serious one to us, and embarrassed us for the remainder of the war, as it put us at once on a running stock."— EDITORS.

☆ In "The Century" magazine for May, 1885, General Johnston, to support his assertion, quoted statements by Major J. B. Washington, Dr. A. M. Fauntleroy, and Colonel E. J. Harvie, which are now omitted for want of space.— EDITORS.

President's letter to me, dated February 28th, 1862. He says ("R. and F.," II., 83):

" The withdrawal of our forces across the Rappahannock was fatal to the [Federal] programme of landing on that river and marching to Richmond before our forces could be in position to resist an attack on the capital."

This withdrawal was expressly to enable the army to unite with other Confederate troops to oppose the expected invasion. I supposed that General McClellan would march down the Potomac on the Maryland side, cross it near the mouth of Aquia Creek, and take the Fredericksburg route to Richmond. The position of Hooker, about midway between Washington and this crossing-place, might well have suggested that he had this intention.

POSTCRIPT.— In the first paragraph of General Beauregard's postcript, it is asserted that I did not claim to have commanded in the first battle of Manassas until May, 1885, and that my official report of that action contains no such claim. It is, nevertheless, distinctly expressed in that report — thus:

"In a brief and rapid conference, General Beauregard was assigned to the command of the left, which, as the younger officer, he claimed, while I returned to that of the whole field."

And in "Johnston's Narrative," published in 1874, it is expressed in these words, on page 49:

" After assigning General Beauregard to the command of the troops *immediately engaged*, which he properly suggested belonged to the second in rank, not to the commander of the army, I returned to the supervision of the whole field."

So much for my not having claimed to have commanded at the "first Manassas" until May, 1885.

General Beauregard in his official report states the circumstance thus:

". . . I urged General Johnston to leave the immediate conduct of the field to me, while he, repairing to Portici, the Lewis house, should urge reënforcements forward."

This language would certainly limit his command as mine does. He did not attempt to command the army, while I did command it, and disposed of all the troops not engaged at the time of his assignment.

In his official report of the battle, General Beauregard further states:

" Made acquainted with my plan of operations and dispositions to meet the enemy, he gave them his entire approval, and generously directed their execution under my command."

The only "plan" that he offered me [to move *via* Aldie] was rejected — on the 14th, before my arrival. The battle fought was on McDowell's plan, not General Beauregard's. The proof of this is, that at its commencement little more than a regiment of Beauregard's command was on the ground where the battle was fought, and, of his 7 brigades, 1 was a mile and 6 were from 4 to 7 or 8 miles from it. The place of the battle was fixed by Bee's and Jackson's brigades, sent forward by my direction. At my request General Beauregard did write an order of march against the Federal army, finished a little before sunrise of the 21st. In it I am invariably termed commander-in-chief, and he (to command one of the wings) " second in command," or General Beauregard—conclusive proof that the troops were not "under his command."

Two letters, from General Lee and Mr. Walker, Secretary of War, are cited as evidence that General Beauregard commanded. Those gentlemen were not in a position to know if I relinquished the command. But I had this letter from General Lee:

"RICHMOND, July 24th, 1861. MY DEAR GENERAL: I almost wept for joy at the glorious victory achieved by our brave troops. The feelings of my heart could hardly be repressed on learning the brilliant share you had in its achievement. I expected nothing else, and am truly grateful for your safety   "

In conclusion, I cannot discover that my unfavorable opinion of the Federal general's tactics, quoted by General Beauregard, indicates a fear to command against him.

GENERAL EWELL AT BULL RUN.↓

BY MAJOR CAMPBELL BROWN, AIDE-DE-CAMP AND ASSISTANT ADJUTANT-GENERAL TO GENERAL EWELL.

IN General Beauregard's article on Bull Run, in "The Century" for November [1884], is this severe criticism of one of his subordinates, the late Lieutenant-General R. S. Ewell:

"Meanwhile, in rear of Mitchell's Ford, I had been waiting with General Johnston for the sound of conflict to open in the quarter of Centreville upon the Federal left flank and rear (making allowance, however, for the delays possible to commands unused to battle), when I was chagrined to hear from General D. R. Jones that, while he had been long ready for the movement upon Centreville, General Ewell had not come up to form on his right, though he had sent him between 7 and 8 o'clock a copy of his own order, which recited that Ewell had been already ordered to begin the movement. I dispatched an immediate order to Ewell to advance; but within a quarter of an hour, just as I received a dispatch from him informing me that he had received no order to advance in the morning, the firing on the left began to increase so intensely as to indicate a severe attack, whereupon General Johnston said that he would go personally to that quarter."

This contains at least three errors, so serious that they should not be allowed to pass uncorrected among the materials from which history will one day be constructed:

1. That Ewell failed to do what a good soldier would have done — namely, to move forward immediately on hearing from D. R. Jones.

2. That Beauregard was made aware of this supposed backwardness of Ewell by a message from D. R. Jones.

3. That on receiving this message he at once ordered Ewell to advance.

The subjoined correspondence,↓ now [March, 1885] first in print, took place four days after the battle. It shows that Ewell did exactly what Beauregard says he ought to have done — namely, move forward promptly; that his own staff-officer, sent to report this forward movement, carried also to headquarters the first intelligence of the failure

↓ This article appeared substantially as here printed in "The Century " for March, 1885.— EDITORS.

↓ [CORRESPONDENCE.]

UNION MILLS, July 25th, 1861.
GENERAL BEAUREGARD.

SIR: In a conversation with Major James, Louisiana 6th Regiment, he has left the impression on my mind that you think some of your orders on the 21st were either not carried out or not received by me.

My first order on that day was to hold myself in readiness to attack — this at sunrise. About 10, General Jones sent a copy of an order received by him in which it was stated that I had been ordered to cross and attack, and on receipt of this I moved on until receiving the following: 10 & 1-2 A. M.

On account of the difficulties of the ground in our front, it is thought advisable to fall back to our former position.

(Addressed) General Ewell. (Signed) G. T. B.

If any other order was sent to me, I should like to have a copy of it, as well as the name of the courier who brought it.

Every movement I made was at once reported to you at the time, and this across Bull Run, as well as the advance in the afternoon, I thought were explained in my report sent in to-day.

If an order were sent earlier than the copy through General Jones, the courier should be held responsible, as neither General Holmes nor myself received it. I send the original of the order to fall back in the morning. The second advance in the afternoon and recall to Stone Bridge were in consequence of verbal orders.

My chief object in writing to you is to ask you to leave nothing doubtful in your report, both as regards my crossing in the morning and recall — and not to let it be inferred by any possibility that I blundered on that day. I moved forward as soon as notified by General Jones that I was ordered and he had been.

of orders to reach him; that no such message was received from D. R. Jones as is here ascribed to him; and that the order sent back by Beauregard to Ewell was not one to advance, but to retire from an advance already begun.

It is not easy to understand these mistakes, as General Beauregard has twice given a tolerably accurate though meager account of the matter — once in his official report, and once in his biography published by Colonel Roman in 1884. Neither of these accounts can be reconciled with the later attitude.

Upon reading General Beauregard's article, I wrote to General Fitzhugh Lee, who was Ewell's assistant adjutant-general at Manassas, asking his recollection of what took place. I have liberty to make the following extracts from his reply. After stating what troops composed the brigade, he goes on:

"These troops were all in position at daylight on the 21st July, ready for *any* duty, and held the extreme right of General Beauregard's line of battle along Bull Run, at Union Mills. As hour after hour passed, General Ewell grew impatient at not receiving any orders (beyond those to be ready to advance, which came at sunrise), and sent me between 9 and 10 A. M. to see General D. R. Jones, who commanded the brigade next on his left at McLean's Ford, to ascertain if that officer had any news or had received any orders from army headquarters. I found General Jones making preparations to cross Bull Run, and was told by him that, in the order he had received to do so, it was stated that General Ewell had been sent similar instructions.

"Upon my report of these facts, General Ewell at once issued the orders for his command to cross the Run and move out on the road to Centreville."

General Lee then describes the recall across Bull Run and the second advance of the brigade to make a demonstration toward Centreville, and adds that the skirmishers of Rodes's 5th Alabama Regiment, which was in advance, had actually become engaged, when we were again recalled and ordered to "move by the most direct route at once, and as rapidly as possible, for the Lewis house" — the field of battle on the left. Ewell moved rapidly,

If there was an order sent me to advance before the one I received through General Jones, it is more than likely it would have been given to the same express.

Respectfully,

R. S. EWELL, B. G.

MANASSAS, VA., July 26th, 1861.

GENERAL: Your letter of the 25th inst. is received. I do not attach the slightest blame to you for the failure of the movement on Centreville, but to the guide who did not deliver the order to move forward, sent at about 8 A. M. to General Holmes and then to you — corresponding in every respect to the one sent to Generals Jones, Bonham, and Longstreet — only their movements were subordinate to yours. Unfortunately no copy, in the hurry of the moment, was kept of said orders; and so many guides, about a dozen or more, were sent off in different directions, that it is next to impossible to find out who was the bearer of the orders referred to. Our guides and couriers were the worst set I ever employed, whether from ignorance or over-anxiety to do well and quickly I cannot say; but many regiments lost their way repeatedly on their way toward the field of battle, and of course I can attach no more blame to their commanding officers than I could to you for not executing an order which I am convinced you did not get.

I am fully aware that you did all that could have been expected of you or your command. I merely expressed

sending General Lee and another officer ahead to report and secure orders. On his arrival near the field they brought instructions to halt, when he immediately rode forward with them to General Beauregard, "and General Ewell begged General Beauregard to be allowed to go in pursuit of the enemy, but his request was refused."

As to the real causes of the miscarriage of General Beauregard's plan of attack there need be little doubt. They are plainly stated by his immediate superior in command, General Joseph E. Johnston, in his official report, as being the "early movements of the enemy on that morning and the non-arrival of the expected troops" from Harper's Ferry. He adds: "General Beauregard afterward proposed a modification of the abandoned plan, to attack with our right, while the left stood on the defensive. This, too, became impracticable, and a battle ensued, different in place and circumstances from any previous plan on our side."

There are some puzzling circumstances connected with the supposed miscarriage of the order for our advance. The delay in sending it is unexplained. General Beauregard says it was sent "at about 8 A. M.," but D. R. Jones had received his corresponding order at 10 minutes past 7, and firing had begun at half-past 5.

The messenger was strangely chosen. It was the most important order of the day, for the movements of the army were to hinge on those of our brigade. There was no scarcity of competent staff-officers; yet it was intrusted to "a guide," presumably an enlisted man, perhaps even a citizen, whose very name was unknown.

His instructions were peculiar. Time was all-important. He was ordered not to go direct to Ewell, but first to make a détour to Holmes, who lay in reserve nearly two miles in our rear.

His disappearance is mysterious. He was never heard of after receiving the order; yet his route lay wholly within our lines, over well-beaten roads and far out of reach of the enemy.

my regret that my original plan could not be carried into effect, as it would have been a most complete victory with only half the trouble and fighting.

The true cause of countermanding your forward movement after you had crossed was that it was *then* too late, as the enemy was about to annihilate our left flank, and had to be met and checked *there*, for otherwise he would have taken us in flank and rear and all would have been lost. Yours truly,

G. T. BEAUREGARD.

General R. S. EWELL, Union Mills, Va.

P. S. Please read the above to Major James.

N. B. The order sent you at about 8 A. M., to commence the movement on Centreville, was addressed to General Holmes and yourself, as he was to support you, but being nearer Camp Pickens, the headquarters, than Union Mills, where you were, it was to be communicated to him first, and then to you; but he has informed me that it never reached him. With regard to the order sent you in the afternoon to recross the Bull Run (to march toward the Stone Bridge), it was sent you by General J. E. Johnston, as I am informed by him, for the purpose of supporting our left, if necessary. G. T. B.

Do not publish until we know what the enemy is going to do — or reports are out — which I think will make it all right. B.

Lastly, General Beauregard, in his official report, gives as his reason for countermanding the movement begun by Ewell at 10 o'clock, that in his judgment it would require quite three hours for the troops to get into position for attack. Had the messenger dispatched at 8 been prompt, Ewell might have had his orders by 9. But at 9 we find Beauregard in rear of Mitchell's Ford, waiting for an attack which, by his own figures, he should not have expected before 12.

It is not for me to reconcile these contradictions.

THE CONFEDERATE COMMISSARIAT AT MANASSAS.

BY COLONEL L. B. NORTHROP, COMMISSARY-GENERAL, C. S. A.

GENERALS Beauregard, Imboden, and Johnston in the foregoing articles [see pages 221, 239, and 256] criticise the management of my department in the matter of supplies for the Confederate army at Manassas either before or after the first battle. In the statements of these generals, there is some conflict, but they all concur in making me appear a preposterous imbecile, whom Mr. Davis was guilty of retaining. General Imboden in effect charges Mr. Benjamin with suppressing, in order to shield my incapacity, an official report of a board of officers convened by Johnston.

July 29th, 1861, General Beauregard wrote to his aides, Colonels Chesnut and Miles,—the latter read the letter in the Confederate Congress,—about his vision of capturing Washington, and thus laid the foundation of the cabal against Mr. Davis which made the Confederate Government a "divided house." It produced a resolution of inquiry, followed soon by a standing committee, and afterward, in January, 1865, by a unanimous resolution, in secret session of both houses, to appoint a joint select committee to investigate the condition and management of all the Bureaux of the War Department. The session of this committee on commissary affairs was held January 23d, 1865. During the war the investigations of the standing committee into my policy and methods were frequent; several were long taking testimony, for one member, H. S. Foote,—who when I was myself in prison published me as cruel to Federal prisoners,—was ever zealous to attack. Every investigation ended in approval. I have a letter from Mr. John B. Baldwin, chairman of the joint select committee, stating that he had declared in Congress, as the result of their examination, "that the commissary department of subsistence, under the control of Colonel Northrop, the Commissary-General, had been managed with a foresight and sagacity, and a far-reaching, comprehensive grasp of its business, such as we had found in no other bureau connected with the army supply, with perhaps a single exception."

The facts are that the engineer, General Beauregard, neglected his communications, so that "troops for the battle" and "supplies" were "retarded"; but the supplies were at the depot. "Eighteen heavy cannon, called for two weeks before," occupied unloaded cars at Fredericksburg, where there was a large supply of flour that had been accumulating since early June. Numerous cars were retained as stationary storehouses "for provisions," "useless baggage," and "trunks";

one hundred and thirty-three cars were abstracted by the "military" power from the use of the railroads for two weeks and more before the battle until returned by the Quartermaster-General and Mr. Ashe, the Government agent. There was plenty of lumber available to construct a storehouse. General Beauregard was not "urgent on the Commissary-General for adequate supplies before the battle," for there was no ground of complaint. It was *after the battle*, when the vision of capturing Washington had seduced him, that he tried to construct a ground of complaint anterior to the battle.

General Beauregard made but *one* demand on me (July 8th, by a telegram which I have) for a commissary of the old service. Lieutenant-Colonel Richard B. Lee was added; no one was removed. On the 6th day of July I ordered Fowle to buy all the corn-meal, and soon after all the bacon, he could. July 7th, Beauregard ordered him to keep in advance a two weeks' supply for 25,000 men, and Major Noland was ready to supply *any number* of beeves. The findings of the Board (on which Colonel Lee sat) are incoherent as stated by Imboden. The interdictions alleged by him are refuted by Colonel Ruffin (my chief assistant), and by all the letters sent officially to me in August, 1861. I have Fowle's detailed report of the rations at Manassas; there was plenty of provision for a march on Washington. If I had removed his commissaries as he alleges, or had "interdicted" them as General Imboden states, General Beauregard need not have been hampered, in a country which all the generals have declared abounded in the essentials of food.

General Johnston's comments on the commissariat are unfounded. He "requested" an increase of provisions which his commissary alone could determine, and allowed the accumulation to go on for twelve days after he knew that he had more than he wanted. When I was informed, I did what he should have done — telegraphed the shippers to stop. Two weeks before his move he promised my officer, Major Noland, the transportation deemed sufficient, and of which he had assumed direct control. Empty trains passed the meat which had been laid in piles, ready for shipment. Empty trains lay idle at Manassas for days, in spite of Noland's efforts to get them. General Johnston says the stores of the other departments were brought off. Eight hundred new army saddles, several thousand pairs of new shoes, and a large number of new blankets were burned — Quartermaster's stores then difficult of attainment.

THE FIRST YEAR OF THE WAR IN MISSOURI.

BY COLONEL THOMAS L. SNEAD. ☆

A VERY RAW RECRUIT.

SOUTH CAROLINA had just seceded and the whole country was in the wildest excitement when the General Assembly of Missouri met at Jefferson City on the last day of the year 1860. Responding to the recommendations of Governor Jackson and to the manifest will of the people of the State, it forthwith initiated measures for ranging Missouri with the South in the impending conflict. A State Convention was called; bills to organize, arm, and equip the militia were introduced; and the Federal Government was solemnly warned that if it sent an army into South Carolina, or into any other slaveholding State, in order to coerce it to remain in the Union, or to force its people to obey the laws of the United States, "the people of Missouri would instantly rally on the side of such State to resist the invaders at all hazards and to the last extremity."

The most conspicuous leader of this movement was Claiborne F. Jackson, who had just been inaugurated Governor. He had for many years been one of the foremost leaders of the Democrats of Missouri, and had been elected Governor in August. In the late canvass he had supported Douglas for President, not because he either liked him or approved his policy on the slavery question, but because Douglas was the choice of the Missouri Democrats, and to have opposed him would have defeated his own election; for in August, 1860, the people of Missouri were sincerely desirous that the questions at issue between the North and the South should be compromised and settled upon some fair basis, and were opposed to the election to the Presidency of any man — whether Lincoln or Breckinridge — whose success might intensify sectional antipathies and imperil the integrity of the Union.

But while loyally supporting the candidacy of Douglas, Jackson abated none of his devotion to the political principles which had been the constant guide of his life. He was a true son of the South, warmly attached to the land that had given him birth, and to her people, who were his own kindred. He was now nearly fifty-five years of age, tall, erect, and good-looking; kind-hearted, brave, and courteous; a thoughtful, earnest, upright man; a political leader, but not a soldier.

The Governor urged the people of Missouri to elect to the Convention men who would place Missouri unequivocally on the side of the South. He was

☆ Colonel Snead was at different times aide-de-camp to Governor Jackson, acting Adjutant-General of the Missouri State Guard, Chief-of-Staff of the Army of the West, and member of the Confederate Congress. He was made by General Price the custodian of his private and official papers. — EDITORS.

MAP OF
OPERATIONS IN
MISSOURI, 1861.

SCALE OF MILES

disappointed. Francis P. Blair, Jr., banded together the unconditional Union men of the State; while the St. Louis "Republican," Sterling Price, Hamilton R. Gamble, James S. Rollins, William A. Hall, and John B. Clark consolidated the conservatives, and together these elected on the 18th of February a Convention not one member of which would say that he was in favor of the secession of Missouri. To the courage, moderation, and tact of Francis P. Blair this result was greatly due.

Blair was just forty years of age. His father, the trusted friend of Andrew Jackson, had taken him to Washington City when he was about seven years old, and there he had been bred in politics. In 1843 he had come to St. Louis, where his brother Montgomery was already practicing law. For that profession, to which he too had been educated, Frank had no taste, and, having in it no success, quickly turned his attention to politics. In 1852 he was elected to the Legislature as a Benton Democrat. Shortly afterward he and B. Gratz Brown established the St. Louis "Democrat." When the Kansas conflict broke out in 1854, he identified himself with the Free-soil party, and in 1856 supported Frémont for the Presidency, though Senator Benton, Frémont's father-in-law, refused to do this. He was elected to Congress that year, for the first time. In the presidential canvass of 1860 he had been the leader of the Republicans of Missouri, and it was through him chiefly that Lincoln received 17,000 votes in the State. Immediately after the secession of South

Carolina, he had begun to organize his adherents as Home Guards and had armed some of them, and was drilling the rest for the field, when the election of delegates to the State Convention took place. To complete the arming of these men was his first aim. In the city of St. Louis the United States had an arsenal within which were more than enough arms for this purpose— 60,000 stand of arms and a great abundance of other munitions of war. So long as Buchanan was President, Blair could not get them, but the 4th of March was near at hand and he could well wait till then, for the Southern-rights men had been so demoralized by the defeat which they had sustained in the election of delegates to the Convention, that they were in no condition to attack the arsenal, as they had intended to do if the election had gone in their favor. It was, indeed, more than a month after the inauguration of Lincoln before the Southern-rights men ventured to make any move in that direction. The Governor then came to St. Louis to concert with General D. M. Frost (who commanded a small brigade of volunteer militia) measures for seizing the arsenal in the name of the State. While the matter was still under consideration the bombardment of Fort Sumter took place, and the President called for 75,000 troops to support the Government. To his call upon Missouri for her quota of such troops, the Governor replied that the requisition was, in his opinion, "illegal, unconstitutional, and revolutionary in its object, inhuman and diabolical," and that Missouri would not furnish one man "to carry on such an unholy crusade."

GOVERNOR CLAIBORNE F. JACKSON.
FROM A PHOTOGRAPH.

A few days later he convened the General Assembly, to adopt measures for the defense of the State.

In the consultation with Frost it had been decided that the Governor, in pursuance of an existing law of the State, should order all its militia into encampment for the purpose of drill and discipline; and that, under cover of this order, Frost should camp his brigade upon the hills adjacent to and commanding the arsenal, so that when the opportunity occurred he might seize it and all its stores. A great difficulty in the way of the execution of this plan was the want of siege-guns and mortars. To remove this difficulty the Governor sent Captains Colton Greene and Basil W. Duke to Montgomery, Alabama, and Judge Cooke to Virginia to obtain these things By Mr. Davis's order the arms were turned over to Duke and Greene at Baton Rouge, and were by them taken to St. Louis. Before they arrived there, however, the scheme to seize the arsenal had been completely frustrated by its commandant, Captain Nathaniel Lyon, who distributed a part of the coveted arms to Blair's Home Guards and removed the rest to Illinois, and then occupied with his own troops the hills around the arsenal. Frost consequently established Camp Jackson in a grove in the western part of the city, remote from the arsenal, and was drilling and disciplining his men there in conformity to the laws of the State and under the flag of the Union, when Jefferson Davis's gift to Missouri was taken into the camp.

Blair and Lyon, to whom every detail of the Governor's scheme had been made known, had been waiting for this opportunity. They had made up their minds to capture the camp and to hold the officers and men as prisoners of war. Frost went into camp on the 6th of May. The arms from the Confederacy were taken thither on the 8th. On Saturday, the 11th, the camp was to break up. Lyon had no time to lose. On Thursday he attired himself in a dress and shawl and other apparel of Blair's mother-in-law, Mrs. Alexander, and having completed his disguise by hiding his red beard and weather-beaten

BRIGADIER-GENERAL D. M. FROST, C. S. A.
FROM A PHOTOGRAPH.

features under a thickly veiled sun-bonnet, took on his arm a basket, filled, not with eggs, but with loaded revolvers, got into a barouche belonging to Blair's brother-in-law, Franklin A. Dick, and was driven out to Camp Jackson and through it. Returning to the city, he called the Union Safety Committee together, and informed them that he intended to capture the camp the next day. Some of the committee objected, but Blair and James O. Broadhead sustained him, and he ordered his men to be in readiness to move in the morning. Just as they were about to march, Colonel John S. Bowen came to Lyon with a protest from Frost. Lyon refused to receive it, and, marching out to the camp with about 7000 men, surrounded it and demanded its surrender. Frost, who had only 635 men, was obliged to comply.

While the surrender was taking place a great crowd of people, among whom were U. S. Grant and W. T. Sherman, hurried to the scene. Most of the crowd sympathized with the prisoners, and some gave expression to their indignation. One of Lyon's German regiments thereupon opened fire upon them, and twenty-eight men, women, and children were killed. The prisoners were then marched to the arsenal, and paroled the next day.

The capture of Camp Jackson and the bloody scenes that followed — the shooting down then and the next day of unoffending men, women, and children — aroused the State.⏀ The General Assembly, which had reconvened in extra session, enacted instantly a law for organizing, arming, and equip-

⏀ Lyon officially states that on both days the firing was in response to attacks by mobs. — EDITORS.

ping the Missouri State Guard, created a military fund, and conferred dictatorial power upon the Governor.

Hardly less important than these things — for it was what gave effect to them all — was the fact that the capture of the camp caused ex-Governor Sterling Price, President of the State Convention, and up to that time a Union man, to tender his services to the Governor. The General Assembly forthwith authorized the Governor to appoint a major-general to command all the forces which the State might put into the field, and Price was appointed to that position. ⚓

In the Convention Price had been opposed under all circumstances to the secession of Missouri, but just as earnestly opposed to the invasion and conquest of the South by the Federal Government. To that position he still adhered even when Mr. Lincoln, after the bombardment of Fort Sumter, had called for troops with which to repossess the Federal forts and enforce the laws of the Union within the seceded States. But considering Lyon's attack upon the State militia and his killing peaceable citizens an "unparalleled insult and wrong to the State," he believed it was the duty of Missouri to resent such wrongs.

The State now sprang to arms. Volunteers began to crowd the streets of Jefferson City, and everything indicated the opening of hostilities. Blair and Lyon would have met these demonstrations with force, would have driven Jackson and Price from the capital, would have dispersed the militia wherever it dared to show itself, would have occupied the State with Federal garrisons, and would have held her in unresisting obedience to the Union; but, unfortunately for the execution of their plans, General William S. Harney, who commanded the Military Department of the West, of which Missouri was part, had returned to St. Louis the day after the capture of Camp Jackson, and had resumed command there. Instead of using force Harney used conciliation. Instead of making war he made a truce with Price.

Blair now caused Harney to be relieved of the command of the Federal troops in Missouri, and on the 31st of May he was superseded by Lyon. As soon as this was made known to the Governor and General Price, they ordered the militia to be gotten in readiness for the field, for they knew that

⚓ Born in Prince Edward County, Virginia, in 1809, Price was now fifty-one years of age. He had been carefully educated in the schools of his native State and at Hampden-Sidney College, and had afterward attended the Law School of one of the most eminent jurists of Virginia, the venerable Chancellor Creed Taylor. He removed with his father's family to Chariton County, Missouri, in 1831, and had resided there ever since. Elected to the Legislature in 1840, he was at once chosen Speaker of the House, an honor rarely conferred upon so young a man, and particularly upon one who had never before been a member of a deliberative assembly. But he was preëminently fitted for the position. Well born and well bred, courteous and dignified, well educated, and richly endowed with that highest of all mental faculties, common sense; tall, straight, handsome, and of a commanding presence, — he was also a parliamentarian by instinct, understood intuitively the rules that govern deliberative bodies, and knew how to enforce them with promptness and vigor. He occupied this position till 1844, and was then elected to Congress. He took his seat in December, 1845; but when the war with Mexico broke out, a few months later, he left Congress, returned to Missouri, raised a regiment and led it to New Mexico, where he was placed in command. For his good conduct and gallantry in several battles that he fought and won there, and in recognition of the military and civic ability which he displayed in completing the conquest of that part of the Mexican territory, he was appointed brigadier-general by President Polk. In 1852 he was elected Governor of Missouri, and he held that office till the beginning of 1857.—T. L. S.

FAC-SIMILE OF WAR SCRIP ISSUED BY THE CONFEDERATE LEGISLATURE OF MISSOURI.

Blair and Lyon would quickly attack them. Some well-meaning gentlemen, who vainly imagined that Missouri could maintain her neutrality in the midst of war, now sought to establish a truce between Price and Lyon. Through them a conference was agreed upon, and the Governor and General Price came to St. Louis under Lyon's safe conduct. They met him and Blair at the Planters' House. Lyon was accompanied by his aide-de-camp, Major Horace A. Conant, and I was present as the Governor's aide. The interview, which lasted several hours, was at last terminated by Lyon's saying that he would see every man, woman, and child in Missouri under the sod before he would consent that the State should dictate to "his Government" as to the movement of its troops within her limits, or as to any other matter however unimportant. "This," said he, "means war. One of my officers will conduct you out of my lines in an hour." So saying, he left without another word, without even a salutation.

He had hardly left us when he was issuing orders for the movement of his troops. Sweeny and Sigel were sent with about 3000 men to the south-west to intercept the retreat of Jackson and Price if they should undertake to effect a junction with General Ben. McCulloch, who was believed to be concentrating a Confederate army in north-western Arkansas for the invasion of Missouri. Lyon would himself move up the Missouri after Jackson.

The conference was held on the 11th of June. On the 13th Lyon was on his way to Jefferson City with about 2000 men. Arriving there the next day, he found that the Governor had fled to Boonville. Leaving a garrison at Jefferson City, he pushed on to Boonville, where some 1300 militia had rendezvoused. Attacking these on the 17th, he dispersed them and drove the Governor southward with some two or three hundred men who still adhered to him and to the cause which he represented. General Price had meanwhile gone to Lexington, where several thousand militia had assembled.

From a military standpoint the affair at Boonville was a very insignificant thing, but it did in fact deal a stunning blow to the Southern-rights men of

Missouri, and one which weakened the Confederacy during all of its brief existence.   It was indeed the consummation of Blair's statesmanlike scheme to make it impossible for Missouri to secede, or out of her great resources to contribute liberally of men and material to the South, as she would have done could her people have had their own way.   It was also the most brilliant achievement of Lyon's well-conceived campaign.   The capture of Camp Jackson had disarmed the State, and completed the conquest of St. Louis and all the adjacent counties.   The advance upon Jefferson City had put the State government to flight and taken away from the Governor the prestige which sustains established and acknowledged authority.   The dispersion of the volunteers that were flocking to Boonville to fight under Price for Missouri and the South extended Lyon's conquest at once to the borders of Iowa, closed all the avenues by which the Southern men of North Missouri could get to Price and Jackson, made the Missouri River a Federal highway from its source to its mouth, and put an end to Price's hope of holding the rich and friendly counties in the vicinity of Lexington till the Confederacy could send an army to his support, and arms and supplies for the men whom he was concentrating there.

Price had, indeed, no alternative now but to retreat in all haste to the south-western part of the State, so as to organize his army within supporting distance of the force which McCulloch was assembling in western Arkansas for the protection of that State and the Indian Territory.   He accordingly ordered Brigadier-General James S. Rains to take command of the militia at and near Lexington, and to move southward so as to effect a junction with the Governor in the vicinity of Lamar, toward which place the latter was retreating with Generals M. M. Parsons and John B. Clark and what was left of their commands.   General Price himself, accompanied by his staff and a small escort, hastened rapidly toward Arkansas in order to bring McCulloch to the rescue of both the Governor and Rains.   On the way he was joined, almost daily, by squads or companies, and by the time he reached Cowskin Prairie, in the extreme south-western corner of the State, he had collected about 1200 men.

On the 3d of July Rains reached Lamar, near which place the Governor and his followers were already encamped.   The combined force amounted to about 6000 men, of whom 4000 were armed, and they had seven pieces of artillery.   Halting until the 5th in order to rest and organize, they pushed on that morning toward Carthage, having heard that a Federal force had occupied that place, which lay in their line of retreat.   They had marched but a few miles when, as they were passing through the open prairie, they descried, some three miles away, on the declivity of a hill over which they had themselves to pass, a long line of soldiers with glistening bayonets and bright guns.   These were part of the force which Lyon, on marching against Jefferson City, had sent under General Sweeny and Colonel Sigel to the south-west to intercept the Governor's retreat toward Arkansas.   Sigel, in executing this plan, had first attempted to intercept Price.   Failing in that, he had now, with more boldness than discretion, thrown himself, with about 1100 men and eight pieces of artillery, in front of the Governor, hoping either to defeat him or to hold him in check till Lyon could arrive and destroy him. Halting his column in the prairie, and deploying his armed men (about 4000), the Governor awaited Sigel's attack. The fight (known as the battle of Carthage) did not last long, for Sigel was outnumbered four to one, and the Missourians quickly put him to flight. He retreated, however, in perfect order, carrying off almost everything that he had brought with him. But he did not stop running till he had made forty miles. That night the State troops rested in Carthage. The next day they resumed their southward march, and soon met Price and McCulloch. Price now assumed command of the Missourians and led them to Cowskin Prairie, in the south-western corner of the State, while McCulloch went into camp near Maysville in Arkansas.

Lyon left Boonville in pursuit of the Governor, on the 3d of July, with about 2350 men, and directed his course toward Clinton in Henry county, where he had ordered Major Sturgis, who was following Rains with about 2500 regulars and Kansas troops, to unite with him. The two columns came together near Clinton on the 7th of July and pushed on after the Missourians. Lyon did not learn till the 9th that they had defeated Sigel and effected a junction with McCulloch. He then made in all haste for Springfield, fearing that the Confederates would attack that place. Arriving there on the 13th of July, he made it his headquarters.

Lyon, on the one hand, and Price on the other now began to get their armies in readiness for active operations. For Lyon this was a simple undertaking; for Price it was one of great complexity and great difficulty. Of the 7000 or 8000 men that he had, only a few had been organized into regiments. Several thousand of them had no arms of any kind. The rest were for the most part armed with the shot-guns and rifles which they had brought from their homes. Of powder and lead they had an abundance, but no fixed ammunition for either their seven pieces of artillery or for their small-arms. Tents they had none, nor camp equipage of any kind. There were no quartermasters' supplies, nor subsistence; and neither the quartermaster-general nor the chief commissary had a dollar of funds. The men were not fighting for pay, they wanted none, nor did they get any; but they and their thousands of horses and mules had to be fed. For their animals there was nothing but the grass of the prairies, and for themselves nothing but a scant supply of lean beef and coarse corn-meal. There were enough good officers to organize and command the men; but it would have puzzled almost any one to drill a company of raw recruits, armed, some with shot-guns, some with rifles, a few with old-fashioned flint-lock muskets, and here and there a man with a percussion musket. No better proof could be given of the dearth of material for the Staff, than the fact that I was myself assigned to duty by General Price as chief of ordnance of the army, though I told him at the time that I did not know the difference between a howitzer and a siege-gun, and had never seen a musket-cartridge in all my life; and a few days later I was assigned to the still more important position of acting Adjutant-General of the State Guard, though I had never then heard of a "morning report," and did not know the right of a company from its left. Had Hardee or any other West Pointer been in command, he would have kept us in camp six months, drilling and disciplining us, getting together wagons and teams, tents and cartridge-boxes, uniforms and haversacks, quartermasters and red tape, and all the other equipments and *impedimenta* of an army in the field, and then we would have gone into winter quarters; Lyon would have had his own way in Missouri, and the Federal armies that were sent thither to whip us would have been sent to fight in Virginia or in Tennessee instead, and the Confederacy might have been vanquished sooner than it was. But Price had us all ready for the field in less than three weeks. We had no tents, it is true, but tents would only have been in our way; we had no uniforms, but a bit of flannel or calico fastened to the shoulder of an officer designated his rank sufficiently for all practical purposes; the ripening corn-fields were our depots of subsistence; the prairies furnished forage, and the people in defense of whose homes we were eager to fight gladly gave us of all their stores.

McCulloch, one of the bravest of men and best of scouts, looking at us through the eyes of the young army officers whom Mr. Davis had sent to teach him how to organize, equip, and fight an army scientifically, saw in the Missourians nothing but a half-armed mob, led by an ignorant old militia general, but he consented to go with Price in search of Lyon, who was at Springfield and not hard to find. General N. B. Pearce, commanding a brigade of Arkansas State troops, agreed to go along with them.

Hardee, who was at Pitman's Ferry, Arkansas, within a few hundred yards of the Missouri line, and almost as near to Springfield as were Price and McCulloch, and who had with him several thousand good soldiers, was begged by both Price and McCulloch to coöperate in the movement against Lyon, but he replied that he "did not wish to march to their assistance with less than 5000 men, well appointed, and a full complement of artillery"!

By order of General Polk, made at the earnest personal solicitation of Governor Jackson, who had gone to Memphis for that purpose, General Pillow moved into Missouri from Tennessee, with twelve thousand men, and occupied New Madrid on the 28th of July, with the intent to unite in the effort to repossess the State.

On the same day, Price, McCulloch, and Pearce, relying upon the coöperation of both Hardee and Pillow, concentrated their forces at Cassville, within about fifty miles of Springfield. There Price was reënforced by General McBride's command, consisting of two regiments of foot and three companies of mounted men, about 700 in all. They had come from the hill country lying to the south and south-east of Springfield, and were a unique body of soldiers. Very few of the officers had any knowledge whatever of military principles or practices, and only the most superficial experience in company tactics. The staff was composed chiefly of country lawyers who took the ways of the court-room with them into the field. Colonels could not drill their regiments, nor captains their companies; a drum and a fife—the only ones in the entire command—sounded all the calls, and companies were paraded by the sergeant's calling out, "Oh, yes! Oh, yes! all you who belong to Captain Brown's company fall in here." Officers and men messed together, and all approached McBride without a salute, lounged around his quarters, listened to all that was said, and when they spoke to him called him "Jedge." Their only arms were the rifles with which they hunted the squirrels and other small game that abounded in their woods, but these they knew how to use. A powder-horn, a cap-pouch, "a string of patchin'," and a hunter's knife completed their equipment. I doubt whether among them all there was a man that had ever seen a piece of artillery. But, for all this, they were brave and intelligent. Like all frontiersmen, they were shrewd, quick-witted, wary, cunning, and ready for all emergencies, and like all backwoodsmen, their courage was serene, steady, unconscious. While there was no attempt at military discipline, and no pretense of it, the most perfect order was maintained by McBride's mere force of character, by his great good sense, and by the kindness with which he exercised his patriarchal authority.

Leaving Cassville on the 31st of July, the combined Southern armies, nearly 11,000 strong, advanced toward Springfield. On the way they encountered Lyon, who had come out to meet them. McCulloch, who could not comprehend the Missourians or the able soldier who commanded them, refused to attack unless Price and Pearce would confer upon him the chief command. Price had been a brigadier-general in Mexico, when McCulloch was but a captain of scouts, and had won more battles there than McCulloch had ever witnessed; he was now a major-general with more than 5000 men, and McCulloch had barely 3000; and in intellect, in experience, and in generalship he was worth a dozen McCullochs; nevertheless, he cheerfully placed himself and his army under the Texan's command. The order to advance was then given. Lyon had been encamped six miles in front with between 5000 and 6000 men. McCulloch moved at midnight, hoping to fall upon him unexpectedly, and to defeat him. To his amazement he learned, on approaching the spot, that Lyon had left twenty hours before, and must now be almost in sight of Springfield. The Confederates kept on, and on the 6th of August went into camp on Wilson's Creek, within ten miles of Springfield. They were still lying there on the morning of the 10th of August, when they were surprised and suddenly attacked on the north by Lyon, and on the south by Sigel.⸸

One of the stubbornest and bloodiest battles of the war now took place. Lyon's main attack was met by Price with about 3200 Missourians, and Churchill's regiment and Woodruff's battery, both from Arkansas. His left was met and driven back by McIntosh with a part of McCulloch's brigade (the Third Louisiana and McIntosh's regiment). McCulloch then took some companies of the Third Louisiana and parts of other commands, and with them attacked and routed Sigel (who had been sent to attack the rear), capturing five of his guns. This done, Pearce's Arkansas brigade, which up to this time had not fired a gun, was sent to reënforce Price. Lyon, seeing that

⸸ For maps and more specific descriptions of the three chief engagements of this "first year," — Wilson's Creek, Lexington, and Pea Ridge, — see the papers by Generals Pearce and Wherry, Colonel Mulligan, and General Sigel, to follow.— EDITORS.

MAJOR-GENERAL STERLING PRICE, C. S. A. FROM A PHOTOGRAPH.

the supreme moment had come, and that the day would be surely lost if he did not overwhelm Price before the Arkansans could reënforce him, now brought forward every available man, and was putting them into the fight, when his horse was killed, and himself wounded in the head. Dazed by the blow, dazed and stunned, his heart gave way for a moment under the sudden shock, but quickly coming to his senses he mounted another horse, and, swinging his hat in the air, called on his men to follow. Closing around him they dashed with him into the thick of the fight. But a moment later a bullet pierced his heart, and he fell from his horse into the arms of his orderly, and in an instant was dead. It was vain that the Federals tried to prolong the battle. Sturgis, on whom the command devolved, ordered a retreat, and before the Confederates knew that the battle was ended he was a mile away, having withdrawn his men unseen through the dense undergrowth of the woods in which the battle mainly was fought. In the haste of their retreat, the Federals left Lyon's dead body on the field. I delivered it myself an hour or two later to a flag-of-truce party that had been sent to ask for it. I saw it again the next day in Springfield, where it had been again abandoned by his men. [See foot-note, page 297.]

Rarely have I met so extraordinary a man as Lyon, or one that has interested me so deeply. Coming to St. Louis from Kansas on the 6th of February, this mere captain of infantry, this little, rough-visaged, red-bearded, weather-beaten Connecticut captain, by his intelligence, his ability, his energy, and his zeal, had at once acquired the confidence of all the Union men of Missouri, and had made himself respected, if not feared, by his enemies. In less than five months he had risen to the command of the Union armies in Missouri, had dispersed the State government, had driven the Governor and his adherents into the extremest corner of the State, had almost conquered the State, and would have completely conquered it had he been supported by his Government; and now he had given his life willingly for the Union which he revered, and to the cause of Human Freedom to which he was fanatically devoted.

The Federal force in the battle amounted to about 5400 officers and men. The Confederates had over 10,000 armed men on the ground, but 3000 of them took little or no part in the fight. The Confederates lost 279 killed and 951 wounded. The Federal loss was 258 killed, 873 wounded, and 186 captured or missing.

McCulloch refused to pursue, and Price resumed command of the Missouri troops. The next day he took possession of Springfield, and sent Rains with a mounted force to clear the western counties of the State of the marauding bands that had come into them from Kansas. On the 25th of August he moved northward with his army. On the 2d of September he met a part of Lane's Kansas Brigade under Colonel Montgomery on the banks of the Big Dry Wood. Montgomery had about 500 men and gave battle, but was forced to retreat before Price's superior force. The loss on either side was trifling.

Price now hastened toward Lexington, joined at every step by recruits. Reaching the city on the 12th of September with his mounted men, he drove Colonel Mulligan within his intrenchments, and as soon as his main body came up, completed the investment of the place. On the 20th he caused a number of hemp-bales saturated with water to be rolled to the front and converted them into movable breastworks, behind which his men advanced unharmed against the enemy. Colonel Mulligan was forced to surrender the next day. Price's loss was 25 killed and 72 wounded. Frémont reported to the War Department that the Union loss was 39 killed and 120 wounded. The Missourians captured about 3500 prisoners, five pieces of artillery, two mortars, 3000 stand of small-arms, a large number of sabers, about 750 horses, many sets of cavalry equipments, ammunition, many wagons and teams, more than $100,000 worth of commissary stores, and a large amount of other property. Price also recovered $900,000 that had been taken by the enemy from the Bank at Lexington, and restored it to the Bank. His force amounted to about 18,000 men, Mulligan's to about 3600.

In order to obtain the coöperation of the Confederate armies, the Governor and General Price sent me to Richmond, after the capture of Lexington, as a special commissioner to explain to President Davis the condition of affairs in Missouri, and to negotiate a treaty of alliance with the Confederate States, inasmuch as Missouri had not seceded nor been admitted into the Confederacy.

By their direction I went by way of McCulloch's headquarters, in order to make one more effort to secure his coöperation, and failing in that, to get from him certain supplies which General Price greatly needed, particularly caps for the muskets which we had captured at Lexington. To all my entreaties McCulloch replied that Price had gone to the Missouri against his advice; that the movement was unwise and would result in disaster, and that he would not endanger his own army by going to his assistance; and that as for musket-caps, he had none to spare.

General John C. Frémont, who had assumed command of the Union armies in the West on the 25th of July,

MAJOR-GENERAL DAVID HUNTER. FROM A PHOTOGRAPH.

now began to concentrate his forces against Price. Sending about 40,000 men, with 100 pieces of artillery, to attack him in front, and others to cut off his retreat, he took the field himself. His plan was magnificent—to capture or disperse Price's army; march to Little Rock and occupy the place; turn the Confederates under Polk, Pillow, Thompson, and Hardee, and compel them to fall back southward; push on to Memphis with his army and Foote's flotilla; capture that city; and *then* make straight for New Orleans.

Price left Lexington on the 29th of September, after advising his unarmed men to return to their homes, and to wait for a more convenient time to rise. Marching as rapidly as his long train would permit, he reached the Osage on the 8th of October with about 7000 men. To cross his troops and trains over that difficult river on a single flat-boat was a tedious operation, but Frémont gave him all the time that he needed, and he got them safely over.

After crossing the Osage, Price marched quickly to Neosho, where the General Assembly had been summoned by Governor Jackson to meet. Frémont continued to follow till the 2d of November, when he was superseded by Major-General David Hunter, who immediately stopped the pursuit and turned the army back to St. Louis. On the 19th of November Major-General Halleck assumed command of the Federal Department.

When I returned from Richmond, Price had gone into winter quarters on the Sac River near Osceola. Many of his men had been furloughed so that they might go to their homes, where they could subsist themselves during the winter and provide for their families. McCulloch's brigade was on the Arkansas River, and Pearce's had been disbanded. Under the treaty which had been negotiated at Richmond, the enlistment of Missourians in the Confederate army was at once begun and was continued at Springfield, whither Price moved his army just before Christmas. Before the end of January, 1862, two regiments of infantry (Burbridge's and Rives's), one regiment of cavalry (Gates's), and two batteries (Wade's and Clark's) had been mustered into the Confederate service, and on the 28th I started to Richmond to deliver the muster-rolls to the Secretary of War, and to inform the President as to the strength and condition of the army in Missouri, and to communicate to him Price's views as to the future conduct of the war in that State.

On the way I met Major-General Earl Van Dorn at Jacksonport in Arkansas. He had just assumed command (January 29th) of the District of the Trans-Mississippi, constituting a part of General Albert Sidney Johnston's extensive department. He was a dashing soldier, and a very handsome man, and his manners were graceful and fascinating. He was slight of stature and his features were almost too delicately refined for a soldier, but this defect, if it was a defect, was converted into a charm by the martial aspect of his mustache and imperial, and by an exuberant growth of brownish hair. Quitting the United States army when Mississippi seceded, he first entered her service, and was afterward appointed to that of the Confederacy and placed in command of Texas. Transferred thence to Virginia in September, 1861, he was commissioned major-general and ordered to report to General J. E. Johnston, commanding the Army of the Potomac. Johnston ordered him to Beauregard, and Beauregard assigned him to the command of a division, October 4th, 1861. He was assigned to the command of the Trans-Mississippi District, January 10th, 1862. We Missourians were delighted; for he was known to be a fighting man, and we felt sure he would help us to regain our State. I explained to him the condition of affairs in Missouri, and General Price's views.

Van Dorn had already decided upon a plan of campaign, and in execution of it ordered General Albert Pike, a few days afterward, to Lawrence county, Missouri, with a mixed command of whites and Indians estimated at 7000 men; ordered McIntosh to report to Price at Springfield with McCulloch's infantry; ordered McCulloch to Pocahontas with his mounted men; and called upon Louisiana, Arkansas, and Texas to send reënforcements. Hopeful and enthusiastic by nature, he believed that Price would have 15,000 effective men at Springfield by the last of March, and himself 18,000 at Pocahontas, and that they could then march against St. Louis. The two columns were to effect a junction north of Ironton, and, moving thence rapidly without tents or baggage, take the city by assault. Possession of the city would give him possession of the State, and the enemy would supply the arms for the thousands of volunteers that would flock to his standard.

From this day-dream he was rudely awakened a few days later by news that Price had been driven from Springfield on the 12th of February, and was hotly pursued by a Federal army which Halleck had sent against him under General S. R. Curtis. With this army was Captain P. H. Sheridan, doing duty

MAJOR-GENERAL HENRY W. HALLECK.   FROM A PHOTOGRAPH.

as quartermaster. Price sought refuge in the mountains of Arkansas, and February 21st was within thirty miles of Van Buren, near which place was McCulloch.

On learning all this Van Dorn hastened to Van Buren and thence to Price's headquarters, which he reached on the 1st of March. After a hurried consultation with Price and McCulloch, he decided to instantly attack Curtis, who had taken a strong position among the mountains near Bentonville. He moved on the 4th of March with about 16,000 men, of whom 6800 were Missourians under Price, and the rest Confederates under McCulloch and Pike. When almost within reach of Curtis (who reported his own strength at 10,500 infantry and cavalry and forty-nine pieces of artillery) Van Dorn unwisely divided his army, and leaving McCulloch with his own command and Pike's to attack Curtis in front, himself made with Price and the Missourians a long circuit to the rear of Curtis, and out of communication with McCulloch. Both columns attacked about the same time on the 7th. Price was completely successful and carried everything before him, taking during the afternoon seven pieces of cannon and about 200 prisoners, and at night bivouacked near Elkhorn Tavern. But morning revealed the enemy in a new and strong position, their forces united and offering battle. The Confederates soon learned that McCulloch and McIntosh had been killed the day before and their force routed and dispersed. The battle was renewed nevertheless, and the Missourians fought desperately and were still holding their ground when about 10 o'clock Van Dorn ordered a retreat, and the army leaving Missouri to her fate began to fall back toward Van Buren.

In this battle, sometimes called the battle of Pea Ridge, and at other times the battle of Elkhorn, the Federal general reported his losses at 203 killed, 980 wounded, and 201 missing. Van Dorn's were probably greater, and he lost heavily in good officers. McCulloch and McIntosh were killed; General Price was again wounded and narrowly escaped death; General W. Y. Slack, whom his men idolized and whom the whole army held in honor, was fatally wounded; and Colonel B. A. Rives, one of the knightliest of soldiers and bravest of gentlemen, and Churchill Clark, a heroic boy, were killed.

Halleck, who had determined to make the Tennessee "the great strategic line of the Western campaign," now began to concentrate all of his forces on that river and the Mississippi, in order "to fight a great battle on the Tennessee," one which would "settle the campaign in the West." He consequently ordered Curtis not to advance any farther into Arkansas; and sent out of Missouri all the troops that could be safely taken thence, some of them to Pope on the Mississippi, and others to Grant on the Tennessee.

The concentration of Federal armies on the Mississippi portended such danger to Beauregard, who had lately assumed command of the defenses of that river, that General Albert Sidney Johnston ordered Van Dorn to move his army to within supporting distance of Beauregard. This Van Dorn began to do on the 17th of March, on which day he wrote to General Johnston that he would soon "relieve Beauregard by giving battle to the enemy near New Madrid," or, by marching "boldly and rapidly toward St. Louis, between Ironton and the enemy's grand depot at Rolla."

While he was executing this plan, and while the greater part of the army that had survived Elkhorn was on the march across the mountains of North Arkansas toward Jacksonport, Van Dorn was suddenly ordered by General Johnston on the 23d of March to move his entire command by "the best and most expeditious route" to Memphis. His forces, to which he had given the name of "the Army of the West," were accordingly concentrated in all haste at Des Arc, on the White River, whence they were to take boats for Memphis. The first division of this army, to the command of which General Price had been assigned, was the first to move, Little's Missouri Brigade embarking on the 8th of April for Memphis, just as Pope was taking possession of Island No. 10, and Beauregard was leading Johnston's army back to Corinth from the fateful field of Shiloh.

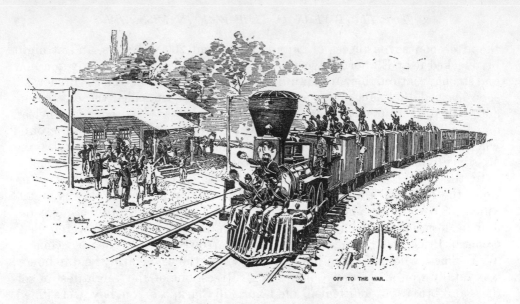

OFF TO THE WAR.

IN COMMAND IN MISSOURI.

BY JOHN C. FRÉMONT, MAJOR-GENERAL, U. S. A.

AT the outbreak of the war, in the spring of '61, being then in England, I offered my services to the Government, and was appointed one of the four major-generals of the regular army. General McClellan and myself were commissioned of even date, ranking next after General Scott. On my arrival I reported to the President, using a few days to arrange in some order the business which had carried me abroad. There was great confusion and indecision in affairs, and the people in power were slow to realize the actuality of war; it was long before they realized its magnitude. Several commands in the East were suggested to me, but I preferred the West, which I knew, and I held the opinion that the possession of the immediate valley of the Mississippi river would control the result of the war. Who held the Mississippi would hold the country by the heart.

A command was agreed upon between President Lincoln, Montgomery Blair, his Postmaster-General, who was a graduate of West Point, and myself, of which the great object was the descent of the Mississippi river. Necessary to this was first the firm possession of the State of Missouri, freed and protected from the secession forces within and around it. In pursuance of this plan "The Western Department" was created, comprehending, with Illinois, the states and territories west of the Mississippi river to the Rocky Mountains, including New Mexico. For reasons not wholly military, the President reserved the State of Kentucky, but assured me that so soon as I had succeeded in raising and organizing an army for the descent of the Mississippi river, he would extend my command over that State and the left bank of the Mississippi.

The President had gone carefully over with me the subject of my intended campaign, and this with the single desire to find out what was best to do and how to do it. This he did in the unpretending and kindly manner which invited suggestion, and which with him was characteristic. When I took leave of him he accompanied me down the stairs, coming out to the steps of the portico. I asked him then if there was anything further in the way of instruction that he wished to say to me. "No," he answered. "I have given you *carte blanche.* You must use your own judgment and do the best you can. I doubt if the states will ever come back."

Governor Yates, of Illinois, then in Washington, informed me fully of the unarmed and unprepared condition of the West. I immediately began a search for arms at Washington, and out of those at hand was able to obtain an order for only seven thousand stand.

Arriving at New York, I found that the order for the seven thousand stand of arms had been countermanded. Upon my complaint to Washington, and through the personal interposition of the President, Major Peter V. Hagner was sent to aid me in procuring what I judged immediately necessary for my department. With him I arranged for gathering from various arsenals and forwarding to St. Louis arms and equipments for 23,000 men. This detained me some weeks in New York. Before leaving, I telegraphed to Lieutenant-General Scott, to ask if he had any instructions to give me. He replied that he had none.

At Philadelphia we heard the news of the disaster of Bull Run. On the 25th of July I reached St. Louis, and at the start I found myself in an enemy's country, the enemy's flag displayed from houses and recruiting offices. St. Louis was in sympathy with the South, and the State of Missouri was in active rebellion against the national authority. The Bull Run defeat had been a damaging blow to the prestige of the Union.

In this condensed sketch I can give only the strong outline of the threatening situation I found, and, in part, the chief measures I adopted to convert our *defensive* position into one that was vigorously *offensive*, going into detail only enough to show some of the difficulties that beset me.

There was a wide difference between the situation here and that at Washington. The army of the East was organized under the eyes of the President and Congress; in the midst of loyal surroundings and loyal advisers where there was no need to go outside of prescribed military usage, or to assume responsibilities. But in Missouri all operations had to be initiated in the midst of upturned and revolutionary conditions and a rebellious people, where all laws were set at defiance. In addition to the bodies of armed men that swarmed over the State, a Confederate force of nearly 50,000 men was already on the Southern frontier: Pillow, with 12,000, advancing upon Cairo; Thompson, with 5000, upon Girardeau; Hardee, with 5000, upon Ironton; and Price, with an estimated force of 25,000, upon Lyon, at Springfield. Their movement was intended to overrun Missouri, and, supported by a friendly population of over a million, to seize upon St. Louis and make that city a center of operations for the invasion of the loyal States.

To meet this advancing force I had 23,000 men of all arms. Of this only some 15,000 were available, the remainder being three-months men whose term of service was expiring. General John Pope was fully occupied in North Missouri with nearly all my disposable force, which was required to hold in check rebellion in that quarter. For the defense of Cairo B. M. Prentiss had 8 regiments, but 6 were three-months men, at the end of their term, unpaid, and unwilling to reënlist. At Springfield General Lyon had about 6000 men, unpaid and badly fed, and in need of clothing. In this condition he was in hourly expectation of being attacked by the enemy, who was advancing in three times his nominal strength.

This was the situation to be met at the outset. The arms and equipments for 23,000 men which I had gathered at New York I now found had been diverted from my department and sent to Virginia. I had no money and the Government no credit; but the chief difficulty was the want of arms. There was no want of men. The loyal population of the North-western States flocked to the Union standard; the German population with a noble unanimity.

Having these conditions to face, on the 26th of July I telegraphed my needs to Montgomery Blair, whom I had known intimately. In reply he telegraphed, "I find it impossible to get any attention to Missouri or Western matters from the authorities here. You will have to do the best you can and take all needful responsibility to defend and protect the people over whom you are specially set." Two days afterward Secretary Seward telegraphed to ask what disposition I had made of the arms I had purchased in Europe, asking for an invoice. I telegraphed him that I needed to use these arms for my department, that I had absolutely no arms, and that the situation of the State was critical. On the 30th I sent to the President, as had been arranged, an unofficial letter setting forth the condition of my command. I informed him that the treasurer of the United States at St. Louis had $300,000 entirely unappropriated, but had refused my request for $100,000 to be delivered to my paymaster-general. I said to him that there were three courses open to me: "First, to let the enemy possess himself of some of the strongest points in the State and threaten St. Louis, which is insurrectionary; second, to force a loan from the secession banks here; third, to use the money belonging to the Government which is in the treasury. . . . This morning I will order the treasurer to deliver the money in his possession to General Andrews and will send a force to the treasury to take the money, and will direct such payments as the exigency requires. I will hazard everything for the defense of the department you have confided to me, and I trust to you for support." To the propositions of this letter the President gave the tacit approval of not replying, and I acted upon it.

I had no time to lose. The situation of Lyon at Springfield was critical, and the small disintegrating garrison at Cairo was hourly exposed to assault by an overpowering force. Among the various points threatened, Cairo was the key to the success of my operations. The waterways and the district around Cairo were of first importance. Upon the possession of this district depended the descent and control of the Mississippi Valley by the Union armies, or the inroad by the Confederate forces into the loyal States.

MAJOR-GENERAL FRANCIS P. BLAIR, JR. FROM A PHOTOGRAPH.

I now sent within the Confederate lines a capable engineer officer possessed of the necessary military knowledge, with instructions to go into the States of Kentucky and Tennessee to observe the situation of the enemy, ascertain his strength and probable plans, and make rough maps of important localities occupied by troops or likely to be.

Five days after my arrival, hearing that Pillow was moving upon Cairo, I left St. Louis for that place, with all my available force, 3800 men. I distributed my command over a transport fleet of eight large steamboats, in order to create in the enemy an impression of greater strength than I possessed. I found the garrison demoralized. From the chief of artillery I learned there were only about six hundred effective men under arms. These troops had enlisted for three months, which had now expired. They had not been paid, and there was much sickness among them. The reënforcement I brought, and such assurances as I was able to give, restored confidence; and I prevailed on one of the garrison regiments to remain.

Cairo was the most unhealthy post within my command. Fever and dysentery were prevailing. The roomy, shaded decks and convenient cabins of the large steamboats which brought the reënforcements, and the breeze from the water blowing through them, were in strong contrast with the steaming heat of the low, moist grounds of Cairo. This suggested the idea of floating hospitals. Before the sun went down the greater number of the sick were carried to one of the roomiest boats, thus securing good ventilation and perfect drainage.

The sudden relief of Cairo and the exaggerated form in which the news of it reached Pillow had the intended effect. He abandoned his proposed attack, and gave time to put it effectually beyond reach of the enemy, and eventually to secure a firm hold on the whole of that important district.

Having secured the initial point in my campaign, I returned to St. Louis on August 4th. Meantime I had ordered Stevenson's 7th Missouri regiment from Boonville, and Montgomery's Kansas regiment near Leavenworth, to the support of Lyon at Springfield. Amidst incessant and conflicting demands, my immediate care was to provide aid for him.

Governor Oliver P. Morton, of Indiana, answering my urgent request for troops, telegraphed that if leave were granted from Washington he would send five regiments made up of river boatmen, well adapted for the Mississippi expedition. In answer to my request they were ordered to me. But the order was changed, and instead of joining me they were sent to General Robert Anderson, then in command at Louisville. The same day I asked Senator Latham, at Washington, to aid my application for three thousand men from California, to be placed at El Paso, to operate against Texas troops moving into Arkansas. On the 5th Marsh reported from Girardeau that the enemy was close upon him, 5000 strong, and would attack him before morning. At midnight a heavy battery of 6 twenty-four-pounders and 1000 men were embarked to his aid under experienced officers, and Prentiss further reënforced him from below the same morning.

On the 6th General Scott telegraphed me that he had ordered all the troops out of New Mexico, and directed me to confer immediately with the governor of Kansas, and arrange for the safety of New Mexico, sending two regiments "without delay," as the first detachment would leave on the 15th.

On the 9th I informed the Government that the greater part of the old troops were going out of service, while the new levies, totally unacquainted with the rudiments of military training, would be unmanageable before an enemy. Therefore, I asked authority from the President to collect throughout the states educated officers who had seen service. With them I could make a framework on which to organize an army. My request was granted, and I acted upon it at once.

On the 10th Prentiss reported from Cairo that the enemy were again concentrating and intrenching at New Madrid about ten thousand strong.

Before my arrival at St. Louis General Lyon had borne a decisive and important part in Missouri. Together with Francis P. Blair, the younger, he had saved Missouri from secession. For this reason I had left his movements to his own discretion, but had myself made every possible effort to reënforce him. The defeat at Bull Run had made a change in affairs from that which was existing when General Lyon left Boonville for Springfield on the 5th of July. To any other officer in his actual situation, I should have issued peremptory orders to fall back upon the railroad at Rolla.

On the 6th I had sent an officer by special engine to Rolla, with dispatches for Lyon, and for news of him. In his letter of August 9th, the day before the battle, Lyon states, in answer to mine of the 6th, that he was unable to determine whether he could maintain his ground or would have to retire. At a council of war a fortnight before the battle, the opinion of his officers was unanimous for retreating upon Rolla.

On the 13th news reached me of the battle fought at Wilson's Creek on the 10th between about 6000 Union troops, under Lyon, and a greatly superior force under Price and McCulloch. I was informed that General Lyon had been killed, and that the Union troops under Sigel were retreating unmolested upon Rolla. In telegraphing a report of the battle to Washington, I informed the Department of the need of some organized force to repel the enemy, reported to be advancing on other points in considerable strength. I again asked the Secretary of War for Groesbeck's 39th Ohio regiment, and to order from the governors of Indiana, Illinois, and Wisconsin their disposable force. I informed him that we were badly in want of field artillery and that few small-arms had arrived. I also asked the President to read my dispatches.

Dissensions in the camp of the enemy prevented them from using their success, and I made and pushed forward as rapidly as possible dispositions for the defense of the city and State. I reënforced Rolla, which was the receiving-place for troops destined for the South-west. The plan of defense adopted was to fortify Girardeau and the termini of the railroads at Ironton, Rolla, and Jefferson City, with St. Louis as a base; holding these places with sufficient garrisons and leaving the army free for operations in the field. These points I connected by telegraph lines centering at headquarters. St. Louis was the base and center of operations and depot of reserves. Six thousand men, working night and day, were employed upon the fortifications, which commanded the city itself, as well as the surrounding country, upon a line of about ten miles. All the railroads entering the city I connected at one depot, more cars were added, and on twenty-four hours' notice 10,000 men could have been moved upon them from any one point to the opposite side of the State.

The officer who had been sent within the Confederate lines had returned, bringing important information concerning the position of the enemy, together with the rough maps required, indicating, among other points, the positions of Forts Henry and Donelson, then in course of construction. I sent him back immediately to make examinations of the Tennessee and Cumberland with reference to the use of those rivers by gun-boats, and also to watch the enemy's moves toward the Cairo district.

In answer to my appeal to the loyal governors for troops, regiment after regiment arrived at St. Louis from the whole North-west, but they were entirely without tents or camp equipage. The chief quartermaster of my department was an officer of the regular army, Major McKinstry, experienced, able, and energetic. But there were no supplies on hand, of any kind, to meet the necessities of the troops arriving without notice, and entirely unprovided. In this exigency he made requisition on the head of his department in Washington, but was informed in reply that the department could not meet the requisitions that were being made by the Army of the Potomac; that the preservation of the capital was deemed of more importance than the State of Missouri; that their entire time and attention was devoted to meeting requisitions made upon them; that General Frémont had full power, and that he, as Frémont's chief quartermaster, must use his own judgment and do the best he could toward meeting the wants of the department.

In July, at Washington, the subject of mortar-boats for the Mississippi expedition had been discussed between General M. C. Meigs, Gustavus V. Fox, afterward the Assistant Secretary of the Navy, and myself, and had been referred to me for decision, as having in charge military operations on the Mississippi. On the 31st of July the Secretary of War directed that the 16 nine-inch guns made at Pittsburg for the navy should be forwarded to me with the greatest dispatch, and that 30 thirteen-inch mortars be made as soon as possible and forwarded to me, together with shells for both guns and mortars. On the 24th of August I directed the construction of 38 mortar-boats, and later of 8 steam-tugs to move them, and the purchase and alteration into gun-boats of two strongly built river vessels,—the *New Era*, a large ferry-boat, and the *Submarine*, a powerful snag-boat; they were re-named *Essex* and *Benton*. At my suggestion and order, the sides of all these vessels were to be clad with iron. On the 3d of September General Meigs advised me to order from Pittsburg fifteen-inch guns for my gun-boats, as "able to empty any battery the enemy could make." Work on these gun-boats was driven forward night and day. As in the case of the fortifications, the work was carried on by torchlight.

August 25th an expedition was ordered under Colonel G. Waagner with one regiment, accompanied by Commander John Rodgers with two gun-boats, to destroy the enemy's fortifications that were being constructed at Belmont. [See map, page 263.]

BRIGADIER-GENERAL NATHANIEL LYON.
FROM A PHOTOGRAPH.

August 28th I assigned Brigadier-General U. S. Grant to the command of South-east Missouri, with headquarters at Cairo. He was fully instructed concerning the actual and intended movements on the Mississippi and the more immediate movements upon the Kentucky shore, together with the intention to hold the mouths of the Tennessee and Cumberland rivers. In his written instructions General Grant was directed to act in concert with Commander Rodgers and Colonel Waagner, and to take possession of points threatened by the Confederates on the Missouri and Kentucky shores.

August 31st Captain Neustadter was ordered to Cairo, to select a site opposite Paducah for a battery to command the mouth of the Tennessee river.

September 4th I sent heavy guns and an artillery officer to Cairo, where General Grant had just arrived from Girardeau. I telegraphed the President informing him that the enemy was beginning to occupy, on the Kentucky shore, every good point between Paducah and Hickman, and that Paducah should be occupied by us. I asked him now to include Kentucky in my command.

September 5th I sent to General Grant a letter of instruction, in which I required him to push forward with the utmost speed all work on the point selected on the Kentucky shore ten miles from Paducah, to be called Fort Holt. In this letter I directed him to take possession of Paducah if he felt strong enough to do so; but if not, then to plant a battery opposite Paducah on the Illinois side to command the Ohio River and the mouth of the Tennessee. On the evening of the day on which this letter was sent to General Grant, the officer who had been sent by me within the Confederate lines reached Cairo on his way to St. Louis to let me know that the enemy was advancing on Paducah. He judged it right to inform General Grant, urging him to take Paducah without delay. General Grant decided to do so, and in accordance with his instructions of the 28th immediately moved on Paducah with an adequate force and two gun-boats. He reached the town on the morning of the 6th, having only about six hours' advance of the enemy. Taking undisputed possession, he returned to Cairo the same day.

In answer to my persistent application for Colonel C. F. Smith he was ordered to join me, having meantime been made by the President a brigadier-general at my special request. I at once sent him forward to the command I had designed for him,—Paducah and the Kentucky shore of the Mississippi. His letter of instructions made known to him all the previous measures taken to hold the Kentucky shore and the mouths of the Tennessee and Cumberland. The execution of this part of my plans broke in upon the Confederate lines, drove them back, and dispersed their combinations for transferring the war to the loyal States.

I now on the 8th of September wrote to the President, giving him in the following extract the general features of my plan of campaign:

. . . . "As the rebel forces outnumber ours, and the counties of Kentucky between the Mississippi and Tennessee rivers, as well as those along the latter and the Cumberland, are strongly secessionist, it becomes imperatively necessary to have the coöperation of the loyal Union forces under Generals Anderson and Nelson, as well as of those already encamped opposite Louisville, under Colonel Rousseau. I have reënforced, yesterday, Paducah with two regiments, and will continue to strengthen the position with men and artillery. As soon as General Smith, who commands there, is reënforced sufficiently to enable him to spread his forces, he will have to take and hold Mayfield and Lovelaceville, to be in the rear and flank of Columbus, and to occupy Smithland, controlling in this way the mouths of both the Tennessee and the Cumberland rivers. At the same time Colonel Rousseau should bring his force, increased if possible, by two Ohio regiments, in boats to Henderson, and, taking the Henderson and Nashville railroad, occupy Hopkinsville; while General Nelson should go with a force of five thousand by railroad to Louisville, and from there to Bowling Green. As the population in all the counties through which the above railroads pass are loyal, this movement could be made without delay or molestation to the troops. Meanwhile General Grant would take possession of the entire Cairo and Fulton railroad, Piketon, New Madrid, and the shore of the Mississippi opposite Hickman and Columbus. The foregoing disposition having been effected, a combined attack will be made upon Columbus, and, if successful in that, upon Hickman, while Rousseau and Nelson will move in concert by railroad to Nashville, Tenn., occupying the State capital, and, with an adequate force, New Providence. The conclusion of this movement would be a combined advance toward Memphis, on the Mississippi, as well as the Memphis and Ohio railroad."

Meantime the untoward and obstructing conduct of the people of Missouri had decided me to assert the power of the Government. Accordingly, on the 30th of August, I issued a proclamation affixing penalties to rebellion and extending martial law over the State of Missouri. By this proclamation the property of persons in rebellion against the United States was held to be confiscated, and their slaves were declared free. As a war measure this, in my opinion, was equal to winning a deciding battle. The President disapproved it, as likely to lose us Kentucky, the loyalty of which was so strained and the temper of which was so doubtful, that he had agreed to the neutral attitude Kentucky demanded. He desired me to withdraw it as of my own motion. Unwilling to put myself in this position, I asked him to order it withdrawn, which he did. Shortly following upon this act, I was in many ways made to feel the withdrawal from me of the confidence and support of the Administration, but, acceding to strong representations from leading citizens of St. Louis, I did not resign my command.

MAJOR-GENERAL FRANZ SIGEL.
FROM A PHOTOGRAPH.

I had already been brought into collision with the intrigues of men who were in confidential relations with the President, and the occasion was promptly seized by them to urge misrepresentations which were readily accepted as reasons for my removal. The visits of high officers charged with inquiry into the affairs of my department, and the simultaneous and sustained attacks of leading journals, accumulated obstructions and weakened my authority. In fact, my command at the end of August had virtually existed little over a month; but the measures which I had initiated had already taken enduring shape, and eventually worked their intended result.

The inadequate space to which I am restricted compels me to pass over here the circumstances which made inevitable the loss of Lexington, upon which Price advanced after his victory at Wilson's Creek. All possible efforts were made to relieve Colonel Mulligan, but, notwithstanding the large concentration of troops for his relief, these efforts were baffled by absolute want of transportation and by river obstructions. To the Confederate general it was a barren success, and he was shortly forced to retreat to the south-west. As a military position Lexington was of no value to him. In the midst of the demand for troops for Lexington, I was on the 14th ordered by General Scott to "send five thousand well-armed infantry to Washington without a moment's delay." Two thousand were sent.

At the end of September I left St. Louis to take the field against Price. The army numbered 38,000 men. To complete the defenses of St. Louis, after the advance of the army, I left 5 regiments of infantry, with 1 battalion of cavalry, and 2 batteries of field artillery. The five divisions which composed it were assigned positions, their lines of march converging to Springfield; and in the beginning of October I moved against Price. Transportation and, consequently, supplies were very inadequate; but in exigencies an army sometimes moves without either. The September rains were over; the fine weather of the Indian summer had come; the hay was gathered, and the corn was hardening, and we were about to carry out the great object of the campaign with fewer hardships from exposure, and fewer impediments from want of transport, than could have been expected at any other season. The spirit of the army was high. A finer body of men could not have been brought together, and we had every reason to believe that the campaign would open with a signal victory in the defeat or dispersion of the enemy, with a move on Memphis as the immediate result. Had I possessed means of transport when Price moved on Lexington I should have compelled him to give me battle on the north side of the Osage; as he could not cross the Missouri without exposing himself to certain defeat, no other course would have remained open to him. In fact, when I did go forward, the appearance of my advance at Sedalia was the signal for his precipitate retreat. The first contact now with the enemy was at Fredericktown and Springfield,— the former one of the most admirably conducted engagements of the war, and the latter action a glorious victory. Along the whole extent of our lines we were uniformly successful against the enemy.

At the end of October I was in Springfield with 21,000 effective men. Price had terminated his retreat, and his movements showed that he had decided to offer battle. This was confirmed by information obtained from his headquarters that the Missourians were refusing to leave the State.

Recognizing the rights of humanity, and remembering that this conflict was among our own people, and that the whole State of Missouri was a battle-field, General Price and myself had been engaged in arranging the terms of a convention which was concluded and signed by us on the 1st of November. It provided: 1st, for an exchange of prisoners, hitherto refused by our Government; 2d, that guerrilla fighting should be suppressed, and the war confined to the organized armies in the field; 3d, that there should be no arrests for opinion, the preservation of order being left to the State courts.

Generals Asboth and Sigel, division commanders, now reported that the enemy's advance-guard was at Wilson's Creek, nine miles distant, several thousand strong; his main body occupying the roads in the direction of Cassville, at which place General Price had his headquarters with his reserves. On November 2d the dispositions for the expected battle were being planned, when late in the evening a messenger arrived bearing an order from General Scott which removed me from my command. This order had been hurried forward by General Hunter, who superseded me, and who was behind with his division. The next day, Hunter not arriving, the plan of battle was agreed on, the divisions were assigned conformably, and in the evening the troops began to occupy their positions. About 10 o'clock at night

MAJOR-GENERAL JOHN C. FRÉMONT. FROM A STEEL PLATE IN POSSESSION OF MRS. FRÉMONT.

Hunter arrived at my headquarters, where the officers were assembled. I handed to him the plan of battle and turned over my command.

The order which gave my command to General Hunter was dated October 24th, and had been sent to one of my subordinate officers in St. Louis, to be served on me at his discretion. Accompanying it was a letter from the President in which he directed that it should not be served on me if I had fought a battle or was about to fight one. His intention was disregarded; the order was put in force when both ourselves and the enemy were ready and intending battle. In the face of positive knowledge, General Hunter assumed that there was no enemy near and no battle possible, and withdrew the army. ✩

The correctness of the operations in this campaign to meet the intended movements of the enemy, have all been corroborated and proved by subsequent information. My expenditures to raise and equip this army were vindicated and sustained by decisions of the United States courts. The establishment of martial law at St. Louis, which was denounced as arbitrary and unnecessary, was maintained and acted upon by all my successors until peace was declared; and the fortifications of that city, upon which all lines of defense rested, aided its enforcement and made the dyke between the Northwest and the South. The taking of Paducah, for which I was censured, has since been made the pivot of success to others. And the gun-boats, for the preparation of which, also, I was censured, the work being countermanded as a "useless extravagance," became historic in the progress of the war.

✩ In support of the facts, I quote from the report of General McCulloch to his Secretary of War, at the close of this Missouri campaign: "We met next day at a point between the two armies where it was agreed upon by all the Missouri generals that we should wait an attack from the enemy, the ground to be selected by General Price and myself." Official Records, III., 748.—J. C. F.

Hunter's withdrawal was in pursuance of instructions of a general nature from President Lincoln, dated October 24th, 1861, and accompanying the orders relieving General Frémont.— EDITORS.

WILSON'S CREEK, AND THE DEATH OF LYON.

BY WILLIAM M. WHERRY, SIXTH U. S. INFANTRY, BREVET BRIGADIER-GENERAL, U. S. V.,
AT WILSON'S CREEK AIDE-DE-CAMP TO GENERAL LYON.

CAVALRYMAN OF THE UNITED STATES
REGULARS, IN 1861.

ABOUT the middle of July, 1861, the Army of the Union in south-west Missouri, under General Nathaniel Lyon, was encamped in and near the town of Springfield, and numbered approximately 6200 men, of whom about 500 were ill-armed and undisciplined "Home Guards." The organized troops were in all 5868, in four brigades. By the 9th of August these were reduced to an aggregate of about 5300 men, with the 500 Home Guards additional. Of these troops, the 1st Iowa regiment was entitled to discharge on the 14th of August, and the 3d and 5th Missouri, Sigel's and Salomon's, at different periods, by companies, from the 9th to the 18th of August. All except the regulars had been enrolled since the attack on Sumter in April, and but little time had been possible for drill and instruction. They had been moved and marched from St. Louis and points in Kansas, taking part in several spirited but minor engagements, and were ill-provided with clothing and food, but their spirits were undaunted, and they were devoted to their leader.

The latter part of July was spent by Lyon in drilling his troops and procuring supplies, the mills in the neighborhood having been seized and employed in grinding flour for the troops. He continued to send urgent appeals to St. Louis for reënforcements.

On the 1st of August, however, having received information of an advance by the enemy, in superior numbers, Lyon moved down the Fayetteville road (also known as the Cassville road) to meet and attack the largest and most advanced force, hoping to drive it back and then strike the others in detail. A lively skirmish with Price's advance-guard, under Rains, took place at Dug Springs on the 2d of August; and on the 3d a more insignificant affair occurred with the rear-guard of Rains's forces at McCullah's farm, which had been his headquarters, but from which he retired without resistance. Here Lyon became convinced he was being drawn farther and farther from his base, without supplies, and he determined to fall back to Springfield, which place he reached on the 5th. During those blistering August days the men marched with bleeding feet and parched lips, Lyon himself urging forward the weary and footsore stragglers.

On the 8th a march in force was planned for the following night, to make an attack on the enemy's front at Wilson's Creek at daylight. From this intention General Lyon was dissuaded, after having called together the principal officers to receive their instructions. Many of the troops were exhausted, and all were tired; moreover, some supplies having arrived from

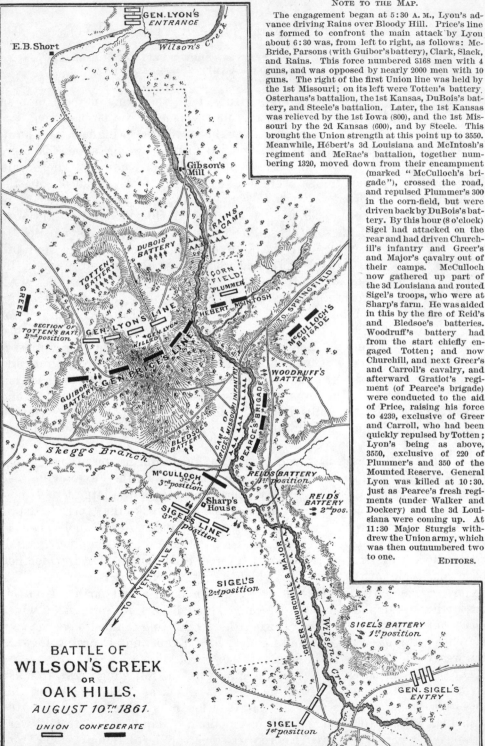

BATTLE OF
WILSON'S CREEK
OR
OAK HILLS.
AUGUST 10TH 1861.

UNION   CONFEDERATE

NOTE TO THE MAP.

The engagement began at 5:30 A. M., Lyon's advance driving Rains over Bloody Hill. Price's line as formed to confront the main attack by Lyon about 6:30 was, from left to right, as follows: McBride, Parsons (with Guibor's battery), Clark, Slack, and Rains. This force numbered 5168 men with 4 guns, and was opposed by nearly 2000 men with 10 guns. The right of the first Union line was held by the 1st Missouri; on its left were Totten's battery, Osterhaus's battalion, the 1st Kansas, DuBois's battery, and Steele's battalion. Later, the 1st Kansas was relieved by the 1st Iowa (800), and the 1st Missouri by the 2d Kansas (600), and by Steele. This brought the Union strength at this point up to 3550. Meanwhile, Hébert's 3d Louisiana and McIntosh's regiment and McRae's battalion, together numbering 1320, moved down from their encampment (marked "McCulloch's brigade"), crossed the road, and repulsed Plummer's 300 in the corn-field, but were driven back by DuBois's battery. By this hour (8 o'clock) Sigel had attacked on the rear and had driven Churchill's infantry and Greer's and Major's cavalry out of their camps. McCulloch now gathered up part of the 3d Louisiana and routed Sigel's troops, who were at Sharp's farm. He was aided in this by the fire of Reid's and Bledsoe's batteries. Woodruff's battery had from the start chiefly engaged Totten; and now Churchill, and next Greer's and Carroll's cavalry, and afterward Gratiot's regiment (of Pearce's brigade) were conducted to the aid of Price, raising his force to 4239, exclusive of Greer and Carroll, who had been quickly repulsed by Totten; Lyon's being as above, 3550, exclusive of 220 of Plummer's and 350 of the Mounted Reserve. General Lyon was killed at 10:30, just as Pearce's fresh regiments (under Walker and Dockery) and the 3d Louisiana were coming up. At 11:30 Major Sturgis withdrew the Union army, which was then outnumbered two to one. — EDITORS.

Rolla, it was deemed wise to clothe and shoe the men as far as practicable, and to give them another day for recuperation.

On the 9th it was intended to march that evening with the whole force united, as agreed upon the 8th, and attack the enemy's left at daylight, and Lyon's staff were busied in visiting the troops and seeing that all things were in order. During the morning Colonel Sigel visited Lyon's headquarters, and had a prolonged conference, the result of which was that Colonel Sigel was ordered to detach his brigade, the 3d and 5th Missouri, one six-gun battery, one company of the 1st U. S. Cavalry, under Captain Eugene A. Carr, and one company of the 2d Dragoons, under Lieutenant Charles E. Farrand, for an attack upon the enemy from the south, while Lyon with the remainder of his available force should attack on the north.

The troops were put in march in the evening; those about Springfield immediately under General Lyon moving out to the west on the Little York road until joined by Sturgis's command from their camps, when they turned to the south across the prairie. The head of the main column reached the point where the enemy's pickets were expected to be found, about 1 A. M., and went into bivouac. Sigel's force, consisting of 1200 men and six pieces of artillery, moved four miles down the Fayetteville road, and then, making a long détour to the left by a by-road, arrived within a mile of the enemy's camp and rear at daylight.

In the vicinity of the Fayetteville road crossing, the creek acquires considerable depth, and in most places has rough, steep, and rather high banks, rendering fording difficult. On the left side the hills assume the proportion of bluffs; on the right or western bank the ground is a succession of broken ridges, at that time covered for the most part with trees and a stunted growth of scrub oaks with dense foliage, which in places became an almost impenetrable tangle. Rough ravines and deep gullies cut up the surface.

The Confederates were under command of General Ben. McCulloch. On the west side of the stream, "Old Pap" Price, with his sturdy Missourians, men who in many later battles bore themselves with a valor and determination that won the plaudits of their comrades and the admiration of their foes, was holding the point south of Wilson's Creek, selected by Lyon for attack. Price's command consisted of five bodies of Missourians, under Slack, Clark, Parsons, McBride, and Rains, the last-named being encamped farther up the stream. On the bluffs on the east side of the creek were Hébert's 3d Louisiana and McIntosh's Arkansas regiment, and, farther south, Pearce's brigade and two batteries, while other troops, under Greer, Churchill, and Major, were in the valley along the Fayetteville road, holding the extreme of the Confederate position.

Lyon put his troops in motion at early dawn on the 10th, and about 4 o'clock struck Rains's most advanced picket, which escaped and gave warning of the attack, of which General Price was informed just as he was about to breakfast. Captain Plummer's battalion of regular infantry was the advance, followed by Osterhaus's two companies of the 2d Missouri Volunteers, and Totten's battery. A body of 200 mounted Home Guards was on Plummer's left.

Having reached the enemy's pickets, the infantry was deployed as skirmishers, Plummer to the left and Osterhaus to the right, and Lieutenant-Colonel Andrews, with the 1st Missouri Infantry, was brought up in support of the battery. Advancing a mile and a half and crossing a brook tributary to the creek, the Union skirmishers met and pushed the Confederate skirmishers up the slope. This disclosed a considerable force of the enemy, along a ridge perpendicular to the line of march and to the valley of the creek, which was attacked by the 1st Missouri and the 1st Kansas, assisted by Totten's battery, who drove back the Confederates on the right to the foot of the slope beyond.

Plummer on the left early became separated from the main body by a deep ravine terminating in a swampy piece of ground, beyond which lay a corn-field which he entered, encountering a large force, the main part of which was the Louisiana regiment. These troops fought with determined valor and checked Plummer's progress. DuBois's battery was moved up to a hill on the left, supported by Osterhaus's battalion, the 1st Iowa, and the 2d Kansas, and opened a deadly fire with shells upon the corn-field, with such marked effect as to throw the Confederates into disorder and enable Plummer to draw off his command in good order across the ravine.

A momentary lull occurred at this time, except on our extreme right, where Price's Missourians opposed the 1st Missouri and attempted to turn that flank, but the 2d Kansas by its timely arrival and gallant attack bore back Price's overwhelming numbers and saved the flank. Meanwhile Totten's battery, which had been brought into action by section and by piece as the conformation of the ground would admit, performed extraordinary service. Steele's regular infantry was added to its support. Price's troops had fought with great bravery and determination, advancing and retiring two or three times before they were compelled to give way on the lower slope of the ridge they had occupied. Many times the firing was one continuous roar.

The lull enabled the enemy to re-adjust his lines and bring up fresh troops, having accomplished which, Price made a determined advance along nearly the whole of Lyon's front. He charged fiercely in lines of three or four ranks, to within thirty or forty yards, pouring in a galling fire and directing his most determined efforts against Totten's battery, for which Woodruff's, which was pitted against it, was no match at all.↓

Every available man of Lyon's was now brought into action and the battle raged with redoubled energy on both sides. For more than an hour the balance was about even, one side gaining ground only to give way in its turn to the advance of the other, till at last the Confederates seemed to yield, and a suspension of the fury took place.

General Lyon had bivouacked near the head of his column on the night of the 9th, sharing a rubber-coat with Major (now Major-General) John M. Schofield, his chief of staff, between two rows of corn in a field by the roadside, his other staff-officers near by. He did not seem hopeful, but was

↓ Woodruff's Little Rock battery was composed of guns which had been captured at the seizure of the Little Rock arsenal, of which Captain Totten had been in command. Woodruff and his gunners had, in fact, been drilled and instructed by Totten.— EDITORS.

MAJOR-GENERAL JOHN M. SCHOFIELD. FROM A PHOTOGRAPH.

oppressed with the responsibility of his situation, with anxiety for the cause, and with sympathy for the Union people in that section, when he should retreat and leave to their fate those who could not forsake their homes. He repeatedly expressed himself as having been abandoned by his superiors. When the troops were put in motion, he went at the head of the column, and when the action opened he kept his place at the front, entering the heat of the engagement with the line, near Totten's battery. He maintained an imperturbable coolness, and his eye shone with the ardor of conflict. He directed, encouraged, and rallied his troops in person, sending his staff in all directions, and was frequently without an attendant except one or two faithful orderlies. Early in the attack while on the line to the left of Totten's battery, rallying a part of the 1st Missouri Infantry, his horse, which he was leading, was killed and he received a slight wound in the leg. Shortly afterward he was wounded in the head. He continued dismounted during the contest above described, and walking a few paces toward the rear with his chief of staff, Major Schofield, who had also lost his horse, shot under him, Lyon said, "I fear the day is lost." Schofield encouraged him to take a more hopeful view of the case, assuring him that the troops were easily rallied and were gaining confidence, and that the disorder was only temporary, and then proceeded to another part of the line in search of a mount.

About 9 o'clock, during a brief cessation in the firing, Lyon started toward the top of the ridge, accompanied by an aide, who was urging him to accept his horse, when they met Major Sturgis and a few troopers. One of these was dismounted, and his horse was given to General Lyon. Lyon also expressed himself despondingly to Sturgis, and was by him encouraged. Sturgis proceeded to another quarter, and Lyon toward DuBois's battery.

About this time great anxiety began to be felt for the fate of Sigel's command. Shortly after Lyon's attack the sound of battle had been heard in the rear of the enemy's line. It continued but a short time, and was renewed shortly afterward for a very brief period only, when it ceased altogether. Sigel had proceeded to within a mile of the camps, and his cavalry had cut off the enemy's small parties and thus suppressed information of his coming. He then

advanced his infantry toward the point
where the by-road crosses the creek, his
flanks supported by the cavalry on the
right and dragoons on the left, four
guns being placed on a hill overlooking
the tents. At about 5:30 A. M., hearing the musketry on Lyon's front, he
opened fire with his guns, pushing his
infantry across the creek and into the
lower camp, whence they had fled, overwhelmed by the suddenness of the attack. Sigel crossed his guns and pushed
with infantry and artillery forward a
short distance in pursuit, meeting with
slight resistance. He advanced from his
first position near the creek, by a road
west of the deserted camp, and formed
line of battle in a field between the
road and the camp. Afterward he
advanced to Sharp's house. The Arkansans and Texans retired to the
northward, fell in with Price's Missouri
line, and assisted in the fight against
Lyon. Meanwhile McCulloch called
upon a battalion of mounted Missourians, and upon a part of the Louisiana
regiment which had been confronting
Plummer in the corn-field, and with
these attacked Sigel's men, who were
in line at Sharp's farm, and drove them
from the field. When the attack by
the Confederates, from the direction of
Lyon's front, was made, the confusion
of Sigel's men was brought about by
the enfilading fire of Reid's battery east
of the creek, and by the belief that
the infantry in their front were friends.
Sigel went back the way he came with
a part of his command, including Carr's
cavalry. All but the cavalry, who were
ahead, were ambuscaded and, for the
most part, killed or captured; Sigel
narrowly escaped capture. Colonel Salomon with 450 of the troops retreated,
by a détour to the west, to the Little
York road, as did also Lieutenant Far-

BLOODY HILL, IN THE DISTANCE.

SHARP'S HOUSE (SIGEL'S POSITION).

THE BATTLE-FIELD OF WILSON'S CREEK AS SEEN FROM BEHIND PEARCE'S CAMP ON THE EAST SIDE OF THE CREEK—SEE MAP, PAGE 290. FROM PHOTOGRAPHS.

rand, with the dragoons. The latter, finding himself with his company alone, forcibly detained a guide, and made up teams for one gun and one caisson of the abandoned artillery, He was finally compelled to unhorse and leave the caisson, in order to put the animals to the gun. Thus by 10 o'clock Sigel was out of the fight, and the enemy could turn his whole force upon Lyon.

Meantime a body of troops was observed moving down the hill on the east bank of Wilson's Creek toward Lyon's left, and an attack by other troops from that direction was anticipated. Schofield deployed eight companies of the 1st Iowa and led them in person to repel this. They did so most gallantly after a sanguinary contest, effectually assisted by the fire from DuBois's battery, which alone drove back the column on the opposite side of the stream before it began a crossing.

Lyon, accompanied by an aide↓ and his six or eight orderlies, followed closely the right of the Iowa regiment. After proceeding a short distance, his attention was called by the aide to a line of men drawn up on the prolongation of the left of our main line and nearly perpendicular to the 1st Iowa as it moved to the eastward. A party of horsemen came out in front of this line of the enemy and proceeded to reconnoiter. General Price and Major Emmett Mac Donald (who had sworn that he would not cut his hair till the Confederacy was acknowledged) were easily recognized. General Lyon started as if to confront them, ordering his party to "draw pistols and follow" him, when the aide protested against his exposing himself to the fire of the line, which was partly concealed by the mass of dense underbrush, and asked if he should not bring up some other troops. To this Lyon assented, and directed the aide to order up the 2d Kansas. The general advanced a short distance, joining two companies of the 1st Iowa, left to protect an exposed position.

Colonel Mitchell of the 2d Kansas, near DuBois's battery, sent his lieutenant-colonel, Blair, to Lyon to ask to be put in action, and the two messengers passed each other without meeting. Lyon repeated his order for the regiment to come forward. The regiment moved promptly by the flank, and as it approached Lyon he directed the two companies of Iowa troops to go forward with it, himself leading the column, swinging his hat. A murderous fire was opened from the thick brush, the 2d Kansas deployed rapidly to the front and with the two companies of the 1st Iowa swept over the hill, dislodging the enemy and driving them back into the next ravine; but while he was at the head of the column, and pretty nearly in the first fire, a ball penetrated Lyon's left breast, inflicting a mortal wound. He slowly dismounted, and as he fell into the arms of his faithful orderly, Lehmann, he exclaimed, "Lehmann, I am killed," and almost immediately expired. Colonel Mitchell was also severely wounded about the same time and removed to the rear.

Lieutenant Gustavus Schreyer and two of his men of the 2d Kansas bore the body of Lyon through the ranks, Lehmann bearing the hat and loudly bemoaning the death of his chief. In the line of file-closers the returning aide was met, who, apprehensive of the effect upon the troops, stopped the clamor

↓ The writer.—EDITORS.

of the orderly, covered the general's features with his coat, and had the body carried to a sheltered spot near DuBois's battery. Surgeon Florence M. Cornyn was found and called upon to examine the lifeless body of the dead general, and having pronounced life extinct, the aide went to seek Schofield and inform him of the calamity. He was met return-ing from the successful charge he had led, and at once announced that Major Sturgis should assume command, but vis-ited the remains of Lyon on his way to find Sturgis. These were taken charge of by the aide, and conveyed to the field-hospital, where the body was placed in a wagon and carefully covered. Strict or-ders were given that under no circum-stances was the body to be removed till the army returned to Springfield, after which the aide returned to the front to report to Major Sturgis for duty.

BRIGADIER-GENERAL N. B. PEARCE, C. S. A.
FROM A PHOTOGRAPH.

The engagement on different parts of the line lasted about half an hour after Lyon's death, when the Confederates gave way, and silence reigned for nearly the same length of time. Many of the senior officers having been disabled, Sturgis as-sumed command, and the principal officers were summoned for consultation. This council and the suspended hostilities were soon abruptly terminated by the appearance of the Confederates along our entire front, where the troops had been readjusted in more compact form and were now more determined and cooler than ever. A battery planted on a hill in the front began to use shrapnel and canister, a species of ammunition which, so far as I know, the enemy had not fired before at the troops who were with General Lyon.

DuBois's battery continued on the left supported by Osterhaus's battalion and the 1st Missouri; the 1st Iowa, 1st Kansas, and the regular infantry sup-ported Totten's battery in the center, and the 2d Kansas held the extreme right. With unabated ardor and impetuosity the Confederates assailed this front and endeavored to gain the rear of the right flank, but Totten's battery in the center was the main point of assault. For the first time during this bloody day, the entire line maintained its position without flinching, the inexperienced volunteers vieing with the seasoned regulars in tenacity and coolness. ♭ The flash and roar were incessant, and the determined Southrons repeatedly advanced nearly to the muzzles of the pieces of their foes, only to

♭ This engagement is considered one of the se-verest of the war. Colonel Snead (in "The Fight for Missouri") says: "Never before—considering the number engaged—had so bloody a battle been fought upon American soil; seldom has a bloodier one been fought on any modern field." Another participant, a Confederate officer, described it as "a mighty mean-fowt fight."—EDITORS.

be hurled back before the withering fire as from the blast of a furnace and to charge again with a like result.

At a moment when the contest seemed evenly balanced, except for the overwhelming numbers of the Confederates on the field, Captain Gordon Granger, noted for his daring and intrepidity, rushed to the rear and brought up the supports of DuBois's battery, hurling them upon the enemy's right flank, into which they poured a murderous, deadly volley, which created a perfect rout along the whole front.\ Our troops continued to send a galling fire into the disorganized masses as they fled, until they disappeared, and the battle was ended.

The order to withdraw was then given, and DuBois's battery with its supports was moved to a hill and ridge in rear to cover the movement. Before the withdrawal of the main body took place, Captain Granger and others urged remaining on the ground, but Sturgis had received information of Sigel's rout, and in view of his depleted, worn-out forces and exhausted ammunition, persisted in a return to Springfield. The infantry and artillery, as soon as Totten's disabled horses were replaced, left the scene of conflict, and, passing through the troops placed in rear, took up the march for Springfield. On reaching the Little York road, a body of horsemen was seen to the west, which proved to be Lieutenant Farrand with his dragoons, leading in a remnant of Sigel's brigade, with the one piece of artillery he had saved. In his hand he carried a captured flag, which he trailed by his side. He was received with vociferous cheering, and became for the time the admiration of all, having marched around both armies and brought his command in safe. ☆

On reaching Springfield, Sturgis found that Sigel had arrived there half an hour earlier. Regarding him as the senior, the command was given over to him. On the following morning the army withdrew.

\ In his report Major Sturgis gave great praise to Gordon Granger, saying that he was "now sighting a gun of DuBois's battery, and before the smoke had cleared away sighting one of Totten's; at one moment reconnoitering the enemy, and the next either bringing up reënforcements or rallying some broken line. To whatever part of the field I might direct my attention, there would I find Captain Granger, hard at work at some important service."—EDITORS.

☆ About this time, too, it was discovered that in order to gather up the wounded on the field the body of General Lyon had been taken from the wagon in which it was placed and had been left at the field-hospital. Lieutenant Canfield with his company B, 1st Cavalry, was dispatched with a wagon to recover the general's body, and the army moved on into Springfield, arriving about 5 P. M. Lieutenant Canfield proceeded to the battle-field, and before reaching there found the Confederates had returned and engaged in gathering their own wounded, and had found General Lyon's body. It was delivered by the enemy and was brought into the town to the house occupied as Lyon's headquarters, and was placed in charge of the late general's staff, who carefully cared for it. The house belonged to Governor John S. Phelps, and as it had been determined early in the evening that the troops would take up the retreat for Rolla before daylight the next morning, Mrs. Phelps, a warm personal friend of General Lyon during his sojourn in the town, was communicated with at her home in the country, and asked to have the remains buried on her farm till they could be removed. To this she gladly consented. The body was left in custody of surgeons who were to remain behind, and the next day Mrs. Phelps took possession of it, and General Lyon was laid to rest in her garden, just outside the town. His body was subsequently removed to his home in Connecticut and buried with military and civic honors.—W. M. W.

Lyon was born in Ashford, Conn., July 14th, 1818. He was graduated at West Point in 1841, and served in the army in Florida and in the war with Mexico. He was brevetted captain for gallant conduct at Churubusco and Contreras. From 1849 to 1853 he served in California, winning special mention for his services in frontier warfare. He served afterward in Kansas, and from that State was ordered to St. Louis in January, 1861.—EDITORS.

"BLOODY HILL," FROM THE EAST. FROM A RECENT PHOTOGRAPH.

ARKANSAS TROOPS IN THE BATTLE OF WILSON'S CREEK.

BY N. B. PEARCE, BRIGADIER-GENERAL, C. S. A.

I STYLE this short account of my personal recollections of the battle of "Oak Hills" (as the Confederates named the engagement) as above, because I was identified with the State of Arkansas and her soldiers. I also believe that subsequent events, developed by the prominence of some of the commanders engaged in this fight, have had a tendency to obscure that just recognition which the Arkansas troops so nobly earned in this, one of the first great battles of our civil war.

The ninth day of August, 1861, found the Confederate army under General Ben. McCulloch, camped on Wilson's Creek, ten miles south of Springfield, in south-west Missouri. It consisted of a Louisiana regiment under Colonel Louis Hébert (a well-drilled and well-equipped organization, chiefly from the north part of the State); Greer's Texas regiment (mounted); Churchill's Arkansas cavalry, and McIntosh's battalion of Arkansas mounted rifles (Lieutenant-Colonel Embry), under the immediate charge of the commanding general; General Price's command of Missouri State Guards, with Bledsoe's and Guibor's batteries, and my three regiments of Arkansas infantry, with Woodruff's and Reid's batteries. More than half the Missourians were mounted, and but few of the troops in the whole command were well armed. The army numbered in all about 11,500 men,— perhaps, 6000 to 7000 of whom were in semi-fighting trim, and participated in the battle.

The Federal forces under General Nathaniel Lyon, between 5000 and 6000 strong, occupied the town of Springfield, and General McCulloch was expecting them to advance and give him battle. General McCulloch's headquarters were on the right of the Springfield road, east of Wilson's Creek, rather in advance of the center of the camp. General Price occupied a position immediately west, and in the valley of the creek, with his command mostly north of the Springfield road. I had established my headquarters on the heights east and south of Wilson's Creek and the Springfield road, with my forces occupying the elevated ground immediately adjacent.

Detailed reports as to the strength and movements of Lyon's command were momentarily expected, through spies sent out by General Price, as

McCulloch relied upon the native Missourians to furnish such knowledge; but it was not until late in the afternoon that two "loyal" ladies succeeded in passing out of the Federal lines, by permission of General Lyon, and, coming in a circuitous route by Pond Springs, reached General Price's head-quarters with the desired information. General McCulloch at once called a council of war of the principal officers, where it was decided, instead of wait-ing for the enemy, to march with the whole command, at 9 o'clock that night, and attack General Lyon at Springfield. As soon as the orders of General McCulloch had been properly published by his adjutant-general, Colonel McIntosh, the camp was thrown into a ferment of suppressed excitement. It was ordered that the advance be made in three divisions, under the separate commands of General Price, Adjutant-General McIntosh, and myself. The scene of preparation, immediately following the orders so long delayed and now so eagerly welcomed by the men, was picturesque and animating in the extreme. The question of ammunition was one of the most important and serious, and as the Ordnance Department was imperfectly organized and poorly supplied, the men scattered about in groups, to impro-vise, as best they could, ammunition for their inefficient arms. Here, a group would be molding bullets — there, another crowd dividing percussion-caps, and, again, another group fitting new flints to their old muskets. They had little thought then of the inequality between the discipline, arms, and accouterments of the regular United States troops they were soon to engage in battle, and their own homely movements and equipments. It was a new thing to most of them, this regular way of shooting by word of command, and it was, per-haps, the old-accustomed method of using rifle, musket, or shot-gun as game-sters or marksmen that won them the battle when pressed into close quarters with the enemy. All was expectancy, and as the time sped on to 9 o'clock, the men became more and more eager to advance. What was their disappointment when, as the hour finally arrived, instead of the order to march, it was announced that General McCulloch had decided, on account of a threatened rain, which might damage and destroy much of their ammuni-tion, to postpone the movement. The men did not "sulk in their tents," but rested on their arms in no amiable mood. This condition of uncertainty and suspense lasted well through the night, as the commanding officers were better informed than the men of the risks to be encountered, and of the prob-able result, in case they should make an aggressive fight against disciplined forces when only half prepared. Daybreak, on the 10th of August, found the command still at Wilson's Creek, cheerlessly waiting, many of the troops remaining in position, in line of march, on the road, and others returning to camp to prepare the morning meal.

Perhaps it was 6 o'clock when the long-roll sounded and the camp was called to arms. A few minutes before this, Sergeant Hite, of my body-guard, dashed up to my headquarters, breathless with excitement, hatless, and his horse covered with foam, exclaiming hurriedly, "General, the enemy is com-ing!" "Where?" said I, and he pointed in the direction of a spring, up a ravine, where he had been for water. He had been fired at, he said, by a picket of some troops advancing on the right flank. I ordered the sergeant to ride in haste to General McCulloch with this information, and proceeded to place my command in position. I was the better enabled to do this without delay, because I had on the day before, with Colonel R. H. Weightman, made a careful reconnoissance of the ground in the direction from which the enemy was said to be approaching. The colonels commanding were imme-

diately notified, and the regiments were formed and posted so as to meet his advance. Captain Woodruff's Little Rock (Ark.) battery was ordered to occupy a hill commanding the road to Springfield, and the 3d Arkansas Infantry (Colonel John R. Gratiot) was ordered to support him. I placed Captain Reid's Fort Smith (Ark.) battery on an eminence to command the approaches to our right and rear, and gave him the 5th Arkansas Infantry (Colonel T. P. Dockery) as a support. I then advanced the 4th Arkansas Infantry (Colonel J. D. Walker) north of this battery to watch the approach down the ravine, through which Sergeant Hite had reported that the enemy was coming. Thus, the Arkansas troops under my command had all been

MAJOR-GENERAL BEN. McCULLOCH, C. S. A., KILLED IN
THE BATTLE OF PEA RIDGE, MARCH 7, 1862.
FROM A PHOTOGRAPH.

placed in favorable position, ready for action, within a very short time after the first alarm.

While these events were taking place under my immediate notice, General McCulloch had been actively making disposition of the troops more nearly opposed to the first advance of the enemy, under General Lyon. He had posted the 3d Louisiana Infantry (Colonel Hébert) and McIntosh's 2d Arkansas Rifles (dismounted) to meet the earliest demonstration from the direction of Springfield. General Price had also been industriously engaged in placing his troops to intercept the advancing foe. General Rains's (Missouri) command had the honor of giving the first reception to the main column under General Lyon. He was ably supported by the gallant Missouri generals, Slack, McBride, Parsons, and Clark, with their respective brigades. The fighting at this juncture — perhaps about 7 o'clock — was confined to the corn-field north of Wilson's Creek, where the Louisiana infantry, with Lieutenant-Colonel Embry's 2d Arkansas Mounted Rifles (dismounted), all under the immediate command of Colonel McIntosh, effectually charged and drove back the enemy. Simultaneously the battle opened farther west and south of Wilson's Creek, where the Missouri troops were attacked by the main column or right wing of the enemy. Totten's (Federal) battery was pushed forward, and took its first position on the side of Oak Hill, north of where the main fight afterward took place. I had directed Captain Woodruff, who was posted within easy range, to give attention to Totten, and the two batteries were soon engaged in a lively artillery duel, being well matched in skill and mettle. Lieutenant Weaver, of Woodruff's battery, was killed, and 4 of Totten's men were killed and 7 wounded in this engagement. General Lyon's right, although it had gained a temporary advantage in the early morning by surprising the Missourians, was roughly handled when they had recovered themselves. They were reënforced by Churchill's regiment, which had moved up from the extreme right, and the battle raged several hours while they held their ground. At this juncture a gallant charge was made by Greer's and Carroll's mounted regiments on Totten's battery, but it was not a complete success, as the gunners turned about and recovered their guns.

In the early morning, perhaps simultaneously with the advance of Lyon, General Sigel, commanding the left column of the advance from Springfield, came upon our right and rear, first attacking Colonel Churchill's camp, as the men were preparing for breakfast, obliging them to retreat to an adjacent wood, where they were formed in good order. The surprise resulted from the movement of the night before, when pickets had been withdrawn that were not re-posted in the morning. Sigel did not wait for a fight, however, but advanced to, and had his battery unlimbered near, the Fayetteville road, west of Wilson's Creek, opposite and within range of Reid's battery as it was then in position as originally placed. Before he had discovered us, and perhaps in ignorance of our position, Reid attacked him, under my personal orders and supervision. Sigel's movement was a bold one, and we really could not tell, on his first appearance (there having been no fight with Churchill), whether he was friend or foe. An accidental gust of wind having unfurled his flag, we were no longer in doubt. Reid succeeded in getting his range accurately, so that his shot proved very effective. At this juncture, General McCulloch in person led two companies of the Louisiana infantry in a charge and captured five of the guns.☆ General Sigel was himself in command, and made vain attempts to hold his men, who were soon in full retreat, back over the road they came, pursued by the Texas and Missouri cavalry. This was the last of Sigel for the day, as his retreat was continued to Springfield. As a precaution, however, not knowing how badly we had defeated Sigel, I immediately posted the 4th Arkansas Infantry (Colonel Walker) along the brow of the hill, commanding the road over which he had fled, which regiment remained on duty until the battle was over.

There seemed now to be a lull in the active fighting; the bloody contest in the corn-field had taken place; the fight "mit Sigel" had resulted satisfactorily to us, but the troops more immediately opposed to General Lyon had not done so well. General Price and his Missouri troops had borne the brunt of this hard contest, but had gained no ground. They had suffered heavy

---

☆ General McCulloch's report says: "When we arrived near the enemy's battery we found that Reid's battery had opened upon it, and it was already in confusion. Advantage was taken of it, and soon the Louisianians were gallantly charging among the guns and swept the cannoneers away. Five guns were here taken."

losses, and were running short of ammunition. I had watched anxiously for signs of victory to come from the north side of the creek, but Totten's battery seemed to belch forth with renewed vigor, and was advanced once or twice in its position. The line of battle on our left was shortening, and the fortunes of war appeared to be sending many of our gallant officers and soldiers to their death. There was no de-moralization—no signs of wavering or retreat, but it was an hour of great anxiety and suspense. No one then knew what the day would bring forth. As the sun poured down upon our devoted comrades, poised and resting, as it were, between the chapters of a mighty struggle not yet completed, the stoutest of us almost weakened in our anxiety to know the outcome.

Just at this time, General Lyon appeared to be massing his men for a final and decisive movement. I had been relieved of Sigel, and Reid's battery was inactive because it could not reach Totten. This was fortunate, for my command, in a measure fresh and enthusiastic, was about to embrace an opportunity—such a

BRIGADIER-GENERAL WM. Y. SLACK, C. S. A., MORTALLY WOUNDED AT PEA RIDGE. FROM A PHOTOGRAPH.

one as will often win or lose a battle—by throwing its strength to the weakened line at a critical moment and winning the day. Colonel McIntosh came to me from General McCulloch, and Captain Greene from General Price, urging me to move at once to their assistance. General Lyon was in possession of Oak Hill; his lines were forward, his batteries aggressive, and his charges impetuous. The fortunes of the day were balanced in the scale, and something must be done or the battle was lost. My men were eager to go forward, and when I led the 3d Arkansas Infantry (Colonel Gratiot) and the right wing of the 5th Arkansas Infantry (Lieutenant-Colonel Neal) across the creek, and pushed rapidly up the hill in the face of the enemy, loud cheers went up from our expectant friends that betokened an enthusiasm which, no doubt, helped to win the fight. Colonel McIntosh, with two pieces of Reid's battery, and with a part of Dockery's 5th Arkansas Infantry, supported my right; the Federal forces occupied two lines of battle, reaching across the crest of Oak Hill; and at this juncture our troops in front were composed of the Missouri forces, under General Price (occupying the center); Texas and Louisiana troops, under General McCulloch (on the right), and my forces thrown forward (on the left), when a combined advance was ordered by General McCulloch. This proved to be the decisive engagement, and as volley after volley was poured against our lines, and our gallant boys were cut down like grass, those who survived seemed to be nerved to greater effort and a determination to win or die. At about this time (11:30 A. M.) the first line of battle before us gave way. Our boys charged the second line with a yell, and were soon in possession of the field, the enemy slowly withdrawing toward Springfield. This hour decided the contest and won for us the day. It was in our front here, as was afterward made known, that the brave commander of the Federal forces, General Lyon, was killed, gallantly leading his men to what he and they supposed was victory, but which proved (it may be because they were deprived of his enthusiastic leadership) disastrous defeat. In the light of the present day, even, it is difficult to measure the vast results had Lyon lived and the battle gone against us.

General McCulloch, myself, and our staff-officers now grouped ourselves together upon the center of the hill. Woodruff's battery was again placed in position, and Totten, who was covering the retreat of Sturgis (who had assumed command of the Federal forces after the death of General Lyon), received the benefit of his parting shots. We watched the retreating enemy through our field-glasses, *and were glad to see him go.* Our ammunition was exhausted, our men undisciplined, and we feared to risk pursuit. It was also rumored that reënforcements were coming to the Federal army by forced marches, but it was found the next day that the disaster to the retreating army was greater than we had supposed, and a few fresh cavalry troops could doubtless have followed and captured many more stragglers and army stores. Next day the enemy evacuated Springfield, and Price, with his Missouri troops, occupied it, and had his supplies and wounded moved to that point.

The Arkansans in this battle were as brave, as chivalrous, and as successful as any of the troops engaged. They bore out, on many a hard-fought field later on in the struggle, the high hopes built upon their conduct here.

The body of the army remained at Springfield until the beginning of General Price's march upon Lexington, on the 25th of August. A few days after the battle Pearce's brigade of Arkansas militia was disbanded on the expiration of their term of enlistment. General McCulloch moved westward with his own brigade, and then to Maysville, Arkansas, being influenced in his return by the general tenor of his instructions from the Confederate Government to avoid, if possible, operating in the State of Missouri, which had not seceded. General Price, upon being informed of his decision, issued an order re-assuming command, and the operations in the State which followed, including the capture of Lexington, were conducted with Missouri troops alone. At this time the Federal troops held the Missouri river by a cordon of military posts. The object of this line was to prevent the crossing of the river by the secessionists of north Missouri, who, to the number of 5000 or 6000, were armed and organized and desirous of joining the army of General Price in south-west Missouri. To break this blockade became the object of General Price. Of the four Federal posts, Jefferson City, Boonville, Lexington, and Kansas City, Lexington was the easiest and most important one to take. General Price left Springfield on the 25th of August, dispersed Lane's forces at Drywood, September 2d, and reached Warrensburg in pursuit of Colonel Peabody at daybreak, September 10th; Peabody getting into Lexington first, Price, after a little skirmishing with Mulligan's outpost, bivouacked within 2½ miles of Lexington. In the morning (12th) Mulligan sent out a small force which burnt a bridge in Price's path. Price then crossed to the Independence Road, and waited for his infantry and artillery. These came up in the afternoon, and Price then advanced toward Lexington, and drove Mulligan behind his defenses. There was a little skirmishing in a corn-field and in a cemetery through which Price advanced, and in the streets of Lexington, where he opened upon Mulligan with 7 pieces of artillery. Price's movement into Lexington in the afternoon of September 12th was only a reconnoissance in force. Toward dark he retired to the Fair Ground, and waited for his trains to come up, and for reënforcements that were hurrying to him from all directions, including Harris's and Green's commands from north of the Missouri. The investment of Mulligan's position was made as shown on the map, page 309.— Editors.

THE FLANKING COLUMN AT WILSON'S CREEK.

BY FRANZ SIGEL, MAJOR-GENERAL, U. S. V.

ON August 9th, 1861, the day before the battle at Wilson's Creek, my brigade, consisting of the 3d and 5th Missouri Infantry, commanded respectively by Lieutenant-Colonel Anselm Albert and Charles E. Salomon, and two batteries of artillery, each of 4 pieces, under the command of Lieutenants Schaefer and Schuetzenbach, was encamped on the south side of Springfield, near the Yokermill road. On our right was encamped the 1st Iowa Infantry, a regiment clad in militia gray. The bulk of General Lyon's forces were on the west side of the city. During the morning I sent a staff-officer to General Lyon's headquarters for orders, and on his return he reported to me that a forward movement would take place, and that we must hold ourselves in readiness to march at a moment's warning directly from our camp, toward the south, to attack the enemy from the rear. I immediately went to General Lyon, who said that we would move in the evening to attack the enemy in his position at Wilson's Creek, and that I was to be prepared to move with my brigade; the 1st Iowa would join the main column with him, while I was to take the Yokermill (Forsyth) road, then turn toward the south-west and try to gain the enemy's rear. At my request, he said that he would procure guides and some cavalry to assist me ; he would also let me know the exact time when I should move. I then asked him whether, on our arrival near the enemy's position, we should attack immediately or wait until we were apprised of the fight by the other troops. He reflected a moment and then said : " Wait until you hear the firing on our side." The conversation did not last longer than about ten minutes. Between 4 and 5 o'clock in the afternoon I received the order to move at 6:30 P. M. At 6 o'clock two companies of cavalry, under Captain Eugene A. Carr and Lieutenant Charles E. Farrand, joined us, also several guides. My whole force now consisted of 8 companies of the 3d and 9 companies of the 5th Missouri (912 men), 6 pieces of artillery (85 men), and the 2 companies of cavalry (121),— in all, 1118 men.

Precisely at 6:30 o'clock the brigade moved out of its camp ; after following the Yokermill road for about five miles we turned south-west into the woods, and found our way, with difficulty, to a point south of the enemy's camp, where we arrived between 11 and 12 o'clock at night. There we rested. It was a dark, cloudy night, and a drizzling rain began to fall. So far no news of our movement had reached the enemy's camp, as the cavalry in advance had arrested every person on the road, and put guards before the houses in its neighborhood.

At the first dawn of day we continued our advance for about a mile and a half, the cavalry patrols in front capturing forty men who had strolled into our line while looking for food and water, and who said that twenty regiments of Missouri, Arkansas, and Louisiana troops were encamped not far distant in the valley beyond. Moving on, we suddenly found ourselves near a hill, from which we gained a full view of the camp. We halted a few moments, when I directed four pieces of our artillery to take position on the top of the hill, commanding the camp, while the infantry, with the other two pieces and preceded by Lieutenant Farrand's cavalry company, continued its march down the road to the crossing of Wilson's Creek.

It was now 5:30 A. M. At this moment some musket-firing was heard from the north-west, announcing the approach of General Lyon's troops ; I therefore ordered the four pieces to open fire against the camp, which had a " stirring " effect on the enemy, who were preparing breakfast. The surprise was complete, except that one of the enemy's cavalrymen made good his retreat from Lieutenant Farrand's dragoons and took the news of our advance to the other side (General Pearce's headquarters). I became aware of his escape, and believing that no time should be lost to lend assistance to our friends, we crossed Wilson's Creek, took down the fences at Dixon's farm, passed through it and crossed Terrel (or Tyrel) Creek. (See map, page 290.) Not knowing whether it would be possible to bring all our pieces along, I left the four pieces on the hill, with a support of infantry, and continued our march until we reached the south side of the valley, which extends northward to Sharp's house, about 3000 paces, and from west to east about 1000. We took the road on the west side of the valley, along the margin of the woods, and within a fence running nearly parallel with the open fields.

During this time a large body of the enemy's cavalry, about 2500 strong, was forming across the valley, not far distant from its northern extremity ; I therefore halted the column on the road, sent for the four pieces left on the other side of the creek, and, as soon as their approach was reported to me, I directed the head of our column to the right, left the road, and formed the troops in line of battle, between the road and the enemy's deserted camp,— the infantry on the left, the artillery on the right, and the cavalry on the extreme right, toward Wilson's Creek. A lively cannonade was now opened against the dense masses of the hostile cavalry, which lasted about twenty minutes, and forced the enemy to retire in disorder toward the north and into the woods. We now turned back into the road, and, advancing, made our way through a number of cattle near Sharp's house, and suddenly struck the Fayetteville road, leading north to that part of the battlefield on which General Lyon's troops were engaged. We were now on the principal line of retreat of the enemy, and had arrived there in perfect order and discipline. Up to this time we had made fifteen miles, had been constantly in motion, had had a successful engagement, and the troops felt encouraged by what they had accomplished. It is, therefore, totally false, as rumor had it after the battle, that "Sigel's men" gave themselves up to plundering the camp, became scattered, and were for this reason surprised by the "returning enemy."

When we had taken our position on the plateau near Sharp's, a cannonade was opened by me against a part of the enemy's troops, evidently forming the left of their line, confronting Lyon, as we could observe from the struggle going on in that direction. The firing lasted about 30 minutes.J

Suddenly the firing on the enemy's side ceased, and it seemed as if we had directed our own fire against Lyon's forces. I therefore ordered the pieces to cease firing. Just at this time — it was between 9 and 10 o'clock — there was a lull in the fight on the north side, and not a gun was heard, while squads of the enemy's troops, unarmed, came streaming up the road from Skegg's Branch toward us and were captured. Meanwhile a part of McCulloch's force was advancing against us at Sharp's farm, while Reid's battery moved into position on the hill east of Wilson's Creek, and opposite our right flank, followed by some cavalry.

All these circumstances — the cessation of the firing in Lyon's front, the appearance of the enemy's deserters, and the movement of Reid's artillery and the cavalry toward the south — led us into the belief that the enemy's forces were retreating, and this opinion became stronger by the report of Dr. Melcher, who was in advance on the road to Skegg's Branch, that "Lyon's troops" were coming up the road and that we must not fire. So uncertain was I in regard to the character of the approaching troops, now only a few rods distant, that I did not trust to my own eyes, but sent Corporal Tod, of the 3d Missouri, forward to challenge them. He challenged as ordered, but was immediately shot and killed. I instantly ordered the artillery and infantry to fire. But it was too late — the artillery fired one or two shots, but the infantry, as though paralyzed, did not fire; the 3d Louisiana, which we had mistaken for the gray-clad 1st Iowa, rushed up to the plateau, while Bledsoe's battery in front and Reid's from the heights on our right flank opened with canister at point-blank against us. As a matter of precaution I had during the last moment brought four of our pieces into battery on the right against the troops on the hill and Reid's battery; but after answering Reid's fire for a few minutes, the horses and drivers of three guns suddenly left their position, and with their caissons galloped down the Fayetteville road, in their tumultuous flight carrying panic into the ranks of the infantry, which turned back in disorder, and at the same time received the fire of the attacking line.

On our retreat the right wing, consisting mostly of the 3d Missouri Infantry and one piece of artillery, followed the road we came, while the left

wing, consisting of the 5th Missouri Infantry and another piece, went down the Fayetteville road, then, turning to the right (north-west), made its way toward Little York and Springfield; on its way the latter column was joined by Lieutenant Farrand's cavalry company. Colonel Salomon was also with this column, consisting in all of about 450 men, with 1 piece and caisson. I remained with the right wing, the 3d Missouri, which was considerably scattered. I re-formed the men during their retreat into 4 companies, in all about 250 men, and, turning to the left, into the Fayetteville road, was joined by Captain Carr's company of cavalry. After considering that, by following the left wing toward Little York, we might be cut off from Springfield and not be able to join General Lyon's forces, we followed the Fayetteville road until we reached a road leading north-east toward Springfield. This road we followed. Captain Carr, with his cavalry, was leading; he was instructed to remain in advance, keep his flankers out, and report what might occur in front. One company of the 3d Missouri was at the head of our little column of infantry, followed by the piece of artillery and two caissons, behind them the remainder of the infantry, the whole flanked on each side by skirmishers. So we marched, or rather dragged along as fast as the exhausted men could go, until we reached the ford at James Fork of the White River. Carr had already crossed, but his cavalry was not in sight; it had hastened along without waiting for us; ⚓ a part of the infantry had also passed the creek; the piece and caissons were just crossing, when the rattling of musketry announced the presence of hostile forces on both sides of the creek. They were detachments of Missouri and Texas cavalry, under Lieutenant-Colonel Major, Captains Mabry and Russell, that lay in ambush, and now pounced upon our jaded and extended column. It was in vain that Lieutenant-Colonel Albert and myself tried to rally at least a part of them; they left the road to seek protection, or make good their escape in the woods, and were followed and hunted down by their pursuers. In this chase the greater part of our men were killed, wounded, or made prisoners, among the latter Lieutenant-Colonel Albert and my orderly, who were with me in the last moment of the affray. I was not taken, probably because I wore a blue woolen blanket over my uniform and a yellowish slouch-hat, giving me the appearance of a Texas Ranger. I halted on horseback, prepared for defense, in a small strip of corn-field on the west side of the creek, while the hostile cavalrymen swarmed around and several times passed close by me. When we had resumed our way toward the north-east, we were immediately recognized as enemies, and pursued by a few horsemen, whose number increased rapidly. It was a pretty lively race for about six miles, when our pursuers gave up the chase. We reached Spring-

J Colonel Graves, commanding the First Brigade, Mo. State Guards, says in his report: "Colonel Rosser, commanding the 1st Regiment and Fourth Battalion, with Captain Bledsoe's artillery, being stationed on the extreme left, was attacked by Colonel Sigel's battery, and his men exposed to a deadly fire for thirty minutes."—F. S.

⚓ Colonel Carr says in his official report: "It is a subject of regret with me to have left him [Sigel] behind, but I supposed all the time that he was close behind me till I got to the creek, and it would have done no good for my company to have been cut to pieces also."— EDITORS.

field at 4:30 in the afternoon, in advance of Sturgis, who with Lyon's troops was retreating from the battle-field, and who arrived at Springfield, as he says, at 5 o'clock. The circumstance of my arrival at the time stated gave rise to the insinuation that I had forsaken my troops after their repulse at Sharp's house, and had delivered them to their fate. Spiced with the accusation of "plunder," this and other falsehoods were repeated before the Committee on the Conduct of the War, and a letter defamatory of me was dispatched to the Secretary of War (dated February 14th, 1862, six months after the battle of Wilson's Creek). I had no knowledge of these calumnies against me until long after the war, when I found them in print.

In support of my statements, I would direct attention to my own reports on the battle and to the Confederate reports, especially to those of Lieutenant-Colonel Hyams and Captain Vigilini, of the 3d Louisiana; also to the report of Captain Carr, in which he frankly states that he abandoned me immediately before my column was attacked at the crossing of James Fork, without notifying me of the approach of the enemy's cavalry. I never mentioned this fact, as the subsequent career of General Carr, his coöperation with me during the campaigns of General Frémont, and his behavior in the battle of Pea Ridge vindicated his character and ability as a soldier and commander.

THE OPPOSING FORCES AT WILSON'S CREEK, MO.

The composition and losses of each army as here stated give the gist of all the data obtainable in the official records. K stands for killed; w for wounded; m w mortally wounded; m for captured or missing; c for captured.—EDITORS.

COMPOSITION AND LOSSES OF THE UNION ARMY.

Brig.-Gen. Nathaniel Lyon (k), Major Samuel D. Sturgis.

First Brigade, Major Samuel D. Sturgis: Regular Battalion (B, C, and D, 1st Infantry and Wood's company Rifle Recruits), Capt. Joseph B. Plummer; Battalion 2d Mo. Infantry, Major P. J. Osterhaus; F, 2d U. S. Arty., Capt. James Totten; Kansas Rangers, Capt. S. N. Wood; B, 1st U. S. Cavalry, Lieut. Charles W. Canfield. *Second Brigade*, Lieut.-Col. George L. Andrews: Regular Battalion (B and E, 2d Infantry, Lothrop's company General Service Recruits, and Morine's company Rifle Recruits), Capt. Frederick Steele; DuBois's Battery (improvised), Lieut. John V. DuBois; 1st Mo. Infantry, Lieut.-Col. Geo. L. Andrews. *Third Brigade*, Col. Geo. W. Deitzler: 1st Kansas, Col. Geo. W. Deitzler (w), Major J. A Halderman; 2d Kansas, Col. R. B. Mitchell (w), Lieut.-Col. Chas. W. Blair. *Missouri Volunteers, Second Brigade*, Colonel Franz Sigel: 3d Mo., Lieut.-Col. Anselm Albert; 5th Mo., Col. C. E. Salomon; I, 1st U. S. Cavalry, Capt. Eugene A. Carr; C, 2d U. S. Dragoons, Lieut. C. E. Farrand; Backof's Mo. Arty. (detachment), Lieutenants G. A. Schaefer and Edward Schuetzenbach. *Unattached Organizations:* 1st Iowa Infantry, Lieut.-Col. William H. Merritt; Wright's and Switzler's Mo. Home Guard Cavalry; detachment D, 1st U. S. Cavalry; Mo. Pioneers, Capt. J. D. Voerster.

The Union loss, as officially reported, was 223 killed, 721 wounded, and 291 missing,— total, 1235.*

COMPOSITION AND LOSSES OF THE CONFEDERATE ARMY.

Brig.-Gen. Ben. McCulloch.

MISSOURI STATE GUARD, Major-Gen. Sterling Price. RAINS'S DIVISION, Brig.-Gen. James S. Rains. *First Brigade*, Col. R. H. Weightman (m w), Col. John R. Graves: 1st Infantry, Lieut.-Col. Thomas H. Rosser; 3d Infantry, Col. Edgar V. Hurst; 4th Infantry (battalion), Major Thomas H. Murray; 5th Infantry, Col. J. J. Clarkson; Graves's Infantry, Col. John R. Graves, Major Brashear; Bledsoe's Battery, Capt. Hiram Bledsoe. *Second Brigade*, Col. Cawthon (m w). [Composition of brigade not given in the official records.] PARSONS'S BRIGADE, Brig.-Gen. M. M. Parsons: Kelly's Infantry, Col. Kelly (w); Brown's Cavalry, Col. Ben. Brown (k); Guibor's Battery, Capt. Henry Guibor. CLARK'S DIVISION, Brig.-Gen. John B. Clark: Burbridge's Infantry, Col. J. Q. Burbridge (w), Major John B. Clark, Jr.; 1st Cavalry (battalion), Lieut.-Col. J. P. Major. SLACK'S DIVISION, Brig.-Gen. W. Y. Slack (w): Hughes's Infantry, Col. John T. Hughes; Thornton's Infantry (battalion), Major J. C. Thornton; Rives's Cavalry, Col. B. A. Rives. McBRIDE'S DIVISION, Brig.-Gen. James H. McBride: Wingo's Infantry, Foster's Infantry, Col. Foster (w); Campbell's Cavalry, Capt. Campbell.

ARKANSAS FORCES, Brig.-Gen. N. B. Pearce, 1st Cavalry, Col. De Rosey Carroll; Carroll's Company Cavalry, Capt. Charles A. Carroll; 3d Infantry, Col. John R. Gratiot; 4th Infantry, Col. J. D. Walker; 5th Infantry, Col. Tom P. Dockery; Woodruff's Battery, Capt. W. E. Woodruff; Reid's Battery, Capt. J. G. Reid.

McCULLOCH'S BRIGADE: 1st Ark. Mounted Riflemen, Col. T. J. Churchill; 2d Ark. Mounted Riflemen, Col. James McIntosh, Lieut.-Col. B. T. Embry; Arkansas Infantry (battalion), Lieut.-Col. Dandridge McRae; South Kansas-Texas Mounted Regiment, Col. E. Greer; 3d La. Infantry, Col. Louis Hébert.

The Confederate loss, as officially reported, was 265 killed, 800 wounded, and 30 missing,— total, 1095.*

STRENGTH OF THE OPPOSING FORCES.

The Union forces are estimated from official returns at 5400 (with 16 guns). Of these 1118 were with Sigel and 350 mounted reserve. The Confederate forces are more difficult to estimate, but Colonel Snead, General Price's adjutant-general during the battle, gives in his volume,

"The Fight for Missouri" (Charles Scribner's Sons), the following estimate, which is doubtless as near the facts as it is possible to get: Price's force (Missouri State Guard), 5221; McCulloch's brigade, 2720, and Pearce's brigade, 2234,— total, 10,175 (with 15 guns).

* NOTE.— Colonel Snead, with unusual facilities for ascertaining the facts, gives the losses as follows: Union, (k), 258; (w), 873; (m), 186,—total, 1317. Confederate, (k), 279; (w), 951,—total, 1230. The Union reports do not include Osterhaus's battalion, which lost (k), 15; (w), 40; and give Sigel's loss at 26 less than Colonel Snead's estimate.— EDITORS.

CONFEDERATES FIGHTING BEHIND HEMP BALES AT LEXINGTON. SEE PAGE 312.

THE SIEGE OF LEXINGTON, MO.⸗

BY COLONEL JAMES A. MULLIGAN.

ON the night of the 30th of August, 1861, as the "Irish Brigade" (23d Illinois Volunteers) lay encamped just outside of Jefferson City, Mo., I received orders to report to General Jefferson C. Davis, commanding in the town. On doing so, I was informed by General Davis that the cavalry regiment of Colonel Thomas A. Marshall, which had left for the South-west some days before, had reached Tipton, where it was hemmed in by the enemy, and could neither advance nor return, and that he wished me to go to Tipton, join Colonel Marshall, take command of the combined forces, cut my way through the enemy, go to Lexington, and hold it at all hazards.

The next morning the "Irish Brigade" started with forty rounds of ammunition and three days' rations for each man. We marched for nine days without meeting an enemy, foraging upon the country for support. We reached Tipton, but found neither Colonel Marshall nor the enemy, and we passed on to a pleasant spot near Lexington where we prepared for our entry into the city. The trouble was not so much the getting into Lexington as the getting out. At Lexington we found Colonel Marshall's cavalry regiment and about 350 of a regiment of Home Guards. On the 10th of September we received a letter from Colonel Everett Peabody, of the 13th Missouri Regiment, saying that he was retreating from Warrensburg, 34 miles distant, and that the rebel General Price was in full pursuit with an army of 10,000 men. A few hours later Colonel Peabody joined us.

There were then at this post the "Irish Brigade," Colonel Marshall's Illinois cavalry regiment (full), Colonel Peabody's regiment, and a part of the 14th Missouri—in all about 2780 men, with one six-pounder,‡ forty rounds of

⸗ Reprinted, with revision, from newspaper reports of a lecture by Colonel Mulligan, who was killed during the war (see page 313). In certain important particulars, the text has been altered to free it from clearly demonstrable errors.— EDITORS.

‡ Doubtless an accidental mistake. Colonel Mulligan had 7 six-pounders (Waldschmidt, 2 ; Adams, 3, and Pirner, 2); Pirner also had 2 brass mortars for throwing six-inch spherical shells, of which he had but 40, which were soon exhausted. The Confederate artillery consisted of 16 guns in five

ammunition, and but few rations. We then dispatched a courier to Jefferson City to inform General Davis of our condition, and to pray for reënforcements or even rations, whereupon we would hold out to the last. At noon of the 11th we commenced throwing up intrenchments on College Hill, an eminence overlooking Lexington and the broad Missouri. All day long the men worked untiringly with the shovel. That evening, but six or eight hours after we had commenced, our pickets were driven in and intimation was given that the enemy were upon us. Colonel Peabody was ordered out to meet them, and two six-pounders were planted in a position to command a covered bridge by which the enemy were obliged to enter the town. It was a night of fearful anxiety; none knew at what moment the enemy would be upon our devoted little band, and the hours passed in silence. We waited until the morning of the 12th, vigilantly and without sleep, when a messenger rushed in, saying, " Colonel, the enemy are pushing across the bridge in overwhelming force." With a glass we could see them as they came, General Price riding up and down the lines, urging his men on. Two companies of the Missouri 13th were ordered out, and, with Company K of the Irish Brigade, quickly checked the enemy, drove him back, burned the bridge, and gallantly ended their work before breakfast.

The enemy now made a détour, and approached the town once more, by the Independence road. Six companies of the Missouri 13th and the Illinois Cavalry were ordered out, and met them in the Lexington Cemetery, just outside the town, where the fight raged furiously over the dead. We succeeded in keeping the enemy in check, and in the mean time the work with the shovel went bravely on until we had thrown up breastworks three or four feet high.

At 3 o'clock in the afternoon the engagement opened with artillery. A volley of grape from the enemy was directed at a group of our officers who were outside the breastworks. Our men returned the volley. The contest raged about an hour and a half, when we had the satisfaction, by a lucky shot, of knocking over the enemy's big gun, exploding a powder caisson, and otherwise doing much damage. The fight was continued until dusk, and, as the moon rose, the enemy retired to camp in the Fair Ground, two miles away, and Lexington was our own again.

On Friday, the 13th, though a drenching rain had set in, the work of throwing up intrenchments went on, and the men stood almost knee-deep in mud and water, at their work. We had taken the basement of the Masonic College, a building from which the eminence took its name; powder was obtained, and the men commenced making cartridges. A foundry was fitted up, and 150 rounds of shot — grape and canister — were cast for each of our six-pounders.

batteries, as follows : Bledsoe, 4 guns ; Churchill Clark, 2 ; Guibor, 4 ; Kelly, 4 ; Kneisley, 2.—("History of Lafayette County, Missouri.")

The lack of agreement between the numbers of the Union forces as here stated, and as given by Colonel Snead on page 273, is accounted for by the latter on the supposition that Colonel Mulligan did not include in his estimate either his officers or the body of Home Guards who assisted in the defense. Colonel Snead states positively that, as adjutant-general of the Missouri troops, he paroled about 3500 prisoners. Among these may have been many not reckoned as effectives by Colonel Mulligan.—EDITORS.

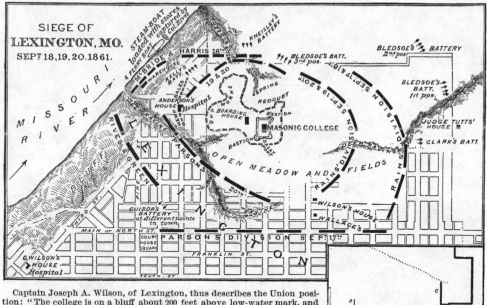

SIEGE OF
LEXINGTON, MO.
SEPT 18, 19, 20, 1861.

Captain Joseph A. Wilson, of Lexington, thus describes the Union position: "The college is on a bluff about 200 feet above low-water mark, and from 15 to 30 feet higher than North or Main street. Third street runs along the top of the bluff. Close to and surrounding the college building was a rectangular fort of sods and earth about 12 feet thick and 12 feet high; with bastions at the angles and embrasures for guns. At a distance of 200 to 800 feet was an irregular line of earthworks protected by numerous traverses, occasional redoubts, a good ditch, trous-de-loup, wires, etc., etc. Still farther on the west and north were rifle-pits. The works would have required 10,000 or 15,000 men to occupy them fully. All the ground from the fortifications to the river was then covered with scattering timber. The spring just north and outside of fortifications, was in a deep wooded ravine, and was the scene of some sharp skirmishing at night, owing to the attempts of the garrison to get water there when their cisterns gave out."

DIAGRAM OF THE HOSPITAL POSITION.
FROM THE "HISTORY OF LAFAYETTE COUNTY, MISSOURI."

Explanation of the Diagram of the Hospital Position: "a is the Anderson house or hospital; b a smaller brick house back of it; c an outlying low earthwork, projecting down nearly into the ravine, represented by the dotted line, while the inclosed earthwork was built up around the head of the ravine, as shown by the plain line; d the sally-port in the earthworks, about one hundred yards from the hospital; e a canal-like carriageway leading up to the house, and in which the sharp-shooters lay secure, only about eighty feet from the front door of the hospital; the brackets represent Federal picket-guard stations with a little dirt thrown up for protection; the dotted line sss shows deep gorge or ravine which was full of Confederate sharp-shooters."

Sunday had now arrived. We had found no provisions at Lexington, and our 2700 men were getting short of rations. Father Thaddeus J. Butler, our chaplain, celebrated mass on the hillside, and all were considerably strengthened and encouraged by his words, and after services were over we went back to work, actively casting shot and stealing provisions from the inhabitants round about. Our pickets were all the time skirmishing with the enemy, while we were making preparations for defense against the enemy's attack, which was expected on the morrow.

At 9 o'clock on the morning of the 18th the enemy were seen approaching. The Confederate force had been increased to 18,000 men with 16 pieces of cannon. They came as one dark moving mass, their guns beaming in the sun, their banners waving, and their drums beating — everywhere, as far as we could see, were men, men, men, approaching grandly. Our earthworks covered an area of about eighteen acres, surrounded by a ditch, and protected in front by what were called "confusion pits," and by mines. Our men stood firm behind the breastworks, none trembled or paled, and a solemn

THE HOSPITAL.   THE COLLEGE, FRONTING SOUTH.

THE BATTLE OF LEXINGTON, MO., AS SEEN FROM GENERAL PARSONS' POSITION.   AFTER A CONTEMPORARY DRAWING.

silence prevailed.   As Father Butler went round among them, they asked his blessing, received it with uncovered heads, then turned and sternly cocked their muskets.

The enemy opened a terrible fire with their cannon on all sides, which we answered with determination and spirit.   Our spies had brought intelligence, and had all agreed that it was the intention of the enemy to make a grand rush, overwhelm us, and bury us in the trenches of Lexington.

At noon, word was brought that the enemy had taken the hospital.   We had not fortified that; it was situated outside the intrenchments, and I had supposed that the little white flag was sufficient protection for the wounded and dying soldiers who had finished their service and were powerless for harm. The hospital contained our chaplain, our surgeon, and a number of wounded. The enemy took it without opposition, filled it with their sharp-shooters, and from every window, every door, from the scuttles in the roof, poured right into our intrenchments a deadly drift of lead.   A company of the Home Guards, then a company of the Missouri 14th, were ordered to retake the hospital, but refused.   The Montgomery Guards, a company of the Irish Brigade, was then ordered out.   Their captain admonished them to uphold the gallant name they bore, and the order was given to charge.   The distance across the plain from the intrenchments to the hospital was about eighty yards.   They started; at first quick, then double-quick, then on a run, then faster. Still the deadly fire poured into their ranks. But on they went; a wild line of steel, and, what is better than steel, irresistible human will. They reached the hospital, burst open the door, without shot or shout, until they encountered the enemy within, whom they hurled out and sent flying down the hill. ♭

Our surgeon was held by the enemy, although we had released the Confederate surgeon on his mere pledge that he was such. It was a horrible thing to see those brave fellows, mangled and wounded, without skillful hands to bind their ghastly wounds; and Captain David P. Moriarty, who had been a physician in civil life, was ordered to lay aside his sword and go into the hospital. He went, and through all the siege worked among the wounded with no other instrument than a razor. Our supply of water had given out and the scenes in the hospital were fearful to witness, wounded men suffering agonies from thirst and in their frenzy wrestling for the water in which the wounded had been bathed.∖

On the morning of the 19th the firing was resumed, and continued all day. Our officers had told the men that if they could hold out until the 19th we should certainly be reënforced, and all through that day the men watched anxiously for the appearance of the friendly flag under which aid was to reach them, and listened eagerly for the sound of friendly cannon. But they looked and listened in vain, and all day long they fought without water, their parched lips cracking, their tongues swollen, and the blood running down their chins when they bit their cartridges and the saltpeter entered their blistered lips. But not a word of murmuring.

The morning of the 20th broke, but no reënforcements had come, and still the men fought on. ☆ The enemy appeared that day with an artifice which

♭ The Union force held the building an hour or two, when they were again dislodged. In regard to the capture of the hospital by the Confederates, and to its recapture by the Union forces, we find the following in the "History of Lafayette County, Missouri" (St. Louis: Missouri Historical Company, 1881), a work which, in its treatment of the siege of Lexington, exhibits impartiality and a painstaking research, the more valuable by reason of the meagerness of the official reports of the engagement:

"This hospital matter has been much animadverted upon by partisan writers on both sides. Colonel Mulligan *assumed* that the Confederates were guilty of a breach of civilized warfare in firing on a hospital; and, consequently, when his men retook the building, having this belief firmly fixed in their minds, they gave no quarter, but killed every armed man caught in the building. Some of the minor Confederate officers seemed to labor under the same impression, and claimed, as an excuse or justification for the capture, that the Federals had fired upon them from inside the building; but this was positively denied at the time by the surgeon, Dr. Cooley, and the priest, Father Butler, who were in the hospital, and by Major Meet, Mr. H. Boothman, and others, still living in Lexington, who were at the time in that part of the intrenchment nearest the hospital. But, aside from this, the official report of General Harris, made at the time, shows that there was no such reason for the capture; but that it was deliberately planned and ordered as a rightful military movement. The Fed-

erals had no military right to expect that a strategic position so important to their opponents as the Anderson house and premises manifestly were, would or should be left in quiet possession merely because they had seen fit to use some part of it for hospital purposes. Nevertheless, that first false scent has been followed and barked after for twenty years—the Federals erroneously claiming an unjustifiable attack on the hospital, and the Confederates erroneously claiming that they were first fired on by Federals from inside the building, and that *for that reason* the attack was made." EDITORS.

∖ After the investment, the Union forces being entirely cut off from the river, "Marshall's cavalrymen and some of the teamsters had watered their horses out of the cisterns at the college, and there was but little water left, what there was being muddy. Two springs at the foot of the bluffs— one on the north and one on the south — were closely guarded by the enemy. . . . One of Colonel Mulligan's men, in an account of the battle, said: 'On the morning of the 19th it rained heavily for about two hours, saturating our blankets, which we wrung out into our canteens for drinking'" ("History of Lafayette County, Missouri").—EDITORS.

☆ No reënforcements reached Colonel Mulligan, though efforts were made to relieve him. September 16th, Sturgis with 1100 men, but without artillery or cavalry, was ordered by General Pope to

was destined to overreach us and secure to them the possession of our intrenchments. They had constructed a movable breastwork of hemp bales, rolled them before their lines up the hill, and advanced under this cover. All our efforts could not retard the advance of these bales. Round-shot and bullets were poured against them, but they would only rock a little and then

settle back. Heated shot were fired with the hope of setting them on fire, but they had been soaked and would not burn. Thus for hours the fight continued. ⎮ Our cartridges were now nearly used up, many of our brave fellows had fallen, and it was evident that the fight must soon cease, when at 3 o'clock an orderly came, saying that the enemy had sent a flag of truce. With the flag came a note from General Price, asking "why the firing had ceased." I returned it, with the reply written on the back, "General, I hardly know, unless you have surrendered." He at once took pains to assure me that this was not the case. I then discovered that the major of another regiment, in spite of orders, had raised a white flag.

Our ammunition was about gone. We were out of rations, and had been without water for days, and many of

COLONEL JAMES A. MULLIGAN.

the men felt like giving up the post, which it seemed impossible to hold longer. They were ordered back to the breastworks, and told to use up all their powder, then defend themselves as best they could, but to hold their place. Then a council of war was held in the college, and the question of

proceed from Macon City for the purpose. He did so, but his messenger to Mulligan being intercepted by General Price, the latter, on the 19th, dispatched a force of 3000 men or more under General Parsons and Colonel Congreve Jackson across the river to repel Sturgis's advance, then within fifteen miles of Lexington. Sturgis, being informed of Mulligan's situation, retreated to Fort Leavenworth. Parsons recrossed the river and took part in the fighting during the afternoon.—EDITORS.

⎮ There are many claimants for the credit of having first suggested the hemp-bale strategy. General Harris's official report says:

"I directed the bales to be wet in the river to protect them against the casualties of fire of our troops and of the enemy, but it was soon found that the wetting so materially increased the weight as to prevent our men, in their exhausted condition, from rolling it to the crest of the hill. I then adopted the idea of wetting the hemp after it had been transported to its position."

As to the date of the use of these, which is given both by Colonel Mulligan and by Colonel Snead as the morning of the 20th, we quote the following circumstantial account from the official report of Colonel Hughes:

"On the morning of the 19th, we arose from our 'bivouac' upon the hills to renew the attack. This day we continued the fighting vigorously all day, holding possession of the hospital buildings, and throwing large wings from both sides of the house, built up of bales of hemp saturated with water, to keep them from taking fire. These portable hemp-bales were extended, like the wings of a partridge net, so as to cover and protect several hundred men at a time, and a most terrible and galling and deadly fire was kept up from them upon the works of the enemy by my men. I divided my forces into reliefs and kept some three hundred of them pouring in a heavy fire incessantly upon the enemy, supplying the places of the weary with fresh troops. On the night of the 19th we enlarged and advanced our defensive works very near to the enemy's intrenchments, and at daybreak opened upon their line with most fatal effect."
EDITORS.

surrender was put to the officers, and a ballot was taken, only two out of six votes being cast in favor of fighting on. Then the flag of truce was sent out with our surrender.

Colonel Snead (see page 262) writes us as follows in regard to the circumstances of the surrender:

"The surrender of Lexington was negotiated on the part of Colonel Mulligan by Colonel Marshall of the 1st Illinois Cavalry, and on the part of General Price by me. We met inside of the Union lines. Of course I demanded the unconditional surrender of the post, with its officers and men and material of war. Colonel Marshall hesitated, and at last said that he would have to submit the matter to Colonel Mulligan. As we knew that reënforcements were on the way to Mulligan, and as I feared that Mulligan was only practicing a ruse in order to gain time, I said to Colonel Marshall that if the terms which I offered were not accepted within ten minutes I should return to our lines and order fire to be reopened. He left me, but returned just as the ten minutes were expiring, and said that the surrender would be made as demanded. I immediately sent one of the officers, whom I had taken with me, to announce the fact to General Price and to ask when he would accept the surrender. He came over at once, and notified Colonel Mulligan that he would himself accept the surrender of him and his field-officers forthwith, and assign one of his division commanders to accept the surrender of the men and their company officers. Mulligan and his field-officers came forward immediately, on foot, and offered to surrender their swords. General Price (next to whom I was sitting) replied instantly, 'You gentlemen have fought so bravely that it would be wrong to deprive you of your swords. Keep them. Orders to parole you and your men will be issued, Colonel Mulligan, without unnecessary delay.' The only officer or man that was not paroled, and the only one who was taken South, was Colonel Mulligan."

Colonel Mulligan was held as a prisoner until the 30th of October, being accompanied by his wife, who had been an eye-witness of the siege from the town. They journeyed in General Price's private carriage, and (Mrs. Mulligan says) received "every possible courtesy from the general and his staff." They returned to St. Louis under escort of forty men and a flag of truce. In Chicago and elsewhere Colonel Mulligan was received with enthusiastic honors.

Colonel Mulligan, after his exchange, was placed in command along the Baltimore and Ohio Railroad, in western Virginia. During this period he engaged in many skirmishes with the enemy. In the battle of Winchester, July 24th, 1864, Colonel Mulligan received three mortal wounds. Some of the officers, among whom was his brother-in-law, Lieutenant James H. Nugent, nineteen years of age, attempted to carry him from the field. Seeing the colors in danger the colonel said: "Lay me down and save the flag." Lieutenant Nugent rescued the colors and returned to the colonel's side,

but in a few moments fell, mortally wounded. Colonel Mulligan died forty-eight hours after, at the age of thirty-four. After his death, his widow received from President Lincoln Colonel Mulligan's commission of Brevet Brigadier-General, U. S. V., dated July 24th, "for gallant and meritorious services at the battle of Winchester."— EDITORS.

NOTE: The seizure of the money of the Lexington Bank referred to by Colonel Snead on page 273 is treated in full in the "History of Lafayette County," from which we condense the following statement: Governor Jackson having appropriated the school fund of the State to the arming and equipment of the State troops, and the proposal having been made to force loans from certain banks for the same purpose, General Frémont, in order to checkmate this action of the Governor, ordered the funds of certain banks to be sent to St. Louis, not for the use of the Federal authorities, but to prevent their employment to aid the enemy. By his order, Colonel Marshall secured the funds of the State Bank of Lexington against the protest of the officers, giving a receipt for the amount, which was $960,159.60, of which $165,659.60 was in gold. The money was buried in the fort under Colonel Mulligan's tent, and upon the surrender every dollar of the gold was delivered to General Price, but $15,000 in notes of the bank was missing. Governor Jackson and General Price ordered all the money to be restored to the bank, but on the 30th of September made a demand upon the bank for, and under threat of force received, the sum of $37,337.20 in gold, claimed to be due to the State under an act of the Legislature of Missouri, which permitted of the suspension of certain banks on the condition that they should loan the State on its bonds a certain portion of their fund. At the time of the capture of Lexington the State Convention of Missouri had deposed Governor Jackson and elected in his place Hamilton R. Gamble. The Union State Government made demand afterward for the same sum, which was paid and bonds of the State issued therefor, which were redeemed at their face value when due. The sum given to Governor Jackson was charged by the bank to "profit and loss." See also page 280 for General Frémont's declaration of policy in this respect. "The funds of other banks of the State were taken possession of by the Federal authorities, transported to St. Louis, and in due time every dollar returned."— EDITORS.

THE PEA RIDGE CAMPAIGN.

BY FRANZ SIGEL, MAJOR-GENERAL, U. S. V.

UNIFORM OF THE UNITED STATES
REGULARS IN 1861.

THE battle of Pea Ridge (or Elkhorn Tavern, as the Confederates named it) was fought on the 7th and 8th of March, 1862, one month before the battle of Shiloh. It was the first clear and decisive victory gained by the North in a pitched battle west of the Mississippi River, and until Price's invasion of 1864 the last effort of the South to carry the war into the State of Missouri, except by abortive raids. Since the outbreak of the rebellion, Missouri, as a border and slave State, had represented all the evils of a bitter civil strife. The opening events had been the protection of the St. Louis arsenal, the capture of Camp Jackson, the minor engagements at Boonville and Carthage, the sanguinary struggle at Wilson's Creek on the 10th of August, forever memorable by the heroic death of General Lyon. The retreat of our little army of about 4500 men to Rolla, after that battle, ended the first campaign and gave General Sterling Price, the military leader of the secessionist forces of Missouri, the opportunity of taking possession of Springfield, the largest city and central point of south-west Missouri, and of advancing with a promiscuous host of over 15,000 men as far as Lexington, on the Missouri River, which was gallantly defended for three days by Colonel Mulligan. Meanwhile, General Frémont, who on the 25th of July had been placed in command of the Western Department, had organized and put in motion an army of about 30,000 men, with 86 pieces of artillery, to cut off Price's forces, but had only succeeded in surprising and severely defeating about a thousand recruits of Price's retiring army at Springfield by a bold movement of 250 horsemen (Frémont's body-guard and a detachment of "Irish Dragoons") under the lead of Major Zagonyi. Our army, in which I commanded a division, was now concentrated at Springfield, and was about to follow and attack the forces of Price and McCulloch, who had taken separate positions, the one (Price) near Pineville in the south-western corner of Missouri, the other (McCulloch) near Keetsville, on the Arkansas line. Although McCulloch was at first averse to venturing battle, he finally yielded to the entreaties of Price, and prepared himself to coöperate in resisting the further advance of Frémont. Between Price and McCulloch it was explicitly understood that Missouri should not be given up without a struggle. Such was the condition of things when the intended operations of General Frémont were cut short by his removal from the command of the army (November 2d), his successor being General David Hunter. The result of this change was an immediate and uncommonly hasty retreat of our army in a northerly and easterly direction, to Sedalia on the 9th, and to Rolla on the 13th; in fact, the abandonment of the whole south-west of the State by the Union troops, and the occupation of

314

the city of Springfield for the second time by the enemy, who were greatly in need of more comfortable winter quarters. They must have been exceedingly glad of the sudden disappearance of an army which by its numerical superiority, excellent organization, and buoyant spirit had had a very good chance of at least driving them out of Missouri. As it was, the new-fledged "Confederates" ⚓ utilized all the gifts of good fortune, organized a great portion of their forces for the Confederate service, and provided themselves with arms, ammunition, and equipments for the field, while the Northern troops were largely reduced by the hardships of miserable winter quarters, and the Union refugees who had left their homes were in great part huddled together in tents in the public places and streets of Rolla and St. Louis, and were dependent on the charity of their sympathizing friends or on municipal support. The whole proceeding was not only a most deplorable military blunder, but also a political mistake. To get rid of Frémont, the good prospects and the honor of the army were sacrificed. It would be too mild an expression to say that the Union peo-

MAJOR-GENERAL SAMUEL R. CURTIS.
FROM A PHOTOGRAPH.

ple of Missouri, or rather of the whole West, felt disappointed; there was deep and bitter indignation, even publicly manifesting itself by demonstrations and protests against the policy of the Administration, and especially against its political and military advisers and intriguers, who sacrificed the welfare of the State to their jealousy of an energetic and successful rival.

To regain what was lost, another campaign — the third in the course of eight months — was resolved upon. It was undertaken by the very same army, but under a different commander, and greatly reduced on account of the prevalence of diseases and the extraordinary mortality in the different camps during the months of inactivity; in truth, the campaign from September to November had "to be done over again" in January, February, and March, in the midst of a very severe winter, and with the relations of numerical strength reversed. Toward the end of December, '61, when not fully restored from a severe illness, I was directed by General Halleck (who, on November 9th, had succeeded General Hunter, the command now being called the Department of the Missouri) to proceed to Rolla, to take command of the troops encamped there, including my own division (the Third, afterward the First)

⚓ On the 29th of October, when I was engaged in a reconnoissance on Bloody Hill, at Wilson's Creek, I heard the salute of one hundred guns fired at Neosho in celebration of the act of secession, and of the sending of delegates to the Confederate Congress by the Rump Legislature of Missouri.— F. S.

This body was composed of 39 representatives and 10 senators — each number being far short of a lawful quorum.— EDITORS.

and General Asboth's (the Fourth, afterward the Second), and to prepare them for active service in the field. I arrived at Rolla on the 23d of December, and on the 27th, when the organization was completed, I was superseded by General Samuel R. Curtis, who had been appointed by Halleck to the command of the District of South-west Missouri, including the troops at Rolla. The campaign was opened by the advance of a brigade of cavalry under Colonel E. A. Carr on the 29th of December from Rolla to Lebanon, for the purpose of initiating a concentration of forces, and to secure a point of support for the scouting parties to be pushed forward in the direction of Springfield, the supposed headquarters of the enemy. (See map, p. 263.)

On January 9th, after toilsome marching, all the disposable forces were assembled at Lebanon. Here, by order of General Curtis, the army was organized into 4 divisions of 2 brigades each, besides a special reserve.↓

Before we reached Lebanon I was doubtful about my personal relations to General Curtis, which had been somewhat troubled by his sudden appearance at Rolla and the differences in regard to our relative rank and position, but the fairness he showed in the assignment of the commands before we left Lebanon, and his frankness and courtesy toward me, dispelled all apprehensions on my part, and with a light heart and full confidence in the new commander, I entered into the earnest business now before us.

The army left Lebanon on the 10th of February, arrived at Marshfield on the 11th, at McPherson's Creek, about 12 miles from Springfield, on the 12th, where a light engagement with the rear-guard of the enemy's troops occurred, and took possession of Springfield on the 13th. Price's army of Missourians, about 8000 strong, had retired and was on its way to Cassville. On entering Springfield we found it pitifully changed,—the beautiful "Garden City" of the South-west looked desolate and bleak; most of the houses were empty, as the Union families had followed us to Rolla after the retreat of General Hunter in November, 1861, and the secessionists had mostly followed Price. The streets, formerly lined with the finest shade trees, were bereft of their ornament, and only the stumps were left. General Price had applied his vacation-time well in organizing two brigades under Colonel Little and General Slack for the Southern Confederacy, had spread out his command as far as, and even beyond, the Osage River, and would have been reënforced by several thousand recruits from middle Missouri, if they had not been intercepted on their way South by Northern troops. As it was, he took whatever he found to his purpose, destroyed what he could not use, and feeling himself not strong enough to venture battle, withdrew to Arkansas to seek assistance from McCulloch. We followed him in two columns, the left wing (Third and Fourth Divisions) by the direct road to Cassville, the right wing (First and Second Divisions), under my command, by the road to Little York, Marionsville, and Verona, both columns to unite at McDowell's, north of Cassville.

I advanced with the Benton Hussars during the night of the 13th to Little York, and as it was a very cold night, the road being covered with a

↓ For details of the composition and losses of both armies, see page 337.—EDITORS.

crust of ice, we had to move slowly. On this night march about eighteen horsemen, including myself, had their feet frozen. In the neighborhood of Marionsville we captured a wagon train and 150 stragglers of the enemy, and arrived at McDowell's just at the moment when, after a short engagement, the left wing had driven Price's rear-guard out of the place. From this time our army moved, united, to Cassville and Keetsville, forced without great trouble Cross Timber Hollows, a defile of about ten miles in length across the Missouri-Arkansas State line, leading to Elkhorn Tavern, and arrived at Sugar Creek on the 18th of February. We were now over 320 miles from St. Louis, and 210 miles from our base at Rolla. The Third and Fourth Divisions advanced from this position 12 miles farther south to Cross Hollows, where also the headquarters of General Curtis were established, and the First and Second to Bentonville, 12 miles to the south-west, while a strong cavalry force under General Asboth went to Osage Springs. On the 23d General Asboth made a dash into Fayetteville, twenty miles in advance, found the city evacuated, and planted the Union flag on the court-house. To balance things somewhat, a raiding party of the enemy surprised our foragers near Huntsville, and another party ventured as far as Keetsville, in our rear, playing havoc with the drowsy garrison of the place.

On March 1st Colonel Jeff. C. Davis's division withdrew from Cross Hollows and took position immediately behind Little Sugar Creek, covering the road which leads from Fayetteville, Arkansas, by Elkhorn Tavern to Springfield, and as an approach of the enemy was expected to take place on that road from the south, Colonel Davis made his position as strong as possible by crowning the hills north of the creek with abatis and parapets of felled trees; he also protected one of his batteries in the rear of the bridge with intrenchments. As we shall see, these works never became of any practical value.

On the 2d of March the First and Second Divisions moved 4½ miles south of Bentonville to McKissick's farm. Colonel Schaefer, with the 2d Missouri Infantry and a detachment of cavalry, was sent to Smith's Mills (Osage Mills), 7 miles east of McKissick's farm, as a post of observation toward Elm Springs, and for the purpose of protecting and working the mill — at that time and under our circumstances a very important " strategic object."

Another detachment of cavalry was stationed at Osage Springs to hold connection with the division at Cross Hollows (south of Elkhorn Tavern), and to scour the country toward Fayetteville and Elm Springs. On the 5th, a detachment under Major Conrad was on its way from McKissick's farm to Maysville, 30 miles west of McKissick's farm; by order of General Curtis, another detachment under Major Mezaros went to Pineville, 25 miles north-west, while from Carr's division a detachment under Colonel Vandever had been sent as far east as Huntsville, 40 miles from Cross Hollows, making the line of our front about seventy miles from Maysville in the west to Huntsville in the east. Since the 18th of February, when we took our first position at Sugar Creek, Price had made his way to the Boston Mountains (Cove Creek), between Fayetteville and the Arkansas River, where he united with McCulloch.

Although serving the same cause, there never existed an *entente cordiale* between the two champions of Missouri and Arkansas; the two men were too different in their character, education, and military policy to understand each other perfectly, to agree in their aims and ends, and to subordinate themselves cheerfully one to the other. McCulloch was a "rough-and-ready" man, not at all speculative, but very practical, to the point, and rich in resources to reach it. In his youth he was a hunter and trapper; he served under Sam Houston, with the artillery, in the battle of San Jacinto, participated in the Mexican war as captain of a company of Texas rangers, and when the war for the Union broke out, he was very active in Texas in securing much war material from the United States, and forcing United States troops to surrender. He was a good fighter, energetic in battle, and quick in discerning danger or espying the weak point of his antagonist; an excellent organizer, disciplinarian, and administrator, indefatigable in recruiting and equipping troops. His care for them was proverbial, and his

MAJOR-GENERAL EARL VAN DORN, C. S. A.
FROM A PHOTOGRAPH.

ability in laying out encampments was extraordinary, and challenged the admiration of our troops.

In a strategical point of view, McCulloch was more bent to the defense of the Trans-Mississippi region, especially Arkansas and the Indian Territory, which district had been put under his command, than to aggressive movements beyond the borders of Arkansas. Price had also had military experience in the Mexican war, which circumstance, combined with his political position, his irreproachable personal character and sincere devotion to the cause which he embraced, after the catastrophe of Camp Jackson, had made him the military head of the secession forces in the State. Brave, and gifted with the talent of gaining the confidence and love of his soldiers, he was undoubtedly

GENERAL VAN DORN'S SIGNATURE.

the proper man to gather around him and hold together the heterogeneous military forces; but, having no organized State or Government to back him, he seldom could rise above the effectiveness of a guerrilla chief, doing business on a large scale and almost on his own account. His army was an ever-changing body, varying from week to week, advancing and retreating, without stability of quarters and security of resources, and therefore not disciplined in a manner to be desired. Sometimes there were men and no arms for them, or muskets without caps and horses without riders; at other times the army of camp-followers and poorly mounted infantry was almost as large as the fighting force of infantry. No wonder then that in spite of the great popularity of the champion of Missouri, McCulloch became disgusted in meeting the half-starved "State Guards" of Missouri with their "huckleberry" cavalry and their great crowd of unarmed, noisy camp-followers.

It was therefore fortunate for the Confederates that on the 10th of January, 1862, Major-General Earl Van Dorn was appointed by Jefferson Davis to the command of the Trans-Mississippi Department, and that he took charge of the combined forces about to confront Curtis. He was a graduate of West Point and had served with honors in the Mexican war as lieutenant of infantry, and was in the United States service as major at the opening of the war. Having joined the Confederacy, he was appointed colonel, and already in Texas had been of great service to his cause. On the 14th of February, 1862,—the very day when the Army of the South-west took possession of Springfield,— he wrote to Price from his headquarters at Pocahontas, stating in detail his plan for "attempting St. Louis and carrying the war into Illinois." Our appearance in Arkansas suddenly changed the situation. Van Dorn at once hastened from Jacksonport to Van Buren on the 24th of February, issued a very flourishing proclamation on the 2d of March, and on the 3d the Confederate army was on its way from the Boston Mountains to Fayetteville and Elm Springs, at which latter place its advance arrived on the evening of the 5th. On this march Price's troops were leading, followed by the division of McCulloch, while General Albert Pike, who had come from the Indian Territory by way of Evansville with a brigade of Indians, brought up the rear. The secrecy of the movement was so well kept that positive news did not reach us until the 5th, when the Confederates were about a day's march from my position at McKissick's farm. It was the intention of Van Dorn to move early on the 6th and "gobble up" my two divisions before they could prepare for defense or make good their retreat; I had, however, ample time to guard myself against the attempted capture, as I had not only been advised by General Curtis on the 5th, after nightfall, of the advance of the enemy, but also had received positive proof of the movement from Colonel Schaefer at Smith's Mill, whose outposts had been attacked on the evening of the same day, which fact he immediately reported. It was now necessary for us to concentrate to meet the enemy's advance, and Colonel Schaefer was then directed to fall back during the night to Bentonville and await further instructions. The time for the two divisions to leave McKissick's farm and march by Bentonville to Sugar Creek was fixed for 2 o'clock A. M. of the 6th, but, before the movement began, the commanders of divisions and brigades, with their staff-officers, met at my headquarters at 1 o'clock A. M. of that day, to be informed of the enemy's movements and to receive verbal instructions respecting the order of march, and the precautions to be taken during the retreat. At precisely 2 o'clock A. M. of the 6th, General Asboth's division left McKissick's farm with the whole train, followed by the division of Colonel Osterhaus. They passed through Bentonville from 4 to 8 o'clock A. M., and arrived at the camp behind Sugar Creek at 2 P. M., where the Union army was to concentrate.

For the purpose of defending the main column on its retreat, and with the intention of finding out whether the enemy was approaching in strong force, and whether he was advancing from Smith's Mill on the road to Bentonville, or by Osage Springs, or on both roads at the same time, I remained at Bentonville with about 600 men, and a battery of 6 pieces, after all the troops had left the place. ♭

During this time Colonel Nemett, who had been sent out with the Benton Hussars to reconnoiter, reported to me that he had met the enemy's cavalry, and that several thousand men, cavalry, and infantry were forming in line of battle about a mile from Bentonville on the open fields south of the village. From personal observation I found out that this was correct, and, therefore, had not the least doubt that we had the advance of an army before us. This was at precisely 10 o'clock. I state these facts to show how egregiously Van Dorn was mistaken in supposing that if he had arrived an hour sooner—Maury says 30 minutes sooner—"he would have cut me off with my whole force [of 7000 men], and certainly have beaten the enemy [our army at Sugar Creek] the next day." As it really was, he only found my rear-guard of 600 men in his front, because at the hour when his troops advanced against Bentonville, the leading division (Asboth's) of our retreating column crossed Sugar Creek, 10 miles from Bentonville. Van Dorn officially says, "We followed him [Sigel], our advance skirmishing with his rear-guard, which was admirably handled, until we gained a point on Sugar Creek, about 7 miles beyond Bentonville, and within 1 or 2 miles of the strongly intrenched camp of the enemy." Van Dorn then ascertained, in a conference with McCulloch and McIntosh, that by making a détour of eight miles he could outflank our position on Sugar Creek, and reach the Telegraph road in our rear, which movement he commenced soon after dark, Price's division leading. He expected to reach the point in our rear, north of Elkhorn Tavern, before daylight, but on account of obstructions placed on the road by Colonel Dodge's Iowa regiment his march was so impeded that Price's division did not gain the Telegraph road until nearly 10 A. M. of the 7th, the first day of the battle, while McCulloch's division, and the Indian brigade under Pike,

♭ Colonel Frederick Schaefer's 2d Missouri regiment was also to be retained, to form a part of the rear-guard, but by some misunderstanding he followed the division of Colonel Osterhaus toward Sugar Creek; he was ambuscaded on the way, and lost thirty-seven men.—F. S.

had only reached a point opposite Leetown, about five miles distant from where Price struck the Telegraph road. (See map, p. 322.)

During the night of the 6th our army rested quietly in its position behind Sugar Creek. General Asboth's division held the extreme right, on the entrance of the Bentonville road, Colonel Osterhaus's was on his left, Colonel Davis's in the center, and Colonel Carr's, which during the 5th had retreated from Cross Hollows (Camp Halleck) behind Sugar Creek, was posted on the extreme left. Asboth's division was facing west and south-west, the other two divisions were facing toward the south. Curtis expected to be attacked from the south, and had made all his preparations accordingly. I was, however, doubtful whether the enemy would knock his head against a position naturally so strong, and for this reason expected the main attack from the direction of Bentonville against Asboth's division, *i. e.*, against our right flank and rear. To ascertain, therefore, what was going on during the night in the direction mentioned, I sent out two of my scouts (Brown and Pope) with some cavalry, to proceed as far as possible toward the west and north-west, and report any movement of hostile troops immediately. Toward morning they reported that during the night troops and trains were moving on the back road, around our position toward Cross Timber; that they had heard the noise of wagons or artillery, but they had not seen the troops. I then ordered Lieutenant Schramm, of my staff, to go out with an escort and bring in more information. This was at 5 o'clock in the morning. His report, made a little after 6 o'clock, left no doubt in my mind that the enemy was moving around our position toward the north-east (Springfield road). I now went out myself and saw clearly trains and troops moving in the direction mentioned. At about the same time when the flanking movement of the enemy was discovered on our right, Major Weston of the 24th Missouri Infantry, who was posted in our rear, at Elk-horn Tavern, was informed by his outposts of the advance of some of the enemy's cavalry on the roads from Bentonville and Cassville, toward his position. Between 6 and 7 in the morning, skirmishing had begun near the tan-yard, on the Cassville road, north of Elkhorn Tavern, so that his reports and those sent in by myself reached General Curtis during the early morning of the 7th. A meeting of the division commanders was called by him for 8 o'clock at Pratt's store, and after a short consultation he directed Colonel Carr to take position at Elkhorn Tavern, while Colonel Bussey was directed to proceed with the cavalry of the different commands (except the 3d Illinois), and with three pieces of Elbert's battery to move by Leetown against the enemy, supposed to be advancing in that direction. Colonel Osterhaus was also requested to accompany Colonel Bussey for the purpose of taking control of the movement. As up to that time not even a demonstration had been made against our front on Little Sugar Creek, and there was no doubt in my mind that the main forces of the enemy were working around our flank, I suggested the necessity of supporting our cavalry by at least a brigade of infantry and another battery of my command, because a repulse of the cavalry might lead to serious consequences. The proposition was immediately accepted,

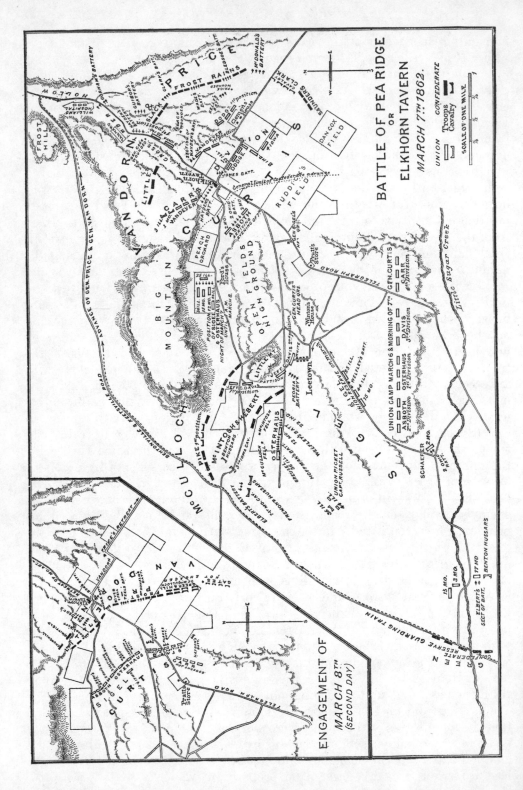

BATTLE OF PEA RIDGE
OR
ELKHORN TAVERN
MARCH 7TH 1862.

UNION   CONFEDERATE

Troops

Cavalry

SCALE OF ONE MILE

ENGAGEMENT OF
MARCH 8TH
(SECOND DAY)

[Mr. Hunt P. Wilson, who was a member of Guibor's Confederate battery, has given the following description in the "St. Louis Republican" of the contest on the Confederate right in the first day's fight. He also describes the ground where the principal fighting on both days took place, for which reason his account is useful in connection with the map on the preceding page and the cut on page 330:

"The Missouri army by a long night march had passed completely around the Federal right flank, marching to the north-east of Big Mountain, then forming line of battle facing south on the Keetsville and Fayetteville or 'Wire' road, directly in General Curtis's rear. The country on this side of the hill is broken with high ridges and deep hollows through which the Wire road runs. The column entered by what is called Cross Timber Hollow. Some of the ridges are 150 feet high. In the valley of this defile is located what is known as the tan-yard, three-quarters of a mile from Elkhorn Tavern. From the tan-yard there is a gradual ascent, and alongside the road runs a deep hollow reaching up to the spring near the tavern. At the head of this and crossing it is a 'bench' along the base of the mountain. Along this bench was the United States Cavalry under General Carr. Along the road leading down from the tavern were the Iowa troops with artillery, and on their right, reaching to the east of the Van Winkle road, on which there are a few clearings, General Curtis prolonged his line of battle. Another hollow leads from the tan-yard to the south-east, and at the head of this hollow rested the Federal right. . . . The battle was opened by the Iowa Battery [Hayden's] of 4 guns, on the Wire road, supported by the Iowa troops with 2 guns 150 feet further up the road, to which Guibor's battery responded from the opposite ridge at a distance of 250 yards. The other Confederate batteries with the infantry arriving by the same road, took position further to the left, and opened on the enemy's right wing."

Mr. Wilson says of the first Confederate line:

"Some State Guard Cavalry under Bob McCulloch and Congreve Jackson formed on the extreme left. Then on their right came Bledsoe's and Clark's and McDonald's batteries, Rains's infantry, Wade's battery, a regiment of infantry, and then Guibor's battery. This filled out the ridge. Little's Confederate brigade was on the right across the tan-yard hollow. Within an hour the Iowa Battery was obliged to withdraw. Soon after, Gates's regiment of cavalry came up the hollow in front of the guns, and went half-way up the slope, dismounted, every fourth man holding the horses, then formed and moved up the brow of the hill. At the same time, Little's Confederate brigade, which had by this time come into line, opened on the Iowa troops in their rear, with Gates in their front. After a fierce contest of musketry, Little's brigade swung around and cut off part of the Federal line, the remainder retreating up to the tavern. Guibor's battery now moved around to the position which had been held by the Iowa Battery. Guibor's battery had gone up with Little's line and the fight was renewed on the new line."

He thus describes the Confederate advance:

"The fire in front began to lull, and Slack's brigade with Rives's and Burbridge's regiments came up on a left-wheel, with Rains on their left, across to the hollow, and the whole line charged up with a wild cheer. Captain Guibor, who well understood how to fight artillery in the brush, took all the canister he could lay his hands on, and with two guns went up in the charge with the infantry. General Rains's brigade on the left, led by Colonel Walter Scott O'Kane, and Major Rainwater made a brilliant dash at the redoubt and battery which had been throwing on them for an hour or more from its position in an old field. Eight guns were captured along the line. The Federal troops being dislodged from the woods began forming in the fields and planted some new

batteries back of the knobs in the rear. And now the fight grew furious. Gorham's battery could not hold its position, and fell back to its old place. Guibor planted his two guns directly in front of the tavern and opened at close quarters with grape and canister on the Federal line, in which great confusion was evident, as officers could be seen trying to rally and re-form their men.

"The entire Confederate line was charging up to the Elkhorn Tavern; Colonel Carr, the Federal cavalry commander, had withdrawn his command from the bench of the mountain on the Confederate right. The Illinois Battery, at first planted in the horse-lot west of the tavern, had limbered to the rear and taken a new position in the fields. The Federal Mountain Howitzer Battery had also moved away. The 8th Iowa Battery, which had poured such a hot fire down the road upon Guibor and Gorham, had by this time lost the use of two of its guns, dismounted by the fire of Guibor's battery, but continued to fight its two remaining guns until the Confederate regiment of Colonel Clint Burbridge was upon them; when, their horses being killed, that regiment took them in, and at nightfall brought them down the road. To the left on the Van Winkle road the [Confederate] batteries of McDonald, Bledsoe, and Wade had been engaged in a severe artillery duel in which the Federal batteries held their own until the Confederate infantry got within range, when they were forced back, leaving two guns captured by Rains's men led by the gallant O'Kane. The cavalry on the extreme left, under General John B. Clark and Colonel Robert McCulloch, had turned the Federal right wing, and the latter's entire line was falling back to meet reënforcements hurrying to their assistance from Sugar Creek on their left rear. The Federals placed 18 or 20 guns to command the tavern. Guibor moved up with the Confederate line, or a little in advance, and formed in battery in the narrow road in front of the tavern, losing several horses in the movement. And now commenced a hot fight. The rapid fire of the twenty pieces of Federal artillery . . . commenced waving and blazing in his front, while the two guns were replying with grape and canister. Now came the crisis. A regiment of United States infantry moved out of the timber on the left front of the guns, about one hundred yards distant, with a small field intervening, the fences around it leveled to the ground. On Guibor's right was the tavern, on his left a blacksmith's shop, and in the lot some corn-cribs. Behind these buildings 'Rock' Champion had placed his company of cavalry to protect their horses from thickly flying bullets. Rock's quick eye saw the bright bayonets as they were pushing through the brush, and, riding up, he yelled in his rough-and-ready style, 'Guibor, they're flankin' you!' 'I know it, but I can't spare a gun to turn on them,' was the reply. There was no supporting infantry on his left. Said Rock, 'I'll charge them!' This meant to attack a full regiment of infantry advancing in line, 700 or 800 strong, with 22 men. . . . Galloping back a few paces to his little band, his clear, ringing voice could be heard by friend and enemy. 'Battalion, forward, trot, march, gallop, march, charge!' and with a wild yell in they went, their gallant chief in the lead, closely followed by 'Sabre Jack' Murphy, an old regular dragoon; Fitzsimmons, Coggins, O'Flaherty, Pomeroy, and the others. The last named were old British dragoons; three of them had ridden with the heavy squadrons at Balaklava and all well knew what was in front of them. . . . Within thirty seconds they were right in the midst of the surprised Federal infantry, shouting, slashing, shooting. Corporal Casey charged on foot. Guibor's two guns were at the same time turned left oblique and deluged the Federal left with canister. The result was precisely what Champion had foreseen, and proved his reckless courage was directed by good judgment. The attack was a clear surprise, the result a stampede; the infantry fired an aimless, scattering volley, then, expecting a legion of horsemen to fall on them, fled in confusion. Champion did not follow. Knowing when to stop as well as to commence, he secured their flag and quickly returned to the battery which he had saved, with a loss of only three of his gallant rough-riders."]

and so it happened that after the disaster which befell our cavalry,⸢ the advance and onslaught of McCulloch's troops were checked by the command of Osterhaus. The speedy arrival of Colonel Jeff. C. Davis's division on the right of Osterhaus, and its energetic advance, turned a very critical moment into a decisive victory of our arms. McCulloch and McIntosh fell while leading their troops in a furious attack against Osterhaus and Davis. Hébert and a number of his officers and men were captured by pickets of the 36th Illinois (cavalry) under Captain Smith and of the 44th Illinois infantry under Captain Russell. Thus the whole of Mc-Culloch's column, deprived of its leaders and without unity of command, was thrown into confusion and beaten back. During the night of the 7th scarcely two-thirds of it reached the wing under Price, near Elkhorn Tavern. ☆

MAJOR-GENERAL PETER J. OSTERHAUS.
FROM A PHOTOGRAPH.

Though a great advantage was gained on our side by the death or capture of those leaders, the principal cause of our success was rather the quick rallying and the excellent manœuvring of Osterhaus's and Davis's forces, as well as the coolness and bravery of their infantry, supported by Welfley's, Hoffmann's, and Davidson's batteries. Osterhaus changed his front twice under the fire of the enemy, to meet the dangerous flank attack and pressure of Hébert's Louisiana and Arkansas infantry, while the brigades of Davis, by striking the left of McCulloch's advancing column, threw it into disorder and forced it to retreat. It was during this conflict that two officers, Major John C. Black of the 37th Illinois and Major Sidney Post of the 59th Illinois, although both severely wounded in the right arm, refused to leave the field until peremptorily ordered to do so. Here fell Lieutenant-Colonel John A. Hendricks of the 22d Indiana, receiving two mortal wounds.

While our left wing was thus successful against about 11,500 of the enemy, the right wing under Carr had been sorely pressed by the 6500 Missourians under Van Dorn and Price. In spite of the heroic resistance of the two brigades of Dodge and Vandever, and the reënforcements sent to them during

⸢ Elbert, Bussey, and the Hussars were repulsed by Pike with Drew's and Stand Watie's Indian regiments, and Sims's and Welch's cavalry. Mc-Culloch was farther to the left with Hébert and McIntosh, who became engaged with Davis's division — at first with the brigade of Julius White, who retired a short distance when Pattison came up and aided him in flanking McCulloch's line.—EDITORS.

☆ Of McCulloch's column, Drew retreated to the south-west toward Bentonville. Watie, Welch, and Greer joined Van Dorn in the night, but Watie retreated to Bentonville during the next day's fight. Pike himself remained. Greer, who succeeded McCulloch in command of the wing, moved with the remainder of the force and joined Van Dorn, taking position on the left, as shown on the map, page 322.— EDITORS.

the afternoon,] they were forced back from position to position, until Elkhorn Tavern was taken by the enemy, and our crippled forces, almost without ammunition, their artillery reduced by losses of guns, men, and horses, their infantry greatly reduced, had to seek a last shelter in the woods and behind the fences, separated from the enemy's position by open fields, but not farther than a mile from our trains. There they formed a contracted and curved line, determined to resist, not disheartened, but awaiting with some apprehension another attack. Fortunately, the enemy did not follow up his success, and night fell in, closing this terrible conflict. While this engagement of our right wing was in progress, I received an order from General Curtis at 2 o'clock P. M. to reënforce Colonels Osterhaus and Davis with the remainder of the troops of the First and Second Divisions, held in reserve near our original position, between Sugar Creek and Elkhorn Tavern. Before receiving this order I sent Major Poten with the 17th Missouri, 2 companies of the 15th, 2 companies of the 3d Missouri, a section of artillery (Elbert's 2 pieces), and a squadron of Benton Hussars under Major Heinrich, toward the south-

MAJOR-GENERAL EUGENE A. CARR.
FROM A PHOTOGRAPH.

west, to try to gain the rear of a hostile force stationed there. Leaving a small detachment as a guard in our camp, I moved with all the other troops by Leetown to the battle-field, north of the town. We arrived just in time to give a send-off to the retreating hostile forces, and, joined by Osterhaus's brigade, advanced toward the east, parallel with the curve formed by the chain of hills called Pea Ridge, with the intention of bringing assistance to our right wing, where the noise of the engagement with Van Dorn and Price was unabating.

We had to move slowly and cautiously, as a part of the enemy's forces evidently tried to rally on our left flank but withdrew after some little skirmishing with the 44th Illinois. Reaching finally an open field about half a mile from the last spur of the hills, looking down upon Elkhorn Tavern, we halted, and report was sent to General Curtis's headquarters, describing our position and asking for orders. At that time it had become dark, firing on the right had almost ceased, and as we had not sufficient knowledge of the position of the enemy, or our own troops on the right, I concluded to

---

] Five companies of the 8th Indiana and 3 pieces of Klauss's Indiana battery; part of the Second Division, 4 companies of the 2d Missouri, 4 pieces of Chapman's battery, 5 companies of the 25th Illinois, a section of Hoffmann's battery, Bowen's cavalry battalion, and mountain howitzers.—F. S.

stay where we were, and took the necessary precautions to make our position secure. To conceal it as much as possible, no camp-fires were allowed, and the troops lay silently on the field resting on their arms. Between 12 and 1 o'clock the outposts reported some noise at a distance from our left, as if troops were moving toward the north-east. I therefore went out with one of my staff-officers as far as our line of outposts, and remained there about half an hour, but could hear nothing. I, however, saw distinctly the camp-fires of Price's troops extending from the heights near Elkhorn Tavern far down toward the south-east. Toward the west and south-west the sky was illumined by two large, isolated camp-fires, one about midway between Elkhorn Tavern and Leetown, and the other four or five miles farther off in the direction of Bentonville. This, in

BRIGADIER-GENERAL JAMES McINTOSH.
FROM A PHOTOGRAPH.

connection with what we had seen during the afternoon, when some of the enemy's troops were moving along the heights of Pea Ridge toward Elkhorn Tavern, and others toward the south-west, and with what the outposts had reported, made it clear to my mind that the enemy would not venture battle again near Leetown, but that McCulloch's troops would join those of Price, and by a united effort try to overwhelm our right wing at Elkhorn Tavern. For this reason, and to give our worn-out and hungry troops something to eat, good camp-fires and rest, I resolved to withdraw them from their position, move them back to our camp, and lead them forward again in the morning to the same ground, to fall upon the enemy's right flank and rear, as soon as he should begin his attack. Leaving the Benton Hussars and a line of outposts with a reserve of infantry on the field, to guard our position, I marched off from the left, called in all the detachments from wherever they were, and formed the two divisions in such a manner on the road leading from my headquarters to the ground we had left, that, by reaching it with the head of our column, we could bring it in the shortest possible time on the right into line, and come into action at the very moment the first regiment and battery had taken their position. All these preparations were completed before daybreak of the 8th.

During the night of the 7th the division of Colonel Davis had been called in by General Curtis from Leetown, and in the morning it took position on the Telegraph road, in place of Carr's division, which had borne the brunt of the battle of the day before, and was now withdrawn, and the greater part of it held in reserve. Pattison's brigade, of Davis's division, formed on the right of the Telegraph road, with Klauss's battery before the center of the line; the second brigade (the 37th and 59th Illinois), under Colonel White, formed on the left of the road, supported by Davidson's battery. Colonel Carr, although wounded, assisted in placing these troops.

It was a little after 6 o'clock in the morning when I sent out Colonel Osterhaus with Captain Asmussen of my staff to reconnoiter the ground on which I intended to deploy, and to find the nearest road leading to it. The 44th Illinois followed the two officers for the purpose of marking the right of the position to be taken, but with orders to keep concealed as much as possible, and not to enter into an engagement unless attacked. Half an hour later, I was standing in front of my tent, ready to mount, and anxiously awaiting the return of the staff-officers, when suddenly a few cannon-shots in our front, from Davidson's Union battery, announced the conflict. At this moment General Curtis, to whom I had sent word during the night where my two divisions were assembling, and that they would be ready for action in the morning, rode toward me from the direction where the firing had begun, and, somewhat excitedly, said: "General, I have opened the battle; it will be a hard fight; Davis is already there. Please bring your troops in line as quickly as possible." I confess that I did not understand the reason why a cannonade was commenced on our side when we were not ready to meet a counter-attack of the enemy with a good chance of success, the more so, as I had been out in our front before General Curtis met me, and had found that our line was weak, stretched out in an open field, the Telegraph road obstructed by artillery, ammunition-wagons, and other vehicles, and that there was no room to deploy my divisions, except behind the first line and masked by it; nor on the left, unless immediately exposed to and raked by the fire of the enemy, whose batteries were supposed to be posted in the margin of the woods, whence they could reach my troops at point-blank range. I explained this to General Curtis, made him acquainted with the object in view, told him that I expected Colonel Osterhaus and Captain Asmussen back every moment, and finally asked him to give me ten minutes' time to wait for them, when I would move immediately to the position selected and commence the attack. Even if our troops on the right should be compelled to yield, it could only be momentarily, as the enemy would have to direct his whole attention to my attack on his flank and rear. I never felt more relieved than when General Curtis, evidently encouraged by this proposition, said: "Well, General, do what you propose." I must add here that I had not seen General Curtis during the night and before I met him near my tent; he could, therefore, not have been fully aware of what I had experienced in my position away from him on the left, and what my intention was to do in the morning, although I had sent Captain Asmussen to his headquarters to report to him, receiving, however, no orders from him in return. After our conversation, which lasted only a few minutes, the two officers came back in all haste, and reported that they had found an excellent position; that no enemy was in sight, and that Colonel Knobelsdorff, with his regiment, was posted as directed. General Curtis declared himself satisfied and rode off, but scarcely had he left me when the cannonade in front became very brisk, some of the hostile missiles bursting over our heads.

I mounted, told Colonel Osterhaus to take charge of our column and move it to the position to be occupied; then, accompanied by Captain Asmussen, I rode to the front, where Davis's division had formed into line, to see what was going on. I found one of our batteries hotly engaged, but compelled to withdraw, which exposed the infantry on the right to an enfilading fire, and also forced it to change its position. One of the regiments—I think it was the 22d or the 8th Indiana— was thrown into momentary disorder by this surprise, and the men fell back toward an eminence on the right of the road on which I was halting. I assisted their brave commander to rally them, which did not take long, and spoke a few words to them, saying that if the right could hold out for half an hour, assistance would come, and all would be well. Meanwhile another regiment had formed on the left, the battery had taken position again and was supported by four other guns (of White's brigade), farther to the left, diverting the enemy's fire. The line stood firm,

PRATT'S STORE.   RESERVE.   GUARD-HOUSE.   TROTT'S HILL.
3D IOWA CAVALRY.   GEN. CURTIS'S HEADQUARTERS.   PEORIA BATTERY.

THE UNION RIGHT WING UNDER GENERAL CARR AT
PRATT'S STORE, SECOND DAY OF THE BATTLE.
FROM A PANEL TO THE PICTURE ON PAGE 330.

and as no hostile infantry appeared, I took leave of the commander of the "Indiana boys," and hastened to my own troops. I reached the head of the column when it was just debouching from the woods, and the first battery that arrived took position on the left of the 44th Illinois, which was kneeling behind a fence. In about 15 minutes the First Division (Osterhaus's) was formed into line, with the artillery in the intervals between the infantry, the Second Division in reserve, about 250 paces behind our right, with General Asboth at its head, who, in spite of his wound received on the 7th, was again in the saddle. Our position, in full view of the open fields, which sloped gently down toward the long skirt of woods, where the enemy's artillery and infantry were posted, was excellent, and allowed the full development of our forces. The enemy's batteries received us well, but many of their shots were either aimed too high, or struck the ground and were buried a short distance in front of us. When well in action, we advanced slowly from position to position, at the same time contracting our line, the infantry following, rising quickly, and as soon as they had reached a new position lying down again. During this time the whole cavalry force of the two divisions had formed behind the extreme left of our line, supported by the 2d Missouri and Elbert's flying battery of General Asboth's command. The 17th Missouri, under Major Poten, also came up from the Bentonville road, and was posted on the left. On our right, communication was established with the right wing, and the two batteries of Klauss and Davidson were brought into line with our own, while the two brigades of Colonels Julius White and Thomas Pattison held the left of the enemy's line in check until our whole line advanced.

It was now a little after 11 o'clock; most of the enemy's batteries (about fifty guns) were silenced one after another, by our concentric fire; his infantry, not venturing out of the woods into the open fields, was now treated with a shower of shell and shrapnel. Opposite our extreme left, however, near Elkhorn Tavern, Van Dorn made a determined effort to hold the high spur of hills, the top of which was crowned and protected by rocks and bowlders. Some of Price's infantry had already taken possession of it, and a battery was being placed in position, when Hoffmann's and Elbert's batteries were ordered to direct their fire against them chiefly with solid shot. Not more than fifteen minutes elapsed before the enemy evacuated this last stronghold, while our infantry on the left — the 36th Illinois, and the 2d, 3d, and 17th Missouri — rushed up the steep hill and forced the remnants of the enemy's troops down into Cross Timber Hollow. Almost simultaneously the 12th Missouri, the 25th and the 44th Illinois advanced in double-quick from the center and right into the woods, engaged the enemy's infantry, drove it back, and one of our regiments (the 12th Missouri) captured the " Dallas Battery." On the extreme right, where General Curtis had directed the movements of the troops, Davis's division and a part of Carr's, assisted by Hayden's and Jones's batteries (the latter commanded by Lieutenant David), pushed forward against the left wing of the enemy and forced it to leave the field. The army of Van Dorn and Price, including about two-thirds of McCulloch's troops under Churchill and Greer, and one-third of Pike's Indian Brigade, all of whom had joined Price during the night, were now in precipitate retreat in all directions, pursued by the First and Second Divisions as far as Keetsville, 9 miles to the north, and by a cavalry force under Colonel Bussey with 2 mountain howitzers to the south-west beyond Bentonville. So ended the battle of Pea Ridge, and our little army, instead of being " beaten and compelled to surrender," had gained a decisive victory. ⚓

⚓ The picture on the next page shows Big Mountain in the right background, as it appeared in March, 1862. When I visited the battle-field a few weeks ago (July 6th, 1887) the whole range of mountains was covered by a dense forest, and the rocky summits of Big Mountain were not discernible from the fields below, where our troops had been posted. In other respects there were not great changes. The rising ground stretching across the fields from east to west, with its highest elevation in the center, and on which my artillery was posted, shows at once how great our advantage must have been against the hostile batteries, which were planted behind the margin of the woods in the lower ground. The surface of the cultivated fields is now widened by the clearing of the adjacent woods, so that the whole interior space of the battle-field seems much larger. The house and barn

DIVISION OF JEFF. C. DAVIS.   DIVISIONS OF ASBOTH AND OSTERHAUS UNDER SIGEL.   ROSSER'S CONFEDERATE BRIGADE ON BIG MOUNTAIN.

HILL'S ARKANSAS AND TEXAS TROOPS.   GENERAL STERLING PRICE.   GUIBOR'S BATTERY.   ELKHORN TAVERN.

FROST'S BRIGADE.   BURBRIDGE'S, WHITFIELD'S, AND BLACK'S REGIMENTS.   CHURCHILL'S ARKANSAS AND TEXAS TROOPS.   BLEDSOE'S AND GORHAM'S BATTERIES.

LAST HOUR OF THE BATTLE OF PEA RIDGE, MARCH 8, 1862 — ADVANCE OF THE UNION FORCES TO RETAKE THE POSITION AT ELKHORN TAVERN.

FROM A PAINTING BY HUNT P. WILSON, IN POSSESSION OF THE SOUTHERN HISTORICAL SOCIETY, ST. LOUIS.

The losses of our army were: killed, 203; wounded, 980; missing, 201,—total, 1384. The enemy's losses on the battle-field were about equal, if not greater than, ours, but they have never been accurately stated. On the 7th we lost more on our right, against Price, than he did; the enemy (McCulloch's troops) more on his right against our left. On the 8th, when our forces were concentrated against Van Dorn and Price, the enemy's loss was much more severe than ours.

In reviewing the period from the 13th of June, 1861, when the first expeditions started from St. Louis to the north-west and south-west of Missouri, and comprising the three campaigns under Generals Lyon, Frémont, and Curtis, we must acknowledge the extraordinary activity represented in these movements. As war in its ideal form is nothing else than a continuous series of action and reaction, that side which develops the greater energy will, other conditions being equal, become master of the situation. It was the energy of the South in the first period of the War of the Rebellion which in less than three months organized a powerful insurrection and threatened the existence of the Union. And so, on a smaller scale, isolated and left almost to its own resources at the beginning of the conflict, the Union element of Missouri, led by a few energetic men, saved the city of St. Louis, then the chief city of the West, and by successive, rapid blows became master of the whole State. In no other State of the North was greater activity shown, or more undertaken, endured, or accomplished. There were regiments which traversed the State three times in 8 months, forward and backward, a distance of over 1200 miles (the line of railroad from St. Louis to Rolla not taken into account), and this, especially during the first few months, with the most miserable outfit,—without tents, without knapsacks and other accouterments, the men carrying their cartridges in their pockets and sleeping on the bare ground, braving hunger and disease.

The battle of Pea Ridge was the first respite gained by the almost incessant activity and the unflinching courage of our little army,— the Army of the South-west. It was not a "great" battle, like that of Gettysburg or Chattanooga; it was not of such preponderating national importance; it did not "break the backbone of the Rebellion," but it virtually cleared the South-west of the enemy, gave peace to the people of Missouri, at least for the next two years, and made it possible for our veterans to reënforce the armies under Buell, Rosecrans, Grant, and Sherman. It was a battle of all kinds of surprises and accidents, of good fighting and good manœuvring. Van Dorn was evidently "surprised" when he found that his plan to take St. Louis, and to carry the war into Illinois in April, 1862, was anticipated by our

to which our extreme left extended on the second day (March 8th) are still standing, and even the new Elkhorn Tavern stands on the old site. Mr. Cox, who lived there in 1862, was obliged, with his mother and his young wife, to seek protection in the cellar, where they remained for two days, being under fire thirteen hours. Late in the war the tavern was burned, but Mr. Cox rebuilt it after the plan of the old one, and still lives there. He is, of course, familiar with the battle-field, and tramped over it with me and my driver. Pratt's store, near which General Curtis's headquarters tent was pitched, is still there.— F. S.

NOTE.— The cut opposite, the reader may be reminded, represents also the *ground* of the first day's fighting by Price's troops.— EDITORS.

BRIGADIER-GENERAL ALBERT PIKE, C. S. A.,
COMMANDER OF THE INDIAN FORCES AT PEA RIDGE.
FROM A PHOTOGRAPH.

unexpected appearance; he was badly "surprised" when on the 6th of March, instead of "gobbling up" my two divisions at McKissick's farm, as he confidently expected, he only met a rear-guard of 600 men, which he could not gobble up during nearly 6 hours of its march of 6 miles; he was also surprised to find, on his détour around our left flank and rear, that the road was at different places so blocked up, that instead of arriving in our rear, on the road to Springfield, with the divisions of Price, at daylight of the 7th, he did not reach that point before 10 o'clock in the morning, by which delay Price's and McCulloch's forces became separated and could not assist each other at the decisive moment, while we gained time to make our preparations for the reception of both. Finally, on the 8th, Van Dorn was greatly "surprised to find himself suddenly confronted by a new, unexpected force," attacked in flank and rear, and compelled to retreat. On the other hand, Curtis was "surprised" by the sudden turn things had taken, and much disappointed because the enemy did not make the attack against our front, a position not only very strong by nature, presenting a chain of high hills, but also strengthened by intrenchments and abatis, the access to it being also protected and impeded by a deep creek running along our line of defense. He would have been much more "surprised" had it not been for the discovery, by our scouting parties, of the enemy's flanking movement. ↓

↓ The reports of Generals Van Dorn and Price make it evident that they intended and were prepared to renew the battle, or, as Van Dorn says, "to accept the gage," on the morning of the 8th; the determination to retreat was therefore forced upon them during the course of the morning by the advantages we gained. The results obtained in this three-days struggle consisted not only in the immediate losses, which, as mentioned before, were about equal, but also, and much more so, in the condition into which the Southern forces were thrown at the beginning of and after their retreat from the battle-field; their separation by following diverging lines, the disorganization of their artillery, the dissolution of the "Indian Brigade," and of a part of the Arkansas troops, and finally by the impossibilty of restoring order and bringing together all their forces north of the Boston Mountains. A report of the actual strength of McCulloch's division on March 11th, three days after the battle, shows only 2894 men out of a total effective of 8384, present at "Strickler's," March 2d, four days before the battle. On the 12th of March Van Dorn wrote or telegraphed from Van Buren to Colonel B. W. Share, 3d Texas Cavalry, to join "the army" at its encampment on the Frog Bayou road, about seven miles from that town (Van Buren), which shows that the Southern army was very considerably scattered for several days after the battle, and that Curtis could have followed it as far as the Boston Mountains without meeting any serious resistance. If Van Dorn had succeeded in his bold manœuvre against us, had "cornered" our army and forced it to surrender, he would have come into possession of such material of war as would have enabled him to move with thirty thousand men to Springfield and Rolla, and, by at least "threatening" St. Louis, he might have seriously disconcerted the plans of Halleck. The consideration of such an exigency lends additional importance to the success of the Union forces at Pea Ridge.—F. S.

In a strategical and tactical point of view, the battle of Pea Ridge forms a counterpart to the battle of Wilson's Creek. In the latter battle *we* were the outflanking party, approaching the camp of McCulloch and Price, by a night march, completely surprising and attacking their forces in the morning, but making our attack in front and rear, without being able to communicate with and assist each other. My own brigade of 1118 men, which had gained the enemy's rear, was beaten first, and then the forces of General Lyon, 4282 men, after a heroic resistance were compelled to leave the field. The enemy held the "interior lines," and could throw readily his forces from one point to the other. At Pea Ridge the same advantage was with *our* army, although the enemy had better facilities of communication between his left and right wing, by the road leading from Bentonville to Elkhorn Tavern, than we had had at Wilson's Creek. There we had had to meet substantially the same troops we encountered at Pea Ridge, with the exception of the Indian Brigade under Pike.

BRIGADIER-GENERAL STAND WATIE, C. S. A., OF THE INDIAN FORCES. FROM A PHOTOGRAPH.

From the result of the battles of Wilson's Creek and Pea Ridge, it will be seen that the manœuvre of outflanking and "marching into the enemy's rear" is not always successful. It was not so at Wilson's Creek, when we had approached, unobserved, within cannon-shot of the enemy's lines; however, we were only 5400 against about 11,000, while at Pea Ridge the enemy had 16,202 men in action against our 10,500. In a manœuvre of that kind, the venture of a smaller army to surprise and "bag" an enemy, whose forces are concentrated and who holds the "interior lines" or "inside track," will always be great, unless the enemy's troops are inferior in quality, or otherwise at a disadvantage. ♭

♭ During the war there was not, I believe, a single case where an army tried such a "bagging" process and succeeded in it, except in the attack of posts and intrenched positions, as, for instance, at Harper's Ferry during the advance of Lee into Maryland in September, 1862, and with partial success at Winchester, June 15th, 1863. There are instances where flanking manœuvres of great detachments from the main army have been successful, but more through non-interference with them than for other reasons. Jackson's détour into the rear of the Army of Virginia, in August, 1862, was a strategical surprise, that was only successfully executed because it was not discovered in time, or rather because, when discovered, it was not properly met. The flanking movement and attack by Jackson, against the Eleventh Corps at the battle of Chancellorsville, was very successful from a strategical and tactical point of view, as

the enemy not only gained the right flank of our army without being interfered with, but also fell on the Eleventh Corps before proper arrangements were made to meet the attack. It may therefore be said, that in all such manœuvres going on at a reaching distance from our own position, we are as much on the flank of the enemy as he is on ours. The case is similar, when an army has succeeded in gaining the rear of another, at the same time giving up its own base; because the two parties have then simply exchanged their positions and are in each other's rear. So it was at Pea Ridge, when, after the defeat of McCulloch, Van Dorn and Price had "settled down" on our line of communication with Springfield, while we held theirs to Fayetteville. The chances were equal, relative to position, and it was only by good fortune that the Confederates came off as well as they did.—F. S.

The movement of Van Dorn during the night of the 6th was bold, well conceived, and would probably have been more successful if it had not been pushed too far out. If Van Dorn had formed his line with the left of Price's forces resting on the heights, west of Elkhorn Tavern, and McCulloch's immediately on its right, he would have gained three or four hours' time, and could have swept down upon us before 8 o'clock in the morning, when no preparations had been made to receive him; his two wings (Price's and McCulloch's) would not have been separated from each other by an interval of several miles, and his communications between Bentonville and his position would have been protected. Instead of following this course of action demanded by the unforeseen impediment on the road, he passed several miles farther to the north-east, and after gaining the Springfield road, he shifted the whole of Price's forces around to the south-east (toward the Huntsville road), consuming again much valuable time. In fact, instead of commencing his attack by the left at daylight on the 7th, as he expected to do, he did not commence it earnestly before 2 P. M., and instead of gaining the desirable position on the heights and fields which my divisions occupied the next day, he made his attack in Cross Timber Hollow, where our inferior forces had the advantage of defense and of concealing their weakness in the woods, ravines, and gullies of that wilderness. Price's troops fought very bravely, but so did ours; it therefore happened that when Carr's division had been forced back, even half a mile beyond Elkhorn Tavern, the assailants had spent so much of their force and sustained so great a loss, that they were unable to follow up their success by a last assault on our reduced and contracted line. Price's 6500 men with 38 guns could not overwhelm about 4500 with 23 guns (including the reënforcements from the First and Second Divisions). The fight on this part of the field was, at the beginning, a wild, isolated, irregular struggle of single batteries and their supports, sometimes almost hand to hand, instead of in serried and well-defined lines;—this accounts for the great losses on both sides. It was here that the two brigades of Vandever and Dodge, with the 9th and 4th Iowa, the 35th Illinois, the 24th and Phelps's Missouri regiment, Hayden's and Jones's batteries, and two mountain howitzers of Bowen's battalion, assisted by a part of the 1st Missouri and 3d Illinois Cavalry, withstood the incessant onslaught of the two Confederate brigades of Colonel Little and General Slack and the Missouri State Guards with the greatest tenacity, yielding only step by step, when exhausted by losses and without ammunition.

The death of McCulloch was not only fatal to his troops, but also a most serious blow to Van Dorn. Until 2 o'clock on the 7th, the latter had confidently expected to hear of successful action against our left wing; but he received no answer to the dispatch he had sent, and began to push forward his own wing. He succeeded, and when night fell made his headquarters at Elkhorn Tavern, where Carr and Major Weston of our army had been in the morning. But here he stopped. He says that by some misunderstanding the troops in the advance were called back (as they were at Shiloh); the true reason for their withdrawal, however, seems to have been their satisfaction with what they had done, and the assurance of completing the work in the morning.

UNION AND CONFEDERATE INDIANS IN THE CIVIL WAR.

BY WILEY BRITTON.

ELKHORN TAVERN, PEA RIDGE.
FROM A RECENT PHOTOGRAPH.

THE Cherokee, Creek, Choctaw, Chickasaw, and Seminole tribes were the only Indian tribes who took an active part in the civil war. Before the war very few of the Indians of these tribes manifested any interest in the question of slavery, and only a small number owned slave property. Slavery among them was not regarded in the same light as among the whites, for in many instances the slaves acted as if they were on an equality with their masters. But the tribes named occupied valuable territory, and the Confederate authorities lost no time in sending agents among them to win them over. When the Confederate agents first approached the full-blood leaders of the Cherokee and Creek tribes on the subject of severing their relations with the United States, the Indians expressed themselves cautiously but decidedly as preferring to remain neutral.

Conspicuous among those who took a decided stand against organizing the Indians to oppose the Federal Government was Hopoeithleyohola, the old chief of the Creek tribe. The Confederate agents had succeeded in winning over ex-Chief McIntosh, by appointing him colonel, but, perhaps, two-thirds of the people preferred to be guided by the advice of their venerable old chief, Hopoeithleyohola.

In the fall of 1861, Colonel Douglas H. Cooper, commanding the department of Indian operations under authority from the Confederate Government, made several ineffectual efforts to have a conference with the old chief for the purpose of effecting a peaceful settlement of the difficulties that were dividing the nation into two hostile camps. Finding Hopoeithleyohola unwavering in his loyalty to the United States, Colonel Cooper determined to force him into submission, destroy his power, or drive him out of the country, and at once commenced collecting forces, composed mostly of white troops, to attack him. In November and December, 1861, the battles of Chusto Talasah and Chustenahlah were fought, and the loyal Indians finally were defeated and forced to retire to Kansas in midwinter.

In the spring of 1862 the United States Government sent an expedition of five thousand men under Colonel William Weer, 10th Kansas Infantry, into the Indian Territory to drive out the Confederate forces of Pike and Cooper, and to restore the refugee Indians to their homes. After a short action at Locust Grove, near Grand Saline, Cherokee Nation, July 2d, Colonel Weer's cavalry captured Colonel Clarkson and part of his regiment of Missourians. On the 16th of July Captain Greeno, 6th Kansas Cavalry, captured Tahlequah, the capital of the Cherokee Nation, and on the 19th of July Colonel Jewell, 6th Kansas Cavalry, captured Fort Gibson, the most important point in the Indian Territory.

The Confederate forces were now driven out of all that part of the Indian country north of the Arkansas River, and the loyal Indians of the Cherokee, Creek, and Seminole nations were organized, by authority of the United States Government, into three regiments, each fully a thousand strong, for the defense of their country. The colonel and part of the field and line officers of each regiment were white officers. Most of the captains of companies were Indians. Colonel William A. Phillips, of Kansas, who was active in organizing these Indian regiments, commanded the Indian brigade from its organization to the close of the war. He took part with his Indian troops in the action at Locust Grove, C. N., and in the battles of Newtonia, Mo., Maysville, Ark., Prairie Grove, Ark., Honey Springs, C. N., Perryville, C. N., besides many other minor engagements.

In all the operations in which they participated they acquitted themselves creditably, and to the satisfaction of the Federal commander in the Indian Territory.

On the Confederate side, General Albert Pike and Colonel Douglas H. Cooper, in the fall and winter of 1861, organized three regiments of Indians from the Choctaw, Chickasaw, Cherokee, Creek, and Seminole nations or tribes, for service in the Indian Territory. These regiments, under General Pike, participated in the battle of Pea Ridge, Ark., on the 7th and 8th of March, 1862. In the five tribes named a battalion and parts of four regiments were raised for the Confederate service, but these amounted in all to perhaps not over 3500 men.

At the close of Mr. Buchanan's administration nearly all the United States Indian agents in the Indian Territory were secessionists, and the moment the Southern States commenced passing ordinances of secession, these men exerted their influence to get the five tribes committed to the Confederate cause. Occupying territory south of the Arkansas River, and having the secessionists of Arkansas on the east and those of Texas on the south for neighbors, the Choctaws and Chickasaws offered no decided opposition to the scheme. With the Cherokees, the most powerful and most civilized of the tribes of the Indian Territory, it was different. Their chief, John Ross, was opposed to hasty action, and at first favored neutrality, and in the summer of 1861 issued a proclamation, enjoining his people to observe a strictly neutral attitude during the war between the United States and the Southern States. In June, 1861, Albert Pike, a commissioner of the Confederate States, and General Ben. McCulloch, commanding the Confederate forces in western Arkansas and the Department of Indian Territory, visited Chief Ross with the view of having him make a treaty with the Confederacy. But he declined to make a treaty, and in the conference expressed himself as wishing to occupy, if possible, a neutral position during the war. A majority of the Cherokees, nearly all of whom were full-bloods, were known as Pin Indians, and were opposed to the South.

Commissioner Pike went away to make treaties with the less civilized Indian tribes of the plains, and in the mean time the battle of Wilson's Creek was fought, General Lyon killed, and the Union army defeated and forced to fall back from Springfield to Rolla.

Chief Ross now thought that the South would probably succeed in establishing her independence, and expressed a willingness to enter into a treaty with the Confederate authorities. On his return from the West in September, 1861, Commissioner Pike, at the request of Mr. Ross, went to Park Hill and made a treaty with the Cherokees. The treaties made with each tribe provided that the troops it raised should be used for home protection, and should not be taken out of the Indian Territory. Even before the treaty with Commissioner Pike, Chief Ross had commenced to organize a regiment composed nearly altogether of Pin Indians. John Drew, a stanch secessionist, was commissioned colonel, and William P. Ross lieutenant-colonel, of this regiment. Colonel Stand Watie, the leader of the secession party, had also commenced to raise a regiment of half-breeds for General McCulloch's division. As already stated, there were two factions among the Creeks, one of which was led by Hopoeithleyohola and the other by D. N. and Chitty McIntosh, who were sons of General William McIntosh, killed in 1825 by Hopoeithleyohola and his followers in Georgia, for making the treaty of Indian Springs. It is asserted by General Pike and others that with Hopoeithleyohola it was not a question of loyalty or disloyalty to the United States, but simply one of self-preservation;

that when he found the Confederate authorities had commissioned D. N. McIntosh as colonel of a Creek regiment, and Chitty McIntosh as lieutenant-colonel of a battalion of Creeks, he felt certain that the Indian troops thus being raised would be used to persecute and destroy him and his followers. In November, 1861, he started for Kansas, and was pursued and overtaken by the Confederate Creeks, Choctaws, Chickasaws, Cherokees, and Texans under Colonel Douglas H. Cooper. A fight took place in the night, and Colonel Drew's regiment of Cherokees, which had been raised by Chief Ross, went over to Hopoeithleyohola, and fought with him in the next day's desperate battle (known as the battle of Chusto Talasah), in which five hundred of the Union Indians were reported by Colonel Cooper to have been killed and wounded. ⸯ The Confederate Indians of Colonel Stand Watie's regiment, and those of Colonel Drew's regiment who had returned to the Confederate service under Pike and Cooper, also participated in the battle of Pea Ridge in March, 1862, where they were charged with scalping and mutilating the Federal dead on the field. General Pike, hearing of the scalping, called on the surgeon and assistant-surgeon of his field-hospital for reports, and in their reports they stated that they found one of the Federal dead who had been scalped. General Pike then issued an order, denouncing the outrage in the strongest language, and sent a copy of the order to General Curtis. General Pike claimed that part of the Indians were in McCulloch's corps in the first day's battle; and that the scalping was done at night in a quarter of the field not occupied by the Indian troops under his immediate command. After Pea Ridge the operations of the Confederate Indians under General Cooper and Colonel Stand Watie were confined, with a few exceptions, to the Indian Territory. In connection with white troops from Texas, they participated in several engagements with the Federal Indian brigade under Colonel Phillips, after he recaptured Fort Gibson in the spring of 1863; and they made frequent efforts to capture Federal supply trains from Fort Scott to Fort Gibson and Fort Smith, but were always unsuccessful. They fought very well when they had an opportunity to take shelter behind trees and logs, but could not easily be brought to face artillery, and a single shell thrown at them was generally sufficient to demoralize them and put them to flight.

ⸯ The position chosen by Hopoeithleyohola at Chusto Talasah, where he determined to make a stand and fight the Confederate forces, was naturally a very strong one to resist an attack made with small-arms. It was at a gorge of a bend of Bird Creek, the bend being in the form of a horse-shoe, and four hundred yards in length. The creek made up to the prairie on the side approached by the Confederate forces in an abrupt and precipitous bank about thirty feet high. On the opposite side of this precipitous bank was the inside of the horse-shoe or bend, which was densely covered with heavy timber, cane, and tangled thickets. The position was also strengthened by felled trees and by the creek forming the bend or horse-shoe. The creek was deep and was fordable only at certain places known to the Union Indians.

In this bend Hopoeithleyohola's forces were posted after they were obliged to fall back in the preliminary skirmish. A house and crib at the mouth of the bend served as a shelter for a while, from which his sharp-shooters kept back the Confederates. The Union Indians, however, were finally driven from this position back into the bend, contesting the ground with much obstinacy. The Confederate troops made repeated efforts to dislodge them from the bend, but without success. Every time a detachment of Hopoeithleyohola's warriors showed themselves in an opening or in the prairie, the Confederates charged them to the timber, when a volley from the concealed Union Indians threw the charging column into confusion and sent it back in a hasty retreat. Night coming on put an end to the fight.— W. B.

THE OPPOSING FORCES AT PEA RIDGE, ARK.

The composition and losses of each army as here stated give the gist of all the data obtainable in the Official Records. K stands for killed; w for wounded; m w for mortally wounded; m for captured or missing; c for captured.—EDITORS.

COMPOSITION AND LOSSES OF THE UNION ARMY.

Brig.-Gen. Samuel R. Curtis.

FIRST AND SECOND DIVISIONS, Brig.-Gen. Franz Sigel. *First Division,* Col. Peter J. Osterhaus. *First Brigade:* 25th Ill., Col. William N. Coler; 44th Ill., Col. Charles Knobelsdorff; 17th Mo., Major August H. Poten. Brigade loss: k, 4; w, 22; m, 11 = 37. *Second Brigade,* Col. Nicholas Greusel. 36th Ill., Col. Nicholas Greusel; 12th Mo., Major Hugo Wangelin; Illinois Cavalry (2 Cos.), Captains Albert Jenks and Henry A. Smith. Brigade loss: k, 7; w, 66; m, 36 = 109. *Artillery:* Mo. Battery, Capt. Martin Welfley; 4th Ohio Battery, Capt. Louis Hoffmann. Loss: w, 6; m, 4 = 10. *Second Division,* Brig.-Gen. Alexander Asboth (w). Staff loss: w, 1. *First Brigade,* Col. Frederick Schaefer: 2d Mo., Lieut.-Col. Bernard Laiboldt; 15th Mo., Col. Francis J. Joliat. Brigade loss: k, 8; w, 34; m, 22 = 64. *Unattached:* Frémont Hussars Mo. Cavalry, Major Emeric Meszaros; 5th Mo. Cavalry (Benton Hussars), Col. Joseph Nemett; 1st Mo. Horse Battery, Capt. G. M. Elbert; 2d Ohio Battery, Lieut. W. B. Chapman. Loss: k, 12; w, 29: m, 14 = 55.

THIRD DIVISION, Col. Jefferson C. Davis. *First Brigade,* Col. Thomas Pattison : 8th Ind., Col. William P. Benton: 18th Ind., Lieut.-Col. Henry D. Washburn; 22d Ind., Lieut.-Col. John A. Hendricks (m w), Major David W.

Daily, Jr.; 1st Ind. Battery, Capt. Martin Klauss. Brigade loss: k, 17; w, 88; m, 6 = 111. *Second Brigade,* Col. Julius White; 37th Ill., Lieut.-Col. M. S. Barnes; 59th Ill., Lieut.-Col. C. H. Frederick; Peoria Ill. Battery, Capt. P. Davidson. Brigade loss: k, 29; w, 195; m, 3 = 227. *Cavalry:* 1st Mo., Col. C. A. Ellis. Loss: k, 2; w, 2; m, 2 = 6.

FOURTH DIVISION, Col. Eugene A. Carr (w). Staff loss : w, 1. *First Brigade,* Col. Grenville M. Dodge: 35th Ill., Col. Gustavus A. Smith (w), Lieut.-Col. William P. Chandler (c); 4th Iowa, Lieut.-Col. John Galligan (w) ; 1st Iowa Battery, Capt. Junius A. Jones (w), Lieut. V. J. David. Brigade loss: k, 35 ; w, 200; m, 55 = 290. *Second Brigade,* Col. William Vandever: 9th Iowa, Lieut.-Col. Francis J. Herron (w and c), Major William H. Coyl (w) ; Phelps's Mo., Col. John S. Phelps (w); 3d Ill. Cavalry, Major John McConnell ; 3d Iowa Battery, Captain Mortimer M. Hayden. Brigade loss: k, 61; w, 300; m, 30 = 391. *Unattached:* 3d Iowa Cavalry, Col. Cyrus Bussey (during a part of the battle Col. Bussey had command of other troops in addition to his own regiment), Lieut.-Col. Henry H. Trimble (w); Bowen's Battalion Mo. Cavalry, Major Wm. D. Bowen; 3d Mo. Infantry, Major Joseph Conrad ; 24th Mo. Infantry, Major Eli W. Weston. Loss: k, 28 ; w, 36 ; m, 18 = 82.

Total loss in the Union Army (revised returns) : 203 killed, 980 wounded, and 201 captured or missing,— total, 1384.

COMPOSITION AND LOSSES OF THE CONFEDERATE ARMY.

Major-General Earl Van Dorn.

MISSOURI STATE GUARD, Major-General Sterling Price. CONFEDERATE VOLUNTEERS: *Escort,* Cearnal's Battalion Cavalry, Lieut.-Col. J. T. Cearnal (w). *First Brigade,* Col. Henry Little : 1st Cavalry, Col. Elijah Gates; 1st Infantry, Col. John Q. Burbridge ; 2d Infantry, Col. Benjamin A. Rives (m w), Lieut.-Col. J. A. Pritchard; 1st Battery, Capt. William Wade; 2d Battery, Capt. S. Churchill Clark (k), Lieut. James L. Farris. *Second Brigade,* Brig.-Gen. William Y. Slack (m w), Col. Thomas H. Rosser: Battalion Infantry, Col. John T. Hughes; Battalion Infantry, Major R. S. Bevier ; Battalion Infantry, Col. Thomas H. Rosser; Battalion Cavalry, Col. G. W. Riggins; Light Battery, Capt. Wm. Lucas. Brigade loss : k, 5; w, 37 = 42. *Third Brigade,* Col. Colton Greene. Brigade loss: k, 6; w, 59 = 65. STATE TROOPS, *Second Division,* Brig.-Gen. Martin E. Green. *Third Division,* Col. John B. Clark, Jr. : 1st Infantry, Major Rucker (w) ; 2d Infantry, Col. Congreve Jackson ; 3d Infantry, Major Hutchinson ; 4th and 5th Infantry (consolidated), Col. J. A. Poindexter (w) ; 6th Infantry, Lieut.-Col. Peacher. Division loss: k, 11 ; w, 101; m, 35 = 147. *Fifth Division,* Col. James P. Saunders: detachments of infantry, cavalry, and Kelly's battery of artillery. Division loss: k, 9; w, 32 = 41. *Sixth Division,* Major D. H. Lindsay: detachments of infantry and Gorham's battery of artillery. Division loss: w, 13 ; m, 34 = 47. *Seventh and Ninth Divisions,* Brig.-Gen. D. M. Frost: detachments of infantry and cavalry and Guibor's and MacDonald's batteries of artillery ; also included the Third Brigade

of Volunteers given above. *Eighth Division,* Brig.-Gen. James S. Rains: Infantry under Col. William H. Erwin, Lieut.-Cols. John P. Bowman, A. J. Pearcy, and Stemmons ; Bledsoe's battery, and Shelby's company of cavalry. Division loss: k, 2 ; w, 26 = 28.

McCULLOCH'S DIVISION, Brig.-Gen. Ben. McCulloch (k), Col. E. Greer. *Infantry Brigade,* Col. Louis Hébert (c), Col. Evander McNair: 4th Ark., Col. Evander McNair, Lieut.-Col. Samuel Ogden; 14th Ark., Col. M. C. Mitchell; 16th Ark., Col. J. .F Hill; 17th Ark., Col. F. A. Rector; 21st Ark., Col. D. McRae; 3d Louisiana, Major W. F. Tunnard (c), Capt. W. S. Gunnell. *Cavalry Brigade,* Brig.-Gen. James McIntosh (k): 1st Ark. Mounted Rifles, Col. J. T. Churchill; 2d Ark. Mounted Rifles, Col. B. T. Embry; 3d Texas, Col. E. Greer, Lieut.-Col. Walter P. Lane; 4th Texas, Col. Wm. B. Sims (w), Lieut.-Col. William Quayle; 6th Texas, Col. B. W. Stone ; 11th Texas, Lieut.-Col. James J. Dimond. *Artillery:* Hart's, Provence's, Gaines's, and Good's batteries.

PIKE'S COMMAND, Brig.-Gen. Albert Pike. Cherokee Regiment, Col. Stand Watie; Cherokee Regiment, Col. John Drew; Creek Regiment, Col. D. N. McIntosh; Squadron Texas Cavalry, Capt. O. G. Welch.

OTHER TROOPS (not included in preceding roster): 1st Battalion Ark. Cavalry, Major W. H. Brooks; Battalion Texas Cavalry, Major R. P. Crump; Battalion Texas Mounted Rifles, Major J. W. Whitfield; Teel's Texas Battery; 19th Ark. Infantry, Lieut.-Col. P. R. Smith ; 22d Ark. Infantry, Col. G. W. King.

The Confederate loss is reported at 800 to 1000 killed and wounded, and between 200 and 300 prisoners.

STRENGTH OF THE OPPOSING FORCES.

The effective force of the Union Army did not exceed 10,500 infantry and cavalry, with 49 pieces of artillery. (See "Official Records," VIII., p. 196.)

The effective strength of the Confederate Army was as follows: Price's command, 6818, with 8 batteries of

artillery ("Official Records," VIII., p. 305); McCulloch's command, 8384, with 4 batteries of 18 pieces ("Official Records," VIII., p. 763); and Pike's command, 1000 ("Official Records," VIII., p. 288), making an aggregate of 16,202 infantry and cavalry.

BUILDING THE EADS GUN-BOATS AT CARONDELET. FROM A PHOTOGRAPH.

RECOLLECTIONS OF FOOTE AND THE GUN–BOATS.

BY CAPTAIN JAMES B. EADS. |

SOON after the surrender of Fort Sumter, while in St. Louis, I received a letter from Attorney-General Bates, dated Washington, April 17th, in which he said: "Be not surprised if you are called here suddenly by telegram. If called, come instantly. In a certain contingency it will be necessary to have the aid of the most thorough knowledge of our Western rivers and the use of steam on them, and in that event I have advised that you should be consulted." The call by telegraph followed close upon the letter. I hurried

| Of the services of Captain Eads to the Western flotilla, the Reverend C. B. Boynton says, in his "History of the Navy":

"During the month of July, 1861, the Quartermaster-General advertised for proposals to construct a number of iron-clad gun-boats for service on the Mississippi River. The bids were opened on the 5th of August, and Mr. Eads was found to be the best bidder for the whole number, both in regard to the time of completion and price. . . . On the 7th of August, 1861, Mr. Eads signed a contract with Quartermaster-General Meigs to construct these seven vessels ready for their crews and armaments in sixty-five days. At this early period the people in the border States, especially in the slave States, had not yet learned to accommodate themselves to a state of war. The pursuits of peace were interrupted; but the energy and enterprise which were to provide the vast material required for an energetic prosecution of the war had not then been aroused. None could foresee the result, and a spirit of doubt and distrust pervaded financial and commercial circles. It was at this time that the contractor returned to St. Louis with an obligation to perform what, under ordinary circumstances, would have been deemed by most men an impossibility. Rolling-mills, machine-shops, foundries, forges, and saw-mills were all idle. The demands of peace had ceased for months before, and the working-men were enlisting, or seeking in States more quiet their accustomed employment. The engines that were to drive this our first iron-clad fleet were yet to be built. The timber to form their hulls was uncut in the forests, and the huge rollers and machinery that were to form their iron armor were not yet constructed. The rapidity with which all these various parts were to be supplied forbade depending alone on any two or three establishments in the country, no matter how great were their resources. The signatures were scarcely dry upon this important contract before persons in different parts of the country were employed upon the work through telegraphic orders issued from Washington. Special agents were dispatched in every direction, and saw-mills were simultaneously occupied in cutting the timber required in the construction of the vessels, in Kentucky, Tennessee, Illinois, Indiana, Ohio, Minnesota, and Missouri; and railroads, steamboats, and barges were engaged for its immediate transportation. Nearly all of the largest machine-shops and foundries in St. Louis, and many small ones, were at once set at work day and night, and the telegraph lines between St. Louis and Pittsburgh and Cincinnati were occupied frequently for hours in transmitting instructions to similar establishments in those cities for the construction of the twenty-one steam-engines and the five-and-thirty steam-boilers that were to propel the fleet. . . . Within two weeks not less than four thousand men were engaged in the various details of its construction. Neither the sanctity of the Sabbath nor the darkness of night was permitted to interrupt it. The workmen on the hulls were promised a handsome bonus in money for each one who stood steadfastly at the work until it was completed, and many thousands of dollars were thus gratuitously paid by Mr. Eads when it was finished. On the 12th of October, 1861, the first United States iron-clad,

to Washington, where I was introduced to the Secretary of the Navy, the Hon. Gideon Welles, and to Captain G. V. Fox, afterward Assistant Secretary. In the August following I was to construct 7 gun-boats, which, according to the contract, were to draw 6 feet of water, carry 13 heavy guns each, be plated with 2½-inch iron, and have a speed of 9 miles an hour. The *De Kalb* (at first called the *St. Louis)* was the type of the other six, named the *Carondelet*, *Cincinnati*, *Louisville*, *Mound City*, *Cairo*, and *Pittsburgh*. They were 175 feet long, 51½ feet beam; the flat sides sloped at an angle of about thirty-five degrees, and the front and rear casemates corresponded with the sides, the stern-wheel being entirely covered by the rear casemate. Each was pierced for three bow guns, eight broadside guns (four on a side), and two stern guns. Before these seven gun-boats were completed, I engaged to convert the snag-boat *Benton* into an armored vessel of still larger dimensions.

After completing the seven and dispatching them down the Mississippi to Cairo, I was requested by Foote (who then went by the title of "flag-officer," the title of admiral not being recognized at that time in our navy), as a special favor to him, to accompany the *Benton*, the eighth one of the fleet, in her passage down to Cairo. It was in December, and the water was falling rapidly.

The *Benton* had been converted from the U. S. snag-boat *Benton* into the most powerful iron-clad of the fleet. She was built with two hulls about twenty feet apart, very strongly braced together. She had been purchased by General Frémont while he was in command of the Western Department, and had been sent to my ship-yard for alteration into a gun-boat. I had the space between the two hulls planked, so that a continuous bottom extended from the outer side of one hull to the outer side of the other. The upper side was decked over in the same manner; and by extending the outer sides of the two hulls forward until they joined each other at a new stem, which received them, the twin boats became one wide, strong, and substantial hull. The new bottom did not extend to the stern of the hull, but was brought up to the deck fifty feet forward of the stern, so as to leave a space for

with her boilers and engines on board, was launched in Carondelet, Missouri, in forty-five days from the laying of her keel.* She was named the *St. Louis*, by Rear-Admiral Foote, in honor of the city. When the fleet was transferred from the War Department to the Navy, this name was changed to *Baron de Kalb*, there being at that time a vessel commissioned in the Navy called the *St. Louis*. In ten days after the *De Kalb* the *Carondelet* was launched, and the *Cincinnati*, *Louisville*, *Mound City*, *Cairo*, and *Pittsburgh* followed in rapid succession. An eighth vessel [the *Benton*], larger, more powerful and superior in every respect, was also undertaken before the hulls of the first seven had fairly assumed shape. . . . Thus one individual put in construction and pushed to completion within one hundred days a powerful squadron of eight steamers, aggregating five thousand tons, capable of steaming at nine knots per hour, each heavily armored, fully equipped, and all ready for their armament of one hundred and seven large guns. The fact that such a work was done is nobler praise than any that can be bestowed by words.

It is to be regretted, however, that the promptness and energy of the man who thus created an iron-clad navy on the Mississippi were not met on the part of the Government with an equal degree of faithfulness in performing its part of the contract. On one pretext or another, the stipulated payments for the work were delayed by the War Department until the default assumed such magnitude that nothing but the assistance rendered by patriotic and confiding friends enabled the contractor, after exhausting his own ample means, to complete the fleet. Besides the honorable reputation which flows from success in such a work, he has the satisfaction of reflecting that it was with vessels at the time his own property that the brilliant capture of Fort Henry was accomplished, and the conquest of Donelson and Island Number Ten achieved. The ever-memorable midnight passage of Number Ten by the *Pittsburgh* and *Carondelet*, which compelled the surrender of that powerful stronghold, was performed by vessels furnished four or five months previous by the same contractor, and at the time unpaid for."   EDITORS.

* It was stipulated in the contract that the gun-boats should be delivered, October 10th, at Cairo. As a matter of fact, they were not sent to Cairo until the latter part of November, and considerable work still remained to be done before their completion. They were finished and accepted, January 15th, 1862, and put in commission the next day. The delay was in part due to lack of funds and in part to the necessity of alteration in the design of the vessels. Had they been completed in the time specified, the Mississippi campaign, from Island Number Ten to Vicksburg, would probably have been over before Farragut passed the forts at New Orleans.

EDITORS.

THE "DE KALB," FORMERLY THE "ST. LOUIS" (TYPE OF THE "CARONDELET," "CINCINNATI," "LOUISVILLE,"
"MOUND CITY," "CAIRO," AND "PITTSBURGH"). FROM A PHOTOGRAPH.

a central wheel with which the boat was to be propelled. This wheel was
turned by the original engines of the snag-boat, each of the engines having
formerly turned an independent wheel on the outside of the twin boat. In
this manner the *Benton* became a war vessel of about seventy-five feet beam,
a greater breadth, perhaps, than that of any war vessel then afloat. She was
about two hundred feet long. A slanting casemate, covered with iron plates,
was placed on her sides and across her bow and stern; and the wheel was
protected in a similar manner. The casemate on the sides and bow was covered with iron 3½ inches thick; the wheel-house and stern with lighter plates,
like the first seven boats built by me. She carried 16 guns,—7 32-pounders,
2 9-inch guns, and 7 army 42-pounders.

The wish of Admiral Foote to have me see this boat safely to Cairo was
prompted by his knowledge that I had had experience in the management of
steamboats upon the river, and his fear that she would be detained by
grounding. Ice had just begun to float in the Mississippi when the *Benton*
put out from my ship-yard at Carondelet for the South. Some 30 or 40 miles
below St. Louis she grounded. Under the direction of Captain Winslow, who
commanded the vessel, Lieutenant Bishop, executive officer of the ship, an
intelligent and energetic young man, set the crew at work. An anchor was
put out for the purpose of hauling her off. My advice was not asked with
reference to this first proceeding, and although I had been requested by
Admiral Foote to accompany the vessel, he had not instructed the captain,
so far as I knew, to be guided by my advice in case of difficulty. After they
had been working all night to get the boat afloat, she was harder on than
ever; moreover, the water had fallen about six inches. I then volunteered
the opinion to Captain Winslow that if he would run hawsers ashore in a cer-

tain direction, directly opposite to that in which he had been trying to move the boat, she could be got off. He replied, very promptly, "Mr. Eads, if you will undertake to get her off, I shall be very willing to place the entire crew under your direction." I at once accepted the offer; and Lieutenant Bishop was called up and instructed to obey my directions. Several very large hawsers had been put on board of the boat for the fleet at Cairo. One of the largest was got out and secured to a large tree on the shore, and as heavy a strain was put upon it as the cable would be likely to bear. As the water was still falling, I ordered out a second one, and a third, and a fourth, until five or six eleven-inch hawsers were heavily strained in the effort to drag the broad-bottomed vessel off the bar. There were three steam capstans on the bow of the vessel, and these were used in tightening the strain by luffs upon the hawsers. One of the hawsers was led through a snatch-block fastened by a large chain to a ring-bolt in the side of the vessel. I was on the upper deck of the vessel near Captain Winslow when the chain which held this block broke. It was made of iron one and one-eighth inches in diameter, and the link separated into three pieces. The largest, being one-half of the link, was found on the shore at a distance of at least five hundred feet. Half of the remainder struck the iron

plating on the bow of the boat, making an indentation half the thickness of one's finger in depth. The third piece struck Captain Winslow on the fleshy part of the arm, cutting through his coat and the muscles of his arm. The wound was a very painful one, but he bore it as might be expected. The iron had probably cut an inch and a half into the arm between the shoulder and the elbow. In the course of the day the *Benton* was floated, and proceeded on her voyage down the river without further delay. Captain Winslow soon after departed for his home on leave of absence. On his recovery he was placed in command of the *Kearsarge*, and to that accident he owed, perhaps, the fame of being the captor of the *Alabama*.

When the *Benton* arrived at Cairo she was visited by all the officers of the army and navy stationed there, and was taken, on that or the following day, on a trial trip a few miles down the river. The *Essex*, in command of Captain William D. Porter, was lying four or five miles below the mouth of the Ohio on the Kentucky shore. As the *Benton* passed up, on her return from this little expedition, Captain Porter offered his congratulations to Foote on the apparent excellence of the boat. "Yes," replied Foote, "but she is almost too slow."

"Plenty fast enough to fight with," was Porter's rejoinder.

Very soon after this (early in the spring of 1862) I was called to Washington, with the request to prepare plans for still lighter iron-clad vessels, the draught of those which I had then completed being only about six feet. The later plans were for vessels that should be capable of going up the Tennessee and the Cumberland. As rapidly as possible I prepared and presented for the inspection of Secretary Welles and his able assistant, Captain

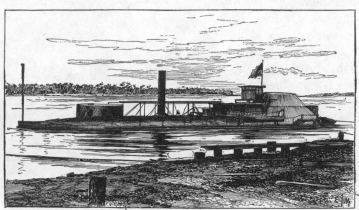

Fox, plans of vessels drawing five feet. They were not acceptable to Captain Fox, who said: "We want vessels much lighter than that."

"But you want them to carry a certain thickness

THE "OSAGE" (TWIN OF THE "NEOSHO"). FROM A PHOTOGRAPH.

of iron?" I replied.

"Yes, we want them to be proof against heavy shot—to be plated and heavily plated,—but they must be of much lighter draught."

THE "CHICKASAW" (TYPE OF THE "MILWAUKEE," "WINNEBAGO," AND "KICKAPOO"). FROM A PHOTOGRAPH.

After the interview I returned with the plans to my hotel, and commenced a revision of them; and in the course of a few days I presented the plans for the *Osage* and the *Neosho*. These vessels, according to my recollection, were about forty-five feet beam on deck, their sides slanting outward, and the tops of the gunwales rising only about six inches above the surface of the water, so as to leave very little space to be covered with the plating, which extended two and a half feet down under water on these slanting sides. The deck of the vessel, rising from six inches above water, curved upward about four feet higher at center; and this was covered all over with iron an inch thick. The plating on the sides was two and a half inches thick. Each vessel had a rotating turret, carrying two eleven-inch guns, the turret being six inches thick, but extending only a few feet above the deck of the vessel. I was very anxious to construct these turrets after a plan which I had devised, quite different from the Ericsson or Coles systems, and in which the guns should be operated by steam. But, within a month after the engagement at Fort Donelson, the memorable contest between the *Merrimac* and the *Monitor* occurred, whereupon the Navy Department insisted on Ericsson turrets being placed upon these two vessels.

At the same time the department was anxious to have four larger vessels for operations on the lower Mississippi River, which should have two turrets each, and it consented that I should place one of my turrets on each of two of these vessels (the *Chickasaw* and the *Milwaukee*) at my own risk, to be replaced with Ericsson's in case of failure. These were the first turrets in which the guns were manipulated by steam, and they were fired every forty-five seconds. The *Osage* and *Neosho*, with their armaments, stores, and everything on board, drew only three and a half feet of water, and steamed about nine miles an hour. While perfecting those plans, I prepared the designs for the larger vessels (the *Chickasaw, Milwaukee, Winnebago,* and *Kickapoo*), and when these were approved by Captain Fox and the officers of the navy to whom they were submitted at Washington, Mr. Welles expressed the wish that I should confer with Admiral Foote about them before proceeding to build them, inasmuch as the experience which he had had at Forts Henry and Donelson and elsewhere would be of great value, and might enable him to suggest improvements in them. I therefore hastened from Washington to Island Number Ten, a hundred miles below Cairo, on the Mississippi River, where Foote's flotilla was then engaged.

In the railway train a gentleman who sat in front of me, learning that I had constructed Foote's vessels, introduced himself as Judge Foote of Cleveland, a brother of the Admiral. Among other interesting matters, he related an anecdote of one of his little daughters who was just learning to read. After the capture of Fort Henry the squadron was brought back to Cairo for repairs, and, on the Sunday following, the crews, with their gallant flag-officer, attended one of the churches in Cairo. Admiral Foote was a thorough Christian gentleman and an excellent impromptu speaker. Upon this occasion, after the congregation had assembled, some one whispered to him that the minister was ill and would be unable to officiate; whereupon the admiral went up into the pulpit himself, and after the usual prayer and hymn he selected as the text John xiv. 1, "Let not your heart be troubled: ye believe in God, believe also in me." Upon this text he delivered what was declared to be an excellent sermon, or exhortation, after which he dismissed the congregation. An account of the sermon was widely published in the papers at the time, and came into the hands of the little niece just referred to. After she had read it, she exclaimed to her father: "Uncle Foote did not say that right." "Say what right?" asked the father. "Why, when he preached." "What did he say?" "He said, 'Let not your heart be troubled: ye believe in

FROM A PHOTOGRAPH.

REAR-ADMIRAL ANDREW HULL FOOTE.

God, believe also in *me.*'" "Well, what should he have said?" inquired the father. "Why, he ought to have said, 'Let not your heart be troubled: ye believe in God, believe also in *the gun-boats.*'"

On arriving at Cairo, I found Representative Elihu B. Washburne, afterward our minister to France, waiting for an opportunity to visit the army, then in Missouri, in the neighborhood of Island Number Ten, coöperating with Admiral Foote in the reduction of that stronghold. We embarked together on a small tug-boat which carried the mail down to the fleet. We arrived and landed alongside the flag-ship *Benton*, and were cordially greeted by Admiral Foote. I presented a letter which I had brought from the Secretary of the Navy. We withdrew to his cabin to consider the plans of the four new gun-boats. Mr. Washburne was sent to the Missouri shore. After discussing the plans of the new boats for fifteen or twenty minutes, we returned to the deck.

At the time we landed, the *Benton* and the other boats of the fleet were anchored between two and three miles above the Confederate forts, and were then throwing their shells into the enemy's works. When we boarded the *Benton* Admiral Foote had his lorgnette in his hand, and through it was watching the flight of each shell discharged from the guns of his ship. He resumed this occupation when we came up on deck, until, after a shot or two had been fired, one of his officers approached and handed him a dozen or more letters which had been brought down in the mail. While still conversing with me, his eye glanced over them as he held them in his hand, and he selected one which he proceeded to open. Before reading probably four lines, he turned to me with great calmness and composure, and said, "Mr. Eads, I must ask you to excuse me for a few minutes while I go down to my cabin. This letter brings me the news of the death of my son, about thirteen years old, who I had hoped would live to be the stay and support of his mother."

Without further remark, and without giving the slightest evidence of his feelings to any one, he left me and went to his cabin. I was, of course, deeply grieved; and when he returned after an absence of not more than fifteen minutes, still perfectly composed, I endeavored to divert his mind from his affliction by referring to the plans and to my interview with his brother. I told him also the anecdote of his little niece which his brother had related, and this served to clothe his face with a temporary smile. I then asked him if he would be kind enough to assign me some place where I could sleep on the *Benton* that night. It was then probably 3 o'clock in the day. He replied that I must not stay on board. I said that I had come down for that very purpose, since I wanted to see how the *Benton* and the other boats worked under fire. I was not particular where I slept; any place would do for me; I did not want to turn any of the officers out of their rooms.

With a look of great gravity and decision, he replied:

"Mr. Eads, I cannot permit you to stay here a moment after the tug is ready to return. There is no money in the world which would justify me in risking my life here; and you have no duty here to perform, as I have, which requires you to risk yours. You *must not* stay," emphasizing the words very distinctly! "You must return, both you and Mr. Washburne, as soon as the tug is ready to go."

I felt somewhat disappointed at this, for I had fully expected to spend a day at least on board the *Benton*, and to visit the other vessels of the fleet, with many of the officers of which I was well acquainted. I did not believe there was much danger in remaining, for the shells of the enemy seemed to fall short;

REAR-ADMIRAL HENRY WALKE, COMMANDER OF THE "TYLER," AND AFTERWARD OF THE "CARON-DELET." FROM A PHOTOGRAPH.

but, within fifteen minutes after this, one of these interesting missiles struck the water fifty or a hundred feet from the side of the *Benton*. This satisfied me that Foote was right, and I did not insist on staying.

The Admiral was a great sufferer from sick headache. I remember visiting him in his room at the Planter's House in St. Louis, a day or two after the battle of Belmont, when he was suffering very severely from one of these attacks, which lasted two days. He was one of the most fascinating men in company that I have ever met, being full of anecdote, and having a graceful, easy flow of language. He was likewise, ordinarily, one of the most amiable-looking of men; but when angered, as I once saw him, his face impressed me as being most savage and demoniacal, and I can imagine that at the head of a column or in an attack he would have been invincible. Some idea of the moral influence that he possessed over men may be gained from the fact that, long before the war, when commanding the United States fleet of three vessels in Chinese waters, he converted every officer and man in the fleet to the principles of temperance, and had every one of them sign the pledge. I believe that this was the beginning of the reform movement in the navy which led to the disuse of the rations of grog which used to be served to the sailors on shipboard at stated hours every day.

From my knowledge of Foote, I think that there is no doubt that if his health had not given way so early in the war, he would have gained laurels like those so gallantly won by Farragut. And, aside from his martial character, no officer ever surpassed him in those evidences of genuine refinement and delicacy which mark the true gentleman.

NOTES ON THE LIFE OF ADMIRAL FOOTE.

BY HIS BROTHER, JOHN A. FOOTE.

THERE were six boys and no girls in my father's family. I was the eldest and am the only survivor. The Admiral was next to me in age. We were brought up, I think, upon purely patriarchal and Puritan principles, so I was surprised that my father, on taking me to the law school at Litchfield, should so far unbend as to say to me, " John, I think I have been able to control my family pretty well, all except Andrew — I have never tried to do more than to guide him." In subsequent life I have thought that in that avowal I find the secret of the Admiral's unconquerable will and of his success as a naval commander. He was very genial and good-natured, and as a subaltern implicitly obedient. His interest in the Christian religion transformed him by subduing his will. There never was any cant about him, and he seemed to enjoy life and to get much out of it. A younger brother of ours said to me, " The world is a clog to me, but it seems to be a help to Andrew." This justly expressed my opinion of his very decided and cheerful Christian character. I once visited him when he was stationed at the Naval Asylum at Philadelphia. Asking of the sentinel before the door for Lieutenant Foote, I was answered that he was in his *church*, which proved to be only a large room, at the end of the hall, where I halted to catch his earnest entreaties to his hearers to become good men. Such meetings, or a Sunday-school, or both, he sustained at all his stations ashore or afloat. At one time he doubted whether he could conscientiously continue in the navy. My father having asked him if he did not think a navy necessary, he replied, " Certainly, the seas must be policed." Then added my father, " Should the navy be in charge of good or bad men ?" " Of good men," he replied — and declared that this view removed his doubts.

Later in life he got bravely over such doubts. It was enough for him that as an officer of the Government he was bound to do and dare everything to put down the rebellion. I was trying still further to intensify him, by other reasons, when he turned on me and said : " John, will you fight ?" He saw that I hesitated, and at once added : " I will fight — my life is in my hand for this cause ; and if you won't fight, don't talk quite so loud."

When he began to descend the Mississippi I noticed that he went very slowly, and lay off at a distance when attacking any position. I informed him that I thought the people wanted dash and close fighting — something sharp and decisive. He replied : " Don't you know that my boats are the only protection you have upon your rivers against the rebel gun-boats — that without my flotilla everything on your rivers, your cities and towns would be at the mercy of the enemy ? My first duty then is to care for my boats, if I am to

protect you. Now when I ran up the Tennessee and the Cumberland, and attacked Fort Henry and Fort Donelson, if my boats were rendered unmanageable as my flag-ship was at Donelson, the current took care of me by carrying me away from the enemy's works. But all this is changed when I descend the Mississippi. Then my boats, if they become unmanageable, are carried directly into the hands of the enemy." I saw the point and had to give in. As to the comparative value of the two arms of the service — the Army and the Navy — in clearing the Western rivers of the Confederates, my brother said they were like blades of shears — united, invincible ; separated, almost useless.

About the middle of May, 1862, being much enfeebled by his wounds received at Fort Donelson and by illness, he made his home at my house in Cleveland, Ohio, until about midsummer of that year. During this time he retained his command, and was in constant receipt of reports from the fleet.

June 17th he wrote to the Navy Department :

" If it will not be considered premature, I wish further to remark, that when this rebellion is crushed and a squadron is fitted out to enforce the new treaty for the suppression of the African slave-trade, I should be pleased to have command. But so long as the rebellion continues, it will be my highest ambition to be actively employed in aiding its suppression."

His interest in Africa was intense. His one book was called " Africa and the American Flag."

In a message to Congress, dated July 6th, 1862, President Lincoln recommended a vote of thanks to Admiral Foote, which was given. After his return to duty he was for several months at the head of one of the new bureaus of the Navy Department, and notwithstanding the state of his health, after the failure of the attack with monitors and iron-clads upon the Charleston defenses, Admiral Foote was appointed, June 4th, 1863, to the command of the South Atlantic Squadron ; but he was stricken down on his way to his command. I was told that Professor Bache — of the Medical Staff at the New York Navy Yard, where Foote had been stationed at the commencement of the war — said that he dreaded to tell the Admiral that his attack was a fatal one, as he thought his heart was set upon attempting to take Charleston. But, instead of his being affected by the solemn intelligence, Foote replied that he felt he was prepared and that he was glad to be through with guns and war. He died at the Astor House, in the city of New York, on the 26th of the same month. The mother of General Tilghman, who surrendered Fort Henry, was at the hotel, and, learning of his illness, tendered her sympathies. His native city of New Haven gave a public funeral, which was attended by the governor and legislature.

GENERAL POLK AND THE BATTLE OF BELMONT.

BY HIS SON, DR. WILLIAM M. POLK, CAPTAIN, C. S. A.

ON the 1st of November, 1861, General Frémont ordered General Grant at Cairo, and General C. F. Smith at Paducah, to hold their commands in readiness for a demonstration upon Columbus, Kentucky, a strong position then occupied by about ten thousand Confederate troops under General Leonidas Polk. The object of the proposed demonstration was to cover an effort to be made to drive General Jeff. Thompson from south-east Missouri; and at the same time to check the sending of reënforcements to Price. In accordance with this general plan, on the 4th and 6th Grant moved Colonels R. J. Oglesby, W. H. L. Wallace, and J. B. Plummer in the direction of the town of Sikeston, Mo. Next he ordered the garrison at Fort Holt opposite Cairo to advance in the direction of Columbus, and early on the morning of the 7th, with a force of about 3500 men of all arms, convoyed by the gun-boats *Lexington* and *Tyler*, he steamed down the Mississippi River toward the same objective point. Smith meanwhile from the direction of Paducah threw forward his column of 2000 men.

The mobilization of these various commands, some 12,000 men in all, was duly reported to Polk, and with the report came rumors of the enemy's designs. Polk, however, did not believe that so extensive a movement was directed against Thompson, whose entire force numbered not more than 1500 men, then encamped far down toward Arkansas. Nor could he think that the plea of preventing the sending of reënforcements to Price was genuine, as he knew that there were no troops then (nor were there likely to be any) in motion to join Price. On the other hand, having for some weeks had every reason to expect a determined effort on Grant's part to dislodge him, he naturally supposed that the looked-for attack was at hand.

The force at his disposal, including the garrison of Columbus, was then about 10,000 men of all arms. At Belmont, opposite Columbus, Polk had established a camp of observation, which was then occupied by one regiment of infantry, a battery of artillery, and a squadron of cavalry. In order to command the approaches to this position by the batteries on the high ground at Columbus, the trees had been felled for some distance along the west bank, and the fallen timber had been so placed as to form an abatis capable of obstructing the advance of an enemy. This camp Grant decided to attack.

Accordingly, at about 8 o'clock on the morning of the 7th he disembarked his force on the Missouri shore, some five miles above Belmont, and ordered the gun-boats to drop below and engage the batteries at Columbus. Quickly forming his column, Grant pushed for the Confederate camp.

Polk meanwhile sent General McCown with a force of infantry and artillery up the east bank of the river, and, learning of the landing of the enemy on the west shore, dispatched General Pillow with four regiments to the aid of the camp, thus providing this officer with a force (2700 of all arms) but little

PORTRAITS OF CONFEDERATE PRIVATES OF THE WEST.—I.

From tintypes found at the close of the war in the dead-letter office, Richmond. Letters accompanying the tintypes suggest that the warlike attitude was a favorite pose for pictures intended for sisters and sweethearts.

inferior to that which was about to attack him. Anxious, however, to give Pillow all the men that he deemed necessary, Polk moved over another regiment (five hundred men), which landed on the Missouri shore just as the battle began (10:30 A. M.) Thus in all fairness it must be stated, that when the battle of Belmont commenced the opposing forces were virtually equal. The engagement became general a few minutes before 11 o'clock. With his line well extended Grant bore down upon the Confederate position, and, though stubbornly resisted, he gradually fought his way forward, driving the Confederates to the river bank and capturing the camp.

Polk had been deterred from sending in the first instance a larger force to meet Grant's attack by the reports which his scouts made of the movements of the transports upon the river, and of the position and numbers of the columns from Fort Holt and Paducah,— all tending to show that the landing upon the opposite side of the river was a mere feint, while the real design was an attack upon Columbus. In spite of this, however, as we have seen, he placed at Belmont a force fully equal to that with which Grant was acting. Finding now that this force was being defeated, and learning at the same time that there was no enemy upon the Kentucky shore near enough to threaten seriously his position, he promptly moved over to Belmont additional reënforcements. Striking Grant upon the flank and rear, he drove him from

PORTRAITS OF CONFEDERATE PRIVATES OF THE WEST.—II.

the field and pursued him to his transports. The heavy guns upon the high ground at Columbus aided materially in Grant's discomfiture; as, after the Confederates were driven to the river bank, they were able to rake the Federal position.⚓ These batteries also had an opportunity to test their fire upon gun-boats, and the ease with which they repulsed the two attacks which the

⚓ General Grant, in his "Personal Memoirs" (New York: C. L. Webster & Co.), says: "The officers and men engaged at Belmont were then under fire for the first time. Veterans could not have behaved better than they did up to the moment of reaching the rebel camp. At this point they became demoralized from their victory and failed to reap its full reward. The enemy had been followed so closely that when he reached the clear ground on which his camp was pitched he beat a hasty retreat over the river bank, which protected him from our shots and from view. This precipitate retreat at the last moment enabled the National forces to pick their way without hindrance through the abatis — the only artificial defense the enemy had. The moment the camp was reached our men laid down their arms and commenced rummaging the tents to pick up trophies. Some of the higher officers were little better than the privates. They galloped about from one cluster of men to another, and at every halt delivered a short eulogy upon the Union cause and the achievements of the command. All this time the troops we had been engaged with for four hours lay crouched under cover of the river bank, ready to come up and surrender if summoned to do so; but,

finding that they were not pursued, they worked their way up the river and came up on the bank between us and our transports. I saw at the same time two steamers coming from the Columbus side toward the west shore, above us, black, or gray, with soldiers from boiler-deck to roof. Some of my men were engaged in firing from captured guns at empty steamers down the river, out of range, cheering at every shot. I tried to get them to turn their guns upon the loaded steamers above and not so far away. My efforts were in vain. At last I directed my staff-officers to set fire to the camps. This drew the fire of the enemy's guns located on the heights of Columbus. They had abstained from firing before, probably because they were afraid of hitting their own men; or they may have supposed, until the camp was on fire, that it was still in the possession of their friends. About this time, too, the men we had driven over the bank were seen in line up the river between us and our transports. The alarm 'surrounded' was given. The guns of the enemy and the report of being surrounded brought officers and men completely under control. At first some of the officers seemed to think that to be surrounded was to be placed in a hopeless position, where there was

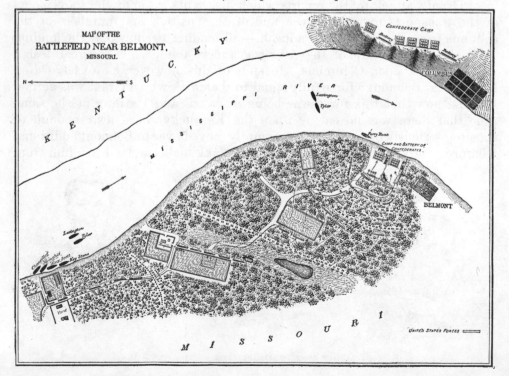

MAP OF THE
BATTLEFIELD NEAR BELMONT,
MISSOURI.

boats attempted argued well for the efficiency of their service. In closing his report of this battle, General Polk says:

"On landing I was met by General Pillow and General Cheatham, whom I directed, with the regiments of General Cheatham's command and portions of others, to press the enemy to his boats. This order was executed with alacrity and in double-quick time. The route over which we passed was strewn with the dead and wounded of the conflicts of Colonel Marks and General Cheatham, already alluded to, and with arms, knapsacks, overcoats, etc. On arriving at the point where his transports lay, I ordered the column, headed by the 154th Regiment of Tennessee Volunteers, under cover of a field thickly set with corn, to

GENERAL LEONIDAS POLK, BISHOP OF LOUISIANA (KILLED NEAR KENESAW, JUNE, 1864). FROM A PHOTOGRAPH.

be deployed along the river bank within easy range of the boats. This being accomplished, a heavy fire was opened upon them simultaneously, riddling them with balls, and, as we have reason to believe, with heavy loss to the enemy. Under this galling fire he cut his lines and retreated from the shore, many of his soldiers being driven overboard by the rush of those behind them. Our fire was returned by heavy cannonading from his gun-boats, which discharged upon our lines showers of grape, canister and shell, as they retired with their convoy in the direction of Cairo."

General Polk was mistaken in concluding that all the Federal force had reëmbarked. The 27th Illinois regiment, whose colonel, N. B. Buford, was one of Polk's old West Point friends, had been separated from the rest of the command in the hurry of the retreat, and, taking a road that lay some little distance from the river, made its way northward. Coming back to the river at a point above that at which General Grant had so precipitately taken to his boats, it succeeded, at about dark, in getting on board a transport without molestation. The absence of the Confederate cavalry and the confusion of the pursuit alone prevented the discovery and capture of this force. ↓

nothing to do but surrender. But when I announced that we had cut our way in and could cut our way out just as well, it seemed a new revelation to officers and soldiers. They formed line rapidly and we started back to our boats, with the men deployed as skirmishers as they had been on entering camp. The enemy was soon encountered, but his resistance this time was feeble."

↓ General Grant thus describes the return to the

boats: "The corn-field in front of our transports terminated at the edge of a dense forest. Before I got back the enemy had entered this forest and had opened a brisk fire upon the boats. Our men, with the exception of details that had gone to the front after the wounded, were now either aboard the transports or very near them. Those who were not aboard soon got there, and the boats pushed off. I was the only man of the National army be-

BRIGADIER-GENERAL U. S. GRANT. FROM A PHOTOGRAPH TAKEN IN 1861.

In a note to the editors Colonel Frederick D. Grant says of this picture: "It was taken in Cairo, Ill., in 1861, and is a remarkably good picture of General Grant as he looked at that time. He had always worn his beard trimmed short until he was appointed colonel of the 21st Illinois; but during the time that he was serving in Missouri he did not trim his beard, nor did he do so on being stationed at Cairo after his appointment as brigadier-general. After he had fought the battle of Belmont, he sent for his family to come on from Galena and make him a visit. This picture had been taken just before the visit, and one of the first things that my mother said to him was, that she did not like the length of his beard. Later in the winter, and a short time after our arrival in Cairo, General Grant got permission to go to St. Louis on business connected with his command. During that visit he was shaved—the first time in my recollection that he ever was shaved; the second and only other instance was when he was President.

The battle of Belmont was long and severe. Beginning at half-past 10 o'clock in the morning, it did not end until sunset. The losses on both sides bear evidence of the character of the fighting. The Confederate loss was

tween the rebels and our transports. The captain of a boat that had just pushed out, but had not started, recognized me and ordered the engineer not to start the engine; he then had a plank run out for me. My horse seemed to take in the situation. There was no path down the bank, and every one acquainted with the Mississippi River knows that its banks, in a natural state, do not vary at any great angle from the perpendicular. My horse put his fore feet over the bank without hesitation or urging, and, with his hind feet well under him, slid down the bank and trotted aboard the boat, twelve or fifteen feet away, over a single gang-plank."—["Personal Memoirs."]

642 in killed, wounded, and missing. That of the Federals, owing to the differences in their figures, is more difficult to determine; but, accepting the reports of the brigade and regimental commanders as correct, it must be placed at about six hundred [see page 355]. It is, however, not easy to place entire confidence in these figures. One thing is certain: the Federal dead and nearly all their wounded were left upon the field. General Pillow reports that he buried 295 of them, and that, under a flag of truce, the Federals were similarly engaged "a good part of the day." General Grant states that he carried 175 prisoners from the field, and General Polk, that after a liberal exchange, by which he recovered all of his own men, he had still 100 prisoners in his hands. The substantial fruits of victory were, therefore, with the Confederates, and their Congress, in acknowledgment of the fact, passed resolutions commending Polk, his commanders, and the troops for the service rendered.

The chief objects of General Grant's attack, as stated by himself, had been, first to assist a movement against General Thompson's command, and second, to break up the camp at Belmont. He failed in both, for the camp was continued, and the disaster to his command caused him to recall the troops sent after Thompson. He carried off two cannon and a number of the sick and wounded Confederates found in their camp; but he fled the field, virtually abandoning one of his regiments, leaving his dead and wounded, a large preponderance of prisoners, a stand of his colors, one thousand stand of arms, and the caissons of his battery in the hands of the Confederates. His fight had, however, been a gallant one, and, at one time, the entire Confederate line was swept before his onset.

THE GUN-BOATS "TYLER" AND "LEXINGTON" FIGHTING THE COLUMBUS BATTERIES DURING THE
BATTLE OF BELMONT. FROM A DRAWING BY REAR-ADMIRAL WALKE.

He has estimated his force at 3114 men, while the commander of his First Brigade states it as 3500. The discrepancy is, no doubt, accounted for by the fact that five companies were left to guard the transports, thus leaving, for the actual engagement, the number of troops stated by himself. When the battle began General Pillow had in line 2500 men, exclusive of a squadron of cavalry and a battery, and by 11 o'clock he was joined by Walker's regiment, numbering about 500, thus giving the Confederates a force fully equal to that of their antagonists; and yet they were driven in much confusion from their position. To account for this three reasons have been assigned: It has been said, first, that the Federal force was largely superior in numbers; secondly, that the Confederates were insufficiently supplied with ammunition; and thirdly, that they were at a disadvantage owing to the exposed position in which their line was formed. The first of these reasons is, as has just been shown, clearly incorrect; the second is equally so, as regards the infantry, although the field-battery certainly was short of powder and ball. Proof of this may be found in the reports of the several regimental commanders who took part in the engagement. On the third point the evidence shows that

CONFEDERATE FORTIFICATIONS AT COLUMBUS, KY.
FROM A WAR-TIME SKETCH.

most of the line of battle, especially the center, was placed in an exposed position, in an open field, with a heavy wood only about eighty yards distant in its front. Under the cover of this wood the Federal force moved forward its line of battle and, halting at the timber's edge, raked the field with its fire. The Confederates had been on the ground for several weeks, and the advantageous positions should have been familiar to them. The force sent over to aid in opposing Grant was on the ground quite long enough before the battle began to have found out a better position on which to form, and it stood in line of battle one hour before the Federal attack was made. There were several positions at hand, any one of which would have been better. This was especially the case with the ground in the rear of the abatis of felled trees. It is difficult to account for this error, without taking into consideration the characteristics of General Pillow, the officer commanding upon the field. Pillow was a man of unlimited personal courage, and upon this occasion, the first, in this war, in which he had had an opportunity to come to blows with his enemy, he no doubt mentally invested his soldiers with the same capacity for resistance that he felt within himself, overlooking the fact that they were fresh levies and that it was their first engagement. Be this as it may, he soon found that he was unable to hold his position and therefore attempted to dislodge the concealed foe by a series of gallant charges. These proved of no avail, and, after losing heavily, he had to give way. In the mean time he must have inflicted heavy loss upon the enemy, for it required the pressure of but two additional regiments, which ar-

CAPTAIN JOHN A. RAWLINS, ASSISTANT-ADJUTANT-GENERAL ON BRIG.-GEN. GRANT'S STAFF. FROM A PHOTOGRAPH TAKEN IN 1861.

rived about 12 o'clock, and numbered together but 1000 men, to drive Grant from the field. The force which won the battle of Belmont was, then, about 4000 men. It is true that an additional reënforcement of 2 regiments of about 500 men each was sent across the river, but they arrived after the Federal force had been defeated, and took part only in the pursuit.

In short, it may be said that the battle was fought by 3114 Federals against 4000 Confederates, the result being a victory for the latter; and that, subsequently, the Confederates were reënforced by 1000 men with whom they took up the pursuit, thus bringing the total upon the field to 5000 of all arms.♭ In

♭ A recent revision of the official tables of losses shows that the estimates as given in the official records are under the mark. The official records and the officially revised estimates furnish the following data:

The Union forces engaged at Belmont, Mo., under Brig.-Gen. U. S. Grant, were composed of the *First Brigade*, Brig.-Gen. John A. McClernand: 27th Illinois, Col. N. B. Buford; 30th Illinois, Col. Philip B. Fouke; 31st Illinois, Col. John A. Logan; Dollins' Co. Illinois Cavalry, Capt. J. J. Dollins; Delano's Co. Illinois Cavalry, Lieut. J. K. Catlin; Battery B, 1st Illinois Lt. Artillery, Capt. Ezra Taylor. *Second Brigade*, Col. Henry Dougherty: 22d Illinois, Lieut.-Col. H. E. Hart, and 7th

Iowa, Col. J. G. Lauman,— the whole command numbering 3114 men.

The gun-boats *Tyler*, Capt. Henry Walke, and *Lexington*, Capt. R. N. Stembel, also bore a part in the engagement.

The loss sustained by the Union troops, according to the revised official returns, was 120 killed, 383 wounded, and 104 captured or missing,— total, 607. The navy lost 1 killed and 2 wounded.

The superior officer on the Confederate side was Maj.-Gen. Leonidas Polk, with Brig.-Gens. G. J. Pillow and B. F. Cheatham in subordinate command. The troops under them immediately engaged consisted of the 13th Arkansas, Col. James C. Tappan; 11th Louisiana, Col. S. F. Marks (com-

comparing this engagement with other battles of the war the points of resemblance between it and that of Shiloh, fought six months later and upon a much more extended scale, must strike every observer. If Shiloh was a defeat for the Confederates, then, by a similar chain of occurrences and conclusions, Grant was defeated at Belmont.

Soon after the battle of Belmont a painful accident occurred at Columbus by which the commanding general nearly lost his life. During the progress of the battle a 128-pounder rifled gun had been charged while hot; but, no opportunity offering to use it to advantage, it was allowed to cool and remain charged four days. When fired it burst. This caused the explosion of its magazine, killing seven persons and severely wounding General Polk and other officers.

In a letter to his wife, dated November 12th, General Polk says:

"I and others of my officers have spent pretty much the whole day in my boat on the river with Buford [Colonel N. B. Buford, 27th Illinois] and his officers, discussing the principles of exchange, and other matters connected with the war. He is as good a fellow as ever lived, and most devotedly my friend — a true Christian, a true soldier, and a gentleman every inch of him. He said it did him good to come down and talk with me, and hoped it might be the means of peace and so on. I was very plain and clear in my position, as you may know, but very kind.

"After completing my exchange, I had still about 100 of their prisoners in my keeping, and among them 15 or 20 of his regiment. These he was very anxious I should let him take back. He urged me in every way, even on the score of our friendship, but I could not yield, especially to such a plea, which would have subjected me to the charge of consulting individual preference to public duty. He admitted it, and was obliged to leave without them, but we had a very pleasant day. I went up with him nearly to Cairo. He wanted me to go and spend the night with him; so you see how much we have done on this line toward ameliorating the severities of this unfortunate and wretched state of things."

In another letter to Mrs. Polk, dated November 15th, he says:

"Since the accident I have been up the river on two occasions to meet flags of truce; once to meet Grant, and to-day to meet my friend Buford. My interview with General Grant was, on the whole, satisfactory. It was about an exchange of prisoners. He looked rather grave, I thought, like a man who was not at his ease. We talked pleasantly and I succeeded in getting a smile out of him and then got on well enough. I discussed the principles on which I thought

manding brigade), Lieut.-Col. R. H. Barrow; Blythe's Mississippi, Col. A. K. Blythe; 2d Tennessee, Col. J. Knox Walker (commanding brigade), Lieut.-Col. W. B. Ross; 12th Tennessee, Col. R. M. Russell (commanding brigade), Lieut.-Col. T. H. Bell; 13th Tennessee, Col. John V. Wright; 15th Tennessee, Maj. J. W. Hambleton; 21st Tennessee, Col. Ed. Pickett, Jr.; 22d Tennessee, Col. Thomas J. Freeman; 154th Senior Tennessee, Col. Preston Smith (commanding brigade), Lieut.-Col. Marcus J. Wright; Watson (La.) Battery, Lieut.-Col. D. Beltzhoover; Mississippi and Tennessee Cavalry, Lieut.-Cols. John H. Miller and T. H. Logwood.

The Point Coupée (Louisiana) Battery, Captain R. A. Stewart; Mississippi Battery, Captain Melancthon Smith; Siege Battery, Captain S. H. D. Hamilton, and the Fort Artillery, Major A. P. Stewart, all of Brigadier-General John P. Mc-

Cown's command on the Kentucky side of the river, also participated.

The Confederate loss was 105 killed, 419 wounded, and 117 missing,— in all, 641.

The whole number of Confederates on the field is not officially reported. The 5 regiments originally engaged numbered about 2500 men. Allowing the same average of strength for the reënforcements subsequently sent across the river, and more or less engaged, the Confederates may be estimated at not less than five thousand.— EDITORS.

Of the result of the battle, General Grant says: "Belmont was severely criticised in the North as a wholly unnecessary battle, barren of results or the possibility of them from the beginning. If it had not been fought, Colonel Oglesby would probably have been captured or destroyed with his three thousand men. Then I should have been culpable indeed."— ["Personal Memoirs."]

REËMBARKATION OF GRANT'S TROOPS AFTER THE BATTLE. FROM A DRAWING BY REAR-ADMIRAL WALKE.

the war should be conducted; denounced all barbarity, vandalism, plundering, and all that, and got him to say that he would join in putting it down. I was favorably impressed with him; he is undoubtedly a man of much force. We have now exchanged five or six flags, and he grows more civil and respectful every time."

It was at one of these conferences that an amusing incident occurred which, so far from marring the harmony of the occasion, afforded much merriment to all present. The jest chanced to be at Colonel Buford's expense. The matters of the flag of truce had all been discussed, and the party had adjourned to partake of a simple luncheon which the Confederates had provided. As the company rose from the table the gallant colonel, raising his glass, proposed: "George Washington, the Father of his Country." General Polk, with a merry twinkle in his eye, quickly added: "And the first Rebel!" The Federal officers, caught in their own trap, gracefully acknowledged it by drinking the amended toast.

A little later General Cheatham, who was an ardent follower of the turf, discovered symptoms of a like weakness in General Grant. After they had been conversing for some time upon official matters, the conversation drifted upon the subject of horses. This congenial topic was pursued to the satisfaction of each until it finally ended in a grave proposition from Cheatham to Grant that, as this thing of fighting was a troublesome affair, they had best settle the vexing questions about which they had gone to war, by a grand, international horse-race over on the Missouri shore. Grant laughingly answered that he wished it might be so.

ARMY TRANSPORTS AT THE CAIRO LEVEE. FROM A WAR-TIME SKETCH.

THE GUN-BOATS AT BELMONT AND FORT HENRY.

BY HENRY WALKE, REAR-ADMIRAL, U. S. N.

FLAG-OFFICER FOOTE IN THE WHEEL-HOUSE OF THE "CINCINNATI" AT FORT HENRY.

AT the beginning of the war, the army and navy were mostly employed in protecting the loyal people who resided on the borders of the disaffected States, and in reconciling those whose sympathies were opposed. But the defeat at Manassas and other reverses convinced the Government of the serious character of the contest, and of the necessity of more vigorous and extensive preparations for war. Our navy yards were soon filled with workmen; recruiting stations for unemployed seamen were established, and we soon had more sailors than were required for the ships that could be fitted for service. Artillerymen for the defenses of Washington being scarce, five hundred of these sailors, with a battalion of marines (for guard duty), were sent to occupy the forts on Shuter's Hill, near Alexandria. The *Pensacola* and the Potomac flotilla and the seaboard navy yards required nearly all of the remaining unemployed seamen.

While Foote was improvising a flotilla for the Western rivers he was making urgent appeals to the Government for seamen. Finally some one at the Navy Department thought of the five hundred tars stranded on Shuter's Hill, and obtained an order for their transfer to Cairo, where they were placed on the receiving ship *Maria Denning*. There they met fresh-water sailors from our great lakes, and steamboat hands from the Western rivers. Of the seamen from the East, there were Maine lumbermen, New Bedford whalers, New York liners, and Philadelphia sea-lawyers. The foreigners enlisted were mostly Irish, with a few English and Scotch, French, Germans, Swedes, Norwegians, and Danes. The Northmen, considered the hardiest race in the world, melted away in the Southern sun with surprising rapidity.

On my gun-boat, the *Carondelet*, were more young men perhaps than on any other vessel in the fleet. Philadelphians were in the majority; Bostonians came next, with a sprinkling from other cities, and just enough men o' war's men to leaven the lump with naval discipline. The *De Kalb* had more than its share of men-o'-war's men, Lieutenant-Commander Leonard Paulding having had the first choice of a full crew, and having secured all the frigate *Sabine's* reënlisted men who had been sent West.

WHARF-BOAT AT CAIRO.
FROM A WAR-TIME PHOTOGRAPH.

During the spring and summer of 1861, Commander John Rodgers purchased, and he, with Commander Roger N. Stembel, Lieutenant S. L. Phelps, and Mr. Eads, altered, equipped, and manned, for immediate service on the Ohio and Mississippi rivers, 3 wooden gun-boats—the *Tyler*, of 6 8-inch shell-guns and 2 32-pounders; the *Lexington*, of 4 8-inch shell-guns and 2 32-pounders, and the *Conestoga*, of 4 32-pounder guns. This nucleus of the Mississippi flotilla (like the fleets of Perry, Macdonough, and Chauncey in the war of 1812) was completed with great skill and dispatch; they soon had full possession of the Western rivers above Columbus, Kentucky, and rendered more important service than as many regiments could have done. On October 12th, 1861, the *St. Louis*, afterward known as the *De Kalb*, the first of the seven iron-clad gun-boats ordered of Mr. Eads by the Government, was launched at Carondelet, near St. Louis. The other iron-clads, the *Cincinnati*, *Carondelet*, *Louisville*, *Mound City*, *Cairo*, and *Pittsburgh*, were launched soon after the *St. Louis*, Mr. Eads having pushed forward the work with most commendable zeal and energy. Three of these were built at Mound City, Ill. To the fleet of iron-clads above named were added the *Benton* (the largest and best vessel of the Western flotilla), the *Essex*, and a few smaller and partly armored gun-boats.

Flag-Officer Foote arrived in St. Louis on September 6th, and assumed command of the Western flotilla. He had been my fellow-midshipman in 1827, on board the United States ship *Natchez*, of the West India squadron, and was then a promising young officer. He was transferred to the *Hornet*, of the same squadron, and was appointed her sailing-master. After he left the *Natchez*, we never met again until February, 1861, at the Brooklyn Navy Yard, where he was the executive officer. Foote, Schenck, and myself were then the only survivors of the midshipmen of the *Natchez*, in her cruise of 1827, and now I am the only officer left.

During the cruise of 1827, while pacing the deck at night, on the lonely seas, and talking with a pious shipmate, Foote became convinced of the truth of the Christian religion, of which he was an earnest professor to the last. He

THE GUN-BOATS "TYLER" AND "LEXINGTON" ENGAGING THE BATTERIES OF COLUMBUS, KY., DURING THE BATTLE OF BELMONT. AFTER A SKETCH BY REAR-ADMIRAL WALKE.

In a letter written early in January, 1862, General Polk says of the works at Columbus : "We are still quiet here. I am employed in making more and more difficult the task to take this place. . . . I have now, mounted and in position, all round my works, 140 cannon of various calibers, and they look not a little formidable. Besides this, I am paving the bottom of the river with submarine batteries, to say nothing of a tremendous, heavy chain across the river. I am planting mines out in the roads also."

rendered important service while in command of the brig *Perry*, on the coast of Africa, in 1849, in suppressing the slave-trade, and he greatly distinguished himself by his skill and gallantry in the attack upon the Barrier Forts, near Canton (1856), which he breached and carried by assault, leading the assailing column in person. He was slow and cautious in arriving at conclusions, but firm and tenacious of purpose. He has been called "the Stonewall Jackson of the Navy." He often preached to his crew on Sundays, and was always desirous of doing good. He was not a man of striking personal appearance, but there was a sailor-like heartiness and frankness about him that made his company very desirable.

Flag-Officer Foote arrived at Cairo September 12th, and relieved Commander John Rodgers of the command of the station. The first operations of the Western flotilla consisted chiefly of reconnoissances on the Mississippi, Ohio, Cumberland, and Tennessee rivers. At this time it was under the control of the War Department, and acting in coöperation with the army under General Grant, whose headquarters were at Cairo.

On the evening of the 6th of November, 1861, I received instructions from General Grant to proceed down the Mississippi with the wooden gun-boats *Tyler* and *Lexington* on a reconnoissance, and as convoy to some half-dozen transport steamers; but I did not know the character of the service expected of me until I anchored for the night, seven or eight miles below Cairo. Early the next morning, while the troops were being landed near Belmont, Missouri, opposite Columbus, Kentucky, I attacked the Confederate batteries, at the request of General Grant, as a diversion, which was done with some effect. But the superiority of the enemy's batteries on the bluffs at Columbus, both in the number and the quality of his guns, was so great that it would have been too hazardous to have remained long under his fire with such frail vessels as the *Tyler* and *Lexington*, which were only expected to protect the land forces in case of a repulse. Having accomplished the object of the attack, the gun-boats withdrew, but returned twice during the day and renewed the contest. During the last of these engagements a cannon-ball passed obliquely through the side, deck, and scantling of the *Tyler*, killing one man and wounding others. This convinced me of the necessity of withdrawing my vessels, which had been moving in a circle to confuse the enemy's gunners. We fired a few more broadsides, therefore, and, perceiving that the firing had ceased at Belmont, an ominous circumstance, I returned to the landing, to protect the army and transports. In fact, the destruction of the gun-boats would have involved the loss of our army and our depot at Cairo, the most important one in the West.

Soon after we returned to the landing-place our troops began to appear, and the officers of the gun-boats were warned by General McClernand of the approach of the enemy. The Confederates came *en masse* through a cornfield, and opened with musketry and light artillery upon the transports, which were filled or being filled with our retreating soldiers. A well-directed fire from the gun-boats made the enemy fly in the greatest confusion.

Flag-Officer Foote was at St. Louis when the battle of Belmont was fought, and made a report to the Secretary of the Navy of the part which the gun-boats took in the action, forwarding my official report to the Navy Department. The officers of the vessels were highly complimented by General Grant for the important aid they rendered in this battle; and in his second official report of the action he made references to my report. It was impossible for me to inform the flag-officer of the general's intentions, which were kept perfectly secret.

During the winter of 1861–62, an expedition was planned by Flag-Officer Foote and Generals Grant and McClernand against Fort Henry, situated on the eastern bank of the Tennessee River, a short distance south of the line between Kentucky and Tennessee. In January the iron-clads were brought down to Cairo, and great efforts were made to prepare them for immediate service, but only four of the iron-clads could be made ready as soon as required.

On the morning of the 2d of February the flag-officer left Cairo with the

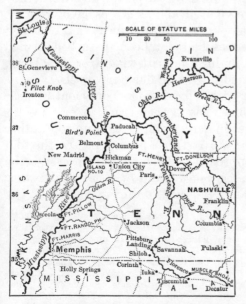

MAP OF THE REGION OF FOOTE'S OPERATIONS.

four armored vessels above named, and the wooden gun-boats *Tyler*, *Lexington*, and *Conestoga*, and in the evening reached the Tennessee River. On the 4th the fleet anchored six miles below Fort Henry. The next day, while reconnoitering, the *Essex* received a shot which passed through the pantry and the officers' quarters and visited the steerage.☆ On the 5th the flag-officer inspected the officers and crew at quarters, addressed them, and offered a prayer.

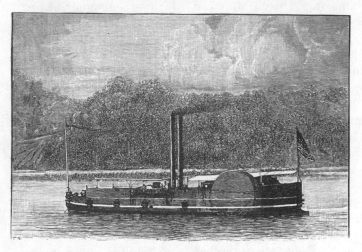

UNITED STATES GUN-BOAT "TYLER." FROM A DRAWING BY
REAR-ADMIRAL WALKE.

Heavy rains had been falling, and the river had risen rapidly to an unusual height; the swift current brought down an immense quantity of heavy drift-wood, lumber, fences, and large trees, and it required all the steam-power of the *Carondelet*, with both anchors down, and the most strenuous exertions of the officers and crew, working day and night, to prevent the boat from being dragged downstream. This adversity appeared to dampen the ardor of our crew, but when the next morning they saw a large number of white objects, which through the fog looked like polar bears, coming down the stream, and ascertained that they were the enemy's torpedoes forced from their moorings by the powerful current, they took heart, regarding the freshet as providential and as a presage of victory. The overflowing river, which opposed our progress, swept away in broad daylight this hidden peril; for if the torpedoes had not been disturbed, or had broken loose at night while we were shoving the drift-wood from our bows, some of them would surely have exploded near or under our vessels.

The 6th dawned mild and cheering, with a light breeze, sufficient to clear away the smoke. At 10:20 the flag-officer made the signal to prepare for battle, and at 10:50 came the order to get under way and steam up to Panther Island, about two miles below Fort Henry. At 11:35, having passed the foot of the island, we formed in line and approached the fort four abreast,— the *Essex* on the right, then the *Cincinnati*, *Carondelet*, and *St. Louis*. For want of room the last two were interlocked, and remained so during the fight.

☆ Composition and losses of the Union fleet at Fort Henry: Flag-Officer A. H. Foote, commanding. *First Division:* Flagship *Cincinnati*, Commander R. N. Stembel: 6 32-pounders, 3 8-inch, 4 rifled army 42-pounders, 1 12-pounder boat-howitzer; *Essex*, Commander W. D. Porter: 1 32-pounder, 3 11-inch, 1 10-inch, 1 12-pounder boat-howitzer; *Carondelet*, Commander H. Walke (same armament as the *Cincinnati*); *St. Louis*, Lieut.-Commanding L. Paulding: 7 32-pounders, 2 8-inch, 4 rifled 42-pounders, 1 rifled boat-howitzer. *Second Division:* Lieut. S. L. Phelps, commanding: *Conestoga*, Lieut.-Commanding S. L. Phelps: 4 32-pounders; *Tyler*, Lieut.-Commanding William Gwin: 1 32-pounder, 6 8-inch; *Lexington*, Lieut.-Commanding J. W. Shirk: 2 32-pounders, 4 8-inch. The Union loss as officially reported was: *Cincinnati*, killed, 1; wounded, 9. *Essex*, killed, 6; wounded, 18; missing, 5. Total killed, 7; wounded, 27; missing, 5. Total, 39.—EDITORS.

As we slowly passed up this narrow stream, not a sound could be heard nor a moving object seen in the dense woods which overhung the dark and swollen river. The gun-crews of the *Carondelet* stood silent at their posts, impressed with the serious and important character of the service before them. About noon the fort and the Confederate flag came suddenly into view, the barracks, the new earth-works, and the great guns well manned. The captains of our guns were men-of-war's men, good shots, and had their men well drilled.

The flag-steamer, the *Cincinnati*, fired the first shot as the signal for the others to begin. At once the fort was ablaze with the flame of her eleven heavy guns. The wild whistle of their rifle-shells was heard on every side of us. On the *Carondelet* not a word was spoken more than at ordinary drill, except when Matthew Arthur, captain of the starboard bow-gun, asked permission to fire at one or two of the enemy's retreating vessels, as he could not at that time bring his gun to bear on the fort. He fired one shot, which passed through the upper cabin of a hospital-boat, whose flag was not seen, but injured no one. The *Carondelet* was struck in about thirty places by the enemy's heavy shot and shell. Eight struck within two feet of the bow-ports, leading to the boilers, around which barricades had been built — a precaution which I always took before going into action, and which on several occasions prevented an explosion. The *Carondelet* fired 107 shell and solid shot; none of her officers or crew was killed or wounded.

The firing from the armored vessels was rapid and well sustained from the beginning of the attack, and seemingly accurate, as we could occasionally see the earth thrown in great heaps over the enemy's guns. Nor was the fire of the Confederates to be despised; their heavy shot broke and scattered our iron-plating as if it had been putty, and often passed completely through the casemates. But our old men-of-war's men, captains of the guns, proud to show their worth in battle, infused life and courage into their young comrades. When these experienced gunners saw a shot coming toward a port, they had the coolness and discretion to order their men to bow down, to save their heads. After nearly an hour's hard fighting, the captain

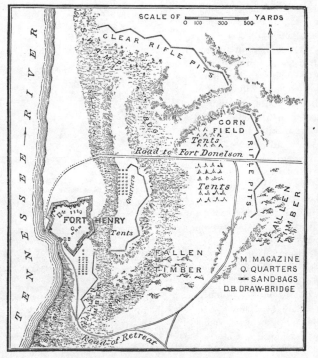

MAP OF FORT HENRY, FEBRUARY 6, 1862.

of the *Essex*, going below, and complimenting the First Division for their splendid execution, asked them if they did not want to rest and give three cheers, which were given with a will. But the feelings of joy on board the *Essex* were suddenly changed by a calamity which is thus described in a letter to me from James Laning, second master of the *Essex*:

"A shot from the enemy pierced the casemate just above the port-hole on the port side, then through the middle boiler, killing in its flight Acting Master's Mate S. B. Brittan, Jr., and opening a chasm for the escape of the scalding steam and water. The scene which followed was almost indescribable. The writer, who had gone aft in obedience to orders only a few moments before (and was thus providentially saved), was met by Fourth Master Walker, followed by a crowd of men rushing aft. Walker called to me to go back; that a shot from the enemy had carried away the steam-pipe. I at once ran to the stern of the vessel, and, looking out of the stern-port, saw a number of our brave fellows struggling in the water. The steam and hot water in the forward gun-deck had driven all who were able to get out of the ports overboard, except a few who were fortunate enough to cling to the casemate outside. When the explosion took place Captain Porter was standing directly in front of the boilers, with his aide, Mr. Brittan, at his side. He at once rushed for the port-hole on the starboard side, and threw himself out, expecting to go into the river. A seaman, John Walker, seeing his danger, caught him around the waist, and supporting him with one hand, clung to the vessel with the other, until, with the assistance of another seaman, who came to the rescue, they succeeded in getting the captain upon a narrow guard or projection which ran around the vessel, and thus enabled him to make his way outside to the after-port, where I met him. Upon speaking to him, he told me he was badly hurt, and that I must hunt for Mr. Riley, the First Master, and if he was disabled I must take command of the vessel, and man the battery again. Mr. Riley was unharmed, and already in the discharge of his duties as Captain Porter's successor. In a very few minutes after the explosion our gallant ship (which, in the language of Flag-Officer Foote, had fought most effectively through two-thirds of the engagement) was drifting slowly away from the scene of action; her commander badly wounded, a number of her officers and crew dead at their post, while many others were writhing in their last agony. As soon as the scalding steam would admit, the forward gun-deck was explored. The pilots, who were both in the pilot-house, were scalded to death. Marshall Ford, who was steering when the explosion took place, was found at his post at the wheel, standing erect, his left hand holding the spoke and his right hand grasping the signal-bell rope. A seaman named James Coffey, who was shot-man to the No. 2 gun, was on his knees, in the act of taking a shell from the box to be passed to the loader. The escaping steam and hot water had struck him square in the face, and he met death in that position. When I told Captain Porter that we were victorious, he immediately rallied, and, raising himself on his elbow, called for three cheers, and gave two himself, falling exhausted on the mattress in his effort to give the third. A seaman named Jasper P. Breas, who was badly scalded, sprang to his feet, exclaiming: 'Surrender! I must see that with my own eyes before I die.' Before any one could interfere, he clambered up two short flights of stairs to the spar-deck. He shouted 'Glory to God!' and sank exhausted on the deck. Poor Jasper died that night."

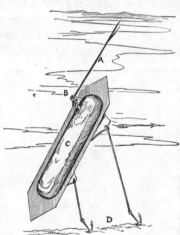

CROSS-SECTION OF A CONFEDERATE TORPEDO FOUND IN THE TENNESSEE RIVER.

A, iron rod armed with prongs to fasten upon the bottom of boats going up-stream and act upon B, a lever connecting with trigger to explode a cap and ignite the powder. C, canvas bag containing 70 lbs. of powder. D, anchors to hold torpedo in place.

This torpedo consisted of a stout sheet-iron cylinder, pointed at both ends, about 5½ feet long and 1 foot in diameter. The iron lever was 3½ feet long, and armed with prongs to catch in the bottom of a boat. This lever was constructed to move the iron rod on the inside of the cylinder, thus acting upon the trigger of the lock to explode the cap and fire the powder. The machine was anchored, presenting the prongs in such a way that boats going down-stream should slide over them, but those coming up should catch.

BETWEEN DECKS — SERVING THE GUNS. AFTER A SKETCH BY REAR-ADMIRAL WALKE.

The *Essex* before the accident had fired seventy shots from her two 9-inch guns. A powder boy, Job Phillips, fourteen years of age, coolly marked down upon the casemate every shot his gun had fired, and his account was confirmed by the gunner in the magazine. Her loss in killed, wounded, and missing was thirty-two.

The *St. Louis* was struck seven times. She fired one hundred and seven shots during the action. No one on board the vessel was killed or wounded.

Flag-Officer Foote during the action was in the pilot-house of the *Cincinnati*, which received thirty-two shots. Her chimneys, after-cabin, and boats were completely riddled. Two of her guns were disabled. The only fatal shot she received passed through the larboard front, killing one man and wounding several others. I happened to be looking at the flag-steamer when one of the enemy's heavy shot struck her. It had the effect, apparently, of a thunder-bolt, ripping her side-timbers and scattering the splinters over the vessel. She did not slacken her speed, but moved on as though nothing unexpected had happened.

From the number of times the gun-boats were struck, it would appear that the Confederate artillery practice, at first, at least, was as good, if not better, than ours. This, however, was what might have been expected, as the Confederate gunners had the advantage of practicing on the ranges the gun-boats would probably occupy as they approached the fort. The officers of the gun-boats, on the contrary, with guns of different caliber and unknown range, and without practice, could not point their guns with as much accuracy. To counterbalance this advantage of the enemy, the gun-boats were much better protected by their casemates for distant firing than the fort by its fresh earth-works. The Confederate soldiers fought as valiantly and as skillfully as the Union sailors. Only after a most determined resistance, and after all his heavy guns had been silenced, did Gen-eral Tilghman lower his flag. The Con-federate loss, as reported, was 5 killed, 11 wounded, and 5 missing. The pris-oners, including the general and his staff, numbered 78 in the fort and 16 in a hospital-boat; the remainder of the garrison, a little less than 2600, having escaped to Fort Donelson.

Our gun-boats continued to approach the fort until General Tilghman, with two or three of his staff, came off in a small boat to the *Cincinnati* and sur-rendered the fort to Flag-Officer Foote, who sent for me, introduced me to General Tilghman, and gave me orders to take command of the fort and hold it until the arrival of General Grant.

General Tilghman was a soldierly-looking man, a little above medium height, with piercing black eyes and a resolute, intelligent expression of coun-tenance. He was dignified and courte-ous, and won the respect and sympathy of all who became acquainted with him. In his official report of the battle he said that his officers and men fought with the greatest bravery until 1:50 P. M., when seven of his eleven guns were disabled; and, finding it impos-

GENERAL LLOYD TILGHMAN. FROM A PHOTOGRAPH.

sible to defend the fort, and wishing to spare the lives of his gallant men, after consultation with his officers he surrendered the fort.

It was reported at the time that, in surrendering to Flag-Officer Foote, the Confederate general said, "I am glad to surrender to so gallant an offi-cer," and that Foote replied, "You do perfectly right, sir, in surrendering, but you should have blown my boat out of the water before I would have surrendered to you." I was with Foote soon after the surrender, and I can-not believe that such a reply was made by him. He was too much of a gentle-man to say anything calculated to wound the feelings of an officer who had defended his post with signal courage and fidelity, and whose spirits were clouded by the adverse fortunes of war.

When I took possession of the fort the Confederate surgeon was laboring with his coat off to relieve and save the wounded; and although the officers and crews of the gun-boats gave three hearty cheers when the Confederate flag was hauled down, the first inside view of the fort sufficed to suppress every feeling of exultation and to excite our deepest pity. On every side the blood of the dead and wounded was intermingled with the earth and their implements of war. Their largest gun, a 128-pounder, was dismounted and filled with earth by the bursting of one of our shells near its muzzle; the carriage of another was broken to pieces, and two dead men lay near it, almost covered with heaps of earth; a rifled gun had burst, throwing its mangled gunners into the water. But few of the garrison escaped unhurt.

General Grant, with his staff, rode into the fort about 3 o'clock on the same day, and relieved me of the command. The general and staff then accompanied me on board the *Carondelet* (anchored near the fort), where he complimented the officers of the flotilla in the highest terms for the gallant manner in which they had captured Fort Henry. He had expected his troops to take part in a land attack, but the heavy rains had made the direct roads to the fort almost impassable.

The wooden gun-boats *Conestoga*, Commander S. L. Phelps, *Tyler*, Lieutenant-Commander William Gwin, and *Lexington*, Lieutenant J. W. Shirk, engaged the enemy at long range in the rear of the iron-clads. After the battle they pursued the enemy's transports up the river, and the *Conestoga* captured the steamer *Eastport*. The news of the capture of Fort Henry was received with great rejoicing all over the North.

Following upon the capture of Fort Henry (February 6th, 1862) and of Fort Donelson (February 16th), the fortifications at Columbus on the Mississippi were evacuated February 20th. In January General Halleck reached the conclusion that the object for which General Polk had labored in fortifying Columbus had been accomplished, for on the 20th he wrote General McClellan: "Columbus cannot be taken without an immense siege-train and a terrible loss of life. I have thoroughly studied its defenses — they are very strong; but it can be turned, paralyzed, and forced to surrender." In accordance with the idea suggested in this dispatch, the Federal movement upon Forts Henry and Donelson was decided upon.

In the latter part of January General Beauregard was ordered to report to General Johnston for assignment to duty at Columbus. He arrived at Jackson, Tennessee, about the middle of February, but, being too ill to proceed to Columbus, he requested General Polk to visit him at Jackson. The fall of Forts Henry and Donelson, and the declared purpose of the Federals to push their forces up the Tennessee River, made the further occupation of Columbus a serious question. General Beauregard had sent his chief of staff, Colonel Jordan, and his engineer officer, Captain Harris, up to Columbus, and they had made such reports to him concerning the nature of the works that he was inclined to doubt their efficiency. This, together with the necessity he was under to gather as large a force as possible which with to meet the enemy's movement up the Tennessee, convinced him that Columbus should be evacuated, and the defense of the river made at Island Number Ten and Fort Pillow. These points he considered not only more defensible than Columbus, but defensible with a smaller force, which would enable him to take a part of the command then holding the river for operations in conjunction with the troops he was gathering along the line of the Memphis and Charleston railroad. When, in the conference at Jackson, Beauregard unfolded these views to General Polk, the latter was not disposed to yield a ready assent to all of them. He recognized the necessity for gathering a force for field operations. It was, indeed, exactly what he and every other prominent officer in the department had, for six months, been urging upon the authorities. He, however, questioned the advisability of giving up Columbus. The works had been accepted by Colonel Gilmer, the chief engineer of the department, an officer who subsequently became the head of the Corps of Engineers in the Confederacy. In spite of the strategical fault which might be committed in an attempt to hold it, General Polk maintained that, just at that time, the moral effect of a determined stand at Columbus would be of great service to the Confederate arms.— Dr. Wm. M. Polk.

THE ATTACK UPON FORT HENRY. AFTER A DRAWING BY REAR-ADMIRAL WALKE.

THE DEFENSE OF FORT HENRY.

BY CAPTAIN JESSE TAYLOR, C. S. A.

ABOUT the 1st of September, 1861, while I was in command of a Confederate "camp of artillery instruction," near Nashville, Tenn., I received a visit from Lieutenant-Colonel Milton A. Haynes of the 1st Regiment Tennessee Artillery, who informed me of the escape of a number of our steamers from the Ohio River into the Tennessee, and of their having sought refuge under the guns of Fort Henry; that a "cutting-out" expedition from Paducah was anticipated, and that as there was no experienced artillerist at the fort the governor (Isham G. Harris) was anxious that the deficiency should immediately be supplied; that he had no one at his disposal unless I would give up my light battery (subsequently Porter's and later still Morton's), and take command at Fort Henry. Anxious to be of service, and convinced that the first effort of the Federals would be to penetrate our lines by the way of the Tennessee River, I at once, in face of the loudly expressed disapproval and wonder of my friends, consented to make the exchange.

Arriving at the fort, I was convinced by a glance at its surroundings that extraordinarily bad judgment, or worse, had selected the site for its erection. I found it placed on the east bank of the river in a bottom commanded by high hills rising on either side of the river, and within good rifle range. This circumstance was at once reported to the proper military authorities of the State at Nashville, who replied that the selection had been made by competent engineers and with reference to mutual support with Fort Donelson on the Cumberland, twelve miles away; and knowing that the crude ideas of a sailor in the navy concerning fortifications would receive but little consideration when conflicting with those entertained by a "West Pointer," I resolved quietly to acquiesce, but the accidental observation of a water-mark left on a tree caused me to look carefully for this sign above, below, and in the rear of the fort; and my investigation convinced me that we had a more dangerous force to contend with than the Federals,—namely, the river itself. Inquiry among old residents confirmed my fears that the fort was not only subject to overflow, but that the highest point within it would be—in an ordinary February rise—at least two feet under water. This alarming fact was also communicated to the State authorities, only to evoke the curt notification that the State forces had been transferred to the Confederacy, and that I should apply to General Polk, then in command at Columbus, Ky. This suggestion was at once acted on,—not once only, but with a frequency and urgency commensurate with its seeming importance,— the result being that I was again referred, this time to General A. S. Johnston, who at once dispatched an engineer (Major Jeremy F. Gilmer) to investigate and remedy; but it was now too late to do so effectually, though an effort was made looking to that end, by beginning to fortify the heights on the west bank (Fort Heiman). The armament of the fort at the time I assumed command consisted of 6 smooth-bore 32-pounders and 1 6-pounder iron-gun; February 1st, 1862, by the persistent efforts of General Lloyd Tilghman and Colonel A. Heiman, this had been increased to 8 32-, 2 42-, 1 128-pounders (Columbiad), 5 18-pounder siege guns, all smooth-bore, and 1 6-inch rifle; we also had 6 12-pounders, which looked so much like pot-metal that it was deemed best to subject them to a test, and as two of them burst with an ordinary charge, the others were set aside as useless incumbrances. The powder supplied was mostly of a very inferior quality, so much so that it was deemed necessary to adopt the dangerous expedient of adding to each charge a proportion of quick-burning powder. That this was necessary will, I think, be admitted when it is understood that with the original charge it was almost impossible to obtain a random shot of a little over one mile (that being the distance to a small island below the fort).

During the winter of 1861 and 1862 the Federal gun-boats, notably the *Lexington* and *Conestoga*, made frequent appearances in the Tennessee, and coming up under the cover of this island would favor the fort with an hour or more of shot and shell, but, as their object was to draw our fire and thus obtain the position of our guns, we, though often sorely tempted by the accuracy of their fire, deemed it best not to gratify them. On the 4th of February the Federal fleet of gun-boats, followed by countless transports, appeared below the fort. Far as eye could see, the course of the river could be traced by the dense volumes of smoke issuing from the flotilla—indicating that the long-threatened attempt to break our lines was to be made in earnest. The gun-boats took up a position about three miles below and opened a brisk fire, at the same time shelling the woods on the east bank of the river, thus covering the debarkation of their army. The 5th was a day of unwonted animation on the hitherto quiet waters of the Tennessee; all day long the flood-tide of arriving and the ebb of returning transports continued ceaselessly. Late in the afternoon three of the gun-boats, two on the west side and one on the east at the foot of the island, took position and opened a vigorous and well-directed fire, which was received in silence until the killing of one man and the wounding of three provoked an order to open with the Columbiad and the rifle. Six shots were fired in return,—three from each piece,—and with such effect that the gun-boats dropped out of range and ceased firing.

At night General Tilghman called his leading officers in consultation— Colonels Heiman, Forrest, and Drake are all that I can now recall as having been present. The Federal forces were variously estimated by us, 25,000 being, I think, the lowest. To oppose this force General Tilghman had less than four thousand men,— mostly raw regiments armed with shot-guns and hunting-rifles; in fact, the best-equipped regiment of his command, the 10th Tennessee, was armed with old flint-lock "Tower of London" muskets that had "done the state some service" in the war of 1812. The general opinion and final decision was that successful resistance to such an overwhelming force was an impossibility, that the army must fall back and unite with Pillow and Buckner at Fort Donelson. General Tilghman, recognizing the difficulty of withdrawing undisciplined troops from the front of an active and superior opponent, turned to me with the question, "Can you hold out for one hour against a determined attack?" I replied that I could. "Well, then, gentlemen, rejoin your commands and hold them in readiness for instant motion." The garrison left at the fort to cover the withdrawal consisted of part of Company B, 1st Tennessee Artillery, Lieutenant Watts, and fifty-four men.

The forenoon of February 6th was spent by both sides in making needful preparations for the approaching struggle. The gun-boats formed line of battle abreast under the cover of the island. The *Essex*, the *Cincinnati*, the *Carondelet*, and the *St. Louis*, the first with 4 and the others each with 13 guns, formed the van; the *Tyler*, *Conestoga*, and *Lexington*, with 15 guns in all, formed the second or rear line. Seeing the formation of battle I assigned to each gun a particular vessel to which it was to pay its especial compliments, and directed that the guns be kept constantly trained on the approaching boats. Accepting the volunteered services of Captain Hayden (of the engineers) to assist at the Columbiad, I took personal supervision of the rifle. When they were out of cover of the island the gun-boats opened fire, and as they advanced they increased the rapidity of their fire, until as they swung into the main channel above the island they showed one broad and leaping sheet of flame. At this point, the van being a mile distant, the command was given to commence firing from the fort; and here let me say that as pretty and as simultaneous a "broadside" was delivered as I ever saw flash from the sides of a frigate. The action now became general, and for the next twenty or thirty minutes was, on both sides, as determined, rapid, and accurate as heart could wish, and apparently inclined in favor of the fort. The iron-clad *Essex*, disabled by a shot through her boiler, dropped out of line; the fleet seemed to hesitate, when a succession of untoward and unavoidable accidents happened in the fort; thereupon the flotilla continued to advance. First, the rifle gun, from which I had just been called, burst, not only with destructive effect to those working it, but with disabling effect on those in its immediate vicinity. Going to the Columbiad as the only really effective gun left, I met General Tilghman and for the first time knew that he had returned to the fort; I supposed that he was with his retreating army. While consulting with him a sudden exclamation drew me to the Columbiad, which I found spiked with its own priming wire, completely disabled for the day at least. The Federal commander, observing the silence of these two heavy guns, renewed his advance with increased precision of fire. Two of the 32-pounders were struck almost at the same instant, and the flying fragments of the shattered guns and bursted shells disabled every man at the two guns. His rifle shot and shell penetrated the earth-works as readily as a ball from a navy Colt would pierce a pine board, and soon so disabled other guns as to leave us but four capable of being served.

General Tilghman now consulted with Major Gilmer and myself as to the situation, and the decision was that further resistance would only entail a useless loss of life. He therefore ordered me to strike the colors, now a dangerous as well as a painful duty. The flag-mast, which had been the center of fire, had been struck many times; the top-mast hung so far out of the perpendicular that it seemed likely to fall at any moment; the flag halyards had been cut by shot, but had fortunately become "foul" at the cross-trees. I beckoned—for it was useless to call amid the din—to Orderly-Sergeant Jones, an old "man-o'-war's man," to come to my assistance, and we ran across to the flag-staff and up the lower rigging to the cross-trees, and by our united efforts succeeded in clearing the halyards and lowering the flag. The view from that elevated position at the time was grand, exciting, and striking. At our feet the fort with her few remaining guns was sullenly hurling her harmless shot against the sides of the gun-boats, which, now apparently within two hundred yards of the fort, were, in perfect security, and with the coolness and precision of target practice, sweeping the entire fort; to the north and west, on both sides of the river, were the hosts of "blue coats," anxious and interested spectators, while to the east the feeble forces of the Confederacy could be seen making their weary way toward Donelson.

On the morning of the attack, we were sure that the February rise of the Tennessee had come; when the action began, the lower part of the fort was already flooded, and when the colors were hauled down, the water was waist-deep there; and when the cutter came with the officers to receive the formal surrender, she pulled into the "sally-port"; between the fort and the position which had been occupied by the infantry support was a sheet of water a quarter of a mile or more wide, and "running like a mill-race." If the attack had been delayed forty-eight hours, there would hardly have been a hostile shot fired; the Tennessee would have accomplished the work by drowning the magazine.

The fight was over; the little garrison were prisoners; but our army had been saved. We had been required to hold out an hour; we had held out for over two.

We went into the fight with nine guns bearing on the river approach,—we had two more 42-pounders, but neither shot nor shell for them; of these all were disabled but four. Of the 54 men who went into action [see General

Tilghman's report], 5 were killed, 11 wounded or disabled, and 5 missing. When the *Essex* dropped out of the fight I could see her men wildly throwing themselves into the swollen river. Admiral Foote reported that his flag-ship was struck thirty-eight times, and the commanding officers of gun-boats (with several of whom I had enjoyed a warm personal acquaintance) complimented me highly on what they termed the extraordinary accuracy of the fire. I believe that with effective guns the same precision of fire would have sunk or driven back the flotilla.

The formal surrender was made to the naval forces; Lieutenant-Commander Phelps acting for Flag-Officer Foote, and I representing General Tilghman. The number captured, including Tilghman and staff, hospital attendants and some stragglers from the infantry, amounted to about seventy.

During the evening a large number of army officers came into the fort, to whom I was introduced by my old messmates, Lieutenant-Commanders Gwin and Shirk. Here I first saw General Grant, who impressed me, at the time, as a modest, amiable, kind-hearted but resolute man. While we were at headquarters an officer came in to report that he had not as yet found any papers giving information of our forces, and, to save him further looking, I informed him that I had destroyed all the papers bearing on the subject, at which he seemed very wroth, fussily demanding, " By what authority ?" Did I not know that I laid myself open to punishment, etc., etc. Before I could reply fully, General Grant quietly broke in with, " I would be very much surprised and mortified if one of my subordinate officers should allow information which he could destroy to fall into the hands of the enemy."

We were detained for several days at the fort and were confined to the same steamer on which General Grant had established his headquarters, and as the officers, Confederate and Federal, messed together, I saw much of the general during that time. We were treated with every courtesy; so our confinement was less irksome than we had anticipated and was only marred by one incident. Two of the younger Confederate officers having obtained liquor became vociferous. At dinner General Grant did not take his seat with the rest, and this restraint being removed, the young men, despite frowns and nudges, persisted in discussing politics, military men and movements, etc. While they were thus engaged General Grant, unobserved by them, entered, took his seat, and dined without appearing to notice their conversation, but when the youngsters left the table they were dumfounded to meet a corporal and file of men, who ceremoniously conducted them to the " nursery " and left them under guard, where I shortly visited them. At last I promised to intercede, which I did, carrying with me regrets, explanations, and apologies. The general smiled and said that he had confined them partly for their own sakes, lest they might fall in with some of his own men in a similar condition ; that he did not believe the young men knew of his presence, and that he would order their release so soon as they became sober, which he did.

HOLDING KENTUCKY FOR THE UNION.

BY R. M. KELLY, COLONEL, U. S. V

MILITARY WATER-SLED. FROM A WAR-TIME
SKETCH.

THE military situation in Kentucky in September, 1861, cannot be properly understood without a brief sketch of the initial political struggle which resulted in a decisive victory for the friends of the Union. The State Legislature had assembled on the 17th of January in called session. The governor's proclamation convening it was issued immediately after he had received commissioners from the States of Alabama and Mississippi, and was followed by the publication of a letter from Vice-President Breckinridge advising the calling of a State convention and urging that the only way to prevent war was for Kentucky to take her stand openly with the slave States. About this time the latter's uncle, the Rev. Dr. Robert J. Breckinridge, an eminent Presbyterian minister, addressed a large meeting at Lexington in favor of the Union. The division of sentiment is further illustrated by the fact that one of his sons, Colonel W. C. P. Breckinridge, followed his cousin into the Confederate army, while another son, Colonel Joseph C. Breckinridge, fought for the Union. The position of the Union men was very difficult. They knew that Governor Magoffin was in sympathy with the secession movement and that the status of the Legislature on the question was doubtful. The governor had under his orders a military force called the State Guard, well armed and disciplined, and under the immediate command of General Simon B. Buckner, a graduate of West Point. There was a small Union element in it, but a large majority of its membership was known to be in favor of secession. Suspicious activity in recruiting for this force began as soon as the governor issued his call for the Legislature, and it was charged that new companies of known secession proclivities could get arms promptly from the State arsenal, while those supposed to be inclined toward the Union were subjected to annoying delays. The State Guard at its strongest numbered about only four thousand men, but it was organized and ready while the Union men had neither arms nor organization to oppose it.

When the Legislature assembled it was soon ascertained that it was very evenly divided in sentiment. Old party lines promptly disappeared, and members were classed as "Union" or "Southern Rights." In the Senate there was a safe majority against calling a convention. In the house on a test question the Union men prevailed by only one vote. There were some half-dozen waverers who always opposed any decisive step toward secession but were equally unwilling to give any active support to the Government. Outside pressure was brought to bear. Large delegations of secessionists assembled at Frankfort, to be speedily confronted by Union men, just as determined, summoned by telegraph from all parts of the State. Argument was met by argument, threat by threat, appeals to sentiment and prejudice on one side by similar appeals on the other. The leading public men of the State, however, had been trained in a school of compromises, and they long cherished themselves, and kept alive in the people, the hope that some settlement would be reached that would avert war and save Kentucky from becoming the battle-field of contending armies. This hope accounts in a large degree for the infrequency of personal affrays during those exciting days.

The struggle, kept up during three sessions of the Legislature, demonstrated that the State could not be carried out of the Union by storm, and terminated in adopting the policy of neutrality as a compromise. The Union men, however, had gained some decided advantages. They had consented to large appropriations for arming the State, but on condition that the control of military affairs should be taken from the governor and lodged in a military board of five members, the majority being Union men; they provided for organizing and arming Home Guards, outside of the militia force, and not subject, as such, to the governor's orders, and they passed an act requiring all the State Guard to take the oath required of officers, this measure being mainly for the purpose of allowing the Union members of that organization to get rid of the stringent obligations of their enlistment.

THE REV. ROBERT J. BRECKINRIDGE, D. D.
FROM A PHOTOGRAPH.

As in most compromises, the terms of the neutrality compromise were differently interpreted by the parties, but with both the object was to gain time. The secessionists believed that neutrality, as they interpreted it, would educate the people to the idea of a separation from the Union and result in alliance with the new Confederacy; the Union men expected to gain time to organize their forces, elect a new legislature in sympathy with their views, and put the State decisively on the side of the Government. Events soon showed that the Union men best understood the temper of the people. The Legislature adjourned May 24th, four days after the governor had issued his neutrality proclamation. At the special congressional election, June 20th, nine Union representatives were chosen to one secessionist by an aggregate majority of over 54,000 votes. The legislative election in August resulted in the choice of a new body three-fourths of whose members in each house were Union men.

Under the first call for troops, Kentucky was required to furnish four regiments for the United States service. These Governor Magoffin indignantly refused to furnish. Shortly afterward he was asked by the Secretary of War of the Confederacy for a regiment. He declined this request as beyond his power to grant. His course did not suit the more ardent of the young men on either side. Blanton Duncan had already procured authority to recruit for the Confederacy, and in various portions of the State men were publicly engaged in raising companies for him. Before the end of April he had started with a regiment for Harper's Ferry by way of Nashville. An incident connected with this movement shows how strong the belief still was that the war was to be short, and that Kentucky might keep out of it. As Desha's company of Duncan's regiment was leaving Cynthiana, Ky., by rail, one of the privates said to a friend who was bidding him farewell: "Be sure to vote for Crittenden [then the Union candidate for delegate to the Border State Conference] and keep Kentucky out of the fuss. We are just going to Virginia on a little frolic and will be back in three months." On the other side, immediately after Magoffin's refusal to furnish troops, J. V. Guthrie, of Covington, went to Washington and got authority for himself and W. E. Woodruff, of Louisville, to raise two regiments. They established a camp just above Cincinnati, on the Ohio side of the river, and began recruiting in Kentucky. They soon filled two regiments, afterward known as the 1st and 2d Kentucky, which were sent early in July to take part in the West Virginia campaign.

The Union Club in Louisville was an important factor in organizing Union sentiment. Originating in May, in six weeks it numbered six thousand members in that city, and spread rapidly through the State and into East Tennessee. It was a secret society, the members of which were bound by an oath to be true to the flag and Government of the United States.

One of the most striking figures of the period was Lieutenant William Nelson of the navy. He was a man of heroic build, six feet four inches high, and carrying lightly his weight of three hundred pounds; he had many accomplishments, spoke several languages, and was endowed with a strong intellect and a memory which enabled him to repeat, verbatim, page after page of his favorite authors. A fluent and captivating talker, when he wished to please, no man could be more genial and companionable, but he had a quick and impetuous temper and an overbearing disposition, and when irritated or opposed was offensively dictatorial and dogmatic. A native of Kentucky and an ardent friend of the Union, he visited the State several times in the course of the spring to watch the course of events. As a result of his observations he reported to Mr. Lincoln that the arms of the State were in the hands of the secessionists, and that the Union men could not maintain themselves unless they were also furnished with arms. Mr. Lincoln placed at his disposal ten thousand muskets with means for their transportation. Toward the end of April he met in consultation at Frankfort a number of the leading Union men of the State and arranged for the distribution of the arms. When, shortly afterward, the organization of the Union Home Guards began, it was from this source they were armed. In Louisville, on the initiative of J. M. Delph, the Union mayor, a brigade of

MAJOR-GENERAL WILLIAM NELSON. FROM A PHOTOGRAPH.

On the morning of Sept. 29th, 1862, General Nelson had an altercation with General Jefferson C. Davis in the Galt House, Louisville. General Davis shot General Nelson, who died almost instantly.— EDITORS.

two full regiments and a battery were organized, which were destined to play a very useful part.

When the Legislature of which he was a member had finally adjourned, Lovell H. Rousseau went to Washington and obtained authority to recruit a brigade, and, in order to avoid possibly injurious effects on the approaching election, established his camp on the Indiana shore, opposite Louisville.

Nelson, after making arrangements for the distribution of guns to the Union men of the State, was authorized by the President to do a similar service for the Union men of East Tennessee, and for an escort was empowered to recruit three regiments of infantry and one of cavalry in eastern Kentucky. He selected his colonels, commissioning them "for the Tennessee expedition" and appointing a rendezvous at Hoskin's Cross Roads, in Garrard county, on the farm of Richard M. Robinson, a stanch Union man, for the day after the legislative elections in August.

During this period of neutrality Kentucky history seemed to be repeating itself. As before its occupation by white men it was the common hunting-ground for the Indian of the North and of the South on which by tacit agreement neither was to make a permanent home, so now it had become the common recruiting-ground of Northern and Southern armies on which neither was to establish a camp. The Kentucky secessionists had opened a recruiting rendezvous near Clarksville, Tennessee, a few miles from the Kentucky border, which they called Camp Boone, and recruits began to gather there early in July. Buckner resigned from the State Guard a few days after the battle of Bull Run and soon took his way southward.‖ His example was followed by most of the higher officers, and the State Guard began rapidly to disintegrate. It was no uncommon sight in Louisville, shortly after this, to see a squad of recruits for the Union service marching up one side of a street while a squad destined for the Confederacy was moving down the other.

JOHN C. BRECKINRIDGE, MAJOR-GENERAL, C. S. A.; VICE-PRESIDENT OF THE UNITED STATES, 1857–61; CONFEDERATE SECRETARY OF WAR, APPOINTED JAN. 28, 1865. FROM A DAGUERREOTYPE TAKEN ABOUT 1850.

In the interior, a train bearing a company destined for Nelson's camp took aboard at the next county town another company which was bound for Camp Boone. The officers in charge made a treaty by which their men were kept in separate cars.

On the day after the August election Nelson's recruits began to gather at his rendezvous. Camp Dick Robinson was situated in a beautiful blue-grass country, near where the pike for Lancaster and Crab Orchard leaves the Lexington and Danville Pike, between Dick's River and the Kentucky. By September 1st, there had gathered at this point four full Kentucky regiments and nearly two thousand East Tennesseeans, who had been enlisted by Lieutenant

---

‖ During the neutrality period it would appear that the Union authorities were in doubt as to which side General Buckner would espouse, since on August 17th, 1861, President Lincoln wrote to the Secretary of War: "Unless there be reason to the contrary, not known to me, make out a commission for Simon [B.] Buckner, of Kentucky, as a brigadier-general of volunteers. It is to be put into the hands of General Anderson, and delivered to General Buckner or not, at the discretion of General Anderson. Of course it is to remain a secret unless and until the commission is delivered." This letter bears the indorsement, "this day made."—EDITORS.

S. P. Carter. This officer, like Nelson, belonging to the navy, was a native of East Tennessee, and it was part of the original plan of the East Tennessee expedition that he should enter that section and organize men to receive the arms that Nelson was to bring. This was found to be impracticable, and he opened his camp at Barboursville and the men began to come to him.

In August, W. T. Ward, a prominent lawyer of Greensburg, commenced recruiting a brigade and soon had twenty-two companies pledged to rendezvous when he should obtain the necessary authority from Washington. In Christian county, Colonel J. F. Buckner, a wealthy lawyer and planter, recruited a regiment from companies which organized originally as Home Guards, but soon determined to enter the volunteeer service. He established a camp five miles north of Hopkinsville, where a few companies remained at a time. Christian county was strongly Unionist, while all the counties west of it were overwhelmingly secessionist. Camp Boone was only a few miles from its southern border, and Fort Donelson about twenty miles south-west. Colonel Buckner had a 6-pounder cannon, which could be heard at Camp Boone and made his vicinity additionally disagreeable to those neighbors.

The neutrality proclaimed by Governor Magoffin on the 20th of May had been formally recognized by the Confederate authorities and treated with respect by those of the United States, but it was destined to speedy termination. It served a useful purpose in its time, and a policy that had the respectful consideration of the leading men of that day could not have been so absurd as it seems now.

On the 3d of September General Polk, who was in command in western Tennessee, caused Columbus, Kentucky, to be occupied, on account of the appearance of a body of Union troops on the opposite side of the Missis-

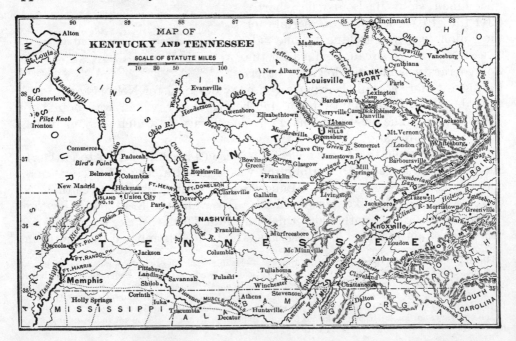

sippi.✠ Hearing of this, on the 5th General Grant moved from Cairo and occupied Paducah. A few days afterward General Zollicoffer advanced with four Confederate regiments through Cumberland Gap to Cumberland Ford. The Union Legislature had met on the 2d. Resolutions were passed on the 11th requiring the governor to issue a proclamation ordering the Confederate troops to leave the State. They were promptly vetoed and promptly passed over the veto, and the proclamation was issued. In spite of the governor's opposition, acts were passed putting the State in active support of the Government. The governor was reduced to a nullity. General Robert Anderson, who was assigned on May 28th to command the Department of Kentucky, was invited to remove his headquarters to Louisville, and the State's full quota of volunteers was called for. Recruiting was pushed with energy, and by the end of the year 28 regiments of infantry, 6 of cavalry, and 3 batteries had been organized.

On September 15th General Albert Sidney Johnston assumed command of the Confederate forces in the West, and at once ordered General Buckner with five thousand men from Camp Boone and another camp in the vicinity to proceed by rail and occupy Bowling Green. Buckner reached that point early on the 18th, having sent in advance one detachment by rail to seize the bridge over Green River at Munfordville, and another to go as far as Elizabethtown and bring back all the rolling-stock possible. This was successfully accomplished, a part of the advance detachment going as far as the bridge over the Rolling Fork of Salt River, within thirty-three miles of Louisville, and burning the bridge.

Buckner's movement was supposed in Louisville to have that city for its objective, and great excitement prevailed there. Rumor magnified his forces, but there was abundant ground for apprehension without that. General Anderson was in command, but he was without troops. The only forces in his department in Kentucky were the unorganized regiment of Colonel Buckner near Hopkinsville, the few hundred recruits gathered at Greensburg by General Ward, and Nelson's forces at Camp Dick Robinson,— none of which were ready for service,— the Home Guard Brigade of Louisville, and the scattered companies of Home Guards throughout the State. Opposite Louisville was Rousseau's camp, in which were some two thousand men not yet prepared for the field. Very few troops were in reach. Owing to the neutrality of Kentucky, the regiments recruited in Ohio, Indiana, and the North-west generally had been sent as fast as organized to the Potomac or Missouri armies. Fortunately, Governor Oliver P. Morton, of Indiana, had received information, about the 1st, which had led him to reserve a few regiments for Kentucky, and in response to General Anderson's appeal he hurried them forward. Anderson had learned of Buckner's intended advance the day it was made, and the non-arrival of the regular train from the south showed him that it had begun. The Home Guards of Louisville were at once ordered out for ten days, and, assembling at midnight, eighteen hundred of them under Colonel A. Y. Johnson, Chief of the Fire Department, started by rail for Mul-

✠ Thus the neutrality of Kentucky was first broken by the Confederates.— EDITORS.

JOHN J. CRITTENDEN, DURING FOUR TERMS UNITED STATES SENATOR FROM KENTUCKY; TWICE
ATTORNEY-GENERAL OF THE UNITED STATES; EX-GOVERNOR OF KENTUCKY.
FROM A DAGUERREOTYPE TAKEN ABOUT 1851.

In the session of 1860–61 Senator Crittenden introduced resolutions called the "Crittenden Compromise," proposing as an unalterable Constitutional Amendment that slavery be prohibited north of the parallel of 36° 30′, and never interfered with by Congress south of that line. Though this was the most promising of the numerous plans for a compromise, the resolutions failed for want of agreement.— EDITORS.

draugh's Hill. Rousseau, with twelve hundred men, followed in a few hours. The whole force was under Brigadier-General W. T. Sherman, who had shortly before, at Anderson's request, been assigned to duty with him. On arriving at Lebanon Junction Sherman learned that Rolling Fork Bridge, a few miles farther on, had just been destroyed. The Home Guards debarked at the junction, and Rousseau moved forward to the bridge, finding it still smoking. A reconnoissance in force, carried for some distance beyond the river, found no enemy, and the burning of the bridge indicated that no farther advance was intended immediately.

General Sherman's army was rather a motley crew. The Home Guards did not wear regulation uniforms, and Rousseau's men were not well equipped. Muldraugh's Hill had been occupied for six weeks or more during the summer by a regiment of the State Guard, and the people in the vicinity were generally in sympathy with the rebellion. Sherman's attention was attracted to a young man, without any uniform, who was moving around with what he considered suspicious activity, and he called him up for question. The young fellow gave a prompt account of himself. His name was Griffiths, he was a medical student from Louisville acting as hospital steward, and he had been called out in such a hurry that he had had no time to get his uniform. As he moved away he muttered something in a low tone to an officer standing by, and Sherman at once demanded to know what it was. "Well, General," was the reply, "he said that a general with such a hat as you have on had no right to talk to him about a uniform." Sherman was wearing a battered hat of the style known as "stovepipe." Pulling it off, he looked at it, and, bursting into a laugh, called out: "Young man, you are right about the hat, but you ought to have your uniform."

On the 20th, the 38th Indiana (Colonel B. F. Scribner) arrived, and soon after four other regiments. Sherman moved forward to Elizabethtown, not finding any available position at Muldraugh's Hill. A few days afterward, having on October 8th suc-

CAMP DICK ROBINSON — THE FARM-HOUSE.
FROM A PHOTOGRAPH TAKEN IN 1887.

ceeded Anderson, who had been relieved by General Scott in these terms, "To give you rest necessary to restoration of health, call Brigadier-General Sherman to command the Department of the Cumberland," Sherman ordered Rousseau to advance along the railroad to Nolin, fifty-three miles from Louisville, and select a position for a large force.

While Sherman was at Elizabethtown, Buckner, with several thousand men, moved rapidly to Rochester, on Green River, and destroyed the locks there, and then moved against Colonel Buckner's camp near Hopkinsville. Warned of his approach, Colonel Buckner directed his men, who had not yet been regularly enrolled, to disperse and make their way to the Union camp near Owensboro'. They succeeded, but Colonel Buckner himself was taken prisoner. Occupying Hopkinsville after a slight skirmish with the Home Guards, Buckner left a garrison there under General Alcorn and returned to Bowling Green.

Rousseau's advance to Nolin and the arrival of large reënforcements there induced Johnston to move his headquarters from Columbus to Bowling Green, and on October 15th he sent Hardee with 1200 men from that place against Ward at Greensburg, who, hearing of Hardee's approach, fell back with his recruits 20 miles to Campbellsville.

No material change in this position of affairs in western Kentucky occurred while General Sherman remained in command, though there were several sharp skirmishes between bodies of Kentucky recruits and Confederate scouting parties in the Lower Green River country.

In the mean time the East Tennessee expedition was not progressing. Nelson, whose arbitrary temper had made him enemies among influential politicians, was sent to eastern Kentucky to superintend recruiting camps, and Brigadier-General George H. Thomas took command at Camp Dick Robinson. Thomas was an ardent advocate of the movement on East Tennessee and bent all his energies to getting ready for it, but his command was not half equipped and was wholly without transportation; staff-officers were scarce, and funds were not furnished. More patient than Nelson, he was yet greatly tried by the importunities of the East Tennessee troops, and of the prominent politicians from that region, who made his camp their rendezvous, as well as by military suggestions from civilians more zealous than wise in such matters. The speech-making of distinguished visitors became a burden to

MAJOR-GENERAL LOVELL H. ROUSSEAU.
FROM A PHOTOGRAPH.

him. On one occasion, when General Sherman visited his camp, Ex-Senator J. J. Crittenden, Senator Andrew Johnson, and Horace Maynard were there. A band came from the camp to serenade them, and the soldiers, not yet rid of their civilian characteristics, began calling for speeches from one after another. Thomas withdrew from the orators to the seclusion of a little room used as an office, on one side of the piazza from which they were speaking. One of his aides was writing in a corner, but Thomas did not see him, and began striding up and down the floor in growing irritation. At last Sherman, who was not then such an orator as he is now, finished speaking, and cries arose for "Thomas." He blurted out, "—— this speech-making! I won't speak! What does a man want to make a speech for, anyhow?" Observing that he had an auditor, he strode from the room slamming the door behind him, and kept his own quarters for the rest of the evening.

Accustomed to the discipline of the regular army, and fresh from the well-organized army of General Patterson on the upper Potomac, Thomas had little confidence in the raw recruits whom, for lack of a mustering officer, he mustered in himself. He was willing to advance into East Tennessee with half a dozen well-drilled regiments, and asked for and obtained them, but they came without transportation, and he had none for them. While he was struggling to get ready for an advance, Zollicoffer had made several demonstrations, and to oppose him Garrard's regiment had been thrown forward to a strong position on Wild Cat Mountain just beyond Rockcastle River, supported by a detachment of Wolford's cavalry. On the 17th of October, Garrard reported that Zollicoffer was advancing in force, and asked for reënforcements. Thomas hurried forward several regiments under General Schoepf, who had reported to him shortly before. Schoepf arrived with the 33d Indiana, in time to help in giving Zollicoffer, who had attacked vigorously with two regiments, a decisive repulse. Zollicoffer retired, apparently satisfied with developing Garrard's force, and Thomas moved Schoepf with Carter's East Tennesseeans and several other regiments forward in pursuit, till stopped by order of General Sherman, at London.

On the 12th of November, Sherman, having received information from his advance that a large force was moving between him and Thomas, apparently toward Lexington, ordered the latter to withdraw all his forces north of the Kentucky River. Making arrangements to obey, Thomas at the same time sent an officer to Sherman, urging the impolicy of the move unless absolutely necessary, and controverting the information on which it was based. The order was revoked, but the revocation did not reach Schoepf until his troops had begun the movement. The East Tennessee regiments had received it with an indignation that carried them to the verge of mutiny. They threw their guns to the ground and swore they would not obey. Many actually left the command, though they returned in a few days. It required all of Carter's influence to keep them to their standards, and hundreds of them wept as they turned their backs on their homes. Andrew Johnson was with them, and his indignation had added fuel to their discontent. He was so indiscreet that Thomas seriously contemplated his arrest. On the revocation of the order Carter returned to London, while Schoepf took position soon after at Somerset.

In September Colonel John S. Williams had begun to gather a Confederate force at Prestonburg, in eastern Kentucky, threatening incursions into the central part of the State. On the 8th of November

MAJOR-GENERAL GEORGE B. CRITTENDEN, C. S. A.
FROM A PHOTOGRAPH.

General Crittenden was a son of Senator John J. Crittenden. His brother, Thomas L. Crittenden, was a major-general in the Union army.

General Nelson, who had advanced against him with two Ohio and detachments of several Kentucky regiments, with a part of his force encountered a large detachment thrown forward by Williams to cover his retreat, in a strong position on Ivy Creek. After a well-contested engagement Williams was forced from his position, and retired through Pound Gap [see map, page 394]

FROM A PHOTOGRAPH.

D. C. Buell

into Virginia. Nelson with the Ohio regiments was then ordered to join the column in front of Louisville, where he was assigned to command the Fourth Division. On this expedition Nelson reported as part of his force, "thirty-six gentlemen volunteers," probably the latest appearance in history of that description of soldier. One of them, of strong bibulous propensities, acting as his private secretary, brought about an altercation between Nelson and a wagoner nearly as large, which narrowly missed fatal results. He was anxious to get the driver away from his wagon in which there was a jug of whisky, and directed him to Nelson's tent to find a big fellow who was employed to unhitch teams for tired drivers. He warned him that the big fellow was cross, but told him he must insist on his rights. The driver was just tipsy enough to be reckless, and he roused Nelson with little ceremony.

There was a terrible outburst of fury on both sides, which brought inter-ference just in time to prevent a conflict between the two giants, one armed with a sword, and the other with a loaded whip-handle. The aide, not reporting next morning, was, after some search, found sound asleep in a wagon with the jug beside him. He was a noted wag, and Nelson, recognizing him at once as the author of the trick, dismissed him to his home.

A visit from Secretary Cameron and Adjutant-General Lorenzo Thomas, on their return from St. Louis in the latter part of October, resulted in the removal of General Sherman. In explaining the needs of his department to the Secretary, Sherman expressed the opinion that two hundred thousand men would be required for successful operations on his line. This estimate, which, as events showed, evinced remarkable foresight, then discredited his judgment. On their way to St. Louis, on the same tour, the Secretary had ordered General O. M. Mitchel to take charge of the East Tennessee expedition, superseding General Thomas, but General Sherman succeeded in having the order recalled.

On November 15th, General Don Carlos Buell assumed command of the Department of the Ohio, enlarged so as to include the States of Ohio, Mich-igan, and Indiana.‡ He was given the advantage, not enjoyed by his prede-cessors, of controlling the new troops organized in those States. By one of his first orders, General Thomas was directed to concentrate his command at Lebanon. The new commander began at once the task of creating an efficient army out of the raw material at hand. He organized the regiments into bri-gades and divisions, and subjected them to a system of drill and discipline the beneficial effects of which endured throughout the war.

The advance into East Tennessee remained a favorite project with the author-ities at Washington. Buell's instructions presented Knoxville as the objective of his first campaign. McClellan wrote several times urging that the seizing of the East Tennessee and Virginia railroad was essential to the success of his plans, and that the political results likely to follow success in that direction made the movement of the first importance. Buell did not consider East Tennessee important enough to be his principal objective; he wanted it to be a subordinate feature in a great campaign. He submitted his plans to McClellan in a personal letter. They were comprehensive and required a large force, and it was already seen that Sherman's estimate was not so far out of the way. Buell proposed that a heavy column should be moved up the Ten-nessee and Cumberland rivers by steamer, to unite with another moving on Nashville, to the eastward of Bowling Green. Demonstrations were to be made in front of Columbus and Bowling Green, sufficient to keep the forces holding them fully occupied until their retreat was cut off by the marching columns. At the same time an expedition from Lebanon, moving by way of Somerset, was to be directed against East Tennessee. Until he was ready to move, he desired to do nothing to put the enemy on the alert. His bri-gades and regiments were allowed to remain in apparently objectless dispersion. He did not care if some isolated posts were occasionally raided by the enemy. But his regiments were frequently inspected and required to keep constantly ready for a movement the day and hour of which he proposed to keep to himself. The notion that Buckner or Zollicoffer contemplated an advance, which so frequently agitated the military mind before he came, was dismissed by him as idle. "I would as soon," he wrote to McClellan, "expect to meet the Army of the Potomac marching up the road, as Johnston."

His policy of quiet had to be laid aside when, early in December, Morgan and Helm burned the Bacon Creek bridge in his front. He advanced his lines to Munfordville and threw forward a small force beyond Green River. This resulted in a skirmish between a portion of the 32d Indiana, deployed as skirmishers, and Terry's Texas Cavalry—notable as one of the few fights of the war between infantry skirmishers in the open and cavalry.

Nothing else of moment occurred on Buell's main line until the capture of Forts Henry and Donelson compelled Johnston to retire from Bowling Green and leave the road to Nashville open.) During November Buell reviewed Thomas's command at Lebanon, and advised with him about an attack on Zollicoffer, who to meet a rumored advance had left Cumberland Gap in charge of a strong garrison, had made his appearance on the Cumberland at Mill Springs, a few miles south-west of Somerset, had crossed the river, and after some picket-firing with Schoepf had intrenched himself on the north side.

General Thomas left Lebanon on the 1st of January. As far as Columbia there was a good turnpike; beyond, only mud roads. It rained incessantly, and artillery carriages and wagons sank to their axles in the soft soil. On one part of the route eight days were consumed in advancing forty miles.

) The letter which follows shows Mr. Lincoln's ideas of what was demanded by the situation:

"Executive Mansion, Washington, January 13th, 1862. BRIGADIER-GENERAL BUELL: My dear sir,—Your dispatch of yesterday is received, in which you say, 'I have received your letter and General McClellan's, and will at once devote all my efforts to your views and his.' In the midst of my many cares, I have not seen or asked to see General McClellan's letter to you. For my own views, I have not offered, and do not now offer them, as orders; and while I am glad to have them respectfully considered, I would blame you to follow them contrary to your own clear judgment, unless I should put them in the form of orders. As to General McClellan's views, you understand your duty in regard to them better than I do. With this preliminary I state my general idea of this war to be that we have the greater numbers and the enemy has the greater facility of concentrating forces upon points of collision; that we must fail unless we can find some way of making our advantage an over-match for his; and that this can only be done by menacing him with superior forces at different points at the same time, so that we can safely attack one or both if he makes no change; and if he weakens one to strengthen the other, forbear to attack the strengthened one, but seize and hold the weakened one, gaining so much. To illustrate: Suppose last summer, when Winchester ran away to reënforce Manassas, we had forborne to attack Manassas, but had seized and held Winchester. I mention this to illustrate, and not to criticise. I did not lose confidence in McDowell, and I think less harshly of Patterson than some others seem to. In application of the general rule I am suggesting, every particular case will have its modifying circumstances, among which the most constantly present and most difficult to meet will be the want of perfect knowledge of the enemy's movements. This had its part in the Bull Run case; but worse in that case was the expiration of the terms of the three-months men. Applying the principle to your case, my idea is that Halleck shall menace Columbus, and 'down-river' generally, while you menace Bowling Green and East Tennessee. If the enemy shall concentrate at Bowling Green, do not retire from his front, yet do not fight him there either, but seize Columbus and East Tennessee, one or both, left exposed by the concentration at Bowling Green. It is a matter of no small anxiety to me, and one which I am sure you will not overlook, that the East Tennessee line is so long and over so bad a road. Yours, very truly, A. LINCOLN. [Indorsement]: January 13th, 1862. Having to-day written General Buell a letter, it occurs to me to send General Halleck a copy of it. A. LINCOLN."

On February 5th, the day before the capture of Fort Henry, General Buell wrote thus to General Halleck in a correspondence with regard to coöperation:

"I think it is quite plain that the center of the enemy's line — that part which you are now moving against — is the decisive point of his whole front, as it is also the most vulnerable. If it is held, or even the bridges on the Cumberland and Tennessee rivers destroyed, and your force maintains itself near those points, Bowling Green will speedily fall, and Columbus will soon follow. The work which you have undertaken is therefore of the very highest importance, without reference to the injurious effects of a failure. There is not in the whole field of operations a point at which every man you can raise can be employed with more effect or with the prospect of as important results." EDITORS.

On the 17th of January Thomas reached Logan's Cross Roads, ten miles north of Zollicoffer's intrenched camp (on the north side of the Cumberland, opposite Mill Springs) and about the same distance west of Somerset, with the 9th Ohio and 2d Minnesota of Robert L. McCook's brigade, the 10th Indiana of Manson's brigade, Kenny's battery, and a battalion of Wolford's cavalry. The 4th Kentucky, 10th Kentucky, the 14th Ohio, Wetmore's battery, and the 18th regulars were still detained in the rear by bad roads. Halting at the cross roads, Thomas communicated with Schoepf and ordered him to send across Fishing Creek to his camp the 12th Kentucky, the 1st and 2d East Tennessee regiments, and Standart's battery, to remain until the arrival of his delayed force. Hearing that a large wagon train, sent on a foraging expedition by Zollicoffer, was on a road about six miles from the camp of Steedman, of the 14th Ohio, he ordered that officer to take his own regiment and Harlan's 10th Kentucky and attempt its capture. On the evening of the 18th the 4th Kentucky, the battalion of Michigan Engineers, and the battery arrived and went into camp near the 10th Indiana.

THE BATTLE OF LOGAN'S CROSS ROADS (MILL SPRINGS).

A FEW days before this General George B. Crittenden had arrived at Zollicoffer's camp and assumed command. Hearing of the arrival of Thomas with part of his command, and believing that Fishing Creek, which was a troublesome stream at any stage of water, was unfordable from recent rains, he called a council of his brigade and regimental commanders to consider the propriety of making an attack on Thomas before he could be reached by Schoepf or his regiments in the rear. There was little delay in coming to a decision. Their camp on the north side of the river was not tenable against a strong attack, and the means of crossing the river were so insufficient that a withdrawal without great loss could not have been effected, in the face of an enterprising enemy. The only chance for a satisfactory issue was to attack Thomas before he could concentrate. Crittenden ordered a movement to begin at midnight on the 18th in the following order: General Zollicoffer's brigade, consisting of two cavalry companies, a Mississippi regiment, three Tennessee regiments, and a battery in front; next, the brigade of General Carroll, composed of three Tennessee regiments and a section of artillery. An Alabama regiment and two cavalry regiments, intended as a reserve, closed the column. After a march of nine miles over muddy roads and through the rain, his cavalry about daylight encountered Wolford's pickets, who after firing fell back on the reserve, consisting of two companies of the 10th Indiana, and with them made a determined stand, in which they were promptly supported by Wolford with the rest of his battalion, and soon after by the rest of the 10th Indiana, ordered up by Manson, who had been advised by courier from Wolford of the attack. Colonel Manson proceeded in person to order forward the 4th Kentucky and the battery of his brigade and to report to General Thomas. On his way he notified Colonel Van Cleve, of the 2d Minnesota. As Manson dashed through the camp of the 4th Kentucky shouting for Colonel Speed S. Fry, and giving warning of the attack, the men, wearied with the muddy march of the day before, were just beginning to crawl out of their tents to roll-call. Forming rapidly, Fry led them at double-quick in the direction of the firing. Having no one to place him, on coming in sight of the enemy, he took position along a fence in the edge of the woods, with his right resting near the Mill Springs road. In front of him was an open field, across which the enemy were advancing from the shelter of woodland on the opposite side. A ravine ran through the open field parallel to Fry's front, heading near the road on his right, with steep sides in his front, but sloping gradually beyond his left. Before Fry's arrival Zollicoffer had deployed his brigade, and had forced Wolford and the 10th Indiana to fall back, almost capturing the horses of Wolford's men, who were fighting on foot. A portion of Wolford's command, under his immediate charge, and Vanarsdall's company of the 10th Indiana, rallied on the 4th Kentucky when it appeared, the remainder of the 10th falling back to its encampment, where it re-formed its lines. Fry was at once subjected to a severe attack. The enemy in his front crawled up under shelter of the

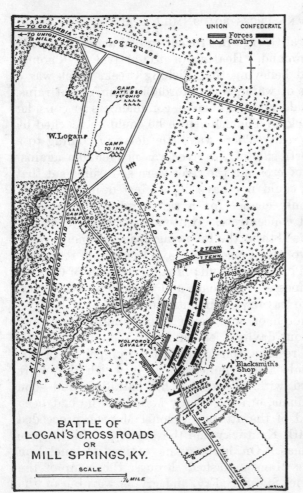

BATTLE OF
LOGAN'S CROSS ROADS
OR
MILL SPRINGS, KY.

SCALE

¼ MILE

ravine to within a short distance of his lines before delivering their fire, and Fry, mounting the fence, in stentorian tones denounced them as dastards, and defied them to stand up on their feet and come forward like men.

A little lull in the firing occurring at this juncture, Fry rode a short distance to the right to get a better view of the movement of the enemy in that direction. The morning was a lowering one, and the woods were full of smoke. As Fry turned to regain his position he encountered a mounted officer whose uniform was covered with a water-proof coat. After approaching till their knees touched, the stranger said to Fry: "We must not fire on our own men"; and nodding his head to his left, he said, "Those are our men." Fry said, "Of course not. I would not do so intentionally"; and he began to move toward his regiment, when turning he saw another mounted man riding from the trees who fired and wounded Fry's horse. Fry at once fired on the man who had accosted him, and several of his men, observing the incident, fired at the same time. The shots were fatal, and the horseman fell dead, pierced by a pistol-shot in his breast and by two musket-balls. It was soon ascertained that it was Zollicoffer himself who had fallen. In the mean time, the enemy were pressing Fry in front and overlapping his right. On his right front only the fence separated the combatants. The left of his regiment not being assailed, he moved two companies from that flank to his right. As he was making this change General Thomas appeared on the field, and at once placed the 10th Indiana in position to cover Fry's exposed flank.

The fall of Zollicoffer and the sharp firing that followed caused two of his regiments to retreat in confusion. Crittenden then brought up Carroll's brigade to the support of the other two, and ordered a general advance. Thomas met this by placing a section of Kenny's battery on the left of the 4th Kentucky, which was overlapped by Carroll's line, ordered the 12th Kentucky to the left of Kenny's two guns, and Carter with the two East Tennessee regiments, and Wetmore's battery still farther to the left, in front of the Somerset road. Standart's battery and Kenny's remaining

BRIG.-GEN. FELIX K. ZOLLICOFFER, C. S. A.
FROM A PHOTOGRAPH.

guns were held in the rear of the center, and McCook's two regiments were ordered up, the 9th Ohio on the right of the 10th Indiana, and the 2d Minnesota in reserve behind the latter regiment and the 4th Kentucky. During these movements Kenny's section was so threatened that it was withdrawn some distance to the rear. There was little opportunity for the effective use of artillery on either side, and that arm played an insignificant part in the engagement, Thomas's superiority in that particular availing him little. Carroll's attack was pressed with great courage, and the ammunition of the 4th Kentucky and 10th Indiana beginning to fail, the 2d Minnesota was ordered to relieve them, which it did under severe fire. Both of McCook's regiments were admirably drilled and disciplined, and moved to the attack with the order and steadiness of veterans. Thomas's disposition of his troops had begun to tell. The advance of the 12th Kentucky on the left, the firing of Wetmore's battery, and the movement of Carter's East Tennesseeans checked the enemy's right, and it soon began to give back. The 2d Minnesota was slowly pushing forward over the ground that had been the scene of the most persistent fighting from the first, and the 9th Ohio, on the right, was forcing back the enemy through open ground, when, slightly changing direction, it made a bayonet charge against the enemy's left, which gave way in confusion. Their whole line then broke into a disorderly retreat. After replenishing cartridge-boxes, Thomas pushed forward in pursuit. Within a few miles, a small body of the enemy's cavalry attempted to make a stand, but were scattered by a few shells from Standart. The road which the retreating force followed was strewn with evidences that the retreat had degenerated into a panic. A piece of artillery was found abandoned in a mud hole, hundreds

of muskets were strewn along the road and in the fields, and, most convincing proof of all, the flying foe had thrown away their haversacks filled with rations of corn pone and bacon. Those were the days when stories of "rebel atrocities" in the way of poisoning wells and food were current, and the pursuers, who had gone into the fight breakfastless, were doubtful about tasting the contents of the first haversacks they observed. Their great number, however, soon became a guarantee of good faith, and the hungry soldiers seized on them with avidity. As Crittenden in his report mentioned the loss of all the cooked rations carried to the field as enhancing the distress of his subsequent retreat, the abundance of the supply obtained by the pursuing force may be inferred. On arriving near the enemy's intrenchments the division was deployed in line of battle,

BRIGADIER-GENERAL SPEED S. FRY.
FROM A PHOTOGRAPH.

advancing to the summit of the hill at Moulden's, which commanded the enemy's intrenchments. From this point Standart and Wetmore's batteries kept up a cannonade till dark, while Kenny's on the left, at Russell's house, fired upon their ferry to keep them from crossing. The 14th Ohio and the 10th Kentucky had come up during the pursuit, and were placed in advance for the assault ordered for daybreak. General Schoepf arrived about dark with the 17th, 31st, and 38th Ohio. [See also pp. 546, 547.]

At daybreak next morning Wetmore's Parrott guns, which had been moved to Russell's, began firing on the steamer which was evidently engaged in crossing troops, and it was soon abandoned and set on fire by the enemy. The assaulting columns moved forward, the 10th Kentucky and the 14th Ohio in advance, and reaching the intrenchments found them abandoned. In the bottom near the ferry-crossing were found 11 pieces of artillery, with their caissons, battery-wagons, and forges, hitched up and ready to move but abandoned by the artillerymen, more than 150 wagons, and over 1000 horses and mules. All the troops had escaped. The steep road on the other bank was strewn with abandoned baggage and other evidences of disorderly flight. The boats used for crossing having been destroyed by the retreating enemy, no immediate pursuit was possible; but during the day means were improvised for getting the 14th Ohio across for a reconnoissance and to secure abandoned property.

Thomas reported his loss in action as 39 killed and 207 wounded, the casualties being confined entirely to the 10th Indiana, 4th Kentucky, 2d Minnesota, 9th Ohio, and Wolford's cavalry. Colonels McCook and Fry were among the wounded. The enemy's loss he reported as 192 killed, 89 prisoners not wounded, and 68 prisoners wounded. Crittenden's report stated his own loss at 125 killed, 309 wounded, and 99 missing, much the heaviest loss being in the 15th Mississippi (Lieutenant-Colonel E. C. Walthall), of Zollicoffer's brigade, which had led the attack on Fry and fought through the whole engagement.

Besides the property mentioned above, a large amount of ammunition, commissary stores, intrenching tools, camp and garrison equipage and muskets, and five stands of colors were found in the camp. The demoralization was acknowledged by Crittenden in his report, in which he says: "From Mill Springs and on the first steps of my march officers and men, frightened by false rumors of the movements of the enemy, shamefully deserted, and, stealing horses and mules to ride, fled to Knoxville, Nashville, and other places in Tennessee." Of one cavalry battalion, he reported that all had deserted except twenty-five. On his retreat his sick-list increased greatly from lack of food and fatigue, and the effective force of his army was practically destroyed.

After entrance into his intrenchments had demonstrated the panic that existed in the enemy's forces, Fry said to Thomas: "General, why didn't you send in a demand for surrender last night?" Looking at him a moment as if reflecting, Thomas replied: "Hang it, Fry, I never once thought of it." At this time originated a saying often heard in the Western army afterward. A sprightly young prisoner slightly wounded was allowed the freedom of the camp.

NATIONAL CEMETERY AT LOGAN'S CROSS ROADS.
FROM A PHOTOGRAPH TAKEN IN 1887.

To some soldiers chaffing him about his army being in such a hurry as even to throw away their haversacks, he replied: "Well, we were doing pretty good fighting till old man Thomas rose up in his stirrups, and we heard him holler out: 'Attention, Creation! By kingdoms right wheel!' and then we knew you had us, and it was no time to carry weight."

Thomas's victory was complete, and the road was opened for the advance into East Tennessee which he had so long endeavored to make and which was

VIEW ON THE BATTLE-FIELD OF LOGAN'S CROSS ROADS. FROM A PHOTOGRAPH, 1887.

contemplated by his instructions, but the scarcity of provisions, the badness of the roads, and the difficulty of crossing the river made progress on that line impracticable, and shortly afterward Carter was ordered with his brigade against Cumberland Gap and Thomas to rejoin Buell's main column, and the East Tennessee expedition, which Nelson had devised and McClellan had strongly urged and Thomas had labored so to put in motion, was definitively abandoned.

While Thomas was marching against Zollicoffer, Colonel Garfield was driving Humphrey Marshall from the mountainous region along the Virginia border. With Marshall's retreat the last Confederate force was driven from the State, and Garfield with his brigade joined the army in Tennessee.

THE OPPOSING FORCES AT LOGAN'S CROSS ROADS, KNOWN AS MILL SPRINGS AND ALSO AS FISHING CREEK, KY.

The composition and losses of each army as here stated give the gist of all the data obtainable in the Official Records. K stands for killed; w for wounded; m w for mortally wounded; m for captured or missing; c for captured.—EDITORS.

THE UNION ARMY, Brig.-Gen. George H. Thomas. *Second Brigade*, Col. Mahlon D. Manson: 10th Ind., Lt.-Col. William C. Kise; 4th Ky., Col. Speed S. Fry (w); 10th Ky., Col. John M. Harlan; 14th Ohio, Col. James B. Steedman. [The two latter regiments were engaged only in the pursuit of the enemy.] Brigade loss: k, 19; w, 127 = 146. *Third Brigade*, Col. Robert L. McCook (w): 2d Minn., Col. Horatio P. Van Cleve; 9th Ohio, Major Gustave Kammerling. Brigade loss: k, 18; w, 61 = 79; *Twelfth Brigade*, Acting Brig.-Gen. Samuel P. Carter: 12th Ky., Col. William A. Hoskins; 1st Tennessee, Col. Robert K. Byrd; 2d Tennessee, Col. J. P. T. Carter; 1st Ky. Cavalry, Col. Frank Wolford. Brigade loss: k, 3; w, 19; m, 15 = 37. *Artillery:* Battery B, 1st Ohio, Capt. William E. Standart; Battery C, 1st Ohio, Capt. Dennis Kenny, Jr.; 9th Ohio Battery, Capt. Henry S. Wetmore. *Camp Guard:* D, F, and K, Michigan Engineers and Mechanics, Lieut.-Col. K. A. Hunton; A, 38th Ohio, Capt. Charles Greenwood.

Brig.-Gen. A. Schoepf joined Thomas on the evening of the battle, after the fighting had ceased, with the 17th, 31st, and 38th Ohio.

The total loss of the Union forces was 40 killed, 207 wounded, and 15 captured or missing,—aggregate, 262.

In the Official Records, vol. VII., p. 86, Col. Manson reports that "the Federal force actually engaged did not exceed at any time over 2500." Gen. Thomas's entire command on the field during the engagement probably numbered about four thousand effectives.

THE CONFEDERATE ARMY, Major-Gen. George B. Crittenden. *First Brigade*, Brig.-Gen. F. K. Zollicoffer (k), Col. D. H. Cummings: 15th Miss., Lieut.-Col. E. C. Walthall; 19th Tenn., Col. D. H. Cummings, Lieut.-Col. Francis M. Walker; 20th Tenn., Col. Joel A. Battle; 25th Tenn., Col. S. S. Stanton (w); Tenn. Battery, Capt. A. M. Rutledge; Ind'p't Co. Tenn. Cav., Capt. W. S. Bledsoe; Ind'p't Co. Tenn. Cav., Capt. T. C. Sanders. Brigade loss: k, 98; w, 265; m, 66 = 429. *Second Brigade*, Brig.-Gen. Wm. H. Carroll: 16th Ala., Col. Wm. B. Wood; 17th Tenn., Lieut.-Col. T. C. H. Miller; 28th Tenn., Col. J. P. Murray; 29th Tenn., Col. Saml. Powell (w), Major Horace Rice; Tenn. Battery (2 guns), Capt. Hugh L.W. McClung; 4th Battalion Tenn. Cav., Lieut.-Col. B. M. Branner. Brigade loss: k, 28; w, 46; m, 29 = 103. *Reserve:* 5th Battalion Tenn. Cav., Lieut.-Col. George R. McClellan.

The total Confederate loss was 125 killed, 309 wounded, and 99 captured or missing,—aggregate, 533.

Gen. Crittenden says: "In the then condition of my command I could array for battle about 4000 effective men."

MARSHALL AND GARFIELD IN EASTERN KENTUCKY.

BY THE REV. EDWARD O. GUERRANT, ASSISTANT ADJUTANT-GENERAL TO GENERAL MARSHALL.

CONFEDERATE PRIVATE. FROM AN AMBROTYPE.

ON the 10th of September, 1861, General Albert Sidney Johnston, one of the five officers who then held the rank of "General" in the Confederate army, was assigned to the command of Department No. 2, embracing the States of Tennessee and Arkansas, and that part of the State of Mississippi west of the New Orleans, Jackson and Great Northern and Central Railroad; also, the military operations in Kentucky, Missouri, Kansas, and the Indian country immediately west of Missouri and Arkansas. Tennessee had entered into a league with the Confederacy on the 7th of May, 1861, and although the efforts of the Confederates to take Kentucky out of the Union had been defeated, the State contained a large element friendly to secession, from which was recruited at an early day a number of regiments. In order to afford securer opportunities for such enlistments, it was necessary to make an effort to occupy eastern Kentucky. This was desirable, also, in order to protect vital interests of the Confederacy in south-western Virginia, where were situated the great salt-works and lead-mines of the South, and where ran the chief line of railway, connecting Virginia with the Gulf States.

With these objects in view, on the 1st of November, 1861, Brigadier-General Humphrey Marshall was sent by the Confederate Government to take command of certain troops at Prestonburg, Ky., then under command of Colonel (afterward General) John S. Williams. These consisted of a regiment and a battalion in a camp on the Big Sandy, which had been organized in the fall of 1861, by Colonel Williams. The regiment was the 5th Kentucky, the famous "Ragamuffin Regiment," composed almost exclusively of mountain men, and one of the finest corps of soldiers ever enlisted in the army. They were hardy, raw-boned, brave mountaineers, trained to hardships, and armed with long rifles. Colonel Williams had also organized a battalion of mounted riflemen from the famous "Blue Grass" country in central Kentucky, composed of young men of education and fortune,—the class of men who afterward made John Morgan famous as a raider. This force was further increased by the 54th Virginia, under Colonel John H. Trigg, the 29th Virginia, under Colonel A. C. Moore, and a battery of field artillery, under Captain W. C. Jeffress. In General Marshall's official reports, he states that during the campaign of 1861–62 his force never exceeded 1800 effective men of all arms.⸗ The force assigned to him was very small, considering the interests involved and the objects to be attained. The

---

⸗ Yet, on the 30th of December, 1861, General Marshall had reported his force as "equal to 3000," including "battery of four pieces, equal to 600 men."—EDITORS.

MAP OF BIG SANDY RIVER AND
MIDDLE-CREEK BATTLE-FIELD
(JANUARY 10, 1862).

occupation of eastern Kentucky would have required an army of several thousand men. In response to his request for reënforcements, President Davis wrote to General Marshall that they "were sorely pressed on every side," and were unable to send him any troops.

It was a very severe winter, and Marshall's men were poorly clad, and many of the soldiers were nearly naked. One regiment had 350 barefooted men and not over 100 blankets for 700 men. General Albert Sidney Johnston, observing their condition, sent them one thousand suits of clothes, including hats and shoes. These supplies reached the army at Whitesburg, Ky. An incident connected with the distribution of them will serve to illustrate the poverty of the Quartermaster's Department, and the ready genius of General Marshall. When the quartermaster distributed the clothing among the soldiers, it was noticed that they examined with suspicion the peculiar color and texture of the cloth. General Marshall discovering that it was *cotton*, and fearing the result of such a discovery by his men, rose to the occasion with a stirring speech, in which he eulogized the courage, endurance, and patriotism of his men, and commended the Government for its thoughtful care of them, and relieved their fears as to the quality of the goods by assuring them that they were "woven out of the *best quality of Southern wool, with which, doubtless, many of the Kentuckians were not acquainted.*" The men took the general's word for it (with a grain of salt) and walked off to their quarters with their cottonade suits. The general often remarked afterward that the deception nearly choked him, adding, "but something had to be done."

The army was not only badly clothed, but in general badly armed. Many of the men had only shot-guns and squirrel rifles. Requisitions on the War Department were not filled for want of supplies; and General Lee wrote that owing to the scarcity of arms he was having *pikes* made, which he offered to furnish General Marshall for his unarmed troops.

The field of operations lay in the Cumberland Mountains, along the sources of the Big Sandy River,—a poor, wild, thinly settled country. The roads ran along the water-courses between the mountains, and were often rendered impassable by the high waters, and during this winter were ruined by the passage of cavalry, wagons, and artillery. Captain Jeffress was three days moving his battery from Gladesville to Pound Gap, only sixteen miles. General Marshall's report states that his wagons were sometimes unable to make over four miles a day. An unusual amount of rain fell, drenching the unprotected soldiers, most of them raw recruits, and keeping the roads deep and the waters high. This first winter was the worst of the war, and the scanty rations and great hardships made hundreds of the men sick. Besides, the measles and mumps broke out in the camps, and many died from these diseases and from exposure. The command at Prestonburg was over one hundred miles from its base of supplies at Abingdon, Va., with the Cumberland Mountains between. The farms were generally small and poor, lying along the mountain-sides or in narrow valleys. During January, 1862, corn was worth ten dollars per barrel, and had to be hauled thirty miles over desperate roads. For weeks they subsisted upon mountain beef and parched corn. These privations General Marshall shared, giving up his tent to the sick and wounded, and sleeping beneath a wagon.

BRIGADIER-GENERAL JAMES A. GARFIELD.
FROM A WAR-TIME PHOTOGRAPH.

On the 17th of December, 1861, General Don Carlos Buell, then in command of the Department of the Ohio, including Kentucky, assigned Colonel (afterward General and President) James A. Garfield, of Ohio, to command his Eighteenth Brigade, and sent him against General Marshall. Colonel Garfield concentrated his forces at Louisa, at the forks of the Sandy, from which place he began his advance movement on the 23d of December. His army consisted of his own regiment, the 42d Ohio, under Lieutenant-Colonel L. A. Sheldon, the 1st Squadron Ohio Cavalry, Major William McLaughlin, the 14th Kentucky, Colonel L. T. Moore, the 22d Kentucky, Colonel D. W. Lindsey, 2d Virginia Cavalry (6 companies), Lieutenant-Colonel W. M. Bolles, the 40th Ohio, Colonel Jonathan Cranor, and 300 of the 1st Kentucky Cavalry, Lieutenant-Colonel J. W. Letcher, numbering in all some three thousand men. Garfield having found the road up the river impassable for wagons, many were taken to pieces and conveyed on boats; others, that were empty, were pulled by the men. His supplies were brought up on steam-boats and push-boats.

On the 6th of January, 1862, Garfield arrived within seven miles of Paintsville, where Marshall had established his camp and headquarters. It had been Marshall's intention to offer battle at Hagar's farm, near Paintsville, but he had intercepted a letter from Garfield to Cranor, who, with his regiment and some 400 cavalry, was advancing upon Marshall's left and rear from the direction of Salyersville. He then decided to fall back to the forks of Middle Creek, where he awaited the approach of the Federal forces. Garfield and Cranor made a junction near Paintsville, and all moved up to Marshall's front on the 10th of January.

General Marshall had selected a strong position along a high ridge south of Middle Creek, and covering the road to Virginia by way of Beaver Creek. Jeffress's battery was placed in a gorge of the left fork of Middle Creek; the 5th Kentucky and 29th Virginia regiments and part of the Kentucky Battalion of Mounted Riflemen occupied the spurs and heights to the right of the artillery; the 54th Virginia occupied a height covering the battery, with two cavalry companies in reserve; two other cavalry companies (dismounted and armed with Belgian rifles) were placed across Middle Creek, on a height commanding the valley. Skirmishing between the two commands began about 10 A.M., but the action began in earnest about noon by a charge of Federal cavalry, supported by infantry. This attack was repulsed, the artillery putting the cavalry to flight, and it appeared no more during the engagement. The men probably dismounted and fought on foot, as the ground was not suitable for cavalry operations. Colonel Garfield then endeavored to take the ridge occupied by the 5th Kentucky and 29th Virginia, on the right wing of General Marshall's position. He moved his infantry up the side of the mountain, above Spurlock's Branch, and made a desperate attempt to dislodge the Confederate forces, commanded by Colonel Williams, but was repulsed. The attack was renewed

BRIGADIER-GENERAL HUMPHREY MARSHALL.
FROM A PHOTOGRAPH.

three times, with the same result. The ascent was steep, the top of the mountain was covered with trees and rocks affording good protection to the Confederate forces. The engagement lasted until dark, both sides claiming the victory, and both withdrawing from the field of battle.

General Marshall estimated Colonel Garfield's forces at 5000, ⚓ and states his own at *not over* 1500. In his official report to the War Department he gives his losses at 11 killed and 15 wounded.

General Marshall withdrew his forces next day, taking three days to reach Martin's Mill on Beaver Creek,—sixteen miles from the battle-field. This was the nearest point at which he could get provisions for his men, some of whom had fasted for thirty hours before the action.

Colonel Garfield withdrew his forces, February 22d, to the Big Sandy River, where he remained until March. This was the only engagement between the

⚓ Garfield's strength on the field did not exceed 1700 men. He says in his report: "Not more than 900 of my force were actually engaged." Marshall's estimate of his own (1500) is probably correct. The Union loss was 2 killed and 25 wounded. Garfield's reports exhibit no doubt of his success in the engagement. He says: "At 4.30 he ordered a retreat. My men drove him down the slopes of the hills, and at 5 o'clock he had been driven from every point. . . . . It was growing dark, and I deemed it unsafe to pursue him." Garfield withdrew to Paintsville on the 12th and 13th, to procure supplies, having on the 11th occupied Prestonburg, which the enemy had abandoned.'—EDITORS.

two forces. The next month General Marshall sent the bulk of his command south of the Cumberland Mountains, to go into winter quarters, because all supplies were exhausted in the mountains of Kentucky. General Marshall's forces would probably have been compelled to return to Virginia in order to secure supplies, even if they had not been opposed by an enemy. The occupation of the Sandy Valley by a largely superior force so crippled his resources that he could hardly have subsisted his troops among the impoverished mountains. Indeed, Colonel Garfield could not have maintained his position a week, without the aid of the river, by which supplies were brought on steamboats. On the 16th of March, 1862, Garfield with 750 men made an attack on a battalion of Virginia militia, occupying Pound Gap, and drove them away and burned the log-huts built for winter quarters. Soon after this he was ordered to report to General Buell, who had gone to the relief of General Grant at Pittsburg Landing. This he did on the 7th of April, 1862, in time to take part in the second day's contest.

General Marshall was born January 13th, 1812, in Frankfort, Ky., and came of a most distinguished family, which included Chief-Justice John Marshall of Virginia, the historian Humphrey Marshall of Kentucky, and the orator and lawyer Thomas F. Marshall. He was four times elected to Congress from the Louisville District, and was Minister to China under President Fillmore. In his profession of law Humphrey Marshall had probably no superior and few equals among the jurists of Kentucky. As an orator he fully inherited the talent of a family which was famous in the forum. As a soldier he enjoyed the confidence of General Lee, who wrote him frequently in reference to military operations, and earnestly opposed his retirement from the army. He was a graduate of West Point, and both he and General Williams had won distinction in the Mexican war—Marshall at Buena Vista and Williams at Cerro Gordo.

General Marshall personally was not adapted to mountain warfare, owing to his great size; nor was he qualified to command volunteers, being the most democratic of men. Moreover, his heart was tender as a woman's. For these reasons he could not enforce the rigorous discipline of an army. So well known was his leniency, that an officer of his staff made a standing offer to eat the first man the general should shoot for any crime. Speaking to Colonel Leigh about military dignity and discipline, Marshall said he " regarded these things as the decrepitudes of the military art." General Williams, who was his ablest lieutenant, was a man of very different mold, proud, imperious, a born soldier, who believed in discipline to its last extremity.

With his little command Marshall afterward successfully defended the vital interests of the Confederacy in south-west Virginia, so long as he remained in the service. In the summer of 1863 he was transferred to the Mississippi Department, but resigned his commission because he believed that he had been badly treated by President Davis in not having received the governmental support which he thought he deserved and which the necessities of his command required.

THE CAPTURE OF FORT DONELSON.

BY LEW WALLACE, MAJOR-GENERAL, U. S. V.

HEADQUARTERS IN THE FIELD.

THE village of Dover was — and for that matter yet is — what our English cousins would call the "shire-town" of the county of Stewart, Tennessee. In 1860 it was a village unknown to fame, meager in population, architecturally poor. There was a court-house in the place, and a tavern, remembered now as double-storied, unpainted, and with windows of eight-by-ten glass, which, if the panes may be likened to eyes, were both squint and cataractous. Looking through them gave the street outside the appearance of a sedgy slough of yellow backwater. The entertainment furnished man and beast was good of the kind; though at the time mentioned a sleepy traveler, especially if he were of the North, might have been somewhat vexed by the explosions which spiced the good things of a debating society that nightly took possession of the bar-room, to discuss the relative fighting qualities of the opposing sections.

If there was a little of the romantic in Dover itself, there was still less of poetic quality in the country round about it. The only beautiful feature was the Cumberland River, which, in placid current from the south, poured its waters, ordinarily white and pure as those of the springs that fed it, past the village on the east. Northward there was a hill, then a small stream, then a bolder hill round the foot of which the river swept to the west, as if courteously bent on helping Hickman's Creek out of its boggy bottom and cheerless ravine. North of the creek all was woods. Taking in the ravine of the creek, a system of hollows, almost wide and deep enough to be called valleys, inclosed the town and two hills, their bluffest ascents being on the townward side. Westward of the hollows there were woods apparently interminable. From Fort Henry, twelve miles north-west, a road entered the village, stopping first to unite itself with another wagon-way, now famous as the Wynn's Ferry road, coming more directly from the west. Still another road, leading off to Charlotte and Nashville, had been cut across the low ground near the river on the south. These three highways were the chief reliances of the people of Dover for communication with the country, and as they were more than supplemented by the river and its boatage, the three were left the year round to the guardianship of the winds and rains.

However, when at length the Confederate authorities decided to erect a military post at Dover, the town entered but little into consideration. The real inducement was the second hill on the north — more properly a ridge. As it rose about a hundred feet above the level of the inlet, the reconnoitering engineer, seeking to control the navigation of the river by a fortification, adopted it at sight. And for that purpose the bold bluff was in fact a happy gift of nature, and we shall see presently how it was taken in hand and made terrible.

It is of little moment now who first enunciated the idea of attacking the rebellion by way of the Tennessee River; most likely the conception was simultaneous with many minds. The trend of the river; its navigability for large steamers; its offer of a highway to the rear of the Confederate hosts in Kentucky and the State of Tennessee; its silent suggestion of a secure passage into the heart of the belligerent land, from which the direction of movement could be changed toward the Mississippi, or, left, toward Richmond; its many advantages as a line of supply and of general communication, must have been discerned by every military student who, in the summer of 1861, gave himself to the most cursory examination of the map. It is thought better and more consistent with fact to conclude that its advantages as a strategic line, so actually obtrusive of themselves, were observed about the same time by thoughtful men on both sides of the contest. With every problem of attack there goes a counter problem of defense.

A peculiarity of the most democratic people in the world is their hunger for heroes. The void in that respect had never been so gaping as in 1861. General Scott was then old and passing away, and the North caught eagerly at the promise held out by George B. McClellan; while the South, with as much precipitation, pinned its faith and hopes on Albert Sidney Johnston. There is little doubt that up to the surrender of Fort Donelson the latter was considered the foremost soldier of all who chose rebellion for their part. When the shadow of that first great failure fell upon the veteran, President Davis made haste to reassure him of his sympathy and unbroken confidence. In the official correspondence which has survived the Confederacy there is nothing so pathetic, and at the same time so indicative of the manly greatness of Albert Sidney Johnston, as his letter in reply to that of his chief. |

| In this letter dated Decatur, Ala., March 18th, 1862, General Johnston says in part :

"The blow [Fort Donelson] was most disastrous and almost without remedy. I therefore in my first report remained silent. This silence you were kind enough to attribute to my generosity. I will not lay claim to the motive to excuse my course. I observed silence, as it seemed to me the best way to serve the cause and the country. The facts were not fully known, discontent prevailed, and criticism or condemnation were more likely to augment than to cure the evil. I refrained, well knowing that heavy censures would fall upon me, but convinced that it was better to endure them for the present, and defer to a more propitious time an investigation of the conduct of the generals ; for in the mean time their services were required and their influence useful. For these reasons Generals Floyd and Pillow were assigned to duty, for I still felt confidence in their gallantry, their energy, and their devotion to the Confederacy. . . . The test of merit, in my profession, with the people, is success. It is a hard rule, but I think it right. If I join this corps to the forces of Beauregard (I confess a hazardous experiment), those who are now declaiming against me will be without an argument."

EDITORS.

THE TOWN OF DOVER FROM ROBINSON'S HILL.
FROM A PHOTOGRAPH TAKEN IN 1884.

This view was taken from the site of a house on McClernand's right, which was destroyed for camp purposes after the surrender. The house is said to have been used by McClernand as headquarters. It was near the Wynn's ferry road, which reaches the river perhaps a quarter of a mile to the right of the picture.

When General Johnston assumed command of the Western Department, the war had ceased to be a new idea. Battles had been fought. Preparations for battles to come were far advanced. Already it had been accepted that the North was to attack and the South to defend. The Mississippi River was a central object; if opened from Cairo to Fort Jackson (New Orleans), the Confederacy would be broken into halves, and good strategy required it to be broken. The question was whether the effort would be made directly or by turning its defended positions. Of the national gun-boats afloat above Cairo, some were formidably iron-clad. Altogether the flotilla was strong enough to warrant the theory that a direct descent would be attempted; and to meet the movement the Confederates threw up powerful batteries, notably at Columbus, Island Number Ten, Memphis, and Vicksburg. So fully were they possessed of that theory that they measurably neglected the possibilities of invasion by way of the Cumberland and Tennessee rivers. Not until General Johnston established his headquarters at Nashville was serious attention given to the defense of those streams. A report to his chief of engineers of November 21st, 1861, establishes that at that date a second battery on the Cumberland at Dover had been completed; that a work on the ridge had been laid out, and two guns mounted; and that the encampment was then surrounded by an abatis of felled timber. Later, Brigadier-General Lloyd Tilghman was sent to Fort Donelson as commandant, and on January 25th he reports the batteries prepared, the entire field-works built with a trace of 2900 feet, and rifle-pits to guard the approaches were begun. The same officer speaks further of reënforcements housed in four hundred log-cabins, and adds that while this was being done at Fort Donelson, Forts Henry and Heiman, over on the Tennessee, were being thoroughly strengthened. January 30th, Fort Donelson was formally inspected by Lieutenant-Colonel Gilmer, chief engineer of the Western Department, and the final touches were ordered to be given it.

It is to be presumed that General Johnston was satisfied with the defenses thus provided for the Cumberland River. From observing General Buell at Louisville, and the stir and movement of multiplying columns under General U. S. Grant in the region of Cairo, he suddenly awoke determined to fight for Nashville at Donelson. To this conclusion he came as late as the beginning of February; and thereupon the brightest of the Southern leaders proceeded to make a capital mistake. The Confederate estimate of the Union force at that time in Kentucky alone was 119 regiments. The force at Cairo, St. Louis, and the towns near the mouth of the Cumberland River was judged to be about as great. It was also known that we had unlimited means of transportation for troops, making concentration a work of but few hours. Still General Johnston persisted in fighting for Nashville, and for that purpose divided his thirty thousand men. Fourteen thousand he kept in observation of Buell at Louisville. Sixteen thousand he gave to defend Fort Donelson. The latter detachment he himself called " the best part of his army." It is difficult to think of a great master of strategy making an error so perilous.

Having taken the resolution to defend Nashville at Donelson, he intrusted the operation to three chiefs of brigade — John B. Floyd, Gideon J. Pillow, and Simon B. Buckner. Of these, the first was ranking officer, and he was at the time under indictment by a grand jury at Washington for malversation as Secretary of War under President Buchanan, and for complicity in an embezzlement of public funds. As will be seen, there came a crisis when the recollection of the circumstance exerted an unhappy influence over his judgment. The second officer had a genuine military record; but it is said of him that he was of a jealous nature, insubordinate, and quarrelsome. His bold attempt to supersede General Scott in Mexico was green in the memories of living men. To give pertinency to the remark, there is reason to believe that a personal misunderstanding between him and General Buckner, older than the rebellion, was yet unsettled when the two met at Donelson. All in all, therefore, there is little doubt that the junior of the three commanders was the fittest for the enterprise intrusted to them. He was their equal in courage; while in devotion to the cause and to his profession of arms, in tactical knowledge, in military bearing, in the faculty of getting the most service out of his inferiors, and inspiring them with confidence in his ability,—as a soldier in all the higher meanings of the word,—he was greatly their superior.

The 6th of February, 1862, dawned darkly after a thunder-storm. Pacing the parapets of the work on the hill above the inlet formed by the junction of Hickman's Creek and the Cumberland River, a sentinel, in the serviceable butternut jeans uniform of the Confederate army of the West, might that

MAP OF FORT DONELSON, AS INVESTED BY GENERAL GRANT; BASED ON THE OFFICIAL MAP
BY GENERAL J. B. McPHERSON.

day have surveyed Fort Donelson almost ready for battle. In fact, very little was afterward done to it. There were the two water-batteries sunk in the northern face of the bluff, about thirty feet above the river; in the lower battery 9 32-pounder guns and 1 10-inch Columbiad, and in the upper another Columbiad, bored and rifled as a 32-pounder, and 2 32-pounder carronades. These guns lay between the embrasures, in snug revetment of sand in coffee-sacks, flanked right and left with stout traverses. The satisfaction of the sentry could have been nowise diminished at seeing the backwater lying deep in the creek; a more perfect ditch against assault could not have been constructed. The fort itself was of good profile, and admirably adapted to the ridge it crowned. Around it, on the landward side, ran the rifle-pits, a continuous but irregular line of logs, covered with yellow clay. From Hickman's Creek they extended far around to the little run just outside the town on the south. If the sentry thought the pits looked shallow, he was solaced to see that they followed the coping of the ascents, seventy or eighty feet in height, up which a foe must charge, and that, where they were weakest, they were strengthened by trees felled outwardly in front of them, so that the interlacing limbs and branches seemed impassable by men under fire. At points inside the outworks, on the inner slopes of the hills, defended thus from view of an enemy as well as from his shot, lay the huts and log-houses of the garrison. Here and there groups of later comers, shivering in their wet blankets, were visible in a bivouac so cheerless that not even morn-ing fires could relieve it. A little music would have helped their sinking spirits, but there was none. Even the picturesque effect of gay uniforms was wanting. In fine, the Confederate sentinel on the ramparts that morning, taking in the whole scene, knew the jolly, rollicking picnic days of the war were over.

To make clearer why the 6th of February is selected to present the first view of the fort, about noon that day the whole garrison was drawn from their quarters by the sound of heavy guns, faintly heard from the direction of Fort Henry, a token by which every man of them knew that a battle was on. The occurrence was in fact expected, for two days before a horseman had ridden to General Tilghman with word that at 4:30 o'clock in the morn-ing rocket signals had been exchanged with the picket at Bailey's Landing, announcing the approach of gun-boats. A second courier came, and then a third; the latter, in great haste, requesting the general's presence at Fort Henry. There was quick mounting at headquarters, and, before the camp could be taken into confidence, the general and his guard were out of sight. Occasional guns were heard the day following. Donelson gave itself up to excitement and conjecture. At noon of the 6th, as stated, there was continuous and heavy cannonading at Fort Henry, and greater excitement at Fort Donel-son. The polemicists in Dover became uneasy and prepared to get away. In the evening fugitives arrived in groups, and told how the gun-boats ran straight upon the fort and took it. The polemicists hastened their departure from town. At exactly midnight the gallant Colonel Heiman marched into Fort Donelson with two brigades of infantry rescued from the ruins of Forts Henry and Heiman. The officers and men by whom they were received then knew that their turn was at hand; and at daybreak, with one mind and firm of purpose, they set about the final preparation.

Brigadier-General Pillow reached Fort Donelson on the .9th; Brigadier-General Buckner came in the night of the 11th; and Brigadier-General Floyd on the 13th. The latter, by virtue of his rank, took command.

The morning of the 13th — calm, spring-like, the very opposite of that of the 6th — found in Fort Donelson a garrison of 28 regiments of infantry: 13 from Tennessee, 2 from Kentucky, 6 from Mississippi, 1 from Texas, 2 from Alabama, 4 from Virginia. There were also present 2 independent battalions, 1 regiment of cavalry, and artillerymen for 6 light batteries, and 17 heavy guns, making a total of quite 18,000 effectives. [See page 430.]

General Buckner's division — 6 regiments and 2 batteries — constituted the right wing, and was posted to cover the land approaches to the water-bat-

GLIMPSE OF THE CUMBERLAND RIVER WHERE THE GUN-BOATS FIRST APPEARED, LOOKING NORTH FROM THE HIGHEST EARTH-WORKS OF FORT DONELSON. FROM A PHOTOGRAPH TAKEN IN 1884.

teries. A left wing was organized into six brigades, commanded respectively by Colonels Heiman, Davidson, Drake, Wharton, McCausland, and Baldwin, and posted from right to left in the order named. Four batteries were distributed amongst the left wing. General Bushrod R. Johnson, an able officer, served the general commanding as chief-of-staff. Dover was converted into a depot of supplies and ordnance stores. These dispositions made, Fort Donelson was ready for battle.

It may be doubted if General Grant called a council of war. The nearest approach to it was a convocation held on the *New Uncle Sam*, a steamboat that was afterward transformed into the gun-boat *Blackhawk*. The morning of the 11th of February, a staff-officer visited each commandant of division and brigade with the simple verbal message: "General Grant sends his compliments, and requests to see you this afternoon on his boat." Minutes of the proceedings were not kept; there was no adjournment; each person retired when he got ready, knowing that the march would take place next day, probably in the forenoon.

There were in attendance on the occasion some officers of great subsequent notability. Of these Ulysses S. Grant was first. The world knows him now; then his fame was all before him. A singularity of the volunteer service in that day was that nobody took account of even a first-rate record of the Mexican War. The battle of Belmont, though indecisive, was a much better reference. A story was abroad that Grant had been the last man to take boat at the end of that affair, and the addendum that he had lingered in face of the enemy until he was hauled aboard with the last gang-plank, did him great good. From the first his silence was remarkable. He knew how to keep his temper. In battle, as in camp, he went about quietly, speaking in a conversational tone; yet he appeared to see everything that went on, and was always intent on business. He had a faithful assistant adjutant-general, and appreciated him; he preferred, however, his own eyes, word, and hand. His aides were little more than messengers. In dress he was plain, even negligent; in partial amendment of that his horse was always a good one and well kept. At the council — calling it such by grace — he smoked, but never said a word. In all probability he was framing the orders of march which were issued that night.

Charles F. Smith, of the regular army, was also present. He was a person of superb physique, very tall, perfectly proportioned, straight, square-shoul-dered, ruddy-faced, with eyes of perfect blue, and long snow-white mus-taches. He seemed to know the army regulations by heart, and caught a tac-tical mistake, whether of command or execution, by a kind of mental *coup d'œil.* He was naturally kind, genial, communica-tive, and never failed to answer when information was sought of him; at the same time he believed in "hours of service" regu-larly published by the adjutants as a rabbi be-lieves in the Ten Tables, and to call a court-martial on a "bummer" was in his eyes a sinful waste of sta-tionery. On the occasion

MAJOR-GENERAL JOHN A. McCLERNAND. FROM A PHOTOGRAPH.

of a review General Smith had the bearing of a marshal of France. He could ride along a line of volunteers in the regulation uniform of a briga-dier-general, plume, chapeau, epaulets and all, without exciting laughter — something nobody else could do in the beginning of the war. He was at first accused of disloyalty, and when told of it, his eyes flashed wickedly; then he laughed, and said, "Oh, never mind! They'll take it back after our first battle." And they did. At the time of the meeting on the *New Uncle Sam* he was a brigadier-general, and commanded the division which in the land operations against Fort Henry had marched up the left bank of the river against Fort Heiman.

Another officer worthy of mention was John A. McClernand, also a briga-dier. By profession a lawyer, he was in his first of military service. Brave, industrious, methodical, and of unquestioned cleverness, he was rapidly acquiring the art of war.

There was still another in attendance on the *New Uncle Sam* not to be passed — a young man who had followed General Grant from Illinois, and was seeing his first of military service. No soldier in the least familiar with headquarters on the Tennessee can ever forget the slender figure, large black eyes, hectic cheeks, and sincere, earnest manner of John A. Rawlins, then assistant adjutant-general, afterward major-general and secretary of war. He had two special devotions—to the cause and to his chief. He lived to see the first triumphant and the latter first in peace as well as in war. Probably no officer of the Union was mourned by so many armies.

Fort Henry, it will be remembered, was taken by Flag-Officer Foote on the 6th of February. The time up to the 12th was given to reconnoitering the country in the direction of Fort Donelson. Two roads were discovered: one of twelve miles direct, the other almost parallel with the first, but, on account of a slight divergence, two miles longer.

By 8 o'clock in the morning, the First Division, General McClernand commanding, and the Second, under General Smith [see page 429], were in full march. The infantry of this command consisted of twenty-five regiments in all, or three less than those of the Confederates. Against their six field-batteries General Grant had seven. In cavalry alone he was materially stronger. The rule in attacking fortifications is five to one; to save the Union commander from a charge of rashness, however, he had also at control a fighting quality ordinarily at home on the sea rather than the land. After receiving the surrender of Fort Henry, Flag-Officer Foote had hastened to Cairo to make preparation for the reduction of Fort Donelson. With six of his boats, he passed into the Cumberland River; and on the 12th, while the two divisions of the army were marching across to Donelson, he was hurrying, as fast as steam could drive him and his following, to a second trial of iron batteries afloat against earth batteries ashore. The *Carondelet*, Commander Walke, having preceded him, had been in position below the fort since the 12th. By sundown of the 12th, McClernand and Smith reached the point designated for them in orders.

On the morning of the 13th of February General Grant, with about twenty thousand men, was before Fort Donelson.⚓ We have had a view of the army in the works ready for battle; a like view of that outside and about to go into position of attack and assault is not so easily to be given. At dawn the latter host rose up from the bare ground, and, snatching bread and coffee as best they could, fell into lines that stretched away over hills, down hollows, and through thickets, making it impossible for even colonels to see their regiments from flank to flank.

Pausing to give a thought to the situation, it is proper to remind the reader that he is about to witness an event of more than mere historical interest; he is about to see the men of the North and North-west and of the South and South-west enter for the first time into a strife of arms; on one side, the best blood of Tennessee, Kentucky, Alabama, Mississippi, and Texas, aided materially by fighting representatives from Virginia; on the other, the best blood of Illinois, Ohio, Indiana, Iowa, Missouri, and Nebraska.

⚓ General Grant estimates his available forces at this time at about 15,000, and on the last day at 27,000, 5000 or 6000 of whom were guarding transportation trains in the rear.— EDITORS.

We have now before us a spectacle seldom witnessed in the annals of scientific war—an army behind field-works erected in a chosen position waiting quietly while another army very little superior in numbers proceeds at leisure to place it in a state of siege. Such was the operation General Grant had before him at daybreak of the 13th of February. Let us see how it was accomplished and how it was resisted.

In a clearing about two miles from Dover there was a log-house, at the time occupied by a Mrs. Crisp. As the road to Dover ran close by, it was made the headquarters of the commanding general. All through the night of the 12th, the coming and going was incessant. Smith was ordered to find a position in front of the enemy's right wing, which would place him face to face with Buckner. McClernand's order was to establish himself on the enemy's left, where he would be opposed to Pillow.

A little before dawn Birge's sharp-shooters were astir. Theirs was a peculiar service. Each was a preferred marksman, and carried a long-range Henry rifle, with sights delicately arranged as for target practice. In action each was perfectly independent. They never manœuvred as a corps. When the time came they were asked, "Canteens full?" "Biscuits for all day?" Then their only order, "All right; hunt your holes, boys." Thereupon they dispersed, and, like Indians, sought cover to please themselves behind rocks and stumps, or in hollows. Sometimes they dug holes; sometimes they climbed into trees. Once in a good location, they remained there the day. At night they would crawl out and report in camp. This morning, as I have said, the sharp-shooters dispersed early to find places within easy range of the breastworks.

The movement by Smith and McClernand was begun about the same time. A thick wood fairly screened the former. The latter had to cross an open valley under fire of two batteries, one on Buckner's left, the other on a high point jutting from the line of outworks held by Colonel Heiman of Pillow's command. Graves commanded the first, Maney the second; both were of Tennessee. As always in situations where the advancing party is ignorant of the ground and of the designs of the enemy, resort was had to skirmishers, who are to the main body what antennæ are to insects. Theirs it is to unmask the foe. Unlike sharp-shooters, they act in bodies. Behind the skirmishers, the batteries started out to find positions, and through the brush and woods, down the hollows, up the hills the guns and caissons were hauled. Nowadays it must be a very steep bluff in face of which the good artillerist will stop or turn back. At Donelson, however, the proceeding was generally slow and toilsome. The officer had to find a vantage-ground first; then with axes a road to it was hewn out; after which, in many instances, the men, with the prolongs over their shoulders, helped the horses along. In the gray of the dawn the sharp-shooters were deep in their deadly game; as the sun came up, one battery after another opened fire, and was instantly and gallantly answered; and all the time behind the hidden sharp-shooters, and behind the skirmishers, who occasionally stopped to take a hand in the fray, the regiments marched, route-step, colors flying, after their colonels.

LIEUT.-GENERAL SIMON B. BUCKNER, C. S. A. FROM A PHOTOGRAPH.

About 11 o'clock Commander Walke, of the *Carondelet*, engaged the water-batteries. The air was then full of the stunning music of battle, though as yet not a volley of musketry had been heard. Smith, nearest the enemy at starting, was first in place; and there, leaving the fight to his sharp-shooters and skirmishers and to his batteries, he reported to the chief in the log-house, and, like an old soldier, calmly waited orders. McClernand, following a good road, pushed on rapidly to the high grounds on the right. The appearance of his column in the valley covered by the two Confederate batteries provoked a furious shelling from them. On the double-quick his men passed through it; and when, in the wood beyond, they resumed the route-step and saw that nobody was hurt, they fell to laughing at themselves. The real baptism of fire was yet in store for them.

When McClernand arrived at his appointed place and extended his brigades, it was discovered that the Confederate outworks offered a front too great for him to envelop. To attempt to rest his right opposite their extreme left would necessitate a dangerous attenuation of his line and leave him without reserves. Over on their left, moreover, ran the road already mentioned as passing from Dover on the south to Charlotte and Nashville, which it was of the highest importance to close hermetically so that there would be no communication left General Floyd except by the river. If the road to Charlotte were left to the enemy, they might march out at their pleasure.

The insufficiency of his force was thus made apparent to General Grant, and whether a discovery of the moment or not, he set about its correction. He knew a reënforcement was coming up the river under convoy of Foote; besides which a brigade, composed of the 8th Missouri and the 11th Indiana infantry and Battery A, Illinois, had been left behind at Forts Henry and Heiman under myself. A courier was dispatched to me with an order to bring my command to Donelson. I ferried my troops across the Tennessee in the night, and reported with them at headquarters before noon the next day. The brigade was transferred to General Smith; at the same time an order was put into my hand assigning me to command the Third Division, which was conducted to a position between Smith and McClernand, enabling the latter to extend his line well to the left and cover the road to Charlotte.

Thus on the 14th of February the Confederates were completely invested, except that the river above Dover remained to them. The supineness of General Floyd all this while is to this day incomprehensible. A vigorous attack on the morning of the 13th might have thrown Grant back upon Fort Henry. Such an achievement would have more than offset Foote's conquest. The *morale* to be gained would have alone justified the attempt. But with McClernand's strong division on the right, my own in the center, and C. F. Smith's on the left, the opportunity was gone. On the side of General Grant, the possession of the river was all that was wanting; with that Grant could force the fighting, or wait the certain approach of the grimmest enemy of the besieged — starvation.

DOVER TAVERN — GENERAL BUCKNER'S HEADQUARTERS AND THE SCENE OF THE SURRENDER. FROM A PHOTOGRAPH TAKEN IN 1884.

It is now — morning of the 14th — easy to see and understand with something more than approximate exactness the oppositions of the two forces. Smith is on the left of the Union army opposite Buckner. My division, in the center, confronts Colonels Heiman, Drake, and Davidson, each with a brigade. McClernand, now well over on the right, keeps the road to Charlotte and Nashville against the major part of Pillow's left wing. The infantry on both sides are in cover behind the crests of the hills or in thick woods, listening to the ragged fusillade which the sharp-shooters and skirmishers

MAJOR-GENERAL MORGAN L. SMITH. FROM A PHOTOGRAPH.

maintain against each other almost without intermission. There is little pause in the exchange of shells and round shot. The careful chiefs have required their men to lie down. In brief, it looks as if each party were inviting the other to begin.

These circumstances, the sharpshooting and cannonading, ugly as they may seem to one who thinks of them under comfortable surroundings, did in fact serve a good purpose the day in question in helping the men to forget their sufferings of the night before. It must be remembered that the weather had changed during the preceding afternoon: from ˌsuggestions of spring it turned to intensified winter. From lending a gentle hand in bringing Foote and his iron-clads up the river, the wind whisked suddenly around to the north and struck both armies with a storm of mixed rain, snow, and sleet. All night the tempest blew mercilessly upon the unsheltered, fireless soldier, making sleep impossible. Inside the works, nobody had overcoats; while thousands of those outside had marched from Fort Henry as to a summer fête, leaving coats, blankets, and knapsacks behind them in the camp. More than one stout fellow has since admitted, with a laugh, that nothing was so helpful to him that horrible night as the thought that the wind, which seemed about to turn his blood into icicles, was serving the enemy the same way; they, too, had to stand out and take the blast. Let us now go back to the preceding day, and bring up an incident of McClernand's swing into position.

About the center of the Confederate outworks there was a V-shaped hill, marked sharply by a ravine on its right and another on its left. This Colonel Heiman occupied with his brigade of five regiments — all of Tennessee but one. The front presented was about 2500 feet. In the angle of the V, on the summit of the hill, Captain Maney's battery, also of Tennessee, had been planted. Without protection of any kind, it nevertheless completely swept a large field to the left, across which an assaulting force would have to come in order to get at Heiman or at Drake, next on the south.

Maney, on the point of the hill, had been active throughout the preceding afternoon, and had succeeded in drawing the fire of some of McClernand's guns. The duel lasted until night. Next morning it was renewed with increased sharpness, Maney being assisted on his right by Graves's battery of Buckner's division, and by some pieces of Drake's on his left.

McClernand's advance was necessarily slow and trying. This was not merely a logical result of unacquaintance with the country and the dispositions of the enemy; he was also under an order from General Grant to avoid everything calculated to bring on a general engagement. In Maney's well-served guns he undoubtedly found serious annoyance, if not a positive obstruction. Concentrating guns of his own upon the industrious Confederate, he at length fancied him silenced and the enemy's infantry on the right thrown into confusion — circumstances from which he hastily deduced a favorable chance to deliver an assault. For that purpose he reënforced his Third Brigade, which was nearest the offending battery, and gave the necessary orders.

Up to this time, it will be observed, there had not been any fighting involving infantry in line. This was now to be changed. Old soldiers, rich with experience, would have regarded the work proposed with gravity; they would have shrewdly cast up an account of the chances of success, not to speak of the chances of coming out alive; they would have measured the distance to be passed, every foot of it, under the guns of three batteries, Maney's in the center, Graves's on their left, and Drake's on their right — a direct line of fire doubly crossed. Nor would they have omitted the reception awaiting them from the rifle-pits. They were to descend a hill entangled for two hundred yards with under-brush, climb an opposite ascent partly

MAJOR-GENERAL C. F. SMITH. FROM A PHOTOGRAPH.

shorn of timber; make way through an abatis of tree-tops; then, supposing all that successfully accomplished, they would be at last in face of an enemy whom it was possible to reënforce with all the reserves of the garrison — with the whole garrison, if need be. A veteran would have surveyed the three regiments selected for the honorable duty with many misgivings. Not so the men themselves. They were not old soldiers. Recruited but recently from farms and shops, they accepted the assignment heartily and with youthful confidence in their prowess. It may be doubted if a man in the ranks gave a thought to the questions, whether the attack was to be supported while making, or followed up if successful, or whether it was part of a general advance. Probably the most they knew was that the immediate objective before them was the capture of the battery on the hill.

The line when formed stood thus from the right: the 49th Illinois, then the 17th, and then the 48th, Colonel Haynie. At the last moment, a question of seniority arose between Colonels Morrison and Haynie. The latter was of opinion that he was the ranking officer. Morrison replied that he would conduct the brigade to the point from which the attack was to be made, after which Haynie might take the command, if he so desired.

Down the hill the three regiments went, crashing and tearing through the undergrowth. Heiman, on the lookout, saw them advancing. Before they cleared the woods, Maney opened with shells. At the foot of the descent, in the valley, Graves joined his fire to Maney's. There Morrison reported to Haynie, who neither accepted nor refused the command. Pointing to the hill, he merely said, "Let us take it together." Morrison turned away, and rejoined his own regiment. Here was confusion in the beginning, or worse, an assault begun without a head. Nevertheless, the whole line went forward. On a part of the hillside the trees were yet standing. The open space fell to Morrison and his 49th, and paying the penalty of the exposure, he outstripped his associates. The men fell rapidly; yet the living rushed on and up, firing as they went. The battery was the common target. Maney's gunners, in relief against the sky, were shot down in quick succession. His first lieutenant (Burns) was one of the first to suffer. His second lieutenant (Massie) was mortally wounded. Maney himself was hit; still he staid, and his guns continued their punishment; and still the farmer lads and shop boys of Illinois clung to their purpose. With marvelous audacity they pushed through the abatis and reached a point within forty yards of the rifle-pits. It actually looked as if the prize were theirs. The yell of victory was rising in their throats. Suddenly the long line of yellow breastworks before them, covering Heiman's five regiments, crackled and turned into flame. The forlorn-hope stopped — staggered — braced up again — shot blindly through the smoke at the smoke of the new enemy, secure in his shelter. Thus for fifteen minutes the Illinoisans stood fighting. The time is given on the testimony of the opposing leader himself. Morrison was knocked out of his saddle by a musket-ball, and disabled; then the men went down the hill. At its foot they rallied round their flags and renewed the assault. Pushed down again, again they rallied, and a third time climbed to the enemy. This time the battery set fire to the dry leaves on the ground, and the heat and smoke became stifling. It was not possible for brave men to endure more. Slowly, sullenly, frequently pausing to return a shot, they went back for the last time; and in going their ears and souls were riven with the shrieks of their wounded comrades, whom the flames crept down upon and smothered and charred where they lay.

Considered as a mere exhibition of courage, this assault, long maintained against odds,—twice repulsed, twice renewed,—has been seldom excelled. One hundred and forty-nine men of the 17th and 49th were killed and wounded. Haynie reported 1 killed and 8 wounded.

There are few things connected with the operations against Fort Donelson so relieved of uncertainty as this: that when General Grant at Fort Henry became fixed in the resolution to undertake the movement, his primary object was the capture of the force to which the post was intrusted. To effect their complete environment, he relied upon Flag-Officer Foote and his gun-boats, whose astonishing success at Fort Henry justified the extreme of confidence.

THE CRISP FARM — GENERAL GRANT'S
HEADQUARTERS.

Foote arrived on the 14th, and
made haste to enter upon his work.
The *Carondelet* (Commander Walke)
had been in position since the 12th.
Behind a low output of the shore,
for two days, she maintained a fire
from her rifled guns, happily of
greater range than the best of those
of the enemy.

At 9 o'clock on the 14th, Captain
Culbertson, looking from the para-

FRONT VIEW OF MRS. CRISP'S HOUSE.
FROM PHOTOGRAPHS TAKEN IN 1884.

pet of the upper battery, beheld the river below the first bend full of transports,
landing troops under cover of a fresh arrival of gun-boats. The disembarkation concluded, Foote was free. He waited until noon. The captains in the
batteries mistook his deliberation for timidity. The impinging of their shot
on his iron armor was heard distinctly in the fort a mile and a half away.
The captains began to doubt if he would come at all. But at 3 o'clock
the boats took position under fire: the *Louisville* on the right, the *St. Louis*
next, then the *Pittsburgh*, then the *Carondelet*, all iron-clad.

Five hundred yards from the batteries, and yet Foote was not content! In
the Crimean war the allied French and English fleets, of much mightier ships,
undertook to engage the Russian shore batteries, but little stronger than those
at Donelson. The French on that occasion stood off 1800 yards. Lord Lyons
fought his *Agamemnon* at a distance of 800 yards. Foote forged ahead within
400 yards of his enemy, and was still going on. His boat had been hit
between wind and water; so with the *Pittsburgh* and *Carondelet*. About the
guns the floors were slippery with blood, and both surgeons and carpenters
were never so busy. Still the four boats kept on, and there was great cheering; for not only did the fire from the shore slacken; the lookouts reported
the enemy running. It seemed that fortune would smile once more upon the
fleet, and cover the honors of Fort Henry afresh at Fort Donelson. Unhap-
pily, when about 350 yards off the hill a solid shot plunged through the pilot-
house of the flag-ship, and carried away the wheel. Near the same time the

tiller-ropes of the *Louisville* were disabled. Both vessels became unmanageable and began floating down the current. The eddies turned them round like logs. The *Pittsburgh* and *Carondelet* closed in and covered them with their hulls.

Seeing this turn in the fight, the captains of the batteries rallied their men, who cheered in their turn, and renewed the contest with increased will and energy. A ball got lodged in their best rifle. A corporal and some of his men took a log fitting the bore, leaped out on the parapet, and rammed the missile home. "Now, boys," said a gunner in Bidwell's battery, "see me take a chimney!" The flag of the boat and the chimney fell with the shot.

When the vessels were out of range, the victors looked about them. The fine form of their embrasures was gone; heaps of earth had been cast over their platforms. In a space of twenty-four feet they had picked up as many shot and shells. The air had been full of flying missiles. For an hour and a half the brave fellows had been rained upon; yet their losses had been trifling in numbers. Each gunner had selected a ship and followed her faithfully throughout the action, now and then uniting fire on the *Carondelet*. The Confederates had behaved with astonishing valor. Their victory sent a thrill of joy through the army. The assault on the outworks, the day before, had been a failure. With the repulse of the gun-boats the Confederates scored success number two, and the communication by the river remained open to Nashville. The winds that blew sleet and snow over Donelson that night were not so unendurable as they might have been.

The night of the 14th of February fell cold and dark, and under the pitiless sky the armies remained in position so near to each other that neither dared light fires. Overpowered with watching,

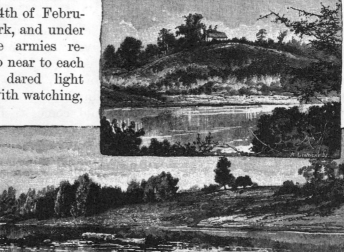

THE POSITION OF THE GUN-BOATS AND THE WEST BANK. FROM A PHOTOGRAPH TAKEN IN 1884.

Fort Donelson is in the farther distance on the extreme left — Hickman's Creek empties into the Cumberland in the middle distance — midway are the remains of the obstructions placed in the river by the Confederates. The upper picture, showing Isaac Williams's house, is a continuation of the right of the lower view.

fatigue, and the lassitude of spirits which always follows a strain upon the faculties of men like that which is the concomitant of battle, thousands on both sides lay down in the ditches and behind logs and whatever else would in the least shelter them from the cutting wind, and tried to sleep. Very few closed their eyes. Even the horses, after their manner, betrayed the suffering they were enduring.

That morning General Floyd had called a council of his chiefs of brigades and divisions. He expressed the opinion that the post was untenable, except with fifty thousand troops. He called attention to the heavy reënforcements of the Federals, and suggested an immediate attack upon their right wing to reopen land communication with Nashville, by way of Charlotte. The proposal was agreed to unanimously. General Buckner proceeded to make dispositions to cover the retreat, in the event the sortie should be successful. Shortly after noon, when the movement should have begun, the order was countermanded at the instance of Pillow. Then came the battle with the gun-boats.

In the night the council was recalled, with general and regimental officers in attendance. The situation was again debated, and the same conclusion reached. According to the plan resolved upon, Pillow was to move at dawn with his whole division, and attack the right of the besiegers. General Buckner was to be relieved by troops in the forts, and with his command to support Pillow by assailing the right of the enemy's center. If he succeeded, he was to take post outside the intrenchments on the Wynn's Ferry road to cover the retreat. He was then to act as rear-guard. Thus early, leaders in Donelson were aware of the mistake into which they were plunged. Their resolution was wise and heroic. Let us see how they executed it.

Preparations for the attack occupied the night. The troops for the most part were taken out of the rifle-pits and massed over on the left to the number of ten thousand or more. The ground was covered with ice and snow; yet the greatest silence was observed. It seems incomprehensible that columns mixed of all arms, infantry, cavalry, and artillery, could have engaged in simultaneous movement, and not have been heard by some listener outside. One would think the jolting and rumble of the heavy gun-carriages would have told the story. But the character of the night must be remembered. The pickets of the Federals were struggling for life against the blast, and probably did not keep good watch.

Oglesby's brigade held McClernand's extreme right. Here and there the musicians were beginning to make the woods ring with reveille, and the numbed soldiers of the line were rising from their icy beds and shaking the snow from their frozen garments. As yet, however, not a company had "fallen in." Suddenly the pickets fired, and with the alarm on their lips rushed back upon their comrades. The woods on the instant became alive.

The regiments formed, officers mounted and took their places; words of command rose loud and eager. By the time Pillow's advance opened fire on Oglesby's right, the point first struck, the latter was fairly formed to receive it. A rapid exchange of volleys ensued. The distance intervening between

THE BIVOUAC IN THE SNOW ON THE LINE OF BATTLE—QUESTIONING A PRISONER.

the works on one side and the bivouac on the other was so short that the action began before Pillow could effect a deployment. His brigades came up in a kind of echelon, left in front, and passed " by regiments left into line," one by one, however; the regiments quickly took their places, and advanced without halting. Oglesby's Illinoisans were now fully awake. They held their ground, returning in full measure the fire that they received. The Confederate Forrest rode around as if to get in their rear, ⟩ and it was then give and take, infantry against infantry. The semi-echelon movement of the Confederates enabled them, after an interval, to strike W. H. L. Wallace's brigade, on Oglesby's left. Soon Wallace was engaged along his whole front, now prolonged by the addition to his command of Morrison's regiments. The first charge against him was repulsed; whereupon he advanced to the top of the rising ground behind which he had sheltered his troops in the night. A fresh assault followed, but, aided by a battery across the valley to his left, he repulsed the enemy a second time. His men were steadfast, and clung to the brow of the hill as if it were theirs by holy right. An hour passed, and yet another hour, without cessation of the fire. Meantime the woods rang with a monstrous clangor of musketry, as if a million men were beating empty barrels with iron hammers.

Buckner flung a portion of his division on McClernand's left, and supported the attack with his artillery. The enfilading fell chiefly on W. H. L. Wallace. McClernand, watchful and full of resources, sent batteries to meet Buckner's batteries. To that duty Taylor rushed with his Company B; and McAllister pushed his three 24-pounders into position and exhausted his ammunition in the duel. The roar never slackened. Men fell by the score, reddening the snow with their blood. The smoke, in pallid white clouds, clung to the underbrush and tree-tops as if to screen the combatants from each other. Close to the ground the flame of musketry and cannon tinted everything a lurid red. Limbs dropped from the trees on the heads below, and the thickets were shorn as by an army of cradlers. The division was under peremptory orders to hold its position to the last extremity, and Colonel Wallace was equal to the emergency.

It was now 10 o'clock, and over on the right Oglesby was beginning to fare badly. The pressure on his front grew stronger. The "rebel yell," afterward a familiar battle-cry on many fields, told of ground being gained against him. To add to his doubts, officers were riding to him with a sickening story that their commands were getting out of ammunition, and asking where they could go for a supply. All he could say was to take what was in the boxes of the dead and wounded. At last he realized that the end was come. His right companies began to give way, and as they retreated, holding up their empty cartridge-boxes, the enemy were emboldened, and swept more fiercely around his flank, until finally they appeared in his rear. He then gave the order to retire the division.

⟩ Colonel John McArthur, originally of General C. F. Smith's division, but then operating with McClernand, was there, and though at first discomfited, his men beat the cavalry off, and afterward shared the full shock of the tempest with Oglesby's troops.— L. W.

W. H. L. Wallace from his position looked off to his right and saw but one regiment of Oglesby's in place, maintaining the fight, and that was John A. Logan's 31st Illinois. Through the smoke he could see Logan riding in a gallop behind his line; through the roar in his front and the rising yell in his rear, he could hear Logan's voice in fierce entreaty to his "boys." Near the 31st stood W. H. L. Wallace's regiment, the 11th Illinois, under Lieutenant-Colonel Ransom. The gaps in the ranks of the two were closed up always toward the colors. The ground at their feet was strewn with their dead and wounded; at length the common misfortune overtook Logan. To keep men without cartridges under fire sweeping them front and flank would be cruel, if not impossible; and seeing it, he too gave the order to retire, and followed his decimated companies to the rear. The 11th then became the right of the brigade, and had to go in turn. Nevertheless, Ransom changed front to rear coolly, as if on parade, and joined in the general retirement. Forrest charged them and threw them into a brief confusion. The greater portion clung to their colors, and made good their retreat. By 11 o'clock Pillow held the road to Charlotte and the whole of the position occupied at dawn by the First Division, and with it the dead and all the wounded who could not get away.

BRANCH OF HICKMAN'S CREEK NEAR JAMES CRISP'S HOUSE — THE LEFT OF GENERAL C. F. SMITH'S LINE. FROM A PHOTOGRAPH TAKEN IN 1884.

Pillow's part of the programme, arranged in the council of the night before, was accomplished. The country was once more open to Floyd. Why did he not avail himself of the dearly bought opportunity, and march his army out?

Without pausing to consider whether the Confederate general could now have escaped with his troops, it must be evident that he should have made the effort. Pillow had discharged his duty well. With the disappearance of W. H. L. Wallace's brigade, it only remained for the victor to deploy his regiments into column and march into the country. The road was his. Buckner was in position to protect Colonel Head's withdrawal from the trenches opposite General Smith on the right; that done,

McALLISTER'S BATTERY IN ACTION.

Captain Edward McAllister's Illinois battery did good service on the 13th. In his report he describes the manner of working the battery: "I selected a point, and about noon opened on the four-gun battery [see map, page 402] through an opening in which I could see the foe. Our fire was promptly returned with such precision that they cut our right wheel on howitzer number three in two. I had no spare wheel, and had to take one off the limber to continue the fight. I then moved all my howitzers over to the west slope of the ridge and loaded under cover of it, and ran the pieces up by hand until I could get the exact elevation. The recoil would throw the guns back out of sight, and thus we continued the fight until the enemy's battery was silenced."

he was also in position to cover the retreat. Buckner had also faithfully performed his task.

On the Union side the situation at this critical time was favorable to the proposed retirement. My division in the center was weakened by the dispatch of one of my brigades to the assistance of General McClernand; in addition to which my orders were to hold my position. As a point of still greater importance, General Grant had gone on board the *St. Louis* at the request of Flag-Officer Foote, and he was there in consultation with that officer, presumably uninformed of the disaster which had befallen his right. It would take a certain time for him to return to the field and dispose his forces for pursuit. It may be said with strong assurance, consequently, that Floyd could have put his men fairly *en route* for Charlotte before the Federal commander could have interposed an obstruction to the movement. The real difficulty was in the hero of the morning, who now made haste to blight his laurels. General Pillow's vanity whistled itself into ludicrous exaltation. Imagining General Grant's whole army defeated and fleeing in rout for Fort Henry and the transports on the river, he deported himself accordingly. He began by ignoring Floyd. He rode to Buckner and accused him of shameful conduct. He sent an aide to the nearest telegraph station with a dispatch to Albert Sidney Johnston, then in command of the Department, asseverating, " on the honor of a soldier," that the day was theirs. Nor did he stop at that. The victory, to be available, required that the enemy should be followed with energy. Such was a habit of Napoleon. Without deigning even to consult his chief, he ordered Buckner to move out and attack the Federals. There was a gorge, up which a road ran toward our central position, or rather what had been our central position. Pointing to the gorge and the road, he told Buckner that was his way and bade him attack in force. There was nothing to do but obey ; and when Buckner had begun the movement, the wise programme decided upon the evening before was wiped from the slate.

When Buckner reluctantly took the gorge road marked out for him by Pillow, the whole Confederate army, save the detachments on the works, was virtually in pursuit of McClernand, retiring by the Wynn's Ferry road — falling back, in fact, upon my position. My division was now to feel the weight of Pillow's hand ; if they should fail, the fortunes of the day would depend upon the veteran Smith.

When General McClernand perceived the peril threatening him in the morning, he sent an officer to me with a request for assistance. This request I referred to General Grant, who was at the time in consultation with Foote. Upon the turning of Oglesby's flank, McClernand repeated his request, with such a representation of the situation that, assuming the responsibility, I ordered Colonel Cruft to report with his brigade to McClernand. Cruft set out promptly. Unfortunately a guide misdirected him, so that he became involved in the retreat, and was prevented from accomplishing his object.

I was in the rear of my single remaining brigade, in conversation with Captain Rawlins, of Grant's staff, when a great shouting was heard behind me on the Wynn's Ferry road, whereupon I sent an orderly to ascertain the cause. The man reported the road and woods full of soldiers apparently in rout. An officer then rode by at full speed, shouting, " All's lost! Save yourselves ! " A hurried consultation was had with Rawlins, at the end of which the brigade was put in motion toward the enemy's works, on the very road by which Buckner was pursuing under Pillow's mischievous order. It happened also that Colonel W. H. L. Wallace had dropped into the same road with such of his command as staid by their colors. He came up riding and at a walk, his leg over the horn of his saddle. He was perfectly cool, and looked like a farmer from a hard day's plowing. " Good-morning," I said. " Good-morning," was the reply. " Are they pursuing you ? " " Yes." " How far are they behind ? " That instant the head of my command appeared on the road. The colonel calculated, then answered : " You will have about time to form line of battle right here." " Thank you. Good-day." " Good-day."

At that point the road began to dip into the gorge ; on the right and left there were woods, and in front a dense thicket. An order was dispatched to bring Battery A forward at full speed. Colonel John A. Thayer, commanding the brigade, formed it on the double-quick into line ; the 1st Nebraska

and the 58th Illinois on the right, and the 58th Ohio, with a detached com
pany, on the left. The battery came up on the run and swung across the road,
which had been left open for it. Hardly had it unlimbered, before the enemy
appeared, and firing began. For ten minutes or thereabouts the scenes of the
morning were reënacted. The Confederates struggled hard to perfect their
deployments. The woods rang with musketry and artillery. The brush on
the slope of the hill was mowed away with bullets. A great cloud arose and

VIEW ON THE LINE OF PILLOW'S DEFENSES IN FRONT OF McCLERNAND, SHOWING WATER IN THE OLD TRENCHES.
FROM A PHOTOGRAPH TAKEN IN 1884.

shut out the woods and the narrow valley below. Colonel Thayer and his
regiments behaved with great gallantry, and the assailants fell back in confusion and returned to the intrenchments. W. H. L. Wallace and Oglesby
re-formed their commands behind Thayer, supplied them with ammunition,
and stood at rest waiting for orders. There was then a lull in the battle.
Even the cannonading ceased, and everybody was asking, What next?

Just then General Grant rode up to where General McClernand and I were
in conversation. He was almost unattended. In his hand there were some

papers, which looked like telegrams. Wholly unexcited, he saluted and received the salutations of his subordinates. Proceeding at once to business, he directed them to retire their commands to the heights out of cannon range, and throw up works. Reënforcements were *en route*, he said, and it was advisable to await their coming. He was then informed of the mishap to the First Division, and that the road to Charlotte was open to the enemy.

In every great man's career there is a crisis exactly similar to that which now overtook General Grant, and it cannot be better described than as a crucial test of his nature. A mediocre person would have accepted the news as an argument for persistence in his resolution to enter upon a siege. Had General Grant done so, it is very probable his history would have been then and there concluded. His admirers and detractors are alike invited to study him at this precise juncture. It cannot be doubted that he saw with painful distinctness the effect of the disaster to his right wing. His face flushed slightly. With a sudden grip he crushed the papers in his hand. But in an instant these signs of disappointment or hesitation — as the reader pleases — cleared away. In his ordinary quiet voice he said, addressing himself to both officers, "Gentlemen, the position on the right must be retaken." With that he turned and galloped off.

Seeing in the road a provisional brigade, under Colonel Morgan L. Smith, consisting of the 11th Indiana and the 8th Missouri Infantry, going, by order of General C. F. Smith, to the aid of the First Division, I suggested that if General McClernand would order Colonel Smith to report to me, I would attempt to recover the lost ground; and the order having been given, I reconnoitered the hill, determined upon a place of assault, and arranged my order of attack. I chose Colonel Smith's regiments to lead, and for that purpose conducted them to the crest of a hill opposite a steep bluff covered by the enemy. The two regiments had been formerly of my brigade. I knew they had been admirably drilled in the Zouave tactics, and my confidence in Smith and in George F. McGinnis, colonel of the 11th, was implicit. I was sure they would take their men to the top of the bluff. Colonel Cruft was put in line to support them on the right. Colonel Ross, with his regiments, the 17th and 49th, and the 46th, 57th, and 58th Illinois, were put as support on the left. Thayer's brigade was held in reserve. These dispositions filled the time till about 2 o'clock in the afternoon, when heavy cannonading, mixed with a long roll of musketry, broke out over on the left, whither it will be necessary to transfer the reader.

The veteran in command on the Union left had contented himself with allowing Buckner no rest, keeping up a continual sharp-shooting. Early in the morning of the 14th he made a demonstration of assault with three of his regiments, and though he purposely withdrew them, he kept the menace standing, to the great discomfort of his *vis-à-vis*. With the patience of an old soldier, he waited the pleasure of the general commanding, knowing that when the time came he would be called upon. During the battle of the gunboats he rode through his command and grimly joked with them. He who never permitted the slightest familiarity from a subordinate, could yet indulge in fatherly pleasantries with the ranks when he thought circumstances justified them. He never for a moment doubted the courage of volunteers; they were not regulars — that was all. If properly led, he believed they would storm the gates of his Satanic Majesty. Their hour of trial was now come.

From his brief and characteristic conference with McClernand and myself, General Grant rode to General C. F. Smith. What took place between them is not known, further than that he ordered an assault upon the outworks as a diversion in aid of the assault about to be delivered on the right. General Smith personally directed his chiefs of brigade to get their regiments ready. Colonel John Cook by his order increased the number of his skirmishers already engaged with the enemy.

Taking Lauman's brigade, General Smith began the advance. They were under fire instantly. The guns in the fort joined in with the infantry who were at the time in the rifle-pits, the great body of the Confederate right wing being with General Buckner. The defense was greatly favored by the ground, which subjected the assailants to a double fire from the beginning of the abatis. The men have said that "it looked too thick for a rabbit to get through." General Smith, on his horse, took position in the front and center of the line. Occasionally he turned in the saddle to see how the alignment was kept. For the most part, however, he held his face steadily toward the enemy. He was, of course, a conspicuous object for the sharp-shooters in the rifle-pits. The air around him twittered with minie-bullets. Erect as if on review, he rode on, timing the gait of his horse with the movement of his colors. A soldier said: "I was nearly scared to death, but I saw the old man's white mustache over his shoulder, and went on."

On to the abatis the regiments moved without hesitation, leaving a trail of dead and wounded behind. There the fire seemed to get trebly hot, and there some of the men halted, whereupon, seeing the hesitation, General Smith put his cap on the point of his sword, held it aloft, and called out, "No flinching now, my lads? — Here — this is the way! Come on!" He picked a path through the jagged limbs of the trees, holding his cap all the time in sight; and the effect was magical. The men swarmed in after him, and got through in the best order they could — not all of them, alas! On the other side of the obstruction they took the semblance of re-formation and charged in after their chief, who found himself then between the two fires. Up the ascent he rode; up they followed. At the last moment the keepers of the rifle-pits clambered out and fled. The four regiments engaged in the feat — the 25th Indiana, and the 2d, 7th, and 14th Iowa — planted their colors on the breastwork. Later in the day, Buckner came back with his division; but all his efforts to dislodge Smith were vain.

We left my division about to attempt the recapture of the hill, which had been the scene of the combat between Pillow and McClernand. If only on account of the results which followed that assault, in connection with the heroic performance of General C. F. Smith, it is necessary to return to it.

Riding to my old regiments,— the 8th Missouri and the 11th Indiana,— I asked them if they were ready. They demanded the word of me. Waiting

MAJOR-GENERAL GIDEON J. PILLOW, C. S. A.   FROM A PHOTOGRAPH.

a moment for Morgan L. Smith to light a cigar, I called out, "Forward it is, then!" They were directly in front of the ascent to be climbed. Without stopping for his supports, Colonel Smith led them down into a broad hollow, and catching sight of the advance, Cruft and Ross also moved forward. As the two regiments began the climb, the 8th Missouri slightly in the lead, a line of fire ran along the brow of the height. The flank companies cheered while deploying as skirmishers. Their Zouave practice proved of excellent service to them. Now on the ground, creeping when the fire was hottest, running when it slackened, they gained ground with astonishing rapidity, and at the same time maintained a fire that was like a sparkling of the earth. For the most part the bullets aimed at them passed over their heads and took effect in the ranks behind them. Colonel Smith's cigar was shot off close to his lips. He took another and called for a match. A soldier ran and gave him one. "Thank you. Take your place now. We are almost up," he said, and, smoking, spurred his horse forward. A few yards from the crest of the height the regiments began loading and firing as they advanced. The defenders gave way. On the top there was a brief struggle, which was ended by Cruft and Ross with their supports.

The whole line then moved forward simultaneously, and never stopped until the Confederates were within the works. There had been no occasion to call on the reserves. The road to Charlotte was again effectually shut, and the battle-field of the morning, with the dead and wounded lying where they had fallen, was in possession of the Third Division, which stood halted within easy musket-range of the rifle-pits. It was then about half-past 3 o'clock in the afternoon. I was reconnoitering the works of the enemy preliminary to charging them, when Colonel Webster, of General Grant's staff, came to me and repeated the order to fall back out of cannon range and throw up breastworks. "The general does not know that we have the hill," I said. Webster replied: "I give you the order as he gave it to me." "Very well," said I, "give him my compliments, and say that I have received the order." Webster smiled and rode away. The ground was not vacated, though the assault was deferred. In assuming the responsibility, I had no doubt of my ability to satisfy General Grant of the correctness of my course; and it was subsequently approved.

When night fell, the command bivouacked without fire or supper. Fatigue parties were told off to look after the wounded; and in the relief given there was no distinction made between friend and foe. The labor extended through the whole night, and the surgeons never rested. By sunset the conditions of the morning were all restored. The Union commander was free to order a general assault next day or resort to a formal siege.

A great discouragement fell upon the brave men inside the works that night. Besides suffering from wounds and bruises and the dreadful weather, they were aware that though they had done their best they were held in a close grip by a superior enemy. A council of general and field officers was held at headquarters, which re- sulted in a unanimous resolution that if the position in front of General Pillow had not been reoccupied by the Federals in strength, the army should effect its retreat. A reconnoissance was ordered to make the test. Colonel Forrest conducted it. He report- ed that the ground was not only reoccupied, but that the enemy were extended yet farther around the Confederate left. The council then held a final session.

General Simon B. Buckner, as the junior officer present, gave his opinion first; he thought he could not successfully resist the assault which would be made by daylight by a vastly superior force. But he further remarked, that as he understood the principal

ROWLETT'S MILL (SEE MAP, PAGE 402). FROM A PHOTOGRAPH TAKEN IN 1884.

object of the defense of Donelson was to cover the movement of General Albert Sidney Johnston's army from Bowling Green to Nashville, if that movement was not completed he was of opinion that the defense should be continued at the risk of the destruction of the entire force. General Floyd replied that General Johnston's army had already reached Nashville, where- upon General Buckner said that "it would be wrong to subject the army to a virtual massacre, when no good could result from the sacrifice, and that the general officers owed it to their men, when further resistance was una-vailing, to obtain the best terms of capitulation possible for them."

Both Generals Floyd and Pillow acquiesced in the opinion. Ordinarily the council would have ended at this point, and the commanding general would have addressed himself to the duty of obtaining terms. He would have called for pen, ink, and paper, and prepared a note for dispatch to the commanding general of the opposite force. But there were circumstances outside the mere military situation which at this juncture pressed themselves into consideration. As this was the first surrender of armed men banded together for war upon the general government, what would the Federal authorities do with the prisoners? This question was of application to all the gentlemen in the council. It was lost to view, however, when General Floyd announced his purpose to leave with two steamers which were to be down at daylight, and to take with him as many of his division as the steamers could carry away.

General Pillow then remarked that there were no two persons in the Con-federacy whom the Yankees would rather capture than himself and General Floyd (who had been Buchanan's Secretary of War, and was under indict-ment at Washington). As to the propriety of his accompanying General Floyd, the latter said, coolly, that the question was one for every man to decide for himself. Buckner was of the same view, and added that as for himself he regarded it as his duty to stay with his men and share their fate, whatever it might be. Pillow persisted in leaving. Floyd then directed Gen-eral Buckner to consider himself in command. Immediately after the council was concluded, General Floyd prepared for his departure. His first move was to have his brigade drawn up. The peculiarity of the step was that, with the exception of one, the 20th Mississippi regiment, his regiments were all Virginians. A short time before daylight the two steamboats arrived. Without loss of time the general hastened to the river, embarked with his Virginians, and at an early hour cast loose from the shore, and in good time, and safely, he reached Nashville. He never satisfactorily explained upon what principle he appropriated all the transportation on hand to the use of his particular command.

Colonel Forrest was present at the council, and when the final resolution was taken, he promptly announced that he neither could nor would surren-der his command. The bold trooper had no qualms upon the subject. He assembled his men, all as hardy as himself, and after reporting once more at headquarters, he moved out and plunged into a slough formed by backwater from the river. An icy crust covered its surface, the wind blew fiercely, and the darkness was unrelieved by a star. There was fearful floundering as the command followed him. At length he struck dry land, and was safe. He was next heard of at Nashville.

General Buckner, who throughout the affair bore himself with dignity, ordered the troops back to their positions and opened communications with General Grant, whose laconic demand of " unconditional surrender,"

Hd Qrs. Army in the Field
Camp near Donelson, Feby 16th 1862

Gen. S. B. Buckner,
Confed. Army

Sir: Yours of this date proposing armistice, and appointment of Commissioners to settle terms of Capitulation is just received. No terms except an unconditional and immediate surrender can be accepted.

I propose to move immediately upon your works.

I am sir: very respectfully
Your obt. svt.
U. S. Grant
Brig. Gen.

FAC-SIMILE OF THE ORIGINAL "UNCONDITIONAL SURRENDER" DISPATCH.

The original of the dispatch was obtained by Charles L. Webster & Co., publishers of General Grant's "Memoirs," from Dr. James K. Wallace, of Litchfield, Conn., who received it, November 28th, 1868, from his relative by marriage, General John A. Rawlins, who, as chief of staff to General Grant, had the custody, after the capture, of General Buckner's papers. General Rawlins told Dr. Wallace that it was the original dispatch. The above is an exact reproduction of the original dispatch in every particular, except that, in order to adapt it to the width of the page, the word, "Sir," has been lowered to the line beneath, and the words, "I am, sir, very respectfully," have been raised to the line above.—EDITORS.

in his reply to General Buckner's overtures, became at once a watchword of the war.

The Third Division was astir very early on the 16th of February. The regiments began to form and close up the intervals between them, the intention being to charge the breastworks south of Dover about breakfast-time. In the midst of the preparation a bugle was heard and a white flag was seen coming from the town toward the pickets. I sent my adjutant-general to meet the flag half-way and inquire its purpose. Answer was returned that General Buckner had capitulated during the night, and was now sending information of the fact to the commander of the troops in this quarter, that there might be no further bloodshed. The division was ordered to advance and take possession of the works and of all public property and prisoners. Leaving that agreeable duty to the brigade commanders, I joined the officer bearing the flag, and with my staff rode across the trench and into the town, till we came to the door of the old tavern already described, where I dismounted. The tavern was the headquarters of General Buckner, to whom I sent my name; and being an acquaintance, I was at once admitted.

I found General Buckner with his staff at breakfast. He met me with politeness and dignity. Turning to the officers at the table, he remarked: "General Wallace, it is not necessary to introduce you to these gentlemen; you are acquainted with them all." They arose, came forward one by one, and gave their hands in salutation. I was then invited to breakfast, which consisted of corn bread and coffee, the best the gallant host had in his kitchen. We sat at the table about an hour and a half, when General Grant arrived and took temporary possession of the tavern as his headquarters. Later in the morning the army marched in and completed the possession.

VIEW FROM THE NATIONAL CEMETERY, WITHIN THE HEDGE ON THE RIGHT, ACROSS TO THE HILL
WHERE WERE SITUATED THE INTERIOR WORKS OF FORT DONELSON (SEE MAP, PAGE 402).
FROM A PHOTOGRAPH TAKEN IN 1884.

THE OPPOSING FORCES AT FORT DONELSON, TENN.

The composition and losses of each army as here stated give the gist of all the data obtainable in the Official Records. **K** stands for killed; w for wounded; m w for mortally wounded; m for captured or missing; c for captured.—EDITORS.

COMPOSITION AND LOSSES OF THE UNION ARMY.
Brig.-Gen. Ulysses S. Grant.

FIRST DIVISION, Brig.-Gen. John A. McClernand. *First Brigade*, Col. Richard J. Oglesby: 8th Ill., Lieut.-Col. Frank L. Rhoads; 18th Ill., Col. Michael K. Lawler (w), Capt. Daniel H. Brush (w), Capt. Samuel B. Marks; 29th Ill., Col. James S. Rearden; 30th Ill., Lieut.-Col. Elias S. Dennis; 31st Ill., Col. John A. Logan (w); Battery A, Ill. Lt. Arty., Capt. Jasper M. Dresser; Battery E, 2d Ill. Lt. Artillery, Lieut. G. C. Gumbart; A and B, 2d Ill. Cavalry, Capts. John R. Hotaling and Thomas J. Larrison; C, 2d, and I, 4th U. S. Cavalry, Lieut. James Powell; Ind'p't companies Ill. Cavalry, Capts. E. Carmichael, James J. Dollins, M. J. O'Harnett, and Lieut. Ezra King. Brigade loss: k, 184; w, 603; m, 66 = 853. *Second Brigade*, Col. W. H. L. Wallace: 11th Ill., Lieut.-Col. T. E. G. Ransom (w), Major Garrett Nevins (temporarily); 20th Ill., Col. C. Carroll Marsh; 45th Ill., Col. John E. Smith; 48th Ill., Col. Isham N. Haynie (temporarily commanding Third Brigade), Lieut.-Col. Thomas H. Smith (k); Battery B, 1st Ill. Lt. Artillery, Capt. Ezra Taylor; Battery D, 1st Ill. Lt. Artillery, Capt. Edward McAllister; 4th Ill. Cavalry, Col. T. Lyle Dickey. Brigade loss: k, 99; w, 350; m, 98 = 547. *Third Brigade*, Col. Wm. R. Morrison (w), Col. Leonard F. Ross: 17th Ill., Major Francis M. Smith, Capt. Henry H. Bush; 49th Ill., Lieut.-Col. Phineas Pease. Brigade loss: k, 28; w, 105; m, 19 = 152.

SECOND DIVISION, Brig.-Gen. Charles F. Smith. *First Brigade*, Col. John McArthur: 9th Ill., Lieut.-Col. Jesse J. Phillips; 12th Ill., Lieut.-Col. Augustus L. Chetlain; 41st Ill., Col. Isaac C. Pugh. Brigade loss: k, 69; w, 340; m, 20 = 429. *Third Brigade*, Col. John Cook: 7th Ill., Lieut.-Col. Andrew J. Babcock; 50th Ill., Col. Moses M. Bane; 52d Ind., Col. James M. Smith; 12th Iowa, Col. J. J. Woods; 13th Mo., Col. Crafts J. Wright; Batteries D, H, and K, 1st Mo. Lt. Artillery, Capts. Henry Richardson, F. Welker, and George H. Stone. Brigade loss: k, 10; w,

109; m, 2 = 121. *Fourth Brigade*, Col. Jacob G. Lauman: 25th Ind., Col. James C. Veatch; 2d Iowa, Col. James M. Tuttle; 7th Iowa, Lieut.-Col. James C. Parrott; 14th Iowa, Col. William T. Shaw; Birge's Mo. Sharp-shooters. Brigade loss: k, 55; w, 301; m, 1 = 357. *Fifth Brigade*, Col. Morgan L. Smith: 11th Ind., Col. George F. McGinnis; 8th Mo., Major John McDonald. Brigade loss: k, 11; w, 69 = 80.

THIRD DIVISION, Brig.-Gen. Lew Wallace. *First Brigade*, Col. Charles Cruft: 31st Ind., Lieut.-Col. John Osborn, Major Fred. Arn; 44th Ind., Col. Hugh B. Reed; 17th Ky., Col. John H. McHenry, Jr.; 25th Ky., Col. James M. Shackelford. Brigade loss: k, 35; w, 182; m, 16 = 233. *Second Brigade* [attached to the Third Brigade]: 46th Ill., Col. John A. Davis; 57th Ill., Col. Silas D. Baldwin; 58th Ill., Col. William F. Lynch; 20th Ohio, Col. Charles Whittlesey. Brigade loss: k, 6; w, 15; m, 1 = 22. *Third Brigade*, Col. John M. Thayer: 1st Neb., Lieut.-Col. Wm. D. McCord; 58th Ohio, Lieut.-Col. F. F. Rempel; 68th Ohio, Col. S. H. Steedman; 76th Ohio, Col. Wm. B. Woods. Brigade loss: k, 3; w, 24; m, 1 = 28. *Unattached*: Battery A, 1st Ill. Lt. Artillery, Lieut P. P. Wood; A, 32d Ill. Infantry, Capt. Henry Davidson. Loss: w, 10.

IRON-CLADS AND GUN-BOATS, Flag-Officer Andrew H. Foote (w). *St. Louis* (flag-ship), Lieut. Leonard Paulding, k, 2; w, 8; *Carondelet*, Commander Henry Walke, k, 5; w, 28; *Louisville*, Commander Benjamin M. Dove, k, 4; w, 5; *Pittsburgh*, Lieut. Egbert Thompson, w, 2; *Tyler*, Lieut.-Com. William Gwin; *Conestoga*, Lieut.-Com. S. L. Phelps. Total loss: k, 11; w, 43 = 54. The vessels which had been in action at Fort Henry (see page 362) carried the same armament at Fort Donelson. The *Louisville* and *Pittsburgh* were each armed with 6 32-pounders, 3 8-inch, and 4 rifled 42-pounders. The *Louisville* had also 1 12-pounder boat-howitzer.

The total loss of the Union forces (army and navy) was 510 killed, 2152 wounded, 224 captured or missing = 2886.

COMPOSITION AND LOSSES OF THE CONFEDERATE ARMY.

1 Brig.-Gen. Gideon J. Pillow, 2 Brig-Gen. John B. Floyd, 3 Brig-Gen. Simon B. Buckner (c).

BUCKNER'S DIVISION. *Second Brigade*, Col. Wm. E. Baldwin: 2d Ken., Col. R. W. Hanson; 14th Miss., Maj. W. L. Doss; 20th Miss., Maj. W. N. Brown; 26th Miss., Col. A. E. Reynolds; 26th Tenn., Col., John M. Lillard; 41st Tenn., Col. Robert Farquharson. *Third Brigade*, Col. John C. Brown: 3d Tenn., Lieut.-Col. T. M. Gordon (w), Maj. N. F. Cheairs; 18th Tenn., Col. J. B. Palmer; 32d Tenn., Col. E. C. Cook. *Artillery:* Kentucky Battery, Capt. R. E. Graves; Tenn. Battery, Capt. T. K. Porter (w), Lieut. John W. Morton; Jackson's Va. Battery. Division loss: k and w, 577 (approximate).

JOHNSON'S COMMAND (left wing), Brig.-Gen. Bushrod R. Johnson. *Heiman's Brigade*, Col. A. Heiman: 27th Ala., Col. A. A. Hughes; 10th Tenn., Lieut.-Col. R. W. MacGavock; 42d Tenn., Col. W. A. Quarles; 48th Tenn., Col. W. M. Voorhies; 53d Tenn., Col. A. H. Abernathy, Lieut.-Col. Thomas F. Winston; Tenn. Battery, Capt. Frank Maney (w). *Davidson's Brigade*, Col. T. J. Davidson, Col. J. M. Simonton: 8th Ky., Lieut.-Col. H. B. Lyon; 1st Miss., Col. J. M. Simonton, Lieut.-Col. A. S. Hamilton; 3d Miss., Lieut.-Col. J. M. Wells; 7th Texas,

Col. John Gregg. Brigade loss: k, 68; w, 218 = 286. *Drake's Brigade*, Col. Joseph Drake: Ala. Battalion, Maj. John S. Garvin; 15th Ark., Col. J. J. Gee; 4th Miss., Maj. T. N. Adair; Tenn. Battalion, Col. B. M. Browder.

FLOYD'S DIVISION. *First Brigade*, Col. G. C. Wharton: 51st Va., Lieut.-Col. J. M. Massie; 56th Va., Capt. G. W. Davis. Brigade loss : k, 17; w, 80; m, 120 = 217. *Second Brigade*, Col. John McCausland: 36th Va., Lieut.-Col. L. W. Reid; 50th Va., Maj. Thomas Smith. Brigade loss: k, 24; w, 91 = 115. *Artillery:* Va. Batteries, Captains D. A. French and J. H. Guy; Green's Ken. Battery.

GARRISON FORCES, Col. J. W. Head, Col. J. E. Bailey: 30th Tenn., Maj. J. J. Turner; 49th Tenn., Col. J. E. Bailey; 50th Tenn., Col. C. A. Sugg. *Fort Batteries*, Capt. Joseph Dixon (k), Capt. Jacob Culbertson: A, 30th Tenn., Capt. B. G. Bidwell; A, 50th Tenn., Capt. T. W. Beaumont; Maury (Tenn.) Battery, Capt. R. R. Ross.

CAVALRY: Tenn. Regiment, Col. N. B. Forrest; 9th Tenn. Battalion, Lieut.-Col. George Gantt; Milton's Company Tennessee. *Unattached:* Tennessee Battalion Infantry, Major S. H. Colms.

The total loss of the Confederate army is not definitely stated. General Gideon J. Pillow says, in his report, that in killed and wounded it was about two thousand. With regard to the number of Confederates captured, General Grant says in his "Memoirs": "I asked General Buckner about what force he had to surrender. He replied that he could not tell with any degree of accuracy; that all the sick and weak had been sent to Nashville while we were about Fort Henry; that Floyd and Pillow had left during the night, taking many men with them; and that Forrest, and probably others, had also escaped during the preceding night; the number of casualties he could not tell; but he said I would not find fewer than 12,000, nor more than 15,000." But General Buckner says, in his official report, that "the aggregate of the army, never greater than 12,000, was now reduced to less than 9000 after the departure of General Floyd's brigade."

THE "CARONDELET" FIGHTING FORT DONELSON, FEBRUARY 13, 1862.   FROM A SKETCH BY REAR-ADMIRAL WALKE.

THE WESTERN FLOTILLA AT FORT DONELSON, ISLAND NUMBER TEN, FORT PILLOW AND MEMPHIS.

BY HENRY WALKE, REAR-ADMIRAL, U. S. N.

ON the 7th of February, the day after the capture of Fort Henry, I received on board the *Carondelet* Colonels Webster, Rawlins, and McPherson, with a company of troops, and under instructions from General Grant proceeded up the Tennessee River, and completed the destruction of the bridge of the Memphis and Bowling Green Railroad.

On returning from that expedition General Grant requested me to hasten to Fort Donelson with the *Carondelet*, *Tyler*, and *Lexington*, and announce my arrival by firing signal guns. The object of this movement was to take possession of the river as soon as possible, to engage the enemy's attention by making formidable demonstrations before the fort, and to prevent it from being reënforced. On February 10th the *Carondelet* alone (towed by the transport *Alps*) proceeded up the Cumberland River, and on the 12th arrived a few miles below the fort.

Fort Donelson occupied one of the best defensive positions on the river. It was built on a bold bluff about 120 feet in height, on the west side of the river, where it makes a slight bend to the eastward. It had 3 batteries, mounting in all 15 guns: the lower, about twenty feet above the water; the second, about fifty feet above the water; the third, on the summit.⌡

⌡ The armament of the fort consisted of "ten 32-pounder guns (two of them ship carronades), one 8-inch howitzer, two nondescript 9-pounders, one 10-inch Columbiad, and one rifled gun throwing a conical shell of 128 pounds." The garrison was commanded by Colonel J. E. Bailey, the artillery by Captain Joseph Dixon, and after his death by Captain Jacob Culbertson, with Captains Ross, Beaumont, and Bidwell in separate command of the guns of the lower batteries. Captain Dixon was killed in the action of the 13th with the *Carondelet* by a shot which dismounted one of his guns — "the only damage done to the batteries during the siege." (Captain Culbertson's report.) — EDITORS.

When the *Carondelet*, her tow being cast off, came in sight of the fort and proceeded up to within long range of the batteries, not a living creature could be seen. The hills and woods on the west side of the river hid part of the enemy's formidable defenses, which were lightly covered with snow; but the black rows of heavy guns, pointing down on us, reminded me of the dismal-looking sepulchers cut in the rocky cliffs near Jerusalem, but far more repulsive. At 12:50 P. M., to unmask the silent enemy, and to announce my arrival to General Grant, I ordered the bow guns to be fired at the fort. Only one shell fell short. There was no response except the echo from the hills. The fort appeared to have been evacuated. After firing ten shells into it, the *Carondelet* dropped down the river about three miles and anchored. But the sound of her guns aroused our soldiers on the southern side of the fort into action; one report says that when they heard the guns of the *avant-courrier* of the fleet, they gave cheer upon cheer, and rather than permit the sailors to get ahead of them again, they engaged in skirmishes with the enemy, and began the battle of the three days following. On the *Carondelet* we were isolated and beset with dangers from the enemy's lurking sharp-shooters.

On the 13th a dispatch was received from General Grant, informing me that he had arrived the day before, and had succeeded in getting his army in position, almost entirely investing the enemy's works. "Most of our batteries," he said, "are established, and the remainder soon will be. If you will advance with your gun-boat at 10 o'clock in the morning, we will be ready to take advantage of any diversion in our favor."

I immediately complied with these instructions, and at 9:05, with the *Carondelet* alone and under cover of a heavily wooded point, fired 139 70-pound and 64-pound shells at the fort. We received in return the fire of all the enemy's guns that could be brought to bear on the *Carondelet*, which sustained but little damage, except from two shots. One, a 128-pound solid, at 11:30 struck the corner of our port broadside casemate, passed through it, and in its progress toward the center of our boilers glanced over the temporary barricade in front of the boilers. It then passed over the steam-drum, struck the beams of the upper deck, carried away the railing around the engine-room and burst the steam-heater, and, glancing back into the engine-room, "seemed to bound after the men," as one of the engineers said, "like a wild beast pursuing its prey." I have preserved this ball as a souvenir of the fight at Fort Donelson. When it burst through the side of the *Carondelet*, it knocked down and wounded a dozen men, seven of them severely. An immense quantity of splinters was blown through the vessel. Some of them, as fine as needles, shot through the clothes of the men like arrows. Several of the wounded were so much excited by the suddenness of the event and the sufferings of their comrades, that they were not aware that they themselves had been struck until they felt the blood running into their shoes. Upon receiving this shot we ceased firing for a while.

After dinner we sent the wounded on board the *Alps*, repaired damages, and, not expecting any assistance, at 12:15 we resumed, in accordance with General Grant's request, and bombarded the fort until dusk, when nearly all

EXPLOSION OF A GUN ON BOARD THE "CARÓNDELET" DURING THE ATTACK ON FORT DONELSON. AFTER A SKETCH BY REAR-ADMIRAL WALKE.

our 10-inch and 15-inch shells were expended. The firing from the shore having ceased, we retired.

At 11:30 on the night of the 13th Flag-Officer Foote arrived below Fort Donelson with the iron-clads *St. Louis*, *Louisville*, and *Pittsburgh*, and the wooden gun-boats *Tyler* and *Conestoga*. On the 14th all the hard materials in the vessels, such as chains, lumber, and bags of coal, were laid on the upper decks to protect them from the plunging shots of the enemy. At 3 o'clock in the afternoon our fleet advanced to attack the fort, the *Louisville* being on the west side of the river, the *St. Louis* (flag-steamer) next, then the *Pittsburgh* and *Carondelet* on the east side of the river. The wooden gun-boats were about a thousand yards in the rear. When we started in line abreast at a moderate speed, the *Louisville* and *Pittsburgh*, not keeping up to their positions, were hailed from the flag-steamer to "steam up." At 3:30, when about a mile and a half from the fort, two shots were fired at us, both falling short. When within a mile of the fort the *St. Louis* opened fire, and the other iron-clads followed, slowly and deliberately at first, but more rapidly as the fleet advanced. The flag-officer hailed the *Carondelet*, and ordered us not to fire so fast. Some of our shells went over the fort, and almost into our camp beyond. As we drew nearer, the enemy's fire greatly increased in force and effect. But, the officers and crew of the *Carondelet* having recently been long under fire, and having become practiced in fighting, her gunners were as cool and composed as old veterans. We heard the deafening crack of the bursting shells, the crash of the solid shot, and the whizzing of fragments of shell and wood as they sped through the vessel. Soon a 128-pounder struck our anchor, smashed it into flying bolts, and bounded over the vessel, taking away a part of our smoke-stack; then another cut away the iron boat-davits as if they were pipe-stems, whereupon the boat dropped into the water. Another ripped up the iron plating and glanced over; another went through the plating and lodged in the heavy casemate; another struck the pilot-house, knocked the plating to pieces, and sent fragments of iron and splinters into the pilots, one of whom fell mortally wounded, and was taken below; another shot took away the remaining boat-davits and the boat with them; and still they came, harder and faster, taking flag-staffs and smoke-stacks, and tearing off the side armor as lightning tears the bark from a tree. Our men fought desperately, but, under the excitement of the occasion, loaded too hastily, and the port rifled gun exploded. One of the crew, in his account of the explosion soon after it occurred, said: "I was serving the gun with shell. When it exploded it knocked us all down, killing none, but wounding over a dozen men and spreading dismay and confusion among us. For about two minutes I was stunned, and at least five minutes elapsed before I could tell what was the matter. When I found out that I was more scared than hurt, although suffering from the gunpowder which I had inhaled, I looked forward and saw our gun lying on the deck, split in three pieces. Then the cry ran through the boat that we were on fire, and my duty as pump-man called me to the pumps. While I was there, two shots entered our bow-ports and killed four men and wounded several others. They were borne past me, three with their heads off. The sight almost sickened me, and I turned my head away. Our master's mate came soon after and ordered us to our quarters at the gun. I told him the gun had burst, and that we had caught fire on the upper deck from the enemy's shell. He then said: 'Never mind the fire; go to your quarters.' Then I took a station at the starboard tackle of another rifled bow-gun and remained there until the close of the fight." The carpenter and his men extinguished the flames.

When within four hundred yards of the fort, and while the Confederates were running from their lower battery, our pilot-house was struck again and another pilot wounded, our wheel was broken, and shells from the rear boats were bursting over us. All four of our boats were shot away and dragging in the water. On looking out to bring our broadside guns to bear, we saw that the other gun-boats were rapidly falling back out of line. The *Pittsburgh* in her haste to turn struck the stern of the *Carondelet*, and broke our starboard rudder, so that we were obliged to go ahead to clear the *Pittsburgh* and the point of rocks below. The pilot of the *St. Louis* was killed, and the pilot of the *Louisville* was wounded. Both vessels had their wheel-ropes shot away, and the men were prevented from steering the *Louisville* with the tiller-ropes at the stern by the shells from the rear boats bursting over them. The *St. Louis* and *Louisville*, becoming unmanageable, were compelled to drop out of battle, and the *Pittsburgh* followed; all had suffered severely from the enemy's fire. Flag-Officer Foote was wounded while standing by the pilot of the *St. Louis* when he was killed. We were then about 350 yards from the fort.

There was no alternative for the *Carondelet* in that narrow stream but to keep her head to the enemy and fire into the fort with her two bow-guns, to prevent it, if possible, from returning her fire effectively. The enemy saw that she was in a manner left to his mercy, and concentrated the fire of all his batteries upon her. In return, the *Carondelet's* guns were well served to the last shot. Our new acting gunner, John Hall, was just the man for the occasion. He came forward, offered his services, and with my sanction took charge of the starboard-bow rifled gun. He instructed the men to obey his warnings and follow his motions, and he told them that when he saw a shot coming he would call out " Down " and stoop behind the breech of the gun as he did so; at the same instant the men were to stand away from the bow-ports. Nearly every shot from the fort struck the bows of the *Carondelet*. Most of them were fired on the ricochet level, and could be plainly seen skipping on the water before they struck. The enemy's object was to sink the gun-boat by striking her just below the water-line. They soon succeeded in planting two 32-pound shots in her bow, between wind and water, which made her leak badly, but her compartments kept her from sinking until we could plug up the shot-holes. Three shots struck the starboard casemating; four struck the port casemating forward of the rifle-gun; one struck on the starboard side, between the water-line and plank-sheer, cutting through the planking; six shots struck the pilot-house, shattering one section into pieces and cutting through the iron casing. The smoke-stacks were riddled.

THE GUN-BOATS AT FORT DONELSON (FEBRUARY 14, 1862) —
THE LAND ATTACK IN THE DISTANCE.
AFTER A SKETCH BY REAR-ADMIRAL WALKE.

Our gunners kept up a constant firing while we were falling back; and the warning words, "Look out!" "Down!" were often heard, and heeded by nearly all the gun-crews. On one occasion, while the men were at the muzzle of the middle bow-gun, loading it, the warning came just in time for them to jump aside as a 32-pounder struck the lower sill, and glancing up struck the upper sill, then, falling on the inner edge of the lower sill, bounded on deck and spun around like a top, but hurt no one. It was very evident that if the men who were loading had not obeyed the order to drop, several of them would have been killed. So I repeated the instructions and warned the men at the guns and the crew generally to bow or stand off from the ports when a shot was seen coming. But some of the young men, from a spirit of bravado or from a belief in the doctrine of fatalism, disregarded the instructions, saying it was useless to attempt to dodge a cannon-ball, and they would trust to luck. The warning words, "Look out!" "Down!" were again soon heard; down went the gunner and his men, as the whizzing shot glanced on the gun, taking off the gunner's cap and the heads of two of the young men who trusted to luck, and in defiance of the order were standing up or passing behind him. This shot killed another man also, who was at the last gun of the starboard side, and disabled the gun. It came in with a hissing sound; three sharp spats and a heavy bang told the sad fate of three brave comrades. Before the decks were well sanded, there was so much blood on them that our men could not work the guns without slipping.

We kept firing at the enemy so long as he was within range, to prevent him from seeing us through the smoke.

MAP OF THE REGION OF THE FLOTILLA
OPERATIONS.

The *Carondelet* was the first in and the last out of the fight, and was more damaged than any of the other gun-boats, as the boat-carpenters who repaired them subsequently informed me. She was much longer under fire than any other vessel of the flotilla; and, according to the report of the Secretary of the Navy, her loss in killed and wounded was nearly twice as great as that of all the other gun-boats together. She fired more shot and shell into Fort Donelson than any other gun-boat, and was struck fifty-four times. These facts are given because a disposition was shown by correspondents and naval historians to ignore the services of the *Carondelet* on this and other occasions.

In the action of the 14th all of the armored vessels were fought with the greatest energy, skill, and courage, until disabled by the enemy's heavy shot. In his official report of the battle the flag-officer said: "The officers and men in this hotly contested but unequal fight behaved with the greatest gallantry and determination." [For losses, see p. 429.]⚓

Although the gun-boats were repulsed in this action, the demoralizing effect of their cannonade, and of the heavy and well-sustained fire of the *Carondelet* on the day before, must have been very great, and contributed in no small degree to the successful operations of the army on the following day.

After the battle I called upon the flag-officer, and found him suffering from his wounds. He asked me if I could have run past the fort, something I should not have ventured upon without permission.

The 15th was employed in the burial of our slain comrades. I read the Episcopal service on board the *Carondelet*, under our flag at half-mast; and the sailors bore their late companions to a lonely field within the shadows of

⚓ From the report of Captain B. G. Bidwell, "the only officer connected with the heavy batteries of Fort Donelson who was fortunate enough to escape," we take this account of the engagement:

"All was quiet until the evening of the 14th (Friday), when 4 boats came around the point, arranged themselves in line of battle, and advanced slowly, but steadily, up the river to within 200 yards of our battery, and halted, when a most incessant fire was kept up for some time. We were ordered to hold our fire until they got within range of our 32-pounders. We remained perfectly silent, while they came over about one and a half miles, pouring a heavy fire of shot and shell upon us all the time. Two more boats came around the point and threw shell at us. Our gunners were inexperienced and knew very little of the firing of heavy guns. They, however, did some excellent shooting. The rifled gun was disabled by the ramming of a cartridge while the wire was in the vent, it being left in there by a careless

gunner,—being bent, it could not be got out,—but the two center boats were both disabled, the left-center (I think) by a ricochet shot entering one of the port-holes, which are tolerably large. The right-center boat was very soon injured by a ball striking her on top, and also a direct shot in the port hole, when she fell back, the two flank boats closing in behind them and protecting them from our fire in retreat. I think these two were not seriously injured. They must have fired near two thousand shot and shell at us. Our Columbiad fired about 27 times, the rifled gun very few times, and the 32-pounders about 45 or 50 rounds each. A great many of our balls took effect, being well aimed. I am confident the efficiency of the gun-boat is in the gun it carries rather than in the boat itself. We can whip them always if our men will only stand to their guns. Not a man of all ours was hurt, notwithstanding they threw grape at us. Their fire was more destructive to our works at 2 miles than at 200 yards. They over-fired us from that distance."

the hills. When they were about to lower the first coffin, a Roman Catholic priest appeared, and his services being accepted, he read the prayers for the dead. As the last service was ended, the sound of the battle being waged by General Grant, like the rumbling of distant thunder, was the only requiem for our departed shipmates.

On Sunday, the 16th, at dawn, Fort Donelson surrendered and the gunboats steamed up to Dover. After religious services the *Carondelet* proceeded back to Cairo, and arrived there on the morning of the 17th, in such a dense fog that she passed below the town unnoticed, and had great difficulty in finding the landing. There had been a report that the enemy was coming from Columbus to attack Cairo during the absence of its defenders; and while the *Carondelet* was cautiously feeling her way back and blowing her whistle, some people imagined she was a Confederate gun-boat about to land, and made hasty preparations to leave the place. Our announcement of the victory at Fort Donelson changed their dejection into joy and exultation. On the following morning an order congratulating the officers and men of the *Carondelet* was received from Flag-Officer Foote.

A few days later the *Carondelet* was taken up on the ways at Mound City, Illinois,—six or seven miles above Cairo on the Ohio River,—for repairs; and a crowd of carpenters worked on her night and day. After the repairs were completed, she was ordered to make the experiment of backing

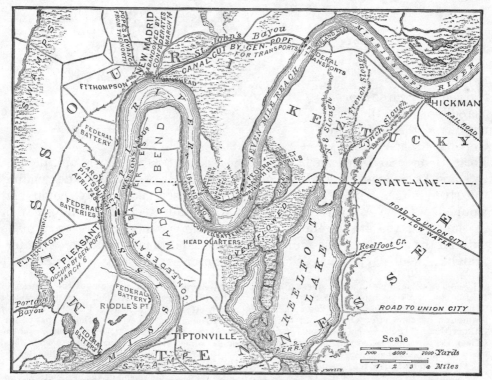

MAP OF MILITARY AND NAVAL OPERATIONS ABOUT ISLAND NUMBER TEN. (BASED ON THE TWO MAPS BY CAPTAIN A. B. GRAY, C. S. A., MADE IN MARCH, 1862, AND ON OFFICIAL REPORTS.) FOR CORRECTION OF THE LINE OF THE CANAL, SEE PAGE 461.

up-stream, which proved a laughable failure. She would sheer from one side of the river to the other, and with two anchors astern she could not be held steady enough to fight her bow-guns down-stream. She dragged both anchors alternately, until they came together, and the experiment failed completely.

On the morning of the 23d the flag-officer made a reconnoissance to Columbus, Kentucky, with four gun-boats and two mortar-boats, accompanied by the wooden gun-boat *Cones-* *toga,* convoying five transports. The fortifications looked more formidable than ever. The enemy fired two guns, and sent up a transport with the pretext, it was said, of effecting an exchange

of prisoners.‡ But at that time, as we learned afterward from a credible source, the evacuation of the fort (which General Grant's successes at

THE MORTAR-BOATS AT ISLAND NUMBER TEN.

Forts Henry and Donelson had made necessary) was going on, and the last raft and barge loads of all the movable munitions of war were descending the river, which, with a large quantity previously taken away, could and would have been captured by our fleet if we had received this information in time. On the 4th of March another reconnoissance in force was made with all the gun-boats and four mortar-boats, and the fortress had still a formidable, life-like appearance, though it had been evacuated two days before. ♭

‡ The ostensible object was a request to permit the families of officers captured at Fort Donelson to pass through the Union lines. The request was granted on the following day, but General George W. Cullum (General Halleck's chief of staff) and Flag-Officer Foote remonstrated with General Polk for the use made of the flag of truce.— EDITORS.

♭ On the 3d of March the evacuated works had been occupied by a scouting party of the 2d Illinois Cavalry, sent from Paducah by Brigadier-General W. T. Sherman, who had succeeded Briga-dier-General Grant in command of the District of Cairo (February 14, 1862) on the assignment of General Grant to the command of the District of West Tennessee. The fact of the occupation was not known at the time of the gun-boat reconnoissance, which included a land force accompanied by General Sherman and by Brigadier-General Cullum. This detachment landed and took formal possession. In his report of the occupation, General Cullum speaks of Columbus as "the Gibraltar of the West." See also note, p. 367.— EDITORS.

On the 5th of March, while we were descending the Mississippi in a dense fog, the flag-steamer leading, the Confederate gun-boat *Grampus*, or *Dare-devil Jack*, the sauciest little vessel on the river, suddenly appeared across our track and "close aboard." She stopped her engines and struck her colors, and we all thought she was ours at last. But when the captain of the *Grampus* saw how slowly we moved, and as no gun was fired to bring him to, he started off with astonishing speed and was out of danger before the flag-steamer could fire a gun. She ran before us yawing and flirting about, and blowing her alarm-whistle so as to announce our approach to the enemy who had now re-tiréd to Island Number Ten, a strong position sixty miles below Columbus (and of the latitude of Forts Henry and Donelson), where General Beauregard, who was now in general command of our opponents, had determined to con-test the possession of the river.

On March 15th the flotilla and transports continued on their way to Island Number Ten, arriving in its vicinity about nine in the morning. The strong and muddy current of the river had overflowed its banks and carried away every movable thing. Houses, trees, fences, and wrecks of all kinds were being swept rapidly down-stream. The twists and turns of the river near Island Number Ten are certainly remarkable. Within a radius of eight miles from the island it crosses the boundary line of Kentucky and Tennessee three times, running on almost every point of the compass. We were greatly surprised when we arrived above Island Number Ten and saw on the bluffs a chain of forts extending for four miles along the crescent-formed shore, with the white tents of the enemy in the rear. And there lay the island in the lower corner of the crescent, with the side fronting the Missouri shore lined with heavy ordnance, so trained that with the artillery on the opposite shore almost every point on the river between the island and the Missouri bank could be reached at once by all the enemy's batteries.

On the 17th an attack was made on the upper battery by all the iron-clads and mortar-boats. The *Benton* (flag-steamer), lashed between the *Cincinnati* and *St. Louis*, was on the east side of the river; the *Mound City, Carondelet,* and *Pittsburgh* were on the west side; the last, however, changed her position to the east side of the river before the firing began. We opened fire on the upper fort at 1:20, and by order of the flag-officer fired one gun a minute. The enemy replied promptly, and some of his shot struck the *Benton*, but, owing to the distance from which they were fired, did but little damage. We silenced all the guns in the upper fort except one. During the action one of the rifled guns of the *St. Louis* exploded, killing and wounding several of the gunners,—another proof of the truth of the saying that the guns furnished the Western flotilla were less destructive to the enemy than to ourselves.

From March 17th to April 4th but little progress was made in the reduc-tion of the Confederate works — the gun-boats firing a few shot now and then at long range, but doing little damage. The mortar-boats, however, were daily throwing 13-inch bombs, and so effectively at times that the Confederates were driven from their batteries and compelled to seek refuge in caves and other places of safety. But it was very evident that the

THE "CARONDELET" RUNNING THE CONFEDERATE
BATTERIES AT ISLAND NUMBER TEN (APRIL 4, 1862).
AFTER A SKETCH BY REAR-ADMIRAL WALKE.

great object of the expedition—the
reduction of the works and the capture of the Confederate forces—
could not be effected by the gun-boats alone, owing to their mode of
structure and to the disadvantage under which they were fought in the
strong and rapid current of the Mississippi. This was the opinion not only
of naval officers, but also of General Pope and other army officers.

On the 23d of March the monotony of the long and tedious investment
was unfortunately varied in a very singular manner. The *Carondelet* being
moored nearest the enemy's upper fort, under several large cottonwood trees,
in order to protect the mortar-boats, suddenly, and without warning, two of
the largest of the trees fell across her deck, mortally wounding one of the
crew and severely wounding another, and doing great damage to the vessel.
This was twelve days before I ran the gauntlet at Island Number Ten with
the *Carondelet*.

To understand fully the importance of that adventure, some explanation
of the military situation at and below Island Number Ten seems necessary.
After the evacuation of New Madrid, which General Pope had forced by
blockading the river twelve miles below, at Point Pleasant, the Confederate
forces occupied their fortified positions on Island Number Ten and the eastern shore of the Mississippi, where they were cut off by impassable swamps
on the land side. They were in a *cul-de-sac*, and the only way open for them
to obtain supplies or to effect a retreat was by the river south of Island
Number Ten. General Pope, with an army of twenty thousand men, was on

the western side of the river below the island. Perceiving the defect in the enemy's position, he proceeded with great promptness and ability to take advantage of it. It was his intention to cross the river and attack the enemy from below, but he could not do this without the aid of a gun-boat to silence the enemy's batteries opposite Point Pleasant and protect his army in cross- ing. He wrote repeatedly to Flag-Officer Foote, urging him to send down a gun-boat past the enemy's batteries on Island Number Ten, and in one of his letters expressed the belief that a boat could pass down at night under cover of the darkness. But the flag-officer invariably declined, saying in one of his letters to General Pope that the attempt "would result in the sacrifice of the boat, her officers and men, which sacrifice I would not be justified in making."

During this correspondence the bombardment still went on, but was attended with such poor results that it became a subject of ridicule among the officers of Pope's army, one of whom (Colonel Gilmore, of Chillicothe, Ohio) is reported to have said that often when they met, and inquiry was made respecting the operations of the flotilla, the answer would generally be: "Oh! it is still bombarding the State of Tennessee at long range." And a Confederate officer said that no casualties resulted and no damage was sus- tained at Island Number Ten from the fire of the gun-boats.

On March 20th Flag-Officer Foote consulted his commanding officers, through Commander Stembel, as to the practicability of taking a gun-boat past the enemy's forts to New Madrid, and all except myself were opposed to the enterprise, believing with Foote that the attempt to pass the batteries would result in the almost certain destruction of the boat. I did not think so, but believed with General Pope that, under the cover of darkness and other favorable circumstances, a gun-boat might be run past the enemy's

THE LEVEE AT NEW MADRID. FROM A SKETCH MADE SOON AFTER THE CAPTURE OF ISLAND NUMBER TEN.

batteries, formidable as they were with nearly fifty guns. And although fully aware of the hazardous nature of the enterprise, I knew that the aid of a gun-boat was absolutely necessary to enable General Pope to succeed in his operations against the enemy, and thought the importance of this success would justifiy the risk of running the gauntlet of the batteries on Island Number Ten and on the left bank. The army officers were becoming impatient, and it was well known that the Confederates had a number of small gun-boats below, and were engaged in building several large and powerful vessels, of which the renowned *Arkansas* was one. And there was good reason to apprehend that these gun-boats would ascend the river and pass or silence Pope's batteries, and relieve the Confederate forces on Island Number Ten and the eastern shore of the Mississippi. That Pope and Foote apprehended this, appears from the correspondence between them. ⏐

The flag-officer now called a formal council of war of all his commanding officers. It was held on board the flag-steamer, on the 28th or 29th of March, and all except myself concurred in the opinion formerly expressed that the attempt to pass the batteries was too hazardous and ought not to be made. When I was asked to give my views, I favored the undertaking, and advised compliance with the requests of General Pope. When asked if I was willing to make the attempt with the *Carondelet,* I replied in the affirmative. Foote accepted my advice, and expressed himself as greatly relieved from a heavy responsibility, as he had determined to send none but volunteers on an expedition which he regarded as perilous and of very doubtful success.

Having received written orders from the flag-officer, under date of March 30th, I at once began to prepare the *Carondelet* for the ordeal. All the loose material at hand was collected, and on the 4th of April the decks were covered with it, to protect them against plunging shot. Hawsers and chain cables were placed around the pilot-house and other vulnerable parts of the vessel, and every precaution was adopted to prevent disaster. A coal-barge laden with hay and coal was lashed to the part of the port side on which there was no iron plating, to protect the magazine. It was truly said that the *Carondelet* at that time resembled a farmer's wagon prepared for market. The engineers led the escape-steam, through the pipes aft, into the wheel-house, to avoid the puffing sound it made when blown through the smoke-stacks.

All the necessary preparations having been made, I informed the flag-officer of my intention to run the gauntlet that night, and received his approval. Colonel N. B. Buford, who commanded the land forces temporarily with the flotilla, assisted me in preparing for the trip, and on the night of the 4th brought on board Captain Hottenstein, of the 42d Illinois, and twenty-three sharp-shooters of his command, who volunteered their services, which were gratefully accepted. Colonel Buford remained on board until the last moment, to encourage us. I informed the officers and crew of the character of the

⏐ An interesting and important enterprise in this campaign was the sawing out, under great difficulties, of a channel, twelve miles in length, to complete a water-way for the Union transports across Madrid Bend. See paper by Colonel J. W. Bissell and corrected map, page 460.— EDITORS.

undertaking, and all expressed a readiness to make the venture. In order to resist boarding parties, in case of being disabled, the sailors were well armed, and pistols, cutlasses, muskets, boarding-pikes, and hand-grenades were within reach. Hose was attached to the boilers for throwing scalding water over any who might attempt to board. If it should be found impossible to save the vessel, it was designed to sink rather than burn her. During the afternoon there was a promise of a clear, moonlight night,

MAJOR-GENERAL JOHN POPE.
FROM A PHOTOGRAPH TAKEN EARLY IN THE WAR.

and it was determined to wait until the moon was down, and then to make the attempt, whatever the chances. Having gone so far, we could not abandon the project without an effect on the men almost as bad as failure.

At 10 o'clock the moon had gone down, and the sky, the earth, and the river were alike hidden in the black shadow of a thunder-storm, which had now spread itself over all the heavens. As the time seemed favorable, I ordered the first master to cast off. Dark clouds now rose rapidly over us and enveloped us in almost total darkness, except when the sky was lighted up by the welcome flashes of vivid lightning, to show us the perilous way we were to take. Now and then the dim outline of the landscape could be seen, and the forest bending under the roaring storm that came rushing up the river.

With our bow pointing to the island, we passed the lowest point of land without being observed, it appears, by the enemy. All speed was given to the vessel to drive her through the tempest. The flashes of lightning continued with frightful brilliancy, and "almost every second," wrote a correspondent, "every brace, post, and outline could be seen with startling distinctness, enshrouded by a bluish white glare of light, and then her form for the next minute would become merged in the intense darkness." When opposite Battery No. 2, on the mainland, the smoke-stacks blazed up, but the fire was soon subdued. It was caused by the soot becoming dry, as the escape-steam, which usually kept the stacks wet, had been sent into the wheel-house, as already mentioned, to prevent noise. With such vivid lightning as prevailed during the whole passage, there was no prospect of escaping the vigilance of the enemy, but there was good reason to hope that he would be unable to point his guns accurately. Again the smoke-stacks took fire, and were soon put out; and then the roar of the enemy's guns began, and from Batteries Nos. 2, 3, and 4 on the mainland came the continued crack and scream of their rifle-shells, which seemed to unite with the electric batteries of the clouds to annihilate us.

BRIGADIER-GENERAL W. W. MACKALL, C. S. A., IN COMMAND AT ISLAND NUMBER TEN, PREVIOUSLY ASSISTANT ADJUTANT-GENERAL TO GENERAL ALBERT SIDNEY JOHNSTON.
FROM A PHOTOGRAPH.

While nearing the island or some shoal point, during a few minutes of total darkness, we were startled by the order, "Hard a-port!" from our brave and skillful pilot, First Master William R. Hoel. We almost grazed the island, and it appears were not observed through the storm until we were close in, and the enemy, having no time to point his guns, fired at random. In fact, we ran so near that the enemy did not, probably could not, depress his guns sufficiently. While close under the lee of the island and during a lull in the storm and in the firing, one of our pilots heard a Confederate officer shout, "Elevate your guns!" It is probable that the muzzles of those guns had been depressed to keep the rain out, and that the officers ordered the guns elevated just in time to save us from the direct fire of the enemy's heaviest fort; and this, no doubt, was the cause of our remarkable escape.

The Confederate land batteries above New Madrid were ten in number—five on the eastern side of Island Number Ten; four (Batteries No. 5, 4, 3, and 2) opposite the island on the mainland, as shown on the map (p. 437), besides Battery No. 1, two miles above the island.—EDITORS.

During the dark and stormy night of April 1st Colonel George W. Roberts, of the 42d Illinois Regiment, executed a brilliant exploit. Forty picked men, in five barges, with muffled oars, left for Battery No. 1. They proceeded in silence, and were unobserved until within a few rods of the fort, when a flash of lightning discovered them to the sentries, who fired. Our men, who did not reply, were soon climbing up the slippery bank, and in three minutes more the six guns were spiked, Colonel Roberts himself spiking a huge 80-pounder pivot-gun. Some of these guns had been previously dismounted by our fleet, and were now rendered doubly useless.—H. W.

Having passed the principal batteries, we were greatly relieved from suspense, patiently endured, however, by the officers and crew. But there was another formidable obstacle in the way—a floating battery, which was the great "war elephant" of the Confederates, built to blockade the Mississippi permanently. As we passed her she fired six or eight shots at us, but without effect. One ball struck the coal-barge, and one was found in a bale of hay; we found also one or two musket-bullets. We arrived at New Madrid about midnight with no one hurt, and were most joyfully received by our army. At the suggestion of Paymaster Nixon, all hands "spliced the main brace."

On Sunday, the 6th, after prayers and thanksgiving, the *Carondelet*, with General Gordon Granger, Colonel J. L. Kirby Smith of the 43d Ohio, and Captain Louis H. Marshall of General Pope's staff on board, made a reconnoissance twenty miles down, nearly to Tiptonville, the enemy's forts firing on her all the way down. We returned their fire, and dropped a few shells into their camps beyond. On the way back, we captured and spiked the guns of a battery of one 32-pounder and one 24-pounder, in about twenty-five minutes, opposite Point Pleasant. Before we landed to spike the guns, a tall Confederate soldier, with cool and deliberate courage, posted himself behind a large cottonwood tree, and repeatedly fired upon us, until our Illinois sharpshooters got to work on him from behind the hammock nettings. He had two rifles, which he soon dropped, fleeing into the woods with his head down. The next day he was captured and brought into camp at Tiptonville, with the tip of his nose shot off. After the capture of this battery, the enemy prepared to evacuate his positions on Island Number Ten and the adjacent shores, and thus, as one of the historians of the civil war says, the *Carondelet* struck the blow that secured that victory.

Returning to New Madrid, we were instructed by General Pope to attack the enemy's batteries of six 64-pounders which protected his rear; and besides, another gun-boat was expected. The *Pittsburgh* (Lieutenant-Commander Thompson) ran the gauntlet without injury, during a thunder-storm, at 2 in the morning of April 7th, and arrived at 5 o'clock; but she was not ready for service, and the *Carondelet* attacked the principal batteries at Watson's Landing alone and had nearly silenced them when the *Pittsburgh* came up astern and fired nearly over the *Carondelet's* upper deck, after she and the Confederates had ceased firing. I reported to General Pope that we had cleared the opposite shores of the enemy, and were ready to cover the crossing of the river and the landing of the army. Seeing themselves cut off, the garrison at Island Number Ten surrendered to Foote on the 7th of April, the day of the Confederate repulse at Shiloh. The other Confederates retreating before Pope's advance, were nearly all overtaken and captured at 4 o'clock on the morning of the 8th; and about the same time the cavalry under Colonel W. L. Elliott took possession of the enemy's deserted works on the Tennessee shore.

The result of General Pope's operations in connection with the services of the *Carondelet* below Island Number Ten was the capture of three generals (including General W. W. Mackall, who ten days before the surrender had succeeded General John P. McCown in the command at Madrid Bend), over

THE "CARONDELET" AND "PITTSBURGH" CAPTURING THE CONFEDERATE BATTERIES BELOW NEW MADRID.
AFTER A DRAWING BY REAR-ADMIRAL WALKE.

5000 men, 20 pieces of heavy artillery, 7000 stand of arms, and a large quantity of ammunition and provisions, without the loss of a man on our side.

On the 12th the *Benton* (flag-steamer), with the *Cincinnati, Mound City, Cairo,* and *St. Louis,* passed Tiptonville and signaled the *Carondelet* and *Pittsburgh* to follow. Five Confederate gun-boats came up the next day and offered battle; but after the exchange of a few shots at long range they retired down the river. We followed them all the way to Craighead's Point, where they were under cover of their fortifications at Fort Pillow. I was not aware at the time that we were chasing the squadron of my esteemed shipmate of the U. S. Frigates *Cumberland* and *Merrimac*, Colonel John W. Dunnington, who afterward fought so bravely at Arkansas Post.

On the 14th General Pope's army landed about six miles above Craighead's Point, near Osceola, under the protection of the gun-boats. While he was preparing to attack Fort Pillow, Foote sent his executive officer twice to me on the *Carondelet* to inquire whether I would undertake, with my vessel and two or three other gun-boats, to pass below the fort to coöperate with General Pope, to which inquiries I replied that I was ready at any time to make the attempt. But Pope and his army (with the exception of 1500 men) were ordered away, and the expedition against Fort Pillow was abandoned. Between the 14th of April and the 10th of May two or three of the mortar-boats were towed down the river and moored near Craighead's Point, with a gun-boat to protect them. They were employed in throwing 13-inch bombs across the point into Fort Pillow, two miles distant. The enemy returned our bombardment with vigor, but not with much accuracy or effect. Several of their bombs fell near the gun-boats when we were three miles from the fort.

The Confederate fleet called the " River Defense" having been reënforced, they determined upon capturing the mortar-boats or giving us battle. On the 8th three of their vessels came to the point from which the mortar-boats had thrown their bombs, but, finding none, returned. Foote had given special orders to keep up steam and be ready for battle any moment, day or night. There was so much illness at that time in the flotilla that about a third of the officers and men were under medical treatment, and a great many were unfit for duty. On the 9th of May, at his own request, our distinguished commander-in-chief, Foote, was relieved from his arduous duties. He had become very much enfeebled from the wounds received at Fort Donelson and from illness. He carried with him the sympathy and regrets of all his command. He was succeeded by Flag-Officer Charles Henry Davis, a most excellent officer.

This paper would not be complete without some account of the naval battles fought by the flotilla immediately after the retirement of Flag-Officer Foote, under whose supervision and amid the greatest embarrassments it had been built, organized, and equipped. On the morning of the 10th of May a mortar-boat was towed down the river, as usual, at 5 A. M., to bombard Fort Pillow. The *Cincinnati* soon followed to protect her. At 6:35 eight Confederate rams came up the river at full speed.☆ The *Carondelet* at once prepared for action, and slipped her hawser to the " bare end," ready for orders to " go ahead." No officer was on the deck of the *Benton* (flag-steamer) except the pilot, Mr. Birch, who informed the flag-officer of the situation, and passed the order to the *Carondelet* and *Pittsburgh* to proceed without waiting for the flag-steamer. General signal was also made to the fleet to get under way, but it was not visible on account of the light fog.

The *Carondelet* started immediately after the first verbal order; the others, for want of steam or some other cause, were not ready, except the *Mound City*, which put off soon after we were fairly on our way to the rescue of the *Cincinnati*. We had proceeded about a mile before our other gun-boats left their moorings. The rams were advancing rapidly, and we steered for the leading vessel, *General Bragg*, a brig-rigged, side-wheel steam ram, far in advance of the others, and apparently intent on striking the *Cincinnati*. When about three-quarters of a mile from the *General Bragg*, the *Carondelet* and *Mound City* fired on her with their bow-guns, until she struck the *Cincinnati* on the starboard quarter, making a great hole in the shell-room, through which the water poured with resistless force. The *Cincinnati* then retreated up the river and the *General Bragg* drifted down, evidently disabled. The *General Price*, following the example of her consort, also rammed the *Cincinnati*. We fired our bow-guns into the *General Price*, and she backed off, disabled also. The *Cincinnati* was again struck by one of the enemy's rams, the *General Sumter*. Having pushed on with all speed to the rescue of the *Cincinnati*, the *Carondelet* passed her in a sinking condition, and, rounding to, we fired our bow and starboard broadside guns into the retreating *General Bragg* and the advancing rams, *General Jeff. Thompson*, *General Beauregard*,

☆ The mortar-boat, No. 16, which was the first object of attack, was defended with great spirit by Acting-Master Gregory, who fired his mortar eleven times, reducing the charge and diminishing the elevation. (See cut, p. 450.) — EDITORS.

and *General Lovell.* Heading up-stream, close to a shoal, the *Carondelet* brought her port broadside guns to bear on the *Sumter* and *Price,* which were dropping down-stream. At this crisis the *Van Dorn* and *Little Rebel* had run above the *Carondelet;* the *Bragg, Jeff. Thompson, Beauregard,* and *Lovell* were below her. The last three, coming up, fired into the *Carondelet;* she returned their fire with her stern-guns; and, while in this position, I ordered the port rifled 50-pounder Dahlgren gun to be leveled and fired at the center of the *Sumter.* The shot struck the vessel just forward of her wheel-house, and the steam instantly poured out from her ports and all parts of her casemates, and we saw her men running out of them and falling or lying down on her deck. None of our gun-boats had yet come to the assistance of the *Carondelet.* The *Benton* and *Pittsburgh* had probably gone to aid the *Cincinnati,* and the *St. Louis* to relieve the *Mound City,* which had been badly rammed by the *Van Dorn.* The smoke at this time was so

FLAG-OFFICER CHARLES HENRY DAVIS (AFTERWARD REAR-ADMIRAL AND CHIEF OF THE BUREAU OF NAVIGATION). FROM A PHOTOGRAPH.

dense that we could hardly distinguish the gun-boats above us. The upper deck of the *Carondelet* was swept with grape-shot and fragments of broken shell; some of the latter were picked up by one of the sharp-shooters, who told me they were obliged to lie down under shelter to save themselves from the grape and other shot of the *Pittsburgh* above us, and from the shot and broken shell of the enemy below us. Why some of our gun-boats did not fire into the *Van Dorn* and *Little Rebel* while they were above the *Carondelet,* and prevent their escape, if possible, I never could make out.↓

As the smoke rose we saw that the enemy was retreating rapidly and in great confusion. The *Carondelet* dropped down to within half a mile above Craighead's Point, and kept up a continual fire upon their vessels, which were very much huddled together. When they were nearly, if not quite, beyond gunshot, the *Benton,* having raised sufficient steam, came down and passed the *Carondelet;* but the Confederates were under the protection of Fort Pillow before the *Benton* could reach them. Our fleet returned to Plum Point, except the *Carondelet,* which dropped her anchor on the battle-field, two miles or more below the point, and remained there two days on voluntary

↓ Flag-Officer Davis says in his report: "All of these vessels might easily have been captured if we had possessed the means of towing them out of action; but the steam-power of our gun-boats is so disproportionate to the bulk of the vessels that they can accomplish but little beyond overcoming the strength of the current, even when unincumbered."— EDITORS.

guard duty. This engagement was sharp, but not decisive. From the first to the last shot fired by the *Carondelet*, one hour and ten minutes elapsed. After the battle, long-range firing was kept up until the evacuation of Fort Pillow.

On the 25th seven of Colonel Ellet's rams arrived,—a useful acquisition to our fleet. During the afternoon of June 4th heavy clouds of smoke were observed rising from Fort Pillow, followed by explosions. which continued through the night; the last of which, much greater than the others, lit up the heavens and the Chickasaw bluffs with a brilliant light, and convinced us that this was the parting salute of the Confederates before leaving for the lower Mississippi. At dawn next morning the fleet was all astir to take possession of Fort Pillow, the flag-steamer leading. We found the casemates, magazines, and breastworks blown to atoms.

On our way to Memphis the enemy's steamer *Sovereign* was intercepted by one of our tugs. She was run ashore by her crew, who attempted to blow her up, but were foiled in their purpose by a boy of sixteen whom the enemy had pressed into service, who, after the abandonment of the vessel, took the extra weights from the safety-valves, opened the fire-doors and flue-caps, and put water on the fires, and, having procured a sheet, signaled the tug, which came up and took possession. It may be proper to say that on our way down the river we respected private property, and did not assail or molest any except those who were in arms against us.

The morning of the 6th of June we fought the battle of Memphis, which lasted one hour and ten minutes. It was begun by an attack upon our fleet by the enemy, whose vessels were in double line of battle opposite the city. We were then at a distance of a mile and a half or two miles above the city. Their fire continued for a quarter of an hour, when the attack was promptly met by

FORT PILLOW AND THE WATER-BATTERY. AFTER A SKETCH BY REAR-ADMIRAL WALKE.

"MOUND CITY."   "CARONDELET."   "CINCINNATI."   "PRICE."   "BRAGG."   "SUMTER."
        MORTAR NO. 16.   "VAN DORN."   "LITTLE REBEL."

THE BATTLE OF FORT PILLOW, MAY 10, 1862 (LOOKING NORTH). AFTER A SKETCH BY REAR-ADMIRAL WALKE.

two of our ram squadron, the *Queen of the West* (Colonel Charles Ellet) leading, and the *Monarch* (Lieutenant-Colonel A. W. Ellet, younger brother of the
leader).   These vessels fearlessly dashed ahead of our gun-boats, ran for the
enemy's fleet, and at the first plunge succeeded in sinking one vessel and disabling another.   The astonished Confederates received them gallantly and
effectively.   The *Queen of the West* and *Monarch* were followed in line of battle
by the gun-boats, under the lead of Flag-Officer Davis, and all of them opened
fire, which was continued from the time we got within good range until the
end of the battle—two or three tugs keeping all the while a safe distance astern.
The *Queen of the West* was a quarter of a mile in advance of the *Monarch*,
and after having rammed one of the enemy's fleet, she was badly rammed
by the *Beauregard*, which then, in company with the *General Price*, made a
dash at the *Monarch* as she approached them.   The *Beauregard*, however,
missed the *Monarch* and struck the *General Price* instead on her port side,
cutting her down to the water-line, tearing off her wheel instantly, and
placing her *hors de combat*.   The *Monarch* then rammed the *Beauregard*,
which had been several times raked fore and aft by the shot and shell of
our iron-clads, and she quickly sank in the river opposite Memphis.   The
General Lovell, after having been badly rammed by the *Queen of the West*,
was struck by our shot and shell, and, at about the same time and place
as the *Beauregard*, sank to the bottom so suddenly as to take a considerable number of her officers and crew down with her, the others being saved
by small boats and our tugs.   The *Price, Little Rebel* (with a shot-hole

through her steam-chest), and our *Queen of the West*, all disabled, were run on the Arkansas shore opposite Memphis; and the *Monarch* afterward ran into the *Little Rebel* just as our fleet was passing her in pursuit of the remainder of the enemy's fleet, then retreating rapidly down the river. The *Jeff. Thompson*, below the point and opposite President's Island, was the next boat disabled by our shot. She was run ashore, burned, and blown up. The Confederate ram *Sumter* was also disabled by our shell and captured. The *Bragg* soon after shared the same fate and was run ashore, where her officers abandoned her and disappeared in the forests of Arkansas. All the Confederate rams which had been run on the Arkansas shore were captured. The *Van Dorn*, having a start, alone escaped down the river. The rams

"CARONDELET."   "BENTON."   "ST. LOUIS."   "CAIRO."   "LOUISVILLE."   "QUEEN OF THE
        IN THE DISTANCE CONFEDERATE FLEET ADVANCING.   WEST."   "MONARCH."

THE BATTLE OF MEMPHIS (JUNE 6, 1862), LOOKING SOUTH. AFTER A DRAWING BY REAR-ADMIRAL WALKE.

Monarch and *Switzerland* were dispatched in pursuit of her and a few transports, but returned without overtaking them, although they captured another steamer.⚓

The scene at this battle was rendered most sublime by the desperate nature of the engagement and the momentous consequences that followed very speedily after the first attack. Thousands of people crowded the high bluffs overlooking the river. The roar of the cannon and shell shook the houses on shore on either side for many miles. First wild yells, shrieks, and clamors, then loud, despairing murmurs, filled the affrighted city. The screaming, plunging shell crashed into the boats, blowing some of them and their crews into fragments, and the rams rushed upon each other like wild beasts in

⚓ See paper on "Ellet and his Steam-rams at Memphis," page 453.—EDITORS.

BRIGADIER-GENERAL M. JEFF. THOMPSON.
FROM A PHOTOGRAPH.

deadly conflict. Blinding smoke hovered about the scene of all this confusion and horror; and, as the battle progressed and the Confederate fleet was destroyed, all the cheering voices on shore were silenced. When the last hope of the Confederates gave way, the lamentations which went up from the spectators were like cries of anguish.

Boats were put off from our vessels to save as many lives as possible. No serious injury was received by any one on board the United States fleet. Colonel Ellet received a pistol-shot in the leg; a shot struck the *Carondelet* in the bow, broke up her anchor and anchor-stock, and fragments were scattered over her deck among her officers and crew, wounding slightly Acting-Master Gibson and two or three others who were standing at the time on the forward deck with me. The heavy timber which was suspended at the water-line, to protect the boats from the Confederate rams, greatly impeded our progress, and it was therefore cut adrift from the *Carondelet* when that vessel was in chase of the *Bragg* and *Sumter*. The latter had just landed a number of her officers and crew, some of whom were emerging from the bushes along the bank of the river, unaware of the *Carondelet's* proximity, when I hailed them through a trumpet, and ordered them to stop or be shot. They obeyed immediately, and by my orders were taken on board a tug and delivered on the *Benton*.

General Jeff. Thompson, noted in partisan or border warfare, having signally failed with those rams at Fort Pillow, now resigned them to their fate. It was said that he stood by his horse watching the struggle, and seeing at last his rams all gone, captured, sunk, or burned, he exclaimed, philosophically, "They are gone, and I am going," mounted his horse, and disappeared.

An enormous amount of property was captured by our squadron; and, in addition to the Confederate fleet, we captured at Memphis six large Mississippi steamers, each marked "C. S. A." We also seized a large quantity of cotton in steamers and on shore, and the property at the Confederate Navy Yard, and caused the destruction of the *Tennessee*, a large steam-ram, on the stocks, which was to have been a sister ship to the renowned *Arkansas*. About one hundred Confederates were killed and wounded and one hundred and fifty captured. Chief of all results of the work of the flotilla was the opening of the Mississippi River once for all from Cairo to Memphis, and the complete possession of Western Tennessee by the Union forces.

IN THE DISTANCE : " PRICE," " LITTLE REBEL," " QUEEN OF THE WEST," AND " MONARCH."   UNION GUN-BOATS.
" VAN DORN "   " JEFF. THOMPSON."   " BRAGG."   " SUMTER."   " BEAUREGARD "   (SINKING).   " LOVELL "   (SUNK).
THE BATTLE OF MEMPHIS, JUNE 6, 1862 (LOOKING NORTH).   RETREAT OF THE CONFEDERATE FLEET. AFTER A SKETCH BY REAR-ADMIRAL WALKE.

ELLET AND HIS STEAM-RAMS AT MEMPHIS.

BY ALFRED W. ELLET, BRIGADIER-GENERAL, U. S. V. ↓

ON the 8th of March, 1862, occurred the memorable catastrophe at Hampton Roads. The possibility of such a disaster had been repeatedly urged in warning terms by a gentleman who had vainly endeavored to avert it. I refer to the late eminent civil engineer, Charles Ellet, Jr., the inventor of the steam-ram as a vehicle of war destruction. On the 6th of February, 1862, Mr. Ellet wrote in a pamphlet as follows:

" It is not generally known that the rebels now have *five steam-rams* nearly ready for use. Of these five, two are on the lower Mississippi, two are at Mobile, and one is at Norfolk. The last of the five, the one at Norfolk, is doubtless the most formidable, being the United States steam-frigate *Merrimac*, which has been so strengthened that, in the opinion of the rebels, it may be used as a ram. But we have not yet a single vessel at sea, nor, so far as I know, in course of construction, able to cope at all with a well-built ram. If the *Merrimac* is permitted to escape from Elizabeth River, she will be almost certain to commit great depredations on our armed and unarmed vessels in Hampton Roads, and may even be expected to pass out under the guns of Fortress Monroe and prey upon our commerce in Chesapeake Bay. Indeed, if the alterations have been skillfully made, and she succeeds in getting to sea, she will not only be a terrible scourge to our commerce, but may prove also to be a most dangerous visitor to our blockading squadrons off the harbors of the southern coasts. I have attempted to call the attention of the Navy Department and the country so often to this subject during the last seven years, that I almost hesitate to allude to it again ; and I would not do so here but that I think the danger from these tremendous engines *is very imminent but not at all appreciated*. Experience,

↓ After the death of Colonel Ellet, the command of the ram-fleet was conferred upon the writer, by order of the Secretary of War.— EDITORS.

COLONEL CHARLES ELLET, JR. FROM A PHOTOGRAPH.

derived from accidental collisions, shows that a vessel struck in the waist by a steam-ram at sea will go down almost instantaneously, and involve, as has often happened, the loss of nearly all on board."

Upon the startling verification of his neglected admonitions afforded by the *Merrimac*, Mr. Ellet was called to the War Department, and, after a short conference with Secretary Stanton, was given authority to purchase, refit, man, and command, with the rank of colonel, any number of vessels deemed, in his judgment, necessary to meet and defeat the fleet of iron-clad rams then known to be in process of construction on the lower Mississippi River.

Never was work more promptly or more effectually performed. Colonel Ellet purchased a number of steamboats at different points on the Ohio River, the best he could find in the short time at his disposal. He took some old and nearly worn-out boats, strengthened their hulls and bows with heavy timbers, raised bulkheads of timber around the boilers, and started them down the river to Cairo as fast as they could be got off the ways. They were the *Dick Fulton, Lancaster, Lioness, Mingo, Monarch, Queen of the West, Samson, Switzerland*, and *T. D. Horner*.

While the work was progressing, and before any one of the rams was nearly completed, information was received that the Confederate fleet had come out from under the batteries of Fort Pillow, had attacked our fleet of gun-boats lying near Craighead's Point, and had disabled two of them.♭ Colonel Ellet received most urgent telegrams from the Secretary of War to hurry the rams forward at the earliest possible moment. In consequence of these demands, five of them were immediately dispatched down the river under my command, work upon them being continued as they proceeded and for several days after their arrival at Fort Pillow. The other rams followed, and about the 25th of May Colonel Ellet joined the fleet on board the *Switzerland*, and the ram-fleet was now ready for action.

Colonel Ellet at once conferred with Flag-Officer Charles H. Davis on the propriety of passing Fort Pillow, and engaging the enemy's fleet wherever found. Flag-Officer Davis did not approve the plan suggested, but offered no objection to Colonel Ellet's trying the experiment. Accordingly, imme-

♭ The *Cincinnati* and the *Mound City*. See page 447.—EDITORS.

diate preparations were begun for running the batteries with the entire ram-fleet. During this period of preparation, constant watch was kept upon the fort and the enemy's fleet. On the night of the 4th of June I crossed the timber point in front of the fort, and reported to the colonel commanding my conviction that the fort was being evacuated. About 2 o'clock in the morning I obtained permission, with many words of caution from Colonel Ellet, to run down opposite the fort in a yawl and, after lying off in order to become assured that the place was abandoned, to land, with the assurance that the rams would follow in case my yawl did not return before daylight.

"SUMTER" AND "BRAGG" "THOMPSON" (BLOWING UP). MEMPHIS. "BENTON." "CAIRO." BURNING OF
  (CAPTURED). "LOUISVILLE." "ST. LOUIS." UNFINISHED CONFEDERATE RAM.
  "CARONDELET."

CLOSE OF THE BATTLE OF MEMPHIS, JUNE 6, 1862 (LOOKING NORTH).
AFTER A DRAWING BY REAR-ADMIRAL WALKE.

I landed with my little band, only to find the fort entirely deserted; and after planting the National colors upon the ruins of one of the magazines, we sat down to wait for the coming of daylight and the rams. They came, followed by the entire fleet, and after a short stop all proceeded down the river, the rams taking the lead, to Fort Randolph, where they delayed long enough to plant the National flag and to examine the abandoned fortifications, the gun-boats at this point taking the advance.↓

After leaving Fort Randolph the ram-fleet proceeded without incident to within about twenty-five miles of Memphis, where they all rounded to and

↓ The advance of Halleck upon Corinth after Shiloh, and its evacuation on May 30th, gave the Union forces possession of the Memphis and Charleston railroad, broke the second line of Confederate defense, and turned all the positions on the river above Memphis. Fort Pillow and Fort Randolph were thus made untenable (just as Columbus had become untenable after the fall of Forts Henry and Donelson on the Confederate first line of defense) and hence were evacuated.—EDITORS.

tied up for the night, with orders of sailing issued to each commander; instructions to be ready to round out at the signal from the flag-ship, and that "each boat should go into the anticipated fight in the same order they maintained in sailing." At the first dawn of day (June 6th) the fleet moved down the river, and at sunrise the flag-ship rounded the bend at "Paddy's Hen and Chickens," and immediately after came in sight of the Federal gun-boats anchored in line across the river, about a mile above Memphis. Colonel Ellet promptly signaled his vessels to tie up on the Arkansas shore, in the order of their sailing, as he desired to confer with Flag-Officer Davis before passing further.

The *Queen of the West* came to first, followed by the *Monarch* and other rams in regular succession. The *Queen of the West* had made the land, and passed out line to make fast; the *Monarch* was closing in just above, but had not yet touched the shore. At this moment, and as the full orb of the sun rose above the horizon, the report of a gun was heard from around the point and down the river. It was the first gun from the Confederate River Defense Fleet moving to attack us. Colonel Ellet was standing on the hurricane-deck of the *Queen of the West*. He immediately sprang forward, and, waving his hat to attract my attention, called out: "It is a gun from the enemy! Round out and follow me! Now is our chance!" Without a moment's delay, the *Queen* moved out gracefully, and the *Monarch* followed. By this time our gun-boats had opened their batteries, and the reports of guns on both sides were heavy and rapid.

The morning was beautifully clear and perfectly still; a heavy wall of smoke was formed across the river, so that the position of our gun-boats could only be seen by the flashes of their guns. The *Queen* plunged forward, under a full head of steam, right into this wall of smoke and was lost sight of, her position being known only by her tall pipes which reached above the smoke. The *Monarch*, following, was greeted, while passing the gun-boats, with wild huzzas from our gallant tars. When freed from the smoke, those of us who were on the *Monarch* could see Colonel Ellet's tall and commanding form still standing on the hurricane-deck, waving his hat to show me which one of the enemy's vessels he desired the *Monarch* to attack,—namely, the *General Price*, which was on the right wing of their advancing line. For himself he selected the *General Lovell* and directed the *Queen* straight for her, she being about the middle of the enemy's advancing line. The two vessels came toward each other in most gallant style, head to head, prow to prow; and had they met in that way, it is most likely that both vessels would have gone down. But at the critical moment the *General Lovell* began to turn; and that moment sealed her fate. The *Queen* came on and plunged straight into the *Lovell's* exposed broadside; the vessel was cut almost in two and disappeared under the dark waters in less time than it takes to tell the story. The *Monarch* next struck the *General Price* a glancing blow which cut her starboard wheel clean off, and completely disabled her from further participation in the fight.\

ⸯ It is impossible to reconcile this statement with that of Admiral Walke, on page 450, *q. v.* The reports of the engagement are meager and conflicting, but it has always been the general impression that the *Price* received her disabling blow in an accidental collision with the *Beaure-*

As soon as the *Queen* was freed from the wreck of the sinking *Lovell*, and before she could recover headway, she was attacked on both sides by the enemy's vessels, the *Beauregard* on one side and the *Sumter* on the other. In the *mêlée* one of the wheels of the *Queen* was disabled so that she could not use it, and Colonel Ellet, while still standing on the hurricane-deck to view the effects of the encounter with the *General Lovell*, received a pistol-ball in his knee, and, lying prone on the deck, gave orders for the *Queen* to be run on her one remaining wheel to the Arkansas shore, whither she was soon followed by the *General Price* in a sinking condition. Colonel Ellet sent an officer and squad of men to meet the *General Price* upon her making the shore, and received her entire crew as prisoners of war. By this time consternation had seized upon the enemy's fleet, and all had turned to escape. The fight had drifted down the river, below the city.✩

The *Monarch*, as soon as she could recover headway after her conflict with the *General Price*, drove down upon the *Beauregard*, which vessel, after her encounter with the *Queen of the West*, was endeavoring to escape. She was thwarted by the *Monarch* coming down upon her with a well-directed blow which crushed in her side and completely disabled her from further hope of escape. Men on the deck waved a white flag in token of surrender, and the *Monarch* passed on down to intercept the *Little Rebel*, the enemy's flag-ship. She had received some injury from our gun-boats' fire, and was making for the Arkansas shore, which she reached at the moment when the *Monarch*, with very slight headway, pushed her hard and fast aground; her crew sprang upon shore and ran into the thick woods, making their escape. Leaving the *Little Rebel* fast aground, the *Monarch* turned her attention to the sinking *Beauregard*, taking the vessel in tow, and making prisoners of her crew. The *Beauregard* was towed by the *Monarch* to the bar, where she sank to her boiler-deck and finally became a total loss.

The others of the enemy's fleet were run ashore and fired by the crews before they escaped into the adjoining Arkansas swamps. The *Jeff. Thompson* burned and blew up with a tremendous report; the *General Bragg* was secured by our gun-boats before the fire gained headway, and was saved. The *Van Dorn* alone made her escape, and was afterward burned by the enemy at Liverpool Landing, upon the approach of two of our rams in Yazoo River, in order to prevent her from falling into our hands. Two other rebel boats were burned at the same time,— the *Polk* and the *Livingston*.

After the *Monarch* had towed the *Beauregard* into shoal water, from which, it was hoped, she might be raised, I received the first intelligence, from a dis-

---

gard, as has been stated by Captain Hurt, commander of the *Beauregard*. The reports of Flag-Officer Davis and of General M. Jeff. Thompson, commander of the Confederate troops at Memphis, agree in saying that the *Price* was rammed by one of her consorts,— General Thompson adding that the blow, which he states was delivered by the *Beauregard*, knocked off the *Price's* wheel and entirely disabled her.— EDITORS.

✩ The gun-boat flotilla, under Flag-Officer Davis, had weighed anchor at 4:30 A. M. and

proceeded immediately to quarters. The Confederate fleet opened at 5, and at 5 : 20 the gun-boats were returning the fire and steaming down the river. The higher speed of Colonel Ellet's rams enabled them to pass through the intervals in Davis's flotilla, and the latter, coming after them, completed with its batteries the work which the rams had so successfully begun. The guns of the flotilla were well served, and both the *Beauregard* and *Little Rebel* were disabled by shots in their boilers.— EDITORS.

patch-boat bearing orders, that Colonel Ellet was wounded. The orders I received from him were: "Continue the pursuit as long as there is any hope of overtaking the flying enemy."

One other episode of this day should not be omitted. Toward the close of the engagement, Colonel Ellet was informed that a white flag had been raised in Memphis, and he immediately sent his young son, Medical Cadet Charles Rivers Ellet, ashore with a party of three men and a flag of truce, to demand the surrender of the city. They landed in a row-boat and delivered Colonel Ellet's dispatch to the mayor, and received his reply; then, surrounded by an excited and threatening crowd, they proceeded to the post-office, ascended to the top of the building, and, while stoned and fired upon by the mob below, young Ellet lowered the Confederate colors and raised the National flag over the city of Memphis. This incident occurred a considerable length of time before the formal surrender of the city into the possession of the United States troops under command of Colonel G. N. Fitch.

At first, Colonel Ellet's wound was not considered necessarily dangerous, but a few days showed us all how futile was the hope that our brave commander would ever again tread the decks of his victorious fleet. He continued to send dispatches and issue necessary orders from his bed as long as he could receive the reports of his subordinates. Finally, his rapidly failing strength gave way; the *Switzerland*, to which he had been removed, and on board which he had been joined by his heart-broken wife and his young daughter, left Memphis on the night of the 18th of June, and as the vessel neared Cairo on the 21st, his gallant spirit passed away. He was accorded a state funeral in Independence Hall. |

The boats constituting the ram-fleet of the Mississippi River were not built for the purpose they were to serve; they were simply such river steamers as could be purchased under the urgency then pressing. Some were side-wheelers, others stern-wheel tugs, with strong machinery and great power, and were hurriedly strengthened and braced to sustain a severe headlong blow. In a letter to the Secretary of War respecting the rams, while they were being fitted out, Colonel Ellet wrote: "The boats I have purchased are illy adapted for the work I shall require of them; it is not their strength upon which I rely, but upon the audacity of our attack, for success."

His idea of an effective "steam-ram" was not a hermaphrodite thing, half ram, half gun-boat, nor did he favor those sharp knife-like prows which, if they cut a hole in an enemy, would plug it at the same time. He wanted a vessel of medium size, easy to handle, and of great speed; she should be built very strongly, fitted with machinery of great power, and have weight sufficient when projected against an enemy to crush the side of any vessel that could float. Colonel Ellet did not rely on heavy ordnance, and did not recommend arming his rams. At the battle of Memphis there were no fire-arms on board the ram-fleet except a few short carbines and some pocket-

| His devoted wife, stricken by grief, survived him but a few days. Both are buried at Laurel Hill Cemetery, Philadelphia.— A. W. E.

revolvers; his reliance was upon the prow of his vessel. ⚓ He desired, as far as possible, to protect the vulnerable parts of his ship, the boilers and engines, and with simply enough men as crew to handle the boat with certainty and dispatch, to run the gauntlet of any fire that could be precipitated upon him, and drive his ram deep into his unwieldy adversary. At the battle of Memphis the enemy concentrated their fire upon the *Queen of the West* and the *Monarch*, but their missiles passed harmlessly by. Not a splinter was raised off either of the rams, and not a man sustained the slightest injury except Colonel Ellet, whose fatal wound was received from a pistol-ball.

The battle of Memphis was, in many respects, one of the most remarkable naval victories on record. For *two* unarmed, frail, wooden river steamboats, with barely men enough on board to handle the machinery and keep the furnace-fires burning, to rush to the front, between two hostile fleets, and *into* the enemy's advancing line of eight iron-clad, heavily armed, and fully manned steam-rams, sinking one, disabling and capturing three, and carrying consternation to the others, was a sight never before witnessed.

The River Defense Fleet was composed of strong, well-built ocean steamers, well strengthened and protected with railroad iron so as to be almost invulnerable to shot when advancing. The intention was apparent to repeat at Memphis the tactics which had proved so successful at Fort Pillow,— to ram the Union gun-boats at anchor; and had the rams *Queen of the West* and *Monarch* not run through the line of gun-boats and attacked the Defense Fleet as it approached, sinking, disabling, and scattering its vessels, and thus removing the fight half a mile below, the result of the affair might have been very different. The Defense Fleet was advancing up-stream, thus exposing the strongest and best-protected portions of each vessel; the gun-boats, relying upon their guns, were at anchor, with their sterns, their most vulnerable part, pointing down-steam and consequently exposed to the tremendous attack of the enemy. Had the Confederate commanders trusted only to the strength of their vessels, ceased firing, and with every pound of steam on plunged at full speed into our anchored gun-boat fleet, who could doubt what the result would have been?

⚓ The *Monarch* had 11 sharp-shooters out of a detail of 50 from the 59th Illinois regiment, who constituted the sole armed force of the ram-fleet.— EDITORS.

PRACTICING ON A RIVER PICKET.

METHOD OF CUTTING THE CHANNEL.

SAWING OUT THE CHANNEL ABOVE ISLAND NUMBER TEN.

BY J. W. BISSELL, COLONEL, U. S. V., IN CHARGE OF THE WORK.

THE Engineer Regiment of the West was an organization composed of twelve full companies of carefully selected workmen, chiefly mechanics, and officered by men capable of directing such skilled labor. Most of the officers and about six hundred of the men were engaged in the operations about New Madrid and Island Number Ten. In all the operations of that regiment I am not aware that any of its officers ever made a report beyond a verbal notification to the general in command that the work required of it was done. This narrative is therefore made entirely from memory, aided by reference to letters written to my family.

It is perhaps proper to state here that the term "canal," as used in all the letters and reports relating to the opening of this waterway, conveys an entirely wrong idea. No digging was done except by way of slightly widening a large break in the levee, and those who speak of "working waist-deep in the water" knew nothing of it.

The enemy held Island Number Ten and the left bank opposite, and the same bank from New Madrid down to Tiptonville, a ridge of high land between the back swamp and the river. In rear of their position was Reelfoot Lake and the overflow, extending from above them to a point below Tiptonville. Escape by land was impossible, New Madrid and the right bank below being occupied by General Pope. The gun-boats under Foote held the river above, and our heavy batteries commanded the only place of debarkation below. Having accomplished this much, the problem for General Pope to solve was to cross his army to make an attack, for which purpose he judged that two gun-boats, to be used as ferry-boats, would be sufficient. The general was so confident that his letter to Foote would bring the boats that he directed me to go back to the fleet at Island Number Eight by dug-out across the overflow, and come down with them past the batteries.

I reached the flag-ship in the afternoon about dark, and that evening Foote called together all his commanders in council. One or two wanted to run the blockade, but the commodore flatly refused. He explained that his boats, since they were armored solely about the bows, were invincible fighting up-stream, but fighting down-stream were of little account; and that if one of them should be boarded and captured, she could be turned against us, and could whip the whole fleet and place Cairo, Louisville, and St. Louis at her mercy! One of the captains said that if he were allowed to go, he would blow the vessel out of water if the enemy got on board. Another, I think, was quite as emphatic, but Foote was firm.

The next day, with two of the tugs of the fleet, I explored the shore carefully on each side: first on the eastern shore, to see if the enemy were securely shut in, which I found to be the case; and then on the western, to see if St. James's Bayou, which emptied into the river seven miles above Island Number Eight, in any way communicated with St. John's Bayou, which débouched at New Madrid. Here I found no possible way across.

Early the next morning while standing on the levee, chagrined at my failure to obtain a gun-boat, and while waiting for the guide to get the dug-out ready to take me back to camp, I spied, directly opposite me across the submerged fields, an opening in the timber; and the thought flashed upon me that there was the place to take the transports through. This proved to be an old wagon-road extending half a mile into the woods; beyond and around was a dense forest of heavy timber. The guide said it was two miles to the nearest bayou. I asked him to make a map upon my memorandum-book, which he did, showing a straight cut to the first bayou and the general route of the bayous to New Madrid. This route we carefully explored, and I reached Pope's headquarters about dark. When in my report of the interview I mentioned Foote's refusal, the general gave vent to his disappointment and indignation. Some officer present making some suggestion about a "canal," I immediately pulled out my memorandum-book, and, showing the sketch, said the whole thing was provided for, and that I would have the boats through in fourteen days.

General Pope then gave me an order on the authorities at Cairo for steamboats and material. That evening Captain William Tweeddale, Lieutenant Mahlon Randolph, and I sat up till a late hour arranging all the details, including barges to be fitted with heavy artillery to be used as gun-boats, and the next morning they started with one hundred men for Cairo, to meet me at Island Number Eight with all the materials they could get

CORRECTED LINE OF THE CHANNEL ABOVE ISLAND NO. TEN CUT BY THE ENGINEER REGIMENT. (See p. 437.)

the first day. Other officers and men started by the same route daily, until the six hundred men of my force had returned, and my stock of supplies was complete. I returned in the dug-out through the selected channel, and in due time found at the proposed starting-point four stern-wheel steam-boats, drawing thirty to thirty-six inches of water, and six large coal-barges, besides one Columbiad, three large siege-guns with carriages and ammunition, saws, lines, and all kinds of tools and tackle, and fully two million feet of timber and lumber.

The way through the submerged corn-field and the half-mile of road was easy enough, but when we reached the timber the labor of sawing out a channel commenced. The one steamer which had a powerful steam-capstan was put in the lead, and the others having hand-capstans were fastened single file in the rear, and then the six barges in like order, so that the progress of the first controlled all the others. Captain Tweeddale took charge of the cutting in front, while Lieutenant Randolph was fitting up the improvised gun-boats astern. About three hundred men were assigned to each, and they worked in relays from dawn until dark.

First of all, men standing on platforms on small rafts cut off the trees about eight feet above the water. As soon as a tree was down, another set of men, provided with boats and lines, adjusted about it a line which ran through a snatch-block and back to the steam-capstan, and hauled it out of the way; thus a partial cut was made forward,

the lines always working more than two hundred feet ahead of the capstan, so as to leave plenty of room for the saws. It took about four sets of lines to keep pace with twelve saws.

When the space about the stumps allowed sufficient room, a raft about forty feet long was lashed to a stump, and the saw set at work in a frame attached by a pivot and working in an arc as shown in the sketch [page 460]—two men working the saw at opposite ends by a rope, and a fifth on the farther side of the tree guiding its teeth into the tree. Where the stumps were too close, or irregular, three yawl-boats were used instead of the raft. No trouble was experienced with stumps a foot or less in diameter. With the larger ones it was different; the elms spread out so much at the bottom that the saw almost always would run crooked and pinch. If it ran up, we notched the top and set the frame farther in; if down, we put in powerful tackle, and pulled the top of the stump over.

Here was where the ingenuity of the officers and men was exercised; as the saws were working four and a half feet beneath the surface, and the water was quite turbid, the question was how to ascertain what was interfering with the saw, and then to apply the remedy. But I found Captain Tweeddale equal to the most obstinate stump. I think two and a half hours was the longest time ever expended upon any one, while about two minutes would dispose of some small ones when the saw was ready. It took eight days to cut the two miles.

When we reached the bayous the hard and wet work began. The river had begun to fall, and the water was running very rapidly. We had to get rid of great drift-heaps from the lower side with our machinery all on the upper side. Small pieces of drift would be disposed of by the yawl-boats, or a single line and snatch-block would take them right out; but sometimes a great swamp-oak, three feet through, and as heavy as lignum-vitæ, lying right across our channel a foot or so under water, would try our tackle. We had then to raise them up to the surface, and hold them there till they could be chopped in pieces. In one of the bayous for about two miles the current was so swift that all the men who were out on logs, or in exposed places, had safety-lines tied around them; and as the timber was slippery, some were indebted to these lines for their lives. During the whole work not a man was killed, injured, or taken sick.

While all this was being done in front of the boats, Lieutenant Randolph was at work with his detachment in the rear in improvising gun-boats to supply the lack of Foote's. The barges used were coal-barges, about eighty feet long and twenty wide, scow-shaped, with both ends alike. The sides were six inches thick, and of solid timber. The original plan was to use three of the steamboats with a barge on each side — the other steamer to be kept as a reserve. One Columbiad and three 32-pounders were mounted on platforms, and arrangements were made to use a considerable number of field-guns to be taken on board at New Madrid. Six hundred men of the Engineer Regiment, using one of the steamers with her two barges, were to land at break of day at the mouth of the slough about a mile below and opposite Fort Thompson, and with their intrenching tools dig a line of rifle-pits as soon as possible. About the same number of picked men were to be with them to help fight or dig, as occasion might require. The other two sections of the flotilla were to be filled with men, and landed just below, as best could be done when the resistance was developed. The reserve steamer with her men, not being incumbered with barges, could move rapidly and take advantage of any opening to land the force.

When about half-way through the channel, I left the flotilla and reported progress to General Pope. Upon a reëxamination of the ground from Fort Thompson, he concluded that it would be best to make the leading boat a fighting boat that could not be disabled; so he telegraphed to Cairo and St. Louis for a great number of coal-oil barrels, which were laid in two tiers all over the bottoms of two barges; the interstices were filled with dry rails, the whole well secured in place by a heavy floor. In the mean time the steamer was so bulkheaded with lumber that her engines and boilers were secure from damage from field-artillery, and the forward part of the hull, which projected beyond the barges, was bulkheaded off and filled with dry rails, to keep her from being disabled. On the steamer and barges protection was prepared for a large number of sharp-shooters.

The boats and barge gun-boats were kept concealed in the bayou, just back from New Madrid, for a day or two, till the soldiers could be prepared for the passage and attack. Meanwhile Foote concluded to risk the passage of the island with the *Carondelet* and afterward with the *Pittsburgh*, and the whole plan was changed; the gun-boats could move so much more rapidly that they were to silence the Confederate field-guns, while the transports could land the troops wherever an opening could be found. The barges were not used at all; nor did any of the Engineer Regiment cross; they were kept on the right bank, ready in case of disaster.

Several of the captured officers told me that after the gun-boats had run their batteries, nearly their whole force was withdrawn from about Island Number Ten and kept concealed in the woods back of the practicable landing-places, and they were prepared to pick off all the men that could be landed; but when they saw the four transports, loaded with troops, steam out from the bayou, the word was given for each man to take care of himself. A few hundred did manage to make their way through the swamps in the rear, but the most of them quietly yielded to the inevitable. So well had the movement been concealed that they had not the least idea of what was being done. ☆

POSTSCRIPT: The Official Records, which, since writing the above, I have just seen for the first time, contain a letter from General Pope to me, which I never before heard of (dated the day I was on my way back from the gun-boat with the plan fully matured), asking if I could not dig a *canal*, a "mere ditch of a foot wide which the water of the river would soon wash out," from a point one mile above Island Number Ten to a point one mile below. That land was at this time ten feet under water.—J. W. BISSELL.

DECEMBER, 1884.

☆ The effort to cut the canal was known to the Confederates as early as March 31st, the day General Mackall relieved General McCown of the command at Madrid Bend; for General Mackall says in his report, that General McCown then informed him "that they [the Union forces] were endeavoring to cut a canal across the opposite peninsula for the passage of transports, in order to land below the bend; that they would fail, and that the position was safe until the river fell, and no longer."—EDITORS.

COMMENT BY GENERAL SCHUYLER HAMILTON, MAJOR-GENERAL, U. S. V.

I have read Colonel J. W. Bissell's article on the "Sawing out a Channel above Island Number Ten." I desire to call attention to what he says:

"Some officer making some suggestion about a 'canal,' I immediately pulled out my memorandum-book, and, showing the sketch, said the whole thing was provided for."

This on the evening of March 19th, 1862, which is the date of General Pope's letter to which Colonel Bissell refers in a foot-note, saying he did not receive the letter because he (Colonel Bissell) was on his return from the reconnoissance he had been ordered to make. To the public this reads as though the plan originated with Colonel Bissell, while I am ready to show that while the colonel directed the work, "some officer," as he says,— or to be exact I myself,—was the sole inventor of the project. My own official report, dated Headquarters Second Division Army of the Mississippi, Pittsburg Landing, April 22d, 1862, reads as follows:

"Transports having reached us through a *channel* cut with enormous labor under the direction of Colonel Bissell, on a suggestion advanced by the subscriber, March 17th, 1862, the Second Division embarked on them, April 7th, to cross the Mississippi, which was accomplished in gallant style, but without opposition, the gun-boats *Carondelet* and *Pittsburgh*, under Captain Walke, having in dashing style silenced the enemy's shore batteries."

General Pope wrote to General Halleck, under date New Madrid, Mo., April 9th, 1862:

"The canal across the peninsula opposite Island Number Ten, and for the idea of which I am indebted to General Schuyler Hamilton, was completed by Colonel Bissell's Engineer Regiment, and four steamers brought through on the night of the 6th."

General Pope again, in his official report to General Halleck of May 2d, 1862, writes:

"On the 16th of March I received your dispatch, directing me, if possible, to construct a road through the swamps to a point on the Missouri shore opposite Island Number Ten, and transfer a portion of my force sufficient to erect batteries at that point to assist in the artillery practice on the enemy's batteries. I accordingly dispatched Colonel J. W. Bissell, Engineer Regiment, to examine the country with this view, directing him at the same time, if he found it impracticable to build a road through the swamps and overflow of the river, to ascertain whether it were possible to dig a canal across the peninsula from some point above Island Number Ten to New Madrid, in order that steam transports might be brought to me, which would enable my command to cross the river. The idea of the canal was suggested to me by General Schuyler Hamilton in a conversation upon the necessity of crossing the river and assailing the enemy's batteries near Island Number Ten in the rear."

The New York "Herald," in its issue of April 13th, 1862, published an article in reference to this channel, entitled "The Schuyler Hamilton Canal."

NEW YORK, June 16th, 1885.

THE OPPOSING FORCES AT NEW MADRID (ISLAND NUMBER TEN), FORT PILLOW, AND MEMPHIS.

The composition and losses of each army as here stated give the gist of all the data obtainable in the Official Records. K stands for killed; w for wounded; m w mortally wounded; m for captured or missing; c for captured.— EDITORS.

UNION ARMY AT NEW MADRID. Major-Gen. John Pope. FIRST DIVISION, Brig.-Gen. David S. Stanley. *First Brigade*, Col. John Groesbeck: 27th Ohio, Col. John W. Fuller; 39th Ohio, Major Edward F. Noyes. Brigade loss: k, 2; w, 5=7. *Second Brigade*, Col. J. L. Kirby Smith: 43d Ohio, Lieut.-Col. Wager Swayne; 63d Ohio, Col. John W. Sprague. Brigade loss: w, 5.

SECOND DIVISION, Brig.-Gen. Schuyler Hamilton. *First Brigade*, Col. W. H. Worthington: 59th Ind., Col. J. I. Alexander; 5th Iowa, Lieut.-Col. Charles L. Matthies. Brigade loss: k, 2; w, 4 = 6. *Second Brigade*, Col. Nicholas Perczel: 10th Iowa, Lieut.-Col. William E. Small; 26th Mo., Col. George B. Boomer. *Artillery:* 11th Ohio Battery, Capt. Frank C. Sands. Loss: k, 1.

THIRD DIVISION, Brig.-Gen. John M. Palmer. *First Brigade*, Col. James R. Slack: 34th Ind., Col. Townsend Ryan; 47th Ind., Lieut.-Col. Milton S. Robinson. *Second Brigade*, Col. Graham N. Fitch: 43d Ind., Col. William E. McLean; 46th Ind., Lieut.-Col. Newton G. Scott. *Cavalry:* 7th Ill., Col. Wm. P. Kellogg. Loss: w, 1; m, 2 = 3. *Artillery:* G, 1st Mo., Capt. Henry Hescock.

FOURTH DIVISION, Brig.-Gen. E. A. Paine. *First Brigade*, Col. James D. Morgan: 10th Ill., Lieut.-Col. John Tillson; 16th Ill., Col. Robert F. Smith. Brigade loss: k, 1; w, 1 = 2. *Second Brigade*, Col. Gilbert W. Cumming: 22d Ill., Lieut.-Col. Harrison E. Hart; 51st Ill., Lieut.-Col. Luther P. Bradley. *Cavalry:* H and I, 1st Ill., Major D. P. Jenkins. *Sharp-shooters:* 64th Ill., Major F. W. Matteson.

FIFTH DIVISION, Brig.-Gen. Joseph B. Plummer. *First Brigade*, Col. John Bryner: 47th Ill., Lieut.-Col. Daniel L. Miles; 8th Wis., Lieut.-Col. George W. Robbins. *Second Brigade*, Col. John M. Loomis: 26th Ill., Lieut.-Col. Charles J. Tinkham; 11th Mo., Lieut.-Col. William E. Panabaker. *Artillery:* M, 1st Mo., Capt. Albert M. Powell.

CAVALRY DIVISION, Brig.-Gen. Gordon Granger: 2d Mich., Lieut.-Col. Selden H. Gorham; 3d Mich., Lieut.-Col. R. H. G. Minty, Col. John K. Mizner.

ARTILLERY DIVISION, Major Warren L. Lothrop: 2d Iowa, Capt. N. T. Spoor; 5th Wis., Capt. Oscar F. Pinney; 6th Wis., Capt. Henry Dillon; 7th Wis., Capt. Richard R. Griffiths; C, 1st Mich., Capt. A. W. Dees; H, 1st Mich., Capt. Samuel De Golyer; C, 1st Ill., Capt. Charles Houghtaling; F, 2d U. S., Lieut. John A. Darling, Lieut. D. P. Walling.

UNASSIGNED TROOPS: Engineer Regt. of the West, Col. Josiah W. Bissell; 22d Mo., Lieut.-Col. John D. Foster; 2d Iowa Cav., Col. W. L. Elliott; 2d Ill. Cav. (4 cos.), Lieut.-Col. Harvey Hogg; 4th U. S. Cav. (3 cos.), Lieut. M. J. Kelly; 1st U. S. Infantry (6 cos.), Capt. George A. Williams. Loss of latter regiment: k, 2; w, 5; m, 1 = 8.

FLOTILLA BRIGADE, Col. Napoleon B. Buford: 27th Ill., Lieut.-Col. F. A. Harrington; 42d Ill., Col. George W. Roberts; 15th Wis., Col. Hans C. Heg; G, 1st Ill. Artillery, Capt. Arthur O'Leary; G, 2d Ill. Artillery, Capt. Frederick Sparrestrom.

UNION NAVAL FORCES AT ISLAND NUMBER TEN. Flag-Officer A. H. Foote: *Benton* (flag-ship), Lieut.-Comr. S. L. Phelps; *St. Louis*, Lieut.-Comr. Leonard Paulding *Cincinnati*, Comr. R. N. Stembel; *Pittsburgh*, Lieut.-Comr. Egbert Thompson; *Mound City*, Comr. A. H. Kilty; *Carondelet*, Comr. Henry Walke; Eleven *Mortarboats*, Capt. Henry E. Maynadier.

The total Union loss (including 2 killed and 13 wounded on the *St. Louis*, by the bursting of a gun March 17) was 17 killed, 34 wounded, and 3 captured or missing.

CONFEDERATE ARMY AT ISLAND NUMBER TEN. (1) Major-Gen. John P. McCown; (2) Brig.-Gen. W. W. Mackall. *Subordinate General Officers:* Brig.-Generals A. P. Stewart, L. M. Walker, E. W. Gantt, and James

Trudeau. *Infantry:* 1st Ala., Tenn., and Miss., Col. Alpheus Baker; 1st Ala., Col. J. G. W. Steedman; 4th Ark. Battalion, Major M. M. McKay; 5th Ark. Battalion, Lieut.-Col. F. A. Terry; 11th Ark., Col. J. M. Smith; 12th Ark., Lieut.-Col. W. D. S. Cook; 11th La., Col. S. F. Marks; 12th La., Col. Thomas M. Scott; 5th La. Battalion, Col. J. B. G. Kennedy; 4th Tenn., Col. R. P. Neely; 5th Tenn., Col. W. E. Travis; 31st Tenn., Col. W. M. Bradford; 40th Tenn., Col. C. C. Henderson; 46th Tenn., Col. John M. Clark; 55th Tenn., Col. A. J. Brown. *Cavalry:* Hudson's and Wheeler's companies, Miss.; Neely's and Haywood's companies, Tenn. *Light Artillery:* Point Coupée, La. Battery, Capt. R. A. Stewart; Tenn. Battery, Capt. Smith P. Bankhead. *Tenn. Heavy Artillery:* Companies of Captains Jackson, Sterling, Humes, Hoadley, Caruthers, Jones, Dismuke, Rucker, Fisher, Johnston, and Upton. *Engineer Corps:* Captains A. B. Gray and D. B. Harris. *Sappers and Miners:* Capt. D. Wintter.

CONFEDERATE NAVAL FORCES AT ISLAND NUMBER TEN. Flag-Officer George N. Hollins. *McRae* (flag-ship), Lieut. Thomas B. Huger, 6 32-pounders, 1 9-inch, 1 24-pounder rifle; *Livingston*, Comr. R. F. Pinkney; *Polk*, Lieut.-Comr. J. H. Carter, 5 guns; *Pontchartrain*, Lieut.-Comr. John W. Dunnington; *Maurepas*, Lieut. Joseph Fry, 5 rifled guns; *Jackson*, Lieut. F. B. Renshaw, 2 guns; Floating Battery, *New Orleans*, Lieut. S. W. Averett. No loss reported. The fleet, with the exception of the Floating Battery, was not actively engaged.

The total Confederate loss in killed and wounded is estimated at about 30. Of the number of Confederates captured the Confederate and Union reports range from 2000 to 7000, respectively.

UNION FLEET AT FORT PILLOW, MAY 10TH, 1862. Capt. Charles Henry Davis, commanding pro tem. *Benton* (flagship), Lieut. S. L. Phelps; *Carondelet*, Comr. Henry Walke; *Mound City*, Comr. A. H. Kilty; *Cincinnati*, Comr. R. N. Stembel (w); *St. Louis*, Lieut. Henry Erben; *Cairo*, Lieut. N. C. Bryant; *Pittsburgh*, Lieut. Egbert Thompson.

The Union loss as officially reported was: *Cincinnati*, wounded, 3 (1 mortally). *Mound City*, wounded, 1. Total, 4.

UNION FLEET AT MEMPHIS, JUNE 6TH, 1862. Flag-Officer Charles Henry Davis, commanding. *Gun-boats — Benton* (flagship), Lieut. S. L. Phelps; *Louisville*, Comr. B. M. Dove; *Carondelet*, Comr. Henry Walke; *Cairo*, Lieut. N. C. Bryant; *St. Louis*, Lieut. Wilson McGunnegle. *Ram fleet — Queen of the West* (flag-ship), Col. Charles Ellet, Jr.; *Monarch*, Lieut.-Col. Alfred W. Ellet; *Switzerland*, First Master David Millard.

The Union loss as officially reported was: *Gun-boats —* wounded, 3. *Ram fleet —* wounded, 1 (Col. Ellet, who subsequently died). Total, 4.

CONFEDERATE RIVER DEFENSE FLEET, AT FORT PILLOW AND MEMPHIS. Capt. J. E. Montgomery, commanding. *Little Rebel* (flag-ship), Capt. Montgomery; *General Bragg*, Capt. William H. H. Leonard, *General Sterling Price*, First Officer, J. E. Henthorne; *Sumter*, Capt. W. W. Lamb; *General Earl Van Dorn*, Capt. Isaac D. Fulkerson; *General M. Jeff. Thompson*, Capt. John H. Burke; *General Lovell*, Capt. James C. Delancy; *General Beauregard*, Capt. James Henry Hurt. Each vessel carried one or more guns, probably 32-pounders.

The Confederate loss in the action off Fort Pillow, May 10th, as officially reported, was: killed, 2; wounded, 1 = 3. No report was made of the Confederate loss in the action at Memphis of June 6th, nor is it possible, in view of the irregular organization of the fleet, the nature of the conflict, and the dispersal of the survivors, to form even an approximate estimate of it.

FROM A PHOTOGRAPH TAKEN, PROBABLY, IN 1863.

THE BATTLE OF SHILOH.

BY ULYSSES S. GRANT, GENERAL, U. S. A.

ON THE SKIRMISH LINE.

THE battle of Shiloh, or Pittsburg Landing, fought on Sunday and Monday, the 6th and 7th of April, 1862, has been perhaps less understood, or, to state the case more accurately, more persistently misunderstood, than any other engagement between National and Confederate troops during the entire rebellion. Correct reports of the battle have been published, notably by Sherman, Badeau, and, in a speech before a meeting of veterans, by General Prentiss; but all of these appeared long subsequent to the close of the rebellion, and after public opinion had been most erroneously formed.

Events had occurred before the battle, and others subsequent to it, which determined me to make no report to my then chief, General Halleck, further than was contained in a letter, written immediately after the battle, informing him that an engagement had been fought, and announcing the result. The occurrences alluded to are these: After the capture of Fort Donelson, with over fifteen thousand effective men and all their munitions of war, I believed much more could be accomplished without further sacrifice of life.

Clarksville, a town between Donelson and Nashville, in the State of Tennessee, and on the east bank of the Cumberland, was garrisoned by the enemy. Nashville was also garrisoned, and was probably the best-provisioned depot at the time in the Confederacy. Albert Sidney Johnston occupied Bowling Green, Ky., with a large force. I believed, and my information justified the belief, that these places would fall into our hands without a battle, if threatened promptly. I determined not to miss this chance. But being only a district commander, and under the immediate orders of the department commander, General Halleck, whose headquarters were at St. Louis, it was my duty to communicate to him all I proposed to do, and to get his approval, if possible. I did so communicate, and, receiving no reply, acted upon my own judgment. The result proved that my information was correct, and sustained my judgment. What, then, was my surprise, after so much had been accomplished by the troops under my immediate command between the time of leaving Cairo, early in February, and the 4th of March, to receive from my chief a dispatch of the latter date, saying: "You will place Major-General C. F. Smith in command of expedition, and remain yourself at Fort Henry. Why do you not obey my orders to report strength and positions of

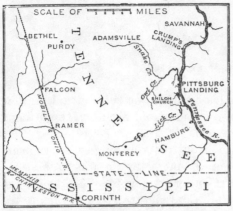

OUTLINE MAP OF THE SHILOH CAMPAIGN.

your command?" I was left virtually in arrest on board a steamer, without even a guard, for about a week, when I was released and ordered to resume my command.

Again : Shortly after the battle of Shiloh had been fought, General Halleck moved his headquarters to Pittsburg Landing, and assumed command of the troops in the field. Although next to him in rank, and nominally in command of my old district and army, I was ignored as much as if I had been at the most distant point of territory within my jurisdiction; and although I was in command of all the troops engaged at Shiloh, I was not permitted to see one of the reports of General Buell or his subordinates in that battle, until they were published by the War Department, long after the event. In consequence, I never myself made a full report of this engagement.

When I was restored to my command, on the 13th of March, I found it on the Tennessee River, part at Savannah and part at Pittsburg Landing, nine miles above, and on the opposite or western bank. I generally spent the day at Pittsburg, and returned by boat to Savannah in the evening. I was intending to remove my headquarters to Pittsburg, where I had sent all the troops immediately upon my reassuming command, but Buell, with the Army of the Ohio, had been ordered to reënforce me from Columbia, Tenn. He was expected daily, and would come in at Savannah. I remained, therefore, a few days longer than I otherwise should have done, for the purpose of meeting him on his arrival.

General Lew Wallace, with a division, had been placed by General Smith at Crump's Landing, about five miles farther down the river than Pittsburg, and also on the west bank. His position I regarded as so well chosen that he was not moved from it until the Confederate attack in force at Shiloh.

The skirmishing in our front had been so continuous from about the 3d of April up to the determined attack, that I remained on the field each night until an hour when I felt there would be no further danger before morning. In fact, on Friday, the 4th, I was very much injured by my horse falling with me and on me while I was trying to get to the front, where firing had been heard. The night was one of impenetrable darkness, with rain pouring down in torrents; nothing was visible to the eye except as revealed by the frequent flashes of lightning. Under these circumstances I had to trust to the horse, without guidance, to keep the road. I had not gone far, however, when I met General W. H. L. Wallace and General (then Colonel) McPherson coming from the direction of the front. They said all was quiet so far as the enemy was concerned. On the way back to the boat my horse's feet slipped from under him, and he fell with my leg under his body. The extreme softness of the ground, from the excessive rains of the few preceding days, no doubt saved me from a severe injury and protracted lameness. As it was, my ankle was very much injured; so much so, that my boot had to be cut off. During the battle, and for two or three days after, I was unable to walk except with crutches.

On the 5th General Nelson, with a division of Buell's army, arrived at Savannah, and I ordered him to move up the east bank of the river, to be in a position where he could be ferried over to Crump's Landing or Pittsburg Landing, as occasion required. I had learned that General Buell himself would be at Savannah the next

MRS. CRUMP'S HOUSE.

day, and desired to meet me on his arrival. Affairs at Pittsburg Landing had been such for several days that I did not want to be away during the day. I determined, therefore, to take a

THE LANDING BELOW THE HOUSE. FROM PHOTOGRAPHS TAKEN IN 1884.

Crump's Landing is, by river, about five miles below (north of) Pittsburg Landing. Here one of General Lew Wallace's three brigades was encamped on the morning of the battle, another brigade being two miles back, on the road to Purdy, and a third brigade half a mile farther advanced. The Widow Crump's house is about a quarter of a mile above the landing.

very early breakfast and ride out to meet Buell, and thus save time. He had arrived on the evening of the 5th, but had not advised me of the fact, and I was not aware of it until some time after. While I was at breakfast, however, heavy firing was heard in the direction of Pittsburg Landing, and I hastened there, sending a hurried note to Buell, informing him of the reason why I could not meet him at Savannah. On the way up the river I directed the dispatch-boat to run in close to Crump's Landing, so that I could communicate with General Lew Wallace. I found him waiting on a boat, apparently expecting to see me, and I directed him to get his troops in line ready to execute any orders he might receive. He replied that his troops were already under arms and prepared to move.

Up to that time I had felt by no means certain that Crump's Landing might not be the point of attack. On reaching the front, however, about 8 A. M., I found that the attack on Shiloh was unmistakable, and that nothing more than a small guard, to protect our transports and stores, was needed at Crump's. Captain A. S. Baxter, a quartermaster on my staff, was accordingly directed to go back and order General Wallace to march immediately to Pittsburg, by the road nearest the river. Captain Baxter made a memorandum of his order. About 1 P. M., not hearing from Wallace, and being much in need of reënforcements, I sent two more of my staff, Colonel James B. McPherson and Captain W. R. Rowley, to bring him up with his division. They reported finding him marching toward Purdy, Bethel, or some point west from the river, and farther from Pittsburg by several miles than when he started. The road from his first position was direct, and near the river. Between the two points a bridge had been built across Snake Creek by our troops, at which Wallace's command had assisted, expressly to enable the troops at the two places to support each other in case of need. Wallace did not arrive in time to take part in the first day's fight. General Wallace has since claimed that the order delivered to him by Captain Baxter was simply to join the right of the army, and that the road over which he marched would have taken him to the road from Pittsburg to Purdy, where it crosses Owl Creek, on the right of Sherman; but this is not where I had ordered him nor where I wanted him to go. I never could see, and do not now see, why any order was necessary further than to direct him to come to Pittsburg Landing, without specifying by what route. His was one of three veteran divisions that had been in battle, and its absence was severely felt. Later in the war, General Wallace would never have made the mistake that he committed on the 6th of April, 1862. I presume his idea was that by taking the route he did, he would be able to come around on the flank or rear of the enemy, and thus perform an act of heroism that would redound to the credit of his command, as well as to the benefit of his country.⚓

⚓ Since the publication in "The Century" of my article on "The Battle of Shiloh" I have received from Mrs. W. H. L. Wallace, widow of the gallant general who was killed in the first day's fight at that battle, a letter from General Lew Wallace to him, dated the morning of the 5th. At the date of this letter it was well known that the Confederates had troops out along the Mobile and Ohio railroad west of Crump's Landing and Pittsburg Landing, and were also collecting near Shiloh. This letter shows that at that time General Lew Wallace was making preparations for the emergency that might happen for the passing of reënforcements between Shiloh and his position, extending from Crump's Landing westward; and he sends the letter over the road running from Adamsville to the Pittsburg Landing and Purdy road. These two roads intersect nearly a mile west of the crossing of the latter over Owl Creek, where our right rested. In this letter General Lew Wallace advises General W. H. L. Wallace that he will send "to-morrow" (and his letter also says "April 5th," which is the same day the letter was dated and which, therefore, must have been written on the 4th) some cavalry to report to him at his headquarters, and suggesting the propriety of General W. H. L. Wallace's sending a company back with them for the purpose of having the cavalry at the two landings familiarize themselves with the road, so that they could "act promptly in case of emergency as guides to and from the different camps."

This modifies very materially what I have said, and what has been said by others, of the conduct of General Lew Wallace at the battle of Shiloh. It shows that he naturally, with no more experience than he had at the time in the profession of arms, would take the particular road that he did

NEW SHILOH CHURCH, ON THE SITE OF THE LOG CHAPEL WHICH WAS DE-STROYED AFTER THE BATTLE.

Shiloh was a log meeting-house, some two or three miles from Pittsburg Land-ing, and on the ridge which divides the waters of Snake and Lick creeks, the former entering into the Tennes-see just north of Pittsburg Landing, and the latter south. Shiloh was the key to our position, and was held by Sherman. His di-vision was at that time wholly raw, no part of it ever having been in an en-gagement, but I thought this deficiency was more than made up by the superiority of the commander. McCler-nand was on Sherman's left, with troops that had been engaged at Fort Don-elson, and were therefore veterans so far as Western troops had become such at that stage of the war. Next to McClernand came Prentiss, with a raw division, and on the extreme left,

SHILOH SPRING, IN THE RAVINE SOUTH OF THE CHAPEL. FROM PHOTOGRAPHS TAKEN IN 1884.

The spring is on the Confederate side of the ravine. Hard fighting took place here, in the early morning of Sunday, between Sherman's and Hardee's troops.

Stuart, with one brigade of Sherman's division. Hurlbut was in rear of Prentiss, massed, and in reserve at the time of the onset. The division of General C. F. Smith was on the right, also in reserve. General Smith was start upon in the absence of orders to move by a different road.

The mistake he made, and which probably caused his apparent dilatoriness, was that of ad-vancing some distance after he found that the firing, which would be at first directly to his front and then off to the left, had fallen back until it had got very much in rear of the position of his advance. This falling back had taken place before I sent General Wallace orders to move up to Pittsburg Landing, and, naturally, my order was to follow the road nearest the river. But my order was verbal, and to a staff-officer who was to deliver it to Gen-eral Wallace, so that I am not competent to say just what order the general actually received.

General Wallace's division was stationed, the First Brigade at Crump's Landing, the Second out two miles, and the Third two and a half miles out. Hearing the sounds of battle, General Wallace early ordered his First and Third brigades to concen-trate on the Second. If the position of our front had not changed, the road which Wallace took would have been somewhat shorter to our right than the River road.

U. S. GRANT.

MOUNT McGREGOR, N. Y., June 21, 1885.

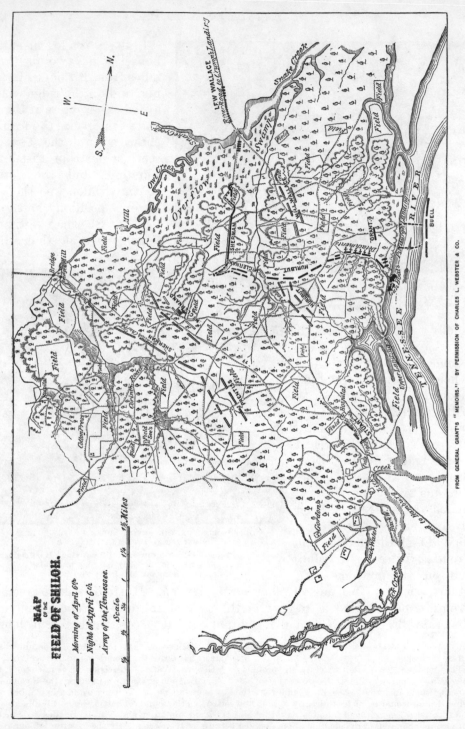

MAP
OF THE
FIELD OF SHILOH.

Morning of April 6th
Night of April 6th

Army of the Tennessee.

Scale

½   ¾   1   1¼   1½ Miles

FROM GENERAL GRANT'S "MEMOIRS." BY PERMISSION OF CHARLES L. WEBSTER & CO.

The map used with General Grant's article on Shiloh, as first printed in "The Century" Magazine for February, 1885, was a copy of the official map (see page 508) which was submitted by the editors to General Grant and was approved by him. Sub-sequently General Grant, through his son, Colonel Frederick D. Grant, furnished the editors with a revision of the official map, agreeing in every respect with the map printed in the "Memoirs," here reproduced. In response to an inquiry by the

470

FIRST POSITION OF WATERHOUSE'S BATTERY. FROM A SKETCH MADE SHORTLY AFTER THE BATTLE.

Major Ezra Taylor, General Sherman's chief of artillery, says in his report: "Captain A. C. Waterhouse's battery [was placed] near the left of the division [Sherman's] — four guns on the right bank of the Owl Creek [to the left and front of General Sherman's headquarters] and two guns on the left bank of Owl Creek [about 150 yards to the front]. The enemy appearing in large masses, and opening a battery to the front and right of the two guns, advanced across Owl Creek. I instructed Captain Waterhouse to retire the two guns to the position occupied by the rest of his battery, about which time the enemy appeared in large force in the open field directly in front of the position of this battery, bearing aloft, as I supposed, the American flag, and their men and officers wearing uniforms so similar to ours that I hesitated to open fire on them until they passed into the woods and were followed by other troops who wore a uniform not to be mistaken. I afterward learned that the uniform jackets worn by these troops were black. As soon as I was certain as to the character of the troops, I ordered the firing to commence, which was done in fine style and with excellent precision." Both Captain Waterhouse and Lieutenant A. R. Abbott were severely wounded.— EDITORS.

sick in bed at Savannah, some nine miles below, but in hearing of our guns. His services on those two eventful days would no doubt have been of inestimable value had his health permitted his presence. The command of his division devolved upon Brigadier-General W. H. L. Wallace, a most estimable and able officer,— a veteran, too, for he had served a year in the Mexican war, and had been with his command at Henry and Donelson. Wallace was mortally wounded in the first day's engagement, and with the

editors for the reasons which influenced General Grant in making the substitution, Colonel Grant wrote as follows, under date of Chicago, Ill., March 20th, 1887: "Father was very ill when the map used with his article, on Shiloh, by 'The Century' Co., was submitted to him. He looked at the topography and found it about as he remembered the ground; but after you published it, he read some of the criticisms upon both the article and the map. Thus having his attention called to the subject, he revised the article, making it more *forcible*, and directed me to get for his book the map which was in the possession of Colonel Dayton, Secretary of the Society of the Army of the Tennessee, and which he had heard of or seen.

"This map proved to be more satisfactory to him than the one he had first used, as it agreed more perfectly with his statements and recollection of the positions occupied by the troops at the end of the first day's battle. Therefore, the only reason that can be assigned for General Grant's change of maps is that the one used in his book ['Memoirs'] was more *satisfactory to him*, his delicate health having prevented his thorough investigation of the map in the first place."

CONFEDERATE CHARGE UPON PRENTISS'S CAMP ON SUNDAY MORNING.

Of the capture of General Prentiss's camp, Colonel Francis Quinn (Twelfth Michigan Infantry) says in his official report dated April 9th: "About daylight the dead and wounded began to be brought in. The firing grew closer and closer, till it became manifest a heavy force of the enemy was upon us. The division was ordered into line of battle by General Prentiss, and immediately advanced in line about one-quarter of a mile from the tents, where the enemy were met in short-firing distance. Volley after volley was given and returned, and many fell on both sides, but their numbers were too heavy for our forces. I could see to the right and left. They were visible in line, and every hill-top in the rear was covered with them. It was manifest they were advancing, in not only one, but several lines of battle. The whole division fell back to their tents and again rallied, and, although no regular line was formed, yet from behind every tree a deadly fire was poured out upon the enemy, which held them in check for about one half-hour, when, reënforcements coming to their assistance, they advanced furiously upon our camp, and we were forced again to give way. At this time we lost four pieces of artillery. The division fell back about one half-mile, very much scattered and broken. Here we were posted, being drawn up in line behind a dense clump of bushes."—EDITORS.

change of commanders thus necessarily effected in the heat of battle, the efficiency of his division was much weakened.

The position of our troops made a continuous line from Lick Creek, on the left, to Owl Creek, a branch of Snake Creek, on the right, facing nearly south, and possibly a little west. [See map, page 470.] The water in all these streams was very high at the time, and contributed to protect our flanks. The enemy was compelled, therefore, to attack directly in front. This he did with great vigor, inflicting heavy losses on the National side, but suffering much heavier on his own.

The Confederate assaults were made with such disregard of losses on their own side, that our line of tents soon fell into their hands. The ground on which the battle was fought was undulating, heavily timbered, with scattered clearings, the woods giving some protection to the troops on both sides. There was also considerable underbrush. A number of attempts were made by the enemy to turn our right flank, where Sherman was posted, but every effort was repulsed with heavy loss. But the front attack was kept up so vigorously that, to prevent the success of these attempts to get on our flanks, the National troops were compelled several times to take positions to the rear, nearer Pittsburg Landing. When the firing ceased at night, the National line was all of a mile in rear of the position it had occupied in the morning.

In one of the backward moves, on the 6th, the division commanded by General Prentiss did not fall back with the others. This left his flanks exposed, and enabled the enemy to capture him, with about 2200 of his officers and men. General Badeau gives 4 o'clock of the 6th as about the time this capture took place. He may be right as to the time, but my recollection is that the hour was later. General Prentiss himself gave the hour as half-past five. I was with him, as I was with each of the division commanders that day, several times, and my recollection is that the last time I was with him was about half-past four, when his division was standing up firmly, and the general was as cool as if expecting victory. But no matter whether it was four or later, the story that he and his command were surprised and captured in their camps is without any foundation whatever. If it had been true, as currently reported at the time, and yet believed by thousands of people, that Prentiss and his division had been captured in their beds, there would not have been an all-day struggle with the loss of thousands killed and wounded on the Confederate side.

With the single exception of a few minutes after the capture of Prentiss, a continuous and unbroken line was maintained all day from Snake Creek or its tributaries on the right to Lick Creek or the Tennessee on the left, above Pittsburg. There was no hour during the day when there was not heavy firing and generally hard fighting at some point on the line, but seldom at all points at the same time. It was a case of Southern dash against Northern pluck and endurance.

Three of the five divisions engaged on Sunday were entirely raw, and many of the men had only received their arms on the way from their States to the field. Many of them had arrived but a day or two before, and were hardly able to load their muskets according to the manual. Their officers were equally ignorant of their duties. Under these circumstances, it is not astonishing that many of the regiments broke at the first fire. In two cases, as I now remember, colonels led their regiments from the field on first hearing the whistle of the enemy's bullets. In these cases the colonels were constitutional cowards, unfit for any military position. But not so the officers and men led out of danger by them. Better troops never went upon a battle-field than many of these officers and men afterward proved themselves to be who fled panic-stricken at the first whistle of bullets and shell at Shiloh.

During the whole of Sunday I was continuously engaged in passing from one part of the field to another, giving directions to division commanders. In thus moving along the line, however, I never deemed it important to stay long with Sherman. Although his troops were then under fire for the first time, their commander, by his constant presence with them, inspired a confidence in officers and men that enabled them to render services on that bloody battle-field worthy of the best of veterans. McClernand was next to Sherman, and the hardest fighting was in front of these two divisions. McClernand told me on that day, the 6th, that he profited much by having so able a commander supporting him. A casualty to Sherman that would have taken him from the field that day would have been a sad one for the troops engaged at Shiloh. And how near we came to this! On the 6th Sherman was shot twice, once in the hand, once in the shoulder, the ball cutting his coat and making a slight wound, and a third ball passed through his hat. In addition to this he had several horses shot during the day.

The nature of this battle was such that cavalry could not be used in front; I therefore formed ours into line, in rear, to stop stragglers, of whom there were many. When there would be enough of them to make a show, and after they had recovered from their fright, they would be sent to reënforce some part of the line which needed support, without regard to their companies, regiments, or brigades.

On one occasion during the day, I rode back as far as the river and met General Buell, who had just arrived; I do not remember the hour, but at that time there probably were as many as four or five thousand stragglers lying under cover of the river-bluff, panic-stricken, most of whom would have been shot where they lay, without resistance, before they would have taken muskets and marched to the front to protect themselves. This meeting between General Buell and myself was on the dispatch-boat used to run between the landing and Savannah. It was brief, and related specially to his getting his troops over the river. As we left the boat together, Buell's attention was attracted by the men lying under cover of the bank. I saw him berating them and trying to shame them into joining their regiments. He even threatened them with shells from the gun-boats near by. But it was all to no effect. Most of these men afterward proved themselves as gallant as any of those who saved the battle from which they had deserted. I have no doubt that this sight impressed General Buell with the idea that a line of retreat would be a good thing just then. If he had come in by the front instead of through the stragglers in the rear, he would have thought and felt differently. Could he have come through the Confederate rear, he would have witnessed there a scene similar to that at our own. The distant rear of an army engaged in battle is not the best place from which to judge correctly what is going on in front. Later in the war, while occupying the country between the Tennessee and the Mississippi, I learned that the panic in the Confederate lines had not differed much from that within our own. Some of the country people estimated the stragglers from Johnston's army as high as twenty thousand. Of course, this was an exaggeration.

The situation at the close of Sunday was as follows: Along the top of the bluff just south of the log-house which stood at Pittsburg Landing, Colonel J. D. Webster, of my staff, had arranged twenty or more pieces of artillery facing south, or up the river. This line of artillery was on the crest of a hill overlooking a deep ravine opening into the Tennessee. Hurlbut, with his division intact, was on the right of this artillery, extending west and

CHECKING THE CONFEDERATE ADVANCE ON THE EVENING OF THE FIRST DAY.

Above this ravine, near the landing, the Federal reserve artillery was posted, and it was on this line the
Confederate advance was checked, about sunset, Sunday evening. The Confederates
then fell back and bivouacked in the Federal camps.

possibly a little north. McClernand came next in the general line, looking more to the west. His division was complete in its organization and ready for any duty. Sherman came next, his right extending to Snake Creek. His command, like the other two, was complete in its organization and ready, like its chief, for any service it might be called upon to render. All three divisions were, as a matter of course, more or less shattered and depleted in numbers from the terrible battle of the day. The division of W. H. L. Wallace, as much from the disorder arising from changes of division and brigade commanders, under heavy fire, as from any other cause, had lost its organization, and did not occupy a place in the line as a division; Prentiss's command was gone as a division, many of its members having been killed, wounded, or captured. But it had rendered valiant service before its final dispersal, and had contributed a good share to the defense of Shiloh.

There was, I have said, a deep ravine in front of our left. The Tennessee River was very high, and there was water to a considerable depth in the ravine. Here the enemy made a last desperate effort to turn our flank, but was repelled. The gun-boats *Tyler* and *Lexington*, Gwin and Shirk commanding, with the artillery under Webster, aided the army and effectually checked their further progress. Before any of Buell's troops had reached the west bank of the Tennessee, firing had almost entirely ceased; anything like an attempt on the part of the enemy to advance had absolutely ceased. There was some artillery firing from an unseen enemy, some of his shells passing beyond us; but I do not remember that there was the whistle of a single musket-ball heard. As his troops arrived in the dusk, General Buell marched several of his regiments part way down the face of the hill, where they fired briskly for some minutes, but I do not think a single man engaged in this firing received an injury; the attack had spent its force.

PRESENT ASPECT OF THE OLD HAMBURG ROAD (TO THE LEFT OF THE NEW ROAD) WHICH LED UP TO "THE HORNETS' NEST." FROM A PHOTOGRAPH TAKEN IN 1884.

General Lew Wallace, with 5000 effective men, arrived after firing had ceased for the day, and was placed on the right. Thus night came, Wallace came, and the advance of Nelson's division came, but none—unless night—in time to be of material service to the gallant men who saved Shiloh on that first day, against large odds. Buell's loss on the 6th of April was two men killed and one wounded, all members of the 36th Indiana Infantry. The Army of the Tennessee lost on that day at least 7000 men. The presence of two or three regiments of his army on the west bank before firing ceased had not the slightest effect in preventing the capture of Pittsburg Landing.

So confident was I before firing had ceased on the 6th that the next day would bring victory to our arms if we could only take the initiative, that I visited each division commander in person before any reënforcements had reached the field. I directed them to throw out heavy lines of skirmishers in the morning as soon as they could see, and push them forward until they found the enemy, following with their entire divisions in supporting distance, and to engage the enemy as soon as found. To Sherman I told the story of the assault at Fort Donelson, and said that the same tactics would win at Shiloh. Victory was assured when Wallace arrived even if there had been no other support. The enemy received no reënforcements. He had suffered heavy losses in killed, wounded, and straggling, and his commander, General Albert Sidney Johnston, was dead. I was glad, however, to see the reënforcements of Buell and credit them with doing all there was for them to do. During the night of the 6th the remainder of Nelson's division, Buell's army, crossed the river, and were ready to advance in the morning, forming the left wing. Two other divisions, Crittenden's and McCook's, came up the river from Savannah in the transports, and were on the west bank early on the 7th. Buell commanded them in person. My command was thus nearly doubled in numbers and efficiency.

During the night rain fell in torrents, and our troops were exposed to the storm without shelter. I made my headquarters under a tree a few hundred yards back from the river-bank. My ankle was so much swollen from the fall of my horse the Friday night preceding, and the bruise was so painful, that I could get no rest. The drenching rain would have precluded the possibility of sleep, without this additional cause. Some time after midnight, growing restive under the storm and the continuous pain, I moved back to the log-house on the bank. This had been taken as a hospital, and all night wounded men were being brought in, their wounds dressed, a leg or an arm amputated, as the case might require, and everything being done to save life or alleviate suffering. The sight was more unendurable than encountering the enemy's fire, and I returned to my tree in the rain.

The advance on the morning of the 7th developed the enemy in the camps occupied by our troops before the battle began, more than a mile back from the most advanced position of the Confederates on the day before. It is known now that they had not yet learned of the arrival of Buell's command. Possibly they fell back so far to get the shelter of our tents during the rain, and also to get away from the shells that were dropped upon them by the gun-boats every fifteen minutes during the night.

The position of the Union troops on the morning of the 7th was as follows: General Lew Wallace on the right, Sherman on his left; then McClernand, and then Hurlbut. Nelson, of Buell's army, was on our extreme left, next to the river; Crittenden was next in line after Nelson, and on his right; McCook followed, and formed the extreme right of Buell's command. My old command thus formed the right wing, while the troops directly under Buell constituted the left wing of the army. These relative positions were retained during the entire day, or until the enemy was driven from the field.

MAJOR-GENERAL B. M. PRENTISS.
FROM A PHOTOGRAPH.

In a very short time the battle became general all along the line. This day everything was favorable to the Federal side. We had now become the attacking party. The enemy was driven back all day, as we had been the day before, until finally he beat a precipitate retreat. The last point held by him was near the road leading from the landing to Corinth, on the left of Sherman and right of McClernand. About 3 o'clock, being near that point and seeing that the enemy was giving way everywhere else, I gathered up a couple of regiments, or parts of regiments, from troops near by, formed them in line of battle and marched them forward, going in front myself to prevent premature or long-range firing. At this point there was a clearing between us and the enemy favorable for charging, although exposed. I knew the enemy were ready to break, and only wanted a little encouragement from us to go quickly and join their friends who had started earlier. After marching to within musket-range, I stopped and let the troops pass. The command, *Charge*, was given, and was executed with loud cheers, and with a run, when the last of the enemy broke.

During this second day of the battle I had been moving from right to left and back, to see for myself the progress made. In the early part of the afternoon, while riding with Colonel James B. McPherson and Major J. P. Hawkins, then my chief commissary, we got beyond the left of our troops. We were moving along the northern edge of a clearing, very leisurely, toward the river above the landing. There did not appear to be an enemy to our right, until suddenly a battery

BRIGADIER-GENERAL W. H. L. WALLACE.
FROM A PHOTOGRAPH,

with musketry opened upon us from the edge of the woods on the other side of the clearing. The shells and balls whistled about our ears very fast for about a minute. I do not think it took us longer than that to get out of range and out of sight. In the sudden start we made, Major Hawkins lost his hat. He did not stop to pick it up. When we arrived at a perfectly safe position we halted to take an account of damages. McPherson's horse was panting as if ready to drop. On examination it was found that a ball had struck him forward of the flank just back of the saddle, and had gone entirely through. In a few minutes the poor beast dropped dead; he had given no sign of injury until we came to a stop. A ball had struck the metal scabbard of my sword, just below the hilt, and broken it nearly off; before the battle was over, it had broken off entirely. There were three of us: one had lost a horse, killed, one a hat, and one a sword-scabbard. All were thankful that it was no worse.

After the rain of the night before and the frequent and heavy rains for some days previous, the roads were almost impassable. The enemy, carrying his artillery and supply trains over them in his retreat, made them still worse for troops following. I wanted to pursue, but had not the heart to order the men who had fought desperately for two days, lying in the mud and rain whenever not fighting, and I did not feel disposed positively to order Buell, or any part of his command, to pursue. Although the senior in rank at the time, I had been so only a few weeks. Buell was, and had been for some time past, a department commander, while I commanded only a district. I did not meet Buell in person until too late to get troops ready and pursue with effect; but, had I seen him at the moment of the last charge, I should have at least requested him to follow.

The enemy had hardly started in retreat from his last position, when, looking back toward the river, I saw a division of troops coming up in beautiful order, as if going on parade or review. The commander was at the head of the column, and the staff seemed to be disposed about as they would have been had they been going on parade. When the head of the column came near where I was standing, it was halted, and the commanding officer, General A. McD. McCook, rode up to where I was and appealed to me not to send his division any farther, saying that they were worn out with marching and fighting. This division had marched on the 6th from a point ten or twelve miles east of Savannah, over bad roads. The men had also lost rest during the night while crossing the Tennessee, and had been engaged in the battle of the 7th. It was not, however, the rank and file or the junior officers who asked to be excused, but the division commander.⚓ I rode forward several miles the day after the battle, and found that the enemy had dropped much, if not all, of their provisions, some ammunition, and the extra wheels of their caissons, lightening their loads to enable them to get off their guns. About five miles out we found their field-hospital abandoned. An immediate pursuit must have resulted in the capture of a considerable number of prisoners and probably some guns.

Shiloh was the severest battle fought at the West during the war, and but few in the East equaled it for hard, determined fighting. I saw an open field, in our possession on the second day, over which the Confederates had made repeated charges the day before, so covered with dead that it would have been possible to walk across the clearing, in any direction, stepping on dead bodies, without a foot touching the ground. On our side National and Confederate were mingled together in about equal proportions; but on the remainder of the field nearly all were Confederates. On one part, which had evidently not been plowed for several years, probably because the land was

⚓ In an article on the battle of Shiloh, which I wrote for "The Century" magazine, I stated that General A. McD. McCook, who commanded a division of Buell's army, expressed some unwillingness to pursue the enemy on Monday, April 7th, because of the condition of his troops. General Badeau, in his history, also makes the same statement, on my authority. Out of justice to General McCook and his command, I must say that they left a point twenty-two miles east of Savannah on the morning of the 6th. From the heavy rains of a few days previous and the passage of trains and artillery, the roads were necessarily deep in mud, which made marching slow. The division had not only marched through this mud the day before, but it had been in the rain all night without rest. It was engaged in the battle of the second day, and did as good service as its position allowed. In fact, an opportunity occurred for it to perform a conspicuous act of gallantry which elicited the highest commendation from division commanders in the Army of the Tennessee. General Sherman, both in his memoirs and report, makes mention of this fact. General McCook himself belongs to a family which furnished many volunteers to the army. I refer to these circumstances with minuteness because I did General McCook injustice in my article in "The Century," though not to the extent one would suppose from the public press. I am not willing to do any one an injustice, and if convinced that I have done one, I am always willing to make the fullest admission. U. S. GRANT.

MOUNT MCGREGOR, N.Y., June 21, 1885.

FORD WHERE THE HAMBURG ROAD CROSSES LICK CREEK, LOOKING FROM COLONEL STUART'S
POSITION ON THE FEDERAL LEFT.

Lick Creek at this point was fordable on the first day of the battle, but the rains on Sunday night rendered
it impassable on the second day.

poor, bushes had grown up, some to the height of eight or ten feet. There
was not one of these left standing unpierced by bullets. The smaller ones
were all cut down.

Contrary to all my experience up to that time, and to the experience of the
army I was then commanding, we were on the defensive. We were without
intrenchments or defensive advantages of any sort, and more than half the
army engaged the first day was without experience or even drill as soldiers.
The officers with them, except the division commanders, and possibly two or
three of the brigade commanders, were equally inexperienced in war. The
result was a Union victory that gave the men who achieved it great confidence in themselves ever after.

The enemy fought bravely, but they had started out to defeat and destroy
an army and capture a position. They failed in both, with very heavy loss in
killed and wounded, and must have gone back discouraged and convinced
that the "Yankee" was not an enemy to be despised.

After the battle I gave verbal instructions to division commanders to let
the regiments send out parties to bury their own dead, and to detail parties,
under commissioned officers from each division, to bury the Confederate
dead in their respective fronts, and to report the numbers so buried. The
latter part of these instructions was not carried out by all; but they were

by those sent from Sherman's division, and by some of the parties sent out by McClernand. The heaviest loss sustained by the enemy was in front of these two divisions.

The criticism has often been made that the Union troops should have been intrenched at Shiloh; but up to that time the pick and spade had been but little resorted to at the West. I had, however, taken this subject under consideration soon after reassuming command in the field. McPherson, my only military engineer, had been directed to lay out a line to intrench. He did so, but reported that it would have to be made in rear of the line of encampment as it then ran. The new line, while it would be nearer the river, was yet too far away from the Tennessee, or even from the creeks, to be easily supplied with water from them; and in case of attack, these creeks would be in the hands of the enemy. Besides this, the troops with me, officers and men, needed discipline and drill more than they did experience with the pick, shovel, and axe. Reënforcements were arriving almost daily, composed of troops that had been hastily thrown together into companies and regiments — fragments of incomplete organizations, the men and officers strangers to each other. Under all these circumstances I concluded that drill and discipline were worth more to our men than fortifications.

General Buell was a brave, intelligent officer, with as much professional pride and ambition of a commendable sort as I ever knew. I had been two years at West Point with him, and had served with him afterward, in garrison

BRIDGE OVER SNAKE CREEK BY WHICH GENERAL LEW WALLACE'S TROOPS REACHED THE FIELD, SUNDAY EVENING. FROM A PHOTOGRAPH TAKEN IN 1884.

Pittsburg Landing is nearly two miles to the left. Owl Creek empties from the left into Snake Creek, a short distance above the bridge.

BIVOUAC OF THE FEDERAL TROOPS, SUNDAY NIGHT.

and in the Mexican war, several years more. He was not given in early life or in mature years to forming intimate acquaintances. He was studious by habit, and commanded the confidence and respect of all who knew him. He was a strict disciplinarian, and perhaps did not distinguish sufficiently between the volunteer who "enlisted for the war" and the soldier who serves in time of peace. One system embraced men who risked life for a principle, and often men of social standing, competence, or wealth, and independence of character. The other includes, as a rule, only men who could not do as well in any other occupation. General Buell became an object of harsh criticism later, some going so far as to challenge his loyalty. No one who knew him ever believed him capable of a dishonorable act, and nothing could be more dishonorable than to accept high rank and command in war and then betray the trust. When I came into command of the army, in 1864, I requested the Secretary of War to restore General Buell to duty.

After the war, during the summer of 1865, I traveled considerably through the North, and was everywhere met by large numbers of people. Every one had his opinion about the manner in which the war had been conducted; who among the generals had failed, how, and why. Correspondents of the press were ever on hand to hear every word dropped, and were not always disposed to report correctly what did not confirm their preconceived notions, either about the conduct of the war or the individuals concerned in it. The opportunity frequently occurred for me to defend General Buell against what

I believed to be most unjust charges. On one occasion a correspondent put in my mouth the very charge I had so often refuted—of disloyalty. This brought from General Buell a very severe retort, which I saw in the New York " World " some time before I received the letter itself. I could very well understand his grievance at seeing untrue and disgraceful charges apparently sustained by an officer who, at the time, was at the head of the army. I replied to him, but not through the press. I kept no copy of my letter, nor did I ever see it in print, neither did I receive an answer.

General Albert Sidney Johnston, who commanded the Confederate forces at the beginning of the battle, was disabled by a wound in the afternoon of the first day. His wound, as I understood afterward, was not necessarily fatal, or even dangerous. But he was a man who would not abandon what he deemed an important trust in the face of danger, and consequently continued in the saddle, commanding, until so exhausted by the loss of blood that he had to be taken from his horse, and soon after died. The news was not long in reaching our side, and, I suppose, was quite an encouragement to the National soldiers. I had known Johnston slightly in the Mexican war, and later as an officer in the regular army. He was a man of high character and ability. His contemporaries at West Point, and officers generally who came to know him personally later, and who remained on our side, expected him to prove the most formidable man to meet that the Confederacy would produce. Nothing occurred in his brief command of an army to prove or disprove the high estimate that had been placed upon his military ability.↓

General Beauregard was next in rank to Johnston, and succeeded to the command, which he retained to the close of the battle and during the subsequent retreat on Corinth, as well as in the siege of that place. His tactics have been severely criticised by Confederate writers, but I do not believe his fallen chief could have done any better under the circumstances. Some of these critics claim that Shiloh was won when Johnston fell, and that if he had not fallen the army under me would have been annihilated or captured. *Ifs* defeated the Confederates at Shiloh. There is little doubt that we would have been disgracefully beaten *if* all the shells and bullets fired by us had passed harmlessly over the enemy, and *if* all of theirs had taken effect. Commanding generals are liable to be killed during engagements; and the fact that when he was shot Johnston was leading a brigade to induce it to make a charge which had been repeatedly ordered, is evidence that there was neither the universal demoralization on our side nor the unbounded confidence on theirs which has been claimed. There was, in fact, no hour during the day when I doubted the eventual defeat of the enemy, although I was disappointed that reënforcements so near at hand did not arrive at an earlier hour.

The Confederates fought with courage at Shiloh, but the particular skill claimed I could not, and still cannot, see; though there is nothing to criticise

↓ In his " Personal Memoirs " General Grant says: " I once wrote that 'nothing occurred in his brief command of an army to prove or disprove the high estimate that had been placed upon his military ability'; but after studying the orders and dispatches of Johnston I am compelled to materially modify my views of that officer's qualifications as a soldier. My judgment now is that he was vacillating and undecided in his actions."

WOUNDED AND STRAGGLERS ON THE WAY TO THE LANDING, AND AMMUNITION-WAGONS GOING TO THE FRONT.

except the claims put forward for it since. But the Confederate claimants for superiority in strategy, superiority in generalship, and superiority in dash and prowess are not so unjust to the Union troops engaged at Shiloh as are many Northern writers. The troops on both sides were American, and united they need not fear any foreign foe. It is possible that the Southern man started in with a little more dash than his Northern brother; but he was correspondingly less enduring.

The endeavor of the enemy on the first day was simply to hurl their men against ours—first at one point, then at another, sometimes at several points at once. This they did with daring and energy, until at night the rebel troops were worn out. Our effort during the same time was to be prepared to resist assaults wherever made. The object of the Confederates on the second day was to get away with as much of their army and material as possible. Ours then was to drive them from our front, and to capture or destroy as great a part as possible of their men and material. We were successful in driving them back, but not so successful in captures as if further pursuit could have been made. As it was, we captured or recaptured on the second day about as much artillery as we lost on the first; and, leaving out the one great capture of Prentiss, we took more prisoners on Monday than the enemy gained from us on Sunday. On the 6th Sherman lost 7 pieces of artillery, McClernand 6, Prentiss 8, and Hurlbut 2 batteries. On the 7th Sherman captured 7 guns, McClernand 3, and the Army of the Ohio 20.

At Shiloh the effective strength of the Union force on the morning of the 6th was 33,000. Lew Wallace brought five thousand more after nightfall. Beauregard reported the enemy's strength at 40,955. According to the custom of enumeration in the South, this number probably excluded every man enlisted as musician, or detailed as guard or nurse, and all commissioned officers,— everybody who did not carry a musket or serve a cannon. With us everybody in the field receiving pay from the Government is counted. Excluding the troops who fled, panic-stricken, before they had fired a shot, there was not a time during the 6th when we had more than 25,000 men in line. On the 7th Buell brought twenty thousand more. Of his remaining two divisions, Thomas's did not reach the field during the engagement; Wood's arrived before firing had ceased, but not in time to be of much service.

Our loss in the two-days fight was 1754 killed, 8408 wounded, and 2885 missing. Of these 2103 were in the Army of the Ohio. Beauregard reported a total loss of 10,699, of whom 1728 were killed, 8012 wounded, and 959 missing. This estimate must be incorrect. We buried, by actual count, more of the enemy's dead in front of the divisions of McClernand and Sherman alone than here reported, and four thousand was the estimate of the burial parties for the whole field. Beauregard reports the Confederate force on the 6th at over 40,000, and their total loss during the two days at 10,699; and at the same time declares that he could put only 20,000 men in battle on the morning of the 7th.

The navy gave a hearty support to the army at Shiloh, as indeed it always did, both before and subsequently, when I was in command. The nature of the ground was such, however, that on this occasion it could do nothing in aid of the troops until sundown on the first day. The country was broken and heavily timbered, cutting off all view of the battle from the river, so that friends would be as much in danger from fire from the gun-boats as the foe. But about sundown, when the National troops were back in their last position, the right of the enemy was near the river and exposed to the fire of the two gun-boats, which was delivered with vigor and effect. After nightfall, when firing had entirely ceased on land, the commander of the fleet informed himself, proximately, of the position of our troops, and suggested the idea of dropping a shell within the lines of the enemy every fifteen minutes during the night. This was done with effect, as is proved by the Confederate reports.

Up to the battle of Shiloh, I, as well as thousands of other citizens, believed that the rebellion against the Government would collapse suddenly and soon if a decisive victory could be gained over any of its armies. Henry and Donelson were such victories. An army of more than 21,000 men was captured or destroyed. Bowling Green, Columbus, and Hickman, Ky., fell in consequence, and Clarksville and Nashville, Tenn., the last two with an immense amount of stores, also fell into our hands. The Tennessee and Cumberland rivers, from their mouths to the head of navigation, were secured. But when Confederate armies were collected which not only attempted to hold a line farther south, from Memphis to Chattanooga, Knoxville and on to the Atlantic, but assumed the offensive, and made such a gallant effort to regain what had been lost, then, indeed, I gave up all idea of saving the Union except by complete conquest. Up to that time it had been the policy of our army, certainly of that portion commanded by me, to protect the property of the citizens whose territory was invaded, without regard to their sentiments, whether Union or Secession. After this, however, I regarded it as humane to both sides to protect the persons of those found at their homes but to consume everything that could be used to support or supply armies. Protection was still continued over such supplies as were within lines held by us, and which we expected to continue to hold. But such supplies within the reach of Confederate armies I regarded as contraband as much as arms or ordnance stores. Their destruction was accomplished without bloodshed, and tended to the same result as the destruction of armies. I continued this policy to the close of the war. Promiscuous pillaging, however, was discouraged and punished. Instructions were always given to take provisions and forage under the direction of commissioned officers, who should give receipts to owners, if at home, and turn the property over to officers of the quartermaster or commissary departments, to be issued as if furnished from our Northern depots. But much was destroyed without receipts to owners when it could not be brought within our lines, and would otherwise have gone to the support of secession and rebellion. This policy, I believe, exercised a material influence in hastening the end.

ABOVE THE LANDING — THE STORE, AND A PART OF THE NATIONAL CEMETERY.
FROM A PHOTOGRAPH TAKEN IN 1884.

SHILOH REVIEWED.

BY DON CARLOS BUELL, MAJOR-GENERAL, U. S. V.

BATTERY, FORWARD !

TWENTY-THREE years ago the banks of the Tennessee witnessed a remarkable occurrence. There was a wage of battle. Heavy blows were given and received, and the challenger failed to make his cause good. But there were peculiar circumstances which distinguished the combat from other trials of strength in the rebellion: An army comprising 70 regiments of infantry, 20 batteries of artillery, and a sufficiency of cavalry, lay for two weeks and more in isolated camps, with a river in its rear and a hostile army claimed to be superior in numbers 20 miles distant in its front, while the commander made his headquarters and passed his nights 9 miles away on the opposite side of the river. It had no line or order of battle, no defensive works of any sort, no outposts, properly speaking, to give warning, or check the advance of an enemy, and no recognized head during the absence of the regular commander. On a Saturday the hostile force arrived and formed in order of battle, without detection or hindrance, within a mile and a half of the unguarded army, advanced upon it the next morning, penetrated its disconnected lines, assaulted its camps in front and flank, drove its disjointed members successively from position to position, capturing some and routing others, in spite of much heroic individual resistance, and steadily drew near the landing and depot of its supplies in the pocket between the river and an impassable creek. At the moment near the close of the day when the remnant of the retrograding army was driven to refuge in the midst of its magazines, with the triumphant enemy at half-gunshot distance, the advance division of a reënforcing army arrived on the opposite bank of the river, crossed, and took position under fire at the point of attack; the attacking force was checked, and the battle ceased for the day. The next morning at dawn the reënforcing army and a fresh division belonging to the defeated force advanced against the assailants, followed or accompanied by such of the broken columns of the previous day as had not lost all cohesion, and after ten hours of conflict drove the enemy from the captured camps and the field.

Such are the salient points in the popular conception and historical record of the battle of Shiloh. Scarcely less remarkable than the facts themselves are the means by which the responsible actors in the critical drama have endeavored to counteract them. At society reunions and festive entertainments, in newspaper interviews and dispatches, in letters and contributions to periodicals, afterthought official reports, biographies, memoirs, and other popular sketches, the subject of Shiloh, from the first hour of the battle to the present time, has been invaded by pretensions and exculpatory statements which revive the discussion only to confirm the memory of the grave faults that brought an army into imminent peril. These defenses and assumptions, starting first, apparently half suggested, in the zeal of official attendants and other partisans, were soon taken up more or less directly by the persons in whose behalf they were put forward; and now it is virtually declared by the principals themselves, that the Army of the Ohio was an unnecessary intruder in the battle, and that the blood of more than two thousand of its members shed on that field was a gratuitous sacrifice.

With the origin of the animadversions that were current at the time upon the conduct of the battle, the Army of the Ohio had little to do, and it has not generally taken a willing part in the subsequent discussion. They commenced in the ranks of the victims, and during all the years that have given unwonted influence to the names which they affected, the witnesses of the first reports have without show of prejudice or much reiteration firmly adhered to their earlier testimony. It does not impair the value of that testimony if extreme examples were cited to illustrate the general fact; nor constitute a defense that such examples were not the general rule. I have myself, though many years ago, made answer to the more formal pleas that

PITTSBURG LANDING, VIEWED FROM THE FERRY LANDING ON THE OPPOSITE SHORE.
FROM A PHOTOGRAPH TAKEN IN 1885.

PITTSBURG LANDING. FROM A PHOTOGRAPH TAKEN A FEW DAYS AFTER THE BATTLE.

Of the six transports, the one farthest up stream, on the right, is the *Tycoon*, which was dispatched by the
Cincinnati Branch of the Sanitary Commission with stores for the wounded. The next steamer
is the *Tigress*, which was General Grant's headquarters boat during the Shiloh campaign. On the opposite side of the river is seen the gun-boat *Tyler.*

concerned the army which I commanded, and I am now called upon in the
same cause to review the circumstances of my connection with the battle, and
investigate its condition when it was taken up by the Army of the Ohio.

WHEN by the separate or concurrent operations of the forces of the Department of the Missouri, commanded by General Halleck, and of the Department
of the Ohio, commanded by myself, the Confederate line had been broken, first
at Mill Springs by General Thomas, and afterward at Fort Henry and at Fort
Donelson by General Grant and the navy, and Nashville and Middle Tennessee
were occupied by the Army of the Ohio, the shattered forces of the enemy
fell back for the formation of a new line, and the Union armies prepared to
follow for a fresh attack. It was apparent in advance that the Memphis and
Charleston railroad between Memphis and Chattanooga would constitute the
new line, and Corinth, the point of intersection of the Memphis and Charleston road running east and west, and the Mobile and Ohio road running north
and south, soon developed as the main point of concentration.

While this new defense of the enemy and the means of assailing it by the
Union forces were maturing, General Halleck's troops, for the moment under

the immediate command of General C. F. Smith, were transported up the Tennessee by water to operate on the enemy's railroad communications. It was purely an expeditionary service, not intended for the selection of a rendezvous or depot for future operations. After some attempts to debark at other points farther up the river, Pittsburg Landing was finally chosen as the most eligible for the temporary object; but when the concentration of the enemy at Corinth made that the objective point of a deliberate campaign, and the coöperation of General Halleck's troops and mine was arranged, Savannah, on the east bank of the river, was designated by Halleck as the point of rendezvous. This, though not as advisable a point as Florence, or some point between Florence and Eastport, was in a general sense proper. It placed the concentration under the shelter of the river and the gun-boats, and left the combined force at liberty to choose its point of crossing and line of attack.

On the restoration of General Grant to the immediate command of the troops, and his arrival at Savannah on the 17th of March, he converted the expeditionary encampment at Pittsburg Landing into the point of rendezvous of the two armies, by placing his whole force on the west side of the river, apparently on the advice of General Sherman, who, with his division, was already there. Nothing can be said upon any rule of military art or common expediency to justify that arrangement. An invading army may, indeed, as a preliminary step, throw an inferior force in advance upon the enemy's coast or across an intervening river to secure a harbor or other necessary foothold; but in such a case the first duty of the advanced force is to make itself secure by suitable works. Pittsburg Landing was in no

THE LANDING AT SAVANNAH, NINE MILES BELOW (NORTH OF) PITTSBURG LANDING.

General Grant's headquarters were in the Cherry mansion, on the right; the portico has since been added. The building on the left is a new hotel. The town lies about a quarter of a mile back from the bluff, and is much changed since the war.— EDITORS.

sense a point of such necessity or desirability as to require any risk, or any great expenditure of means for its occupation. If the force established there was not safe alone, it had no business there; but having been placed there, still less can any justification be found for the neglect of all proper means to make it secure against a superior adversary. General Grant continued his headquarters at Savannah, leaving General Sherman with a sort of control at Pittsburg Landing. Sherman's rank did not allow him the command, but he was authorized to assign the arriving regiments to brigades and divisions as he might think best, and designate the camping-grounds. In these and other ways he exercised an important influence upon the fate of the army.

The movement of the Army of the Ohio from Nashville (which I had occupied on February 25th) for the appointed junction was commenced on the night of the 15th of March by a rapid march of cavalry to secure the bridges in advance, which were then still guarded by the enemy. It was followed on the 16th and successive days by the infantry divisions, McCook being in advance with instructions to move steadily forward; to ford the streams where they were fordable, and when it was necessary to make repairs on the roads, such as building bridges over streams which were liable to frequent interruption by high water, to leave only a sufficient working party and guard for that purpose; to use all possible industry and energy, so as to move forward steadily and as rapidly as possible without forcing the march or straggling; and to send forward at once to communicate with General Smith at Savannah, and learn his situation.

MAJOR-GENERAL ALEXANDER M^CD. M^CCOOK.
FROM A PHOTOGRAPH.

When the cavalry reached Columbia the bridge over Duck River was found in flames, and the river at flood stage. General McCook immediately commenced the construction of a frame bridge, but finding, after several days, that the work was progressing less rapidly than had been expected, I ordered the building of a boat bridge also, and both were completed on the 30th. On the same day the river became fordable. I arrived at Columbia on the 26th. General Nelson succeeded in getting a portion of his division across by fording on the 29th, and was given the advance. Most of his troops crossed by fording on the 30th. The other divisions followed him on the march with intervals of six miles, so as not to incommode one another— in all 5 divisions; about 37,000 effective men. On the first day of April, General Halleck and General Grant were notified that I would concentrate at Savannah on Sunday and Monday, the 6th and 7th, the distance being ninety miles. On the 4th General Nelson received notification from General Grant that he need not hasten his march, as he could not be put across the river before the following Tuesday; but the rate of march was not changed.

After seeing my divisions on the road, I left Columbia on the evening of the 3d, and arrived at Savannah on the evening of the 5th with my chief of staff, an aide-de-camp (Lieutenant C. L. Fitzhugh), and an orderly, leaving the rest of my staff to follow rapidly with the headquarters train. Nelson had already arrived and gone into camp, and Crittenden was close in his rear. We were there to form a junction for the contemplated forward movement under the command of General Halleck in person, who was to leave St. Louis the first of the following week to join us. General Grant had been at Nelson's camp before my arrival, and said he would send boats for the division "Monday or Tuesday, or some time early in the week." "There will," he said, "be no fight at Pittsburg Landing; we will have to go to Corinth, where the rebels are fortified. If they come to attack us we can whip them, as I have more than twice as many troops as I had at Fort Donelson." I did not see General Grant that evening—probably because he was at Pittsburg Landing when I arrived, but he had made an appointment to meet me next day.

We were finishing breakfast at Nelson's camp Sunday morning, when the sound of artillery was heard up the river. We knew of no ground to apprehend a serious engagement, but the troops were promptly prepared to march, and I walked with my chief of staff, Colonel James B. Fry, to Grant's quarters at Savannah, but he had started up the river. I there saw General C. F. Smith, who was in his bed sick, but apparently not dangerously ill. He had no apprehension about a battle, thought it an affair of outposts, and said that Grant had sixty thousand men. This would agree approximately with the estimate which Grant himself made of his force, at Nelson's camp.

As the firing continued, and increased in volume, I determined to go to the scene of action. Nelson only waited for the services of a guide to march by land. The river bottom between Savannah and Pittsburg Landing was a labyrinth of roads from which the overflows had obliterated all recent signs of travel, and left them impassable except in certain places, and it was with great difficulty that a guide could be obtained. The artillery had to be left behind to be transported by water. After disposing of these matters and sending orders for the rear divisions to push forward without their trains, I took a small steamer at the landing and proceeded up the river, accompanied only by my chief of staff. On the way we were met by a descending steamer which came alongside and delivered a letter from General Grant addressed to the "Commanding Officer, advanced forces, near Pittsburg, Tenn.," and couched in the following words:

"PITTSBURG, April 6, 1862.

"GENERAL: The attack on my forces has been very spirited since early this morning. The appearance of fresh troops on the field now would have a powerful effect, both by inspiring our men and disheartening the enemy. If you will get upon the field, leaving all your baggage on the east bank of the river, it will be a move to our advantage, and possibly save the day to us. The rebel forces are estimated at over one hundred thousand men. My headquarters will be in the log-building on the top of the hill, where you will be furnished a staff-officer to guide you to your place on the field.   Respectfully, &c.,   U. S. GRANT, Maj.-Gen."

About half-way up we met a stream of fugitives that poured in a constantly swelling current along the west bank of the river. The mouth of Snake Creek was full of them swimming across. We arrived at the landing about 1 o'clock. I inquired for General Grant and was informed that he was on his headquarters boat, nearly against which we had landed. I went on board, and was met by him at the door of the ladies' cabin, in which there were besides himself two or three members of his staff. Other officers may have entered afterward. He appeared to realize that he was beset by a pressing danger, and manifested by manner more than in words that he was relieved by my arrival as indicating the near approach of succor; but there was nothing in his deportment that the circumstances would not have justified without disparagement to the character of a courageous soldier. Certainly there was none of that masterly confidence which has since been assumed with reference to the occasion. After the first salutation, and as I walked to a seat, he remarked that he had just come in from the front, and held up his sword to call my attention to an indentation which he said the scabbard had received from a shot. I did not particularly notice it, and after inquiring about the progress of the battle and requesting him to send steamers to bring up Crittenden's division, which was coming into Savannah as I left, I proposed that we should go ashore. As we reached the gangway I noticed that the horses of himself and his staff were being taken ashore. He mounted and rode away, while I walked up the hill; so that I saw him no more until the attack occurred at the landing late in the evening. I state these particulars of our meeting with so much detail because a totally incorrect version of the place, manner, and substance of the interview has been used to give a false impression of the state of the battle, and a false coloring to personal traits which are assumed to have had the issue in control. ▷

▷ About two weeks after the battle of Shiloh there appeared in some newspaper that was shown to me a report of a conversation assumed to have taken place between General Grant and myself soon after the battle, in which I was represented as rallying him upon the narrowness of his escape, and saying that he had not transports enough to carry off ten thousand men; to which he was reported as replying, in substance, that when it came to retreating transportation would not have been required for more than ten thousand.

The story had been colored for popular effect, but was traceable to a conversation in a vein of pleasantry that occurred at my camp, after the battle, among a party of officers in which I had taken but little part.

Some time afterward it took on a modification which suited the alleged conversation, to my meeting with General Grant on my arrival at Pittsburg Landing during the battle. This changed materially the character of the report, but I continued to treat it with the indifference which I thought it deserved, though the story has been freely circulated. I never knew until within a few months past, through the publication of the "War Records," that in its modified form it had the indorsement of an official authorship.

From that publication it appears that a year after the battle General Grant called upon three of his staff-officers to make reports concerning the movements of General Lew Wallace's division on the day of the battle, in answer to a complaint of the latter officer that injustice had been done him in General Grant's reports. Two of the officers, namely, General McPherson and Captain Rowley, in their replies confined themselves to that sub-

ject. The third, Colonel Rawlins, on the other hand, made it the occasion of a specific defense, or explanation, or commendation, or whatever it may be called, of General Grant's relation to the battle. Among other things that have since been more or less disputed, he said:

"General Nelson's division of the Army of the Ohio reached Savannah on the afternoon of the 5th of April, but General Buell himself did not arrive. . . . You [General Grant] then rode back to the house near the river that had been designated for headquarters, to learn what word if any had been received from General Nelson, whose division you expected soon to arrive at the landing on the opposite side of the river; and you there met Maj.-Gen. D. C. Buell, who had arrived at Savannah and taken a steamer and come up to see you, and learn how the battle was progressing in advance of his force. Among his first inquiries was: 'What preparations have you made for retreating?' To which you replied, 'I have not yet despaired of whipping them, general'; and went on to state to him your momentary expectation of the arrival of General Wallace, to whom orders had been timely and repeatedly sent, and that General Nelson's division might soon be expected by the wagonroad from Savannah," etc.

This statement, ridiculous and absurd in its principal feature, is incorrect in every particular.

It is well known that I arrived at Savannah on the 5th of April; General Grant did not, as might be inferred, find *me* at the landing at Pittsburg—I found *him* there; we did not meet at "the house near the river," but on his headquarters steamer.

I mention these points only to show the tendency of the statement to error, and I aver that no such conversation as is described ever occurred, and that the contingency of a retreat was not brought forward by General Grant or by me.

My attention has within a few days been called

PITTSBURG LANDING IN THE SUMMER OF 1884.   FROM A PHOTOGRAPH.

The central or main landing is here shown. On the hill to the right is seen the flag-staff of the National
Cemetery; in the rear and to the left of the cemetery is the steamboat-store and
post-office, where the roads from the landings meet.

On the shore I encountered a scene which has often been described. The
face of the bluff was crowded with stragglers from the battle. The number
there at different hours has been estimated at from five thousand in the
morning to fifteen thousand in the evening. The number at nightfall would
not have fallen short of fifteen thousand, including those who had passed
down the river, and the less callous but still broken and demoralized fragments about the camps on the plateau near the landing. At the top of the
bluff all was confusion. Men mounted and on foot, and wagons with their
teams and excited drivers, all struggling to force their way closer to the
river, were mixed up in apparently inextricable confusion with a battery of
artillery which was standing in park without men or horses to man or move
it. The increasing throng already presented a barrier which it was evidently
necessary to remove, in order to make way for the passage of my troops when
they should arrive. In looking about for assistance I fell upon one officer,
the quartermaster of an Ohio regiment, who preserved his senses, and was
anxious to do something to abate the disorder. I instructed him to take control of the teams, and move them down the hill by a side road which led to
the narrow bottom below the landing, and there park them. He went to
work with alacrity and the efficiency of a strong will, and succeeded in clear-

to the fact that an article, in a recent number of
"The Century" magazine [General Adam Badeau's
paper on "General Grant," in the number for
May, 1885], has given fresh circulation to the
story, and has combined the official and the original phraseology of it. I have regarded it as a

trivial question, of little moment to either General
Grant or myself; but perhaps the value attached
to it by others makes it proper for me to give it an
attention which I have not heretofore chosen to
bestow upon it.—D. C. BUELL.

AIRDRIE, Kentucky, July 10th, 1885.

ing the ground of the wagons. It proved before night to have been a more important service than I had expected, for it not only opened the way for Nelson's division, but extricated the artillery and made it possible to get it into action when the attack occurred at the landing about sunset.

It is now time to glance at the circumstances which had brought about and were urging on the state of affairs here imperfectly portrayed.

Upon learning on the 2d of April of the advance of the Army of the Ohio toward Savannah, General Sidney Johnston determined to anticipate the junction of that army with General Grant's force, by attacking the latter, and at once gave orders for the movement of his troops on the following day. It was his expectation to reach the front of the army at Pittsburg Landing on Friday, the 4th, and make the attack at daylight on Saturday; but the condition of the roads, and some confusion in the execution of orders, prevented him from getting into position for the attack until 3 o'clock P. M. on Saturday. This delay and an indiscreet reconnoissance which brought on a sharp engagement with the Federal pickets, rendered it so improbable that the Union commander would not be prepared for the attack, that General Beauregard advised the abandonment of the enterprise, to the success of which a surprise was deemed to be essential. General Johnston overruled the proposition, however, and the attack was ordered for the following morning. The army was drawn up in three parallel lines, covering the front of the Federal position. Hardee commanded the first line, Bragg the second, and Polk and Breckinridge the third, the latter being intended as a reserve.

The locality on which the storm of battle was about to burst has often been described with more or less of inaccuracy or incompleteness. It is an undulating table-land, quite broken in places, elevated a hundred feet or thereabout above the river; an irregular triangle in outline, nearly equilateral, with the sides four miles long, bordered on the east by the river, which here runs nearly due north, on the north-west by Snake Creek and its tributary, Owl Creek, and on the south, or south-west, by a range of hills which immediately border Lick Creek on the north bank, two hundred feet or more in height, and sloping gradually toward the battle-field. In these hills rise the eastern tributaries of Owl Creek, one of them called Oak Creek, extending half-way across the front or south side of the battle-field, and interlocking with a ravine called Locust Grove Creek, which runs in the opposite direction into Lick Creek a mile from its mouth. Other short, deep ravines start from the table-land and empty into the river, the principal among them being Dill's Branch, six hundred yards above the landing. Midway in the front, at the foot of the Lick Creek hills, start a number of surface drains which soon unite in somewhat difficult ravines and form Tillman's Creek, or Brier Creek. It runs almost due north, a mile and a quarter from the river, in a deep hollow, which divides the table-land into two main ridges. Tillman's Creek empties into Owl Creek half a mile above the Snake Creek bridge by which the division of Lew Wallace arrived. Short, abrupt ravines break from the main ridges into Tillman's Hollow, and the broad surface of the west ridge is further broken by larger branches which empty into Owl Creek. Tillman's Hollow, only about a mile long, is a marked feature in the topography, and is identified with some important incidents of the battle.

Pittsburg Landing is three-quarters of a mile above the mouth of Snake Creek, and two and a quarter miles below the mouth of Lick Creek. Shiloh Church is on Oak Creek two miles and a half south-west of Pittsburg Landing. The table-land comes up boldly to the river at the landing and for a mile south. Beyond those limits the river bends away from the high land, and the bottom gradually widens.

The principal roads are the River road, as it will here be called, which crosses Snake Creek at the bridge before mentioned, and running a mile west of Pittsburg Landing, obliquely along the ridge east of Tillman's Creek, crosses Lick Creek three-quarters of a mile from the river at the east end of the Lick Creek hills; the Hamburg and Purdy road, which branches from the River road a mile and two-thirds in a straight line south of Pittsburg Landing, and extends north-west 400 yards north of Shiloh Church; and two roads that start at the landing, cross the River road two-thirds of a mile apart, and also cross or run into the Hamburg and Purdy road nearly

MAP SHOWING THE UNION CAMPS AT SHILOH, Obtained from Gen. W. T. Sherman on the evening of the first day of the battle. (This map is a fac-simile in every respect, except as to the words "*To Crump's Landing,*" which in the original are outside the limits of the magazine page; and except as to the signs referring to errors, and the division into two parts.)

Errors in the Original Map,

As indicated by Gen. D. C. Buell.

* Should be 43 Ill. instead of 41 Ill.
†   "   " 25 Ind.   "   " 25 Io.
‡‡   "   " 13 Mo.   "   " 12 Mo.
§   "   " 32 Ill.   "   " 52 Ill.
‡ Withdrawn before the battle.

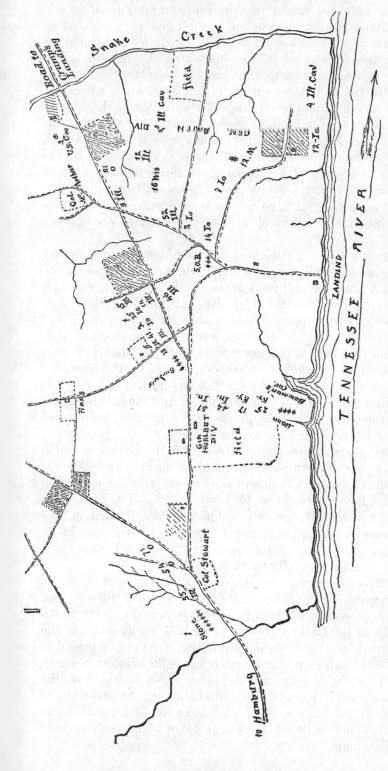

opposite the church. In the official reports these various roads are called with some confusion, but not altogether inaccurately, Crump's Landing road, Hamburg road, Corinth road or Purdy road, even over the same space, according to the idea of the writer. The Corinth road from the landing has two principal branches. The western branch passes by the church, and the eastern passes a mile east of the church into the Bark road, which extends along the crest of the Lick Creek hills. The military maps show many other roads, some of them farm-roads, and some only well-worn tracks made in hauling for the troops. In some places the old roads were quite obliterated, and are improperly represented on the maps, as in the case of the River road, which is not shown on the official map between McArthur's and Hurlbut's headquarters, immediately west of the landing. It is shown on Sherman's camp map, and its existence is not doubtful. At the time of the battle, much the largest part of the ground was in forest, sometimes open, sometimes almost impenetrable for horsemen, with occasional cleared fields of from 20 to 80 acres; and these variations operated in a signal manner upon the fortune of the combatants. There was not a cleared field within the limits of the battle that has not its history.

We may now locate the troops in their encampments, for there is where the battle found them, and its currents and eddies will frequently be discovered by the reference to certain camps in the official reports. The camp map which I received from General Sherman will serve as a useful guide, subject to some necessary modifications, to make a field sketch agree with an actual survey. But the regimental camps did not always conform to the lines laid down for the brigades and divisions. Sometimes they were in front, sometimes in rear of the general line. I have not pretended generally to introduce these variations into the map which I have prepared to accompany this article.

Starting at the landing, we find the Second Division, commanded by W. H. L. Wallace, in the space bounded by the river, Snake Creek, the River road, and the right-hand road leading west from the landing. Along that road are, in this order, the camps of the 12th, 7th, 14th, and 2d Iowa, and the 52d and 9th Illinois. At the point where that road crosses the River road, in the south-west angle of the intersection, are the headquarters of General McArthur. On the east side of the River road, north of McArthur are, first, the 14th Missouri, called "Birge's sharp-shooters" (not on the Sherman camp map), and next the 81st Ohio. The 16th Wisconsin has been assigned to Prentiss's division since the Sherman map was made, and the 13th Missouri has probably taken that ground. All these points are particularly mentioned in the reports of the battle and have been verified.

On the left-hand road where it crosses the River road, three-quarters of a mile from the landing, is the Fourth Division (Hurlbut's), its Third Brigade between the road and the river, and the line of the two other brigades bearing off to the north-west. I have located the 3d Iowa, of that division, on the ground just in front of which Crittenden's division was first formed in line Monday morning, because it was stated to me at the time that General Prentiss was killed at that camp; the fact being that near that point Prentiss was captured and W. H. L. Wallace mortally wounded.

At the fork of the River road and the Hamburg and Purdy road, is the camp of Sherman's Second Brigade, commanded by Colonel Stuart, two miles from the division to which it belongs, and one mile from Hurlbut's division. On both sides of the eastern Corinth road, half a mile south of the Hamburg and Purdy road, is Prentiss's division (the Sixth) of 2 brigades. It is not shown on the Sherman map. Stretching across the western Corinth road at the church, along Oak Creek, are the other three brigades of the Fifth Division (Sherman's)—Hildebrand's brigade being on the east side of the road, Buckland's next on the west side, and John A. McDowell's next on Buckland's right. Only one regiment (the 6th Iowa) of McDowell's brigade is shown on the Sherman map.

The official reports and other authority locate the First Division (McClernand's) as follows: The right of the Third Brigade is at the point where the western Corinth road crosses the Hamburg and Purdy road, 500 yards from the church, and the left is 200 yards from Hildebrand's brigade, which is thus obliquely in its front. The other 2 brigades, on a general line starting from the right of the Third, form an obtuse angle with the Third, and are along the ridge nearly parallel with Tillman's Creek, the extreme right being not far from the bluff overlooking Owl Creek bottom. The First Brigade is on the east side of the adjacent field instead of the west side, as the Sherman map, according to the road, would seem to place it, though that map does not show the field. It remains to be added that 3 of the 5 divisions were for that period of the war old and experienced troops. Hurlbut's Third Brigade belonged to the Army of the Ohio, and had been sent to reënforce Grant before Donelson. Eight other regiments were furnished by me for the first movement up the Tennessee, and remained with Grant's army. Sherman's division, one of the newest, had been under his command more than a month, and ought to have been in a tolerably efficient state of discipline. Prentiss's division, composed largely of raw regiments, had only been organized a few days; yet it was posted in the most exposed and assailable point on the front. The effective force at the date of the battle, exclusive of Lew Wallace's division, which was at or near Crump's Landing, 6 miles below, is stated by General Sherman at 32,000 men; by General Grant at 33,000. General Wallace left 2 regiments of his division and a piece of artillery at Crump's Landing, and joined the army Sunday evening, with, as he states, not more than 5000 men.

I proceed now, in the light of the official reports and other evidence, to explain briefly what happened: the object being not so much to criticise the manner of the battle, or give a detailed description of it, as to trace it to its actual condition at the close of the first day, and outline its progress during the second. With this object the question of a surprise has little to do. I stop, therefore, only to remark that each revival of that question has placed the fact in a more glaring light. The enemy was known to be at hand, but no adequate steps were taken to ascertain in what force or with what design. The call to arms blended with the crash of the assault, and when the whole forest on the rising ground in front flashed with the gleam of bayonets, then General Sherman, as he reports, " became satisfied for the first time that the enemy designed a determined attack." Yet among the more watchful officers in the front divisions, there was a nervous feeling that their superiors were not giving due heed to the presence of hostile reconnoitering parties, though they little imagined the magnitude of the danger that impended. On Saturday General Sherman was notified of these parties. He answered that the pickets must be strengthened, and instructed to be vigilant; that he was embarrassed for the want of cavalry; his cavalry had been ordered away, and the cavalry he was to have instead had not arrived; as soon as they reported he would send them to the front and find out what was there. In one of his brigades the regimental commanders held a consultation, at which it was determined to strengthen the pickets. These are curious revelations to a soldier's ear.

Prentiss's vigilance gave the first warning of the actual danger, and in fact commenced the contest. On Saturday, disquieted by the frequent appearance of the enemy's cavalry, he increased his pickets, though he had no evidence of the presence of a large force. Early Sunday morning one of these picket-guards, startled no doubt by the hum of forty thousand men half a mile distant, waking up for battle, went forward to ascertain the cause, and soon came upon the enemy's pickets, which it promptly attacked. It was then a quarter past 5 o'clock, and all things being ready, the Confederate general, accepting the signal of the pickets, at once gave the order to advance. Previously, however, General Prentiss, still apprehensive, had sent forward Colonel Moore of the 21st Missouri, with five companies to strengthen the picket-guard. On the way out Colonel Moore met the guard returning to camp with a number of its men killed and wounded. Sending the latter on to camp and calling for the remaining companies of his regiment, he proceeded to the front in time to take a good position on the border of a cleared field and opened fire upon the enemy's skirmishers, checking them for a while; but the main body forced him back upon the division with a considerable list of wounded, himself among the number. All this occurred in front of Sherman's camp, not in front of Prentiss's. This spirited beginning, unexpected on both sides, gave the first alarm to the divisions of Sherman and Prentiss. The latter promptly formed his division at the first news from the front, and moved a quarter of a mile in advance of his camp, where he was attacked before Sherman was under arms. He held his position until the enemy on his right passed him in attacking Sherman, whose left regiment immediately broke into rout. He then retired in some disorder, renewing the resistance in his camp but forced back in still greater disorder, until at 9 o'clock he came upon the line which Hurlbut and W. H. L. Wallace were forming half a mile in rear.

Upon the first alarm in his camp, which was simultaneous with the attack upon Sherman, McClernand rapidly got under arms, and endeavored to support Sherman's left with his Third Brigade, only two hundred yards in rear, while he placed his First and Second Brigades in inverted order still farther to the rear and left, to oppose the enemy's columns pouring in upon his left flank through the opening on Sherman's left; but his Third Brigade was forced back with the fugitives from Sherman's broken line by the advancing enemy, and endeavored with only partial success to form on the right of McClernand's line, which at first was formed with the left a little south, and the center north of the Corinth road. Before the formation was completed the line was compelled to retire by the pressure on its front and left flank, with the loss of 6 pieces of artillery, but it re-formed 300 yards in rear.

Hildebrand's brigade had now disappeared in complete disorder from the front, leaving three pieces of artillery in the hands of the enemy. Buckland formed promptly at the first alarm, and in order to keep the enemy back endeavored by Sherman's direction to throw a regiment beyond Oak Creek, which covered his front at a distance of two hundred yards, but on reaching the brow of the low hill bordering the stream the enemy was encountered on the hither side. Nevertheless the brigade resisted effectively for about two hours the efforts of the assailants to cross the boggy stream in force. The enemy suffered great loss in these efforts, but succeeded at last. Before being quite forced back, Buckland received orders from Sherman to form line on the Purdy road four hundred yards in rear, to connect with McClernand's right. Orders were also given to McDowell, who had not yet been engaged, to close to the left on the same line. These orders were in effect defeated in both cases, and five pieces of artillery lost by faults in the execution and the rapid advance of the enemy. Sherman's division as an organized body disappeared from the field from this time until the close of the day. McDowell's brigade preserved a sort of identity for a while. Sherman reports that at "about 10:30 A. M. the enemy had made a furious attack on General McClernand's whole front. Finding him pressed, I moved McDowell's brigade against the left flank of the enemy, forced him back some distance, and then directed the men to avail themselves of every cover — trees, fallen timber, and a wooded valley to our right." It sounds like the signal to disperse, and a little after 1 o'clock the brigade and regiments are seen no more. Some fragments of the division and the commander himself attached themselves to McClernand's command, which now, owing to its composite and irregular organization, could hardly be denominated a division.

The contest which raged in McClernand's camp was of a fluctuating character. The ground was lost and won more than once, but each ebb and flow of the struggle left the Union side in a worse condition. In his fifth position McClernand was driven to the camp of his First Brigade, half of his command facing to the south and half to the west, to meet the converging attack of the enemy. His nominal connection with the left wing of the army across the head of Tillman's Hollow had been severed, by the dispersion or defeat of the detached commands that formed it. Another reverse to his thinned ranks would drive him over the bluff into Owl Creek bottom, and perhaps cut him off from the river. He determined, therefore, between 2 and 3 o'clock to retire across Tillman's Hollow in the direction of the landing. That movement was effected with a good deal of irregularity, but with the repulse of a small body of pursuing cavalry, and a new line was formed on the opposite ridge along the River road, north of Hurlbut's headquarters. I shall have occasion farther along to remark upon the display of force on the right of this line in the vicinity of McArthur's headquarters. The movement must have been completed about 3 o'clock. Leaving the right wing, as it may be called, in this position prior to the attack of 4 o'clock, which drove it still farther back, we will return to the current of events in the left wing.

With Stuart on the extreme left, as with the other commanders, the presence of the enemy was the first warning of danger. He was soon compelled to fall back from his camp to a new position, and presently again to a third, which located him on the prolongation and extreme left of the line formed

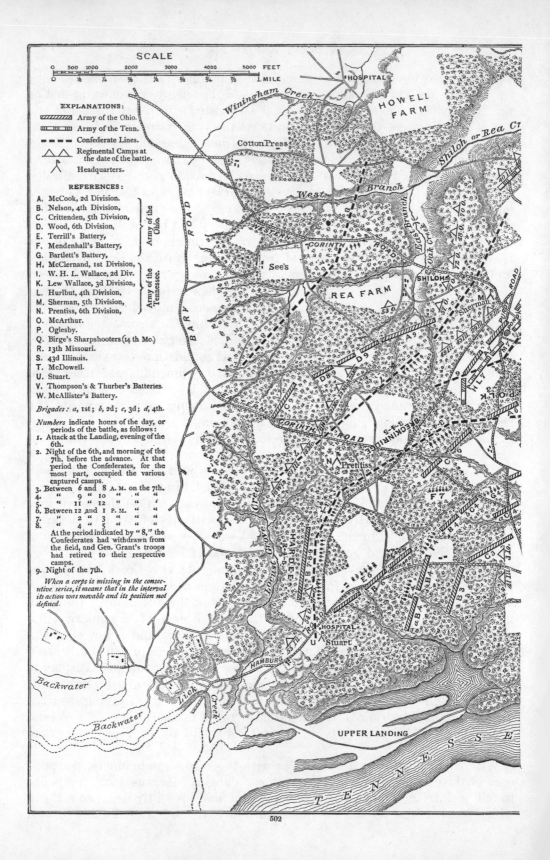

SCALE

0 500 1000   2000   3000   4000   5000 FEET
0   ⅛   ¼   ⅜   ½   ⅝   ¾   ⅞   1 MILE

EXPLANATIONS:

⬚⬚⬚⬚ Army of the Ohio.
⬚⬚⬚⬚ Army of the Tenn.
▬ ▬ ▬ Confederate Lines.
△△ Regimental Camps at the date of the battle.
⚐ Headquarters.

REFERENCES:

A. McCook, 2d Division. ⎫
B. Nelson, 4th Division. ⎪
C. Crittenden, 5th Division, ⎬ Army of the Ohio.
D. Wood, 6th Division, ⎪
E. Terrill's Battery, ⎪
F. Mendenhall's Battery, ⎪
G. Bartlett's Battery, ⎭

H. McClernand, 1st Division, ⎫
I. W. H. L. Wallace, 2d Div. ⎬ Army of the Tennessee.
K. Lew Wallace, 3d Division, ⎪
L. Hurlbut, 4th Division, ⎭
M. Sherman, 5th Division,
N. Prentiss, 6th Division,
O. McArthur.
P. Oglesby.
Q. Birge's Sharpshooters (14th Mo.)
R. 13th Missouri.
S. 43d Illinois.
T. McDowell.
U. Stuart.
V. Thompson's & Thurber's Batteries.
W. McAllister's Battery.

Brigades: a, 1st; b, 2d; c, 3d; d, 4th.

Numbers indicate hours of the day, or periods of the battle, as follows:
1. Attack at the Landing, evening of the 6th.
2. Night of the 6th, and morning of the 7th, before the advance. At that period the Confederates, for the most part, occupied the various captured camps.
3. Between 6 and 8 A. M. on the 7th.
4.   "   9 " 10 "   "   "
5.   "   11 " 12 "   "   "
6. Between 12 and 1 P. M. "   "
7.   "   2 " 3 "   "   "
8.   "   4 " 5 "   "   "
   At the period indicated by "8," the Confederates had withdrawn from the field, and Gen. Grant's troops had retired to their respective camps.
9. Night of the 7th.

When a corps is missing in the consecutive series, it means that in the interval its action was movable and its position not defined.

502

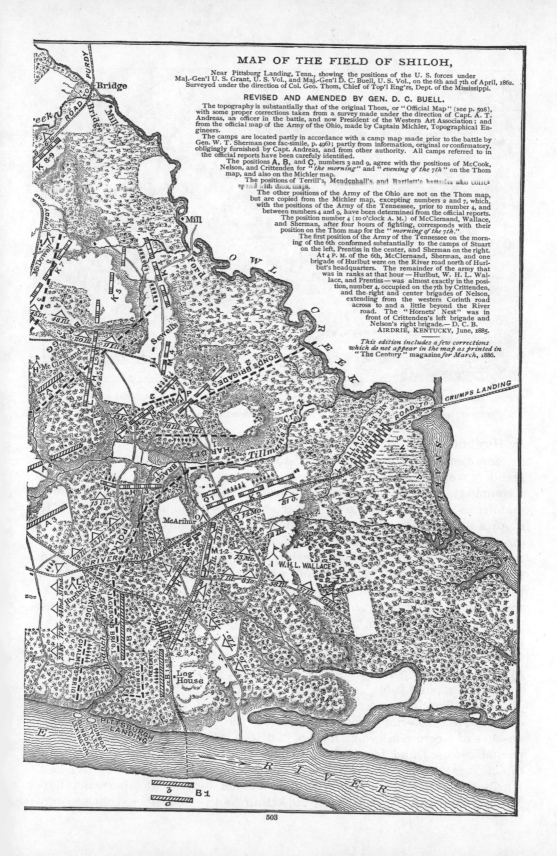

MAP OF THE FIELD OF SHILOH,

Near Pittsburg Landing, Tenn., showing the positions of the U. S. forces under
Maj.-Gen'l U. S. Grant, U. S. Vol., and Maj.-Gen'l D. C. Buell, U. S. Vol., on the 6th and 7th of April, 1862.
Surveyed under the direction of Col. Geo. Thom, Chief of Top'l Eng'rs, Dept. of the Mississippi.

REVISED AND AMENDED BY GEN. D. C. BUELL.

The topography is substantially that of the original Thom, or "Official Map" (see p. 508),
with some proper corrections taken from a survey made under the direction of Capt. A. T.
Andreas, an officer in the battle, and now President of the Western Art Association; and
from the official map of the Army of the Ohio, made by Captain Michler, Topographical Engineers.

The camps are located partly in accordance with a camp map made prior to the battle by
Gen. W. T. Sherman (see fac-simile, p. 496); partly from information, original or confirmatory,
obligingly furnished by Capt. Andreas, and from other authority. All camps referred to in
the official reports have been carefully identified.

The positions A, B, and C, numbers 3 and 9, agree with the positions of McCook,
Nelson, and Crittenden for "the morning" and "evening of the 7th" on the Thom
map, and also on the Michler map.

The positions of Terrill's, Mendenhall's, and Bartlett's batteries also correspond with those maps.

The other positions of the Army of the Ohio are not on the Thom map,
but are copied from the Michler map, excepting numbers 2 and 7, which,
with the positions of the Army of the Tennessee, prior to number 4, and
between numbers 4 and 9, have been determined from the official reports.

The position number 4 (10 o'clock A. M.) of McClernand, Wallace,
and Sherman, after four hours of fighting, corresponds with their
position on the Thom map for the "morning of the 7th."

The first position of the Army of the Tennessee on the morning of the 6th conformed substantially to the camps of Stuart
on the left, Prentiss in the center, and Sherman on the right.

At 4 P. M. of the 6th, McClernand, Sherman, and one
brigade of Hurlbut were on the River road north of Hurlbut's headquarters. The remainder of the army that
was in ranks at that hour — Hurlbut, W. H. L. Wallace, and Prentiss — was almost exactly in the position, number 4, occupied on the 7th by Crittenden,
and the right and center brigades of Nelson,
extending from the western Corinth road
across to and a little beyond the River
road. The "Hornets' Nest" was in
front of Crittenden's left brigade and
Nelson's right brigade.— D. C. B.

AIRDRIE, KENTUCKY, June, 1885.

*This edition includes a few corrections
which do not appear in the map as printed in
"The Century" magazine for March, 1886.*

THE "HORNETS' NEST" — PRENTISS'S TROOPS AND HICKENLOOPER'S BATTERY REPULSING HARDEE'S TROOPS.

This cut and the one on the next page form one picture relating to the battle of the first day.

by Hurlbut and W. H. L. Wallace, but without having any connection with it. As soon as the first advance of the enemy was known, these two commanders were called upon by those in front for support. In the absence of a common superior it was sent forward by regiments or brigades in such manner as seemed proper to the officer appealed to, and after that was left to its own devices. It seldom formed the connection desired, or came under the direction of a common superior. Indeed, the want of cohesion and concert in the Union ranks is conspicuously indicated in the official reports. A regiment is rarely overcome in front, but falls back because the regiment on its right or left has done so, and exposed its flank. It continues its backward movement at least until it is well under shelter, thus exposing the flank of its neighbor, who then must also needs fall back. Once in operation, the process repeats itself indefinitely. In a broken and covered country which affords occasional rallying-points and obstructs the pursuit, it proceeds step by step. On an open field, in the presence of light artillery and cavalry, it would run rapidly into general rout.

This outflanking, so common in the Union reports at Shiloh, is not a mere excuse of the inferior commanders. It is the practical consequence of the absence of a common head, and the judicious use of reserves to counteract partial reverses and preserve the front of battle. The want of a general direction is seen also in the distribution of Hurlbut's and Wallace's divisions. Hurlbut sent a brigade under Colonel Veatch to support Sherman's left; Wallace sent one under General McArthur to the opposite extreme to sup-

GIBSON'S BRIGADE CHARGING HURLBUT'S TROOPS IN THE "HORNETS' NEST."

From the Cyclorama of Shiloh at Chicago. By permission.

port Stuart; and the two remaining brigades of each were between the extremes—Wallace on Veatch's left but not in connection with it, and Hurlbut on McArthur's right, also without connection. Stuart himself with his brigade was two miles to the left of Sherman's division to which he belonged. When the three Confederate lines were brought together successively at the front, there was, of course, a great apparent mingling of organizations; but it was not in their case attended with the confusion that might be supposed, because each division area was thereby supplied with a triple complement of brigade and division officers, and the whole front was under the close supervision of four remarkably efficient corps commanders. The evils of disjointed command are plainly to be seen in the arrangement of the Federal line, but the position of the left wing after the forced correction of the first faulty disposition of Hurlbut's brigades was exceedingly strong, and in the center was held without a break against oft-repeated assaults from 9 o'clock until 5 o'clock. From 12 until 2 it was identical with the second position taken by Nelson and Crittenden on Monday, and it was equally formidable against attack from both directions. Its peculiar feature consisted in a wood in the center, with a thick undergrowth, flanked on either side by open fields, and with open but sheltering woods in front and rear. The Confederates gave the name of "Hornets' Nest" to the thicket part of it on Sunday, and it was in the open ground on the east flank that General Sidney Johnston was killed.

On this line, between and under the shelter of Hurlbut and W. H. L. Wallace, Prentiss rallied a considerable force, perhaps a thousand men, of his routed division at 9 o'clock, and fought stubbornly until near the close of the day. By 3 o'clock the withdrawal of the right wing, accompanied by Veatch's brigade, exposed W. H. L. Wallace's right flank, which also partially crumbled away; and the retirement of Stuart about the same hour before the strong attack brought against him, and of Hurlbut at 4 o'clock under the same powerful pressure upon his left flank, left Prentiss and Wallace with his remaining regiments isolated and unsupported. Still they held their ground while the enemy closed upon each flank. As they were about being completely enveloped, Wallace endeavored to extricate his command, and was mortally wounded in the attempt at 5 o'clock. Some of his regiments under Colonel Tuttle fought their way through the cross-fire of the contracting lines of the enemy, but 6 regiments of the 2 divisions held fast until the encompassment was complete, and one by one with Prentiss, between half-past 5 and 6 o'clock, they were forced to surrender. This gallant resistance, and the delay caused by the necessary disposition of the captives, weakened the force of the attack which McClernand sustained in his seventh position on the River road at 4 o'clock, and retarded the onward movement of the enemy for nearly 3 hours after the retirement of the right wing from the west side of Tillman's Creek.

Before the incumbrance of their success was entirely put out of the way the Confederates pressed forward to complete a seemingly assured victory, but it was too late. John K. Jackson's brigade and the 9th and 10th Mississippi of Chalmers's brigade crossed Dill's ravine, and their artillery on the south side swept the bluff at the landing, the missiles falling into the river far beyond. Hurlbut had hurriedly got into line in rear of the siege-guns, as they are called in the official reports posted half a mile from the river, but for five hundred yards from the landing there was not a soldier in ranks or any organized means of defense.\ Just as the danger was perceived, Colonel Webster, Grant's chief of artillery, rapidly approached Colonel Fry and myself. The idea of getting the battery which was standing in park into action was expressed simultaneously by the three, and was promptly executed by Colonel Webster's immediate exertion. General Grant came up a few minutes later, and a member of his escort was killed in that position. Chalmers's skirmishers approached to within one hundred yards of the battery. The number in view was not large, but the gunners were already abandoning their pieces, when Ammen's brigade, accompanied by Nelson, came into action. The attack was repelled, and the engagement ended for the day.

In his report of April 9th, to Halleck, General Grant says of this incident:

"At a late hour in the afternoon a desperate effort was made by the enemy to turn our left and get possession of the landing, transports, etc. This point was guarded by the gun-boats *Tyler* and *Lexington*, Captains Gwin and Shirk, U. S. Navy, commanding, four 20-pounder Parrott guns, and a battery of rifled guns. As there is a deep and impassable ravine for artillery or cavalry, and very difficult for infantry, at this point, no troops were stationed here, except the necessary artillerists and a small infantry force for their support. Just at this moment the

\ In studying the Official Reports these "siege-guns" must not be confounded with the battery of rifle field-guns nearer the river; to all of these the term "Reserve Artillery" has been given on the map (page 503).— D. C. B.

advance of Major-General Buell's column (a part of the division under General Nelson) arrived, the two generals named both being present. An advance was immediately made upon the point of attack and the enemy soon driven back. In this repulse, much is due to the presence of the gun-boats *Tyler* and *Lexington,* and their able commanders, Captains Gwin and Shirk."

My own official report is to the same effect. In a calm review of the battle, not unfriendly to General Grant, and written some years after the occurrence, General Hurlbut said:

"About 6 P. M. this movement (for a final attack at the landing) was reported to General Hurlbut. He at once took measures to change the front of 2 regiments, or parts of regiments, of which the 55th Illinois was one, and to turn 6 pieces of artillery to bear upon the point of danger. At that instant, he being near the head of the Landing road, General Grant came up from the river, closely followed by Ammen's brigade of Nelson's division. Information of the expected attack was promptly given, and two of Ammen's regiments deployed into line, moved rapidly forward, and after a few sharp exchanges of volleys from them, the enemy fell back, and the bloody series of engagements of Sunday at Pittsburg Landing closed with that last repulse."

The reports of all the officers who took part in the action at the landing, Nelson, Ammen, and the regimental commanders, fully sustain the main point in these accounts, and are totally at variance with General Grant's statement in his "Century" article [see page 465]. I have myself never described the attack at the landing as "a desperate effort" of the enemy; but I have said that the condition of affairs at that point made the occasion critical. We know from the Confederate reports that the attack was undertaken by Jackson's and Chalmers's brigades as above stated; that the reserve artillery could effect nothing against the attacking force under the shelter of Dill's ravine; that the fire of the gun-boats was equally harmless on account of the elevation which it was necessary to give the guns in order to clear the top of the bluff; and that the final assault, owing to the show of resistance, was delayed. Jackson's brigade made its advance without cartridges. When they came to the crest of the hill and found the artillery supported by infantry, they shrank from the assault with bayonets alone, and Jackson went in search of coöperation and support. In the meantime the attack was superseded by the order of the Confederate commander calling off his troops for the night. The attack was poorly organized, but it was not repelled until Ammen arrived, and it cannot be affirmed under the circumstances that the action of his brigade in delaying and repelling the enemy was not of the most vital importance. Had the attack been made before Nelson could arrive, with the means which the enemy had abundantly at hand, it would have succeeded beyond all question.

As fast as Nelson's division arrived it was formed in line of battle in front of Grant's troops, pickets were thrown across Dill's ravine, and the dawn of another day was awaited to begin the second stage in the battle; or, speaking more correctly, to fight the second battle of Shiloh. Let us in the meantime examine more in detail the condition in which the first day had left General Grant's command, and its prospects unaided for the morrow.

THE evidence relied upon to refute the accepted belief in the critical condition of General Grant's command on Sunday evening is of two sorts: first,

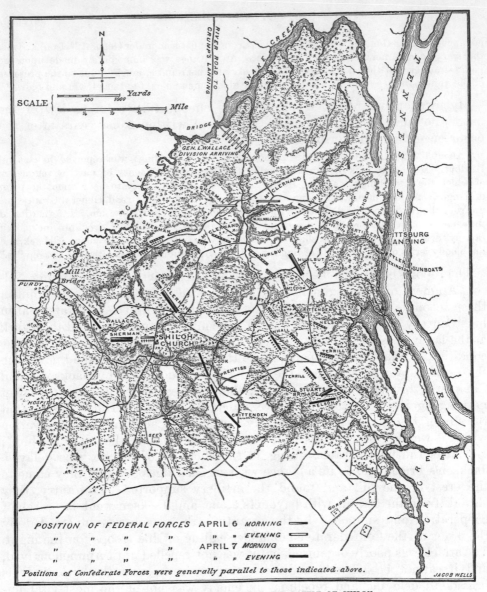

SCALE

500   1000   Yards

¼   ½   ¾   Mile

POSITION OF FEDERAL FORCES   APRIL 6   MORNING ━━━

"   "   "   "   "   "   EVENING ═══

"   "   "   "   APRIL 7   MORNING ▬▬▬

"   "   "   "   "   "   EVENING ━━━

Positions of Confederate Forces were generally parallel to those indicated above.

JACOB WELLS

THE OFFICIAL, OR THOM, MAP OF THE BATTLE OF SHILOH.

On Nov. 28th, 1884, two weeks before the Official Map was sent to press with General Grant's Shiloh article (in "The Century" magazine for February, 1885), inquiry was made of General George Thom concerning its history. He replied, Dec. 5th, that it was prepared under his direction as Chief of Topographical Engineers on Halleck's staff soon after the battle, while the Union troops were still encamped on and near the battle-ground, and that Generals Grant, Buell, and Sherman furnished him with information as to the positions occupied by the troops in the battle. On Dec. 15th, General Thom "called the attention of General Grant to certain criticisms which General Sherman published on the Official Map . . . of that battle-field, at a meeting of the Army of the Tennessee held in Cincinnati on the 6th and 7th of April, 1881." In reply, General Grant wrote:

"3 E. 66th St., N. Y. City, Dec. 30th, 1884.

"MY DEAR GENERAL THOM: Your letter of the 15th instant was duly received, and I now have yours of the 28th. In

regard to the matter of the map which 'The Century' magazine is to use in illustration of the article which I have furnished on the battle of Shiloh, I have examined it, and see nothing to criticise. I was not aware before the receipt of your first letter that General Sherman had ever criticised your map of the battle-field of Shiloh. I have not spoken to Sherman on that particular subject recently, nor ever that I remember of. 'The Century,' as I understand, has taken the Official Map to illustrate my article. Very truly yours, U. S. GRANT."

General Grant's approval of the use of the Official Map with his article was given in an interview with one of the editors over the map, at his house early in Nov., 1884. On June 24th, 1885, five months after the appearance of the article, Colonel F. D. Grant wrote to the editor from Mount McGregor, inclosing notes for the revision of the map, and saying: "He [General Grant] would like you to make the changes in the map, indicated." For General Grant's map and Colonel Grant's explanation, see page 470.— EDITORS.

the *official map*, as it is called, and second, the personal statements and assumptions of General Grant and General Sherman. I shall examine these data upon the evidence of the official reports and my own observation.

The official map was prepared, after the arrival of General Halleck at Pittsburg Landing, by his topographical engineer, General George Thom. The topographical part of it was made from an approximate survey, and, though not strictly accurate, is sufficiently so for an intelligent study of the battle. For the errors in the location of the troops General Thom cannot be supposed to be responsible, since he could have no knowledge of the facts except what he derived from the statements of others; but in what is given and what is withheld they are of a very misleading nature. They consist, first, in the extension of Grant's line on the evening of the 6th a full half-mile to the west of its true limit — placing Hurlbut's division on the front actually occupied by McClernand, McClernand on and four hundred yards beyond Sherman's ground, and Sherman entirely on the west side of Tillman's Hollow on the right of the camping-ground of McClernand's division, and within the lines occupied by the Confederates. On the morning of the 7th they place from left to right, McClernand, then Sherman, then Lew Wallace, along the bluff bordering Owl Creek bottom, all west of Tillman's Creek, and on ground which we did not possess until after four hours of fighting; followed on the left by Hurlbut's division; thus occupying a solid front of a mile and a third, in comparison with which the undeveloped front of my army presents a very subordinate appearance. They give no account of the positions during the battle, in which the right of that army was substantially in contact with Wallace's division on the extreme right. They give two of its positions,— one in the first formation before its front was developed, and the other at the close of the day, when Grant's troops had taken possession of their camps again, and mine had been withdrawn from the ground on which they fought. These two positions are taken from my official map, but not the intermediate positions shown on that map. Below the copy of the Thom map, as published with General Grant's article in the February number of "The Century" (1885), it was stated that "the positions of the troops were indicated in accordance with information furnished at the time by Generals Grant, Buell, and Sherman." It would be presumed that Grant and Sherman, the latter especially, in consequence of his intimate relations with Halleck's headquarters, were consulted about the location of the troops; and it is not to be doubted that their information was the guide. If any information of mine was adopted, it was only through the map that accompanied my report, and with reference to the position of my own troops.

Nineteen years after the battle General Sherman revised the official map, and deposited his version with the archives of the Society of the Army of the Tennessee for historical use. Ostensibly it accepts the topography of the Thom map, but modifies the positions of the troops in the most radical manner. On the Thom map the line of battle Sunday evening is represented as being along the right-hand road leading west from the landing, with the reserve artillery and Nelson's and Crittenden's divisions on the left, and

CONFEDERATES.

IN THE "HORNETS' NEST"—W. H. L. WALLACE'S LINE.

This cut and the one on the next page form one picture relating to the first day's battle.

Hurlbut, McClernand, and Sherman in the order mentioned, toward the right. The modification of this position of the troops by the Sherman edition, may be described as follows [see map, page 470]: Looking west over the map, we see a line on the east bank of the river marked "Buell." No part of my army is represented on the west bank. On the west side of the river, 400 yards back from the landing and parallel with the river, is a line 100 yards long marked "Grant." Extending back from the river along Dill's Branch, is a line half a mile long marked "Detachments." This might mean the reserve artillery. From the outer extremity of the "Detachments" is a line two-thirds of a mile long running west, but swelling in the center well to the south, with its right resting on Tillman's Creek, and marked "Hurlbut." On the right of Hurlbut extending in the same west course, and entirely on the west side of Tillman's Creek, is a double line one-eighth of a mile long marked "McClernand." Then commencing one hundred yards north-west of McClernand's right and extending due north, along the edge of the field in front of the camp of McClernand's First Brigade, is a line two-thirds of a mile long marked "Sherman." On the right of this line are three houses covered in front by a sort of demi-lune and wing, between which and the main Sherman line is a bastion-like arrangement. The demi-lune figure Sherman designates as a "strong flank," and says it was occupied by Birge's sharp-shooters. Off to the right is seen Lew Wallace's division crossing Snake Creek bridge, and marching toward the demi-lune by a road which had no existence in fact or on the original Thom map. At the angle between Sherman and McClernand is a

GEN. W. H. L. WALLACE.
IN THE "HORNETS' NEST"—W. H. L. WALLACE'S LINE.

From the Cyclorama of Shiloh at Chicago. By permission.

ravine which extends into the camp of McClernand's division, and along the sides of this ravine from the right and left respectively of McClernand and Sherman are two dotted lines terminating in a point at the head of the ravine. In his speech submitting his map to the society, Sherman explains how that horn-like projection was formed, with other particulars, as follows:

"In the very crisis of the battle of April 6, about 4 o'clock P. M., when my division occupied the line from Snake Creek bridge to the forks of the Corinth and Purdy road, there occurred an incident I have never seen recorded. Birge's sharp-shooters, or 'Squirrel Tails,' occupied the stables, granaries, and house near the bridge as a strong flank. My division occupied a double line from it along what had once been a lane with its fences thrown down, and the blackberry and sassafras bushes still marking the border of an open cotton-field in front, and the left was in a ravine near which Major Ezra Taylor had assembled some ten or twelve guns. This ravine was densely wooded and extended to the front near two hundred yards, and I feared it might be occupied by the enemy, who from behind the trees could drive the gunners from their posts. I ordered the colonel of one of my regiments to occupy that ravine to anticipate the enemy, but he did not quickly catch my meaning or comprehend the tactics by which he could fulfill my purpose. I remember well that Colonel Thomas W. Sweeny, a one-armed officer who had lost an arm in the Mexican War and did not belong to my command, stood near by and quickly spoke up: 'I understand perfectly what you want; let me do it.' 'Certainly,' said I, 'Sweeny, go at once and occupy that ravine, converting it into a regular bastion.' He did it, and I attach more importance to that event than to any of the hundred achievements which I have since heard 'saved the day,' for we held that line and ravine all night, and the next morning advanced from them to certain victory."

And yet it will be seen that this new line, prepared with such elaboration of detail and introduced with such richness of anecdotal embellishment, was a thorough delusion; that Birge's sharp-shooters were not there, and that General Sherman was in a different place! Setting aside historical accuracy, however, the advantage of the revised arrangement is obvious. It extended General Grant's territory a half-mile to the south, fully as much to the west, taking in Tillman's Hollow, one-third of McClernand's captured camp, and a large part of the Confederate army, giving a battle front of two miles and a half instead of one mile, and requiring no greater power of imagination to man it than to devise it. In presenting his map to the Society, Sherman said: "The map as thus modified tells the story of the battle!"

There can be no doubt that General Sherman's position will carry unhesitating credence to his naked assertion in the minds of a considerable number of persons; while the more cautious but still unsearching readers will say that until the accuracy of the official map is disproved, it must be accepted as the standard representation of the battle. It is proper, therefore, to cite the proof which rejects both, and establishes a materially different version. The investigation may be confined, for the present, to the location of the Federal line of battle on Sunday evening. The other errors in the maps will be developed incidentally as the general subject progresses. Moreover, the inquiry will be directed specifically to the Sherman map, as that includes the faults of the Thom map as well as its own peculiar errors.

It is unnecessary to remark upon the exclusion of Nelson's leading brigade from the west bank of the river on the Sherman map. Its presence there at the time in question is as notorious as the battle itself. The distance from the landing to Dill's Branch is six hundred yards. Sherman places his "Detachments," i. e., the "reserve artillery," exactly on the line of that branch, whereas they were five hundred yards north of it. During the engagement the Confederates passed the ravine and reached the crest of the hill on the north side. After the engagement Nelson's division occupied the ravine, and his pickets held ground beyond it during the night. None of Grant's troops were ever in that position.

In adducing evidence from the official reports to determine the further position of the Union line, the extracts will be somewhat extended when the context is pertinent, in order to show at the same time the number and condition of the troops occupying it. The reader will be spared the impression of some irrelevancy if he will keep these additional objects in mind.

Of the position of General Hurlbut's division, the next on the right of the "Detachments," that officer says in his official report:

"On reaching the 24-pounder siege-guns in battery near the river, I again succeeded in forming line of battle *in rear of the guns.*"

That brought his division on the line of the right-hand road leading back from the river, but not entirely to the right of the artillery where the Thom map places it. He adds:

"I passed to the right *and found myself in communication with General Sherman,* and received his instructions. In a short time the enemy appeared *on the crest of the ridge,* led by the 18th Louisiana," etc. . . . "*General Sherman's artillery also was rapidly engaged,* and after an artillery contest of some duration, the enemy fell back." . . . "About dark the firing ceased. I advanced my division one hundred yards to the front, threw out pickets, and officers and men bivouacked in a heavy storm of rain. About 12 P. M. *General Nelson's leading columns passed through my line and went to the front,* and I called in my advance-guard."

The next division in the regular order is McClernand's, though the reader will not have failed to observe the presence of General Sherman, with at least a portion of his command, in communication with Hurlbut's right. General Sherman, it will be remembered, locates this division (McClernand's) on the west side of Tillman's Creek. We trace its retrogression step by step, from its permanent camp, across Tillman's Hollow, at the close of the day, by the following extracts from General McClernand's report:

"Continuing this sanguinary conflict until several regiments of my division had exhausted their ammunition, and its right flank had been borne back, and it was in danger of being turned, the remainder of my command . . . also fell back to the camp of the First Brigade. Here the portion that had first fallen back re-formed parallel with the camp, and fronting the approach of the enemy from the west, while the other portion formed at right angles with it, still fronting the approach of the enemy from the south. . . . It was 2 o'clock when my fifth line had been thus formed. . . . Deterred from direct advance, he (the enemy) moved a considerable force by the right flank, with the evident intention of turning my left. To defeat this purpose, *I ordered my command to fall back in the direction of the landing, across a deep hollow, and to re-form on the east side of another field, in the skirts of a wood. This was my sixth line.* Here we rested a half-hour, continuing to supply our men with ammunition, until the enemy's cavalry were seen rapidly crossing the field to the charge. Waiting until they approached within some thirty paces of our line, I ordered a fire, which was delivered with great coolness and destructive effect. First halting, then wavering, they turned and fled in confusion, leaving behind a number of riders and horses dead on the field. The 29th Illinois Infantry, inspired by the courageous example of their commanding officer, Lieutenant-Colonel Ferrell, bore the chief part in this engagement. . . . In the meantime, under cover of this demonstration strengthened by large additions from other portions of the field yielded by our forces, the enemy continued his endeavors to turn the flanks of my line, and to cut me off from the landing. To prevent this I ordered my left wing to fall back a short distance and form an obtuse angle with the center, opposing a double front to the enemy's approach. Thus disposed, my left held the enemy in check, *while my whole line slowly fell back to my seventh position. Here I re-formed the worn and famished remnant of my division, on favorable ground along a north and south road, supported on my right by fragments of General Sherman's division, and on my left by the* [14th *Illinois* and 25th *Indiana*] *under command of Colonel Veatch, acting brigadier-general.*"

The identity of this seventh position of McClernand is determined by the following extracts. Colonel Marsh, commanding McClernand's Second Brigade, says:

"At this time, *my command having been reduced to a merely nominal one,* I received orders to fall a short distance to the rear and form a new line, detaining all stragglers, portions of commands, and commands which should attempt to pass. In obedience to this, though with some difficulty as regarded portions of some commands, whose officers seemed little inclined to halt short of the river, . . . I had gathered quite a force, *and formed a line near the camp of the Second Division, concealing my men in the timber facing an open field. I here requested Colonel Davis, of the 46th Illinois, to take position on my right. He promptly and cheerfully responded. . . . In a short time General McClernand, with portions of the First and Third Brigades of his own division, and two regiments of Ohio troops,* came up and formed on the left of the line I had already established."

Colonel Davis, of the 46th Illinois, says:

"It being now 1 o'clock, my ammunition exhausted, the men tired and hungry, and myself exhausted, having lost my horse in the first engagement, and compelled to go on foot the

THE SIEGE-BATTERY, ABOVE THE LANDING, THAT WAS A PART OF THE "LAST LINE" IN THE FIRST
DAY'S BATTLE. FROM A PHOTOGRAPH TAKEN A FEW DAYS AFTER THE BATTLE.

balance of the time, *and finding myself within one-half mile of my regimental encampment, I marched my men to it and got dinner for them. Calling my men into line immediately after dinner, I formed them upon the right of the brigade commanded by Colonel C. C. Marsh, at his request, in front and to the left of my camp,* where we again met the enemy on Sunday evening."

Colonel Engelmann, of the 43d Illinois, whose report in many respects is a remarkably clear and interesting one, says:

"We now fell back by degrees [from McClernand's sixth position], and a new line being formed, *we found ourselves posted between the 46th Illinois and the 13th Missouri, our position being midway between the encampments of the 46th and 9th Illinois.*"

Colonel Wright, 13th Missouri, of McArthur's brigade, Second Division, but attached during the battle to Sherman's division, says:

"After advancing and falling back several times, the regiment was forced to retire, with all the others there, *to the road which crosses the Purdy road at right angles near General McArthur's headquarters. We here took up quarters for the night, bivouacking without fires within four hundred yards of our regimental camp.*"

The "Purdy road" here mentioned is the continuation of the right-hand road leading from the landing. The camp of the 9th Illinois was in the north-east angle of the intersection of that road with the River road, and General McArthur's headquarters were in the south-west angle of the same intersection. The camp of the 46th Illinois was located in the south-east angle of the intersection of the River road and a middle road leading west from the landing, about five hundred yards from McArthur's headquarters. These reports plainly identify General McClernand's seventh position, of which General Sherman formed part, with the River road between McArthur's and Hurlbut's headquarters. It is a full half-mile in rear of the position given to Sherman's division on the Thom map, and of the position which

General Sherman assigns to himself on his edition, with the deep hollow of Tillman's Creek intervening.

The struggle which drove General McClernand from his seventh position is described by that officer as follows:

" The enemy renewed the contest by trying to shell us from our position. . . . Advancing in heavy columns led by the Louisiana Zouaves to break our center, we awaited his approach within sure range, and opened a terrific fire upon him. The head of the column was instantly mowed down ; the remainder of it swayed to and fro for a few seconds, and turned and fled. This second success of the last two engagements terminated a conflict of ten and a half hours' duration, from 6 o'clock A. M. to 4:30 o'clock P. M., and probably saved our army, transports and all, from capture. Strange, however, at the very moment of the flight of the enemy, the right of our line gave way, and immediately after, notwithstanding the indignant and heroic resistance of Colonel Veatch, the left, comprising the [14th Illinois and 25th Indiana] was irresistibly swept back by the tide of fugitive soldiers and trains seeking vain security at the landing. . . . *Left unsupported and alone, the 20th and 17th Illinois, together with other portions of my division not borne back by the retreating multitude, retired in good order under the immediate command of Colonel Marsh and Lieutenant-Colonel Wood, and re-formed under my direction, the right resting near the former line, and the left at an acute angle with it. A more extended line, comprising portions of regiments, brigades, and divisions, was soon formed on this nucleus by the efforts of General Sherman, myself, and other officers. Here, in the eighth position occupied by my division during the day, we rested in line of battle upon our arms, uncovered and exposed to a drenching rain during the night.*"

This last position would locate McClernand, excepting his First Brigade, perhaps three hundred yards south of, and obliquely with reference to the right-hand road leading from the landing, facing a little to the west. His First Brigade is traced to within half a mile of the river, where it was rallied by its commander " in front of the camp-ground of the 14th Iowa," on the road to the landing. It did not join the division again until after the battle, but acted in connection with my troops. Colonel Veatch, who was on McClernand's left with the 14th Illinois and 25th Indiana in the seventh position, fell back and took " position on the road leading to the landing near the heavy siege-guns," and became reunited there with Hurlbut's division, to which he belonged. The space along the road in rear of McClernand was filled in with various fragments which constituted Sherman's command, including at last Buckland's two regiments. General Sherman says that Colonel Sweeny was with him. No doubt some of Sweeny's men also were there. It was the camp-ground of his brigade—the camp of his own regiment, the 52d Illinois, being immediately on the road. Two of his regiments were captured with Prentiss, and the remainder had been driven back from W. H. L. Wallace's right and virtually broken up. One of his regiments, the 50th Illinois, was sent in the morning to support Colonel Stuart on the extreme left, and shared the fate of the sufferers in that quarter. The space along the road between Sherman and Hurlbut was occupied by the remnant of Colonel Tuttle's brigade and a portion of McClernand's First Brigade which united itself to Tuttle. It was Tuttle's camp-ground. Two of his regiments had been captured with Prentiss.

From the reports of the 13th Missouri and 43d Illinois it is inferred that those two regiments did not move from their position on the River road in the last falling back. But that, if certain, is not important. They were at any rate substantially on the general line above indicated. The same, in a careless reading, might be presumed of the 46th Illinois, which was immediately on the left of the 43d. The report of that regiment says: "The regiments both *on my right and left fell back*, but my line did not *waver under the fire of the enemy*." But it evidently fell back at last, for the report continues: "After breakfast on Monday morning, still retaining my position on the right of Colonel Marsh's brigade, I moved with him until *I reached* and *went beyond* the ground of *our last engagement of Sunday*, where our pickets were driven in," etc. It remains now to determine the question of the extreme right of the general line.

General Sherman says, and his statement on that point is sustained by the reports, that Birge's sharp-shooters were immediately on his right and constituted the extreme right of the line. The official report of that regiment shows that during the afternoon it occupied a *"position near Colonel McArthur's headquarters" in an open field*. Its camp was in its rear along the opposite or east side of the River road. This would fix General Sherman's right at the cross-roads near McArthur's headquarters. It is more than a mile from the Snake Creek bridge. Other evidence confirms these positions. The official reports of Lew Wallace's division show that he marched along the River road from the bridge, and formed in line of battle. facing Tillman's Creek in front of the camp of Birge's sharp-shooters and the 81st Ohio, the right of the division being in front of the latter, and the left in front of the former; and that it came in actual contact with the " sharp-shooters," who occupied their camp that night and received the new-comers with cheers. This is clearly and more circumstantially explained by General Force in his book entitled " From Fort Henry to Corinth," page 163. He was present and commanded the right regiment of Lew Wallace's division on that occasion. The position thus assigned to Wallace must have taken his left well up to the cross-road at McArthur's headquarters, and covered the entire field toward the north; for the distance from the cross-road to the right of the camp of the 81st Ohio was only half a mile.

It is particularly to be observed that in no report, either from Sherman's division or from Lew Wallace's, is there any mention of actual contact or of any definite proximity of these two divisions on the evening of the 6th, or earlier than 10 o'clock on the morning of the 7th. The inference is, that at the time of Wallace's arrival and subsequently, no part of Sherman's division was on the River road, or anywhere along the heights of Tillman's Creek north of McArthur's headquarters. General Sherman, in his report, says: "General Wallace arrived from Crump's Landing shortly after dark and formed his line to my right and rear." That relative position could only exist by assuming that Sherman's command was on the road leading to the landing east of McArthur's headquarters, and nearly at right angles with Wallace,—a supposition which is strengthened by the condition indicated in Sherman's revised map, that Birge's sharp-shooters were on his right— not entirely in his front, as they would have been if his front had been on the River road. It is also sustained by General Buckland's statement in the

"Journal of the Society of the Army of the Tennessee" for 1881, p. 82. "About dark," he says, "General Wallace's division commenced arriving, and formed to the right of my brigade." Buckland states in his report and in the "Journal" that he lay "on the road." If he had been on the River road, Wallace would have come in contact with him, and when he formed in line would have been entirely in his front—not in rear or on his right. Buckland seems to know nothing about Birge's sharp-shooters. The probable explanation is that when he came along the road from the bridge they were on the west side of the road, in the field near McArthur's headquarters. After Lew Wallace arrived and formed in front of them, they probably retired to their camp on the east side of the road. The explanation of Buckland's position is that, after the retreat across Tillman's Creek from the west side, he found himself, as he says, near Snake Creek bridge "late in the afternoon, after the repulse of the right of the line," entirely apart from the rest of the army, and that to reëstablish his connection with it he started on the road to the landing, where one of his regiments actually went and remained overnight; and that he came upon the outer flank of the new line where General Sherman soon after found him, east of McArthur's headquarters, and thus placed himself where he is described by Sherman as being, between Birge's sharp-shooters and the rest of the line.

The Confederate reports mention a considerable appearance of force in a camp opposite their extreme left in the afternoon, evidently referring to McArthur's camp. The student of the reports will not be misled by this appearance; it was the force that clustered with Sherman on McClernand's right near McArthur's headquarters; by the 9th Illinois, 81st Ohio, and Birge's sharp-shooters, all belonging to McArthur's brigade; and by the movement of Buckland's regiments from the bridge as already explained. The sharp-shooters and the 81st Ohio had been posted at the bridge, and returned to their camps probably at the time of the retreat from the west side of Tillman's Creek. The 9th Illinois had during the morning been engaged on the extreme left under its brigade commander. It had lost 250 men out of 550, and was ordered to its camp "to replenish cartridge-boxes, clean guns, and be ready for action." While there at 3 o'clock it was ordered "to support the right wing of General Sherman's division," as the report expresses it, and in the subsequent engagements retired to within half a mile of the landing. Birge's sharp-shooters retained their position at or in front of their camp. The movements of the 81st Ohio are not very clearly defined, but in the advance next morning it is found on McClernand's left. The "10 or 12 guns" mentioned by General Sherman in his map-presentation speech as being near a ravine on his left, Sunday afternoon, were Taylor's battery, as it was called, though commanded by Captain Barrett, and Bouton's battery. The former had retired for ammunition from McClernand's camp, probably to near McArthur's headquarters, but afterward evidently went near the river, where it received "1 lieutenant and 24 men with 3 horses" from Fitch's battery. Bouton's battery was taken into action in the field in front of McClernand's right about 4 o'clock, and was forced to retire,

its support helping to draw off its guns. Both the battery and the support
went back toward the river, for in the advance next morning the support is
found on McClernand's left, and the battery was brought into service with
McCook in the afternoon. Sherman had no artillery with him on Monday
until about 10 o'clock. Major Taylor then brought up three pieces of an Illinois battery under Lieutenant Wood, not belonging to Sherman's command.
The final retreat from McClernand's seventh position, Sunday evening,
undoubtedly carried with it all of the fragments connected with Sherman
near McArthur's headquarters, along the road toward the river, where I
found him about dark, excepting Birge's sharp-shooters, the 13th Missouri,
and the 43d Illinois. The latter belonged to McClernand's Third Brigade,
but remained with the 13th Missouri Sunday night. After crossing Tillman's Creek next morning, both were brought into line on McClernand's
left, and did not form with Sherman, though the 13th Missouri subsequently
joined him.

My own observation as to the position and extent of General Grant's line
accords substantially with the evidence of the reports. In the dusk of the
evening after the close of the engagement on Sunday, I walked out with my
chief-of-staff, following the road and the line of
the troops. My object was to gain information
by which to determine the formation of my
divisions, and I not only observed all that I
could see at such an hour, but I made inquiry as
I passed along. I came to Hurlbut's left five
hundred yards from the river; I passed along
its front and came to troops that answered as
McClernand's, and which I supposed at the time
to constitute his division, but which were probably his First Brigade
only; I passed to
the front of these
troops, and when I
turned in toward the
road again, I came
upon Sherman's line,
as it happened, not
far from where he
was, and I was con-
ducted to him. It was
then growing dark.
I judge the distance
to have been about
three-quarters of a
mile from the river
— less than half a
mile from Hurlbut's

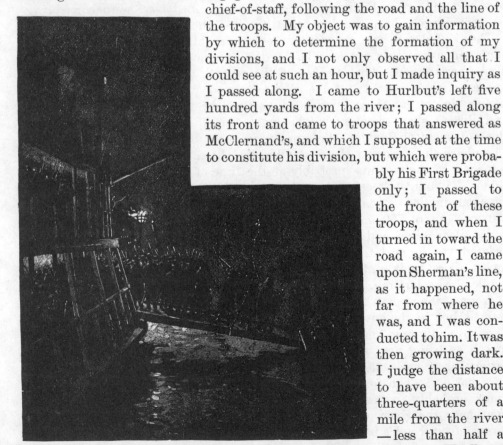

BUELL'S TROOPS DEBARKING AT PITTSBURG LANDING, SUNDAY NIGHT.

left, and I think now that it was near the camp of Colonel Sweeny's regiment, the 52d Illinois, that I found General Sherman.

The impression made upon my mind by that interview has remained as vivid as the circumstances were peculiar. I had no thought of seeing General Sherman when I set out, but on every score I was glad to meet him, and I was there to gain information. By what precise words I sought and he gave it, I would not pretend at this day to repeat. It is sufficient for the present to say that I learned the nature of the ground in front; that his right flank was some three hundred yards from us; and that the bridge by which Lew Wallace was to cross Snake Creek was to his right and rear at an angle, as he pointed, of about forty degrees. I do not know whether I asked the question, but I know now that it was a mile and a quarter from his flank, and that he did not cover it in any practical sense, though in advancing Wallace would approach by his right and rear. I also see now that I was mistaken in supposing that these several commands retained a regular organization and had distinct limits; whereas they were in fact much intermixed.

Of course we talked of other incidental matters. In all his career he has, I venture to say, never appeared to better advantage. There was the frank, brave

MAJOR-GENERAL THOMAS J. WOOD.
COPIED FROM AN ENGRAVING.

soldier, rather subdued, realizing the critical situation in which causes of some sort, perchance his own fault chiefly, had placed him, but ready, without affectation or bravado, to do anything that duty required of him. He asked me what the plans were for the morrow. I answered that I was going to attack the enemy at daylight, and he expressed gratification at my reply, though apparently not because of any unmixed confidence in the result. I had had no consultation with General Grant, and knew nothing of his purpose. I presumed that we would be in accord, but I had been only a few hours within the limits of his authority, and I did not look upon him as my commander, though I would zealously have obeyed his orders. General Sherman allowed me to take with me the map of which a fac-simile accompanies this article [page 496]. I never imagined that in the future it would have the interest which now attaches to it, and after the battle it was laid aside and forgotten.

Within two years after that meeting, quite contrary opinions developed themselves between General Sherman and myself concerning the battle of Shiloh, and his Memoirs give a different account of the interview above described. He says that he handed the map to my engineer-officer, Captain

Michler, who, in fact, was not present, and complains that it was never returned to him. He says that I grumbled about the stragglers, and that he feared I would not bring my army across the river. One would suppose that his fears would have been allayed by the fact that, at that very moment, my troops were arriving and covering his front as fast as legs and steamboats could carry them.

In the execution of the retreat described in the reports of McClernand and Sherman, from the west to the east side of Tillman's Creek, there was a quite thorough disintegration of divisions and brigades, lacking nothing but the pressure of a vigorous pursuit to convert it into a complete rout. In its seventh position, McClernand's division recovered some force and preserved a recognized organization; but not so with Sherman's. Indeed, in that division the disorganization occurred, as has already been stated, at an earlier period. In Hildebrand's brigade it was almost coincident with the enemy's first assault. With McDowell's it commenced with the unsuccessful attempt to form line of battle along the Purdy road, and was complete very soon after 1 o'clock; and these two brigades never recovered their aggregation again until after the battle. With Buckland's brigade also it occurred at the miscarriage at the Purdy road about 10 o'clock, but it was not so thorough as in the other brigades—at least it was afterward partially repaired during the first day, as his report explains. He says, after the retreat from his camp about 10 o'clock:

"We formed line on the Purdy road, but the fleeing mass from the left broke through our lines, and many of our men caught the infection and fled with the crowd. Colonel Cockerill became separated from Colonel Sullivan and myself, and was afterward engaged with part of his command at McClernand's camp. Colonel Sullivan and myself kept together, and made every effort to rally our men, but with very poor success. They had become scattered in all directions. We were borne considerably to the left, but finally succeeded in forming a line, and had a short engagement with the enemy, who made his appearance soon after our line was formed. The enemy fell back, and we proceeded to the road where you [General Sherman] found us. At this point I was joined by Colonel Cockerill, and we there formed line of battle and slept on our arms Sunday night. Colonel Sullivan, being out of ammunition, marched to the landing for a supply, and while there was ordered to support a battery at that point."

It is only after a close examination of the records that we can understand the full significance of the following passage in General Sherman's report:

"In this position we rested for the night. My command had become decidedly of a mixed character. Buckland's brigade was the only one with me that retained its organization. Colonel Hildebrand was personally there, but his brigade was not. Colonel McDowell had been severely injured by a fall from his horse, and had gone to the river, and the three regiments of his brigade were not in line. The 13th Missouri, Colonel Crafts J. Wright, had reported to me on the field, and fought well, retaining its regimental organization, and it formed part of my line during Sunday night and all of Monday; other fragments of regiments and companies had also fallen into my division, and acted with it during the remainder of the battle."

It thus appears that from about 1 o'clock until the time when General Sherman found Colonel Buckland with two regiments on the road from the bridge to the landing, not a single regiment of his division excepting Cockerill's, and not one prominent individual representative of it excepting that officer and

Colonel Hildebrand, was present with him. The only body of troops besides Cockerill's regiment having any recognized organization was the 13th Missouri, which belonged to another division. All the rest were squads or individual stragglers. In all the official reports, not a regiment or part of a regiment is described as being with him at this juncture or for several hours before. Of the 9 regiments that composed the 3 brigades under his immediate command at the church, only 5 rendered reports, and 3 of these were from Buckland's brigade. The division did not exist except in the person of its commander. Such is the story of the official reports. The number of men present could not have been large. Less than 1000, including Buckland's 2 regiments after they were found, would have told the number that lay on their arms in Sherman's ranks on Sunday night.

This explains the close relation of McClernand and Sherman during the last five hours of Sunday, and the identity of their experiences. General Sherman has nothing to report of his own command distinctively. Everything is conjunctive and general as between McClernand and himself. "*We* held this position, General McClernand and myself acting in perfect concert." "*General McClernand and I,* on consultation, selected a new line." "*We* fell back as well as we could." "The enemy's cavalry charged *us*, and was handsomely repulsed." General McClernand's account of this incident has been quoted on a preceding page. When Colonel Hildebrand lost his brigade, it is not with General Sherman that he is identified, but with McClernand, on whose staff he served part of the day. Hildebrand seems to have been active, but not under the direction of his division commander. "About 3 o'clock," he says, "I assumed command of a regiment already formed of fragmentary regiments. I marched in a north-western direction, where I aided a regiment of sharp-shooters in defeating the enemy in an attempt to flank our rear." This movement was evidently made from McClernand's and Sherman's seventh position, and the troops assisted were Birge's sharp-shooters. General Sherman makes no mention of this significant if not important occurrence. His right flank was threatened, and the regiment of sharp-shooters posted in the field near McArthur's headquarters met, and, in conjunction with Hildebrand's temporary regiment, repelled the danger.

We have in the official reports a good clew to the condition of McClernand's division also. It was in a far better state. It was shattered and worn, but it was represented by at least some recognized following of regiments and brigades. One of the brigades had five hundred men, and another, the commander reports, was "merely nominal," not long before McClernand took up his seventh position. In the last collision, one of the brigades became entirely separated from the division, and did not return to it until after the battle. Fifteen hundred, exclusive of that brigade, would cover the number of men that rested that night under McClernand's colors.

Hurlbut's division was in a somewhat better condition than either of the others. Its loss in killed and wounded was greater than McClernand's, but it had not, like the latter, been affected in its organization by oft-repeated shocks sustained in a cramped and embarrassing position, and his command had received some accessions from the driftings of other divisions. The estimate which he makes of his force is wholly fallacious. It could not have stood on the space which he occupied. There may have been two thousand men in his line on the night of the 6th. These three divisions, if they may be so called, and Tuttle's command, with Birge's sharp-shooters on the extreme right, and the reserve artillery on the left, which, according to General Grant's report, consisted of "four 20-pounder Parrott guns and a battery of rifled guns," constituted the line of battle, which extended a mile from the river. Five thousand men occupied it. Other partially organized fragments were crowded together about the river and the camps on the plateau, and with proper effort could have been fitted for good service; but no steps to that end were taken. The defect in the command that opened the way for the disaster, facilitated its progress at every step—the want of a strong executive hand guided by a clear organizing head. Some of these fragmentary commands sought places for themselves in the advance next day. The remnant of the Second Division under Colonel Tuttle was one of these. Indeed, it deserves a higher name. It presented itself to me on the field without orders, and rendered efficient service with my divisions. There may have been 1500 or 2000 men of these unrecognized commands that went to the front on Monday without instructions. Seven thousand men at the utmost, besides Lew Wallace's 5000, were ready Sunday night to take part in the struggle which was to be renewed in the morning. Of the original force, 7000 were killed or wounded, 3000 were prisoners, at least 15,000 were absent from the ranks and hopelessly disorganized, and about 30 pieces of artillery were in the hands of the enemy.

The physical condition of the army was an exact type of its moral condition. The ties of discipline, not yet of long enough duration or rigidly enough enforced to be very strong, were in much the largest part of the army thoroughly severed. An unbroken tide of disaster had obliterated the distance between grades, and brought all men to the standard of personal qualities. The feeble groups that still clung together were held by force of individual character more than by discipline, and a disbelief in the ability of the army unaided to extricate itself from the peril that environed it, was, I do not hesitate to affirm, universal. In my opinion, that feeling was shared by the commander himself. A week after the battle the army had not recovered from its shattered and prostrated condition. On the 14th, three days after Halleck's arrival, he instructed Grant: "Divisions and brigades should, where necessary, be reorganized and put in position, and all stragglers returned to their companies and regiments. Your army is not now in condition to resist an attack." We are told that the enemy had stragglers too. Yes, every cause which demands effort and sacrifice will have them; but there is a difference between the straggling which is not restrained by the smile of fortune, and that which tries to elude the pursuit of fate — it is the difference between victory and defeat. The Confederates in their official reports make no concealment of their skeletons, but when the time for action arrived they were vital bodies, and, on Sunday, always in sufficient force to do the work at last.

General McClernand, it will have been observed, ascribes the breaking up of his seventh position to a panic among the troops, but the other reports show a different reason. Colonel Veatch on McClernand's left says:

"Our men were much encouraged by the strength of our position, and our fire was telling with terrible effect. Our forces were eager to advance and charge him [the enemy], when we were surprised by his driving back the whole left wing of our army, and advancing close to our rear near General Hurlbut's headquarters. A dense mass of baggage wagons and artillery crowded upon our ranks, while we were exposed to a heavy fire of the enemy both in front and rear."

General Hurlbut thus describes the crisis at that stage of the battle:

"I had hoped to make a stand on the line of my camp, but masses of the enemy were pressing rapidly on each flank, while their light artillery was closing rapidly in the rear. On reaching the 24-pounder siege-guns in battery near the river, I again succeeded in forming line of battle in rear of the guns."

We see here that there was a stern cause for the falling back. It was the tide of defeat and pursuit from the left wing of the army, and was compulsory in the strictest sense. How fortunate that it did not set in an hour earlier, and strike in flank the disorganized material of the right wing as it struggled across the ravines of Tillman's Creek! How more than fortunate that the onward current of the victor was obstructed still an hour longer by the unyielding tenacity of the remaining regiments of Wallace and Prentiss! From the self-assuring interview in which, according to one of General Sherman's reminiscences, it was "agreed that the enemy had expended the furor of his attack" at 4 o'clock, and General Grant told the "anecdote of his Donelson battle," that officer was aroused by the renewal of the din of the strife, and made his way to the river through the disorganized throng of his retreating army. While those mutual felicitations were in progress, the enemy, a mile to the left, was disarming and marching six captured regiments to the rear. Thus disembarrassed, his *furor* revived, and manifested itself at last at the very landing. What worse state of affairs than this could have existed when at noon General Grant wrote: "If you will get upon the field, leaving all your baggage on the east bank of the river, it will be a move to our advantage, and possibly save the day to us"?

Under the circumstances here described, General Grant and General Sherman have said that reënforcements other than Lew Wallace's division were in nowise necessary at the close of the first day, and that, without reference to them, General Grant would have assumed the offensive and defeated the Confederate army next morning. Those who study the subject attentively will find no ground to accept that declaration as regards either the purpose or the result. The former indeed presents an intangible question which it would seem to be useless to discuss. At the time it is alleged to have been entertained, the reënforcements were actually at hand, and their presence gives to the announcement the semblance of a vain boast, which could never have been put to the test of reality. That with the reënforcements from my army, General Grant confidently expected that the enemy would be defeated the following day, it is impossible to doubt; but it was not known, Sunday night, that the enemy had withdrawn from our immediate front, and the evidence establishes that General Grant had not determined upon or had not promulgated a plan of action in the morning. Not an order was given or a note of preparation sounded for the struggle which, with or without his assistance, was to begin at daybreak. To my certain knowledge, if words and actions were not wholly misleading, General Sherman, when I saw him on the night of the 6th, did not consider that any instructions had been given for battle, and if he had such instructions he did not obey them. His report sustains the impression which I derived from our interview. "At daylight on Monday," he says, "I received General Grant's orders to advance and recapture our original camps." Then only it was that he dispatched several members of his staff to bring up all the men they could find. Is that the way in which General Sherman would have acquitted himself of the obligation of orders received the day before to engage in battle? I answer unhesitatingly, No! The reports of the other division commanders are to the same effect. General McClernand says: "Your [General Grant's] order of the morning of the 7th for a forward movement," etc. The hour of the delivery of this order is indicated approximately by the following passage in the report of Colonel Marsh:

"At daylight on Monday morning the men in line were supplied with some provisions. While this was being done firing opened on our right, afterwards ascertained to come from a portion of General Lew Wallace's command. Directly afterwards, firing commenced to our left and front, both artillery and musketry, supposed by me to be a portion of General Buell's command, who, I had been informed during the night, had taken position on our left and considerably in advance. I now received orders from General McClernand to throw out skirmishers and follow with my whole command."

We must presume that General McClernand proceeded to the execution of General Grant's order as soon as it was received, which must then have been after the commencement of the battle in front of Nelson.

General Hurlbut says: "On Monday, about 8 A. M., my division was formed in line close to the river-bank, and I obtained a few crackers for my men. About 9 A. M. I was ordered by General Grant to move up to the support of General McClernand." Colonel Tuttle, commanding the Second Division, acted without any orders. He says: "On Monday morning I collected all of the division that could be found, and such other detached regiments as volunteered to join me, and formed them in column by battalion closed in mass as a reserve for General Buell." The action of General Lew Wallace was not the result of orders, but proceeded from his own motion on discovering the enemy in his front at daylight across Tillman's Hollow. While that action was in progress, General Grant came up and gave Wallace "the direction of his attack." Nelson had been in motion an hour, and was sharply engaged before these orders were given.

General Grant's official reports of the battle are in accord with the subordinate reports upon this question. In his first telegraphic announcement of the battle to General Halleck, he says:

"Yesterday the rebels attacked us here with an overwhelming force, driving our troops in from their advanced position to near the landing. General Wallace was immediately ordered up from Crump's Landing, and in the evening, one division of General Buell's army and General Buell in person arrived. During the night one other division arrived, and still another to-day. *This morning, at the break of day, I ordered an attack,* which resulted in a fight, which continued until late this afternoon, with severe loss on both sides, but a complete repulse of the enemy. *I shall follow to-morrow far enough to see that no immediate renewal of an attack is contemplated.*"

In his more detailed report of April 9th he says:

"During the night [Sunday] all was quiet, and *feeling that a great moral advantage would be gained by becoming the attacking party, an advance was ordered as soon as day dawned.* The result was a gradual repulse of the enemy at all parts of the line from morning until probably 5 o'clock in the afternoon, when it became evident that the enemy was retreating. Before the close of the action the advance of General T. J. Wood's division arrived in time to take part in the action. *My force was too much fatigued, from two days' hard fighting and exposure in the open air to a drenching rain during the intervening night, to pursue immediately.* Night closed in cloudy and with heavy rain, making the roads impracticable for artillery by the next morning. General Sherman, however, followed the enemy, *finding that the main part of the army had retreated in good order.*"

Several points worthy of note present themselves in these dispatches of General Grant. There is still, at the close of the second day, the impression of the enemy's overwhelming force, which the day before he "estimated at over one hundred thousand men." He felt on Monday, after the arrival of reënforcements to the number of 25,000 fresh troops, that "a great moral advantage would be gained by becoming the attacking party." There was, then, a question in his mind, namely, to attack, or to await attack; it was necessary to consider all the advantages, moral and physical; he concluded to secure the former at least, and accordingly gave the order, not on Sunday, but on Monday "at break of day," to attack. The severity of the contest on Monday is affirmed in both dispatches; it was of such a nature as to prevent an immediate pursuit, which at any rate he would only make the next morning after the battle, far enough to see that no immediate renewal of the attack was contemplated. The pursuit was made on that plan, and found "that the main part of the army had retreated in good order." If the fact were not duly authenticated, one would wonder whether these dispatches were actually written by an officer who, twenty-three years afterward, said with boastful assurance over his own signature, "Victory was assured when Wallace arrived with his division of 5000 effective veterans, even if there had been no other support!"

With this tedious but necessary review of the results of the first day, I take up the story of the second.

THE engagement was brought on, Monday morning, not by General Grant's order, but by the advance of Nelson's division, along the River road in line of battle, at the first dawn of day, followed by Crittenden's division in column. The enemy was encountered at 5:20 o'clock, and a little in advance of Hurlbut's camp Nelson was halted while Crittenden came into line on his right. By this time the head of McCook's division came up and was formed on the right of Crittenden. Before McCook's rear brigade was up the line moved forward, pushing back the enemy's light troops, until Nelson and Crittenden reached the very position occupied by Hurlbut, Prentiss, and W. H. L. Wallace at 4

MAJOR-GENERAL THOMAS L. CRITTENDEN.
FROM A PHOTOGRAPH.

o'clock the previous day, where the enemy was found in force. McCook was on the north side of the western Corinth road, and eventually swept across half of McClernand's camp and released his headquarters from the grasp of the enemy. The "Hornets' Nest" was in front of Crittenden's left brigade, and "the peach orchard" and the ground where Albert Sidney Johnston fell were in front of Nelson.

Without following the vicissitudes of the struggle in this part of the field, I enter with a little more detail, but still cursorily, upon the operations of Grant's troops, which have not been connectedly explained in any official report. The action here was commenced by Lew Wallace, one of whose batteries at half-past 5 o'clock opened fire on the enemy, who was discovered on the high ground across Tillman's Hollow. There is some diversity of statement among the official reports as to the priority of artillery firing in front of Nelson and Wallace. Colonel Hovey, who was in immediate support of Wallace's battery, gives the priority to Nelson, while Colonel Marsh, who was half a mile farther to the left, gives it to Wallace. But this is unimportant. Nelson was in motion three-quarters of an hour before that time, and had been engaged with the enemy's light troops. The first artillery fire was from the enemy, Nelson at first having no artillery. Wallace's action was not yet aggressive, no orders having been given for his advance; but while the firing was in progress General Grant came up, and gave him his "direction of attack, which was formed at a right angle with the river, with which at the time his line ran almost parallel." The enemy's battery and its supports having been driven from the opposite height by the artillery of Wallace, the latter moved his line forward about 7 o'clock, crossed the hollow, and gained the crest of the hill almost without opposition. "Here," he says, "as General Sherman's division, next on my left, had not made its appearance to support my advance, a halt was ordered for it to come up." Wallace was now on the edge of the large oblong field which was in front of the encampment of McClernand's right brigade.

The next of Grant's commands to advance was McClernand's. The orders to that effect have already been cited, and their execution is explained by Colonel Marsh, into whose brigade what was present of McClernand's division seems to have merged. He says:

"Moving steadily forward for half a mile, I discovered a movement of troops on the hill nearly a quarter of a mile in front. Dispatching scouts to ascertain who they were, they were met by a message from Colonel Smith, commanding a [the left] brigade of the Third Division [Wallace's], informing me that he would take position on the right and wait my coming up."

Sherman, it thus appears, was not yet in motion. Hurlbut moved out about 9 o'clock, and formed one brigade on McClernand's left.

When Lew Wallace advanced across Tillman's Hollow, followed next on the left by McClernand, the force opposed to him fell gradually back upon reënforcements beyond the field on the edge of which was the encampment of McClernand's First Brigade; the enemy's left then clinging a little to the bluffs of Owl Creek in that quarter, but yielding without a very stubborn resistance, chiefly because of McCook's vigorous pressure along the western Corinth road, until it fell into a general line running through the center of McClernand's camp, and nearly parallel with the Hamburg and Purdy road. This swinging back of the enemy's left, and the direction of the Owl Creek bluffs, naturally caused a change in the direction of Wallace's front, until about 10 o'clock it faced south, at right angles to its direction in the beginning. A sharp artillery contest and some infantry fighting had been going on all the time. It was at 10 o'clock, according to Sherman's report, that McClernand formed line obliquely in rear of the camp of his First Brigade, to advance against the enemy's position. Here for the first time Sherman's division appears in the movement, from which its absence at an earlier period is mentioned by both McClernand and Wallace. The statement in General Sherman's report, in regard to its movements, is as follows:

CAPTURE OF A CONFEDERATE BATTERY.

Colonel Robert H. Sturgess (8th Illinois Infantry) says in his official report that while awaiting orders on the Purdy road, during the morning of the second day's fight, "General Crittenden ordered the Eighth and Eighteenth (Illinois) to take a rebel battery which some regiment had endeavored to capture, but had been driven back with heavy loss. The men received the order with a cheer, and charged on a double-quick. The enemy, after firing a few shots, abandoned his guns and retreated to the woods. My color-bearer rushed up and planted his colors on one of the guns, and the color-bearer of the Eighteenth took possession of another."

"At daylight I received General Grant's orders to advance and recapture our original camps. I dispatched several members of my staff to bring up all the men they could find, and especially the brigade of Colonel Stuart, which had been separated from the division all the day before; and at the appointed time the division, or, rather, what remained of it, with the 13th Missouri and other fragments, marched forward and reoccupied the ground on the extreme right of General McClernand's camp, where we attracted the fire of a battery located near Colonel McDowell's former headquarters. Here I remained patiently waiting for the sound of General Buell's advance upon the main Corinth road. About 10 A. M. the heavy firing in that direction and its steady approach satisfied me, and General Wallace being on our right flank with his well-conducted division, I led the head of my column to General McClernand's right, formed line of battle, facing south, with Buckland's brigade directly across the ridge, and Stuart's brigade on its right in the woods, and thus advanced slowly and steadily under a heavy fire of musketry and artillery."

The contest thus inaugurated in and around McClernand's camp involved the whole of Grant's available force and McCook's division of the Army of the Ohio, and continued with great violence from 10 until 4 o'clock. The significant facts connected with it are, the narrowness of the space covered by the interior divisions,—McClernand's, Hurlbut's, and Sherman's,—the lapping over them by McCook, so as to form, in fact, a connection with the division of Wallace on the extreme right, and the decisive part ascribed to McCook's division in that part of the field in the reports of McClernand, Wallace, and Sherman. General McClernand says:

"Here one of the severest conflicts ensued that occurred during the two days. We drove the enemy back . . . to the edge of a field . . . where reserves came to his support. Our position at this moment was most critical, and a repulse seemed inevitable; but fortunately the Louisville Legion, forming part of General Rousseau's brigade, came up at my request and succored me. Extending and strengthening my line, this gallant body poured into the enemy's ranks one of the most terrible fires I ever witnessed. Thus breaking its [his] center, it [he] fell back in disorder, and thenceforth he was beaten at all points."

Wallace mentions particularly an important service rendered to the left of his division at a crisis in its operations, by one of McCook's regiments.

Colonel McGinnis, of the 11th Indiana, whose regiment was on Wallace's extreme left, describes this incident as follows:

"At 2:30 o'clock I discovered that the Federal forces on our left were falling back and the rebels advancing, and that they were nearly in rear of our left flank. I immediately notified you [the brigade commander] of their position, changed front with our left wing, opened our fire upon them, and sent to you for assistance. During this the most trying moment to us of the day, I received your order to fall back if it got too hot for us. . . . Fortunately and much to our relief, at this critical moment the 32d Indiana, Colonel Willich, came up on our left, and with their assistance the advancing enemy was compelled to retire."

General Sherman says:

"We advanced until we reached the point where the Corinth road crosses the line of McClernand's camp, and here I saw for the first time the well-ordered and compact columns of General Buell's Kentucky forces, whose soldierly movements at once gave confidence to our newer and less-disciplined forces. Here I saw Willich's regiment advance upon a point of water-oaks and thicket, behind which I knew the enemy was in great strength, and enter it in beautiful style. Then arose the severest musketry fire I ever heard, which lasted some twenty minutes, when this splendid regiment had to fall back. This green point of timber is about five hundred yards east of Shiloh Meeting House, and it was evident that here was to be the struggle. The enemy could be seen forming his lines to the south. . . . This was about 2 o'clock P. M. Willich's regiment had been repulsed, but a whole brigade of McCook's division advanced beautifully, deployed, and entered this dreaded woods. . . . Rousseau's brigade moved in splendid order steadily to the front, sweeping everything before it."

This occurred in front of Sherman, who was between McClernand and Wallace, for he says: "I ordered my Second Brigade . . . to form on its right, and my Fourth Brigade, Colonel Buckland, on its right, all to advance abreast with this Kentucky brigade." Of the action of McCook's division, General Sherman further says: "I concede that General McCook's splendid division from Kentucky drove back the enemy along the Corinth road, which was the great central line of this battle."

The conclusion to be drawn from these several reports is that at this stage of the battle McCook's division reached across and practically connected the Army of the Ohio with Wallace's division, which formed the extreme right of Grant's force, and that its steady valor and effective service, not without the coöperation of McClernand's, Hurlbut's, and Sherman's commands, decided the issue of the conflict on that portion of the field. The result, however, was not brought about without the concurrence of decisive action at other points.

While the battle was going on in McClernand's camp, it raged with great fury from an earlier hour in front of Nelson and Crittenden on the left, and vigorously but with less destructive effects in front of Wallace on the right. As soon as the enemy's right began to yield, the splendid batteries of Mendenhall and Terrill directed an enfilading fire upon the Confederate batteries playing fiercely upon McCook, and they were soon silenced. General Sherman ascribes that result to the action of two pieces of artillery to which he says he gave personal direction, but it is probable that he mistook the principal cause. A Confederate view of the contest in front of Nelson and Crittenden is seen in the report of Colonel Trabue, whose brigade at a certain stage of the battle (about 1 o'clock) was moved with Anderson's brigade to their right, in front of Crittenden. The report describes the conflict at this point as terrific, the ground being crossed and recrossed four times in the course of it. I refer to it, chiefly because in some accounts of the battle it has erroneously been identified with McCook's front, where Trabue's brigade was first engaged.

Without going further into details in which the official reports abound, it may be sufficient to add briefly, that at 4 o'clock the flag of the Union floated again upon the line from which it had been driven the previous day, and General Grant's troops at once resumed their camps.

What more need be said? Must I sketch the scenes with twenty thousand of the soldiers of the Army of the Ohio left out of their place in the combat, as it is described by General Grant and his own officers? Shall I not, indeed, already have wearied the reader with the citation of evidence to substantiate a view of the case which unbiased intelligence is forbidden to deny?

But if the Army of the Ohio had not arrived, and General Grant had remained on the defensive, what then? Some of those who frankly acknowledge the reality of their discomfiture on Sunday, like now to believe with natural pride, the difficulties that beset them then being far in the past, that they would have been more successful the second day; and it has been argued that the withdrawal of the Confederates from their advanced positions on the night of the 6th threw doubt upon the final result. A newspaper interviewer has even said for General Grant that they were then preparing to retreat. The inconsistency of that observation is evident. A general who stops to fight a fresh army is not likely to have had it in contemplatation to flee before one that he had already defeated on the same ground. The published reports show that the withdrawal on Sunday night did not proceed from any faltering of the Confederate commander. On the contrary, he believed the victory to have been substantially won, and that the fruit would certainly be gathered the following day. His confidence in that respect was shared in the fullest manner by his entire army, backed by a particularly able body of high officers. All demanded to be led against the last position: not one doubted the result. We can imagine the effort such an army would have put forth when animated by such a spirit.

With the usual apologies for defeat on Monday, they rated their strength at 20,000 men, but, with the fruits of victory in view, it will be safe to say they would have brought at least 25,000 into action; and it has been claimed that 25,000, according to the Confederate method of computation, would have been equal to about 28,000 according to the Federal method. Their relative strength would have been materially increased by the large accession of captured cannon. They had also improved their condition by having exchanged their inferior arms for better ones which they had captured. Comparatively, the enemy was in a more efficient state than before the battle.

The Union ranks might have been swelled to 15,000 — not more. That force on such ground could not have ventured to cover a line of more than a mile — its left at the river, and its right near the ravines of Tillman's Creek. The high ground beyond the creek would have enfiladed it, and the ravines would have afforded a lodgment and shelter for the enemy. Dill's ravine on the left might also have proved an element of weakness, and though that flank could not be turned, the peculiar advantage of position that aided the Union troops on the left so much on Sunday, would not have existed on Monday — the field of action in front was a uniform wooded surface.

Nowhere in history is the profane idea that, in a fair field fight, Providence is on the side of the strongest battalions, more uniformly sustained than in our Civil War. It presents no example of the triumph of 15,000 or even 20,000 men against 25,000. It affords some such instances where the stronger force was surprised by rapid and unexpected movements, and still others where it was directed with a want of skill against chosen positions strengthened by the art of defense; but nowhere else. The weaker force is uniformly defeated or compelled to retire. In this case the missiles of the assailant would have found a target in the battle-line of the defense, and in the transportation and masses of stragglers crowded together about the landing. The height of the bluff would have rendered the gun-boats powerless; the example of Belmont could only have been partially repeated, if at all; the bulk of the defeated force must have laid down its arms. There are those who argue that General Grant's personal qualities were a guarantee for his triumph. That is a poor sort of logic, and thousands of patriotic citizens, not unfriendly to General Grant, would draw back in alarm from the contemplation of any contingency that would have deprived the Union cause of its superior numbers at more than one period of his career.

In the usual extravagant newspaper dispatches from the field of battle, there was a statement of charges led by General Grant and his staff, which were assumed to have decided the fate of the day on Monday, or at least to have given a crowning touch to the victory. It would be a satire to reproduce that statement in its original form at this time. Its adoption, however, by various books and sketches, and especially the reference to such an incident by General Grant in his recent " Century " article [see page 465], makes it properly an object of inquiry. Such an act as leading a charge is a conspicuous incident rarely resorted to by the commander of an army. General Grant in some former newspaper interview is made to assume that General Sidney Johnston lost his life under such circumstances, from which he argues the failing fortune of the Confederate attack on Sunday. General Johnston's conduct in that affair is described in the Confederate reports. It was an outburst of impatient valor not caused by any crisis in the battle, though an attack by his troops at a certain point had been repulsed. He did not lose his life in the attack, and the most substantial successes of the Confederates were achieved at a later hour. We likewise naturally look in the official reports for a circumstantial account of the charge said to have been led by General Grant, for no colonel of a regment is likely to overlook the honor of having been led in a charge by the commander of the army.

In the report of Colonel Veatch of Hurlbut's division, there occurs the following passage: " Maj.-Gen. Grant now ordered me forward to charge the enemy. I formed my brigade in column of battalions, and moved forward in double-quick through our deserted camps and to the thick woods beyond our lines in pursuit of the retreating enemy, following until we were in advance of our other forces, and were ordered to fall back by General Buell." It is proper to remark that I witnessed this movement. I was in advance on the line toward which it was made, and understand its bearing. It does not answer the description of a charge led by General Grant, since he is not said to have been present in it.

In the report of General Rousseau occurs the following:

" When thus repulsed, the enemy fell back and his retreat began ; soon after which I saw two regiments of Government troops advancing in double-quick time across the open fields in our front, and saw that one of them was the 1st Ohio, which had been moved to our left to wait for ammunition. I galloped to the regiment and ordered it to halt, as I had not ordered the movement, but was informed that it was advancing by order of General Grant, whom I then saw in rear of the line with his staff. I ordered the regiment to advance with the other, which it did some two or three hundred yards farther, when it was halted, and a fire was opened upon it from one of our camps, then occupied by the enemy. The fire was instantly returned, and the enemy soon fled, after wounding eight men of the 1st Ohio."

There is in the official reports no other mention of such an occurrence. This must have been the charge referred to, though it does not satisfy the description, since it appears that General Grant was not taken into the enemy's fire ; and there is nothing in it which fills the definition of a charge. The professional soldier at least understands that the term implies something more serious than a movement of troops upon the field of battle, even at a rapid pace, in the presence of an enemy. But putting out of the question all appropriate distinctions in the use of terms, there was nothing in the occasion or in these simple movements which promised any advantage, or entitled them to the slightest prominence. The enemy had retired from the last line, and was believed to be in retreat; but he had withdrawn in good order, and it is known that he halted a half-mile beyond, fully prepared to repel a careless pursuit. The topographical feature of larger fields and intervening woods, made the left and left-center of the battle-field more difficult for attack than the ground about McClernand's camp, as was illustrated by the battle of the previous day. The antagonists, except when in immediate contact, were kept at a greater distance apart, and were more screened from the observation of each other. The resistance, quelled for the moment, would be renewed unexpectedly by reënforcements or on a new line with increased vigor, and did not always allow the assailant to retain the advantage he had gained.

Nelson and Crittenden were working their way step by step over this difficult ground, when the cheers of victory commenced on the right where the enemy could be better observed. It was my misfortune to know nothing about the topography in front, and when at that moment the enemy on the left was found to be yielding readily to our advance, it was my mistake to suppose that the retirement was more precipitate and disordered than proved to be the case. On that supposition Nelson was ordered rapidly to the lower ford of Lick Creek, by which I supposed a part of the enemy had advanced and would retreat, and was thus out of position for the state of the case as it turned out. The last attack of Crittenden was made through thick woods, and his division had become a good deal scattered; but a brigade of Wood's division came up just then and was pushed forward on the eastern Corinth road. It soon came upon and engaged the enemy's skirmishers, and was attracting a flank fire from a battery a considerable distance off on the right. The orderly withdrawal of the enemy was now discovered, and indicated that a single brigade unsupported would be insufficient for a pursuit. Wood's brigade was therefore halted while its skirmishers occupied the enemy's cavalry, and orders were sent to McCook and Crittenden to form on the new line. Just at that moment a feeble column was seen to the right and rear of Wood's brigade, moving in a direction which would bring it into the flank fire of the enemy's artillery on the right. I therefore ordered it to be halted until other dispositions were made; but, misapprehending the object of the order, or deeming perhaps that enough had been done for one day, it withdrew altogether, and, like the rest of Grant's troops, retired to its camp. Following the same example, and most probably with General Grant's authority, McCook's division had started to the river. Before these misconceptions could be corrected, and my divisions got into position, night came on, and the time for a further forward movement passed for the day. Indeed, while my troops were being called up, I received from General Grant, who had retired to the landing, the following letter:

"HEADQUARTERS DIST. OF W. TENN., PITTSBURG, April 7, 1862. MAJOR-GENERAL D. C. BUELL. GEN.: When I left the field this evening, my intention was to occupy the most advanced position possible for the night, with the infantry engaged through the day, and follow up our success with cavalry and fresh troops expected to arrive during my last absence on the field. The great fatigue of our men — they having been engaged in two days' fight, and subject to a march yesterday and a fight to-day — would preclude the idea of making any advance to-night without the arrival of the expected reënforcements. My plan, therefore, will be to feel out in the morning, with all the troops on the outer lines, until our cavalry force can be organized (one regiment of your army will finish crossing soon), and a sufficient artillery and infantry support to follow them are ready for a move. Under the instructions which I have previously received, and a dispatch also of to-day from Major-General Halleck, it will not then do to advance beyond Pea Ridge, or some point which we can reach and return in a day. General Halleck will probably be here himself to-morrow. Instructions have been sent to the division commanders not included in your command, to be ready in the morning either to find if an enemy was in front, or to advance. Very respectfully, your obedient servant,

U. S. GRANT, Major-General Commanding."

This letter implies the hypothesis expressed also in General Grant's dispatch of the same evening to General Halleck, that the enemy might still be in our front with the intention of renewing the attack. I make no comment on that point further than to contrast it with the later pretensions with which the battle has been reviewed by General Grant and his friends. The idea is again indicated in his orders to his division commanders on the 8th:

" I have instructed Taylor's cavalry to push out the road toward Corinth to ascertain if the enemy have retreated. . . . Should they be retreating, I want all the cavalry to follow them."

Something in the same vein, which I would by no means be understood as dwelling upon censoriously, is seen in a dispatch of the next day to Halleck.

" I do not " [he says] " like to suggest, but it appears to me that it would be demoralizing upon our troops here to be forced to retire upon the opposite bank of the river, and unsafe to remain on this many weeks without large reënforcements."

The passage is chiefly noteworthy as showing that the fault of Shiloh was not in an excess of rashness or contempt for the adversary, and that the lesson of the occasion had not yet pointed out a means of security other than in reënforcements or retreat. The introduction of the evidence is not to be ascribed to any motive of disparagement. It is entirely pertinent to the subject under consideration.

General Grant has recently admitted that a pursuit ought to have been made, and vaguely intimates that somebody else than himself was responsible that it was not done. The reason given in his letter to me is, of course, insufficient. General McCook may have told him that his men were hungry and tired; but if the order had been issued, both McCook and his troops would cheerfully have shown how much tired and hungry soldiers can do when an emergency demands it. If General Grant meant to imply that I was responsible that the pursuit was not made, I might perhaps answer that it is always to be expected that the chief officer in command will determine the course to be pursued at such a juncture, when he is immediately upon the ground; but I inwardly imposed upon myself the obligation of employing the army under my command as though the whole duty of the occasion rested upon it. There was no doubt in my mind or hesitation in my conduct as to the propriety of continuing the action, at least as long as the enemy

SCENE IN A UNION FIELD-HOSPITAL.

was in our presence, as I considered him still to be; and I make no attempt
to excuse myself or blame others when I say that General Grant's troops, the
lowest individual among them not more than the commander himself, appear
to have thought that the object of the battle was sufficiently accomplished
when they were reinstated in their camps; and that in some way that idea
obstructed the reorganization of my line until a further advance that day
became impracticable.

MUCH harsh criticism has been passed upon General Lew Wallace for having failed to reach the field in time to participate in the battle on Sunday.
The naked fact is apt to be judged severely, and the reports made a year
afterward by General Grant's staff-officers — the report of Colonel Rawlins
especially — are calculated to increase the unfavorable impression. But some
qualification of that evidence must be made, on account of the anxiety produced in the minds of those officers by their peculiar connection with the
exciting circumstances of the battle. The statement of Rawlins is particularly to be received with reservation. They found Wallace on a different
road from the one by which they expected him, and assumed that he was
wrongfully there. Rawlins pretends to give the words of a verbal order that
would have taken him to a different place. Wallace denies that version of
the order, and the circumstances do not sustain it. [See page 607.] He was

on the road to and not far from the upper ford of Owl Creek, which would have brought him on the right flank of the Federal line, as it was in the morning, and as he presumed it still to be. It would have been at least an honest if not a reasonable interpretation of the order, that took him to a point where the responsibility and danger were liable to be greatly increased. The impression of Major Rowley, repeated more strongly by General Grant in his "Century" article, that when found he was farther from the battle-field than when he started, the map shows to have been incorrect. The statement of Rawlins, that he did not make a mile and a half an hour, is also not correct of the whole day's march. He actually marched nearly 15 miles in six hours and a half. That is not particularly rapid marching, but it does not indicate any loitering. At the same time it must be said that, under the circumstances, the manner in which the order was given to Wallace is liable to unqualified disapproval, both as it concerned the public interest and the good name of the officer.

To these qualifying facts it must be added that a presumption of honest endeavor is due to Wallace's character. He did good service at Donelson, and at Shiloh on the 7th, and on no other occasion have his zeal and courage been impugned. The verdict must perhaps remain that his action did not respond to the emergency as it turned out, but that might fall far short of a technical criminality, unless under a more austere standard of discipline than prevailed at that, or indeed at any other period of the war. If he had moved energetically after McPherson and Rawlins arrived and informed him of the urgency of the occasion, no just censure could be cast upon his conduct. The reports of those officers imply that he did not do so; but McPherson, who was more likely to be correct, is least positive on that point. It would probably be easy in any of the armies to point to similar examples of a lack of ardent effort which led to grave disappointment without being challenged, and to many more that would have been attended with serious consequences if any emergency had arisen. It was a defect in the discipline which it was not possible at that time to remedy completely.

WHEN this article was urged upon me by the recent revival of the discussion, I was advised by friends in whose judgment I have great confidence, to write an *impersonal* account of the battle. The idea was perfectly in harmony with my disposition, but a moment's reflection showed me that it was impracticable. It would ignore the characteristics which have made the battle of Shiloh the most famous, and to both sides the most interesting of the war. The whole theme is full of personality. The battle might be called, almost properly, a personal one. It was ushered in by faults that were personal, and the resistance that prolonged it until succor came was personal. This does not pretend to be a history of it, but only a review of some of the prominent facts which determined its character and foreshadowed its result. Even this fragmentary treatment of the subject would be incomplete without a revision of the roll of honor. The task is not difficult, for the evidence is not meager or doubtful. It says of McClernand, that, crippled at the start by the rudeness of the unexpected attack and the wreck of the division in his front, before he had time well to establish his line, he struggled gallantly and long with varying fortune to keep back the columns of the enemy; and though he failed in that, he was still able to present an organized nucleus which attracted the disrupted elements of other divisions: of Hurlbut, that he posted the two brigades under his immediate command, not in the strongest manner at first, but with judgment to afford prompt shelter to the defeated division of Prentiss, and maintained his front with some serious reverses to his left flank, for 7 hours and until his left was turned, with a greater list of mortality than any other division sustained: of W. H. L. Wallace, that, never dislodged, he sacrificed his life in a heroic effort with Prentiss to maintain his front between the enemy and the landing: of Prentiss, that with the rawest troops in the army his vigilance gave the earliest warning of the magnitude of the danger, and offered a resolute resistance to its approach; that, though overwhelmed and broken in advance, he rallied in effective force on the line of Hurlbut and Wallace, and firmly held his ground until completely surrounded and overpowered: and of Sherman, that he, too, strove bravely, but from an early hour with a feeble and ineffective force, to stay the tide of disaster for which his shortcoming in the position of an advanced guard was largely responsible; but it discloses no fact to justify the announcement of General Halleck that he "saved the fortune of the day on the 6th." On the contrary it shows, that, of all the division commanders, not one was less entitled to that distinction. This will be a strange and may seem like a harsh utterance to many readers, but it is the verdict of the record. The similar indorsement of General Grant a year later, that "he held the key-point to the landing," is equally alien to the evidence, and still further without intelligent meaning. If the key-point was any other than the landing itself, it was on the left where the attack was strongest and the resistance longest maintained.

Into the list of brave men in the inferior grades — captains and even lieutenants who for the moment led the wrecks of regiments and brigades, and field-officers who represented brigades and divisions, and who poured out their lives on the field or survived its carnage — I cannot here pretend to enter, though it is a most interesting chapter in the battle.

And of Grant himself — is nothing to be said? The record is silent and tradition adverse to any marked influence that he exerted upon the fortune of the day. The contemporaneous and subsequent newspaper accounts of personal adventure are alike destitute of authenticity and dignity. If he could have done anything in the beginning, he was not on the ground in time. The determining act in the drama was completed by 10 o'clock. From Sherman's report and later reminiscences we learn that he was with that officer about that hour, and again, it would seem, at 3 and 5 o'clock, and he was with Prentiss between 10 and 11; but he is not seen anywhere else in front. We read of some indefinite or unimportant directions given without effect to straggling bodies of troops in rear. That is all. But he was one of the many there who would have resisted while resistance could avail. That is all that can be said, but it is an honorable record.

AIRDRIE, Kentucky, June, 1885.

THE SKIRMISHING IN SHERMAN'S FRONT.

Robert W. Medkirk, of Co. E, 72d Ohio Vols., wrote, March 22d, 1886, from Indianapolis, Ind.:

"On Friday afternoon, April 4th, two days before the battle of Shiloh, while our regiment of Buckland's brigade was drilling on the west side of Rea Creek [see map, page 502], about a mile from our camp, rapid firing was heard from the direction of our brigade pickets, from the 70th Ohio, Colonel Cockerill. Our commander, Major Crockett, was conversing with Colonel Buckland, who soon rode rapidly in the direction of the firing. Major Crockett ordered the regiment to double quick toward the outposts. When we arrived at the picket post, we found that it had been captured. Major Crockett, with part of our regiment, started in pursuit of the enemy. In a little while a soldier came back, out of breath, and asked that the rest of the regiment be sent to the major's aid. Then we heard the roar of artillery, and felt that the enemy was there in force. Colonel Cockerill sent an orderly back to camp, with orders for the 70th Ohio to hurry out to the front. The remainder of our regiment pushed on to the assistance of Major Crockett. After wandering in the woods for a time, night came on, and we returned to the outpost. There we found the 70th Ohio, and General Sherman with them. The general was enraged at what he designated indiscreet conduct, and ordered us all back to camp. That portion of the 72d Ohio which had been with Major Crockett came straggling in. Then it was that we learned of the capture of the major and eight men.

"The next day, Saturday, my company, 'E,' and Company 'C' constituted the brigade picket. We were stationed on the east side of the Howell farm [see page 502]. All day the enemy kept in our front. We fired on them frequently, but they did not return the fire until toward evening, when they had a brush with a squadron of the 5th Ohio Cavalry. Late Saturday afternoon, a Confederate officer with his staff rode up on a knoll on the west side of the Howell farm, and with his glass began to take observations; in a few minutes we opened fire on them and they rode rapidly away. To show that no serious attack was expected, a detail from Colonel Buckland's brigade worked all day Saturday, April 5th, *building two bridges in front of Buckland's brigade,* one over the east branch of Oak Creek and one over the west branch of Rea Creek, which bridges were used by the enemy to cross their artillery on Sunday, after our brigade fell back from its first line."

General Sherman's report of the affair of April 4th to Grant's headquarters, written on the 5th, says: "I infer that the enemy is in some considerable force at Pea Ridge," or Monterey, about eight miles from Shiloh Church.— EDITORS.

THE OPPOSING FORCES AT SHILOH.

The composition, losses, and strength of each army as here stated give the gist of all the data obtainable in the Official Records. K stands for killed; w for wounded; m w for mortally wounded; m for captured or missing; c for captured.

THE UNION ARMY.

ARMY OF THE TENNESSEE.— Brigadier-General Ulysses S. Grant.

FIRST DIVISION, Major-Gen. John A. McClernand. Staff loss: w, 2.
First Brigade, Col. A. M. Hare (w), Col. M. M. Crocker; 8th Ill., Capt. James M. Ashmore (w), Capt. William H. Harvey (k), Capt. R. H. Sturgess; 18th Ill., Major Samuel Eaton (w), Capt. Daniel H. Brush (w), Capt. William J. Dillon (k), Capt. J. J. Anderson; 11th Iowa, Lieut.-Col. William Hall; 13th Iowa, Col. Marcellus M. Crocker; Battery D, 2d Ill. Artillery, Capt. James P. Timony. Brigade loss: k, 104; w, 467; m, 9 = 580. *Second Brigade,* Col. C. Carroll Marsh; 11th Ill., Lieut.-Col. T. E. G. Ransom (w), Major Garrett Nevins (w), Capt. Lloyd D. Waddell, Major Garrett Nevins; 20th Ill., Lieut.-Col. Evan Richards (w), Capt. Orton Frisbie; 45th Ill., Col. John E. Smith; 48th Ill., Col. Isham N. Haynie (w), Maj. Manning Mayfield. Brigade loss: k, 80; w, 475; m, 30 = 585. *Third Brigade,* Col. Julius Raith (m w), Lieut.-Col. Enos P. Wood, Col. C. Carroll Marsh: 17th Ill., Lieut.-Col. Enos P. Wood, Maj. Francis M. Smith; 29th Ill., Lieut.-Col. Charles M. Ferrell; 43d Ill., Lieut.-Col. Adolph Engelmann; 49th Ill., Lieut.-Col. Phineas Pease; Company Ill. Cavalry, Capt. E. Carmichael. Brigade loss: k, 96; w, 393; m, 46 = 535. *Unattached:* Stewart's Co. Ill. Cav., Lieut. Ezra King; D, 1st Ill. Artillery, Capt. Edward McAllister (w); E, 2d Ill. Artillery, Lieut. George L. Nispel; 14th Ohio Battery, Capt. J. B. Burrows (w). Unattached loss: k, 5; w, 35 = 40.
SECOND DIVISION, Brig.-Gen. W. H. L. Wallace (m w), Col. James M. Tuttle. Staff loss: w, 1.
First Brigade, Col. James M. Tuttle: 2d Iowa, Lieut.-Col. James Baker; 7th Iowa, Lieut.-Col. James C. Parrott; 12th Iowa, Col. Joseph J. Woods (w), Capt. Samuel R. Edgington; 14th Iowa, Col. William T. Shaw. Brigade loss: k, 39; w, 143; m, 676 = 858. (A number of the captured or missing were also wounded.) *Second Brigade,* Brig.-Gen. John McArthur (w), Col. Thomas Morton: 9th Ill., Col. August Mersy; 12th Ill., Lieut.-Col. Augustus L. Chetlain, Capt. James R. Hugunin; 81st Ohio, Col. Thomas Morton; 13th Mo., Col. Crafts J. Wright; 14th

Mo. (Birge's Sharp-shooters), Col. B. S. Compton. Brigade loss: k, 99; w, 470; m, 11 = 580. *Third Brigade,* Col. Thomas W. Sweeny (w), Col. Silas D. Baldwin: 8th Iowa, Col. James L. Geddes (w and c); 7th Ill., Maj. Richard Rowett; 50th Ill., Col. Moses M. Bane (w); 52d Ill., Maj. Henry Stark, Capt. Edwin A. Bowen; 57th Ill., Col. Silas D. Baldwin, Lieut.-Col. F. J. Hurlbut; 58th Ill., Col. William F. Lynch (c). Brigade loss: k, 127; w, 501; m, 619 = 1247. (A number of the captured or missing were also wounded.) *Cavalry:* C, 2d, and I, 4th U. S., Lieut. James Powell; A and B, 2d Ill., Capt's John R. Hotaling and Thomas J. Larrison. Cavalry loss: k, 1; w, 5 = 6. *Artillery:* A, 1st Ill., Lieut. Peter P. Wood; D, 1st Mo., Capt. Henry Richardson; H, 1st Mo., Capt. Frederick Welker; K, 1st Mo., Capt. George H. Stone. Artillery loss: k, 4; w, 53 = 57.
THIRD DIVISION, Major-General Lew Wallace.
First Brigade, Col. Morgan L. Smith: 11th Ind., Col. G. F. McGinnis; 24th Ind., Col. Alvin P. Hovey; 8th Mo., Lieut.-Col. James Peckham. Brigade loss: k, 18; w, 114 = 132. *Second Brigade,* Col. John M. Thayer: 23d Ind., Col. W. L. Sanderson; 1st Neb., Lieut.-Col. William D. McCord; 56th Ohio (at Crump's Landing), Col. Peter Kinney; 58th Ohio, Col. Valentine Bausenwein. Brigade loss: k, 20; w, 99; m, 3 = 122. *Third Brigade,* Col. Charles Whittlesey: 20th Ohio, Lieut.-Col. Manning F. Force; 68th Ohio (at Crump's Landing), Col. S. H. Steedman; 76th Ohio, Col. Charles R. Woods; 78th Ohio, Col. M. D. Leggett. Brigade loss: k, 2; w, 32; m, 1 = 35. *Artillery:* 9th Ind. Battery, Capt. N. S. Thompson; I, 1st Mo., Lieut. Charles H. Thurber. Artillery loss: k, 1; w, 6 = 7. *Cavalry:* 3d Battalion, 11th Ill., Maj. James F. Johnson; 3d Battalion, 5th Ohio, Maj. C. S. Hayes.
FOURTH DIVISION, Brig.-Gen. Stephen A. Hurlbut.
First Brigade, Col. N. G. Williams (w), Col. Isaac C. Pugh: 28th Ill., Col. A. K. Johnson; 32d Ill., Col. John Logan (w); 41st Ill., Col. Isaac C. Pugh, Lieut.-Col. Ansel Tupper (k), Maj. John Warner, Capt. John H. Nale; 3d Iowa, Maj. William M. Stone (c), Lieut. G. W.

Crosley. Brigade loss: k, 112; w, 532; m, 43 = 687. *Second Brigade*, Col. James C. Veatch: 14th Ill., Col. Cyrus Hall; 15th Ill., Lieut.-Col. E. F. W. Ellis (k), Capt. Louis D. Kelley, Lieut.-Col. William Cam; 46th Ill., Col. John A. Davis (w), Lieut.-Col. John J. Jones; 25th Ind., Lieut.-Col. William H. Morgan (w), Maj. John W. Foster. Brigade loss: k, 130; w, 492; m, 8 = 630. *Third Brigade*, Brig.-Gen. Jacob G. Lauman: 31st Ind., Col. Charles Cruft (w), Lieut.-Col. John Osborn; 44th Ind., Col. Hugh B. Reed; 17th Ky., Col. John H. McHenry, Jr.; 25th Ky., Lieut.-Col. B. H. Bristow, Maj. Wm. B. Wall (w), Col. John H. McHenry, Jr. Brigade loss: k, 70; w, 384; m, 4 = 458. *Cavalry:* 1st and 2d Battalions, 5th Ohio, Col. W. H. H. Taylor. Loss: k, 1; w, 6 = 7. *Artillery:* 2d Mich. Battery, Lieut. C. W. Laing; Mann's Mo. Battery, Lieut. Edward Brotzmann; 13th Ohio Battery, Capt. John B. Myers. Artillery loss: k, 4; w, 27; m, 56 = 87.

FIFTH DIVISION, Brig.-Gen. William T. Sherman (w). Staff loss: w, 1.

First Brigade, Col. John A. McDowell: 40th Ill., Col. Stephen G. Hicks (w), Lieut.-Col. James W. Boothe; 6th Iowa, Capt. John Williams (w), Capt. Madison M. Walden; 46th Ohio, Col. Thomas Worthington; 6th Ind. Battery, Capt. Frederick Behr (k). Brigade loss: k, 137; w, 444; m, 70 = 651. *Second Brigade*, Col. David Stuart (w), Lieut.-Col. Oscar Malmborg (temporarily), Col. T. Kilby Smith: 55th Ill., Lieut.-Col. Oscar Malmborg; 54th Ohio, Col. T. Kilby Smith, Lieut.-Col. James A. Farden; 71st Ohio, Col. Rodney Mason. Brigade loss: k, 80; w, 380; m, 90 = 550. *Third Brigade*, Col. Jesse Hildebrand: 53d Ohio, Col. J. J. Appler, Lieut.-Col. Robert A. Fulton; 57th Ohio, Lieut.-Col. Americus V. Rice; 77th Ohio, Lieut.-Col. Wills De Hass, Maj. Benjamin D. Fearing. Brigade loss: k, 70; w, 222; m, 65 = 356. *Fourth Brigade*, Col. Ralph Buckland: 48th Ohio, Col. Peter J. Sullivan (w), Lieut.-Col. Job R. Parker; 70th Ohio, Col. Joseph R. Cockerill; 72d Ohio, Lieut.-Col. Herman Canfield (k), Col. Ralph P. Buckland. Brigade loss: k, 36; w, 203; m, 74 = 313. *Cavalry:* 1st and 2d

Battalions, 4th Ill., Col. T. Lyle Dickey. Cavalry loss: w, 6. *Artillery*, Maj. Ezra Taylor: B, 1st Ill., Capt. Samuel E. Barrett; E, 1st Ill., Capt. A. C. Waterhouse (w), Lieut. A. R. Abbott (w), Lieut. J. A. Fitch. Artillery loss: k, 2; w, 22 = 24.

SIXTH DIVISION, Brig.-Gen. Benjamin M. Prentiss (c). Staff loss: k, 1; m, 2 = 3.

First Brigade, Col. Everett Peabody (k): 12th Mich., Col. Francis Quinn; 21st Mo., Col. David Moore (w), Lieut.-Col. H. M. Woodyard; 25th Mo., Col. Robert T. Van Horn; 16th Wis., Col. Benjamin Allen (w). Brigade loss: k, 113; w, 372; m, 236 = 721. *Second Brigade*, Col. Madison Miller (c): 61st Ill., Col. Jacob Fry; 16th Iowa, Col. Alexander Chambers (w), Lieut.-Col. A. H. Sanders; 18th Mo., Lieut.-Col. Isaac V. Pratt (c). Brigade loss: k, 44; w, 228; m, 178 = 450. *Cavalry:* 11th Ill. (8 co's), Col. Robert G. Ingersoll. Cavalry loss: k, 3; w, 3 = 6. *Artillery:* 1st Minn. Battery, Capt. Emil Munch (w), Lieut. William Pfaender; 5th Ohio Battery, Capt. A. Hickenlooper. Artillery loss: k, 4; w, 27 = 31. *Unattached Infantry:* 15th Iowa, Col. Hugh T. Reid; 23d Mo., Col. Jacob T. Tindall (k), Lieut.-Col. Quin Morton (c); 18th Wis., Col. James S. Alban (k). Loss Unattached Infantry: k, 71; w, 298; m, 592 = 961. (Some of the captured or missing [1008] of this division were also wounded.)

UNASSIGNED TROOPS: 15th Mich., Col. John M. Oliver; 14th Wis., Col. David E. Wood; H, 1st Ill. Artillery, Capt. Axel Silfversparre; I, 1st Ill. Artillery, Capt. Edward Bouton; B, 2d Ill. Artillery, Capt. Relly Madison; F, 2d Ill. Artillery, Capt. John W. Powell (w); 8th Ohio Battery, Capt. Louis Markgraf. Loss unassigned troops: k, 39; w, 159; m, 17 = 215. The total loss of the Army of the Tennessee was 1513 killed, 6601 wounded, and 2830 captured or missing = 10,944.

UNION GUN-BOATS. *Tyler*, Lieut.-Com. William Gwin; *Lexington*, Lieut.-Com. James W. Shirk.

ARMY OF THE OHIO — Major-General Don Carlos Buell.

SECOND DIVISION. Brig.-Gen. Alexander McD. McCook. *Fourth Brigade*, Brig.-Gen. Lovell H. Rousseau: 6th Ind., Col. Thomas T. Crittenden; 5th Ky., Col. H. M. Buckley; 1st Ohio, Col. B. F. Smith; 1st Battalion, 15th U. S. (Capt. Peter T. Swaine), and 1st Battalion, 16th U. S. (Capt. Edwin F. Townsend), Major John H. King; 1st Battalion, 19th U. S., Maj. S. D. Carpenter. Brigade loss: k, 28; w, 280; m, 3 = 311. *Fifth Brigade*, Col. Edward N. Kirk (w): 34th Ill., Maj. Charles N. Levanway (k), Capt. Hiram W. Bristol; 29th Ind., Lieut.-Col. David M. Dunn; 30th Ind., Col. Sion S. Bass (m w), Lieut.-Col. Joseph B. Dodge; 77th Pa., Col. Fred. S. Stumbaugh. Brigade loss: k, 24; w, 310; m, 2 = 346. *Sixth Brigade*, Col. William H. Gibson: 32d Ind., Col. August Willich; 39th Ind., Col. Thomas J. Harrison; 15th Ohio, Maj. William Wallace; 49th Ohio, Lieut.-Col. Albert M. Blackman. Brigade loss: k, 25; w, 220; m, 2 = 247. *Artillery:* H, 5th U. S., Capt. William R. Terrill. Artillery loss: k, 1; w, 13 = 14.

FOURTH DIVISION, Brig.-Gen. William Nelson. *Tenth Brigade*, Col. Jacob Ammen: 36th Ind., Col. William Grose; 6th Ohio, Lieut.-Col. Nicholas L. Anderson; 24th Ohio, Lieut.-Col. Frederick C. Jones. Brigade loss: k, 16; w, 106; m, 8 = 130. *Nineteenth Brigade*, Col. William B. Hazen: 9th Ind., Col. Gideon C. Moody; 6th Ky., Col. Walter C. Whitaker; 41st Ohio, Lieut.-Col. George S. Mygatt. Brigade loss: k, 48; w, 357; m, 1 =

406. *Twenty-second Brigade*, Col. Sanders D. Bruce: 1st Ky., Col. David A. Enyart; 2d Ky., Col. Thomas D. Sedgewick; 20th Ky., Lieut.-Col. Charles H. Hanson. Brigade loss: k, 29; w, 138; m, 11 = 178. *Cavalry:* 2d Ind. (not actively engaged), Lieut.-Col. Edward M. McCook.

FIFTH DIVISION, Brig.-Gen. Thomas L. Crittenden. *Eleventh Brigade*, Brig.-Gen. Jeremiah T. Boyle: 9th Ky., Col. Benjamin C. Grider; 13th Ky., Col. Edward H. Hobson; 19th Ohio, Col. Samuel Beatty; 59th Ohio, Col. James P. Fyffe. Brigade loss: k, 33; w, 212; m, 18 = 263. *Fourteenth Brigade*, Col. William Sooy Smith: 11th Ky., Col. Pierce B. Hawkins; 26th Ky., Lieut.-Col. Cicero Maxwell; 13th Ohio, Lieut.-Col. Joseph G. Hawkins. Brigade loss: k, 25; w, 157; m, 10 = 192. *Artillery:* G, 1st Ohio, Capt. Joseph Bartlett; H and M, 4th U. S., Capt. John Mendenhall. Artillery loss: k, 2; w, 8 = 10. *Cavalry:* 3d Ky. (not actively engaged), Col. James S. Jackson.

SIXTH DIVISION, Brig.-Gen. Thomas J. Wood. *Twentieth Brigade*, Brig.-Gen. James A. Garfield: 13th Mich., Col. Michael Shoemaker; 64th Ohio, Col. John Ferguson; 65th Ohio, Col. Charles G. Harker. *Twenty-first Brigade*, Col. George D. Wagner: 15th Ind., Lieut.-Col. Gustavus A. Wood; 40th Ind., Col. John W. Blake; 57th Ind., Col. Cyrus C. Hines; 24th Ky., Col. Lewis B. Grigsby. Brigade loss: w, 4.

The total loss of the Army of the Ohio was 241 killed, 1807 wounded, and 55 captured or missing = 2103.

The grand total of Union loss was 1754 killed, 8408 wounded, and 2885 captured or missing = 13,047.

The only official statement of Grant's strength at Shiloh is on page 112, Vol. X., "Official Records," which is compiled from division returns of April 4th and 5th, and shows (exclusive of two regiments and one battery not reported), an aggregate, "present for duty," of 44,895. Included, however, in these figures are such non-combatants as medical officers, quartermasters, chaplains, musicians, hospital stewards, buglers, etc., etc. Deducting from the total above given the "present for duty" of Lew Wallace's division (7564), leaves 37,331 as the "present for duty" (combatant and non-combatant) in Grant's army on the morning of April 6th. The actual number of effectives is nowhere officially reported, nor do the "Official Records" afford any information as to the number of men brought by Buell to Grant's assistance. General Buell speaks in a general way of "25,000 reënforcements," including "Lew Wallace's 5000." General Grant says: "At Shiloh, the effective strength of the Union forces on the morning of the 6th was 33,000 men. Lew Wallace brought 5000 more after nightfall. . . . Excluding the troops who fled, panic-stricken, before they had fired a shot, there was not a time during the 6th when we had more than

25,000 men in line. On the 7th Buell brought 20,000 more (Nelson's, Crittenden's, and McCook's divisions). Of his remaining two divisions Thomas's did not reach the field during the engagement; Wood's arrived before firing had ceased, but not in time to be of much service." General M. F. Force, in "From Fort Henry to Corinth" (Charles Scribner's Sons), says: "The reënforcements of Monday numbered, of Buell's army about 25,000; Lew Wallace's 6500; other regiments about 1400." General Lew Wallace says in his report that his command "did not exceed 5000 men of all arms."

THE CONFEDERATE ARMY.

ARMY OF THE MISSISSIPPI.— General Albert Sidney Johnston (k). General G. T. Beauregard.

FIRST ARMY CORPS.— Major-Gen. Leonidas Polk.

FIRST DIVISION, Brig.-Gen. Charles Clark (w), Brig.-Gen. Alexander P. Stewart. Staff loss: w, 1.

First Brigade, Col. R. M. Russell: 11th La., Col. S. F. Marks (w), Lieut.-Col. Robert H. Barrow; 12th Tenn., Lieut.-Col. T. H. Bell, Major R. P. Caldwell; 13th Tenn., Col. A. J. Vaughan, Jr.; 22d Tenn., Col. T. J. Freeman (w); Tenn. Battery, Capt. Smith P. Bankhead. Brigade loss: k, 97; w, 512 = 609. *Second Brigade*, Brig.-Gen. Alexander P. Stewart: 13th Ark., Lieut.-Col. A. D. Grayson (k), Major James A. McNeely (w), Col. J. C. Tappan; 4th Tenn., Col. R. P. Neely, Lieut.-Col. Q. F. Strahl; 5th Tenn., Lieut.-Col. C. D. Venable; 33d Tenn., Col. Alexander W. Campbell (w); Miss. Battery, Capt. T. J. Stanford. Brigade loss: k, 93; w, 421; m, 3 = 517.

SECOND DIVISION, Major-Gen. B. F. Cheatham (w). Staff loss: w, 1.

First Brigade, Brig.-Gen. Bushrod R. Johnson (w), Col. Preston Smith (w): Blythe's Miss., Col. A. K. Blythe (k), Lieut.-Col. D. L. Herron (k), Major James Moore; 2d Tenn., Col. J. Knox Walker; 15th Tenn., Lieut.-Col. R. C. Tyler (w), Major John F. Hearn; 154th Tenn. (senior), Col. Preston Smith, Lieut.-Col. Marcus J. Wright; Tenn. Battery, Capt. Marshall T. Polk (w). Brigade loss: k, 120; w, 607; m, 13 = 740. *Second Brigade*, Col. William H. Stephens, Col. George Maney: 7th Ky., Col. Charles Wickliffe (m w), Lieut.-Col. W. D. Lannom; 1st Tenn. (battalion), Col. George Maney, Major H. R. Field; 6th Tenn., Lieut.-Col. T. P. Jones, Col. W. H. Stephens; 9th Tenn., Col. H. L. Douglass; Miss. Battery, Capt. Melancthon Smith. Brigade loss: k, 75; w, 413; m, 3 = 491. *Cavalry*: 1st Miss., Col. A. J. Lindsay; Miss. and Ala. Battalion, Lieut.-Col. R. H. Brewer. Cavalry loss: k, 5; w, 12; m, 2 = 19. *Unattached*: 47th Tenn., Col. M. R. Hill.

SECOND ARMY CORPS, Major-Gen. Braxton Bragg. *Escort*: Alabama Cavalry, Capt. R. W. Smith.

FIRST DIVISION, Brig.-Gen. Daniel Ruggles. *First Brigade*, Col. Randall L. Gibson: 1st Ark., Col. James F. Fagan; 4th La., Col. H. W. Allen (w), Lieut.-Col. S. E. Hunter; 13th La., Major A. P. Avegno (m w), Capt. S. O'Leary (w), Capt. E. M. Dubroca; 19th La., Col. Benjamin L. Hodge, Lieut.-Col. J. M. Hollingsworth. Brigade loss: k, 97; w, 488; m, 97 = 682. *Second Brigade*, Brig.-Gen. Patton Anderson: 1st Fla. Battalion, Major T. A. McDonell (w), Capt. W. G. Poole, Capt. W. C. Bird; 17th La., Lieut.-Col. Charles Jones (w); 20th La., Col. August Reichard; 9th Texas, Col. W. A. Stanley; Confederate Guards Response Battalion, Major Franklin H. Clack; 5th Company Washington (La.) Artillery, Capt. W. I. Hodgson. Brigade loss: k, 69; w, 313; m, 52 = 434. *Third Brigade*, Col. Preston Pond, Jr.: 16th La., Maj. Daniel Gober; 18th La., Col. Alfred Mouton (w), Lieut.-Col. A. Roman; Crescent (La.) Regt., Col. Marshall J. Smith; Orleans Guard Battalion, Major Leon Querouze (w); 38th Tenn., Col. R. F. Looney; Ala. Battery, Capt. Wm. H. Ketchum. Brigade loss: k, 89; w, 336; m, 169 = 594. *Cavalry*: Ala. Battalion, Capt. T. F. Jenkins. Cavalry loss, k, 2; w, 6; m, 1 = 9.

SECOND DIVISION, Brig.-Gen. Jones M. Withers. *First Brigade*, Brig.-Gen. A. H. Gladden (m w), Col. Daniel W. Adams (w), Col. Z. C. Deas (w): 21st Ala., Lieut.-Col. S. W. Cayce, Maj. F. Stewart; 22d Ala., Col. Z. C. Deas, Lieut.-Col. John C. Marrast; 25th Ala., Col. J. Q. Loomis (w), Maj. George D. Johnston; 26th Ala., Col. J. G. Col-

tart (w), Lieut.-Col. William D. Chadick; 1st La., Col. Daniel W. Adams, Maj. F. H. Farrar, Jr.; Ala. Battery, Capt. F. H. Robertson. Brigade loss: k, 129; w, 597; m, 103 = 829. *Second Brigade*, Brig.-Gen. James R. Chalmers: 5th Miss., Col. A. E. Fant; 7th Miss., Lieut.-Col. H. Mayson; 9th Miss., Lieut.-Col. William A. Rankin (m w); 10th Miss., Col. R. A. Smith; 52d Tenn., Col. B. J. Lea; Ala. Battery, Capt. Charles P. Gage. Brigade loss: k, 83; w, 343; m, 19 = 445. *Third Brigade*, Brig.-Gen. John K. Jackson: 17th Ala., Lieut.-Col. Robert C. Farris; 18th Ala., Col. Eli S. Shorter; 19th Ala., Col. Joseph Wheeler; 2d Tex., Col. John C. Moore, Lieut.-Col. W. P. Rogers, Maj. H. G. Runnels; Ga. Battery, Capt. I. P. Girardey. Brigade loss: k, 86; w, 364; m, 194 = 644.

THIRD ARMY CORPS, Maj.-Gen. Wm. J. Hardee (w). *First Brigade*, Brig.-Gen. T. C. Hindman (commanded his own and the Third Brigade), Col. R. G. Shaver: 2d Ark., Col. D. C. Govan, Maj. R. F. Harvey; 6th Ark., Col. A. T. Hawthorn; 7th Ark., Lieut.-Col. John M. Dean (k), Maj. James T. Martin; 3d Confederate, Col. John S. Marmaduke; Miss. Battery, Capt. Charles Swett. Brigade loss: k, 109; w, 546; m, 38 = 693. *Second Brigade*, Brig.-Gen. P. R. Cleburne: 15th Ark., Lieut.-Col. A. K. Patton (k); 6th Miss., Col. J. J. Thornton (w), Capt. W. A. Harper; 2d Tenn., Col. W. B. Bate (w), Lieut.-Col. D. L. Goodall; 5th Tenn., Col. Ben. J. Hill; 23d Tenn., Lieut.-Col. James F. Neill (w); 24th Tenn., Lieut.-Col. Thomas H. Peebles; Ark. Batteries, Capts. J. T. Trigg and J. H. Calvert. Brigade loss: k, 188; w, 790; m, 65 = 1043. *Third Brigade*, Brig.-Gen. S. A. M. Wood, Col. W. K. Patterson (temporarily): 16th Ala., Lieut.-Col. J. W. Harris; 8th Ark., Col. W. K. Patterson; 9th Ark. (battalion), Maj. J. H. Kelly; 3d Miss. Battalion, Maj. A. B. Hardcastle; 27th Tenn., Col. Chris. H. Williams (k), Maj. Samuel T. Love (m w); 44th Tenn., Col. C. A. McDaniel; 55th Tenn., Col. James L. McKoin; Miss. Battery, Capt. W. L. Harper (w), Lieut. Put. Darden; Ga. Dragoons, Capt. I. W. Avery. Brigade loss: k, 107; w, 600; m, 38 = 745.

RESERVE CORPS, Brig.-Gen. John C. Breckinridge. *First Brigade*, Col. Robert P. Trabue: 4th Ala. Batt., Maj. J. M. Clifton; 31st Ala., Lieut.-Col. —— Galbraith; 3d Ky., Lieut.-Col. Ben. Anderson (w); 4th Ky., Lieut.-Col. A. R. Hynes (w); 5th Ky., Col. Thomas H. Hunt; 6th Ky., Col. Joseph H. Lewis; Tenn. Battalion, Lieut.-Col. J. M. Crews; Ky. Battery, Capt. Edward P. Byrne; Ky. Battery, Capt. Robert Cobb. Brigade loss: k, 151; w, 557; m, 92 = 800. *Second Brigade*, Brig.-Gen. John S. Bowen (w), Col. John D. Martin: 9th Ark., Col. Isaac L. Dunlop; 10th Ark., Col. T. D. Merrick; 2d Confederate, Col. John D. Martin, Maj. Thomas H. Mangum; 1st Mo., Col. Lucius L. Rich; Miss. Battery, Capt. Alfred Hudson. Brigade loss: k, 98; w, 498; m, 28 = 624. *Third Brigade*, Col. W. S. Statham: 15th Miss.; 22d Miss.; 19th Tenn., Col. D. H. Cummings; 20th Tenn., Col. J. A. Battle (c); 28th Tenn.; 45th Tenn., Lieut.-Col. E. F. Lytle; Tenn. Battery, Capt. A. M. Rutledge. Brigade loss: k, 137; w, 627; m, 45 = 809.

TROOPS NOT MENTIONED IN THE FOREGOING LIST. *Cavalry*: Tenn. Regt., Col. N. B. Forrest (w); Ala. Regt., Col. James H. Clanton; Texas Regt., Col. John A. Wharton (w); Ky. Squadron, Capt. John H. Morgan. *Artillery*: Ark. Battery, Capt. George T. Hubbard; Tenn. Battery, Capt. H. L. W. McClung.

The total Confederate loss, as officially reported, was 1728 killed, 8012 wounded, and 959 missing = 10,699.

According to a field return for April 3d, 1862 ("Official Records," Vol. X, 398), the effective strength of the Confederate forces that marched from Corinth was as follows: Infantry, 34,727; artillery, 1973; cavalry, 2073,— or an aggregate of 38,773. The 47th Tennessee Regiment reached the field on the 7th with probably 550 men, making in all 39,323. Another return ("Official Records," Vol. X., 396) gives the following "effective total before the battle": Infantry and artillery, 35,953; cavalry, 4382,— grand total, 40,335.

ALBERT SIDNEY JOHNSTON AT SHILOH.

BY HIS SON, WILLIAM PRESTON JOHNSTON, COLONEL, C. S. A.

ALBERT SIDNEY JOHNSTON AT THE AGE OF 35.
FROM A MINIATURE BY THOMAS CAMPBELL, PAINTED IN
LOUISVILLE, KY., IN 1838 OR 1839.

DURING the angry political strife which preceded the contest of arms, General Albert Sidney Johnston ⚓ remained silent, stern, and sorrowful. He determined to stand at his post in San Francisco, performing his full duty as an officer of the United States, until events should require a decision as to his course. When Texas—his adopted State—passed the ordinance of secession from the Union, the alternative was presented, and, on the day he heard the news, he resigned his commission in the army. He kept the fact concealed, however, lest it might stir up disaffection among the turbulent population of the Pacific Coast. He said, "I shall do my duty to the last, and, when absolved, shall take my course." All honest and competent witnesses now accord that he carried out this purpose in letter and spirit. General Sumner, who relieved him, reported that he found him "carrying out the orders of the Government."

Mr. Lincoln's Administration treated General Johnston with a distrust which wounded his pride to the quick, but afterward made such amends as it could, by sending him a major-general's commission. He was also assured through confidential sources that he would receive the highest command in the Federal Army. But he declined to take part against his own people, and retired to Los Angeles with the intention of farming. There he was subjected to an irritating surveillance; while at the same time there came

⸸ For extended treatment of this subject, see "The Life of General Albert Sidney Johnston," by William Preston Johnston (D. Appleton & Co.), upon which Colonel Johnston has drawn freely in the preparation of this paper.— EDITORS.

⚓ General Johnston was of New England descent, though both he and his mother were of pioneer stock and natives of Kentucky. His father was the village physician. He was born February 3d, 1803, in Mason County, Kentucky. He was "a handsome, proud, manly, earnest, and self-reliant boy," "grave and thoughtful." His early education was desultory, but was continued at Transylvania and at West Point, where he evinced superior talents for mathematics, and was graduated in 1826. He was a lieutenant of the 6th Infantry, from 1827 to 1834, when he resigned. His only active service during this period was the Black Hawk war, in which he won considerable distinction. In 1829 he married Miss Henrietta Preston, who died in 1835. In 1836 he joined the army of the young republic of Texas,

and rapidly rose to the chief command. In 1839 he was Secretary of War, and expelled the intruding United States Indians, after two battles on the River Neches. He served one campaign in Mexico under General Taylor, and was recommended by that commander as a brigadier-general for his conduct at Monterey, but was allowed no command by the Administration. In 1843 he married Miss Eliza Griffin, and retired to a plantation in Brazoria County, Texas, where he spent three years in seclusion and straitened circumstances. In 1849 he was appointed a paymaster by President Taylor, and served in Texas until 1855, when he was made colonel of the 2d Cavalry by President Pierce. In 1857 he conducted the remarkable expedition to Utah, in which he saved the United States army there from a frightful disaster by his prudence and executive ability. He remained in command in Utah until the summer of 1860, which he passed with his family in Kentucky. In December of that year he was assigned to the command of the Pacific Coast.—W. P. J.

across mountain and desert the voice of the Southern people calling to him for help in their extremity.↓ His heart and intellect both recognized their claim upon his services, and he obeyed. At this time he wrote, "No one could feel more sensibly the calamitous condition of our country than myself, and whatever part I may take hereafter, it will always be a subject of gratulation with me that no act of mine ever contributed to bring it about. I suppose the difficulties now will only be adjusted by the sword. In my humble judgment, that was not the remedy."

When he arrived in the new Confederacy, his coming was welcomed with a spontaneous outburst of popular enthusiasm, and deputations from the West preceded him to Richmond, entreating his assignment to that department. President Davis said that he regarded his coming as of more worth than the accession of an army of ten thousand men; and on the 10th of September, 1861, he was intrusted with the defense of that part of the Confederate States which lay west of the Alleghany Mountains, except the Gulf Coast (Bragg having control of the coast of West Florida and Alabama, and Mansfield Lovell of the coast of Mississippi and Louisiana). His command was

↓ The following statement was written in response to an inquiry by the editors as to the details of the offer of high command referred to by Colonel Johnston:

"The circumstances which gave rise to the expressed desire of the Administration in 1861 to retain General Albert Sidney Johnston in the Federal army were as follows:

"Early in April, 1861, while on duty in the adjutant-general's office in Washington, I learned that Colonel Sumner had been dispatched *incog.* to California, with secret orders to assume command of the Department of the Pacific, and that this unusual course had been prompted by the fear that the forts and arsenals and garrisons on that coast would be placed in the hands of the secessionists by General Johnston, the then commander, who was reported to be arranging to do so.

"I had just received a letter from General Johnston expressing his pleasure at the large and handsome parade of State troops in San Francisco, on February 22d, and at the undoubted loyalty to the Union cause of the whole Pacific coast, and also his earnest hope that the patriotic spirit manifested in California existed as strongly in all other States, and would as surely be maintained by them as it would be in the Pacific States in case of attempted secession.

"Fearing the effect of the superseding orders upon a high-toned and sensitive officer, one whom I esteemed as a brother, and earnestly desired to be secured to our cause, I induced Major McDowell to show the letter to Secretary Cameron, and to urge every effort to keep General Johnston from leaving the service. His superior qualifications, his influence among prominent citizens at the South, and especially among his relatives in his native State, Kentucky,— which it was exceedingly desirable to keep in the Union,— were strong

inducements to these efforts. My desire was met as cordially and earnestly as it existed, and I was authorized to send, as I did through my friend 'Ben' Holliday, in New York, for transmission by telegraph to St. Louis, and thence by his 'pony express' to San Francisco, the following message: 'I take the greatest pleasure in assuring you, for the Secretary of War, that he has the utmost confidence in you, and will give you the most important command and trust on your arrival here. Sidney is appointed to the Military Academy.' This message reached General Johnston after the arrival of Colonel Sumner.

"In response to the above, and by the same channel of communication, I received this message: 'I thank you and my friends for efforts in my behalf. I have resigned, and resolved to follow the fortunes of my State.' His letter of resignation was soon received, and put an end to all hope, especially as Texas — which had then seceded — was his adopted State.

"I felt in 1861, as I now know, that the assertion that General Johnston intended to turn over to the secessionists the defenses of California, or any part of the regular army, was false and absurd. Under no circumstances, even if intended, could such a plan have succeeded, especially with the regular army. But no such breach of trust was intended, nor would any graduate of West Point in the army have committed or permitted it. It had no better foundation than the statement of Senator Conness of California, who three years later urged and secured the assignment of General McDowell to command on the Pacific coast, on the ground that after the war for the Union should have ended there would be in California a more powerful rebellion than that then existing among the Southern States.

"FITZ JOHN PORTER.

"NEW YORK, December 8, 1884."

GENERAL ALBERT SIDNEY JOHNSTON AT THE AGE OF FIFTY-SEVEN.
FROM A PHOTOGRAPH TAKEN IN SALT LAKE CITY IN 1860.

The appearance of General Albert Sidney Johnston before the war is described as both commanding and attractive. In some respects the bust of Alexander Hamilton is the best extant likeness of him, a resemblance very frequently remarked. His cheek-bones were rather high, and with his nose and complexion gave him a Scotch look. His chin was delicate and handsome; his teeth were white and regular, and his mouth was square and firm. In the portrait by Bush taken about this time, his lips seem rather full, but as they are best remembered, they were somewhat thin and very firmly set. Light-brown hair clustered over a noble forehead, and from under heavy brows his deep-set but clear, steady eyes looked straight at you with a regard kind and sincere, yet penetrating. In repose his eyes were as blue as the sky, but in excitement they flashed to a steel-gray, and exerted a remarkable power over men. He was six feet and an inch in height, of about one hundred and eighty pounds weight, straight as an arrow, with broad, square shoulders and a massive chest. He was strong and active, and of a military bearing.—W. P. J.

imperial in extent, and his powers and discretion as large as the theory of the Confederate Government permitted. He lacked nothing except men, munitions of war, and the means of obtaining them. He had the right to ask for anything, and the State Executives had the power to withhold everything.

The Mississippi River divided his department into two distinct theaters of war. West of the river, Frémont held Missouri with a force of from 60,000 to 80,000 Federals, confronted by Price and McCulloch in the extreme south-west corner of the State with 6000 men, and by Hardee, in north-eastern Arkansas, with about as many raw recruits down with camp diseases and unable to move. East of the Mississippi, the northern boundary of Tennessee was barely in his possession, and was held under sufferance from an enemy who, for various reasons, hesitated to advance. The Mississippi opened the way to a ruinous naval invasion unless it could be defended and held. Grant was at Cairo and Paducah with 20,000 men; and Polk, to oppose his invasion, had seized Columbus, Ky., with about 11,000 Confederates, and had fortified it. Tennessee was twice divided: first by the Tennessee River, and then by the

AUTOGRAPH FOUND INSIDE THE COVER OF GENERAL JOHN-STON'S POCKET-MAP OF TENNESSEE, AND WRITTEN THREE DAYS BEFORE THE BATTLE OF SHILOH— PROBABLY HIS LAST AUTOGRAPH.

Cumberland, both of which invited the advance of a hostile force. Some small pretense of fortifications had been made on both rivers at Forts Henry and Donelson, near the boundary line, but practically there was nothing to prevent the Federal army from capturing Nashville, then the most important depot of supplies west of the Alleghanies. Hence the immediate and pressing question for General Johnston was the defense of the Tennessee border. The mock neutrality of Kentucky, which had served as a paper barrier, was terminated, on the 13th of September, by a formal defiance from the Union Legislature of Kentucky. The United States Government had about 34,000 volunteers and about 6000 Kentucky Home Guards assembled in the State under General Robert Anderson, of Fort Sumter fame, who had with him such enterprising corps commanders as Sherman, Thomas, and Nelson.

The Confederacy had some four thousand ill-armed and ill-equipped troops at Cumberland Gap under General Zollicoffer, guarding the only line of railroad communication between Virginia and Tennessee, and overawing the Union population of East Tennessee. This hostile section penetrated the heart of the Confederacy like a wedge and flanked and weakened General Johnston's line of defense, requiring, as it did, constant vigilance and repression.

Besides Zollicoffer's force, General Johnston found only 4000 men available to protect his whole line against 40,000 Federal troops. There were, it is true, some four thousand more raw recruits in camps of

BIRTHPLACE OF ALBERT SIDNEY JOHNSTON, WASHINGTON, KY. FROM A PHOTOGRAPH.

FORT ANDERSON, PADUCAH, IN APRIL, 1862. FROM A LITHOGRAPH.

instruction, but they were sick and not half armed. Of course he might have abandoned the Mississippi River to Grant and brought Polk to his aid, but he had no thought of that; that would have been all which the Federals could have asked. The boldest policy seemed to him the best, and he resolved on a daring step. On September 17th he threw forward his whole force of four thousand men under Buckner by rail into Kentucky and seized Bowling Green. It was a mere skirmish line to mask his own weakness.   But if he could maintain it, even temporarily, it gave him immense strategic and political advantages, and, most of all, time to collect or create an army.   And then (I hold in spite of some dilettante criticism) it gave him a formidable line, with Cumberland Gap and Columbus as the extremities and Bowling Green as the salient.

The result more than answered his expectations.   Buckner's advance produced the wildest consternation in the Federal lines.   Even Sherman, writing thirteen years later, speaks of a picket which burned a bridge thirty miles from Louisville as a " division." As late as November 10th, 1861, he said: " If Johnston chooses, he could march into Louisville any day." The effect of the movement was for a time to paralyze the Federal army and put it on the defensive.

CAMP BURGESS, BOWLING GREEN — THE 70TH INDIANA ON DRESS PARADE. FROM A LITHOGRAPH.
On the hill are seen the Confederate fortifications erected by General Buckner.

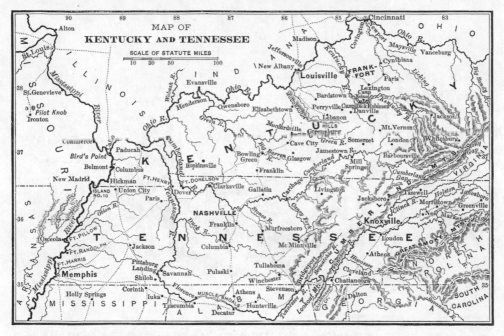

General Johnston had made the opportunity required by the South, if it meant seriously to maintain its independence. He had secured time for preparation; but it neglected the chance, and never recovered it. He at once strongly fortified Bowling Green, and used every measure to stir up and rally the Kentuckians to his standard. He brought Hardee with four thousand men from Arkansas, and kept his little force in such constant motion as to produce the impression of a large army menacing an attack. Even before Buckner advanced, General Johnston had sent to the Southern governors an appeal for arms and a call for fifty thousand men. Harris of Tennessee alone responded heartily, and the Government at Richmond seemed unable to reënforce him or to arm the troops he had. Many difficulties embarrassed it, and not half his men were armed that winter; while up to the middle of November he received only three new regiments. General Johnston realized the magnitude of the struggle, but the people of the South only awoke to it when it was too late. Calamity then stirred them to an ineffectual resistance, the heroism of which removed the reproach of their early vainglory and apathy. General Johnston never was able to assemble more than 22,000 men at Bowling Green, to confront the 100,000 troops opposed to him on that line.

The only battle of note that occurred that fall was at Belmont, opposite Columbus, in which Polk scored a victory over Grant. General Johnston wrote as follows to the Secretary of War, on Christmas Day, from Bowling Green: "The position of General Zollicoffer on the Cumberland holds in check the meditated invasion and hoped-for revolt in East Tennessee; but I can neither order Zollicoffer to join me here nor withdraw any more force from Columbus without imperiling our communications toward Richmond

COL. SPEED S. FRY.   DEATH OF GENERAL ZOLLICOFFER.

BATTLE OF LOGAN'S CROSS ROADS, OR MILL SPRINGS (SEE MAP, PAGE 388). FROM A LITHOGRAPH.

or endangering Tennessee and the Mississippi Valley. This I have resolved not to do, but have chosen, on the contrary, to post my inadequate force in such a manner as to hold the enemy in check, guard the frontier, and hold the Barren [River] till the winter terminates the campaign; or, if any fault in his movements is committed, or his lines become exposed when his force is developed, to attack him as opportunity offers." This sums the situation.

In January, 1862, General Johnston found himself confronted by Halleck in the West, and by Buell, who had succeeded Sherman, in Kentucky. With the exception of the army under Curtis in Missouri, about twelve thousand strong, the whole resources of the North-west, from Pennsylvania to the plains, were turned against General Johnston's lines in Kentucky. Halleck, with armies at Cairo and Paducah, under Grant and C. F. Smith, threatened equally Columbus, the key of the Mississippi River, and the water-lines of the Cumberland and Tennessee, with their defenses, at Forts Donelson and Henry. Buell's right wing also menaced Donelson and Henry, while his center was directed against Bowling Green, and his left was advancing against Zollicoffer at Mill Springs, on the Upper Cumberland. If this last-named position could be forced, the way seemed open to East Tennessee on the one hand, and to Nashville on the other.

The campaign opened with the defeat of the Confederates under Crittenden and Zollicoffer, January 19th, 1862, by General Thomas, at Mill Springs, or Fishing Creek. The fighting was forced by the Confederates, but the whole affair was in disregard of General Johnston's orders. The loss was not severe, but it ended in a rout which left General Johnston's right flank exposed.

There has been much discussion as to who originated the movement up the Tennessee River. Grant *made* it, and it made Grant. It was obvious enough to all the leaders on both sides. General Johnston wrote, January 22d:

" To suppose, with the facilities of movement by water which the well-filled rivers of the Ohio, Cumberland, and Tennessee give for active operations, that they will suspend them in Tennessee and Kentucky during the winter months is a delusion. All the resources of the Confederacy are now needed for the defense of Tennessee."

Great efforts were made to guard against it, but the popular fatuity and apathy prevented adequate preparations. General Polk says in a report, "The principal difficulty in the way of a successful defense of the rivers in question was the want of an adequate force." It was only one of a number of possible and equally fatal movements, which could not have been properly met and resisted except by a larger force than was to be had. General Johnston could not reduce the force at Columbus without imperiling the Mississippi River, and this was not even debatable. Nor could he hazard the loss of Nashville, if it could be saved. He was compelled, therefore, to take the risk at Forts Henry and Donelson. The thrust was made at Henry, and it fell.

As soon as General Johnston learned of the movement against Fort Henry he resolved to fall back to the line of the Cumberland, and make the defense of Nashville at Donelson. Buell was in his front with 90,000 men, and to save Nashville—Buell's objective point—he had to fall back upon it with part of his army. He kept for this purpose 14,000 men, including his sick,—only 8500 effectives in all,—to confront Buell's 90,000 men, and concentrated at Fort Donelson 17,000 men under Floyd, Pillow, and Buckner, his three most experienced generals, to meet Grant, who had 28,000 troops, but was reported

COLONEL SCHOEPF'S TROOPS CROSSING FISHING CREEK ON THE WAY TO JOIN GENERAL THOMAS AT LOGAN'S CROSS ROADS, OR MILL SPRINGS. FROM A LITHOGRAPH.

as having only 12,000. He certainly reserved for himself the more difficult task, the place of greater hazard, leaving the chance of glory to others. The proposition that he should have left Nashville open to capture by Buell, and should have taken all his troops to Donelson, could not have been seriously considered by any general of even moderate military capacity. General Beauregard alleges that he urged General Johnston to concentrate all

CONFEDERATE TYPES OF 1862.

his available forces and attack Grant at Fort Henry. Conclusive contemporary evidence demonstrates that General Beauregard's memory is at fault. But, this aside, no more fatal plan of campaign could have been proposed. Such a concentration was impracticable within the limits of the time required for success. The Confederates would have been met by a superior force under General Grant, whose position, flanked by the batteries of Fort Henry, covered by gun-boats, and to be approached only over causeways not then con-

structed, was absolutely impregnable. It requires an utter disregard of facts seriously to consider such a project. Moreover, this movement would have been an abandonment to Buell of Nashville, the objective point of the Federal campaign. And, finally, this desperate project, commended by General Beauregard, was exactly what the Union generals were striving, hoping, planning, to compel General Johnston to do. The answer to any criticism as to the loss of the army at Donelson is *that it ought not to have been lost.* That is all there is of it.

At midnight of February 15th–16th General Johnston received a telegram announcing a great victory at Donelson, and before daylight information that it would be surrendered. His last troops were then arriving at Nashville from Bowling Green. His first words were: "I must save this army." He at once determined to abandon the line of the Cumberland, and concentrate all available forces at Corinth, Mississippi, for a renewed struggle. He had indicated this movement as a probable event to several distinguished officers some time previous; it was now to be carried into effect. He had remaining only his little army from Bowling Green, together with the fragments of

Crittenden's army, and the fugitives from Donelson. These he reorganized at Murfreesboro' within a week. He saved the most of his valuable stores and munitions, which fully absorbed his railroad transportation to Stevenson, Alabama, and moved his men over the mud roads to Corinth, Mississippi, by way of Decatur, in a wet and stormy season. Nevertheless, he assembled his army of 23,000—about 16,000 effectives—at Corinth, on the 25th day of March, full of enthusiasm and the spirit of combat. In the meantime the Confederate Government lent him all the aid in its power, reënforcing him with an army ten thousand strong, from the Southern coast, under General Braxton Bragg, who had been in command at Pensacola [see note, page 32], and with such arms as could be procured.

General Beauregard has claimed that he raised, concentrated, and organized the army which fought at Shiloh; that he persuaded General Johnston to turn aside from a retreat toward Stevenson and join him at Corinth, and substituted an offensive campaign for a defensive one projected by General Johnston; and that he likewise planned the battle of Shiloh, induced General Johnston to fight it, and executed all the general movements on the field, and that General Johnston was merely the ostensible commander. I have elsewhere fully confuted each of these absurd pretenses; and as this rapid survey is historical, not controversial, the space at my disposal does not permit me to argue here the points involved; I shall, therefore, merely state the facts, which rest upon unimpeachable contemporary evidence. The final verdict I am satisfied to leave to the soldiers of both armies who fought there, to the careful analysis of impartial military criticism, or to the ultimate arbitrament of history.

When the capture of Fort Henry separated Tennessee into two distinct theaters of war, General Johnston assigned the district west of the Tennessee River to General Beauregard, who had been sent to him for duty. This officer had suddenly acquired a high reputation at the battle of Bull Run, and General Johnston naturally intrusted him with a large discretion. He sent him with instructions to concentrate all available forces near Corinth, a movement previously begun. His own plan was to defend Columbus to the last extremity with a reduced garrison, and withdraw Polk and his army for active movements. Beauregard made the mistake, however, of evacuating Columbus, and making his defense of the Mississippi River at Island Number Ten, which proved untenable and soon surrendered with a garrison of 6000 or 7000 men. He was ill most of the time and intrusted the actual command to Bragg, but did what he could from his sick-bed.

Besides the reënforcements brought by Bragg, General Beauregard found in the western district 17,500 effectives under Polk, and at or near Corinth 3000 men under Pope Walker and Chalmers, and 5000 under Ruggles sent from Louisiana by Lovell. He made eloquent appeals, which brought him several regiments more. Thus he had nearly 40,000 men collected for him, 10,000 of whom he disposed in river defenses, and the remainder to protect the railroads from Grant's force which was concentrating at Pittsburg

Landing.   General Johnston's arrival increased the force at Corinth to about 50,000 men, about 40,000 of whom were effectives.

After the surrender at Donelson, the South, but especially the important State of Tennessee, was in a delirium of rage and terror.   As the retreat from Nashville to the Tennessee River went on, the popular fury rose to a storm everywhere.   The people who had refused to listen to his warnings, or answer his appeals for aid, now denounced General Johnston as an idiot, coward, and traitor.   Demagogues joined in the wild hunt for a victim, and deputations waited on President Davis to demand his removal.   To such a committee of congressmen he replied: "If Sidney Johnston is not a general, I have none." General Johnston was too calm, too just, and too magnanimous to misapprehend so natural a manifestation.   His whole life had been a training for this occasion.   To encounter suddenly and endure calmly the obloquy of a whole nation is, to any man, a great burden.   To do this with a serenity that shall not only not falter in duty, but restore confidence and organize victory, is conclusive proof of greatness of soul.

But while the storm of execration raged around him, the men who came into immediate contact with General Johnston never for a moment doubted his ability to perform all that was possible to man in the circumstances. To a friend who urged him to publish an explanation of his course he replied: "I cannot correspond with the people.   What the people want is a battle and a victory.   That is the best explanation I can make.   I require no vindication.   I trust that to the future." ⌡

General Johnston's plan of campaign may be summed up in a phrase.   It was to concentrate at Corinth and interpose his whole force in front of the great bend of the Tennessee, the natural base of the Federal army: this effected, to crush Grant in battle before the arrival of Buell.   This meant immediate and decisive action.   The army he had brought from Nashville was ready for the contest, but Generals Beauregard and Bragg represented to him that the troops collected by them were unable to move without thorough reorganization.   Ten days were consumed in this work of reorganization.   Moments were precious, but there was the hope of reënforcement by Van Dorn's army, which might arrive before Buell joined Grant, and which did arrive only a day or two later.   [See page 277.]   But Buell's movements were closely watched, and, hearing of his approach on the 2d of April, General Johnston resolved to delay no longer, but to strike at once a decisive blow.

In the reorganization of the army, he assigned General Bragg as chief of staff, with command of a corps.   To Beauregard he tendered the immediate command of the army in the impending battle.   Though General Beauregard declined the offer, he evidently misinterpreted its spirit and intention.   He imagined it was a confession of inadequacy for the duty, in which case he ought to have accepted it.   The truth was that, coming into this district which he had assigned to Beauregard, Johnston felt disinclined to deprive him of any reputation he might acquire from a victory.   He had not the

⌡ For part of his much-quoted letter of March 18th to President Davis, written at Decatur, in regard to the loss of Donelson, see foot-note, page 399.— EDITORS.

slightest idea, however, of abdicating the supreme command, and said to friends who remonstrated with him: "I will be there to see that all goes right." He was willing to yield to another the glory, if thereby anything was added to the chance of victory. The offer was rather quixotic, but characteristic; he

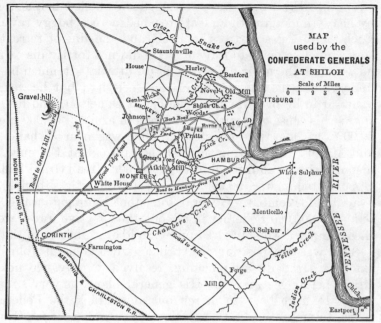

FROM THE "LIFE OF GENERAL A. S. JOHNSTON," BY W. P. JOHNSTON.   (D. APPLETON & CO.)

had done the same thing in his victories on the Neches in 1840. He then gave General Beauregard the position of second in command, without special assignment. Indeed, as is shown by his own frequent statements, General Beauregard was, from severe and protracted ill-health, inadequate to any more serious duty.

General Grant's army had been moved up the Tennessee River by boat, and had taken position on its left bank at Pittsburg Landing. It had been landed by divisions, and Bragg had proposed to Beauregard to attack Grant before he assembled his whole force. Beauregard forbade this, intending to await events, and attack him away from his base if possible, though he now insists that his plan of campaign was offensive. Grant's first object was to destroy the railroads which centered at Corinth, and, indeed, to capture that place if he could. But his advance was only a part of a grand plan for a combined movement of his own and Buell's army. With Pittsburg Landing as a base, this army was to occupy North Mississippi and Alabama, command the entire railroad system of that section, and take Memphis in the rear, while Halleck forced his way down the Mississippi River. General Johnston divined the movement before it was begun, and was there to frustrate it. Indeed, Grant's army was assembled at Pittsburg Landing only one week before Johnston completed the concentration.

Grant has been severely criticised for placing his army with the river at its back. But he was there to take the initiative. He had the larger army, under cover, too, of his gun-boats; he was expecting Buell daily; and the ground was admirable for defense. Indeed, his position was a natural stronghold. Flanked by Owl and Lick creeks, with their marshy margins, and with his front protected by a swampy valley, he occupied a quadrilateral of great strength. His troops were stationed on wooded heights, generally screened by heavy undergrowth and approached across boggy ravines or open fields. Each camp was a fortress in itself, and the line of retreat afforded at each step some like point to rally on. He did not fortify his camps, it is true; but he was not there for defense, but for attack. It must be admitted that he undervalued his enemy's daring and celerity; but he was a young general, exultant in his overwhelming victory at Donelson; and his generals and army shared his sense of security. He had an army of 58,000 men in camp, nearly 50,000 of whom were effectives. Buell was near at hand with 37,000 more, and Mitchel was moving against the railroad at Florence, Alabama, not far distant, with an additional force of 18,000. In all Grant had 105,000 effectives. Opposed to him were 50,000 Confederate troops, less than 40,000 of whom were available for combat. General Johnston's aggregate was 60,000 men, opposed to about 200,000 Federals in all, but the effective forces were as above. As these figures are disputed I invite a rigid examination of the Official Records.\

Such was the position on April 2d, when General Johnston, learning that Buell was rapidly approaching, resolved to advance next day and attack Grant before his arrival. His general plan was very simple in outline. It seems to have been to march out and attack the Federals by columns of corps, to make the battle a decisive test, and to crush Grant utterly or lose all in the attempt; this effected, to contend with Buell for the possession of Tennessee, Kentucky, and possibly the North-west.

General Beauregard also, it seems, had a plan, which, however, must have differed widely from that of General Johnston, as it was evidently tentative in its nature,—"a reconnoissance in force," with a retreat on Corinth as one of its features,— and which admitted the possibility of finishing on Monday a battle which had to be won on Sunday or never. This was not in any sense General Johnston's plan, and much useless discussion has arisen from a confusion of the two. But, as General Johnston intended to fight, and did fight, on his own plan as long as he lived, the battle may be considered his until Beauregard's order of retreat, about 5 o'clock Sunday evening, substituted "the reconnoissance in force" in place of the decisive test of victory or defeat.

General Beauregard had been on the ground some six weeks, and his prestige as an engineer and a victor of Bull Run warranted General Johnston in committing to him the elaboration of the details of the march and order of battle. Unfortunately he changed what seems evidently General Johnston's original purpose of an assault by columns of corps into an array in three parallel lines of battle, which produced extreme confusion when the second and third lines advanced to support the first and intermingled with it. Johnston's original plan is summed up in the following dispatch to President Davis:

"CORINTH, April 3d, 1862. General Buell in motion thirty thousand strong, rapidly from Columbia by Clifton to Savannah. Mitchel behind him with ten thousand. Confederate forces— forty thousand — ordered forward to offer battle near Pittsburg. Division from Bethel, main

\ By careful and thorough examination of the Official Records we have not been able to verify Colonel Johnston's estimates of forces. In important particulars the Records are not explicit, and in places they indicate that Colonel Johnston greatly overestimates the Union strength. Before January, 1863 (when a new form was adopted), the Union returns did not show the number of *effectives* separate from the "present for duty," a term that included the non-combatants.—EDITORS.

body from Corinth, reserve from Burnsville, converging to-morrow near Monterey on Pittsburg. Beauregard second in command, Polk the left, Bragg the center, Hardee the right wing, Breckinridge the reserve. *Hope engagement before Buell can form junction.*"

In the original dispatch, the words italicised are in General Johnston's own handwriting. The words, "the left," "the center," "the right wing," "the reserve," clearly point to a formation by columns of corps. Moreover, owing to ignorance of the country, the march was so ordered that the corps interfered with each other in their advance, and by a detention the battle was delayed an entire day, an almost fatal loss of time.

If it be asked why General Johnston accepted and issued an order of march and battle which he had not contemplated, the reply is that it had been prepared by his second in command, who was presumably more familiar with the country and the roads than himself, and hence with the necessities of the case. But the overruling reason was the question of *time*. Buell was at hand, and Johnston's plan was not to manœuvre, but to attack; and *any* plan which put him front to front with Grant was better than the best two days later. Besides, the written orders were not shown him until the morning of

LIEUTENANT-GENERAL W. J. HARDEE, C. S. A.
FROM A PHOTOGRAPH.

the 4th, after he had mounted to start to the front, and when his advance was near its position on the field. It was then obviously too late to apply a remedy.

General Johnston did not undervalue the importance of details. No man regarded more closely all the details subsidiary to a great result than he. But, important as were the preliminaries,— the maps, the roads, the methods of putting his army face to face with the enemy, which General Johnston had to take on trust,— he knew that the chief *strategy* of the battle was in the decision to fight. Once in the presence of the enemy, he knew that the result would depend *on the way in which his troops were handled.* This was his part of the work, and he felt full confidence in his own ability to carry it out successfully. The order was issued, as elaborated by Beauregard, and the army was moved against the enemy, April 3d, 1862. Said General Bragg:

"The details of that plan, arranged after General Sidney Johnston decided on delivering battle, and had given his instructions, were made up and published to the army in full from the adjutant-general's office. My first knowledge of them was derived from this general order, the authorship of which has been claimed by General Beauregard. . . . In this case, as I understood then, and still believe, Johnston gave verbal instructions for the general movement. . . . Over his [Colonel Jordan, the adjutant-general's] signature, they reached the army. The general plan (General Johnston's) was admirable — *the elaboration simply execrable.*

"When the time arrived for execution, you know well what occurred. In spite of opposition and prediction of failure, Johnston firmly and decidedly ordered and led the attack in the execution of his general plan, and, notwithstanding the faulty arrangement of troops, was eminently successful up to the moment of his fall. *The victory was won.* How it was lost, the official reports will show, and history has recorded." [Bragg to W. P. Johnston, December 16th, 1874.]

The President of the Confederate States has repeatedly and positively asserted that he received from General Johnston a dispatch which gave the plan of battle, exactly as it was fought, and that this dispatch was not that of April 3d already quoted, but was lost. General Beauregard and his staff-officer, Colonel Jordan, have taken issue with Mr. Davis on this point, vehemently insisting that no such dispatch was, or could have been, sent. Their denial rests merely upon *a priori* objections to the probability of Mr. Davis's assertion. On the other hand, Mr. Davis's clear and positive statement made many years ago, and often repeated since, is confirmed by contemporary documentary evidence. On April 5th he sent a telegram to General Johnston, in which he acknowledges his telegram of " yesterday," April 4th. This telegram of " yesterday" was plainly the "lost dispatch," for " yesterday" was April 4th, not April 3d. If, as I have sought to show, important changes had occurred in the plan of battle, nothing could be more natural and proper for the commanding general than instantly to inform his friend and commander-in-chief ; and even if no change had occurred, still it would have been right for him to keep his chief fully advised of the progress of the movement. I have always said that General Johnston's *original* plan was probably to attack by columns of corps, as indicated in his telegram of April 3d. Special Orders, No. 8 directed an attack in three lines parallel to the enemy's front. Jordan tells us General Johnston did not see these orders as published until the morning of the 4th. What more natural than that he should then communicate the changes made, and add his purpose to turn the enemy's left, not mentioned in the telegram of April 3d. A curious corroboration, hitherto unobserved, occurs in Mr. Davis's telegram of April 5th, that it was in reply to a lost dispatch. On April 2d General Beauregard wrote to General Johnston, saying that he had telegraphed to the War Department for generals, and adding, "Would it not be well for you to telegraph also for the generals you may require ?" We have no record of any such request made upon this suggestion, but Mr. Davis, in his telegram of April 5th, says: " Brigadiers have been recently appointed ; among them, Bowen. Do you require others ?" This seems to be a response to a request ; Bowen was commanding a brigade in General Johnston's army. But as there was no request in General Johnston's telegram of April 3d, it is reasonable to suppose that it was contained in one of the 4th, which has been lost. But I am giving an importance to this question which it would not merit except for the prominence given it in the pages of "The Century Magazine." Whether sent or not, it is entirely irrelevant to the main issue. Its whole importance consists in showing, not who made the plan of battle, but that the plan having been given to his subordinates, General Johnston, so long as he lived, held them to the steady and successful execution of it. When General Beauregard succeeded to the command he abandoned the vital principle of that plan, which was to push the contest to a final decision that day, and took a course of his own, not embraced or contemplated in General Johnston's designs — a policy of withdrawal and delay which led to defeat instead of victory.

General Johnston gave orders about 1 o'clock on the night of Wednesday, the 2d of April, for the advance. But much time was spent in their elaboration, and the troops did not receive them from the adjutant-general's office until the next afternoon. When the soldiers learned that they were going out to fight, their long-restrained ardor burst into a blaze of enthusiasm, and they did all that was possible for inexperienced troops in both marching and fighting. Some of the arms were not distributed till that afternoon. With hasty preparations the movement began, and Hardee's corps was at Mickey's, within four or five miles of Pittsburg, next morning. But some of the troops did not move until the morning of Saturday, the 5th, owing to a still further delay in the delivery of orders by the adjutant-general's office, and all were impeded by the heavy condition of the roads, through a dense forest, and across sloughs and marshes.

The order was to attack at 3 o'clock on the morning of Saturday, the 5th; but the troops were not in position until late that afternoon. All day Friday the advancing columns had pushed on over the tangled, miry roads, hindered and embarrassed by a pelting rain. After midnight a violent storm broke upon them as they stood under arms in the pitch darkness, with no shelter but the trees. From detention by the rain, ignorance of the roads, and a confusion produced by the order of march, some divisions failed to get into line, and the day was wasted.

As they were waiting the disposition of troops late Saturday afternoon, a council of war occurred, in which Johnston, Beauregard, Bragg, Polk, Breckinridge and Gilmer took part, which added greatly to General Johnston's responsibilities, and the heavy burden he had already incurred by his experiment of concentration, and his resolve to fight a pitched battle. The Confederate army was in full battle array, within two miles of Shiloh Church and Grant's line, when General Beauregard suddenly proposed that the army should be withdrawn and retreat to Corinth. He maintained that the delay and noise must have given the enemy notice, and that they would be found intrenched "to their eyes" and ready for attack. General Johnston seemed to be much surprised at the suggestion. Polk and Bragg differed with Beauregard, and a warm discussion ensued between him and Polk, in which General Johnston took little part, but closed it with the simple remark, "Gentlemen, we shall attack at daylight to-morrow," which he uttered with great decision. Turning to one of his staff-officers, he said, "I would fight them if they were a million. They can present no greater front between these two creeks than we can, and the more men they crowd in there, the worse we can make it for them. Polk is a true soldier and a friend."

General Bragg, in a monograph prepared for the use of the writer, says: "The meeting then dispersed upon an invitation of the commanding general to meet at his tent that evening. At that meeting a further discussion elicited the same views, and the same firm, decided determination. The next morning, about dawn of day, the 6th, as the troops were being put in motion, several generals again met at the camp-fire of the general-in-chief. The discussion was renewed, General Beauregard again expressing his dissent, when, rapid firing in front indicating that the attack had commenced, General Johnston closed the discussion by remarking, 'The battle has opened, gentlemen; it is too late to change our dispositions.' He proposed to move to the front, and his subordinates promptly joined their respective commands, inspired by his coolness, confidence, and determination. Few men have equaled him in the possession and display at the proper time of these great qualities of the soldier."

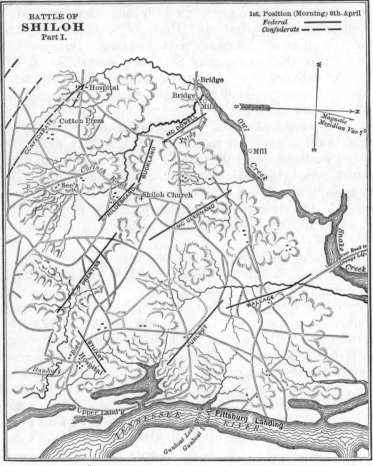

FROM THE "LIFE OF GENERAL A. S. JOHNSTON," BY W. P. JOHNSTON.   (D. APPLETON & CO.)

It will readily be seen how much General Beauregard's urgent opposition to fighting must have added to the weight of General Johnston's responsibility. Beauregard was in the full tide of popular favor, while Johnston was laboring under the load of public obloquy and odium. Nothing short of complete and overwhelming victory would vindicate him in differing with so famous a general. A reverse, even a merely partial success, would leave him under condemnation. Nevertheless, without a moment's hesitation, he resolved to fight.

The sun set on Saturday evening in a cloudless sky, and night fell calm, clear, and beautiful. Long before dawn the forest was alive with silent preparations for the ensuing contest, and day broke upon a scene so fair that it left its memory on thousands of hearts. The sky was clear overhead, the air fresh, and when the sun rose in full splendor, the advancing host passed the word from lip to lip that it was the "sun of Austerlitz."

General Johnston, usually so self-contained, felt the inspiration of the scene, and welcomed with exultant joy the long-desired day. His presence inspired all who came near him. His sentences, sharp, terse, and clear, had the ring of victory in them. Turning to his staff, as he mounted, he exclaimed: "To-night we will water our horses in the Tennessee River." It was thus that he formulated his plan of battle; it must not stop short of entire victory. To Randall L. Gibson, who was commanding a Louisiana brigade, he said: "I hope you may get through safely to-day, but *we must win a victory.*" To Colonel John S. Marmaduke, who had served under him in Utah, he said, placing his hand on his shoulder: "My son, we must this day conquer or perish." To the ambitious Hindman, who had been in the vanguard from the beginning, he said: "You have *earned* your spurs as a major-general. Let this day's work win them." With such words, as he rode from point to point, he raised a spirit in that host which swept away the serried lines of the conquerors of Donelson. Friend and foe alike testify to the enthusiastic courage and ardor of the Southern soldiers that day.

General Johnston's strategy was completed. He was face to face with his foe, and that foe all unaware of his coming. His front line, composed of the Third Corps and Gladden's brigade, was under Hardee, and extended from Owl Creek to Lick Creek, more than three miles. (See maps.) Hindman's division of two brigades occupied the center, Cleburne's brigade had the left, and Gladden's the right wing — an effective total in the front line of 9024. The second line was commanded by Bragg. He had two divisions: Withers's, of two brigades, on the right, and Ruggles's, of three brigades, on the left. The brigades were, in order from right to left, as follows: Chalmers, Jackson, Gibson, Anderson, Pond. This second line was 10,731 strong. The third line, or reserve, was composed of the First Corps, under Polk, and three brigades under Breckinridge. Polk's command was massed in columns of brigades on the Bark road near Mickey's, and Breckinridge's on the road from Monterey toward the same point. Polk was to advance on the left of the Bark road, at an interval of about eight hundred paces from Bragg's line; and Breckinridge, to the right of that road, was to give support wherever it should become necessary. Polk's corps, 9136 strong in infantry and artillery, was composed of two divisions: Cheatham's on the left, made up of Bushrod R. Johnson's and Stephens's brigades, and Clark's on his right, formed of A. P. Stewart's and Russell's brigades. It followed Bragg's line at a distance of about eight hundred yards. Breckinridge's reserve was composed of Trabue's, Bowen's, and Statham's brigades, with a total, infantry and artillery, of 6439. The cavalry, about 4300 strong, guarded the flanks or was detached on outpost duty; but, both from the newness and imperfection of their organization, equipment, and drill, and from the rough and wooded character of the ground, they could do little service that day. The effectives of all arms that marched out to battle were about 39,630, or, exclusive of cavalry, 35,330.

The Federal army numbered present 49,232, and present for duty 41,543. But at Crump's Landing, five or six miles distant, was General Lew Wallace's division with 8820 present, and 7771 men present for duty. [See page 538.] General Nelson's division of Buell's army had arrived at Savannah on Saturday morning, and was now about five miles distant; Crittenden's division also had arrived on the morning of the 6th. So that Grant, with these three divisions, may be considered as having about 22,000 men in immediate reserve, without counting the remainder of Buell's army, which was near by.│

As General Johnston and his staff were taking their coffee, the first gun of the battle sounded. "Note the hour, if you please, gentlemen," said General Johnston. It was fourteen minutes past 5. They immediately mounted and galloped to the front.

Some skirmishing on Friday between the Confederate cavalry and the Federal outposts, in which a few men were killed, wounded, and captured on both sides, had aroused the vigilance of the Northern commanders to some extent. Sherman reported on the 5th to Grant that two regiments of infantry and one of cavalry were in his front, and added: "I have no doubt that nothing will occur to-day more than some picket-firing. . . . I do not apprehend anything like an attack on our position." In his "Memoirs" he says: "I did not believe they designed anything but a strong demonstration." He said to Major Ricker that an advance of Beauregard's army "could not be possible. Beauregard was not such a fool as to leave his base of operations and attack us in ours,— *mere reconnoissance in force.*" This shows a curious coincidence with the actual state of General Beauregard's mind on that day. And Grant telegraphed Halleck on Saturday night: "The main force of the enemy is at Corinth. . . . One division of Buell's column arrived yesterday. . . . I have scarcely the faintest idea of an attack (general one) being made upon us."

Nevertheless, some apprehension was felt among the officers and men of the Federal army, and General Prentiss had thrown forward Colonel Moore, with the 21st Missouri regiment, on the Corinth road. Moore, feeling his way cautiously, encountered Hardee's skirmish-line under Major Hardcastle, and, thinking it an outpost, assailed it vigorously. Thus really the Federals began the fight. The struggle was brief, but spirited. The 8th and 9th Arkansas came up. Moore fell wounded. The Missourians gave way, and Shaver's brigade pursued them. Hindman's whole division moved on, following the ridge and drifting to the right, and drove in the grand guards and outposts until they struck Prentiss's camps. Into these they burst, overthrowing all before them.

To appreciate the suddenness and violence of the blow, one must read the testimony of eye-witnesses. General Bragg says, in a sketch of Shiloh made for the writer: "Contrary to the views of such as urged an abandonment of the attack, the enemy was found utterly unprepared, many being surprised and captured in their tents, and others, though on the outside, in costumes better fitted to the bedchamber than to the battle-field." General Preston says: "General Johnston then went to the camp assailed, which was carried between 7 and 8 o'clock. The enemy were evidently surprised. The breakfasts were

---

│ General Grant takes no account of these in his narratives of the battle, and talks as though he were outnumbered instead of outgeneraled. It was his business to get these troops there in time, especially if he was not surprised.—W. P. J.

on the mess tables, the baggage unpacked, the knapsacks, stores, colors, and ammunition abandoned."

The essential feature of General Johnston's strategy had been to get at his enemy as quickly as possible, and in as good order. In this he had succeeded. His plan of battle was as simple as his strategy. It had been made known in his order of battle, and was thoroughly understood by every brigade commander. The orders of the 3d of April were, that "every effort should be made to turn the *left flank of the enemy,* so as to cut off his line of retreat to the Tennessee River and *throw him back on Owl Creek, where he will be obliged to surrender.*" It is seen that, from the first, these orders were carried out in letter and spirit; and, so long as General Johnston lived, the success of this movement was complete. *The battle was fought precisely as it was planned.* The first, and almost only, censure of this plan was made by Colonel Jordan, confidential adviser and historian of General Beauregard, who now claims to have made this plan. The instructions delivered to General Johnston's subordinates on the previous day were found sufficient for their conduct on the battle-field. But, to accomplish this, his own personal presence and inspiration and direction were often necessary with these enthusiastic but raw troops. He had personal conference on the field with most of his generals, and led several brigades into battle. The criticism upon this conduct, that he exposed himself unnecessarily, is absurd to those who know how important rapid decision and instantaneous action are in the crisis of conflict.

His lines of battle were pushed rapidly to the front, and as gaps widened in the first lines, they were filled by brigades of the second and third. One of Breckinridge's brigades (Trabue's) was sent to the left to support Cleburne and fought under Polk the rest of the day; and the other two were led to the extreme right, only Chalmers being beyond them. Gladden, who was on Hindman's right, and had a longer distance to traverse to strike some of Prentiss's brigades further to the left, found them better prepared, but, after a sanguinary resistance, drove them from their camps. In this bitter struggle Gladden fell mortally wounded. Chalmers's brigade, of Bragg's line, came in on Gladden's right, and his Mississippians drove the enemy, under Stuart, with the bayonet half a mile. He was about to charge again, when General Johnston came up, and moved him to the right, and brought John K. Jackson's brigade into the interval. Prentiss's left and Stuart's brigade retreated sullenly, not routed, but badly hammered.

With Hindman as a pivot, the turning movement began from the moment of the overthrow of Prentiss's camps. While the front attacks were made all along the line with a desperate courage which would have swept any ordinary resistance from the field, and with a loss which told fearfully on the assailants, they were seconded by assaults in flank which invariably resulted in crushing the Federal line with destructive force and strewing the field with the wounded and the dead. The Federal reports complain that they were flanked and outnumbered, which is true; for, though fewer, the Confederates were probably stronger at every given point throughout the day except at the center called the Hornets' Nest, where the Federals eventually massed nearly two divisions.   The iron flail of war beat upon the Federal front and right flank with the regular and ponderous pulsations of some great engine, and these assaults resulted in a crumbling process which was continually but slowly going on, as regiment and brigade and division yielded to the continuous and successive blows.   There has been criticism that there were no grand assaults by divisions and corps.   In a broken, densely wooded and unknown country, and with the mode of attack in parallel lines, this was impossible, but the attack was unremitting and the fact is that there were but few lulls in the contest. The fighting was a grapple and a death-struggle all day long, and, as one brigade after another wilted before the deadly fire of the stubborn Federals, still another was pushed into the combat and kept up the fierce assault. A breathing-spell, and

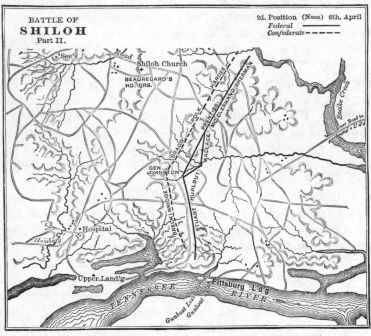

BATTLE OF
SHILOH
Part II.

2d. Position   (Noon) 6th. April
Federal ————
Confederate – – – – –

FROM THE "LIFE OF GENERAL A. S. JOHNSTON," BY W. P. JOHNSTON.   (D. APPLETON & CO.)

the shattered command would gather itself up and resume its work of destruction.   These were the general aspects of the battle.

When the battle began Hindman, following the ridge, had easy ground to traverse; but Cleburne's large brigade, on his left, with its supports, moving over a more difficult country, was slower in getting upon Sherman's front. That general and his command were aroused by the long roll, the advancing musketry, and the rush of troops to his left, and he got his division in line of battle and was ready for the assault of Cleburne, which was made about 8 o'clock.   General Johnston, who had followed close after Hindman, urging on his attack, saw Cleburne's brigade begin its advance, and then returned to where Hindman was gathering his force for another assault.   Hardee said of Cleburne that he "moved quickly through the fields, and, though far outflanked by the enemy on our left, rushed forward under a terrific fire from the serried ranks drawn up in front of the camp.   A morass covered his front, and, being difficult to pass, caused a break in this brigade.   Deadly volleys were poured upon the men from behind bales of hay and other defenses, as they advanced; and after a series of desperate charges they were compelled to fall back.

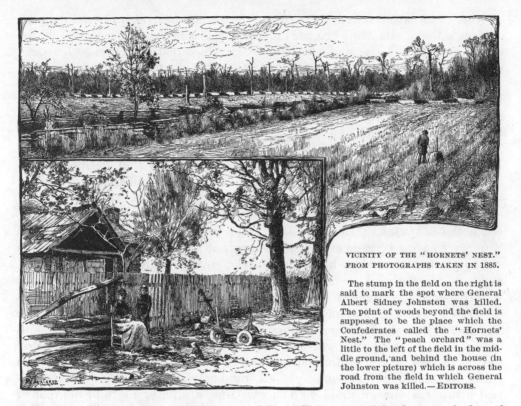

VICINITY OF THE "HORNETS' NEST."
FROM PHOTOGRAPHS TAKEN IN 1885.

The stump in the field on the right is said to mark the spot where General Albert Sidney Johnston was killed. The point of woods beyond the field is supposed to be the place which the Confederates called the "Hornets' Nest." The "peach orchard" was a little to the left of the field in the middle ground, and behind the house (in the lower picture) which is across the road from the field in which General Johnston was killed.— EDITORS.

Supported by the arrival of the second line, Cleburne, with the remainder of his troops, . . . entered the enemy's encampment, which had been forced on the center and right by . . . Gladden's, Wood's, and Hindman's brigades."

While Sherman was repelling Cleburne's attack, McClernand sent up three Illinois regiments to reënforce his left. But General Polk led forward Bushrod R. Johnson's brigade, and General Charles Clark led Russell's brigade, against Sherman's left, while General Johnston himself put A. P. Stewart's brigade in position on their right. Supported by part of Cleburne's line, they attacked Sherman and McClernand fiercely. Polk said: "The resistance at this point was as stubborn as at any other point on the field." Clark and Bushrod R. Johnson fell badly wounded. Hildebrand's Federal brigade was swept from the field, losing in the onslaught 300 killed and wounded, and 94 missing.

Wood's brigade, of Hindman's division, joined in this charge on the right. As they hesitated at the crest of a hill, General Johnston came to the front and urged them to the attack. They rushed forward with the inspiring "rebel yell," and with Stewart's brigade enveloped the Illinois troops. In ten minutes the latter melted away under the fire, and were forced from the field. In this engagement John A. McDowell's and Veatch's Federal brigades, as well as Hildebrand's, were demolished and heard of no more. Buckland retreated and took position with McClernand. In these attacks Anderson's and Pond's Confederate brigades joined with great vigor and severe loss, but with unequal fortune. The former had one success after another; the latter suffered a series of disasters; and yet an equal courage animated them. Gladden's brigade made a final desperate and successful charge on Prentiss's line. The whole Federal front, which had been broken here and there, and was getting ragged, gave way under this hammering process on front and flank, and fell back across a ravine to another strong position behind the Hamburg and Purdy road in rear of Shiloh. Sherman's route of retreat was marked by the thick-strewn corpses of his soldiers. At last, pressed back toward both Owl Creek and the river, Sherman and McClernand found safety by the interposition on their left flank of W. H. L. Wallace's fresh division. Hurlbut and Wallace had advanced about 8 o'clock, so that Prentiss's command found a refuge in the intervals of the new and formidable Federal line, with Stuart on the left and Sherman's shattered division on the right.

General Johnston had pushed Chalmers to the right and front, sweeping down the left bank of Lick Creek, driving in pickets, until he encountered Stuart's Federal brigade on the Pittsburg and Hamburg road. Stuart was strongly posted on a steep hill near the river, covered with thick undergrowth, and with an open field in front. McArthur was to his right and rear in the woods. Jackson attacked McArthur, who fell back; and Chalmers went at Stuart's brigade. This command reserved its fire until Chalmers's men were within forty yards, and then delivered a heavy and destructive volley; but, after a hard fight, the Federals were driven back. Chalmers's right rested on the Tennessee River bottom-lands, and he fought down the bank toward Pittsburg Landing. The enemy's left was completely turned, and the Federal army was now crowded on a shorter line, a mile or more to the rear of its first position, with many of their brigades *hors de combat*. The new line of battle was established before 10 o'clock. All the Confederate troops were then in the front line, except two of Breckinridge's brigades, Bowen's and Statham's, which were moving to the Confederate right, and soon occupied the interval to the left of Chalmers and Jackson. Hardee, with Cleburne and Pond, was pressing Sherman slowly but steadily back. Bragg and Polk met about half-past 10 o'clock, and by agreement Polk led his troops against McClernand, while Bragg directed the operations against the Federal center. A gigantic contest now began which lasted more than five hours. In the impetuous rush forward of regiments to fill the gaps in the front line, even the brigade organization was broken; but, though there was dislocation of commands, there was little loss of effective force. The Confederate assaults were made by rapid and often unconnected charges along the line. They were repeatedly checked, and often repulsed. Sometimes counter-charges drove them back for short distances; but, whether in assault or recoil, both sides saw their bravest soldiers fall in frightful numbers. The Confederates came on in motley garb, varying from the favorite gray and domestic "butternut" to the blue of certain Louisiana regiments, which paid dearly the penalty of doubtful colors. Over them waved flags and pennons as various as their uniforms. At each charge there went up a wild yell, heard above the roar of artillery; only the Kentuckians, advancing with measured step, sang in chorus their war-song: "Cheer, boys, cheer; we'll march away to battle."

SCENE OF GENERAL
ALBERT SIDNEY
JOHNSTON'S DEATH.

FROM A PHOTOGRAPH TAKEN
IN THE SUMMER OF
1884.

On the Federal left center W. H. L. Wallace's and Hurlbut's divisions were massed, with Prentiss's fragments, in a position so impregnable, and thronged with such fierce defenders, that it won from the Confederates the memorable title of the "Hornets' Nest." [See pages 504–5, 510, and 588.] Here, behind a dense thicket on the crest of a hill, was posted a strong force of as hardy troops as ever fought, almost perfectly protected by the conformation of the ground, and by logs and other rude and hastily prepared defenses. To assail it an open field had to be passed, enfiladed by the fire of its batteries. No figure of speech would be too strong to express the deadly peril of assault upon this natural fortress. For five hours brigade after brigade was led against it. Hindman's brigades, which earlier had swept everything before them, were reduced to fragments, and paralyzed for the remainder of the day. A. P. Stewart's regiments made fruitless assaults. Then Bragg ordered up Gibson's brigade. Gibson himself, a knightly soldier, was aided by colonels three of whom afterward became generals. The brigade made a gallant charge; but, like the others, recoiled from the fire it encountered. Under a cross-fire of artillery and musketry it at last fell back with very heavy loss. Gibson asked that artillery should be sent him; but it was not at hand, and Bragg sent orders to charge again. The colonels thought it hopeless; but Gibson led them again to the attack, and again they suffered a bloody repulse.

The brigade was four times repulsed, but maintained its ground steadily, until W. H. L. Wallace's position was turned, when, renewing its forward movement in conjunction with Cheatham's command, it helped to drive back its stout opponents. Cheatham, charging with Stephens's brigade on Gibson's right, across an open field, had been caught under a murderous cross-fire, but fell back in good order, and, later in the day, came in on Breckinridge's left in the last assault when Prentiss was captured. This bloody fray lasted till nearly 4 o'clock, without making any visible impression on the Federal center. But when its flanks were turned, these assaulting columns, crowding in on its front, aided in its capture.

General Johnston was with the right of Statham's brigade, confronting the left of Hurlbut's division, which was behind the crest of a hill, with a depression filled with chaparral in its front. Bowen's brigade was further to the right in line with Statham's, touching it near this point. The Confederates held the parallel ridge in easy musket-range; and "as heavy fire as I ever saw during the war," says Governor Harris, was kept up on both sides for an hour or more. It was necessary to cross the valley raked by this deadly ambuscade and assail the opposite ridge in order to drive the enemy from his stronghold. When General Johnston came up and saw the situation, he said to his staff: "They are offering stubborn resistance here. I shall have to put the bayonet to them." It was the crisis of the conflict. The Federal key was in his front. If his assault were successful, their left would be completely turned, and the victory won. He determined to charge. He sent Governor Harris, of his staff, to lead a Tennessee regiment; and, after a brief conference with Breckinridge, whom he loved and admired, that officer, followed by his staff, appealed to the soldiers. As he encouraged them with his fine voice and manly bearing, General Johnston rode out in front and slowly down the line. His hat was off. His sword rested in its scabbard. In his right hand he held a little tin cup, the memorial of an incident that had occurred earlier in the day. Passing through a captured camp, he had taken this toy, saying, "Let this be my share of the spoils to-day." It was this plaything which, holding it between two fingers, he employed more effectively in his natural and simple gesticulation than most men could have used a sword. His presence was full of inspiration. He sat his thoroughbred bay, "Fire-eater," with easy command. His voice was persuasive, encouraging, and compelling. His words were few; he said: "Men! they are stubborn; we must use the bayonet." When he reached the center of the line, he turned. "I will lead you!" he cried, and moved toward the enemy. The line was already thrilling and trembling with that irresistible ardor which in battle decides the day. With a mighty shout Bowen's and Statham's brigades moved forward at a charge. A sheet of flame and a mighty roar burst from the Federal stronghold. The Confederate line withered; but there was not an instant's pause. The crest was gained. The enemy were in flight.

General Johnston had passed through the ordeal seemingly unhurt. His horse was shot in four places; his clothes were pierced by missiles; his boot-sole was cut and torn by a minie; but if he himself had received any severe wound, he did not know it. At this moment Governor Harris rode up from the right. After a few words, General Johnston sent him with an order to Colonel Statham, which having delivered, he speedily returned. In the meantime, knots and groups of Federal soldiers kept up a desultory fire as they retreated upon their supports, and their last line, now yielding, delivered volley after volley as they sullenly retired. By the chance of war, a minie-ball from one of these did its fatal work. As he sat there, after his wound, Captain Wickham says that Colonel O'Hara, of his staff, rode up, and General Johnston said to him, "We must go to the left, where the firing is heaviest," and then gave him an order, which O'Hara rode off to obey. Governor Harris returned, and, finding him very pale, asked him, "General, are you wounded?" He answered, in a very deliberate and emphatic tone: "Yes, and, I fear, seriously." These were his last words. Harris and Wickham led his horse back under cover of the hill, and lifted him from it. They searched at random for the wound, which had cut an artery in his leg, the blood flowing into his boot. When his brother-in-law, Preston, lifted his head, and addressed him with passionate grief, he smiled faintly, but uttered no word. His life rapidly ebbed away, and in a few moments he was dead.

His wound was not necessarily fatal. General Johnston's own knowledge of military surgery was adequate for its control by an extemporized tourniquet had he been aware or regardful of its nature. Dr. D. W. Yandell, his surgeon, had attended his person during most of the morning; but, finding a large number of wounded men, including many Federals, at one point, General Johnston had ordered Yandell to stop there, establish a hospital, and give them his services. He said to Yandell: "These men were our enemies a moment ago; they are our prisoners now. Take care of them." Yandell remonstrated against leaving him, but he was peremptory. Had Yandell remained with him, he would have had little difficulty with the wound.

Governor Harris, and others of General Johnston's staff, promptly informed General Beauregard of his death, and General Beauregard assumed command, remaining at Shiloh Church, awaiting the issue of events.

Up to the moment of the death of the commander-in-chief, in spite of the dislocation of the commands, there was the most perfect regularity in the development of the plan of battle. In all the seeming confusion there was the predominance of intelligent design; a master mind, keeping in clear view its purpose, sought the weak point in the defense, and, by massing his troops upon the enemy's left, kept turning that flank. With the disadvantage of inferior numbers, General Johnston brought to bear a superior force on each particular point, and, by a series of rapid and powerful blows, broke the Federal army to pieces.

Now was the time for the Confederates to push their advantage, and, closing in on the rear of Prentiss and Wallace, to finish the battle. But, on the contrary, there came a lull in the conflict on the right, lasting more than an hour from half-past 2, the time at which General Johnston fell. It is true that the Federals fell back and left the field, making some desultory resistance, and the Confederates went forward deliberately, occupying their positions, and thus helping to envelop the Federal center; but Breckinridge's two brigades did not make another charge that day, and there was no further general direction or concerted movement. The determinate purpose to capture Grant that day was lost sight of. The strong arm was withdrawn, and the bow remained unbent. Elsewhere there were bloody, desultory combats, but they tended to nothing.

About half-past 3 the contest, which had throbbed with fitful violence for five hours, was renewed with the utmost fury. While an ineffectual struggle was going on at the center, a number of batteries opened upon

Prentiss's right flank, the center of what remained of the Federals. The opening of so heavy a fire, and the simultaneous though unconcerted advance of the whole Confederate line, resulted at first in the confusion of the enemy, and then in the death of W. H. L. Wallace and the surrender of Prentiss.

These generals have received scant justice for their stubborn defense. They agreed to hold their position at all odds, and did so until Wallace received

BATTLE OF
SHILOH
Part III.

3rd. Position (Sunset) 6th. April
Federal ————
Confederate - - - - -

FROM THE "LIFE OF GENERAL A. S. JOHNSTON," BY W. P. JOHNSTON. (D. APPLETON & CO.)

his fatal wound and Prentiss was surrounded and captured with nearly three thousand men. This delay was the salvation of Grant's army.

General Breckinridge's command closed in on the Federal left and rear; General Polk crushed their right center by the violence of his assault, and in person, with Marshall J. Smith's Crescent regiment, received the surrender of many troops. General Prentiss gave up his sword to Colonel Russell. Bragg's troops, wrestling at the front, poured in over the Hornets' Nest, and shared in the triumph. Polk ordered his cavalry to charge the fleeing enemy, and Colonel Miller rode down and captured a 6-gun battery.

His men "watered their horses in the Tennessee River." All now felt that the victory was won. Bragg, Polk, Hardee, Breckinridge, all the corps commanders, were at the front, and in communication. Their generals were around them. The hand that had launched the thunder-bolt of war was cold, but its influence still nerved this host and its commanders. A line of battle was formed, and all was ready for the last fell swoop, to compel an "unconditional surrender" by General Grant.

The only position on the high grounds left to the Federals was held by Colonel Webster, of Grant's staff, who had collected some twenty guns or more and manned them with volunteers. Soon after 4 o'clock Chalmers and Jackson, proceeding down the river-bank while Prentiss's surrender was going on, came upon this position. The approaches were bad from that direction; nevertheless, they attacked resolutely, and, though repeatedly repulsed, kept up their assaults till nightfall. At one time they drove some gunners from their guns, and their attack has been generally mistaken by Federal writers for the final assault of the Confederate army—*which was never made.* The Federal generals and writers attribute their salvation to the repulse of Chalmers, and the honor is claimed respectively for Webster's artillery and for Ammen's brigade of Buell's army, which came up at the last moment. But neither they nor all that was left of the Federal army could have withstood five minutes the united advance of the Confederate line, which was at hand and ready to deal the death-stroke. Their salvation came from a different quarter. Bragg, in his monograph written for the use of the writer in preparing the "Life of A. S. Johnston," gives the following account of the close of the battle:

"Concurring testimony, especially that of the prisoners on both sides,— our captured being present and witnesses to the demoralization of the enemy, and their eagerness to escape or avoid further slaughter by surrender,— left no doubt but that a persistent, energetic assault would soon have been crowned by a general yielding of his whole force. About one hour of daylight was left to us. The enemy's gun-boats, his last hope, took position opposite us in the river, and commenced a furious cannonade at our supposed position. From the elevation necessary to reach the high bluff on which we were operating, this proved 'all sound and fury signifying nothing,' and did not in the slightest degree mar our prospects or our progress. Not so, however, in our rear, where these heavy shells fell among the reserves and stragglers; and to the utter dismay of the commanders on the field, the troops were seen to abandon their inspiring work, and to retire sullenly from the contest when danger was almost past, and victory, so dearly purchased, was almost certain."

Polk, Hardee, Breckinridge, Withers, Gibson, Gilmer, and all who were there confirm this statement. General Buell says of Grant's army that there were "not more than five thousand men in ranks and available on the battle-field at nightfall. . . . The rest were either killed, wounded, captured, or scattered in inextricable and hopeless confusion for miles along the banks of the river." General Nelson describes them as "cowering under the river-bank, . . . frantic with fright and utterly demoralized."

At this crisis came from General Beauregard an order for the withdrawal of the troops, of which his chief of staff says: "General Beauregard, in the meantime, observing the exhausted, widely scattered condition of his army, directed it to be brought out of battle, collected and restored to order as far as practicable, and to occupy for the night the captured encampments of the enemy. This, however, had been done in chief part by the officers in immediate command of the troops before the order was generally distributed." For this last allegation, or that the army was exhausted, there is not the slightest warrant. When Beauregard's staff-officer gave Bragg this order he said: "Have you promulgated this order to the command?" The officer replied: "I have." General Bragg then said: "If you had not I would not obey it. *The battle is lost.*"

The concurrent testimony of the generals and soldiers *at the front* is at one on all essential points. General Beauregard at Shiloh, two miles in the rear, with the *débris* of the army surging back upon him, the shells bursting around him, sick with his two months' previous malady, pictured in his imagination a wreck at the front, totally different from the actual condition there. Had this officer been with Bragg, and not greatly prostrated and suffering from severe sickness, I firmly believe his order would have been to advance, not to retire. And this in spite of his theory of his plan of battle, which he sums up as follows, and which is so different from General Johnston's: "By a rapid and vigorous attack on General Grant, it was expected he would be beaten back into his transports and the river, or captured in time to enable us to profit by the victory, and remove to the rear all the stores and munitions that would fall into our hands in such an event before the arrival of General Buell's army on the scene. It was never contemplated, however, to retain the position thus gained and abandon *Corinth, the strategic point of the campaign.*" Why, then, did General Beauregard stop short in his career? Sunday evening it was not a question of retaining, but of gaining, Pittsburg Landing. Complete victory was in his grasp, and he threw it away. General Gibson says: "General Johnston's death was a tremendous catastrophe. There are no words adequate to express my own conception of the immensity of the loss to our country. Sometimes the hopes of millions of people depend upon one head and one arm. The West perished with Albert Sidney Johnston, and the Southern country followed."

Monday was General Beauregard's battle, and it was well fought. But in recalling his troops from the heights which commanded the enemy's landing, he gave away a position which during the night was occupied by Buell's twenty thousand fresh troops, who thus regained the high grounds that had been won at such a cost. Lew Wallace, too, had come up 6500 strong.☆ Moreover, the orders had been conveyed by Beauregard's staff to brigades and even regiments to withdraw, and the troops wandered back over the field, without coherence, direction, or purpose, and encamped where chance provided for them. All array was lost, and, in the morning, they met the attack of nearly thirty thousand fresh and organized troops, with no hope of success except from their native valor and the resolute purpose roused by the triumph of Sunday. Their fortitude, their courage, and the free offering of their lives were equal to the day before. But it was a retreat, not an assault. They retired slowly and sullenly, shattered, but not overthrown, to Corinth, *the strategic point of General Beauregard's campaign.*

☆ General Wallace, in his report to General Halleck, says that his whole command "did not exceed 5000 men of all arms."— EDITORS.

PREACHING AT THE UNION CAMP DICK ROBINSON, KENTUCKY (SEE PAGE 377).   SKETCHED FROM A LITHOGRAPH.

THE CAMPAIGN OF SHILOH.

BY G. T. BEAUREGARD, GENERAL, C. S. A.

ON the 22d of January, 1862, Colonel Roger A. Pryor, a member of the Mili- tary Committee of the lower branch of the Confederate Congress, visited my headquarters at Centreville, Virginia, and in his own name, as also for the representatives in Congress of the Mississippi Valley States, urged me to consent to be transferred from the Army of the Potomac to the command of the Confederate forces at Columbus, Kentucky, within the Department of Kentucky and Tennessee, under the superior command of General Albert Sidney Johnston,— a transfer which he said Mr. Davis would not direct unless it was agreeable to me, but which was generally desired at Richmond because of the recent crushing disaster at Mill Springs, in eastern Kentucky: the defeat and death of Zollicoffer. Against the monitions of some of my friends at Richmond, and after much hesitation and disinclination to sever my relations with such an army as that of the Potomac, but upon the assurance that General Johnston's command embraced an aggregate of at least seventy thousand men of all arms, which, though widely scattered, might, by virtue of the possession of the "interior lines," be concentrated and operated offensively, I gave Colonel Pryor authority to inform Mr. Davis of my readiness to be thus transferred. Upon the return of Colonel Pryor to Richmond, I was, on the 26th of January, ordered to proceed at once "to report to General A. S. Johnston at Bowling Green, Kentucky," and thence

⌡ Recast and revised from the "North American Review" for January and February, 1886.—EDITORS.

as promptly as possible to assume my new command at Columbus, "which," said my orders, "is threatened by a powerful force, and the defense of which is of vital importance."

Dispatching Colonel Thomas Jordan, my chief of staff, to Richmond, with a view to secure from the War Department certain aids to the proper organization of the troops I was to command, I left Centreville on the 2d of February and reached Bowling Green about the 5th. General Johnston, whom I had never seen before, welcomed me to his department with a cordiality and earnestness that made a deep impression on me at the time. As he informed me, General Buell's army, fully 75,000 strong, was on the line of Bacon Creek, on the Louisville and Nashville railroad, about 40 miles from Bowling Green. General Grant had about 20,000 men in hand at or about Cairo, ready to move either upon Fort Henry or Fort Donelson. General Pope, having a force of not less than 30,000 men in Missouri, was menacing General Polk's positions, including New Madrid, while General Halleck, exercising command over the whole of this force of 125,000 men of all arms, had his headquarters at St. Louis.

On the other hand, General Johnston (as he stated, to my surprise) had an "aggregate effective" of not over 45,000 men of all arms, thus distributed: at Bowling Green, his headquarters, not over 14,000; at Forts Henry and Donelson, 5500; in the quarter of Clarksville, Tennessee, 8000; besides 17,000 under General Polk, chiefly at Columbus, and for the most part imperfectly organized, badly armed and equipped. As may be seen from any map of the region, the chief part of this force occupied a defensive line facing northwardly, the two salient extremities of which were Bowling Green, some 70 miles by railway in advance of Nashville, and Columbus, about 110 miles west of Bowling Green. This line was penetrated, almost centrally, by the Cumberland and Tennessee rivers, respectively, at points in Tennessee just south of the Kentucky line, twelve miles apart, at which Fort Henry had been established on the east bank of the Tennessee, and Fort Donelson on the west bank of the Cumberland, thus constituting the reëntering angle of the line. These vital works General Johnston described as defective in more than one respect and unready, but said that he had sent his chief engineer to improve their effectiveness as far as possible. So unpromising was the situation and so different from what had been represented before I left Virginia, that my first impulse was to return at once; but this idea was abandoned at the earnest request of General Johnston. However, after an inspection of the works at and around Bowling Green, I found that while strong against any direct attack, they could be readily turned on their right, and I so stated to General Johnston. His reply was, that in the event of a serious flank movement he must evacuate the position, having no relieving army to support it. In the face of this self-evident military proposition, I recommended the immediate evacuation of a position so salient as Bowling Green, that must fall from its own weight if turned,—leaving there only a cavalry force in observation, and concentrating at once all our available strength at Henry and Donelson, information having just reached us of the aggressive presence of General

Grant on the Tennessee River. That recommendation was not adopted, for the alleged reason that, in the event of a failure to defeat General Grant as proposed, our forces thus assembled might be caught and crushed between the armies of Grant and Buell, and that it would also expose to capture the large stock of military supplies collected so far in advance as Bowling Green and Clarksville, as well as at Nashville. In this decision sight was certainly lost of the facts that, having no pontoon-train, General Buell could not possibly throw his army across the Cumberland, between Donelson and Nashville, so as to prevent the Confederates from falling safely back behind Duck River, or retreating upon Nashville behind the Cumberland, as we would hold the interior or shorter lines.

Fort Henry having fallen after an ineffective but gallant defense of twenty-four hours, immediately thereafter the railroad bridge across the Tennessee, about twelve miles southward of the surrendered fortress, was destroyed. The direct line of communication between our forces eastward of that stream and those at Columbus having thus been broken, on the 7th of February I again urged as imperative the swift concentration of all our then available forces upon Donelson. General Johnston, however, asserting that Fort Donelson was not "tenable," would only support the position by directing the force at Clarksville to cross to the south side of the Tennessee River, and ordered immediate "preparations" to be made for the "removal" of the army at Bowling Green, "to Nashville, in rear of the Cumberland River."⚓ He also prescribed that, "from Nashville, should any further retrograde movement become necessary," it should be "made to Stevenson and thence according to circumstances."⚓ He further declared that as "the possession of the Tennessee River by the enemy, resulting from the fall of Fort Henry, separated the army at Bowling Green from the one at Columbus," henceforth the forces thus sundered must "act independently of each other until they can again be brought together."⚓

Fort Henry fell on the 6th of February, but General Grant, failing to press the signal advantage thus gained, did not advance against Fort Donelson until the 12th, and then with but 15,000 men, having dispatched, at the same time, 6 regiments under General Lew Wallace by water. The investment of the position was not completed, however, until early on the 13th of February, the Confederate commander having had a whole week for preparation. On the 6th of February the Confederate garrison at Fort Donelson embraced about 600 artillerists and 3 regiments of infantry, or at most 2350 officers and men; to this force Heiman's brigade and other troops, some 2500 men, were added that night, having been detached that morning from Fort Henry. Between the morning of the 7th of February and the investment of the position by the Federal army of 15,000 men, on the morning of the 13th, it was further increased from the troops on the east and north side of the Cumberland, under Brigadier-General Floyd, to whom the command of the defense was now intrusted, so as to be, in numbers, about equal to that of the enemy on the land side, until the latter was reënforced by General Wallace's

⚓ See p. 487, "Life of General A. S. Johnston," by W. P. Johnston. New York: D. Appleton & Co.

division, nearly 10,000 strong, later in the afternoon of the 14th. By that time the evacuation of Bowling Green, determined upon, as I have said, on the 7th,—and commenced on the 11th of February,—had been completed, the Confederate rear-guard having marched out of the town at 3:30 P. M. on the 14th.

Satisfied, as affairs stood, that Nashville and the Valley of the Cumberland could only be defended successfully at Donelson and by the crushing defeat of General Grant in that quarter, an end to which all other considerations were evidently of minor military importance, I had insisted, as I may repeat, upon that as the one evident exigent operation. That the resolution to give up Bowling Green and to begin such a movement as early as the 11th of February ought to have removed every possible objection on the part of General Johnston to going at once in person with fully ten thousand of his Bowling Green army, I am very sure must be the ultimate professional lesson taught by the history of that most disastrous Confederate campaign! Nothing were easier in the exigency than the transfer from Bowling Green to Donelson by the night of the 13th of February of ten thousand men, after General Johnston had decided that the immediate abandonment of Kentucky was an *imperative necessity.*↓ Thus, on the morning of the 14th, General Grant's army of 15,000 men could and should have been confronted with nearly if not quite 25,000 men, who, promptly handled, must have so effectually beaten their adversary, taken at such disadvantage, before the advent of Lew Wallace that afternoon, as to have enhanced the victory for the Confederates by the immediate defeat of Wallace also.

What happened from the policy adopted by the Confederate general in chief may be briefly stated: Fort Donelson was surrendered at 2 A. M. on the 16th of February, and with it 11,600 men. In the expressive words of General Johnston's telegram, which reached me at Corinth, "We lost all." And as in the business of war, as in all other material human affairs, "the omission to do that which is necessary seals a commission to a blank of dangers," so was it now. The failure to employ opportunely all possible available resources against General Grant, and the consequent loss of Donelson, with its invaluable garrison, carried immediately in its train the irrevocable loss of Nashville also, with the early abandonment of Middle Tennessee. Another irrevocable consequence was the evacuation of Columbus, with incalculable moral detriments. And had the stroke consummated at Donelson been vigorously pressed to its proper military corollary,—Buell being left to look after the remains of Johnston's army,—General Grant's victorious army of 25,000 men, with the resources of transportation at its disposal, might have been thrown within ten days, at latest, after the fall of Donelson, upon the rear of General Polk's forces at Columbus and their easy capture thus have been assured.

Going no farther in the direction of Columbus than Jackson, in West Tennessee, fifty-seven miles north of Corinth, I there established my headquarters, and called thither Colonel Jordan, my chief of staff, who had gone to Columbus direct from Virginia (with Captain D. B. Harris, my chief engi-

---

↓ It is noteworthy that in the movement to Nashville from Bowling Green, Breckinridge's division was marched twenty-seven miles one day. — G. T. B.

neer) to inspect the command. His report upon rejoining me about the 17th of February, and that of Captain Harris, regarding the exaggerated extension of the lines, coupled with a faulty location, imperfect command of the river, and defective organization of the troops, confirmed my opinion that the place could not be evacuated too soon. General Polk, whom I also called to Jackson, I found possessed with a belief in the defensive capacity of the position and averse to its abandonment. However, upon my exposition of its saliency, and the ease with which its communications, both by railway and water, might be broken, he changed his views. As, meanwhile General Johnston had telegraphed that I must do with respect to Columbus as my "judgment dictates"; and also, that "the separation of our armies is now complete"; and further, as upon my report of the situation at Columbus the Confederate War Department had consented, on the 19th of February General Polk was directed to prepare to evacuate the position without delay. It was only to be held long enough to remove its invaluable ordnance to the batteries erected or under construction at Island Number Ten and Madrid Bend, to New Madrid and to Fort Pillow, upon which the ultimate defense of the Mississippi River must depend thereafter. The preparation of these works for the vital service hoped from them was now intrusted to Captain D. B. Harris, who subsequently left so brilliant a record as a consummate engineer at Charleston and Savannah, Drewry's Bluff and Petersburg.

On the 25th of February commenced the evacuation of a position the attempt to hold which must have resulted in the loss by capture of the corps of at least 13,000 men thus isolated, or, on the other hand, if left intact or unassailed by the enemy, must have been rendered wholly unavailable in the formation of a Confederate army for the recovery of what had been lately lost,— a corps without which no such army could have been possibly assembled at Corinth as early as the 1st of April, 1862.

Because of a severe bronchial affection contracted by exposure before leaving Bowling Green, I had not assumed formal command of the military district assigned to me, though virtually directing all the movements within it, and arduously endeavoring to become acquainted with the chief points within its limits,— a course specially requested of me by General Johnston through his adjutant-general, in the event that I should not feel "well enough to assume command."

Meanwhile, threatened by Buell's presence with a large army in front of Nashville, General Johnston, following the line of retreat (marked out as early as February 7th) to Stevenson, in north-eastern Alabama, had moved as far in that direction as Murfreesboro', where he assembled about 17,000 men by the 23d of February, who were there subdivided into 3 divisions each of 2 brigades, with a "reserve" under Brigadier-General Breckinridge, and several cavalry regiments unattached.

As the system of the "passive defensive" hitherto pursued had only led us to disaster,— the natural fruits, in fact, of the system,— encouraged by the latitude that was given me in General Johnston's telegram of February 18th,

I resolved to exert myself to the utmost, despite all that was so unpromising, to secure the means for an aggressive campaign against the enemy, of whose early movement up the Tennessee there were already such indications that there should be no doubt as to its objective.

But as General Johnston's projected line of retrograde upon Stevenson must with each day's march widen the distance between that army and the corps of General Polk, while General Grant, naturally flushed with his recent signal successes, would be left free at any moment to move up the Tennessee to Hamburg or, indeed, to Eastport, and thus, by seizing the Memphis and Charleston railroad, effectually separate and virtually neutralize the two Confederate armies,—my sole force left available for the protection of that important railway, exclusive of General Polk's forces at Columbus and elsewhere, would be but 2500 men under Chalmers, in the quarter of Iuka, with 3000 men recently arrived at Corinth from New Orleans, under Ruggles.

With a view to avoiding such a catastrophe as the enforced permanent separation of our two armies, I urged General Johnston, about the 22d of February, to abandon his line of march toward Stevenson, and to hasten to unite his army with such troops as I might be able to assemble, meanwhile, at the best point to cover the railroad center at Corinth together with Memphis, while holding Island Number Ten and Fort Pillow. This plan, of course, required more troops than our united armies would supply. Therefore, on the 22d of February, I dispatched staff-officers with a circular addressed to the governors of Alabama, Louisiana, Mississippi, and Tennessee respecting the supreme urgency and import of the situation, in all its phases, and invoking their utmost exertions to send me, each of them, from 5000 to 10,000 men as well armed and equipped as possible, enrolled for 90 days, within which period, by timely, vigorous action, I trusted we might recover our losses, and assure the defense of the Mississippi River. ⁾ At the same time I appealed to General Bragg for such troops as he could possibly spare temporarily in such an exigency, from Mobile and Pensacola; and to General Lovell for the like aid from New Orleans. To General Van Dorn, represented to have an army twenty thousand strong in Arkansas, I likewise sent, on the 21st of February, a most pressing invitation to come in haste to our aid with as many men as possible, by way of New Madrid. To him I wrote ("O. R.," VII., 900): "The fate of Missouri necessarily depends on the successful defense of Columbus and of Island Number Ten; hence we must, if possible, combine our operations not only to defend those positions, but also to take the offensive as soon as practicable to recover some lost ground."

General Johnston acceded to my views and request, though he did not put his troops in motion until the 28th of February, and although he regarded the projected attempt to unite his army with mine a "hazardous experiment."⸝

⸝ See "Military Operations of General Beauregard" (N. Y.: Harper & Brothers), I., 240–241.

⸝ "If I join this corps to the forces of Beauregard (I confess a hazardous experiment), then those who are declaiming against me will be without an argument."—"Life of General A. S. Johnston." Letter dated Decatur, Alabama, March 18th, 1862, p. 521.—G. T. B.

The evacuation of Columbus was successfully completed on the 2d of March, apparently without any suspicion on the part of our adversary in that quarter that such an operation had been going on, or without the least show of that vigilance and vigor that were to be apprehended from him after the series of most serious disasters for the Confederate arms which had characterized the month of February, 1862. About seven thousand men were now placed at New Madrid, and in the quarter of Island Number Ten, under the command of General McCown, while the rest of General Polk's force was withdrawn along the line of the Mobile and Ohio railroad as far south as Humboldt, and there held in observation, with a small detachment of infantry left at Union City, and some five hundred cavalry thrown well out toward Hickman, on the Mississippi below Columbus, and extending across to the Tennessee River in the quarter of Paris, to watch and report all material movements upon either river.

Reliable information reached me that while General Pope was on his march on the Missouri side of the Mississippi, to strike at New Madrid, such was the urgency of the danger impending by way of the Tennessee River that it threatened the fatal hindrance of the conjunction of our forces, as already arranged about the 23d of February, in response to my dispatch through my aide-de-camp, Captain Ferguson. Growing profoundly apprehensive, on the 2d of March I dispatched Captain Otey, an assistant adjutant-general on my staff, with a note to General Johnston which contained these words: "I send herewith inclosed a slip showing intended movements of the enemy, no doubt against the troops in Western Tennessee. I think you ought to hurry up your troops to Corinth by railroad, as soon as practicable, for [t]here ☆ or thereabouts will be fought the great battle of this controversy."

I thus fixed upon Corinth as the Confederate base, because the recent movements of our enemy up the Tennessee could only be intelligently construed as having the Memphis and Charleston railroad primarily, and such a railway center as Corinth later, as their immediate objectives. ⌡

☆ Evidently the word "here," as it appears in the original letter as it reached General Johnston, did not refer and could not possibly have referred to Jackson, but to Corinth, as is shown by the context of that letter and of others relative to Corinth as the evident Federal objective.— G. T. B.

⌡ To say, as has been done, with apparent seriousness, by Colonel W. P. Johnston [see p. 549 of the present work], that his father "sent" me at any time, "with instructions to concentrate all available forces near Corinth,— a movement previously begun,"—is a sheer invention that is twin-born with the fable concerning General Johnston and the map upon which in January, 1862, it is alleged, he pointed out a position which had been marked by the engineers "Shiloh Church," and said in effect: "Here the great battle of the South-east will be fought" ("Life of General A. S. Johnston," by W. P. Johnston, pp. 488–490). Now, to be able to foretell in January, 1862, that a battle would be fought at "Shiloh Church," General Johnston must also have foreseen at that moment that within the next thirty days General Grant would strike and capture the Confederate center at Forts Henry and Donelson, with one-fourth of the entire force under General Johnston's command at the time, as also obtain the control of both the Tennessee and Cumberland rivers as far as navigable; thus forcing the immediate loss by abandonment of the Confederates in turn of Bowling Green, Nashville, and Columbus; foreseen also that General Grant would straightway establish himself at so unfavorable a base of operations as Pittsburg Landing rather than at Hamburg, which was really about to be made the Federal base of operations when the battle of Shiloh interrupted the movement. Under no other conditions could there have been a battle at Shiloh Church, a mere log-cabin, unmarked on any map existing in January, 1862.— G. T. B.

LIEUTENANT-GENERAL JOHN C. BRECKINRIDGE, C. S. A.
FROM A PHOTOGRAPH. (SEE ALSO PAGE 377.)

On the 5th of March I formally assumed command of the district, retaining my headquarters for the time at Jackson as the most central point of observation and the junction of two railroads. General Bragg's forces began to arrive at Corinth on the 6th, when they, with the other troops reaching there from other quarters, were organized as fast as possible into brigades and divisions.

As a material part of the history of the campaign, I might here dwell upon the perplexing, inexplicable lack of cordial coöperation, in many ways, in the essential work of organizing the Confederate army being assembled at Corinth, as efficiently and speedily as possible for the work ahead, that was manifested by the War Department at Richmond, but it must suffice to say that a drawback was encountered from that quarter which served to delay us, while helping to make the operation which we finally took in hand fall greatly short of its momentous aim.

Five Federal divisions (reënforced a few days later) had reached Savannah, twelve miles below Pittsburg Landing, on the east bank of the Tennessee, by the 13th of February. This force, aggregating some 43,000 men of all arms, was under the direct command of General C. F. Smith, and embraced the greater part of the army that had triumphed at Donelson. One division, without landing at Savannah, was dispatched, under General W. T. Sherman, to endeavor to land, and to reach and cut some trestle-work near Burnsville, on the Memphis and Charleston railroad. Effecting a landing, short, however, of Eastport, the intervening country was found so inundated as to be seemingly impracticable. So, this expedition, hardly characterized by a really vigorous effort to reach the railroad, was abortive—a result aided somewhat by the opportune presence on the ground of Brigadier-General Chalmers with a Confederate force of 2500 infantry. On his way upon this expedition, General Sherman had wisely sent back from Pittsburg Landing a request that a Federal division should be dispatched at once to that point, to prevent the Confederate forces from occupying it and obstructing his return; consequently Hurlbut's division was sent thither, and it was found on its transports at that point by Sherman on his return that far down the river on the 16th of March. Sherman, landing there his own division, made an apparently objectless short march into the interior and back on the 17th of March. Making his report the same day to General Grant, who had just reached Savannah, General Sherman stated that he was "strongly impressed with the position" of Pittsburg Land-

SLAVES LABORING AT NIGHT ON THE CONFEDERATE EARTHWORKS AT CORINTH.

ing, "for its land advantages and its strategic character. The ground itself admits of easy defense by a small command, and yet affords admirable camping-ground for one hundred thousand men." Unquestionably, it was upon this report that Pittsburg, rather than Hamburg, was made the Federal base; for Hurlbut's and Sherman's divisions were immediately ordered ashore to encamp upon a prescribed line, while, on the same day General Grant directed all the other troops at Savannah except one division to be immediately sent to the same point; Wallace's division being left, however, at Crump's Landing. About the position thus taken by the Federal army, there can hardly be two professional opinions. It gave their adversary an opportunity for an almost fatal counterstroke such as has rarely been afforded to the weaker of two belligerents in all the sinews and resources of war. A narrow *cul de sac*, formed by Snake Creek and Lick Creek, with the broad bank-full river forming its bottom, tactically as well as strategically it was a false position for an invading army, and I may add that, having been occupied, the exigent precaution, under the circumstances, of making a *place d'armes* of it was wholly overlooked, though it was barely twenty-three miles distant from Corinth, where, according to the Federal general's reports of the period, a supposed Confederate army of from 50,000 to 60,000 men were concentrated.

Previously, or as early as the 3d of March, Pope, with about 19,000 " present for duty," had appeared before New Madrid, in Missouri, the essentially weak or most vulnerable point of our upper Mississippi defenses.‡ Delaying

‡ Five divisions each of 2 brigades, 3 regiments of cavalry, a body of unattached troops, including some "regulars," and 11 batteries of field-artillery. "Official Records," VIII., 94.—G. T. B.

his attack, however, until the 12th,—until siege-guns could be brought up,—the works there were easily made so untenable that General McCown abandoned them and transferred his forces, at night, across the river to support the heavy batteries at Madrid Bend and Island Number Ten.

About the time Pittsburg Landing was made General Grant's base, I had collected within easy marches of Corinth about 23,000 men of all arms of the service, independent of the forces of General Polk,—giving, with his troops and including those at Forts Pillow and Madrid Bend, an aggregate of at most 44,000 men, of excellent personality but badly armed—particularly the cavalry, some of whom had no arms at all. The new forces, with the exception of those from Mobile, Pensacola, and New Orleans, were raw and undisciplined. Made aware by the great number of transports↓ that were now plying up and down the Tennessee of the magnitude of the invasion that clearly threatened the seizure of the Memphis and Charleston railroad, the delay on the part of the Bowling Green forces filled both General Bragg and myself with great solicitude. Meanwhile, on the 15th of March, General Johnston addressed me by telegraph: "Have you had the south bank of the Hatchee examined near Bolivar? I recommend it to your attention. It has, besides the other advantages, that of being further from the enemy's line,"—that is, Pittsburg Landing. As the essential point for us, however, was to strike a blow at General Grant so soon as General Johnston's troops were united with mine, but before Buell's junction with the exposed army at Pittsburg, I could see no possible advantage in the least increase of distance from our real objective so soon as the advent of General Johnston's troops should give us the power to undertake the offensive. Exposing these features of the situation, I again urged General Johnston to hurry his forces forward.

On the 22d of March he reached Corinth with his staff, and I went down from Jackson to meet him. Proceeding at once to explain to him what resources had been collected and all that was known of the position and numbers of our adversary at Pittsburg, as also my views of the imperative necessity for an immediate movement against that adversary lest Buell's forces should become a fatal factor in the campaign, to my surprise General Johnston, with much emotion, informed me that it was his purpose to turn over to me the command of the entire force being assembled at Corinth, and thereafter confine himself to the duties of department commander, with his headquarters either at Memphis or Holly Springs, in Mississippi. This course, as he explained, he felt called upon to take in order to restore confidence to the people and even the army, so greatly impaired by reason of recent disasters. Thoroughly understanding and appreciating his motives (and about these and his words there could be no possible misinterpretation), I declined as altogether unnecessary the unselfish tender of the command, but agreed, after some further exchange of views touching the military situation, to draw up a plan for the organization of our forces, and, as second in command, to supervise the task of organization.

↓ Sixty-one of these transports were reported to have passed by a point known as Coffee. — G. T. B.

By the 27th of March the last of General Hardee's corps reached the vicinity of Corinth,—about 8000 men,—while Crittenden's division of 5000 men was halted at Burnsville and Iuka, eastward of Corinth. The order of organization, signed by General Johnston, was published on the 29th of March. Based on my notes, it had been drawn up by Colonel Jordan, and subdivided the armies of Kentucky and Mississippi, now united, into three army corps, with reserves of cavalry, artillery, and infantry, the corps under Major-Generals Polk, Bragg, and Hardee respectively, and the reserve (two brigades) under Major-General G. B. Crittenden. On the 30th of March, Colonel Mackall having been promoted and assigned to the command of the river defenses at Madrid Bend, Colonel Jordan was formally announced as the adjutant-general of the "Army of the Mississippi," and on the following day Brigadier-General Breckinridge was substituted for General Crittenden in the command of the reserve.

So much longer time than I had anticipated had been taken in effecting the junction of the "Central Army" with mine, agreed upon as far back as the 23d of February, that we were scarcely as ready for assuming the offensive as I had hoped to be, at latest by the 1st of April.

However, on the night of the 2d of April, after 10 o'clock, a dispatch from Brigadier-General Cheatham, in command at Bethel Station, twenty odd miles north of Corinth, reached me through General Polk, to the effect that he was being menaced by General Lew Wallace's division. Assuming that the enemy had divided his forces for an operation against the Mobile and Ohio railroad at Bethel, I thus indorsed the dispatch: "Now is the moment to advance and strike the enemy at Pittsburg Landing." Colonel Jordan was then asked to carry it at once to General Johnston, who, after reading both dispatch and indorsement, accompanied by Colonel Jordan, went to General Bragg's quarters near by. That officer, already in bed, immediately agreed with my recommendation. General Johnston presented objections in effect that our forces were not as yet ready for the movement, and that we could not move up our reserve in time. Colonel Jordan, however, was able to reassure him on these points by expressing my conviction that we were as ready now as we could hope to be for some time to come, whereas the union of Buell's forces with Grant, which might be anticipated at an early day, would make any offensive operation on our side out of the question. Thereupon, General Johnston instructed Colonel Jordan to issue the orders for the movement. This was done in General Bragg's bed-chamber, in a "circular" to the three corps commanders directing them "to hold their commands in hand, ready to advance upon the enemy in the morning by 6 A. M., with 3 days' cooked rations in haversacks, 100 rounds of ammunition for small arms, and 200 rounds for field-pieces. Carry 2 days' cooked subsistence in wagons and 2 tents to the company." These orders reached the hands of Generals Polk and Hardee by 1:30 A. M., and General Breckinridge was notified to the same effect by telegraph that night.

As it had been agreed between General Johnston and myself, the day after his arrival at Corinth, that all orders relating to our operations in that

quarter, as, also, touching re-organization, should be left in my hands, during the night of the 2d of April I had made notes regulating the order of march from Corinth to Pitts-burg, and the manner of bring-

ing on the battle, which I hand-ed to Colonel Jordan soon after daylight the next morning. Those notes served as the basis of Special Orders, No. 8 of that date, issued in the name of General Johnston. However, before these orders were finally

CORINTH DWELLINGS.

1. Bragg's headquarters, afterward Halleck's, later Hood's. 2. Beauregard's headquarters. 3. Grant's headquarters, June, 1862. 4. Rosecrans's headquarters, October, 1862. 5. House in which Albert Sidney Johnston's body lay in state after the battle of Shiloh.

written, all the details were explained to and discussed by me with General Johnston, who came early to my headquarters; next, before 10 A. M., I explained to and instructed Generals Polk, Bragg, and Hardee, also, at my headquarters, in the presence of General Johnston and of one another, precisely what each of them had to do with their respective corps that day, and they were severally directed to put their corps in motion by the described roads in the direction of the enemy, by 12 meridian, without further order.

Though the distance to be traversed was barely twenty-three miles, it was no easy matter to move an army of thirty odd thousand essentially raw troops, with their artillery, through so densely wooded a country as that intervening between Corinth and our objective. Of the two narrow country roads that existed, the shorter was assigned to Bragg's corps, because it was the one immediately contiguous to it; while to Hardee's corps was given the initiation of the movement, with the longest line of march as well as the front line in the approaching onset, because it was made up of troops most hardened by long marches, and the best trained in field service. Polk's corps followed Hardee's necessarily, because there was no other way for it, ⟩

⟩ As for marching upon Pittsburg in three separate columns of corps, as would seem to be indicated in the cipher dispatch to Mr. Davis of the 3d of April, the *terrain* to be passed over made such a movement an absolute impossibility. And I must add, that another pretension set up by Colonel Johnston, supported by Mr. Davis, is flatly contradicted by the official reports of the corps commanders, which show that they entered battle exactly as prescribed in Special Orders, No. 8.

Apropos of the alleged missing dispatch of April 4th, Mr. Davis has asseverated as recently as the spring of 1887, that it was in a different cipher from that of April 3d, which erroneously described the manner of march, not only in date and matter, but in the character of cipher used, being in a cipher that he had sent General Johnston specially for such a dispatch: a fatal statement in view of the fact that there is to be found (p. 365, Vol. X., Part II., "Official Records") this *postscriptum* to a letter from Mr. Davis to General Johnston, dated as late as March 26th, 1862:

"I send you [by Mr. Jack] a dictionary, of which I have the duplicate, so that you may communicate with me by cipher, telegraphic or written, as follows: First give the page by its number; second, the column by the letter L, M, or R, as it may be, in the left-hand, middle, or right-hand column; third, the number of the word in the column, counting from the top. Thus, the word junction would be designated by 146, L, 20."

That is, Mr. Davis sent him the very dictionary which supplied the cipher into which the original of General Johnston's dispatch to Mr. Davis of April 3d was translated, by one of my staff, for transmission, having been handed over to me for that purpose by General Johnston; and a copy of the translation into that cipher is to be seen, in its due order of date, in my telegraph-book of the period. That Captain Jack reached Corinth before General Johnston advanced against Pittsburg is stated, page 522 of Col. Johnston's Life of

his father, on which page, I may notice, is the very letter from Davis of the 26th of March, but with the material *postscriptum* omitted. After General Johnston's death, the original of the telegram of April 3d was found, but no record of another later one, which Mr. Davis claims to have received, basing that claim, manifestly, only on the fact that in his own reply, dated April 5th, he had referred to a telegram "of yesterday," which plainly could only be that of April 3d, received, however, on the 4th, which he erroneously supposed to be of that date. That Mr. Davis's telegram was an answer to no other dispatch than that of the 3d of April is plain from the text of that answer, for it clearly echoes its language. For the clear understanding of this much-mooted matter, I give the exact cipher text of the dispatch of April 3d, as it reached Mr. Davis, as I insist, not until April 5th, and as it is of record in my official telegram-book in its regular order of date as follows:

"CORINTH, April 3d, 1862, 3 P. M.
"TO THE PRESIDENT, RICHMOND, VA.

"General Buell 132. R. 5 — 166 L 26 — 250. M 20 — 250 R g — 239 M 32 — 111 M 28 — Columbia 43 M 6 — Clifton 252 M 6. — 218 M. 26. Mitchell 32. R. 22 — 124. R. 32. — 276 R 27 — 248 M, 1 — 250 R. 9 — 59 R. 17 — 108 — M. 20 — 109. R.16 — 175 R 6 ed — 109 R.18 — 252. M 6 — 174 L. 28 — 31 M. 10 — 69. L. 12 — Pittsburg — 84 M. 4 — 111. M. 28 — Bethel — 156 M. 4 — 37 M. 20 — 111. M. 28 Corinth — 210 M. 16 111 M. 28 — Burnsville — 63 R. 25 — 252 R. 11 — 169. L 12 — Monterey — 174. R. 14 — Pittsburg. Beauregard, 221 R. 10 — 132 R. 5 — 56, M. 14 — Polk 150. M. 7 — Hardee, 48. M. 3 — Bragg 213 M. 6 — 276. M. 22. Breckinridge 210 M. 16 — 126 M. 4 — 92. R. 18 — 32. M. 28 — Buell 44. M 13 — 109 M. 6 — 146. L. 20 — (Signed) A. S. JOHNSTON, General C. S. A."

The translated text, as given both by Mr. Davis

and next to Hardee's troops those under Polk · had been most seasoned by marching.

Although our troops were under arms at an early hour on the 3d of April, as prescribed in the "circular" order, it is a part of the history of the campaign that the commanders of the two leading corps not only failed to put their troops in motion at least as early as meridian on the 3d of April, but did not move until so late in the afternoon as in effect to cause our army to reach the presence of its objective twenty-four hours later than there was every reason to expect, considering the shortness of the distance to be overcome. What led to this delay of the outset of the Second and Third corps has certainly never been explained in any official document which has yet seen the light. Their preparations necessary for such a movement were of the slightest, or only to cook five days' rations, and to load a few wagons, for the amount of ammunition to be carried was no more than they had been directed some days previously to have and keep in possession of the troops. Moreover, Hardee's corps (Polk's also), "with all detached brigades," had been under orders of "readiness for a field movement" ever since the 1st of April ("Official Records," Vol. X., Part II., p. 381). Be this as it may, Bragg's corps did not quit the vicinage of Corinth until so late that afternoon that none of it reached Monterey, twelve miles away, until the next morning at 8:30, and one division (Withers's) was not there until late on the 4th of April. Hardee's corps, though dilatory in quitting Corinth, would have easily reached its destination early enough on the second day's march to have been deployed on the same ground that it occupied on the night of the 5th, twenty-four hours later, had not General Bragg interposed his authority to check its advance. The march on the 4th was unaccountably slow and confused, especially that of the Second Corps, in view of the numerous staff attached to the headquarters of each corps. The roads were extremely narrow and rendered excessively bad for artillery in some places by the rains, while the Second Corps was unused to marching; but all this hardly made it out of the power of that army to reach its objective by the night of April 4th, had there been a closer personal attention given to the movement during that day by those whose duty it was to execute Special Orders, No. 8. And the cost was an irremediable loss of twenty-four hours. Another misadventure, that might have brought us sore disaster, was a cavalry reconnoissance with two pieces of artillery pushed forward without authority on the 4th, from Bragg's corps into

and Colonel Johnston, is in these words: "CORINTH, April 3d, 1862. General Buell in motion 30,000 strong, rapidly from Columbia by Clifton to Savannah. Mitchel behind him with 10,000. Confederate forces — 40,000 — ordered forward to offer battle near Pittsburg. Division from Bethel, main body from Corinth, reserve from Burnsville, converging to-morrow near Monterey on Pittsburg. Beauregard second in command, Polk the left, Bragg the center, Hardee the right wing, Breckinridge the reserve. Hope engagement before Buell can form junction.

"TO THE PRESIDENT, RICHMOND."

In publishing it as found among his father's papers, the son presents this telegram as "containing the plan of battle as General Johnston had originally devised, but not as he had fought it; doubtless in deference to General Beauregard's opinion in the matter, and for reasons which seemed sufficient at the time." On the other hand, Mr. Davis gives it not as a plan of battle, but merely of the march from Corinth to the field,— while the alleged missing dispatch of the 4th of April gave not only the plan of battle as devised, but as it was fought up to the moment of General Johnston's death.— G. T. B.

collision with the enemy with such aggressiveness that it ought to have given the Federal general full notice that an offensive army was close behind it, and led to immediate preparation for our onset, including intrenchments.

After the Third Corps had reached its assigned position, on the afternoon of the 5th of April, and the other corps were in supporting distance, including the reserve that had encountered a much more difficult road between Burnsville and Monterey than had been traversed by the other troops, naturally their commanders were called together at a point not two miles distant from Shiloh Church,—as it turned out, not far in the rear of Hardee's line.

Of course, it was recognized to be too late for an attack that day. Moreover, it was reported that the First Corps was already nearly out of provisions, and that the ammunition train was still so far to the rear as to be unpromising. The loss of twenty-four hours, when every hour was precious because of the imminent danger of Buell's conjunction, the maladroit manner in which our troops had been handled on the march, and the blunder of the noisy, offensive reconnoissance, coupled with these reports of corps commanders, served to satisfy me that the purpose for which we had left Corinth had been essentially frustrated and should be abandoned as no longer feasible. The military essence of our projected operation was that it should be a surprise, whereas, now, I could not believe the enemy was still ignorant of our near presence with an aggressive intention, and if now attacked would be found intrenched beyond the possibility of being beaten in assault by so raw and undisciplined an army as ours was, however intrepid. Hence, an imperative prudence that included the necessity for preserving that army essentially intact for further operations forced me to advise against any attempt now to attack the enemy in position and to retrace our steps toward our base with the possible result of leading him to follow us away from his own and thus giving us a probable opening to the retrieval of the present lost opportunity.

General Johnston listened heedfully to what I said, but answered that he hoped not only we should find our enemy still unready for a sudden onslaught, but that there was yet time for it before Buell could come up; therefore, he should decide to adventure the enterprise as early after dawn the next day as possible, adding his opinion that now our troops were partly in line of battle it were " better to make the venture." The opinions of the corps commanders, I may add, were neither asked nor given. That my views were based on sound military principles it seems to me could be readily deduced from what followed at the battle of Shiloh itself, were this the place for such a discussion.

So soon as General Johnston's decision was announced, the conference ended with the understanding on all sides that the battle should be ventured at dawn on the 6th of April, according to the manner already prescribed in Special Orders, No. 8, to which end every exertion should be made to place our troops in the best shape possible for the attack. No further conference was held that night by General Johnston with myself, or with the reserve or corps commanders; nor did he issue any order at all concerning the impending battle.

At the first flush of dawn on the 6th, the Confederate army was promptly formed in the three lines directed in Special Orders, No. 8, except that untowardly the left of Hardee's corps, which, reënforced by Gladden's division of Bragg's corps, constituted the advance, did not rest on Owl Creek, as prescribed. Nine thousand and twenty-four men were in this line, deployed for battle, and formed, as it were, a heavy skirmish line thrown forward to embrace the whole Federal front. Five hundred yards rearward was Bragg's corps (less Gladden's division), 10,731 men, exclusive of cavalry, in a line, as far as the nature of the ground admitted, of regiments massed in double columns at half distance—not deployed in line of battle, as some writers have stated, coupled with criticisms based thereon. General Polk's corps of 9036 men, exclusive of cavalry, came next, some 800 yards behind Bragg in a column of brigades deployed in line of battle on the left of the Pittsburg road, each brigade having its own battery, and there was cavalry protecting the left of his line. The reserve, under Breckinridge, of 7062 men, exclusive of cavalry, marched in the rear of Bragg's right or between the Pittsburg road and Lick Creek. The troops of the third line were to be thrown forward according to the exigencies of the battle. The total force thus sent forward against the Federal position numbered 40,335 rank and file, of all arms, including 4382 cavalry, more than half of whom were of no other military value except for observation or outpost service that did not involve skirmishing. [See estimates, page 557.]

On the other hand, the force to be assailed occupied "a continuous line from Lick Creek, on the [Federal] left, to Owl Creek, a branch of Snake Creek, on the [Federal] right, facing nearly south, and possibly a little west," says General Grant. Their first line, reaching from the bridge on Owl Creek to the Lick Creek ford, was held by the divisions of Generals Sherman and Prentiss; three of Sherman's brigades holding the Federal right, while the other (Stuart's) was on the extreme left, with its left resting on Lick Creek. This division had from 16 to 18 guns, and also a cavalry support. Prentiss occupied the intervening space. These two divisions numbered at least seventeen thousand men, exclusive of cavalry.\

About half a mile behind Sherman and Prentiss came McClernand's division of 7028 effectives; nearer the river were the divisions of C. F. Smith, (under W. H. L. Wallace) and of Hurlbut, aggregating 16,000 men with 34 guns. There was also a cavalry force including detachments from two "regular" regiments. Thus the force encountered must have numbered forty thousand men, infantry and artillery, supported by sixty odd guns. The ground occupied was an undulating table-land embraced between Owl Creek and Lick Creek, that run nearly in the same general direction and are about four miles apart at their mouths. This area, rising in some places about one hundred feet above the low-water level of the river, was from three to five miles

\ Prentiss's division is reported ("Official Records," Vol. X., Part I., 112) as numbering but 5463 men "present for duty" April 5th, but 2 regiments and a battery joined during the battle.— G. T. B.

broad. Interlaced by a network of ravines, which, near the river, are deep, with abrupt sides, the ground rises somewhat ridge-like in the quarter of Lick Creek, and recent rains had made all these depressions boggy and difficult for the movement of artillery across them. A primitive forest, dense with undergrowth, spread over the whole space except a few scattered farm fields of from fifty to seventy-five acres. Pittsburg Landing, near the mouth of Snake Creek, was about three miles from that of Lick Creek. The two roads from Corinth, while crossing Lick Creek about a mile asunder, come together two miles from Pittsburg. A road from Purdy, crossing Owl Creek by a bridge near Sherman's right, gave one way to reach the field from Crump's Landing, but the shortest road between the two landings was one near the river leading over a bridge across Snake Creek.

As it has been denied in the highest quarters that the Con-

MAJOR-GENERAL BUSHROD R. JOHNSON, C. S. A.
FROM A WAR-TIME PHOTOGRAPH.

federate attack on the 6th of April was of the nature of a surprise, it belongs to the history of the day's operations to give here these words of a note from General Sherman to his chief, in the afternoon of the 5th. The "enemy is saucy, but got the worst of it yesterday. . . . I do not apprehend anything like an attack upon our position." General Grant thereupon wrote to his superior, General Halleck: "Our outposts have been attacked in considerable force. I immediately went up, but found all quiet. . . . I have scarcely the faintest idea of an attack upon us." Moreover, at 3 o'clock P. M., having visited the encampment of Colonel Ammen near Savannah, General Grant informed that officer that water transportation would be furnished for his brigade of Nelson's division, Army of the Ohio, on the 7th or 8th of April, or some time early in the week, and also that there would be "no fight" at Pittsburg, but at "Corinth, where the rebels were fortified."☆ Further, even when leaving Savannah the next morning, General Grant scarcely at first can have believed that his army was being seriously attacked, for instead of dispatching to the field the whole of Nelson's division by steamers, he ordered it to march thither by a wretched road, a march that occupied nearly the whole day. Aside, however, from such documentary evidence, or did none exist, the absence of all those ordinary precautions that habitually shield an army in the field must forbid the historian from regarding it as other than one of the most surprising surprises ever achieved.

About 5 A. M. the Confederate lines were set in motion. The first collision was in the quarter of Gladden's brigade, on our right, and with a battalion of five companies of the 21st Missouri of Prentiss's division dispatched well to the front by General Prentiss, of his own motion, as early as 3 A. M. But for this incident, due solely to the intelligent, soldierly forethought of an officer not trained to the business of war, the whole Federal front would have been struck wholly unawares, for nowhere else had such prudence been shown.

Exactly at 6 A. M. Prentiss's whole division was under fire, and the battle of Shiloh began in earnest.

As soon as the outburst of musketry and artillery gave notice that Hardee's line was engaged, General Johnston said that he should go to the front, leaving me in the general direction, as the exigencies of the battle might arise.⌡ Then he rode forward with his personal staff and the chief engineer of the army, Colonel Gilmer, the only officer of the general staff in his suite, Colonel Jordan, remaining with me. At 7:30 A. M., by which time the battle was in full tide, as was evident from the play of artillery and the heavy, continuous rattle of small arms, I ordered Generals Polk and Breckinridge to hasten forward, the first to the support of our now engaged left, and the latter in a like service affecting our right. Adjutant-General Jordan, whom I had early in the morning directed to impress personally on the corps commanders the value of fighting their artillery massed twelve guns at a point, was also now dispatched forward to overlook the field and urge on the attack continuously at as many points as possible.

When our attack reached Sherman's division, owing to the failure of Hardee to keep his left near Owl Creek as was intended, only the left brigade of that division on the Federal right was struck, leaving intact the other two to the left of our left flank, which were swiftly formed by General Sherman on strong ground with a small watercourse in his front. But the other stricken brigade was swept out of its encampment, scattered, and took no further part as an organization in the battle of either day.

While Hardee's left failed to touch the enemy's right, on his own right there was left a vacant space between it and Lick Creek, to fill which Chalmers's brigade of Withers's division, Bragg's corps, was ordered up from the second line, with a battery; and a hot, urgent conflict ensued in that quarter, in which General Johnston was present, after Chalmers had carried at least

---

☆ Diary of Col. Jacob Ammen, "Official Records," Vol. X., Part I., p. 331.
⌡ See report of Col. Thompson, A. D. C., p. 570, "Life of General A. S. Johnston," by W. P. Johnston.

one encampment. In the same quarter of the field all of Withers's division, including Gladden's brigade, reënforced by Breckinridge's whole reserve, soon became engaged, and Prentiss's entire line, though fighting stoutly, was pressed back in confusion. We early lost the services of the gallant Gladden, a man of soldierly aptitudes and experience, who, after a marked influence upon the issue in his quarter of the field, fell mortally wounded. His immediate successor, Colonel D. W. Adams, was also soon seriously disabled. Meantime, on our left (Federal right) Ruggles's division of Bragg's corps was so strenuously pressing the two brigades of Sherman's division, that at the moment McClernand's division came up, Sherman was giving way with the loss of five or six guns. McClernand could not stay the retrograde, and the Federal right was forced back to the line of the road from Purdy to Hamburg. There a foothold was gained on a thickly wooded ridge, with a ravine in front, from which two favorably posted batteries were used with deadly effect for a time upon our assailing force, now composed of Ruggles's three brigades reënforced by several of Polk's. Here, again, the Federal line had to give way, with the loss of some guns.

By 7:30 Hurlbut, sending Veatch's brigade of his division to the help of Sherman and McClernand, had gone, in person with his two other brigades, to the support of Prentiss, and with him went 8 companies of cavalry and 3 batteries. Prentiss's division was met, however, in a somewhat fragmentary condition, but was rallied in the immediate rear of a line which Hurlbut formed along the edge of a field on favorable ground on the Hamburg road, southward of the position last taken up by McClernand. Meanwhile (9:30 A. M.) I had advanced my headquarters to a point about a quarter of a mile in advance of the Shiloh Meeting House, whence I dispatched my staff in all directions to gather reports of the progress of the battle with its exigencies and needs on our side, as, also, in quest of stragglers, whose numbers had become dangerously large under the temptations of the abundant stores of food and other articles left in the abandoned Federal camps.‡ In the work of cleaning these encampments of stragglers and dispatching them to the front, my cavalry escort was also effectively employed.

As designated by Special Orders, No. 8, Hardee's corps having developed the enemy's position, Bragg's troops first and then Polk's on our left and left center, Withers's division of Bragg's corps and Breckinridge's reserves on the right, had been thrown forward to fill intervening gaps and to aid the onset. At all points from the right to the left, the opposing forces had been stoutly engaged on ground in rear of the line of McClernand's encampment since 9 A. M., when W. H. L. Wallace had carried forward his division into action; a division that, trained by so thorough a soldier as General C. F. Smith, had done most soldierly work at Donelson, and which Wallace now handled with marked vigor. Its influence seemed to stiffen the Federal

‡ At the conference in the afternoon of April 5th, I had said in support of my recommendations to retire without attacking the enemy: "Nature has claims that cannot be disregarded. The best-disciplined troops do not fight well on empty stomachs. And this is all the more true of raw troops unaccustomed to the hardships of war."— G. T. B.

WOOD AND UNDERBRUSH CALLED THE "HORNETS' NEST." FROM A PHOTOGRAPH TAKEN IN 1885.

center and left center. Stuart, commanding one of Sherman's brigades strongly posted on the extreme Federal left, also, had made so obstinate a stand that he was not forced from the position until three times his numbers, of Withers's division, diverted from the main current of the attack, were brought to bear against him. For some time General Johnston was with that division, but he shifted to Breckinridge's division about 11 A. M., and remained closely in rear alternately of either Bowen's or Statham's brigade until mortally wounded near the latter, a little after 2 P. M. He took post and remained on our extreme right, and at no time does it appear from the reports of subordinates in any other part of the field that, either personally or by his staff, General Johnston gave any orders or concerned himself with the general movements of our forces. In fact, engrossed as he soon became with the operations of two or three brigades on the extreme right, it would have been out of his power to direct our general operations, especially as he set no machinery in motion with which to gather information of what was being done elsewhere, or generally, by the Confederate army, in order to enable him to handle it intelligently from his position on the field.

Learning about 1 P. M. that the Federal right (Sherman and McClernand) seemed about to give way, I ordered General Hardee to employ his cavalry (Wharton's Texas Rangers) to turn their flank and cut off their retreat to the river, an operation not effected because a proper or sufficient détour to the left was not made; and the gallant Texans under a heavy fire became involved in ground impracticable for cavalry, and had to fall back. But Colonel Wharton soon afterward dismounted half of his regiment and, throwing it forward on foot, drove his adversary from the position.

The falling back of Sherman's and McClernand's troops under stress from several brigades of Hardee's corps with a part of Ruggles's division of Bragg's, aided by some of Polk's troops, left Wallace (W. H. L.) on the advanced Federal right, where, with Hurlbut and Prentiss on his left, in a strong, sheltered position, well backed by artillery, and held with great resolution, they repulsed a series of uncombined assaults made against them. Here General Bragg was directing operations in person; and it was here that, after Hindman had suffered severely in several ineffectual efforts, Gibson's brigade of Bragg's own corps was employed in four unavailing assaults, when finding himself unable to carry the position, General Bragg, as he reports, desisted from any further attempt, leaving that part of the field in charge of a staff-officer with authority to act in his name, and going farther to the right to find that General Johnston was dead. However, having previously learned, from his aide-de-camp, Colonel Urquhart, that Adjutant-General Jordan was near by, he requested that officer, through Colonel Urquhart, to collect and employ some of our troops to turn the left of the position that obstructed his advance toward the river, as just described. Upon that service Colonel Jordan, in a few moments, employed Statham's brigade, which was fortunately found near by, resting at ordered arms, General Breckinridge, to whom the order was given, being with it at the time. This happened, be it noted, at 2:30 P. M., or about the moment that General Johnston was bleeding to death in the covert of a deep ravine a very short distance from Statham's brigade, in the immediate rear of which it was that his wound had been inflicted. ‡

General Breckinridge quickly became engaged with the enemy in his front, covered by a thick underbrush that edged an open field over which the Confederate advance was made. The conflict was sharp for a few moments, but the Federals had to give way. ♭ About this time, under my orders, Cheatham came up with his Second Brigade on the left of Breckinridge. Moreover, a few moments later, or as early as 3 P. M., Withers, of Bragg's corps, having found that his adversary (Stuart's brigade) which had so long occupied him on the extreme right had disappeared toward Pittsburg Landing, and having moved across the intervening ravines and ridges with his division to where the sound of artillery and musketry showed the main battle was now raging,—was brought opportunely into coöperation with Cheatham's and Breckinridge's operations directly upon Hurlbut's left flank—a movement which Hurlbut resisted stoutly until, justly apprehensive of being cut off, he fell back, after 4 P. M., upon Pittsburg Landing.⸗ This left Prentiss's left flank exposed; Wallace, whose unflinching handling of his division had done so much to keep the Federal army from being driven to the river-side by midday, now also, to

‡ General Johnston was not wounded while leading a charge, as has been so frequently asserted, but while several hundred yards in the rear of Statham's brigade after it had made a successful advance, and during the absence of Governor Harris of his staff, whom he had dispatched to Colonel Statham, some two hundred yards distant, with orders to charge and take a Federal battery on his left. (See letter of Isham G. Harris, April 13th, 1876, p. 537, Vol. I. "The Military Operations of General Beauregard.")— G. T. B.

♭ Colonel W. P. Johnston has sought to make it appear that immediately upon the death of his father [see page 565], and in consequence of that event, there was in effect a lull in the operations on the Confederate right of which General Johnston had hitherto been the soul—a lull of an hour; whereas it is manifest there cannot have been a cessation of the operations of General Breckinridge's troops for more than fifteen minutes at most,—the only troops whom General Johnston had been directing in any way since 11 A. M.—G. T. B.

⸗ This saved him from sharing the fate of Prentiss, for the strength of the Confederate force that had now been brought to bear upon the remains of Wallace's, Hurlbut's, and Prentiss's divisions was sufficient to assure their environment and capture.—G. T. B.

avoid being surrounded, gave orders for it to retire, and soon fell mortally wounded; but a part of his division remained with Prentiss.

Sometime previously I had ordered General Hardee to gather all the forces he could and press the enemy on our own left. Stragglers that had been collected by Colonels Brent and Chisolm and others of my staff, were also sent forward extemporized into battalions, and Colonel Marshall J. Smith with the New Orleans Crescent Regiment was added, with orders to " Drive the enemy into the Tennessee."

Meantime, or shortly after 3 P. M., Governor Harris and Captain Wicliffe, both of General Johnston's staff, had reached me with information of his death. Staff-officers were immediately dispatched to acquaint the corps commanders of this deplorable casualty, with a caution, however, against otherwise promulgating the fact. They were also urged to push the battle with renewed vigor and, if possible, to force a speedy close, to which end my staff were energetically employed in pushing up the stragglers or regiments or parts of regiments that had become casually separated from their organizations because of the nature of the battle-field.

As I have said, by five o'clock the whole Federal army except Prentiss's division, with a part of Wallace's, had receded to the river-bank, and the indomitable force which under Prentiss still contested the field was being environed on its left by brigades from the divisions of Breckinridge, Cheatham, and Withers in that quarter. It remains to be said that Prentiss was equally encompassed on the other flank by a part of Ruggles's division, together with some of General Polk's corps. Thus surrounded on all sides, that officer, whose division had been the first to come into collision with us that morning, stoutly keeping the field to the last, was now forced to surrender in person, just after 5:30 P. M., with some 2200 officers and men.

We had now had more than eleven hours of continuous fighting, fighting without food except that hastily snatched up in the abandoned Federal encampments. In the meantime Colonel J. D. Webster, the Federal chief of staff, had massed his reserve artillery, some sixty guns, on a ridge about three hundred yards in advance of the landing which commanded all the approaches thereto from the landward, with a deep ravine on the side facing the Confederates. Moreover, much of the ground in front of this position was swept by the guns of the steamers *Lexington* and *Tyler*, properly posted for that purpose. Near by had gathered the remnants of Wallace's, Hurlbut's, and McClernand's divisions, from which gunners had been taken to man the artillery. At this critical instant, Colonel Ammen's brigade of Nelson's division of Buell's army was brought across the Tennessee and placed as a support, on the ridge, in a position selected by General Buell himself, just at the instant that the Confederates attempted to storm this last foothold to which they had finally driven their adversary after eleven hours of unceasing battle.

This was the situation at 6 P. M., and that the Confederate troops were not in a condition to carry such a position as that which confronted them at that late hour becomes clearly apparent from the official reports. After the capture of General Prentiss no serious effort was made to press the victory by the corps commanders. In fact the troops had got out of the hands either of corps, divisional, or brigade commanders, and for the most part, moreover, at the front, were out of ammunition. Several most gallant uncombined efforts (notably by Chalmers) were made to reach and carry the Federal battery, *but in every instance the effort failed.*

Comprehending the situation as it was, at six P. M. I dispatched staff-officers with orders to cease hostilities, withdraw the troops from under fire of the Federal gun-boats, and to sleep on their arms. However, before the order was received many of the regiments had already been withdrawn out of action, and really the attack had practically ceased at every point. ☆

My headquarters for the night were established at the Shiloh Meeting House, in the tent that General Sherman had occupied. There several of the corps and division commanders called for orders, and all evinced and expressed much satisfaction with the results, while no one was heard to express or suggest that more might have been achieved had the battle been prolonged. All seemed to believe that our troops had accomplished as much as could have been hoped for.

Of the second day's battle my sketch shall be very brief. It began with daylight, and this time Buell's army was the attacking force.

Our widely scattered forces, which it had been impossible to organize in the night after the late hour at which they were drawn out of action, were gathered in hand for the exigency as quickly as possible. Generals Bragg, Hardee, and Breckinridge hurried to their assigned positions,— Hardee now to the extreme right, where were Chalmers's and Jackson's brigades of Bragg's corps; General Bragg to the left, where were assembled brigades and fragments of his own troops, as also of Clark's division, Polk's corps, with Trabue's brigade of Kentuckians; Breckinridge was on the left of Hardee. This left a vacant space to be occupied by General Polk, who during the night had gone with Cheatham's division back nearly to Hardee's position on the night of the 5th of April. But just at the critical time, to my great pleasure, General Polk came upon the field with that essential division.

By 7 P. M. the night before, all of Nelson's division had been thrown across the Tennessee, and during the night had been put in position between General Grant's disarrayed forces and our own; Crittenden's division, carried from Savannah by water and disembarked at midnight, was forced through the mob of demoralized soldiers that thronged the river-side and established half a mile in advance, to the left of Nelson. Lew Wallace's division of General Grant's army also had found its way after dark on the 6th across Snake Creek from Crump's Landing to the point near the bridge where General Sherman had rallied the remains of two of his brigades. Rousseau reached the field by water, at daylight, while two other brigades of the same division

---

☆ Colonel William Preston Johnston has in effect asserted [see page 567] that my order to retire out of action prevented a concentrated organized operation on the part of the corps commanders about to be launched at the Federal position, a statement that flies in the face of all the reports of the division, brigade, and regimental commanders but one (Withers), as may be readily seen from the official documentary history of the battle.— G. T. B.

THE UNION GUN-BOATS AT SHILOH ON THE EVENING OF THE FIRST DAY. FROM A LITHOGRAPH.

(McCook's) were close at hand. Thus, at the instant when the battle was opened we had to face at least 23,000 fresh troops, including 3 battalions of regulars, with at least 48 pieces of artillery.↓ On the Confederate side there was not a man who had not taken part in the battle of the day before. The casualties of that day had not been under 6500 officers and men, independent of stragglers; consequently not more than 20,000 infantry could be mustered that morning. The Army of the Ohio in General Buell's hands had been made exceptionally well-trained soldiers for that early period of the war.

The extreme Federal right was occupied by General Lew Wallace's division, while the space intervening between it and Rousseau's brigade was filled with from 5000 to 7000 men gathered during the night and in the early morning from General Grant's broken organizations.

After exchanging some shots with Forrest's cavalry, Nelson's division was confronted with a composite force embracing Chalmers's brigade, Moore's Texas Regiment, with other parts of Withers's division, also the Crescent Regiment of New Orleans and the 26th Alabama, supported by well-posted batteries, and so stoutly was Nelson received that his division had to recede somewhat. Advancing again, however, about 8 o'clock, now reënforced by Hazen's brigade, it was our turn to retire with the loss of a battery. But rallying and taking the offensive, somewhat reënforced, the Confederates were

↓General Lew Wallace's division numbered "5000 men of all arms," with 12 guns; Nelson's division, "4541 strong," officers and men, with 18 guns. The strength of Crittenden's division may be estimated at 6750, rank and file, and Rousseau's brigade of McCook's division at 2250.— G. T. B.

able to recover their lost ground and guns, inflicting a sharp loss on Hazen's brigade, that narrowly escaped capture. Ammen's brigade was also seriously pressed and must have been turned but for the opportune arrival and effective use of Terrill's regular battery of McCook's division.

In the meantime Crittenden's division became involved in the battle, but was successfully kept at bay for several hours by the forces under Hardee and Breckinridge, until it was reënforced by two brigades of McCook's division which had been added to the attacking force on the field, after the battle had been joined, the force of fresh troops being thus increased by at least five thousand men.⚓ Our troops were being forced to recede, but slowly; it was not, however, until we were satisfied that we had now to deal with at least three of Buell's divisions as well as with General Lew Wallace's, that I determined to yield the field in the face of so manifestly profitless a combat.

By 1 o'clock General Bragg's forces on our left, necessarily weakened by the withdrawal of a part of his troops to reënforce our right and center, had become so seriously pressed that he called for aid. Some remnants of Louisiana, Alabama, and Tennessee regiments were gathered up and sent forward to support him as best they might, and I went with them personally. General Bragg, now taking the offensive, pressed his adversary back. This was about 2 P. M. My headquarters were still at Shiloh Church.

The odds of fresh troops alone were now too great to justify the prolongation of the conflict. So, directing Adjutant-General Jordan to select at once a proper position in our near rear, and there establish a covering force including artillery, I dispatched my staff with directions to the several corps commanders to prepare to retreat from the field, first making a show, however, at different points of resuming the offensive. These orders were executed, I may say, with no small skill, and the Confederate army began to retire at 2:30 P. M. without apparently the least perception on the part of the enemy that such a movement was going on. There was no flurry, no haste shown by officers or men; the spirit of all was admirable. Stragglers dropped into line; the caissons of the batteries were loaded up with rifles; and when the last of our troops had passed to the rear of the covering force, from the elevated ground it occupied and which commanded a wide view, not a Federal regiment or even a detachment of cavalry was anywhere to be seen as early as 4 P. M.

General Breckinridge, with the rear-guard, bivouacked that night not more than two miles from Shiloh. He withdrew three miles farther on the 8th, and there remained for several days without being menaced.

Our loss in the two days was heavy, reaching 10,699. [See page 539.]

The field was left in the hands of our adversary, as also some captured guns, which were not taken away for want of horses, but in exchange we carried off at least 30 pieces of his artillery with 26 stands of colors and nearly 3000 prisoners of war, also a material acquisition of small arms and accouterments which our men had obtained on Sunday instead of their inferior weapons.

⚓ The fresh Federal troops now engaged aggregated at least 25,000 rank and file, further increased, about 1 o'clock, by Wagner's brigade of Wood's division, say 2500 strong.— G. T. B.

NOTES OF A CONFEDERATE STAFF-OFFICER AT SHILOH.

BY THOMAS JORDAN, BRIGADIER-GENERAL (AT SHILOH, ADJUTANT-GENERAL OF THE CONFEDERATE ARMY).

A CONFEDERATE PRIVATE OF THE WEST.
FROM A TINTYPE.

AFTER 10 o'clock at night, on the 2d of April, 1862, while in my office as adjutant-general of the Confederate army assembled at Corinth, a telegram was brought to me from General Cheatham, commanding an outpost on our left flank at Bethel, on the Mobile and Ohio railway, some twenty odd miles northward of Corinth. General Cheatham had addressed it to General Polk, his corps commander, informing him that a Federal division, under General Lew Wallace, had been manœuvring in his proximity during the day. General Polk had in due course sent the message to General Beauregard, from whom it came to me with his indorsement, addressed to General A. S. Johnston, in substance: "Now is the time to advance upon Pittsburg Landing." And below were these words, in effect, if not literally: "Colonel Jordan had better carry this in person to General Johnston and explain the military situation.—G. T. B."

At the time Colonel Jacob Thompson, formerly Secretary of the Interior of the United States, was in my office. I read the telegram aloud to him and immediately thereafter proceeded to General Johnston's quarters, nearly a quarter of a mile distant, where I found the general surrounded by his personal staff, in the room which the latter habitually occupied. I handed him the open dispatch and the indorsements, which he read without comment. He then asked me several questions about matters irrelevant to the dispatch or what might naturally grow out of it, and rose, saying that he would cross the street to see General Bragg. I asked if I should accompany him. "Certainly," was his answer. We found that General Bragg had already gone to bed, but he received us in dishabille, General Johnston handing him the dispatch at once, without remark. Bragg, having read it, immediately expressed his agreement with Beauregard's advisement. General Johnston thereupon very clearly stated strongly some objections, chiefly to the effect that as yet our troops were too raw and incompletely equipped for an offensive enterprise, such as an attack upon the Federal army in a position of their own choosing, and also that he did not see from what quarter a proper reserve could be assembled in time.

As General Beauregard had discussed with me repeatedly within a week the details of such an offensive operation in all its features, and the necessity for it before the Federal army was itself ready to take the offensive, I was able to answer satisfactorily the objections raised by General Johnston, including the supposed difficulty about a reserve—for which use I pointed out that the Confederate forces posted under General Breckinridge at several points along the line of the Memphis and Charleston railroad, to the eastward of Corinth, could be quickly concentrated at Burnsville, and be moved thence direct to Monterey, and there effect a junction with our main force. General Johnston at last assented to the undertaking. Thereupon I turned to a table in General Bragg's chamber, and wrote a circular order to the three corps commanders, Major-Generals Polk, Bragg, and Hardee, directing that each should hold his corps under arms by 6 A. M., on the 3d of April, ready to march, with one hundred rounds of ammunition; three days' cooked provisions per man in their haversacks, with two more to be transported in wagons. This circular also prescribed the ammunition for the artillery, and the number of tents each company should be provided with; all of which was approved by General Johnston when I read the rough draught of it. Afterward the copies were made by an aide-de-camp on the staff of General Bragg.

These orders were delivered to Generals Polk and Hardee by 1:40 A. M., as shown by their receipts, which I required to be taken. The orders to General Breckinridge were given by telegraph, he having been called by me to the military telegraph office nearest his headquarters to receive them and to answer queries regarding his command. ⌡ Thus did it happen that the Confederate army was brought to undertake the offensive at Pittsburg Landing.

II.

Upon quitting General Bragg's quarters I proceeded immediately to the tent of Colonel A. R. Chisolm, aide-de-camp to General Beauregard, separated from my office by some thirty or forty yards, roused him from sleep, and asked him to inform the general at daylight that the order to advance at midday had been issued.

Soon after sunrise I was called to the quarters of General Beauregard, whom I found with the notes of the plan of operations and orders of engagement. These, I may add, had just been copied by Colonel Chisolm from the backs of telegrams and envelopes upon which the general had made them during the night while in bed. Taking these notes and the general's sketch-map of the roads leading from all surrounding quarters to Monterey and thence to Pittsburg Landing, I returned to my office and began to draw up the order for the battle (Special Orders, No. 8), which will be found in the "Official Records," X., 392–395. ⌢

Called to my breakfast before the order could be framed, I met General Johnston en route for General Beauregard's quarters, where I said I would meet him as quickly as possible, and where I soon joined him. General Beauregard was explaining the details as to the roads by which the several corps would have to move through the somewhat difficult, heavily wooded country, both before and after leaving Monterey; and to make this clear, as

⌡ As I find from a paper officially signed by me April 21st, 1862, this reserve consisted of 6436 rank and file effectives. ("Official Records," Series I., Vol. X., p. 396.)—T. J.

⌢ As I framed this order, I had before me Napoleon's order for the battle of Waterloo, and, in attention to ante-battle details, took those of such soldiers as Napoleon and Soult for model — a fact which I here mention because the ante-Shiloh order has been hypercriticised.—T. J.

I had from General Beauregard the only sketch extant, General Beauregard drew a rough sketch on his camp-table top. Meanwhile, General Bragg and afterward Generals Polk and Hardee had joined the conference. As I remarked that it would take me some time to formulate the order and issue all the requisite copies, General Beauregard explained orally to the three generals their routes of march for the first day, so that they might not wait for receipt of the written orders, which would be in all proper hands before night. Accordingly, these explanations were carefully made, and the corps commanders went away with distinct instructions to begin the movement at midday, as prescribed in the written orders subsequently issued. Pursuant to the terms of the circular order which I had written and issued from General Bragg's headquarters the night before, the troops were brought under arms before noon, by which time the streets and all approaches to the railway station, as well as the roads leading from Corinth, were densely packed with troops, wagons, and field-batteries ready for the march. But no movement was made; General Polk's corps in some way blocked the line of march,— as was reported to General Beauregard at a late hour in the afternoon by General Hardee in person. Thereupon, an aide-de-camp was sent to General Polk, who, to the surprise of all, explained that he had kept his corps at a stand awaiting the written order. Thus it was so late before the movement actually began, that, coupled with the really inexplicable tardiness with which Bragg's corps was moved, it caused the arrival of the Confederate army in the near presence of their adversary twenty-four hours later than was intended, as, by reason of this tardiness, it was not until the late afternoon of the 5th of April that the head of the Confederate column reached a point within less than two miles of the Federal lines, instead of on the 4th, in which case the battle would have been fought with General Grant alone, or without the material and moral help derived from the advent of Buell on the field, as happened on the night of April 6th and morning of the 7th.

III.

GENERAL BEAUREGARD with his staff left Corinth the afternoon of the 4th of April, and reaching Monterey, twelve miles distant, found the Confederate corps massed in that quarter. He was hardly encouraged, however, by the manner in which they had been handled to that stage in the operation. General Johnston and his staff were already at the same point, in occupation of a house at which we dismounted just as some cavalry brought from the front a soldierly young Federal volunteer officer, Major Le Roy Crockett, of the 72d Ohio, who had been captured a few hours before in a sharp skirmish in close proximity to the Federal lines, brought on by a Confederate reconnoitering force pressed most indiscreetly from General Bragg's corps almost upon the Federal front line. As this officer rode beside his captors through the mass of Confederate infantry and batteries, and his eyes rested intelligently on the warlike spectacle, he exclaimed, "This means a battle"; and he involuntarily added, "They don't expect anything of this kind back yonder." He was taken in charge by myself, and, assisted by Major Gilmer, chief engineer on the staff, I interrogated him with the least possible semblance of so doing, with the result of satisfying me, as I reported to Generals Johnston and Beauregard, that we should have no earth-works to encounter, and an enemy wholly unaware of what was so near at hand.

IV.

It has more than once been represented with pencil, as well as with pen, that there was a somewhat dramatic conference of the Confederate generals around the camp-fire the night before the battle of the 6th of April. The simple fact is this: Hardee, whose corps was to be in the advance in the attack, having reached a point known to be somewhat less than two miles from our adversary, was halted and deployed in line of battle across the Pittsburg road to await the arrival and formation in his rear of the rest of the army as prescribed in the battle order. As this was not effected until after 3 o'clock, it was too late to make the attack that day. As a matter of course in such a contingency, the corps commanders were called to meet Generals Johnston and Beauregard, who, having gone from Monterey together with the general staff and their respective personal staffs, had taken a position, dismounted, on the Pittsburg road, somewhat to the rear of Hardee's corps. The meeting took place about 4 o'clock. General Polk now reported that his men were almost destitute of provisions, having either already consumed or thrown them away. General Bragg reported that his own men had been more provident, and therefore could spare enough for the emergency. Deeply dissatisfied with the inexplicable manner in which both Bragg's and Polk's corps had been delayed, both before reaching and after leaving Monterey, as well as by the injudicious manner in which a reconnoissance had been made with such aggressiveness and use of artillery as ought to have apprised any sharp-sighted enemy that an offensive army was not far distant, General Beauregard — though it had been upon his urgent instance that the advance had been made — did not hesitate to say that, inasmuch as it was scarcely possible for the enemy to be unaware of our presence and purpose, should we attack next morning we would find the Federals ready for us intrenched to the eyes; whereas the whole success of the movement had depended on our ability to assail our enemy unexpectedly. Therefore he advised the return of the Confederate army to Corinth, as it assuredly was not in a condition to attack an army superior in numbers and behind the intrenchments that would now be thrown up in expectation of our approach.

General Johnston listened attentively to what General Beauregard said, and at length replied in substance that he recognized its weight; nevertheless, as he hoped the enemy was not suspecting our proximity, he felt bound, as he had put the army in motion for a battle, to venture the hazard. Whereupon the officers rapidly dispersed to their respective commands for that venture. As I have seen it intimated, among others by General Bragg, that this conference was a mere casual or " partly accidental meeting of general

A UNION BATTERY TAKEN BY SURPRISE.   (SEE PAGE 601.)

officers," it may not be amiss to recall that such a conference was the inevitable consequence of the arrival of the Confederate army at the point from which it was to spring upon the enemy, as it were from an ambush. Naturally, moreover, by a conference with their corps commanders, Johnston and Beauregard could best ascertain the condition of all the troops and determine the best course to be pursued. It was after the reports thus made with the mutual blame of each other of two of the corps commanders for the delay, that Beauregard, confirmed in his apprehension that the campaign had miscarried, urged that its objective should be given up,— much as Wellington once, in Spain, after taking the field to attack Massena, finding the latter more strongly posted and prepared than he had been misled to believe, had not hesitated to retire without fighting. The course of events demonstrated the correctness of Beauregard's judgment.

V.

THAT night, soon after supper, an aide-de-camp from General Johnston informed me of the general's desire to see me, and guided me to where he was bivouacking in the open air. I was wanted to issue the order for the immediate transfer of Maney's regiment of Tennessee infantry from a brigade in

Bragg's corps to a certain brigade in Polk's corps, of which Colonel Maney would have the command as senior officer, which order I wrote, in the absence of any table or other convenience, outstretched upon General Johnston's blankets, which were spread at the foot of a tree. After this was done, and the order dispatched by a special courier so that the transfer might be made in time to place Colonel Maney at the head of the brigade in the coming battle, something led us to talk of the Pacific Coast, in which quarter I had served eight years. Having been at Washington during the momentous winter of 1860–61, I spoke of the fact that when Colonel Sumner had been sent *via* the Isthmus of Panama to supersede him (Johnston) in the command of the Department of the Pacific in April, 1861, Sumner's berth in the steamer had been taken under an assumed name, so that the newspapers might not get and divulge the fact of his departure on that errand in time for intelligence of it to reach the Pacific Coast by the overland route, and lead General Johnston to act with a supposed powerful disunion party in California in a revolt against the Federal authority before Sumner's arrival. "Yes," answered the general, with much quiet feeling in his manner, "while distrusting me sufficiently to act thus toward me, my former adjutant-general, Fitz John Porter, was induced to write me of their great confidence in me, and to say that it was their purpose to place me in command of the Federal army, immediately next to General Scott." He had evidently been deeply hurt that his personal character had not shielded him from the suspicion of doing aught while holding a commission that could lead his superiors to suppose it necessary to undertake his supersedure by stealth. [See p. 541.]

VI.

THE next morning, as the Confederate army, deployed in the three lines prescribed in the order of march and battle, moved before sunrise down the gentle wooded slope toward Shiloh Chapel, Generals Johnston and Beauregard, with the general staff as well as aides-de-camp, stood upon a slight eminence, delighted with the evident alacrity, animated faces, and elastic gait with which all moved forward into action. Hardly had the last line passed them before the rattle of musketry announced that Hardee's corps was engaged. General Johnston now informed General Beauregard that he would go to the front with the troops engaged, leaving General Beauregard to take the proper central position from which to direct the movement as the exigencies of the battle might require. Then General Johnston rode off with his personal staff exclusively, except possibly Major Gilmer, the chief engineer. Soon the sound of battle became general; and, as during the battle of Manassas, I had been left at headquarters to send reënforcements into action as they came up by rail, I reminded General Beauregard of the fact, and requested to be dispatched to join General Johnston. He assented, and I set off, accompanied by my friend Colonel Jacob Thompson. In a little time I found that the corps commanders were ahead of or separated from a material part of their troops, whom I repeatedly found halted for want of orders. In all

THE LAST STAND MADE BY THE CONFEDERATE LINE.

General Beauregard at Shiloh Chapel sending his aides to the corps commanders with orders to begin the
retreat.   This was at two o'clock on Monday (see page 603).   The tents are part of
Sherman's camp, which was reoccupied by him Monday evening.

such cases, assuming the authority of my position, I gave the orders in the
name of General Johnston.   At one time I had with me the chiefs-of-staff of
Polk, Bragg, and Hardee, Colonel David Urquhart, the chief aide-de-camp of
Bragg, and Colonel William Preston, the chief aide-de-camp of General Johnston, all of whom I employed in assisting to press the Confederate troops
toward the heaviest firing, and to keep the batteries advancing.   Colonels
Preston and Urquhart remained with me the longer time and assisted greatly.
Finally, however, Urquhart, learning from some of the troops encountered
that he was in proximity to his chief, General Bragg, left me to join him,

while I, accompanied by Colonel Preston, rode to the right wing in the direction of sharp battle. Soon we came in near view of a deserted Federal encampment in an open field, with a Federal battery of four or six guns unlimbered and horseless, while in advance of it were to be seen a brigade of Confederate troops at a halt. Urquhart now galloped up and informed me that General Bragg had sent him to me with the request that I should find and order forward some troops to turn and capture some batteries just in his front which obstructed his advance. I at once pushed across a deep ravine with Urquhart and Preston to the troops in view, which proved to be Statham's brigade of the reserve under General Breckinridge; but because it belonged to the reserve, I hesitated to take the responsibility to employ it, and said so; however, asking Colonel Preston — the brother-in-law as well as aide-de-camp of General Johnston — the hour, he replied, from his watch, twenty minutes after 2 o'clock. I then said that the battle ought to be won by that time, and "I think the reserve should be used." Colonel Preston expressed his agreement with me, and I rode at once to General Breckinridge, who was not far to the rear of his troops, surrounded by a number of officers.

Accosting him, I said, "General Breckinridge, it is General Johnston's order that you advance and turn and take those batteries," pointing in the direction indicated by Urquhart, and where was to be heard the din of their discharges. As the order was given, General Breckinridge, clad in a well-fitting blouse of dark-colored Kentucky jeans, straightened himself in his stirrups. His dark eyes seemed to illuminate his swarthy, regular features, and as he sat in his saddle he seemed to me altogether the most impressive-looking man I ever had seen.

I then turned, accompanied both by Urquhart and Preston, with the purpose of going to the camp and battery previously mentioned, and from that point to observe the movement. On reaching the ravine, which we had crossed, Colonel Preston, who possibly had just heard from some of the officers of the command just set in motion of General Johnston's recent presence with them, said to me, "I believe I will make another attempt to find General Johnston," and rode down the ravine toward the left, and as it so happened, did find General Johnston, but already unconscious, if not dead.

General Johnston had received his death-wound near the very troops I had found standing at ordered arms, but who were unaware of the fact, and therefore were not, as has been written, brought to a stand-still by reason of that catastrophe, and who undeniably were put in effective forward movement by me within twenty minutes after his wounding.

A striking incident of the first day's battle may be here mentioned for its novelty on battle-fields. A completely equipped Federal battery was so suddenly turned and environed by the Confederates, that it was captured with all the guns limbered up *en règle* for movement as upon drill, before its officers could possibly unlimber and use its guns in self-defense. The drivers were in their saddles, the gunners seated side by side in their places upon the ammunition-boxes of the caissons, grinning over the situation, and the officers with their swords drawn were mounted on their horses. Not a horse had been disabled.

VII.

At the time of the reception of the order given as the sun was setting on the 6th of April by General Beauregard for his greatly disarranged and scattered troops to withdraw from action and reorganize for the next day's operations, I had reached a point very close to the Tennessee River where it was densely wooded. The large ordnance of the gun-boats was raking this position, creating more noise in some quarters than harm to the Confederates, as the heavy projectiles tore and crashed in all directions through the heavy forest.

Riding slowly backward to the point at which I understood I should find General Beauregard, it was after sunset when I dismounted at the tent of a Federal officer, before which the general was standing with some of his staff and with an officer in the uniform of a Federal general, to whom I was introduced. It was General Prentiss. Several hours previously a telegraphic dispatch addressed by Colonel Helm to General Johnston (as well as I now remember, from the direction of Athens, in Tennessee) was brought me from Corinth by a courier, saying that scouts employed in observing General Buell's movements reported him to be marching not toward a junction with Grant, but in the direction of Decatur, North Alabama. This assuring dispatch I handed to General Beauregard, and then, at his order, I wrote a telegraphic report to the Confederate adjutant-general, Cooper, at Richmond, announcing the results of the day, including the death of Johnston.

Meanwhile, it had become so dark that I could barely see to write, and it was quite dark by the time Generals Hardee and Breckinridge came to see General Beauregard for orders for the next day's operations. General Bragg, who had also come from the front, had taken up his quarters for the night in a tent which General Sherman had previously occupied at the Shiloh Chapel. This chapel, a rude log-hut of one story, was only two or three hundred yards distant from the spot at which I had found General Beauregard. Leaving General Prentiss in my charge, General Beauregard soon after dark took up his quarters for the night with General Bragg. The corps commanders had meanwhile been personally directed to assemble their respective commands at the earliest possible moment in the morning to be ready for the final stroke.

Colonel Thompson and myself, with General Prentiss sandwiched between us, shared a rough makeshift of a bed made up of tents and captured blankets. Prentiss and Thompson had been old acquaintances, and the former talked freely of the battle, as also of the war, with a good deal of intelligence and good temper. With a laugh, he said: "You gentlemen have had your way to-day, but it will be very different to-morrow. You'll see! Buell will effect a junction with Grant to-night, and we'll turn the tables on you in the morning."

This was said evidently with sincerity, and was answered in the same pleasant spirit, and I showed him the dispatch that had reached me on the field. He insisted, however, that it was a mistake, as we would see. Tired as we were with the day's work, sleep soon overtook and held us all until early dawn, when the firing first of musketry and then of field-artillery roused us, and General Prentiss exclaimed: "Ah! didn't I tell you so! There is Buell!" And so it proved.

VIII

UP to half-past two o'clock on the 7th of April, or second day's conflict, General Beauregard had his headquarters at the Shiloh Chapel, or immediately at Sherman's former headquarters. The Confederate troops, now hardly 20,000 men, were all either directly in advance of that position, or, to the right and left of it, somewhat in advance, hotly engaged, having only receded from the places occupied during the night sufficiently to be better massed and organized for fighting. But our losses were swelling perilously, and the straggling was growing more difficult to restrain. A little after two o'clock, Governor Harris of Tennessee, who, after the death of General Johnston, had joined the staff of Beauregard in action, taking me aside, asked if I did not regard the day as going against us irremediably, and whether there was not danger in tarrying so long in the field as to be unable to withdraw in good order. I answered that I thought it would soon be our proper course to retreat. Having an opportunity a moment later to speak to General Beauregard in private, I brought the subject before him in almost these words:

"General, do you not think our troops are very much in the condition of a lump of sugar thoroughly soaked with water, but yet preserving its original shape, though ready to dissolve? Would it not be judicious to get away with what we have?"

"I intend to withdraw in a few moments," was his reply.

Calling upon his aides-de-camp present, he dispatched them with orders to the several corps commanders to begin the rearward movement. He also directed me to collect as many of the broken organizations as I could,—both of infantry and artillery,—post them in the best position I might find, and hold it until the whole army had passed to the rear of it. Such a position I quickly found on an elevated ridge in full view of the chapel and the ground to the right and left of it, and also somewhat more elevated, rising abruptly toward the enemy but receding gently toward Corinth. There I collected and posted some two thousand infantry, making them lie down at rest. I also placed in battery some twelve or fifteen guns, so as to command and sweep the approach from the direction of the enemy. There also I remained until after 4 o'clock, or until the entire Confederate force had retired, General Breckinridge's troops being the last, and without seeing a single Federal soldier within the wide range of my eyes. I then retired, carrying from the field the caissons loaded down with muskets and rifles picked up on the field.

SURPRISE AND WITHDRAWAL AT SHILOH.

BY S. H. LOCKETT, COLONEL, C. S. A. (AT SHILOH GENERAL BRAGG'S CHIEF ENGINEER).

AT the time of the battle of Shiloh I was on General Bragg's staff as his chief engineer, with the rank of captain. On the night of April 5th I accompanied him to General Johnston's headquarters, where the last council of war was held. I was not present at the meeting of the generals, but with a number of other staff-officers remained near by. We could hear the low, earnest discussion of our superiors, but could not distinguish the words spoken.

When the council closed, and General Bragg started to his own bivouac, I joined him, and received the following instructions: That as the attack would be made at daylight, the next morning at 4 o'clock I should proceed to the front along the Bark road, with Lieutenant Steel, of the engineers, and a squad of cavalry, until I came to the enemy's camp; that I should very carefully and cautiously reconnoiter the camp from where I struck it toward the enemy's left flank; that I should by no means allow any firing by my little force, or do anything to attract attention; that my duty was to get all the information possible about the enemy's position and condition, and send it back by couriers from point to point, as my judgment should suggest. Those orders I carried out the next morning. Lieutenant S. M. Steel, now Major Steel, of Nashville, Tenn., had been a civil engineer and surveyor in that section of the country, had already made several daring and valuable reconnoissances of the Federal camps, and knew the country thoroughly. He was a splendid scout, and as brave a man as ever lived. Under his skillful guidance I reached in safety a point which he said was not more than a few hundred yards from the Federal camps. Here our cavalry escort and our own horses were left, and we two, leaving the road, passed down a narrow valley or gorge, got beyond the Federal pickets, and came within a few rods of a sleepy camp sentinel leaning against a tree. In front of us was a large camp as still and silent as the grave; no signs of life except a few smoldering fires of the last night's supper. Noting these facts and without disturbing the man at the tree, we returned to our cavalry squad, and I dispatched a courier to General Bragg with a note telling what I had seen. We then moved by our right flank through the woods, from a quarter to half a mile, and repeated our former manœuvre. This time we found the cooks of the camp astir preparing breakfast. While we were watching the process reveille was sounded, and I saw one or two regiments form by companies, answer to roll-call, and then disperse to their tents. Once more I returned to my cavalry and dispatched a courier.

A third time I made a descent from the hills, down a narrow hollow, still farther to our right, and saw Federal soldiers cleaning their guns and accouterments and getting ready for Sunday morning inspection. By this time firing had begun on our left, and I could see that it caused some commotion in the camps, but it was evident that it was not understood. Soon the firing became more rapid and clearer and closer, and I saw officers begin to stir out of their tents, evidently anxious to find out what it all meant. Then couriers began to arrive, and there was great bustle and confusion; the long roll was beaten; there was rapid falling in, and the whole party in front of me was so thoroughly awake and alarmed that I thought my safest course was to retreat while I could and send another courier to the rear.

How long all this took I cannot now recall, but perhaps not more than an hour and a half or two hours. When I reached my cavalry squad I knew that the battle had opened in earnest, but I determined to have one more look at the Federal position, and moved once more to the right. Without getting as near as our former positions, I had a good view of another camp with a line of soldiers formed in front of it. Meantime the Confederate troops had moved on down the hills, and I could plainly see from the firing that there was hot and heavy work on my left and in advance of my present position. I then began to fear that the division in front of me would swing around and take our forces in flank, as it was manifest that the Federal line extended farther in that direction than ours. I therefore disposed my little cavalry force as skirmishers, and sent a courier with a sketch of the ground to General Bragg, and urged the importance of having our right flank protected. How long I waited and watched at this point it is hard to say. Finally, becoming very uneasy at the state of affairs, I left Lieutenant Steel with the cavalry and rode to the left myself to make a personal report. In this ride I passed right down the line of battle of the Confederate forces, and saw some splendid duels both of artillery and infantry. Finally, as I have always thought about 11 o'clock, I came to General A. S. Johnston and his staff standing on the brow of a hill watching the conflict in their front. I rode up to General Johnston, saluted him, and said I wished to make a report of the state of affairs on our extreme right. He said he had received that report and a sketch from Captain Lockett, of the engineers. I told him I was Captain Lockett. He replied, "Well, sir, tell me as briefly and quickly as possible what you have to say." When my report was finished he said, "That is what I gathered from your note and sketch, and I have already ordered General Breckinridge to send forces to fill up the space on our right. Ride back, sir, toward the right, and you will probably meet General Breckinridge; lead him to the position you indicate, and tell him to drive the enemy he may find in his front into the river. He needs no further orders." The words are, as near as I can remember them, exactly the ones General Johnston used. I obeyed the order given, met General Breckinridge, conducted him to the place where I had left my cavalry, but found both them and the Federal division gone. I rode with General Breckinridge a few hundred yards forward, and we soon received a volley which let us know that the Federal forces had retired but a very short distance from their original position. General Breckinridge deployed Bowen's and Statham's brigades, moved them forward, and soon engaged the Federal forces. I bade the General good-day and good luck, and once more rode down the line of battle until I found General Bragg. With him I remained, excepting when carrying orders and making reconnoissances, until the close of the first day's fight.

I witnessed the various bloody and unsuccessful attacks on the "Hornets' Nest." During one of the dreadful repulses of our forces, General Bragg directed me to ride forward to the central regiment of a brigade of troops that was recoiling across an open field, to take its colors and carry them forward. "The flag must not go back again," he said. Obeying the order, I dashed through the line of battle, seized the colors from the color-bearer, and said to him, "General Bragg says these colors must not go to the rear." While I was talking to him the color-sergeant was shot down. A moment or two afterward I was almost alone on horseback in the open field between the two lines of battle. An officer came up to me with a bullet-hole in each cheek, the blood streaming from his mouth, and asked, "What are you doing with my colors, sir?" "I am obeying General Bragg's orders, sir, to hold them where they are," was my reply. "Let me have them," he said. "If any man but my color-bearer carries these colors, I am the man. Tell General Bragg I will see that these colors are in the right place. But he must attack this position in flank; we can never carry it alone from the front." It was Colonel H. W. Allen, afterward Governor Allen of Louisiana. I returned, miraculously preserved, to General Bragg, and reported Colonel Allen's words. I then carried an order to the same troops, giving the order, I think, to General Gibson, to fall back to the fence in the rear and reorganize. This was done, and then General Bragg dispatched me to the right, and Colonel Frank Gardner (afterward Major-General) to the left, to inform the brigade and division commanders on either side that a combined movement would be made on the front and flanks of that position. The movements were made, and Prentiss was captured.

As Colonel William Preston Johnston says, that capture was a dear triumph to us — dear for the many soldiers we had lost in the first fruitless attacks, but still dearer on account of the valuable time it cost us. The time consumed in gathering Prentiss's command together, in taking their arms, in marching them to the rear, was inestimably valuable. Not only that; the news of the capture spread, and grew as it spread; many soldiers and

officers believed we had captured the bulk of the Federal army, and hundreds left their positions and came to see the "captured Yanks." But after a while the Confederates were gotten into ranks, and a perfect line of battle was formed, with our left wing resting on Owl Creek and our right on the Tennessee River. General Polk was on the left, then Bragg, then Hardee, then Breckinridge. In our front only one single point was showing fight, a hill crowned with artillery. I was with General Bragg, and rode with him along the front of his corps. I heard him say over and over again, "One more charge, my men, and we shall capture them all." While this was going on a staff-officer (or rather, I think, it was one of the detailed clerks of General Beauregard's headquarters, for he wore no uniform) came up to General Bragg, and said, "The General directs that the pursuit be stopped; the victory is sufficiently complete; it is needless to expose our men to the fire of the gun-boats." General Bragg said, "My God, was a victory ever sufficiently complete?" and added, "Have you given that order to any one else?" "Yes, sir," was the reply, "to General Polk, on your left; and if you will look to the left, you will see that the order is being obeyed." General Bragg looked, and said, "My God, my God, it is too late!" and turning to me, he said, "Captain, carry that order to the troops on the right"; and to Captain Frank Parker, "You carry it to the left." In a short time the troops were all falling back — *and the victory was lost*. Captain Parker and myself were the only members of General Bragg's staff who were with him at that time. Captain Parker, I think, is still living in South Carolina, and will surely remember all that I have narrated.

In this hasty sketch I have intentionally omitted everything but the beginning and end of that day's operations, to throw what light I can upon the two great points of dispute: Was the Federal army surprised by our attack? and whose fault was it that the victory was not sufficiently complete on the first day?

In regard to the second day's fight, I will touch upon but one point. I, as a great many other staff-officers, was principally occupied in the early hours of the second day in gathering together our scattered men and getting them into some sort of manageable organization. In this duty I collected and organized a body of men about a thousand strong. They were composed of men of at least a half-dozen different regiments. The 7th Kentucky, with a tattered flag, and the 9th Arkansas were the most numerously represented. We had not one single field-officer in the command. When I reported to General Beauregard that I had the troops divided into companies, had assigned a captain to duty as lieutenant-colonel and a first lieutenant as major, he himself put me in command of them as colonel. In order that my command might have a name, I dubbed it the "Beauregard Regiment,"—a name that was received with three rousing cheers. Not long after my regiment was thus officered and christened, a message came from General Breckinridge on our extreme right that he was hard pressed, and needed reënforcements. My regiment, which was at the time just behind General Beauregard, held in reserve by his orders, was sent by him to General Breckinridge's assistance. We marched down the line of battle to the extreme right, passed beyond General Breckinridge's right, wheeled by companies into line of battle, and went in with the "rebel yell." The men on our left took up the yell and the charge, and we gained several hundred yards of ground. From this point we fought back

slowly and steadily for several hours, until word came that the army was ordered to retreat, that the commands would fall back in succession from the left, and that the right wing would be the rear-guard. This order was carried out, and when night came the right wing was slowly falling back with face to the foe. We halted on the same ground we had occupied on the morning of the 6th, just before the battle began. If there was any "breaking" and "starting," as General Grant expresses it, I did not witness it.

THE SHILOH BATTLE-ORDER AND THE WITHDRAWAL SUNDAY EVENING.

BY ALEXANDER ROBERT CHISOLM, COLONEL, C. S. A. (AT SHILOH ON GENERAL BEAUREGARD'S STAFF).

In the paper published in "The Century" for February, 1885, Colonel William Preston Johnston, assuming to give the Confederate version of the campaign and battle of Shiloh, at which he was not present, has adventured material statements regarding operations on that field, which must have been based on misinformation or misunderstanding in essential particulars, as I take occasion to assert from personal knowledge acquired as an eye-witness and aide-de-camp on the staff of General Beauregard. My personal knowledge runs counter to many of his statements and deductions, but I shall here confine myself to two points.

First, I must dispute that the battle-order as promulgated was in any wise different from the one submitted by General Beauregard at his own quarters at Corinth, early in the morning of the 3d of April, to General A. S. Johnston, and which was accepted without modification or suggestion. This assertion I base on these facts: About 1 o'clock in the morning the adjutant-general of the Confederate forces, Colonel Jordan, aroused me from sleep in my tent, close by General Beauregard's chamber, and desired me to inform the general at dawn that General Johnston had agreed to his recommendation to move offensively against Pittsburg Landing early that same day, and that the circular orders to the corps commanders had been already issued by Colonel Jordan to that effect. Acting upon this request, I found that General Beauregard had already during the night made full notes on loose scraps of paper of the order of march and battle, from which he read aloud for me to copy — my copy being given to Colonel Jordan as soon as completed, as the basis of the official order which he was to frame, and did frame and issue in the name of General Johnston. And that is the order which Colonel Johnston erroneously alleges upon the posthumous authority of General Bragg to differ essentially from the plan settled upon by General Johnston for the battle. This allegation I know to be unfounded, as the order as issued varies in no wise from the notes dictated to me by General Beauregard, excepting the mere wording and some details relating to transportation and ordnance service added by Colonel Jordan; that is to say, the plan explained by General Beauregard and accepted by General Johnston at the quarters of the former.

Being limited as to space, I shall pass over a throng of facts within my personal knowledge,

which would establish that General Beauregard was as actively and directly handling the Confederate forces engaged in their general conduct of the battle before the death of General Johnston as he was after that incident. I shall confine myself on this occasion to relating that after General Beauregard became cognizant of the death of General Johnston, he dispatched me to the front with orders that led to the concentration of the widely scattered and disarrayed Confederate forces, which resulted in the capture of General Prentiss and so many of his division after 5 o'clock on the 6th.

I also, later in the day, carried orders to Hardee, who was engaged on our extreme left, or Federal right, where I remained with that officer until almost dark, up to which time no orders had reached him to cease fighting. On the contrary, he was doing his best to force back the enemy in his front. As he was without any of his staff about him, for the nonce I acted as his aide-de-camp. Meantime the gun-boats were shelling furiously, and their huge missiles crushed through the branches of the trees overhead with so fearful a din, frequency, and closeness that, despite the excitement of our apparently complete victory, there was room left in our minds for some most unpleasant sensations, especially when the top of some lofty tree, cut off by a shell, would come toppling down among the men.

Possibly, had Colonel Johnston been present on the field at that last hour of the battle of the 6th, a witness of the actually fruitless efforts made to storm the last position held by the enemy upon the ridge covering the immediate landing-place, known as Pittsburg, he might be better informed why it was that that position was not carried, and be less disposed to adduce such testimony as that of General Bragg, to the effect that but for the order given by Beauregard to withdraw from action he would have carried all before him.

It so happened that I rejoined General Beauregard at a point near Shiloh-Chapel (having escorted General Prentiss from the field to General Beauregard), when General Bragg rode up from the front, and I heard him say in an excited manner: "General, we have carried everything before us to the Tennessee River. I have ridden from Owl to Lick Creek, and there is none of the enemy to be seen." Beauregard quietly replied: "Then, General, do not unnecessarily expose your command to the fire of the gun-boats."

THE MARCH OF LEW WALLACE'S DIVISION TO SHILOH.

CIRCUMSTANCES AND CHARACTER OF THE ORDER.

As GENERAL GRANT passed up from Savannah on the *Tigress* on the 6th of April to the battle-field of Shiloh, he found General Lew Wallace awaiting him at Crump's Landing, the troops of his division having been ordered under arms at the sound of the battle. [For General Grant's statements, see pages 467–8.] General Wallace in his official report places the hour at which General Grant reached Crump's at about 9, while General Grant gives the hour of his arrival at Pittsburg Landing as about 8. Grant left Wallace a direction to hold himself in readiness for orders. In anticipation of the receipt of them, a horse was saddled at Crump's for the use of the expected messenger, the First Brigade having been already sent from Crump's to join the Second at Stony Lonesome (marked A on the map), General Wallace following about 9:15. To this point, at an hour which has been variously stated by the officers of the command as from 11 o'clock to noon (Wallace says, "exactly 11:30"), came Captain A. S. Baxter, quartermaster on Grant's staff, with the order. Concerning the time, dispatch, and character of this order there is much disagreement. General Grant says that the order was verbal; that it was given after riding out to the front, and that Baxter made a memorandum of it, though he does not say that he saw Baxter. Furthermore Rawlins says that the order was taken by him back to the Landing, half a mile away, and given verbally to Baxter, and afterward dictated to him, at the latter's request, and that Baxter started on the steamer not later than 9 o'clock. Rowley states that Grant gave the order verbally and in person to Baxter at once upon arriving at the Landing, and then rode immediately to the front. Wallace states that Baxter delivered an unsigned order and said that "it had been given to him verbally, but that in coming down the river he had reduced it to writing."

Concerning the circumstances and character of the order Captain Baxter made the following statement in the New-York "Mail and Express" for November 4th, 1886:

"I will give my own recollection of the event at Pittsburg Landing. On Sunday, between the hours of 8 and 9 o'clock A. M., April 6th, 1862, Adjutant-General Rawlins, of General Grant's staff, requested me to go to Crump's Landing (five miles below) and order General Lew Wallace to march his command at once by the River Road to Pittsburg Landing, and join the army on the right. At the same time General Rawlins dictated the order to General Wallace, which was written by myself and signed by General Rawlins.

"On meeting General Wallace I gave the order verbally, also handed to him the written order. General Wallace said 'he was waiting for orders, had heard the firing all the morning, and was ready to move with his command immediately — knew the road and had put it in good order.'

"My stay with Lew Wallace did not exceed three minutes. I had no further conversation with him, and I returned immediately to Pittsburg Landing."

As to the character of the order: General Grant's statement (see page 468) is that the order as given was "to march immediately to Pittsburg by the road nearest the river." Captain Rowley says, "to march with his division up the river, and into the field on the right of our line, as rapidly as possible." Rawlins says it read "substantially as follows: 'Major-General Wallace: You will move forward your division from Crump's Landing, leaving a sufficient force to protect the public property at that place, to Pittsburg Landing, on the road nearest to and parallel to the river, and form in line at right angles with the river, immediately in rear of the camp of Major-General C. F. Smith's division on our right [W. H. L. Wallace's], and there wait further orders.'" General Wallace says, that as received, it directed him "to come up and take position on the right of the army, and form my line of battle at a right angle with the river," and "to leave a force to prevent surprise at Crump's Landing." Colonel James R. Ross says, "I very distinctly remember that this order directed you to move forward and join General Sherman's right on the Purdy Road, and form your line of battle at right angles with the river, and then act as circumstances would dictate." ☆ General Fred. Knefler says, "It was a written order to march and form a junction with the right of the army." ⟍ Captain Addison Ware says it was "to move your division up and join General Sherman's right on the road leading from Pittsburg Landing to Purdy." ⚓ General Knefler adds, "The order was placed in my hands as Assistant Adjutant-General; but where it is now, or what became of it, I am unable to say. Very likely, having been written on a scrap of paper, it was lost." ⟍

ROUTE AND LIMIT OF THE MARCH.

All reports agree that the march of the two brigades began at 12 o'clock, along the road A B C. Wallace not arriving at Pittsburg Landing, General Grant sent Captain Rowley of his staff to hurry him forward. Rowley went by the River Road almost to Crump's Landing, and then "a distance of between five and six miles," when he reached the rear of Wallace's division by the road A B C, and passing the resting troops continued to the head of the column, where he found Wallace and delivered the orders, and gave him the first information that the right of the army had been driven back. Wallace then ordered a countermarch of the troops. The point at which this turning took place is fixed by General Wallace at D, half-way between the Purdy crossing and the Owl Creek bridge. (This identification is fully confirmed by letters of October 5th and 6th, 1887, written by Generals Fred. Knefler and G. F. McGinnis, Captains Thomas C. Pursel and George F. Brown, and Dr. S. L. Ensminger, all of whom took part in the march, and the last two of whom examined the ground in 1884 to determine the point.) In the "Official Records" is a sketch map, without scale, by Colonel James B. McPherson, placing the

---

☆ Ross to Wallace, January 25th, 1868.   ⟍ Knefler to Wallace, February 19th, 1868.   ⚓ Ware to Wallace [1868].

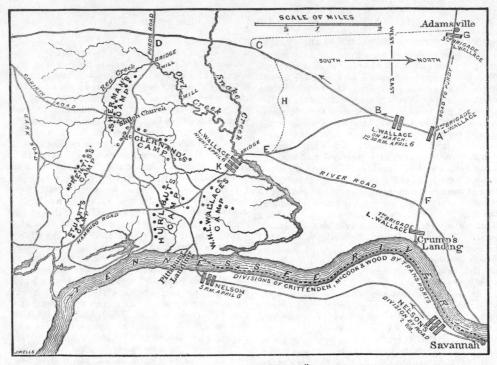

MAP OF THE ROUTES BY WHICH GENERAL GRANT WAS REËNFORCED AT PITTSBURG LANDING.

Authorities: (1.) The Official or Thom map (p. 508), for roads and distances on the south side of Snake Creek; (2.) the Union Camp map (pp. 496–7), for the location of camps morning of April 5th, 1862; (3.) the Shiloh map in General Badeau's "Military History of U. S. Grant," for the main roads on the north side of Snake Creek, that map also agreeing with General McPherson's sketch map without scale in "Official Records," Vol. X., p. 183; (4.) General Wallace's statement to the editors, 1887, based on investigations and measurements in 1884, by Captain George F. Brown and Dr. S. L. Ensminger, for the roads from G to C and from C to E, and for the point D as the limit of the march toward Owl Creek. N. B.—No detailed survey appears to have been made.

Key to routes of Wallace's division:
Route of First Brigade, morning of April 6th — F A.
Route of First and Second brigades to the battlefield, afternoon—A B C D C H E K.
Route of Third Brigade, afternoon — G C H E K.

limit of march at C. This was probably intended for the point where Rowley came up with the rear of the column, which must have covered a distance of two miles or more; but if intended for the limit of the advance, it could not have been fixed on McPherson's own knowledge, for when Rawlins and McPherson, who were also sent by General Grant (McPherson says at 2:30) to hasten the movement, following Rowley's course, came up with the division (Rawlins says about 3:30), the First Brigade had passed across toward E and the Second was passing. Some mystery attaches to the inaction of the Third Brigade during the morning. General Wallace states in his report that it was concentrated on the Second, meaning, as he explains to the editors, that the order for the concentration had been sent, and, he presumed, obeyed. Colonel Ross delivered the order to Colonel Charles R. Woods, then in command at Adamsville, and Captain Ware, Wallace's second aid, carried a repetition of it —both during the morning. [Ross to Wallace, January 25th, 1868, and Ware to Wallace, 1868.] Yet Colonel Whittlesey, who during the day, by seniority of commission, succeeded to the command of the brigade, says in his report that three of the four regiments "received orders to march with their trains about 2 P. M., and to advance toward Pittsburg Landing in advance of the trains at 4 P. M." This they did (General Wallace informs us) by the route shown on the map. The fourth regiment went to Crump's to guard the public property.

The "Official Records" (Vol. X., p. 177) also tain a rough sketch map, submitted by General con-Wallace to General Halleck, accompanying a memorandum dated March 14th, 1863. That map is manifestly imperfect in representing but one bridge between A and the right of the army, the junction of Owl and Snake creeks being placed above the upper Snake creek bridge, instead of below it. General Wallace himself has informed the editors that that map is incorrect, and that its inaccuracy arose from a prevalent confusion of the names of Snake and Owl creeks. That map, however, faithfully represents General Wallace's claim that the head of his column advanced to within a mile of what had been the right of the army. This confusion of the two creeks has given ambiguity to General Wallace's statement in his report, made five days after the battle, which he informs us should read as bracketed:

"Selecting a road that led directly to the right of the lines, as they were established around Pittsburg Landing on Sunday morning, my column started immediately, the distance being about six miles. The cannonading, distinctly audible, quickened the steps of the men. Snake Creek [Owl Creek], difficult of passage at all times on account of its steep banks and swampy bottoms, ran between me and the point of junction. Short way from it [Owl Creek] Captain Rowley, from General Grant, . . . overtook me. . . . . It seemed, on his representation, most prudent to carry the column across to what is called the 'River Road.' . . . This movement occasioned a counter-march, which delayed my junction with the main army until a little after nightfall."

CHARACTER OF THE MARCH.

Rowley, McPherson, and Rawlins report that they represented the need of haste, and that the march was slow:

"Of the character of the march, after I overtook General Wallace, I can only say that to *me* it appeared intolerably slow, resembling more a reconnoissance in the face of an enemy than a forced march to relieve a hard-pressed army. So strongly did this impression take hold of my mind, that I took the liberty of repeating to General Wallace that part of General Grant's order enjoining haste." [Rowley.]

"After I had reached the head of the column, I must say it seemed to me that the march was not as rapid as the urgency of the case required. Perhaps this arose in a great measure from my impatience and anxiety to get this force on the field before dark. . . ." [McPherson]

" Colonel McPherson and I came up to him about 3:30 o'clock P. M. He was then not to exceed four or four and a half miles [two and a half miles ?] from the scene of action ; the roads were in fine condition ; he was marching light ; his men were in buoyant spirits, within hearing of the musketry, and eager to get forward. He did not make a mile and a half an hour, although urged and appealed to, to push forward. Had he moved with the rapidity his command were able and anxious to have moved after we overtook him, he would have reached you [Grant] in time to have engaged the enemy before the close of Sunday's fight." [Rawlins.]

General Wallace denies this last conclusion and the statement about the condition of the road. General Knefler says [letter to Wallace]: "After some hard marching over execrable roads, we reached our position about dusk." Col. James R. Ross says [letter to Wallace, January 25th, 1868]: "We had to march over the worst road I ever remember to have seen. In many places it was almost impossible to get artillery through."

The head of the column did not arrive at K until after dark, probably at 7:15, sunset being at 6 : 30. The total time of the march was about 7 hours. The total distance traveled to the lower bridge (K) was, according to our map, 11 miles. It is possible that a detailed survey of the field would indicate the distance as somewhat greater. General Wallace estimates it as " over 14 miles, of which quite 5 miles were through mire so deep that the axles of my guns left wakes behind them as if mud-scows had been dragged that way." Captain Brown, who studied the route in 1884, estimates it at between 13 and 14 miles. Not considering the comparative difficulties of the two marches, the map indicates little difference in the speed of Wallace's division and that of Nelson's leading brigade (Ammen) from Savannah to Pittsburg Landing (1:30 to 5). Ammen in his diary dwells on the extreme difficulties of his route, which lay largely through swamps impassable by artillery.

DOCUMENTS SUBMITTED BY GENERAL WALLACE.

I.—Letter found on the person of General W. H. L. Wallace, after he had received a mortal wound at Shiloh, and sent by his widow to General Grant [see foot-note, page 468; printed also in THE CENTURY and in the "Personal Memoirs of U. S. Grant"]:

" HEADQUARTERS THIRD DIVISION, ADAMSVILLE, April 5th, 1862. GENERAL W. H. L. WALLACE, commanding Second Division. SIR: Yours received. Glad to hear from you. My cavalry from this point has been to and from your post frequently. As my Third Brigade is here, five miles from Crump's Landing, my Second two and a half miles from it, I thought it would be better to open communication with you from Adamsville. I will to-morrow order Major Hays, of the 5th Ohio Cavalry, to report to you at your quarters; and, if you are so disposed, probably you had better send a company to return with him, that they may familiarize themselves with the road, to act in case of emergency as guides to and from our camps.—I am, very respectfully, your obedient servant, LEWIS WALLACE, General Third Division."

General Wallace says : " As I was ignorant of the position of W. H. L. Wallace's camp, this letter was sent by way of Owl Creek. I knew Wallace, and did not know Sherman, whose camp was nearer."

II. — Letter from General Grant to General Lew Wallace, in 1868, after examining statements by the latter and by the following officers of his command, touching the character of the order and march: Generals Fred. Knefler, George F. McGinnis, Daniel Macauley, John A. Strickland, John M. Thayer, Colonel James R. Ross, and Captain Addison Ware:

" HEADQUARTERS ARMY OF THE UNITED STATES, WASHINGTON, D. C., March 10th, 1868. MY DEAR GENERAL: Inclosed herewith I return you letters from officers of the army who served with you at the battle of Shiloh, Tennessee, giving their statement of your action on that occasion. I can only state that my orders to you were given verbally to a staff-officer to communicate, and that they were substantially as given by General Badeau in his book. I always understood that the staff-officer referred to, Captain Baxter, made a memorandum of the orders he received, and left it with you. That memorandum I never saw.

"The statements which I now return seem to exonerate you from the great point of blame, your taking the wrong road, or different road from the one directed, from Crump's Landing to Pittsburg Landing. All your subsequent military career showed you active and ready in the execution of every order you received. Your promptness in moving from Baltimore to Monocacy, Maryland, in 1864, and meeting the enemy in force far superior to your own when Washington was threatened, is a case particularly in point. There you could scarcely have hoped for a victory, but you delayed the enemy, and enabled me to get troops from City Point, Virginia, in time to save the city. That act I regarded as most praiseworthy. I refer you to my report of 1865, touching your course there. In view of the assault made upon you now, I think it due to you that you should publish what your own staff and other subordinate officers have to say in exoneration of your course. —Yours truly, U. S. GRANT, General.

"To MAJOR-GENERAL L. WALLACE."

III. — Letter from General Wallace to General Grant, in 1884, referring to the whole controversy. The omissions are made by the editors, for lack of space :

"CRAWFORDSVILLE, IND., September 16th, 1884. DEAR GENERAL: The Century Co. people inform me that they have engaged you to write a paper for them on Pittsburg Landing. Such a contribution from your hand will be important as well as most interesting. Probably I ought not to trouble you touching the subject; still, I trust you will appreciate the anxieties natural to one who has been so bitterly and continuously criticised in the connection, and pardon me a few lines of request.

"The letter of exoneration you gave me some years ago is not permitted to be printed in the volume of reports published by the Government, though I earnestly sought the favor of the Secretary of War. The terrible reflections in your indorsement on my official report of the battle, and elsewhere, go to the world wholly unqualified. It is not possible to exaggerate the misfortune thus entailed upon me. But now you have it in power to make correction, in a paper which will be read far more generally than the compilation of the department. May I hope you will do it?

"Since my return from Europe I have for the first time read the reports of Generals Rawlins and McPherson, and Major Rowley, touching my march the first day of the battle. I shall regret all my remaining days not previously knowing their tenor; for I think I could have explained to the satisfaction of those gentlemen every mystery of my conduct during their ride with me the afternoon of the 6th April. They did not understand that there was a mistake in your order as it was delivered to me, and while with them I supposed they knew why I was where they found me. Consequently, no explanation took place between us. I see now, they really supposed me lost, and wandering aimlessly about. Had the correctness of the order been mooted, no doubt the order itself could have been produced. I would not have rested until my adjutant-general had produced it. Is it to be supposed for an instant that, knowing their thoughts of me during the hours of that ride, I could have been indifferent to them? As it is, you will observe that neither of them pretends to explain my behavior. Neither makes allusion to a theory of explanation. The truth is, I all the time supposed the necessity for the change of direction in my movement was simply due to the bad turn of the battle after the order was dispatched to me. The whole time I was in their company I thought myself entitled to credit for the promptness with which I was obeying your orders. It never occurred to me that there was anything to explain, and I was wholly given up to the movement of the division, which was urgent business in hand.

"With reference to Major Rowley's statement, that I had no knowledge of any other road than that by the old mill, and his other statement, that I retained him as a guide, the explanation is that I was speaking of a cross-road to the River Road. I had no knowledge of such a road. In hopes of finding one, I countermarched instead of facing column to the rear. One of my captains of artillery has since gone over the entire route we took, from Stony Lonesome, the place at which I received your order to march, to Pittsburg Landing, and he finds me mistaken in saying we countermarched back nearly to the initial point of movement. He not only found the cross-road taken, but measured the whole march, chain in hand, making it a little more than fifteen miles. . . .

"As to my requiring a written order from you, I repeat my absolute denial of the statement. The order I acted upon was *unsigned*, and it is susceptible of proof that when the young Illinois cavalryman overtook me I was already on the march.

"As to the slowness referred to by McPherson, Rawlins and Rowley, please try that point by comparisons. . . . . From 11 : 30 o'clock till just dusk my march was quite fifteen miles. I refer the argument to your calm judgment. I do not wonder my movement seemed slow to your officers. With their anxieties quickened by what they had seen on the field, it must have seemed intolerable to them. They describe me correctly as *at the head of the column,* and I did several times dismount, but only to wait the closing up of the division and reports of my own staff-officers, who were kept urging the column through the mud and mire.

"There is another point your officers seem not to have understood, and that was my determination not to send the division piecemeal into the battle. The *whole* division was what I supposed you wanted, and I was resolved to bring you the whole division. I paid no attention to contrary suggestions from anybody. I think you will justify this pertinacity of purpose by the fact that it was impossible to tell the moment I might be attacked *en route.* The chances of such an occurrence grew sharper as I drew nearer Pittsburg Landing. For you must remember, general, that from the moment Major Rowley overtook me with the information, then first received, that our army had been driven from the line it occupied in the morning, and was back far towards the river, I supposed it utterly unable to help me. Then whether the enemy attacked me or I them, it was only my *division,* and not a part of it, that could have achieved your desires. . . .

"At your table at City Point we one day sat listening to the comments of some officers upon the battle of Pittsburg Landing. After a while you remarked to me in a low tone, 'If I had known then what I know now, I would have ordered you where you were marching when stopped.' The remark was made at your table, and in a confidential manner, so that I have never felt at liberty to repeat, much less publish, it. But times innumerable since then I have wished that Rowley had not overtaken me for another hour that afternoon. The enemy had used the last of his reserves. I would have taken the bluff on which Sherman had been camped in the morning and, without opposition, effected my deployment. The first of the rebels struck would have been the horde plundering the sutlers and drinking in the streets of the camp. Their fears would have magnified my command, and rushing to their engaged lines they would have carried the word that Buell's army was up and on their lines of retreat. For your sake and my own, general, and for the cause generally, it was unfortunate that Rowley had not lost his way, as it was said I had mine.

"Finally, general, did you ever ask yourself what motive I could have had to play you falsely that day? It couldn't have been personal malice. Only a few weeks before I had been promoted major-general on your recommendation. It couldn't have been cowardice. You had seen me under fire at Donelson, and twice the second day at Pittsburg Landing you found me with my division under fire. It couldn't have been lack of resolution. I certainly showed no failing of that kind at Monocacy Junction, where my situation was quite as trying as at any hour of the 6th of April of which I am writing. The fact is, I was the victim of a mistake. Captain Baxter's omission from the order you gave him for transmission to me—the omission of the road you wanted me to take in coming up—viz., the *lower or River Road to Pittsburg Landing,* was the cause of my movement at noon. It is also the key of explanation of all that followed. That I took the directest and shortest road to effect a junction with the right of the army, and marched promptly upon receipt of the order, are the best evidence I could have furnished of an actual desire to do my duty, and share the fortunes of the day with you, whether they were good or bad.

"In all the years that have followed I have been patient and uncomplaining, because, as you had shown the will to exonerate me, I believed you would follow it up on all proper occasions. And I submit to you if this is not one of them. For the sake of the hundreds of survivors of my old division, as well as that justice may be finally and completely done to me individually, I presume to present the matter to you in this letter.

"Very respectfully, your friend, LEW WALLACE."

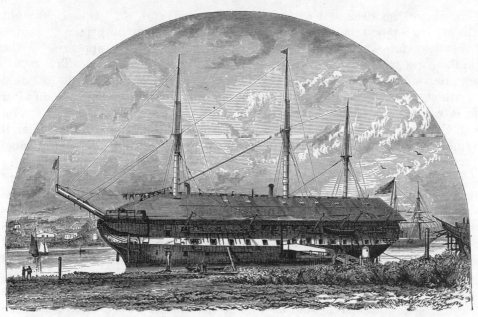

A FRIGATE OF THE OLDEN TIME — THE "INDEPENDENCE," BUILT IN 1814.   RECEIVING-SHIP AT THE MARE ISLAND NAVY YARD IN 1872.

THE UNION AND CONFEDERATE NAVIES.

BY JAMES RUSSELL SOLEY, PROFESSOR, U. S. N.

IN order to understand the condition of the United States navy in 1861, it is necessary to glance at the state of affairs during the twenty years before the war. Until the year 1840, naval science during a long period had made but little progress. The various improvements in construction, in equipment, and in ordnance that had been introduced before this date had come about very slowly and gradually, and though numerous small mechanical devices had been adopted from time to time, and old ones had been rendered more efficient, no marked changes had taken place in the art of naval war. Ships were essentially what they had been for two hundred years, and they were rigged, propelled, armed, and fought upon essentially the same principles. But toward the year 1840, the introduction of steam as a motive power marked the beginning of a new era,—an era of developments so rapid and of changes so radical that only the most progressive and elastic minds could follow them. The sailing vessel was about to be laid aside, except for purposes of training. In the next few years it was replaced, first by the paddle-wheel steamer, then by the screw, then by the twin-screw. The rig of the ship was next altered, and her spars and sail-spread reduced until they were merely auxiliary. Gradually it was realized that the danger from falling spars in an engagement was a disadvantage often out of all proportion to the benefits of auxiliary sail-power, and vessels were built with no spars above the deck but a signal-pole forward and aft. Steam brought with it also a new weapon. The ram, which had been the principal engine of naval warfare in the Greek and Roman galleys, had disappeared in the Middle Ages when galleys were superseded by sailing ships. The latter, being dependent upon the wind for their motive power and direction, could not attack an enemy end-on, and hence the ram became useless. Soon after the introduction of steam a few men of inquiring and fertile minds, among them Commodore Matthew Perry and Mr. Charles Ellet, a distinguished civil engineer, perceived that the steam-engine placed a ship-of-war in the same situation as the galleys of the classical period, and that the ram might be employed on the modern vessel to much greater advantage than in ancient times. Presently, the whole system of naval tactics underwent a change, due to the same cause. The close-hauled line ahead, the order of battle for two hundred years and more, gave place to the direct attack in line abreast. To utilize the guns in this new order of battle, they must no longer be mounted in broadside, but upon elevated citadels, giving them a wider sweep around the horizon. Meantime the guns had undergone a change, and were becoming vastly more powerful. First they were adapted to fire shells, which had hitherto been confined to mortars; next the calibers were increased, then rifling was adopted, giving greater range, accuracy, and penetration, and finally breech-loaders came into use. Following closely upon the improvements in guns, came the idea of protecting the sides of vessels with a light armor, at first of bar iron or of two-inch plates, developed by experiment after experiment into masses of solid steel, twenty-two inches in thickness. Last of all came the torpedo, of which a slight and tentative use had been made as early as 1776, but which only made its way into successful and general employment in the war of 1861.

There were signs of the dawn of this revolution before 1840, and its culmination was only reached during the war. But the twenty years between 1840 and 1860 were those in which the movement was really accomplished. During this period the naval administration had endeavored to follow the changes that were taking place, but it had not fully caught up with them. It had begun by building heavy side-wheelers, first the *Mississippi* and *Missouri* and next the *Powhatan* and *Susquehanna*. Efficient as these latter vessels were considered in 1847, when they were begun, and even in 1850, when they were launched, their model was promptly dropped when the submarine screw was introduced in place of the vulnerable paddle-wheel. The six screw-frigates were accordingly built in 1855, and they were regarded with admiration by naval men abroad as well as at home. The *Niagara*, the largest of these, was a ship of 4500 tons. The other five, the *Roanoke, Colorado, Merrimac, Minnesota,* and *Wabash,* had a tonnage somewhat over 3000. All of them were heavily armed, and they formed, or were supposed to form,

ROMAN WAR-GALLEY.
FROM ANCIENT TERRA-COTTA MODEL.

LINE-OF-BATTLE SHIP OF THE SEVENTEENTH CENTURY.

the chief element of naval strength of the United States. This reliance of the Government upon its large frigates would seem to have been well grounded, and if a war had arisen with a maritime enemy supplied with vessels of the same general type, they would have given a good account of themselves. In the civil war, however, the enemy had no ordinary vessels of war to be met and conquered in ocean duels, and the waters upon his coast at points vulnerable to naval attack were too shallow to admit the frigates. Hence none of them performed any service at all proportionate to their size and cost of maintenance, except in two or three isolated cases of bombardment, as at Hatteras Inlet, Port Royal, and Fort Fisher.

Of a much more useful type for general service were the twelve screw sloops-of-war built in 1858. There were five of these of the first class, among them the *Hartford*, *Brooklyn*, and *Richmond*, which gave and took so many heavy blows while fighting in Farragut's West Gulf Squadron. Hardly less important were the sloops of the second class, of which the *Iroquois* and *Dacotah* were the largest and most typical examples. To the same group belonged the *Pawnee*, a vessel of peculiar construction, whose constant service was hardly surpassed in efficiency and importance by any other ship of her size on the Atlantic coast. Besides the sloops, there were a few other steamers of miscellaneous dimensions and character, some of which had been purchased and altered for naval use; and these comprised all that the Government had secured toward the creation of a modern steam fleet.

The normal strength of the United States navy, if it is to be a navy at all, cannot be figured at much less than from 80 to 100 vessels, and this was the number in 1861. But of the actual total of 90, as shown by the navy list, 50 were sailing ships,—line-of-battle ships, frigates, sloops, and brigs,—which, splendid vessels as they had been in their day, were now as obsolete as the galleys of Themistocles. It was in placing a false reliance upon these vessels that the Government was at fault: it should have recognized in the course of twenty years that their day was gone forever, that they were of no more use than if they did not exist, that they would only be the slaughter-houses of their gallant crews in an encounter with a modern antagonist; and it should by that time have replaced every one of them by war-ships of the period.

At the beginning of President Lincoln's administration, out of the forty vessels composing the steam-fleet, one, the *Michigan*, was stationed on the lakes, and five were from one cause or another unserviceable. The remaining thirty-four, which comprised the whole of the effective force, were in the scattered situation that is usual in time of profound peace. Nine were laid up in ordinary, and with the traditional methods prevailing at the Navy Department, it would have taken some months to fit them out for sea. No orders had been issued for the general recall of the seventeen ships on foreign service, an operation requiring considerable time in those days, when no submarine cable existed. In the Home Squadron there were seven steamers, two of which, the sloop-of-war *Brooklyn* and the small steamer *Wyandotte*, were at Pensacola; two others, the gun-boats *Mohawk* and *Crusader*, were at New York; the *Pawnee*, a second-class sloop, was at Washington; and the *Powhatan*, a side-wheeler of 1850, was on her way home from Vera Cruz in company with the gun-boat *Pocahontas*. Five sailing ships were also attached to this squadron,—the frigate *Sabine* and the sloop *St. Louis*, at Pensacola; the sloops *Cumberland* and *Macedonian*, at Vera Cruz or returning thence, and the store-ship *Supply*, at New York. These twelve vessels, together with the *Anacostia*, a small screw-tender, at the Washington Navy Yard, were all that could be said to be at the immediate disposal of the Administration.

When the vessels abroad were gathered in, and those in ordinary were fitted out, the Government had a little squadron of about 30 steamers, of which the most important were 5 screw-frigates (the sixth, the *Merrimac*, having been abandoned at Norfolk), 6 sloops of

THE UNITED STATES FRIGATE "MERRIMAC" BEFORE AND AFTER CONVERSION INTO AN IRON-CLAD.

the first or *Hartford* class, 4 large side-wheelers, and 8 sloops of the second or *Iroquois* class. All these were exceedingly valuable as the nucleus of a fleet, but for the war which the Government had now on hand they could be considered as nothing more than this. According to the position which the Administration was very soon compelled to take, the struggle was one *à outrance.* In a foreign war the conflict usually springs from a collision of rights or of interests, involving only a particular branch of the relations of the two contestants, and the question is ultimately settled by some form of compromise, as soon as financial or military exhaustion leads one party or the other to conclude that a protraction of the contest is not worth its while. In the civil war, however, no compromise was possible, and with the resolution shown by the Southern people, nothing short of complete subjugation would insure the restoration of the Union. In such a war, a little fleet capable of raids upon the enemy's commerce or sea-ports might be advantageous to the insurgents, but the Federal Government required materials and methods of a totally different character. No mere raids would profit it a jot. It must blockade the insurgent territory; and to do this it was not enough to keep a few ships cruising in neighboring waters, but a cordon of fast and efficient steamers must be stretched from end to end, without so much as a gap in the whole four thousand miles of coast. The reduction or even the passage of fortifications required powerful and well-equipped fleets engaged solely in these enterprises. The vast net-work of interior waterways in which the army's base and communications must be protected, could only be occupied successfully by another and equally numerous fleet. Finally, the protection of commerce demanded, from the very nature of things, far more vessels than its destruction.

Had the material of the navy of 1861 been such as it ought to have been,—composed, let us say, of ninety modern war-steamers of fair quality; with such an organization that those laid up in ordinary could have been fitted out in two weeks at farthest, as should always be the case; with a reserve of a hundred, or even of fifty merchant-steamers, constructed with a view to conversion into war-vessels at short notice, which is an easy matter to accomplish; with some system by which the latest problems in naval science, especially in reference to iron-clads, had been considered and, in part at least, carried to solution; and finally, with a corps of officers graded more or less by merit, or the promise of growing fitness for command, instead of by age, or the promise of growing unfitness,— had all these plain, practicable, and sensible measures found a place in the naval administration, it is perfectly safe to say that a single year would have seen the opening of the Mississippi, the occupation of North Carolina, the fall of Richmond, Charleston, Savannah, and Mobile, and probably the end of the Confederacy. During the first six months of the war, there was really nothing to oppose the vigorous attack of such a force, and there was little more during the six months following.

As the naval material was not on a respectable peace-footing, and as no provision had been made for its conversion to a war-footing, the measures adopted for its increase were chiefly makeshifts to which the Government was driven by the exigencies of the moment. The vessels purchased by the

Department during the war amounted to 418, and included every variety of merchantman and river steamboat roughly adapted in the navy yards for war service. Three types of wooden vessels were built: 14 screw sloops of the *Kearsarge, Shenandoah,* and *Ossipee* classes; 23 screw gun-boats, called from the rapidity of their construction the "ninety-day" gun-boats; and 47 side-wheel steamers, known as "double-enders," for service in narrow channels, where they could move ahead or astern without turning.⹁ Later in the war forty-eight additional sloops or corvettes of various sizes were projected, but few of these were ever finished, and hardly any before the close of the struggle.

In the matter of iron-clads, the extreme slowness with which the Navy Department moved shows that it failed to comprehend the magnitude of the struggle, and that it was unfamiliar with the recent progress of naval warfare. The advantages of a light armor-plating for vessels-of-war had been demonstrated by the experience of the French floating batteries *Devastation, Lave,* and *Tonnante,* in the attack on Kinburn in 1855, during the Crimean war. These vessels were protected by 4½-inch plates, and the experiment had been deemed so conclusive that both France and England had already constructed new war-ships incased in armor. It was to be expected that a navy with a war on its hands would have directed its attention from the first moment when it was convinced of the probability of hostilities to securing some of these formidable vessels; and if a hesitation due to the want of statutory authority had led the Department to defer building until after Congress met, it would at least by that time have digested its plans so thoroughly that the work could begin at once. Nevertheless, for four months after Mr. Welles entered upon his office no steps were taken, even of the most elementary character, toward procuring iron-clads. In his report of July 4th, 1861, at the opening of the special session of Congress, the Secretary, by way of calling attention to the subject, makes the following somewhat ponderous observations:

"Much attention has been given within the last few years to the subject of floating batteries, or iron-clad steamers. Other governments, and particularly France and England, have made it a special object in connection with naval improvements; and the ingenuity and inventive faculties of our own countrymen have also been stimulated by recent occurrences toward the construction of this class of vessel. The period is, perhaps, not one best adapted to heavy expenditures by way of experiment, and the time and attention of some of those who are most competent to investigate and form correct conclusions on the subject are otherwise employed. I would, however, recommend the appointment of a proper and competent board to inquire into and report in regard to a measure so important; and it is for Congress to decide whether, on a favorable report, they will order one or more iron-clad steamers, or floating batteries, to be constructed, with a view to perfect protection from the effects of present ordnance at short range, and make an appropriation for that purpose."

In consequence of this recommendation, which, it must be confessed, was hardly such as the urgency of the measure demanded, Congress, a whole month later, on the 3d of August, passed an act authorizing the Secretary to appoint a board of officers to investigate the subject, a thing which was certainly within the scope of ministerial powers without any special legislation,

⹁ Eight of the "double-enders" were built of iron.

THE NAVY YARD, WASHINGTON, IN 1861.

and appropriating $1,500,000 for the work. After another delay of five precious days, on the 8th of August the board was appointed, composed of Commodores Smith and Paulding and Commander Davis. The board took occasion to remark that it approached the subject "with diffidence, having no experience, and but scanty knowledge in this branch of naval architecture." Inconceivable as it seems, this statement was literally true; for although five months had elapsed since the new administration had come in; although it knew, or should have known, what the Confederates were doing at Norfolk, and that time was of vital moment, the very best men whom it could select took six weeks to reach a conclusion on the subject. Even at the close of its protracted deliberations, so little did the board understand the tremendous importance of its work that in its final report it sagely remarked:

"Opinions differ amongst naval and scientific men as to the policy of adopting the iron armature for ships-of-war. For coast and harbor defense they are undoubtedly formidable adjuncts to fortifications on land. As cruising vessels, however, we are skeptical as to their advantages and ultimate adoption. But whilst other nations are endeavoring to perfect them, we must not remain idle. . . . We, however, do not hesitate to express the opinion, notwithstanding all we have heard or seen written on the subject, that no ship or floating battery, however heavily she may be plated, can cope successfully with a properly constructed fortification of masonry."

The same inability to understand the situation is shown in the Secretary's report transmitted to Congress in December, in which he contents himself with this perfunctory utterance:

"The subject of iron armature for ships is one of great general interest, not only to the navy and country, but is engaging the attention of the civilized world."

The board selected three plans, offered respectively by Bushnell & Co., of New Haven, Merrick & Sons, of Philadelphia, and John Ericsson, of New York, from which were subsequently built the *Galena*, the *New Ironsides*, and the *Monitor*. The choice of plans was wise, although the *Galena* totally failed to accomplish what was expected of her, and neither she nor the *Ironsides* was afterward duplicated. The *Ironsides*, however, proved a very efficient vessel within her sphere of action; but so overwhelming was the success of the *Monitor* that hardly any other model was afterward adopted.

The main features of the *Monitor* were the revolving turret, the low freeboard, and the projecting overhang. By means of these devices the ship was made to present a very small target, and her engines, battery, screw, rudder, and anchor, as well as her crew, were thoroughly protected, and neither rams nor guns could make much impression on her. On the other hand, the low freeboard had also one distinctive disadvantage, in that it reduced the vessel's reserve of flotation, thus making it possible for a small influx of water to sink her. The idea of mounting guns in a revolving circular turret had been suggested before at various times, but had never been carried to the point of useful application. In 1842 Timby had proposed a system of coast fortification based on this idea, but the plan had been found defective, and had been rejected. In 1854 Captain Ericsson had submitted to the Emperor Napoleon III. a design of an iron-clad battery with a hemispherical turret. In the next year Captain Cowper Coles, R. N., had suggested a vessel in the form of a raft with a stationary shield for protecting the guns; and in 1859 he had improved upon this design by adding a revolving cupola. But it was left to the genius of Ericsson to develop by itself the perfected application of the principle, and to construct a navigable turret iron-clad which should be nearly invulnerable to every weapon but the torpedo.

When the Navy Department finally understood Ericsson's plan, it immediately adopted it. According to Captain Ericsson, "The Committee of Naval Commanders . . . occupied me less than two hours in explaining my new system. In about two hours more the committee had come to a decision. After their favorable report had been [made] to the Secretary I was called into his office, where I was detained less than five minutes. In order not to lose any

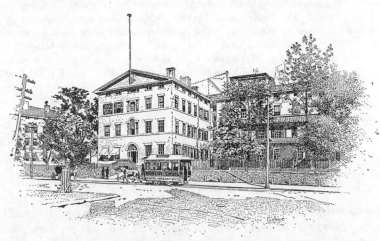

THE OLD NAVY DEPARTMENT BUILDING, WASHINGTON.   FROM A PHOTOGRAPH.

time, the Secretary ordered me to 'go ahead at once.' Consequently, while the clerks of the department were engaged in drawing up the formal contract, the iron which now forms the keel-plate of the *Monitor* was drawn through the rolling-mill."

The contract for the *Monitor* was finally signed on the 4th of October. The extraordinary energy of the contractors when they had once undertaken the work pushed it to completion with unexampled speed. But the time which had been of the greatest value, namely, the six months from March to September, had been lost, and thus it happened that the new iron-clad was not finished in season to prevent the raid of the *Merrimac* in Hampton Roads, and the obliteration of the *Congress* and the *Cumberland*. In the battle of the 9th of March the presence of the *Monitor*, which had arrived late the night before, saved the rest of the fleet from a like fate, to say nothing of other disasters whose magnitude can only be conjectured.

It must be remembered that the Navy Department had possessed from the beginning five frigates, sister ships of the *Merrimac*, any one of which could have been armored more efficiently than she was, in half the time and with half the money, and without waiting for congressional action. Evidently the department little imagined, while it was dallying for six months with the question of iron-clads, that the first twenty-four hours of the *Monitor's* career would be so big with fate.

In addition to the three vessels selected by the board of 1861, there were built or projected during the war nearly sixty iron-clads, all of which were of the *Monitor* type except three,—the huge ram *Dunderberg*, which was sold to the French Government, and afterward called the *Rochambeau;* the *Keokuk*, which sank off Charleston, immediately after the battle of April 7th, 1863, and the converted frigate *Roanoke*. Of the fourteen double-turreted monitors, including the *Puritan*, the *Onondaga*, the *Kalamazoo* class, the *Monadnock* class, and the *Winnebago* class, only six were finished in time to take part in the war. The single-turreted monitors which saw the most service were those of the *Passaic* class, most of which were stationed in the South Atlantic Squadron. Besides these there were the *Dictator*, the nine vessels of the *Canonicus* class, and the twenty light-draft monitors. The last were never of any use, the calculations for their displacement having been so faulty that they could not float their guns and coal.

Hitherto we have been speaking of vessels for service on the coast or in the waters adjacent to the coast. The Mississippi flotilla deserves a place by itself. This force, which included all the vessels operating on the Ohio, the Mississippi, the Red River, and their tributaries, comprised altogether over a hundred vessels, of the greatest variety in construction and character,— propellers, side-wheelers, stern-wheelers, rams, iron-clads, "tin-clads," unarmored boats, mortar-vessels. As the first demand for a flotilla came from the army, its early organization was directed by the War Department, although a naval officer was placed in command. The complications resulting from this arrangement, under which, as Foote said, "every brigadier could interfere with him," were obviated, October 1st, 1862, by the transfer of the force to the Navy Department.

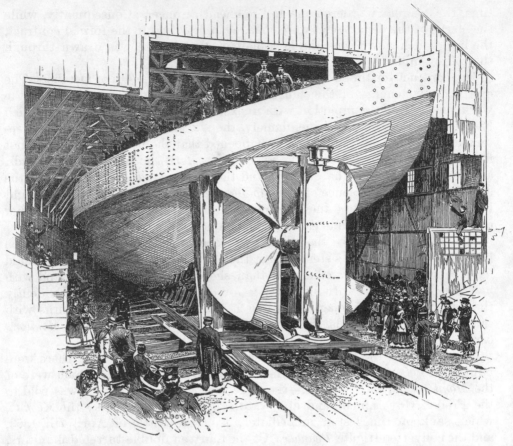

LAUNCH OF THE "DICTATOR" FROM THE DELAMATER IRON WORKS, NEW YORK, DECEMBER 27, 1863.

The first step in the creation of the Mississippi flotilla was taken in May, 1861, by Commander John Rodgers, who, acting under the authority of the War Department, purchased at Cincinnati three river-steamboats, the *Conestoga*, *Lexington*, and *Tyler*, and altered them into gun-boats by strengthening their frames, lowering their machinery, and protecting their decks by heavy bulwarks. In August, the War Department made a contract with James B. Eads [see page 338], the famous engineer of the Mississippi jetties, to build in two months seven gun-boats, propelled by a central paddle-wheel, and covered with armor two and a half inches thick, on the forward end of the casemates and on the sides abreast of the engines. These may be said to have been our first iron-clads, light as their plating was, and imperfectly as it covered the vessels. In spite of all their defects, they performed constant service of incalculable importance throughout the war; and there is not one among them all — the *Cairo*, *Carondelet*, *Cincinnati*, *Louisville*, *Mound City*, *Pittsburgh*, and *St. Louis* or *De Kalb* — which failed to make her name famous in the incessant conflicts of the Mississippi. Two larger vessels purchased by the Government, the *Benton* and the *Essex*, of one thousand tons each, and somewhat more heavily armored, together with thirty-eight mortar-boats, complete the list of vessels of the Mississippi flotilla during the period of Foote's command, which extended to the summer of 1862. [See pages 358 and 430.]

During the following year important additions were made to the flotilla. These were of two classes, light-draft boats and iron-clads. The light-drafts were small stern-wheel boats armed with howitzers, which were peculiarly useful for vedette and other light, flying service, but which in addition took their full share of the brunt of battle in the numerous contests that took place in the shoal waters of the Yazoo and the Red River. Drawing less than two feet of water, they could go almost anywhere, and with their howitzer batteries, and their light, bullet-proof plating, they were efficient vessels for clearing the river-banks of field batteries and sharp-shooters. Their armor, less than an inch in thickness, gave them the colloquial name of "tin-clads." Many of them, such as the *Forest Rose, Juliet, Marmora, Rattler, Romeo,* and *Signal,* became famous in the annals of the squadron, and the tiny *Cricket,* under Gorringe, fought in the Red River one of the hottest and most gallant little battles of the Western campaign.

The second class of new acquisitions, which may be called by comparison the heavily armored vessels, though more pretentious than their older consorts, were hardly, as a whole, more efficient. Three of them, the *Tuscumbia, Indianola,* and *Chillicothe,* were side-wheel casemate iron-clads, carrying a somewhat thicker plating than the earlier boats and a much more formidable armament, but owing to poor and hasty workmanship they were occasionally found unequal to the demands that were made upon them. Of a more satisfactory performance were two large steamers, the *Lafayette* and *Choctaw,* of one thousand tons each, well-built side-wheelers, which the Government purchased and altered into casemate iron-clads fitted with rams. Still later, three turreted iron-clads of light draft, the *Osage, Ozark,* and *Neosho* [see page 342], were added to the squadron. The above, together with a number of captured gun-boats, the foremost of which was the *Eastport,* and a few wooden steamers of various size and miscellaneous description, made up the force with which Admiral Porter conducted his wonderful series of operations from the autumn of 1862 until his transfer to the North Atlantic Squadron in 1864.

In addition to these vessels, which constituted the regular naval force, special mention must be made of the Ram Fleet, as it was called. This fleet was the really brilliant conception of Colonel Charles Ellet, Jr., a civil engineer who, as has been already said, had called attention, some years before the war, to the renewed importance of the ram as a naval weapon. Having been vested with rank and authority by the War Department, Colonel Ellet, who was no less ready in execution than brilliant in conception, bought nine river-boats, which he strengthened and altered into rams on a plan of his own. They were called the *Queen of the West, Monarch, Samson, Lioness, Switzerland, Lancaster, Mingo, T. D. Horner,* and *Dick Fulton.* Though they were hastily and imperfectly prepared, yet under the leadership of Ellet and other members of his remarkable family, who shared with him a native military instinct that was little short of genius, and a superb courage

MONITOR "WEEHAWKEN" IN A STORM.

that bordered upon recklessness, they performed services that gave them a place apart in the history of the river operations.   [See page 453.]

In its personnel, the navy was by no means so well prepared for war as it should have been.   Several circumstances combined to weaken the strength of the corps.   As there was no system of retirement, and as promotion for many years had been made solely on the basis of seniority, the upper part of the list was filled with officers who had grown too old for active service, but who nevertheless felt that their position entitled them to important commands at sea, or to high places in council or in administration.   For these duties most of them were peculiarly unfitted.   At a time when conservatism meant stagnation, the seventy-eight commodores and captains who were the senior officers of the navy, through long adherence to routine had, with few exceptions, become doubly conservative, and owing to the rapid development of their profession, those whose early training belonged to the sail period seemed almost the relics of a bygone age.

The consciousness of ignorance in some men begets modesty, but it seldom has this effect upon the older members of a military hierarchy.   Obedience to the orders of a superior is, of course, the essence of military discipline, without which it could not exist, and rank is the primary source of authority. But a system which combines reliance upon rank as the sole source of authority, and reliance upon age as the sole qualification for rank, contains essential elements of weakness.   Its tendency is to make the seniors grow less capable and more despotic, while the juniors gradually lose all sense of responsibility and all power of initiative, and when they at last reach a position of command, their faculties have become paralyzed from long disuse.   Especially is this the case in a long period of peace, such as followed the war of 1812, and lasted, with only a brief intermission, until 1861. During this time the navy was always grasping at the shadow and losing the substance. The commodore of the period was an august personage, who went to sea in a great flag-ship, surrounded by a conventional grandeur which was calculated to inspire a becoming respect and awe. As the years of peace rolled on, this figure became more and more august, more and more conventional. The fatal defects of the system were not noticed until 1861, when the crisis came and the service was unprepared to meet it; and to this cause was largely due the feebleness of naval operations during the first year of the war.

In addition to the other elements of weakness, the junior grades at this time were short of officers, owing to the recent establishment of the Naval Academy and the limitation of the power of appointment; and at the very moment when stress was put upon the service, it lost through resignation a large number of its members, many of them men of high professional reputation. To fill these gaps, the course at the Academy was for the moment curtailed, and the upper classes were ordered into active service. On the 1st of August, 1861, the total number of officers of all grades and corps holding regular appointments in the navy was 1457. This number was inadequate to supply the demands of the newly expanded fleet, and it became necessary to employ volunteer officers, 7500 of whom were enrolled in the navy during the war. These came chiefly from the merchant marine. Many of them were brave and capable, but their want of naval (as distinguished from merely nautical) training delayed their development. A still larger increase took place in the force of enlisted men. The normal strength of the corps of seamen was 7600, which rose during the war to 51,500, although the utmost difficulty was found in obtaining recruits, and it became necessary toward the end of the war to offer enormous bounties. The same want of training was apparent in the blue-jackets as in the volunteer officers, and while the army was able to rely from the beginning upon a trained militia, the navy was compelled to create its militia after the war had begun. Although the organization of a trained naval reserve presents no serious difficulties, and although it is evident that such a reserve is of prime importance in any considerable war, no steps had ever been taken to form it.

This was, however, only one of the many points in which the workings of the department were defective. There seems to have been a total want of information at the central office of administration in reference to the existing demands of naval war, and the measures necessary to put the machine into efficient operation. Everything in relation to the plan of a campaign, to the vulnerability of points on the coast,— and it must be remembered that this was our own coast, whose capacity for resisting attack should have been better known to the Navy Department than any other,— to the increase of the force of officers and men, to the expansion of the fleet, to the acquisition of the most modern instruments of warfare,— in short, all problems relating to the conduct of hostilities, the only purpose for which a navy really exists, had to be worked out and solved after the war had begun. Indeed, it would seem that the one subject with which the direction of naval affairs had never concerned itself was the subject of making war.

These circumstances placed the Secretary, at the opening of his administration, in a situation of peculiar difficulty. Although Mr. Welles had at one time been connected with the Navy Department, having been the civil chief of the Bureau of Provisions and Clothing from 1846 to 1849, he was in no sense a naval expert, and he was obliged to rely upon others for expert advice and assistance in his office. There was no one, however, at his office to give such advice and assistance, except the five chiefs of bureau, who were concerned only with the business of supplying materials, and who had really nothing to do with the general direction of the fleet,— meaning thereby the working force of ships, officers, and men actually employed in naval operations. To meet this difficulty, the Secretary wisely called Captain Gustavus V. Fox to the post of chief professional adviser. Captain Fox had formerly been an officer of the navy, and had borne a high reputation for professional skill. His connection with manufacturing enterprises during the few years preceding the war had emancipated him from the slavery of routine and had given him a knowledge of affairs which naval officers in general could not easily acquire. He had shown great intelligence and zeal in the second relief-expedition to Fort Sumter, where he acted in a semi-private capacity, and Mr. Welles decided to take him into the department. The duties for which he was wanted, and which he ultimately performed with such success, were those which are commonly assigned to an officer known as the chief of staff, namely, the disposition and direction of the fleet, and the conduct of naval operations. It is hardly necessary to add that without his previous experience as a naval officer he could not have performed these duties for a day. A temporary place was made for him on May 9th, 1861, as chief clerk. When Congress met in July, it created the office of Assistant Secretary, to which Fox was appointed on August 1st, and which he retained until after the close of the war. He was succeeded in the chief clerkship by William Faxon.

THE South entered upon the war without any naval preparation, and with very limited resources by which its deficiencies could be promptly supplied. Indeed, it would hardly be possible to imagine a great maritime country more destitute of the means for carrying on a naval war than the Confederate States in 1861. No naval vessels, properly speaking, came into their possession, except the *Fulton*, an old side-wheeler built in 1837, and at this time laid up at Pensacola, and the sunken and half-destroyed hulks at Norfolk, of which only one, the *Merrimac*, could be made available for service. The seizures of other United States vessels included six revenue-cutters, the *Duane* at Norfolk, the *William Aiken* at Charleston, the *Lewis Cass* at Mobile, the *Robert McClelland* and the *Washington* at New Orleans, and the *Henry Dodge* at Galveston ;‡ three coast-survey vessels, the schooners *Petrel* and *Twilight*, and the steam-tender *Firefly ;* and six or eight light-house tenders. As all of these were small, and most of them were sailing vessels, they were of little value.

Several coasting or river steamers belonging to private owners, which were lying in Southern waters when the war broke out, were taken or pur-

‡ The *James C. Dobbin* was also seized at Savannah, but was soon afterward released.— J. R. S.

chased by the Confederate Government. The most important were the *Jamestown* and the *Yorktown* (afterward the *Patrick Henry*) at Richmond; the *Selden* at Norfolk; the *Beaufort, Raleigh, Winslow*, and *Ellis*, screw-tugs plying on the Chesapeake and Albemarle Canal; the side-wheel passenger boats *Seabird* and *Curlew*, in the North Carolina Sounds; the *Nashville* at Charleston, and the *Everglade* at Savannah.

The *Star of the West*, whose name had been on everybody's lips after the attack made upon her in January, 1861, while she was attempting to relieve Fort Sumter, had subsequently sailed on transport service to Indianola, Texas, where she was seized in April by a party of Texan volunteers. In the Confederate navy she became the *St. Philip*. She was stationed at New Orleans as a receiving-ship when Farragut passed the forts, and fled with other vessels up the

GIDEON WELLES, SECRETARY OF THE UNITED STATES NAVY DURING THE WAR. FROM A PHOTOGRAPH.

Mississippi River, taking refuge finally in the Yazoo. In March, 1863, when the ships of the Yazoo Pass expedition descended the windings of the Tallahatchie to attack Fort Pemberton, they found the river barricaded by the hull of a sunken vessel, which was no other than the once-famous *Star of the West*.

The purchases and seizures made at New Orleans enabled the Confederate Government to equip at that point its only considerable fleet. The vessels fitted out successively by Commodores Rousseau and Hollins included the *Habana*, afterward the *Sumter*, in which Semmes made his first commerce-destroying cruise; the *Enoch Train*, which was altered into a ram and called the *Manassas*; the *Florida* and *Pamlico*, employed on Lake Pontchartrain; the *Marques de la Habana (McRae)*, the *Webb, Yankee (Jackson), Gros-tête (Maurepas), Lizzie Simmons (Pontchartrain), Ivy, General Polk*, and a few others of smaller size. The State of Louisiana and the citizens of New Orleans also made purchases of vessels on their own account. Thus the *Governor Moore* and the *General Quitman*, which took part in the action at the forts, were State vessels; and the *Enoch Train* was originally purchased by private subscription. There were also a large number of flat-boats or coal-barges, destined for use as fire-ships, upon which Commodore George N. Hollins placed great reliance.

Another measure of defense adopted by the Confederate Government deserves mention here, although the navy was in no way connected with it. On the 14th of January, 1862, Secretary Benjamin, of the War Department, telegraphed orders to General Lovell, who was in command at New Orleans, to impress certain river steamboats, fourteen in number, for the public service. On the 15th the vessels designated were seized. They were intended to form a flotilla of rams for the defense of the Mississippi, in accordance with a plan suggested by two steamboat captains, Montgomery and Townsend, who had secured the adoption of their project at Richmond through the influence of political friends in Congress. In the words of Secretary Benjamin, they were "backed by the whole Missouri delegation." The scheme had its origin partly in jealousy or distrust of the navy, and the direction of the "River Defense Fleet," as it was called, was therefore intrusted to the army. The projectors of the enterprise had taken care, however, to limit the authority of the army officers over the fleet, and the War Department wrote that when it sailed it would be "subject to the orders of General Beauregard, as regards the service required of it, but of course without any interference in its organization." The original cost of the vessels was $563,000, and the cost of equipping and fitting them out was $800,000.

GUSTAVUS V. FOX, ASSISTANT SECRETARY, UNITED STATES NAVY.
FROM A PHOTOGRAPH.

The River Defense Flotilla hardly accomplished results that justified this heavy outlay. Its organization, as might have been expected, was seriously defective. In January, Lovell was apprehensive that "fourteen Mississippi River captains and pilots will never agree about anything after they once get under way." These fears were afterward realized. April 15th, Lovell wrote:

"The river pilots (Montgomery and Townsend), who are the head of the fleet, are men of limited ideas, no system, and no administrative capacity whatever. I very much fear, too, that their powers of execution will prove much less than has been anticipated,— in short, unless some competent person of education, system, and brains is put over each division of this fleet, it will, in my judgment, prove an utter failure. No code of laws or penalties has been established, and it is difficult to decide how deserters from the fleet are to be tried and punished. There is little or no discipline or subordination — too much 'steamboat' and too little of the 'man-of-war' to be very effective."

When the River Defense Fleet was ready, eight of the vessels, commanded by Captain J. E. Montgomery, were sent up the river to meet the Union fleet, then on its way down, under Flag-Officer Davis. After a gallant but ineffectual brush near Fort Pillow, Montgomery's flotilla had a pitched battle at Memphis, on the 6th of June, with the Union force, now strengthened by the addition of Colonel Ellet's ram-fleet, and was literally wiped out of existence,—four of the vessels being captured and three destroyed. The *Van Dorn* alone escaped, and fleeing to the Yazoo River was soon afterward burnt. The six vessels of the River Defense Fleet, which had been retained by General Lovell at New Orleans, were sent down to assist in the defense of the forts, but the only part they took in the battle was to get out of the way as quickly as possible. All of them were captured or destroyed.

WILLIAM FAXON, CHIEF CLERK OF THE UNITED STATES NAVY DEPARTMENT DURING THE WAR. FROM A PHOTOGRAPH.

In addition to the vessels purchased and altered, the Confederate authorities built several new ones at New Orleans. Of these there were three wooden boats, the *Livingston, Bienville,* and *Carondelet,* and two iron-clads, the *Louisiana* and the *Mississippi.* The *Bienville* and *Carondelet* were substantially built side-wheelers of light draft, built on the lakes, and were only finished in March and April, 1862. They were unable to fill up their crews, and hence took no part in the action at the forts. ♭ The *Livingston,* which had been attached some time before to the flotilla in the upper Mississippi, made its way to the Yazoo River, and was burnt there with the *Polk* and *Van Dorn.* The two new iron-clads, however, were intended to be by far the most important factors in the defense of New Orleans. If they had been finished in time, this intention would doubtless have been realized. The *Louisiana,* built by contract with E. C. Murray, was not begun until the middle of October, and her machinery was transferred from the steamer *Ingomar,* which the contractors had bought for the purpose. She was 264 feet long, and from 400 to 500 tons of railroad iron were used in plating her with armor. The ship was in several ways badly designed, and on the 20th of April, when she was sent from New Orleans down the river to the forts, her engines would not work. During the battle she could only serve as a stationary floating battery, and she was blown up by Captain J. K. Mitchell on the day of the surrender of the forts. The other iron-clad, the *Mississippi,* a still larger and more heavily armored vessel, was constructed by the Messrs. Tift upon a very novel and peculiar design. To obviate the want of ship-builders and designers, she was built

♭ Report of Joint Confederate Committee on the affairs of the Navy Department, p. 28.

like a house, in straight lines and with pointed ends. Though there was apparently no lack of steamers to tow the unfinished vessel up the river, she was burnt just before the Federal fleet reached the city.

The total failure of the Confederate fleet on the Mississippi was largely due to bad management and to the want of a proper organization. Authority was divided between the State Government and the Confederate Government, and still further between the army, the navy, and the steamboat captains. The War and Navy Departments at Richmond did not work together. There were some differences of opinion between General Lovell, in command at New Orleans, and General Duncan, in command of the exterior defenses. Four naval officers, Rousseau, Hollins, Mitchell, and Whittle, were successively in command of the " Naval Station," a command of vague and indeterminate limits, and there were plenty of sources of disagreement between them and their colleagues of the army. They were perplexed and worried by confusing orders, and by the presence of independent agents in their own field of operations. They had no authority over the work of building the iron-clads, although constantly urged to hurry their completion. The organization of the River Defense Fleet, under Montgomery, was a direct and intentional blow at their authority, and left them without the aid of reserves whose disposition they could direct. The naval operations suffered from the lack of funds, so much so that on the 26th of February Governor Moore telegraphed to Richmond, "The Navy Department here owes nearly a million. Its credit is stopped." This condition of affairs was all the more remarkable, since the strategic position of New Orleans and the river was of vital importance to the Confederacy, and the post required above all things unity of command,—indeed, one might well say a dictatorship. Had one man of force and discretion been in full command and provided with sufficient funds, the defense would at least not have presented a spectacle of complete collapse.

The construction and equipment of vessels for the Confederate Government at other points were executed with great difficulty, owing to the want of iron and the absence of properly equipped workshops. In 1861 the only foundry or rolling-mill of any size in the Confederacy was the Tredegar Iron Works, at Richmond, and here the principal work in ordnance and armor was done. By dint of great efforts, foundries and rolling-mills were established at Selma, Atlanta, and Macon; smelting-works and a rope-walk at Petersburg; a powder-mill at Columbia, and an ordnance-foundry and chemical works at Charlotte. These works supplied what was needed in the way of ordnance and equipment, but they could not build vessels. The spring of 1862 saw the loss of Norfolk, Pensacola, and New Orleans, and after this date the Confederacy had no well-appointed ship-yard. Nevertheless, numerous contracts were entered into with business firms all over the country, and the construction of small vessels went on actively during the war. On March 15th, 1861, the Provisional Congress had authorized the construction or purchase of 10 steam gun-boats, of from 750 to 1000 tons. By the latter part of 1862 the Navy Department had purchased and altered 44 vessels, and had built and completed 24, while 32 others were in process of construction.

Most of these vessels were small craft, only suitable for detached local employment in rivers and harbors. Of the more formidable ships, the *Tennessee* and *Arkansas* were built at Memphis in the winter of 1861–62. They were covered with railroad iron. The *Arkansas* was completed and taken to the Yazoo River in April, 1862. After a short and brilliant career under Lieutenant Isaac N. Brown, she finally fell a victim in August to the defects of her engines. The *Tennessee*, being still on the stocks at Memphis when Davis's fleet descended the river, was burnt where she lay. At Mobile, the second *Tennessee*, a much more powerful vessel, but with engines transferred, like those of the *Louisiana*, from a river steamboat, was captured in her first and only engagement, when she attacked single-handed the whole Federal squadron. At Savannah, the *Atlanta*, a converted blockade-runner with a casemate covered with four inches of armor, was disabled and defeated by four shots from the monitor *Weehawken*. At Charleston, four casemate iron-clads were built, the *Palmetto State* and *Chicora* in 1862, the *Charleston* in 1863, and the *Columbia*; the last, however, was still unfinished at the close of the war, and was captured by Admiral Dahlgren at the evacuation of the city. The other three were blown up at the same time. In the sounds of North Carolina two iron-clads were projected, one to be built on the Neuse River, the other on the Roanoke. The first was destroyed before completion, but the second, the *Albemarle*, which the Union forces, through most culpable negligence, suffered to remain undisturbed until she was fully armed and equipped, captured the town of Plymouth, and fought a drawn battle with the squadron of double-enders in the sound. After a career of six months, she was destroyed by the expedition under Lieutenant Cushing.

The last, and in some ways the most useful naval force of the Confederates, was the James River Squadron. After the destruction of the *Merrimac* in May, 1862, and the abortive attempt of the Union vessels to pass up the James River, a fleet was gradually constructed and fitted out for the defense of Richmond. There were still in the river the *Patrick Henry*, which was soon after assigned to the use of the Confederate Naval Academy, and the *Beaufort* and *Raleigh*, which had come to Hampton Roads from the North Carolina Sounds after the battles of Roanoke Island and Elizabeth City. All three had taken part in the first day's engagement off Newport News, when the *Merrimac (Virginia)* had destroyed the *Congress* and the *Cumberland*, after which they withdrew to the James River. To these were added the gun-boats *Nansemond, Hampton,* and *Drury*. But by far the most important division of the squadron consisted of the three iron-clads *Richmond*, the second *Virginia*, and *Fredericksburg*. Of these the *Fredericksburg* was the weakest and the *Virginia* the strongest. In fact, the *Virginia* was one of the strongest vessels that the Confederates got afloat at any point, having six inches of armor on the sides of her casemate and eight inches on the ends. This fleet was an important element in the military situation in Virginia in 1864–65, though never brought into decisive action. At the evacuation of

Richmond it was burned, and with its destruction the coast navy of the Confederates came to an end.

In order to make war on the commerce of the United States, the Confederacy early resorted to privateering, which was then, as it is now, a legitimate practice with all States not parties to the Declaration of Paris. In accordance with the President's proclamation of April 17th, and the Act of Congress of May 6th, letters of marque were issued by the ·Confederate Government to owners of private vessels, authorizing them to cruise against the United States. Under this authority, more than twenty privateers were fitted out and made cruises during the summer and autumn of 1861, taking sixty or more prizes. The exact number either of privateers or of prizes will probably never be known. Charleston, New Orleans, and Hatteras Inlet were the principal centers of privateering operations. Three of the privateers were captured,—the *Savannah* by the brig *Perry*, the *Petrel* by the frigate *St. Lawrence*, and the *Beauregard* by the bark *W. G. Anderson*. The cessation of privateering after the first year was brought about by the blockade, which took away the profits of the sale of prizes, and such of the privateers as were not taken into the Government service were converted into blockade-runners.

After privateering came to an end, the Confederate Government depended almost wholly upon Europe for sea-going cruisers. These were not privateers, however, but commissioned ships-of-war of the Confederacy. Captain James D. Bulloch resided in England as the Confederate naval agent, and his skill and enterprise resulted in the acquisition of the *Florida, Alabama, Georgia* and *Shenandoah*, all of which made successful commerce-destroying cruises. Attempts to secure other vessels, including the *Alexandra*, the *Pampero*, the iron-clad contracted for by Captain North on the Clyde, and the two armored rams built by the Messrs. Laird, failed through the intervention of the British Government. Of the six vessels built in France, including four corvettes and two iron-clads, only one of the latter, *Stonewall*, passed into the hands of the Confederates, and this was acquired so late in the war as to be of no value.

In its personnel, the Confederate navy was more fortunate than in its vessels. The Secretary was Stephen R. Mallory [see p. 106], who had been for several years before the war the chairman of the Naval Committee in the Senate,— a position much better calculated to give its holder a knowledge of the demands of a modern navy than that which Mr. Welles had filled from 1846 to 1849. He entered upon his task with vigor and intelligence, and he was ably seconded by the officers around him, many of whom had been men of conspicuous ability in the old navy. In the branches of ordnance and torpedoes he relied largely upon two men, Commander John M. Brooke and Lieutenant Hunter Davidson. To Brooke were due the banded guns which proved of such signal use during the war, while Davidson did much to develop the torpedo service, which probably contributed more to the defense of the Confederacy than all the vessels of its navy. In 1862, some impatience was shown by the press and the public of the South at the continued succession of naval disasters, and a Congressional committee made an exhaustive investigation of the department. Nothing of importance was disclosed except the condition of affairs at New Orleans in 1861–62, already referred to, for which the Navy Department was partly responsible, but which was largely owing to the poverty of Confederate resources.

It was especially in his quick perception of the demands of modern naval war, and his prompt and bold action to meet these demands, that Secretary Mallory showed his ability and decision of character. No doubt this was in great part due to good advisers, but it is not every man who has the wisdom to perceive what good advice is, and the courage to act upon it, where his action involves heavy responsibilities. Mr. Mallory's emphatic recommendations in reference to iron-clads contrast favorably with the halting suggestions of Mr. Welles on the same subject. In a letter of May 8th, 1861, to Mr. Conrad, the chairman of the Naval Committee, Mallory presents with precision and force the history of the development of armored vessels, stating accurately the essential facts, which certainly were either not known or not appreciated at Washington. He closes his letter with these remarkable words:

"I regard the possession of an iron-armored ship as a matter of the first necessity. Such a vessel at this time could traverse the entire coast of the United States, prevent all blockade, and encounter, with a fair prospect of success, their entire navy.

"If, to cope with them upon the sea, we follow their example, and build wooden ships, we shall have to construct several at one time, for one or two ships would fall an easy prey to her comparatively numerous steam-frigates. But inequality of numbers may be compensated by invulnerability, and thus not only does economy, but naval success, dictate the wisdom and expediency of fighting with iron against wood without regard to first cost.

"Naval engagements between wooden frigates as they are now built and armed will prove to be the forlorn hopes of the sea—simply contests in which the question, not of victory, but who shall go to the bottom first is to be solved.

"Should the committee deem it expedient to begin at once the construction of such a ship, not a moment should be lost."

The result was that early in July the *Merrimac* had been raised and docked, the details of the plan of reconstruction had been completed, and the work had been begun without waiting for an appropriation. This early start enabled her to destroy the *Congress* and the *Cumberland* unopposed.

The number of officers who left the United States navy, either by resignation or dismissal, to join the Southern cause, was 322, of whom 243 were line-officers. In the beginning they were attached to the separate State organizations, but during the spring of 1861 they were gradually enrolled in the navy of the Confederate States. In 1863 a naval academy was established under the command of Captain W. H. Parker, on board the *Patrick Henry* in the James River, which turned out excellent junior officers. The personnel of the Confederate navy was distinguished by enterprise, originality, and resource, and to it were due some of the most gallant episodes of the war.

In seamen the South was deficient, not having a seafaring population. The number of enlisted men in the navy at any given time was probably less than four thousand, but as it took the offensive only in detached enterprises, no very extensive force was required. The four principal commerce-destroyers were chiefly manned by foreign sailors.

EARLY COAST OPERATIONS IN NORTH CAROLINA.⸗

BY RUSH C. HAWKINS, BREVET BRIGADIER-GENERAL, U. S. V.

UNIFORM OF HAWKINS'S ZOUAVES,
THE 9TH N. Y.

ONE sultry afternoon in the last third of the month of August, 1861, while stationed at Newport News, Virginia, with my regiment, the 9th New York (Zouaves), a message from General Benjamin F. Butler came through the signal corps station from Fort Monroe asking if I would like to go upon an expedition. An affirmative answer brought General Butler to my headquarters the same afternoon, and he explained the objects of the proposed expedition, which was to be composed of military and naval forces for joint offensive action on the coast of North Carolina.

CAPTURE AND DEFENSE OF HATTERAS ISLAND.

AT 11 o'clock in the forenoon of August 26th, 1861, all arrangements having been completed, the combined forces set sail for Hatteras Inlet, North Carolina, with Flag-Officer Silas H. Stringham in command of the fleet and Major-General B. F. Butler of the land forces. The same afternoon the fleet arrived off Hatteras, and at 10 o'clock on the morning of the 28th began the bombardment of Forts Clark and Hatteras (the latter mounting twenty-five guns), which was continued throughout a part of the day, until several of the ships were compelled to put out to sea for fear of being blown too near the shore. During the bombardment, efforts were being made about three miles north of the inlet to land the troops through the Hatteras breakers; in these efforts all the available boats were smashed. Two hulks, which had been towed from Fort Monroe for the purpose of assisting the landing, were then filled with troops and slowly allowed to drift into the breakers by means of a cable attached to an anchor and passed around a windlass fixed in the deck of each hulk. Late in the afternoon, when the wind came to blow fresh from the east, the position of the troops upon the hulks became most perilous, and for a time there were serious doubts about a successful rescue. Finally

⸗ "The State of North Carolina, immediately after passing the ordinance of secession, began the work of defending the possession of the sounds. The steamer *Winslow*, a small side-wheel steamboat, was fitted out by the governor of the State, and on the outside of Hatteras began to annoy and destroy the commerce of the United States, under Thomas M. Crossan, formerly of the United States Navy. The *Winslow* captured and brought into the sounds for condemnation many prizes. . . . The outcry that went up from commercial circles at the North may have had no little to do in influencing the naval authorities to block the outlet from which the little *Winslow* inflicted such damages. After the State united herself to the Confederate States her navy, consisting of the *Winslow*, the *Ellis*, the *Raleigh*, and the *Beaufort*, all ordinary steamboats armed with one gun each, was turned over to the Confederate States. The defense of the entrances to these sounds was undertaken by the erection of batteries at Hatteras and Ocracoke Inlet, and at Beaufort; on the interior waters New Berne, Roanoke Island, and the mouth of the Neuse River were defended under the State by small batteries, which were not completed when the State adopted the constitution of the Confederate States.

"Major R. C. Gatlin was commander of the Southern Department Coast Defenses, with headquarters at Wilmington, North Carolina. Promoted to Brigadier-General in August, 1861, he was assigned to the command of the Department of North Carolina and the coast defenses of the State." [Scharf's "History of the Confederate States Navy." New-York: Rogers and Sherwood.]

the *Fanny*, after several unsuccessful backings into the breakers, which every moment were becoming more dangerous, succeeded in getting lines on board the hulks and towing them to calmer water. But the few troops (318) who had effected a landing were left on shore in face of an enemy twice their numbers. The next day the vessels came in from sea and recommenced the action as early as 8 o'clock A. M., and by 11 o'clock the last gun on Fort Hatteras had ceased firing, and before noon the white flag had taken the place of the Confederate colors. During the bombardment our troops on shore gained possession of Fort Clark, but were driven out by our own guns, a fragment of a shell striking private Lembrecht, of Company G, 9th New York, making a painful wound in the hand. This was the only casualty among the Union forces.

The immediate results of this expedition were the capture of 670 men, 1000 stand of arms, 35 cannon, and 2 strong forts; the possession of the best sea entrance to the inland waters of North Carolina; and the stoppage of a favorite channel through which many supplies had been carried for the use of the Confederate forces. ⚓

The whole affair was conceived and carried out with simplicity and pro-

REAR-ADMIRAL SILAS H. STRINGHAM.
FROM A PHOTOGRAPH.

⚓ The vessels detailed were the *Minnesota* (flagship), Captain G. J. Van Brunt; *Wabash*, Captain Samuel Mercer; *Susquehanna*, Captain I. S. Chauncey; *Pawnee*, Commander S. C. Rowan; *Monticello*, Commander J. P. Gillis; *Harriet Lane*, Captain John Faunce; and the *Cumberland* (sailing-ship), Captain John Marston,— carrying in all 143 guns. For the transportation of troops there were the chartered steamers *Adelaide*, Commander H. S. Stellwagen, and *George Peabody*, Lieutenant R. B. Lowry, and the tug *Fanny*, Lieutenant Pierce Crosby. Upon these were embarked detachments of infantry from the 9th and 20th New York Volunteers, the Union Coast Guard, and a company of the 2d U. S. Artillery,— in all numbering about 880 men.

Both the forts were under command of Major W. S. G. Andrews, the North Carolina troops being under Colonel Wm. F. Martin. Flag-Officer Samuel Barron, C. S. N., who was charged with the defense of this coast, arrived during the attack,

and, taking command, was included in the capitulation, of which he says in his report made on board the *Minnesota*:

"During the first hour the shells of the ships fell short, we only firing occasionally to ascertain whether our shots would reach them, and wishing to reserve our very limited supply of ammunition until the vessels might find it necessary to come nearer in; but they, after some practice, got the exact range of the 9, 10, and 11 inch guns, and did not find it necessary to alter their positions, while not a shot from our battery reached them with the greatest elevation we could get. This state of things—shells bursting over and in the fort every few seconds—having continued for about three hours, the men were directed to take shelter under the parapet and traverses, and I called a council of officers, at which it was unanimously agreed that holding out longer could only result in a greater loss of life. . . . The *personnel* of the command are now prisoners of war on board this ship, where everything is done to make them as comfortable as possible under the circumstances, Flag-Officer Stringham, Captain Van Brunt, and Commander Case extending to us characteristic courtesy and kindness." EDITORS.

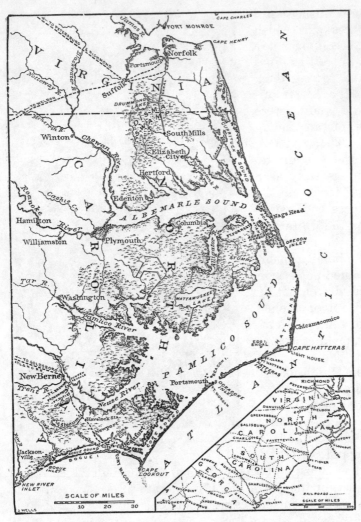

MAP OF EARLY COAST OPERATIONS IN NORTH CAROLINA.

fessional directness, and the valuable results attained cost the Government only a small expenditure for coal and ammunition. Flag-Officer Stringham fought this action with admirable skill, worthy of a great commander. Instead of anchoring his ships, he kept them moving during the whole engagement and, as he came within range of the enemy's works, delivered his fire, generally with surprising accuracy, while the gunners in the forts were compelled to make an on-the-wing shot with pieces of heavy ordnance, and in most instances their shot fell short.↓

On the 29th of August articles of full capitulation were signed interchangeably by officers representing both forces, and General Butler and Flag-Officer Stringham sailed away with the prisoners, leaving the *Pawnee*, Captain S. C. Rowan, the *Monticello*, Lieutenant D. L. Braine, and the tug *Fanny*, Lieutenant Pierce Crosby, as the sea forces; and detachments of the 9th and 20th New York Volunteers and Union Coast Guard to garrison the captured forts, of which I was left in command. Just before the squadron sailed, General Butler sent word on shore that the three schooners left by the enemy inside the inlet were loaded with provisions that could be used

↓Boynton, in his "History of the Navy," says:

"So far as known this was the first trial in our navy of this movement, and the honor of introducing it belongs to Commodore Stringham. The little that was known of the real character of the Hatteras expedition prevented the public from paying any attention to the commodore's strategy, but when it was repeated soon after by Commodore DuPont in a more brilliant affair, its merit was duly recognized."

While DuPont rose to the highest point in public estimation, Stringham was relegated to an obscure official background and never after had a sea-service command.—R. C. H.

by the troops.   An examination proved that the only food-materials were fruits from the West Indies, which were fast decaying.   For the next ten days the diet of the stranded soldiers consisted of black coffee, fresh fish, and a "sheet-iron pancake" made of flour and salt-water.   This diet was neither luxurious nor nutritious, and it produced unpleasant scorbutic results.   On the 10th of September relief arrived, and with it, under Lieut.-Colonel George

F. Betts, six more companies of the 9th New York.

Until September 16th, nothing occurred to disturb the uneventful routine work incident to military occupation of an enemy's territory.   On that day a mixed expedition of land and sea forces under com-

FORTS HATTERAS AND CLARK. FROM WAR-TIME SKETCHES.

mand of Lieutenant James G. Maxwell, of the United States navy, was sent to destroy the forts of Beacon Island and Portsmouth, near Ocracoke Inlet. They were found to have been deserted by the Confederates, but twenty-two guns of heavy caliber, that were left intact, were made useless by the Union forces.

Soon after the capture of the forts the "intelligent contraband" began to arrive, often bringing news of important military activity in several directions.

Before the first week of our occupation had expired I became convinced that the enemy was fortifying Roanoke Island, with the intention of making it a base for immediate operations, and that his first offensive work would be against the forces stationed at Hatteras Inlet, with the further purpose of destroying the Hatteras light; and that they would land a considerable force at the upper end of the island, at a point near Chicamacomico, and march down.

Seeing the necessity of counter-action on the part of the Union forces, on the 6th of September I wrote a full account of the situation to General John

E. Wool, commanding the Department of Virginia, in which occurred the following suggestions:

"*First.* Roanoke Island, which commands the Croatan Channel between Pamlico and Albemarle sounds, should be occupied at once. It is now held by the rebels. They have a battery completed at the upper end of the island and another in course of erection at the southern extremity. *Second.* A small force should be stationed at Beacon Island, which is in the mouth of Ocracoke Inlet and commands it. *Third.* Two or three light-draught vessels should be stationed between the mouths of the Neuse and Pamlico rivers. This would shut out all commerce with New Berne and Washington. *Fourth.* There should be at least eight light-draught gun-boats in Pamlico Sound. *Fifth.* Beaufort should be occupied as soon as possible. All of these recommendations should be attended to immediately. Seven thousand men judiciously placed upon the soil of North Carolina would, within the next three weeks, draw 20,000 Confederate troops from the State of Virginia.

"I wish, if you agree with me and deem it consistent with your duty, that you would impress upon the Government the importance and necessity of immediate action in this department."

General Wool gave this letter the strongest possible indorsement, and sent a copy to the Secretary of War.

In my next report (September 11th) I sent an account of the marked enterprise on the part of the enemy, setting forth that since the capture of Fort Hatteras they had strengthened Fort Macon, obstructed the Neuse and Pamlico rivers, mounted seventeen heavy guns at Roanoke Island and landed a considerable number of troops at that place. I urged my former suggestions and called for immediate action and reënforcements. A copy of this letter, with a very strong approval, was also sent to the Secretary of War, but neither brought any response beyond a merely formal acknowledgment.

My policy from the moment of assuming command on Hatteras Island had been to cultivate friendly relations with the inhabitants. As they were mostly of a seafaring race, I concluded they could not have much sympathy with the revolt against a government which had been their constant friend. Within ten days after the landing, nearly all of the male adults had taken the oath of allegiance, and several professed their willingness to carry proclamations to the mainland, and to bring back such news of military movements as they could obtain. One of these volunteer spies succeeded in opening communication with a relative, who lived at Roanoke Island, and from him I learned that, as I had suspected, a force was to start from that point to make the attack upon Hatteras Island. In the meantime we had done what we could to place the forts at the inlet in a better condition for defense, and General Wool, of his own volition, had sent reënforcements,— the seven remaining companies of the 9th New York, the 20th Indiana Volunteers,

THE UNITED STATES SLOOP "CUMBERLAND" SAILING INTO ACTION AT THE BOMBARDMENT OF FORTS HATTERAS AND CLARK. FROM A WAR-TIME SKETCH.

FORT HATTERAS.　　　　　FLAG-SHIP "MINNESOTA."　　　　　"SUSQUEHANNA."　"PAWNEE."

THE UNION FLEET BOMBARDING FORTS HATTERAS AND CLARK. FROM A WAR-TIME SKETCH.

Colonel W. L. Brown, and one company of the 1st U. S. Artillery, under Captain Lewis O. Morris.

In the latter days of September, information of the intended movement from Roanoke Island made immediate action necessary. I had already apprised General Wool of my intention to establish a post near Chicamacomico for the purpose of protecting the natives who had taken the oath, and also to prevent a surprise by the landing of a large force of the enemy to march down the island. Accordingly, on the 29th of September, I embarked the 20th Indiana regiment upon the gun-boats *Putnam* and *Ceres*, and accompanied it to a point opposite Chicamacomico, saw the troops safely disembarked, and returned with the gun-boats to the inlet. On the first day of October, the *Fanny* was dispatched with supplies, and arrived at the point of disembarkation the same afternoon. After preparations for landing had commenced, a force of the enemy's gun-boats was discovered. The *Fanny* tried to escape, but got aground and was captured, not, however, until after a spirited resistance by the men and officers with the two small guns which were mounted on her deck.

Flag-Officer W. F. Lynch, C. S. N., in his report says:

" Colonel Wright, of the 8th Georgia regiment, who commands the military forces of the island, had agreed with me to make an attempt to destroy Hatteras Light-house, and we only waited the return of an emissary I had sent to glean intelligence as to the force of the enemy in that vicinity. But early in the forenoon of the 1st instant intelligence came that one of the Federal steamers was at Chicamacomico, about forty miles distant on the eastern shore of Pamlico Sound, and I determined to get after her. As Colonel Wright was anxious, however, to make the contemplated attempt, I would not, in courtesy, refuse to wait for the embarkation of troops, although two precious hours were thereby lost.   We left here at 2:30 P. M. with about two hundred of the 8th Georgia regiment, Colonel W——, who is a man after my own heart in such matters, accompanying them.   A little before 5 P. M. we came in sight and soon after opened fire upon the enemy, which was returned at first with spirit; but in about twenty minutes he attempted to escape, and in the attempt ran aground, and shortly after surrendered."

The *Fanny* had on board, when captured, a captain and 30 men of the 20th Indiana regiment, and the sergeant-major and 11 men of the 9th New York. The Confederate vessels engaged were the *Curlew, Raleigh*, and the little tug *Junaluski*.   As soon as I heard of the disaster I sent an order for Colonel Brown to retreat.   On the 4th of October a large body of Confederates, under Colonel A. R. Wright, assisted by gun-boats, landed at Chicamacomico, and Colonel Brown commenced a successful retreat down the island.   Having received early news, by a native messenger, of the landing and Brown's march, I moved, with my regiment, toward the north, and met Colonel Brown's command early the next morning at the light-house.   Colonel Wright was closely following the retreating troops, but as soon as he saw the reënforcements he faced about and commenced a retreat which only ended in the landing of his forces at Roanoke Island.   During the march back the steamer *Monticello*, from the ocean side, with her heavy guns, maintained a fire at the Confederates across the low sand-fields, which may have annoyed them without doing any serious damage.   This was the end of an elaborately conceived plan on the part of the enemy to capture our troops, destroy Hatteras Light, and recapture the forts of the inlet.   From that time until the arrival of the "Burnside expedition," the Federal forces at the inlet pursued the even quiet of routine duty.

The news of the loss of the *Fanny* created some excitement both at Fort Monroe and at Washington, and I was severely censured for having divided so small a force, and was superseded by Brigadier-General J. K. F. Mansfield. I am still of the opinion that my course was right, as no other disposition of the small force at my command would have saved the light-house and prevented the landing, opposite the light-house, where there was a wharf and deep water, of the whole Confederate force of about two thousand men. That landing would have given them a safe base for a decisive movement against the Union troops at the inlet.   I afterward heard that Colonel

RETREAT OF THE CONFEDERATES TO THEIR BOATS AFTER THEIR ATTACK UPON HATTERAS.

LANDING OF THE UNION TROOPS AT HATTERAS UNDER COVER OF THE FLEET. FROM A WAR-TIME SKETCH.

Wright intended to land part of his force above and the balance below the camp of Colonel Brown, capture his regiment, destroy the light-house, and then, in his discretion, move upon Hatteras Inlet. The prompt retreat frustrated the first part of the design, and Colonel Wright, seeing what he believed to be a large reënforcement, retreated without undertaking the other parts of his plan.

Until October 13th we had peace at the inlet. That day Brigadier-General Thomas Williams relieved General Mansfield, and assumed command of the post. The new commander was a man of many idiosyncrasies, and outside of his staff was cordially disliked for his severe treatment of the men. ♭

On the 5th of November I was sent by General Wool on a special boat to Washington to urge upon the President the importance of either abandoning Hatteras Inlet or erecting suitable accommodations for the troops. The next morning after my arrival in Washington I reported to the President and presented my letter from General Wool, and was asked by the President to appear before the Cabinet. I did so and explained fully the situation at Hatteras Inlet and urged the importance of undertaking further operations to hold that position, it being the threshold to the

♭ I was arrested by General Williams for refusing to assign to duty, as captain in my regiment, a disreputable officer who had received an appointment from Governor E. D. Morgan. I denied the right of appointment, and I was sustained by General Wool and President Lincoln. — R. C. H.

whole inland water system of North Carolina. At this meeting the Secretary of War was represented by General McClellan, who had one end of the long council-table to himself. After I had finished, he drew me into conversation about operations in the Department of Virginia, and as I had often urged upon General Wool the importance of making Fort Monroe a base for operations against Richmond, I was fully prepared to answer his questions or to combat opposition. At his request I made a rough drawing showing the old road up the peninsula, with a waterway on each side for gun-boats and general transportation. He listened attentively to all I had to say, talked but little himself, and put my drawing in his pocket. I have always suspected that my animated advocacy of that route may have had something to do with his change of base from Washington, and the undertaking of his unfortunate Peninsular Campaign. Before the council dissolved it was decided to hold Hatteras Inlet and to erect suitable quarters for the forces, and I was instructed to wait until necessary orders could be prepared before returning to General Wool and my command.☆

LAND AND WATER FIGHTING AT ROANOKE ISLAND.

THE Burnside expedition, the naval part being under command of Flag-Officer L. M. Goldsborough,⎬ had concentrated in Pamlico Sound by the 4th of February, and on the 5th the welcome signal was hoisted for the whole command to move up toward the Confederate stronghold. About sundown, after a charming day's sail, the fleet came to anchor for the night, and started again early the next morning, but in consequence of the inclemency of the weather was soon compelled to seek another anchorage. On the morning of the 7th the expedition got under way very early, the armed army boats and naval part taking the lead several miles in advance. By 11 o'clock the first division of army gun-boats, under Commander Hazard, arrived opposite the forts on the west side of Roanoke Island, and commenced the bombardment in earnest, and at the same time engaged the enemy's fleet. As the naval vessels arrived they went into action, and by half-past 11 the whole fleet of gun-boats was engaged. The engagement between the heavy guns lasted all day without much damage having been done to either side. At the close the gunners answered each other with about the same spirit displayed at the commencement. The Confederate forts had, however, fared better than their fleet. The latter was protected from an assault on the part of our vessels by a row of piles driven across the navigable part of the channel, and by sunken vessels; but, notwithstanding this protection, the accurate fire of the Union fleet soon compelled it to retire out of range, with the loss

☆ Captain W. H. Parker, C. S. N., who commanded the *Beaufort* in these waters, says in his "Recollections of a Naval Officer" (N. Y.: Charles Scribner's Sons):

"The enemy made a great mistake in not taking possession of the sounds immediately after capturing Hatteras. There was nothing to prevent it but two small gun-boats, carrying one gun each. Two of the small steamers, under Flag-Officer Stringham, should have swept the sounds, and a force should have occupied Roanoke Island."

⎬ For details of the origin and composition of this expedition, see the article by General Burnside, p. 660.—EDITORS.

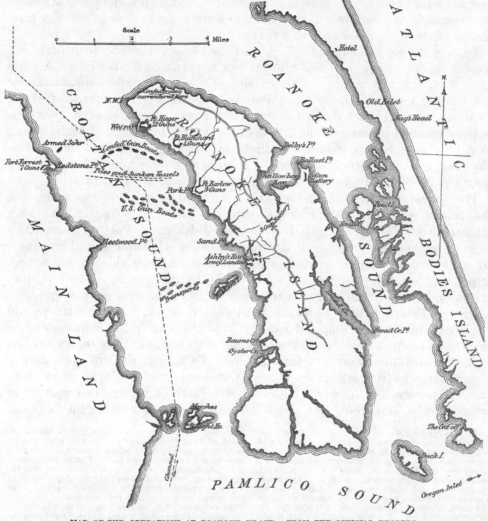

MAP OF THE OPERATIONS AT ROANOKE ISLAND — FROM THE OFFICIAL RECORDS.

Captain W. H. Parker, in his "Recollections of a Naval Officer" (Charles Scribner's Sons), thus describes the later Confederate defenses of Croatan Sound:

"Three forts had been constructed on the [Roanoke] island to protect the channel. The upper one was on Weir's Point, and was named Fort Huger. It mounted 12 guns, principally 32-pounders of 33 cwt., and was commanded by Major John Taylor, formerly of the navy. About one and three-quarter miles below, on Pork Point, was Fort Bartow; it mounted 7 [9?] guns, 5 of which were 32-pounders of 33 cwt., and 2 were rifled 32-pounders. This fort, which was the only one subsequently engaged in the defense, was in charge of Lieut. B. P. Loyall, of the navy. Between these two points was a small battery. On the mainland opposite the island, at Redstone Point, was a battery called Fort Forrest. The guns, which were 32-pounders, were mounted on the deck of a canal-boat which had been hauled up in the mud and placed so that the guns would command the channel. The channel itself was obstructed a little above

Fort Huger by piling. It was hoped that these batteries, with the assistance of Commodore Lynch's squadron, would be able to prevent the enemy's ships from passing the island. The great mistake on our part was in not choosing the proper point at which to dispute the entrance to the sound. The fortifications and vessels should have been at the 'marshes,' a few miles below, where the channel is very narrow."

The attack by the Union fleet is thus described by Captain Parker:

"At daylight the next morning, February 7th, the *Appomattox* was dispatched to Edenton, and as she did not return till sunset, and the *Warrior* did not take any part in the action, this reduced our [Confederate] force to seven vessels and eight guns. [See list, p. 670.] At 9 A. M. we observed the enemy to be under way and coming up, and we formed 'line abreast,' in the rear of the obstructions. At 11:30 the fight commenced at long range. The enemy's fire was aimed at Fort Bartow and our vessels, and we soon became warmly engaged. The commodore at first directed his vessels to fall back, in

of one of its vessels. A short time before sunset the Confederate boats came near enough to fire a few more shots, but were again driven off, this time making their last appearance as a fleet.

During the fight between the forts and the vessels the army transport fleet was at anchor about three miles to the south, prepared for landing. A little after 4 o'clock the troops began to land, General Foster's brigade taking the lead, followed by Reno's and Parke's. By 10 o'clock a force of about 7500 strong had been landed. One of the two sections of a boat-gun battery manned by men of the Union Coast Guard, in charge of Midshipman Porter, was stationed well out to the front, supported by the 21st Massachusetts; the other troops bivouacked in an open field, where before morning they were thoroughly drenched by a most uncomfortable cold rain.

The morning was cold and cheerless and the breakfast was poor, but the troops were in fine spirits. Foster was the first to move, the 25th Massachusetts in the advance, followed by Midshipman Porter's guns. The enemy's pickets gradually retired into an earth-work mounting three guns, situated in the center of a morass, flanked on each side by an almost impenetrable swamp, and protected in front by an open field of deep mud, in part covered by fallen trees with their limbs cut short and sharpened.

General Foster, as soon as he reached the earth-work, placed his troops and the boat-guns in position, and by 8 o'clock the attack had commenced in earnest. But no effective work was done until General Reno came up and with the 21st Massachusetts, the 51st New York, and the 9th New Jersey began his effective attack upon the Confederate right. With great difficulty he penetrated the swamp, covered with its thick interwoven growth of briers, shrubs, and trees. At length he succeeded in delivering his fire from

the hope of drawing the enemy under the fire of Forts Huger and Forrest; but as they did not attempt to advance, and evidently had no intention of passing the obstructions, we took up our first position and kept it during the day. At 2 P. M. the firing was hot and heavy, and continued so until sunset. Our gunners had had no practice with their rifled guns, and our firing was not what it should have been. It was entirely too rapid, and not particularly accurate. Early in the fight the *Forrest* was disabled in her machinery, and her gallant young captain, Lieutenant Hoole, badly wounded in the head by a piece of shell. She got in under Fort Forrest and anchored. Some time in the afternoon, in the hottest of the fire, reënforcements arrived from Wise's brigade, and were landed on the island. The Richmond Blues, Captain O. Jennings Wise, were, I think, a part of this force. Pork Point Battery kept up a constant fire on the fleet, and the enemy could not silence it. The garrison stood to their guns like men, encouraged by the spirited example of their instructor, Lieutenant B. P. Loyall. Forts Huger and Forrest did not fire, the enemy being out of range; but the small battery between Pork Point and Weir's Point fired an occasional gun during the day. Toward 4 o'clock in the afternoon a shot or shell struck the hurricane-deck of the *Curlew* [Captain Hunter] in its descent, and went through her decks and bottom as though they had been made of paper. Hunter put his vessel ashore, immediately in front of Fort Forrest, completely masking its guns, and we could not fire her for fear of burning up the battery, which, as I have said, was built on an old canal-boat. . . . We, in the *Beaufort*, did our best in maintaining our position. About 4 P. M. I observed

that the enemy's troops were landing to the southward of Pork Point, under the guns of a division of their fleet, and could not perceive that any successful resistance was being made to it. A little after sunset the firing ceased on both sides, and as we felt sure the enemy would not attempt to pass the obstructions by night, as he had declined to attempt them by day, we ran in and anchored under Fort Forrest. . . . Soon after we anchored signal was made by the flag-ship for the captains to report on board. Upon my entering the cabin I was informed by Commodore Lynch that we must retreat from Roanoke Island. Much surprised and mortified, I asked why, and was told that the vessels generally were out of ammunition. A council was held as to whether the vessels should retreat to Norfolk, through the Chesapeake and Albemarle Canal, or go to Elizabeth City, on the Pasquotank River. We would have saved the vessels by going to the former place, but the commodore's orders were to do his utmost to defend the waters of North Carolina; so we decided to go to the latter, where it was understood a fort had been built to protect the town. Elizabeth City was the terminus of the Dismal Swamp Canal, and we hoped to get ammunition that way from Norfolk in time to act in conjunction with the fort. I was sent to Roanoke Island to communicate all this to Colonel Shaw, and confess did not relish my mission. It looked too much like leaving the army in the lurch, and yet to have remained without ammunition would have been mere folly. . . . I met Colonel Shaw at his quarters, and stated the facts in relation to the vessels, and then returned to the *Beaufort*. All lights were now extinguished, and the squadron got under way for Elizabeth City."

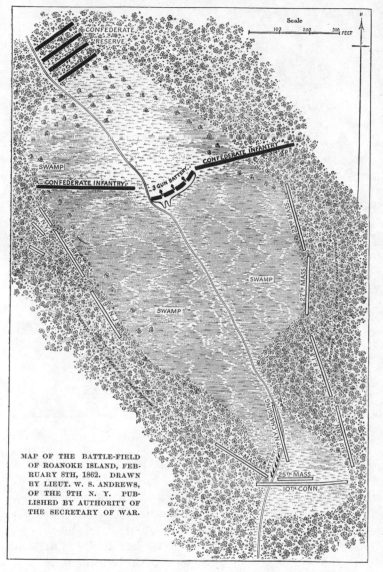

MAP OF THE BATTLE-FIELD OF ROANOKE ISLAND, FEBRUARY 8TH, 1862. DRAWN BY LIEUT. W. S. ANDREWS, OF THE 9TH N. Y. PUBLISHED BY AUTHORITY OF THE SECRETARY OF WAR.

an unexpected direction upon the enemy inside the work. They turned their guns upon his troops, but failed to drive them from their position. While General Reno was maintaining the left attack, General Foster, with the 25th Massachusetts and 10th Connecticut, was making a serious demonstration in front; and the 23d and 27th Massachusetts, later with the 51st Pennsylvania, were trying to penetrate the almost impassable wood and swamp in the far-off front of the earth-work for the purpose of getting on the enemy's left. While engaged in this movement, the Massachusetts troops encountered a battalion of the enemy and drove them inside their work.

About 11 o'clock General Parke with his brigade arrived upon the field, and the 4th Rhode Island was ordered to follow the regiments making the demonstration on the enemy's left. "The 9th New York regiment, arriving upon the ground, was ordered to follow." . . . "The regiment, under the lead of the colonel, Rush C. Hawkins, entered the clearing with great spirit." Nearly two companies had succeeded in getting into the clearing immediately in front of the earth-work, where the mud was more than ankle-deep, and where they were receiving the undivided attention of the enemy's three pieces of artillery, and getting a shot now and then from the infantry. It

UNION ASSAULT UPON THE THREE-GUN BATTERY, ROANOKE ISLAND.   (SEE MAP, PAGE 642.)
FROM A WAR-TIME SKETCH.

was at this point that Colonel De Monteil was killed.   Seeing that it would
be almost impossible to get through the deep mud, I had made up my mind
to face to the front and make an effort to charge the work, and after a
moment's consultation with Lieutenant-Colonel Betts and Captain Jardine,
who commanded the right company, I ordered my bugler to sound the charge.
At that moment I heard a great cheer down the line, and, looking in that
direction, discovered that Major Kimball had broken the regiment in two
parts and was heading the left companies in a direct charge up a causeway
running through the center of the field of fallen timber directly to the sally-
port covered by a 24-pounder howitzer.   Soon the right companies joined,
and all entered the work, pell-mell, together.   As the column advanced,
the men crowded each other from the causeway, and soon the whole front of
the work was covered with an animated sea of red fezzes.   The men of Company C were the first to cross the ditch and enter the work.   About the same
time, the 21st Massachusetts and the 51st New York came into the work from
the left.

The officers of those two regiments claimed that their colors were the
first on the parapet; if so, it was because the colors of the 9th New York

were in the center of the column and did not get into the work with the men on the right who led the charge. The regiments sent around to outflank the enemy's left arrived at their objective point about the time the decisive charge was made, and were entitled to a fair share of credit for the successful day's work.

The commands of Generals Foster and Reno pursued the enemy to a point near the northern end of the island, where an unconditional surrender was consummated. Soon after leaving the earth-work my regiment deflected to the right and succeeded in capturing two boat-loads of the Richmond Blues, among them O. Jennings Wise, trying to escape to Nag's Head, on the opposite shore. Company B in the meantime had taken possession of a two-gun battery at Shallowbag Bay. Wise, severely wounded, was carried to a farm-house, where he received the best attention attainable, but died the next morning, defiant to the last, and wishing he had more lives to lose in the defense of the Confederacy. Among the results of these two days' fighting were the capture of 2675 officers and men of the Confederate army and 5 forts mounting 32 heavy guns, the complete possession of Roanoke Island, and with it the control of the inland waters of North Carolina. ⚓ [For losses, see p. 679.]

THE TWO SQUADRONS AT ELIZABETH CITY.

THE Confederate fleet, known as the "mosquito fleet," was under command of Commodore William F. Lynch, who, after firing one of his own steamers, the *Curlew*, and blowing up Fort Forrest, a work situated opposite Roanoke Island on the mainland, retreated up the Pasquotank River, and concentrated his vessels behind a four-gun battery at a point a short distance below Elizabeth City.

At 8 o'clock on the morning of February 10th Commander Rowan came up with the Union fleet, and the rebels opened fire upon him at a long range. The Union forces continued their course uninterrupted by the enemy's fire until within three-fourths of a mile of their position, when they opened fire and dashed on at full speed. In a few minutes five of the enemy's six vessels were either captured or destroyed, and Elizabeth City was in possession of the naval forces. ↓ Two days later a small naval division under Lieutenant Alexander Murray took possession of Edenton.

⚓ The Confederate commander at Roanoke Island was General Henry A. Wise, who, on the 7th of January, 1862, had assumed command of the Chowan district, General Benjamin Huger being in command of the department, that of Norfolk. The official relations of the two generals were somewhat strained, and the responsibility for this disaster was afterward the subject of recrimination between them. General Wise claimed that he had been deprived of his artillery by reason of the countermanding of his orders by General Huger, and that, in general, there had been culpable neglect on the part of the Confederate authorities to aid the defense of Roanoke Island. "Nothing! nothing!! nothing!!!" he said. "That was the disease which brought disaster at Roanoke Island." There was also lack of cordial agreement

between General Wise and Flag-Officer Lynch. General Wise being ill at Nag's Head on the day of the battle, the Confederate troops on the field were under command of Colonel H. M. Shaw, who says in his report: "An unceasing and effective fire was kept up from 7 A. M. until 12:20, when, our artillery ammunition having been exhausted and our right flanks having been turned by an overwhelming force of the enemy, I was compelled to yield the place."

↓ Of this engagement Captain Parker, C. S. N., in his "Recollections of a Naval Officer," writes as follows:

"The enemy were coming up at full speed and our vessels were under weigh ready to abide the shock, when a boat came off from the shore with the bearer of a dis-

The morning of February 9th, having heard that a portion of the command of General Henry A. Wise still remained at Nag's Head, General Parke ordered that I should take a battalion of my regiment, proceed to that point, and, if possible, effect their capture. When we arrived at the place of debarkation we were surprised to meet with no resistance to our landing. The fact was sufficiently accounted for when we learned that Wise with his whole command had retreated northward at sundown the day before.

From the time of the capture of Roanoke Island stories had come frequently to the Union commanders setting forth the loyalty of the citizens of the town of Winton on the Chowan River, and their desire to serve the Union cause. On the 18th of February an expedition of eight gun-boats under Commander Rowan, and a land force of which I had charge, started for the Chowan River, for the purpose of encouraging our friends at Winton and destroying two important bridges of the Seaboard and Roanoke Railroad. The morning of the 19th we began to ascend the river, and as I had never believed in the tales regarding the loyalty of the Wintonians, from the time of entering the river, I assumed the position of volunteer lookout from the cross-trees of the mainmast of the steamer *Delaware*. The day was beautiful, the sail charming, and all went well until about half-past 3 o'clock. The steamer had "slowed down" and taken a sheer in toward the Winton wharf, where a negro woman stood waving a rag, when from my lofty perch I discovered the glistening of many musket-barrels among the short shrubs that covered the high bank, and farther back two pieces of artillery in position. I shouted to the astonished native pilot at the helm, "Ring on, sheer off, rebels on shore!" fully half a dozen times before he could comprehend my meaning. At last he rang on full speed, changed his course, and cleared the wharf by about ten feet. At that moment the enemy opened fire, and

patch for me. It read: 'Captain Parker, with the crew of the *Beaufort*, will at once take charge of the fort.—Lynch.' 'Where the devil,' I asked, 'are the men who were in the fort?' 'All run away,' said the messenger. . . . Upon getting into the fort I hastily commenced stationing the men at the guns, and as quickly as possible opened fire upon the advancing enemy. Some of the officers and men of the *Forrest* made their way to us upon learning that the militia had fled. I must not forget to say that the engineer officer who had been sent from Richmond for service in the fort remained bravely at his post. . . . I found Commodore Lynch on shore; his boat had been cut in two by a shot and he could not get off to his ship, as he informed me; and he furthermore said I was to command the fort without reference to his being there — that if he saw an opportunity to get off to the *Seabird*, he should embrace it. The enemy's vessels came on at full speed under a heavy fire from our vessels and the fort. The fire from the latter was ineffectual. The officers and men were cool enough; but they had not had time to look about them. Everything was in bad working order, and it was difficult to train the guns. . . . Commodore Rowan's steamers did not reply to our fire until quite close; and without slackening their speed they passed the fort and fell upon our vessels. They made short work of them. The *Seabird* was rammed and sunk by the *Commodore Perry*. The *Ellis* was captured after a desperate defense, in which her gallant commander, James Cooke, was badly wounded. The schooner *Black Warrior* was set on fire and abandoned, her crew escaping through the marshes

on their side of the river. The *Fanny* was run on shore and blown up by her commander, who with his crew escaped to the shore. . . . Captain Sims, of the *Appomattox*, kept up a sharp fire from his bow gun until it was accidentally spiked; and he then had to run for it. He had a howitzer aft which he kept in play; but upon arriving at the mouth of the canal he found his vessel was about *two inches* too wide to enter; he therefore set her on fire, and she blew up. The *Beaufort* got through to Norfolk.

"We in the fort saw this work of destruction going on without being able to prevent it. As soon as the vessels passed the fort we could not bring a gun to bear on them, and a shot from them would have taken us in reverse. A few rounds of grape would have killed and wounded all the men in the fort, for the distance was only a few hundred yards. Seeing this, I directed Johnson to spike the guns, to order every man to shoulder his musket, and then to take down the flag.

"All this was promptly and coolly done, and upon the fact being reported to me by Johnson, I pointed to some woods in our rear and told him to make the best of his way there with the command. All this time Commodore Lynch had stood quietly looking on, but without uttering a word. As his command had just been destroyed under his eyes, I knew pretty well what his feelings were. Turning to him I said: 'Commodore, I have ordered the fort evacuated.' 'Why so, sir?' he demanded. I pointed out the condition of affairs I have just stated, and he acquiesced. Arm in arm, we followed the retreating men."

before we passed out of range the low guards, wheel-house, and masts of the *Delaware* were riddled. My descent from the cross-trees, with only the mast to protect my body, was rapid and not graceful; ratlines and shrouds were cut by bullets as I went down, and my escape without injury was one of the every-day miracles of war.

The Union forces withdrew down the river and anchored. Early the next morning we returned, and after some preliminary shelling, my regiment with two boat-howitzers were landed, the enemy was driven out, and the town was occupied. We soon discovered that the court-house and several other buildings were in use for barracks and store-houses for army supplies. They were all fired. Then the expedition returned to Roanoke Island.

VICE-ADMIRAL S. C. ROWAN.

The Winton expedition was, for the time being, the last of active operations having Roanoke Island for a base. The army forces on shore were enjoying a period of luxurious rest, while the naval vessels were making pleasant excursions to the towns on the shores of the sounds before embarking in an enterprise second only in importance to the capture of Roanoke Island. It was an open secret that the next move would be against New Berne, a small city on the Neuse River.

The morning of the 10th of March ♭ a letter was handed to me from General Burnside containing the information that a new brigade, composed of the 9th and 89th New York and the 6th New Hampshire, and designated as the Fourth, had been formed for duty at Roanoke Island, which was to be left under my command for the protection of that post. The formation of this new brigade was the culmination of preparations for the departure of the New Berne expedition.

THE BATTLE OF NEW BERNE.

THE morning of the 11th the force detailed for the attack upon that city embarked and that night, with the naval forces, rendezvoused at Hatteras Inlet. On the 12th an early start was made, and that evening the whole fleet anchored off the mouth of Slocum's Creek, about sixteen miles below New Berne.

The next morning was as unpleasant as a cold penetrating rain and dark sky could make it, but, notwithstanding, at 6:30, after some preliminary shelling of woods near the landing, the troops began to disembark, the majority

---

♭ The 9th of March had been clear and sunny, with a light breeze from the north. Although I was at Roanoke Island, some eighty miles away, I heard, quite distinctly, the roar of the guns engaged in the action between the *Merrimac* and the Union fleet, including the *Monitor.* — R. C. H.

going in small boats, while others in their eagerness for the fray jumped from the transports, which were fast on the mud bottoms, and, holding their cartridge-boxes and muskets over their heads, waded to the land.   In addition to the 13 regiments of infantry, 8 pieces of artillery were landed, 6 in charge of Lieutenant McCook, of the navy, and 2 commanded by Captains Dayton and Bennett, of the Marine Artillery.

The enemy had chosen a strong position, well calculated for defensive purposes.   On Otter Creek, about seven miles up the river from the mouth of Slocum's Creek, they had a line of intrenchments reaching from the Neuse River to the Atlantic and North Carolina Railroad; two miles beyond they had erected a strong field-work for preventing a landing at that point; three miles

BRIGADIER-GENERAL L. O'B. BRANCH, COMMANDING THE CONFEDERATE FORCES AT NEW BERNE. KILLED AT ANTIETAM, SEPT. 17, 1862.
FROM A PHOTOGRAPH.

farther on there was a battery mounting 4 heavy guns, but bearing upon the river; and one mile farther up toward New Berne was their long line of strong works, the chief defense against an attack upon that city.   Fort Thompson, a large and carefully planned flanking bastion, located on the river, and mounting 13 heavy guns, the enemy's extreme left, was the commencement of their main line of breastworks, which extended a mile and a quarter to the railroad; and commencing the other side of the railroad was another series of defensive works, consisting of rifle-pits and detached intrenchments in the form of redans and lunettes, that terminated in a 2-gun battery, about two miles from Fort Thompson.   All were located upon a low, swampy soil.   The line from the river to the railroad was protected by a ditch and clearing in front, and the one

beyond by a swamp and underbrush along its whole length.   These works were armed with 41 heavy guns and 19 field-pieces, and had between 7000 and 8000 men for their defense.   In the river, opposite Fort Thompson, and crossing its channel, were a double row of piles and many sunken vessels, formidable obstructions, to assist the fort in preventing an attack upon New Berne from the river.   The naval forces moved up the river along with the troops while the light guns on shore were being dragged through the deep mud of the road.   The first day's march took the whole Union force beyond the second deserted work, where the advance came in contact with the enemy's pickets.   It being then 8 o'clock, a halt was ordered for the night, and the weary, hungry troops found a soldiers' resting-place in the mud, with no better covering than a continuous downpour of cold water.   The eight pieces of artillery, although assisted on their way by the whole of the 51st Pennsylvania, did not arrive on the ground until 3 o'clock the following morning.   [See map, p. 651.]

During the night it was ascertained from pickets, negroes, and others that the enemy's fortified line was not far off; and early on the morning of the 14th the positions of the Union forces were designated preparatory to a forward movement for attack.   General Foster was to move up the country

FORTS ELLIS AND LANE IN THE DISTANCE.

BOMBARDMENT OF THE CONFEDERATE FORT THOMPSON DURING THE BATTLE OF NEW BERNE.
FROM A WAR-TIME SKETCH.

road and attack the enemy's left; General Reno was to advance by the railroad and attempt to turn the rebel right; while General Parke was to follow on the country road as a reserve, or to operate in the center. The heads of the two advancing columns soon came within range, and a disposition of the troops for a general engagement was immediately consummated. The 25th Massachusetts had the extreme right; second in line came the 24th Massachusetts, its left resting on the country road, which was occupied by the artillery commanded by Captain Dayton and Lieutenant McCook. The 27th Massachusetts, with its right resting on the country road, was joined on its left by the 23d Massachusetts, the whole parallel with the enemy's works. The artillery and right regiments opened the engagement before those on the left of the road got into position. The 10th Connecticut Volunteers, arriving a little after the others, was ordered to the left of the 23d. The action along the whole of General Foster's front had now commenced in earnest. The 27th Massachusetts soon exhausted its short supply of ammunition, and was replaced by the 11th Connecticut, which had been ordered by General Parke to assist in bringing up the guns.

Early in the morning General Reno, on the left, moved his brigade along the railroad in the following order: 21st Massachusetts, 51st New York, 9th New Jersey, and 51st Pennsylvania. The first encounter, about 8 o'clock, was with a large detachment of the enemy who were bringing a gun to bear on the railroad. This move was checked by a well-maintained fire from the Union skirmishers, and soon after the right wing of the 21st Massachusetts, under

Lieutenant-Colonel Clark, charged through an opening and captured a brick-kiln within the enemy's line. The other regiments of the brigade were now brought into line on the left of the 21st Massachusetts, with the 51st Pennsylvania in reserve, supporting the extreme left of the line. On this part of the field the action lasted for about three and a half hours, when the regiments engaged had expended nearly all their ammunition. At that time the right wing of the 51st Pennsylvania, under Lieutenant-Colonel T. S. Bell, was ordered to relieve the 51st New York, which had suffered severely, to pass in front of it, deliver one volley, and then charge the enemy's works. This order was gallantly executed. At the same time the other wing of the 51st Pennsylvania and the 9th New Jersey charged the intrenchments, and the enemy fled from their entire left, leaving fifty prisoners. Just then General Reno discovered the Stars and Stripes waving from the works far off to his right.

MAJOR-GENERAL JOHN G. FOSTER.
FROM A PHOTOGRAPH.

Lieutenant-Colonel Clark, after capturing the brick-kiln, moved along the inside of the works toward the right, came upon a light battery of sixteen pieces which he captured, but was driven back by an overwhelming force of infantry.

General Parke's brigade, consisting of the 4th and 5th Rhode Island and the 8th and 11th Connecticut regiments, was assigned to the center in supporting distance of either end of the line, but this command was destined to play a more important part than merely supporting the troops. Soon after getting under fire Colonel Rodman, with the 4th Rhode Island, offered to charge through an opening left in the intrenchments for the railroad to pass through. The offer was accepted, and the 8th Connecticut and the 5th Rhode Island were ordered to his support. Passing the rifle-pits, he entered the rear of the intrenchments, moving toward the right, capturing nine brass guns and driving the enemy from his intrenched position between the railroad and the river. Simultaneously with the movement of Colonel Rodman, General Foster made a charge along his whole front, when the enemy retreated. During the greater part of the action the gun-boats coöperated by shelling the woods in the rear of the works. Rodman's soldierly movement was the culminating point of the day, and ended a battle most creditable for all the Union troops and the officers who commanded them. Immediately after the close of the action, New Berne was occupied.

When the strength of the position is taken into consideration, the fatigue of the Union forces, and the great difficulties they had to encounter in making an infantry attack against a strong intrenched position, it is astonishing that they came out of the action with a loss of only 90 killed and 380 wounded. The loss to the enemy was 9 forts, mounting 41 heavy guns, over 2 miles of intrenchments, with 19 field-pieces in position, 6 32-pounders not mounted, over 300 prisoners, more than 1000 stand of small arms, tents and barracks for 10,000 troops, a large amount of army supplies and naval stores, and the control of the second commercial city in the State of North Carolina. The enemy's loss in killed, wounded, prisoners, and missing was about 578. This complete success, coming so soon after that of Roanoke Island, created an *esprit de corps* among the troops of the " Coast Division " which they maintained to the end of their army career. ⟨

⟨ The Confederate forces in this engagement were all North Carolinians, and were commanded by General L. O'B. Branch, who gives in his official report this account of the battle :

"The defensive works were located and constructed before I assumed command. The troops under my command had performed a large amount of work, but it was mainly on the river defenses, which were not assailed by the enemy. They had been originally planned for a force much larger than any ever placed at my disposal, and I was for six weeks engaged in making the necessary changes to contract them, but the failure of all my efforts to obtain implements and tools with which the troops could carry on the work prevented me from making satisfactory progress. I had circulated handbills over the State, calling on the citizens generally to assist me, and received from two counties a small party of free negroes without implements. I then inserted in the newspaper an advertisement calling on the slave-owners to hire their slaves, with implements, for a few days, and I got but a single negro. During all this time I continued the troops at work, and when the enemy came into the river, five hundred per day were being detailed to construct breastworks, with less than half that number of worn and broken shovels and axes, without picks or grubbing-hoes. If the fate of New Berne shall prevent a similar supineness on the part of citizens, and especially slave-owners, elsewhere, it will be fortunate for the country. . . . At about 7 : 30 o'clock, Friday morning, the fire opened along the line from the railroad to the river. I soon received a message from Colonel Lee [commanding the Confederate left wing] that the enemy were attempting to turn our left. This proved to be a feint, as I replied to him that I thought it would. The next incident of the battle was the appearance of the enemy's skirmishers in front of Vance [26th N. C.], and consequently on the prolongation of the line held by the militia. It was to drive the enemy from that position that I had directed the 24-pound battery to be placed there, and supposing it was ready for service, I sent Captain Rodman, with his company, to man it, but they found the guns not mounted, and were ordered into position to act as infantry. The skirmishers of the enemy, finding themselves on the flank of the militia, fired at them a few shots from their flank files, which caused a portion of them to flee in great disorder. I instantly ordered Colonel Avery [33d Regiment] to send five companies to dislodge them. He sent them instantly, under Lieutenant-Colonel Hoke; but before Colonel Hoke had fully got into position, though he moved with the greatest promptness and celerity, I received a message from Colonel Clark, of the militia, informing me that the enemy were in line of battle in great force on his right. I instantly ordered up the remaining five companies of Colonel Avery's regiment, and the whole ten opened a terrific fire from their Enfield rifles. The whole militia, however, had now abandoned their positions, and the utmost exertions of myself and my staff could not rally them. Colonel Sinclair's regiment [35th] very quickly followed their example, retreating in the utmost disorder. This laid open Haywood's right [7th], and a large portion of the breastwork was left vacant. I had not a man with whom to reoccupy it, and the enemy soon poured in a column along the railroad and through a portion of the cut-down ground in front, which marched up behind the breastwork to attack what remained of Campbell's command [7th]. The brave 7th met them with the bayonet, and drove them headlong over the parapet, inflicting heavy loss upon them as they fled ; but soon returning with heavy reënforcements, not less than five or six regiments, the 7th was obliged to yield, falling back slowly and in order. Seeing the enemy behind the breastwork, without a single man to place in the gap through which he was entering, and finding the day lost, my next care was to secure the retreat."

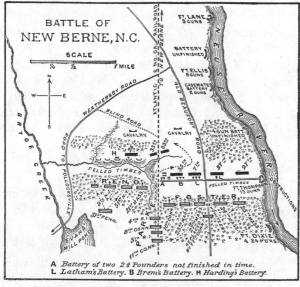

MAP OF THE BATTLE OF NEW BERNE, NORTH CAROLINA,
MARCH 14, 1862.

This map is based upon the sketch map accompanying General Branch's official report of the Confederate operations in this engagement, with the addition of the Union dispositions as indicated by the official reports.

ASSAULT OF THE UNION TROOPS UPON FORT THOMPSON, NEAR NEW BERNE. FROM A WAR-TIME SKETCH.

The enemy in their retreat destroyed bridges, and as they passed through the town set fire to it, and left parts of it in a blaze; and the first work of our troops and sailors after landing was to assist the citizens in putting out the flames, which was not done until much valuable property had been uselessly destroyed. With the military machinery at his command it did not take General Burnside long to establish order and give the captured city such a government as the occasion required. The next and most important business in hand was to make the captured position secure from a land attack; and in order to accomplish this, a portion of the railroad leading to Goldsboro' had to be destroyed, and a line of fortifications built between the Neuse and Trent rivers, which would completely insulate New Berne from the surrounding country.

THE SIEGE OF FORT MACON.

THE next and last objective point of any importance in the new department of North Carolina was the capture of Fort Macon, an old-style, strong, stone, casemated work, mounting 67 guns, garrisoned by above 500 men, commanded by Colonel Moses J. White, located on the eastern extremity of Bogue Island, commanding the channel from the open sea to Beaufort Harbor, and about forty miles from New Berne. [See map, p. 634.] To General Parke was assigned the duty of moving upon this work and undertaking its capture. March 18th, General Burnside and Lieutenant Williamson, of the Engineers, made a reconnoissance to the east as far as Slocum's Creek, and occupied Havelock Station with one company of the 5th Rhode Island Battalion. The 21st,

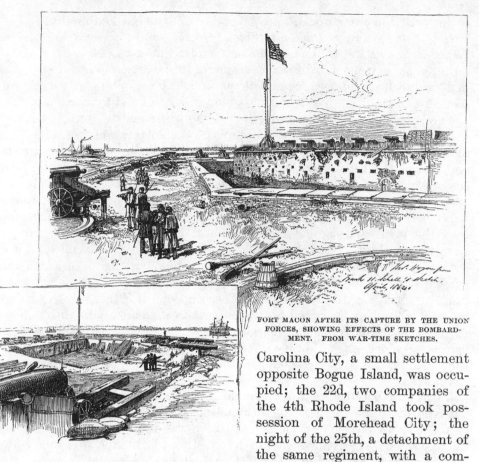

FORT MACON AFTER ITS CAPTURE BY THE UNION FORCES, SHOWING EFFECTS OF THE BOMBARDMENT. FROM WAR-TIME SKETCHES.

Carolina City, a small settlement opposite Bogue Island, was occupied; the 22d, two companies of the 4th Rhode Island took possession of Morehead City; the night of the 25th, a detachment of the same regiment, with a company of the 8th Connecticut, occupied Beaufort; and the night of the 23d, Newport was garrisoned by the 5th Rhode Island. Thus all the important positions around or in the vicinity of Fort Macon had fallen into the possession of the Union forces without contest or the loss of a man. General Parke, who had established his headquarters at Carolina City, demanded a surrender of the fort, which was refused. The evidence of preparations completed and in hand left no doubt upon the mind of General Parke that Colonel White intended to make a desperate defense. It was therefore decided to besiege the fort, and as soon as possible to make a combined land and sea attack.

In this important work General Parke was most ably assisted by Captain Williamson and Lieutenant Flagler, of the Ordnance Corps. On the 29th a part of the Third Brigade was landed upon Bogue Island, and operations for besieging the fort were immediately commenced. The configuration of the sand-hills was singularly well adapted to facilitate the operations of the Union forces. These ridges or hills intervened between the working parties and the fort to such an extent in height as to permit the erection of besieging works to go on by day as well as by night, without any serious inconvenience from the enemy's fire. By April 23d, the fort was entirely cut off from communication with the outer world. On the ocean side the blockading division, consisting of the steamers *Daylight, State of Georgia,* and *Chippewa,* and the bark *Gemsbok,* under the command of Commander Samuel Lockwood, prevented all intercourse from that direction. General Parke announced the works completed, and his readiness for an attack, and Colonel White was again summoned, and again, in the tersest possible terms, declined to surrender.

The preparations for the reduction of the fort consisted of a battery of 3 rifled 30-pounder guns, under Captain L. O. Morris; another of 4 8-inch mortars, under Lieutenant D. W. Flagler; and a third of 4 10-inch mortars, commanded by Lieutenant M. F. Prouty, of the 25th Massachusetts. From these works the bombardment commenced on the morning of the 25th, and continued for ten hours. The fire from the Union batteries was not only vigorous, but also accurate and effective. Shell after shell dropped into the work and exploded. Many breaches were made, the ramparts were swept clean of gunners, and seventeen guns were disabled and dismounted. The naval forces, owing to the sudden coming on of a gale, after participating in the early part of the bombardment, were compelled to seek deeper water. On the morning of the 26th Colonel White, by the hanging out of a white flag, indicated his willingness to surrender. He and his troops received honorable terms and marched out of the fort as the 5th Rhode Island marched in, and so ended, in a comparatively bloodless victory, the siege of Fort Macon, the combined losses of both sides being only 9 killed and 25 wounded.☆

During the bombardment a detachment of the Signal Corps under Lieutenant Andrews rendered most important assistance to the commanders of the batteries. His position on the Bogue banks was nearly at right angles with the line of fire. Early in the action he saw that the 10-inch shells were going three hundred yards beyond the fort, and that the 8-inch shells were falling short. By signaling his observations, the elevations of the pieces were corrected, so that after 12 o'clock every projectile from the mortars fell inside the fort. This was not only one of the first, but among the better, of the achievements of the Signal Corps, proving its usefulness in war operations.

SOUTH MILLS AND OTHER OPERATIONS.

Soon after the capture of Roanoke Island rumors reached us of the building of rebel iron-clads which were to enter Albemarle Sound *via* the Dismal Swamp Canal and Roanoke River. Commander Rowan and I were equally

---

☆ Colonel Moses J. White says in his report:

"At 6 A. M., on the 25th, the enemy's land batteries opened upon the fort, and at 6:30 A. M. their vessels, consisting of three war steamers and one sailing vessel, commenced a cross-fire with rifle and 11-inch shell. The fire from both directions was immediately returned, and at 7 A. M. the ships retired — one disabled and two others in a damaged condition. [No such damage is reported by the commanders of the Union vessels. Commander Lockwood, of the *Daylight,* the senior naval officer, attributed the withdrawal to the rolling of the sea. He speaks, however, of the excellence of the Confederate aim.— EDITORS.] The attack from land was kept up with great vigor, the enemy having immense advantage from their superior force, being able to relieve their men at the guns, while our morning reports showed only 263 men for duty. Our guns were well managed, but being able to do little damage to water batteries and siege guns, firing through very narrow embrasures. The enemy kept up a very vigorous and accurate fire from both rifles and mortars, dismounting guns, disabling men, and tearing the parade, parapet, and walls of the fort. At 6:30 P. M., finding that our loss had been very great, and from the fatigue of our men being unable to keep up the fire with but two guns, a proposition was made to General Parke for the surrender of Fort Macon."

anxious to protect the "pasteboard" vessels composing his fleet. We decided it would be feasible to land a considerable force at Elizabeth City, make a forced march to the south end of the Dismal Swamp Canal, and destroy the lock that connected it with the river. In an interview with General Burnside the plan was submitted and approved; he agreed to detail a necessary additional force from New Berne to take part in the movement, and I was ordered to have my entire command ready for April 14th. On the 17th I received a personal letter from him, saying he had detailed the 21st Massachusetts and the 51st Pennsylvania, and ordering me to embark immediately with at least eighteen hundred men, and closed by saying he would be up at once or send orders. The morning of the 18th I was greatly surprised to receive a call from General Reno, who stated that he had with him two regiments and was in command of the expedition.

The transports were soon under way, and reached the point of debarkation at about 1 o'clock the next morning. My brigade, consisting of the 9th New York, Lieutenant-Colonel Kimball; the 89th New York, Colonel H. S. Fairchild; and the 6th New Hampshire, Colonel S. G. Griffin, was landed and on the march by 3 o'clock. A light mulatto man for a guide came to me from one of the gun-boats and by a circuitous route took us far out of the way, so that we marched 30 miles to get at the rebel position, instead of 16 by the direct road.] This détour led to the meeting of the Union commands where two roads joined, about three or four miles from the enemy's position. It was decided that General Reno should take the advance, and that I should follow as rapidly as the fatigued condition of my men would permit.

Soon after 1 o'clock the rebels were discovered with a small detachment of cavalry thrown to the front, their infantry and artillery in a concealed line along the edge of a wood, facing an open field. The action was commenced by rapid shell-firing from the enemy's guns, which was vigorously answered by the four rifled pieces (two belonging to Company K, 9th New York), commanded by Colonel William A. Howard, of the Marine Artillery. The 21st Massachusetts and the 51st Pennsylvania, coming in range, were deflected out of a road, through a field, to a wood on the right. My command soon arrived, when the 6th New Hampshire was ordered to the left, and the two other regiments followed those on the right. The action had continued for about an hour (chiefly artillery), when I concluded to make an observation in an open corn-field, directly in front of the rebel center. I proceeded to a fence within a hundred yards of the edge of the clearing, heard no firing of infantry, concluded the rebels had been silently outflanked on their left by the 21st Massachusetts and the 51st Pennsylvania, and thought my regiment might get across the corn-field and capture the battery which still continued the action.

I returned, and described what I proposed to do, and asked the men if they thought they were equal to the undertaking. Although greatly fatigued,

---

] When it was discovered that the guide had led my brigade ten miles out of the way, he was quietly taken to a wood out of sight of the troops and shot. A few days after, we heard that he had been sent to us by the enemy for the purpose of leading our troops astray.— R. C. H.

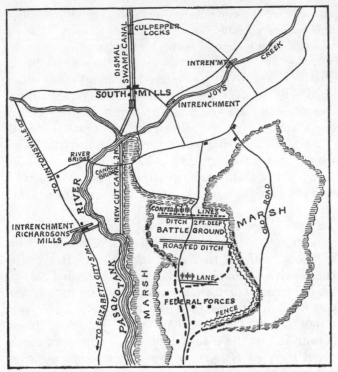

MAP OF THE ENGAGEMENT AT SOUTH MILLS, N. C., BASED ON THE MAP ACCOMPANYING GENERAL HUGER'S REPORT.

they answered, "We will try." Arriving at the fence, the regiment was formed in line of battle, and commenced to move over the field. When within fifty yards of the edge of the clearing, the right companies received the concentrated fire of the whole of the enemy's infantry and artillery, and in less than two minutes lost 9 killed and 58 wounded. I immediately ordered a deflection to the right, when suddenly the rebels ceased firing, and fell back to avoid being outflanked by our force that entered the wood on their left. The 6th New Hampshire gave them a parting vol-

ley, which caused their artillery to retreat, and so ended the battle of South Mills, or Camden, ⚓ as it is now known.

⚓ In his report of the fight at South Mills General Huger thus describes the Confederate position:

"On the 19th, the enemy approaching. . . Colonel Wright moved forward with his three companies, and at 9:30 o'clock was met by Colonel McComas with his battery (1 rifled piece and 3 bronze 6-pounders). After advancing 3 miles from South Mills the road emerged from the woods, and the field on the right and the left extended 160 to 180 yards to thick woods and swamp. On the edge of the woods, on both sides of the road and perpendicular to it, was a small ditch, the earth from which was thrown up on the south side in a ridge, upon which was a heavy rail fence. From this point the road led through a narrow lane for one mile with cleared land on both sides of it. Here he determined to make his stand. About three hundred yards from the woods ran a deep wide ditch parallel with the one first mentioned and extending to the woods on either side of the road, and a short distance beyond it were dwellings and outhouses which would give cover for the enemy. Colonel Wright therefore ordered them burned. The large ditch in his front he filled with fence rails and set them on fire, his object being to have this ditch so hot by the time the enemy came up they could not occupy it. (This ditch is marked on sketch as ' Roasted Ditch.') Two pieces of artillery (the road was too narrow for more) were placed in the road just where it emerged from the woods, which commanded the road — the range of the guns. He also threw down the fences for three hundred yards on each side of the road for three hundred yards in front of the guns, and tossed the rails into the road to destroy the effect of the enemy's ricochet firing, and to deprive him of the cover of the fences. The

fences on the sides of the woods were taken down and laid in heaps on the embankment in front of his men. . . . The smoke from the burning buildings and fences rolled toward the enemy, thus masking the position. . . ."

General Huger speaks of four repulses of the Union troops between 12 and 3:35 P. M., and continues:

"They soon advanced again, two regiments skirting the woods on our left, and approached near enough to engage the skirmishers. One company from the right was moved over, and Colonel Reid ordered to send one company from the reserve. The enemy deployed in the open field and bore down rapidly, but the heavy fire of musketry caused them to waver, and they fell back to the fence. Three regiments and a field-piece were in the center and the 9th New York regiment on the right. The fire was now brisk from one end of the line to the other, and the enemy were held in check, when just at this moment Captain McComas was killed by a minieball, and his men, who for four hours had fought with most indomitable courage, became panic-stricken and left the field, taking their pieces with them. Colonel Wright succeeded in rallying them and getting two pieces and a few men in position, and the enemy had advanced so close that canister was fired on them with effect, and they again fell back. The ammunition in the limberboxes was exhausted, and during the temporary absence of Colonel Wright the artillery left the field. The enemy made a charge upon our line, but the steady fire at close distance . . . caused them to break in confusion, and they fell back."

The Confederate forces were the 3d Georgia,

I was helped off the field to a negro cabin, and heard nothing from General Reno until about 9 o'clock, when he came to me with the information that he had learned that reënforcements were coming from Norfolk; and we agreed, under the circumstances, that it would be better to return to the gun-boats. The command moved at once through the mud and rain, reached the point of debarkation about 4 o'clock the next morning, and returned to Roanoke Island. My brigade had marched about 46 miles in a little less than 26 hours, besides taking part in a severe action. Our entire loss was 14 killed and 100 wounded and missing. Among the former was Lieutenant Charles A. Gadsden, adjutant of the 9th New York, an Americanized Englishman, who had been with his command less than a week. He fell most gallantly at the head of the first company that came under fire, where he had no right to be.

Chaplain Thomas W. Conway, of the 9th New York, who with Surgeon George H. Humphreys remained behind with the wounded, discovered that the rebel infantry, which gave us such a warm reception, were concealed in a broad, deep drain which conformed to the edge of the wood, and was parallel to my line of attack. The lock the expedition was sent to destroy remains to this day intact, and no iron-clad has ever passed through it, and for the best of all reasons, that none was ever built for that purpose.

May 7th, Captain O. W. Parisen, with Company C, 9th New York, embarked on the gun-boat *Shawsheen*, proceeded to Catharine's Creek, which empties into Chowan River, landed his command with a part of the gun-boat's crew, marched about two miles back from the creek and destroyed a large storehouse filled with $50,000 worth of commissary supplies for the rebel army. While returning to the gun-boat, Captain Parisen repelled an attack of rebel cavalry, which after one volley retreated, with the commanding officer mortally wounded.

Immediately after the first occupation of the inland waters of North Carolina by the Union forces, great inconvenience had been experienced, and in several instances movements had been retarded, because the only way of communication with Washington was through the sometimes dangerous and always unreliable channel of Hatteras Inlet. Knowing this, I had constantly urged upon General Burnside the importance of opening connection with Norfolk through the Currituck Sound and Dismal Swamp Canal, and, as a preliminary to such an undertaking, had commenced blowing up the obstructions placed by the enemy in the Currituck Canal. May 28th, I received permission from General Burnside to make an attempt to get to Fort Monroe through my proposed route, for the purpose of having an important conference with General Wool. I embarked Company K of the 9th New York, with its battery of rifled naval boat-guns, on board the small side-wheel steamer *Port Royal*. All the canal obstructions not being removed, I decided to

some drafted militia under Colonel Ferebee, Mc-Comas's battery, and Gillette's company of cavalry. The Confederate loss was 6 killed, 19 wounded, and 3 prisoners. The Union forces were the 6th New Hampshire, 21st Massachusetts, 9th and 89th New York, 51st Pennsylvania, and 1st New York Marine Artillery (4 pieces); and the losses were: killed, 13; wounded, 101; captured, 13,—total, 127. General Jesse L. Reno says in his report that the object of his expedition was to convey the idea that the entire Burnside expedition was marching upon Norfolk.—EDITORS.

PASSAGE OF UNION BOATS THROUGH THE DISMAL SWAMP CANAL. (SEE MAP, PAGE 634.)
FROM A WAR-TIME SKETCH.

pick my way outside in Currituck Sound through a narrow, crooked channel. The result can best be told by a dispatch to the New York "Tribune" from Fort Monroe:

"May 30th, 1862. This morning the side-wheel steamer *Port Royal* arrived here from Roanoke Island, *via* the Currituck Sound and Dismal Swamp Canal. Colonel Hawkins and a company of his gallant Zouaves are the first to open communication between Generals Wood and Burnside. By this movement we can dispense with all seaward transportation, and forward supplies, etc., in a safe and rapid manner to our troops in that vicinity."

When I was left in charge of Roanoke Island, Commander Rowan assigned to the command of the naval division in Albemarle and Croatan sounds Lieutenant Charles W. Flusser, who had been conspicuous for his efficiency upon many occasions. A finer character than this officer possessed it is impossible to imagine,—patriotic, sincere, manly, modest, considerate, and truthful to an extent almost beyond description; and a braver man never lived. Early in June he took possession of the town of Plymouth, situated a short distance above the mouth of the Roanoke River, and held it unaided by land forces until June 15th, when Company F of the 9th New York was detailed for guard and observation duty at that post. It did not take a long time for us to ascertain that there were among the non-slaveholding population many who professed sentiments not hostile to the Union, and that they had expressed a determination never to serve in the ranks of the rebel army. Lieutenant-Commander Flusser constantly urged upon me the importance of enlisting these men in the cause of the United States. Nearly all of the poorer class of inhabitants were still devoted to the old government; and many had successfully resisted rebel conscription, and had never given their allegiance to the rebel government.

Very few of them were slave-owners, and consequently had little interest in aiding the rebellion. They worked in their fields in groups, with arms near at hand during the day, and at night resorted to the swamps for shelter against conscripting parties of rebel soldiers; and by thus constantly being on the alert, they succeeded in rendering unavailing all efforts to force them into the ranks of the Confederate army. In several interviews which I had with Commander Flusser, he urged me in the strongest manner to occupy the town of Plymouth, and to organize the Union men of that vicinity into a regiment of soldiers.

I had several conversations with General Burnside in relation to this matter, and the final result was that he placed the affair entirely in my hands. Accordingly, by appointment, Commodore Rowan and I met some two hundred and fifty Union men; and a free interchange of views in relation to the affairs of the country took place. The matter of great concern with them was, " What will become of us in case we are captured by the rebels ? " We assured them that the Government of the United States would protect them and their families to the last extreme, and that any outrage perpetrated upon them or upon their families would be severely punished. An enlistment-roll was accordingly made out, and about one hundred men signed their names at once. Too much cannot be said of the devotion of these men under peculiar dangers — of these men of the 1st North Carolina. ⬇

Things remained in this condition until July, 1862, when General Burnside, with the Ninth Corps, of which my command was part, was ordered to join the Army of the Potomac.

⬇ On the 1st of February, 1864, a large Confederate force, under the command of Major-General G. E. Pickett, made an advance upon New Berne, N. C., and after destroying the United States gun-boat *Underwriter*, burning a bridge or two, and capturing some prisoners, withdrew to Kinston. Among the prisoners captured were several natives of North Carolina, who had enlisted in our service. A court-martial was convened, composed of Virginians, and twenty-two of these loyal North Carolinians were convicted of and executed for (constructive) desertion. June 1st, 1865, Pickett applied to President Johnson for a pardon. Secretary Stanton and Judge Advocate-General Holt were for trying him, and his application hung fire. March 12th, 1866, he wrote to Lieutenant-General Grant, stating his grievances and again setting forth his claim for a pardon. Upon the back of that letter General Grant made this singular indorsement: " During the rebellion belligerent rights were acknowledged to the enemies of our country, and it is clear to me that the parole given by the armies laying down their arms protects them against punishments for acts lawful for any other belligerents. In this case I know it is claimed that the men tried and convicted for the crime of desertion were Union men from North Carolina, who had found refuge within our lines and in our service. The punishment was a harsh one, but it was in time of war, and when the enemy no doubt felt it necessary to retain by some power the services of every man within their reach. General Pickett I know personally to be an honorable man, but in this case his judgment prompted him to do what cannot well be sustained, though I do not see how good, either to friends of the deceased or by fixing an example for the future, can be secured by his trial now. It would only open up the question whether or not the Government did not disregard its contract entered into to secure the surrender of an armed enemy." And the whole was referred to the President. The indorsement of General Grant was all-powerful, and nothing was done.— R. C. H.

THE BURNSIDE EXPEDITION.[1]

BY AMBROSE E. BURNSIDE, MAJOR-GENERAL, U. S. A.

UNION LOOKOUT, HATTERAS BEACH.
FROM A WAR-TIME SKETCH.

SOON after the 1st Rhode Island regiment was mustered out of service, I was appointed by President
Lincoln to the office of brigadier-general. My commission was given to me on the 6th of August, 1861,
and I was ordered to report to General McClellan,
who placed me in charge of the division and brigades which were formed of the new troops as they
arrived in Washington. My duty was to look after
the drill and discipline of these brigades, with a view
to giving the men the efficiency necessary for assignment to the older divisions of the army, which were
then organizing in Washington under the name of
the Army of the Potomac. The duty was interesting in some respects,
but was in the main somewhat tame, so that I very naturally desired more
active duty.

One evening in the following October, General McClellan and I were chat-
ting together over the affairs of the war, when I mentioned to him a plan for
the formation of a coast division to which I had given some thought. After
giving him a somewhat detailed account of the plan,
he asked me to put it in writing as soon as possible,
which was done. The next day it was presented
to him, and it met his approval. He laid it before
the Secretary of War, by whom it was also approved. The general details of the plan were briefly
as follows: To organize a division of from 12,000
to 15,000 men, mainly from States bordering on the
Northern sea-coast, many of whom would be familiar with the coasting trade, and among whom would
be found a goodly number of mechanics; and to fit
out a fleet of light-draught steamers, sailing vessels,
and barges, large enough to transport the division,
its armament and supplies, so that it could be rapidly thrown from point to point on the coast with
a view to establishing lodgments on the Southern
coast, landing troops, and penetrating into the
interior, thereby threatening the lines of transportation in the rear of the main army then

UNIFORM OF THE 1ST RHODE ISLAND,
COLONEL A. E. BURNSIDE, WHICH
SERVED AT THE BATTLE OF
BULL RUN. (SEE ABOVE.)

[1] This paper was read by General Burnside before the Soldiers' and
Sailors' Historical Society of Rhode Island, July 7th, 1880, and is
included here by permission of the Society, the text being somewhat
abridged to conform to the plan of this work.—EDITORS.

concentrating in Virginia, and holding possession of the inland waters on the Atlantic coast.

After the approval of the plan, I was ordered to New York to fit out the fleet; and on the 23d of October orders were issued establishing my headquarters for the concentration of the troops of the division at Annapolis. Troops arrived from time to time at Annapolis, and all went well in the camp, which was established on beautiful grounds just outside the town. The improvement in drill and discipline was very rapid, but affairs did not progress so smoothly at the headquarters in New York. There was great difficulty in procuring vessels of a light draught, almost everything of that sort having already been called into service; but after much difficulty I was enabled to report to General McClellan on the 12th of December that a sufficient amount of transportation and armament had been secured for the division. It was a motley fleet. North River barges and propellers had been strengthened from deck to keelson by heavy oak planks, and water-tight compartments had been built in them: they were so arranged that parapets of sand-bags or bales of hay could be built upon their decks, and each one carried from four to six guns. Sailing vessels, formerly belonging to the coasting trade, had been fitted up in the same manner. Several large passenger steamers, which were guaranteed to draw less than eight feet of water, together with tug and ferry boats, served to make up the fleet, which gave a capacity to transport 15,000 troops, with baggage, camp-equipage, rations, etc. Light-draught sailing vessels were also added to the fleet, on which were stored building material for bridges, rafts, scows, intrenching implements, quartermasters' stores, tools, extra ordnance stores, etc. All of these vessels were ordered to rendezvous at Fort Monroe. Coal and water vessels were chartered in Baltimore, and ordered to rendezvous at the same place. The transports were ordered to Annapolis Harbor, at which point, after most mortifying and vexatious delays, they all arrived by the 4th of January, 1862, and on this day were promulgated the orders for embarkation, which were received with most enthusiastic cheers from one end of the camp to the other.

I had organized the division into three brigades, which were placed in command of General J. G. Foster, General Jesse L. Reno, and General John G. Parke, three of my most trusted friends. We had been cadets together at West Point, and I had always entertained for them the greatest confidence and esteem. In all future operations in the expedition, our close friendly relations were maintained, and I was never disappointed in any reliance which I placed on their gallantry, skill, and integrity. I had been notified by General McClellan that our destination would be Hatteras Inlet, with a view to operations in the inland waters of North Carolina.

On the 5th of January the troops began to embark. During that day there were some delays, which resulted from inexperience in the manœuvring of the vessels and in the new work to which they were unaccustomed. On that night, snow to the depth of from two to three inches fell, which gave to the camp and surrounding country, on the morning of the 6th, a most picturesque appearance. Regiment after regiment struck their tents and marched to the point of embarkation, with bands playing, colors flying, and the men cheering and singing from lightness of heart. As they passed through the quaint old town of Annapolis, the lines of troops, with their dark uniforms and glittering bayonets, contrasted markedly with the snow-clad fields and trees. The men were not cheered and encouraged by many friendly voices, such as they had heard whilst coming from their homes to the seat of war; but they were not at all chilled by the reception, and cheerfully marched on to the work before them. Embarkation had become more easy to each regiment than it was to the preceding one, owing to the greater facility with which the vessels were handled. The order to break camp had been obeyed with joyful alacrity, and more troops poured into the Academy grounds during the day than could be embarked, so that large numbers remained there for the night. This bivouac was one of the most enlivening and beautiful that I saw during the war. There was very little sleep, but great joyousness. Wednesday morning every regiment was on board except the 6th New Hampshire, which arrived late on the night of the 7th, and was embarked on the next morning. The scene in the harbor was inspiring beyond description. The vessels, as

BREVET BRIGADIER-GENERAL RUSH C. HAWKINS.
FROM A PHOTOGRAPH.

they passed each other from time to time, saluted with their steam-whistles, while the bands played and the troops cheered, the decks being covered with blue-coats, some chattering, some sleeping, others writing their last letters to their loved ones at home. The whole fleet seemed to be under a mixed influence of excitement and contentment.

On the morning of the 9th, each vessel set sail, under orders to rendezvous at Fort Monroe, and there, by the night of the 10th, all had joined the *Supply* and other vessels, making altogether a fleet of more than eighty. The harbor probably never presented a finer appearance than on that night. All the vessels were illuminated, and the air was filled with the strains of martial music and the voices of brave men. Not a man in the fleet knew his destination, except myself, the brigade commanders, and two or three staff-officers, yet there was no complaint or inquisitiveness, but all seemed ready for whatever duty was before them.

Sealed orders were given to the commanders of each vessel, to be opened at sea. Much discouragement was expressed by nautical men and by men high in military authority as to the success of the expedition. The President and General McClellan were both approached, and the President was frequently warned that the vessels were unfit for sea, and that the expedition would be a total failure. Great anxiety was manifested to know its destination, but the secret had been well kept at Washington and at our headquarters. As Mr. Lincoln afterward told me, one public man was very importunate, and, in fact, almost demanded that the President should tell him where we were going. Finally, the President said to him, "Now, I will tell you in great confidence where they are going, if you will promise not to speak of it to any one." The promise was given, and Mr. Lincoln said, " Well, now, my friend, the expedition is going to sea!" The inquirer left him without receiving any further information. In this jocular manner Mr. Lincoln was in the habit of throwing off the cares of state; and it often occurs to me that but for that habit he would have broken down under the great weight of public responsibility which rested upon him from the first day of the war to the termination of his noble life. In my opinion, no man has ever lived who could have gone through that struggle as he did. At no period of his life, I believe, was his heart ever stirred with a feeling of enmity or resentment against any one. He was actuated by the simple desire and determination to maintain the authority of the Government at all hazards.

On the night of the 11th the signal for sailing was given, and very soon the fleet was under way. My headquarters were on board a large steamer, the *George Peabody ;* but, with two or three of my staff-officers, I took for my headquarters during the voyage a small propeller called the *Picket,* in reality the smallest vessel in the fleet. I was moved to do this because of the great criticism which had been made as to the unseaworthiness of the vessels of the fleet, and because of a desire to show my faith in their adaptability to the service. Their weaknesses were known to me, but they were the best that could be procured, and it was necessary that the service should be performed even at the risk of losing life by shipwreck. The weather was threatening, but I did not foresee the storm by which we were afterward overtaken. At that time we had no weather signal reports; but, in any event, the sailing would not have been delayed, because the orders to proceed to our work were imperative. It was, of course, learned by all, after reaching the sea, that the destination of the fleet was Hatteras Inlet.

Just before midnight the *Picket* weighed anchor, and we were soon at sea, and it was not long before the little vessel was called upon to test her sea-going ability. On rounding Cape Hatteras we met a very strong breeze, and the little vessel got into the trough of the sea. It seemed for a time as if she would surely be swamped; but by skillful management the captain brought her head-to, after which she behaved better. We passed a most uncomfortable night. Everything on the deck that was not lashed was swept overboard; and the men, furniture, and crockery below decks were thrown about in a most promiscuous manner. The breeze died away toward morning, soon after which a heavy fog arose, which continued the greater part of the day. The ocean's swell kept one in constant thought that the little vessel was in

REAR-ADMIRAL GOLDSBOROUGH.   FROM A PHOTOGRAPH.

momentary danger of going under. Toward night the wind arose, and within a short time it increased to a terrible gale, and we experienced more discomfort and dread, if possible, than on the preceding night. At times, it seemed as if the waves, which appeared to us mountain high, would ingulf us, but then the little vessel would ride them and stagger forward in her course.

During the day before (the 12th), the fog had hidden the fleet, but at about midnight we discovered a large steamer upon our port bow. We fired a shot astern of her, which she answered by approaching us. It was the *Eastern Queen;* but we dared not go near her, for fear of being crushed. She seemed to us enormous, and we were all delighted when she answered the signal to lay by us until daylight, but to keep off. In the morning more vessels were found to be in sight, and just before noon of the 13th we hove to, off Hatteras Inlet. Soon after, a tug-boat came out from the inlet, which, it will be remembered, had been occupied by General Butler and Commodore Stringham. [See map, p. 634.] The little boat undertook to do the duty of piloting the fleet over the bar. The *Picket* led the way, and bravely fought the breakers until she was safely anchored inside the harbor. Vessel after vessel followed us in, until we were ready to wish that the fleet were not so large. At one time it seemed as if our little boat would be crushed between two of the larger vessels which had dragged their anchors and were coming down upon her. Fortunately, the commanders of the vessels succeeded in checking them just as they came in contact with us. Most of the fleet arrived inside the bar during the afternoon.

The propeller *City of New York*, which was laden with supplies and ordnance stores, grounded on the bar, and proved a total loss. Her officers and crew clung to the rigging until the next day, when they were rescued by surf-boats sent to their assistance. One of the troop-vessels also grounded on the bar, after nightfall, and it seemed for a time as if she and her precious cargo would be lost. Some gallant volunteers went to her relief with a tug-boat, which succeeded in getting her off the bar and into the harbor. The water and coal vessels did not approach the inlet, but went to sea as a matter of safety. Such of the vessels as were of too heavy draught to pass over the bar anchored under the protection of the cape. From one of these vessels, two officers, Colonel Joseph W. Allen and Surgeon Frederick A. Weller, of the 9th New Jersey, started in a surf-boat to report to me. They succeeded in reaching my headquarters, but on their return the boat was swamped by the breakers on the bar, and they were lost.✠ The crew, who were more skilled in such service, clung to the boat and were rescued. Strange to say, these were the only two of our force lost during the entire voyage and entrance into the inlet, notwithstanding the gloomy prognostications touching the seaworthiness of the vessels of the fleet. Besides the propeller, we lost the ship *Pocahontas*, with over a hundred horses on board. The gun-boat *Zouave* was sunk in the inlet after she crossed the bar, and proved a total loss, but no lives were lost. From the 14th until the 26th we had terrific weather, and it required the utmost care on the part of the commanders of the vessels to prevent a general disaster. Many of the vessels were driven from their anchors and grounded on the swash and the bar. Many collisions occurred, which caused great damage to the fleet. At times it seemed as if nothing could prevent general disaster. As I before said, the water and most of the coal vessels were driven to sea by the stress of the weather, and the entire fleet was for many days on short rations of water. Much suffering resulted from this, and at one time a flag of distress was hoisted on many of the vessels in consequence of the want of water. On one of these dreary days I for a time gave up all hope, and walked to the bow of the vessel that I might be alone. Soon after, a small black cloud appeared in the angry gray sky, just above the horizon, and very soon spread so as to cover the entire canopy, and in a few moments a most copious fall of rain came to our relief. Signals were given to spread sails to catch the water, and in a short time an abundance was secured for the entire fleet. I was at once cheered up, but was very much ashamed of the distrust which I had allowed to get the mastery of me.

From time to time we made efforts to cross the fleet from the inlet into Pamlico Sound, over what was called the swash, which separated it from the inlet. We had been led to believe that there were eight feet of water upon the swash, but when we arrived we discovered to our sorrow that there were but six feet; and as most of our vessels, as well as the vessels of the naval

---

✠ The loss of these officers occasioned profound gloom throughout New Jersey, and especially at Trenton, where the colonel was widely known and esteemed. Colonel Joseph W. Allen was born in Bristol, Pa., in 1811. He had been for many years a citizen of New Jersey, residing at Bordentown. Educated as a civil engineer, he had executed with signal ability many important works, including numerous railroad enterprises. He had been prominently identified with political affairs, and for six years had represented his county in the State Senate. From the firing upon Fort Sumter he gave all his thoughts and his time to the cause of the Union, at first in the position of Deputy Quartermaster-General, where his energies were devoted to the forwarding of troops. When asked if he could look at his family and still say, "Country first," he replied: "In these times every man must say, 'Country first,' and that for the sake of his family." An evidence of the attachment and respect of his comrades is furnished in the monument erected to his memory by the officers of his regiment two years after his death. Surgeon Weller was born at Paterson in 1817, and was a gentleman of great intelligence and private worth, and his death was widely mourned.— Condensed from "New Jersey and the Rebellion," by John Y. Foster.

fleet which we found at Hatteras Inlet on our arrival, drew more water than that, it was necessary to deepen the channel by some process. The current upon the swash was very swift, a circumstance which proved to be much in our favor. Large vessels were sent ahead, under full steam, on the bar when the tide was running out, and then anchors were carried out by boats in advance, so as to hold the vessels in position. The swift current would wash

GENERAL BURNSIDE'S HEADQUARTERS, ROANOKE ISLAND. FROM A WAR-TIME SKETCH.

the sand from under them and allow them to float, after which they were driven farther on by steam and anchored again, when the sand would again wash out from under them. This process was continued for days, until a broad channel of over eight feet was made, deep enough to allow the passage of the fleet into the sound. On the 26th, one of our largest steamers got safely over the swash and anchored in the sound, where some of the gun-boats had preceded them. By the 4th of February the entire fleet had anchored and had passed into the sound, and orders were given for the advance on Roanoke Island. Detailed instructions were given for the landing of the troops and the mode of attack.

At an early hour on the morning of the 5th the start was made. The naval vessels, under Commodore Goldsborough, were in advance and on the flanks. The sailing vessels containing troops were taken in tow by the steamers. There were in all sixty-five vessels. The fleet presented an imposing appearance as it started up the sound. The day was most beautiful, and the sail was enjoyed beyond measure by the soldiers, who had long been so penned up in the desolate inlet. At sundown, signal was given to come to anchor within ten miles of Roanoke Island. At 8 o'clock the next morning the signal to weigh anchor was given, but our progress was very much retarded by a gale that sprung up; so we anchored, but very little in advance of our position of the night before. During that night all lights were carefully concealed. The naval vessels were well out in advance to protect the transports from the inroads of the rebel gun-boats.

GENERAL BURNSIDE AT THE CONFEDERATE COTTON BATTERY ON THE WHARF, NEW BERNE.
FROM A WAR-TIME SKETCH.

On the morning of the 7th the gun-boats passed inside the narrow passage known as Roanoke Sound, and were soon abreast of the lower part of Roanoke Island. Soon after the naval fleet had passed through, the transport fleet began its passage. The rebel gun-boats were seen close inshore under the batteries of the island. At half-past 10 o'clock a signal gun was fired from one of the forts, announcing our approach. At half-past 11, one of the naval vessels opened fire, which was replied to by the rebels. Signals were given by the commodore of the fleet to begin the action. By noon the firing became rapid, and soon after, the engagement became general. The rebels had driven a line of piles across the main channel to obstruct the progress of our vessels, leaving a narrow space for themselves to retreat through; and as our naval vessels pressed them, they availed themselves of this means of safety. Our guns soon got the range of their batteries, and, by most extraordinary skill and rapidity of firing, almost silenced them. Just before noon I ordered a reconnoissance by a small boat, with the view of ascertaining a point of landing. A young negro, who had escaped from the island on our arrival at Hatteras Inlet, had given me most valuable information as to the nature of the shore of the island, from which I had determined that our point of landing should be at Ashby's Harbor, which was nearly midway up the shore. [See map, p. 641.]

At 1 o'clock, the quarters of the garrison in one of the forts were fired by one of our shells. The rebel gun-boats retired up the sound, but still continued a brisk fire as they were followed by our vessels. Orders were given for the troops to land at 3 o'clock. The ground in the rear of Ashby's Harbor was cleared by shells from the naval vessels, and our large surf-boats were lowered, rapidly filled with troops, and towed up in long lines by light-draught vessels until they came near to the shore of the harbor, when each of the surf-boats was cut loose and steered for the shore. There was no obstruction to their landing. In less than an hour 4000 troops were ashore, and before midnight the entire force was landed, with the exception of one regiment, which was landed on the morning of the 8th. The advance of our troops was ordered on this morning, General Foster being in the advance and center, General Reno on the left, and General Parke on the right. Just above Ashby's Harbor the island from shore to shore was marshy, swampy ground. A causeway had been built up the center of the island, and on this, about one mile and a half from the harbor, was a fort, which was flanked by what seemed to be impassable ground; but it did not prove to be so to our troops. General Foster pressed the rebels in front, General Reno passed around the left with his brigade, often waist-deep in the marsh, through almost impenetrable thickets, until he gained the right flank of the enemy's line. General Parke performed equally good service on the right, and after advantageous positions had been obtained, the work was carried by a simultaneous assault, and from that time there was no hindrance to the march of our troops to the head of the island and to the forts on the shore, where the entire garrison was captured. The naval fleet pursued the rebel gun-boats, nearly all of which, however, were destroyed by their crews, to prevent capture. The results of this important victory were great, particularly in inspiring the confidence of the country in the efficiency of its armies in the field.

The troops enjoyed their rest at Roanoke Island, but were not allowed to remain idle long. On the 26th of February, orders were given to make arrangements to embark for New Berne, and within four days they were all on board. On the 12th of March, the entire command was anchored off the mouth of Slocum's Creek, and about fourteen miles from New Berne. The approach to the city had been obstructed by piles and sunken vessels. About four miles from New Berne a large fort on the shore had been built, with a heavy armament, and a line of earth-works extended from the fort inland a distance of some two miles, where it ended in almost impassable ground.

On the night of the 12th, orders were given for landing, and on the morning of the 13th the troops were put ashore, in very much the same way that they had been at Roanoke. By 1 o'clock the debarkation was finished, and the troops were put in line of march. About this time the rain began to fall, and the road became almost impassable. No ammunition could be carried except what the men themselves could carry. No artillery could be taken except the small howitzers, which were hauled by the troops with drag-ropes. This was one of the most disagreeable and difficult marches that I witnessed during the war. We came in contact with the enemy's pickets just before dark, when it was decided to delay the attack until morning. That night a most dreary bivouac followed. Early the next morning, notwithstanding the fog, the disposition for the attack was made. General Foster was ordered to engage the enemy on the right, General Reno to pass around on the extreme left, and General Parke to occupy the center. We were much nearer to the enemy than we expected, and were soon in contact with them. General Foster rapidly closed with them, and met with severe resistance. He asked for reënforcements, but was told that every man had been ordered into action, and that there were no reserves. The contest was sharp, but brief. The 4th Rhode Island broke the enemy's line near where it crossed the railroad, after which the enemy wavered, and a general advance of our whole line placed us in possession of the works. The enemy fled to New Berne, burning the bridge behind them. Our troops rapidly pursued, but the fact that they had to cross the river in boats prevented them from capturing the main body of the enemy. As it was, large numbers of prisoners and munitions fell into our hands. In the meantime the naval vessels had worked their way up to the city and aided in the transportation of the troops across, and New Berne was occupied on the afternoon of the 14th.

COLONEL ZEBULON B. VANCE, GOVERNOR OF NORTH CAROLINA, 1862–5; AT THE BATTLE OF NEW BERNE, IN COMMAND OF THE 26TH NORTH CAROLINA REGIMENT. FROM A PHOTOGRAPH.

It still remained for us to reduce Fort Macon, Beaufort. To this work General Parke's brigade was ordered. The country between New Berne and Beaufort was immediately occupied, and a passage by hand-car was made between the two places, all the rolling-stock having been run off the road. By the morning of the 11th of April regular siege operations had been begun by General Parke and were pressed rapidly forward, and by the 26th of April the garrison at Beaufort had been forced to surrender.

Thus another victory was to be inscribed upon our banner. The Rhode Island troops bore a most honorable part in this conflict. After that, several small expeditions were sent into the interior of the country, all of which were successful.

Much to my sorrow, on the 3d of the following July I was ordered to go to the Peninsula to consult with General McClellan, and after that my duties as commanding officer in North Carolina ended; but a large proportion of the troops of the expedition served under me during the remainder of the war, as members of the gallant Ninth Corps.

The Burnside expedition has passed into history; its record we can be proud of. No body of troops ever had more difficulties to overcome in the same space of time. Its perils were both by land and water. Defeat never befell it. No gun was lost by it. Its experience was a succession of honorable victories.

THE OPPOSING FORCES AT ROANOKE ISLAND AND NEW BERNE, N. C.

The composition, losses, and strength of each army as here stated give the gist of all the data obtainable in the Official Records. K stands for killed; w for wounded; m w for mortally wounded; m for captured or missing; c for captured.

THE UNION FORCES.

ARMY.— Major-General Ambrose E. Burnside.
NAVY.—Flag-Officer L. M. Goldsborough.

TROOPS.—*First Brigade*, Brig.-Gen. John G. Foster: 10th Conn., Col. Charles L. Russell (k at Roanoke), Lieut.-Col. Albert W. Drake; 23d Mass., Col. John Kurtz; 24th Mass., Col. Thomas G. Stevenson; 25th Mass., Col. Edwin Upton; 27th Mass., Col. Horace C. Lee. Brigade loss: Roanoke, k, 19; w, 113 = 132. New Berne, k, 37; w, 145 = 182. *Second Brigade*, Brig.-Gen. Jesse L. Reno: 21st Mass., Lieut.-Col. Alberto C. Maggi (at Roanoke), Lieut.-Col. William S. Clark (at New Berne); 9th N. J., Lieut.-Col. Charles A. Heckman; 51st N. Y., Col. Edward Ferrero; 51st Pa., Col. John F. Hartranft. Brigade loss: Roanoke, k, 79; m, 13 = 107. New Berne, k, 30; w, 169 = 199. *Third Brigade*, Brig.-Gen. John G. Parke: 8th Conn., Col. Edward Harland; 11th Conn. (not at Roanoke), Lieut.-Col. Charles Mathewson; 9th N. Y. (not at New Berne), Col. Rush C. Hawkins; 4th R. I., Col. Isaac P. Rodman; 5th R. I. (1st Battalion), Maj. John Wright. Brigade loss: Roanoke, w, 17. New Berne, k, 21; w, 58 = 79. *Unassigned:* Detachment 1st N. Y. Marine Artillery, Col. William A. Howard; Co. B, 99th N. Y. (Union Coast Guard), Lieut. Charles W. Tillotson (c at New Berne). Unassigned loss: Roanoke Island, k, 2; w, 5 = 7. New Berne, k, 2; w, 8; m, 1 = 11.

DIVISION OF ARMED VESSELS, Capt. S. F. Hazard:

Picket, Capt. T. P. Ives; *Vidette*, Capt, John L. Foster; *Hussar*, Capt. Frederick Crocker; *Lancer*, Capt. M. B. Morley; *Ranger*, Capt. Samuel Emerson; *Chasseur*, Capt. John West; *Pioneer*, Capt. Charles E. Baker. [Only the *Picket* appears to have been used offensively in the attack on New Berne.]

NAVAL DIVISION, Commander S. C. Rowan:

Philadelphia (flag-steamer), Acting Master Com. Silas Reynolds; *Stars and Stripes*, Lieut.-Com. Reed Werden; *Louisiana*, Lieut.-Com. A. Murray; *Hetzel*, Lieut.-Com. H. K. Davenport; *Underwriter*, Lieut.-Com. William N. Jeffers (at Roanoke), Lieut.-Com. A. Hopkins (at New Berne); *Delaware*, Lieut.-Com. S. P. Quackenbush; *Commodore Perry*, Lieut.-Com. C. W. Flusser; *Valley City*, Lieut.-Com. J. C. Chaplin; *Commodore Barney*, Acting Lieut.-Com. R. T. Renshaw; *Hunchback*, Acting Vol. Lieut.-Com. E. R. Colhoun; *Southfield* (flag-steamer temporarily at Roanoke), Acting Vol. Lieut.-Com. C. F. W. Behm; *Morse*, Acting Master Com. Peter Hayes; *Whitehead* (at Roanoke), Acting Master Com. Charles A. French; *Lockwood*, Acting Master Com. G. W. Graves; *Brinker*, Acting Master Com. John E. Giddings; *Seymour* (at Roanoke), Acting Master Com. F. S. Wells; *Ceres* (at Roanoke), Acting Master Com. John McDiarmid; *Putnam* (at Roanoke), Acting Master Com. W. J. Hotchkiss; *Shawsheen* (at Roanoke), Acting Master Com. Thomas J. Woodward; *Granite* (at Roanoke), Acting Master's Mate Com. E. Boomer.

The batteries of the Union vessels at Roanoke Island and New Berne are as follows: *Philadelphia*, 2 twelve-pounders; *Stars and Stripes*, 4 eight-inch, 1 twenty-pounder rifle, 2 twelve-pounders; *Louisiana*, 1 eight-inch, 3 thirty-two-pounders, 1 twelve-pounder; *Hetzel*, 1 nine-inch, 1 eighty-pounder rifle; *Underwriter*, 1 eight-inch, 1 eighty-pounder rifle, 2 twelve-pounders; *Delaware*, 1 nine-inch, 1 thirty-two-pounder, 1 twelve-pounder; *Commodore Perry*, 1 one-hundred-pounder rifle, 4 nine-inch, 1 twelve-pounder; *Valley City*, 4 thirty-two-pounders, 1 twelve-pounder; *Commodore Barney*, 4 nine-inch, 1 thirty-two-pounder, 1 twelve-pounder; *Hunchback*, 3 nine-inch, 1 one-hundred-pounder rifle; *Southfield*, 3 nine-inch, 1 one-hundred-pounder rifle; *Morse*, 2 nine-inch; *Whitehead*, 1 nine-inch; *Lockwood*, 1 eighty-pounder rifle, 2 twelve-pounders; *Henry Brinker*, 1 thirty-two-pounder rifle; *Seymour*, 1 thirty-pounder rifle, 1 twelve-pounder; *Ceres*, 1 thirty-pounder rifle, 1 thirty-two-pounder; *Putnam*, 1 twenty-pounder rifle, 1 thirty-two-pounder; *Shawsheen*, 2 twenty-pounder rifles; *Granite*, 1 thirty-two-pounder.

The total Union loss at Roanoke Island was 37 killed, 214 wounded, and 13 missing = 264; and at New Berne 90 killed, 380 wounded, and 1 missing = 471. At the former place the navy lost (exclusive of details from the army) 3 killed and 11 wounded, and at the latter place 4 wounded.

THE CONFEDERATE FORCES.

ROANOKE ISLAND, Brig.-Gen. Henry A. Wise, Col. H. M. Shaw (c), second in command.

Troops: 2d N. C. Battalion, Lieut.-Col. Wharton J. Green; 8th N. C., Col. H. M. Shaw; 17th N. C. (3 co's), Maj. G. H. Hill; 31st N. C., Col. John V. Jordan; 46th Va., Maj. H. W. Fry; 59th Va., Lieut.-Col. Frank P. Anderson.

NAVAL FORCES, Flag-Officer William F. Lynch:

Sea-Bird (flag-steamer), Lieut.-Com. Patrick McCarrick; *Curlew*, Com. Thomas T. Hunter; *Ellis*, Lieut.-Com. J. W. Cooke; *Beaufort*, Lieut.-Com. W. H. Parker; *Raleigh*, Lieut.-Com. J. W. Alexander; *Fanny*, Midshipman Tayloe; *Forrest*, Lieut.-Com. James L. Hoole (w). The *Sea-Bird* was armed with 1 thirty-two-pounder smooth-bore and 1 thirty-pounder rifle. The other vessels carried each 1 thirty-two-pounder rifle.

The total loss of the Confederate army is reported at 23 killed, 58 wounded, 62 missing, and about 2500 captured. The loss of the navy was 6 wounded.

NEW BERNE, Brig.-Gen. L. O'B. Branch.

Troops: 7th N. C., Col. R. P. Campbell (commanded the right wing), Lieut.-Col. E. G. Haywood; 19th N. C. (cavalry), Col. S. B. Spruill; 26th N. C., Col. Zebulon B. Vance; 27th N. C., Maj. John A. Gilmer, Jr.; 28th N. C., Lieut.-Col. Thomas L. Lowe; 33d N. C., Col. Clark M. Avery (c), Lieut.-Col. R. F. Hoke; 35th N. C., Col. James Sinclair; 37th N. C., Col. Charles C. Lee (commanded the left wing), Lieut.-Col. William M. Barbour; Company N. C. Heavy Artillery, Captain C. C. Whitehurst; Special Battalion N. C. Militia, Col. H. J. B. Clark; N. C. Batteries, Capts. T. H. Brem and A. C. Latham.

The total Confederate loss was 64 killed, 101 wounded, 413 captured or missing = 578. Branch says of the missing, "About 200 are prisoners and the remainder at home."

There is no definite statement in the Official Records of the numbers engaged on either side, and the returns furnish no satisfactory basis for an estimate.

HOSPITAL.   FORT WALKER.   POPE'S HOUSE OLD HEADQUARTERS.
MONITOR "WEEHAWKEN."   NEW HEADQUARTERS AND STORES.

GENERAL VIEW OF HILTON HEAD IN 1863. FROM A PHOTOGRAPH.

DU PONT AND THE PORT ROYAL EXPEDITION.|

BY DANIEL AMMEN, REAR-ADMIRAL, U. S. N.

UNION POST-OFFICE, HILTON HEAD.
FROM A WAR-TIME SKETCH.

AFTER the inauguration of Mr. Lincoln as President of the United States, in March, 1861, a painful lethargy seemed to pervade every branch of the Administration, while the South was arming and organizing with extraordinary activity for the avowed purpose of destroying the Government, which apparently supinely awaited that event. The attack on Fort Sumter broke the spell, after which an almost frantic energy manifested itself at the North in raising troops and in the purchase and armament of vessels to blockade the thousands of miles of Southern coasts. Naturally, the Navy Department sought the advice of Professor Alexander D. Bache, Superintendent of the Coast Survey, and it was at his suggestion that the department secured a board of conference composed of Captain S. F. Du Pont, of the Navy, as President, and Major J. G. Barnard, U. S. Engineers, Professor Bache, and Commander Charles H. Davis, U. S. Navy, as members.

In a private letter Captain Du Pont wrote, on the 1st of June: "It may be that I shall be ordered to Washington on some temporary duty, on a board to arrange a programme of blockade—first suggested by Professor Bache." The first memoir of the conference in the confidential letter-book of the Navy Department is written in pencil, has many erasures and interlineations, and is evidently the original draft of a paper, probably referred and never returned. It closes as follows:

"Finally, we will repeat the remark made in the beginning of this report, that we think the expedition to Fernandina should be undertaken simultaneously with a similar expedition having a purely military character. We are preparing a brief report on the latter, which we shall have the honor to submit in a few days."

|Recently, the private correspondence of Admiral Du Pont has been kindly put within the scope of my researches, and his very clear and precise reports of the Port Royal expedition have been carefully examined, together with the reports of officers commanding vessels, the log-books of most of the ships engaged, and other documentary evidence. No labor has been spared in verifying the events narrated, notwithstanding that my presence throughout our operations, in command of the gun-boat *Seneca*, gave me an intelligent personal view of the whole subject.— D. A.

A carefully prepared memoir, evidently the third, dated July 16th, discusses the question of blockade of the coast from Cape Henry to Cape Romain in one section, and from thence to Cape Florida in another section. These were afterward the limits of the North and South Atlantic blockading squadrons. A fourth report, dated July 26th, in treating of the methods to be employed in carrying out the blockade, states:

"Our second memoir, in which we discussed the occupation of Bull's Bay, St. Helena Sound, and Port Royal Bay, has left us little to say on the first of those subsections. When the three anchorages above mentioned are secured, the whole of this part of our coast will be under complete control. But you are better aware than ourselves of the favorable manner in which our foreign political relations would be affected by the possession of one or more of the three points, the seizure of which was the topic of the second memoir.⚓ A preceding discussion would be incomplete, if we were not to repeat at the conclusion that an inland passage from Savannah to Fernandina, long used by steamboats drawing five feet of water, unites in one common interest and intercourse all the bays, sounds, rivers, and inlets of which we have given little more than the names. A superior naval force must command the whole of this division of the coast."

BREVET MAJOR-GENERAL THOMAS W. SHERMAN.
FROM A PHOTOGRAPH.

On July 25th, Captain Du Pont wrote:

"They have our memoirs, and, Mr. Fox tells me, are at them. We are to see the Secretary, Mr. Welles, to-night, at our request, to talk over our labors." . . . [July 26th.] "Last night our conference had a meeting with the Secretary of the Navy and Mr. Fox, when the subject of the expeditions was entered into. The Cabinet had our papers again." [July 28th.] "I sat up last night in the Navy Department until eleven, with Charles Davis, to prepare for this meeting, by condensing into notes the pith of our reports, and to read them to the board when called upon; but General Meigs seemed to desire that our full reports should be read, which I could not, of course, ask to be done, without seeming to attach too much importance to them. General Scott said at the conclusion, they were of singular ability, and he adopted every word of them; and General Totten told me there was not a criticism made. The meeting consisted of General Scott, General Totten, General Meigs, Colonel T. W. Sherman, Captain H. G. Wright, of the Engineers, and Colonel Cullum, aide-de-camp to the general."

Memoirs dated August 9th, September 2d and 3d, follow, giving a discussion of the blockade on the west coast of Florida, and to the border of Mexico.

A memoir dated September 12th discusses a proposition submitted from the department in relation to the taking of Fort Macon, which closes as follows:

"We beg leave to observe that here, and in all our previous reports and memoirs, we have confined ourselves to the treatment of cases, more or less special or general, connected with, and

⚓ As it referred to a purely military expedition, this memoir was probably referred to the War Department, since it is not in the confidential files of the Navy Department.— D. A.

tending to promote, the efficiency and activity of the blockade of the Southern shores. We have not entered upon the exclusive consideration of the great military expeditions alone; we have treated mixed expeditions compounded of military and naval operations, and requiring combined naval and military action."

In the above extracts we can note the inception of the Port Royal expedition, so ably executed and so important in its results, as well as the creation of a systematic plan of blockade, practically extending from Cape Hatteras to the Rio Grande. It seems just to the memory of the late Rear-Admiral Du Pont and his associates in the conference, all of whom have passed away, to present these important facts in a substantial and reliable form.

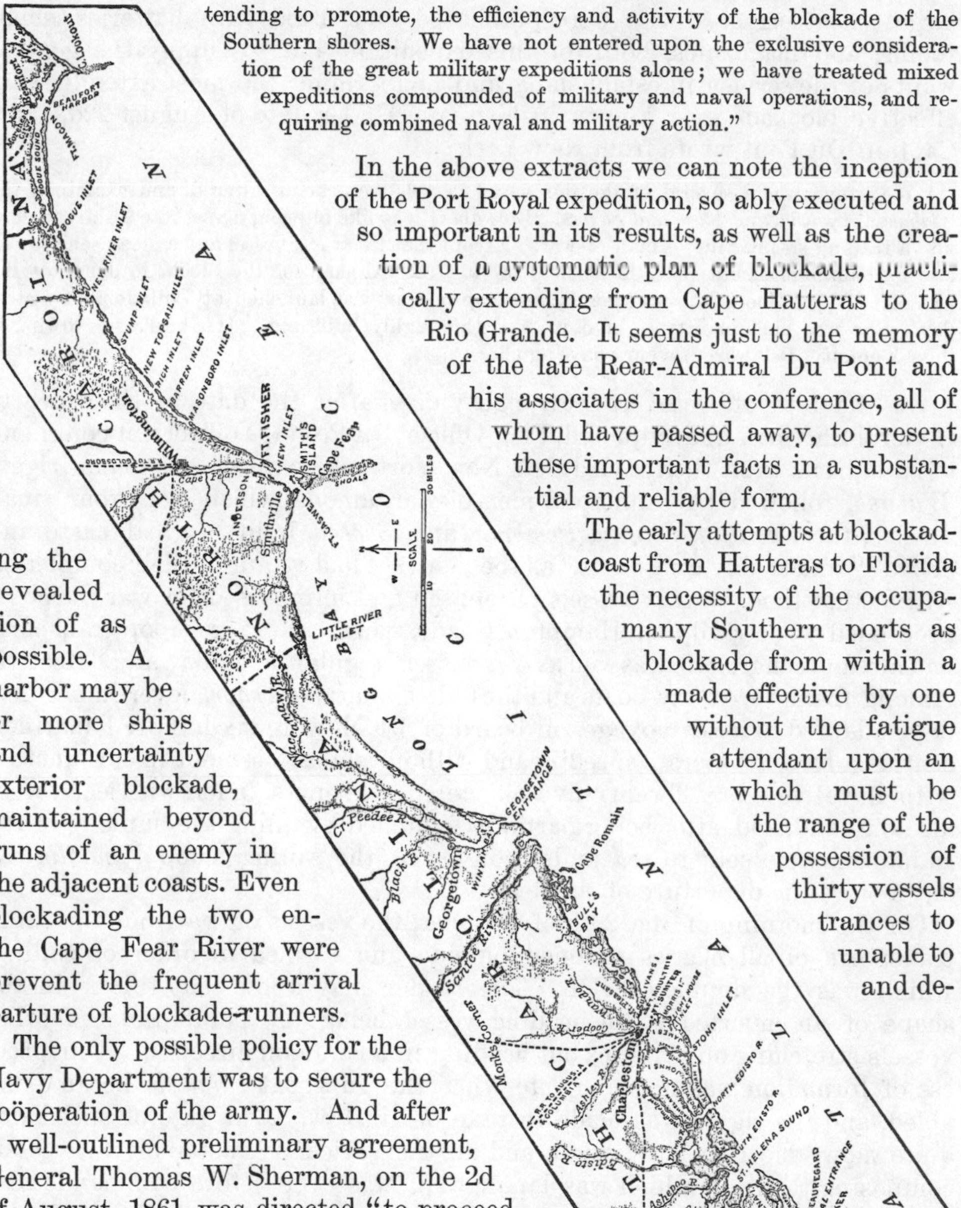

The early attempts at blockad-
coast from Hatteras to Florida
the necessity of the occupa-
many Southern ports as
blockade from within a
made effective by one
without the fatigue
attendant upon an
which must be
the range of the
possession of
thirty vessels
trances to
unable to
and de-

ing the
revealed
tion of as
possible. A
harbor may be
or more ships
and uncertainty
exterior blockade,
maintained beyond
guns of an enemy in
the adjacent coasts. Even
blockading the two en-
the Cape Fear River were
prevent the frequent arrival
parture of blockade-runners.

The only possible policy for the Navy Department was to secure the coöperation of the army. And after a well-outlined preliminary agreement, General Thomas W. Sherman, on the 2d of August, 1861, was directed "to proceed immediately to New York and organize, in connection with Captain Du Pont, of the navy, an expedition of twelve thousand men. Its destination," said his orders, "you and the naval commander will determine after you have sailed."

A dozen or more small gun-boats were then under construction in the Northern States on contract, and vessels of every size, from a canal steamboat to the largest coasting steamers, were purchased and fitted with batteries, shell-rooms, and magazines, both for this expedition and to supply the general wants of the service in establishing and maintaining the most extended and effective blockade ever known in history. Under date of August 22d, 1861, Captain Du Pont wrote from New York:

"We drove where several of the purchased vessels were being altered, and examined the *Alabama, Augusta,* and *Stars and Stripes.* But, alas! it is like altering a vest into a shirt to convert a trading steamer into a man-of-war. Except that there is a vessel and a steam-engine, all else is inadaptable; but there is no help for it—the exigency of the blockade demands it." [August 23d.] "The *Tuscarora* (new steam sloop-of-war) was launched at Philadelphia yesterday. She was built in fifty-eight days, and thoroughly built too. Her keel was growing in Sussex county, Delaware, seventy days ago."

On the 19th of October, 1861, eighty days after the date of the order to General Sherman above quoted, Flag-Officer Du Pont (as officers in command of squadrons were then styled) left New York on board of the steam-frigate *Wabash,* followed by numerous men-of-war, among which were four small vessels, the *Unadilla, Ottawa, Pembina,* and *Seneca,* built in great haste and called "ninety-day gun-boats," as the contract had required their completion within that time. Other vessels purchased and improvised for war purposes proceeded when ready to Hampton Roads, where the large troop transports had already congregated, as well as war vessels, regular, irregular, and defective. Among them were ferry-boats and the old steamer *Governor,* never in her best days adapted to a sea voyage, on board of which were six hundred marines, sent as a force to operate speedily and without embarrassment in conjunction with naval vessels. Twenty-five chartered schooners, laden with coal, were also on hand, and, after being partially lightened by filling the bunkers of the squadron, were sent to sea under convoy of the sailing sloop *Vandalia* the day before the departure of the fleet.

On the morning of the 29th of October, the vessels of war and the army transports of all classes steamed outside and formed in order of sailing, which was the double échelon. The reader may know that this is in the shape of an inverted V, the leading vessel being the point, and the other vessels stretching out in lines but heading in a common direction. Our process of formation was not complete when the gun-boat *Unadilla* became disabled, and the signal was made to take her in tow. Our rate of speed was quite slow, due to a head-wind, and to the varied character of the vessels composing the fleet, which was larger than was ever before commanded by an American officer. Cape Hatteras, little more than a hundred miles from Cape Henry, was not reached until 1 o'clock on the morning of the 31st, when two of the heavier transports struck slightly on the shoals, which caused all of us to make for the south-east; and soon after, when south of the cape, we bore away. The wind had hauled more to the eastward before we reached Hatteras, and that, with a rough sea, had caused considerable indraught; and the drift from the action of the wind on the large hulls, added to our low speed, had set us considerably to leeward.

Hatteras is known to navigators as being subject to great and sudden changes in the weather: there are few nights in the year when lightning cannot be seen from the top of the light-house, usually to seaward, over the Gulf Stream, which here approaches nearer to the coast than at any other point. An ocean depth of 2000 fathoms or more stretches almost in a direct line from the low sand islands east of Nassau to within a distance of 12 miles of the cape; from the shore the water deepens very rapidly to 100 fathoms, and then falls abruptly to a depth of 2500 fathoms. This great depth, so near the land, and the Gulf Stream sweeping even nearer, are the probable causes of the sudden and violent changes of the weather there prevailing, which were discussed in one of the memoirs of the conference.

REAR-ADMIRAL SAMUEL F. DU PONT. FROM A PHOTOGRAPH.

On rounding the cape, the wind gradually rose, the sea became heavy, a dull leaden sky shut out the light, and not long after midday there were assurances of a south-east gale. About 2:30 P. M. the weather was so rough that signal was made from the flag-ship to commanders of vessels to disregard the order of sailing and take care of their individual commands.

In order to make the best of our way, and the better to avoid collisions with other vessels of the fleet, the *Seneca* was kept on the port tack, and "hove to," barely turning the engines, the vessel being under close-reefed fore and main sails. Had she been square-rigged, the other tack would have been necessary to her safety. In the drifting mists and rain, it soon grew dark. The greater part of that night I stood under the lee of the weather bulwark, near the wheel, casting glances to windward, to be in readiness to bear away should a vessel be seen coming down upon us. It was a long, weary, and anxious night. On peering to windward, the rain-drops pelted the face like sleet, and the phosphorescent spray broke over us in superlative grandeur. At 3 o'clock I observed what had been an object of watchfulness— an arch rising in the west, precursor of a sudden change of wind. The mainsail was lowered, and when the squall struck us the foresheet was shifted over. At 9 or 10 A. M. the gale had abated greatly, and the flag-ship was well under our lee; we then wore ship and were soon in her wake. Later in the day several other vessels fell into line.

We will now note the actual losses from the gale, that became known to us some days later. The *Isaac Smith* was disabled and her commander forced

UNION GUN-BOAT "SENECA," CAPTAIN DANIEL AMMEN'S VESSEL AT PORT ROYAL. FROM A WAR-TIME SKETCH.

to throw his battery overboard, with the exception of one 30-pounder rifle, to enable him to go to the assistance of the *Governor*, which foundered at sea. The *Young Rover*, fortunately coming up, was able to signal to the sailing frigate *Sabine* in the distance, and, after most strenuous exertions, the marine battalion and crew of the *Governor*, with the exception of seven who were lost, were transferred to the *Sabine*. Of the army transports, the *Peerless*, laden with stores, went down, the crew being rescued by the *Mohican*. The steamers *Belvidere*, *Union*, and *Osceola*, having army stores on board, but no troops, either sank or never reached their destination. The large army transport *Winfield Scott* was so disabled that she never left Port Royal harbor after entering.

The morning of November 3d was a bright Sunday, with a moderate breeze and a smooth sea. Several others of the small steamers with the *Seneca* were following in the wake of the flag-ship. In obedience to signal, I went on board that vessel, and received orders to be delivered to Captain Lardner of the *Susquehanna*, the senior officer blockading Charleston, distant about thirty miles. These directed certain vessels to rendezvous off Port Royal entrance, but not to leave the line of blockade until after nightfall. No sooner was the *Seneca* fairly in sight of Sumter than the signal guns were fired, to announce the arrival of the *avant-courier* of the fleet that they knew was intended for the attack of Port Royal. After passing Bull's Bay, I had the belief that we were bound for Port Royal, but no actual knowledge of the fact until going on board of the *Wabash*, as my orders were marked "Confidential — not to be opened unless separated from the flag-ship." At the very time we were weathering the gale, the following telegram was sent:

"Richmond, Nov. 1, '61. Gov. Pickens, Columbia, S. C. I have just received information, which I consider entirely reliable, that the enemy's expedition is intended for Port Royal. J. P. Benjamin, Acting Secretary of War."

The same telegram was sent to Generals Drayton and Ripley, commanding respectively at Port Royal and Charleston.

It was a charming mild afternoon when I stepped on the deck of the *Susquehanna*. Captain Lardner was delighted with his orders, and, after giving him such information as would be of interest, I obtained permission to go up to the entrance to the swash channel, which was well known to me previously, when sounding out the bar on Coast Survey duty. After the sun went down, all the vessels designated left the line of blockade, proceeding, like ourselves, to the entrance of Port Royal harbor, some sixty miles away. Following the seven-fathom curve, the *Seneca* rounded the shoal lying east of the main channel, known as "Martin's Industry," at early daylight, and soon after found a small black barrel-buoy, which, we rightly conjectured, had been put there by the enemy. An hour after sunrise, aided by the refraction, the tops of the pine-trees on both sides of the head-lands were plainly in sight, although twelve miles off. At that hour the flag-ship *Wabash* was at anchor with several other vessels about two miles distant, and the eastern horizon was flecked with approaching vessels. We steamed out to the flag-ship at a later hour, reported the finding of the barrel-buoy, and were informed that the entrance would soon be sounded out. About noon, Captain C. A. Boutelle, in the Coast Survey steamer *Vixen*, with the gun-boats *Pawnee, Ottawa, Pembina, Curlew,* and *Seneca,* crossed the bar and went far enough in to have a good view of the faces and embrasures of the earth-works that we were soon to engage, the one on Hilton Head known as Fort Walker and the other on Bay Point as Fort Beauregard.☆

SLOOP OF WAR "VANDALIA," REAR SHIP OF THE LINE AT PORT ROYAL.
FROM A WAR-TIME SKETCH.

After the surveying steamer had planted some buoys, to serve as general guides, the four gun-boats last named anchored in the channel some distance apart, as additional guides, the one farthest in being some three miles from Fort Beauregard, the *Vixen* and the *Pawnee* going out to pilot the vessels across the bar. This was done without delay; all of them that came in had no more than eighteen feet draught. They anchored a mile or so outside of the gun-boats, and from the shoal ground to seaward.

Near sunset three steamers came outside of the headlands and fired at our gun-boats at long range. The steamers were under the command of Josiah Tattnall, a commodore in the Confederate service, who had been a distinguished officer of our navy, and had resigned some time before, on the secession of Georgia, of which State he was a citizen. His vessels were river boats; as men-of-war they were in every respect of the most vulnerable class. The four advanced gun-boats of our squadron got under way, pivoted their heavy shell-guns over the starboard bow, and headed to the westward so as to bring

☆ On Nov. 15th, 1861, General T. W. Sherman changed the name of Fort Walker to Fort Welles (after Secretary Welles), and of Fort Beauregard to Fort Seward (after the Secretary of State).

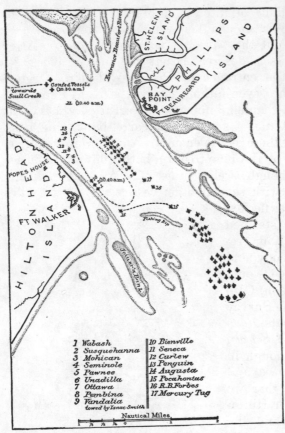

1 Wabash
2 Susquehanna
3 Mohican
4 Seminole
5 Pawnee
6 Unadilla
7 Ottawa
8 Pembina
9 Vandalia
  towed by Isaac Smith

10 Bienville
11 Seneca
12 Curlew
13 Penguin
14 Augusta
15 Pocahontas
16 R.B.Forbes
17 Mercury Tug

Nautical Miles

MAP OF THE NAVAL ATTACK AT HILTON HEAD, NOV. 7, 1861.

their guns to bear. This course with that of the enemy would soon have brought Tattnall's steamers in unpleasant proximity, and in consequence they turned abruptly, passed between the headlands, and disappeared in the distance.

Soon after sunrise the next day, three steamers commanded by Tattnall made their appearance in like manner. It so happened that General H. G. Wright, of the army, and Captain John Rodgers, of the navy, had gone on board of the *Ottawa*, under the instructions of their commanding officers, to make a reconnoissance of the forts, and had brought within supporting distance the *Pawnee*, carrying a heavy battery, and the *Isaac Smith*, carrying one 30-pounder rifle. They were approaching when Tattnall was pretty well out, and had opened fire on the smaller gun-boats. Signal was made to the *Seneca*, *Pembina*, and *Curlew* to follow the movements of the *Ottawa*, and we went in, following Tattnall's steamers, then in retreat, and firing on them, until we were nearly on an air-line between the two earth-works before named. They opened fire on us, at rather too long a range for effective work, with smooth-bore guns; several rifles were also used by the forts, as well as by the Confederate vessels. One of our shells blew up a caisson in Fort Beauregard, and we soon became fairly informed of the number of the enemy's guns bearing on the entrance, and in a measure as to their caliber. On signal, we went out of action and anchored, without having received any material damage; the rigging of all of the vessels was cut more or less. After seven bells, "when the sun is over the foreyard," Tattnall's flag-ship *Savannah*, accompanied by a steamer, came out on the flats, or shoaler waters, to the westward of the channel. They flew about somewhat wildly, had considerable headway, and threw a rifle-shell occasionally, firing "promiscuously," but mostly at the nearest vessel, which was the *Seneca*. Her executive officer was directed to call the eleven-inch pivot gun's crew to quarters and fire a shell at ricochet, the distance supposed to be about 2500 yards. The gun was at once reported ready, and the request made to fire at an elevation. Appreciating the fact that one rarely does well when not doing what he thinks best, I took the matter personally in hand, had the gun leveled and trained as desired, and pulled the lanyard. The huge shell skipped along the surface of a glassy sea, and, as reported from aloft, struck the vessel abaft the starboard wheel-house. In a moment the head of the flag-ship was turned for the harbor, and she lost no time in entering, followed by her consort. It was soon afterward known that the captain of the vessel had availed himself of the temporary absence of Tattnall, and had sallied out to have a little diversion, which would have proved serious had the shell exploded that lodged in the hog-braces.

About the time of this occurrence, the flag-ship *Wabash* crossed the bar, followed by all of the heavy vessels, including the transports, and anchored some two miles outside of Fishing Rip Shoal, some five miles from the forts, the bar being about twelve miles outside of the headlands. Very soon after the flag-ship anchored, signal was made for officers commanding

UNION GUN-BOAT "MOHAWK," THE GUARD-SHIP AT PORT ROYAL. FROM A WAR-TIME SKETCH.

vessels to come aboard. On their arrival, those who commanded vessels detailed for the main line were invited into the cabin, and instructions were given as to position and plan of battle; and afterward those commanding vessels in the flanking line received their instructions, which differed as to the duties to be performed after passing within and beyond the earth-works. It was the intention of the flag-officer at that time to go at once into action, although the hour would of necessity be late.

The main line was to be on the west or Hilton Head side, in line ahead, and the vessels one ship's-length apart. The report of the flag-officer states: "The order of battle comprised a main squadron ranged in line ahead, and a flanking squadron, which was to be thrown off on the northern section of the harbor to engage the enemy's flotilla, and prevent their raking the rear ships of the line when it turned to the southward, or cutting off a disabled vessel."

The leading ship of the main squadron was the frigate *Wabash*, Commander C. R. P. Rodgers, followed by the frigate *Susquehanna*, Captain J. L. Lardner; sloop *Mohican*, Commander S. W. Godon; sloop *Seminole*, Commander J. P. Gillis; sloop *Pawnee*, Lieutenant Commanding R. H. Wyman; gun-boat *Unadilla*, Lieutenant Commanding N. Collins; gun-boat *Ottawa*, Lieutenant Commanding T. H. Stevens; gun-boat *Pembina*, Lieutenant Commanding J. P. Bankhead; and the sailing sloop *Vandalia*, Commander F. S. Haggerty, towed by the *Isaac Smith*, Lieutenant Commanding J. W. A. Nicholson. The

HILTON HEAD, FORT WALKER. ATTACK OF THE UNION FLEET, THE "WABASH" LEADING. FROM A WAR-TIME SKETCH. FORT BEAUREGARD, BAY POINT.

flanking squadron was led by the gun-boat *Bienville*, Commander Charles Steedman, followed by the *Seneca*, Lieutenant Commanding Daniel Ammen; gun-boat *Curlew*, Lieutenant Commanding P. G. Watmough; gun-boat *Penguin*, Lieutenant Commanding T. A. Budd; and the gun-boat *Augusta*, Commander E. G. Parrott.

The plan of attack was to pass up midway between Forts Walker and Beauregard, receiving and returning the fire of both, to about two and one-half miles north of the forts, then to turn toward and close in with Fort Walker, encountering it on its weakest flank, and at the same time enfilading its two water faces. While standing to the southward the vessels would be head to tide, with just enough headway to preserve the order of battle in passing the batteries in slow succession, and to avoid becoming a fixed mark for the enemy's fire. On reaching the extremity of Hilton Head and the shoal ground making off from it, the line was to turn to the north by the east, and, passing northward, to engage Fort Walker with the port battery, but nearer than on entering. These evolutions were to be repeated. A plan of battle was sent to the Navy Department. The "New York

Herald" of November 20th, 1861, contains a diagram in accord with the above statement, and was probably taken from the official one. There was another point in the instructions given by the flag-officer to officers commanding vessels in the flanking line that is not mentioned in his report. He said in substance, if not in words, that, in passing in, the flanking line was to deliver its fire against the fort on Bay Point, and then to guard the fleet of transports within the bar from any attempts of Tattnall; that he knew him well; that he had cour-

age and power to plan, and in the heat of action might try to run out to destroy the transports which it was the special duty of the flanking squadron to protect; and that when Tattnall was disposed of, the vessels would take an enfilading position somewhere to the northward of the Hilton Head fort.

TEN-INCH SHELL GUN WHICH THREW THE OPENING SHOT FROM THE FLAG-SHIP "WABASH." FROM A WAR-TIME SKETCH.

After receiving our instructions, the officers commanding vessels returned without delay to their commands, and made preparations for immediate movement. Soon after, the flag-ship made signal and got under way, as did all of the men-of-war. The *Wabash* stood in toward the forts, and got aground. "In our anxiety to get the outline of the forts before dark," the flag-officer reported, "we stood in too near to Fishing Rip Shoal, and the vessel grounded. By the time she was gotten off it was too late, in my judgment, to proceed, and I made signal for the squadron to anchor out of gunshot of the enemy." The shoal where the *Wabash* grounded was a little short of three miles from the forts. The vessels anchored in convenient positions for the formation of the lines when signaled, and were sufficiently inside of the transports to be unembarrassed by them in forming.

The following day [November 7th] we had a heavy westerly wind. The report of General Thomas F. Drayton, the Confederate commander, states: "On the 6th, the fleet and transports, which had increased to about forty-five sail, would probably have attacked us had not the weather been very boisterous." This conjecture was quite right. The flag-officer was impatiently awaiting the abatement of the wind, and about noon was almost on the point of going in, but wisely deferred the attack until we could make it without disadvantage. Drayton's picturesque report of the engagement continues: "At last the memorable 7th dawned upon us, bright and serene; not a ripple upon the broad expanse of water to disturb the accuracy of fire from the broad decks of that magnificent armada about advancing, in battle array, to vomit forth its iron hail, with all the spiteful energy of long-suppressed rage and conscious strength."

LUNETTE BATTERY.   LUNETTE BATTERY.   FORT BEAUREGARD.

BAY POINT AND FORT BEAUREGARD, AFTER CAPTURE. FROM A WAR-TIME SKETCH.

On the 7th, as soon as the morning light permitted, signals were made indicating that we would soon move. The flag-ship was then at anchor near where she had grounded, nearly three miles from the forts. In consequence of a hawser fouling her propeller, some delay occurred in forming after the vessels were under way, and it was 9 o'clock when signal was made for close order. Tattnall's flotilla at that time was nearly in line between the forts.⹋ As we advanced, at 9:26, the forts, as well as the enemy's vessels, lying right ahead, opened fire on the foremost ships. Soon after, the flag-ship yawed sufficiently to bring a heavy pivot gun on her bow to bear on Tattnall's command, which forced him to retreat, as his vessels would soon have been within reach of our broadside guns. At that time our rate of speed was about six miles, and we were soon making good use of our batteries; the enemy on both sides of the bay had the full benefit of all the shells that both lines could send with precision. So great was the cannons' roar that it was distinctly heard at Fernandina, seventy miles away. There was deafening music in the air, which came from far and near and all around; heavy clouds of dust and smoke, due to our bursting shells and the enemy's fire, partly obscured the earth-works, while our vessels were but dimly seen through the smoke from their own guns which hung over the water. The log-book of the flag-ship states: "At 9:45 the *Bienville* ranged alongside our star-board beam." This was eighteen minutes after the enemy had opened fire on the fleet, and eight minutes before the flag-ship ceased firing and turned toward Hilton Head to repass the fort in heading toward the sea. This was the oppor-tunity for the *Bienville* to open wide her throttles: with her great speed, pos-sibly she might have run down Tattnall's vessels before they could have been pointed fairly and reached the entrance to Scull Creek. The log-book of the *Bienville* states: "At 10:30 the flag-ship winded the line, turning to the southward, when we engaged for a few minutes three steamers that were within long range up the river. We soon put them to flight, and then followed the line in the order of battle, down within close range of the large battery

⹋ A friend of many years, who was in command of one of Tattnall's vessels, writes as follows: "There is one touching incident that I think deserves rec-ord. When the old hero Tattnall got in good range of Du Pont's flag-ship, and was about to receive his fire, he said to the signal quartermaster : 'Dip my broad pennant to my old messmate,' and it was dipped thrice. In the confusion it was not noticed by Du Pont, which I am sure he would have regretted had he known it."—D. A.

on Hilton Head. . . ." The same authority establishes the fact that the *Bienville* thereafter, during the engagement, followed in the main line. ⎰

The report of the *Seneca* states:

"On the morning of the 7th we took position assigned us in the line, and, passing up, delivered our fire at Bay Point, and on arriving out of the fire of the enemy's batteries, made chase, as directed by instructions, on the rebel steamers. They, being river boats, soon left us."

The log-book of the same vessel states that when she turned to join in the attack on Hilton Head, Tattnall's steamers turned also and came toward the fleet, only retreating when she again steamed toward them, so as to make an engagement unavoidable should they advance farther. They then entered the intricate channel to Scull Creek and disappeared behind a wooded point, after which the *Seneca*, with other vessels of the flanking line, took up an enfilading position to the northward of Fort Walker, as previously instructed. Several vessels of the main line were also delivering an enfilading fire, among others the *Mohican*, properly next in the main line to the *Susquehanna*. Godon, who commanded her, was very excitable, and it may be on seeing a strange vessel ahead in his line, imagined that the well-planned attack had been transformed into a "free fight," and the best he could do was to serve his battery well from the most effective point he could take up.

As an exhibition of physical force, allied to human action,

RIFLE-GUN AT FORT BEAUREGARD. FROM A WAR-TIME SKETCH.

⎰ Rear-Admiral Steedman sends to the editors the following explanation of the movements of his vessel: "The *Bienville* was the leading ship in the flanking or starboard column. After the fleet had passed into Port Royal Sound, and as the *Wabash* was turning to pass out, Tattnall's gun-boats were seen approaching from the mouth of Scull Creek. The *Bienville* was at once pointed in that direction, and opened fire from the 30-pounder Parrott on the forecastle. The gun-boats replied with an ineffectual fire at long range. None of the shots reached her. A brisk fire was kept up from the Parrott gun, and as the shells began to fall among the gun-boats they turned and stood up toward Scull Creek. Here the *Bienville* could not safely follow them, as she drew over sixteen feet and had neither chart nor pilot for the channel; while Tattnall's river steamers, with their light draught and the familiarity of the officers with the waters, could retreat to a position where the *Bienville*, in following them, would almost certainly have taken the ground. Moreover, the *Bienville* was within hail of the flag-ship, and a word from the flag-officer would have sent her up Broad River had he desired her to assume the risk. After the second turn within the forts, the *Wabash* was proceeding slowly down, followed by the *Susquehanna*, when the *Mohican* and the vessels astern of her left the line and took up a position above Fort Walker. The position enabled these ships to enfilade the works; but the movement was a departure from the order of battle, and it continued, notwithstanding signals to close up from the flag-ship. The *Bienville* took her position astern of the *Susquehanna*, and these two were the only vessels that followed the *Wabash* on her third circuit; or, to speak more precisely, on her second passage out and her third passage in, under the fire of the forts.

"CHARLES STEEDMAN,
"Rear-Admiral, Retired."

FORT WALKER.   "WABASH."   FORT BEAUREGARD.   "PAWNEE."

1.—BATTLE OF THE UNION FLEET WITH FORTS WALKER AND BEAUREGARD. 2.—HOISTING THE STARS
AND STRIPES OVER FORT WALKER. FROM WAR-TIME SKETCHES.

I can conceive nothing more grand than a view of the main deck of the
Wabash on this occasion. The hatches being battened down, a faint light
only came through the ports, as did the flashes from the discharged guns,
which recoiled violently with a heavy thud. As far as the smoke would

permit, hundreds of men were visible in very rapid motion, loading and running out the guns with the greatest energy. Such a view, accompanied by the noise of battle, is weird and impressive to the highest degree.

The vessels in the main line slowly passed toward the sea, throwing their shells into the earth-work with the utmost precision, and this destruction was supplemented by the fire of ten of the vessels from an enfilading position. As the main line headed seaward, the enemy may have had an idea that his fire was so destructive that the vessels were retreating, and Tattnall, with his three weak vessels, was then disposed to swoop down and pick up "lame ducks"; but, being confronted by one small gun-boat, he thought it best to enter Scull Creek, where at least he would be available for carrying off the Southern troops, if they were defeated. Though Tattnall was a brave and skillful seaman, the law of force was inexorable; and when an officer is a free agent, looking only to the success of his cause, he should not lead his command into destruction without being able to secure a commensurate advantage.

Arriving at the shoal ground off Hilton Head, the flag-ship and her followers turned again within the harbor, and in passing northward availed themselves of the occasion to give Fort Beauregard the benefit of their broadsides. Meantime the enfilading vessels had been steadily throwing their shells into Fort Walker. In relation to this hour [about 10 A. M.], General Drayton states:

"Besides this moving battery, the fort was enfiladed by two gun-boats anchored to the north, off the mouth of Fish Hall Creek, and another at a point on the edge of the shoals to the south. This enfilading fire, on so still a sea, annoyed and damaged us excessively, particularly as we had no gun on either flank of the bastion to reply with."

The vessel near the shoal, to the south, was probably the *Pocahontas*, commanded by Percival Drayton, brother of the general in command of the Confederate forces; she only crossed the bar about noon, having been delayed by deranged machinery.

The main line passed nearer Fort Walker than on entering, and delivered its fire "with all the spiteful energy of long-suppressed rage and conscious strength." Arriving at the turning-point, signal was again made to its vessels to take position, when the *Wabash* led once more, and to within six hundred yards of the fort. The nearness of the ships was the probable cause of their suffering so little damage, the enemy's shots passing over the hulls. The flag-ship was naturally the most conspicuous target, but the shots received by her were high up, the enemy presumably delivering his fire for a distance of a thousand yards or more. At this time a shell was seen to pass between the flag-officer and the captain of the vessel, who were standing on the "bridge" extending across the vessel, just forward of the mainmast.

The flag-officer expressed officially his great admiration of the firing of the batteries of the *Wabash* and of the *Susquehanna*, which was next in line. In a private letter, written just after the engagement, he said of the former:

"In our first attack I was not satisfied with the execution of this ship, though the effect turned out to be much greater than I thought, but in the second attack I can remember nothing in naval history that came up to this ship in the terrific repetitions of her broadsides, and, to use the illustration of the reporter of the 'London News,' 'the rising of the dust on shore in perpendicular columns looked as if we had suddenly raised from the dust a grove of poplars.'"

At 1:15 the *Ottawa* signaled that the enemy was leaving the fort, and fifteen minutes later the same signal was made by the *Pembina*. At this time the flag-ship and her followers had returned from their tour, and were again ready to swoop down and deliver other broadsides. Two pivot guns fired from the flag-ship received no response, and signal was made to cease firing. Captain John Rodgers, who was serving as aide to the flag-officer, was sent on shore with a flag of truce. On landing he found no garrison, and

BRIG.-GEN. THOMAS F. DRAYTON, C. S. A., COMMANDER OF THE CONFEDERATE FORCES AT PORT ROYAL. FROM A PHOTOGRAPH.

at 2:20 P. M. hoisted the Union flag over the fort. When that honored emblem appeared, the rigging was manned in an instant on board the flag-ship and on all of the vessels of war at anchor; three cheers were wafted over the waters, so loud that they startled the defenders of Fort Beauregard. \ Commander C. R. P. Rodgers, with the marines of the flag-ship and a division of small-arm men, landed and threw out pickets. The transports at once steamed in. Soon after sunset the fort was delivered by the naval force to General H. G. Wright, who now held watch and ward as far as the pine-trees some hundreds of yards distant.

Soon after the hoisting of our flag, a vessel was directed to make a reconnoissance of Bay Point, but at nightfall, as nothing had been heard from her, the *Seneca* was sent to ascertain the situation. When we arrived in front of Fort Beauregard, it was so dark that the bow of the vessel was run up on the low beach. There, outlined on the horizon, was the earth-work lying in grim repose, the embrasures being plainly visible. The silence was unbroken; the work had evidently been abandoned. The flood-tide was setting in strongly. The crew of one hundred men were sent as far aft as possible and the engines backed. We at once slid off, and the flag-officer was fully informed as soon as we could steam over. Orders were then given to return to Bay Point at early daylight to reconnoiter, and, if we were not met by force, to hoist our flag at sunrise. This was duly executed, and at noon the fort was turned over to General Isaac I. Ste-

\ Captain Stephen Elliott, Jr., who was at Fort Beauregard, reported: "Colonel Dunovant [who commanded the forces] entered the fort, and said to me: 'Captain Elliott, what is the condition of things over the river?' I replied, 'Fort Walker has been silenced, sir.'—'By what do you judge?' 'By the facts that the fort has been subjected to a heavy enfilade and direct fire, to which it has ceased to reply; that the vessels having terminated their fire, the flag-ship has steamed up and delivered a single shot, which was unanswered, and that thereupon cheering was heard from the fleet.'—'Then, sir, it having been proved that these works cannot accomplish the end for which they were designed (that of protecting the harbor) you will prepare to retire from a position from which our retreat may readily be cut off, and which our small force will not enable us to hold against a land attack.'"

vens, of the army. The flag-staff was on the gable of a small frame-house fifty yards from the fort. I went within, saw some books lying on a table, and went out and toward some tents in the distance. In a few minutes an explosion was heard, and, on turning, I saw a cloud of smoke where the house had stood. A quantity of powder had been put under it, arranged so as to ignite from a friction-tube, and a sailor, in passing along outside, had struck his foot against a small wire attached to the tube, thus causing the explosion. He was knocked over, and partially stunned, but soon revived. It may be said that it is natural in warfare to harm your enemy as much as possible, but it strikes the man who has escaped being blown up that such devices are essentially mean.

The armament found on Fort Walker was as follows: on the right angle of the sea-face, a 6-inch rifled-gun, six 32-pounders (three dismounted and with carriages ruined and another with the cascabel knocked off), one 10-inch and one 8-inch Columbiad, three sea-coast 7-inch howitzers; on the left angle of the sea-front, a 6-inch rifle; on the left wing, one 32-pounder and one sea-coast howitzer; on the outer work, in rear, two 32-pounders, one 8-inch heavy howitzer, and two English siege 12-pounders; on the right wing, three 32-pounders,— total, 23 guns. Twenty guns were found in Fort Beauregard, one of which was a 6-inch rifle, burst, and the carriage entirely destroyed. The heaviest guns were a 10-inch and an 8-inch Columbiad; the other guns mostly 32-pounders. ☆ The armaments of the attacking vessels, and the losses on both sides, will be found on page 691.

In his report General T. W. Sherman states:

"The beautifully constructed work on Hilton Head was severely crippled and many of the guns dismounted. Much slaughter had evidently been made there, many bodies having been buried in the fort, and some twenty or thirty were found some half-mile distant. . . . The number of pieces of ordnance that have fallen into our hands is fifty-two, the bulk of which is of the largest caliber, all with fine carriages, etc., except eight or nine, that were ruined by our fire, which dismounted their pieces."

On the afternoon of the 8th General Sherman made a reconnoissance, on

CAPTAIN PERCIVAL DRAYTON, COMMANDER OF THE U. S. STEAMER "POCAHONTAS" AT PORT ROYAL— BROTHER OF THE COMMANDER OF THE CONFEDERATE FORCES. FROM A PHOTOGRAPH.

☆ General Drayton thus describes the resistance made to the attack of the Union fleet, referring at the outset to the first shot from Fort Walker:

"The shell from the Dahlgren exploded near the muzzle, and was harmless. Other shots followed from both forts, and soon the fire became general on land and water. In spite of our fire, directed with deliberation and coolness, the fleet soon passed both batteries apparently unharmed, and, then returning, delivered in their changing rounds a terrific shower of shot and shell in flank and front. Besides this moving battery, the fort was enfiladed by two gun-boats anchored to the north, off the mouth of Fish Hall Creek, and another at a point on the edge of the shoals to the south. This enfilading fire, on so still a sea, annoyed and damaged us excessively,

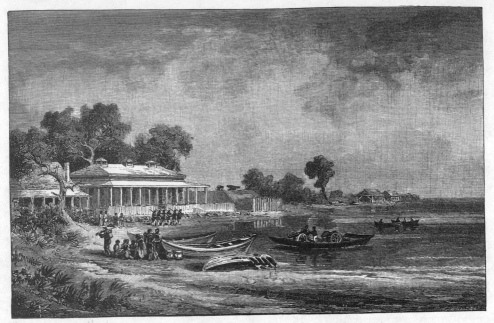

THE OLD HEADQUARTERS, HILTON HEAD. FROM A WAR-TIME SKETCH.

board of the *Seneca*, several miles up the Beaufort River. On the following day that vessel was sent to Beaufort, supported by two gun-boats. This visit brought to view an extraordinary scene. On the wharves were hundreds of negroes, wild with excitement, engaged in carrying movables of every character, and packing them in scows. As the gun-boats appeared, a few mounted white men rode away rapidly. A very beautiful rural town had been abandoned by all of the white inhabitants, quite as though fire and sword awaited them had they remained. Instead of that, I was directed by the flag-officer to assure the peaceable inhabitants that they would be protected in life and property. This

particularly as we had no gun on either flank of the bastion to reply with, for the 32-pounder on the right flank was shattered very early by a round shot, and on the north flank for want of a carriage no gun had been mounted. After the fourth fire the 10-inch Columbiad bounded over the limber and became useless. The 24-pounder rifled cannon was choked while ramming down a shell, and lay idle during nearly the whole engagement. The shells for the 9-inch Dahlgren were also too large. The fourth shell attempted to be rammed home could not be driven below the trunnions, and was then at great risk discharged. Thus far the fire of the enemy had been endured and replied to with the unruffled courage of veterans. At 10:30 our gunners became so fatigued that I left the fort, accompanied by one of my volunteer aides, Captain H. Rose, and went back to Captain Read's battery (one and three-quarter miles to the rear of the fort) and brought the greater part of his men back to take the places of our exhausted men inside the fort. . . . Two o'clock had now arrived, when I noticed our men coming out of the fort, which they had bravely defended for four and a half hours against fearful odds, and then only retiring when all but three of the guns on the water-front had been disabled, and only 500 pounds of powder in the magazine; commencing the action with 220 men inside the fort, afterward increased to 255 by the accession from Read's battery. These heroic men

retired slowly and sadly from their well-fought guns, which to have defended longer would have exhibited the energy of despair rather than the manly pluck of the true soldier."

Of the attack upon Fort Beauregard, General Drayton says:

"The attack upon the fort, though not so concentrated and heavy as that upon Walker, was nevertheless very severe. Its armament was 19 guns, of which the following, viz., 1 8-inch Rodman, bored to 24-pounder and rifled, 2 42-pounders, 1 10-inch Columbiad, 2 42-pounders, reamed to eight inches, and 1 32-pounder in hot-shot battery, were the only guns capable of being used against the fleet. The force on Bay Point was 640 men, commaded by Col. R. G. M. Dunovant, 12th Regiment South Carolina Volunteers. Of the above, 149 garrisoned Fort Beauregard, under the immediate command of Capt. Stephen Elliott, Jr., Beaufort Volunteer Artillery, Company A 9th Regiment South Carolina Volunteers. The infantry force of Colonel Dunovant's regiment was intrusted with the protection of the eastern part of the island, and of the defense of the bastion line at the Island Narrows, where an attack was expected from the enemy."

EDITORS.

message was delivered to the only white man found, who sat in the post-office and seemed quite dazed. At General Drayton's headquarters was found a chart of the coast, and, in red-pencil marks, a very valuable addition, no less than the position of all the earth-works within his command, the number of guns being shown by the number of red marks in each locality. All of the batteries indicated from North Edisto south to Tybee were found to be abandoned; the guns, however, had been removed, with the exception of some inferior pieces. Wherever the gunboats penetrated, into harbors or rivers, huge columns of white smoke were seen on all sides from the burning cotton, far out of our reach, had it been the special object of our visit to secure it. Thus the enemy inflicted upon the inhabitants injuries they would otherwise have escaped, even had it been within the power of the crews of the gun-boats to inflict them.

POPE'S HOUSE, HILTON HEAD, USED BY THE UNION ARMY AS A SIGNAL-STATION. FROM A WAR-TIME SKETCH.

On the 10th, on board the *Seneca*, the flag-officer paid a visit to Beaufort and endeavored, by proclamation printed and distributed, to assure peaceable inhabitants of his protection. A planter whose house was on Paris Island, plainly in view from the anchorage at Port Royal, remained without molestation for weeks, and was then constrained to leave only under threats of dire penalties from his Confederate friends.

After abandoning his works on Hilton Head, the enemy did not succeed in getting off the island, at Seabrook Landing, only six miles from the fort, until 2 A. M. of the 8th. On the Bay Point side, owing to a much longer march and the indifferent means of crossing a small stream, it was not until the following afternoon that the force reached an adjacent island or the mainland.[*] Every man of them, whether in the one fort or the other, was doubtless greatly impressed with the power of gun-boats when brought face to face with those batteries which only a few hours before they had regarded as quite capable of sinking or driving off any force that would be brought against them.

The battle of Port Royal, occurring a little less than seven months after the fall of Fort Sumter, was of surpassing value in its moral and political effect, both at home and abroad. It gave us one of the finest harbors on the Atlantic sea-board, affording an admirable base for future operations; and, by the establishment of coaling stations, shops, and supply depots, made it possible to maintain an effective blockade within the entrances of the whole coast from Charleston to Cape Florida, except at Fernandina. Although

[*] General T. F. Drayton says, in his report: "Notwithstanding the prompt measures adopted by Colonel Dunovant to effect his retreat in the direction of the Narrows, it is surprising that, with the knowledge possessed by the enemy (through Mr. [C. A.] Boutelle and others connected with the Coast Survey), his retreat had not been intercepted by gun-boats passing up toward Beaufort, and mine by other steamers taking the passage through Scull Creek toward the ferry landing. Why they did not adopt this course must be left to time to explain." EDITORS.

the casualties during the engagement were inconsiderable, military men and readers who note results will not measure its importance by the small number of the killed and wounded, indicative, in this case, of the professional ability and tactical skill with which the victory was won. The capture of the forts at Hatteras Inlet, August 28th, 1861, was the result of a bombardment rather than of a battle; owing to shoal water, extending far to seaward, the heavy vessels were held at so long a range that not a single projectile of the enemy reached them. Although 9-inch shells were fired from the broadside guns of the squadron the first day of the bombardment, it is doubtful if they reached the forts: the pivot-guns, being of

UNION SIGNAL-STATION, BEAUFORT, S. C.,—HOME OF
J. G. BARNWELL. FROM PHOTOGRAPHS.

larger caliber and having more elevation, dropped heavy shells on weak bomb-proofs and on insufficient coverings to the magazine, and compelled

FULLER'S HOUSE, BEAUFORT, S. C.

the surrender of the garrison. Nevertheless, the capture of Hatteras Inlet was an event of great military importance.

So far as the relative merits of ships and earth-works were concerned, the battle of Port Royal asserted in such positive terms the power of shell-guns afloat that the enemy at once abandoned all minor points of defense along the coast not covered by difficult water approaches, and ever after seemed to regard the obstruction of channels as the main element in successful defense.

The establishment and maintenance of our most efficient system of blockade along all the Southern coasts was largely due to the intelligence and ability with which Rear-Admiral Du Pont and his co-laborers formulated the principles involved at the very outset of the contest. His long experience in blockade duty during the Mexican war was of the greatest value to the conference, and indeed prompted his selection as its president.

In a private letter, dated on board the *Cyane*, July 27th, 1847, Du Pont stated, quite prophetically, the value of his study of the subject of blockades:

"I have exhausted Kent, Wheaton, and Vattel on the subject,— a right good piece of professional work and study, which may be invaluable in the future. Three or four issues have been started not covered at all by those authorities, of which I have made notes."

Previous to our civil war no higher rank was known in the American navy than that of captain, although the law accorded the title of flag-officer, with additional pay, to captains in command of recognized naval stations. The engagement at Port Royal, the taking of New Orleans, and other successful operations of our navy doubtless led to the creation of the higher grades of commodore and rear-admiral, July 16th, 1862, on which date Flag-Officer Du Pont became a rear-admiral, ranking second on the list.

Eminently adapted to command, he knew well how to secure the best services of his subordinates. Intelligent, cheerful in manner, of tall and commanding mien, he naturally invited and obtained the confidence of those who were fortunate enough to serve under his orders. During the past half century the navy of the United States has not had an officer of more distinguished appearance, or endowed with more manly virtues. Though fitted by nature to be a leader among men, he thoroughly appreciated the necessity for study to make himself equal to every professional requirement. It is not given to man to be preëminent without an earnest exertion to that end, however much nature may have done in his behalf.

In the erection of a statue at Washington, and in the naming of Du Pont Circle, in which it stands, the American people, through Congress, have paid a proper tribute to the memory of this worthy representative of the naval service.

AMMENDALE, MD., September, 1887.

THE OPPOSING FORCES AT PORT ROYAL, NOVEMBER 7TH, 1861.

THE UNION FLEET, Flag-Officer S. F. Du Pont, commanding. Captain Charles Henry Davis, Fleet-Captain.

Flag-ship: frigate *Wabash* (2 10-inch, 28 9-inch, 14 8-inch, 2 12-pounders), Commander C. R. P. Rodgers; side-wheel steamer *Susquehanna* (15 8-inch, 1 24-pounder, 2 12-pounders), Captain J. L. Lardner; sloop *Mohican* (2 11-inch, 4 32-pounders, 1 12-pounder), Commander S. W. Godon; *Seminole* (1 11-inch, 4 32-pounders), Commander J. P. Gillis; *Pocahontas* (1 10-inch, 4 32-pounders), Commander Percival Drayton; *Pawnee* (8 9-inch, 2 12-pounders), Lieutenant R. H. Wyman; gun-boats *Unadilla*, Lieutenant Napoleon Collins; *Seneca*, Lieutenant Daniel Ammen; *Ottawa*, Lieutenant T. H. Stevens; *Pembina*, Lieutenant J. P. Bankhead (each of the four latter carried 1 11-inch, 1 20-pounder rifle, and 2 24-pounders); sailing sloop *Vandalia* (4 8-inch, 16 32-pounders, 1 12-pounder), Commander F. S. Haggerty; steamer *Bienville* (8 32-pounders, 1 30-pounder rifle), Commander Charles Steedman; *Augusta* (8 32-pounders, 1 12-pounder), Commander E. G. Parrott; *Curlew* (6 32-pounders, 1 20-pounder rifle), Lieutenant P. G. Watmough; *Penguin* (4 32-pounders, 1 12-pounder), Lieutenant T. A. Budd; *R. B. Forbes* (2 32-pounders), Lieutenant H. S. Newcomb; *Isaac Smith* (8 8-inch, 1 30-pounder rifle, originally, but the broadside battery was thrown overboard on the way down from Hampton Roads), Lieutenant J. W. A. Nicholson.

The loss in the Union fleet, as officially reported, was 8 killed, and 23 wounded. Total, 31.

UNION LAND FORCES, Brig.-Gen. Thomas W. Sherman.

First Brigade, Brig.-Gen. Egbert L. Vielé: 8th Me., Col. Lee Strickland; 3d N. H., Col. Enoch Q. Fellows; 46th N. Y., Col. Rudolph Rosa; 47th N. Y., Col. Henry Moore; 48th N. Y., Col. James H. Perry. *Second Brigade*, Brig.-Gen. Isaac I. Stevens: 8th Mich., Col. William M. Fenton; 79th N. Y., Lieut.-Col. William H. Nobles; 50th Pa., Col. Benjamin C. Christ; 100th Pa., Col. Daniel Leasure. *Third Brigade*, Brig.-Gen. Horatio G. Wright: 6th Conn., Col. John L. Chatfield; 7th Conn., Col. Alfred H. Terry; 9th Me., Col. Rishworth Rich; 4th N. H., Col. Thomas J. Whipple. *Unattached*: 3d R. I., Col. Nathaniel W. Brown; 1st N. Y. Engineers, Col. Edward W. Serrell; Battery E, 3d U. S. Art'y, Capt. John Hamilton.

CONFEDERATE LAND FORCES, Brig.-Gen. Thomas F. Drayton: 4th Ga. Battalion, Lieut.-Col. W. H. Stiles; 9th S. C. (3 co's), Col. William C. Heyward; 12th S. C., Col. R. G. M. Dunovant; 15th S. C., Col. W. D. De Saussure; Beaufort (S. C.) Guerrillas, Capt. J. H. Screven; Ga. Battery, Capt. Jacob Read; 1st S. C. Militia Art'y (2 co's), Col. John A. Wagener. Loss: k, 11; w, 48; m, 7 = 66.

CONFEDERATE NAVAL FORCES, Flag-Officer Josiah Tattnall: *Savannah* (flag-ship), Lieut. John N. Maffitt; *Sampson*, Lieut. J. S. Kennard; *Resolute*, Lieut. J. Pembroke Jones. They were small side-wheel steamers, and each carried 2 32-pounders (smooth-bore). There were no casualties.

THE FIRST FIGHT OF IRON-CLADS.

BY JOHN TAYLOR WOOD, COLONEL, C. S. A.

THE engagement in Hampton Roads on the 8th of March, 1862, between the Confederate iron-clad *Virginia*, or the *Merrimac* (as she is known at the North), and the United States wooden fleet, and that on the 9th between the *Virginia* and the *Monitor*, was, in its results, in some respects the most momentous naval conflict ever witnessed. No battle was ever more widely discussed or produced a greater sensation. It revolutionized the navies of the world. Line-of-battle ships, those huge, overgrown craft, carrying from eighty to one hundred and twenty guns and from five hundred to twelve hundred men, which, from the destruction of the Spanish Armada to our time, had done most of the fighting, deciding the fate of empires, were at once universally condemned as out of date. Rams and iron-clads were in future to decide all naval warfare. In this battle old things passed away, and the experience of a thousand years of battle and breeze was forgotten. The naval supremacy of England vanished in the smoke of this fight, it is true, only to reappear some years later more commanding than ever. The effect of the news was best described by the London "Times," which said: "Whereas we had available for immediate purposes one hundred and forty-nine first-class war-ships, we have now two, these two being the *Warrior* and her sister *Ironside*. There is not now a ship in the English navy apart from these two that it would not be madness to trust to an engagement with that little *Monitor*." The Admiralty at once proceeded to reconstruct the navy, cutting down a number of their largest ships and converting them into turret or broadside iron-clads.

The same results were produced in France, which had but one sea-going iron-clad, *La Gloire*, and this one, like the *Warrior*, was only protected amidships. The Emperor Napoleon promptly appointed a commission to devise plans for rebuilding his navy. And so with all the maritime powers. In this race the United States took the lead, and at the close of the war led all the others in the numbers and efficiency of its iron-clad fleet. It is true that all the great powers had already experimented with vessels partly armored, but very few were convinced of their utility, and none had been tried by the test of battle, if we except a few floating batteries, thinly clad, used in the Crimean War.

In the spring of 1861 Norfolk and its large naval establishment had been hurriedly abandoned by the Federals, why no one could tell. It is about twelve miles from Fort Monroe, which was then held by a large force of regulars. A few companies of these, with a single frigate, could have occupied and commanded the town and navy yard and kept the channel open. However, a year later, it was as quickly evacuated by the Confederates, and almost with as little reason. But of this I will speak later.

The yard was abandoned to a few volunteers, after it was partly destroyed, and a large number of ships were burnt. Among the spoils were upward of twelve hundred heavy guns, which were scattered among Confederate fortifications from the Potomac to the Mississippi. [See foot-note, p. 712]. Among the ships burnt and sunk was the frigate *Merrimac* of 3500 tons and 40 guns, afterward rechristened the *Virginia*, and so I will call her. During the summer of 1861 Lieutenant John M. Brooke, an accomplished officer of the old navy, who with many others had resigned, proposed to Secretary Mallory to raise and rebuild this ship as an iron-clad. His plans were approved, and orders were given to carry them out. She was raised and cut down to the old berth-deck. Both ends for seventy feet were covered over, and when the ship was in fighting trim were just awash. On the midship section, 170 feet in length, was built at an angle of 45 degrees a roof of pitch-pine and oak 24 inches thick, extending from the water-line to a height over the gun-deck of 7 feet. [See pp. 715–717.] Both ends of the shield were rounded so that the pivot-guns could be

THE BURNING OF THE FRIGATE "MERRIMAC" AND OF THE GOSPORT NAVY-YARD. (SEE FOOT-NOTE, P. 712.)

REMODELING THE
"MERRIMAC" AT THE GOSPORT
NAVY YARD.

[For a statement of the details of the
vessel differing from them as shown in
this picture, see p. 717.]

used as bow and stern chasers or quartering. Over the gun-deck was a light grating, making a promenade about twenty feet wide. The wood backing was covered with iron plates, rolled at the Tredegar works, two inches thick and eight wide. The first tier was put on horizontally, the second up and down,— in all to the thickness of four inches, bolted through the wood-work and clinched. The prow was of cast-iron, projecting four feet, and badly secured, as events proved. The rudder and propeller were entirely unprotected. The pilot-house was forward of the smoke-stack, and covered with the same thickness of iron as the sides. The motive power was the same that had always been in the ship. Both of the engines and boilers had been condemned on her return from her last cruise, and were radically defective. Of course, the fire and sinking had not improved them. We could not depend upon them for six hours at a time. A more ill-contrived or unreliable pair of engines could only have been found in some vessels of the United States navy.

Lieutenant Catesby ap R. Jones was ordered to superintend the armament, and no more thoroughly competent officer could have been selected. To his experience and skill as her ordnance and executive officer was due the character of her battery, which proved so efficient. It consisted of 2 7-inch rifles, heavily reënforced around the breech with 3-inch steel bands, shrunk on. These were the first heavy guns so made, and were the bow and stern pivots. There were also 2 6-inch rifles of the same make, and 6 9-inch smooth-bore broadside,—10 guns in all.

During the summer and fall of 1861 I had been stationed at the batteries on the Potomac at Evansport and Aquia Creek, blockading the river as far as possible. In January, 1862, I was ordered to the *Virginia* as one of the lieutenants, reporting to Commodore French Forrest, who then commanded the navy yard at Norfolk. Commodore Franklin Buchanan was appointed to the command,— an energetic and high-toned officer, who combined with daring courage great professional ability, standing deservedly at the head of his profession. In 1845 he had been selected by Mr. Bancroft, Secretary of the Navy, to locate and organize the Naval Academy, and he launched that institution upon its successful career. Under him were as capable a set of officers as ever were brought together in one ship. But of man-of-war's men or sailors we had scarcely any. The South was almost without a maritime population. In the old service the majority of officers were from the South, and all the seamen from the North. ⚓

Every one had flocked to the army, and to it we had to look for a crew. Some few seamen were found in Norfolk, who had escaped from the gun-boat flotilla in the waters of North Carolina, on their occupation by Admiral Goldsborough and General Burnside. In hopes of securing some men from the army, I was sent to the headquarters of General Magruder at Yorktown, who was known to have under his command two battalions from New Orleans, among whom might be found a number of seamen. The general, though pressed for want of men, holding a long line with scarcely a brigade, gave me every facility to secure volunteers. With one of his staff I visited every camp, and the commanding officers were ordered to parade their men, and I explained to them what I wanted. About 200 volunteered, and of this number I selected 80 who had had some experience as seamen or gunners. Other commands at Richmond and Petersburg were visited, and so our crew of three hundred was made up. They proved themselves to be as gallant and trusty a body of men as any one would wish to command, not only in battle, but in reverse and retreat.

Notwithstanding every exertion to hasten the fitting out of the ship, the work during the winter progressed but slowly, owing to delay in sending the iron sheathing from Richmond. At this time the only establishment in the South capable of rolling iron plates was the Tredegar foundry. Its resources were

⚓ The officers of the *Merrimac* were : *Flag-Officer*, Franklin Buchanan; *Lieutenants*, Catesby ap R. Jones (executive and ordnance officer), Charles C. Simms, R. D. Minor (flag), Hunter Davidson, John Taylor Wood, J. R. Eggleston, Walter Butt; *Midshipmen*, Foute, Marmaduke, Littlepage, Craig, Long, and Rootes; *Paymaster*, James Semple; *Surgeon*, Dinwiddie Phillips; *Assistant-Surgeon*, Algernon S. Garnett; *Captain of Marines*, Reuben Thom; *Engineers*, H. A. Ramsey, acting chief; *Assistants*, Tynan, Campbell, Herring, Jack, and White; *Boatswain*, Hasker; *Gunner*, Oliver; *Carpenter*, Lindsey; *Clerk*, Arthur Sinclair, Jr.; *Volunteer Aides*, Lieutenant Douglas Forrest, C. S. A., Captain Kevil, commanding detachment of Norfolk United Artillery; *Signal Corps*, Sergeant Tabb.

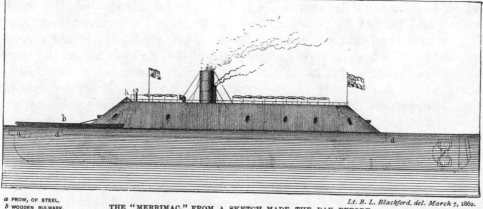

a PROW, OF STEEL.
b WOODEN BULWARK.
h PILOT-HOUSE.

Lt. B. L. Blackford, del. March 7, 1862.

THE "MERRIMAC," FROM A SKETCH MADE THE DAY BEFORE
THE FIGHT.

dd IRON UNDER WATER.
f PROPELLER.

limited, and the demand for all kinds of war material most pressing. And when we reflect upon the scarcity and inexperience of the workmen, and the great changes necessary in transforming an ordinary iron workshop into an arsenal in which all the machinery and tools had to be improvised, it is astonishing that so much was accomplished. The unfinished state of the vessel interfered so with the drills and exercises that we had but little opportunity of getting things into shape.

LIEUTENANT CATESBY AP R. JONES.
FROM A PHOTOGRAPH.

It should be remembered that the ship was an experiment in naval architecture, differing in every respect from any then afloat. The officers and the crew were strangers to the ship and to each other. Up to the hour of sailing she was crowded with workmen. Not a gun had been fired, hardly a revolution of the engines had been made, when we cast off from the dock and started on what many thought was an ordinary trial trip, but which proved to be a trial such as no vessel that ever floated had undergone up to that time. From the start we saw that she was slow, not over five knots; she steered so badly that, with her great length, it took from thirty to forty minutes to turn. She drew twenty-two feet, which confined us to a comparatively narrow channel in the Roads; and, as I have before said, the engines were our weak point. She was as unmanageable as a water-logged vessel.

It was at noon on the 8th of March that we steamed down the Elizabeth River. Passing by our batteries, lined with troops, who cheered us as we passed, and through the obstructions at Craney Island, we took the south channel and headed for Newport News. At anchor at this time off Fort Monroe were the frigates *Minnesota*, *Roanoke*, and *St. Lawrence*, and several gun-boats. The first two were sister ships of the *Virginia* before the war; the last was a sailing frigate of fifty guns. Off Newport News, seven miles above, which was strongly fortified and held by a large Federal garrison, were anchored the frigate *Congress*, 50 guns, and the sloop *Cumberland*, 30. The day was calm, and the last two ships were swinging lazily by their anchors. [The tide was at its height about 1:40 P. M.] Boats were hanging to the lower booms, washed clothes in the rigging. Nothing indicated that we were expected; but when we came within three-quarters of a mile, the boats were dropped astern, booms got alongside, and the *Cumberland* opened with her heavy pivots, followed by the *Congress*, the gun-boats, and the shore batteries.

FRANKLIN BUCHANAN, ADMIRAL, C. S. N.   JOSIAH TATTNALL, COMMODORE, C. S. N.

COMMANDERS OF THE "VIRGINIA" (OR "MERRIMAC"). FROM A PHOTOGRAPH.

COLONEL JOHN TAYLOR WOOD, LIEUTENANT ON THE
"MERRIMAC." FROM AN OIL PORTRAIT.

We reserved our fire until within easy range, when the forward pivot was pointed and fired by Lieutenant Charles Simms, killing and wounding most of the crew of the after pivot-gun of the *Cumberland.* Passing close to the *Congress,* which received our starboard broadside, and returned it with spirit, we steered direct for the *Cumberland,* striking her almost at right angles, under the fore-rigging on the starboard side. The blow was hardly perceptible on board the *Virginia.* Backing clear of her, we went ahead again, heading up the river, helm hard-a-starboard, and turned slowly. As we did so, for the first time I had an opportunity of using the after-pivot, of which I had charge. As we swung, the *Congress* came in range, nearly stern on, and we got in three raking shells. She had slipped her anchor, loosed her foretop-sail, run up the jib, and tried to escape, but grounded. Turning, we headed for her and took a position within two hundred yards, where every shot told. In the meantime the *Cumberland* continued the fight, though our ram had opened her side wide enough to drive in a horse and cart. Soon she listed to port and filled rapidly. The crew were driven by the advancing water to the spar-deck, and there worked her pivot-guns until she went down with a roar, the colors still flying. No ship was ever fought more gallantly.‡ The *Congress* continued the unequal contest for more than an hour after the sinking of the *Cumberland.* Her losses were terrible, and finally she ran up the white flag.

As soon as we had hove in sight, coming down the harbor, the *Roanoke, St. Lawrence,* and *Minnesota,* assisted by tugs, had got under way, and started up from Old Point Comfort to join their consorts. They were under fire from the batteries at Sewell's Point, but the distance was too great to effect much. The first two, however, ran aground not far above Fort Monroe, and took

‡ According to the pilot of the *Cumberland,* A. B. Smith: "Near the middle of the fight, when the berth-deck of the *Cumberland* had sunk below water, one of the crew of the *Merrimac* came out of a port to the outside of her iron-plate roof, and a ball from one of our guns instantly cut him in two. . . . Finally, after about three-fourths of an hour of the most severe fighting, our vessel sank, the Stars and Stripes still waving. That flag was finally submerged, but after the hull grounded on the sands, fifty-four feet below, . . . our pennant was still flying from the top-mast above the waves."

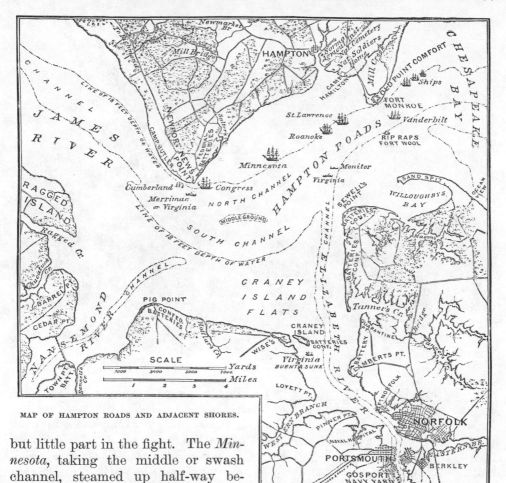

MAP OF HAMPTON ROADS AND ADJACENT SHORES.

but little part in the fight. The *Min-nesota*, taking the middle or swash channel, steamed up half-way between Old Point Comfort and New-port News, when she grounded, but in a position to be actively engaged.

Previous to this we had been joined by the James River squadron, which had been at anchor a few miles above, and came into action most gallantly, passing the shore batteries at Newport News under a heavy fire, and with some loss. It consisted of the *Yorktown* (or *Patrick Henry*), 12 guns, Captain John R. Tucker; *Jamestown*, 2 guns, Lieut.-Commander J. N. Barney; and *Teaser*, 1 gun, Lieut.-Commander W. A. Webb.

As soon as the *Congress* surrendered, Commander Buchanan ordered the gun-boats *Beaufort*, Lieut.-Commander W. H. Parker, and *Raleigh*, Lieut.-Commander J. W. Alexander, to steam alongside, take off her crew, and set fire to the ship. Lieutenant Pendergrast, who had succeeded Lieutenant Smith, who had been killed, surrendered to Lieutenant Parker, of the *Beaufort*. Delivering his sword and colors, he was directed by Lieutenant Parker to return to his ship and have the wounded transferred as rapidly as possible. All this time the shore batteries and small-arm men were keeping up an incessant fire on our vessels. Two of the officers of the *Raleigh*, Lieutenant Tayloe

THE "MERRIMAC" RAMMING THE "CUMBERLAND."

and Midshipman Hutter, were killed while assisting the Union wounded out of the *Congress*. A number of the enemy's men were killed by the same fire. Finally it became so hot that the gun-boats were obliged to haul off with only thirty prisoners, leaving Lieutenant Pendergrast and most of his crew on board, and they all afterward escaped to the shore by swimming or in small boats. While this was going on, the white flag was flying at her mainmast-head. Not being able to take possession of his prize, the commodore ordered hot shot to be used, and in a short time she was in flames fore and aft. While directing this, both himself and his flag-lieutenant, Minor, were severely wounded. The command then devolved upon Lieutenant Catesby Jones.

It was now 5 o'clock, nearly two hours of daylight, and the *Minnesota* only remained. She was aground and at our mercy. But the pilots would not attempt the middle channel with the ebb tide and approaching night. So we returned by the south channel to Sewell's Point and anchored, the *Minnesota* escaping, as we thought, only until morning.

Our loss in killed and wounded was twenty-one. The armor was hardly damaged, though at one time our ship was the focus on which were directed at least one hundred heavy guns, afloat and ashore. But nothing outside escaped. Two guns were disabled by having their muzzles shot off. The ram was left in the side of the *Cumberland*. One anchor, the smoke-stack, and the steam-pipes were shot away. Railings, stanchions, boat-davits, everything was swept clean. The flag-staff was repeatedly knocked over, and finally a boarding-pike was used. Commodore Buchanan and the other wounded were sent to the Naval Hospital, and after making preparations for the next day's fight, we slept at our guns, dreaming of other victories in the morning.)

But at daybreak we discovered, lying between us and the *Minnesota*, a strange-looking craft, which we knew at once to be Ericsson's *Monitor*, which had long been expected in Hampton Roads, and of which, from different sources, we had a good idea. She could not possibly have made her appearance at a more inopportune time for us, changing our plans, which were to destroy the *Minnesota*, and then the remainder of the fleet below Fort Monroe. She appeared but a pigmy compared with the lofty frigate which she guarded. But in her size was one great element of her success. I will not attempt a description of the *Monitor ;* her build and peculiarities are well known.

After an early breakfast, we got under way and steamed out toward the enemy, opening fire from our bow pivot, and closing in to deliver our starboard broadside at short range, which was returned promptly from her 11-inch guns. Both vessels then turned and passed again still closer. The *Monitor* was firing every seven or eight minutes, and nearly every shot struck. Our ship was working worse and worse, and after the loss of the smoke-stack, Mr. Ramsey, chief engineer, reported that the draught was so poor that it was with great difficulty he could keep up steam. Once or twice the ship was on the bottom. Drawing 22 feet of water, we were confined to a narrow channel, while the *Monitor*, with only 12 feet immersion, could take any position, and always have us in range of her guns.

LIEUTENANT GEORGE U. MORRIS, ACTING COMMANDER OF THE "CUMBERLAND."

In the absence of Captain Radford, the command of the *Cumberland* devolved upon the executive officer, Lieutenant Morris, from whose official report we quote the following : "At thirty minutes past three the water had gained upon us, notwithstanding the pumps were kept actively employed to a degree that, the forward-magazine being drowned, we had to take powder from the after-magazine for the ten-inch gun. At thirty-five minutes past three the water had risen to the main hatchway, and the ship canted to port, and we delivered a parting fire—each man trying to save himself by jumping overboard. Timely notice was given, and all the wounded who could walk were ordered out of the cockpit; but those of the wounded who had been carried into the sick-bay and on the berth-deck were so mangled that it was impossible to save them. . . . I should judge we have lost upward of one hundred men. I can only say, in conclusion, that all did their duty, and we sank with the American flag flying at the peak." When summoned to surrender, Morris replied, "Never! I'll sink alongside!"—EDITORS.

Orders were given to concentrate our fire on the pilot-house, and with good result, as we afterward learned. More than two hours had passed, and we had made no impression on the enemy

) Lieutenant Jones reported : "It was not easy to keep a flag flying. The flag-staffs were repeatedly shot away. The colors were hoisted to the smoke-stack and several times cut down from it."—EDITORS.

THE "MERRIMAC" DRIVING THE "CONGRESS" FROM HER ANCHORAGE.

so far as we could discover, while our wounds were slight. Several times the *Monitor* ceased firing, and we were in hopes she was disabled, but the revolution again of her turret and the heavy blows of her 11-inch shot on our sides soon undeceived us.

Coming down from the spar-deck, and observing a division standing " at ease," Lieutenant Jones inquired:

" Why are you not firing, Mr. Eggleston ? "

" Why, our powder is very precious," replied the lieutenant; " and after two hours' incessant firing I find that I can do her about as much damage by snapping my thumb at her every two minutes and a half."

Lieutenant Jones now determined to run her down or board her. For nearly an hour we manœuvred for a position. Now " Go ahead ! " now " Stop ! " now " Astern ! " The ship was as unwieldy as Noah's ark. At last an opportunity offered. " Go ahead, full speed ! " But before the ship gathered headway, the *Monitor* turned, and our disabled ram only gave a glancing blow, effecting nothing. Again she came up on our quarter, her bow against our side, and at this distance fired twice. Both shots struck about half-way up the shield, abreast of the after pivot, and the impact forced the side in bodily two or three inches. All the crews of the after guns were knocked over by the concussion, and bled from the nose or ears. Another shot at the same place would have penetrated. While alongside, boarders were called away; but she dropped astern before they could get on board. And so, for six or more hours, the struggle was kept up. At length, the *Monitor* withdrew over the middle ground where we could not follow, but always maintaining a position to protect the *Minnesota*. \ To have run our ship ashore on a falling tide would have been ruin. We awaited her return for an hour; and at 2 o'clock P. M. steamed to Sewell's Point, and thence to the dockyard at Norfolk, our crew thoroughly worn out from the two days' fight. Although there is no doubt that the *Monitor* first retired,— for Captain Van Brunt, commanding the *Minnesota*, so states in his official report,— the battle was a drawn one, so far as the two vessels engaged were concerned. But in its general results the advantage was with the *Monitor*. Our casualties in the second day's fight were only a few wounded.

This action demonstrated for the first time the power and efficiency of the ram as a means of offense. The side of the *Cumberland* was crushed like an egg-shell. The *Congress* and *Minnesota*, even with our disabled bow, would have shared the same fate but that we could not reach them on account of our great draught.

It also showed the power of resistance of two iron-clads, widely differing in construction, model, and armament, under a fire which in a short time would have sunk any other vessel then afloat.

The *Monitor* was well handled, and saved the *Minnesota* and the remainder of the fleet at Fort Monroe. But her gunnery was poor. Not a single shot struck us at the water-line, where the ship was utterly unprotected [see p. 717], and where one would have been fatal. Or had the fire been concentrated on any one spot, the shield would have been pierced; or had larger charges been used, the result would have been the same. Most of her shot struck us obliquely, breaking the iron of both courses, but not injuring the wood backing. When struck at right angles, the backing would be broken, but not penetrated. We had no solid projectiles, except a few of large windage, to be used as hot shot, and, of course, made no impression on the turret. But in all this it should be borne in mind that both vessels were on their trial trip, both were experimental, and both were receiving their baptism of fire.

On our arrival at Norfolk, Commodore Buchanan sent for me. I found him at the Naval Hospital, badly wounded and suffering greatly. He dictated a short dispatch to Mr. Mallory, Secretary of the Navy, stating the return of the ship and the result of the two days' fight, and directed me to proceed to Richmond with it and the flag of the *Congress*, and make a verbal report of the action, condition of the *Virginia*, etc.

I took the first train for Petersburg and the capital. The news had pre-

---

\ In his official report, Captain Van Brunt says of the fight, as viewed from the *Minnesota*:

"At 6 A. M. the enemy again appeared, . . . and I beat to quarters; but they ran past my ship and were heading for Fortress Monroe, and the retreat was beaten to enable my men to get something to eat. The *Merrimac* ran down near the Rip-Raps and then turned into the channel through which I had come. Again all hands were called to quarters, and opened upon her with my stern-guns, and made signal to the *Monitor* to attack the enemy. She immediately ran down in my wake, right within the range of the *Merrimac*, completely covering my ship, as far as was possible with her diminutive dimensions, and, much to my astonishment, laid herself right alongside of the *Merrimac*, and the contrast was that of a pigmy to a giant. Gun after gun was fired by the *Monitor*, which was returned with whole broadsides from the Rebels, with no more effect, apparently, than so many pebble-stones thrown by a child. . . . The *Merrimac*, finding that she could make nothing of the *Monitor*, turned her attention once more to me. In the morning she had put one eleven-inch shot under my counter, near the water-line, and now, on her second approach, I opened upon her with all my broadside-guns and ten-inch pivot — a broadside which would have blown out of water any timber-built ship in the world. She returned my fire with her rifled bow-gun, with a shell which passed through the chief engineer's state-room, through the engineers' mess-room amidships, and burst in the boatswain's room, tearing four rooms all into one, in its passage exploding two charges of powder, which set the ship on fire, but it was promptly extinguished by a party headed by my first lieutenant."

ESCAPE OF PART OF THE CREW OF THE "CONGRESS."

ceded me, and at every station I was warmly received, and to listening crowds was forced to repeat the story of the fight. Arriving at Richmond, I drove to Mr. Mallory's office and with him went to President Davis's, where we met Mr. Benjamin, who, a few days afterward, became Secretary of State, Mr. Seddon, afterward Secretary of War, General Cooper, Adjutant-General, and a number of others. I told at length what had occurred on the previous two days, and what changes and repairs were necessary to the *Virginia*. As to the future, I said that in the *Monitor* we had met our equal, and that the result of another engagement would be very doubtful. Mr. Davis made many inquiries as regarded the ship's draught, speed, and capabilities, and urged the completion of the repairs at as early a day as possible. The conversation lasted until near midnight. During the evening the flag of the *Congress*, which was a very large one, was brought in, and to our surprise, in unfolding it, we found it in some places saturated with blood. On this discovery it was quickly rolled up and sent to the Navy Department, where it remained during the war; it doubtless burned with that building when Richmond was evacuated.

The news of our victory was received everywhere in the South with the most enthusiastic rejoicing. Coming, as it did, after a number of disasters in the south and west, it was particularly grateful. Then again, under the circumstances, so little was expected from the navy that this success was entirely unlooked for. So, from one extreme to the other, the most extravagant anticipations were formed of what the ship could do. For instance: the blockade could be raised, Washington leveled to the ground, New York laid under contribution, and so on. At the North, equally groundless alarm was felt. As an example of this, Secretary Welles relates what took place at a Cabinet meeting called by Mr. Lincoln on the receipt of the news.☆ "'The *Merrimac*,' said Stanton, 'will change the whole character of the war; she will destroy, *seriatim*, every naval vessel; she will lay all the cities on the seaboard under contribution. I shall immediately recall Burnside; Port Royal must be abandoned. I will notify the governors and municipal authorities in the North to take instant measures to protect their harbors.' He had no doubt, he said, that the monster was at this moment on her way to Washington; and, looking out of the window, which commanded a view of the Potomac for many miles, 'Not unlikely, we shall have a shell or cannon-ball from one of her guns in the White House before we leave this room.' Mr. Seward, usually buoyant and self-reliant, overwhelmed with the intelligence, listened in responsive sympathy to Stanton, and was greatly depressed, as, indeed, were all the members."

I returned the next day to Norfolk, and informed Commodore Buchanan that he would be promoted to be admiral, and that, owing to his wound, he would be retired from the command of the *Virginia*. Lieutenant Jones should have been promoted, and should have succeeded him. He had fitted out the ship and armed her, and had commanded during the second day's fight. However, the department thought otherwise, and selected Commodore Josiah Tattnall;

☆ The " news " was of the first day's battle before the *Monitor* had arrived.—EDITORS.

THE EXPLOSION ON THE BURNING "CONGRESS."

except Lieutenant Jones he was the best man. He had distinguished himself in the wars of 1812 and with Mexico. No one stood higher as an accomplished and chivalrous officer. While in command of the United States squadron in the East Indies, he was present as a neutral at the desperate fight at the Peiho Forts, below Pekin, between the English fleet and the Chinese, when the former lost nearly one-half of a force of twelve hundred engaged. Seeing his old friend Sir James Hope hard pressed and in need of assistance, having had four vessels sunk under him, he had his barge manned, and with his flag-lieutenant, S. D. Trenchard, pulled alongside the flag-ship, through the midst of a tremendous fire, in which his coxswain was killed and several of his boat's crew were wounded. He found the gallant admiral desperately wounded, and all his crew killed or disabled but six. When he offered his services, surprise was expressed at his action. His reply was, "Blood is thicker than water."

Tattnall took command on the 29th of March. In the meantime the *Virginia* was in the dry dock under repairs. The hull four feet below the shield was covered with 2-inch iron. A new and heavier ram was strongly secured to the bow. The damage to the armor was repaired [see p. 717], wrought-iron port-shutters were fitted, and the rifle-guns were supplied with steel-pointed solid shot. These changes, with 100 tons more of ballast on her fan-tails, increased her draught to 23 feet, improving her resisting powers, but correspondingly decreasing her mobility and reducing her speed to 4 knots. The repairs were not completed until the 4th of April, owing to our want of resources and the difficulty of securing workmen. On the 11th we steamed down the harbor to the Roads with six gun-boats, fully expecting to meet the *Monitor* again and other vessels; for we knew their fleet had been largely reënforced, by the *Vanderbilt*, among other vessels, a powerful side-wheel steamer fitted as a ram. We were primed for a desperate tussle; but to our surprise we had the Roads to ourselves. We exchanged a few shots with the Rip-Raps batteries, but the *Monitor* with the other vessels of the fleet remained below Fort Monroe, in Chesapeake Bay, where we could not get at them except by passing between the forts.

The day before going down, Commodore Tattnall had written to Secretary Mallory, "I see no chance for me but to pass the forts and strike elsewhere, and I shall be gratified by your authority to do so." This freedom of action was never granted, and probably wisely, for the result of an action with the *Monitor* and fleet, even if we ran the gauntlet of the fire of the forts successfully, was more than doubtful, and any disaster would have exposed Norfolk and James River, and probably would have resulted in the loss of Richmond. For equally good reasons the *Monitor* acted on the defensive; for if she had been out of the way, General McClellan's base and fleet of transports in York River would have been endangered. Observing three merchant vessels at anchor close inshore and within the bar at Hampton, the commodore ordered Lieutenant Barney in the *Jamestown* to go in and bring them out. This was promptly and successfully accomplished, under a fire from the forts. Two were brigs loaded with supplies for the army. The capture of these vessels, within gun-shot of

LIEUTENANT JOSEPH B. SMITH, ACTING COMMANDER OF THE "CONGRESS." FROM A PHOTOGRAPH.

According to the pilot of the *Cumberland*, Lieutenant Smith was killed by a shot. His death was fixed at 4:20 P. M. by Lieutenant Pendergrast, next in command, who did not hear of it until ten minutes later. When his father, Commodore Joseph Smith, who was on duty at Washington, saw by the first dispatch from Fort Monroe that the *Congress* had shown the white flag, he said, quietly, "Joe's dead!" After speaking of the death of Lieutenant Smith, Lieutenant Pendergrast says, in his official report: "Seeing that our men were being killed without the prospect of any relief from the *Minnesota*, . . . not being able to get a single gun to bear upon the enemy, and the ship being on fire in several places, upon consultation with Commander William Smith we deemed it proper to haul down our colors." Lieutenant Smith's sword was sent to his father by the enemy under a flag of truce.— EDITORS.

their fleet, did not affect its movements. As the *Jamestown* towed her prizes under the stern of the English corvette *Rinaldo*, Captain Hewett (now [1887] Vice-Admiral Sir William Hewett, commanding the Channel Squadron), then at anchor in the Roads, she was enthusiastically cheered. We remained below all day, and at night returned and anchored off Sewell's Point.

A few days later we went down again to within gun-shot of the Rip-Raps, and exchanged a few rounds with the fort, hoping that the *Monitor* would come out from her lair into open water. Had she done so, a determined effort would have been made to carry her by boarding. Four small gun-boats were ready, each of which had its crew divided into parties for the performance of

THE "MONITOR."

THE "MERRIMAC."

THE ENCOUNTER AT SHORT RANGE.

certain duties after getting on board. Some were to try to wedge the turret, some to cover the pilot-house and all the openings with tarpaulins, others to scale with ladders the turret and smoke-stack, using shells, hand-grenades, etc. Even if but two of the gun-boats should succeed in grappling her, we were confident of success. Talking this over since with Captain S. D. Greene, who was the first lieutenant of the *Monitor*, and in command after Captain Worden was wounded in the pilot-house, he said they were prepared for anything of this kind and that it would have failed. Certain it is, if an opportunity had been given, the attempt would have been made.

A break-down of the engines forced us to return to Norfolk. Having completed our repairs on May 8th, and while returning to our old anchorage, we heard heavy firing, and, going down the harbor, found the *Monitor*, with the iron-clads *Galena, Naugatuck,* and a number of heavy ships, shelling our batteries at Sewell's Point. We stood directly for the *Monitor*, but as we approached they all ceased firing and retreated below the forts. We followed close down to the Rip-Raps, whose shot passed over us, striking a mile or more beyond the ship. We remained for some hours in the Roads, and finally the commodore, in a tone of deepest disgust, gave the order: "Mr. Jones, fire a gun to windward, and take the ship back to her buoy."

During the month of April, 1862, our forces, under General J. E. Johnston, had retired from the Peninsula to the neighborhood of Richmond, to defend the city against McClellan's advance by way of the Peninsula, and from time to time rumors of the possible evacuation of Norfolk reached us. On the 9th of May, while at anchor off Sewell's Point, we noticed at sunrise that our flag was not flying over the batteries. A boat was sent ashore and found them abandoned. Lieutenant Pembroke Jones was then dispatched to Norfolk, some miles distant, to call upon General Huger, who was in command, and learn the condition of affairs. He returned during the afternoon, reporting, to our great surprise, the town deserted by our troops and the navy yard on fire. This precipitate retreat was entirely unnecessary, for while the *Virginia* remained afloat, Norfolk was safe, or, at all events, was not tenable by the enemy, and James River was partly guarded, for we could have retired behind the obstructions in the channel at Craney Island, and, with the batteries at that point, could have held the place, certainly until all the valuable stores and machinery had been removed from the navy yard. Moreover, had the *Virginia* been afloat at the time of the battles around Richmond, General McClellan would hardly have retreated to James River; for, had he done so, we could at any time have closed it and rendered any position on it untenable.

Norfolk evacuated, our occupation was gone, and the next thing to be decided upon was what should be done with the ship. Two courses of action were open to us: we might have run the blockade of the forts and done some damage to the shipping there and at the mouth of the York River, provided they did not get out of our way,— for, with our great draught and low rate of speed, the enemy's transports would have gone where we could not have followed them; and the *Monitor* and other iron-clads would have engaged us with every advantage, playing around us as rabbits around a sloth, and the end would have been the certain loss of the vessel. On the other hand, the pilots said repeatedly, if the ship were lightened to eighteen feet, they could take her up James River to Harrison's Landing or City Point, where she could have been put in fighting trim again, and have been in a position to assist in the defense of Richmond. The commodore decided upon this course. Calling all hands on deck, he told them what he wished done. Sharp and quick work was necessary; for, to be successful, the ship must be lightened five feet, and we must pass the batteries at Newport News and the fleet below before daylight next morning. The crew gave three cheers, and went to work with a will, throwing overboard the ballast from the fan-tails, as well as that below,—all spare stores, water, indeed everything but our powder and shot. By midnight the ship had been lightened three feet, when, to our amazement, the pilots said it was useless to do more, that with the westerly wind blowing, the tide would be cut down so that the ship would not go up even to Jamestown Flats; indeed, they would not take the responsibility of taking her up the river at all. This extraordinary

CAPTAIN G. J. VAN BRUNT, COMMANDER OF THE "MINNESOTA." FROM A PHOTOGRAPH.

conduct of the pilots rendered some other plan immediately necessary. Moral: All officers, as far as possible, should learn to do their own piloting.

The ship had been so lifted as to be unfit for action; two feet of her hull below the shield was exposed. She could not be sunk again by letting in water without putting out the furnace fires and flooding the magazines. Never was a commander forced by circumstances over which he had no control into a more painful position than was Commodore Tattnall. But coolly and calmly he decided, and gave orders to destroy the ship; determining if he could not save his vessel, at all events not to sacrifice three hundred brave and faithful men; and that he acted wisely, the fight at Drewry's Bluff, which was the salvation of Richmond, soon after proved. She was run ashore near Craney Island, and the crew landed with their small-arms and two days' provisions. Having only two boats, it took three hours to disembark. Lieutenant Catesby Jones and myself were the last to leave. Setting her on fire fore and aft, she was soon in a blaze, and by the light of our burning ship we pulled for the shore, landing at daybreak. We marched 22 miles to Suffolk and took the cars for Richmond.

The news of the destruction of the *Virginia* caused a most profound feeling of disappointment and indignation throughout the South, particularly as so much was expected of the ship after our first success. On Commodore Tattnall the most unsparing and cruel aspersions were cast. He promptly demanded a court of inquiry, and, not satisfied with this, a court-martial, whose unanimous finding, after considering the facts and circumstances, was: "Being thus situated, the only alternative, in the opinion of the court, was to abandon and burn the ship then and there; which, in the judgment of the court, was deliberately and wisely done by order of the accused. Wherefore, the court do award the said Captain Josiah Tattnall an honorable acquittal."

It only remains now to speak of our last meeting with the *Monitor.* Arriving at Richmond, we heard that the enemy's fleet was ascending James River, and the result was great alarm; for, relying upon the *Virginia,* not a gun had been mounted to protect the city from a water attack. We were hurried to Drewry's Bluff, the first high ground below the city, seven miles distant. Here, for two days, exposed to constant rain, in bottomless mud and without shelter, on scant provisions, we worked unceasingly, mounting guns and obstructing the river. In this we were aided by the crews of small vessels which had escaped up the river before Norfolk was abandoned. The *Jamestown* and some small sailing-vessels were sunk in the channel, but, owing to the high water occasioned by a freshet, the obstructions were only partial. We had only succeeded in getting into position three thirty-twos and two sixty-fours (shell guns) and were without sufficient supply of ammunition, when on the 15th of May the iron-clad *Galena,* Commander John Rodgers, followed by the *Monitor* and three others, hove in sight. We opened fire as soon as they came within range, directing most of it on the *Galena.* This vessel was handled very skillfully. Coming up within six hundred yards of the battery, she anchored, and, with a spring from her quarter, presented her broadside; this under a heavy fire, and in a narrow river with a strong current. The *Monitor,* and others anchored just below, answered our fire deliberately; but, owing to the great elevation of the battery, their fire was in a great measure ineffectual, though two guns were dismounted and several men were killed and wounded. While this was going on, our sharp-shooters were at work on both banks. Lieutenant Catesby Jones, in his report, speaks of this service: "Lieutenant Wood, with a portion of the men, did good service as sharpshooters. The enemy were excessively annoyed by their fire. His position was well chosen and gallantly maintained in spite of the shell, shrapnel, grape, and canister fired at them." Finding they could make no impression on our works, the *Galena,* after an action of four hours, returned down the river with her consorts. Her loss was about forty killed and wounded.|

This was one of the boldest and best-conducted operations of the war, and one of which very little notice has been taken. Had Commander Rodgers been supported by a few brigades, landed at City Point or above on the south side, Richmond would have been evacuated. The *Virginia's* crew alone barred his way to Richmond; otherwise the obstructions would not have prevented his steaming up to the city, which would have been as much at his mercy as was New Orleans before the fleet of Farragut.

| According to the official report, the loss on the *Galena* was 13 killed and 11 wounded; on the *Port Royal,* 1 wounded, and on the *Naugatuck,* 2 wounded. Total, 13 killed and 14 wounded.—EDITORS.

THE "MONITOR" IN BATTLE TRIM.

WATCHING THE "MERRIMAC."

BY R. E. COLSTON, BRIGADIER-GENERAL, C. S. A.

IN March, 1862, I was in command of a Confederate brigade and of a district on the south side of the James River, embracing all the river forts and batteries down to the mouth of Nansemond River. My pickets were posted all along the shore opposite Newport News. From my headquarters at Smithfield I was in constant and rapid communication through relays of couriers and signal stations with my department commander, Major-General Huger, stationed at Norfolk. ⚓

About 1 P. M. on the 8th of March, a courier dashed up to my headquarters with this brief dispatch: "The Virginia is coming up the river." Mounting at once, it took me but a very short time to gallop twelve miles down to Ragged Island.

I had hardly dismounted at the water's edge when I descried the Merrimac approaching. The Congress was moored about a hundred yards below the land batteries, and the Cumberland a little above them. As soon as the Merrimac came within range, the batteries and war-vessels opened

fire. She passed on up, exchanging broadsides with the Congress, and making straight for the Cumberland, at which she made a dash, firing her bow-guns as she struck the doomed vessel with her prow. I could hardly believe my senses when I saw the masts of the Cumberland begin to sway wildly. After one or two lurches, her hull disappeared beneath the water, guns firing to the last moment. Most of her brave crew went down with their ship, but not with their colors, for the Union flag still floated defiantly from the masts, which projected obliquely for about half their length above the water after the vessel had settled unevenly upon the river-bottom. This first act of the drama was over in about thirty minutes, but it seemed to me only a moment.

The commander of the Congress recognized at once the impossibility of resisting the assault of the ram which had just sunk the Cumberland. With commendable promptness and presence of mind, he slipped his cables, and ran her aground upon

---

⚓ "The situation of affairs, both Federal and State, at Norfolk, on the morning of the 19th of April [1861]," says J. T. Scharf in his "History of the Confederate States Navy," "was that the Federal authorities had there the U. S. frigate Cumberland, 24 guns, fully manned, ready for sea, and under orders for Vera Cruz; the brig Dolphin, 4 guns, fully manned, and ready for sea; the sloop Germantown, 22 guns, fully manned, ready for sea; the sloop Plymouth, 22 guns, ready for sea; the marines of the navy yard, and the guards of the frigate Raritan, 60 guns, in ordinary; the frigate Columbia, 50 guns, in ordinary; the frigate United States, 50 guns, in ordinary; the steam-frigate Merrimac, 40 guns, under repairs; the ship of the line Delaware, 74 guns, in ordinary; the ship of the line Columbus, 74 guns, in ordinary; and the ship of the line Pennsylvania, 120 guns, 'receiving-ship';—all lying at the yard or in the stream. The yard was walled around with a high brick inclosure, and protected by the Elizabeth River, and there were over 800 marines and sailors with officers. On the side of Virginia the situation was: that of General Taliaferro with his staff; Captain Heth and Major Tyler, two volunteer companies,—the Blues of Norfolk and the Grays of Portsmouth,— and Captains Pegram and Jones, of the navy. These were the only troops in Norfolk, until after the evacuation of the navy yard and the departure of the Federal ships."

Captain H. G. Wright, of the Engineers, who was on the United States steamer Pawnee that had been sent to secure the ships and property at the Gosport Navy Yard, reached Norfolk after dark on April 20th. He reported thus: "On reaching the yard it was found that all the ships afloat except the Cumberland had been scuttled, by order of Commodore McCauley, the commandant of the yard, to prevent their seizure by the Virginia forces, and that they were fast sinking. One of the objects of the expedition— that of removing those vessels and taking them to sea —was, therefore, frustrated. On reporting to the commodore of the yard, I found him disposed to defend the yard and property to the last, and the troops were accordingly landed and some disposi-

tions for defense taken. It was soon determined, however, by Commodore Paulding, who had come on the Pawnee from Washington, to finish the destruction of the scuttled ships, to burn and otherwise destroy, as far as practicable, the property in the yard, and withdraw with the frigate Cumberland, in tow of the Pawnee and a steam-tug which was lying at the yard. To Commander John Rodgers, of the navy, and myself was assigned the duty of blowing up the dry-dock, assisted by forty men of the volunteers and a few men from the crew of the Pawnee." Captain Wright and Commander Rodgers lighted the matches, but the mine, as was afterward learned, did not explode. The heat from the burning buildings drove the men in the boats from the landing, and the two officers, alone and hemmed in, had to give themselves up to the commander of the Virginia forces. They were taken to Richmond, and released on April 24th.

In his "Recollections," Captain W. H. Parker, C. S. N., says: "The evacuation of Norfolk by the Federals was a most fortunate thing for the Confederates. Why the Federal authorities did this was always beyond my comprehension. They had the place, and with the force at their command could not have been driven out. No batteries could have been put up by the Confederates in the face of the broadsides of their ships, and it being only twelve miles from Fort Monroe (Old Point Comfort) it could have been reënforced to any extent. But they did give it up, and had hardly done so when they commenced making preparations to retake it. The navy yard contained a large number of heavy cannon, and these guns were used not only to fortify Norfolk and the batteries on the York, Potomac, James, and Rappahannock rivers, but were sent to North and South Carolina, Georgia, Florida, Alabama, Mississippi, and Louisiana. They were to be found at Roanoke Island, Wilmington, Charleston, Mobile, New Orleans, Vicksburg, and many other places. These guns, according to J. T. Scharf, numbered 1198, of which 52 were nine-inch Dahlgrens." EDITORS.

THE "MERRIMAC" PASSING THE CONFEDERATE BATTERY ON CRANEY ISLAND, ON HER WAY
TO ATTACK THE FEDERAL FLEET.

the shallows, where the *Merrimac*, at that time drawing twenty-three feet of water, was unable to approach her, and could attack her with artillery alone. But, although the *Congress* had more guns than the *Merrimac*, and was also supported by the land batteries, it was an unequal conflict, for the projectiles hurled at the *Merrimac* glanced harmlessly from her iron-covered roof, while her rifled guns raked the *Congress* from end to end.

A curious incident must be noted here. Great numbers of people from the neighborhood of Ragged Island, as well as soldiers from the nearest posts, had rushed to the shore to behold the spectacle. The cannonade was visibly raging with redoubled intensity; but, to our amazement, not a sound was heard by us from the commencement of the battle. A strong March wind was blowing direct from us toward Newport News. We could see every flash of the guns and the clouds of white smoke, but not a single report was audible.

The *Merrimac*, taking no notice of the land batteries, concentrated her fire upon the ill-fated *Congress*. The latter replied gallantly until her commander, Joseph B. Smith, was killed and her decks were reeking with slaughter. Then her colors were hauled down and white flags appeared at the gaff and mainmast. Meanwhile, the James River gun-boat flotilla had joined the *Merrimac*.

Through my field-glass I could see the crew of the *Congress* making their escape to the shore over the bow. Unable to secure her prize, the *Merrimac* set her on fire with hot shot, and turned to face new adversaries just appearing upon the scene of conflict.

As soon as it was known at Fort Monroe that the *Merrimac* had come out, the frigates *Minnesota*, *Roanoke*, and *St. Lawrence* were ordered to the assistance of the blockading squadron. The *Minnesota*, assisted by two tugs, was the first to reach the scene, but the *Cumberland* and the *Congress* were already past help. As soon as she came within range, a rapid cannonade commenced between her and the *Merrimac*, aided by the *Patrick*

Henry and the *Jamestown*, side-wheel river steamers transformed into gun-boats. The *Minnesota*, drawing nearly as much water as the *Merrimac*, grounded upon a shoal in the North Channel. This at once put an end to any further attacks by ramming; but the lofty frigate, towering above the water, now offered an easy target to the rifled guns of the *Merrimac* and the lighter artillery of the gun-boats. A shot from her exploded the *Patrick Henry's* boiler, causing much loss of life and disabling that vessel for a considerable time.

In the meantime the *Roanoke* and *St. Lawrence* were approaching, aided by steam-tugs. As they passed Sewell's Point, its batteries opened fire upon them, and they replied with broadsides. Just at that moment the scene was one of unsurpassed magnificence. The bright afternoon sun shone upon the glancing waters. The fortifications of Newport News were seen swarming with soldiers, now idle spectators of a conflict far beyond the range of their batteries, and the flames were just bursting from the abandoned *Congress*. The stranded *Minnesota* seemed a huge monster at bay, surrounded by the *Merrimac* and the gun-boats. The entire horizon was lighted up by the continual flashes of the artillery of these combatants, the broadsides of the *Roanoke* and *St. Lawrence* and the Sewell's Point batteries; clouds of white smoke rose in spiral columns to the skies, illumined by the evening sunlight, while land and water seemed to tremble under the thunders of the cannonade.

The *Minnesota* was now in a desperate situation. It is true that, being aground, she could not sink, but, looking through the glass, I could see a hole in her side, made by the *Merrimac's* rifle shells. She had lost a number of men, and had once been set on fire. Her destruction or surrender seemed inevitable, since all efforts to get her afloat had failed. But just then the *Merrimac* turned away from her toward the *Roanoke* and the *St. Lawrence*. These vessels had suffered but little from the distant fire of the Sewell's Point batteries, but both had run aground, and had not been floated off again without great difficulty, for it was very hazardous for vessels of deep draught to manœuvre over these comparatively shallow waters. When the *Merrimac* approached, they delivered broadsides and were then towed back with promptness. The *Merrimac* pursued them but a short distance (for by this time darkness was falling upon the scene of action, the tide was ebbing, and there was great risk of running aground), and then steamed toward Norfolk with the *Beaufort*, leaving her wounded at the Marine Hospital.

And now followed one of the grandest episodes of this splendid yet somber drama. The moon in her second quarter was just rising over the waters, but her silvery light was soon paled by the conflagration of the *Congress*, whose glare was reflected in the river. The burning frigate four miles away seemed much nearer. As the flames crept up the rigging, every mast, spar, and rope glittered against the dark sky in dazzling lines of fire. The hull, aground upon the shoal, was plainly visible, and upon its black surface each port-hole seemed the mouth of a fiery furnace. For hours the flames raged, with hardly a perceptible change in the wondrous picture. At irregular intervals, loaded guns and shells, exploding as the fire reached them, sent forth their deep reverberations. The masts and rigging were still standing, apparently almost intact, when, about 2 o'clock in the morning, a monstrous sheaf of flame rose from the vessel to an immense height. A deep report announced the explosion of the ship's powder-magazine. Apparently all the force of the explosion had been upward. The rigging had vanished entirely, but the hull seemed hardly shattered; the only apparent change in it was that in two places two or three of the port-holes had been blown into one great gap. It continued to burn until the brightness of its blaze was effaced by the morning sun.

During the night I had sent an order to bring down from Smithfield to Ragged Island the twelve-oared barge that I used when inspecting the river batteries, and at the first dawn of day I embarked with some of my staff, and rowed in the direction of the *Minnesota*, confident of witnessing her destruction or surrender; and, in fact, nothing could have saved her but the timely arrival of the anxiously expected *Monitor*.

The sun was just rising when the *Merrimac*, having anchored for the night at Sewell's Point, headed toward the *Minnesota*. But a most important incident had taken place during the night. The *Monitor* had reached Old Point about 10 o'clock; her commander had been informed of the events of the day, and ordered to proceed at once to the relief of the *Minnesota*.

As soon as the *Merrimac* approached her old adversary, the *Monitor* darted out from behind the *Minnesota*, whose immense bulk had effectually concealed her from view. No words can express the surprise with which we beheld this strange craft, whose appearance was tersely and graphically described by the exclamation of one of my oarsmen, "A tin can on a shingle!" Yet this insignificant-looking object was at that moment the most powerful war-ship in the world. The first shots of the *Merrimac* were directed at the *Minnesota*, which was again set on fire, while one of the tugs alongside of her was blown up, creating great havoc and consternation; but the *Monitor*, having the advantage of light draught, placed herself between the *Merrimac* and her intended victim, and from that moment the conflict became a heroic single combat between the two iron-clads. For an instant they seemed to pause, as if to survey each other. Then advancing cautiously, the two vessels opened fire as soon as they came within range, and a fierce artillery duel raged between them without perceptible effect, although the entire fight was within close range, from half a mile at the farthest down to a few yards. For four hours, from 8 to 12 (which seemed three times as long), the cannonading continued with hardly a moment's intermission. I was now within three-quarters of a mile of them, and more than once stray shots came near enough to dash the spray over my barge, but the grandeur of the spectacle was so fascinating that they passed by unheeded. During the evolutions, in which the *Monitor* had the advantage of light draught, the *Merrimac* ran aground. After much delay and difficulty she was floated off. Finding that her shot made no impression whatever upon the *Monitor*, the *Merrimac*, seizing a favorable chance, succeeded in striking her foe with her stem. Soon afterward they ceased firing and separated as if by common consent. The *Monitor* steamed away toward Old Point. Captain Van Brunt, commander of the *Minnesota*, states in his official report that when he saw the *Monitor* disappear, he lost all hope of saving his ship. But, fortunately for him, the *Merrimac* steamed slowly toward Norfolk, evidently disabled in her motive power. The *Monitor*, accompanied by several tugs, returned late in the afternoon, and they succeeded in floating off the *Minnesota* and conveying her to Old Point.

HOW THE GUN-BOAT "ZOUAVE" AIDED THE "CONGRESS."

BY HENRY REANEY, ACTING MASTER, U. S. N.

THE *Zouave* was a tug-boat built in Albany, N. Y., for service on the Hudson River, of great power and speed for that class of vessel. On her purchase by the Government, she was delivered at Hampton Roads by her original owners to Admiral Goldsborough, at that time in command of the North Atlantic Squadron. The en-gineers and firemen who brought her from Albany entered the naval service, both the former being appointed acting second-assistant engineers, and the latter first-class firemen. I was ordered to her February 1st, 1862, and took with me from the store-ship *William Badger*, of which I was executive, ten men, who, with the pilot, H. J. Phillips, who had been previously ordered, comprised the crew. She had for armament a 30-pounder Parrott rifle forward and a 24-pounder howitzer aft. We were ready for service early in February and were assigned to picket duty in the James River, which employed us only from sunset to sunrise. During the daytime we acted as a tender for the *Cumberland* and *Congress*. On the 8th of March, after coming in from picket duty, we went to Fort Monroe for the mail and fresh provisions, which we got on the arrival of the mail-boat from Baltimore. We returned to Newport News about 10 o'clock. After delivering the stores belonging to the *Congress* and *Cumberland*, we went to the wharf to lie until wanted. A little after dinner, about 12:30, the quartermaster on watch called my attention to black smoke in the Elizabeth River, close to Craney Island. We let go from the wharf and ran alongside the *Cumberland*. The officer of the deck ordered us to run down toward Pig Point and find out what was coming down from Norfolk. It did not take us long to find out, for we had not gone over two miles when we saw what to all appearances looked like the roof of a very big barn belching forth smoke as from a chimney on fire. We were all divided in opinion as to what was coming. The boatswain's mate was the first to make out the Confederate flag, and then we all guessed it was the *Merrimac* come at last. When we were satisfied it was the enemy, we went to quarters and fired our 30-pounder Parrott, which was not answered. We fired again, taking deliberate aim, and were rather surprised that it was unnoticed; we fired, I think, about six shots when our recall signal was hoisted on the *Cumberland*. By this time the batteries at Newport News had commenced firing, the *Congress* had gone to quarters and opened fire; when we got close to the *Cumberland* she also began firing. The *Merrimac* kept on until abreast the *Congress*, when she opened fire, pouring a broadside in passing, and came right on for the *Cumberland*, which vessel was using her guns as fast as they could be fired. We were in rather a tight place, being between the fire of the gun-boats from Norfolk and the *Patrick Henry* and *Jamestown* from Richmond, and our own batteries on shore, the shot from which were falling all round us. However, we kept loading and firing as fast as we were able, until, seeing that the *Congress* had loosed her foretopsail and made signal for us to come alongside, we ran down to her, leaving the *Cumberland* just as the *Merrimac* was passing her bows. We made fast to the port side of the *Congress*, passing our tow-line through a scupper, and with our breastlines through a gun-port, she lying headed toward Hampton Roads. There was hardly a breath of

wind, so that her topsail and jib were of no account in moving her. It took us some time to get our lines fast, owing to the horrible condition of affairs on the gun-deck, which was on fire. The cries of the wounded were terrible. The men were not all regular men-of-war's-men — I think some were soldiers; but, anyhow, the tug's crew had to get on board to make our lines fast. When everything was ready, Lieut. Smith ordered me to go ahead, with our helm hard-a-starboard so as to get her into shoal water. When we had her headed toward the shore, the *Merrimac* got right astern of us and opened fire, pouring broadside after broadside, that raked her fore and aft, overthrowing several of the guns and killing a number of the crew. About this time we were in rather a bad plight; the blood was running from the *Congress* scuppers on to our deck, like water on a wash-deck morning; the tallow-cup on top of our cylinder, and the pilot-house and billethead on the stem were shattered by shot; the pilot, Mr. Phillips, was stunned. Our *Zouave* figure-head, which was a fixture on top of the pilot-house, carried away by a shot on its way over the bows, disabled two of the crew of the rifle. It was about this time that the *Congress* grounded and the white flag was hoisted. Firing ceased and a rebel steamer was making for us. I told Lieut. Pendergrast that if he did not want me any more, I'd leave and try to escape. He told me to take care of myself, as they had surrendered. We cut our lines and backed astern, and, as soon as we got clear, commenced firing, which, I think, gave rise to the charge of the *Congress* firing after she had struck her colors. The *Minnesota* was aground in the North Channel, and had my recall signal flying. We headed for her, keeping as close to the beach on our side as possible, when about half-way, after passing all the enemy's vessels, we were struck by a shot which carried away our rudder-post and one of the blades of our propeller-wheel. Being then unable to use our rudder, and heading directly for the enemy, we stopped and backed so as to get her head right, which we did, and with our large hawser out over our port quarter, we kept her going in the right direction, until the gun-boat *Whitehall* came to our assistance. We lay that night alongside the *Minnesota*, and in the morning were towed to Fort Monroe.

I claim for the *Zouave* that she fired the first shot at the *Merrimac*, and that but for her assistance the *Congress* would have been captured; in evidence of which I refer to page 64 of Professor Soley's book, "The Blockade and the Cruisers," also to the "New York Herald" of March 10th, 1862. I held the appointment of acting master's mate, and had been in the service from June, 1861.

DETROIT, March 9th, 1884.

THE PLAN AND CONSTRUCTION OF THE "MERRIMAC."

I.

BY JOHN M. BROOKE, COMMANDER, C. S. N.

EARLY in June, 1861, the Secretary of the Navy of the Confederate States asked me to design an iron-clad. The first idea presenting itself was a shield of timber, two feet thick, plated with three

or more inches of iron, inclined to the horizontal plane at the least angle that would permit working the guns; this shield, its eaves submerged to the depth of two feet, to be supported by a hull of equal length. There was nothing novel in the use of inclined iron-plating. It was apparent that to support such a shield the ends of the vessel would be so full as to prevent the attainment of speed; and that in moving *end on* even a small sea would prevent working the bow or stern gun. It then occurred to me that fineness of line, protection of hull, and buoyancy with light draught, could be obtained by extending the ends of the vessel under water *beyond the shield*, provided the shield were of sufficient length to give the requisite stability. Considering, then, the liability to the banking up of water over these submerged ends, I erected upon each a decked superstructure of ship-iron, carried up from the sides of the submerged parts to a height above water not greater than would permit free use of the guns, and of the usual form of hull above water. Water could be admitted or taken from them.

I submitted to the secretary outline drawings,—sheer, body and deck plans, with explanations,—and he approved and adopted this novel form. In reply to my suggestion that Naval-Constructor John L. Porter and Chief-Engineer William P. Williamson should be called to Richmond, that we might put the plan in execution, he replied that a practical mechanic would be sent from the Norfolk yard. This mechanic—a master ship-carpenter—came; but as he was lacking in confidence and energy, and was averse to performing unusual duty, he was permitted to return to the yard.

Messrs. Porter and Williamson were ordered to Richmond for consultation on the same general subject, and to aid in the work. They met the secretary and myself on the 23d of June, 1861. Mr. Porter brought and submitted to the secretary a model described by the latter in a report dated March 29th, 1862, to the congress of the Confederate States, as "a flat-bottomed light-draught propeller, casemated battery, with inclined iron sides and ends." The hull of this model did not extend beyond the shield. The secretary then called the attention of Messrs. Williamson and Porter to the plan proposed by me, which had been adopted by the department. The drawings were laid before them, the reasons for extending the hull under water beyond the shield were given, and both approved it. As the drawings were in pencil, the secretary directed me to make a clean drawing in ink of the plan, to be filed in the department.

Messrs. Porter and Williamson were directed to ascertain if suitable engines and boilers could be obtained. Mr. Porter offered to make the clean drawing, as "being more familiar with that sort of work." Accepting the offer I went with Williamson to the Tredegar works, where we learned that there were no suitable engines in the South. Williamson then said he thought the engines of the *Merrimac* could be used, but that the vessel would necessarily draw as much water as the *Merrimac*, and it would not be worth while to build a new hull, as enough of the old hull remained to carry out the plan. Mr. Porter and I thought the draught too great, but that we could not do better. We so reported to the secretary, who concurred. That there might be official record of results of consultation, as there was of the original plan, he directed us to consider and report upon the best mode of making the *Merrimac* useful, which we did in accordance with the views above stated. Mr. Williamson and Mr. Porter returned to Norfolk, the former to adapt and repair the engines, the latter to cut the ship down, submerge her ends, etc. To me was assigned the preparation of armor, construction of guns, etc. On the 11th of July Mr. Porter submitted to the secretary drawings, based upon actual measurements of the ship and on the plan of *submerged extended ends*, which I had presented, and which had been unanimously approved. Having reference to this working plan and its details, the secretary issued the following order:

NAVY DEPARTMENT, RICHMOND, July 11, 1861. FLAG-OFFICER F. FORREST. SIR: You will proceed with all practicable dispatch to make the changes in the form of the *Merrimac*, and to build, equip, and fit her in all respects according to the design and plans of the constructor and engineer, Messrs. Porter and Williamson. . . . R. S. MALLORY, Secretary of the C. S. Navy.

This and a similar order were construed by Mr. Porter to credit him with the origin of the plan, and served as a basis to a published claim after the action in Hampton Roads, which led to a call by the Confederate House of Representatives, upon the Secretary of the Navy, for information as to the origin of the plan, and to the settlement of the question by a patent, No. 100, granted me by the Confederate States, 29th July, 1862. This patent is still in my possession.

LEXINGTON, VA., October, 1887.

II.

BY JOHN L. PORTER, NAVAL CONSTRUCTOR, CONFEDERATE STATES.

IN June, 1861, I was ordered to Richmond by Secretary Mallory, and carried up with me a model of an iron-clad for harbor defense. Soon after my arrival I was informed by the secretary that I had been sent for to confer with Chief Engineer W. P. Williamson and Lieutenant J. M. Brooke in arranging an iron-clad. We went into Engineer Williamson's office, and held a consultation, the result of which was this report to the secretary:

"NAVY DEPARTMENT, RICHMOND, June 25th, 1861. SIR: In obedience to your order, we have carefully examined

and considered the various plans and propositions for constructing a shot-proof steam-battery, and respectfully report that in our opinion the steam-frigate *Merrimac*, which is in such condition from the effect of fire as to be useless for any other purpose without incurring a very heavy expense in her rebuilding, can be made an efficient vessel of that character, mounting 10 heavy guns, 2 pivot and 8 broadside guns of her original battery, and from the further consideration that we cannot procure a suitable engine and boilers for any other vessel without building them, which would occupy too much time, it would appear that this is our only chance to get a suitable vessel in a short time. The bottom of the hull, boilers, and heavy and costly parts of the engine being but little injured, reduce the cost of construction to about one-third of the amount which would be required to construct such a vessel anew.

"We cannot, without further examination, make an accurate estimate of the cost of the proposed work, but think it will be about one hundred and ten thousand dollars, the most of which will be for labor, the materials being nearly all on hand in the yard, excepting the iron plating to cover the shield. The plan to be adopted in the arrangement of the shield for glancing shot, mounting guns, arranging the hull, and plating to be in accordance with the plan submitted for the approval of the department. We are, with much respect, your obedient servants, WILLIAM P. WILLIAMSON, Chief Engineer; JOHN M. BROOKE, Lieutenant; JOHN L. PORTER, Naval Constructor."

I returned immediately to the Gosport Navy Yard, and made a working drawing of the whole thing, put my shield on it, which I had in my model, and returned to the secretary, July 11th, 1861, who had the following order made out, and placed in my hands by himself:

"NAVY DEPARTMENT, RICHMOND, July 11th, 1861. FLAG-OFFICER F. FORREST. SIR: You will proceed, with all practicable dispatch, to make the changes in the *Merrimac*, and to build, equip, and fit her in all respects according to the designs and plans of the constructor and engineer, Messrs. Porter and Williamson. As time is of the first importance in the matter, you will see that work progresses without delay to completion. S. R. MALLORY, Secretary of the Confederate States Navy."

I came immediately back to the Navy Yard and commenced this great work, unassisted by mortal man so far as the plans and responsibilities of the hull and its workings were concerned as an ironclad. The second letter which came from the department about this great piece of work is as follows:

"CONFEDERATE STATES NAVY DEPARTMENT, RICHMOND, August 18th, 1861. FLAG-OFFICER F. FORREST, COMMANDING NAVY YARD, GOSPORT. SIR: The great importance of the service expected from the *Merrimac*, and the urgent necessity of her speedy completion, induce me to call upon you to push forward the work with the utmost dispatch. Chief Engineer Williamson and Constructor Porter, severally in charge of the two respective branches of this great work, and for which they will be held personally responsible, will receive, therefore, every possible facility at the expense and delay of every other work on hand if necessary. SECRETARY S. R. MALLORY, Confederate States Navy."

In April, 1846, I had been stationed in Pittsburg superintending an iron steamer, when I conceived the idea of an iron-clad, and made a model with the exact shield which I placed on the *Merrimac*. Lieutenant Brooke tried for over a week to carry out the wish of the department, but failed entirely to produce anything, whereupon I was called on by the secretary.

After I had made the plan of the *Merrimac*, and had submitted it to the department, not to Lieutenant Brooke, and when everything was fresh in the mind of the secretary, he had the order of July 11th made out and placed in my hands, to Flag-Officer Forrest, to proceed with the work with all dispatch. No man save myself had anything to do with the converting of that ship into an ironclad,—I calculated her displacement, weight, etc., and cut her down to suit, and no man save myself knew what she would bear. Lieutenant Brooke came to the yard once while the ship was being prepared, and stated that he had tried experiments on three inches of iron and it would not stand the fire. I then told him to put on another inch, making four inches; he asked me if she would bear it. I told him she would, and the armor was changed to four inches. All the inboard plans and arrangements were made by myself, and the whole working of the ship; Lieutenant Brooke superintended the armor and guns; Engineer Williamson superintended the machinery, and John L. Porter the construction of the hull. The accompanying drawing is a correct representation of a cross-section amidships. She had only decks, gun and berth. Her shield sloped at an angle of 35 degrees; her rudder and propeller were well protected by a heavy fan-tail; her prow was of cast-iron securely fastened to the ship, and so well secured that though it was broken in two by striking the *Cumberland* a glancing blow, the fastenings to the vessel were not broken loose. Her deck ends were two feet below water and not awash, and the ship was as strong and well protected at her center-line as anywhere else, as her knuckle was two feet below her water-line, and her plating ran down to the knuckle and was there clamped. Her draught of water was 21 feet forward and 22 feet aft.

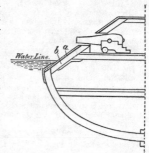

CROSS-SECTION OF "MERRIMAC," FROM A DRAWING BY JOHN L. PORTER, CONSTRUCTOR.

a — 4 inches of iron.
b — 22 inches of wood.

After the engagements of the 8th and 9th of March, 1862, I put her in the dry-dock and found she had 97 indentations on her armor from shot, 20 of which were from the 10-inch guns of the *Monitor*. Six of her top layer of plates were broken by the *Monitor's* shots, and none by those of the other vessels. None of the lower layer of plates were injured. I removed those plates and replaced them by others. Her wood-work underneath was not hurt. Her smoke-stack was full of shot-holes. She never had any boat-davits. Her pilot-house was cast solid, and was not covered with plate-iron like her shield. She had port shutters only at her four quarter port-holes. It will thus be seen that the conversion of the *Merrimac* into an iron-clad was merely accidental, and grew out of the impracticability of building an engine within the time at the disposal of the Confederacy, and no iron-clad, with submerged ends, was afterward built.

PORTSMOUTH, VA., October, 1887.

NOTES ON THE MONITOR – MERRIMAC FIGHT. ☆

BY DINWIDDIE B. PHILLIPS, SURGEON OF THE "MERRIMAC."

THE *Virginia* (or *Merrimac*), with which I was connected during her entire career, bore some resemblance to a huge terrapin with a large round chimney about the middle of its back. She was so built as not to suit high winds and heavy seas, and therefore could not operate outside the capes of Virginia. In fact she was designed from the first as a defense for the harbor of Norfolk, and for that alone. In addition to our guns, we were armed with an iron ram or prow. The prow, not being well put on, was twisted off and lost in our first encounter with the *Cumberland*. I am also satisfied that had not our prow been lost, we should have sunk the *Monitor* when we rammed her on the 9th of March, 1862. Admiral Worden is of contrary opinion. In a private letter to me, dated March 13th, 1882, he says:

"If the prow of the *Merrimac* had been intact at the time she struck the *Monitor*, she could not have damaged her a particle more by the blow with it than she did in hitting her with her stem; and for the following reasons: The hull of the *Monitor* was in breadth, at her midship section, 34 feet, and the armored raft which was placed on the hull was, at the same point, 41 feet 4 inches in breadth, so that the raft extended on either side 3 feet 8 inches beyond the hull. The raft was 5 feet deep and was immersed in the water 3½ feet. The *Merrimac's* prow, according to Jones, was 2 feet below the surface of the water. The prow, therefore, if on, would have struck the armored hull 1½ feet above its lowest part, and could not have damaged it. Further, the prow extended 2 feet forward from the stem, and had it been low enough to reach below the armored raft, it could not have reached the hull by 1 foot 8 inches."

Admiral Worden's theory, given above, like all untested ones, is merely speculation; and I doubt not the commander of the *Cumberland*, previous to a practical demonstration, would have thought it impossible for our prow to have first crushed its way through a strongly constructed raft projected in front of that vessel as a protection against torpedoes, and then to have penetrated her bow — the strongest part of the ship — and to have made a chasm in it large enough, according to Wood, to admit a "horse and cart."

Most of our crew being volunteers from the army and unused to ship-life, about twenty per cent. of our men were usually ashore at the hospital, and our effective force on the 8th of March was about 250 or 260 men.

We left the Norfolk Navy Yard about 11 A. M. of that day. As our engines were very weak and defective, having been condemned just before the war as worthless, we were fortunate in having favorable weather for our purpose. The day was unusually mild and calm for the season, and the water was smooth and glassy; and, except for the unusually large number of persons upon the shores watching our motions, there was nothing to indicate a serious movement on our part. Our vessel never having been tested before, and her model being new and unheard of, many of those who watched us predicted failure, and others suggested that the *Virginia* was an enormous metallic burial-case, and that we were conducting our own funeral.

Though we withdrew on the first day of the battle, at 7 P. M., and went to our anchorage at Sewell's Point, our duties kept us so constantly engaged that it was near midnight before we got our supper, the only meal we had taken since 8 A. M. Afterward the attractiveness of the burning *Congress* was such that we watched her till nearly 1 A. M., when she blew up, before we went to our rest, so that when we were aroused to resume the fight on Sunday morning, it seemed as though we had scarcely been asleep. After a hurried breakfast, and while the crew were getting up the anchor, I landed Captain Buchanan, Lieutenant Minor, and the seriously wounded men at Sewell's Point, for transmission to the naval hospital at Norfolk. Returning, I pulled around the ship before boarding her, to see how she had stood the bombardment of Saturday and to what extent she had been damaged. I found all her stanchions, iron railings, and light work of every description swept away, her smoke-stack cut to pieces, two guns without muzzles, and ninety-eight indentations on her plating, showing where heavy solid shot had struck, but had glanced off without doing any injury. As soon as I had got on deck (about 6:25 A. M.), we started again for Hampton Roads.

On our way to the *Minnesota*, and while we were still too far off to do her much damage, the *Monitor* came out to meet us. For some length of time we devoted our attention to her, but having no solid shot, and finding that our light shell were making but little impression upon her turret, Jones ordered the pilot to disregard the *Monitor* altogether, and carry out his first instructions by placing the *Virginia* as near to the *Minnesota* as possible. Instead, however, of taking us within a half mile of that ship, as we afterward learned he could have done, he purposely ran us aground nearly two miles off. This he did through fear of passing under the *Minnesota's* terrible broadside, as he confessed subsequently to Captain A. B. Fairfax, Confederate States navy, from whose lips I received it.

After fifteen or twenty minutes we were afloat again. We sheered off from the *Monitor* in order to get a chance to turn and ram her. This was the time when Captain Van Brunt was under the impression we were in retreat and "the little battery chasing us." As soon as the move could be effected, we turned and ran into the *Monitor*, and at the same time gave her a shot from our bow pivot-gun. Had our iron prow been intact, as I have already said, we would have sunk her. As it was, she staggered awhile under the shock, and, sheering off from us was for a time inactive [see p. 725]. The battle was renewed, but shortly after noon the *Monitor* again withdrew [see p. 727].

We continued our fire upon the *Minnesota*, at long range, for about half an hour longer, when we took advantage of the flood-tide and returned slowly to Norfolk. That we did not destroy the *Minnesota* was due solely to the fact that our pilot assured us we could get no nearer to her than we then were without grounding again.

☆ Condensed from a paper in "The Southern Bivouac" for March, 1887.

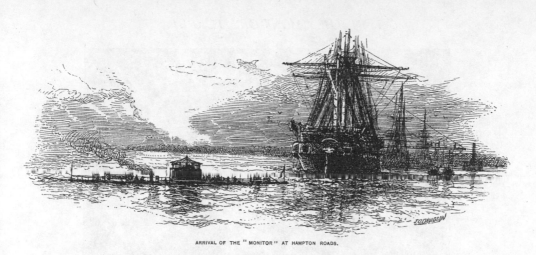

ARRIVAL OF THE "MONITOR" AT HAMPTON ROADS.

IN THE "MONITOR" TURRET.

BY S. DANA GREENE, COMMANDER, U. S. N., EXECUTIVE OFFICER OF THE "MONITOR."

THE keel of the most famous vessel of modern times, Captain Ericsson's first iron-clad, was laid in the ship-yard of Thomas F. Rowland, at Greenpoint, Brooklyn, in October, 1861, and on the 30th of January, 1862, the novel craft was launched. On the 25th of February she was commissioned and turned over to the Government, and nine days later left New York for Hampton Roads, where, on the 9th of March, occurred the memorable contest with the *Merrimac*. On her next venture on the open sea she foundered off Cape Hatteras in a gale of wind (December 29th). During her career of less than a year she had no fewer than five different commanders; but it was the fortune of the writer to serve as her only executive officer, standing upon her deck when she was launched, and leaving it but a few minutes before she sank.

So hurried was the preparation of the *Monitor* that the mechanics worked upon her day and night up to the hour of her departure, and little opportunity was offered to drill the crew at the guns, to work the turret, and to become familiar with the other unusual features of the vessel. The crew was, in fact, composed of volunteers. Lieutenant Worden, having been authorized by the Navy Department to select his men from any ship-of-war in New York harbor, addressed the crews of the *North Carolina* and *Sabine*, stating fully to them the probable dangers of the passage to Hampton Roads and the certainty of having important service to perform after arriving. The sailors responded enthusiastically, many more volunteering than were required. Of the crew Captain Worden said, in his official report of the battle, "A better one no naval commander ever had the honor to command." ↓

↓ The *Monitor's* officers were : Lieut. J. L. Worden, commanding; Lieut. S. D. Greene, executive officer; Acting Master, L. N. Stodder; Acting Master, J. N. Webber; Acting Master's Mate, G. Frederickson; Acting Assistant Surgeon, D. C. Logue; Acting Assistant Paymaster, W. F. Keeler; Chief Engineer, A. C. Stimers (inspector); First Assist-ant Engineer, Isaac Newton (in charge of steam machinery); Second Assist. Engineer, A. B. Campbell; Third Assist. Engineer, R. W. Hands; Fourth Assist. Engineer, M. T. Sunstrom; Captain's Clerk, D. Toffey; Quartermaster, P. Williams; Gunner's Mate, J. Crown; Boatswain's Mate, J. Stocking; and 42 others,—a total of 58.—S. D. G.

FROM A PHOTOGRAPH TAKEN IN 1875.

John D Worden

REAR-ADMIRAL, U. S. N.

The sword was presented to Admiral Worden by the State of New York soon after the engagement
in Hampton Roads.— EDITORS.

We left New York in tow of the tug-boat *Seth Low* at 11 A. M. of Thursday,
the 6th of March.   On the following day a moderate breeze was encountered,
and it was at once evident that the *Monitor* was unfit as a sea-going craft.
Nothing but the subsidence of the wind prevented her from being shipwrecked
before she reached Hampton Roads.   The berth-deck hatch leaked in spite
of all we could do, and the water came down under the turret like a waterfall.
It would strike the pilot-house and go over the turret in beautiful curves, and
it came through the narrow eye-holes in the pilot-house with such force as to
knock the helmsman completely round from the wheel.   The waves also
broke over the blower-pipes, and the water came down through them in such

quantities that the belts of the blower-engines slipped, and the engines consequently stopped for lack of artificial draught, without which, in such a confined place, the fires could not get air for combustion. Newton and Stimers, followed by the engineer's force, gallantly rushed into the engine-room and fire-room to remedy the evil, but they were unable to check the inflowing water, and were nearly suffocated with escaping gas. They were dragged out more dead than alive, and carried to the top of the turret, where the fresh air gradually revived them. The water continued to pour through the hawse-hole, and over and down the smoke-stacks and blower-pipes, in such quantities that there was imminent danger that the ship would founder. The steam-pumps could not be operated because the fires had been nearly extinguished, and the engine-room was uninhabitable on account of the suffocating gas with which it was filled. The hand-pumps were then rigged and worked, but they had not enough force to throw the water out through the top of the turret,— the only opening,— and it was useless to bail, as we had to pass the buckets up through the turret, which made it a very long operation. Fortunately, toward evening the wind and the sea subsided, and, being again in smooth water, the engine was put in operation. But at midnight, in passing over a shoal, rough water was again encountered, and our troubles were renewed, complicated this time with the jamming of the wheel-ropes, so that the safety of the ship depended entirely on the strength of the hawser which connected her with the tug-boat. The hawser, being new, held fast; but during the greater part of the night we were constantly engaged in fighting the leaks, until we reached smooth water again, just before daylight.

It was at the close of this dispiriting trial trip, in which all hands had been exhausted in their efforts to keep the novel craft afloat, that the *Monitor* passed Cape Henry at 4 P. M. on Saturday, March 8th. At this point was heard the distant booming of heavy guns, which our captain rightly judged to be an engagement with the *Merrimac*, twenty miles away. He at once ordered the vessel stripped of her sea-rig, the turret keyed up, and every preparation made for battle. As we approached Hampton Roads we could see the fine old *Congress* burning brightly, and soon a pilot came on board and told of the arrival of the *Merrimac*, the disaster to the *Cumberland* and the *Congress*, and the dismay of the Union forces. The *Monitor* was pushed with all haste, and reached the *Roanoke* (Captain Marston), anchored in the Roads, at 9 P. M. Worden immediately reported his arrival to Captain Marston, who suggested that he should go to the assistance of the *Minnesota*, then aground off Newport News. ♭ As no pilot was available, Captain Worden accepted the

♭ Captain John Marston, of the *Roanoke*, who was the senior officer present during Flag-Officer Goldsborough's absence on the sounds of North Carolina, had received peremptory orders to send the *Monitor* to Washington without delay. Similar orders had been received by Commodore Paulding in New York, but they only arrived after the *Monitor's* departure, and the tug by which Paulding endeavored to communicate with her failed to overtake her. When Worden went on board the *Roanoke* to report his arrival at Hampton Roads, Captain Marston took upon himself the responsibility of retaining the *Monitor* to protect the fleet. Under the circumstances, it is hard to see how he could have done otherwise, although his action involved him in a technical disobedience of orders. In view of the spirit of routine which pervaded the older branch of the service at this time, Captain Marston's action showed commendable spirit and good sense.— EDITORS.

volunteer services of Acting Master Samuel Howard, who earnestly sought the duty.   An atmosphere of gloom pervaded the fleet, and the pygmy aspect of the new-comer did not inspire confidence among those who had witnessed the destruction of the day before. Skillfully piloted by Howard, we proceeded on our way, our path illumined by the blaze of the *Congress*. Reaching the *Minnesota*, hard and fast aground, near midnight, we anchored, and Worden reported to Captain Van Brunt. Between 1 and 2 A. M. the *Congress* blew up,— not instantaneously, but successively. Her powder-tanks seemed to explode, each shower of sparks rivaling the other in its height, until they appeared to reach the zenith,— a grand but mournful sight. Near us, too, at the bottom of the river, lay the *Cumberland*, with her silent crew of brave men, who died while fighting their guns to the water's edge, and whose colors were still flying at the peak.

The dreary night dragged slowly on; the officers and crew were up and alert, to be ready for any emergency. At daylight on Sunday the *Merrimac* and

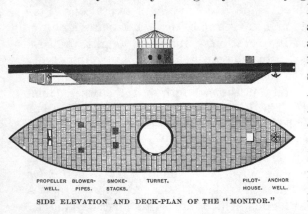

PROPELLER BLOWER- SMOKE- TURRET.   PILOT- ANCHOR
WELL.   PIPES. STACKS.   HOUSE. WELL.

SIDE ELEVATION AND DECK-PLAN OF THE "MONITOR."

her consorts were discovered at anchor near Sewell's Point. At about half-past 7 o'clock the enemy's vessels got under way and steered in the direction of the *Minnesota*. At the same time the *Monitor* got under way, and her officers and crew took their stations for battle. Captain Van Brunt, of the *Minnesota*, officially reports, "I made signal to the *Monitor* to attack the enemy," but the signal was not seen by us; other work was in hand, and Commander Worden required no signal.

The pilot-house of the *Monitor* was situated well forward, near the bow; it was a wrought-iron structure, built of logs of iron nine inches thick, bolted through the corners, and covered with an iron plate two inches thick, which was not fastened down, but was kept in place merely by its weight. The sight-holes or slits were made by inserting quarter-inch plates at the corners between the upper set of logs and the next below. The structure projected four feet above the deck, and was barely large enough inside to hold three men standing. It presented a flat surface on all sides and on top. The steering-wheel was secured to one of the logs on the front side. The position and shape of this structure should be carefully borne in mind.

Worden took his station in the pilot-house, and by his side were Howard, the pilot, and Peter Williams, quartermaster, who steered the vessel through-

The fortune of civil war was illustrated in the case of the *Merrimac*. Commodore Buchanan's brother was an officer of the *Congress*, and each knew of the other's presence. The first and fourth lieutenants of the *Merrimac* had each a brother in the United States army. The father of the fifth lieutenant was also in the United States army. The father of one of the midshipmen was in the United States navy. Lieutenant Butt, of the *Merrimac*, had been the room-mate of Lieutenant S. Dana Greene, of the *Monitor*, at the Naval Academy in Annapolis.— EDITORS.

out the engagement. My place was in the turret, to work and fight the guns; with me were Stodder and Stimers and sixteen brawny men, eight to each gun. John Stocking, boatswain's mate, and Thomas Lochrane, seaman, were gun-captains. Newton and his assistants were in the engine and fire rooms, to manipulate the boilers and engines, and most admirably did they perform this important service from the beginning to the close of the action. Webber had charge of the powder division on the berth-deck, and Joseph Crown, gunner's-mate, rendered valuable service in connection with this duty.

The physical condition of the officers and men of the two ships at this time was in striking contrast. The *Merrimac* had passed the night quietly near Sewell's Point, her people enjoying rest and sleep, elated by thoughts of the victory they had achieved that day, and cheered by the prospects of another easy victory on the morrow. The *Monitor* had barely escaped shipwreck twice within the last thirty-six hours, and since Friday morning, forty-eight hours before, few if any of those on board had closed their eyes in sleep or had anything to eat but hard bread, as cooking was impossible. She was surrounded by wrecks and disaster, and her efficiency in action had yet to be proved.

Worden lost no time in bringing it to test. Getting his ship under way, he steered direct for the enemy's vessels, in order to meet and engage them as far as possible from the *Minnesota*. As he approached, the wooden vessels quickly turned and left. Our captain, to the "astonishment" of Captain Van Brunt (as he states in his official report), made straight for the *Merrimac*, which had already commenced firing; and when he came within short range, he changed his course so as to come alongside of her, stopped the engine, and gave the order, "Commence firing!" I triced up the port, ran out the gun, and, taking deliberate aim, pulled the lockstring. The *Merrimac* was quick to reply, returning a rattling broadside (for she had ten guns to our two), and the battle fairly began. The turrets and other parts of the ship were heavily struck, but the shots did not penetrate; the tower was intact, and it continued to revolve. A look of confidence passed over the men's faces, and we believed the *Merrimac* would not repeat the work she had accomplished the day before.

The fight continued with the exchange of broadsides as fast as the guns could be served and at very short range, the distance between the vessels frequently being not more than a few yards. Worden skillfully manœuvred his quick-turning vessel, trying to find some vulnerable point in his adversary. Once he made a dash at her stern, hoping to disable her screw, which he thinks he missed by not more than two feet. Our shots ripped the iron of the *Merrimac*, while the reverberation of her shots against the tower caused anything but a pleasant sensation. While Stodder, who was stationed at the machine which controlled the revolving motion of the turret, was incautiously leaning against the side of the tower, a large shot struck in the vicinity and disabled him. He left the turret and went below, and Stimers, who had assisted him, continued to do the work.

The drawbacks to the position of the pilot-house were soon realized. We could not fire ahead nor within several points of the bow, since the blast from our own guns would have injured the people in the pilot-house, only

CONFEDERATE BATTERY, SEWELL'S POINT. CONFEDERATE BATTERY, CRANEY ISLAND. CONFEDERATE BATTERIES AT PIG POINT AND BARREL POINT. JAMES RIVER.

CONFEDERATE STEAMERS "YORKTOWN" AND "JAMESTOWN."

"MONITOR" AND "MERRIMAC." "MINNESOTA." WRECKS OF "CONGRESS" AND "CUMBERLAND."

FRENCH MAN-OF-WAR. UNION BATTERIES AND CAMP AT NEWPORT NEWS.

U. S. FRIGATE "ROANOKE" AND TRANSPORTS AND STORE-SHIPS. FORT MONROE.

UNION BATTERY RIP-RAPS.

GOSPORT. PORTSMOUTH. NORFOLK.

BIRD'S-EYE VIEW OF THE ENGAGEMENT.

HAMPTON.

a few yards off. Keeler and Toffey passed the captain's orders and messages to me, and my inquiries and answers to him, the speaking-tube from the pilot-house to the turret having been broken early in the action. They performed their work with zeal and alacrity, but, both being landsmen, our technical communications sometimes miscarried. The situation was novel: a vessel of war was engaged in desperate combat with a powerful foe; the captain, commanding and guiding, was inclosed in one place, and the executive officer, working and fighting the guns, was shut up in another, and communication between them was difficult and uncertain. It was this experience which caused Isaac Newton, immediately after the engagement, to suggest the clever plan of putting the pilot-house on top of the turret, and making it cylindrical instead of square; and his suggestions were subsequently adopted in this type of vessel. [But see p. 736.—EDITORS.]

As the engagement continued, the working of the turret was not altogether satisfactory. It was difficult to start it revolving, or, when once started, to stop it, on account of the imperfections of the novel machinery, which was now undergoing its first trial. Stimers was an active, muscular man, and did his utmost to control the motion of the turret; but, in spite of his efforts, it was difficult, if not impossible, to secure accurate firing. The conditions were very different from those of an ordinary broadside gun, under which we had been trained on wooden ships. My only view of the world outside of the tower was over the muzzles of the guns, which cleared the ports by only a few inches. When the guns were run in, the port-holes were covered by heavy iron pendulums, pierced with small holes to allow the iron rammer and sponge handles to protrude while they were in use. To hoist these pendulums required the entire gun's crew and vastly increased the work inside the turret.

The effect upon one shut up in a revolving drum is perplexing, and it is not a simple matter to keep the bearings. White marks had been placed upon the stationary deck immediately below the turret to indicate the direction of the starboard and port sides, and the bow and stern; but these marks were obliterated early in the action. I would continually ask the captain, "How does the *Merrimac* bear?" He replied, "On the starboard-beam," or "On the port-quarter," as the case might be. Then the difficulty was to determine the direction of the starboard-beam, or port-quarter, or any other bearing. It finally resulted, that when a gun was ready for firing, the turret would be started on its revolving journey in search of the target, and when found it was taken "on the fly," because the turret could not be accurately controlled. Once the *Merrimac* tried to ram us; but Worden avoided the direct impact by the skillful use of the helm, and she struck a glancing blow, which did no damage. At the instant of collision I planted a solid 180-pound shot fair and square upon the forward part of her casemate. Had the gun been loaded with thirty pounds of powder, which was the charge subsequently used with similar guns, it is probable that this shot would have penetrated her armor; but the charge being limited to fifteen pounds, in accordance with peremptory orders to that effect from the Navy Department, the shot rebounded without doing any more damage than possibly to start some of the beams of her armor-backing.

It is stated by Colonel Wood, of the *Merrimac*, that when that vessel rammed the *Cumberland* her ram, or beak, was broken off and left in that vessel. In a letter to me, about two years since, he described this ram as "of castiron, wedge-shaped, about 1500 pounds in weight, 2 feet under water, and projecting 2½ feet from the stem." A ram of this description, had it been intact, would have struck the *Monitor* at that part of the upper hull where the armor and backing were thickest. It is very doubtful if, under any headway that the *Merrimac* could have acquired at such short range, this ram could have done any injury to this part of the vessel. That it could by no possibility have reached the thin lower hull is evident from a glance at the drawing of the *Monitor*, the overhang or upper hull being constructed for the express purpose of protecting the vital part of the vessel.

The battle continued at close quarters without apparent damage to either side. After a time, the supply of shot in the turret being exhausted, Worden hauled off for about fifteen minutes to replenish. The serving of the cartridges, weighing but fifteen pounds, was a matter of no difficulty; but the hoisting of the heavy shot was a slow and tedious operation, it being necessary that the turret should remain stationary, in order that the two scuttles, one in the deck and the other in the floor of the turret, should be in line. Worden took advantage of the lull, and passed through the port-hole upon the deck outside to get a better view of the situation. He soon renewed the attack, and the contest continued as before.

Two important points were constantly kept in mind: first, to prevent the enemy's projectiles from entering the turret through the port-holes,— for the explosion of a shell inside, by disabling the men at the guns, would have ended the fight, as there was no relief gun's crew on board; second, not to

PART OF THE CREW OF THE "MONITOR." ☆ FROM A PHOTOGRAPH TAKEN SOON AFTER THE FIGHT.

fire into our own pilot-house. A careless or impatient hand, during the confusion arising from the whirligig motion of the tower, might let slip one of our big shot against the pilot-house. For this and other reasons I fired every gun while I remained in the turret.

Soon after noon a shell from the enemy's gun, the muzzle not ten yards distant, struck the forward side of the pilot-house directly in the sight-hole, or slit, and exploded, cracking the second iron log and partly lifting the top, leaving an opening. Worden was standing immediately behind this spot, and received in his face the force of the blow, which partly stunned him, and, filling his eyes with powder, utterly blinded him. The injury was known only

☆ The pride of Worden in his crew was warmly reciprocated by his men, and found expression in the following letter, written to him while he was lying in Washington disabled by his wound. We take it from Professor Soley's volume, "The Blockade and the Cruisers" (Charles Scribner's Sons).—EDITORS:

HAMPTON ROADS, April 24th, 1862. U. S. MONITOR. TO OUR DEAR AND HONORED CAPTAIN. DEAR SIR: These few lines is from your own crew of the *Monitor*, with their kindest Love to you their Honored Captain, hoping to God that they will have the pleasure of welcoming you back to us again soon, for we are all ready able and willing to meet Death or anything else, only give us back our Captain again. Dear Captain, we have got your Pilot-house fixed and all ready for you when you get well again; and we all sincerely hope that soon we will have the pleasure of welcoming you back to it. . . . We are waiting very patiently to engage our Antagonist if we could only get a chance to do so. The last time she came out we all thought we would have the Pleasure of sinking her. But we all got disappointed, for we did not fire one shot, and the Norfolk papers says we are cowards in the *Monitor*—and all we want is a chance to show them where it lies with you for our Captain We can teach them who is cowards. But there is a great deal that we would like to write to you but we think you will soon be with us again yourself. But we all join in with our kindest love to you, hoping that God will restore you to us again and hoping that your sufferings is at an end now, and we are all so glad to hear that your eyesight will be spaired to you again. We would wish to write more to you if we have your kind Permission to do so but at present we all conclude by tendering to you our kindest Love and affection, to our Dear and Honored Captain. We remain untill Death your Affectionate Crew.

THE MONITOR BOYS.

To Captain Worden.

to those in the pilot-house and its immediate vicinity. The flood of light rushing through the top of the pilot-house, now partly open, caused Worden, blind as he was, to believe that the pilot-house was seriously injured, if not destroyed; he therefore gave orders to put the helm to starboard and "sheer off." Thus the *Monitor* retired temporarily from the action, in order to ascertain the extent of the injuries she had received. At the same time Worden sent for me, and leaving Stimers the only officer in the turret, I went forward at once, and found him standing at the foot of the ladder leading to the pilot-house.

He was a ghastly sight, with his eyes closed and the blood apparently rushing from every pore in the upper part of his face. He told me that he was seriously wounded, and directed me to take command. I assisted in leading him to a sofa in his cabin, where he was tenderly cared for by Doctor Logue, and then I assumed command. Blind and suffering as he was, Worden's fortitude never forsook him; he frequently asked from his bed of pain of the progress of affairs, and when told that the *Minnesota* was saved, he said, "Then I can die happy."

When I reached my station in the pilot-house, I found that the iron log was fractured and the top partly open; but the steering gear was still intact, and the pilot-house was not totally destroyed, as had been feared. In the confusion of the moment resulting from so serious an injury to the commanding officer, the *Monitor* had been moving without direction. Exactly how much time elapsed from the moment that Worden was wounded until I had reached the pilot-house and completed the examination of the injury at that point, and determined what course to pursue in the damaged condition of the vessel, it is impossible to state; but it could hardly have exceeded twenty minutes at the utmost. During this time the *Merrimac*, which was leaking badly, had started in the direction of the Elizabeth River; and, on taking my station in the pilot-house and turning the vessel's head in the direction of the *Merrimac*, I saw that she was already in retreat. A few shots were fired at the retiring vessel, and she continued on to Norfolk. I returned with the *Monitor* to the side of the *Minnesota*, where preparations were being made to abandon the ship, which was still aground. Shortly afterward Worden was transferred to a tug, and that night he was carried to Washington.

The fight was over. We of the *Monitor* thought, and still think, that we had gained a great victory. This the Confederates have denied. But it has never been denied that the object of the *Merrimac* on the 9th of March was to complete the destruction of the Union fleet in Hampton Roads, and that she was completely foiled and driven off by the *Monitor;* nor has it been denied that at the close of the engagement the *Merrimac* retreated to Norfolk, leaving the *Monitor* in possession of the field.⌡

⌡ "My men and myself were perfectly black with smoke and powder. All my underclothes were perfectly black, and my person was in the same condition. . . . I had been up so long, and been under such a state of excitement, that my nervous system was completely run down. . . . My nerves and muscles twitched as though electric shocks were continually passing through them. . . . I lay down and tried to sleep — I might as well have tried to fly." From a private letter of Lieutenant Greene, written just after the fight.— EDITORS.

In this engagement Captain Worden displayed the highest qualities as an officer and man. He was in his prime (forty-four years old), and carried with him the ripe experience of twenty-eight years in the naval service. He joined the ship a sick man, having but recently left a prison in the South. He was nominated for the command by the late Admiral Joseph Smith, and the result proved the wisdom of the choice. Having accepted his orders against the protests of his physicians and the entreaties of his family, nothing would deter him from the enterprise. He arrived on the battle-ground amidst the disaster and gloom, almost despair, of the Union people, who had little faith that he could beat back the powerful *Merrimac*, after her experience with the *Cumberland* and *Congress*. Without encouragement, single-handed, and without specific orders from any source, he rose above the atmosphere of doubt and depression which surrounded him, and with unflinching nerve and undaunted courage he hurled his little untried vessel against his huge, well-proved antagonist, and won the battle. He was victor in the first iron-clad battle of the world's history.

COMMANDER SAMUEL DANA GREENE, EXECUTIVE OFFICER OF THE "MONITOR." FROM A WAR-TIME PHOTOGRAPH.

The subsequent career of the *Monitor* needs but a few words.

On the day after the fight I received the following letter from Mr. Fox, Assistant Secretary of the Navy:

"U. S. STEAMER *Roanoke*, OLD POINT, March 10th, 1862.

"MY DEAR MR. GREENE: Under the extraordinary circumstances of the contest of yesterday, and the responsibilities devolving upon me, and your extreme youth, ☼ I have suggested to Captain Marston to send on board the *Monitor*, as temporary commanding, Lieutenant Selfridge, until the arrival of Commodore Goldsborough, which will be in a few days. I appreciate your position, and you must appreciate mine, and serve with the same zeal and fidelity. With the kindest wishes for you all, most truly,   G. V. Fox."

For the next two months we lay at Hampton Roads. Twice the *Merrimac* came out of the Elizabeth River, but did not attack. We, on our side, had received positive orders not to attack in the comparatively shoal waters above Hampton Roads, where the Union fleet could not manœuvre. The *Merrimac* protected the James River, and the *Monitor* protected the Chesapeake. Neither side had an iron-clad in reserve, and neither wished to bring on an engagement which might disable its only armored vessel in those waters.

With the evacuation of Norfolk and the destruction of the *Merrimac*, the *Monitor* moved up the James River with the squadron under the command

☼ I was twenty-two years of age, and previous to joining the *Monitor* had seen less than three years of active service, with the rank of midshipman.—S. D. G.

of Commander John Rodgers, in connection with McClellan's advance upon Richmond by the Peninsula. We were engaged for four hours at Fort Darling, but were unable to silence the guns or destroy the earth-works.

Probably no ship was ever devised which was so uncomfortable for her crew, and certainly no sailor ever led a more disagreeable life than we did on the James River, suffocated with heat and bad air if we remained below, and a target for sharp-shooters if we came on deck.

With the withdrawal of McClellan's army, we returned to Hampton Roads, and in the autumn were ordered to Washington, where the vessel was repaired. We returned to Hampton Roads in November, and sailed thence (December 29th) in tow of the steamer *Rhode Island*, bound for Beaufort, N. C. Between 11 P. M. and midnight on the following night the *Monitor* went down in a gale, a few miles south of Cape Hatteras. Four officers and twelve men were drowned, forty-nine people being saved by the boats of the steamer. It was impossible to keep the vessel free of water, and we presumed that the upper and lower hulls thumped themselves apart.

No ship in the world's history has a more imperishable place in naval annals than the *Monitor*. Not only by her providential arrival at the right moment did she secure the safety of Hampton Roads and all that depended on it, but the idea which she embodied revolutionized the system of naval warfare which had existed from the earliest recorded history. The name of the *Monitor* became generic, representing a new type; and, crude and defective as was her construction in some of its details, she yet contained the idea of the turret, which is to-day the central idea of the most powerful armored vessels.↓

↓ On account of the death of the writer of this paper, which occurred December 11th, 1884, soon after its preparation, the proofs did not receive the benefit of his revision. The article appears substantially in the form in which it was written, without changes other than verbal ones and a slight rearrangement of paragraphs.

Of the services of Mr. Greene in connection with the *Monitor*, Captain Worden made the following official record in a letter to the Secretary of the Navy:

" I was ordered to her (the *Monitor*) on the 13th of January, 1862, when she was still on stocks. Prior to that date Lieutenant S. D. Greene had interested himself in her and thoroughly examined her construction and design and informed himself as to her qualities, and, notwithstanding the many gloomy predictions of naval officers and officers of the mercantile marine as to the great probability of her sinking at sea, volunteered to go in her, and, at my request, was ordered. From the date of his orders he applied himself unremittingly and intelligently to the study of her peculiar qualities and to her fitting and equipment. . . . Lieutenant Greene, after taking his place in the pilot-house and finding the injuries there less serious than I had supposed, had turned the vessel's head again in the direction of the enemy to continue the engagement; but before he could get at close quarters with her she retired. He therefore very properly returned to the *Minnesota* and lay by her until she floated. . . . Lieutenant Greene, the executive officer, had charge in the turret, and handled the guns with great courage, coolness, and skill; and throughout the engagement, as in the equipment of the vessel and on her passage to Hampton Roads, he exhibited an earnest devotion to duty unsurpassed in my experience."

EDITORS.

THE BUILDING OF THE "MONITOR."

BY CAPTAIN JOHN ERICSSON, INVENTOR OF THE "MONITOR."

CAPTAIN JOHN ERICSSON. FROM A PHOTOGRAPH.

THE introduction of General Paixhans's brilliant invention, the shell-gun, in 1824, followed, in 1858, by the successful application of armor-plating to the steam-frigate *La Gloire*, under Napoleon III., compelled an immediate change in naval construction which startled the maritime countries of Europe, especially England, whose boasted security behind her "wooden walls" was shown to be a complete delusion. The English naval architects, however, did not overlook the fact that their French rivals, while producing a gun which rendered wooden navies almost useless, had also by their armor-plating provided an efficient protection against the destructive Paixhans shell.

Accordingly, the Admiralty without loss of time laid the keel of the *Warrior*, an armored iron steam-frigate 380 feet long, 58 feet beam, 26 feet draught, and 9200 tons displacement. The work being pushed with extraordinary vigor, this iron-clad ship was speedily launched and equipped, the admiration of the naval world.

Shortly after the adoption of armor-plating as an essential feature in the construction of vessels of war, the Southern States seceded from the Union, some of the most efficient of the United States naval officers resigning their commissions. Their loss was severely felt by the Navy Department at Washington; nor was it long before the presence of great professional skill among the officers of the naval administration of the Confederate States became manifest. Indeed, the utility of the armor-plating adopted by France and England proved to be better understood at Richmond than at Washington. While the Secretary of the Navy, Mr. Welles, and his advisers were discussing the question of armor, news reached Washington that the partly burnt and scuttled steam-frigate *Merrimac*, at the Norfolk Navy Yard, had been raised and cut down to her berth-deck, and that a very substantial structure of timber, resembling a citadel with inclined sides, was being erected on that deck.

The Navy Department at Washington early in August advertised for plans and offers for iron-clad steam-batteries to be built within a stipulated time. My attention having been thus called to a subject which I had thoroughly considered during a series of years, I was fully prepared to present plans of an impregnable steam-battery of light draught, suitable to navigate the shallow rivers and harbors of the Confederate States. Availing myself of the services of a friend who chanced to be in Washington at the time, proposals were at once submitted to a board of naval officers appointed by the President; and the plans presented by my friend being rejected by the board, I immediately set out for Washington and laid the matter personally before its members, all of whom proved to be well-informed and experienced naval experts. Contrary to anticipation, the board permitted me to present a theoretical demonstration concerning the stability of the new structure, doubt of which was the principal consideration which had caused the rejection of the plan presented. In less than an hour I succeeded in demonstrating to the entire satisfaction of the board appointed by President Lincoln that the design was thoroughly practical, and based on sound theory. The Secretary of the Navy accordingly accepted my proposal to build an iron-clad steam-battery, and instructed me verbally to commence the construction forthwith. Returning immediately to New York, I divided the work among three leading mechanical establishments, furnishing each with detailed drawings of every part of the structure; the understanding being that the most skillful men and the best tools should be employed; also that work should be continued during night-time when practicable. The construction of nearly every part of the battery accordingly commenced simultaneously, all hands working with the utmost diligence, apparently confident that their exertions would result in something of great benefit to the national cause. Fortunately no trouble or delay was met at any point; all progressed satisfactorily; every part sent on board from the workshops fitted exactly the place for which it was intended. As a consequence of these favorable circumstances, the battery, with steam-machinery complete, was launched in one hundred days from the laying of the keel-plate. It should be mentioned that at the moment of starting on the inclined ways toward its destined element, the novel fighting-machine was named *Monitor*.|

Before entering on a description of this *fighting-machine* I propose to answer the question frequently asked: What circumstances dictated its size and peculiar construction?

1. The work on the *Merrimac* had progressed so far that no structure of large dimensions could possibly be completed in time to meet her.

2. The well-matured plan of erecting a citadel of considerable dimensions on the ample deck of the razeed *Merrimac* admitted of a battery of heavy ordnance so formidable that no vessel of the ordinary type, of small dimensions, could withstand its fire.

3. The battery designed by the naval authorities of the Confederate States, in addition to the advantage of ample room and numerous guns, presented a

| The origin of the name *Monitor* is given in the following letter to Gustavus V. Fox, Assistant Secretary of the Navy:

"NEW-YORK, January 20th, 1862. SIR: In accordance with your request, I now submit for your approbation a name for the floating battery at Green Point. The impregnable and aggressive character of this structure will admonish the leaders of the Southern Rebellion that the batteries on the banks of their rivers will no longer present barriers to the entrance of the Union forces.

"The iron-clad intruder will thus prove a severe monitor to those leaders. But there are other leaders who will also be startled and admonished by the booming of the guns from the impregnable iron turret. 'Downing Street' will hardly view with indifference this last 'Yankee notion,' this monitor. To the Lords of the Admiralty the new craft will be a monitor suggesting doubts as to the propriety of completing those four steel-clad ships at three-and-a-half millions apiece. On these and many similar grounds I propose to name the new battery *Monitor*. Your obedient servant, J. ERICSSON."

EDITORS.

formidable front to an opponent's fire by being inclined to such a degree that shot would be readily deflected.   Again, the inclined sides, composed of heavy timbers well braced, were covered with two thicknesses of bar iron, ingeniously combined, well calculated to resist the spherical shot peculiar to the Dahlgren and Rodman system of naval ordnance adopted by the United States navy.

4. The shallow waters on the coast of the Southern States called for very light draught; hence the upper circumference of the propeller of the battery would be exposed to the enemy's fire unless thoroughly protected against shot of heavy caliber.   A difficulty was thus presented which apparently could not be met by any device which would not seriously impair the efficiency of the propeller.

5. The limited width of the navigable parts of the Southern rivers and inlets presented an obstacle rendering manœuvring impossible; hence it would not be practicable at all times to turn the battery so as to present a broadside to the points to be attacked.

6. The accurate knowledge possessed by the adversary of the distance between the forts on the river-banks within range of his guns, would enable him to point the latter with such accuracy that unless every part of the sides of the battery could be made absolutely shot-proof, destruction would be certain.   It may be observed that the accurate knowledge of range was an advantage in favor of the Southern forts which placed the attacking steam-batteries at great disadvantage.

7. The difficulty of manipulating the anchor within range of powerful fixed batteries presented difficulties which called for better protection to the crew of the batteries than any previously known.

Several minor points familiar to the naval artillerist and naval architect presented considerations which could not be neglected by the constructor of the new battery; but these must be omitted in our brief statement, while the foregoing, being of vital importance, have demanded special notice.

The plans on pages 732–3 represent a longitudinal section through the center line of the battery, which, for want of space on the page, has been divided into three sections, viz., the aft, central, and forward sections, which for ready reference will be called *aft*, *central*, and *forward*.

Referring particularly to the upper and lower sections, it will be seen that the hull consists of an upper and lower body joined together in the horizontal plane not far below the water-line.   The length of the upper part of the hull is 172 feet, beam 41 feet; the length of the lower hull being 122 feet, beam

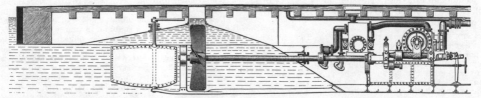

1. AFT SECTION. LONGITUDINAL PLAN THROUGH THE CENTER LINE OF THE ORIGINAL MONITOR.

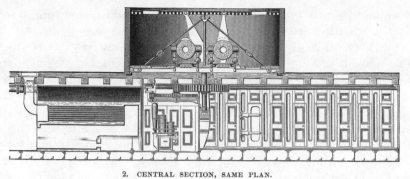

2. CENTRAL SECTION, SAME PLAN.

34 feet. The depth from the underside of deck to the keel-plate is 11 feet 2 inches, draught of water at load-line 10 feet.

Let us now examine separately the three sectional representations.

Forward Section. The anchor-well, a cylindrical perforation of the over-hanging deck, near the bow, first claims our attention. The object of this well being to protect the anchor when raised, it is lined with plate iron backed by heavy timbers, besides being protected by the armor-plating bolted to the outside of the overhang. It should be noticed that this method proved so efficient that in no instance did the anchor-gear receive any injury during the several engagements with the Confederate batteries, although nearly all of the monitors of the *Passaic* class were subjected to rapid fire at short range in upward of twenty actions. It will be remembered that the unprotected anchor of the *Merrimac* was shot away during the short battle with the *Congress* and the *Cumberland*. Having described the method of protecting the anchors, the mechanism adopted for manipulating the same remains to be explained. Referring to the illustration, it will be seen that a windlass is secured under the deck-beams near the anchor-well. The men working the handles of this mechanism were stationed in the hold of the vessel, and hence were most effectually protected against the enemy's shot, besides being completely out of sight. The Confederate artillerists were at first much surprised at witnessing the novel spectacle of vessels approaching their batteries, then stopping and remaining stationary for an indefinite time while firing, and then again departing, apparently without any intervention of anchor-gear. Our examination of this gear and the anchor-well affords a favorable opportunity of explaining the cause of Lieutenant Greene's alarm, mentioned

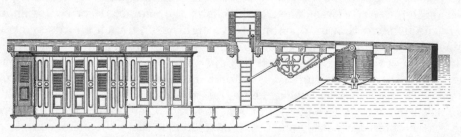

3. FORWARD SECTION, SAME PLAN.

in a statement recently published by a military journal, concerning a mysterious sound emanating from the said well during the passage of the *Monitor* from New York to Fort Monroe. Lieutenant Greene says that the sound from the anchor-well "resembled the death-groans of twenty men, and was the most dismal, awful sound [he] ever heard." Let us endeavor to trace to some physical cause this portentous sound. The reader will find, on close examination, that the chain cable which suspends the anchor passes through an aperture ("hawse-pipe") on the after side of the well, and that this pipe is very near the water-line; hence the slightest vertical depression of the bow will occasion a flow of water into the vessel. Obviously, any downward motion of the overhang will cause the air confined in the upper part of the well, when covered, to be blown through the hawse-pipe along with the admitted water, thereby producing a very discordant sound, repeated at every rise and fall of the bow during pitching. Lieutenant Greene also states that, apart from the reported sound, the vessel was flooded by the water which entered through the hawse-pipe; a statement suggesting that this flooding was the result of faulty construction, whereas it resulted from gross oversight on the part of the executive officer,—namely, in going to sea without stopping the opening round the chain-cable at the point where it passes through the side of the anchor-well.

The pilot-house is the next important object represented in the forward section of the illustration now under consideration. This structure is situated 10 feet from the anchor-well, its internal dimensions being 3 feet 6 inches long, 2 feet 8 inches wide, 3 feet 10 inches high above the plating of the deck; the sides consisting of solid blocks of wrought iron, 12 inches deep and 9 inches thick, firmly held down at the corner by 3-inch bolts passing through the iron-plated deck and deck-beams. The wheel, which by means of ordinary tiller-ropes operates the rudder, is placed within the pilot-house, its axle being supported by a bracket secured to the iron blocks as shown by the illustration. An ordinary ladder resting on the bottom of the vessel leads to the grated floor of the pilot-house. In order to afford the commanding officer and the pilot a clear view of objects before and on the sides of the vessel, the first and second iron blocks from the top are kept apart by packing pieces at the corners; long and narrow sight-holes being thereby formed extending round the pilot-house, and giving a clear view which sweeps round the entire horizon, all but that part which is hidden by the turret, hardly twelve degrees on each side of the line of keel. Regarding the adequacy of the elongated sight-hole formed between the iron blocks in the manner described, it should be borne in mind that an opening of five-eighths of an inch affords a vertical view 80 feet high at a distance of only 200 yards. More is not needed, a fact established during trials instituted by experts before the constructor delivered the vessel to the Government. Unfortunately the sight-holes were subsequently altered, the iron blocks being raised and the opening between them increased to such an extent that at sea, to quote Lieutenant Greene's report, the water entered "with such force as to knock the helmsman completely round from the wheel." It may be shown that but for the injudicious increase of the sight-holes, the commander of the *Monitor* would not have been temporarily blinded during the conflict at Hampton Roads, although he placed his vessel in such an extraordinary position that, according to Lieutenant Greene's report, "a shell from the enemy's gun, the muzzle not ten yards distant [from the side of the *Monitor*], struck the forward side of the pilot-house." The size of the sight-hole, after the injudicious increase, may be inferred from the reported fact that the blast caused by the explosion of the Confederate shell on striking the outside of the pilot-house had the power of "partly lifting the top." This "top," it should be observed, consisted of an iron plate two inches thick, let down into an appropriate groove, but not bolted down—a circumstance which called forth Lieutenant Greene's disapprobation. The object of the constructor

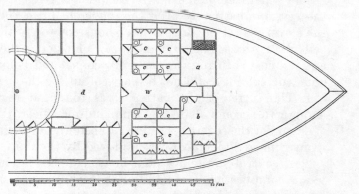

PLAN OF THE BERTH-DECK OF THE ORIGINAL MONITOR, DRAWN TO SCALE.

a, captain's cabin; *b*, his state-room; *c*, state-rooms of the officers; *w*, wardroom; *d*, quarters of the crew, with store-rooms on the sides.

in leaving the top plate of the pilot-house loose, so as to be readily pushed up from below, was that of affording egress to the crew in case of accident. Had the monitor *Tecumseh*, commanded by Captain T. A. M. Craven, when struck by a torpedo during the conflict in Mobile Bay, August 5th, 1864, been provided with a similar loose plate over the main hatch, the fearful calamity of drowning officers and crew would have been prevented. In referring to this untoward event, it should be observed that means had been provided in all the sea-going monitors to afford egress in case of injury to the hull: an opening in the turret-floor, when placed above a corresponding opening in the deck, formed a free passage to the turret, the top of which was provided with sliding hatches. Apparently the officer in charge of the turret-gear of Captain Craven's vessel was not at his post, as he ought to have been during action, or else he had not been taught the imperative duty of placing the turret in such a position that these openings would admit of a free passage from below. ⚓

Lieutenant Greene's report with reference to the position of the pilot-house calls for particular notice, his assertion being that he "could not fire ahead within several points of the bow." The distance between the center of the turret and the pilot-house being fifty-five feet, while the extreme breadth of the latter is only five feet, it will be found that by turning the turret through an angle of only *six degrees* from the center line of the vessel, the shot will clear the pilot-house, a structure too substantial to suffer from

⚓ Under the circumstances of the sinking of the *Tecumseh*, the turret was no doubt being worked to meet the necessities of the battle, not to afford egress for the crew.—EDITORS.

the mere aërial current produced by the flight of the shot. Considering that the *Monitor*, as reported by Lieutenant Greene, was a "quick-turning vessel," the disadvantage of not being able to fire over the bow within *six degrees* of the line of keel is insignificant. Captain Coles claimed for his famous iron-clad turret-ship the advantage of an all-round fire, although the axis of his turret-guns had many times greater deviation from the line of keel than that of the *Monitor*.

The statement published by Lieutenant Greene, that the chief engineer of the vessel immediately after the engagement in Hampton Roads " suggested the clever plan of putting the pilot-house on top of the turret," is incorrect and calls for notice. The obvious device of placing the pilot-house in the center and above the turret was carefully considered before the *Monitor* turret was constructed, but could not be carried out for these reasons:

1. The turret of the battery was too light to support a structure large enough to accommodate the commanding officer, the pilot, and the steering-gear, under the severe condition of absolute impregnability against solid shot from guns of 10-inch caliber employed by the Confederates.

2. A central stationary pilot-house connected with the turret involved so much complication and additional work (see description of turret and pilot-houses further on), that had its adoption not been abandoned the *Monitor* would not have been ready to proceed to Hampton Roads until the beginning of April, 1862. The damage to the national cause which might have resulted from that delay is beyond computation.

The next important part of the battery delineated on the forward section of the illustration, namely, the quarters of the officers and crew, will now be considered; but before entering on a description it should be mentioned that in a small turret-vessel built for fighting, only one-half of the crew need be accommodated at a time, as the other half should be in and on the turret, the latter being always covered with a water-proof awning. Referring again to the forward and to part of the central section, it will be seen that the quarters

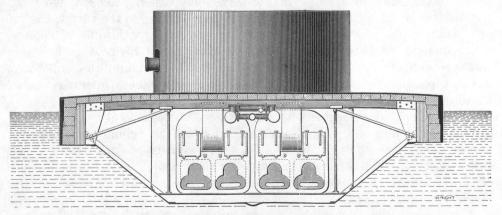

TRANSVERSE SECTION OF THE HULL OF THE ORIGINAL MONITOR.

The diagram gives a front view of the boilers and furnaces; also a side elevation of the rotating cylindrical turret which proved impregnable against ten-inch solid shot fired with battering charges at very short range.

VIEW SHOWING THE EFFECT OF SHOT ON THE "MONITOR" TURRET.
FROM A PHOTOGRAPH TAKEN SOON AFTER THE ENGAGEMENT.

The ridges shown in the nearer port are significant of the haste with which the vessel was built. An opening of this shape is usually made by cutting three circles one above another and intersecting, and then trimming the edges to an oval. In this instance there was no time for the trimming process. Originally the armament was to be 15-inch guns, but as these could not be had in time, the 11-inch Dahlgrens were substituted.—EDITORS.

extend from the transverse bulkhead under the turret to within five feet of the pilot-house, a distance of fifty feet; the forward portion, twenty-four feet in length, being occupied by the officers' quarters and extending across the battery from side to side. The height of the aft part of these quarters is 8 feet 6 inches under the deck-beams; while the height of the whole of the quarters of the crew is 8 feet 6 inches. A mere glance at the illustrations showing a side elevation [p. 733] and top view of internal arrangement [p. 735] gives a correct idea of the nature of the accommodations prepared for the officers and crew of the vessel which Lieutenant Greene regards as a "crude" structure, and of which he says: "Probably no ship was ever devised which was so uncomfortable for the crew." If this opinion were well founded, it would prove that submerged vessels like the monitors are unfit to live in.

Fortunately, the important question whether crews can live permanently below water-line has been set at rest by the report of the chief of the Bureau of Medicine and Surgery to the Secretary of the Navy, 1864. This minute and carefully considered report enabled the naval administration, organized by President Lincoln, to prove the healthfulness of the monitors, by the following clear presentation of the subject: "The monitor class of vessels, it is well known, have but a few inches of their hulls above the water-line, and in a heavy sea are entirely submerged. It has been doubted whether under such circumstances it would be possible long to preserve the health of the men on board, and consequently maintain the fighting material in a condition for effective service. It is gratifying, therefore, to know that an examination of the sick-reports, covering a period of over thirty months, shows that, so far from being unhealthy, there was less sickness on board the monitors than on the same number of wooden ships with an equal number of men and in similar exposed positions. The exemption from sickness upon the iron-clads in some instances is remarkable. There were on board the *Saugus*, from November 25th, 1864, to April 1st, 1865, a period of over four months, but four cases of sickness (excluding accidental injuries), and of these two were diseases with which the patients had suffered for years. On the *Montauk*, for a period of one hundred and sixty-five days prior to the 29th of May, 1865, there was but one case of disease on board. Other vessels of the class exhibit equally remarkable results, and the conclusion is reached that no wooden vessels in any squadron throughout the world can show an equal immunity from disease."

Apart from the ample size of the quarters on board the vessel, shown by the illustration, it should be mentioned that the system adopted for ventilating those quarters furnishes an abundant supply of fresh air by the following means. Two centrifugal blowers, driven by separate steam-engines, furnished seven thousand cubic feet of atmospheric air per minute by the process of suction through standing pipes on deck. Part of the air thus drawn in supported the combustion of the boiler furnaces, the remainder entering the lower part of the hull, gradually expelling the heated and vitiated air within the vessel. It has been imagined that the fresh air supplied by the blowers ought to have been conveyed to the quarters at the forward end of the vessel, by a system of conducting pipes. The laws of static balance, however, render the adoption of such a method unnecessary, since agreeably to those laws the fresh cold air, unless it be stopped by closed doors in the bulkheads, will find its way to every part of the bottom of the hull, gradually rising and expelling the upper heated strata through the hatches, and lastly through the grated top of the turret. Naval constructors who speculate on the cause of the extraordinary healthfulness of the monitors need not extend their researches beyond a thorough investigation of the system of ventilation just described.

Turret Department. The most important object delineated on the *central* section of the illustration, namely, the rotating turret, will now be considered; but before describing this essential part of the monitor system, it will be well to observe that the general belief is quite erroneous that a revolving platform, open or covered, is a novel design. So far from that being the case, this obvious device dates back to the first introduction of artillery. About 1820 the writer was taught by an instructor in fortification and gunnery that under certain conditions a position assailable from all sides should be defended by placing the guns on a turntable. Long before building the *Monitor* I regarded the employment of a revolving structure to operate guns on board ships as a device familiar to all well-informed naval artillerists. But although constructors of revolving circular gun-platforms for naval purposes, open or covered, have a right to

SIDE ELEVATION OF A FLOATING REVOLVING CIRCULAR TOWER, PUBLISHED BY ABRAHAM BLOODGOOD IN 1807.

FLOATING CIRCULAR CITADEL, SUBMITTED TO THE FRENCH DIRECTORY IN 1798.

employ this ancient device, it will be demonstrated further on that the turret of the monitors is a distinct mechanical combination differing from previous inventions.   The correctness of the assumption that revolving batteries for manipulating guns on board floating structures had been constructed nearly a century ago will be seen by the following reference to printed publications.

The "Nautical Chronicle" for 1805 contains an account of a "movable turning impregnable battery, invented by a Mr. Gillespie, a native of Scotland, who completed the model of a movable impregnable castle or battery, impervious to shot or bombs, provided with a cannon and carriage calculated to take a sure aim at any object."   It is further stated that "the invention proposed will be found equally serviceable in floating batteries.   Its machinery is adapted to turn the most ponderous mortars with the greatest ease, according to the position of the enemy."   Again, the Transactions of the Society for the Promotion of Useful Arts in the State of New York, 1807, contains an illustration representing a side elevation of a circular revolving floating battery constructed by Abraham Bloodgood.   The guns of this battery, as the inventor points out, "would be more easily worked than is common, as they would not require any lateral movement."   It is also stated, as a peculiar feature of this floating battery, that "its rotary motion would bring all its cannon to bear successively, as fast as they could be loaded, on objects in any direction"; and that "its circular form would cause every shot that might strike it, not near the center, to glance."   Thirty-five years after the publication of the illustration and description of the circular floating revolving tower of Abraham Bloodgood, Theodore R. Timby proposed to build a tower on land for coast defense, to be composed of iron, with several floors

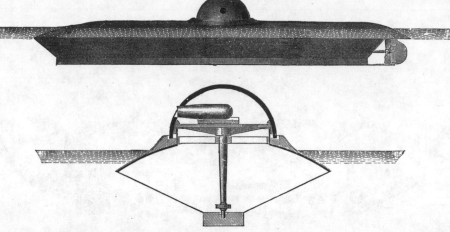

SIDE ELEVATION AND TRANSVERSE SECTION (THROUGH THE CENTER LINE OF ITS REVOLVING SEMI-SPHERICAL
TURRET) OF AN IRON-CLAD STEAM-BATTERY, PLANS OF WHICH WERE SUBMITTED
BY CAPTAIN ERICSSON TO NAPOLEON III. IN SEPTEMBER, 1854.

and tiers of guns, the tower to turn on a series of friction-rollers under its base. The principal feature of Timby's "invention" was that of arranging the guns radially within the tower, and firing each gun at the instant of its coming in line with the object aimed at during the rotary motion of the tower, precisely as invented by Bloodgood. About 1865 certain influential citizens presented drawings of Timby's revolving tower to the authorities at Washington, with a view of obtaining orders to build such towers for coast defense; but the plan was found to be not only very expensive, but radically defective in principle. The slides of the gun-carriages being fixed permanently in a radial direction within the tower, the guns, of course, are directed to all points of the compass. Hence, during an attack by a hostile fleet, with many ships abreast, only one assailant can be fired at, its companions being scot-free in the dead angle formed between the effective gun and the guns on either side. In the meantime the numerous guns, distributed round the tower on the several floors, cannot be fired until their time comes during the revolution of the tower. The enemy's fleet continuing its advance, of course, calls for a change of elevation of the pieces, which, considering the constant revolution of the tower and the different altitudes above the sea of the several tiers, presents perplexing difficulties. Nothing further need be said to explain why the Government did not accept the plans for Timby's revolving towers.

The origin of rotating circular gun-platforms being disposed of, the consideration of the central section of the illustration will now be resumed. It will be seen that the turret which protects the guns and gunners of the *Monitor* consists simply of a short cylinder resting on the deck, covered with a grated iron roof provided with sliding hatches. This cylinder is composed of eight thicknesses of wrought-iron plates, each one inch thick, firmly riveted together, the inside course, which extends below the rest, being accurately faced underneath. A flat, broad ring of bronze is let into the deck, its upper face being very smooth in order to form a water-tight joint with the base of the turret without the employment of any elastic packing, a peculiar feature of the turrets of the monitors, as will be seen further on. Unfortunately, before the *Monitor* left New York for Hampton Roads, it was suggested at the Navy Yard to insert a plaited hemp rope between the base of the turret and the bronze ring, for the purpose of making the joint perfectly water-tight. As might have been supposed, the rough and uneven hemp rope did not form a perfect joint; hence during the passage a great leak was observed at intervals as the sea washed over the decks. "The water came down under the turret like a waterfall," says Lieutenant Greene in his report. It will be proper to observe in this place that the "foundering" of the *Monitor* on its way to Charleston was not caused by the "separation of the upper and lower part of the hull," as was imagined by persons who possessed no knowledge of the method adopted by the builders in joining the upper and lower hulls. Again, those who asserted that the plates had been torn asunder at the junction of the hulls did not consider that severe strain cannot take place in a structure nearly submerged. The easy motion at sea, peculiar to the monitors, was pointed out by several of their commanders. Lieutenant Greene in his report to the Secretary of the Navy, dated on board the *Monitor*, March 27th, 1862, says with reference to sea-going qualities:

ISAAC NEWTON, FIRST ASSIST-ANT-ENGINEER OF THE "MON-ITOR." FROM A MEDALLION PORTRAIT BY LAUNT THOMPSON.

At the time of Mr. Newton's death (September 25, 1884) he had been for several years Chief Engineer of the Croton Aqueduct. The plans which have been adopted for the new aqueduct were his, both in the general features and the details.—EDITORS.

"During her passage from New York her roll was very easy and slow and not at all deep. She pitched very little and with no strain whatever."

Captain John Rodgers's report to the Secretary of the Navy, dated on board of the monitor *Weehawken*, January 22d, 1863, refers specially to the easy motion of his vessel:

"On Tuesday night, when off Chincoteague shoals, we had a very heavy gale from the E. N. E. with a very heavy sea, made confused and dangerous by the proximity of the land. The waves I measured after the sea abated; I found them twenty-three feet high. They were certainly seven feet higher in the midst of the storm. During the heaviest of the gale I stood upon the turret and admired the behavior of the vessel. She rose and fell to the waves, and I concluded that the monitor form had great sea-going qualities. If leaks were prevented no hurricane could injure her."

The true cause of the foundering of the *Monitor* was minutely explained to the writer some time after the occurrence by the engineer, a very intelligent person, who operated the centrifugal pumping-engine of the vessel at the time. According to his statement, oakum was packed under the base of the turret before going to sea, in order to make sure of a water-tight joint; but this expedient failed altogether, the sea gradually washing out the oakum in those places where it had been loosely packed, thereby permitting so large a

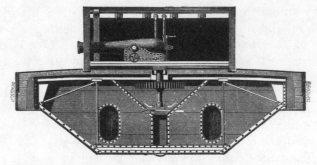

TRANSVERSE SECTION OF THE "MONITOR" THROUGH THE CENTER OF THE TURRET.

quantity of water to enter under the turret, fully sixty-three feet in circumference, that the centrifugal pumping-engine had not sufficient power to expel it. The hull consequently filled gradually and settled, until at the expiration of about four hours the *Monitor* went to the bottom. It will be asked, in view of the preceding explanation of the construction of the monitor turrets, namely, that the smooth base of the turret forms a water-tight joint with the ring on the deck, why was oakum packed under the turret before going to Charleston? The commander of the vessel, Captain Bankhead, in his report of the foundering, adverts to the admission of water under the turret, but does not duly consider the serious character of the leak, sixty-three feet in length. Captain Bankhead evidently had not carefully investigated the matter when he attributed the accident to an imaginary separation of the upper and lower hull.↓ It should be observed, in justice to this officer, that having commanded the *Monitor* only during a brief period he possessed but an imperfect knowledge of his vessel, and probably knew nothing regarding the consequence of employing packing,— namely, that it might cause "water to come down under the turret like a waterfall," as previously reported by the second officer in command. It is proper to mention as a mitigating circumstance in favor of the second officer, Lieutenant Greene, that previous to the battle in Hampton Roads he had "never performed any but midshipman duty." The important question, therefore, must remain unanswered, whether in the hands of an older and more experienced executive officer the *Monitor*, like the other vessels of her type, might not have reached Charleston in safety.

Referring again to the central part of the illustration [p. 733] and the sectional representation of the turret [above], it will be found that the guns are

↓ Captain J. P. Bankhead says in his report:

"Found [in the morning] that the packing of oakum under and around the base had loosened somewhat from the working of the tower as the vessel pitched and rolled . . . towards evening the swell somewhat decreased, the bilge-pumps being found amply sufficient to keep her clear of the water that penetrated through the sight-hole of the pilot-house, hawse-hole, and base of tower (all of which had been well calked previous to leaving). At 7:30 the wind hauled more to the south . . . Found the vessel towed badly, yawing very much, and with the increased motion making somewhat more water around the base of the tower. . . . 8 P. M.; the sea about this time commenced to rise very rapidly, causing the vessel to plunge heavily, completely submerging the pilot-house, and washing over and into the turret, and at times into the blower-pipes. Observed that when she rose to the swell, the flat under-surface of the projecting armor would come down with great force, causing a considerable shock to the vessel and turret, thereby loosening still more the packing around its base. . . . I am firmly of the opinion that the *Monitor* must have sprung a leak somewhere in the forward part, where the hull joins on to the armor, and that it was caused by the heavy shocks received as she came down upon the sea."   EDITORS.

placed across the vessel; consequently only the end of the breech and upper part of the port-hole are seen. The object of the pendulum port-stoppers suspended under the roof is to afford protection to the turret crew while loading the guns. Generally, however, the turret should be moved, and the port-holes thereby turned away from the enemy. Much time was lost during the conflict with the *Merrimac* by closing the port-stoppers in place of merely moving the turret, the latter operation being performed by a small steam-engine controlled by a single hand; while opening and closing the port-stoppers, as reported by Lieutenant Greene, required the entire gun-crew. The slow fire of the *Monitor* during the action, complained of by critics, was no doubt occasioned by an injudicious manipulation of the port-stoppers. There are occasions, however, when the turret should not be turned, in which case the port-stoppers are indispensable. The method adopted for turning the turret will be readily understood. The small steam-engine controlled by one man, before referred to, drives a double train of cog-wheels connected with the vertical axle of the turret, this axle being stepped in a bronze bearing secured to the central bulkhead of the vessel. The mechanism thus described was carefully tested before the *Monitor* left New York for Hampton Roads, and was found to move very freely, the turret being turned and the guns accurately pointed by the sailing-master without aid. The trouble reported by Lieutenant Greene regarding the manipulation of the turret was caused by inattention during the passage from New York, the working-gear having been permitted to rust for want of proper cleaning and oiling while exposed to the action of salt-water entering under the turret, from causes already explained.

Having thus briefly described the turret and its mechanism, our investigation of the central part of the sectional view of the battery will be completed by a mere reference to the steam-boilers placed aft of the turret. There are two of these boilers placed side by side, as shown in the cut on page 736. Two views being thus presented, the nature of the boilers will be understood without further explanation. It should be mentioned, however, that they proved very economical and efficient.

Aft Section. The following brief reference to this section of the sectional illustration, showing the motive engine, propeller, and rudder, will complete our description:

1. The motive engine, the construction of which is somewhat peculiar, consists of only one steam-cylinder with pistons applied at opposite ends, a steam-tight partition being introduced in the middle. The propeller-shaft has only one crank and one crank-pin, the difficulty of " passing the centers " being overcome by the expedient of placing the connecting-rods, actuated by the steam-pistons, at right angles to each other. Much space is saved within the vessel by employing only one steam-cylinder, an advantage of such importance in the short hulls of the monitors that the entire fleet built during the war was provided with engines of the stated type.

2. The propeller, being of the ordinary four-bladed type, needs no description; but the mode of protecting it against shot demands full explanation.

Referring to the illustration, it will be seen that the under side of the over-hang near the stern is cut out in the middle, forming a cavity needed to give free sweep to the propeller-blades; the slope of the cavity on either side of the propeller being considerably inclined in order to favor a free passage of the water to and from the propeller-blades.

3. The extreme beam at the forward side of the propeller-well is 31 feet, while the diameter of the propeller is only 9 feet; it will therefore be seen that the deck and side armor projects 11 feet on each side, thus pro-tecting most effectually the propelling instrument as well as the equipoise rudder applied aft of the same. It will be readily admitted that no other vessel constructed here or elsewhere has such thorough protection to rudder and propeller as that just described.

The foregoing description of the hastily constructed steam-battery proves that, so far from being, as generally supposed, a rude specimen of naval con-struction, the *Monitor* displayed careful planning, besides workmanship of superior quality. Experts who examined the vessel and machinery after com-pletion pronounced the entire structure a fine specimen of naval engineering.

The conflict in Hampton Roads, and the immediate building of a fleet of sea-going monitors by the United States Government, attracted great atten-tion in all maritime countries, especially in the north of Europe. Admiral Lessoffsky, of the Russian navy, was at once ordered to be present during the completion and trial of our sea-going monitors. The report of this talented officer to his government being favorable, the Emperor immediately ordered a fleet of twelve vessels on the new system, to be constructed according to copies of the working-drawings from which the American sea-going monitors had been built. Sweden and Norway also forthwith laid the keels of a fleet of seven vessels of the new type, Turkey rapidly following the example of the northern European nations. It will be remembered that during the naval contest on the Danube the Russian batteries and torpedo-boats subjected the Turkish monitors to severe tests. England, in due course, adopted our turret system, discarding the turn-table and cupola.

SINKING OF THE "MONITOR," DECEMBER 29, 1862.

THE LOSS OF THE "MONITOR." [

BY FRANCIS B. BUTTS, A SURVIVOR OF THE "MONITOR'S" CREW.

AT daybreak on the 29th of December, 1862, at Fort Monroe, the *Monitor* hove short her anchor, and by 10 o'clock in the forenoon she was under way for Charleston, South Carolina, in charge of Commander J. P. Bankhead. The *Rhode Island*, a powerful side-wheel steamer, was to be our convoy, and to hasten our speed she took us in tow with two long 12-inch hawsers. The weather was heavy with dark, stormy-looking clouds and a westerly wind. We passed out of the Roads and rounded Cape Henry, proceeding on our course with but little change in the weather up to the next day at noon, when the wind shifted to the south-south-west and increased to a gale. At 12 o'clock it was my trick at the lee wheel, and being a good hand I was kept there. At dark we were about seventy miles at sea, and directly off Cape Hatteras. The sea rolled high and pitched together in the peculiar manner only seen at Hatteras. The *Rhode Island* steamed slowly and steadily ahead. The sea rolled over us as if our vessel were a rock in the ocean only a few inches above the water, and men who stood abaft on the deck of the *Rhode Island* have told me that several times we were thought to have gone down. It seemed that for minutes we were out of sight, as the heavy seas entirely submerged the vessel. The wheel had been temporarily rigged on top of the turret, where all the officers, except those on duty in the engine-room, now were. I heard their remarks, and watched closely the movements of the vessel, so that I exactly understood our condition. The vessel was making very heavy weather, riding one huge wave, plunging through the next as if shooting straight for the bottom of the ocean, and splashing down upon another with such force that her hull would tremble, and with a shock that would sometimes take us off our feet, while a fourth would leap upon us and break far above the turret, so that if we had not been protected by a rifle-armor that was securely fastened and rose to the height of a man's chest, we should have been washed away. I had volunteered for service on the *Monitor* while she lay at the Washington Navy Yard in November. This going to sea in an iron-clad I began to think was the dearest part of my bargain. I thought of what I had been taught in the service, that a man always gets into trouble if he volunteers.

About 8 o'clock, while I was taking a message from the captain to the engineer, I saw the water pouring in through the coal-bunkers in sudden volumes as it swept over the deck. About that time the engineer reported that the coal was too wet to keep up steam, which had run down from its usual pressure of 80 pounds to 20. The water in the vessel was gaining rapidly over the small pumps, and I heard the captain order the chief engineer to start the main pump, a very powerful one of new invention. This was done, and I saw a stream of water eight inches in diameter spouting up from beneath the waves.

About half-past 8 the first signals of distress to the *Rhode Island* were burned. She lay to, and we rode the sea more comfortably than when we were being towed. The *Rhode Island* was obliged to turn slowly ahead to keep from drifting upon us and to prevent the tow-lines from being caught in her wheels. At one time, when she drifted close alongside, our captain shouted through his trumpet that we were sinking, and asking the steamer to send us her boats. The *Monitor* steamed ahead again with renewed difficulties, and I was ordered to leave the wheel and was kept employed as messenger by the captain. The chief engineer reported that the coal was so wet that he could not keep up steam, and I heard the captain order him to slow down and put all steam that could be spared upon the pumps. As there was danger of being towed under by our consort, the tow-lines were ordered to be cut, and I saw James Fenwick, quarter-gunner, swept from the deck and carried by a heavy sea leeward and out of sight in attempting to obey the order. Our daring boatswain's mate, John Stocking, then succeeded in reaching the bows of the vessel, and I saw him swept by a heavy sea far away into the darkness.

About half-past 10 o'clock our anchor was let go with all the cable, and struck bottom in about sixty fathoms of water; this brought us out of the trough of the sea, and we rode it more comfortably. The fires could no longer be kept up with the wet coal. The small pumps were choked up with water, or, as the engineer reported, were drowned, and the main pump had almost stopped working from lack of power. This was reported to the captain, and he ordered me to see if there was any water in the ward-room. This was the first time I had been below the berth-deck. I went forward, and saw the water running in through the hawse-pipe, an 8-inch hole, in full force, as in dropping the anchor the cable had torn away the packing that had kept this place tight. I reported my observations, and at the same time heard the chief engineer report that the water had reached the ash-pits and was gaining very rapidly. The captain ordered him to stop the main engine and turn all steam on the pumps, which I noticed soon worked again.

The clouds now began to separate, a moon of about half-size beamed out upon the sea, and the *Rhode Island*, now a mile away, became visible. Signals were being exchanged, ¶ and I felt that

[By the courtesy of the Soldiers' and Sailors' Historical Society, of Rhode Island, we are permitted to print the following interesting paper condensed from one of its pamphlets.—EDITORS.

¶ The method of communication from the *Monitor* was by writing in chalk on a black-board which was held up to view; the *Monitor* had no mast on which to hoist the regular naval code used by the *Rhode Island*. As night approached, the captain of the *Monitor* wrote, while we could yet see, that if they were forced to

the *Monitor* would be saved, or at least that the captain would not leave his ship until there was no hope of saving her. I was sent below again to see how the water stood in the ward-room. I went forward to the cabin and found the water just above the soles of my shoes, which indicated that there must be more than a foot in the vessel. I reported this to the captain, and all hands were set to bailing,— bailing out the ocean as it seemed,— but the object was to employ the men, as there now seemed to be danger of excitement among them. I kept employed most of the time, taking the buckets from them through the hatchway on top of the turret. They seldom would have more than a pint of water in them, however, the remainder having been spilled in passing from one man to another [see foot-note, p. 742].

The weather was clear, but the sea did not cease rolling in the least, and the *Rhode Island*, with the two lines wound up in her wheel, was tossing at the mercy of the sea, and came drifting against our sides. A boat that had been lowered was caught between the vessels and crushed and lost. Some of our seamen bravely leaped down on deck to guard our sides, and lines were thrown to them from the deck of the *Rhode Island*, which now lay her whole length against us, ☆ floating off astern, but not a man would be the first to leave his ship, although the captain gave orders to do so. I was again sent to examine the water in the ward-room, which I found to be more than two feet above the deck; and I think I was the last person who saw Engineer G. H. Lewis as he lay seasick in his bunk, apparently watching the water as it grew deeper and deeper, and aware what his fate must be. He called me as I passed his door, and asked if the pumps were working. I replied that they were. "Is there any hope?" he asked; and feeling a little moved at the scene, and knowing certainly what must be his end, and the darkness that stared at us all, I replied, "As long as there is life there is hope." "Hope and hang on when you are wrecked" is an old saying among sailors. I left the ward-room, and learned that the water had gained so as to choke up the main pump. As I was crossing the berth-deck I saw our ensign, Mr. Frederickson, hand a watch to Master's Mate Williams, saying, "Here, this is yours; I may be lost"— which, in fact, was his fate. The watch and chain were both of unusual value. Williams

received them into his hand, then with a hesitating glance at the time-piece said, "This thing may be the means of sinking me," and threw it upon the deck. There were three or four cabin-boys pale and prostrate with seasickness, and the cabin-cook, an old African negro, under great excitement, was scolding them most profanely.

As I ascended the turret-ladder the sea broke over the ship, and came pouring down the hatchway with so much force that it took me off my feet; and at the same time the steam broke from the boiler-room, as the water had reached the fires, and for an instant I seemed to realize that we had gone down. Our fires were out, and I heard the water blowing out of the boilers. I reported my observations to the captain, and at the same time saw a boat alongside. The captain again gave orders for the men to leave the ship, and fifteen, all of whom were seamen and men whom I had placed my confidence upon, were the ones who crowded the first boat to leave the ship. I was disgusted at witnessing the scramble, and, not feeling in the least alarmed about myself, resolved that I, an "old haymaker," as landsmen are called, would stick to the ship as long as my officers. I saw three of these men swept from the deck and carried leeward on the swift current.

Bailing was now resumed. I occupied the turret all alone, and passed buckets from the lower hatchway to the man on the top of the turret. I took off my coat—one that I had received from home only a few days before (I could not feel that our noble little ship was yet lost)—and, rolling it up with my boots, drew the tompion from one of the guns, placed them inside, and replaced the tompion. A black cat was sitting on the breech of one of the guns, howling one of those hoarse and solemn tunes which no one can appreciate who is not filled with the superstitions which I had been taught by the sailors, who are always afraid to kill a cat. I would almost as soon have touched a ghost, but I caught her, and, placing her in another gun, replaced the wad and tompion; but I could still hear that distressing howl. As I raised my last bucket to the upper hatchway no one was there to take it. I scrambled up the ladder and found that we below had been deserted. I shouted to those on the berth-deck, "Come up; the officers have left the ship, and a boat is alongside." As I reached the top of the turret I saw a boat

<hr>

abandon their ship, they would burn a red light as a signal. About 10 o'clock the signal was given. When the steamer stopped to allow the hawsers to be cast off, the *Monitor* forged ahead under the impetus of her headway, and came so close up under the steamer's stern, that there was great danger of her running into and cutting the steamer down. When the engines of the *Rhode Island* were started to go ahead to get out of the way, it was discovered that the hawser had got afoul of the paddle-wheel, and when they were put in motion, instead of getting clear of her, the rope wound up on the wheel and drew the vessels together. This was an extremely dangerous position, for they were being pitched and tossed about so much by the heavy seas that if the iron-clad had once struck the steamer they must both have gone down together. However, a fireman went into the wheel at the risk of his life, and with an axe cut the hawser away so that the steamer was

enabled to get away at a safe distance.— From a letter to the Editors from H. R. SMITH, then of the *Rhode Island*.

☆ The boat lowered was not lost, as I well know, since I was in command of her. The gunwale on the starboard side was crushed by the *Rhode Island* as she tossed helplessly about with two lines wound up in her wheel, but the boat kept above water, and brought off sixteen men, among them Surgeon Weeks. The men did not leap down upon the deck to guard the side, which would have been sheer folly, but remained in the turret, and were with difficulty urged to come on deck and be taken off. The stern of the *Monitor* lay under the *Rhode Island's* quarter— at no time were the vessels parallel. The *Monitor* should not have been lost. She was going against a head-sea. Had she turned back before dark she would have had no difficulty, as all the officers of the *Rhode Island* thought. — A. O. TAYLOR, Acting Ensign of the *Rhode Island*.

made fast on the weather quarter filled with men. Three others were standing on deck trying to get on board. One man was floating leeward, shouting in vain for help; another, who hurriedly passed me and jumped down from the turret, was swept off by a breaking wave and never rose. I was excited, feeling that it was the only chance to be saved. I made a loose line fast to one of the stanchions, and let myself down from the turret, the ladder having been washed away. The moment I struck the deck the sea broke over it and swept me as I had seen it sweep my shipmates. I grasped one of the smoke-stack braces and, hand-over-hand, ascended, to keep my head above water. It required all my strength to keep the sea from tearing me away. As it swept from the vessel I found myself dangling in the air nearly at the top of the smoke-stack. I let myself fall, and succeeded in reaching a life-line that encircled the deck by means of short stanchions, and to which the boat was attached. The sea again broke over us, lifting me feet upward as I still clung to the life-line. I thought I had nearly measured the depth of the ocean, when I felt the turn, and as my head rose above the water I was somewhat dazed from being so nearly drowned, and spouted up, it seemed, more than a gallon of water that had found its way into my lungs. I was then about twenty feet from the other men, whom I found to be the captain and one seaman; the other had been washed overboard and was now struggling in the water. The men in the boat were pushing back on their oars to keep the boat from being washed on to the *Monitor's* deck, so that the boat had to be hauled in by the painter about ten or twelve feet. The first lieutenant, S. D. Greene, and other officers in the boat were shouting, "Is the captain on board?" and, with severe struggles to have our voices heard above the roar of the wind and sea, we were shouting, "No," and trying to haul in the boat, which we at last succeeded in doing. The captain, ever caring for his men, requested us to get in, but we both, in the same voice, told him to get in first. The moment he was over the bows of the boat Lieutenant Greene cried, "Cut the painter! cut the painter!" I thought, "Now or lost," and in less time than I can explain it, exerting my strength beyond imagination, I hauled in the boat, sprang, caught on the gunwale, was pulled into the boat with a boat-hook in the hands of one of the men, and took my seat with one of the oarsmen. The other man, named Thomas Joice, managed to get into the boat in some way, I cannot tell how, and he was the last man saved from that ill-fated ship. As we were cut loose I saw several men standing on top of the turret, apparently afraid to venture down upon deck, and it may have been that they were deterred by seeing others washed overboard while I was getting into the boat. ⸗

After a fearful and dangerous passage over the frantic seas, we reached the *Rhode Island*, which still had the tow-line caught in her wheel and had drifted perhaps two miles to leeward. We came alongside under the lee bows, where the first boat, that had left the *Monitor* nearly an hour before, had just discharged its men; but we found that getting on board the *Rhode Island* was a harder task than getting from the *Monitor*. We were carried by the sea from stem to stern, for to have made fast would have been fatal; the boat was bounding against the ship's sides; sometimes it was below the wheel, and then, on the summit of a huge wave, far above the decks; then the two boats would crash together; and once, while Surgeon Weeks was holding on to the rail, he lost his fingers by a collision which swamped the other boat. Lines were thrown to us from the deck of the *Rhode Island*, which were of no assistance, for not one of us could climb a small rope; and besides, the men who threw them would immediately let go their holds, in their excitement, to throw another — which I found to be the case when I kept hauling in rope instead of climbing.

It must be understood that two vessels lying side by side, when there is any motion to the sea, move alternately; or, in other words, one is constantly passing the other up or down. At one time, when our boat was near the bows of the steamer, we would rise upon the sea until we could touch her rail; then in an instant, by a very rapid descent, we could touch her keel. While we were thus rising and falling upon the sea, I caught a rope, and, rising with the boat, managed to reach within a foot or two of the rail, when a man, if there had been one, could easily have hauled me on board. But they had all followed after the boat, which at that instant was washed astern, and I hung dangling in the air over the bow of the *Rhode Island*, with Ensign Norman Atwater hanging to the cat-head, three or four feet from me, like myself, with both hands clinching a rope and shouting for some one to save him. Our hands grew painful and all the time weaker, until I saw his strength give way. He slipped a foot, caught again, and with his last prayer, "O God!" I saw him fall and sink, to rise no more. The ship rolled, and rose upon the sea, sometimes with her keel out of water, so that I was hanging thirty feet above the sea, and with the fate in view that had befallen our much-beloved companion, which no one had witnessed but myself. I still clung to the rope with aching hands, calling in vain for help. But I could not be heard, for the wind shrieked far above my voice. My heart here, for the only time in my life, gave up hope, and home and friends were most tenderly thought of. While I was in this state, within a few seconds of giving up, the sea rolled forward, bringing with it the boat, and when I would have fallen into the sea, it was there. I can only recollect hearing an old sailor say, as I fell into the bottom of the boat, "Where in —— did he come from?"

When I became aware of what was going on, no one had succeeded in getting out of the boat, which then lay just forward of the wheel-house. Our captain ordered them to throw bow-lines, which was immediately done. The second one I caught, and, placing myself within the loop, was hauled on board. I assisted in helping the others out of the boat, when it again went back to the *Monitor;* it did not reach it, however, and after drifting about on the ocean several days it was picked up by a passing vessel and carried to Philadelphia. ⚓

It was half-past 12, the night of the 31st of December, 1862, when I stood on the forecastle of the *Rhode Island,* watching the red and white lights that hung from the pennant-staff above the turret,

⚓ After making two trips there were still four officers and twelve men on the *Monitor,* and the gallant boat's crew, although well-nigh exhausted by their labors, started for the third time on its perilous trip, but it never reached them, for while all on board the steamer were anxiously watching the light in the turret and vainly peering into the darkness for a glimpse of the

and which now and then were seen as we would perhaps both rise on the sea together, until at last, just as the moon had passed below the horizon, they were lost, and the *Monitor,* whose history is familiar to us all, was seen no more.

The *Rhode Island* cruised about the scene of the disaster the remainder of the night and the next forenoon in hope of finding the boat that had been lost; then she returned direct to Fort Monroe, where we arrived the next day.

rescuing boat, the light suddenly disappeared and forever, for after watching for a long time to try and find it again, they were forced to the conclusion that the *Monitor* had gone to the bottom with all that remained on board. The position of the *Rhode Island* at this time was about eight or ten miles off the coast directly east of Cape Hatteras.—H. R. SMITH.

NEGOTIATIONS FOR THE BUILDING OF THE "MONITOR."

IN 1877, at the request of ex-Secretary Gideon Welles, C. S. Bushnell, of New Haven, one of the associate owners of the *Monitor,* embodied, in a letter to the former, his recollections of the negotiations which led to the building of that vessel. That letter immediately following, and letters of comment by Captain Ericsson and ex-Secretary Welles, have been sent to the editors for publication, by the Reverend Samuel C. Bushnell, son of the builder:

"HONORABLE GIDEON WELLES. DEAR SIR: Some time since, during a short conversation in regard to the little first *Monitor,* you expressed a desire to learn from me some of the unwritten details of her history; particularly, how the plan of the boat came to be presented to the Government and the manner in which the contract for her construction was secured.

"You doubtless remember handing me in August, 1861,↓ at Willard's Hotel in Washington, D. C., the draft of a bill which you desired Congress should pass, in reference to obtaining some kind of iron-clad vessels to meet the formidable preparations the Rebels were making at Norfolk, Mobile, and New Orleans. At that time you stated that you had already called the attention of Congress to this matter, but without effect.

"I presented this bill to the Honorable James E. English, member of Congress from my district, who fortunately was on the Naval Committee and untiringly urged the matter on their attention. The chairman of the committee, A. H. Rice, of Massachusetts, ♭ also coöperated most heartily, so that in about thirty days,♮ if I remember correctly, the bill passed both Houses, and was immediately signed by President Lincoln. The bill required all plans of iron-clad vessels to be submitted to a board of naval officers appointed by yourself. The board consisted of Admirals Smith and Paulding and Captain Davis, who examined hundreds of plans, good and bad, and among others that of a plated iron gunboat called the *Galena,* contrived by Samuel H. Pook, now a constructor in the Navy Department. The partial protection of iron bars proposed for her seemed so burdensome that many naval officers warned me against the possibility of the *Galena's* being able to carry the additional weight of her armament.

"C. H. Delamater, of New York, advised me to consult with the engineer, Captain John Ericsson, on the matter.

This I proceeded at once to do, and on supplying him with the data necessary for his calculations promptly gained the answer, 'She will easily carry the load you propose, and stand a 6-inch shot—if fired from a respectable distance.' At the close of this interview, Captain Ericsson asked if I had time just then to examine the plan of a floating battery absolutely impregnable to the heaviest shot or shell. I replied that the problem had been occupying me for the last three months, and that, considering the time required for construction, the *Galena* was the best result that I had been able to attain. He then placed before me the plan of the *Monitor,* explained how quickly and powerfully she could be built, and exhibited with characteristic pride a medal and letter of thanks received from Napoleon III. For it appears that Ericsson had invented the battery when France and Russia were at war, and out of hostility to Russia had presented it to France, hoping thereby to aid the defeat of Sweden's hereditary foe. The invention, however, came too late to be of service, and was preserved for another issue.

"You no doubt remember my delight with the plan of the *Monitor* when first Captain Ericsson intrusted it to my care; how I followed you to Hartford and astounded you by saying that the country was safe because I had found a battery which would make us master of the situation so far as the ocean was concerned. You were much pleased, and urged me to lose no time in presenting the plan to the Naval Board at Washington. I secured at once the coöperation of wise and able associates in the person of the late Honorable John A. Griswold of [Troy] N. Y., and John F. Winslow of Troy, both of them friends of Governor Seward and large manufacturers of iron plates, etc. Governor Seward furnished us with a strong letter of introduction to President Lincoln, who was at once greatly pleased with the simplicity of the plan and agreed to accompany us to the Navy Department at 11 A. M. the following day, and aid us as best he could. He was on hand promptly at 11 o'clock—the day before you returned from Hartford. Captain Fox, together with a part of the Naval Board, was present. ☆ All were surprised at the novelty of the plan. Some advised trying it; others ridiculed it. The conference was finally closed for that day by Mr. Lincoln's remarking, 'All I have to say is what the girl said when she put her foot into the stocking, "It strikes me there's something in it."' The following day Admiral Smith convened the whole board, when I presented as best I could the plan and its merits, carefully noting the

↓ Mr. Bushnell's recollection of the dates is inexact. The bill (Senate, 36) was introduced July 19th, in the Senate, by Mr. Grimes of Iowa, "at the instance of the Department." (Congressional Globe, 1st Session, 37th Congress, pp. 205, 344). It became a law August 3d.— EDITORS.

♭ As Mr. Welles points out in his letter (see below), this

was an error of Mr. Bushnell's. The chairman of the Naval Committee was Charles B. Sedgwick, of Syracuse, New York. Mr. Rice came second on the committee.— EDITORS.

♮ The time was actually fifteen days.— EDITORS.

☆ Several naval officers were also present unofficially.— EDITORS.

remarks of each member of the board. I then went to my hotel quite sanguine of success, but only to be disappointed on the following day. For during the hours following the last session, I found that the air had been thick with croakings that the department was about to father another Ericsson failure. Never was I more active than now in the effort to prove that Ericsson had *never* made a failure; that, on the contrary, he had built for the Government the first steam war-propeller ever made; that the bursting of the gun was no fault of his, but of the shell, which had not been made strong enough to prevent its flattening up with the pressure of the explosion behind it, making the bursting of the gun unavoidable; that his caloric principle was a triumphant success, but that no metal had yet been found to utilize it on a large scale. I succeeded at length in getting Admirals Smith and Paulding to promise to sign a report advising the building of one trial battery, *provided* Captain Davis would join with them. On going to him, I was informed that I might 'take the little thing home and worship it, as it would not be idolatry, because it was made in the image of nothing in the heaven above or on the earth below or in the waters under the earth.' One thing only yet remained which it was possible to do : this was to get Ericsson to come to Washington and plead the case himself. This I was sure would win the case, and so informed you, for Ericsson is a full electric battery in himself. You at once promised to have a meeting in your room if I could succeed in inducing him to come. This was exceedingly doubtful, for so badly had he been treated and so unmercifully maligned in regard to the *Princeton* that he had repeatedly declared that he would never set foot in Washington again.

"Nevertheless I appeared at his house the next morning precisely at 9 o'clock, and heard his sharp greeting: 'Well! How is it?' 'Glorious,' said I. 'Go on, go on,' said he with much impatience. 'What did they say?' 'Admiral Smith says it is worthy of the genius of an Ericsson.' The pride fairly gleamed in his eyes. 'But Paulding—what did he say of it?' 'He said, "It's just the thing to clear the 'Rebs' out of Charleston with."' 'How about Davis?' he inquired, as I appeared to hesitate a moment. 'Oh, Davis,' said I, 'he wanted two or three explanations in detail which I couldn't give him, and so Secretary Welles proposed that I should come and get you to come to Washington and explain these few points to the entire board in his room to-morrow.' 'Well, I'll go — I'll go to-night.'

"From that moment I knew that the success of the affair was assured. You remember how he thrilled every person present in your room with his vivid description of what the little boat would be and what she could do; and that in ninety days' time she could be built, although the Rebels had already been four months or more on the *Merrimac* with all the appliances of the Norfolk Navy Yard to help them.

"You asked him how much it would cost to complete her. 'Two hundred and seventy-five thousand dollars,' he said. Then you promptly turned to the members of the board, and one by one asked them if they would recommend that a contract be entered into, for her construction, with Captain Ericsson and his associates. Each one answered, 'Yes, by all means.' Then you told Captain Ericsson to start her immediately. On the next day in New York a large portion of every article used in her construction was ordered, and a contract at once entered into between Captain Ericsson and his associates and T. F. Rowland, at Green Point, for the expeditious construction of the most formidable vessel ever made. It was arranged that after a few days I should procure a formal documentary contract from the Naval Board to be signed and executed by the Secretary of the Navy, Captain John Ericsson and associates.

"I regret that this part of the matter has been misunderstood, as though you had made terms heavier or the risk greater than you ought. The simple fact was that after we had entered upon the work of construction, and before the formal contract had been awarded, a great clamor arose, much of it due to interested parties, to the effect that the battery would prove a failure and

disgrace the members of the board for their action in recommending it. For their own protection, therefore, and out of their superabundant caution they insisted on inserting in the contract a clause requiring us to guarantee the complete success of the battery, so that, in case she proved a failure, the Government might be refunded the amounts advanced to us from time to time during her construction. To Captain Ericsson and myself, this was never an embarrassment; but to Mr. Winslow, as indeed to Mr. Griswold also, it appeared that the board had asked too much. But I know that the noble old Admiral Smith never intended that we should suffer, and among the many fortunate things for which the nation had occasion to be grateful — such as the providential selection as President in those dark days of the immortal Lincoln and his wisely chosen Cabinet — was the appointment of Admiral Smith to the charge of the navy yards, who always seemed to sleep with one eye open, so constant was his watchfulness and so eager his desire that the entire navy should be always in readiness to do its part in the overthrow of the rebellion.

"I am confident that no native-born child of this country will ever forget the proud son of Sweden who could sit in his own house and contrive the three thousand different parts that go to make up the complete hull of the steam-battery *Dictator*, so that when the mechanics came to put the parts together not a single alteration in any particular was required to be made. What the little first *Monitor* and the subsequent larger ones achieved is a part of history. . . . Very respectfully, C. S. BUSHNELL."

The date of the following letter from Captain Ericsson to the son of Mr. C. S. Bushnell indicates that the above letter was submitted to Captain Ericsson before it was sent to Ex-Secretary Welles:

"NEW YORK, March 2d, 1877.
"ERICSSON F. BUSHNELL, ESQ., NEW HAVEN. MY DEAR SIR : I have read with much pleasure your father's statement to Mr. Welles concerning the construction of the original *Monitor*. I do not think any changes or additions are needed, the main facts being well stated. . . . Yours very truly,   J. ERICSSON."

Ex-Secretary Welles, under date of Hartford, 19th March, 1877, addressed the following letter to Mr. C. S. Bushnell :

"MY DEAR SIR : I received on the 16th inst. your interesting communication without date—relative to the construction of the *Monitor*. Many of the incidents narrated by you I remember, although more than fifteen years have gone by since they transpired. Some errors, not very essential and caused by lapse of years, occur — Sedgwick, not Rice, was chairman of the Naval Committee; Griswold resided in Troy, not New York, and subsequently represented the Troy District in Congress, etc., etc.

"I well remember asking you to put in writing the facts in your possession concerning the construction of the *Monitor*. Some statements of General Butler, Wendell Phillips, and others, to disparage the Navy Department, pervert the truth and deny us all credit, led Admiral Smith, in the autumn of 1868 to address to me a communication reciting the facts, for he said, when we were gone, those of us who took the responsibility and would have incurred the disgrace had Ericsson's invention proved a failure, would be ignored and history misstated. As you were more intimate with the case at its inception, were the first to bring it to the attention of the department, it seemed to be me proper that your recollection and knowledge of the transaction should be reduced to writing. I am greatly obliged to you for the full and satisfactory manner in which you have complied with my request. Next, after Ericsson himself, you are entitled to bringing his invention to the knowledge of the department. I would not knowingly do injustice to any one, and I am well aware that the official in civil life, and who in administering the government directs movements by which naval and military men acquire renown, is often by the passing multitude little thought of and scarcely known; but the truth should not be suppressed.

"The civilians of the Navy Department who adopted and pursued through ridicule and assault the *Monitor* experiment, Butler and others would slight and defame. In the histories of the war, the Navy Department, which originated, planned, and carried forward the naval achievements from Hatteras to New Orleans, and finally Fort Fisher, is scarcely known or mentioned. The heroes who fought the battles and periled their lives to carry into effect the plans which the department devised have deservedly honorable remembrance — but the originators and movers are little known. I remember, my dear sir, your earnest efforts in the early days of the war and the comfort they gave me.

"Yours,   GIDEON WELLES."

Captain Ericsson's version of the visit to Washington, as given in Colonel William C. Church's paper on "John Ericsson" in "The Century" magazine for April, 1879, is as follows:

"With his previous experience of the waste of time and patience required to accomplish anything at Washington, Captain Ericsson, who is not, it must be said, like the man Moses, 'exceeding meek,' would not himself go to the capital to secure attention to his ideas. There were associated with him three men of practical experience, great energy and wealth, who had become interested in the *Monitor* and were determined that it should have a trial. One of these was Mr. C. S. Bushnell, of Connecticut. He went to Washington, but failed in the attempt to persuade the iron-clad board that the designer of the *Princeton* was worthy of a hearing. Nothing remained except to induce Ericsson to visit Washington in person and plead his own cause with that rude but forcible eloquence which has seldom failed him in an emergency. To move him was only less difficult than to convince the Navy Department without him. At last a subterfuge was adopted. Ericsson was given to understand that Mr. Bushnell's reception at Washington had been satisfactory and that nothing remained but for him to go on and complete the details of a contract for one of his vessels. Presenting himself before the board, what was his astonishment to find that he was not only an unexpected but apparently an unwelcome visitor! It was evident that the board were asking themselves what could have brought him there. He was not left long in doubt as to the meaning of this reception. To his indignation, as well as his astonishment, he was informed that the plan of a vessel submitted by him had already been rejected. The first impulse was to withdraw at once. Mastering his anger, however, he stopped to inquire the reason for the determination of the board. The vessel had not sufficient stability, Commodore Smith exclaimed; in fact, it would upset and place her crew in the inconvenient and undesirable position of submarine divers. Now, if there is anything which especially distinguishes the *Monitor*, with its low free-board, it is the peculiarity which it has in common with the raft it resembles — its inability to upset. In a most earnest and lucid argument, Captain Ericsson proceeded to explain this. Perceiving that his explanation had its effect, and his blood being well warmed by this time, he ended by declaring to the board with great earnestness: 'Gentlemen, after what I have said, I consider it to be your duty to the country to give me an order to build the vessel before I leave this room.' Withdrawing to one corner, the board consulted together and invited Captain Ericsson to call again at 1 o'clock. Promptly at the hour named he appeared at the Navy Department. In the board-room he found Commodore Paulding alone. The commodore received him in the most friendly manner, invited him into his private office, and asked that he would repeat the explanation of the morning as to the stability of the vessel. Between the two interviews, Ericsson had found time to make at his hotel a diagram presenting the question of stability in a form easily understood. With this diagram, he repeated his previous demonstration. Commodore (afterward Admiral) Paulding was thoroughly convinced, and with frankness which did him great credit said: 'Sir, I have learnt more about the stability of a vessel from what you have now said than all I knew before.' This interview ended with a request to call again at 3 o'clock. Calling at 3, Ericsson was at once invited to pass into the room of secretary Welles. Here, without farther parley, the secretary informed him that the board now reported favorably upon his plan of a vessel, and wished him to return to New York and commence work upon it at once. The contract would be sent on for signature. Before this contract was received, the keel-plates for the first *Monitor* had passed through the rolling-mill."   EDITORS.

END OF VOLUME I.

UNION SOLDIER'S CANDLESTICK.